THE OXFORD HANDBOOK OF

SOCIOLINGUISTICS

Oxford Handbooks in Linguistics

THE OXFORD HANDBOOK OF APPLIED LINGUISTICS
Second edition

Edited by Robert B. Kaplan

THE OXFORD HANDBOOK OF CASE
Edited by Andrej Malchukov and Andrew Spencer

THE OXFORD HANDBOOK OF COGNITIVE LINGUISTICS
Edited by Dirk Geeraerts and Hubert Cuyckens

THE OXFORD HANDBOOK OF COMPARATIVE SYNTAX
Edited by Gugliemo Cinque and Richard S. Kayne

THE OXFORD HANDBOOK OF COMPOUNDING
Edited by Rochelle Lieber and Pavol Štekauer

THE OXFORD HANDBOOK OF COMPUTATIONAL LINGUISTICS
Edited by Ruslan Mitkov

THE OXFORD HANDBOOK OF COMPOSITIONALITY
Edited by Markus Werning, Edouard Machery, and Wolfram Hinzen

THE OXFORD HANDBOOK OF FIELD LINGUISTICS
Edited by Nicholas Thieberger

THE OXFORD HANDBOOK OF GRAMMATICALIZATION
Edited by Heiko Narrog and Bernd Heine

THE OXFORD HANDBOOK OF THE HISORY OF LINGUISTICS
Edited by Keith Allan

THE OXFORD HANDBOOK OF JAPANESE LINGUISTICS
Edited by Shigeru Miyagawa and Mamoru Saito

THE OXFORD HANDBOOK OF LABORATORY PHONOLOGY
Edited by Abigail C. Cohn, Cécile Fougeron, and Marie Hoffman

THE OXFORD HANDBOOK OF LANGUAGE EVOLUTION
Edited by Maggie Tallerman and Kathleen Gibson

THE OXFORD HANDBOOK OF LANGUAGE AND LAW
Edited by Peter Tiersma and Lawrence M. Solan

THE OXFORD HANDBOOK OF LINGUISTIC ANALYSIS
Edited by Bernd Heine and Heiko Narrog

THE OXFORD HANDBOOK OF LINGUISTIC INTERFACES
Edited by Gillian Ramchand and Charles Reiss

THE OXFORD HANDBOOK OF LINGUISTIC MINIMALISM
Edited by Cedric Boeckx

THE OXFORD HANDBOOK OF LINGUISTIC TYPOLOGY
Edited by Jae Jung Song

THE OXFORD HANDBOOK OF TRANSLATION STUDIES
Edited by Kirsten Malmkjaer and Kevin Windle

THE OXFORD HANDBOOK OF

SOCIOLINGUISTICS

Edited by

ROBERT BAYLEY,
RICHARD CAMERON,
and
CEIL LUCAS

OXFORD
UNIVERSITY PRESS

Oxford University Press is a department of the University of Oxford.
It furthers the University's objective of excellence in research, scholarship,
and education by publishing worldwide.

Oxford New York
Auckland Cape Town Dar es Salaam Hong Kong Karachi
Kuala Lumpur Madrid Melbourne Mexico City Nairobi
New Delhi Shanghai Taipei Toronto

With offices in
Argentina Austria Brazil Chile Czech Republic France Greece
Guatemala Hungary Italy Japan Poland Portugal Singapore
South Korea Switzerland Thailand Turkey Ukraine Vietnam

Oxford is a registered trade mark of Oxford University Press
in the UK and certain other countries.

Published in the United States of America by
Oxford University Press
198 Madison Avenue, New York, NY 10016

First issued as an Oxford University Press paperback, 2015.

Library of Congress Cataloging-in-Publication Data
The Oxford handbook of sociolinguistics / edited by Robert Bayley,
Richard Cameron, and Ceil Lucas.
p. cm.
Includes bibliographical references and index.
ISBN 978-0-19-974408-4 (hardcover : alk. paper); 978-0-19-023374-7 (paperback : alk. paper)
1. Sociolinguistics—Handbooks, manuals, etc. I. Bayley, Robert, 1943-
II. Cameron, Richard, 1953- III. Lucas, Ceil.
IV. Title: Handbook of sociolinguistics.
P40.O94 2013
306.44—dc23
2012020046

Contents

PART II. METHODOLOGIES AND APPROACHES

PART III. BILINGUALISM AND LANGUAGE CONTACT

PART IV. VARIATION

PART V. LANGUAGE POLICY, LANGUAGE IDEOLOGY, AND LANGUAGE ATTITUDES

PART VI. SOCIOLINGUISTICS, THE PROFESSIONS, AND THE PUBLIC INTEREST

ACKNOWLEDGMENTS

The editors gratefully acknowledge the usual assistance of their institutions in providing appropriate homes for academic activity, even the editing of others' work. We especially thank Brian Hurley of Oxford University Press, who approached us with the idea for this book. We also thank Molly Morrison of Newgen North America for managing the production of this volume, Ginny Faber for copyediting, Janet Mazefsky for producing the extensive index, and University of California, Davis, linguistics students Matt Balvin, Daniel Villarreal, and Kristin Ware, who read drafts of many of the chapters and contributed in a variety of ways to the progress of this volume.

The contributors to this volume constitute a distinguished group of 50 scholars who represent several generations and reside in 10 different countries. We thank them for their timely contributions and their willingness to respond to requests. We also owe a debt of gratitude to our sociolinguistic mentors at Stanford, Penn, and Georgetown: Gregory Guy, John Rickford, William Labov, and Roger Shuy. Finally, we are grateful to our families and significant others for their continued and unwavering support of all our endeavors: Ann Robinson, Beth Andress, Russell Bayley, Stephen Brown, and Diana González-Cameron.

About the Editors

Robert Bayley is Professor of Linguistics at the University of California, Davis. He has conducted research on variation in English, Spanish, Chinese, ASL, and Italian Sign Language as well as studies of language socialization in U.S. Latino communities. His publications include *Language as Cultural Practice* (with Sandra R. Schecter, 2002), and *Sociolinguistic Variation: Theories, Methods, and Applications* (with Ceil Lucas, 2007).

Richard Cameron is Associate Professor of Linguistics in the Department of Hispanic and Italian Studies and the Department of Linguistics at the University of Illinois at Chicago. He has published on Puerto Rican Spanish, Chicago English, age, gender, medical discourse, and sociolinguistic theory. A recently edited book is *Spanish in Context* (with Kim Potowski, 2007).

Ceil Lucas is Professor of Linguistics at Gallaudet University in Washington, DC. Her recent publications include *Language and the Law in Deaf Communities* (2003), *The Linguistics of American Sign Language*, 5th edition (with Clayton Valli et al., 2011), and *The Hidden Treasure of Black ASL: Its History and Structure* (with Carolyn McCaskill, Robert Bayley, and Joseph Hill, 2011).

Contributors

Robert Adam, a Deaf native signer, is Research Associate at the Deafness Cognition and Language Research Centre (DCAL) of University College, London. He has been involved with research projects investigating sign language segmentation and sociolinguistics research at DCAL. He is currently undertaking doctoral studies in language contact between sign languages.

Maciej Baranowski is Senior Lecturer in English Sociolinguistics at the University of Manchester. He received his Ph.D. from the University of Pennsylvania. He conducts research into phonological variation and sound change in progress in dialects of English in the United States and the United Kingdom.

Matthew C. Bronson is Associate Professor of Social and Cultural Anthropology at the California Institute of Integral Studies in San Francisco and a teacher educator at the University of California, Davis. He works in the areas of language socialization, advanced academic literacy, and educational assessment.

Vineeta Chand is a Lecturer in Sociolinguistics at the University of Essex, UK. Her research deals with ideologies, contemporary language practices, and diachronic linguistic change in urban Indian English as well as clinical sociolinguistic research on language practices in the context of aging and dementia.

Anne H. Charity Hudley is Associate Professor of Education, English, Linguistics, and Africana Studies at the College of William & Mary in Williamsburg, Virginia. She is associate editor of Language and directs the William and Mary Scholars Program. With Christine Mallinson, she is author of *Understanding English Language Variation in U.S. Schools* and *We Do Language: English Language Variation in the Secondary English Classroom.*

Alexandra D'Arcy is Assistant Professor and the Director of the Sociolinguistics Research Lab at the University of Victoria. She is interested in both diachronic and synchronic aspects of grammaticalization and variation and change; her research focuses on the morphosyntax and discourse-pragmatics of English.

Jean-Marc Dewaele is Professor of Applied Linguistics at Birkbeck College, University of London. His research focuses on sociolinguistic and sociopragmatic competence and on the communication of emotions in a variety of languages and contexts. His recent publications include *Emotions in Multiple Languages* (2010) and *New Trends in Crosslinguistic and Multilingualism Research* (with Gessica De Angelis, 2011).

Richard M. Frankel is Professor of Medicine and Geriatrics and the statewide professionalism competency director at the Indiana University School of Medicine. He is also the Associate Director of the VA Center of Excellence on Implementing Evidence-Based Practice at the Richard L. Roudebush Veterans Administration Medical Center in Indianapolis and directs its fellowship programs. Dr. Frankel is a qualitative health services researcher whose scholarship has focused on the impact of physician patient communication on processes, outcomes, and quality of care. He is the co-developer of the Four Habits of Highly Effective Clinicians, which has been used to train more than 10,000 physicians in the United States and abroad.

Charlotte Gooskens is Associate Professor of Scandinavian Linguistics at the University of Groningen, the Netherlands. Her research deals with perceptual and communicative effects of language variation, for example, language attitudes, speaker identity, and mutual intelligibility of closely related languages. She uses experimental research methods and exact measurement techniques. She is leader of the project Mutual Intelligibility of Closely Related Languages in Europe: Linguistic and Non-Linguistic Determinants, financed by The Netherlands Organization for Scientific Research at the Center for Language and Cognition, Groningen.

Kyle Gorman is a postdoctoral fellow at the Center for Spoken Language Understanding at the Oregon Health and Science University in Portland, Oregon. He received his Ph.D. in linguistics from the University of Pennsylvania. His research deploys quantitative techniques for the study of phonology, morphology, and language acquisition and variation.

Lenore A. Grenoble is Professor of General and Slavic Linguistics at the University of Chicago. Her publications include *Language Documentation: Practices and Values* (ed. with N. Louanna Furbee, 2010), *Saving Languages* (with Lindsay J. Whaley, 2006) and "Language ecology and endangerment" (Austin & Sallabank, eds., *Handbook of Endangered Languages*, 2011).

François Grin is Professor of Economics at the University of Geneva's School of Translation and Interpretation. He has specialized in language economics and language policy evaluation, has published widely in these fields, and advises regional or national authorities as well as international organizations on language policy issues.

Rainer Enrique Hamel is Professor of Linguistics at the Universidad Autónoma Metropolitana in Mexico City. He has published on bilingualism and bilingual education, language policy, conflict and shift, and multilingualism in science and higher education. Recent publications include "Indigenous language policy and education in Mexico" and "Bilingual education for indigenous communities in Mexico" in the *Encyclopedia of Language and Education* and "L'aménagement linguistique et la globalisation des langues du monde" in *Télescope*.

JOSEPH HILL is Assistant Professor in the Specialized Educational Services Department at the University of North Carolina at Greensboro. He is a coordinator of the ASL Teacher Licensure concentration of the Professions in Deafness program. He is also a co-author of *The Hidden Treasure of Black ASL: Its History and Structure* (2011).

MARTIN HOWARD is Lecturer in French and Director of the Applied Linguistics programme at University College Cork (Ireland). He is currently Vice-President of the European Second Language Association, and has previously served as Director-at-Large of the International Council for Canadian Studies. His research focuses on Second Language Acquisition, sociolinguistics, and Canadian studies.

DANIEL EZRA JOHNSON is Lecturer in Sociophonetics at Lancaster University (UK). He received his Ph.D. in linguistics from the University of Pennsylvania. He is the author of *Stability and Change along a Dialect Boundary: The Low Vowels of Southeastern New England* (Publication of the American Dialect Society 95). His research interests include quantitative methods and dialectology.

TREVOR JOHNSTON is Associate Professor of Linguistics at Macquarie University, Sydney. In the 1980s he identified and named Auslan (Australian Sign Language), securing its recognition by educators and governments. Since then he has led in the documentation and description of the language (sketch grammar, dictionaries, research articles, introductory textbook, and linguistic corpora).

NKONKO M. KAMWANGAMALU is Professor of Linguistics in the Department of English at Howard University, Washington, DC. He is Polity Editor for the Series "Current Issues in Language Planning"; author of the monograph *The Language Planning Situation in South Africa*; and of numerous refereed articles on topics in language planning, codeswitching, multilingualism, and African linguistics.

TYLER KENDALL is Assistant Professor of Linguistics at the University of Oregon. His recent work focuses on the sociophonetics of speech production and perception and corpus and computational methods in the study of language variation and change. He is the developer of several sociolinguistic software projects, including SLAAP (http://ncslaap.lib.ncsu.edu/), and the author of the forthcoming monograph *Speech Rate, Pause, and Sociolinguistic Variation: Studies in Corpus Sociophonetics.*

RUTH KING is Professor of Linguistics at York University, Toronto. Her research deals with patterns of grammatical variation and change in French, as well as general issues around language change, including the process by which language contact leads to grammatical change. She is the author of three books and numerous journal articles and book chapters.

JULIET LANGMAN is Associate Professor of Applied Linguistics in the Department of Bicultural-Bilingual Studies at the University of Texas at San Antonio. Her research focuses on minority youth populations in multilingual settings, exploring the intersection between language use and identity. Her research settings include school and community-based contexts in the United States and Central Europe.

Li Wei is Professor of Applied Linguistics at Birkbeck College, University of London, where he is also Pro-Vice Master for Research and Director of the Birkbeck Graduate School. He is an Academician of the Academy of Social Sciences, UK. His publications include the award-winning *Blackwell Guide to Research Methods in Bilingualism and Multilingualism* (with Melissa Moyer, 2008), *Handbook of Multilingualism and Multilingual Communication* (with Peter Auer, 2007), *Contemporary Applied Linguistics* (with Vivian Cook, 2009), *The Bilingualism Reader* (2000 & 2007), and *The Routledge Applied Linguistics Reader* (2011). He is Principal Editor of the *International Journal of Bilingualism.*

Brandon C. Loudermilk is a Ph.D. candidate in Linguistics at the University of California, Davis. He is a neuro- and psycholinguist with a focus on sociolinguistic cognition. Brandon is completing a dissertation that uses the methods and insights of cognitive neuroscience and psychology to explore the cognitive architecture and neural underpinnings of dialectal variation perception.

Christine Mallinson is Associate Professor of Language, Literacy and Culture at the University of Maryland, Baltimore County. Her publications include *Understanding English Language Variation in U.S. Schools* (with Anne Charity Hudley, 2011) and *Data Collection in Sociolinguistics: Methods and Applications* (ed. with Becky Childs and Gerard Van Herk, forthcoming).

Gregory Matoesian is a Professor in the Department of Criminology, Law and Justice at the University of Illinois at Chicago. He studies verbal and visual conduct, culture and identity in legal contexts. He is the author of *Reproducing Rape: Domination Through Talk in the Courtroom* and *Law and the Language of Identity: Discourse in the William Kennedy Smith Rape Trial.*

Christopher Mcall is Professor of Sociology at the University of Montreal. He is scientific director of the Montreal Centre for Research on Social Inequality and Discrimination (CREMIS) and specializes in the areas of social inequality, alternative citizenship practices and the history of social thought.

Melanie Metzger is Professor and Chair of the Department of Interpretation at Gallaudet University where she also serves as director of the Interpretation and Translation Research Center. She is an interpreter practitioner and educator, and her research focuses on ASL discourse and sociolinguistic examinations of interpreted interaction.

Miriam Meyerhoff is Professor of Linguistics at the University of Auckland. Her research is on language variation, especially in creole speech communities, and often relating to gender ideologies.

Raymond Mougeon is Professor of French Linguistics at York University, Toronto. His research deals with sociolinguistic variation in Canadian French with a special focus on L1 and L2 adolescent speech in a school setting. He is the author of twelve volumes and numerous journal articles and book chapters.

NAOMI NAGY is Assistant Professor of Linguistics at the University of Toronto. She investigates language variation and change, particularly contact effects, in heritage languages in Toronto (Cantonese, Korean, Italian, Russian, Ukrainian, and the endangered Francoprovençal dialect of Faeto), New England dialects, and Montreal Anglophones. See her publications at http://individual.utoronto.ca/ngn/cv.htm.

ANETA PAVLENKO is Professor of TESOL/Applied Linguistics at Temple University (Philadelphia, USA). Her research examines the relationship between language, emotions, and cognition in bilingualism and second language acquisition as well as language management in post-Soviet countries. She won the 2006 BAAL Book Prize and the 2009 TESOL Award for Distinguished Research.

KIM POTOWSKI is Associate Professor of Hispanic linguistics at the University of Illinois at Chicago. Her publications include *Language and Identity in a Dual Immersion School* (2007), *Language Diversity in the USA* (ed., 2010) and *Bilingual Youth: Spanish in English-Speaking Societies* (ed. with Jason Rothman 2011). She is currently studying Spanish dialect contact, including the linguistic features of mixed ethnicity Latinos.

DAVID QUINTO-POZOS is a member of the Linguistics Department at the University of Texas at Austin. His research interests include language contact between sign languages, register variation, the interaction of language and gesture, and signed language interpretation. With respect to child language, he also examines developmental signed language disorders as exhibited by deaf children who are native signers of ASL.

MARTIN REISIGL is Professor of German Linguistics at the University of Bern, Switzerland. His publications include *The Discursive Construction of National Identity*, 2nd ed. (with Ruth Wodak et al. 2009), *Nationale Rhetorik in Fest- und Gedenkreden* (2007), and *Discourse and Discrimination. Rhetorics of Racism and Antisemitism* (with Ruth Wodak 2001).

THOMAS RICENTO is Professor and Research Chair in English as an Additional Language at the University of Calgary, Alberta, Canada. He is founding co-editor of the *Journal of Language, Identity and Education* (Routledge) and has published widely in the field of language policy and language and ideology. His books include *An Introduction to Language Policy* (2006) and *Ideology, Politics and Language Policies: Focus on English* (2000).

SUZANNE ROMAINE is Merton Professor of English Language at the University of Oxford. She has published numerous books and articles on linguistic diversity, multilingualism, language death, change and contact. *Her book Vanishing Voices: The Extinction of the World's Languages*, coauthored with Daniel Nettle, won the British Association for Applied Linguistics Book of the Year Prize in 2001.

CYNTHIA ROY is Professor in the Department of Interpretation at Gallaudet University, Washington, DC. Her doctorate is in sociolinguistics from Georgetown

University and her research focuses on discourse analysis and sociolinguistic examinations of interpreted interaction.

Eric Russell Webb is Associate Professor at the University of California, Davis, where he is affiliated with the Department of French & Italian and the Linguistics Graduate Group. His research looks at phonological issues in French- and Dutch-lexifier Creoles. He is the author of numerous articles and book chapters.

Gillian Sankoff is Professor of Linguistics at the University of Pennsylvania. Her early research focused on multilingualism and creolization in Papua New Guinea; later work dealt with language variation and change in Canadian French. Her current research centers on the relationship between historical change in language, and language change across the lifespans of individuals.

Adam Schembri is Associate Professor and Director of both the National Institute for Deaf Studies and Sign Language and the Centre for Research on Language Diversity at La Trobe University in Melbourne, Australia. He published work on the lexicon, grammar and sociolinguistics of Australian Sign Language and British Sign Language.

Scott Schwenter is Associate Professor of Hispanic Linguistics at The Ohio State University. He has published widely on pragmatics and grammatical variation, and their intersection, in Spanish and Portuguese. His publications include *Pragmatics of Conditional Marking* (1999), and numerous journal articles.

Paul Seedhouse is Professor of Educational and Applied Linguistics at Newcastle University, UK. His 2004 monograph *The Interactional Architecture of the Language Classroom* won the Modern Languages Association of America Mildenberger Prize. He currently has a grant to build a digital kitchen, which teaches users French language and cuisine simultaneously.

Janet S. Shibamoto-Smith is Professor of Anthropology at the University of California, Davis. She is a specialist in Japanese language, society, and culture, with an emphasis on the interaction between ideology and practice. Publications include *Japanese Women's Language* (1985) and the edited volume *Japanese Language, Gender, and Ideology* (with Shigeko Okamoto, 2004).

James A. Walker is Associate Professor in Linguistics at York University (Toronto). He has worked on linguistic variation in African American English, Canadian English, and Caribbean English. He is the author of *Variation in Linguistic Systems* (2010) and the editor of *Aspect in Grammatical Variation* (2010).

Karen Ann Watson-Gegeo is Professor of Language, Literacy and Culture in the School of Education, University of California, Davis. Her work is on first and second language socialization, language policy and indigenous epistemology, in Hawai'i and Kwara'ae (Solomon Islands).

Walt Wolfram is William C. Friday Distinguished University Professor at North Carolina State University, where he also directs the North Carolina

Language and Life Project. He has authored or coauthored more than 20 books and 300 articles, and has served as President of the Linguistic Society of America and the American Dialect Society.

QING ZHANG is Assistant Professor of Anthropology at the University of Arizona. Her research deals with language variation and change in the context of socioeconomic transformation in China. She is currently writing a book manuscript on the emergence of "cosmopolitan Mandarin" in the construction of a new Chinese middle class.

List of Tables

List of Figures

THE OXFORD HANDBOOK OF

SOCIOLINGUISTICS

INTRODUCTION

THE STUDY OF LANGUAGE AND SOCIETY

ROBERT BAYLEY, RICHARD CAMERON, AND CEIL LUCAS

FROM its beginnings as a discipline in the 1960s, sociolinguistics developed several different subfields with distinct methods and interests: the variationist tradition established by Labov (1966, 1972a, 1972b), the anthropological tradition of Hymes (1974; Gumperz & Hymes 1972), interactional sociolinguistics as developed by Gumperz, and the sociology of language represented by the work of Fishman (1971–1972). All these areas have seen a great deal of growth in recent decades. Indeed, with respect to just the study of language variation and change, Chambers and his colleagues commented: "[U]ntil sometime in the 1980s, it was possible for an enterprising graduate student facing comprehensive examinations to read virtually everything in the field of sociolinguistics. That is no longer true, of course" (2002: 2). When we consider the field of sociolinguistics broadly defined, it is even less possible to read everything now than when Chambers and his colleagues wrote in 2002. Hence, there is a need for a handbook that will survey the main areas of the field, point out the lacunae in our existing knowledge base, and provide directions for future research.

Given the proliferation of handbooks focusing on different areas of linguistics, including sociolinguistics (e.g., Ammon et al. 2002–2009; Chambers et al. 2002; Coulmas 1997; Mesthrie 2011), it is reasonable to ask why we need another. How does this volume differ from the works that are already available? Although we have included contributions that cover the main topics or disciplines, this volume differs from existing work in four major respects. First, it emphasizes new methodological developments, particularly the convergence of linguistic anthropology and variationist sociolinguistics. Second, it includes chapters on sociolinguistic developments in areas of the world that have been relatively neglected in the major journals. Third, while many authors include examples from English, contributors have worked in a range of languages and address sociolinguistic issues in bi- and multilingual contexts, that is, the contexts in which a majority of the world's population lives. Finally, the volume includes substantial material on the rapidly growing study of sign language sociolinguistics.

Recently, Nagy and Meyerhoff (2008: 7–10) surveyed two of the major journals in sociolinguistics, the *Journal of Sociolinguistics* (*JoS*) and *Language Variation and Change* (*LVC*), to determine the number of articles dealing with multilingual contexts and the distribution of studies by world region. Their survey included issue two of *LVC* from 1989 to 2007 and all the issues of *JoS* from its initial publication in 1997 to 2008. Their results were sobering. Only 11 percent of the articles surveyed in *LVC*, the leading journal in variationist sociolinguistics, dealt with more than one language. The *JoS* was somewhat better, with 28 percent of the articles published from its inception in 1997 to 2008 dealing with more than one language. Nagy and Meyerhoff's findings for regional distribution also show that articles were heavily weighted toward North America or Europe. In *LVC*, 66 percent of the articles surveyed in a 19-year period dealt with European or North American contexts. Only 8 percent dealt with Asia. In the *JoS*, 76 percent of the articles published from 1997 to 2008 dealt with European or North American contexts. According to Meyerhoff and Nagy, the percentage for speakers residing in Asia or Africa was zero. While this state of affairs is in part a reflection of the concentration of sociolinguistics programs in North American and European universities, a great deal of work has been and continues to be accomplished in many countries. The current volume highlights that work.

For a long time, the study of sign languages and sociolinguistics existed in separate disciplinary realms. However, it is now clear that many sociolinguistic factors are independent of modality and that the study of the sociolinguistics of sign languages provides numerous opportunities to test sociolinguistic theories. Thanks to recent advances in sign language sociolinguistics, articles on sign languages are now included in major reference volumes (e.g., Bayley & Lucas 2011; Quinto-Pozos 2009). Finally, we address the issue of methodology and approaches. For a number of years, sociolinguists seemed divided into camps determined in part by the disciplinary perspectives of the founding figures. Thus, variationists, taking their inspiration from William Labov and focusing on linguistic structure, tended to publish in *LVC*. Anthropological linguists, drawing inspiration from Dell Hymes and John Gumperz, among others, sent their articles to *Language in Society*, while scholars whose interests were more sociological sent their articles to the *International Journal of the Sociology of*

Language. Recent years, however, have seen a change. The *JoS*, which now publishes five issues a year, welcomes studies from all sociolinguistic subfields. Perhaps more importantly, a number of studies have appeared that combine variationist and ethnographic techniques to go beyond the prescribed social categories common in earlier studies of variation (e.g., Eckert 2000; Mendoza-Denton 2008; Zhang 2005). We suggest that such studies, combined with recent work in language and gender, have led to a more broadly inclusive view of sociolinguistics. The current volume reflects that broader view in the chapters on methodology and disciplinary perspectives, in the focus on bi- and multilingual contexts, in its emphasis on developments in numerous areas around the world, and in giving an appropriate place to sign languages.

Sociolinguistics as an Interdisciplinary Enterprise

The first part of the volume examines the approaches of the various disciplines that have contributed to the sociolinguistic enterprise. In chapter 1, Bayley reviews the variationist tradition, beginning with Labov's (1963, 1966) seminal studies of Martha's Vineyard and New York City, and explores new developments, with emphasis on the renewed ties between ethnographic work and rigorous quantitative analysis exemplified by studies such as Eckert's (2000) work in the Detroit area, Zhang's (2005) studies in China, and Mendoza-Denton's (2008) work on Latina gangs in northern California.

In chapter 2, Shibamoto-Smith and Chand focus on twenty-first-century attempts at reengagement between linguistic anthropology and the quantitative strands of sociolinguistics, strands that grew more and more separate between the 1950s and the present. Christopher McAll then explores the relationship between sociology and sociolinguistics in chapter 3. Drawing examples from bi- and multilingual settings, he shows how the sociology of language is a key part of the sociological enterprise.

Chapters 4, 5, and 6 focus on work in three fields allied to sociolinguistics: (1) critical discourse analysis (Martin Reisigl), conversation analysis (Paul Seedhouse), and language socialization (Karen Ann Watson-Gegeo and Matthew Bronson). Reisigl's chapter 4 attends particularly to the theoretical and methodological role of sociolinguistic concepts, and especially to the different traditions that have developed over the past several decades. In chapter 5, Seedhouse illustrates how social action is accomplished by means of linguistic and other resources that coincide with many interests of the broad field of sociolinguistics. Like Shibamoto-Smith and Chand in chapter 6, Watson-Gegeo and Bronson also attend to recent attempts to bring together insights from linguistic anthropology, specifically language socialization, and sociolinguistics. They argue that researchers in language socialization can benefit from incorporating recent developments in sociolinguistics into their work, while at the same time, language socialization deserves the attention of sociolinguists as a source for a critical review of existing models, theories, and methods.

Chapter 7 represents a change in focus from the more qualitatively oriented work discussed in the previous three chapters. Brandon Loudermilk reviews the intersections between psycholinguistics and sociolinguistics. Part 1 concludes with Christine Mallinson and Tyler Kendall's chapter (8) on interdisciplinary approaches. The authors note the benefits as well as the challenges of bringing together scholars from diverse traditions and show how new insights regarding theory, methods, and analysis/interpretation of language and its relationship to the natural and the social worlds emerge when interdisciplinary scholars' perspectives and approaches intersect.

Part II deals with methods, a central concern of a discipline that bases its conclusions on evidence drawn from the real world of social interaction. Using examples from their recent work on the Caribbean island of Bequia, in chapter 9, James Walker and Miriam Meyerhoff examine the relationship between the community and the individual in studies of language variation and change. As Loudermilk's chapter (7) on psycholinguistic approaches in Part I indicates, in recent years experimental approaches have become increasingly common in sociolinguistics. In chapter 10, Charlotte Gooskens provides an extensive discussion of experimental approaches for measuring the intelligibility of closely related languages.

The study of language variation, a central concern of sociolinguistics, is a quantitative discipline, and in recent years there has been considerable debate about methods for modeling the complex data drawn from the speech community. In chapter 11, Kyle Gorman and Daniel Ezra Johnson present the case for using the type of mixed models available in the open source statistical program R as well as other commercially available programs.

While studies of language variation necessarily rely on quantitative methods, in linguistic anthropology and language socialization, ethnographic methods are the norm. In chapter 12, Juliet Langman, using examples from her own work among the Hungarian minority in Slovakia, outlines current perspectives on conducting qualitative research in multilingual contexts.

In chapter 13, Gillian Sankoff addresses issues concerned with longitudinal research. She reviews studies that replicated earlier research by drawing a new population directly comparable to that of the initial study (trend studies) and studies that follow the same individual speakers across time as they age (panel studies). The section concludes with Ceil Lucas's chapter (14) on the special issues that arise in researching signed languages.

Part III deals directly with a number of issues in multilingualism and language contact. In chapter 15, Eric Russell Webb outlines the mutual contributions of the related fields of sociolinguistics and pidgin and creole studies. Kim

Potowski's chapter (16) then takes up the issues of language maintenance and shift, issues that are increasingly important in an era of widespread immigration. Chapter 17, a joint contribution by Martin Howard, Raymond Mougeon, and Jean-Marc Dewaele, focuses on variationist approaches to second language acquisition, with particular emphasis on the acquisition of French as a second language. In the final two chapters in the section, Li Wei (18) examines codeswitching in a number of different languages, and David Quinto-Pozos and Robert Adam (19) outline important work on language contact and signed languages.

Part IV focuses on a core area of sociolinguistics—the study of language variation and change. Maciej Baranowski, in chapter 20, begins with a careful review of advances in sociophonetics. Recent years, particularly with the rise of optimality theory, have witnessed a greater attention by variationists to linguistic theory and by theoretical linguists to studies of language variation and change. Chapter 21, by Naomi Nagy, and chapter 22, by Ruth King, examine these developments in phonology and morphosyntax respectively. Richard Cameron and Scott Schwenter, in chapter 23, examine the intersection between variationist analysis and pragmatics and illustrate how variationist research may draw on pragmatics when identifying variables and constraints and may also provide quantitative tests of predictions derived from the fundamentally qualitative agenda of pragmatics.

The study of language change has long been central to the sociolinguistic enterprise, In chapter 24, Alexandra D'Arcy uses the example of the rise of innovative English quotatives to illustrate how variationists study language change across time and geographical space. The final chapter of this section, by Adam Schembri and Trevor Johnston, deals with variation in sign languages. Using examples from American Sign Language, Australian Sign Language, New Zealand Sign Language, and British Sign Language, they illustrate how many of the factors, both linguistic and social, that constrain variation in spoken languages also constrain variation in sign languages. Schembri and Johnston also illustrate the factors that are unique to sign languages, resulting in large measure from differences between spoken and sign languages in patterns of acquisition and generational transmission..

Part V focuses on macrosociolinguistics and explores language policy, ideology, and attitudes in a wide range of contexts. It opens with Thomas Ricento's detailed examination of language policy and planning in the English-dominant countries of the United States, Canada, the United Kingdom, Australia, and New Zealand. Next, in chapter 27, Nkonko Kamwangamalu focuses on language policies and ideologies in Africa, with a particular focus on issues involved in vernacularization. Qing Zhang, in chapter 28, deals with the development of language policy in modern China. Zhang not only examines developments on the Chinese mainland but also explores recent changes in Hong Kong and Taiwan. The exploration of language policies and ideologies in Asia continues with Vineeta Chand's comprehensive discussion in chapter 29 of the language policies of seven nations in South Asia.

The focus of Part V then shifts to Latin America. In chapter 30, Rainer Enrique Hamel examines policies on both indigenous bilingual education and elite bilingual education. He concludes with a section on plurilingual policies in the era of globalization. In chapter 31, François Grin then explores language policy, ideology, and attitudes in Western Europe, and Aneta Pavlenko in chapter 32 examines the complex language policies in the Russian Empire, the Soviet Union, and in the successor states. Part V concludes with Joseph Hill's chapter (33) on language ideologies, policies, and attitudes toward signed languages, with particular emphasis on ASL.

Lastly, Part VI concerns sociolinguistics in a number of different domains, including law, medicine, and sign language interpreting, among others. In chapter 34, Gregory Matoesian examines the role of power in legal discourse. In chapter 35, Richard Frankel follows with an examination of the culture of a large medical school, while Metzger and Roy's chapter (36) focuses on the relationship between sign language interpreting and sociolinguistics, with emphasis on how "interpretation itself constitutes a sociolinguistic activity."

No one has done more to promote language awareness among the public at large than Walt Wolfram. In chapter 37, Wolfram discusses programs designed to promote language and dialect awareness, with particular emphasis on his work in North Carolina.

Chapters 38, by Suzanne Romaine, and 39, by Lenore Grenoble, deal with the related topics of language and ecological diversity and language revitalization. Romaine shows how the decline in the number of the world's languages closely parallels the loss of biodiversity. Grenoble examines what steps can be taken to reverse some of the loss that Romaine documents. Finally, the last chapter in the book, chapter 40, by Anne Charity Hudley, explores the relationship between sociolinguistics and social activism, with particular emphasis on the role sociolinguistics has had in promoting minority rights in the United States.

Although *The Oxford Handbook of Sociolinguistics* contains 40 chapters dealing with a great variety of topics, we make no claim to completeness. Nevertheless, the major theoretical approaches are represented in particular bilingual and multilingual contexts, and both spoken and signed languages are well represented. The volume offers both an up-to-date guide to the diverse areas of the study of language in society and numerous guideposts to where the field is headed.

References

Ammon, U., Dittmar, N., Mattheier, K., & Trudgill, P. (eds.) 2002–09. *Sociolinguistics/ Soziolinguistik: An international handbook of the science of language and society/ Ein internationales Handbuch zur Wissenschaft von Sprache und Gesellschaft.* 3 vols. Berlin: Mouton de Gruyter.

Bayley, R., & Lucas, C. 2011. Sign languages. In R. Mesthrie (ed.), *The Cambridge handbook of sociolinguistics*, 83–102. Cambridge: Cambridge University Press.

Chambers, J. K., Trudgill, P., & Schilling-Estes, N. (eds.) 2002. *The handbook of language variation and change.* Oxford: Blackwell.

Coulmas, F. (ed.) 1997. *The handbook of sociolinguistics.* Oxford: Blackwell.

Eckert, P. 2000. *Linguistic variation as social practice.* Oxford: Blackwell.

Fishman, J. A. (ed.) 1971–72. *Advances in the sociology of language.* 3 vols. The Hague: Mouton.

Gumperz, J. J., & Hymes, D. (eds.) 1972. *Directions in sociolinguistics: The ethnography of communication.* New York: Holt, Rinehart, and Winston.

Hymes, D. 1974. *Foundations in sociolinguistics: An ethnographic approach.* Philadelphia: University of Pennsylvania Press.

Labov, W. 1963. The social motivation of a sound change. *Word* 19: 273–309.

Labov, W. 1966. *The social stratification of English in New York City.* Washington, DC: Center for Applied Linguistics.

Labov, W. 1972a. *Language in the inner city: Studies in the Black English vernacular.* Philadelphia: University of Pennsylvania Press.

Labov, W. 1972b. *Sociolinguistic patterns.* Philadelphia: University of Pennsylvania Press.

Mendoza-Denton, N. 2008. *Homegirls: Language and cultural practice among Latina youth gangs.* Oxford: Blackwell.

Mesthrie, R. (ed.). 2011. *The Cambridge handbook of sociolinguistics.* Cambridge: Cambridge University Press.

Nagy, N., & Meyerhoff, M. 2008. Introduction: Social lives in language. In M. Meyerhoff & N. Nagy (eds.), *Social lives in language—sociolinguistics and multilingual speech communities: Celebrating the work of Gillian Sankoff*, 1–16. Amsterdam: John Benjamins.

Quinto-Pozos, D. 2009. Code-switching between sign languages. In B. Bullock & J. Toribio (eds.), *The handbook of code-switching*, 221–37. Cambridge: Cambridge University Press.

Zhang, Q. 2005. A Chinese yuppie in Beijing: Phonological variation and the construction of a new professional identity. *Language in Society* 32: 431–66.

PART I

DISCIPLINARY PERSPECTIVES

CHAPTER 1

VARIATIONIST SOCIOLINGUISTICS

ROBERT BAYLEY

SOCIOLINGUISTIC studies of language variation and change in the modern tradition originated in research conducted by William Labov on Martha's Vineyard and in New York City and Philadelphia in the 1960s and 1970s (Labov 1963, 1966, 1969, 1972a, 1972b), as well as in similar work carried out in Detroit by Shuy, Wolfram, and Riley (1968) and Wolfram (1969). This approach to the study of language was subsequently extended to many communities around the world, including Panama City (Cedergren 1973); Norwich, England (Trudgill 1974); Anniston, Alabama (Feagin 1979); and Cane Walk, Guyana (Rickford 1987), to name just a few. The central ideas of this approach are that an understanding of language requires an understanding of variable as well as categorical processes and that the variation we witness at all levels of language is not random. Rather, linguistic variation is characterized by orderly or "structured heterogeneity" (Weinreich, Labov, & Herzog 1968: 99–100). That is, speakers' choices among variable linguistic forms are systematically constrained by multiple linguistic and social factors that reflect underlying grammatical systems and that both reflect and partially constitute the social organization of the communities to which users of the language belong. In addition, synchronic variation is often a reflection of diachronic change (Labov 1994). Indeed, a period when receding and incoming forms vary is a necessary precursor to language change.

This chapter reviews representative studies and outlines the main assumptions underlying the variationist approach. After this initial review, the chapter provides an example of variationist analysis, using the well-known case of variation between Spanish null and overt subject personal pronouns, a variable that has received increasing attention in recent years because it is relevant to a number of theoretical issues and because it figures prominently in studies of Spanish dialect contact in North America. The chapter then considers a number of relatively recent developments in variationist sociolinguistics, including the expansion of the variationist paradigm into new areas such as second language acquisition and sign linguistics as well as recent work that combines ethnographic observation and quantitative analysis.

Foundational Studies

A number of early studies, including Gauchat's (1905) work on linguistic change in the Swiss village of Charmey and Fischer's (1958) study of gender and the (ing) variable among New England school children might be regarded as sociolinguistic. However, most researchers in the field date the modern study of language variation from Labov's (1963, /1972b) study of vowel change on Martha's Vineyard. Labov examined the centralization of /ay/ and /aw/ and found a higher incidence of centralization among younger speakers. However, the change was not uniform among speakers within the different age cohorts. Rather, through careful ethnographic work, Labov found that speakers' orientation to traditional life on Martha's Vineyard corresponded strongly with the degree of centralization. Speakers who identified as Vineyarders, as opposed to the people from the mainland who came during the summer, exhibited a very high degree of centralization.

Labov's Martha's Vineyard study is important for a number of reasons. In particular, it shows that it is possible to study linguistic change using the construct of *apparent time* (Bailey 2002). That is, we can illustrate the direction of language change by examining speakers of different generations. Typically, younger speakers will exhibit more frequent use of an incoming form than their elders, although in Labov's study, speakers under 30 were an exception to the general trend. Labov's study is also important in that it illustrates the limitations of the predetermined social categories sometimes found in other studies of sociolinguistic variation. Speakers' use of traditional Vineyard forms was associated with their orientation toward the traditional way of life on the island rather than only by predefined social categories.

Labov (1963) was soon followed by a number of large-scale studies carried out in urban environments, including Labov's study of the Lower East Side of Manhattan (1966, 2006) and his work in Harlem (1969, 1972a), Wolfram's (1969) study of African American English, and Trudgill's study of Norwich (1974).

In his study of the Lower East Side, Labov (1966) employed many of the concepts, procedures, and methods that were to become standard in later studies.

These include the idea of the sociolinguistic variable, or "two ways of saying the same thing" (e.g., *workin'/working*), and the sociolinguistic interview, a set of procedures designed to elicit (relatively) unmonitored speech by positioning the interviewer in a "one down" position and focusing on topics of interest to the interviewee. The sociolinguistic interview normally also includes a reading passage, a word list, and a set of minimal pairs, tasks designed to elicit different degrees of attention to speech and hence style shifting (see Labov 1984 for a detailed discussion of methods).

Labov examined five different variables from a random sample of Lower East Side residents representing a range of social classes: the final and preconsonantal /r/ in words like *car* or *card*; (aeh), the height of the vowel in words like *bad* and *ask*; (oh), the low-back rounded vowel in *caught* and *talk*; and (th) and (dh), the initial consonants of *thing* and *then*, respectively (2006: 33–36). Space does not permit a full discussion of all five variables; however, the results for (r), shown in table 1.1, illustrate the clear patterning by style and social class. Note that a higher number indicates greater use of /r/.

As presented in table 1.1, the results for (r) appear to divide New Yorkers into three clearly distinct groups. However, as Labov shows in a more detailed analysis, the stratification is much more fine-grained than it initially appears. Figure 1.1, which is perhaps the best-known graph in sociolinguistics, illustrates (r) indices by six social classes and five styles, differentiated according to the amount of attention paid to speech. All speakers move in the same direction, although lower-middle-class speakers overshoot the mark once they move beyond connected speech and focus only on pronunciation in the word lists and minimal pairs.

Results such as those shown in table 1.1 and figure 1.1 served to illustrate the orderly nature of linguistic variation, and, as previously noted, similar results were found in many other cities. Table 1.2, from Wolfram (1969), illustrates the use of negative concord, or multiple negation, by men and women belonging to four social classes in Detroit's African American community. The results

Table 1.1. (r) Indices by social class and style in New York City

	Class		
Style	Lower (0–2)	Working (3–6)	Middle (6–9)
Casual speech	2.5	4.0	12.5
Careful speech	10.5	12.5	25.0
Reading passage	14.5	21.0	29.0
Word list	23.5	35.0	55.5
Minimal pairs	49.5	55.0	70.0

Source: Labov (2006: 140)

Note: A higher number indicates more frequent use of (r).

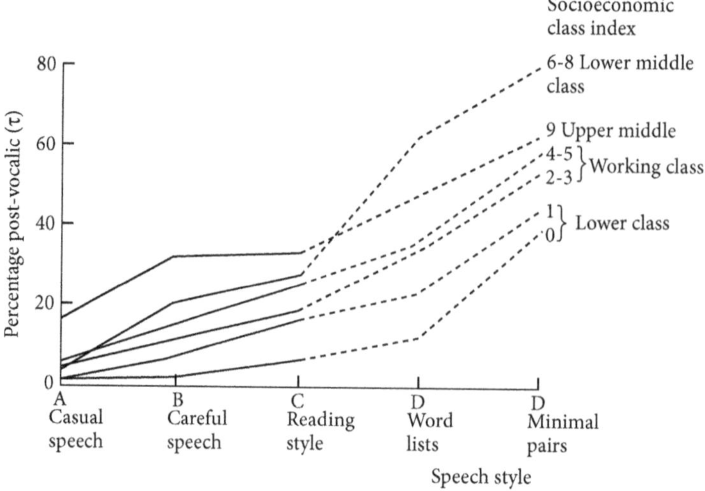

Figure 1.1. The social stratification of (r) in New York City.

Source: Labov (2006: 152)

are interesting for several reasons. First, like Labov's results in New York City, Wolfram's results illustrate the orderly nature of linguistic variation. Second, the Detroit negative concord results illustrate a sociolinguistic generalization: in general, women use fewer stigmatized variants than men of the same social class. Third, it is perhaps not coincidental that the results for women are closer to the results for men in the next-higher social class than the results for men in their own social class.

The examples so far have illustrated the effects of social, or external, constraints—social class, style, and gender—on patterns of variation. However, sociolinguistic variables are also subject to linguistic, or internal, constraints. Table 1.3, from Wolfram and Fasold (1974), summarizes the effect of two linguistic constraints on consonant cluster reduction (CCR), or *-t/d* deletion, in the speech of African Americans in Detroit.

As the data in table 1.3 show, CCR is constrained by the features of the following segment (consonant or vowel) as well as by morphological class. CCR is most likely when the cluster is part of a monomorpheme and followed by a consonant, and least likely when the cluster is a past-tense morpheme and followed by a vowel.

Table 1.2. Negative concord in Detroit African American Vernacular English (AAVE) by gender and social class (percentages)

Sex	Upper Middle	Lower Middle	Upper Working	Lower Working
Male	10.4	22.3	68.2	81.3
Female	6.0	2.4	41.2	74.3

Source: Wolfram (1969: 162).

Table 1.3. -t/d deletion in Detroit African American English (percentages)

	Social Class			
Environment	Upper Middle	Lower Middle	Upper Working	Lower Working
Following vowel				
-t/d is past morpheme (e.g., "missed in")	7	13	24	34
-t/,d is not past morpheme (e.g., "mist in")	28	43	65	72
Following consonant				
-t/d is past morpheme (e.g., "missed by")	49	62	73	76
-t,d is not past morpheme (e.g., "mist by")	79	87	94	97

Source: Wolfram and Fasold (1974: 132)

The systematic conditioning illustrated in table 1.3 has been found for many variables in languages throughout the world and, with the application of more rigorous statistical methods, beginning with but not limited to logistic regression as implemented in the successive versions of the VARBRUL computer program (Bayley 2002; Rousseau & Sankoff 1978), researchers have pursued ever-more fine-grained methods of analysis, including, for example, estimations of the effects of the individual word and the individual speaker (see Gorman & Johnson, chapter 11, this volume). Space does not permit a full treatment of the history of variationist studies (but see Hazen 2007). Indeed, variables such as CCR have been studied in numerous communities throughout the English-speaking world, including, to name just a few, African Americans in New York City (Labov, Cohen, Robins, & Lewis 1968), white Philadelphians and New Yorkers (Guy 1980), Jamaican mesolectal speakers (Patrick 1991), preschool children in Philadelphia (Roberts 1997), Mexican Americans in California and Texas (Bayley 1994; Santa Ana 1992, 1996), and a cross-section of the community in York, England (Tagliamonte & Temple 2006). Studies have revealed a number of differences in the effects of linguistic constraints such as the effect of a following pause in New York and Philadelphia (Guy 1980) or the effect of irregular verbs such as *leave/left* or *tell/told* (Bayley 1994; Guy & Boyd 1990) among Mexican Americans in Texas and children and adolescents in Philadelphia. The main constraints, however, such as those shown in table 1.3, are remarkably consistent across native English dialects, so that CCR is nearly always inhibited when the *-t/d* is a past-tense morpheme or in the environment of a following vowel.

The chapter now turns to a review of the analytical methods scholars have used to uncover the patterns described in the foundational studies.

Variationist Analysis: The Case of Null Pronoun Variation in Spanish

The alternation of Spanish null and overt subject personal pronouns (SPPs) provides a convenient example of how variationists approach linguistic data. In Spanish, a subject pronoun may be realized as overt or null, as shown in examples 1 to 3 taken from Bayley et al. (2012: 49):

(1) Entonces cuando YO/Ø llegué a Panamá, YO/Ø llegué a Panamá en el 87....
'Then when I arrived in Panama, (I) arrived in Panama in 87 [...]'

(2) YO/Ø he vivido en muchas partes....Y como adulto YO/Ø he trabajado mucho con mexicanos.
'I've lived in a lot of places [...] And as an adult I've worked a lot with Mexicans.'

(3) Sí NOSOTROS/Ø hemos platicado de eso y NOSOTROS/Ø queremos que aquí en casa sea el español.
'Yes, we've spoken about this and we want Spanish to be the language of the home.'

Over the past 30 years, the variation illustrated above has been studied in numerous dialects, including those spoken in Caracas, northern and southern California, Madrid, New Jersey, New York, New Mexico, San Juan, Texas, and Puente Genil, Andalucia (see, e.g., Avila-Shah 2000; Bayley & Pease-Alvarez 1996, 1997; Bentivoglio 1987; Cameron 1992, 1993, 1996; Cameron & Flores-Ferrán 2004; Flores-Ferrán 2004, 2007a, 2007b; Hochberg 1986; Otheguy & Zentella 2012; Otheguy, Zentella, & Livert 2007; Ranson 1991; Silva-Corvalán 1994, 1996–97; Travis 2007). SPP variation has aroused intensive interest in sociolinguistics as well as in formal linguistics for a variety of reasons. First, SPP variation marks a clear distinction between Spanish dialects. Spanish varieties spoken in Madrid, most of Mexico, and the Andean region tend to have relatively low rates of overt SPP use. Dialects spoken in the Caribbean, coastal areas of Colombia and Venezuela, and eastern Bolivia tend to use overt SPPs at a higher rate. Thus, SPP variation presents a convenient locus for studying the degree to which different dialects spoken by immigrants to North America are converging or maintaining their linguistic distinctiveness (Otheguy et al. 2007; Bayley et al. 2012).

In addition, SPP variation provides a means to test the influence of functionalism on linguistic variation. Spanish dialects that exhibit relatively high rates of overt SPP use also exhibit high rates of /s/-deletion, which has the effect of neutralizing the distinction between the second-person informal and third-person forms of the verb in most tenses as well as the distinction between all singular forms in some tenses. Thus, following /s/-deletion, *hablas* (you-informal talk) is reduced to *habla/Ø/* and becomes indistinguishable from *habla* (he/she/you-formal talk), while the loss of final /s/ from *hablabas* (you used to talk) results in three-way ambiguity, for example, *hablaba* (I/you-informal/he/she/you-formal used to talk). The study of SPP variation has also contributed to the definition of the envelope of variation, or what variants count as different ways of saying the same thing (Labov 1972b). Finally, like most sociolinguistic variables, SPP variation has been shown to be subject to multiple constraints. Constraints that have proven to be significant in one or more studies are shown in table 1.4.

Table 1.4. Constraints on variable subject personal pronoun expression in Spanish

Constraint	Studies
Switch reference, i.e., a change in subject from the subject of the preceding tensed verb	Bayley & Pease-Alvarez (1996); Cameron (1992, 1995); Flores-Ferrán (2004); Otheguy et al. (2007); Otheguy & Zentella (2012); Silva-Corvalán (1994); Travis (2007).
Discourse connectedness, i.e., continuity of subject, tense, and mood from the preceding tensed verb	Avila-Shah (2000); Bayley & Pease-Alvarez (1997)
Reference chains	Cameron (1992); Travis (2007)
Person/number	Bayley & Pease-Alvarez (1996); Cameron (1992); Cameron & Flores-Ferrán (2004); Flores-Ferrán (2004); Otheguy et al. (2007); Silva-Corvalán (1994)
Semantic features of the verb	Silva-Corvalán (1994); Ranson (1991); Travis (2007)
Tense-mood-aspect	Bayley & Pease-Alvarez (1997); Silva-Corvalán (1996–97)
Potential ambiguity of the verb form	Bayley & Pease-Alvarez (1996); Hochberg (1986)
Genre	Solomon (1999); Travis (2007)
Region	Cameron (1992); Otheguy et al. (2007); Travis (2007)
Length of residence in the United States	Otheguy et al. (2007; but see Bayley & Pease-Alvarez 1996; Flores-Ferrán 2004).
Age	Shin (2010)
Social network	Bayley et al. (2012)

Note: Studies are intended as examples only, not as a comprehensive list.

The multiplicity of possible influences on speakers' choices between an overt and a null SPP illustrates one of the main problems of variationist analysis. That is, with multiple possible constraints, how do we sort out which are significant and what their effects are? Traditionally, sociolinguists have relied upon VARBRUL, a specialized application of the multivariate statistical procedure of logistic regression (Cedergren & Sankoff 1974; Rousseau & Sankoff 1978). VARBRUL enables the researcher to model the many factors that may potentially influence a speaker's choice of one or another variant. Table 1.5, from Bayley and Pease-Alvarez (1997), illustrates the results of a VARBRUL analysis. Factors with weights (sometimes loosely called *probabilities*) between .50 and 1.0 are said to favor the choice of a variant that the researcher has defined as the *application value*, in this case an overt pronoun. Factor weights between 0 and .50 disfavor the use of the application value. Note, however, that the weights must be interpreted in relationship to the overall input value, or corrected mean, that is, the likelihood that a speaker will choose the application value regardless of the presence or absence of any other factor in the environment.

The results in table 1.5 point to a number of conclusions. First, as has been shown in other studies, plural verbs are much less likely to have overt SPPs than singular verbs. Second, Bayley and Pease-Alvarez (1997) argue that the results for discourse connectedness provide a much more fine-grained picture than the usual dichotomous variable of continuity or switch in reference. Also, the results suggest that speakers with greater contact with English are not moving in the direction of greater overt SPP use, the option that is congruent with the dominant language.

Although VARBRUL has been an extremely useful tool in sociolinguistic analysis, it is not the only tool available for multivariate analysis or always the most appropriate tool. In fact, VARBRUL does have a number of limitations. First, the dependent variable is limited to two values. In the case of SPP variation, this is not a problem because a pronoun is either overt or it is null. However, a number of sociolinguistic variables, such as relative pronouns in English or the ASL sign DEAF, have three or more possible variants (Bayley, Lucas, & Rose 2000; Guy & Bayley 1995). Although it is possible to use VARBRUL to analyze such cases, particularly if we can postulate rule ordering in the derivation, it is not convenient. Second, VARBRUL only handles categorical variables. Although, as Guy (2010) points out, many of the variables that linguists are interested in are indeed categorical (e.g., a following segment is either a consonant or a vowel), this is not true of all variables of interest (e.g., formant frequencies, language proficiency scores) and certainly not true of many social factors of interest (see Gorman & Johnson, chapter 11, this volume; Johnson 2009). Finally, VARBRUL is unfamiliar to most scholars outside sociolinguistics. For these reasons, many sociolinguists have adopted Rbrul (Johnson 2009), which is based on the open source program R. Unlike VARBRUL, Rbrul allows the researcher to model both continuous and random variables as well as the categorical variables typically found in variationist analysis. A number of scholars have also turned to the

Table 1.5. Subject personal pronoun variation in Mexican-descent children

Factor group	Factor	% Overt Pronoun	Weight
Person/number	1 pl.	9	.244
	3 pl.	20	.433
	3 sg.	25	.576
	1 sg.	37	.691
Discourse	First degree: continuity of subject, tense, and aspect	12	.293
connectedness	Second degree: continuity of subject, different tense or mood	20	.405
	Third degree: subject continuity interrupted by one or more intervening clauses	21	.490
	Fourth degree: last occurrence of subject in another syntactic function	35	.607
	Fifth degree: change in narrative section or discourse topic	32	.653
Verb type	Preterit	21	.485
	Present	19	.357
	Imperfect, conditional, or subjunctive	31	.575
Immigrant group	Born in Mexico	25	.499
	Born in the US, mother immigrated at age 15 or older	27	.568
	Born in the US: mother immigrated at age 10 or younger or mother born in the US	16	.418
Gender	Male	20	.422
	Female	28	.572
Total/input		24	.198

Note: n = 1549; chi-square/cell = 0.9064; all factor groups significant at $p < .05$.

logistic regression modules now included as part of general statistical programs, such as the Statistical Package for the Social Sciences (SPSS) or R.

Otheguy et al. (2007), for example, used the logistic regression procedure in SPSS to analyze the data from their large-scale study of SPP variation in New York City Spanish. Table 1.6 illustrates the results for the newcomers for person and number. Caribbean newcomers include speakers from Cuba, the Dominican Republic, and Puerto Rico. Mainland newcomers include speakers from Colombia, Ecuador, and Mexico.

Note that the results for person and number in table 1.6 come from a run that included a large number of other independent variables. In interpreting the results, an Exp(B) greater than 1.0 indicates that the application value, in this case an overt SPP, is favored in that environment, while an Exp(B) value of less than 1.0 disfavors the use of an overt SPP. As table 1.6 shows, the two groups differ markedly in the effect of the individual factors within the person/number group, particularly in the effect of second-person *tú*, whether specific or nonspecific.

A full review of the considerable work that has been accomplished on SPP variation, including the large-scale studies of Otheguy and Zentella (2012; Otheguy et al. 2007), is beyond the scope of this chapter (but see Flores-Ferrán 2007a). However, as illustrated in table 1.4 and in the results shown in tables 1.5 and 1.6, the analysis of sociolinguistic variation requires the multivariate analysis of substantial amounts of real data, usually collected in the form of sociolinguistic interviews, from a reasonable cross-section of the community under study. Through the use of such methods, Otheguy et al. (2007), for example, were able to demonstrate in fine detail the clear differences between the Latin American dialects that immigrants brought to New York and to show the effects of contact with English and, to a certain extent, dialect accommodation, in the Spanish of Latinos who were born in New York City. Using similar methods,

Table 1.6. Hierarchies of constraints within the person variable: newcomers

Caribbean newcomers			Mainland newcomers		
	N verbs	Exp (B)		N verbs	Exp (B)
2 sg. specific	716	3.22**	3 sg.	1668	3.21**
2 sg. nonspecific	414	3.13**	1 sg.	3,907	1.98*
3 sg.	1,395	1.09	2 sg. specific	279	1.19
1 sg.	4,458	1.04	2 sg. nonspecific	485	0.61**
3 pl.	1,045	0.30**	3 pl.	1,117	0.58**
1 pl.	555	0.29**	1 pl.	699	0.37**
N verbs = 8583; N speakers = 19			N verbs = 8155; N speakers = 20		

Source: Otheguy et al. (2007: 790).

Notes: Newcomers: Age of arrival > 16; years in New York City < 6.

* p <.05, ** p <.01

Cameron (1996) was able to address the important theoretical question of functional compensation for variable /s/-deletion as an explanation for the relatively high rate of overt SPP use in Caribbean Spanish. In a comparison of the varieties of Spanish spoken in San Juan, Puerto Rico, and Madrid, Cameron used multivariate analysis to show that the difference in rates of overt SPP variation could be explained by the way the two dialects treated specific and nonspecific *tú* rather than by functional compensation, as had previously been proposed by Hochberg (1986) among others.

Studies such as Bayley and Pease-Alvarez (1997), Cameron (1996), and Otheguy et al. (2007) not only highlight the methodological and statistical procedures typical of variationist work, they also illustrate how variationist sociolinguistics can contribute to our understanding of language structure and dialect contact and provide methods to test hypotheses about how language works.

Extending the Variationist Paradigm

Although a fairly small number of sociolinguistic variables, such as English CCR and alveolarization of /ŋ/, the African American English copula, the alternation between overt and null SPPs in Spanish, /s/ aspiration and deletion in Spanish, and *ne* deletion in French, have been examined in a large number of articles, variationist work has extended well beyond a limited set of variables, as a number of the chapters in this volume indicate. The variationist paradigm has been extended to examine a wide range of creole languages (Patrick 1999; Rickford 1987; see also Russell Webb, chapter 15, this volume). Beginning with Dickerson's (1975) study of variation in the pronunciation of /z/ by Japanese learners of English and continuing with work by Adamson (1988), Tarone (1988), and many others, researchers have applied the insights from the variationist paradigm to the process of second language acquisition (for reviews, see Bayley & Tarone 2012; see also Howard, Mougeon, & Dewaele, chapter 17, this volume; and Preston & Bayley 2009). As Howard et al. have shown in chapter 17, studies of learners of many target languages have demonstrated that variation in learner speech, like variation in native speech, is highly systematic and unlikely to be explained by a single cause. Sign languages constitute a third area where variationist approaches have yielded fruitful results. To date, major studies have been carried out or are underway on American Sign Language (ASL), Australian Sign Language, British Sign Language, Italian Sign Language, and New Zealand Sign Language (for reviews, see Lucas & Bayley 2010, 2011; see also Schembri & Johnston, chapter 25, this volume).

The extension of the theories and methods of variationist sociolinguistics has not been limited to new contexts or additional types of languages, such as sign languages. Rather, recent studies have sought to combine ethnographic and variationist methods. Eckert (2005) outlines what she refers to as the "three waves of sociolinguistics." The first wave, typified by Labov's (1966) study of New York's Lower East Side, consisted of surveys that aimed to provide a big picture of a range of variables across a large population. Social class was determined by indices based on objective categories such as occupation, education, and income. Beginning in the 1970s with the Philadelphia neighborhood study, residence value was also considered (Labov 2001). Eckert summarizes the characteristics of the first-wave studies as follows:

> These studies established a regular and replicable pattern of socioeconomic stratification of variables, in which the use of non-standard, and geographically and ethnically distinctive variants, correlates inversely with socioeconomic status. These studies also showed a regular stylistic stratification of variables at all levels in the socioeconomic hierarchy, with the use of non-standard and distinctively regional variants correlating inversely with formality of style. (2005: 2)

Despite the very important contributions of the early surveys, as Eckert notes, these studies do have a number of limitations. First, because the broad coverage and replicability of the early surveys depend upon the use of predetermined social categories and relatively brief contact with a large sample of speakers, "the social significance of variation can only be surmised on the basis of the categories that serve to select and classify speakers" (Eckert 2005: 3). Second, as Eckert notes, the idea that language change proceeds smoothly across the generations has been challenged. Rather, as D'Arcy shows in chapter 24 of this volume, speakers' rate of change tends to peak in adolescence. Third, the early studies treated gender as a binary variable. Such treatment limited the understanding of gendered speech and particularly of the role of gender in language change.

In recent years, scholars have increasingly turned to more ethnographically oriented studies of language variation, and, as Eckert observes, this impulse, which she defines as the "second wave," is not new but can be seen as a return to the earliest roots of the field. As noted in the introductory section of this chapter, Labov (1963), in his study of language change on Martha's Vineyard, found that locally salient categories provided a better explanation of variation in /ay/ and /aw/ than standard social-class descriptors. Other studies that use social categories and analysis drawn from ethnographic observation include Rickford's (1987) work in Guyana; Milroy's (1980) work in Belfast, which introduced and elaborated the idea of social networks; Eckert's (2000) study of adolescents in the suburban Detroit area; and Slomanson and Newman's (2004) study of New York Latino English.

In different ways, these studies showed that the types of indices used to group people into social classes did not capture all the social facts needed to understand the relationship between social structure and linguistic change. Rickford (1986), for example, showed that a consensus model, such as that proposed by Labov (1972b), did not fully explain the variation in the speech of Cane Walk, Guyana, where workers on the sugar plantations espoused a conflictual model. Milroy (1980) and Milroy and Milroy (1992) showed how dense, relatively closed social networks with strong community-based ties tend to maintain non-legitimized linguistic codes, a result of the norm-enforcing power of the network. On the other hand, networks consisting of relatively affluent wage earners with weak community-based ties tend to accept the dominance of legitimized linguistic codes "without hindrance from…alternative vernacular markets" (Milroy & Milroy 1992: 22). Milroy and Milroy further argue that Højrup's (1983) concept of life-modes provides a means to link the influence of the networks observed in their work in Belfast with larger social structures. Life-mode 1 is characteristic of the self-employed, typically "a close-knit family-centered network with little distinction between work and leisure activities and a strong solidarity ideology" (Milroy & Milroy 1992: 19). Life-mode 2 is characteristic of the ordinary wage earner who participates in a complex process of production. Importantly, families are separate from work activities and make up the sphere within which leisure activities occur. Milroy and Milroy observe that the working-class solidarity characteristic of many participants in life-mode 2 is embodied "in the close-knit networks of the traditional working-class society…investigated in Belfast" (20). Finally, in contrast to the working-class wage earners of life-mode 2, life-mode 3 wage earners are professional or managerial employees with high levels of skill. According to Milroy and Milroy, life-mode 3 professionals will form many loose ties, particularly professional ties, "through which innovation may be transmitted" (21). Thus, like Rickford's discussion of social class in Cane Walk, the model proposed by Milroy and Milroy (1992), in contrast to Labov's consensus model, emphasizes conflicts "symbolized by opposing linguistic norms" (23).

Eckert's (2000) own work with adolescents in the Detroit, Michigan, area is one of the best-known recent studies to combine ethnographic analysis and variationist methods. Eckert spent two years engaged in fieldwork at a high school. During the first year, she went virtually every day, while in the second year her visits were more occasional. Because her focus was on adolescent social structure and its relationship to linguistic variation, specifically the Northern Cities vowel shift, she avoided the classroom, the location of most school-based studies. Instead, she spent time in hallways, the cafeteria, and other nonacademic settings in order to avoid being identified in any way with the institution of the school.

Eckert's (2000) study is particularly innovative with respect to social class because she looks at class from the perspective of the adolescent participants and identifies two main groups—*jocks* and *burnouts*—that roughly correspond to middle-class and working-class families. The jocks center their social lives around the school and seldom venture into Detroit. They intend to leave the area for college after finishing high school. The burnouts, in contrast, are focused on the urban scene and have no plans to leave the area after they finish school. The fact that these two groups define the social scene of the school is evident in the fact that a great many of the students define themselves as *in-betweens*, that is, in between the jocks and the burnouts, partaking in some characteristics of each group. Finally, although the social groupings of jocks and burnouts generally follow their fathers' socioeconomic status, the correlation is by no means absolute. Some jocks come from working-class families, while some burnouts come from middle-class families. Importantly, the burnouts are much more advanced in the Northern Cities shift than the jocks, who adhere to a more conservative linguistic norm.

Recent work on US Latinos has also moved beyond ascribed categories of ethnicity and used identity categories that participants find salient to analyze patterns of variation. Slomanson and Newman (2004), for example, examined peer group identification and variation in New York Latino English. Based on extensive ethnographic work in a public high school, they identified three distinct groups of Latino male youth, all of whom had been born in the city or had moved to the United States before starting school. Slomanson and Newman (2004: 202–203) summarize the groups' characteristics as follows:

- Hip-Hop: associated with rap music, graffiti art, and dj-ing...as well as urban styles;
- Skater/Bicycle Moto-Cross: associated with performing tracks using skateboards and special small bicycles;
- Geek: associated with intensive computer gaming, technological sophistication, and sometimes hacking.

Slomanson and Newman also considered students they refer to as "family-oriented," characterized by active bilingualism, pride in national heritage and family, and use of accessories, such as beads in Colombian national colors or Dominican flag pendants. The active bilingualism of the family-oriented students contrasted sharply with the language practices of the other three groups, all of whose members were dominant or exclusive users of English (205–206).

Slomanson and Newman (2004) found that affiliation with a peer group culture that is associated with European American or African American orientations correlated with greater use of European American or African American vowel realizations. However, their data on lateral onsets demonstrated a "robust feature of East Coast Latino English that is traceable to contact with Spanish" (214). Although light onsets were found in the speech of all the Latino English speakers studied, they were most common among the members of the family-oriented group, who had more contact with Spanish than members of other groups. Thus, although, traditionally, the speakers in Slomanson and Newman's study might all be classified as members of the same demographic category—young, male, Latino New Yorkers—it is clear that they engage in very different types of social interactions and have different orientations to other groups in New York. Although it is possible to identify a feature that can be traced to a Spanish substrate, it is clear that the social groupings and activities that groups of youth engage in have consequences for our understanding of linguistic variation, understanding that would remain elusive if the authors had only considered traditional demographic categories.

A number of recent studies, such as Zhang's (2005) study of Chinese yuppies and Mendoza-Denton's (2008) study of Latina gangs, which Eckert (2005) identifies as typifying the "Third Wave" in sociolinguistic variation, have employed a community of practice approach (Lave & Wenger 1991; Wenger 1998). Eckert defines community of practices as follows:

> A community of practice is an aggregate of people who come together on a regular basis to engage in some enterprise.... In the course of their engagement, the community of practice develops ways of doing things—practices. And these practices involve the construction of a shared orientation to the world around them—a tacit definition of themselves in relation to each other, and in relation to other communities of practice.... The individual... is tied into the social matrix through structured forms of engagement. (2005: 16)

Crucially, for studies of linguistic variation, use of particular variants is only one of the practices through which individuals construct an identity. For example, the New York Latino hip-hop group identified by Slomanson and Newman (2004) may be viewed as a community of practice, and their use of vowel variants associated with African American English is one the resources they use, along with styles of dress and participation in particular types of events, to create social meaning. A similar process is at work in Zhang's (2005) study of Beijing yuppies. Zhang contrasts the linguistic and other practices of young Beijing professionals who work for foreign firms with those of their counterparts who work for state-owned enterprises. She notes that the Chinese term for 'yuppies,' *yapíshì*, now connotes "global orientation, trendiness, and sophistication" (436), and that, in contrast to professionals who work in state-owned enterprises, those who work in foreign firms have adopted features of international Mandarin and exhibit less use of Beijing features. For example, professionals who work for foreign firms exhibit less rhotasization of the syllable final, a marker of Beijing speech (e.g., *zhè/zhèr*, 'here') than workers in state enterprises. They are also more likely to realize a neutral tone as a full tone in a weakly stressed syllable (e.g., *míngbai/míngbái*, 'understand'), a feature that is "stereotypically associated with pop stars and business people" (Zhang 2005: 444). Thus, along with styles of dress, use of imported consumer goods, and other lifestyle choices, for the new professionals Zhang studied, the deployment of variable linguistic forms that distinguish them from other Beijingers and even from other speakers of modern standard Mandarin is one among many practices by which they create a new identity.

Similar associations of linguistic variables—and the choice to use English or Spanish—can be seen in the very different world described by Mendoza-Denton (2008) in her study of Latina gang members in a Northern California high school. The two groups Mendoza-Denton focused on, the *norteñas* and *sureñas*, not only exhibit different patterns of language use, but, as the summary in table 1.7 illustrates, they differ in tastes in music and in a range of symbolic resources, including colors, hair styles, and even lipstick colors. Although both groups of girls would be grouped in the same traditional demographic category, Mendoza-Denton, on the basis of extensive ethnographic fieldwork, has shown clearly that the linguistic differences they exhibit are but one means by which they construct distinct styles and identities.

A great deal of recent work in sociolinguistics, like Eckert (2000), Mendoza-Denton (2008), and Zhang (2005), has focused on relatively small groups and combined the rigorous methods of quantitative analysis developed by Labov and others with intensive ethnographic observation and participant observation. However, as Eckert (2005) observed, the waves she describes do not represent a chronological progression but rather a question of emphasis. And, in recent years, a number of studies have appeared that provide the broad outlines of one or more variable features in a large population. Chief among these, of course, is Labov, Ash, and Boberg (2006), which provides an overall picture of the divergent vowel systems in North American English varieties. Moreover, the results of Labov et al. have been confirmed in intensive studies that focus more narrowly on particular areas, for example, Baranowski's (2007) detailed study of Charleston, South Carolina.

Conclusion

Research in the variationist tradition has enabled us to obtain numerous insights into linguistic structure, the social meaning of linguistic variation, and the nature of language change. From a social perspective, variationist sociolinguistics has

Table 1.7. Indexical markers: endpoints on the continua of *norteña* and *sureña* identity

Name	Norteñas	Sureñas
Color	Red, burgundy	Blue, navy
Language	English	Spanish
Numbers	XIV, 14, 4	XIII, 13, 3
Music	Motown oldies	Banda music
Hairdo	Feathered hair	Vertical ponytail
Makeup	Deep-red lipstick	Brown lipstick
Place	Northern hemisphere	Southern hemisphere

Source: Mendoza-Denton (2008: 59)

been particularly important in demonstrating the systematic nature of stigmatized language varieties, including African American Vernacular English (AAVE), Montreal French, popular Puerto Rican, and US Spanish, as well as many others. Current variationist work, in which quantitative analysis is informed by ethnographic fieldwork, promises further insights into the ways in which language users employ variation to construct social identities and the dynamic nature of language change. Finally, the increased interest in bi- and multilingual communities, evident in the work of many of the contributors to this volume, promises additional insights into the language capacities of the majority of the world's population who use more than one language on a daily basis.

References

Adamson, H. D. 1988. *Variation theory and second language acquisition*. Washington, DC: Georgetown University Press.

Avila-Shah, B. 2000. Discourse connectedness in Caribbean Spanish. In A. Roca (ed.), *Research on Spanish in the United States*, 238–51. Somerville, MA: Cascadilla Press.

Bailey, G. 2002. Apparent time. In J. K. Chambers, P. Trudgill, & N. Schilling-Estes (eds.), *The handbook of language variation and change*, 312–42 Oxford: Blackwell.

Baranowski, M. 2007. *Phonological variation and change in the dialect of Charleston, South Carolina*. Publication of the American Dialect Society 92. Durham, NC: Duke University Press.

Bayley, R. 1994. Consonant cluster reduction in Tejano English. *Language Variation and Change* 6: 303–26.

Bayley, R. 2002. The quantitative paradigm. In J. K. Chambers, P. Trudgill, & N. Schilling-Estes (eds.), *The handbook of language variation and change*, 117–41. Oxford: Blackwell.

Bayley, R., Cárdenas, N. L., Schouten, B., T. & Vélez Salas, C. M. (2012). Spanish dialect contact in San Antonio, Texas: An exploratory study. In K. L. Geeslin & M. Díaz-Campos (eds.), *Selected proceedings of the 14th Hispanic Linguistics Symposium*, 48-60. Somerville, MA: Cascadilla Proceedings Project.

Bayley, R., Lucas, C., & Rose, M. 2000. Variation in American Sign Language: The case of DEAF. *Journal of Sociolinguistics* 4: 81–107.

Bayley, R., & Pease-Alvarez, L. 1996. Null and expressed pronoun variation in Mexican-descent children's Spanish. In J. Arnold, R. Blake, B. Davidson, S. Schwenter, & J. Solomon (eds.), *Sociolinguistic variation: Data, theory, and analysis*, 85–99. Stanford, CA: Center for the Study of Language and Information.

Bayley, R., & Pease-Alvarez, L. 1997. Null pronoun variation in Mexican-descent children's narrative discourse. *Language Variation and Change* 9: 349–71.

Bayley, R., & Tarone, E. 2012. Variationist perspectives. In S. M. Gass & A. Mackey (eds.), *The Routledge handbook of second language acquisition*, 41–56. New York: Routledge.

Bentivoglio, P. 1987. *Los sujetos pronominales de primera persona en el habla de Caracas*. Caracas: Universidad Central de Venezuela, Consejo de Desarrollo Cientfíco y Humanístico.

Cameron, R. 1992. Pronominal and null subject variation in Spanish: Constraints, dialects, and functional compensation. Ph.D. dissertation, University of Pennsylvania.

Cameron, R. 1993. Ambiguous agreement, functional compensation, and nonspecific *tú* in the Spanish of San Juan, Puerto Rico, and Madrid, Spain. *Language Variation and Change* 5: 304–34.

Cameron, R. 1995. The scope and limits of switch reference as a constraint on pronominal subject expression. *Hispanic Linguistics* 6–7: 1–27.

Cameron, R. 1996. A community-based test of a linguistic hypothesis. *Language in Society* 25: 61–111.

Cameron, R., & Flores-Ferrán, N. 2004. Perservation of subject expression across regional dialects of Spanish. *Spanish in Context* 1: 41–65.

Cedergren, H. 1973. The interplay of social and linguistic factors in Panama. Ph.D. dissertation, Cornell University.

Cedergren, C., & Sankoff, D. 1974. Variable rules: Performance as a statistical reflection of competence. *Language* 50: 333–55.

Dickerson, L. J. 1975. The learner's interlanguage as a system of variable rules. *TESOL Quarterly* 9: 401–7.

Eckert, P. 2000. *Linguistic variation as social practice: The linguistic construction of identity in Belten High.* Oxford: Blackwell.

Eckert, P. 2005. Variation, convention, and social meaning. Paper presented at the Linguistic Society of America, Oakland, CA, January 5.

Feagin, C. 1979. *Variation and change in Alabama English: A sociolinguistic study of the white community.* Washington, DC: Georgetown University Press.

Fischer, J. L. 1958. Social influences on the choice of a linguistic variant. *Word* 14: 47–56.

Flores-Ferrán, N. 2004. Spanish subject personal pronoun use in New York City Puerto Ricans: Can we rest the case of English contact? *Language Variation and Change* 16: 49–73.

Flores-Ferrán, N. 2007a. A bend in the road: Subject personal pronoun expression in Spanish after thirty years of sociolinguistic research. *Language and Linguistics Compass* 1: 624–52.

Flores-Ferrán, N. 2007b. *Los mexicanos* in New Jersey: Pronominal expression and ethnolinguistic aspects. In J. Holmquist, A. Lorenzino, & L. Sayahi (eds.), *Selected proceedings of the third workshop on Spanish sociolinguistics*, 85–91. Somerville, MA: Cascadilla Proceedings Project.

Gauchat, L. 1905. L'unité phonétique dan le patois d'un commune. In *Aus romanischen sprachen un literaturen: Festschrift Heinrich Morf*, 175–232. Halle, Germany: Max Niemeyer Verlag.

Guy, G. R. 1980. Variation in the group and in the individual: The case of final stop deletion. In W. Labov (ed.), *Locating language in time and space*, 1–36. New York: Academic Press.

Guy, G. R. 2010. The variable rule model: The right tool for explaining linguistic variation…sometimes. Paper presented at NWAV 39, University of Texas, San Antonio.

Guy, G. R., & Bayley, R. 1995. On the choice of relative pronouns in English. *American Speech* 70: 148–62.

Guy, G. R., & Boyd, S. 1990. The development of a morphological class. *Language Variation and Change* 2: 1–18.

Hazen, K. 2007. The study of variation in historical perspective. In R. Bayley & C. Lucas (eds.), *Sociolinguistic variation: Theories, methods, and applications*, 70–89. Cambridge: Cambridge University Press.

Hochberg, J. G. 1986. Functional compensation for /s/ deletion in Puerto Rican Spanish. *Language* 62: 609–21.

Højrup, T. 1983. The concept of life-mode: A form-specifying mode of analysis applied to contemporary western Europe. *Ethnologia Scandinavica* 13: 1–50.

Johnson, D. E. 2009. Getting off the GoldVarb standard: Introducing Rbrul for mixed-effects variable rule analysis. *Language and Linguistics Compass* 3: 359–83.

Labov, W. 1963. The social motivation of a sound change. *Word* 19: 273–309.

Labov, W. 1966. *The social stratification of English in New York City*. Washington, DC: Center for Applied Linguistics.

Labov, W. 1969. Contraction, deletion, and inherent variability of the English copula. *Language* 45: 715–62.

Labov, W. 1972a. *Language in the inner city: Studies in the Black English vernacular*. Philadelphia: University of Pennsylvania Press.

Labov, W. 1972b. *Sociolinguistic patterns*. Philadelphia: University of Pennsylvania Press.

Labov, W. 1994. *Principles of linguistic change*. Vol. 1, *Internal factors*. Oxford: Blackwell.

Labov, W. 2006. *The social stratification of English in New York City*. 2nd ed. New York: Cambridge University Press.

Labov, W. Ash, S., & Boberg, C. 2006. *The atlas of North American English: Phonetics, phonology, and sound change*. Berlin: Mouton de Gruyter.

Labov, W., Cohen, P., Robins, C., & Lewis, J. 1968. *A study of the non-standard English of Negro and Puerto Rican speakers in New York City*. Final report, Cooperative Research Project 3288. Vols. 1 and 2.

Lave, J., & Wenger, E. 1991. *Situated learning: Legitimate peripheral participation*. Cambridge: Cambridge University Press.

Lucas, C., & Bayley, R. 2010. Variation in ASL. In D. Brentari (ed.), *Sign languages*, 451–75. Cambridge: Cambridge University Press.

Lucas, C., & Bayley, R. 2011. Variation in sign languages: Recent research on ASL and beyond. *Language and Linguistics Compass* 5: 677–90.

Mendoza-Denton, N. 2008. *Homegirls: Language and cultural practice among Latina youth gangs*. Oxford: Blackwell.

Milroy, L., & Milroy, J. 1992. Social network and social class: Toward an integrated sociolinguistic model. *Language in Society* 21: 1–26.

Milroy, L. 1980. *Language and social networks*. Oxford: Blackwell.

Otheguy, R., & Zentella, A. C. 2012. *Spanish in New York: Language contact, dialectal leveling, and structural continuity*. Oxford: Oxford University Press.

Otheguy, R., Zentella, A. C., & Livert, D. 2007. Language and dialect contact in Spanish in New York: Toward the formation of a speech community. *Language* 83: 770–802.

Patrick, P. L. 1991. Creoles at the intersection of variable processes: -t, -d deletion and past-marking in the Jamaican mesolect. *Language Variation and Change* 3: 171–90.

Patrick, P. L. 1999. *Urban Jamaican Creole: Variation in the mesolect*. Amsterdam: John Benjamins.

Preston, D. L., & Bayley, R. 2009. Variationist linguistics and second language acquisition. In W. C. Ritchie & T. K. Bhatia (eds.), *The new handbook of second language acquisition*, 89–113. Bingley, UK: Emerald.

Ranson, D. L. 1991. Person marking in the wake of /s/ deletion in Andalusian Spanish. *Language Variation and Change* 3: 133–52.
Rickford, J. R. 1986. The need for new approaches to social class analysis in sociolinguistics. *Language and Communication* 6: 215–21.
Rickford, J. R. 1987. *Dimensions of a creole continuum: History, texts, and linguistic analysis of Guyanese Creole.* Palo Alto, CA: Stanford University Press.
Roberts, J. 1997. Acquisition of variable rules: A study of (-t, d) deletion in preschool children. *Journal of Child Language* 24: 351–72.
Rousseau, P., & Sankoff, D. 1978. Advances in variable rule methodology. In D. Sankoff (ed.), *Linguistic variation: Models and methods*, 57–69. New York: Academic.
Santa Ana, O. 1992. Chicano English evidence for the exponential hypothesis: A variable rule pervades lexical phonology. *Language Variation and Change* 4: 275–88.
Santa Ana, A. O. 1996. Sonority and syllable structure in Chicano English. *Language Variation and Change* 8: 63–89.
Shin, N. L. 2010. A variationist approach to overt and null Spanish subject pronouns in first language acquisition. Paper presented at the 14th Hispanic Linguistics Symposium, Indiana University, Bloomington, IN.
Shuy, R., Wolfram, W., & Riley, W. K. 1968. *A study of social dialects in Detroit.* Washington, DC: Educational Resources Information Center.
Silva-Corvalán, C. 1994. *Language contact and change: Spanish in Los Angeles.* Oxford: Clarendon Press.
Silva-Corvalán, C. 1996–97. Avances en el estudio de la variación sintáctica. *Cuadernos del Sur* 27: 35–49.
Slomanson, P., & Newman, M. 2004. Peer group identification and variation in New York Latino English laterals. *English World-Wide* 15: 199–216.
Solomon, J. 1999. Phonological and syntactic variation in the Spanish of Valladolid, Yucatán. Ph.D. dissertation, Stanford University.
Tagliamonte, S. A., & Temple, R. 2006. New perspectives on an ol' variable. *Language Variation and Change* 17: 281–302.
Tarone, E. 1988. *Variation in interlanguage.* London: Edward Arnold.
Travis, C. E. 2007. Genre effects on subject expression in Spanish: Priming in narrative and conversation. *Language Variation and Change* 19: 101–35.
Trudgill, P. 1974. *The social differentiation of English in Norwich.* Cambridge: Cambridge University Press.
Weinreich, U., Labov, W., & Herzog, M. 1968. Empirical foundations for a theory of language change. In W. P. Lehmann & Y. Malkiel (eds.), *Directions for historical linguistics*, 95–195. Austin: University of Texas Press.
Wenger, E. 1998. *Communities of practice: Learning, meaning, and identity.* Cambridge: Cambridge University Press.
Wolfram, W. 1969. *A sociolinguistic study of Detroit Negro speech.* Washington, DC: Center for Applied Linguistics.
Wolfram, W., & Fasold, R. 1974. *The study of social dialects in American English.* Englewood Cliffs, NJ: Prentice-Hall.
Zhang, Q. 2005. A Chinese yuppie in Beijing: Phonological variation and the construction of a new professional identity. *Language in Society* 32: 431–66.

CHAPTER 2

LINGUISTIC ANTHROPOLOGY

JANET S. SHIBAMOTO-SMITH AND VINEETA CHAND

> Is there...a *sociocultural unconscious* in the mind—wherever that is located in respect of the biological organism—that is both immanent in and emergent from our use of language? Can we ever profoundly study the social significance of language without understanding this sociocultural unconscious that it seems to reveal? And if it is correct that language is the principal exemplar, medium, and site of the cultural, then can we ever understand the cultural without understanding this particular conceptual dimension of language.
>
> —Silverstein (2004: 622)

Can we ever understand language without understanding the cultural? The orientation of linguistic anthropology is, along with other strands of sociocultural anthropology, ethnographic, and our methodology of choice has historically been participant-observation. Investigators immerse themselves in the sociocultural complex in which the subjects of their investigations live, thereby hoping to achieve deeper insights into the motivations for particular linguistic practices in their real time instantiations—in all their particularistic messiness—than survey or other methodologies allow. In recent years, however, linguistic anthropology has been challenged, first, by our own realizations that societies are not now and never were as communicatively isolated as our earlier models of language and culture assumed and, second, by the changing conditions of communication worldwide as globalizing technologies appear to create a language "field" with multiple, often privatized (Iwabuchi 1999) network strands reaching out into a larger world of interaction, out of the reach of the participant-observational anthropological view with its links to the local and the communal. This chapter briefly reviews the development of linguistic anthropology as it relates to sociolinguistics, including some particulars of the concept of fieldwork and ethnography as well as some of the changes in the nature of field sites that have occurred over the last few decades, and then turns to some of the new strands of empirical work and theorizing that have emerged as a result of these changes. The chapter ends with some thoughts on how socially oriented linguistics of all sorts might productively work together toward meshing the concerns of quantitative sociolinguistics in the population-wide, emergent patterns of language use that characterize a community of speakers with the historical, discursive, and ideological understandings of on-the-ground speaking events that remain the core concern of linguistic anthropology.

Foundations

In one fashion or another, linguistic anthropologists have been searching for insights about language in the midst of the social lives of groups around the world and, conversely, for insights about social groups in the structures and patterns of language from the beginning of its emergence as a subfield of North American anthropology in the early years of the twentieth century. The Boasian insistence that command of a group's language is indispensable for anthropologists striving for accurate and thorough ethnographic knowledge, that description of a group's language was a necessary first step toward understanding the wider culture of a particular community, and that language was a privileged site for ethnographic understanding because speakers' knowledge of the grammatical operations of their language, being largely unconscious, were less subject to secondary rationalizations than other cultural phenomena (Boas 1911) offered a foundation for the inclusion of the study of language as a necessary first step in the study of society and culture from the outset. From this approach came Edward Sapir and Benjamin Whorf, from whose work emerged a theory of linguistic relativity (Mandelbaum 1949; Carroll 1967). The original orientation of this field was structural, and largely subscribed to the notion that language was a shared cognitive system, the grammatical structures and lexicons of which served as a filter for speakers' ways of viewing the world they inhabited. This orientation has since given way to a more nuanced vision of the language-culture-society relation, which will be discussed below.

We have not abandoned our anthropological roots in the study of culture, and are insistent on the interconnectivity of the social and the cultural, particularly the level of cultural discourses that we term the ideological (Silverstein 1979: 195) that is the trademark of contemporary linguistic anthropology, and that which distinguishes it from other forms of socially oriented linguistics. In what follows, we address some of the developments that emerged from that early history as they relate to sociolinguistics. Linguistic anthropology today is a very broad-ranging field, so we limit our discussion to points we believe to be significant contributions to sociolinguistic interests.

The mid-twentieth century saw the emergence of a trio of linguistic anthropologists instrumental in developing sociolinguistics in an anthropological style. Charles Ferguson, John Gumperz, and Dell Hymes were early and major figures to call for, and develop, a linguistics inextricably tied to the lives and actions of speakers. Silverstein (2008: 173) cites, in particular, John Gumperz and Dell Hymes as leaders in insisting upon a "concern for the social life of language-in-use." Both Gumperz and Hymes shared a theoretical base that was functional rather than formal, holding that the form and function of linguistic elements are not—and cannot be—independent, and took the position that the goal of linguistic anthropology was to understand and theorize communicative, rather than grammatical, competence (Figueroa 1994: 178). Focusing on the utterance rather than the sentence, and on the appropriateness and meaningfulness of the utterance in specific, contextualized verbal interactions, they set the stage for a linguistic anthropology, or *sociolinguistics* as they often termed what they were doing at the time, that was a socially constitutive linguistics.

This, according to Hymes (1962, 1964, 1972), would require analysts to rethink the fundamental units of linguistic analysis themselves: from the sentence to the speech event. And to Hymes, revealing the nature of these speech events lay in combining ethnography with linguistics (Keating 2001: 285) and speakers and their utterances in a single model for description and analysis; this is the famous SPEAKING model, a list of components of speech events, including but not limited to language, that were intended to be useful in pointing ethnographers of communication toward components of speech events that may be pertinent to analyses cross-culturally.[1] In terms of the subsequent work most relevant for sociolinguistics, key components were participant structures of events (P), norms of interaction and interpretation (N), and genre (G). And, although the SPEAKING model afforded an etic grid to guide researchers toward what to look for, insistence upon the goal of uncovering the emic understanding of events was always foregrounded.

Ethnographers of communication have produced an enormous body of cross-cultural, cross-linguistic work, several strands of which have had tremendous impact on our understanding of the range of ways that routinized events can and do play out in different societies, of how children are socialized into speaking competencies and norms, of how literacy is not simply a tool that is distributed in the same way in and across all societies, of how languages change under the forces of a globalizing spread of Western cultural concepts, and the like. One particularly critical strand of work within the larger frame of the ethnography of speaking that has had a major impact on contemporary linguistic anthropology is the development of a frame for describing and analyzing verbal performance (Bauman 1977; Bauman & Briggs 1990; Briggs 1988), wherein verbal art is not treated as simply text but as text enacted, calling attention to issues of cuing performance and of audience role as they are incorporated into the performed speech event. The insights derived from this strand of the ethnography of communication continue to have relevance for our understanding of performed speech in everyday verbal interactions as well as in performance as more classically construed; see, for example, Besnier (2009) and Rampton (2009). They also have implications for the social validity and both speaker-internal and community-specific stability of the variationist and discourse analytic focus on grammatical and stylistic factors.

And this concern with the relation of text emerging in interaction to decontextualized and portable text artifacts resonates with earlier concerns about the production of texts for linguistic anthropological analysis, with regard both to how the texts are collected (Briggs 1986) and to how they are displayed (Ochs 1979). As Briggs (1986: 27) notes, "[T]he interview presupposes a set of role relations, rules for turn-taking, canons for introducing new topics and judging the relevance of statements, constraints on linguistic form, and so on," and this speech form in not necessarily in the metacommunicative repertoire of all groups. Interviews necessarily decontextualize cultural knowledge, forcing interviewees to pre-entextualize such knowledge in "maximally referentially dense" fashions, suppressing all the indexicality that attends knowledge transmission in everyday social life; and the consequences of this for linguistic form in cases where the interview is not a native genre are unknown. Briggs advises caution in using interviews as our sole source of "data." However our data are collected, moreover, issues of entextualization do not end there.

Struck by the unfittedness of commonly used transcription systems for interactional data between adults for use in adult-child interactions, Ochs (1979) unveils a number of transcription convention that foreclose certain interpretations of data. This pioneering piece on the distorting effects of transcription choices focuses on issues of page layout and the interweaving of information on verbal and nonverbal aspects of the interactional data. The first of these foci has been picked up by other scholars in many fields. The second of these foci has received somewhat less attention, particularly with respect to Ochs's concern for a feature of nonverbal and verbal behavior that had not, at the time, been captured in transcribing: interoccurrence. She notes:

> Verbal behavior may occur one or more times in the course of some other action carried out by a participant. Alternatively, nonverbal actions may be carried out one or several times in the course of any one single utterance. While the property of simultaneity per se has been encoded in transcripts...., the evolution of nonverbal and verbal behavior as it happens in the space of an utterance is not reported. [But] Indeed the notion of simultaneity marks the nature of these interoccurrent acts. (Ochs 1979: 57)

Since we, as linguistic anthropologists, are concerned with the embodied speaker as social actor, this is a critical shortcoming of the transcript as an object of study of the *social life* of language.

The ethnography of communication framework has had a profound impact on the practice of linguistic anthropology, both with respect to ethnographic methodologies for examining linguistic data *in situ* and in theorizing the social, cultural, and semiotic functional underpinnings of linguistic forms as they occur in concrete speech events.[2] Hymes, in developing the insights and frameworks for pursuing ethnographic work on language-in-use forged a new direction for linguistic anthropology and sociolinguistics, drawing on and producing work that offers "insight into the importance of language for an understanding of culture and society and the relevance of cultural and social phenomena for an understanding of language" (Duranti 2009: 1). This dialectic remains the foundation for work in the field of linguistic anthropology today. In sum, lasting contributions to a broadly defined sociolinguistics and a contemporary linguistic anthropology are an insistence on ethnography as a starting point, a commitment to a functionalist vision of language, an understanding of language as performed as critical to an understanding of the nature of language, and in recent decades, a focus on the relationship of language (and literacy) practices to social inequality.

Language beyond Linguistic Form

At mid-twentieth century, sociolinguistics, of which linguistic anthropology was a vital component, was part of a loosely defined coalition of disciplines focused on reintroducing the social into the study of language; this included Labovian variationist sociolinguistics, which later came to define the "core" of sociolinguistics as it developed in the 1970s and 1980s. From the mid-1980s until very recently, linguistic anthropology and sociolinguistics went through a period of increasing separation (Duranti 2009: 6) and developments in linguistic anthropology were largely not incorporated into sociolinguistic thinking until much later.

As noted in the previous section, linguistic anthropology is not as concerned with language exclusively as form (structured form) as it is with language as it functions; that is, language as a social-linguistic hybrid (Bauman & Briggs 2003), rather than language as a form system isolable from its social use. Linguistic anthropologists, by talking about language, are fundamentally talking about society and culture. We search, not so much for the linguistic form, but for the "total linguistic fact" (Silverstein 1985).

Two major breakthroughs in the 1970s were the elaboration of the notion that linguistic signs were not limited to a referential function but were, in fact, pervasively multifunctional (Silverstein 1976) and the development of language ideology as a field of study (Silverstein 1979).[3] Silverstein (1976) drew attention to the limitations of a vision of language forms as serving only a referential function. Others were engaged in similar critique (e.g., Austin's 1967 speech act theory, offering a vision of speaking as doing), but Silverstein's description of "shifters" opened an entirely new vision into the pervasive indexicality of language, one in which contextualizing work is always a part of the meaning of utterances.[4] Examples of shifters in English are first- and second-person pronouns, deictics *this* and *that*, and the like. Such shifters—which presuppose aspects of the context of use—alone serve to challenge the assumed primacy of symbolic reference and theories that accounted only for semantico-referential grammars, but Silverstein's analysis extended beyond these presuppositional indexicals to creative forms, whose use can serve to constitute a situation. Examples of such creative indexicals are Japanese first-person pronouns *boku*, and *ore*, which constitute speakers as male[5] and as less versus more aggressively masculine, respectively. The notion of indexicality expanded the scope of theorizing about how context and linguistic form were linked and our understanding of the agentive role a speaker could have on shaping the context to her or his own social ends. The long-standing linguistic anthropological concern for the styling of self through language by the speaker-as-agent contrasts with the traditional variationist focus on an unconscious use of grammar, and affords a distinct perspective on speech as it constitutes social actors versus speech as it reflects some stable, objectively observable attribute of speakers or singular linguistic systems.

Silverstein's 1979 refiguring of Whorfian theories of linguistic relativity into a theory of linguistic ideology showed how the forms and our beliefs about the links of those forms to "reality-out-there" "unrecognizably distort the object of [linguistic] investigation," be it our own language or another's. And he suggests along the way that this insight from the plane of reference concerning an inevitable disjunction between our language forms and "reality-out-there" is perhaps replicated on a plane of language function more generally, in a disjunction between ideology and structure (Silverstein 1979: 194). Language ideologies are "commonsense" sets of beliefs about language and their links to "reality" and to social value that speakers can and do use to rationalize their language use and their attitudes toward the language use of others, with consequences for language structure and language change; for an early collection of key papers demonstrating the utility of the concept of language ideology across a broad range of settings from Papua New Guinea to U.S. law school classrooms, see Schieffelin, Woolard, and Kroskrity (1998). Language ideology serves as a mediating link between social structure and linguistic structure, and is empirically accessible through metapragmatic statements speakers make about the reasons that certain forms are used in certain ways. Inclusion of ideological considerations in ethnographic work has become a mainstay of linguistic anthropology today, and complexifies our understanding of language practices.

With these conceptual tools, linguistic anthropologists were able to carve out new ways of drawing together data on several planes of language form, function, and belief that are relevant to the "total linguistic fact," now seen as "an unstable mutual interaction of meaningful sign forms contextualized to situations of interested human use, mediated by the fact of cultural ideology" (Silverstein 1985: 220). Linguistic ideology serves as the mediating link between the first and second of these "facts" (for a succinct description of how the concept of the total linguistic fact relates to contemporary work in sociolinguistics, see Chand 2009: 14–16).

Almost immediately, political economy was added to the mix, reflecting a trend in the 1980s to consider the relations between language studies oriented toward the symbolic and political economic issues of power and domination. Irvine (1989) called for linguistic anthropologists to move beyond the materialist/idealist dichotomy in order to achieve a better integration of theorizing about verbal sign values and material values. An *Annual Review of Anthropology* piece on language and political economy appeared the same year (Gal 1989), stressing the need for linguistics to take sufficient heed of how language practices are located within larger systems of inequality. Whether the terms are those of Bourdieu's symbolic domination, Marxist oppositional culture, or Foucault's subjugated discourse, language can no longer be viewed as a neutral tool for representing the world, but must be seen as "fundamentally implicated in relations of domination" (Gal 1989: 348).[6] This insight encouraged linguistic anthropologists to look beyond the analytic unit of the speech community to larger national or, increasingly, global processes impacting linguistic inequality. It also encouraged us to examine how we, as researchers, imposed additional frames of power through processes of, for example, transcription and translation (Bucholtz 2000; Liu 1995.) Language ideology became intertwined with, and is now better able to address, politics and new ways of considering the roles of language ideologies, not only in local speech communities, but also in the formation of states and publics, and the institutions that shape them (Kroskrity 2000). With the addition of political economy to linguistic ideology, a "'practice' anthropology of discourse" became possible (Silverstein 2008: 173). Identification of critical processes that results in certain speakers coming to "stand for" their group (iconicity) while others are rendered invisible (erasure) and that allows oppositions existing on one plane to be projected onto another (fractal recursivity), often with loadings of moral or social value transferring rather freely to linguistic differences or complexities such as bi-/multilingualism (Irvine & Gal 2000), provided additional tools for the analysis of discourse practice and that practice's social effects.

A final important strand of inquiry was the expansion of interest in language from sentence or utterance to text and to the processes of creating text out of moment-to-moment verbal interactions, including those processes that enable chunks of interactive languaging to be extracted from one context (decontextualization) and rendered portable, ready for reinsertion into other speaking contexts (Bauman & Briggs 1990; Briggs & Bauman 1992; Hanks 1989; Silverstein & Urban 1996). Hanks (1989: 95–6) defines a text as "any configuration of signs that is coherently interpretable by some community of users," thus locating textuality less in a text's inherent structure and more in the social field within which it is produced and understood. He goes on to claim (1989: 100) that "the textual issues most fruitful for anthropologists lie in the mid-range between formalism, which dwells on the forms, devices, and constructions of closed artifacts (codes or works), and what might be called sociologism, which dwells on the large-scale fields of production, distribution, and reception of discourse." One key question for linguistic anthropology is how to pin down the textual object; that is, is it to be identified in the process of production or is it best understood in its intertextual life as a finished (and mobile) product? If a text is "a causally consequential structure of relative coherence that emerges in and is precipitated by discourse" and is, thus, a "completely spatio-temporal entity" (Silverstein 2005: 18), then viewing the production of specific linguistic forms on the basis of a text *artifact*, stripped of all its spatiotemporal contextual features, can afford only a limited view of what language is and what it can accomplish in situ. Linguistic anthropology's insistence on an ethnographic approach to decontextualization and recontextualization (a.k.a intertextuality) offers concrete specificity to Bakhtin and his notions of the dialogic (Bauman & Briggs 1990). It further allows us to advance toward elucidating the processes that apply to, and are applied by, language use as it is manipulated in the semiotics of everyday living, rather than delimiting language as an inherently decontextualizable set of structures that relate to social life merely in order to reflect a "sociocultural unconscious" that exists prior to, rather than being "both immanent in and emergent from our use of language," as the quotation from Silverstein (2004) suggests.

Linguistic Anthropology in a Sociolinguistics of the Future

Previous decades armed us with tools that allow simultaneous examination of linguistic form and its functional use, in an ethnographically apprehended and sociohistorically grounded context. While linguistic anthropology's focus on the representativeness of examples and their social contexts results in more time spent on a smaller amount of data than is possible to deal with in quantitative strands of sociolinguistics, it uncovers aspects of language that are invisible (or erased) from the perspective of the decontextualized transcript, and hence divorced from all the messy, globalized interconnections of contemporary speaking practices.[7] But in addition to the continuing focus on the functional and multiply indexical features of language, its commitment to "the total linguistic fact" that includes ideology as it impacts language form and language change, its understanding that language is always firmly embedded in a sociohistorical matrix that both shapes and is shaped by the things speakers do with language, and its techniques for linking all these to political economic regimes of social authority and value making, the field has progressed to incorporate new interests and new research emphases. These take linguistic anthropology, and the sociolinguistics closest to it, from "culture" and "worldview" to engagement with the study of "linguistic forms and people *in motion* across fields of value" (Cody 2010: 201, emphasis added), theorizing *through* discovery and description rather than description and discovering in demonstration of theory.[8]

The work of the past has set the stage, then, for new directions. Work within linguistic anthropology linked to intertextuality, and thus to the dialogic, has expanded beyond the circulation of texts or text artifacts to the linkage with other aspects of the discursive situation, refocusing attention on the metalevel at which "like" interactions are recognized and authorized, negotiated, or rejected. Agha (2005: 1) defines interdiscursivity as the connectivity that results when "features of discourse establish forms of connectivity across events of discourse"; interdiscursivity locates discourse within larger sociohistorical frameworks and sharpens our analyses of how linguistic signs—and co-occurring non-linguistic elements—create links that that result in recognizable social formations.

In a particularly clear exposition of intertextual-to-interdiscursive relations in one specific speech genre, the Japanese wedding [reception] speech, Dunn (2005) exemplifies Silverstein's (2005) type- and token-interdiscursivity distinction; she divides the relations of the elements of on-the-ground speeches into formulaic utterances, such as *Goshinzoku no minasama kyō wa hontō ni omedetō gozaimasu* 'Today I sincerely congratulate the members of both families', wherein the utterance is a formulaic reproduction of a specific "thing to say at a wedding reception" and thus contributes generic identifiability to the speech—type-interdiscursivity—and to quotations, speaker-chosen texts that are presented as "autonomous objects detached from particular contexts of utterance in a way that invites analysis and interpretation" (Dunn 2005: 154). These latter exemplify token-interdiscursivity. Dunn concludes that it is type-interdiscursivity that gives listeners the entree into knowing they are hearing a socially recognized genre, while token-interdiscursivity, individually crafted intertextuality, gives the speaker a chance to give a "good" performance.

As Cody (2010: 200) points out, "among the enduring legacies of the turn to language ideology has been a sustained analysis of the ways in which communicative practice articulates with fields of cultural value to produce regular social effects." Type-interdiscursivity affords us a tool for seeking out those continuities between and among speech events that stabilize our notions—or stereotypes—not only of "what is going on" (genre) but also of who is doing it; interdiscursivity's relation to processes of social stereotypification emerges as a clear focus of linguistic anthropological interest. Agha (2007) draws on semiosis across encounters to develop a model of how language, the vehicle through which social relations are constructed and not merely in which they are reflected, links specific repertoires of linguistic signs to stereotypic pragmatic effects through processes of enregisterment, or social recognition, thus allowing these sets of forms and effects to circulate through social groupings for a variety of purposes, not all reflective of individual speaker social identity. This allows a perspective on language style and stylization that encompasses not only the individual event but the sociohistorical matrix within which it occurs. This vision of style and stylization complements other frameworks for considering style and styling in sociolinguistics (Bell's [2001] audience design framework is very well known; for an alternative framework, see Levon 2009), but we argue it is a particularly critical perspective on speaker style when considering the circulation and reception of language across social and/or geopolitical borders. This is particularly true in cases where it is the sociohistorical matrix, with its expected links to particular statements *that are not made*, that allow meanings to be conveyed through entailments from the socially enregistered but not verbalized discourse. For example, Shuck describes a narrative told by a young woman who woke up on an airplane to find a stranger in her mother's seat. The stranger spoke English but had an accent. The narrative recounts the narrator's inability to understand anything the stranger says—he sounds to her like "*bluh luh luh luh*" she says (Shuck 2004: 198), and her fear that she might be killed (or that her mother had been killed). Shuck claims that what renders this narrative comprehensible (as opposed to merely hysterical) to listeners is the *un*spoken set of propositions that constitute what she terms the "ideology of nativeness" that categorizes "native English speakers" (and thus good, safe people) as Americans or perhaps British speakers of English and "non-native English speakers" as incomprehensible and possibly dangerous foreigners. Understanding of this narrative content and style emerges, thus, from the unspoken understanding of the social matrix within which it is performed.

Envisioning language style and stylization as emergent in individual events but also firmly grounded in the sociohistorical matrix within which they occur has facilitated linguistic anthropology's investigations of media-circulated language, globalization, and social hybridity. This includes attention to the *interactions* between public media and individual negotiations of language as speakers orient themselves differently to global versus local norms and to the construction of multiple personae. The sociolinguistics of globalization begins from the insight that, increasingly, research into many domains of local social life, including language, requires researchers to pay attention to global as well as local forms of social organization (Coupland 2003: 466). Linguistic anthropologists, particularly those working on media and new communication technologies (Ginsburg, Abu-Lughod, & Larkin 2002), are early practitioners of a sociolinguistics of globalization, and, particularly with respect to the anthropological study of globalized communications, attend, in ways much of the media and communication technology scholarship does not, to afford an "empirically grounded picture of individual experience of these technologies, understood in reference to [the] entire range of communicative acts" and attention to "the broader social impacts of these phenomena" (Cook 2004: 107; for a theoretical perspective on these two aspects of globalized, media-circulated language varieties, see also Blommaert 2003). Japanese hip-hop, for example, was clearly inspired by American rap music; in the *genba*[9] of the Japanese hip-hop club, however, it shows itself unmoored from it foundational ideologies of race, class, and gender and reinserted into social frames relevant to Japanese youthful consumers (Condry 2006). Racialized framing shifts—blackness is reconstructed in its import to fit a Japanese fascination with a blackness that, not being internal to Japan, does not threaten Japaneseness in any way—; the politics of class refocus on a middle class, and strongly generational, disdain for elite (political and bureaucratic) corruption. The compositional features of hip-hop are *niched* (Blommaert 2003: 609) into a Japanese hierarchies of ideologies and of musical and social value, not imported complete with the values and ideologies from their source. All strands of sociolinguistics must increasingly turn to questions of how media (over)saturation affects and is recursively negotiated within locally grounded individual attitudes and language practices. Appropriation and use of linguistic varieties that circulate through globalized media streams or mediascapes (Appadurai 1991) is well attested by even the most locally grounded groups; looking at variation in terms of singular group membership in ways that exclude both multiple community participation and influence by media, that is, failing to account for the multi-sitedness of contemporary life, is no longer enough. An individual's total linguistic repertoire can only be apprehended by understanding how that individual makes use of various speech styles, registers, and genres across speaking events, and how those varieties of speaking are shaped by local and supra-local norms and how values and communicative competencies are constructed. The ideological backdrop against which speech functions is a further critical element in this understanding, and one that calls for much more attention across all strands of sociolinguistics.

To look at mediatized communication raises core issues of access (see, e.g., Eisenlohr [2004] for an excellent overview of how issues of access to digitized media affect the politics of language revitalization and lesser-language digital archiving projects). It also raises issues of authorization: What kinds of language can flow through global channels? What kinds of speakers can appropriate and deploy which registers and/or languages? How do language practices change as a function of their redeployment and/or re-enregisterment?

These question are particularly acute in the case of sociolinguistics' treatment of bi- and multilingual communities, which have longstanding programs of privileging the concept of the monolingual speaker as the only "authentic" speaker (Bucholtz 2003) and deny authoritative speech to the non-native or the "accented" one (Chand 2009). The future of a "fourth wave" sociolinguistics,[10] we argue, requires theoretical framing and analytic methods that acknowledge the empirical reality of the fully native speaker who is not equally competent across her or his society's ostensible "linguistic repertoire," the "native" *non*-monolingual speaker who is fully engaged not only with her or his local, lived experience, but who also engages with a mediatized twenty-first-century or transborder communities, and other speakers not fully accommodated within the discourse of "one society–one language" native speakerhood.

Contemporary research on transnational (e.g., Whiteside 2009), diasporic (e.g., Shankar 2008), and bordertown (e.g., Llamas 2007) language and identity negotiations and stylization point to additional contexts where a theoretically grounded sociolinguistics of globalization is central for understanding how voices, resources, and identities are authorized and negotiated to produce novel and reworked social meanings and motivations for language use. Building on this, examinations of linguistic identity as fluid and multifaceted have grown substantially (e.g., Ibrahim 1999; Mendoza-Denton 2002, 2008); yet their meanings, histories, and contemporary usages can be traced—and linked with language—only by attending seriously to both the linguistic and the social aspects of their development and contemporary use, while either alone would fail to correlate language with society. Attention to new and emerging spatial and technological ways of interacting and identities as nuanced, rich and changing demonstrate that the study of globalized communication does not, indeed must not, foreclose careful ethnographic study of locally situated practices, but instead, must now attend to multiple local "heres" that speakers may inhabit.[11]

Attention to local social contextualizations, global and cross-border affiliations and negotiations, technology-mediated communication, and their respective overlapping and discordant emergent (or reworked) speaker identities and practices are but some perspectives among many we need to attend to in a sociolinguistic framework of globalization, while we need to also ground such examination in how access and authority control which discourses and linguistic forms move into new locales, and how authority structures and needs in the new locale then shape their meanings. Indeed, the "meanings" of globally mobile texts and discourses across social space cannot be understood without exploration of the on-the-ground experiences of the social actors involved.

This requires a reorientation toward the potentially permeable boundaries of languages and competencies, a better understanding of how language and competencies are socially constructed,[12] and a tool kit that can deal with the non-finite "messiness" that is language in use; specifically, what is needed is framework that includes principled links between the formal and the functional aspects of language—and as linguistic anthropologists, we follow Hymes (1996: 45) in insisting that the functional, "second linguistic relativity" be privileged in this endeavor—and the macro-sociological context to the micro-interactional one. It is critical for contemporary sociolinguistics to incorporate understanding of the speaker not wholly bound by some etically determined social category(/ies) but rather as a real person enacting multiple personae, whose understanding of language forms at any given moment is also shaded by past personal interactions and experiences and engagement with (or mere awareness of) structures of institutional authority in their society. Linguistic anthropology is well adapted to thinking through these linkages because we have developed methodologies that take as a starting point the embodied speaker equipped with both a language capacity (or mental grammar[s]) and a socialized capacity as a member of some group(s), who comes to any speaking event with a life history of prior verbal interactions and prior contact with locally and supra-locally circulating ideologies and norms of speaking behavior. This prior history and social knowledge simultaneously constrains yet affords resources for building upon and potentially challenging or negotiating ideological regimes and linguistic norms. These complex processes cannot be captured fully in one-time interviews with speakers chosen by objectively measurable (but possibly irrelevant) criteria; rather, they must be discovered ethnographically and over multiple interactions. Recurrence, not only of specific linguistic forms as typifying a particular social category of speaker, but also of forms as feeding, relying upon, and responding to the intertextual and interdiscursive construction of an individual, a society, and a culture at the ideological level is key to this enterprise. Tools for linking on-the-ground practices to ideologies of practice and meaning are equally crucial. As we apply these tools to new contexts—multilingual and/or multi-sited interactional contexts—and in local communities, we head toward a new realm of sociolinguistic inquiry that offers the prospect of theoretical breakthroughs by meshing the ethnographic and social theoretic strengths of linguistic anthropology with the on-the-spot understandings of language variation and change emergent from our more quantitatively oriented sister strands of sociolinguistics.

Notes

1. This model is very well described in Keating (2001), and in a more reflexive framing, in Saville-Troike (2003: 100–23).
2. Whether these be the formal speech events that formed the core of early ethnography of communication investigations, or the more everyday events, such as occur in classroom settings or at home over dinner, that are more prominent in contemporary work.
3. This involved a refiguring of Whorfian notions concerning language and worldview in combination with Peircean semiotics (Hartshorne & Weiss 1931–1935).
4. "The referential values of a shifter is constituted by the speech event itself" (Silverstein 1976: 29), that is, the meaning of some forms can only be known by knowing about the context in which they are used.
5. Hence, useful to female speakers who are experimenting with gender in the middle school classroom (Miyazaki 2004) or who are creating gender transgressive personae in, e.g., lesbian bars in Shinjuku (Abe 2004).

6. Although it should be noted that Woolard (1985) warns us against a too-quick adoption of issues of status, dominance, and authority at the expense of more classic sociolinguistic notions of solidarity and group membership.
7. By more closely comparing findings motivated towards generalizability (e.g., quantitative sociolinguistics) with findings arising through the linguistic anthropological approach, which is less focused on such generalizability as a main directive, we may better understand in what ways generalizability itself may (or may not) limit or capture different realities within sociolinguistic research which attend to the overlapping and locally-situated construction of meaning and positionalities that we find in linguistic data.
8. In the context of the ethnographic turn in quantitative (variationist) sociolinguistics (see, e.g., Eckert 2000; Mendoza-Denton 2008) and the recent attention given to a rapprochement of (variationist) sociolinguistics and linguistic anthropology (Bucholtz & Hall 2008), it is worth mentioning that some sociolinguistic work is carried out in the context of grounded theory (Glaser & Strauss 1967), aided by such new tools for qualitative analysis such as Atlas.ti©. Chand (2009) is a good example of such work.
9. *Genba* may be glossed as 'scene'; more precisely, however, *genba* refers to the "real" place, or the "place where something actually happens, appears, or is made" (Condry 2006: 89).
10. This builds upon Eckert's (2005) historical analysis of three waves in sociolingustic data, methods and analytic goals. The first wave examines linguistic variability vis-à-vis major demographic criteria, the second wave nuances this by using local ethnographically uncovered social divisions to capture local meanings as linked to local identity construction, and the third wave looks at the socially constructed, stylistically exploited use of variation within layered communities.
11. Or, as brilliantly demonstrated in Fabian (1990), the singular local "heres" that are multiply constructed by flexibly multilingual speakers, who seem in their verbal practices not even to acknowledge the boundaries between or among languages.
12. This reorientation may problemtatize the notion of a shared underlying grammar as uniting a speech community, with ramifications for variationist and corpus-based sociolinguistic agendas.

References

Abe, H. 2004. Lesbian bar talk in Shinjuku, Japan. In S. Okamoto & J. S. Shibamoto-Smith (eds.), *Japanese language, gender, and ideology: Cultural models and real people*, 205–21. New York: Oxford University Press.

Agha, A. 2005. Introduction: Semiosis across encounters. *Journal of Linguistic Anthropology* 15(1): 1–5.

Agha, A. 2007. *Language and social relations*. Cambridge: Cambridge University Press.

Appadurai, A. 1991. Global ethnoscapes: Notes and queries for a transnational anthropology. In R. Fox (ed.), *Recapturing anthropology*, 191–210. Santa Fe: School of American Research Press.

Austin, J. 1967 [c. 1962]. *How to do things with words*. Cambridge, MA: Harvard University Press.

Bauman, R. 1977. *Verbal art as performance*. Rowley, MA: Newbury House.

Bauman, R., & Briggs, C. L. 1990. Poetics and performance as critical perspectives on language and social life. *Annual Review of Anthropology* 19: 59–88.

Bauman, R., & Briggs, C. L. 2003. *Voices of modernity: Language ideologies and the politics of inequality.* Cambridge: Cambridge University Press.

Bell, A. 2001. Back in style: Reworking audience design. In P. Eckert & J. R. Rickford (eds.), *Style and sociolinguistic variation*, 139–69. Cambridge: Cambridge University Press.

Besnier, N. 2009. *Gossip and the everyday production of politics.* Honolulu: University of Hawai'i Press.

Blommaert, J. 2003. Commentary: A sociolinguistics of globalization. *Journal of Sociolinguistics* 7: 607–23.

Boas, F. 1911 *Handbook of American Indian languages*, vol. 1. Bureau of American Ethnology, Bulletin 40. Washington: Government Printing Office (Smithsonian Institution, Bureau of American Ethnology).

Briggs, C. L. 1986. *Learning how to ask: A sociolinguistic appraisal of the role of the interview in social science research.* Cambridge: Cambridge University Press.

Briggs, C. L. 1988. *Competence in performance: The creativity of tradition in mexicano verbal art.* Philadelphia: University of Pennsylvania Press.

Briggs, C. L., & Bauman, R. 1992. Genre, intertextuality and social power. Journal of Linguistic Anthropology 2(2): 131–72.

Bucholtz, M. 2000. The politics of transcription. *Journal of Pragmatics* 32: 1439–465.

Bucholtz, M. 2003. Sociolinguistic nostalgia and the authentication of identity. *Journal of Sociolinguistics* 7: 398–416.

Bucholtz, M., & Hall, K. (eds.). 2008. Sociolinguistics and linguistic anthropology: Strengthening the connections. Special issue of the *Journal of Sociolinguistics* 12: 401–532.

Carroll, J. B. (ed.). 1967[1956]. *Language, thought, and reality: Selected writings of Benjamin Lee Whorf.* Cambridge, MA: MIT Press.

Chand, V. 2009. Who owns English? Political, social and linguistic dimensions of urban Indian English practices. Ph.D. dissertation, University of California, Davis.

Cody, F. 2010. Linguistic anthropology at the end of the naughts: A review of 2009. *American Anthropologist* 112(2): 200–07.

Condry, I. 2006. *Hip-hop Japan: Rap and the paths of cultural globalization.* Durham: Duke University Press.

Cook, S. E. 2004. New technologies and language change: Toward an anthropology of linguistic frontiers. *Annual Review of Anthropology* 33: 103–15.

Coupland, N. 2003. Introduction: Sociolinguistics and globalisation. *Journal of Sociolinguistics* 7: 465–72.

Dunn, C. D. 2005. Formulaic expression, Chinese proverbs, and newspaper editorials: Exploring type and token interdiscursivity in Japanese wedding speeches. *Journal of Linguistic Anthropology* 16: 153–72.

Duranti, A. 2009. Linguistic anthropology: History, ideas, and issues. In A. Duranti (ed.), *Linguistic anthropology: A reader*, 2nd ed., 1–59. Malden, MA: Wiley-Blackwell.

Eckert, P. 1995. Variation, convention and social meaning. Talk presented at the Linguistic Society of America Annual Meeting on January 7. Oakland, CA.

Eckert, P. 2000. *Linguistic variation as social practice.* Malden, MA: Blackwell.

Eckert, P. 2005. The third wave in variation. Talk presented to the Institute for Danish Dialectology, Copenhagen University, Copenhagen, Denmark.

Eisenlohr, P. 2004. Language revitalization and new technologies: Cultures of electronic mediation and the refiguring of communities. *Annual Review of Anthropology* 33: 21–45.

Fabian, J. 1990. *Power and performance: Ethnographic explorations through proverbial wisdom.* Madison: University of Wisconsin Press.

Figueroa, E. 1994. *Sociolinguistic metatheory.* Oxford: Pergamon.

Gal, S. 1989. Language and political economy. *Annual Review of Anthropology* 18: 345–67.

Ginsburg, F. D., Abu-Lughod, L. & Larkin, B. (eds.). 2002. *Media worlds: Anthropology on new terrain.* Berkeley: University of California Press.

Glaser, B. G. & Strauss, A. 1967. *Discovery of grounded theory: Strategies for qualitative research.* Chicago, IL: Aldine Publishing Co.

Hanks, W. F. 1989. Text and textuality. *Annual Review of Anthropology* 18: 95–127.

Hartshorne, C. & Weiss, P. 1931–35. *Collected papers of Charles Sanders Peirce.* Vols. 1–6. Cambridge, MA: Harvard University Press.

Hymes, D. 1962. The ethnography of speaking. In T. Gladwin & W. C. Sturtevant (eds.), *Anthropology and human behavior,* 15–53. Washington DC: Anthropological Society of Washington.

Hymes, D. 1964. Introduction: Toward ethnographies of communication. In J. J. Gumperz & D. Hymes (eds.), *The ethnography of communication*, special issue of *American Anthropologist* 66(6): Part 2, 1–34.

Hymes, D. 1972. Models of the interaction of language and social life. In J. J. Gumperz & D. Hymes (eds.), *Directions in sociolinguistics: The ethnography of communication*, 35–71. Madlon, MA: Blackwell.

Hymes, D. 1996. *Ethnography, linguistics, narrative inequality: Toward an understanding of voice.* London: Taylor and Francis.

Ibrahim, A. E. K. M. 1999. Becoming Black: Rap and Hip-hop, race, gender, identity and the politics of ESL learning. TESOL Quarterly 33: 349–69.

Irvine, J. T. 1989. When talk isn't cheap: Language and political economy. *American Ethnologist* 16: 248–67.

Irvine, J. T., & Gal, S.. 2000. Language ideology and linguistic differentiation. In P. V. Kroskrity (ed.), *Regimes of language: Ideologies, polities, and identities*, 35–83. Santa Fe, NM, and Oxford: School of American Research Press/James Currey.

Iwabuchi, K. 1999. Return to Asia? Japan in Asian audiovisual markets. In Y. Kosaku (ed.), *Consuming ethnicity and nationalism: Asian experiences*, 177–99. Richmond: Curzon Press.

Keating, E. 2001. The ethnography of communication. In P. Atkinson, A. Coffey, S. Delamont, L. Lofland & J. Lofland (eds.), *Handbook of ethnography*, 285–301. London: Sage Publications.

Kroskrity, P. V. (ed.). 2000. *Regimes of language: Ideologies, polities, and identities.* Santa Fe, NM, and Oxford: School of American Research Press/James Currey.

Levon, E. 2009. Dimension of style: Context, politics and motivation in gay Israeli speech. *Journal of Sociolinguistics* 13: 29–58.

Liu, L. H. 1995. *Translingual practice: Literature, national culture, and translated modernity-China, 1900–1937.* Palo Alto, CA: Stanford University Press.

Llamas, C. 2007. "A place between places": Language and identities in a border town. *Language in Society* 36: 579–604.

Mandelbaum, D. (ed.). 1949. *Selected writings in language, culture and personality.* Berkeley: University of California Press.

Mendoza-Denton, N. 2002. Language and identity. In J. K. Chambers, P. Trudgill, & N. Schilling-Estes (eds.) *The handbook of language variation and change*, 475–99. Oxford: Blackwell.

Mendoza-Denton, N. 2008. *Homegirls: Language and cultural practice among Latina youth gangs*. Malden, MA: Blackwell.

Miyazaki, A. 2004. Japanese junior high school girls' and boys' first-person pronoun use and their social world. In S. Okamoto & J. S. Shibamoto-Smith (eds.), *Japanese language, gender, and ideology: Cultural models and real people*, 256–74. New York: Oxford University Press.

Ochs, E.. 1979. Transcription as theory. In E. Ochs & B. Schieffelin (eds.), *Developmental pragmatics*, 43–72. New York: Academic Press.

Rampton, B. 2009. Interaction ritual and not just artful performance in crossing and stylization. *Language in Society* 38(2): 149–76.

Saville-Troike, M. 2003. *The ethnography of communication: An introduction*, 3rd ed. Malden, MA: Blackwell.

Schieffelin, B. B., Woolard, K. A., & Kroskrity, P. A. (eds.). 1998. *Language ideologies: Practice and theory*. New York and Oxford: Oxford University Press.

Shankar, S. 2008. *Desiland: Teen culture, class, and success in Silicon Valley*. Durham, NC: Duke University Press.

Shuck, G. 2004. Conversational performance and the poetic construction of an ideology. *Language in Society* 33(2): 195–222.

Silverstein, M. 1976. Shifters, linguistic categories, and cultural description. In K. H. Basso & H. A. Selby (eds.), *Meaning in anthropology*, 11–55. Albuquerque: University of New Mexico Press.

Silverstein, M. 1979. Language structure and linguistic ideology. In P. R. Clyne, W. F. Hanks, & C. L. Hofbauer (eds.), *The elements: A parasession on linguistic units and levels*, 193–247. Chicago: Chicago Linguistic Society.

Silverstein, M. 1985. Language and the culture of gender: At the intersection of structure, usage and ideology. In E. Mertz & R. Parmentier (eds.), *Semiotic mediation*, 220–59. Orlando, FL: Academic Press.

Silverstein, M. 2004. "Cultural" concepts and the language-culture nexus. *Current Anthropology* 45(5): 621–45.

Silverstein, M. 2005. Axels of evals: Token versus type interdiscursivity. *Journal of Linguistic Anthropology* 15(1): 6–22.

Silverstein, M. 2008. From the Associate Editor for *Linguistic Anthropology*. *American Anthropologist* 110(2): 172–73.

Silverstein, M., & Urban, G. (eds.). 1996. *Natural histories of discourse*. Chicago: University of Chicago Press.

Woolard, K. A. 1985. Language variation and cultural hegemony: Toward an integration of sociolinguistic and social theory. *American Ethnologist* 12(4): 738–48.

Whiteside, A. 2009. "We don't speak Maya, Spanish or English": Yucatec Maya-speaking transnationals in California and the social construction of competence. In N. M. Doerr (ed.), *The native speaker concept: Ethnographic investigations of native speaker effects*, 209–32. Berlin: Walter de Gruyter.

CHAPTER 3

DOERS AND MAKERS

THE INTERWOVEN STORIES OF SOCIOLOGY AND THE STUDY OF LANGUAGE

CHRISTOPHER McALL

SOCIOLOGY has had the uneasy task of developing its "global" perspective on society since the nineteenth century, while seeking to maintain its disciplinary frontiers and identity with respect to other, more-specialized disciplines. The problem of interdisciplinary frontiers comes out in the parallel (and at times, interwoven) stories of sociology and the study of language (whether in the form of philology or linguistics). These interwoven stories are considered here in relation to four major paradigms: social evolutionism, biologically inspired organic functionalism, the technical-systems approach, and a social constructivism that places emphasis on individual and collective responsibility for outcomes. These paradigms have played a central role in defining sociological thought, and continue to do so in various ways, even if their relative dominance within the discipline appears to have shifted (in part) from one to the other over time. The existence of these paradigms, grouping together different disciplines, brings up the question of disciplinary frontiers. The frontiers that count may not be where we think they are. To look more closely at this question in relation to sociology and the study of language, I begin with the "certainties" of nineteenth-century social evolutionism and the profound effects of the following century's two world wars on the history of social thought.

Improvement

The interweaving of sociology and the study of language is well underway in the "advancing" societies (to use Malthus's term) of the mid-1800s. Much of nineteenth-century social thought is characterized by the belief that contemporary industrial societies marked a high point in the intellectual, social, and moral development of human beings. Accelerating industrial production and technical innovation support the idea that traditional ways of doing things were gone forever. Historians of law, such as Maine ([1861]1924) set out to chart the "refinement" of law over time while Smith ([1775] 1911), Malthus ([1820] 1964) and Ricardo ([1817] 1966), as political economists, seek to document the "progress toward perfection" in terms of production and exchange. Geology and, increasingly, evolutionary biology, describe the succession of stages that led to the making of the earth's crust (Lyell [1863] 1873) or the competitive development of living organisms that leads, in Darwin's terms, to increasing organic "complexity" and therefore "perfection." While some critical social thinkers regret the passing of the old ways—Cobbett (1967) being nostalgic for the slow pace and social values of traditional peasant society—others criticize the burgeoning industrial towns and the misery of the new "working" classes in the light of a brighter future that is to be brought about by yet another stage in social progress and development. Thus Marx and Engels's hoped-for revolution is a moving on to something new in the light of the iron laws of history and the inevitability of social progress.

Political economy in the first part of the nineteenth century has the attributes of a global social science attempting to make sense of a rapidly changing and increasingly complex social system. The urgent requirements of government in the face of mass poverty, child labor, uncontrolled urbanization, financial crises, problems of public hygiene, and labor unrest (among other pressing issues) lead to a gradual breaking down of the more global approach to understanding society into a variety of specialized disciplines—including economics, political science, psychology, anthropology, and sociology—each focusing on particular aspects of the whole. The emerging focus of what is to become known as "sociology" retains, however, something of the breadth of political economy. In its initial formulations it is also thoroughly evolutionary and sets itself up as the only science capable of identifying and understanding what Comte (1883) describes as the "laws of social development." While Comte recognizes Condorcet as a major source of inspiration for seeing society as having gone through a succession of stages toward "perfection," he goes further in defining the science of sociology and its role in informing "social administrators" as to how they should administer society.

For Comte, the laws of social development admit no exceptions, and societies necessarily pass through the different stages. Thus, he rejects the idea that slavery is a regretable episode in social history, seeing it rather as a necessary stage in social progress. The upshot of his position is that contemporary society can only be properly understood—given its specific characteristics that flow from the laws of social development—by those who are well versed in the new "science" of sociology. The ordinary citizen and the administrator have to trust the bearers of this social science as being capable of producing precise, definite, "positive" (in the sense of "certain") information about society and its problems. The claim to precision and to the fact of having discovered the "natural" laws that underlie social evolution, make sociology (in theory) into as "scientific" a discipline as any other natural science. Spencer (1893) is to build on such ideas, as well as on Darwinian theories of organic evolution, in suggesting that societies develop in a competitive way just as organisms do—becoming more complex and therefore more "perfect" in the process. This he describes as the "survival of the fittest"—a notion that Darwin was to integrate subsequently into his own theories. Comtean sociology is thus evolutionary in aspect, the inevitable progress toward perfection of human societies being as much a cornerstone as it was for most of the theoretical constructions of nineteenth-century social thought. It was also built round the idea that the knowledge about society necessary for purposes of government and administration can only be possessed by those who are well versed in social science, everyone else being condemned to ignorance.

The study of language is at the heart of nineteenth-century social evolutionism, both as furnishing "proof" of improvement, as providing a model for thinking about evolution, and as a key element in romantic nationalism. For Humboldt ([1836] 1968), for example, languages can be seen as being primitive or advanced in terms of their structure, with the family of languages thought (at the time) to derive from Sanskrit representing an advance in terms of their capacity to communicate the world of experience. The development of grammatical and syntactical linkages is the key, along with the use of verbal forms that bring life and movement into the sentence in ways that older, monosyllabic languages were incapable of doing. Humboldt suggests that such improvements in language, allowing for conceptual range and precision as well as flexibility and completeness, contributed to the flowering of Greek civilization. He has more difficulty supporting his theory of continuing improvement given the subsequent development of European languages, but claims that the energy and decisiveness of contemporary English is based on its "wonderful word-construction" that is "deeply rooted in English character."[1] This "deep-rootedness" or "groundedness" is symptomatic of the way in which language is seen as being at the heart of national identity, with the development of the German nation over time and the German "spirit" (*Geist*) and "soul" (*Seele*) being inseparable from the development of the German language.

The discoveries of comparative philology and of the laws governing sound change also directly inspired evolutionary theory, with Darwin ([1871] 1936) understanding the lost connections among varieties and species on the basis of contemporary studies of languages and dialects, according to which the disappearance of intervening dialects between two varieties of a language, leads to those varieties being seen as distinct languages.[2] The key to understanding the provenance of the many varieties of the British blackberry and the common pigeon had been found. The study of language thus not only follows the general tendency to see everything in terms of laws of development and progress toward perfection but also provides some of the "proof" of that development. In the 1860s, Whitney insists that language has to be understood primarily through history. Although language only exists as an institution in so far as it is used by a given "community" in the present, it has to be understood as a cultural heritage: "etymology," as the "historical study of individual words" is the "foundation and substructure of all investigations of language" (Whitney [1867] 1971: 25).

System and Function

Progress toward perfection as the central idea of nineteenth-century social thought was to suffer at the hands of increasing economic crisis, unemployment, and runaway competition among industrial states for the control of markets. In the years prior to the First World War, increasing state interventionism is more than ever fueled by the idea that social science must provide the necessary expertise to government. But the ground is shifting. The inevitability of war is in the air, with schoolchildren being drilled in the new martial patriotisms (E. Weber 1976) and the widespread feeling that tensions are to be released through a form of giant "bloodletting" (Hobsbawm 1987). The experience of the Great War puts paid to what is left of the certainties that characterized the way society was thought of in the nineteenth century. It is no longer possible to claim to be at the pinnacle of intellectual, moral, and social evolution, or on the threshold of something new and better. Another paradigm moves into dominance in social science, according to which the present is not so much a staging point between a backward past and an increasingly brilliant future as a set of urgent problems that have to be resolved, in themselves, in the here and now.

This emerging paradigm frames itself in the accoutrements of biological thought. Society has long been thought of as being like a living organism, and Spencer, as we have seen, makes the parallel between the progressive evolution of societies and of organisms. From the 1880s onward, Durkheim is to go further in applying the ideas of nineteenth-century biology to society. The key idea is that of the body as a set of parts, each of which has its specific function in relation to the whole. Particular organs can become nonfunctional and gradually disappear (over generations), or they can become diseased and threaten the survival of the whole. In applying such ideas to society, individuals can be seen as being like parts of an organic whole and as having varied natural abilities that require them to occupy the functions in society to which they are best adapted (Durkheim [1893] 1973). This revival of the Platonic ideal of the social division of labor based on natural competence, gives rise to what Durkheim describes as "organic solidarity": the solidarity of the living organism. Various "pathologies" can arise by people occupying an inappropriate function in relation to their competence: they may be poorly trained, forced—by social inequality—to do work to which they are not suited, or have inappropriate values.

The organic model becomes paramount after the First World War. People have to be fed, clothed, housed, and put to work. The idea of society as a body composed of individuals, each of whom is more or less suited to the function he or she occupies, has the benefit of allowing social problems to be defined as problems of individual adaptation to function, rather than, for example, of opposed collective interests. The idea that social problems arise from individuals being ill-adapted to the new requirements of industry and society was already developed by Owen in the early 1800s, who sought to better prepare children for the discipline of factory work through education (Owen [1814] 1949). In the 1920s, the idea that social problems consist of individuals being maladapted to contemporary industrial civilization comes to be the corner stone of sociology. While quantitative sociology increasingly provides the State with the statistical information needed to govern (Oberschall 1972), other sociologists observe the individuals who fail to "function" correctly (the "deviants") in the streets and assembly plants of Chicago and elsewhere.

Society as a complex organism requiring attention to, and treatment of, its individual parts, can seem to exist outside time. The differences of "culture" that were seen in the nineteenth century by Tylor ([1871] 1958) and Morgan ([1877] 1964) as exemplary of the "improvement" of societies over time (the goal of anthropology being to arrange them in their proper evolutionary sequence) are now viewed by Malinowski (1960) and others as being the ground rules that allow a given society to survive and "function" in the present. Similar approaches, based on the necessity of understanding the functioning of existing systems are to be found from the First World War onward in economics (Keynes 1936), biology (Needham 1926), and geography (Febvre 1922).

The study of language is at the heart of this shift in perspective. Durkheim, for example, maintained that all social "facts" such as religion, law, and language, need to be understood in terms of their function in society (visualized as an organic whole) rather than in those of origins and historical development (Durkheim [1895] 1927, [1912] 1968). The new emphasis is well exemplified by Meillet (1915), who insists that just seeing Indo-European languages as part of a greater system, changing over time, is inadequate: "each language, at every moment of its history, presents an original system that needs to be described and of which the overall make-up needs to be explained as a whole."[3] Meillet's conception of each language as being a "system" in its own right was inspired by de Saussure's study of the Indo-European vowel system (de Saussure

[1878] 1970). De Saussure's subsequent lectures give form to the new, functionalist perspective that sets out to understand how language works in terms of transmission, reception, and signification. Whereas his theory of the sign echoes the work of seventeenth- and eighteenth-century philosophers such as Hobbes ([1640] 1969) and Hume ([1740] 1978), there is a new practicality, a new emphasis placed on the need to understand the "speech act." A key distinction is now made between the *langue* as the *partie sociale du langage* that exists outside the individual and the spoken word, the *parole*. The "basis for all linguistic studies" for de Saussure is no longer etymology, but the distinction between the value of the sign as part of the "*chaîne syntagmatique*" and within the overall system of signs that makes up the language (de Saussure [1915] 1978).

Studying language "in itself and for itself" (in de Saussure's words) opens the door to the appreciation of different languages for their functional adaptation to different environments. This in turn puts paid to what Sapir describes as the "evolutionary prejudice" that had characterized the social sciences in the nineteenth century "and which is only now beginning to abate its tyrannical hold on our mind" (Sapir 1921: 130). The goal now is to understand how the "bricks" (or "significant elements") that go to make up the "structure" of language are formed out of the "unformed and unburnt clay" of the sounds of speech (Sapir 1921: 24). This is the "inner sound-system" that, along with its "specific association of speech elements with concepts" is part of the "genius" of any given language (Sapir 1921: 57, 22). Not only does language exist for the function it has in social life, but its inner workings are subject to the same scrutiny that is being applied in other sciences with respect to their objects, notably biology (Needham 1926). Trubetzkoy goes further than de Saussure in seeing the sound system as an "organic whole" whose "structure" has to be studied (Trubetzkoy 1933: 233). As in the case of nineteenth-century philology, de Saussure's semiology and Trubetzkoy's phonology are to have profound effects on social science, notably in terms of seeing identity as produced through opposition (in Trubetzkoy's case, among phonemes organized as a system of sounds, each of which is recognized as distinct in a given language) and in terms of "structuralism" as a way of understanding the products, literary and otherwise, of the human mind.

If the interwar period represents the coming-of-age of the organic structural functionalist model of society, the study of language is at the heart of that process. For Hjelmslev, for example, language is both an (underlying) system and a process (in which that system is put to work in communication). Given that a system can exist without a process, but a process cannot exist without a system, it is the underlying system of language that needs to be the primary object of study—language as a "structure *sui generis*," a "self-subsistent, specific structure," an "organized totality" (Hjelmslev [1943] 1963: 8,19). The goal of linguistic theory is to "make possible a simple and exhaustive description of the system behind the text" (Hjelmslev [1943] 1963: 42). The text, as "process," only "comes into existence by virtue of a system's being present behind it, a system which governs and determines it in its possible development" (Hjelmslev [1943] 1963: 39). Some years after the publication of Hjelsmlev's (1963) *Prolegomena* (in Danish), Parsons publishes *The Social System* (1951), but it is Hjelmslev, through the example of language, who most clearly expresses the central idea of organic functionalism (as initially proposed by Durkheim): individual action in the world is "governed" and "determined" by the systems (or structures) that already exist.

Technical Adjustment

At the very moment when organic structural functionalism is being encapsulated in definitive works in linguistics and sociology, the ground is shifting once more. Whereas the organic model comes to the fore after the social catastrophe of the First World War amid fears of social disintegration, another model receives a boost from the centralized command economies put in place during the Second World War and that are to inspire the more developed welfare states of the 1950s and 1960s. Social problems are now defined as technical problems that can be resolved through the advice of experts and, ideally, avoided altogether by social "planning" (on the Soviet model, but without the tyranny, as suggested by Beveridge [1944]). Society is still seen as a set of structures and functions, but rather than being "like" an organism, the image is rather that of a machine with its component parts and built-in corrective mechanisms—along the lines of Wiener's cybernetics (Wiener 1948). Social problems can be seen as resulting from system failure that can be resolved through state action on the basis of expert technical advice (along Comtean lines). The beauty of the technical-systems model is that malfunctioning can be blamed on the inadequacy of previous expert advice or on the mistakes of previous governments, while the organic system model suggests parallels with natural processes that may themselves be largely beyond comprehension.

Sociology has thus moved from an evolutionary perspective, according to which the "laws of social development" operating through time have to be understood in order to act in the present for the advancement of society toward perfection, to seeing society as being like a living organism in the present, with its particular set of structures and functions, facing the threat to its own survival, to the technical-systems approach. This latter approach reintroduces the idea of progress but without the overtones of intellectual and moral superiority that characterized nineteenth-century social thought. Progress is defined in terms of efficiency, productivity, cost-effectiveness and the increase of quality and length of life. Much of contemporary sociological endeavor is devoted to documenting such progress, understanding system failure and proposing the necessary technical adjustments to bring the system back into balance (in cybernetic terms) or to help it meet its goals. In the light of this paradigm, deviant individual behaviors can be seen as system induced (as a result of poorly functioning welfare and education systems, for example) rather than as being rooted in character or "natural" personal defects. Language use, like everything else, can now be planned, based on the idea that the action of the state can alter the social "facts" that determine the action of individuals since existing institutions can be seen as arising from prior technical responses to problems of government. Language planning (in societies where language is an issue) becomes a paradigmatic case of the attempt to remodel human behavior through legislation, even if, according to Cooper (1989) the process of language planning itself is under-theorized and its effectiveness unclear.

Another key area in linguistics illustrates the shift toward the technical-systems approach and the continuing centrality of the study of language for social theory. The hunt for the structure underlying the performance (or the text) narrows down to the mental apparatuses that are at work in the production of language. Just as Foucault (1966) sees the "psy-" sciences as having embarked, at the end of the nineteenth century, on a search for the core area of individual personality formation within the recesses of the mind—a search that leads into "dangerous" areas where the subject seems no longer to exist in any clear sense—so Chomskyan linguistics sets out to explore the innate faculties that are seen as necessary (in theory) to allow the acquisition and use of language. The rules underlying universal grammar that are extrapolated from performance in different languages are seen as making up an "intricately structured system" which can be thought of as being made up of a "finite set of switches each of which has perhaps two positions." Experience is required to "set up the switches" which then allow the system to become functional (Chomsky 1986: 146). The whole consists of a "precisely articulated computational system—fairly simple in its basic principles [. . .] but quite intricate in its consequences" (Chomsky 1986: 204).

Chomsky distances himself from the old structuralism and suggests that the term "language" should be applied to the internal language faculty (or I-language) since external language (E-language) is just an epiphenomenon (Chomsky 1986: 25, 29). This technical-systems approach to language (replacing the organic model with the computer as its principal source of inspiration) is now recognized as being the starting point of the 1950s "cognitive revolution" in linguistics (Boeckx 2010). However, more than a half century later, Boeckx admits that little is known about how the language faculty operates, notably because of difficulties in creating the link between cognitive linguistics and neuroscience. The latter does not pretend to the same degree of precision as the former. Thus cognitive linguistics uses "high resolution concepts" referring to "very detailed aspects of linguistic representation and computation" whereas neurobiological research uses much broader conceptual distinctions: "most well-known phenomena at the neurophysiological level appear to be continuously varying, non discrete (analog) phenomena" (Boeckx 2010: 159). The existence of the innate language faculty as a technical system is thus posited in the Chomskyan tradition (and by Boeckx) as being certain, but as far as its workings are concerned, "all we have are interesting brain-behavior correlations, nothing more" (Boeckx 2010: 176).

The social context, within which the language faculty is put to work, or "triggered" in Chomskyan terms, is largely under-theorized by Boeckx (and indeed hardly mentioned). Thus the social context provides the "nutrition" that allows children to "grow" language—an intrusion of the old organic structural model into technical-systems theory—but it is unclear how this happens: "the experience of language used in a community is what awakens the language faculty. Once awakened, the faculty shapes and guides the growth of grammars in children" (Boeckx 2010: 53). "Awakening" and "growing" (as transitive verbs) do not feature as central concepts in social theory. It is as if the technical-systems approach has difficulty making the connection between the system as posited and the neurobiological and social processes within which it is held to operate.

Staking Claims

In the three paradigms hitherto considered, society tends to be seen as being borne along either by the "laws of social development" operating through time, by the functional necessities implied by existing as an "organism" in the present, or by the operational requirements of a "technical system" built to respond to those same functional necessities. Individuals and groups are necessarily involved in the production of society but tend to be seen as being swept along by the laws of history or reduced to more or less functional parts of a greater whole. As Durkheim suggests, society and its institutions are in place prior to the arrival of any given individual, and the latter just has to fit in with what already exists. These paradigms tend to skirt around the question of the capacity of human beings to step outside historical and functional constraints and "create" a society according to alternative value systems. This question has long haunted social thought and was at the heart of Kant's conception of ethics as the capacity to behave according to values that may go against our "natural" interests.

On the surface, the individual of nineteenth-century liberalism is just such a "free" actor, "freely" entering into contract with others in the market-place, but the driving force of market-oriented individual action for liberals (inspired by Locke (1975 (1690)) among others) is the pursuit of individual benefit and the avoidance of loss or pain, both of which are seen as being part of our nature. As Kant laments, choice here operates within the confines of a presumed natural "determinism" (his term) and does not recognize our capacity to act against nature in the light, for example, of higher values (1867 (1785)). The liberal idea of the "free" individual thus fits in with the evolutionary paradigm according to which social evolution is propelled along by competitive individuals giving vent to their natural drives (a conception that still lies at the heart of much contemporary economics). However, there was doubt lurking at the heart of this conception. For example, in spite of his celebration of individual liberty as the defining characteristic of contemporary "advanced" societies, Mill recognizes that the Irish peasantry is sorely oppressed and that women are subject to grossly unequal treatment on the part of men. He appeals for a change of heart and in so doing suggests that human beings are not quite so locked in to their individual interests as they might appear to be (Mill [1848] 1899, 1859).

While the organic model, divorced from evolution, was on the point of moving center stage in the face of the crises leading up to and following the First World War, a more critical understanding of human action and responsibility was in the making. Simmel, in (1917) 1999, suggests that sociology differs from other "social" and human sciences in having as its object the relationship between individuals rather than the individuals themselves. The problem for the discipline is that relationships are invisible. The solution proposed by Weber is for sociology to have as its object the meaningful "social action" that ties individuals to each other and that can be explored through the meanings and purposes that individuals see as underlying their action. The individual here is conceived in Kantian terms as being a thoughtful, rational actor capable of acting according to values that may go against natural drives. But individuals are also subject to such drives in much of what they do (as suggested by old liberalism and the new science of economics (Jevons [1871] 1931), just as they are prone to emotion and habit (areas explored in the psychologies of James [1890] and McDougall [1908]).

Max Weber ([1921] 1978) can be thought of as bringing together the individuals of Jamesian and instinct psychology, economics, and Kantian philosophy and as suggesting a more rounded individual who exists for sociology, not as an entity in him- or herself, but in relationship to others. The relationship is the coming together of two or more rational, diversely motivated, emotional, purposeful actors capable of creating new meanings and outcomes. More often than not they are acting within the framework of established norms—acting out, for example, what they have been brought up to see as the way in which fathers and daughters should relate to each other—but they may interpret those norms in different ways or wilfully diverge from them. Hence Weber's idea of sociology as an "empirical" social science, interested in what people really think and do as opposed to the world of ideal rules and norms which serve as the principle object of such "dogmatic" sciences as theology and law.

For Weber, social action is unpredictable, value-laden, emotional, potentially creative, and, above all, understandable, given that is fraught with meaning. When individuals combine into larger groups interacting with each other and seek to protect their collective interests against others through, for example, the control of territory and resources, we gain access to the central processes that lead to the making of society and community. Weberian sociology thus opens the door on to an understanding of society as being produced and reproduced through the partly blind and emotional, and partly rational and purposeful action of human beings, for the better or for the worse. It is not just the ghost of Kant who stands behind the Weberian conception of the individual, but that of Weber's contemporary, Nietzsche, who, more than anyone else in pre–First World War Germany, held sway among young intellectuals with his understanding of the individual human being as capable of anything.

At the same moment that anthropology was calling into question the supposed superiority of European culture (according to nineteenth-century evolutionism) and arguing that all cultures are of equivalent value as ways of adapting to given environments, Weberian sociology sees history and culture as being actively produced through individual and collective action in the light of varying interests and goals. What he describes as "modern capitalism" is in itself a radical transformation of traditional relationships and ways of life ("cultures") that derives neither from the laws of history nor from the "functional" requirements of society seen as an organism or a technical system but from the motivated action of historically situated individuals and collectivities. Such an actor-centered approach has been constantly present in the history of social thought but has been as constantly challenged by arguments that seek to displace responsibility on to extra-human factors (notably from the point of view of holders of power). The post–First World War period was no exception, and this fourth "social constructivist" paradigm in the history of sociology, remains on the margins up until the 1960s and 1970s, when feminism, the civil rights movement, postcolonialism, and the antinuclear and emerging environmental movements contribute to an increasingly open focus on relations of power and human responsibility for outcomes.

As in the case of the other paradigms discussed here, the study of language is at the heart of the development of the actor-centered model. While the use of language is often associated with creativity, the creative act itself can be seen as of secondary interest to the system (or "underlying structure" in Hjelmslev's case) that allows the creativity to happen. At an earlier epoch, language is seen by Humboldt as the "external manifestation" (*äusserliche Erscheinung*) of the spirit of the people itself (Humboldt [1836] 1968: 53), the individual speaker or writer being in some sense an instrument for the expression of the creative genius of the *Volk*. At another level, Humboldt attributes the creative potential in language to the existence of the verb form that brings "life" into the sentence (Humboldt [1836] 1968: 267). The relegation of the individual to the status of "end-user" in these different conceptions corresponds to the passive role attributed to individuals in the three major social paradigms of social evolutionism, organic structuralism, and the technical-systems approach.

With the emergence of an approach that places emphasis on the making of society (and its "structures") by actors based on a complex set of motivations that are nonetheless accessible to understanding, the production of language texts as a creative moment takes on new significance. For Ricoeur (1969), for example, the spoken (or written) word, within the context of the sentence, is the moment at which language comes to life. Language is not a closed system or structure, which can be studied in is own right, separated from the *parole*, but comes into existence at the moment of use when it is used to say something to someone about something. The key element to be understood is the coming and going between the system of signs and their use in speech, the latter gradually transforming the former. Austin's "doing" and "saying" also sees certain kinds of speech acts as moments of social performance where statuses are enacted (or "spoken") in relation to specific events or procedures: "I do, I will, I pledge, I name . . . " (Austin 1962). Bourdieu (1982) extrapolates from the examples provided by Austin to extend the idea to society as a whole as a "marketplace" where the value of what one says is related to status or class position. These authors echo Habermas's attempts to identify the ground rules of any successful "communicative action" that requires shared understandings as to what is being talked about, what each party can expect of the other, and whether or not what is being expressed is sincere (Habermas 1976, 1982) . Habermas's more global approach can be compared to empirical "conversational analysis" that charts the to-ing and fro-ing in any given conversational exchange where each participant in turn can "repair" prior misunderstandings and keep the communication open (Schegloff 1992).

Such approaches not only build on the idea that society is made through action and interaction, but that language is an integral part of that making. Labov's studies of the linguistic competence of young blacks in New York, or of dialectal variations in the local speech of islanders on Martha's Vineyard, are cases in point where relations within and between groups are established, in part, through language (Labov 1963, 1972). Claims to territory and status are staked out through language, making known the interests and identities of the people involved, and not just through content, but through form. Language is seen as an instrument for identifying and marginalizing those who do not possess the necessary codes whether as members of a street "gang," as incomers on an island, or as kids in school whose linguistic "incompetence" is demonstrated by procedures so intimidating as to reduce them to silence. Labov's variationist approach brings us into the heart of social processes and into the heart of sociology of the social constructivist variety. Milroy's study of the variations in the speech of Belfast residents from one part of the town to another is a similar foray into the heartland of identities and boundaries, with notable differences between Protestant women working in the center of town and their male counterparts in the shipyards (Milroy 1987). The Labovian approach continues to inspire studies that make the connection between the use of language and the making of identities and relationships, with respect, for example, to what language "indicates" ("indexicality") in relation to "stratified social meaning systems" (or "scales") in the context of globalization (Blommaert 2010). The defining characteristic of this approach is to see language-users as agents involved in "acts of identity" (Llamas & Watt 2010). In the light of such studies it is difficult to maintain the frontier between sociology and (socio)linguistics when both share a critical and constructivist understanding of social relations, given that language is the principal medium through which relations are built and understood. Does this mean that the gradual shift in paradigms over time is calling into question old disciplinary boundaries?

Transdisciplinary Alignments

At the roots of the four paradigms presented in this text are to be found, not disciplinary boundaries as such, but different understandings of society, different conceptions of the role of science and different worldviews relating to context, position and interest. Although there appears to have been a shift over time in the relative dominance of one or other paradigm, there are also striking continuities. It may be the case that the paradigms do not so much replace each other as become superimposed, with one or other of them moving to the top of the heap while the others continue to operate at other levels.

For example, the Comtean idea that society has to be administered on the basis of precise, "positive" knowledge that can only be provided by experts versed in the laws of social development is still the cornerstone of the contemporary technical-systems approach albeit shed of (most of) its nineteenth-century evolutionist attributes. The old utilitarian idea that society is a giant marketplace in which individuals pursue their individual interests motivated by their inborn tendency to maximize happiness and avoid pain is still the foundational dogma of much economic thought. The organic functionalist view of the individual as needing to be adapted to fit in to the greater social whole is also the premise of many contemporary social programs that see the individual as the problem to be resolved. This latter view can be related to the organic functionalist idea that the world is made up of cultures in contact and in conflict, and that social problems can be grounded in cultural misunderstanding and the shock of opposed values. In this case it is not so much the individual who is to blame but the cultural system of which he or she is the carrier.

Something of the defining characteristics of these different worldviews can be seen in relation to the variable significance accorded to "nature" and "culture." For nineteenth-century social evolutionism, progress toward perfection is measurable not just through "improvements" in agriculture and the transformation of natural resources but also through the "improvement" of human beings, who are seen as advancing intellectually and morally. While mainstream social thought saw all human beings as "improvable" (through education, for example), the idea that differences in wealth and power may reflect underlying natural differences (in the case of women, the working classes and the colonized "other," for example) is never far below the surface and emerges toward the end of the century in the form of "social hygiene," "racial betterment," and eugenics.

When evolutionism is challenged by organic functionalism before and after the First World War, the social world is understood as being like a living organism that has to respond to functional constraints relating to its survival in the present. Nature, in the form of the organism, again provides the model for understanding society, and individual human beings are seen as being like functioning or non-functioning body parts. The subsequent move toward seeing society as a technical system coincides with the return to a Cartesian view of nature as a complex set of elements and processes that are open to being understood and, if necessary, "corrected" through intervention. Human behavior is no exception, with the science of mental life being formulated in increasingly technical terms and technical solutions.

The role played by nature in these three paradigms itself becomes the object of critical appraisal in the case of the fourth paradigm, which places the actor at the heart of the "making" of society. As one of the principal sources of inspiration for this paradigm, Max Weber draws attention to the way in which social relationships are "seen" as being natural, based on the nebulous ideas of "race" and "ethnicity," for example, whereas they tend to be rooted in the collective, monopolistic appropriation of territory and resources. In other words, relations of power can clothe and justify themselves in natural difference as an argument of last resort. Natural differences exist, but before explaining social phenomena on the basis of such differences, Weber suggests that all possible social explanations need to be taken into consideration. For sociology, priority has to be given to the social explanation of social phenomena.

A similar reading of these paradigms can be made for culture. For nineteenth-century social evolutionism, cultures (as total ways of life) can be arranged in a hierarchical sequence tending toward the perfection represented by European industrial civilization. For the organic functionalist model, culture is the set of rules and practices that allows a society to be functionally adapted to its environment without there being any difference of value from one culture to another. Bearers of such other cultures can have problems of adaptation when they migrate from one part of the world to another. When society is seen as a technical system, culture as a set of values and ways of doing and being is seen as in some way an irrational factor that has to be kept out of the central operating processes that are defined on the basis of technical goals and means. Culture for the actor-based paradigm, on the other hand, is at the heart of the making of society, both in terms of the "macro-culture" of capitalist modernity or postmodernity and in that of the myriad forms of countercultural expression and cultural hegemony that emerge from within social relations. Claiming "cultural difference" as an explanation for social exclusion or inequality is also subject to critical appraisal in the light of the fourth paradigm.

Rather than seeing an apparent coming-into-dominance of a critical social constructivist paradigm (across disciplines) or a blurring of the frontiers between contemporary sociology and (socio)linguistics, it would seem more appropriate to think in terms of a variety of transdisciplinary alignments based on overlapping or shared paradigms. For example, Chomskyan linguistics (as opposed to Chomskyan social criticism) has a strongly positivistic, naturalistic bias according to which the language faculty as an inborn computational system is a "reality" (Boeckx 2010) whose precise location and functioning has yet to be understood. What could be described as the "social determinants" of language acquisition are as remote from this theory as are the social determinants of mental health in current approaches in psychiatry that place emphasis on the chemistry of the brain. Both are part of the technical-systems approach to the understanding of human behavior that cuts across a variety of disciplinary fields.

Another transdisciplinary alignment relates to culture. Hymes (1974) proposes an "ethnography of speaking" in order to get inside the diversity of cultures apart from which "mankind cannot be understood"—culture being defined, following Tylor ([1871] 1958), as a "whole way of life." Individuals are seen as members of language "communities" that have their own distinct cultures and therefore as "bearers" of those cultures whence the problems that can arise in "interethnic" communication as documented by Gumperz (1982). The idea that the world is made up of distinct cultural groupings and that conflicts can arise from the clash of cultures, holds sway in much contemporary political discourse on interculturalism and multiculturalism, and has its roots in the organic functionalist paradigm.

The fourth paradigm also cuts a swathe through a variety of disciplinary territories, and in so doing opens up a new interdisciplinary space and possibly even a new discipline: constructivist social science. The study of language exemplifies the need for such an interdisciplinary space but also the constraints that make its emergence problematic. The relationship between sociology and psychiatry provides a parallel. In pre–First World War Germany, there was a possibility of combining the insights of the new actor-centered sociology and the new psychiatry that saw individual life histories as the key to understanding the emergence of mental health problems (Mayer-Gross et al. 1954). Neither discipline, however, was sufficiently advanced to make the combination possible. The idea of a "social" psychiatry re-emerged in the 1950s and 1960s, but was to succumb to the technical-systems approach in the 1970s and 1980s, with the reinforcing of the biomedical understanding of mental health. With current emphasis on the social determinants of health (social inequality, poverty, stigmatization, domestic violence, among others) there seem to be new possibilities for the creation of a "preventive psychiatry" rooted in both social and biomedical science.

Just as the critical, social constructivist paradigm creates a space in which sociology and psychiatry can find a common language and purpose, so constructivist sociology and (socio)linguistics appear to be on a (benign) collision course. Hymes suggests that sociolinguistics has to exist, given the lack of understanding of language in sociology and the lack of awareness of social context in linguistics (Hymes 1974). The point made in this chapter, however, is that the social constructivist paradigm necessarily places language at the heart of social relations. In the light of this paradigm, sociologists and linguists no longer have the option of ignoring each other. In prior research on language in the Québec workplace, I came to the conclusion that the two disciplines are distinguished on the basis of their objects: sociology has, as its primary object, the understanding of social relations and needs to take language into account in order to do so; linguistics has, as its primary object, the understanding of language and needs to take social relations into account in order to fulfil its goal (McAll 1992). My subsequent research in the Montreal aerospace industry and elsewhere has led to a blurring of this distinction (McAll 1997, 2003). Language is the principle medium through which social relations are built, transformed and reflected upon, identities are "acted out," people are named and placed, and territories are staked out. Given social constructivism, the disciplinary frontier no longer holds. The study of language brings us into the workshop of the social world.

There is, however, no easy access to such an interdisciplinary space. Critical social constructivism requires the abandoning of the safe havens of social thought that see human beings as mere bearers of cultures, end-users of linguistic codes, and functioning or nonfunctioning parts of greater wholes that have their own systemic logic. It requires the crossing of frontiers, the creation of spaces for dialogue, and the pooling of disciplinary knowledge. Different disciplines may bring to the table their own specific insights on one or other aspect of the social world, but that world remains a complex whole that requires a convergence of views within the framework of a common understanding of human beings as doers and makers. That conjoined effort is required not only for the charting of what exists but for documenting and enabling the expression of "voice" in the public domain. This is another area where the interwoven stories of sociology and the study of language play themselves out. Where people not only make structures work but develop a critical, collective conversation about those same structures. At the heart of this process are the spaces where citizenship "voices" make themselves heard, where people engage in what Kant ([1784] 1967) describes as the "public use of reason."

NOTES

1. The "wundervolle Englische Wortbau" that is "tief in dem Englischen Charakter gegründet" (Humboldt 1836: 176).
2. Lyell, who was a source of considerable inspiration for Darwin, makes the same point in *The antiquity of man* (Lyell [1863] 1973).

3. "Chacune des langues présente à chacun des moments de son histoire un système original qu'il est nécessaire de décrire et dont il faut expliquer la formation dans son ensemble" (Meillet 1915: 469). "*Formation*" in French, although somewhat similar to "formation" in English, is nonetheless difficult to translate, referring both to the "process of being formed" and, by metonymy, to "what is formed." "Overall makeup" captures, I think, in this context, the range of meaning implicit in the French word.

References

Austin, J.L. 1962. *How to do things with words.* Cambridge: Harvard University Press.

Beveridge, W. H. 1944. *Full employment in a free society.* London: George Allen & Unwin.

Blommaert, J. 2010. *The sociolinguistics of globalisation.* Cambridge: Cambridge University Press.

Boeckx, C. 2010. *Language in cognition.* Chichester: Wiley-Blackwell.

Bourdieu, P. 1982. *Ce que parler veut dire.* Paris: Fayard.

Chomsky, N. 1986. *Knowledge of language: Its nature, origin, and use.* New York: Praeger.

Cobbett, W. 1967. *Autobiography: The progress of a plough-boy to a seat in Parliament.* London: Faber.

Comte, A. 1883. Plans des travaux scientifiques nécessaires pour réorganiser la société. In A. Comte, *Opuscules de philosophie sociale 1819—1828*, 60–180. Paris: Ernest Leroux, Éditeur.

Cooper, R. L. 1989. *Language planning and social change.* Cambridge: Cambridge University Press.

Darwin, C. (1871) 1936. *The descent of man.* New York: Modern Library.

Durkheim, É . (1895) 1927. *Les règles de la méthode sociologique.* Paris: Librairie Félix Alcan.

Durkheim, É. (1912) 1968. *Les formes élémentaires de la vie religieuse.* Paris.

Durkheim, É. (1893) 1973. *De la division du travail social.* Paris: Presses Universitaires de France.

Febvre, L. 1922. *La terre et l'évolution humaine: Introduction géographique à l'histoire.* Paris: La Renaissance du livre.

Foucault, M. 1966. *Les mots et les choses, une archéologie des sciences humaines.* Paris: Gallimard.

Gumperz, J. J. 1982. *Discourse strategies.* Cambridge: Cambridge University Press.

Habermas, Jürgen. 1979. "What is Universal Pragmatics?" *Communication and the evolution of society*, 1–68. Boston: Beacon Press.

Habermas, Jürgen. 1982. *Theorie des kommunicativen Handelns: Band 1, Handlungsrationalität und gesellschaftliche Rationalisierung*, Frankfurt: Suhrkamp Verlag.

Hjelmslev, L. 1963. *Prolegomena to a theory of language.* Translated by F. J. Whitfield. Madison: University of Wisconsin Press.

Hobbes, T. (1640) 1969. *The elements of law natural and politic.* New York: Barnes & Noble.

Hobsbawm, E. J. 1987. *The age of empire*. London: Weidenfeld & Nicholson.

Humboldt, W. von. (1836) 1968. *Über die Verschiedenheit des menschlichen Sprachbaues und ihren Einfluß auf der geistigen Entwickelung des Menschengeschlechts*. Bonn: Ferd. Dümmler's Verlag.

Hume, D. (1740) 1978. *A treatise of human nature*. Oxford: Clarendon Press.

Hymes, D. 1974. *Foundations in sociolinguistics: An ethnographic approach*. Philadelphia: University of Pennsylvania Press.

James, W. 1890. *The principles of psychology*. London: MacMillan.

Jevons, W. S. (1871) 1931. *The theory of political economy*. London: MacMillan.

Kant, Immanuel. (1784) 1967. Beantwortung der Frage: Was ist Aufklärung?. In *Was ist Aufklärung? Aufsätze zur Geschichte und Philosophie*, Herausg. u. eingeleitet von Jürgen Zehbe, 55–61. Göttingen: Vandenhoeck & Ruprecht.

Kant, I. (1785) 1867. *Grundlegung zur Metaphysik der Sitten*. In I. Kant, *Sämmtliche Werke*, vol.4, herausg, von G. Hartenstein, 233–312. Leipzig: Leopold Voss.

Keynes, J. M. 1936. *The general theory of employment, interest and money*. London: MacMillan.

Labov, W. 1963. The social motivation of a sound change. *Word* 19: 273–309.

Labov, W. 1972. *Language in the inner city: Studies in the Black English vernacular*. Philadelphia: University of Pennsylvania Press.

Llamas, C., & Watt, D. (eds.) 2010. *Language and identities*. Edinburgh: Edinburgh University Press.

Locke, J. (1690) 1975. *An essay concerning human understanding*. Oxford: Oxford University Press.

Lyell, C. (1863) 1873. *The antiquity of man: The geological evidence*. London: John Murray.

Maine, H. J. S. (1861) 1924. *Ancient Law*. London: John Murray.

Malinowski, B. 1960. *A scientific theory of culture and other essays*. New York: Oxford University Press.

Malthus, T. R. (1820) 1964. *Principles of political economy*. New York: August M. Kelley.

Mayer-Gross, W., Slater, E., & Roth, M. 1954. *Clinical psychiatry*. London: Cassell & Company.

McAll, C. 1992. Langues et silence: les travailleurs immigrés au Québec et la sociologie du langage. *Sociologie et sociétés* 24(2): 117–30.

McAll, C. 1997. The breaking point: Language in Quebec Society. In M. Fournier, M. Rosenberg, & D. White (eds.), *Quebec society: Critical issues*, 61–80. Scarborough: Prentice Hall.

McAll, C. 2003. Language dynamics in the bi- and multilingual workplace. In R. Bayley & S. R. Schecter (eds.), *Language socialization in multilingual societies*, 235–50. Clevedon: Multilingual Matters.

McDougall, W. 1908. *An introduction to social psychology*. London: Methuen.

Meillet, A. 1915. *Introduction à l'étude comparative des langues indo-européennes*. Paris: Hachette.

Mill, J. S. 1859. *On liberty*. London: John W. Parker & Son.

Mill, J. S. (1848) 1899. *Principles of political economy*. New York: The Colonial Press.

Milroy, L. 1987. *Language and social networks*. Oxford: Blackwell.

Morgan, L. H. (1877) 1964. *Ancient society*. Cambridge: The Belknap Press.

Needham, J. 1926. Mechanistic biology and the religious consciousness. In J. Needham (ed.), *Science, religion and reality*. London: Sheldon Press.

Oberschall, A. 1972. The Institutionalization of American Sociology. In A. Oberschall (ed.), *The establishment of empirical sociology*, 187–244. New York: Harper and Row.

Owen, R. (1814) 1949. *A new view of society*. London: Dent.

Parsons, T. 1951. *The social system*. Glencoe: Free Press.

Ricardo, D. (1817) 1966. *On the principles of political economy and taxation*. Cambridge: Cambridge University Press.

Ricoeur, P. 1969. La structure, le mot, l'événement. In Paul Ricoeur (ed.), *Le conflit des interprétations*, 80–97. Paris: Éditions du Seuil.

Sapir, E. 1921. *Language, An introduction to the study of speech*. New York: Harcourt, Brace & Company.

Saussure, F. de . 1970. Mémoire sur le système primitif des voyelles dans les langues Indo-européens. In C. Bally & L. Gauthier (eds.), *Recueil des publications scientifiques* (1922), 1–268. Genève: Slatkine Reprints.

Saussure, F. de. (1915) 1978. *Cours de linguistique générale*. Paris: Payot.

Schegloff, Emanuel A. 1992. Repair after next turn: The last structurally provided defense of intersubjectivity in conversation. *American Journal of Sociology* 97(5): 1295–345.

Simmel, G. (1917) 1999. Grundfragen der Soziologie. In *Georg Simmel, Gesamtausgabe*, Band 16. Frankurt am Main: Sührkamp.

Smith, A. (1775) 1910. *An inquiry into the nature and causes of the wealth of nations* London: J.M. Dent & Sons.

Spencer, H. 1893. *The principles of sociology*. London: Williams & Norgate.

Trubetzkoy, N. 1933. La phonologie actuelle. *Journal de psychologie* 30: 227–46.

Tylor, E. B. (1871) 1958. *Primitive culture*. New York: Harper and Row.

Weber, E. 1976. *Peasants into Frenchmen: The modernization of rural France, 1870–1914*. Palo Alto, CA: Stanford University Press.

Weber, M. (1921) 1978. *Economy and society*. Berkeley: University of California Press.

Whitney, W. D. (1867) 1971. Language and the study of language (1867). In Michael Silverstein (ed.), *Whitney on language*, 7–111. Cambridge, MA: MIT Press.

Wiener, N. 1948. *Cybernetics, or control and communication in the animal and the machine*. Cambridge, MA: MIT Press.

CHAPTER 4

CRITICAL DISCOURSE ANALYSIS

MARTIN REISIGL

Critical Discourse Analysis (CDA) has entered the mainstream of linguistic and social science research with a strong transdisciplinary orientation and social engagement. It developed in the late 1980s and early 1990s, after the critical turn loomed as "critical linguistics" in the 1970s had spread and consolidated in the fields of discourse analysis and sociolinguistics. Until now, CDA has differentiated itself into at least six variants: (1) Fairclough's approach, which is strongly social theoretically embedded, and informed by systemic functional linguistics; (2) van Leeuwen's and Kress's social semiotic and systemic functional approach; (3) van Dijk's socio-cognitive approach; (4) the form of CDA promoted by the Duisburg Group around S. and M. Jäger, who keenly draw on Foucault's approach to discourse analysis and Link's discourse theory; (5) the Oldenburg approach, which is upheld by Gloy, Januschek, and others; (6) and finally the "Viennese" and "Lancaster" tradition of CDA, which is often termed the "discourse-historical approach" and sometimes "discourse sociolinguistics," and which, among many others, Wodak and I myself align with.

These six versions of CDA are introduced in the present chapter. Before focusing on the single variants, the next section will concentrate on the relationship between discourse analysis (particularly CDA) and sociolinguistics, by looking at both the relevance of the different ways of doing CDA for sociolinguistics and the tensions between the two linguistic "branches." In the following section, it will be demonstrated that the subdisciplinary status of (critical) discourse analysis within linguistics and the relationship between (critical) discourse analysis and sociolinguistics is historically dynamic and dependent on scientific culture. The chapter then generally depicts common features of the heterogeneous group of critical approaches to discourse. The crucial concepts of discourse and context, as they are conceived of in the six versions of CDA, are then explained and contrasted with each other. Next, the chapter deals with basic research interests and the steps of research practices, as they are outlined in the various approaches. Remarks on future developments conclude the chapter.

Critical Discourse Analysis and Sociolinguistics

Sociolinguistics and discourse analysis started developing almost simultaneously, but developed out of partly differing scientific traditions in various areas of the world.

The term "sociolinguistics" seems to have been coined by Currie in 1949 to delineate the program of a field of research that is concerned with the study of social functions and significations of speech factors (Currie 1952; see Dittmar 1997: 19f.). From the 1960s—and especially from the 1970s—onward, sociolinguistics established itself as a countermovement (first in the United States and then in Europe and elsewhere) against (American) structuralism or descriptivism, which was formally oriented and neglected the social aspects of language use, and was against conventional dialectology. Sociolinguistics soon became a well-established branch of linguistics committed to the study of the concrete language use of social groups and linguistic varieties in different societies (see Dittmar 1997: 20).

Most of the sociolinguistic approaches consider "discourse" as language in use, as parole, or as utterances in a social context; and "discourse analysis," as a method to analyze this language use. Since "sociolinguistics" was soon conceptualized as a specific field that studies the social aspects of language (use), and since "discourse analysis"—among sociolinguistics—was often "just" seen as a "method," it seemed obvious that "discourse analysis" was simply subordinated to "sociolinguistics."

In the same year in which Currie publicly introduced the notion of "sociolinguistics," that is, in 1952, the American structuralist Harris referred to the term "discourse analysis" in order to designate a formal method for the analysis of language above the sentence level, a method for the analysis of connected speech or writing, that is, of discourses (Harris 1952). Harris indicated two approaches: "One can approach discourse analysis from two types of problems, which turn out to be related. The first is the problem of continuing descriptive linguistics beyond the limits of a single sentence at a time. The other is the question of correlating 'culture' and 'language' (i.e. non-linguistic and linguistic behavior)" (Harris 1952: 1). The distributionalist was particularly concerned with the first problem and tried to develop a sort of text grammar. The second problem was disregarded until the late 1960s, when Pêcheux and Foucault became interested in the relationship between language and culture in France. The Birmingham group (Coulthard, Sinclair, and others) started to deal with the first, but partly also with the second issue in mid-1970s (Sinclair and Coulthard 1975). Since then, the discourse-analytical focus on intertextuality, interdiscursivity, social semiotics, and the social, political, and historical context of language in use has continuously broadened.

However, for a long time, discourse analysis was predominantly seen as part of sociolinguistics or pragmatics. Sinclair and Coulthard (1975: 6) regarded their approach to be mainly sociolinguistic. Stubbs (1988: 1) designed discourse analysis to be "the linguistic analysis of naturally occurring connected spoken or written discourse," and considered discourse analysis to be "sociolinguistic analysis of natural language." Brown and Yule (1983: viiif.) characterized "discourse analysis" as a linguistic approach that encompasses a wide range of activities "at the intersection of disciplines as diverse as sociolinguistics, psycholinguistics, philosophical linguistics and computational linguistics." Since the mid-1980s, discourse analysis has increasingly been attempting to connect linguistics with sociology, philosophy, history, political science, psychology, literary studies, anthropology, pedagogy, and geography. This trans- and interdisciplinary development was particularly fostered after the critical turn. Today, CDA is one of the most influential sections within discourse analysis.

In our day, discourse analysis is emancipating itself both from sociolinguistics and pragmatics. It is no longer just seen as method of language analysis, but conceived of as a multidimensional project incorporating theory, methods, methodology, and empirically based research practices that yield concrete social applications.

Studying sociolinguistic work, we find various theoretical conceptions of the relationship between sociolinguistics, pragmatics, and discourse analysis. In the present context, I just want to focus on three such representations. They tend toward subordinating discourse analysis and including it—mostly completely—within sociolinguistics. According to them, "discourse" is language in social use on the level of parole, and "discourse analysis" is a qualitative method neighboring conversation analysis. If they make a distinction between macro- and microsociolinguistics, they incorporate discourse analysis into the latter (see figure 4.1).

Discourse analysis appears at different, and sometimes opposing, places within sociolinguistic categorizations. Dittmar, for instance, regards "discourse analysis" as one of the five domains of "interactional sociolinguistics." He considers pragmatics to be a hypernym of interactional sociolinguistics (Dittmar 1996: 14f.; see figure 4.2).

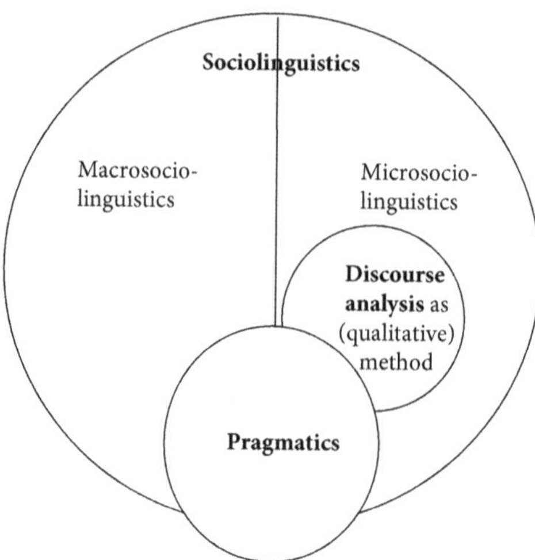

Figure 4.1. A geometrical representation of the relationship between discourse analysis, sociolinguistics, and pragmatics

Sources: Adapted from Stubbs (1983), Boxer (2002), Thibault (1988), and Johnstone (2000).

In contrast, Schiffrin tends toward using "discourse analysis" as a cover term that encompasses a series of linguistic branches. In her 1994 book *Approaches of Discourse*, she distinguishes between six approaches to discourse, namely: (1) speech act theory, (2) interactional sociolinguistics, (3) ethnography of communication, (4) pragmatics, (5) conversation analysis, and (6) variation

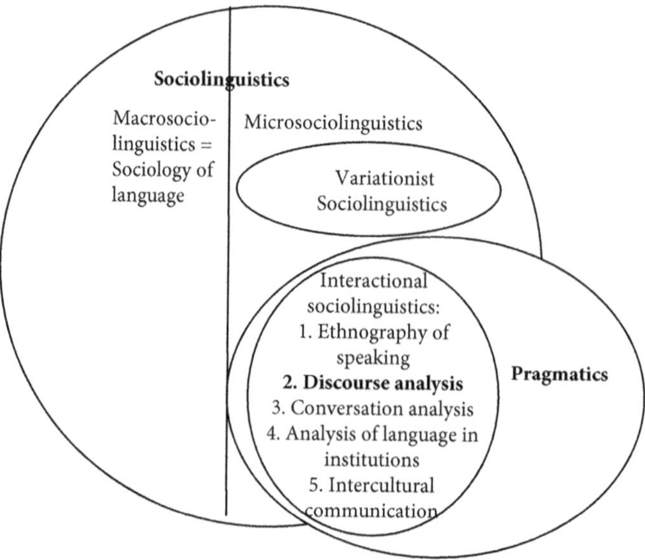

Figure 4.2. A geometrical representation of the relationship between discourse analysis, sociolinguistics, and pragmatics

Source: Extrapolated from Dittmar (1996).

analysis. Here, the relationships between discourse analysis and interactional sociolinguistics go the other way round. Schiffrin's separation of pragmatics and speech act theory can be contested.

The selective synopsis of linguistic handbooks, textbooks, and specialized literature outcrops a variety of relationships of inclusion, subordination, and intersection with respect to the connection of discourse analysis to sociolinguistics. The categorizations often contradict each other, and some scholars—for example, Trudgill (2004: 3)—rightly emphasize that distinctions between different subbranches of linguistics are by no means precise and unambiguous.

Trudgill relates this statement to the subbranches of sociolinguistics. He locates discourse analysis partly within and partly outside sociolinguistics:

> Discourse analysis is a branch of linguistics which deals with linguistic units at levels above the sentence, i.e. texts and conversations. Those branches of discourse analysis which come under the heading of language and society presuppose that language is being used in social interaction and, thus, deal with conversation. (Other non-sociolinguistic branches of discourse analysis are often known as text linguistics.) Discourse analysis is contrasted by some writers with conversation analysis, an area of sociolinguistics which has connections to ethnomethodology and which analyses the structure and norms of conversation such as the relationship between questions and answers, or summonses and responses. (2004: 4)

From Trudgill's (2004: 1–5) explanations emerge rather complex relationships between sociolinguistics and discourse analysis. They can be reproduced schematically (see figure 4.3).

Even though I agree with Trudgill's general claim that distinctions between different subbranches of linguistics are not clear-cut and definite, the arbitrariness of distinctions among various linguistic branches is not satisfactory. Disciplinary monocentrism leads to questionable oversimplification. It leads to a tendency of sociolinguistics considering not only discourse analysis, but also pragmatics and, partly, conversation analysis as well, as parts or "subfields" of sociolinguistics. In turn, from a discourse-analytical point of view, sociolinguistics (especially interactional sociolinguistics) but also pragmatics, conversation analysis, text linguistics, and semantics are often treated as parts of discourse analysis. In contrast to such biased subordinations, I favor a theoretical conceptualization that assumes the relationship among discourse analysis and sociolinguistics, as well as other linguistic branches, as being one of family resemblance. This notion, taken from Wittgenstein's *Philosophische Untersuchungen* (*Philosophical Investigations;* [1952] 1989: 277ff.), permits us to grasp the intersections of linguistic (sub)branches more adequately than unidirectional incorporations. The relationship of family resemblance is illustrated by figure 4.4.

This theoretical modeling is a suggestion developed in the actual version of the discourse-historical approach to CDA, which has been influenced by sociolinguists such as Bernstein (1975, 1996), Labov (1966, 1972) and Hymes

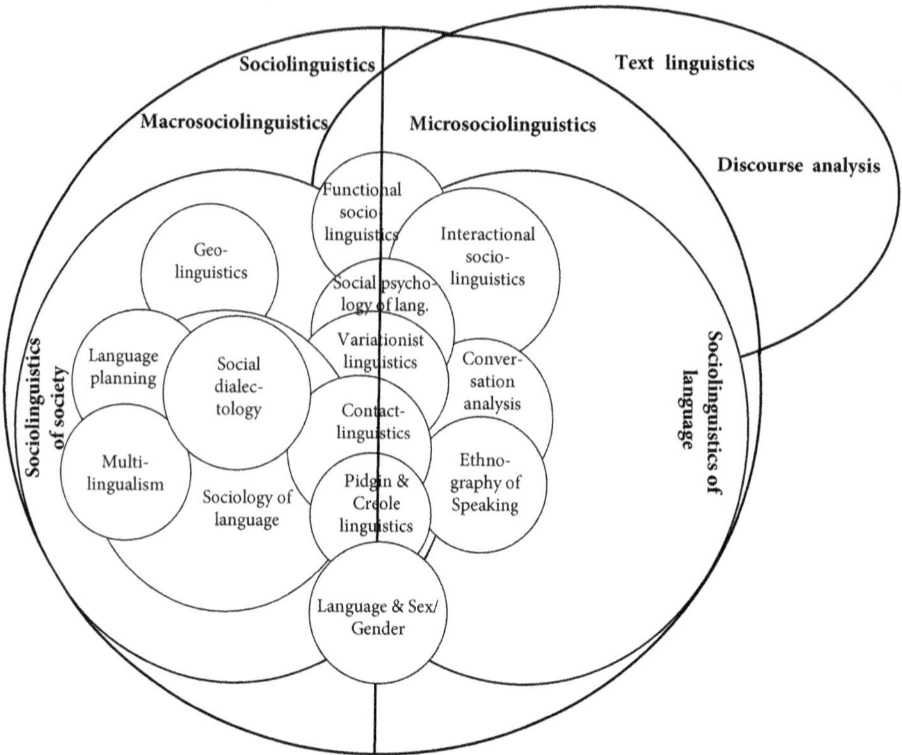

Figure 4.3. A geometrical representation of the relationship between discourse analysis, sociolinguistics, and pragmatics

Source: Adapted from Trudgill (2004: 1–5)

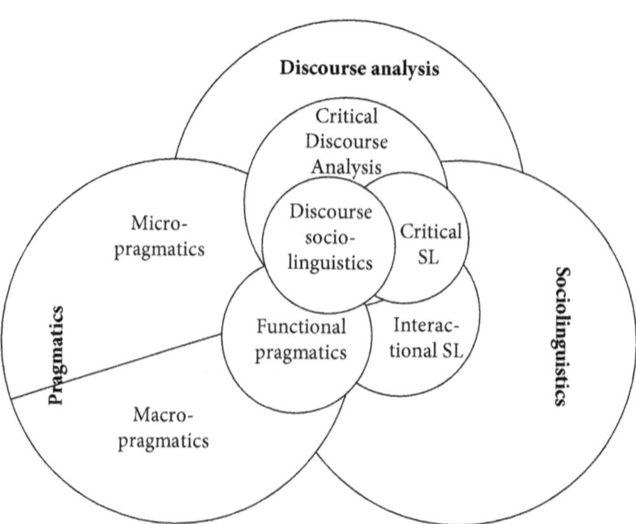

Figure 4.4. A geometrical representation of the relationship of family resemblance

(1974), particularly during the 1970s, 1980s, and 1990s. This is the reason why the term "discourse sociolinguistics" temporarily circulated as a label for this approach, especially between 1993 and 1996 (e.g., Matouschek & Wodak 1995; Wodak 1996: 1–8). Viennese "discourse sociolinguistics" is characterized as sociolinguistics that studies text and context as interdependent factors of equal importance, and that takes an analytical stance both from an "outsider-perspective" and an ethnographic "insider-perspective" (Wodak 1996: 3). It is especially designed for the critical analysis of "language barriers" and "disorders" of institutional discourses, with special attention to doctor-patient interaction, school committee meetings, news broadcasts, and therapeutic communication. In contrast to former sociolinguistic approaches, discourse sociolinguistics introduces an interdisciplinary framework that, among other things, tries to connect its critical claims to Jürgen Habermas's discourse theory as a source for normative standards. Differently from Habermas's abstract theory, discourse sociolinguistics soon became engaged in attempts to contribute to the practical solution of communication problems in the above-mentioned institutions.

As for the relationship between sociolinguistics and discourse analysis in other variants of CDA, the inspiration by sociolinguistic theories is conspicuous in Fairclough's and van Dijk's work, whereas it has been of less significance in van Leeuwen and Kress's research and in the two German approaches.

Fairclough's relationship to "traditional" sociolinguistics is, however, rather broken. Fairclough (1992) refers to early critical linguists (Fowler et al. 1979: 185–195), who reject the dualistic sociolinguistic conception of language and society. Instead of merely trying to establish and insolate single correlations between language and society, analysts should look for deeper causal relations, including the impact and influence of language on society. They should analytically focus on complete texts or discourse fragments, and not just on single linguistic features or elements—an analytical perspective often adopted by variationist sociolinguistics (Fairclough 1992: 26f.). Against Labov and Fanshel (1977), Fairclough stresses the principle of heterogeneity of discourse as a basic element of his theory of "intertextuality." He underlines that the boundaries between styles are less clear cut and that configurations of style in therapeutic discourse are less static than Labov and Fanshel suggest (Fairclough 1992: 22f.). He argues that Labov and Fanshel ignore the reproductive ideological work of therapies, and sums up: "Labov and Fanshel stop short of a *critical* analysis of therapeutic discourse, while providing valuable analytical resources for such an analysis" (Fairclough 1992: 23). Furthermore, Fairclough's criticism of former sociolinguistic, but also pragmatic, work aims at the concept of "context." Partly relying on Foucault's archeology of knowledge, Fairclough argues that the simple appeal to "context" does not allow us to explain what is said or written or how a text or discourse fragment is interpreted. Rather, the analysis of the relationship between "text" and "context" has also to take into consideration that the building up of discursive formations includes the ordered formation of concepts, including the theoretical concepts that are used for specific analytical (e.g., sociolinguistic or discourse-analytical) purposes (Fairclough 1992: 47f.). In this sense, Fairclough, who strongly emphasizes the dialectical relationship between text and context and the diachronic dimension of historically changing discursive practices, rejects the position of a naive sociolinguistic realism or positivism. However, Fairclough still opts for a specific form of realism, that is, for "critical realism" (2006: 12). This epistemic position acknowledges that social relations and "objects" have a materiality that is not just conditioned by human knowledge, but that this materiality is nevertheless heavily influenced by social (co-)constructions performed by social subjects (Fairclough 2006: 12).

As for the Duisburg group, sociolinguistics is even more ostentatiously criticized, although many of Fairclough's points can also be found in S. Jäger's work (1984, 2001a: 28–51). Jäger is strongly influenced by French poststructuralist theories, particularly by Foucault. He rejects positivist sociolinguistic theories that claim to utterly mirror the connections between language and society. Jäger refutes the analytical separation of language and society, which partly is terminologically reflected in the word "sociolinguistics" itself (Jäger 2001a: 28, 46). He contests Bernstein's theory of language barriers (Jäger 2001a: 28–39) and Labov's renunciation of taking content systematically into account in addition to form (Jäger 2001a: 40). Jäger criticizes the sociolinguistic lack of a general social theory that consistently anchors language and language use in a social context (Jäger 2001a: 45). Similarly to Fairclough, Jäger stresses the close interconnections between linguistic and other social conditions and factors (Jäger 2001a: 50f.).

To sum up: CDA emerged as an attempt to abandon some of the traditional dualisms reproduced by older forms of sociolinguistics and to bring language and society closer together, as well as text and context. Its theoretical and methodological framework was designated to include form, function, structure, and content analysis, and related to content analysis, the study of ideological presuppositions. CDA crystallized into an interdisciplinary group of approaches that try to systematically take into account in their analyses the social, political, and historical dimension of language use in context. In addition to the critique of naive epistemic realism, several of the CDA approaches argue against the causal-deterministic belief in the existence of discourse-independent or pre-discursive social factors that monodirectionally control discursive practices. In contrast, they regard sociological variables such as class and gender as discourse dependent, and see the discourse analysts' contribution to the co-construction of discourses and discourse units by their analyses. The discourse-historical variant and Fairclough's CDA assume an epistemic in-between position, since they both stress a dialectical relationship between discursive and other social structures.

General Characteristics of Critical Discourse Analysis

There are a series of commonalities that unite the various approaches to CDA:

(1) They all claim to be "critical," and not just "descriptive," and they found their concepts of critique on ethical (e.g., democratic) principles and norms. They are sociopolitically engaged and very often application oriented—in the sense that their social critique aims at social change toward improvements. They make claims of emancipation and criticize various forms of discursively constituted power abuse and hegemonic social structures that lead to injustice and social discrimination. In addition to these more practical aims, they make epistemic, theory-related claims of exposure or enlightenment: they are concerned with making transparent opaque, contradictory, power-related, manipulative relationships among language and society or social structures.

There have been several controversial intellectual disputes about the differences between "descriptive" and "critical" approaches to language and discourse. These debates encased a lot of misunderstandings and misconceptions. The first and most basic misconception lies in the assumption that there can be such a thing as a purely descriptive science (e.g., linguistics or discourse analysis). If a descriptive science really existed, it would have to be free of any attempt to explain and argue. Obviously, there is no science without explanation and argumentation. Second, the strict opposition must be questioned with respect to the scientific practice of describing itself. Provided that describing means to represent a research object iconically through a scientific metalanguage (including visual metalanguage), an accurate description relies on the recurring procedure of critically comparing the scientific representamen and the represented object—the comparison focusing on the question of adequate structural similarity between object and "sign body." Third, good scientists should always try to reflect on their own conditions, possibilities, and general as well as pragmatic limits of generating scientific knowledge—in the sense that Kant conceived of "critique" as propaedeutics. In short: good science is always critical, even where its task is to describe.

(2) With respect to their understanding of discourse, the six approaches put emphasis on the action-related quality of discourses (discourse is conceived of as social practice), on the situatedness, the context dependence of discourses, and on the socially constructed as well as constructive character of discourses (see number 4 following for more details).

(3) Their epistemological position can be characterized as non- or antipositivist. Critical discourse analysts reject the idea of a "neutral science" and do not believe in the possibility of an objective view of the research object, because they are—to different degrees—constructivist. Their constructivism, however, does not end in voluntarism and radical relativism. An approach such as the

discourse-historical one, for instance, aspires to intersubjectively comprehensible analyses and interpretations of their empirical data.

(4) The research data are mostly composed of corpora of "authentic," "natural" communication that have not been elicited by the analysts for research purposes (except for focus group discussions and interviews). However, it is particularly clear for oral communication that "primary data" (conversations as they are perceived on site) are first transformed into "secondary data" by the semiotic selection of the "camera eye" and "microphone" and then transmuted into "tertiary data" through further selection and abstraction by the analysts who produce transcripts of a specific precision that depends on the analysts research interests.

(5) Research interests of the critical discourse analysts are directed toward various social problems with a linguistic or discourse-related dimension. In this sense, the starting point of critical discourse studies is problem orientation, especially with respect to various forms of social discrimination and their discursive realization, but also with respect to problems of communication in various institutions and with respect to political manipulation through various discursive strategies.

(6) These research interests relate to a social theoretical background that is strongly influenced by a western European neo- or post-Marxist alignment (Critical Theory, Habermas, Gramsci, Althusser, Pêcheux, Laclau, Mouffe), although the specific theoretical background varies from approach to approach.

(7) A last, common feature of all CDA approaches is their trans- or interdisciplinary orientation and, as a result, their multi-methodical and eclectic alignment. This eclecticism is a strength, since it allows for the triangulation of the research object, for its kaleidoscopic inspection. Sometimes, however, it brings along the risk of building theoretical contradictions by hastily mixing Foucault, Habermas, Bourdieu, Giddens, and Luhmann, and so on.

The Concepts of Discourse and Context

Concepts of Discourse

Discourse is the central category of every discourse analysis, although there are approaches that take other concepts as the basic analytical category, as, for example, is the case in Foucault's archaeological approach, which takes "statement" to be the principal notion of discourse analysis (Foucault 1992). In addition to the commonalities that interconnect the six approaches to CDA with respect to their understanding of discourse (see point 2 in the preceding section,

"General Characteristics of Critical Discourse Analysis"), there are also striking differences in their theoretical conceptualizations of the notion.

Fairclough delineates two major usages of the word "discourse." In a general sense, he determines "discourse" to be an abstract collective noun that cannot be made plural and occurs without definite and indefinite articles. In this sense, the noun abstractly denotes any transindividual semiotic form of social practice that is regulated by social conventions and that is both socially constituted and socially constitutive (Fairclough 1992: 63f., 2003: 123f.). According to Fairclough, "discourse" in this sense embraces three dimensions: first, the semiotic aspect of being realized as spoken and written or visualized "text"; second, this understanding of "discourse" includes the dimension of "discursive practice," that is to say, processes of text production, distribution, and consumption; and third, it involves the social-cultural context and practice the discursive practice is linked with or embedded in. This social-cultural practice relates to social conditions, relationships and processes of social organization, especially to institutions, ideologies and power relations (Fairclough 1992: 73).

Fairclough uses the word "discourse" also in a more specific sense as a concrete individualizing count noun that can occur with an indefinite or definite article and in the plural. In this sense, the term serves to characterize a particular oral, written, or somehow differently semiotically realized way of representing aspects of the word (e.g., social life) from a specific perspective (Fairclough 1996: 71, 2001a: 235, 2001b: 123). In other words: discourses are, according to this conceptualization, particular semiotic representations of experience, of specific aspects of the "external" material world or the "internal" world of thoughts, beliefs and emotions, or of interpersonal, social relationships (see Fairclough 2003: 124).

The social semiotic and systemic functional approach advocated by Kress and van Leeuwen regards "discourses," among others, as specific social semiotic acts, as an ongoing flow or process of semiosis that becomes manifest in texts, which have to be understood as concrete material objects, as products of semiosis, as frozen or preserved traces of the rapidly disappearing discourse (Hodge & Kress [1988] 1991: 12, 264). In their book on multimodal discourse, Kress and van Leeuwen characterize "discourses" as socially constructed and socially situated forms of knowledge about (certain aspects of) reality (Kress & van Leeuwen 2001: 4, 20). In part, they consider "discourse" to be an entity that is relatively independent of genre, mode, and design, but—at the same time—they stress that discourses can only be realized in semiotic modes that have developed the means for realizing them. In his *Introduction to Social Semiotics*, van Leeuwen (2005: 275) characterizes discourses as resources for representation and knowledge about ways of representing some aspects of reality. According to this theoretical understanding of discourse, discourses merge two sorts of elements: they connect representations of social practices and evaluations, purposes and legitimations relating to these social practices. Van Leeuwen (2005: 275) further explains that there may be several discourses about a given aspect of reality, making sense of it in different ways and combing semiotic resources and genres in different ways.

Van Dijk, in his socio-cognitive approach to CDA, or "critical discourse studies" (which is the term he actually uses), prefers a rather wide notion of discourse. He designates "discourse" as a complex "communicative event" that becomes manifest and observable in a great variety of semiotic significations, including conversational interaction and written text, as well as associated gestures, facework, typographical layout, images, and any other "semiotic" or multimedia dimension of meaning (van Dijk 2001b: 98; see also van Dijk 2001a: 356). In this meaning, "discourse" is conceived of as part of the discourse–cognition–society triangle. According to van Dijk, "cognition" involves personal and social cognition, beliefs, and goals as well as evaluations and emotions, and any other "mental" or "memory" structures, representations, or processes. As for the concept of society, van Dijk (2001b: 98) explains: "'Society' is meant to include both the local microstructures of situated face-to-face interactions, as well as the more global, societal and political structures variously defined in terms of groups, group-relations, movements, institutions, organisations, social processes, political systems and more abstract properties of societies and cultures."

The Duisburg group around S. and M. Jäger defines "discourse" as an entity that regulates and determines reality and forms consciousness (S. Jäger 2001a: 130). They see discourses as superindividual, institutionally consolidated practices of articulation, which do not simply reflect social reality and relationships in a passive way, but which actively constitute and organize social reality (S. Jäger 2001a: 129). S. Jäger metaphorically qualifies "discourse" as a materialized flow of knowledge and societal knowledge resources stored through the course of time—a flow that determines individual and collective action and thus exercizes power (S. Jäger 2001b: 82; see also Jäger & Meier 2009). S. and M. Jäger comprehend "discourse" as a result of historical processes and, following J. Link, as a "social manner of speaking" that has been institutionalized and that adheres to particular rules that can change over time. S. Jäger theoretically distinguishes between "discourse levels," "discourse strands," and "discourse fragments." A "discourse fragment" is a text or a part of a text that deals with a specific topic, for example, with the topic of "foreigners." "Discourse fragments" appear on different "discourse levels" conceived of as "social places" from which people speak or write, for instance, science, politics, media, education, everyday life, business life, and administration. "Discourse strands" are best explained as thematically interrelated sequences of homogeneous "discourse fragments." Examples of discourse strands would be "migration," "women," "economy," and "social affairs." Discourse strands are, among others, characterized by "collective symbols" in the sense of "cultural stereotypes," which are immediately understood by the members of the same speech community. Finally, S. Jäger poses the category of "discourse positions." Such positions are social class, sex and gender, age, profession, income, and religious affiliation.

The Oldenburg approach shows a series of close links with the Duisburg group, although it distinguishes itself from the Duisburg approach by a stronger linguistic alignment. Gloy (1998: 16) and Januschek (2007: 15) consider discourse to be both a linguistic activity and a complex social system of orientation. Gloy (1998: 8) conceives of discourses as dynamic, continually constituted formations of communicative practices and as supertexts that are specifically formed in historical processes of social conflicts. They are formed through macro-structural relationships established between single texts, although a single text can "belong" to various discourses. This approach regards discourses as networks of thematically, semantically, temporally, and institutionally linked texts that are socio-culturally embedded and that cannot be grasped as being organized in a strict linear manner, because the intertextual, ana-, and catadeictic references are partly constituted by later reception processes (Gloy 1998: 8, 12, 14, 16).

The version of the discourse-historical Approach (DHA) opts for a terminological choice that sees a "discourse" as a specific complex of context-dependent, diachronically changing semiotic practices that are situated within specific fields of social action: "Fields of action" (Girnth 1996) can be understood as segments of the respective societal "reality," which fulfill different socially institutionalized functions of discursive practices (Reisigl & Wodak 2001: 35f.). In accordance with the other approaches to CDA, the DHA regards discourses as both socially constituted and socially constitutive semiotic practices that relate to a particular social issue or problem. In addition, it considers a discourse to be connected with a specific macro-topic and to the argumentation about validity claims, such as truth and normative validity. Not least from the argumentation character, I deduce that a "discourse" prototypically involves various social actors who participate in the discourse and—taken together—bring in different points of view, not only one (see Reisigl 2003: 91ff.). In this respect, the DHA deviates from Fairclough's, van Leeuwen's and S. Jäger's as well as M. Jäger's approaches, which adopt mono-perspectivity as a constitutive element of a discourse.

As we learn from this short overview, which is far from being complete, the theoretical conceptions of "discourse" in CDA are by no means homogeneous, although they all stress the socially constructive as well as constructed character of discourse, the context dependence of discourse, and the actional or "practical" character of discourses.

Concepts of Context

A further key notion of CDA is context. "Context" literally means "with the text." Nevertheless, the word is also used in the sense of "with the discourse": "the term itself suggests that it is all that comes 'with the text', that is, the properties of the 'environment' of discourse" (van Dijk 1998: 211). The notion was introduced in order to abandon the reductionist understanding of language and language analysis as it has been promoted for a long time by decriptivist linguistics. Thus, context has become a defining moment of discourse, because discourse analysts frequently conceive of discourse as "text in context" or "text plus context" or "language use in social context." This understanding, which is based on a container metaphor, implies a twofold relationship of inclusion: text is included in context, and discourse includes both text and context. Most of the approaches to CDA seem to share such a view, although they opt for different accentuations in their understanding of "context" and its operational breakdown into various macro-, meso- and micro-dimensions. All in all, the explicit reference to the term and notion of "context" is performed most empathically in the Viennese approach and in Teun van Dijk's socio-cognitive approach.

Fairclough is very much interested in connecting CDA with critical social theories. This orientation affects his concept of context, which, on the whole, encompasses linguistic, social, political, and economic factors and therein transcends the local understanding of conversation analysis. Fairclough assumes a dialectical relationship of influence between texts or utterances and contexts. He considers social structures and fields, domains, situational variables, and the like, to be contextual features. Fairclough argues that "the relationship between an utterance and its verbal and situational context is not a transparent one: how context affects what is said or written, and how it is interpreted, varies from one discursive formation to another. For instance, aspects of the social identity of a speaker such as gender, ethnicity or age which are likely to substantially affect forms and meanings in a conversation may have little effect in a conference of biologists" (Fairclough 1992: 47). In his methodological outline of how to analyze discourse practices, that is, the production, distribution, and consumption of text, Fairclough distinguishes between context in a narrow sense, as that which precedes (or follows) in a text (i.e., the more or less immediate verbal context), and the "context of situation," that is, the totality of social practice of which the discourse is a part, as the overall social context (Fairclough 1992: 81f). According to Fairclough, context plays a crucial role in the interpretation of text, in reducing its ambivalence of illocutionary force: "Verbal context has two sorts of effect: First, it may eliminate one or more of the senses. Second, it may give relative salience to one of the senses without eliminating the others" (Fairclough 1995: 114).

Kress and van Leeuwen pay particular attention to the context dependence of the discourse construction and to the question of which specific semiotic resources as well as semiotic modes form the basis for a specific production of discourse: "Discourses are socially constructed knowledges of (some aspect of) reality. By 'socially constructed' we mean that they have been developed in specific social contexts, and in ways which are appropriate to the interests of social actors in these contexts. [. . .] Any discourse may be realised in different ways. The 'ethnic conflict' discourse of war, for instance, may be realised as (part of) a dinner-table conversation, a television documentary, a newspaper feature, an airport thriller, and so on. In other words, discourse is relatively independent of genre, of mode, and (somewhat less) of design. Yet discourses can only be realised in semiotic modes which have developed the means for realising them" (Kress & van Leeuwen 2001: 4f.). The semiotic turn in CDA strongly advanced by the seminal work of Kress and van Leeuwen lead to a shifting of the conceptual boundaries among "text," "discourse" and "context." Under the heading of "multimodality," Kress and van Leeuwen started to include various semiotic aspects or dimensions into their discourse analytical framework that formerly were considered to belong to the concept of "context."

The most salient distinguishing feature of van Dijk's conception of context is the cognitive orientation. Van Dijk defines context "as the structured set of all properties of a social situation that are possibly relevant for the production, structures, interpretation and functions of text and talk" (van Dijk 1998: 211). Van Dijk argues that it is not the "context itself" that influences written and spoken discourse, "but rather the *context models* of language users. Such context models are stored in episodic memory" (van Dijk 1998: 212). Among the dimensions of context included in the context models of language users distinguished by van Dijk (1998: 214–227) are the social or institutional domains or fields; the overall interaction or type of speech event; the functions (of genres); the intentions; the props and relevant objects; the participant roles, professional roles, and social roles; the affiliations or memberships; and the ideas about the social other and various social representations (see also van Dijk 2008).

Within the approach of the Duisburg Group, context analysis becomes most relevant with respect to the analysis of the "institutional framework." Every discourse fragment is considered to be embedded in such an institutional framework. This approach primarily analyzes newspaper articles. For the study of newspaper articles, the institutional framework is conceptualized as comprising at least the following contextual elements: media, general orientation of the newspaper or journal, technical quality of the newspaper (paper, print quality, readability), section/column in which the article appears, genre of the article, author of the article and other authors of the newspaper, event(s) linked to the discourse fragment, and occasion of the article (Jäger 2001a: 175). In addition, this form of context analysis includes the analysis of salient intertextual relationships.

The Oldenburg approach shares a lot of features with the Duisburg Approach, but as far as its verbal and contextual analyses are concerned, it is more micro-oriented. The scholars of the Oldenburg approach focus more on the integral analysis of single texts and single pieces of communication than the scholars of the Duisburg Group do. The Oldenburg approach is highly interested in the study of intertextual relationships and textual chains, and of the context of reception. It particularly focuses on the context knowledge required for the analysis of implicit relationships realized by allusions, evocations, and connotations and for the analysis of the semantic polyphony of texts and conversations. Januschek (1986) develops a "linguistics of allusion," Gloy (1998) outlines a program for reception research with respect to talk shows dealing with ethical issues.

The DHA favors a concept of "context" that relates to four dimensions: (1) the immediate, language internal co-text and co-discourse, that is, the thematic and syntactic coherences, lexical solidarities, collocations, connotations, implications, presuppositions, and the local interactive processes (including turn taking, the exchange of speech acts, linguistic activity patterns, etc.); (2) the intertextual and interdiscursive relationship between utterances, texts, genres, and discourses (e.g., discourse representation and allusions or evocations); (3) the extra-linguistic social/sociological variables and institutional frames of a specific "context of situation" (e.g., the formality of situation; the place, time, and occasion of the communicative event; the addressees; the interactive as well as political roles of the participants; their political and ideological orientation, gender, age, profession, and level of education, as well as their ethnic, regional, national, and religious affiliation or membership); and (4) the broader sociopolitical and historical context that the discursive practices are embedded in and related to, that is to say, the fields of action and the history of the discursive event as well as the history to which the discourse topics relate.

As its name tells us, the discourse-historical approach deals intensely with the historical context of discourses and with questions of recontextualization. The importance of historical context knowledge for the interpretation of a discourse fragment can be illustrated by an example taken from the political context of Austria. In the regional election campaign in Carinthia in spring 2009, the Austrian right-wing populist party BZÖ (Bündnis Zukunft Österreich, meaning "Alliance for the Future of Austria") used the poster shown in figure 4.5. The party was founded in 2005 by Jörg Haider, after irreconcilable disagreements within the Austrian Freedom Party (FPÖ), whose leader Haider had been for about 20 years.

The poster realizes an argumentation scheme called "topos of continuity," saying: if you vote for us, we will guarantee you political continuity. Thus, the poster shows how the three leading politicians of the BZÖ in Carinthia—Gerhard Dörfler, Uwe Scheuch, and Harald Dobernig—after Jörg Haider's lethal car incident in October 2008, represented themselves as guarantors of the continuity of Haider's politics and as those who will take care of Carinthia and the Carinthian

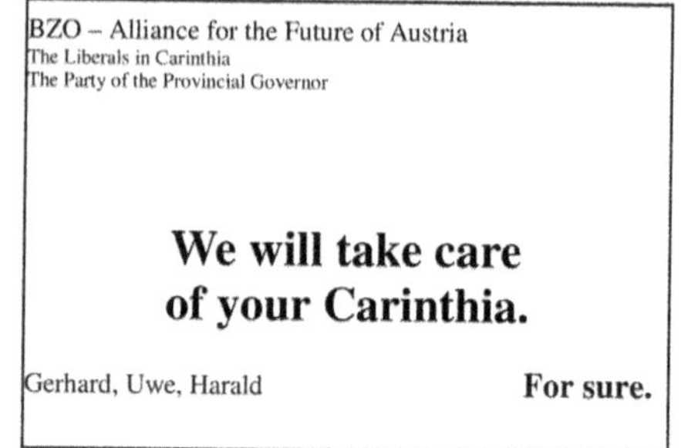

Figure 4.5. "Alliance for the Future of Austria" poster

voters. This topos seems to have been convincing to many voters, because the BZÖ remained by far the strongest party after the last election in Carinthia, in March 2009, but this was also due to the strong compassion effect elicited in Austrians after Haider's accident. The most interesting point about the poster is that—from the perspective of an ahistorical, purely text-internal, and discourse-internal analysis—it looks harmless. But from the perspective of a critical analysis that takes the historical context into account and looks at intertextual as well as interdiscursive relationships, the poster represents a very strange case of—maybe—ambivalence, because it seems to contain various messages at one and the same time. At least for those Austrian voters and critical discourse analysts who know the Austrian history, it clearly relates to National Socialism, although you would not assume this from just looking at the allegedly innocent sentence and commissive speech act "we will take care of your Carinthia," the illocutionary force of which is backed and intensified both verbally and non-verbally. Two verbal intensifiers are (1) the three signature-like first names of the politicians, which serve a nomination strategy aiming to establish an informal interpersonal relationship between the politicians and potential voters, and (2) the elliptic reinforcement "For sure," literally 'Guaranteed.' Nonverbal authentication of the promise is underlined by the seemingly direct eye contact between the visually represented politicians and the viewers of the posters (see van Leeuwen 2008) as well as by the friendly smiling faces. However, the promise "we will take care of your Carinthia" also alludes to an utterance verbalized by Jörg Haider in 1991, when he was forced to resign as the head of the region of Carinthia because he had praised the National Socialist employment policy, describing it as an "orderly employment policy," in contrast to the employment policy of the Austrian government. Haider resigned saying "Passt mir auf mein Kärnten auf!," ('Take care of my Carinthia!'). But this is only half of the story, because in 1945, during the last days of the Second World War, Carinthia had a National Socialist "Gauleiter," that is to say, a National Socialist head of the administrative district of Carinthia, named Friedrich Rainer, and this Gauleiter is said to have pronounced the same directive speech act, "Passt mir auf mein Kärnten auf!" ('Take care of my Carinthia!') in a radio speech broadcast from a bunker when it was clear that the National Socialists had lost the war and the Gauleiter had to resign. The election slogan suggests a pseudo-dialogic answer to Haider's request verbalized in 1991, aiming to feign political continuity, but indirectly it also constitutes a connection with the National Socialist period. This is a recurring feature of both the BZÖ and the FPÖ: they nourish a highly problematic, ambivalent, and partly affirmative relationship to National Socialism. However, this relationship is often not expressed explicitly, but in a coded way, and maybe not even always intentionally so. In the case of the poster, the critical discourse analyst can demonstrate the mimetic, iconic historical link to National Socialism, although it cannot simply be claimed that this link was intentionally constructed by allusion to National Socialism, because such a claim falls under the burden-of-proof rule, and the specific proof of intentionality is difficult in the present case, even though it is possible that the semantic polyphony and the two specific historical links were reckoned with on purpose by the producers of the poster. An element that backs the assumption of calculated ambivalence is the fact that the bunker currently houses a "Haider museum," that is, a memory place dedicated to the former leader of the BZÖ and FPÖ—despite all the controversial discussions about the National Socialist connotations of that place.

Research Interests and Research Practice

CDA is problem oriented and starts its work with the identification of a social problem that includes a linguistic or semiotic dimension. In the best case, an empirical CDA project ends with the application-oriented attempt to contribute to the solution or reduction of the problem in question.

The discourse-related problems dealt with in CDA are manifold. They include:

- discourse and discrimination (racism, antisemitism, "xenophobia," "Islamophobia," and sexism; see Reisigl & Wodak [2001]);
- language barriers in various social institutions (communication in court; language of the law; doctor-patient interaction; therapeutic communication; mass-mediated communication relevant for citizens' political participation, e.g., radio news, press coverage, political TV discussions, etc.; and communication in schools and at universities, etc.; see Wodak, Menz, & Lalouschek [1989]);
- discourse/language and politics/policy/polity, including language policy (language and nationalism, policy for and against linguistic minorities, right-wing populist rhetoric, European integration, European constitution, etc.; see Reisigl [2008)] Wodak [2009]);
- discourse and history (dealing with the past, with special attention to National Socialism and Fascism and the dealing with them in the National Socialist and Fascist successor states; see Heer, Manoschek, Pollak, & Wodak [2008]);
- discourse and economy (e.g., neoliberal policy against public welfare systems, marketization of public institutions such as universities; see e.g., Fairclough [1993] 2000),
- discourse and identity (e.g., identity struggles of various kinds, including national as well as transnational/European identities, ethnic identities, gendered identities, linguistic identities; see Wodak, De Cillia, Reisigl, & Liebhart [2009]),

- discourse-related research on social organizations (e.g., analysis of decision-making procedures in the institutions of the European Union; see Muntigl, Weiss, & Wodak [2000]); and
- discourse in the media and social change (e.g., problems, but also chances arising from mass-mediated globalization processes; Fairclough [2006]; Machin & van Leeuwen [2007]).

In order to analytically deal with these problems, CDA approaches offer helpful methodologies, but not analytical toolboxes that can be applied mechanically, because every convincing analysis should be based on accurate interpretation and scientific creativity and requires the analysts to reflect upon previous topic-related theoretical and practical knowledge as well to carry out pilot analyses that lead to the development of partly new discourse analytical categories and the adaptation of existing discourse analytical categories.

Just to mention two of the methodologies outlining the steps for empirical research. Fairclough (2009: 167–182) sketches a CDA methodology for his approach that includes four research stages:

1. *Focus upon a social wrong, in its semiotic aspect*:
   (a) Select a research topic that relates to or points out a social wrong and that can productively be approached in a transdisciplinary way with a particular focus on dialectical relations between semiotic and other "moments."
   (b) Construct objects of research for initially identified research topics by theorizing them in a transdisciplinary way.
2. *Identify obstacles to addressing the social wrong*:
   (a) Analyze dialectical relations between semiosis and other social elements: between orders of discourse and other elements of social practices, between texts and other elements of events.
   (b) Select texts, focuses, and categories for their analysis, in the light of and appropriate to the constitution of the object of research.
   (c) Carry out analyses of texts, both interdiscursive analysis, and linguistic/semiotic analysis.
3. *Consider whether the social order "needs" the social wrong.*
4. *Identify possible ways past the obstacles* (in this stage, the analysis moves from a negative to a positive critique).

The DHA delineates an idealized sequence of eight stages and steps in research practice. They can be implemented recursively (for more details, see Reisigl [2008] and Reisigl & Wodak [2009: 96ff.]):

1. The starting point of the research is the awareness of a social and political problem that possesses linguistic aspects. The first step of an

investigation consists of *activating preceding theoretical knowledge about the problem* in question.

2. The second step is the *triangulatory collection and "creation" of discursive data to analyze* (by means of observation, audio-visual registration, etc.) and *the research on and gathering of contextual information* (by research in archives, by source research, etc.). Data collection relies on criteria such as the selection of specific discourses and discourse topics, fields of action, semiotic media, genres, social actors, areas of communication, and periods of time, etc.
3. The third phase comprises the *preparation and selection of data for the specific analyses.* The principal tasks to be completed in this phase are to look through the collected data and to further sort it. If required by the research question, registered oral data have to be transcribed according to specific necessities of precision determined by research interests.
4. The fourth step is dedicated to the *specification of the research question* and the *formulation of hypotheses* on the basis of a rapid checking of the data or a part of it.
5. A *qualitative pilot analysis* may follow as the fifth research step. It aims to refine and sharpen, that is, to adjust the analytical instruments.
6. The research proceeds with *detailed case studies* that are chiefly qualitative, but can also be partly quantitative in their character. This stage operates on the macro-, meso- and micro-level of linguistic analysis as well as on the level of context. This step comes to an overall interpretation of the single results of analysis and takes into account the social, historical, and political context of the analyzed discursive data.
7. It follows the *meticulous formulation of a critique* that seeks to reveal problematic discursive strategies, solve specific problems of (institutional) communication, or improve communication by fighting communicative deficits or inefficiencies (e.g., linguistic barriers in different social institutions). The critique points to opaque, contradictory, and manipulative relations among power, language, and social structures and commits itself to cognitive and political emancipation and improvement of communication.
8. The *social utilization and application of the detailed analytical results* on the basis of accurate critique can be seen as the last stage of research. This application consists both of the publication of books and journal articles and of widely accessible recommendations and public commentaries, training seminars, further education courses, didactic expositions, and radio transmissions on the issue in question.

Concluding Remarks

Historical developments show that CDA is quickly gaining scientific elaboration and institutional autonomy. CDA has already reached the linguistic mainstream. This may have implications for the concept of critique, since the formerly oppositional, antihegemonic critique may become part of a hegemonic project, and this may lead to a mitigation of some of the former dimensions of critique. Especially the younger generation of critical discourse analysts is asked to reflect on this development and to resharpen critical tools where they become less sharp in the process of academic establishment (Billig 2003). Another major task for CDA is to further the development of an integrative analytical framework that brings social theory and linguistic analysis even closer together, thus leaving behind a purely additive combination of linguistic and social scientific knowledge. Since the social problems CDA is dealing with are multifaceted and multidetermined, only a convincingly integrative framework can increase the prospects for success of the problem-solving proposals elaborated by critical discourse analysts, which—in the future—will be challenged by a series of new social problems relating to discourses of various kinds.

References

Bernstein, B. 1975. *Class, codes, and control: Theoretical studies towards a sociology of language.* New York: Schocken Books.

Bernstein, B. 1996. *Pedagogy, symbolic control and identity: Theory, research, critique.* London: Taylor & Francis.

Billig, M. 2003. Critical discourse analysis and the rhetoric of critique. In G. Weiss & R. Wodak (eds.), *Critical discourse analysis: Theory and interdisciplinarity*, 35–46. Bassingstoke, UK: Palgrave Macmillan.

Boxer, D. 2002. *Applying sociolinguistics. Domains and face-to-face-interaction.* Amsterdam: John Benjamins.

Brown, G., & Yule, G. 1983. *Discourse analysis.* Cambridge: Cambridge University Press.

Currie, H. C. 1952: A projection of socio-linguistics: The relationship of speech to social status. *Southern Speech Journal* 18: 28–37.

Dittmar, N. 1996. *Soziolinguistik. Studienbibliographie.* Heidelberg: Groos.

Dittmar, N. 1997. *Grundlagen der Soziolinguistik. Ein Arbeitsbuch mit Aufgaben.* Tübingen: Niemeyer.

Fairclough, N. 1992. *Discourse and social change.* Cambridge: Polity Press.

Fairclough, N. 1993. Critical discourse analysis and the marketization of public discourse: The universities. *Discourse & Society* 4: 133–59.

Fairclough, N. 1995. *Critical discourse analysis: The critical study of language.* London: Longman.

Fairclough N. 1996. Technologisation of discourse. In C. R. Caldas-Coulthard & M. Coulthard (eds.), *Texts and practices: Readings in critical discourse analysis, 71–83.* London: Routledge.

Fairclough, N. 2000. *New labour, new language?* London: Routledge.

Fairclough, N. 2001a. The discourse of new Labour: Critical discourse analysis. In M. Wetherell, S. Taylor, & S. J. Yates (eds.), *Discourse as data: A guide for analysis, 229–66.* London: Sage.

Fairclough, N. 2001b. Critical discourse analysis as a method in social scientific research. In R. Wodak & M. Meyer (eds.), *Methods of critical discourse analysis, 121–38.* London: Sage.

Fairclough, N. 2003. *Analysing discourse. Textual analysis for social research.* London: Routledge.

Fairclough, N. 2006. *Language and globalization.* London: Routledge.

Fairclough, N. 2009. A dialectical-relational approach to critical discourse analysis in social research. In R. Wodak & M. Meyer (eds.), *Methods of critical discourse analysis.* 2nd ed., 162–86. London: Sage.

Foucault, M. 1992. *Archäologie des Wissens.* Frankfurt am Main: Suhrkamp.

Fowler, R., Hodge, B. Kress, G., & Tony, T. 1979. *Language and control.* London: Routledge and Kegan Paul.

Girnth, H. 1996. Texte im politischen Diskurs. Ein Vorschlag zur diskursorientierten Beschreibung von Textsorten. *Muttersprache* 1996 (1): 66–80.

Gloy, K. (1998). *Ethik-Diskurse. Praktiken öffentlicher Konfliktaustragung. Skizze eines Forschungsvorhabens.* Oldenburg: University of Oldenburg.

Harris, Z. S. 1952. Discourse analysis. *Language* 28: 1–30.

Heer, H., W. Manoschek, A. Pollak, & R. Wodak (eds.) (2008). *The discursive construction of history: Remembering the Wehrmacht's war of annihilation.* Translated from the German by S. Fligelstone . Basingstoke, UK: Palgrave Macmillan.

Hodge, R., & Kress, G. [1988] 1991. *Social semiotics.* Cambridge: Polity.

Hymes, D. 1974. *Foundations of sociolinguistics: An ethnographic approach.* Philadelphia: University of Pensylvania Press.

Jäger, S. 1984. (W)ENDE der Soziolinguistik? *OBST* 29: 156–81.

Jäger, S. 2001a. *Kritische Diskursanalyse: Eine Einführung,* 3rd ed. Duisburg: DISS.

Jäger, S. 2001b. Diskurs und Wissen. Theoretische und methodische Aspekte einer Kritischen Diskurs- und Dispositivanalyse. In R. A. Keller, W. Hirseland, W. Schneider, & W. Viehöver (eds.), *Handbuch Sozialwissenschaftliche Diskursanalyse,* Vol. 1: *Theorien und Methoden,* 81–112. Opladen: Leske + Budrich.

Jäger, S., & Meier, F. 2009. Theoretical and methodical aspects of Foucauldian critical discourse analysis and dispostitive analysis. In R. Wodak & M. Meyer (eds.), *Methods of critical discourse analysis,* 2nd ed., 34–61. London: Sage.

Januschek, F. 1986. *Arbeit an Sprache. Konzept für die Empirie einer politischen Sprachwissenschaft,* Opladen: Westdeutscher Verlag.

Januschek, F. 2007. Warum sprachwissenschaftliche Analyse unverzichtbar ist. Diskursbegriff und Zielsetzungen des Oldenburger Ansatzes der KDA. *DISS-Journal. Zeitung des Duisburger Instituts für Sprach- und Sozialforschung (DISS)* 16: 15–18.

Johnstone, B. 2000. *Qualitative methods in sociolinguistics.* Oxford: Oxford University Press.

Kress, G., & van Leeuwen, T. 2001. *Multimodal discourse: The modes and media of contemporary communication.* London: Arnold.

Labov, W. 1966. *The social stratification of English in New York City*. Washington, DC: Center for Applied Linguistics.

Labov, W. 1972. *Sociolinguistic patterns*. Philadelphia: University of Pennsylvania Press.

Labov, W., & Fanshel, D. 1977. *Therapeutic discourse: Psychotherapy as conversation*. San Diego. Academic Press.

Machin, D., & van Leeuwen, T. 2007. *Global media discourse: A critical introduction*. London: Routledge.

Matouschek, B., & Wodak, R. 1995. Diskurssoziolinguistik. Theorien, Methoden und Fallanalysen der diskurshistorischen Methode am Beispiel von Ausgrenzungsdiskursen. *Wiener Linguistische Gazette* 55-56 / 1995: 34–71.

Muntigl, P., Weiss, G., & Wodak, R. 2000. *European Union discourses on un/employment: An interdisciplinary approach to employment policy-making and organizational change*. Amsterdam: John Benjamins.

Reisigl, M. 2003. Wie man eine Nation herbeiredet. Eine diskursanalytische Untersuchung zur sprachlichen Konstruktion der österreichischen Nation und österreichischen Identität in politischen Fest- und Gedenkreden. Ph.D. dissertation, University of Vienna.

Reisigl, M. 2008. Analyzing political rhetoric. In R. Wodak & M. Krzyżanowski (eds.), *Qualitative discourse analysis in the social sciences*, 96–120. Bassingstoke, UK: Palgrave Macmillan.

Reisigl, M., & Wodak, R. 2001. *Discourse and discrimination: Rhetorics of racism and antisemitism*. London: Routledge.

Reisigl, M., & Wodak, R. 2009. The discourse-historical approach. In R. Wodak & M. Meyer (eds.), *Methods of Critical Discourse Analysis*, 2nd ed., 87–121. London: Sage.

Schiffrin, D. 1994. *Approaches to discourse*. Oxford: Blackwell.

Sinclair, J. M., & Coulthard, R. M. 1975. *Towards an analysis of discourse: The English used by teachers and pupils*. Oxford: Oxford University Press..

Stubbs. M. 1983. *Discourse analysis. The sociolinguistic analysis of natural language*. Oxford: Blackwell.

Stubbs, M. 1988. *Educational linguistics*. Oxford: Blackwell.

Thibault, P. 1988. Discourse analysis in sociolinguistics. In N. Dittmar & P. Schlobinski (eds.), *The sociolinguistics of urban vernaculars: Case studies an their evaluation*, 154–60. Berlin: de Gruyter.

Trudgill, P. 2004. The subject matter of sociolinguistics/Der Gegenstand der Soziolinguistik. In U. Ammon, N. Dittmar, K. J. Mattheier, & P. Trudgill (eds.), *Sociolinguistics/Soziolinguistik: An International Handbook of the Science of Language and Society /Ein internationales Handbuch zur Wissenschaft von Sprache und Gesellschaft*, vol. 1/1, 1–5. Teilband. Berlin: de Gruyter.

Van Dijk, T. A. 1998. *Ideology: A multidisciplinary approach*. London: Sage.

Van Dijk, T. A. 2001a: Multidisciplinary CDA: A plea for diversity. In R. Wodak & M. Meyer (eds.), *Methods of critical discourse analysis*, 95–120. London: Sage.

Van Dijk, T. A. 2001b. Critical discourse analysis. In D. Schiffrin, D. Tannen, & H. E. Hamilton (eds.), *The handbook of discourse analysis*, 352–71. Oxford: Blackwell.

Van Dijk, T. A. 2008. *Discourse and context: A socio-cognitive approach*. Cambridge: Cambridge University Press.

Van Leeuwen, T. 2005. *Introducing social semiotics*. London: Routledge.

Van Leeuwen, T. 2008. The visual representation of social actors. In T. Van Leeuwen, *Discourse and practice: New tools for critical discourse analysis*, 136–48. Oxford: Oxford University Press.

Wittgenstein, L. 1989. *Tractatus logico-philosophicus. Tagebücher 1914–1916. Philosophische Untersuchungen. Werkausgabe Band 1.* Frankfurt am Main: Suhrkamp.

Wodak, R. 1996. *Disorders of discourse.* London: Longman.

Wodak, R. 2009. *The discourse of politics in action: Politics as usual.* Bassingstoke, UK: Palgrave Macmillan.

Wodak, R., Menz, F., & Lalouschek, J. 1989. *Sprachbarrieren. Die Verständigungskrise der Gesellschaft.* Vienna: Edition Atelier.

Wodak, R., de Cillia, R., Reisigl, M., & Liebhart, K. 2009. *The discursive construction of national identity.* 2nd ed. Edinburgh: Edinburgh University Press.

CHAPTER 5

CONVERSATION ANALYSIS

PAUL SEEDHOUSE

The history of the development of ethnomethodology and conversation analysis (CA) may be found in Heritage (1984). The principal originator of CA was Harvey Sacks (1992), who worked with Emanuel Schegloff on the development of CA at the University of California, Santa Barbara, until Sacks's accidental death in 1975. His most important idea was that there is "order at all points" in interaction, that is, that talk in interaction is systematically organized and deeply ordered and methodic. This was an extremely radical idea in the 1960s, when the dominant linguistic view was the Chomskyan one that "ordinary talk could not be the object of study for linguistics since it is too disordered; it is essentially a degenerate realization of linguistic competence" (Hutchby & Wooffitt 1998: 22). CA was started as a sociological "naturalistic observational discipline that could deal with the details of social action rigorously, empirically and formally" (Schegloff & Sacks 1973: 289–90).[1]

This chapter explicates *why* CA methodology proceeds as it does, and why it is a suitable methodology for sociolinguists to use.

Ethnomethodology

The basic relationship between ethnomethodology and CA is that the first subsumes the second; ethnomethodology studies the principles on which people base their social actions, while CA focuses more narrowly on the principles that people use to interact with each other by means of language.

According to Heritage (1984: 4) "The term 'ethnomethodology' refers to the study of . . . the body of commonsense knowledge and the range of procedures and considerations by means of which the ordinary members of society make sense of, find their way about in, and act on the circumstances in which they find themselves." Garfinkel's (1967) seminal work on ethnomethodology can be seen as a reaction to the previously dominant top-down Parsonian sociology, which assumed the superiority of the sociologist's knowledge over that of members of society, who were seen as cultural and psychological "dopes" who unthinkingly acted out the macro rules of society as explicated by the sociologist. Garfinkel, however, rejected analytical frameworks that assume the superiority of social science knowledge over the lay social actor's knowledge and sought an answer to the question "how do social actors come to know, and know in common, what they are doing and the circumstances in which they are doing it?" (Heritage 1984: 76). This can be understood as a rejection of an *etic*, or external analyst's perspective on human behavior, in favor of an *emic*, or participant's perspective from within a system.

Garfinkel's assumption was that people must make normative use of a number of principles in order to display their actions to each other and allow others to make sense of them. However, these principles are used on a constant basis in everyday life and have become automatized to the extent that they have a taken-for-granted or *seen-but-unnoticed* status. Garfinkel was, then, trying to make explicit and visible those principles that we orient to in everyday life and that we have implicit knowledge of, and CA extended this project in relation to talk. Garfinkel's (1967) famous "breaching experiments" demonstrated that utterances in conversation are not treated literally but are understood by reference to context and assumptions about the other party, as part of an emerging sequence, and with both retrospective and prospective significance. In a counseling experiment, for example, subjects asked 10 questions for advice on personal problems to a "counselor" hidden behind a screen; they were then given yes/no answers without any further explanation. Five *yes* answers and five *no* answers were allocated on a completely random basis, unknown to the subjects. In spite of this, subjects were determined to make sense of the answers. Garfinkel designed experiments like these to breach the norms, to undermine the subject's belief in reciprocity of perspectives in which the conversational partner is cooperating in a shared reality or intersubjectivity. However, Garfinkel found, as in the above-mentioned case, that this was extremely difficult to accomplish, as subjects constantly made adjustments and found ways to maintain their belief in a shared reality in which both participants were orienting to the same norms.

I now introduce five fundamental and interlocked principles that underlie ethnomethodology (Garfinkel 1967) and also CA.

Indexicality. Interactants generally do not make every single aspect of their intended meaning explicit, relying on mutually understood features of the background context to supply additional information. Indexical knowledge is something talked into being by interactants, who display through their utterances which aspects of context they are orienting to at any given time.

The Documentary Method of Interpretation. This treats any actual real-world action as a "document" or an example of a previously known pattern. There are similarities here with schema theory; a schema is a hypothetical mental framework for portraying memorized generic concepts. But we must note that CA does not "psychologize" about cognitive states nor discuss structures such as schemata. In practical terms, if anyone greets us by saying "Hi," we treat that action as a document and relate it to previously known patterns, normally identify it as a greeting, and respond accordingly. This becomes the fundamental method that analysts must use in analyzing social interaction as it is an emic methodology.

When the documentary method of interpretation is applied to sequential interaction, its explanatory power becomes extremely significant. Any turn at talk becomes a document or a display of a cognitive, emotional, and attitudinal state, an analysis of context and of the previous turn(s) in the sequence, and a social action that renews the context.

The Reciprocity of Perspectives. This involves agreeing that we are following the same norms, to show affiliation with the other person's perspective and try to achieve intersubjectivity. This principle does not mean that people actually succeed in reaching the same perspective on everything all of the time; this is obviously not the case. Rather, to follow the principle means to agree that we are following the same norms in interaction, including a structural bias toward cooperation. In many ways, this is similar to Grice's (1975) Cooperative Principle.

Normative Accountability. This is the key to understanding the ethnomethodological basis of CA. The position on norms in ethnomethodology should be clearly differentiated from the descriptivist "rules and units" approach typical of linguistics. Norms are understood in ethnomethodology as constitutive of action rather than regulative. It is by reference to norms that interactants can design their own social actions and interpret those of others. For example, when one social actor greets another, a greeting response is the norm, or has *seen-but-unnoticed* status. Failure to respond in this case, however, may be noticeable, accountable, and sanctionable. Here, we use a norm of behavior as a point of reference or action template for interpretation rather than a rule. An actor may decide to return a greeting, but "the actor who is determined to declare or continue a quarrel can do so by visibly refusing to return a greeting and leaving the other to draw the conclusion" (Heritage 1984: 118).

Reflexivity. This states that the same set of methods or procedures are responsible for both the production of actions/utterances and their interpretation; this underlies the CA mechanism of the adjacency pair.

Aims of CA

From one perspective, CA is the result of applying ethno-methodological principles to naturally occurring talk, which started when Sacks examined data of telephone calls to a suicide prevention centre. *Talk-in-interaction* has become the accepted superordinate term to refer to the object of CA research (Drew & Heritage 1992a: 4). CA studies the organization and order of social action in interaction. This organization and order is one produced by the interactants in situ and oriented to by them, to uncover and describe this organization and order; the main interest is in uncovering the underlying *system* that enables interactants to achieve this organization and order. So one principal aim is to characterize the organization of the interaction by abstracting from exemplars of specimens of interaction and to uncover the emic logic underlying the organization. A further aim is to develop an emic perspective, which in CA is not merely the participants' perspective, but the perspective from within the sequential environment in which the social actions were performed. Another principal aim of CA is to trace the development of intersubjectivity in an action sequence. This does *not* mean that CA provides access to participants' cognitive states. Rather, it means that analysts trace how participants analyze and interpret each others' actions and develop a shared understanding of the progress of the interaction.

Principles of CA

Ethnomethodology provides generic principles that may be used to study any kind of human action. CA focuses solely on human actions that are manifested through talk, as well as nonverbal behavior. As with other forms of qualitative research, the principles are not to be considered as a formula or to be applied in a mechanistic fashion. It is essential to adopt a conversation analytic mentality that "involves more a cast of mind, or a way of seeing, than a static and prescriptive set of instructions which analysts bring to bear on the data" (Hutchby & Wooffitt 1998: 94).

Sacks's most original idea was that there is order at all points in interaction. This idea leads to the concept of *rational* design in interaction, that is, that talk in interaction is systematically organized, deeply ordered, and methodic. A second principle of CA is that contributions to interaction are *context shaped* and *context renewing.* Contributions are context shaped in that they cannot be adequately understood except by reference to the sequential environment in which they occur and in which the participants design them to occur. Contributions are context renewing in that they inevitably form part of the sequential environment in which a next contribution will occur.

The third principle is that no order of detail can be dismissed, a priori, as disorderly, accidental, or irrelevant (Heritage 1984: 241). This principle follows from the first two and can be seen to underlie the development of the highly detailed CA transcription system, its minute analysis of the detail of naturally occurring data, and its highly empirical orientation (ten Have 1999; Hutchby & Wooffitt 1998).

The fourth principle that follows from this is that analysis is bottom up and data driven; we should not approach the data with any prior theoretical assumptions or assume that any background or contextual detail is relevant unless there is evidence in the details of the interaction that the participants themselves are orienting to them. Another way of presenting the principles of CA is in relation to the questions that it asks. The essential question that we must ask at all stages of CA analysis of data is, why that, in that way, right now? This encapsulates the perspective of interaction as action (why that) that is expressed by means of linguistic forms (in that way) in a developing sequence (right now). Talk is conceived of as social action, which is delivered in particular linguistic formatting, as part of an unfolding sequence.

Types of Interactional Organization

We will now look at four different but related types of interactional organization that were uncovered by Sacks and Schegloff. These are *not* the same as "units of analysis" in the linguistic sense. Interactants use them normatively and reflexively both as an action template for the production of their social actions and as a point of reference for the interpretation of their actions.

Adjacency Pairs

Sequence organization is the essential key to understanding how CA analysis works and its links to its ethnomethodological roots. Adjacency pairs are, as Heritage (1984: 256) puts it, "the basic building-blocks of intersubjectivity." They are paired utterances such that on production of the first part of the pair (e.g., question), the second part of the pair (answer) becomes *conditionally relevant.* If, however, the second part is not immediately produced, it may nonetheless remain relevant and accountable and appear later, or its absence may be accounted for.

Extract 1

A: can I have a bottle of Mich? Q1
B: are you over twenty-one? Q2
A: no. A2
B: no A1

(Levinson 1983: 304)

In the above extract in a liquor store, A is not old enough to buy beer, and one question-answer adjacency pair (lines 2 and 3) is embedded in another (lines 1 and 4). Action sequences do not necessarily unroll in a linear fashion (Q1–A1, Q2–A2), and hence that serial order is not necessarily the same thing as sequential order. The adjacency pair concept does not claim that second parts are always provided for first parts. Rather, it is a *normative* frame of reference that provides a framework for understanding actions and providing accountability. So if we ask a question to someone who does not then provide an answer, we may draw conclusions about that person.

Following a first turn, the interaction continues sequentially, with the second speaker's action creating expectations for subsequent speakers, and so on. Moving on to the third turn, this displays an analysis of the second speaker's turn, so the second speaker is able to determine how his or her turn has been interpreted. So the essence of CA is the concept of action sequences or sequence organization, which has been exemplified by the adjacency pair.

Any first action in interaction is an action template that creates a normative expectation for a next action and a template for interpreting it. The second action displays an interpretation of the first action and itself creates an action and interpretational template for subsequent actions, and so on. This can also be termed the *next-turn proof procedure* (Sacks, Schegloff, & Jefferson 1974: 729), the basic tool that analysts can use to develop an emic perspective. The next turn, then, documents an analysis of the previous turn and displays this analysis, not only to the other interactants, but also to us as analysts, providing us with a proof criterion and search procedure.

Extract 2

1 A: where's Bill?
2 J: there's a yellow VW outside Sue's house

(Levinson 1983: 102)

Here, the second part is interpreted as a tentative answer to A's question rather than an unconnected observation. However, it can be interpreted in this way solely by virtue of its sequential location after the first part of an adjacency pair.

Preference Organization

The concept has been frequently misunderstood. It is *not* related to the notion of liking or wanting to do something, but rather involves issues of affiliation and disaffiliation, of seeing, noticeability, accountability, and sanctionability in relation to social actions, and hence the concept derives directly from ethnomethodological principles. The institutionalized norm is for interaction to be affiliative, that is, to achieve reciprocity of perspectives. This structural bias manifests itself in preference organization. For many adjacency pairs, there are alternative second parts, so an invitation may be answered by an acceptance (preferred action) or a rejection (dispreferred action). These two options are performed in different ways. Preferred actions are normally delivered without hesitation or delay at the start of the response turn, as in the extract below.

Extract 3

Child: could you.hh could you put on the light for my.hh room
Father: yep

(Levinson 1983: 307)

Dispreferred responses are generally accompanied by hesitation and delay and are often prefaced by markers such as *well* or *uh* as well as by positive comments and appreciations, for example, "You're very kind." They are frequently mitigated in some way and accounted for by an explanation or excuse of some kind. A's turn in the extract below exemplifies all of the above-mentioned phenomena.

Extract 4

B: uh if you'd care to come over and visit a little while this morning
I'll give you a cup of coffee.
A: hehh well that's awfully sweet of you, I don't think I can make it
this morning. hh uhm I'm running an ad in the paper and -and uh I
have to stay near the phone.

(Atkinson & Drew 1979: 58)

As Heritage (1984: 269) demonstrates, the preferred responses to actions are *affiliative* and conducive to social solidarity, whereas dispreferred responses are *disaffiliative*. This does not mean that the function of agreement is always preferred. In the case of self-deprecating first turns (e.g., "God, I'm stupid") the preferred response is disagreement. For further discussion, see Boyle (2000) and Heritage (1984).

Turn Taking

The following is a simplified version of Sacks et al.'s seminal (1974) account of the organization of turn taking. There is a mechanism governing turn taking that is termed a local management system; this means that decisions can be made by the participants, rather than having the turns allocated in advance (pre-allocated), as is the case in a courtroom. There is a set of norms with options that the participants can select. The basis of the system is turn-constructional units or TCUs, discussed in detail below. Listeners project, then, when a speaker is going to finish a turn, and the point at which speaker change may occur is known as the transition relevance place, or TRP. At a TRP the norms governing transition of speakers come into play; the speakers may change at that point, but they do not necessarily do so.

a. If current speaker selects the next speaker in the current turn, then the current speaker must stop speaking and the next speaker must speak.
b. If the current speaker does not select a next speaker, then any other participant may select him- or herself as the next speaker: the first person to speak at the TRP gains rights to the next turn.
c. If the current speaker has not selected a next speaker, and if no other participant self-selects as per section b, then the current speaker may (but need not) continue. The procedure then loops or recycles until the end of the conversation, for which there are of course further norms.

We will now return to the phenomenon that perhaps best exemplifies the differing attitudes of CA and formal linguistics to language, namely, that of the *turn-constructional unit,* or TCU. A TCU can be understood as a single social action performed in a turn or sequence, and the projectable end of a TCU is a TRP. A single social action can be manifested in a wide variety of language forms, from a single word, discourse marker, or a clause to a sentence, as we can see in the examples that follow. A TCU can also be performed nonverbally. A TCU is essentially a social concept rather than a linguistic one and cannot therefore be delimited in linguistic terms. Since it is an emic, or participant's, concept, it cannot be specified in etic terms. The discussion of extract 5 that follows illustrates these points.

Extract 5

	Marsha:	en Ilene is going to meet im:. becuz the to:p wz ripped
		off'v iz car which is tih say someb'ddy helped th'mselfs.
→	Tony:	stolen.
		(0.4)
	Marsha:	stolen.=right out in front of my house.
	Tony:	oh: f'r crying out loud,...

(Schegloff 1996: 75)

In line 3, we can see that Tony's turn consists of a single TCU of a single word. Yet this single word not only constitutes an entire turn, but it also performs three kinds of sequential work in the past, present, and future. This is possible because interactants orient to a normative sequential framework, a holistic framework consisting of the interlocking organizations of turn taking, sequence, preference, and repair. Since the normative expectation is that a turn will perform these three kinds of sequential work, Tony can design his turn so that a single word is capable of doing so, and Marsha can interpret it as doing so; *this is the principle of reflexivity in action.* The evidence that the participants are actually orienting to the system described is in the next-turn proof procedure. Marsha analyzes Tony's turn as commenting retrospectively on what happened to her car, as performing a new social action of confirming understanding of Marsha's news by summarizing the content in a new linguistic format, and as providing a context for her to take the sequence further. She displays her understanding of the work performed by his turn in her subsequent turn (line 5) by repeating his turn with the same intonation and adding further information on the theft.

TCUs are only analyzable emically as social actions. They are quite heterogenous in terms of linguistic form and do not correspond in any way to single linguistic categories. However, they are packaged in terms of linguistic form, the point is that social actors are able to recognize them in interaction as complete social actions (as we can see in line 5) and hence are able to project when they are likely to end.

So CA is not a system of etically specifiable units and rules to be followed in a regulative sense and does not have an etically specifiable unit of analysis in the sense in which this is understood in linguistics; it would be preferable to say that CA has an emic analytical focus on the sequence. In CA, it does not make any sense to analyze the turn *stolen* in extract 5 in isolation. *Stolen* is a social action embedded in a sequential environment. So in CA we are dealing with a holistic system of analysis, and this is the case because the interactants are using the same holistic system of analysis themselves.

The organizations of the adjacency pair, preference and turn taking constitute the structural organization of talk. However, the fourth element, repair, comes into play whenever there are problems in the accomplishment of talk.

Repair

Repair may be defined as the treatment of trouble occurring in interactive language use. Trouble is anything that the participants judge is impeding their communication, and a repairable item is one that constitutes trouble for the participants. Schegloff, Jefferson, and Sacks (1997: 363) point out that "nothing is, in principle, excludable from the class 'repairable.'" From the ethnomethodological perspective it is a vital mechanism for the maintenance of reciprocity of perspectives and intersubjectivity. It is important to distinguish self-initiated repair (I prompt repair of my mistake) from other-initiated repair (somebody else notices my mistake and initiates repair). Self-repair (I correct myself) must also be distinguished from other-repair (somebody corrects my mistake). There are therefore normally four repair trajectories:

1. Self-initiated self-repair
2. Self-initiated other-repair
3. Other-initiated self-repair
4. Other-initiated other-repair

Now, there is a clear preference structure in the organization of repair that corresponds with the foregoing listing. This is that self-initiated self-repair is most preferred, and other-initiated other-repair, least preferred. This order also corresponds with frequency of usage in normal conversation, with other-initiated other-repair being rare. In the next extract we can see interactants making normative usage of the preference system for repair.

Extract 6

L: but y'know single beds'r awfully thin to sleep on.
S: what?
L: single beds. [they're-
E: [y'mean narrow?
L: they're awfully narrow yeah.

(Schegloff et al. 1977: 378)

In extract 6 we can see the other speakers (S and E) moving down the preference structure in an attempt to repair the problem, which is that L has used a lexical item (*thin*) that does not collocate with *bed*. Since L does not appear to have noticed this problem in that there is no attempt at self-repair, in line 2, S uses the next-preferred option, namely, other-initiation of self-repair. However, S uses an "open" next-turn repair initiator (*what*?), which means that L does not appear to be able to locate the precise problem and seems in line 3 to be starting to repeat the whole of the initial utterance. Therefore, the other speakers are entitled to move further down the preference organization and use other-initiated other-repair in line 4. However, note that the repair form is mitigated and shows affiliation, as it is designed as a question. Framing a correction as a question or confirmation check and offering an alternative gives first speaker the opportunity to self-repair in the next turn. It is an affiliative action in that it portrays second speaker as attempting to help first speaker. Since S and E have moved gradually down the preference organization and mitigated the other-initiated other-repair, L accepts and confirms uptake of the repair in line 5.

So the different types of interactional organization that work together in complementary fashion to create an architecture of intersubjectivity (Heritage 1984: 254). They function as action templates or points of reference that interactants may use to orientate themselves in the pursuit of mutual understanding.

Socially Distributed Cognition

CA is not able to establish the cognitive state of individuals in isolation. It portrays and explicates the progress of intersubjectivity, or socially distributed cognition. In conversation, interactants perform social displays of their cognitive states to each other. A social display of a cognitive state may differ from an actual state, as in the case of lying. For example, A tells B he doesn't know where the money is, when in fact he does know. Extract 7 illustrates how socially distributed cognition works in ordinary conversation.

Extract 7

	Marsha:	en Ilene is going to meet im:. becuz the to:p wz ripped
		off'v iz car which is tih say someb'ddy helped th'mselfs.
→	Tony:	stolen.
		(0.4)
	Marsha:	stolen.=right out in front of my house.
	Tony:	oh: f'r crying out loud,...

(Schegloff 1996: 75)

In line 3, Tony's turn consists of a single word. This provides both an analysis of Marsha's previous turn and a social display of Tony's cognitive state, specifically, that he has understood what has happened to Marsha's car. Marsha in line 5 analyzes Tony's turn as commenting retrospectively on what happened to her car, as performing a new social action of confirming understanding of Marsha's news by summarizing the content in a new linguistic format, and as providing a context for her to take the sequence further. She displays her understanding of the work performed by his turn in her subsequent turn (line 5) by repeating his turn with the same intonation and adding further information on the theft.

Interactants, then, are always producing in their utterances a social display of their own cognitive state at the same time as they are displaying their understanding of a previous speaker's utterance. Interactants are constantly conducting a social displaying to each other (and to us as analysts) of their cognitive states and their understanding of each others' utterances by means of and by reference to the organization of turn taking, sequence and repair. The study of socially shared cognition, then, cannot be separated from the study of interaction. CA analysis not only demonstrates *what* understandings the interactants display to each other, but also *how* they do so by normative reference to the interactional organizations. We gain access to their displays of understanding to each other in the same way that they gain this access, that is, by reference to the interactional organizations; this develops an emic perspective. The organizations of turn and sequence are mechanisms for displaying and checking mutual understanding and the organization of repair is a mechanism for repairing breakdowns in mutual understanding.

CA Procedures

The first stage of CA analysis has been described as *unmotivated looking* or being open to discovering patterns or phenomena. This is an account of a single case analysis focusing on a single data extract. We start the account after recording, transcription, and unmotivated looking have taken place and after we have identified a single extract to focus on.

1. Locate an action sequence or sequences.
2. Characterize the actions in the sequence or sequences. An action sequence can be as short as an adjacency pair or last for hours.
3. Examine the action sequence(s) in terms of the organization of turn taking, focusing especially on any disturbances in the working of the system.
4. Examine the action sequence(s) in terms of sequence organization. Here, we are looking at adjacency pairs and preference organization but more widely at any action undertaken in response to other actions.
5. Examine the action sequence(s) in terms of the organization of repair.
6. Examine how the speakers package their actions in terms of the actual linguistic forms that they select from the alternatives available, and consider the significance of these. We are focusing on the forms that are used to manifest the functions.
7. Uncover any roles, identities, or relationships that emerge in the details of the interaction.
8. Having completed a preliminary analysis that portrays the interactional organization and the participants' orientations, we now attempt to locate this particular sequence within a bigger picture. We are looking for a rational specification of the sequence that can uncover its emic logic and the system that produced it and that places it in a wider matrix of interaction.

Attitude to Context and Identity

CA has a dynamic, complex, highly empirical perspective on context and identity. The basic aim is to establish an emic perspective, that is, to determine which elements of context and identity are relevant to the interactants, as manifested in the details of the interaction. The perspective is also an active one in which participants talk a context or identity into being. The perspective is dynamic in that, as Heritage (1984: 242) puts it, "The context of a next action is repeatedly renewed with every current action" and is transformable at any moment.

CA sees the underlying machinery that generates interaction as being both context free and context sensitive: The structural organizations (e.g., turn taking) can be seen as the context-free resources in that their organization can be specified as a series of norms in isolation from any specific instance of interaction. Nonetheless, the application of these organizations is context sensitive in that interactants use the organization of (for example) turn taking to display their understanding of context. So professionals and lay clients may talk an institutional context into being through the professional taking control of the turn taking system; we understand this by reference to the context-free norms.

Identity has become a crucial construct in social sciences research in general. Recent approaches have revealed that individual identity may be fluid and variable, assuming different and/or multiple identities in relation to different people and contexts; CA is highly compatible with such approaches. The basic problem, when trying to link talk and identity, is that there is an indefinite number of external aspects of cultural, social, or personal identity that could potentially be relevant to any given instance of talk-in-interaction.

The same basic problem exists when we are trying to relate context to talk or human behavior more generally. The number of aspects of context (external to the individual) that may be relevant is without limit and may change instantly. As with identity, the CA position on context is to study how interactants orient to aspects of context in the details of their talk. Let us see how this functions in relation to the following extract.

Extract 8

J: So who'r the boyfriends for the week.
(0.2)
M: 'k'hhhhh- Oh: go::d e-yih this one'n that one yihknow,
I jist, yihknow keep busy en go out when I wanna go
out John it's nothing 'hhh I don'have anybody
serious on the string,
J: So in other words you'd go out if I askedche out
One a' 'these times.
M: Yeah! Why not.

(Paul Drew's data [JGII:(b):8:14])

As stated earlier, the essential question that we must ask at all stages of CA analysis of data is, why that, in that way, right now? In order to understand the relationship between talk, identity, and context, we must examine the reflexive relationship between them. In line 1, J asks, "So who'r the boyfriends for the week." We should examine how the precise linguistic forms used talk identities and context into being. Of course, J could have asked, "Do you have a serious boyfriend?" What J actually says, however, proposes a particular identity to M, namely, that she is likely to have multiple boyfriends (plural) and that they are not likely to last long (for the week). It also talks into being an identity for J as someone who is interested in whether M has a boyfriend or is available, and therefore also a context, namely, of J and M negotiating the possibility of going out together, but in a light-hearted, jocular way. This is an example of CA analysts' interest in linguistic forms; the interest is not in the linguistic forms themselves, but rather in the way in which they are used to embody and express subtle differences in social actions. M's response in lines 3 through 6 to some extent accepts the proposed identity by saying "this one'n that one yihknow, I jist, yihknow keep busy en go out when I wanna go out." M does not actually answer J's question directly in that she does not name her current boyfriends. Her response displays her analysis of the context as being discussion of the possibility of going out together by saying "it's nothing 'hhh I don'have anybody serious on the string," thus indicating her potential availability.

The identity components of gender and sexuality are relevant to the participants themselves in this extract. This is evident in the topic of the talk and in the social actions performed by the participants. The topic is sexual interest and availability, specifically, whether M currently has a boyfriend and whether she is interested in going out with J if he were to ask her. The first move by J aims to determine potential availability of M and can be seen as a pre-invitation. M's response indicates that she has no serious boyfriend and is available and potentially not averse to an invitation. J follows up with an inquiry as to whether M would go out with him and M indicates that she would.

From a CA perspective we are only able to bring the constructs of gender and sexuality into the discussion because it is evident in the details of the interaction that the participants are orienting to these constructs. Essentially, there are no features of context or identity that are *always* relevant to a CA analysis. We need to determine which features of identity or context the participants are making relevant in their talk—if they are elevant to them, then it is relevant to us as analysts. From a CA perspective, any utterance is a display of the speaker's analysis of the prior utterance of another speaker; it performs a social action in response, and it positions the speaker in a social system. It creates an identity for the speaker, may try to create an identity for the other speaker. and creates a relationship between the speakers. It displays an understanding of the current sequential and social context and also renews it. Through their talk, interactants are constantly negotiating identity and context. To do this, they employ a wide range of resources, including choice of lexis, syntax, phonological and prosodic features, the interactional resources of turn taking, sequence and repair, social action, and nonverbal communication. These resources are combined and deployed with sophistication and precision to create intricate positioning in relation to context and identity, as we saw earlier in extract 7.

Institutional and Professional Discourse

A major development in CA during the 1990s was a perspective on institutional and professional discourse. Studies of institutional interaction (e.g., Drew & Heritage 1992b) have focused on how the organization of the interaction is related to the institutional aim and on the ways in which this organization differs from the benchmark of ordinary conversation. Institutional discourse displays goal orientation and rational organization. CA institutional discourse methodology attempts to relate not only the overall organization of the interaction but also individual interactional devices to the core institutional goal. Such studies embrace not only traditional professions such as medicine or law (see Frankel, chapter 35, and Matoesian, chapter 34, this volume), but also fields such as business, broadcasting, and counseling.

Gafaranga and Britten's (2005) study exemplifies how CA is able to link interactional sequences on the microlevel to the macrolevel of the institutional goal. Gafaranga and Britten focus on topic initial elicitors, such as *How are you?* or *What can I do for you?* which occur at the start of medical consultations and which may at first be taken to be insignificant social preliminaries. However, their analysis of sixty-two consultations shows *How are you?* to be used in follow-up consultations, and *What can I do for you?* in new consultations. This difference is shown to be institutionally significant in relation to the concepts of continuity of care and the doctor-patient relationship. and the authors conclude that "through orderly openings, doctors and patients talk the institution of General Practice into being." The study neatly captures the reflexive relationship between talk and its social and institutional context.

With the development of studies of professional settings, it was only natural that professional interest should extend beyond description and toward the potential of such research in terms of interventions, encouraging the emergence of *applied CA* almost by default. However, the concept of application is by no means straightforward. According to Richards and Seedhouse (2005), the model of application that is most consistent with the nature of CA is that of description leading to informed action.

Vinkhuyzen and Szymanski (2005) uncover a reflexive relationship between grammatical formatting and social/institutional context in an "applied CA" study. They recorded interactions between employees of a local reprographics business and customers who made a request for a copying service at the "drop-off" counter. In the case of small, unprofitable jobs, they generally redirect the customer to the do-it-yourself area. Vinkhuyzen and Szymanski found that the grammatical formatting of these customer requests had an impact on how employees were able to respond. When customers format their requests as self-oriented declaratives that state a customer's desire or need, it proved simple for staff to redirect them to the do-it-yourself area. However, when customers formatted their requests as other-oriented interrogatives that inquire after the organization's willingness or capability to produce a document, problems often ensued, since the staff appeared to be rejecting a request. On the institutional level, this exposes the inherently conflicting goals of many service industries, namely. those of making a profit and satisfying diverse customer needs. In terms of applications, the authors suggest altering the spatial organization of the store to guide customers to the appropriate location. Examination of successful interaction has implications for staff training.

CA as a Research Method

At this point, I will attempt to position CA in relation to social science research methods and concepts, such as validity, reliability, generalizability, epistemology, quantification, and triangulation.

Key factors in relation to *reliability* are the selection of what is recorded, the technical quality of recordings, and the adequacy of transcripts; ten Have (1999) provides a very detailed account of this area. However, another aspect of reliability is the question of whether the results of a study are repeatable or replicable, and the way CA studies present their data is of crucial significance here. It is standard practice for CA studies to include the transcripts of the data and, increasingly, to make audio and video files available electronically via the Internet. Furthermore, the analyst makes transparent the process of analysis for the reader, which enables readers to analyze the data themselves, to test the analytical procedures that the author has followed, and the validity of his/her analysis and claims.

We will now consider four kinds of validity in relation to qualitative research: internal, external, ecological, and construct validity. *Internal validity* is concerned with the soundness, integrity, and credibility of findings. The crucial point in CA is to develop an emic perspective. CA analysts develop the participants' perspective by tracing how the participants document their social actions to each other in the details of the interaction by normative reference to the interactional organizations. Clearly, the details of the interaction provide the only justification for claiming to be able to develop a valid emic perspective. and this is why analysts must stick so tightly to the data.

External validity is concerned with *generalizability*, that is, the extent to which the findings can be generalized beyond the specific research context. CA studies of institutional discourse are often analyzing on the micro and macro level, on the particular and the general simultaneously; by analyzing individual instances, the system that produced these individual instances is revealed, as in the Gafaranga and Britten example given earlier.

Ecological validity is concerned with whether findings are applicable to people's everyday life; laboratory experiments in the social sciences can often be weak in terms of ecological validity. CA practitioners typically record naturally occurring talk in its authentic social setting. Therefore CA studies tend to be exceptionally strong in terms of ecological validity. *Construct validity* is a vital concept in an etic paradigm. However, in an emic paradigm the question is, whose construct is it? In some social science research methods, researchers look for etically specifiable methods of description, so that an analyst can match surface features of the interaction to constructs and categories. In an emic perspective, however, we are looking for organizations to which participants orient during interaction, hich is not at all the same thing. The best example of this different orientation is the TCU, as we saw earlier.

In relation to *epistemology*, CA is based on ethnomethodology, whose fundamental principles were described earlier. From a broader perspective, ethnomethodology can be located in a phenomenological paradigm, which considers that "it is the job of the social scientist to gain access to people's 'common-sense thinking' and hence to interpret their actions and their social world from their point of view" (Bryman 2001: 14). Ethnomethodology's *ontological* position can be associated with constructionism or the belief that social phenomena and their meanings are constantly being generated by social actors.

The CA attitude to *quantification* is that CA is a qualitative methodology that tries to develop an emic perspective, so it is generally of peripheral interest to CA practitioners. However, CA and quantification can be combined, as in Gardner's (2005) study. Gardner examines a mother and a therapist working on speech with the same child and identifies two phenomena (length of bout and the focus of repair initiation) as constituting significant differences in approach by the two adults, the CA analysis uncovering an emic logic that connects the two phenomena. Quantification then confirms that there is an overall significant difference in length of bout in relation to the two adults. Furthermore, Gardner quantifies different turn types that had previously been identified during the CA stage, relating these findings to the therapeutic outcomes achieved by the therapist and the mother. It has often been mistakenly reported that quantification is prohibited in CA. However, Schegloff (1993) warns specifically against premature quantification in relation to superficially identifiable interactional phenomena.

Given the aim of CA to develop an emic perspective within an interactional environment, there is no substitute for detailed analysis of individual sequences; interviews and questionnaires are not able to provide this, which is why *triangulation* is not generally undertaken. However, Silverman (1999) argues that the two approaches are compatible and may be applied to the same instances of talk. A CA analysis of *how* participants locally produce context for their interaction can be followed by an ethnographic analysis of *why* questions about institutional and cultural constraints, thus moving from the micro to the macro levels.

An "applied CA" study demonstrates the possibility of combining CA and ethnography in a mutually reinforcing way. Vinkhuyzen and Szymanski (2005) recorded data that derive from one stage of a three-year ethnographic study, the other two stages being ethnographic observation, shadowing, and interviewing as well as participant observation. The expert knowledge that they obtained of the economics of the business helps the authors explain the institutional significance of the different ways in which customers package their requests.

Conclusions

The applicability of CA to sociolinguistics is limited to the study of naturally occurring spoken interaction. Its perspective on interaction, as social action that is expressed by means of linguistic forms in a developing sequence, is in general very compatible with sociolinguistic approaches. CA is able to portray the complex, reflexive relationship between language and social action, context, identity and institutions. CA is now frequently presented in introductions to sociolinguistics as a suitable methodology (e.g., Holmes 2008). It has so far had no relevance to work on sociolinguistic variables, but there are indications that it may be employed in developing complex systems approaches to researching nonlinear systems (e.g., Larsen-Freeman & Cameron 2008).

CA has proved able to grow organically to accommodate new dimensions. Its current stage of growth is marked by linguistic and cultural diversity and multimodality. Keeping pace with globalization, there are now CA studies of interaction in a number of different languages, bilingual and multilingual settings. Examples include those in German (Egbert 2005), Finnish (Sorjonen 1996), Dutch (ten Have 1999), Japanese (Tanaka 1999), Chinese (Hopper & Chen 1996), and Thai (Moerman 1988). Early criticisms that CA was biased because it was based almost exclusively on English native-speaker interaction are therefore no longer valid. CA has also been employed to analyze cross-cultural communication (e.g., Mori 2003) and lingua franca interaction (e.g., Firth 1996).

An issue that is receiving increasing prominence is the question of the multimodal nature of spoken interaction and what constitutes adequate primary data for CA studies. At the start of CA in the 1960s, the new technology of audio recording was the only one available. However, with the rise of video recording, it has become possible to include nonverbal communication and gaze in multimodal analysis. The importance of nonverbal features of talk in analysis is exemplified in numerous studies (e.g., Goodwin 2007; Heath & Luff 2007). Because of the variety of software, hardware, and techniques that may be employed to portray the multimodal nature of interaction, there is at present no standard procedure.

Notes

1. The discussion is partly based on Richards and Seedhouse (2005), Seedhouse (2004), and Seedhouse (2005).

References

Atkinson, J., & Drew, P. 1979. *Order in court.* London: Macmillan.

Boyle, R. 2000. Whatever happened to preference organisation? *Journal of Pragmatics* 32: 583–604.

Bryman, A. 2001. *Social research methods.* Oxford: Oxford University Press.

Drew, P., & Heritage, J .. 1992a. Analyzing talk at work: An introduction. In P. Drew & J. Heritage (eds.), *Talk at work: Interaction in institutional settings*, 3–65. Cambridge: Cambridge University Press.

Drew, P., & Heritage, J . 1992b. *Talk at work: Interaction in institutional settings.* Cambridge: Cambridge University Press.

Egbert, M. 2005. Discrimination due to non-native speech production? In K. Richards & P. Seedhouse (eds.), *Applying conversation analysis*, 174–96. Basingstoke, UK: Palgrave Macmillan.

Firth, A. 1996. The discursive accomplishment of normality: On 'lingua franca' English and conversation analysis. *Journal of Pragmatics* 26: 237–59.

Gafaranga, J., & Britten, N. 2005. Talking an institution into being: the opening sequence in general practice consultations. In K. Richards & P. Seedhouse (eds.), *Applying conversation analysis*, 75–90. Basingstoke, UK: Palgrave Macmillan.

Gardner, H. 2005. A comparison of a mother and a therapist working on child speech. In K. Richards & P. Seedhouse (eds.), *Applying conversation analysis*, 56–74. Basingstoke, UK: Palgrave Macmillan.

Garfinkel, H. 1967. *Studies in ethnomethodology.* Englewood Cliffs, NJ: Prentice Hall.

Goodwin, C. 2007. Environmentally coupled gestures. In S. Duncan, J. Cassell, & E. Levy (eds.), *Gesture and the dynamic dimensions of language*, 195–212. Amsterdam: John Benjamins.

Grice, H. P. 1975. Logic and conversation. In P. Cole & J. L. Morgan (eds.), *Syntax and semantics 3: Speech acts*, 41–58. New York: Academic Press.

Have, P. ten. 1999. *Doing conversation analysis: A practical guide.* London: Sage.

Heath, C., & Luff, P. 2007. Gesture and institutional interaction: Figuring bids in auctions of fine art and antiques. *Gesture* 7: 215–41.

Heritage, J. 1984. *Garfinkel and ethnomethodology.* Cambridge: Polity Press.

Holmes, J. 2008. *An introduction to sociolinguistics.* Harlow: Pearson.

Hopper, P., & Chen, C-H. 1996. Languages, cultures, relationships: Telephone openings in Taiwan. *Research on Language and Social Interaction* 29(4): 291–313.

Hutchby, I., & Wooffitt, R. 1998. *Conversation analysis.* Cambridge: Polity Press.

Larsen-Freeman, D., & Cameron, L. 2008. Research methodology on language development from a complex systems perspective. *Modern Language Journal* 92: 200–13.

Levinson, S . 1983. *Pragmatics.* Cambridge: Cambridge University Press.

Moerman, M . 1988. *Talking culture: Ethnography and Conversational Analysis.* Philadelphia: University of Pennsylvania Press.

Mori, J. 2003. Construction of interculturality: A study of initial encounters between Japanese and American students. *Research on Language and Social Interaction,* 36: 143–84.

Richards, K., & Seedhouse, P. (eds.) 2005. *Applying conversation analysis.* Basingstoke, UK: Palgrave Macmillan.

Sacks, H. 1992. *Lectures on conversation,* vols. 1 and 2. Oxford: Blackwell.

Sacks, H., Schegloff, E. A., & Jefferson, G . 1974. A simplest systematics for the organisation of turn-taking in conversation. *Language* 5: 696–735.

Schegloff, E.A. 1993. Reflections on quantification in the study of conversation. *Research on Language and Social Interaction* 26: 99–128.

Schegloff, E. A. 1996. Turn organization: One intersection of grammar and interaction. In E. Ochs, E. A. Schegloff, & S. A. Thompson (eds.), *Interaction and grammar,* 52–133. Cambridge: Cambridge University Press.

Schegloff, E. A., Jefferson, G., & Sacks, H. 1977. The preference for self-correction in the organization of repair in conversation. *Language* 53: 361–82.

Schegloff, E.A., & Sacks, H. 1973. Opening up closings. *Semiotica* 7: 289–327.

Seedhouse, P. 2004. *The interactional architecture of the language classroom: A conversation analysis perspective.* Malden, MA: Blackwell.

Seedhouse, P. 2005. Conversation Analysis and language learning. *Language Teaching* 38(4): 165–87.

Silverman, D. 1999. Warriors or collaborators: Reworking methodological controversies in the study of institutional interaction. In: C. Roberts & S. Sarangi (eds.), *Talk, work and institutional order,* 401–25. Berlin: Mouton de Gruyter.

Sorjonen, M. 1996. On repeats and responses in Finnish conversations. In E. Ochs, E.A. Schegloff, & S. A. Thompson (eds.), *Interaction and grammar,* 277–327. Cambridge: Cambridge University Press.

Tanaka, H. 1999. *Turn-taking in Japanese conversation: A study in grammar and interaction.* Amsterdam: John Benjamins.

Vinkhuyzen, E. & Szymanski, P. 2005. Would you like to do it yourself? Service requests and their non-granting responses. In K. Richards & P. Seedhouse (eds.), *Applying Conversation Analysis,* 91–106. Basingstoke, UK: Palgrave Macmillan.

CHAPTER 6

THE INTERSECTIONS OF LANGUAGE SOCIALIZATION AND SOCIOLINGUISTICS

KAREN ANN WATSON-GEGEO AND MATTHEW C. BRONSON

In their introduction to the *Journal of Sociolinguistics* theme issue on sociocultural linguistics, Bucholtz and Hall (2008: 403) called for a new coalition among sociolinguistics, linguistic anthropology, and related subfields.[1] Arguing that recent advances in sociolinguistics "reaffirm the importance of interdisciplinary connections," they proposed a *sociocultural linguistics* to address issues of identity, agency, language change, and micro- (individual speaker) and macrolevels (social structures and processes) in hybridized, urban, globalized settings. Their article was a platform for interdisciplinary work and an acknowledgment of the cross-connections already happening in a contemporary sociolinguistics increasingly focused on bilingual and multilingual settings.

Bucholtz and Hall emphasized the distinctions among theoretical perspectives, but Gumperz and Cook-Gumperz (2008: 524) countered that perspectives have always been intertwined. They pointed to examples of "disciplinary boundary crossing" in which researchers "shared a theoretical view of the local community as the site of language use and a methodological commitment to using fieldwork as the best way to obtain information." The process of building subdisciplines has sometimes obscured the underlying connections.

As a theoretical paradigm for the study of first and second language learning, language socialization (LS) exemplifies the kinds of boundary crossing and integration of (socio)linguistics and culture that Gumperz and Cook-Gumperz described. LS grew from the same roots discussed in both of the foregoing articles, and views the acquisition of language and culture as a mutually constitutive process (Ochs & Schieffelin 2008). Methodologically, a longitudinal, ethnographic design not always present in sociolinguistics has characterized LS since its inception. First and second language acquisition researchers have increasingly adopted LS as a productive and realistic strategy for examining the intertwined relationships among language, culture, and learning. LS integrates micro- and macrolevels of analysis in a broad and deep explanatory framework applicable to a variety of problems and settings (Watson-Gegeo 1992).

Here, we review recent developments in LS in relation to sociolinguistics, with an emphasis on work in bilingual and multilingual situations cross culturally. We argue for the value of accelerating the current shift in sociolinguistics from interdisciplinary toward transdisciplinary inquiry. *Interdisciplinary* work is interactive, combining theory, methods, and practices to address questions difficult to tackle with the tools of a single discipline (Frodeman & Mitcham 2007; Klein 1996). Interdisciplinary work adapts but does not challenge existing boundaries. In contrast, *transdisciplinary* inquiry problematizes disciplinary compartmentalization as imposing limits in creating useful knowledge to address complex issues (Klein 1998; Nicolescu 2002, 2003; Stokols 2006). The centrality of the research questions and the need to reconcile seemingly incommensurable methods for constructing knowledge require greater rigor than is typical of interdisciplinary inquiry, including a nuanced engagement with the researcher's positionality (Alcott & Potter 1993; Montuori 2005).

Following a review of recent work in the intersection of sociolinguistics and LS, we suggest a framework for evaluating sociolinguistic LS research, and for moving toward higher methodological and ethical ground as transdisciplinary inquiry. As researchers increasingly address settings and language issues created by the dislocations of late modernity, a transciplinary stance supports holistic, detailed, and realistic inquiry. We conclude that the best LS research always involves a commitment to benefit the communities studied.

Early Intersections between Sociolinguistics and LS

Although the labels placed on work at the intersection of language, learning, socialization, and enculturation index varying theoretical positions, researchers have long been in conversation. Ochs and Schieffelin (2008, 1984) trace the origins of LS to the mid-1960s, when a team of psycholinguists, linguists, and anthropologists at the Language Behavior Research Laboratory at the University of California, Berkeley, wrote the field manual for cross-cultural research on children's language learning (Slobin 1967). The manual bridged work in child development, first language acquisition, and sociolinguistics, especially Hymes's (1967) notion of communicative competence, and Gumperz's (1968) of speech community. Ervin-Tripp first used the term LS in a 1966 prospectus, arguing for longitudinal "comparative language socialization" (Murray 1998: 129).[2]

The mid-1960s were an awakening to the complexities of language use, evolving from work of various "theory groups" (Murray 1998) on lexicons, dialect studies, sociology of language, and sociolinguistics of bi- and multilingual societies (Gumperz 1964), predated by work in anthropology. In the late 1960s and early 1970s, a new generation of scholars was shaped in an academic milieu that included human development, pidgin and creole linguistics, variationist studies (Labov 1972), child discourse, and educational anthropology. LS was an outgrowth of this milieu. Schieffelin and Ochs's (1986) first edited volume on LS included work undertaken by several researchers (e.g., Watson-Gegeo & Gegeo 1986). A few years later, Schieffelin (1990) published the exemplary book-length study by the initial generation of LS scholars.

Although early LS studies were typically conducted in small-scale societies and/or rural settings, some were concerned with urban settings, especially in the (linguistic) anthropology of education (Rymes 2008; Wortham 2008), in the wake of US court decisions mandating schools to address the needs of language minority children. Because studies often focused on educational issues for ethnic minorities or children in decolonizing societies, they involved bidialectal, bilingual, or multilingual contexts (Boggs et al. 1985; Gilmore & Glatthorn 1982; Heath 1983; Philips 1972; Trueba, Guthrie, & Au 1981; Watson 1975; Watson-Gegeo & Boggs 1977).

In the following, we first present a representative survey of recent work organized thematically, leading to a discussion of lessons learned for robust sociolinguistic LS studies that capture the complexity of language developmental and multilingual contexts.

Recent Bilingual/Multilingual Sociolinguistic Research in LS

Several comprehensive reviews of recent LS work have appeared (Duff 2008, 2010, 2011; Duff & Hornberger 2008; Garrett & Baquedano-López 2002; Watson-Gegeo & Nielsen 2003), and one excellent collection of LS studies in bilingual and multilingual settings (Bayley & Schecter 2003). Since the early

1990s, first and second LS studies undertaken in bi- and multilingual contexts have informed and been informed by increasingly sophisticated sociolinguistic studies on codeswitching (Bullock & Toribio 2009; see also Li, chapter 18, this volume), language variation and change (Bayley & Lucas 2007; Chambers, Trudgill & Schilling-Estes 2002; see also D'Arcy, chapter 24, this volume), language shift and revitalization (Howard 2007; Farfan & Ramallo 2010; see also Potowski, chapter 16, this volume), language ideology (Eckert & Rickford 2001; Mesthrie 2006; Tollefson 2001; Woolard & Schieffelin 1994), gender (Coates 1998; Eckert & McConnell-Ginet 2003), academic discourse (Duff 1995) and educational linguistics (Spolsky & Hult 2010). Pursuing these and related issues, and their connection to education and power, has meant that while many LS studies on young children continue, increasingly researchers are focusing on adolescence—the critical age in processes of language shift and the success or failure of language revitalization efforts (see Duff, Heath, Gordon, and Morita & Kobayashi in Duff & Hornberger 2008, for reviews on LS among adolescents and young adults internationally; work has also been done among young adult lesbians in the Middle East [Khayatt 2003] and elderly Taiwanese women learning Mandarin [Shumin 2009]).

The interrelationships among language ideology, shift, persistence, and revitalization is a theme in several recent LS studies, including Caribbean creoles in Dominica (Paugh 2001, 2005) and St. Lucia (Garrett 2005); creole in Panama (Snow 2004); trilingual LS in home, public, and Koranic schools, Cameroon (Moore 2004); French-Marquesan bilingualism in the Marquesas (Riley 2007); speech styles in bilingualism in northern Thailand (Howard 2003); language ideology in Khmer literacy instruction (Needham 1996); heritage language learning of Chinese American adolescents (Lei 2007); Zapotec and Spanish in Mexico (Augsburger 2004); Aymara, Spanish and gender socialization in Bolivia (Luykx 2003); Spanish-heritage language, shift, and codeswitching in the United States (Delgado 2009); bilingual LS of Finnish children in Sweden (Tryggvason 2002); and LS in Native American efforts to maintain or revitalize indigenous languages ("Navajo," Field 2001; "Kaska," Meek 2001).

In an early study, Kulick (1992) examined language shift and construction of selves in LS among Gapun speakers, Papua New Guinea. He found the Gapun were motivated to shift to Tok Pisin because they associated knowledge and social sensitivity with Tok Pisin and Christianity, versus ignorance, egotism, and stubbornness with Gapun and traditional religion. In contrast, Watson-Gegeo and Gegeo's (1991) sociolinguistic LS study of Kwara'ae, an indigenous language of the Solomon Islands, found that parents emphasized children's learning of formal (high-rhetoric) Kwara'ae, but language rankings depended on church denomination. Evangelicals ranked English highest, Solomon Islands Pijin second, and Kwara'ae lowest; Anglicans and Catholics ranked high-rhetoric Kwara'ae first for in-group contexts and English first for out-group contexts. These examples have implications for child and adolescent LS, codeswitching, "modern" versus "traditional" identities, and trajectories for long-term survival of indigenous languages. They also indicate the importance of understanding indigenous/local epistemologies (Gegeo & Watson-Gegeo 1999, 2001, 2002) in lifelong LS in a time of rapid social change.

As in other cases of indigenous language revitalization (Bronson 2002; Henze & Davis 1999), in her LS study in Canada, Meek (2011) found that English-language ideologies are shaping the way in which Kaska is represented and taught in Yukon schools. Kaska, a Northern Athabaskan language, is verb-based (like Blackfoot and Navajo), and prominent with verbs for handling and carrying. But Kaska grammar as taught in school is shaped by English, a noun-based language. As argued in the case of Hawaiian language immersion, in this and other ways the validity of a school-taught "indigenous" language is suspect, and may continue the "silencing" and undermining of Native languages and cultures (Warner 1999; Wong 1999).

Fellin's (2001) LS study examined language ideologies and revival of Nones, a local dialect rapidly disappearing on the Italian peninsula. She found that in caregiver interactions with young children, speakers used overt and covert communicative strategies to support Nones as a marker of cultural identity, while promoting Italian bilingualism as an advantage in prestigious domains. Interestingly, Wyman (2004) found, in a cross-generational study of Yup'ik speakers in southwestern Alaska, that youth were socialized in peer groups into strategic moment-to-moment emphasis or erasure of language boundaries, using metamessages in situations where they wanted to mark Yup'ik group identity.

Lamarre and Paredes (2003: 68) interviewed trilingual university students in Montreal to explore, across childhood and adolescence, how youth were socialized into French, English, and one of several immigrant languages. Language use in the home was "not stable," shifting over time with household membership, evolving language attitudes, and children's ages. Similarly, in a two-year ethnographic LS study using discourse analysis, Bersola-Nguyen (2004) examined an intergenerational, trilingual family in California. The two focal children were learning Tagalog, Vietnamese, and English. The parents, Pilipino and Vietnamese grandparents, and nearby relatives differed significantly in LS practices and language attitudes. Some were committed to teaching their heritage language, others not—but all emphasized the cultural value of respect. The children actively negotiated communicative practices in the household. The complex language environment may have inspired the six-year-old's decision to attend Spanish-language immersion classes after kindergarten, as she claimed agency to shape her linguistic knowledge and connect in her own way to a California heritage.

The construction of identity, and its overlap with language ideology and change, is a second theme running through many LS studies in bilingual and multilingual settings: He's (2004) of a Chinese heritage class; Alim's (2004) of style shifting in the African American speech community; Nguyen's (2002) on children's gender and social identity LS in a North Vietnamese village; Song's (2007) on "imagined communities" and identity in American Korean children's bilingual LS; Gordon (2003)'s on gender identity shifts and second LS among Lao-American women (see also Gordon 2008); Fogle's (2009) on Russian children's agentic identity formation in their American adoptive family's LS; Langman's (2003) of minority Hungarian identity formation through LS practices in Slovakia; Lotherington's (2003) on Khmer and Vietnamese immigrant youths' multiliteracy practices in Australia; and Aminy's (2004) two-year LS study of language and literacy practices in two Islamic schools and a women's Islamic study circle.

Identity emerged as a theme in several other studies, including the social construction of language and literacy in a Mexican immigrant household (Piedra & Romo 2003); creation of social networks of speech and silence in Hong Kong–born Chinese students in a Canadian classroom (Pon, Goldstein, & Schecter 2003); formation of language attitudes in Inuit-English-French Arctic communities in Quebec (Patrick 2003); the dys-socialization toward English in South Indian identities (Atkinson 2003); narrating community and identity in Mexican-immigrant *doctrina* classes (Baquedano-López 2000); changes in personhood and community in Deaf signing in Nicaragua (Senghas 2003); and linguistic variation, semantic reference, and pronouns for constructing identity in mother-child conflict talk in Guatemala (Comparini 2000).

In her data-rich LS study of bilingual Maya child and adolescent performances in playful speech activities with caregivers and peers in Guatemala, Reynolds (2002) examined the youths' contesting and negotiating their socially constrained lives through verbal art. Youth used images from mass media and local cultural schemas to create a feeling of belonging to "home-place" in a changing national context. Emphasizing the rapid rate of social change, Sandel (2000) studied folk theories and communicative practices in child LS in a small community of central Taiwan. Caregiver practices indexed the dramatic alterations that have occurred in the status of women, economic conditions, and political liberalization in two generations. The majority ethnic group's desire to maintain its Taiwanese language in a context where official language policies have changed from Japanese to Mandarin—despite the more liberalized atmosphere—adversely impacted parent-child and grandparent-grandchild interactions.

In an excellent ethnographic-sociolinguistic study of diverse LS practices in Latino (Mexican American and immigrant) families, focusing on upper-middle-class families in Northern California and rural families in southern Texas, Schecter and Bayley (2002) examined how speakers used Spanish and English in self-definitions of ethnicity, gender, and class. They found that LS is a fluid, dynamic process of linguistic choices and practices tied to contexts with sociohistorical meaning, ambiguity, and constant change. Their analysis clearly demonstrated that maintenance of Spanish does not interfere with learning English, providing further evidence that bilingualism does not inhibit immigrants' English acquisition.

Homegirls, Mendoza-Denton's (2008) groundbreaking study of *norteña* and *sureña* gang-affiliated Latina adolescent girls in a Northern California urban community, integrated variationist and ethnographic analysis. Based on a four-year ethnography that included in-depth interviews and detailed analysis of linguistic and discourse features, Mendoza-Denton showed Mexican American *norteña* girls and Mexican-immigrant *sureña* girls to be linguistically creative in their contributions to linguistic variation and change. Beyond dress, music, and appearance as identity practices, the girls' phonological variation of vowel realizations correlated with how deeply embedded they were in the gang. Although not specifically framed as an LS study, Mendoza-Denton's study illustrates the power of peer language socialization. (A related ethnographic study of *norteño/sureño* youth in a Northern California rural community is Sepúlveda 2007).

Rieschild (2007) also examined linguistic features (phonology, intonation contours, syntax, morphology) in her fascinating study of language proficiency, bilingual LS, and identity of Arabic-heritage urban youth from heterogeneous national origins, in Australia. She found two social varieties of Australian English created by the youth: Arabizi, a playful codeswitching that performed bilingual/bicultural skill; and Lebspeak, that integrated global hip-hop with Arabic in an English matrix, and expressed Australian identity. Lebspeakers assumed they were viewed positively in the larger Australian national society, despite the post–September 11, 2001, atmosphere of hostility toward Muslims. Rieschild (2007: 1) showed that there is no single "Arabic-background ethnolect of Australian English"; rather "there are differently motivated language patterns" related to a group's learning of English and identity construction—a point applying to many immigrant situations.

In an ethnographic study of LS in two fifth-grade Ukrainian classrooms, Friedman (2006) investigated the processes of Ukrainians seeking their "true" identity post–Soviet control. School oral assessments of children's verbal behavior and knowledge of Ukrainian and Russian were central to the children's (re) imagining their nation. Assessment for adherence to "pure" language forms, affective and poetic uses of Ukrainian, and participation in assessing their own verbal performances shaped students' LS. Through the assessments, children were socialized into taking responsibility for their and their classmates' appropriate verbal behavior, and were led into voicing the language ideologies taught in the classroom.

Rampton (2006) examined hybrid emergent identities and language crossing among multiethnic adolescents at an urban school in the United Kingdom. The youth, of white, South Asian, and Caribbean background, mixed features of Panjabi, Caribbean creole, and stylized Asian English, choosing linguistic forms to take on voices of other ethnolinguistic groups in claiming identity. The connection between linguistic variation and identity in adolescence was also the focus of Eckert's (2000, 2006) high school study on social categories and vowel realization among youth.

All these studies on children and youth's identity construction using language varieties they know or hear are consistent in showing children and youth as linguistically creative and as major players in the evolution of language variation and change. The studies also demonstrate the value of integrating sociolinguistic and LS theoretical perspectives and methodologies for constructing a deeper understanding of language use and language learning.

Lessons for a Transdisciplinary Sociolinguistics

Researchers necessarily make simplifying assumptions in their choices of questions, participants, methods, analysis, and reporting. Their choices are based on training, social networks in which they are embedded, practical concerns of time and money, and philosophical assumptions about language, human nature, and learning. All of these pose special challenges when one is attempting to make a principled crossing of disciplinary boundaries. As mentioned earlier, a transdisciplinary perspective foregrounds the philosophical and methodological issues at stake in such border crossing, and demands greater transparency in choice making than is typically required. To this end, we address some of the issues, using as a guide the framework we proposed previously (Bronson & Watson-Gegeo 2008) for the way in which given research aligns with the LS paradigm—LS as topic, approach, method, and intervention. Our taxonomy and placement of studies within it is not intended as *criticism*, but rather as *commentary* on the standards toward which sociolinguistics and LS work should aspire going forward.

LS as Topic

Many studies treat LS as a topic guiding the study; that is, they "touch on aspects of the LS process without necessarily embodying an [LS] approach or methods in the way the inquiry is actually conceived and conducted" (Bronson & Watson-Gegeo 2008: 48). Thus, research may be sociolinguistic, using established methods, investigating language use and learning, and produce important findings, but may not represent a full realization of the LS paradigm. Harklau's (2003) examination of multimedia based interpretations of identity among immigrant students in the United States, Khayatt's (2003) study of lesbian identity in Egypt, Luykx's (2003) study of Aymara-Spanish code-mixing in Bolivia, and Pease-Alvarez's (2003) study of lexical and discoursal indices of language shift and English-Spanish bilingual identity, are topic-oriented LS studies. Topic-oriented research may depend on examples and vignettes without intensive analysis of discourse data in a longitudinal frame.

LS topic studies do not explicitly embrace multiple levels. Thus, Lamarre and Paredes's (2003) interview study of Canadian bilinguals about when and why they use their languages was a highly useful preliminary study to the broad LS study they intend to conduct, and revealed interesting detail about codeswitching and speaker classification of places and contexts. This kind of preliminary study allows researchers to design a full sociolinguistic-LS transdisciplinary study with more precision and depth. As Lamarre and Paredes understand, a reliance on self-reports would exclude extensive information about the backgrounds of speakers, and be unable to account for how speakers actually behave in various settings over time. LS as topic research can be valuable in examining aspects of language shift, ideology, attitudes, and teaching situations, even when it lacks an empirical record of sufficient depth to meet the requirements of a rigorous design.

LS as Approach

LS as approach includes studies that embrace LS ontology and epistemology, in that these studies attempt to "take into account the lived realities of learners and social conditions in which their learning is occurring" (Bronson & Watson-Gegeo 2008: 49) but do not necessarily follow a longitudinal or ethnographic design. LS as approach begins with embracing the full humanity of research participants, who are positioned as active agents in the (re)construction of identity and language use, and interactive with the researcher in providing feedback to researcher interpretations of data (e.g., Bronson 2004, 2009). In this respect, researcher epistemology for creating knowledge is, at the least, participant observation, as in interactional sociolinguistics (Gumperz 1982) and ethnographic research.

Classroom research framed by a sociolinguistic LS as approach can serve as a counterpoint to the aggregate and positivist view of learning embodied in the current shift to standardized testing in education worldwide. Research protocols generated by the LS approach necessarily take into account the political, economic, and social conditions in which learning is taking place, and attempt to connect the micro and macro even when these are not available in the primary record, as do researchers in a critical perspective. Brown (2007), for example, followed such an approach in her critical discourse analysis home/school LS study of the development of identity and literacy practices for Latino English language learners. In her collaborative study with the primary classroom teacher, she integrated critical pedagogy into the design.

The complexity of an issue such as language transfer can be illuminated as more than the interference of one language system on the acquisition of another. In Bronson's (2004) study, for instance, a Japanese student who became his co-researcher struggled with the grammatical category of articles in English. Together they found that her struggle to correctly use "the" in written English was directly related to her struggle to maintain her Japanese identity. As work on the centrality of metaphor in thinking and understanding indicates (Lakoff & Johnson 1980, 1999), how we imagine the sociolinguistic, sociocultural, and political diversity of learners is essential in a time when standardization of education by assessment and stereotyping of populations are increasingly the norm. LS research can help restore the view of students as multidimensional "active agents" (Baquedano-López 2000) who negotiate their identities in a dance of alignment and resistance strategies (Candela 2005, Prior 1998).

LS as Method

LS as method refers to studies that display "a high degree of transparency about the nature of context, participants, setting, data and analysis" (Bronson & Watson-Gegeo 2008: 50), and that meet the criteria set out elsewhere (Watson-Gegeo 2004: 341–342). Specifically, these studies combine ethnographic, sociolinguistic, and discourse analytic (especially critical discourse analysis [CDA]) methods; engage all relevant micro- and macrodimensions of context; describe whole events and behavior (rather than relying on short strips of time, coded into preset categories); generate categories from data; systematically document interactions via observation and multiple forms of recording; include in-depth interviews with participants; and evolve questions and theory primarily from data.

Several studies mentioned earlier are exemplary models for sociolinguistic LS research (e.g., Baquedano-López 1998; Schecter & Bayley 2002; Aminy 2004; Wyman 2004; Mendoza-Denton 2008; Meek 2011). Here we briefly review Zentella (1997) as an example of best practices in transdisciplinary sociolinguistic work. Zentella's LS research centered on *el bloque*, a block in the South Bronx populated almost exclusively by Puerto Ricans whose language repertoire included varieties of Standard English, Hispanicized English, Nonstandard Puerto Rican Spanish, and African American Vernacular English. She examined LS in 20 families, following five focal children for a decade as they navigated the complexities of language and literacy. As secondary data, Zentella drew on previous ethnographies of the neighborhood and of Puerto Ricans in New York; census data; and socioeconomic, cultural, and bilingual history of Nuyoricans from a postcolonial perspective. As primary data, she collected detailed accounts of the circulation of participants between New York and Puerto Rican educational systems, information on the LS context of originating communities in Puerto Rico, and extensive follow-up interviews with the study participants. She compiled 103 hours of naturally occurring discourse to investigate codeswitching between Spanish and English in a primary social network of the five girls aged 6 through 11 years. She carried out quantitative analyses of codeswitching, including a functional taxonomy of every example in the main corpus of 1383 switches. She examined verbal constructions by speech situation, among other aspects of Spanish idiolects. Zentella (1997: 5) chose LS as her primary method to address the fact that "research on Spanish-English code-switching has established its rule-governed nature but the methodology has been disparate with little unity between quantitative and qualitative approaches." Few studies can be as comprehensive as Zentella's, or integrate as many methods, but the transdisciplinary ethos requires responsible researchers to acknowledge the gaps in their work, as Zentella did throughout.

Mainstream social science is on a search for regularities and stable categories. However, as Zentella (1997: 58) argued, she found that "there were almost as many language patterns as families because of the unique configurations of several variables, including the number of caregivers and children, and differences in language proficiency, education, bilingual literacy skills, years in the U.S., gender, and age of each speaker." Sociolinguistic research and educational anthropology have long challenged taken-for-granted, general "truths" about ethnic/linguistic minority children, and shown that perceived "deficits" in achievement are a social construction (e.g., Labov 1969).

In LS and several strands of sociolinguistics, discourse analysis is fundamental to discovery and evidence. The way speech and action are represented in a transcription or coded in the record is key to the quality of analysis, whether the primary record is audio, video, photographic, or document-based. The decision of which features to code is a theoretical as well as a methodological issue (Ochs 1979), and an analyst is responsible for justifying the "delicacy" (DuBois 2006) of transcription, in the case of audio and video records. Even in exemplary studies, we have noticed that researchers often fail to code for paralinguistic and other prosodic features, body orientation, and eye gaze, all of which are essential to communicating and inferring social meaning (Gumperz & Berenz 1993). Exquisite detail in transcription would be characteristic of a transdisciplinary sociolinguistics and LS.

LS as Intervention

We believe that transdisciplinary sociolinguistic-LS studies should also be *criticalist*, by which we mean work that examines issues of race, ethnicity, class, gender, and power as at least part of the agenda, and pursues research for social justice (Bronson & Watson-Gegeo 2008). From the beginning of sociolinguistics and anthropology of education (Gumperz 1964; Hymes 1974; Cazden et al. 1972; Gilmore & Glatthorn 1982), there was a concern with research that made a difference for disadvantaged groups, and that talks back to power. Methodologically, that concern finds full expression in critical discourse analysis (CDA; Fairclough 1989; Chouliaraki & Fairclough 2001; Van Dijk 1993) when combined with other forms of discourse analysis that account for details of paralinguistics, prosody, and so on (e.g., interactional sociolinguistics; Gumperz & Berenz 1993). Criticalist theoretical perspectives that have usefully framed or supported sociolinguistics and LS studies include community of practice theory (Lave & Wenger 1991; Wenger 1998; e.g., Eckert 2000 and Langman 2003); social/"new"/local literacies based on the work of Street (1995; e.g., Piedra & Romo 2003); social practice theory (Bourdieu 1977; e.g., Lamarare & Paredes 2003 and Atkinson 2003); and language heteroglossia (Bakhtin 1981, 1986; e.g., Garrett 2005). Brown (2007) integrated CDA with critical pedagogy. Other LS scholars have integrated several critical perspectives to expand, for example, identity theory (e.g., Mendoza-Denton 2008).

Social justice is a motivating force for LS and sociolinguistic research in its most robust transdisciplinary manifestations that align with interventions in education and society (e.g., Heath 1983, with schools for black and white working-class children in the Carolinas; Schecter & Bayley 2002, with the education of Mexican Americans in California; Watson-Gegeo & Gegeo 1996, and Watson-Gegeo 2009, with schools and communities in Solomon Islands; see also Bronson & Fields 2009). Critical transdisciplinary research focuses on pressing sociopolitical questions, with the researcher as an ally and advocate providing a clear account of his or her own role(s) and motives. Zentella's (1997) nuanced treatment of her positionality is an example, allowing readers to assess her actions and impact as a community member, unofficial family member, advocate, and teacher in the contexts and lives of the Puerto Rican community in which she worked. Zentella did this without undermining her credibility as an "objective" observer, and without fetishizing the self or descending into extreme subjectivity (Montuori 2005). Her vulnerability and transparency as subject adds to the rigor of her study, and thus supports the value of her proposed interventions—among them, a critical bilingual education program to replace the English-only regime now predominant in New York City schools.

LS is fully realized as intervention when those who are the focus of research become full collaborators from the beginning (as in Bronson 2004), and are empowered to participate in research decisions—to have the agency to question researcher assumptions and to bracket any deterministic or essentialist thinking in interpretations and analysis of data.

Conclusion: Toward Higher Ground

The foregoing review of recent studies shows that sociolinguistic work, which has tended in the past to focus on synchronic and/or intermittent samples of adult or adolescent populations, is enriched by LS studies that follow the development of linguistic features and language varieties through the socialization process, as embedded in the ethnography of speakers, networks, and communities. In turn, LS studies gain precision and rigor by examining sociolinguistic and linguistic features such as phonological variation and change, using sociolinguistic perspectives and research tools. A move to a transdisciplinary stance would strengthen research on language use across the life-span in communities and networks.

Finally, by acknowledging the need to address issues of race, class, gender, and power, Zentella (1997: 13–14) spoke to her colleagues in linguistic anthropology on the issue of a critical positioning. She argued for an "anthro*political* linguistics," pointing out that "there is no language without politics" (14). A transdisciplinary sociolinguistics holds significance as a way of restoring otherwise silenced voices into discourses about opportunity and access to society's resources. By taking a broad approach to the intricacies of language, culture, society, and people's experiences, it elevates the humanity and human rights of those with whom it works as collaborator and ally, and depends on the cultivation of a long-term rapport with communities where researchers work. A transdisciplinary sociolinguistics is essential given global problems of language shift and death, challenges to language rights of indigenous and immigrant peoples, and the narrowing of language education through misguided efforts at standardizing education.

Notes

1. The important emergence of *linguistic ethnography* in the United Kingdom and Europe (Rampton 2007), an interdisciplinary field, lies beyond the specific focus of this paper.
2. Cook-Gumperz used the term "language socialization" in the title of a 1974 paper that later appeared in Ervin-Tripp and Mitchell-Kernan's (1977) volume, which redirected the attention from children's *language* to children's *discourse.*

References

Alcott, L., & Potter, E. (eds.). 1993. *Feminist epistemologies.* New York: Routledge.

Alim, H. S. 2004. *You know my steez: An ethnographic and sociolinguistic study of styleshifting in a Black American speech community.* Publications of the American Dialect Society 89. Durham, NC: Duke University Press.

Aminy, M. 2004. Constructing the moral identity: Literacy practices and language socialization in a Muslim community. Ph.D. dissertation, University of California, Berkeley.

Atkinson, D. 2003. Language socialization and dys-socialization in a South Indian college. In R. Bayley & S. R. Schecter (eds.), *Language socialization in bilingual and multilingual societies,* 147–63. Clevedon: Multilingual Matters.

Ausburger, D. 2004. Language socialization and shift in an Isthmus Zapotec community of Mexico. Ph.D. dissertation, University of Pennsylvania.

Bakhtin, M. M. 1981. *The dialogic imagination: Four essays.* Austin: University of Texas Press.

Bakhtin, M. M. 1986. *Speech genres and other late essays.* Austin: University of Texas Press.

Baquedano-López, P. 1998. *Language socialization of Mexican children in a Los Angeles Catholic parish.* Ph.D. dissertation, University of California, Los Angeles.

Baquedano-López, P. 2000. Narrating the community in *Doctrina* classes. *Narrative Inquiry* 10(2): 1–24.

Bayley, R., & Lucas, C. (eds.). 2007. *Sociolinguistic variation: Theories, methods, and applications.* New York: Cambridge University Press.

Bayley, R., & Schecter, S. R. (eds.). 2003. *Language socialization in bilingual and multilingual societies.* Clevedon: Multilingual Matters.

Bersola-Nguyen, I. A. 2004. Transformative participation in an intergenerational Vietnamese-Pilipino-American household community. Ph.D. dissertation, University of California, Davis.

Boggs, S. T., with Watson-Gegeo, K. A. & McMillan. G. 1985. *Speaking, relating and learning: A study of Hawaiian children at home and at school.* Norwood, NJ: Ablex.

Bourdieu, P. 1977. *Outline of a theory of practice.* Cambridge: Cambridge University Press.

Bronson, M. C. 2002. Rekindling the flutes of fire: Why indigenous languages matter to humanity. *ReVision* 25(2): 5–10.

Bronson, M. C. 2004. Writing passage: Academic literacy socialization among ESL graduate students, a multiple case study. Ph.D. dissertation, University of California, Davis.

Bronson, M. C. 2009. The grammar of transformation: What ESL graduate students can teach the anthropology of consciousness. In M. C. Bronson & T. R. Fields (eds.), *So what? Now what? The anthropology of consciousness responds to a world in crisis,* 232–53. Newcastle-upon-Tyne: Cambridge Scholars Press.

Bronson, M. C., & Fields, T. R. (eds.). 2009. *So what? Now what? The anthropology of consciousness responds to a world in crisis.* Newcastle-upon-Tyne: Cambridge Scholars Press.

Bronson, M. C., & Watson-Gegeo, K. A. 2008. The critical moment: Language socialization and the (re)visioning of first and second language acquisition. In P. A. Duff & N. H. Hornberger (eds.), *Encyclopedia of language education,* vol. 8, *Language socialization,* 43–56. New York: Springer.

Brown, S. A. 2007. A critical discourse analysis of identity development and literacy practices: Latino English language learners at home and in the primary classroom. Ph.D. dissertation, University of South Carolina.

Bucholtz, M., & Hall, K. 2008. All of the above: New coalitions in sociocultural linguistics. *Journal of Sociolinguistics* 12: 401–31.

Bullock, B. E., & Toribio, A. J. 2009. Themes in the study of code-switching. In B. E. Bullock & A. J. Toribio (eds.), *The Cambridge handbook of code-switching,* 1–19. New York: Cambridge University Press.

Candela, A. 2005. Students' participation as co-authoring of school institutional practices. *Culture and Psychology* 11: 321–37.

Cazden, C. B., John, V. P., & Hymes, D. (eds.). 1972. *Functions of language in the classroom.* New York: Teachers College Press.

Chambers, J. K., Trudgil, P., & Schilling-Estes, N. (eds.). 2002. *The handbook of language variation and change.* Oxford: Blackwell.

Chouliaraki, L, & Fairclough, N. 2001. *Discourse in late modernity: Rethinking critical discourse analysis*. Edinburgh: University of Edinburgh Press.

Coates, J. (ed.). 1998. *Language and gender: A reader*. Hoboken, NJ: John Wiley.

Comparini, L. 2000. Constructing self and other: A language socialization approach to Latin mother-child conflict talk. Ph.D. dissertation, Clark University.

Cook-Gumperz, J. 1977. Situated instructions: Language socialization of school age children. In S. Ervin-Tripp & C. Mitchell-Kernan (eds.), *Child discourse*, 103–21. New York: Academic Press.

Delgado, M. R. 2009. Spanish heritage language socialization practices of a family of Mexican origin. Ph.D. dissertation, University of Arizona.

Dubois, J. W. 2006. Transcription delicacy hierarchy. Hand-out for conference presentation at the Linguistics Society of America Annual Meeting, Albuquerque, New Mexico. http://www.linguistics.ucsb.edu/projects/transcription/representing. Accessed 8/8/10.

Duff, P. A. 1995. An ethnography of communication in immersion classrooms in Hungary. *TESOL Quarterly* 29: 505–37.

Duff, P. A. 2008. Language socialization, higher education and work. In P. A. Duff & N. H. Hornberger (eds.), *Encyclopedia of language education*, vol. 8, *Language socialization*, 257–70. New York: Springer.

Duff, P. A. 2010. Language socialization into academic discourse register. *Annual Review of Applied Linguistics* 30: 169–92.

Duff, P. A. 2011. Second language socialization. In A. Duranti, E. Ochs, & B. B. Schieffelin (eds.), *Handbook of language socialization*. Malden, MA: Blackwell.

Duff, P. A., & Hornberger, N. H. (eds.). 2008. *Encyclopedia of language education*, vol. 8, *Language socialization*. New York: Springer.

Eckert, P. 2000. *Linguistic variation as social practice: The linguistic construction of identity in Belten High*. Malden, MA: Blackwell.

Eckert, P. 2006. California vowels. http://www.stanford.edu/~eckert/vowels.html. Accessed 8/13/2010.

Eckert, P., & McConnell-Ginet, S. 2003. *Language and gender*. New York: Cambridge University Press.

Eckert, P., & Rickford, J. R. (eds.). 2001. *Style and sociolinguistic variation*. New York: Cambridge University Press.

Ervin-Tripp, S., & Mitchell-Kernan, C. (eds.). 1977. *Child discourse*. New York: Academic Press.

Fairclough, N. 1989. *Language and power*. New York: Longman.

Farfan, J. A. F., & Ramallo, F. (eds.). 2010. *New perspectives on endangered languages: Bridging gaps between sociolinguistics, documentation and language revitalization*. Amsterdam: Johns Benjamins.

Fellin, L. 2001. Language ideologies, language socialization and language revival in an Italian alpine community. Ph.D. dissertation, University of Arizona.

Field, M. 2001. Triadic directives in Navajo language socialization. *Language in Society* 30: 249–63.

Fogle, E. W. 2009. Language socialization in the internationally adoptive family: Identities, second languages, and learning. Ph.D. dissertation, Georgetown University.

Friedman, D. A. 2006. (Re)imagining the nation: Language socialization in Ukrainian classrooms. Ph.D. dissertation, University of California, Los Angeles.

Frodeman, R., & Mitcham, C. 2007. New directions in interdisciplinarity: Broad, deep, and critical. *Bulletin of Science, Technology, and Society* 2: 506–14.

Garrett, P. B. 2005. What a language is good for: Language socialization, language shift, and the persistence of code-specific genres in St. Lucia. *Language in Society* 34: 327–61.
Garrett, P. B., & Baquedano-López, P. 2002. Language socialization: Reproduction and continuity, transformation and change. *Annual Review of Anthropology* 31: 339–61.
Gegeo, D. W., & Watson-Gegeo, K. A. 1999. Adult education, language change, and issues of identity and authenticity in Kwara'ae (Solomon Islands). *Anthropology and Education* 30: 22–36.
Gegeo, D. W., & Watson-Gegeo, K. A. 2001. "How we know": Kwara'ae rural villagers doing indigenous epistemology. *Journal of the Contemporary Pacific* 13: 55–88.
Gegeo, D. W., & Watson-Gegeo, K. A. 2002. Whose knowledge? Epistemological collisions in Solomon Islands community development. *Journal of the Contemporary Pacific* 14: 377–409.
Gilmore, P., & Glatthorn, A. A. (eds.). 1982. *Children in and out of school: Ethnography and education.* Washington, DC: Center for Applied Linguistics.
Gordon, D. M. 2003. "I'm tired, you clean and cook": Shifting gender identities and language socialization in a Lao-American community. Ph.D. dissertation, University of Pennsylvania.
Gordon, D. M. 2008. Gendered second language socialization. In P. A. Duff & N. H. Hornberger (eds.), *Encyclopedia of language education,* vol. 8, *Language socialization,* 231–42. New York: Springer.
Gumperz, J. J. 1964. Hindi-Punjabi code-switching in Delhi. In H. G. Lunt (ed.), *Proccedings of the Ninth International Conference of Linguists,* 1115–124. The Hague: Mouton.
Gumperz, J. J. 1968. The speech community. In *Encyclopedia of the social sciences* 9.3: 381–86. New York: Macmillan.
Gumperz, J. J. 1982. *Discourse strategies.* Cambridge: Cambridge University Press.
Gumperz, J. J., & Berenz, N. 1993. Transcribing conversational exchanges. In J. A. Edwards & M. D. Lampert (eds.), *Talking data: Transcription and coding in discourse research,* 91–122. Hillsdale, NJ: Lawrence Erlbaum.
Gumperz, J. J., & Cook-Gumperz, J. 2008. Studying language, culture, and society: Sociolinguistics or linguistic anthropology? *Journal of Sociolinguistics* 12: 532–45.
Harklau, L. 2003. Representational practices in multi-modal communication in U.S. high schools: Implications for adolescent immigrants. In R. Bayley & S. R. Schecter (eds.), *Language socialization in bilingual and multilingual societies,* 83–97. Clevedon: Multilingual Matters.
He, A. W. 2004. Identity construction in Chinese heritage language classes. *Pragmatics* 14(2/3): 199–216.
Heath, S. B. 1983. *Ways with words: Language, life and work in communities and classrooms.* Cambridge: Cambridge University Press.
Heath, S. B. 2008. Language socialization in the learning communities of adolescence. In P. A. Duff & N. H. Hornberger (eds.), *Encyclopedia of language education,* vol. 8, *Language socialization,* 217–30. New York: Springer.
Henze, R., & Davis, K. A. (eds.). 1999. Authenticity and identity: Lessons from indigenous language education. *Anthropology and Education Quarterly* 30(1): 3–124.
Howard, K. M. 2003. Language socialization in a Northern Thai bilingual community. Ph.D. dissertation, University of California, Los Angeles.

Howard, K. M. 2007. Language socialization and language shift among school- aged children. In P. A. Duff & N. H. Hornberger (eds.), *Encyclopedia of language education*, vol. 8, *Language socialization*, 187–99. New York: Springer.

Hymes, D. 1967. Models of the interaction of language and social setting. *Journal of Social Issues* 23(2): 8–28.

Hymes, D. 1974. *Foundations in sociolinguistics: An ethnographic approach.* Philadelphia: University of Pennsylvania Press.

Khayatt, D. 2003. Terms of desire: Are there lesbians in Egypt? In R. Bayley & S. R. Schecter (eds.), *Language socialization in bilingual and multilingual societies*, 218–34. Clevedon: Multilingual Matters.

Klein, J. T. 1996. *Crossing boundaries: Knowledge, disciplinarities, and interdisciplinarities.* Charlottesville: University Press of Virginia.

Klein, J. T. 1998. Notes toward a social epistemology of transdisciplinarity. Rencontres transdisciplinaires, 12. http://basarab.nicolescu.perso.sfr.fr/ciret/bulletin/b12/b12c2.htm. Accessed 8/3/2012.

Kulick, D. 1992. *Language shift and cultural reproduction: Socialization, self, an syncretism in a Papua New Guinean village.* New York: Cambridge University Press.

Labov, W. 1969. The logic of Non-Standard English. *Georgetown Monograph on Languages and Linguistics* 22: 1–44.

Labov, W. 1972. *Language in the inner city: Studies in the Black English Vernacular.* Philadelphia: University of Pennsylvania Press.

Lakoff, G., & Johnson, M. 1980. *Metaphors we live by.* Chicago: University of Chicago Press.

Lakoff, G., & Johnson, M. 1999. *Philosophy in the flesh: The embodied mind and its challenge to Western thought.* New York: Basic Books.

Lamarre, P., & Paredes, J. R.. 2003. Growing up trilingual in Montreal: Perceptions of college students. In R. Bayley & S. R. Schecter (eds.), *Language socialization in bilingual and multilingual societies*, 62–80. Clevedon: Multilingual Matters.

Langman, J. 2003. Growing a *báyavirág* (Rock Crystal) on barren soil: Forming a Hungarian identity in Eastern Slovakia through joint (inter)action. In R. Bayley & S. R. Schecter (eds.), *Language socialization in bilingual and multilingual societies*, 182–99. Clevedon: Multilingual Matters.

Lave, J., & Wenger, E. 1991. *Situated learning: Legitimate peripheral participation.* Cambridge: Cambridge University Press.

Lei, J. 2007. A language socialization approach to the interplay of ethnic revitalization and heritage language learning: Case studies of Chinese American adolescents. Ph.D. dissertation, State University of New York, Albany.

Lotherington, H. 2003. Multiliteracies in Springvale: Negotiating language, culture and identity in suburban Melbourne. In R. Bayley & S. R. Schecter (eds.), *Language socialization in bilingual and multilingual societies*, 200–17. Clevedon: Multilingual Matters.

Lukyx, A. 2003. Weaving languages together: Family language policy and gender socialization in bilingual Aymara households. In R. Bayley & S. R. Schecter (eds.), *Language socialization in bilingual and multilingual societies*, 218–34. Clevedon: Multilingual Matters.

Meek, B. A. 2001. Kaska language socialization, acquisition and shift. Ph.D. dissertation, University of Arizona, Tucson.

Meek, B. A. 2011. *We are our language: An ethnography of language revitalization in a Northern Athabaskan community.* Tucson: University of Arizona Press.

Mendoza-Denton, N. 2008. *Homegirls: Language and cultural practice among Latina youth gangs.* Malden, MA: Blackwell.

Mesthrie, R. 2006. *English in language shift: The history, structure and sociolinguistics of South African Indian English.* New York: Cambridge University Press.

Montuori, A. 2005. The quest for a new education: From oppositional identities to creative inquiry. *ReVision* 28(3): 4–20.

Moore, L. C. 2004. Learning languages by heart: Second language socialization in a Fulbe community (Maroua, Cameroon). Ph.D. dissertation, University of California, Los Angeles.

Morita, N., & Kobayashi, M. 2008. Academic discourse socialization in a second language. In P. A. Duff & N. H. Hornberger (eds.), *Encyclopedia of language education,* vol. 8, *Language socialization,* 243–56. New York: Springer.

Murray, S. O. 1998. *American sociolinguistics: Theorists and theory groups.* Philadelphia: John Benjamins.

Needham, S. 1996. Literacy, learning and language ideology: Intracommunity variation in Khmer literacy instruction. Ph.D. dissertation, University of California, Los Angeles.

Nguyen, T. B. T. 2002. The diversity in language socialization: Gender and social stratum in a North Vietnamese village. Ph.D. dissertation, University of Toronto.

Nicolescu, B. 2002. *Manifesto of transdisciplinarity.* Translated by K.-C. Voss. Albany: State University of New York.

Nicolescu, B. 2003. Definition of transdisciplinarity. Rethinking interdisciplinarity, 29, May. http://www.caosmose.net/candido/unisinos/textos/textos/nicolescu1.pdf. Accessed 8/3/2012

Ochs, E. 1979. Transcription as theory. In E. Ochs & B. B. Schieffelin (eds.), *Developmental pragmatics,* 43–72. New York: Academic Press.

Ochs, E., & Schieffelin, B. B. 1984. Language acquisition and socialization: Three developmental stories. In R. A. Shweder & R. A. LeVine (eds.), *Culture theory: Essays on mind, self, and emotion,* 276–320. Cambridge: Cambridge University Press.

Ochs, E., & Schieffelin, B. B. 2008. Language socialization: An historical overview. In P. A. Duff & N. H. Hornberger (eds.), *Encyclopedia of language education,* vol. 8, *Language socialization,* 3–15. New York: Springer.

Patrick, D. 2003. Language socialization and second language acquisition in a multilingual Arctic Quebec community. In R. Bayley & S. R. Schecter (eds.), *Language socialization in bilingual and multilingual societies,* 165–81. Clevedon: Multilingual Matters.

Paugh, A. L. 2001. "Creole day is every day": Language socialization, shift, and ideologies in Dominica, West Indies. Ph.D. dissertation, New York University.

Paugh, A. L. 2005. Multilingual play: Children's code-switching, role play and agency in Dominica, West Indies. *Language in Society* 43.1.63–86.

Pease-Alvarez, L. 2003. Transforming perspectives on bilingual language socialization. In R. Bayley & S. R. Schecter (eds.), *Language socialization in bilingual and multilingual societies,* 9–24. Clevedon: Multilingual Matters.

Philips, S. U. 1972. Participant structures and communicative competence: Warm Springs children in community and classroom. In C. B. Cazden, V. P. John, & D. Hymes (eds.), *Functions of language in the classroom,* 370–94. New York: Teachers College Press.

Piedra, M. de la, & Romo, H. D. 2003. Collaborative literacy in a Mexican immigrant household: The role of sibling mediators in the socialization of pre-school learners. In R. Bayley & S. R. Schecter (eds.), *Language socialization in bilingual and multilingual societies*, 44–61. Clevedon: Multilingual Matters.

Pon, G., Goldstein, & Schecter, S. R. 2003. Interrupted by silences: The contemporary education of Hong Kong-born Chinese Canadians. In R. Bayley & S. R. Schecter (eds.), *Language socialization in bilingual and multilingual societies*, 114–227. Clevedon: Multilingual Matters.

Prior, P. A. 1998. *Writing disciplinarity: A sociohistorical account of literate activity in the academy.* Mahwah, NJ: Lawrence Erlbaum.

Rampton, B. 2006. *Language in late modernity: Interaction in an urban school.* New York: Cambridge University Press.

Rampton, B. 2007. Neo-Hymesian linguistic ethnography in the United Kingdom. *Journal of Sociolinguistics* 11(5): 584–607.

Reynolds, J. F. 2002. Maya children's practices of the imagination: (Dis)playing childhood and politics in Guatemala. Ph.D. dissertation, University of California, Los Angeles.

Rieschild, V. R. 2007. Influences of language proficiency, bilingual socialization, and urban youth identities on producing different Arabic-English voices in Australia. *Novitas-Royal* 1(1): 1–20. http://www.novitasroyal.org/archives/vol-1-issue-1. Accessed 8/3/2012

Riley, K. C. 2007. To tangle or not to tangle: Shifting language ideologies and the socialization of *Chabaria*, in the Marquesas, French Polynesia. In M. Makihara & B. B. Schieffelin (eds.), *Consequences of contact: Language ideologies and sociocultural transformations in Pacific societies*, 70–95. New York: Oxford University Press.

Rymes, B. 2008. Language socialization and the linguistic anthropology of education. In P. A. Duff & N. H. Hornberger (eds.), *Encyclopedia of language education*, vol. 8, *Language socialization*, 29–42. New York: Springer.

Sandel, T. L. 2000. Leading children in Chhan-Chng: Language socialization in a Taiwanese community. Ph.D. dissertation, University of Illinois at Urbana-Champaign.

Schecter, S. R., & Bayley, R. 2002. *Language as cultural practice: Mexicanos en el norte.* Mahwah, NJ: Lawrence Erlbaum.

Schieffelin, B. B. 1990. *The give and take of everyday life: Language socialization of Kaluli children.* New York: Cambridge University Press.

Schieffelin, B. B., & Ochs, E. (eds.). 1986. *Language socialization across cultures.* New York: Cambridge University Press.

Senghas, R. J. 2003. New ways to be Deaf in Nicaragua: Changes in language, personhood, and community. In L. Monaghan, C. Schmaling, K. Nakamura, & G. H. Turner (eds.), *Many ways to Be Deaf: International variation in Deaf communities*, 260–82. Washington, DC: Gallaudet University Press.

Sepúlveda, E. 2007. Migrating youth, identity, and the pedagogy of *accompañamiento.* Ph.D. dissertation, University of California, Davis.

Shumin, L. 2009. Education at last! Taiwanese grandmothers "go to school." Ph.D. dissertation, University of Illinois at Urbana-Champaign.

Slobin, D. I. (ed.). 1967. *A field manual for the study of the acquisition of communicative competence.* Berkeley: Language Behavior Research Laboratory, University of California.

Snow, P. M. 2004. What happen: Language socialization and language persistence in a Panamanian Creole village. Ph.D. dissertation, University of California, Los Angeles.

Song, J. 2007. Language ideologies and identity: Korean children's language socialization in a bilingual setting. Ph.D. dissertation, Ohio State University.

Spolsky, B., & Hult, F. M. (eds.). 2010. *Handbook of educational linguistics*. Malden, MA: Wiley-Blackwell.

Stokols, D. 2006. Toward a science of transdisciplinary action research. *American Journal of Community Psychology* 38: 63–77.

Street, B. V. 1995. *Social literacies: Critical approaches to literacy development, ethnography and education*. London: Longman.

Tollefson, J. W. (ed.). 2001. *Language policies in education*. Mahwah, NJ: Lawrence Erlbaum.

Trueba, H. T., Guthrie, G. P., & Au, K. P.-H. (eds.). 1981. *Culture and the bilingual classroom*. Rowley, MA: Newbury House Publishers.

Tryggvason, M.-T. 2002. Language—mirror of culture: A case study on language socialization with Finns living in Finland and Sweden, and Swedes living in Sweden. Ph.D. dissertation, Stockholms Universitet.

Van Dijk, T. A. 1993. Principles of critical discourse analysis. *Discourse and Society* 4(2): 249–83.

Warner, S. L. N. 1999. *Kuleana*: The right, responsibility, and authority of indigenous peoples to speak and make decisions for themselves in language and cultural revitalization. *Anthropology and Education Quarterly* 30(1): 68–93.

Watson, K. A. 1975. Transferable communicative routines: Strategies and group identity in two speech events. *Language in Society* 4: 53–72.

Watson-Gegeo, K. A. 1992. Thick explanation in the ethnographic study of child socialization: A longitudinal study in the problem of schooling for Kwara'ae (Solomon Islands) children. *New Directions for Child Development* 58: 51–66.

Watson-Gegeo, K. A. 2004. Mind, language, and epistemology: Toward a language socialization paradigm for SLA. *Modern Language Journal* 88(3): 331–50.

Watson-Gegeo, K. A. 2009. Finding a path through silver rain: Steps towards at anthropology of conscience. In M. C. Bronson & T. R. Fields (eds.), *So what? Now what? The anthropology of consciousness responds to a world in crisis*, 30–53. Newcastle-upon-Tyne: Cambridge Scholars Press.

Watson-Gegeo, K. A., & Boggs, S. T. 1977. From verbal play to talk story: The role of routines in speech events among Hawaiian children. In S. Ervin-Tripp & C. Mitchell-Kernan (eds.), *Child discourse*, 67–90. New York: Academic Press.

Watson-Gegeo, K. A., & Gegeo, D. W. 1986. Calling-out and repeating routines in Kwara'ae children's language socialization. In B. B. Schieffelin & E. Ochs (eds.), *Language socialization across cultures*, 17–50. New York: Cambridge University Press.

Watson-Gegeo, K. A., & Gegeo, D. W. 1991. The impact of church affiliation on language use in Kwara'ae (Solomon Islands). *Language in Society* 20: 533–55.

Watson-Gegeo, K. A., & Gegeo, D. W. 1996. Keeping culture out of the classroom in rural Solomon Islands schools: A critical analysis. *Educational Foundations* 8(2): 27–55.

Watson-Gegeo, K. A., & Nielsen, S. E. 2003. Language socialization in ESL. In C. J. Doughty & M. H. Long (eds.), *Handbook of second language acquisition*, 155–77. Oxford: Blackwell.

Wenger, E. 1998. *Communities of practice: Learning, meaning and identity.* Cambridge: Cambridge University Press.

Wong, L. 1999. Authenticity and the revitalization of Hawaiian. *Anthropology and Education Quarterly* 30: 94–115.

Woolard, K. A., & Schieffelin., B. B. 1994. Language ideology. *Annual Review of Anthropology* 23: 55–82.

Wortham, S. 2008. Linguistic anthropology of education. *Annual Review of Anthropology* 37: 37–51.

Wyman, L. T. 2004. Language shift, youth culture, and ideology: A Yup'ik example. Ph.D. dissertation, Stanford University.

Zentella, A. C. 1997. *Growing up bilingual: Puerto Rican children in New York.* Oxford: Blackwell.

CHAPTER 7

PSYCHOLINGUISTIC APPROACHES

BRANDON C. LOUDERMILK

THE factors influencing sociolinguistic variation have been well described across languages and dialects, yet open questions remain: How is sociolinguistic variation perceived during real-time language processing? What is the nature of the cognitive representation? How do linguistic and social stereotypes influence perception? A more nuanced understanding of these mechanisms would play an important role in addressing some of the fundamental issues in sociolinguistics, including how children acquire social constraints; how interlocutors "converge" on similar styles; and how individuals develop attitudes toward speakers of different language varieties. This chapter seeks to highlight some of the key developments and methods used in the emerging field of *sociolinguistic cognition* (Campbell-Kibler 2010).

The fundamental goal of the study of sociolinguistic cognition is to characterize the computational stages and cognitive representations underlying the perception and production of sociolinguistic variation. Work in this field has focused on three issues: (1) understanding the manner and degree to which social knowledge, beliefs, and stereotypes influence perceptual processing of spoken language; (2) identifying the cognitive stages, representations, and time course of processing; and (3) characterizing the way in which language and language variants engender attitudes and bias language processing.

This chapter is organized into four sections. The first section discusses different methods for examining how dialectal variation is represented, perceived, and learned. The second section reviews studies investigating the role of sociolinguistic stereotypes in speech processing. The third explores the attitudinal aspects of language variation by presenting two recent studies using innovative variations of the matched-guise technique. This section concludes by introducing a promising technique, the implicit association test, which may be able to address some of the limitations of alternative methods. The fourth section reports on studies that use eye-tracking and event-related brain potentials to investigate sociolinguistic cognition.

Dialectal Variation

One important line of research involves characterizing what naïve language users know about dialectal variation and how they come to learn it. Two approaches are used: (1) perceptual categorization studies in which participants listen to recordings of speakers of different dialects and attempt to categorize them; and (2) perceptual learning experiments that attempt to characterize how dialectal variation affects learning.

Perceptual Categorization of Dialects

In perceptual categorization experiments participants listen to speech that contains dialect-specific features (e.g., vowel variants). In order to tease out the effects of prior dialect exposure on perception, participants with different regional backgrounds are recruited (Clopper 2010).

Forced-Choice Perceptual Categorization

During forced-choice perceptual categorization tasks, participants listen to speech and then identify "where they think the speaker is from" by selecting from a predefined dialect category. Preston (1993) used this technique to investigate how regional background influences dialect classification. Participants from Michigan and Indiana listened to speakers from nine different cities in the United States on a north-to-south continuum. Although participants had difficulty distinguishing between north and midland speakers, they were better at distinguishing between northern and southern speakers. Preston also reported an effect for participant region: Michigan listeners distinguished northern from southern speakers at a more northern boundary than did the Indiana listeners. Early results such as these underscored the importance of linguistic exposure in cognitive processes.

More recently, Clopper and Pisoni (2004b) examined how geographical mobility influenced dialect identification. Here, participants listened to speech from six dialect regions and then classified that speech into one of six dialect regions presented on a map. Participants comprised two groups: "homebodies" who had only lived in Indiana, and "army brats" who had lived in three or more states. On average, participants performed quite poorly on this task (~30 percent accuracy), but were still statistically above chance performance. Army brats outperformed homebodies, and army brats who had lived in a given region categorized talkers from that region more accurately than army brats who had not lived there.

While listeners seem to perform rather poorly on forced-choice dialect classification tasks, these findings highlight the importance of linguistic background by showing how exposure to regional variation affects how well regional accents of unfamiliar talkers are identified. One of the primary limitations of the forced-choice task is that the number of sorting categories and category labels are predefined by the researcher. As such, there may be a poor fit between the participants' actual mental representations of dialectal variation and the categories they choose from.

Auditory Free Classification

One technique that overcomes a limitation of forced-choice classification is the auditory free classification task (Clopper 2008). In this task, participants are presented a screen that allows them to play speech snippets. The graphical representation of the sound stimuli can then be dragged on a grid to form participant-defined groupings of speakers who "speak the same dialect" (figure 7.1). Aggregate results can be interpreted by submitting them to clustering analysis (which identifies how objects group together perceptually) and multidimensional scaling (which identifies the most salient perceptual dimensions). Importantly, the number of categories and category labels need not be pre-specified, thus eliminating one limitation of forced-choice categorization.

Given these more relaxed constraints, Clopper and Pisoni (2007) examined how listeners would freely classify the same speakers from the six dialect regions previously used in the forced-choice experiment (Clopper & Pisoni 2004b). Results showed that participants classified speakers into an average of ten dialect groups, suggesting that listeners do indeed have the ability to make finer discriminations of regional varieties. However, despite this, clustering analysis identified three broad dialect categories (i.e., New England, South, and Midwest/West), which corresponded to the three categories identified by their previous forced-choice study. Multidimensional scaling revealed that linguistic markedness, geographic region, and gender were the primary dimensions by which listeners classified dialects.

Synthesized Speech

Rather than use natural speech, some researchers use synthesized speech in order to exercise greater control over their experimental manipulations.

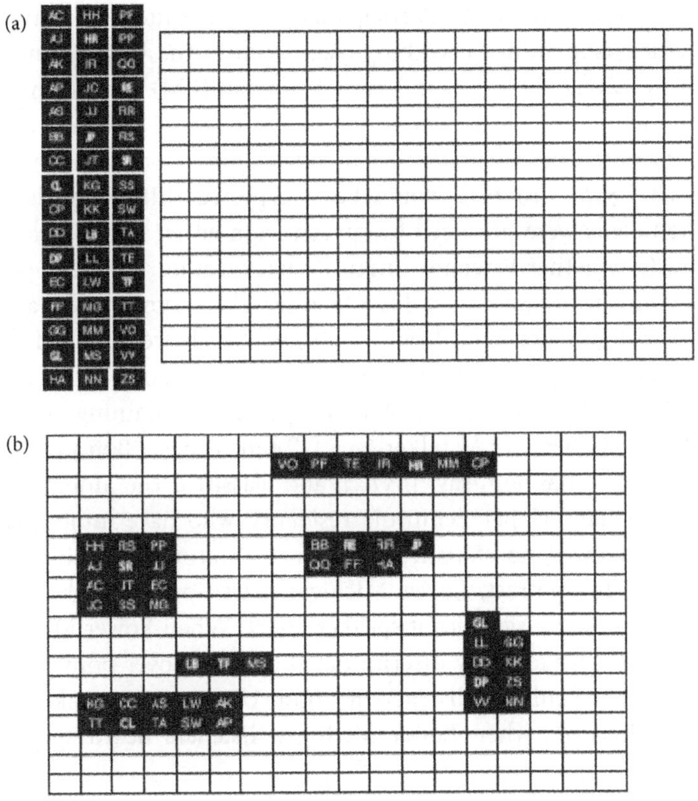

Figure 7.1. Free classification task, with 48 stimulus items. A 16 x 16 grid (A) before the task and (B) after the task

Source: Clopper (2008)

Plichta and Preston (2005) administered a perception test to subjects from 20 regions of the United States. Their study focused on a southern dialect feature, monophthongization of /ay/, and sought to measure participants' ability to use acoustic information to distinguish speaker origin on a north-south continuum. Seven resynthesized vowel tokens were embedded in a [gVd] frame, to create words ranging from a fully diphthongal "guide" to fully monophthongal "god." Participants listened to these words and clicked a map to indicate one of seven locations on a north-south continuum. Although participants reported being unable to discriminate between tokens, results showed otherwise. There were significant differences in "southernness" between every step of the continuum, with the most monophthongal tokens being rated most southern and the fully diphthongal tokens being rated most northern.

Plichta and Rakerd (2010) investigated how listeners' region of origin influences the perception of a change in progress, the Northern Cities Chain Shift (NCCS). In the NCCS, multiple vowels are shifted: /a/ fronting, /æ/ fronting and raising, and /ɛ/ lowering. Participants were recruited from two different Michigan cities: Ishpeming, a working-class town in the Upper Peninsula (UP), and Detroit, a metropolitan city in Lower Michigan (LM). Importantly, residents of Detroit exhibit advanced stages of the NCCS, whereas residents of the Upper Peninsula do not. The researchers set to determine (1) whether vowel tokens subject to NCCS /a/ fronting would be interpreted differently depending on whether the tokens were preceded by speech from either a LM speaker or a UP speaker and (2) whether listeners' linguistic background impacted perception.

By varying the frequency of F2, the researchers synthesized a continuum of seven vowel tokens ranging from /a/ to /æ/, which were embedded in /hVt/ and /sVt/ syllable frames to create words that varied from "hot" to "hat" and "sock" to "sack." Participants listened to sentences containing the ambiguous words spoken by either an LM talker or a UP talker (e.g., "Bob was positive that he heard his wife, Shannon, say: [hVt]"), and classified the ambiguous word as either "hot" or "hat." Upper Peninsula residents, who have limited exposure to NCCS speech, showed no statistical difference in crossover points for speaker (figure 7.2, left). In contrast, Lower Michigan participants highly familiar with NCCS speech, showed a significant speaker effect. When Lower Michigan listeners heard the UP speaker, they discriminated at a crossover point similar to the one used by Upper Peninsula listeners for both UP and LM speakers (figure 7.2, upper right). However, when Lower Michigan listeners heard speech from an

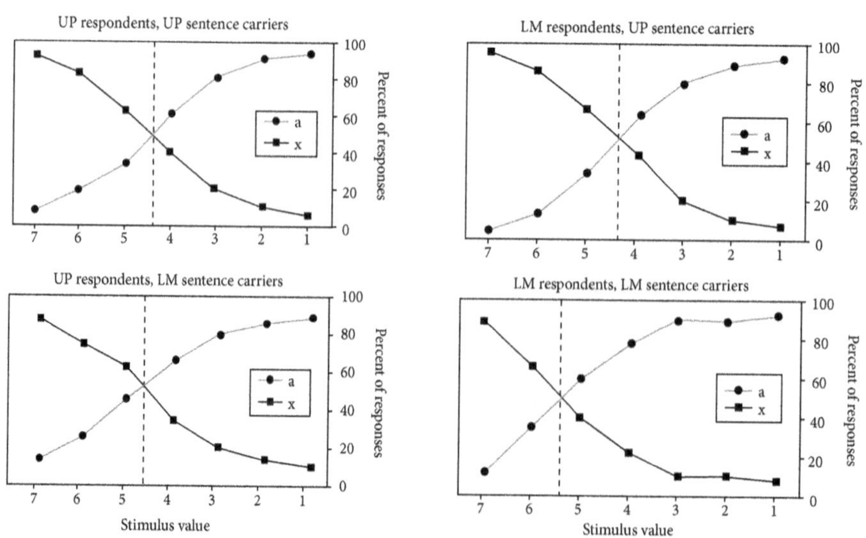

Figure 7.2. Upper Peninsula listeners (*left*) show no difference in perceptual boundaries for ambiguous /a/-/æ/ tokens. Lower Michigan listeners (*upper right*) use the same perceptual boundary /a/-/æ/ as Upper Peninsula speakers when they encounter non-NCCS speech. When Lower Michigan listeners (*bottom right*) encounter NCCS speech, they shift their perceptual boundary is the direction of the shift.

Source: Plichta & Rakerd (2010).

LM talker, they shifted their discrimination threshold a full step further to the front (i.e., a higher F2 value) (figure 7.2, bottom right). These results demonstrate that information about a speaker's dialect plays an important role in vowel identification which is influenced by dialect exposure.

Priming

Sumner and Samuel (2005, 2009) investigated how dialectal variants are processed and represented over different time spans. In their 2005 study, they investigated how the realization of coda /t/ affects language processing. In the Long Island dialect of American English, word-final /t/ is variably realized as a fully articulated [t], a coarticulated glottalized form [ʔt̚], and a singly articulated glottal stop [ʔ]. In order to determine the immediate and long-term processing consequences of these variants, the researchers used an auditory semantic priming paradigm. In this paradigm, participants listen to prime-target word pairs and make a lexical decision on the target word. The prime word "flute," for example, primes, or speeds the reaction time, for the *related* target word "music" compared to the *unrelated* target word "money." In this study, participants heard prime words consisting of the three regular variants of a word (e.g., basic [flut], coarticulated [fluʔt̚], and glottal [fluʔ]). Also included were primes with an arbitrary feature mismatch (e.g., [flus]) that paralleled the place of articulation mismatch for the glottal variant (e.g., [fluʔ]). Target words were semantically related or unrelated to the prime (e.g., "music" or "money"). Results showed that participants were equally primed for all three variants compared to the feature mismatch condition. Interestingly, this shows that at least in terms of immediate processing, there are no cognitive costs associated with processing noncanonical regular variants.

A second experiment by Sumner and Samuel (2005) used a long-term repetition priming paradigm, in which all prime words were presented in a first block of trials and all target words were presented in a second block of trials. This experiment additionally differed from the first, in that it used a repetition priming paradigm in which target words were repeats of prime words. Prior work has shown that participants respond faster and more accurately if they have already encountered the same stimulus. Using this design allowed the researchers to investigate the degree to which one variant primes another variant relative to itself. The temporal lag in the blocked design allowed them to identify which form is encoded in memory over the intervening interval. Results showed that of all the possible combinations of variants, only the Basic [t]—Basic [t] prime-target pairs showed a strong priming effect. Although the partially glottalized variant is more frequent in actual production, it did not show a priming effect. This evidence argues against frequency-based exemplar models of representation, suggesting that the canonical form serves as the underlying representation.

In a subsequent study Sumner and Samuel (2009) investigated the effects of dialectal experience on the perception and representation of phonetic variation, specifically the alternative realization of –er final words (e.g., "baker"). Speakers of the New York City dialect (NYC) often produce r-less variants (bak[ə]), while speakers from other parts of the country (General American—GA) produce r-ful variants (bak[ɚ]). Three groups of participants were identified: (1) Overt-NYC participants were third-generation New York City residents who were primarily r-less; (2) Covert-NYC participants were second-generation New York City residents who were r-ful; and (3) GA participants who were born and raised outside New York City and were r-ful in their speech.

To examine how well dialectal surface features are processed by these groups, several priming experiments were conducted. As expected, results showed that the r-less variant posed difficulties for the GA speakers but not for the Overt-NYC participants. Interestingly, the Covert-NYC speakers patterned with the Overt-NYC speakers on the immediate perceptual tasks (figure 7.3, left panel). Specifically, both groups showed facilitated priming effects for the r-less variant in the short-term repetition priming and the semantic priming experiments. However, in contrast to the Overt-NYC participants, the Covert-NYC speakers showed no r-less priming effect on the long-term repetition priming experiment, in which primes presented in blocks were preceded by targets about 20 to 30 minutes beforehand (figure 7.3, right panel). Apparently, for these Covert-NYC speakers, only the GA form is encoded in memory; the Overt-NYC speakers appear to encode both variants of final –er equally well. These findings suggest there are multiple ways of "having" a dialect: in speech production, in speech perception, and in long-term encoding.

Squires (2011) used a syntactic priming paradigm to explore how social information such as talker gender and social status affects sentence processing. Previous syntactic priming studies have shown that priming participants with one syntactic alternant (e.g., passive voice) makes that alternant more likely in production and increases expectations during perception. Squires' experiments tested whether exposing participants to a nonstandard agreement pattern (e.g., *The dog don't bark; There's dogs in the yard*) in the prime sentence made it more likely that participants would perceive nonstandard agreement in the subsequent target sentence. Prime trials included the full realization of the subject-verb construction with a non-subject noun masked. Critically, target trials masked the subject noun, and participants chose between singular and plural noun photos (e.g., *dog/dogs*).

Squires found that priming was effective for these sociolinguistically variable agreement patterns: exposing participants to nonstandard agreement in a prime stimulus increased the likelihood that they interpreted the target stimulus as nonstandard. Because syntactic priming is argued to reflect speakers' cognitive representations of linguistic structures, these results suggest that speakers store knowledge of grammatical variation as part of linguistic competence and apply that knowledge during processing. Squires' experiments also found differential priming effects of the gender, social status, and individual identity of

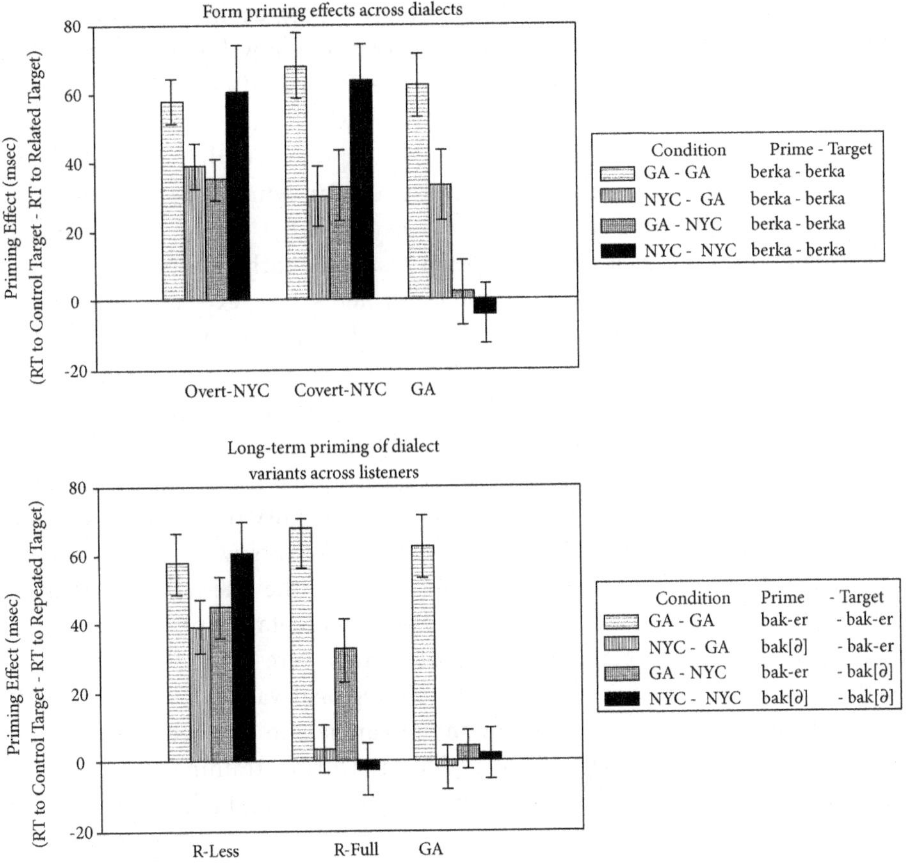

Figure 7.3. Short-term repetition priming by dialect group (*top panel*). Long-term repetition priming by dialect group (*bottom panel*)

the prime and target talkers, suggesting that at least some social knowledge is also recruited during sentence processing.

Perceptual Learning

Recent work has investigated how exposure to phonetic variation can influence "perceptual learning" and alter the nature of linguistic and sociolinguistic representations. Perceptual learning is indicated by improved performance following language exposure, and the studies reported here directly bear on issues germane to sociolinguistics, speech perception, and dialect learning. Perceptual learning experiments generally comprise two parts: an initial learning phase followed by a testing phase. During learning, subjects perform a lexical decision task while they hear an assortment of control words, non-words, and critical words that contain an ambiguous segment.

A study by Maye, Aslin, and Tanenhaus (2008) examined how listeners adjust perceptual boundaries after brief exposure to a novel dialect. Participants first listened to a 20-minute recording of the *Wizard of Oz* read in a synthesized standard American English accent, after which they were given a lexical decision test. Several days later, subjects were presented the same 20-minute story, but this time read in a synthesized dialect in which all the front vowels were systematically lowered (e.g., *witch* → *wetch* [wɛʧ]). Again, after exposure, participants were given a lexical decision test. The authors found a nearly 20 percent increase in acceptance rate for *wetch* items after exposure to the novel dialect. This increase was significant even for stimuli that did not occur in the story, suggesting that adaptation is not purely lexical in nature. The findings highlight the rapidity with which listeners may re-map their perceptual spaces in order to accommodate the speech they encounter.

Clopper and Pisoni (2004a) also used a perceptual learning dialect categorization task to investigate the role of speaker variability on the learning of six regional varieties of English. Two groups of participants were used: one-talker listeners and three-talker listeners. During training the one-talker participants listened to sentences read by a single talker representative of each of the six dialects. In contrast, the three-talker participants were exposed to the speech of three talkers representing each of the six regional varieties. The three talkers from each variety were chosen by the researchers to be good, medium, and poor representatives of their regional dialect. During training, subjects indicated dialect region on an interactive map, with feedback highlighting the correct response. Training was divided into three blocks: (a) talkers reading the same sentence multiple times, (b) talkers reading an alternative multiple times, and (c) talkers reading a number of different novel sentences.

Following training, the two groups of participants were tested on their ability to (1) identify the training talkers on novel sentences, and (2) generalize their dialect knowledge to novel speakers. The single-talker listeners outperformed the three-talker listeners on all training phases and the test phase. However, the three-talker group outperformed the single-talker group on generalization to novel speakers. This crossover effect suggests that talker variability encountered during perceptual learning makes it more difficult to learn specific exemplars, but that it facilitates more robust dialect representations that enable learners to generalize these features to novel speakers.

Sociolinguistic Stereotypes and Language Processing

Over the past decade, a number of studies have examined how sociolinguistic stereotypes impact language processing. These studies seek to identify the extent to which listeners use extra-linguistic information (e.g., age, gender, and region) while processing speech. The questions addressed by this research are, what sort of tacit knowledge do naïve listeners have regarding variation and its social and linguistic correlates; and how does this knowledge influence language processing. These studies manipulate the perceived social characteristics of the speaker, while holding the auditory stimulus constant. This allows researchers to tease apart which aspects of social information listeners rely upon while attending to speech.

Perceived Speaker Origin

In an early study, Niedzielski (1999) examined the relationship between regional linguistic stereotypes and speech perception by using a vowel matching task. Her study focused on Canadian Raising, a phonetic process in which the /aw/ diphthong (as in the word *house*) is pronounced with the tongue raised and fronted compared to canonical /a/. Canadian Raising is a linguistic stereotype that the residents of Detroit hold about the speech of Canadians. Canadian Raising is also found in the speech of white, middle-class Detroit residents, but they themselves do not report any awareness of it in their own speech.

In this study, Detroit area participants heard sentences and were asked to choose from a list of re-synthesized vowels, the token that best matched the vowel in a critical word. All of the sentences were spoken by the same Detroit speaker who had raised /aw/ in her speech. However, whereas one group of subjects believed that the speaker was from Detroit, the other group believed that the speaker was from a nearby Canadian city. When subjects believed a Canadian had spoken the word *house*, 60 percent of the participants chose the raised token. In contrast, when participants believed a fellow Detroiter had spoken the same word, only 11 percent chose the raised /aw/ token. The results for all /aw/ words were similar: if the speaker was perceived to be Canadian, 53 percent chose the raised token in contrast to the 15 percent who chose the raised token for the perceived Detroiter. This suggests that perceived speaker origin is sufficient to bias phonological processing.

In a similar study by Hay and colleagues (2006), participants listened to the speech of a New Zealander but were provided an answer sheet with the word "Australia" or "New Zealand" written on the top of the form. The study focused on the /I/ vowel, which is realized differently in the two dialects—raised and fronted in Australian English and centralized in New Zealand English. Findings were similar to those reported in Niedzielski—when given the Australia answer sheet, listeners perceived more raised and fronted variants than when given the New Zealand answer form. Interestingly, these effects were observed even when listeners reported that they knew that the speaker was in fact a New Zealander. This suggests that instead of a dialect expectation bias per se, these results might be more attributable to a low-level priming mechanism in which "mere exposure" to the concept of Australia is enough to induce a perceptual shift.

Perceived Speaker Race

A study by Staum Casasanto (2008) examined whether listeners use knowledge of speaker race to resolve lexical ambiguities. Her study focused on coronal stop deletion, a characteristic of African American English (Rickford 1999), among other dialects. Stimuli were sentences that contained a lexical ambiguity caused by deleting an underlying /t,d/. For example, the word "mast" pronounced with a deleted –t and the word "mass" are homophonous and thus ambiguous without a supporting context. Participants were visually presented pictures of black or white faces while they listened to short passages containing one of these ambiguous critical words. In one trial they heard

1.) The [mæs] probably lasted…

The audio clip then was followed by a visually presented continuation, either:

a. through the storm
b. an hour on Sunday

The "through the storm" continuation is more likely with a deleted-t interpretation of [mæs], while the "an hour on Sunday" continuation is more consistent with no deletion. Participants responded by button press to indicate whether the continuation was plausible.

Findings revealed a significant interaction of speaker race and deletion. Participants responded faster for continuations that were consistent with a deleted-t (the *mast* interpretation) when accompanied with a black face. Likewise, participants responded faster for a nonunderlying –t continuation (the *mass* interpretation) when accompanied with a white face. These findings demonstrate that listeners use knowledge of correlations or probabilities related to race and variation.

Gender Stereotypes

Work by Strand and Johnson (1996) has examined how perceptual processes are influenced by gender-based stereotypes. Their first study examined the discrimination boundary between /ʃ/ and /s/, the latter of which has a higher-frequency spectrum reflective of the smaller size resonating cavity in front of the constriction. Importantly, variation in spectra for men and women is often attributed to relative differences in vocal tract length. Four speakers whose voices were judged to be prototypically male/female and nonprototypically male/female were recorded. Ambiguous /s/-/ʃ/ tokens were generated and spliced to a following

VC coda spoken by each of the four speakers to form the words *sod* and *shod*. Participants listened to these ambiguous stimuli and categorized them.

Results showed that the discrimination boundary was determined by both the gender and the gender prototypicality of the speaker, with the largest differences observed between prototypical male and prototypical female voices. A second experiment accompanied the ambiguous tokens with video clips of a male or female face. Results showed that the same fricative was perceived differently depending upon whether it was accompanied by a male or female face. Results showed that the /s/-/ʃ/ boundary was shifted up for a female face and shifted down for a male face. These results show that complex social expectations can influence relatively low-level cognitive mechanisms, challenging purely bottom-up modular accounts of processing.

Language Attitude

In the study of language attitude researchers have typically relied on three broad approaches: the societal treatment approach, which typically involves participant observation and ethnography; the direct approach in which participants are directly questioned about their language beliefs and attitudes; and the indirect approach, or matched-guise technique (Garrett, Coupland, & Williams 2003; Lambert, Hodgson, Gardner, & Fillenbaum 1960). The societal treatment approach is qualitative in nature and has been criticized on the grounds that the researcher is inferring attitude from behavior. Likewise, the direct approach has been criticized on "whether subjects" [overt] verbal statements of their attitudes" accurately reflect their "underlying disposition" (Knops & van Hout 1988). The matched-guise technique (MGT) developed by Lambert and colleagues (1960) addresses these shortcomings by trying to covertly elicit language attitudes.

Matched-Guise Experiments

In MGT studies, participants listen to repeated passages of speech read by a single speaker under different guises (e.g., language, dialect, etc.), and are asked to make judgments on some aspect of the speaker (e.g., intelligence, friendliness, etc.). Because the speaker and the content of the recording are held constant, and because the listeners *believe* they are listening to different speakers, any attitudinal differences can be attributed to the manipulation (i.e., guise) under study.

Although the MGT has been used to investigate gross features of language, finer distinctions can be made. Labov et al. (2011), for example, conducted a series of experiments that manipulated the frequency of (ING) variants—the alternation of velar [Iŋ] and apical [In] pronunciations (e.g., *working* vs. as in *workin'*). Subjects were asked to rate the speech of a newscaster-in-training on measures of professionalism. Across excerpts, the ratio of *-ing* and *-in* tokens were manipulated. The researchers found a logarithmic progression between the frequency of apical *-in* and the negative evaluation of speaker professionalism. Consistent with the production literature (Labov 1966; Trudgill 1974), they also reported an effect of gender—females evaluated the vernacular variant more harshly than males. Moreover, subjects from South Carolina were found to be more tolerant of *-in* use than subjects from Philadelphia. In the experiment manipulating speaker dialect, they found no differences in overall evaluation, suggesting that the frequency of the apical variant alone was the determining factor in eliciting these overt attitudes.

Campbell-Kibler (2006, 2007) conducted a single-variable study on (ING) using a novel variation of the MGT. Rather than have speech actors read written scripts, Campbell-Kibler recorded hour-long informal interviews then identified stretches of natural discourse with sufficient (ING) tokens. The speakers were brought back into the recording studio and instructed to produce two versions of the passage (one with apicals and one with velars) while mimicking the intonation and rate of the original recording. In contrast to typical MGT manipulations in which the content of the speech remains the same, the use of spontaneous speech does not allow the content to be controlled. Importantly, however, this technique does allow a unique perspective on the complex interactions between speech style and message content.

Findings revealed a complex interplay between (ING), social perceptions, and attitude. The apical *-in* variant increased the perceived "Southerness" of most speakers, but it also reduced the perceived "gay" accent of another speaker. The velar *-ing* variant also interacted with the perceived socioeconomic status and education of the speaker; for listeners who believed the speaker to be from a working-class background, *-ing* increased the perceived intelligence/education of the speaker. These findings reconfirm many of the results of traditional production studies of (ING). Importantly, however, they also shed light on the flexible nature of perception by showing how a single variant can realize multiple social meanings.

Although MGT studies are pervasive in the field of sociolinguistics, the validity of the technique remains questioned. Lee (1971) has argued that repeating the message forces subjects to focus on form in a manner that may not be commensurate with more naturalistic processing. Gardner and Lambert (1972) acknowledge that the measured attitudes may not accurately reflect underlying mental states, but rather what the participants *think* they should say. Moreover, it is possible that subjects have underlying attitudes they might not be consciously aware of or have overt access to (Greenwald, et al. 2002). Another limitation of the MGT is that it is an off-line measure of attitude. That is to say, there is a temporal lag between the presentation of the linguistic stimulus and the attitudinal behavioral response. As such, the semantic differentials used in MGT studies tap more into deliberative, controlled processes rather than more instantaneous, implicit associations.

Implicit Association Test

One way researchers are attempting to more tightly couple the stimulus and attitudinal response is by using real-time measures. Labov (2008), for example, has run a version of his newscaster experiments using a computer interface that allows participants to register their moment-by-moment attitudinal response by sliding a knob back and forth between two attitudinal poles. One promising technique that we have used in our laboratory[1] is the Implicit Association Test (IAT; Greenwald, McGhee, & Schwartz 1998). Because the IAT uses response latency to measure the implicit strength of association between concepts, it circumvents the limitations of other measures of language attitude which require explicit reporting.

During IAT experiments, subjects press buttons in response to the words they read and hear. The difference in mean response latencies measures the strength of the association and its automatic evaluation (Greenwald, et al. 2002). In our sociolinguistic IAT experiments (table 7.1), subjects are randomly presented spoken words (that end in *–ing* or *–in*) and visual words (associated with our response categories Intelligence vs. Stupidity). If a strong association exists between velar *–ing* and the concept intelligence, then subjects will respond faster when the sorting categories are ING or Intelligence versus IN' or Stupidity (block 4) than when the sorting categories are IN' or Intelligence versus ING or Stupidity (block 7).

We have run undergraduate participants on several different IAT measures (i.e., Intelligence, Gender, and Socioeconomic Status). Results show weak to strong associations between Intelligence and *–ing*, female and *–ing*, and high SES and *–ing*. These results are largely consistent with previous research on (ING) attitude and production. In terms of intelligence, people who use the apical variant are described as *uneducated* and *ignorant*. In regard to socioeconomic status, apical use elicits descriptions that are socially lower (e.g., *working class, blue collar;* Wald & Shopen 1985), the velar form is associated with higher status speakers and production studies show that apical use is indeed greater

Table 7.1. Illustration of Implicit Association Test (IAT) to measure implicit associations between (ING) and intelligence

Block	No. of trials	Function	Items assigned to left-key response	Items assigned to right-key response
1	20	Practice	Intelligence	Stupidity
2	20	Practice	ING	IN'
3	20	Practice	ING or Intelligence	IN' or Stupidity
4	20	Test	ING or Intelligence	IN' or Stupidity
5	20	Practice	Stupidity	Intelligence
6	20	Practice	ING or Stupidity	IN' or Intelligence
7	20	Test	ING or Stupidity	IN' or Intelligence

for lower SES speakers (e.g., Labov 1966). In terms of gender, women have a stated preference for *-ing* (Wald & Shopen 1985), and production studies show that women do indeed use the velar variant in greater frequency than men. The consistency of these preliminary IAT findings with the established literature shows promise for using the IAT in sociolinguistic inquiry.

Importantly, however, IAT results can differ from explicit measure of attitude. Pantos (2010), for example, investigated attitudes toward US- and foreign-accented speech to determine its impact on speaker credibility in a mock medical malpractice trial. Two different measures of attitude were employed: an explicit semantic differential and an auditory IAT. For the explicit task, participants listened to recordings of US- and foreign-accented speech in the mock trial context. After each physician's testimony, participants rated the speaker on a number of traits (e.g., believability, expertise, etc.) and rated the "fairness" of the verdict. Results revealed an explicit bias in favor of the foreign-accented speaker.

For the IAT, participants heard short auditory snippets (e.g., "it is my opinion"; "I have frequently encountered") and categorized visually presented words that were Good (e.g., marvelous, superb, etc.) or Bad (tragic, horrible, etc.). These results indicated an implicit bias in favor of the US-accented speaker, showing that during automatic evaluative processing, participants are biased toward US-accented speech. One interpretation of these diverging results suggests that participants may have used strategic responding on the explicit measure in order to create a socially desirable persona (e.g., by asserting they are not biased against foreigners). In contrast, implicit measures such as the IAT, are argued to be relatively immune from strategic responding. The contrasting results of Pantos (2010) highlight the dual nature of language attitude and give credence to using multiple measures in experimental design.

Newly Emerging Methods

In recent years, a number of studies have adopted techniques from cognitive psychology in order to address topics of sociolinguistic relevance. Like the IAT, these techniques allow a tighter coupling between stimulus and response, providing real-time measures of language processing.

Eye-Tracking Measures

Two studies have successfully used eye-tracking measures to investigate perceptual processing of dialect and age-graded phonological variation. Eye tracking, which involves monitoring participants' eye movements, is one of the most widely used techniques in the cognitive sciences. In terms of language processing, eye tracking has traditionally been used in reading paradigms, though it can be adapted to spoken language. The assumption linking subjects' eye fixations to *spoken* word recognition is that as a word temporally unfolds "the probability that the listener's attention will shift to a potential referent of a referring expression [e.g., a picture or a written word] increases with the activation . . . of its lexical representation" (Tanenhaus & Brown-Schmidt 2008).

Dahan and colleagues (2008) used a dialect manipulation to adjudicate between two competing accounts of talker accommodation during speech processing. In some dialects of English the vowel /æ/ is raised toward /ɛ/ before voiced velars, so that the word *bag* sounds more like *beg*. Because raising is limited to voiced velars, this reduces the phonetic overlap of minimal pairs such as *bag* and *back*. The primary question is whether prior exposure to raised /æ/ in words like *bag* influences processing of unaffected counterparts (e.g., *back*). Such an effect would demonstrate the influence of speaker-specific dialect representations on the evaluation of standard "unaccented" input, providing strong support for the dynamic adjustment of representations based on context.

Listeners were exposed to /g/ final words with either a standard /æ/ or a raised variant. On the monitor, participants were presented with four words (e.g., *bag*, *back*, *wig*, *wick*) and were asked to click on the word they heard. Eye gaze was used as a dependent measure of listeners" interpretation of [bæ…]. That is to say, in a word such as *back*, what is the degree to which listeners entertain the competing alternative *bag*? Error rates on the same standard *back*-like words showed that participants' exposure to standard *bag*-like words made significantly more errors (17.9 percent) than participants exposed to dialect *bag*-like words (7.3 percent). Analysis showed that starting around 600 milliseconds after vowel onset, the standard pronunciation group fixated significantly longer on competitor words than the group exposed to the raised variant. These results provide strong support that listeners evaluate speech representations that are dynamically adjusted to take into account context.

A study by Koops, Gentry, and Pantos (2008) used eye tracking to investigate whether listeners have tacit knowledge of age-graded variation in the PIN~PEN vowel merger —front high and mid lax vowels /I/ and /ɛ/ are merged before nasals. Although the PIN~PEN merger is a long recognized characteristic of Southern American English, recent evidence suggests that an "unmerger" is occurring in large metropolitan urban areas of the southern United States.

To test whether Houstonians have knowledge of this age distribution (i.e., that older speakers are merged and younger speakers are unmerged), participants were given a forced-choice word identification task. On each trial, a photo of a young, middle-aged, or older female was presented in the center of the screen, surrounded by four word choices including the target (e.g., *rinse*), a PIN or PEN competitor (e.g., *rent*), and two distracters (e.g., *rack* and *rough*). Importantly, the target and the competitor are temporarily ambiguous (up to and including the nasal) when spoken by somebody with a merged system (i.e., an older speaker). In contrast, the target and competitor are disambiguated at the vowel for un-merged speakers (i.e., younger speakers).

In the experiment, participants listened to words (e.g., "rinse") and clicked on their response as quickly as possible. Of interest was the length of time subjects fixated on the PIN or PEN competitor. If subjects have tacit knowledge of the social distribution of the merger, then PIN or PEN competitors should get more fixations for older speakers compared to younger speakers. Indeed, Koops et al. (2008) found that listeners assume a merged system for "old" compared to "middle-aged" speakers. However, no significant differences were found between "middle-aged" and "young" speakers, a finding at odds with the production literature that shows that middle-aged speakers align with old speakers.

Event-Related Potentials

For the past 30 years, psycholinguists have successfully used electrophysiological measures of brain activity to investigate various aspects of language processing. Event-related potentials (ERPs) are averaged, scalp-recorded measurements of brain activity that are time-locked to the onset of a critical stimulus, such as the last word of a sentence. Because of their excellent temporal resolution (i.e., millisecond processing) and the fact that ERPs can be recorded in the absence of an overt behavioral response, the technique has been widely used to characterize the cognitive processes in language perception and comprehension (Luck 2005).

A study by Conrey, Potts, and Niedzielski (2005) used the ERP technique to investigate cognitive processing of the PIN~PEN vowel merger in two different populations of speakers: those with merged vowels and those with unmerged vowels. Prior behavioral studies have reported that speakers with merged vowels in production are less able to perceptually discriminate these vowels during perception (Labov, Karan, & Miller 1991). In the PIN~PEN ERP study, subjects read visually presented sentences that concluded with an expected terminal word, for example, "Sign the check with a *pen*." Following the presentation of the terminal word, a synthesized voice spoke a critical word that was either congruent (/pɛn/) or incongruent (/pIn/) with the visually presented word. Subjects then responded via button press to indicate whether the word they heard matched the word they read.

As expected, behavioral data revealed that the merged dialect group made significantly more errors identifying incongruent merger stimuli compared to the unmerged group. The electrophysiological data revealed that the unmerged group showed increased waveform amplitude for incongruent, compared to congruent critical words. In contrast, the merged dialect speakers showed no differences in amplitude for congruent or incongruent words. This pattern of results suggest that the two dialect groups differentially process stimuli at a conscious, decisional stage of processing that requires explicit memory of previously encountered tokens.

A recent study by Loudermilk, Gutierrez, and Corina (submitted) used ERPs to investigate how sociolinguistic variation affects sentence processing during language comprehension. Specifically, we were interested in determining the time course by which the social information indexed by variation is integrated into higher-order representations. We focused our study on the N400 component, a negative deflection of the ERP waveform that occurs when a semantically anomalous or unexpected word is encountered (Hagoort & Brown 1994; Kutas & Hillyard 1984). For example, given the sentence: "I like my coffee with cream and *sugar/sweetener/socks*," the semantically anomalous *socks* would elicit a large N400 response, the semantically appropriate but unexpected *sweetener* would elicit a slightly smaller amplitude N400, and the highly expected *sugar* would elicit the smallest amplitude N400. Researchers believe that N400 amplitude reflects the amount of difficulty involved in integrating a word's meaning into higher-order (i.e., sentence-level) conceptual representations (Hagoort & Van Berkum 2007).

In our study, we sought to determine (1) how listeners handle sociolinguistic variation during real-time language comprehension and (2) the time course by which this social information is integrated into higher-order representations. We focused on the English morpheme (ING) whose variants are associated with formal (*-ing*) and informal (*-in*) registers. In our study we pitted these speech register expectations against semantic expectations. Our stimuli were short, semantically rich passages read by six different speakers. Each passage contained five different (ING) words. The first four (ING) words used the same variant (*-ing* or *–in*) and defined the speech register as either formal (all *–ing*) or informal (all *–in*). The critical fifth (ING) word was sentence-final and was either congruent or incongruent with the preceding register formality. We also manipulated the semantic expectancy of the final word; half of the words were highly expected (high cloze) and half were unexpected (low cloze)—"...when dark clouds rolled in the game was cancelled because it started *raining/storming*." Participants listened to these passages for comprehension and were presented true/false questions about the passages.

We observed two primary effects: (1) an expected N400 effect for cloze probability, with low cloze words eliciting a posterior negativity between 230 and 510 milliseconds after word onset, and (2) an effect of sociolinguistic variant, with vernacular variants engendering a similar negativity between 170 and 440 milliseconds after the acoustic onset of the morpheme. Researchers believe that these posterior negativities reflect processing difficulties that result from semantically anomalous or unexpected words (Brown & Hagoort 1993; Osterhout & Holcomb 1992). Our findings further suggest that the social information indexed by variation can also pose processing difficulties for listeners. Specifically, encountering noncanonical variants (e.g., "the game was canceled because it started *rainin*'") poses integration difficulties similar to those observed for encountering semantically unexpected words (e.g., "the game was canceled because it started *storming*"). This latter finding suggests, at least as far as the brain is concerned, there may be few putative differences between formal semantic meaning and the indexical social meaning conveyed by sociolinguistic variation.

Summary

Less than a decade ago, Erik Thomas (2002) lamented that perception was the "neglected stepsister of production in sociolinguistics." In the following years this statement, research investigating the perception of sociolinguistic variation has slowly but assuredly emerged. In this chapter, I have reviewed a number of studies in sociolinguistic cognition that are beginning to cast light on issues that are fundamental to sociolinguistics, including the relationship between perception and production, how dialect exposure influences processing, how dialects are learned, the nature of sociolinguistic stereotypes, and how social stereotypes influence perceptual processes.

Note

1. Cognitive Neurolinguistics Laboratory (Primary Investigator, David P. Corina), Center for Mind and Brain, University of California, Davis.

References

Brown, C., & Hagoort, P. 1993. The processing nature of the N400: Evidence from masked priming. *Journal of Cognitive Neuroscience* 5: 34–44.

Campbell-Kibler, K. 2006. Listeners perception of sociolinguistic variables: The case of (ING). Ph.D. dissertation, Stanford University.

Campbell-Kibler, K. 2007. Accent, (ING), and the social logic of listener perceptions. *American Speech* 82: 32–64.

Campbell-Kibler, K. 2010. New directions in sociolinguistic cognition. *University of Pennsylvania Working Papers in Linguistics* 15(2): 31–39.

Clopper, C. G. 2008. Auditory free classification: Methods and analysis. *Behavior Research Methods* 40: 575–81.

Clopper, C. G. 2010. Phonetic detail, linguistic experience, and the classification of regional language varieties in the United States. In D. R. Preston & N. A. Niedzielski (eds.), *A reader in sociophonetics*, 203–22. New York: Mouton de Gruyter.

Clopper, C. G., & Pisoni, D. B. 2004a. Effects of talker variability on perceptual learning of dialects. *Language and Speech* 47: 207–38.

Clopper, C. G., & Pisoni, D. B. 2004b. Homebodies and army brats: Some effects of early linguistic experience and residential history on dialect categorization. *Language Variation and Change* 16: 31–48.

Clopper, C. G., & Pisoni, D. B. 2007. Free classification of regional dialects of American English. *Journal of Phonetics* 35: 421–38.

Conrey, B., Potts, G., & Niedzielski, N. 2005. Effects of dialect on merger perception: ERP and behavioral correlates. *Brain and Language* 95: 435–49.

Dahan, D., Drucker, S. J., & Scarborough, R. A. 2008. Talker adaptation in speech perception: Adjusting the signal or the representations? *Cognition* 108: 710–18.

Gardner, R. G., & Lambert, W. 1972. *Attitudes and motivation in second-language learning.* Rowley MA: Newbury House.

Garrett, P., Coupland, N., & Williams, A. 2003. *Investigating language attitudes: Social meanings of dialect, ethnicity, and performance.* Cardiff: University of Wales Press.

Greenwald, A. G., McGhee, D. E., & Schwartz, J. L. K. 1998. Measuring individual differences in implicit cognition: The Implicit Association Test. *Journal of Personality and Social Psychology* 74: 1464–480.

Greenwald, A. G., Rudman, L. A., Nosek, B. A., Banaji, M. R., Farnham, S. D., & Mellot, D. S. 2002. A unified theory of implicit attitudes, stereotypes, self-esteem, and self-concept. *Psychological Review* 109: 3–25.

Hagoort, P., & Brown, C. M. 1994. Brain responses to lexical ambiguity resolution and parsing. In C. Clifton, L. Frazier & K. Rayner (eds.), *Perspectives on sentence processing*, 45–81. Hillsdale, NJ: Lawrence Erlbaum.

Hagoort, P., & Van Berkum, J. 2007. Beyond the sentence given. *Philosophical Transactions of the Royal Society* 362: 801–11.

Hay, J., Nolan, A., & Drager, K. 2006. From fush to feesh: Exemplar priming in speech perception. *Linguistic Review* 23: 351–79.

Knops, U., & van Hout, R. 1988. Language attitudes in the Dutch language area: An introduction. In R. van Hout & U. Knops (eds.), *Language attitudes in the Dutch language area*, 1–24. Dordrecht: Foris.

Koops, C., Gentry, E., & Pantos, A. 2008. The effect of perceived speaker age on the perception of PIN and PEN vowels in Houston, Texas. *University of Pennsylvania Working Papers in Linguistics* 14(2): 91–101.

Kutas, M., & Hillyard, S. A. 1984. Brain potentials during reading reflect word expectancy and semantic association. *Nature* 307(5947): 161–63.

Labov, W. 1966. *The social stratification of English in New York City.* Washington DC: Center for Applied Linguistics.

Labov, W. 2008. *The cognitive status of sociolinguistic variables. Cognitive capacities of the sociolinguistic monitor.* Paper presented at the Sociolinguistics Symposium 17. Amsterdam: Micro and Macro Connections.

Labov, W., Ash, S., Ravindranath, M., Weldon, T., Baranowski, M., & Nagy, N. 2011. Listeners' sensitivity to the frequency of sociolinguistic variables. *Journal of Sociolinguistics* 15: 431–63.

Labov, W., Karan, M., & Miller, C. 1991. Near-mergers and the suspension of phonemic contrast. *Language Variation and Change* 3: 33–74.

Lambert, W., Hodgson, R. C., Gardner, R. C., & Fillenbaum, S. 1960. Evaluational reactions to spoken languages. *Journal of Abnormal and Social Psychology* 60: 44–51.

Lee, R. R. 1971. Dialect perception: A critical review and re-evaluation. *Quarterly Journal of Speech* 57: 410–17.

Loudermilk, B., Gutierrez, E., & Corina, D. Submitted. What are you talkin' about? Perception of sociolinguistic variation: Evidence from event-related potentials

Luck, S. 2005. *An introduction to the event-related potential technique*. Cambridge, MA: MIT Press.

Maye, J., Aslin, R. N., & Tanenhaus, M. K. 2008. The weckud wetch of the wast: Lexical adaptation to a novel accent. *Cognitive Science* 32: 543–62.

Niedzielski, N. A. 1999. The effect of social information on the perception of sociolinguistic variables. *Journal of Language and Social Psychology* 18: 62–85.

Osterhout, L., & Holcomb, P. 1992. Event-related potentials elicited by syntactic anomaly. *Journal of Memory and Language* 31: 785–806.

Pantos, A. 2010. *Measuring implicit and explicit attitudes toward foreign-accented speech*. Ph.D. dissertation. Rice University.

Plichta, B., & Preston, D. R. 2005. The /ay/s have it: The perception of /ay/ as a North-South stereotype in US English. *Acta Linguistica Hafniensia*, 243–85.

Plichta, B., & Rakerd, B. 2010. Perceptions of /a/ fronting across two Michigan dialects. In D. R. Preston & N. A. Niedzielski (eds.), *A reader in sociophonetics*, 223–40. New York: Mouton de Gruyter.

Preston, D. R. 1993. Folk dialectology. In D. R. Preston (ed.), *American dialect research*, 333–77. Amsterdam: John Benjamins.

Rickford, J. R. 1999. *African American Vernacular English: Features, evolution, educational implications*. Oxford: Blackwell.

Squires, L. M. 2011. *Sociolinguistic priming and the perception of agreement variation: Testing predictions of exemplar-theoretic grammar*. Ph.D. dissertation. University of Michigan.

Staum Casasanto, L. 2008. *Experimental investigation of sociolinguistic knowledge*. Ph.D. dissertation. Stanford University.

Strand, E. A., & Johnson, K. 1996. Gradient and visual speaker normalization in the perception of fricatives. In D. Gibbon (ed.), *Natural language processing and speech technology*, 14–26. Berlin: Mouton de Gruyter.

Sumner, M., & Samuel, A. G. 2005. Perception and representation of regular variation: The case of final /t/. *Journal of Memory and Language* 52: 322–38.

Sumner, M., & Samuel, A. G. 2009. The effect of experience on the perception and representation of dialect variants. *Journal of Memory and Language* 60: 487–501.

Tanenhaus, M. K., & Brown-Schmidt, S. 2008. Language processing in the natural world. *Philosophical Transactions of the Royal Society B: Biological Sciences* 363(1493): 1105–122.

Thomas, E. 2002. Sociophonetic applications of speech perception experiments. *American Speech* 77: 115–47.

Trudgill, P. 1974. *The social differentiation of English in Norwich*. Cambridge: Cambridge University Press.

Wald, B., & Shopen, T. 1985. A researcher's guide to the sociolinguistic variable (ING). In V. P. Clark, P. A. Eschholz, & A. G. Rosa (eds.), *Language: Introductory readings*, 4th ed., 515–541. New York: St. Martin's Press.

CHAPTER 8

INTERDISCIPLINARY APPROACHES

CHRISTINE MALLINSON AND TYLER KENDALL

Historiographers often have narrated sociolinguistics as an interdisciplinary field that originated at the intersection of sociology, anthropology, and linguistics (Fishman 1997; Lévi-Strauss 1963; Shuy 2003). Sociolinguistics holds broad appeal for other linguists and scholars from other fields interested in exploring the language, individual, culture, and society interface. Interest in variation and cognition has also increased across diverse approaches to the study of language and linguistic theory, reflecting greater convergence with sociolinguistics.

Still, some sociolinguists suggest the need for further interdisciplinary engagement. One rationale is that doing so will help us better understand "the structure of language" (Chambers 2003: 11). Another position is that learning about other theoretical frameworks, methodologies, and analytic strategies will advance our modeling of relationships among social, linguistic, and cultural factors (Williams 1992; Woolard 1985). A third take is that sociolinguistics should become more interdisciplinary in order to more fully contribute to social theory, as broadly relevant to social science and the humanities (Coupland 2001: 6–8; Hambye & Siroux 2009: 133–134; Woolard 1985).

Regardless of the position taken, the concept of "doing interdisciplinarity" raises complicating questions. To what extent is sociolinguistics a hybrid discipline? How should theories from other disciplines inform sociolinguistic theory and research design? How can sociolinguists avoid selectively choosing and naively importing theoretical elements from other fields, without considering their underlying assumptions (Coupland 2001; Fishman 1991; Horvath 1998; Woolard, 1985)? As Wardhaugh (2006: 11) cautions, "mixing" other disciplines with linguistics by attempting to relate concepts and findings from each will not yield a "worthwhile sociolinguistics." Paradigms from other disciplines do not always have "added-value" for sociolinguistics (Hambye & Siroux 2009: 135) and/or may require careful theoretical and methodological calibrating (Mallinson & Dodsworth 2009).

Finally, the term "interdisciplinarity" implies a two-way exchange and a process of cultivating engagement (Carlin 2002). How might sociolinguistics not only benefit from incorporating concepts, theories, and methods from other disciplines but also lend insight into the complexities of language and society, with the goal of mutual advancement? To that end, in this chapter we review interdisciplinary literature that speaks to the topics, techniques, and extent to which sociolinguists, other linguists, and other scholars have converged. We focus on three sites of inquiry: (1) language, computation, and the mind; (2) language, identity, and culture; and (3) language and social stratification. We do not consider these sites mutually exclusive or collectively exhaustive however, as research on these topics overlaps and intersects, and other scholars might well uncover different themes. We leave consideration of many omitted but important areas (e.g., literary analysis, translation, media studies) to the reader.

We find narrating interdisciplinary approaches to sociolinguistics vis-à-vis these three thematic areas to be a useful tool, organizationally and intellectually. Taylor (2010) advocates that scholars from different disciplines combat academic separation and specialization by converging to work within "emerging zones" of inquiry organized around broad topics, such as "language," in order to analyze common problems. Drawing upon this model, within the topic "language," our three themes constitute fecund zones of inquiry within which to explore language and its interdisciplinary relationship to social, cultural, psychological, and cognitive structures and processes.

Three Sites of Interdisciplinary Inquiry

Language, Computation, and the Mind

Sociolinguistic understandings of language have recently become more central to general linguistic theorizing. Variation in language is also increasingly of interest for what it tells us about general properties of human cognition, and these intersections have generated greater contact between sociolinguistics and the cognitive sciences.

Probabilistic, usage-based, and exemplar-based models of language (Bod, Hay, & Jannedy 2003; Bybee 2001; Goldinger 1998; Johnson 1997; Pierrehumbert

2001) are centrally concerned with variation and often attend to the role of social information in language processing. Exemplar models, which posit that speaker-hearers store "exemplars" in memory and use these exemplars for comprehension and language production, are rooted in the understanding that experience influences speaker-hearers' linguistic systems. In phonological terms, these approaches acknowledge that "exact phonetic targets and patterns of variation must accordingly be learned during the course of language acquisition" and propose "that mental representations of phonological targets and patterns are gradually built up through experience with speech" (Pierrehumbert 2001: 137). There are clear overlaps with sociolinguistics. Pierrehumbert (2006) describes the variable rule paradigm of early variationist sociolinguistics as a precursor to current exemplar theories and notes that "acquisition appears to depend on social information" (527). Areas in syntax also show interest in variation and probabilitistics (Bresnan & Ford 2010). Sociolinguistics offers data and methods to assess the extent to which (social) orientation filters experience (Foulkes & Docherty 2006; Ochs & Schieffelin 1995).

Psycholinguistics and the psychology of language are, like sociolinguistics, often focused on understanding variation in language. One key difference, however, is their orientation to what that variation means. Sociolinguists are typically interested in language variation because of its extralinguistic meanings and its ability to indicate and express social differences. Psycholinguists see variation as symptomatic of processing and as an indicator of cognitive activity in the process of speech production, as well as a central problem to be addressed in theories of speech perception. Yet, much psycholinguistic and psychological research, for example, on accommodation and convergence, asks questions directly of interest to and influential upon sociolinguistic work (Giles, N. Coupland, & J. Coupland 1991). Other work, for instance, on personality including extroversion and introversion (Eysenck 1967; Pennebaker & King 1999), has not as directly influenced sociolinguistics. Meanwhile, these areas could likely benefit from sociolinguistic insights about individual, cultural, and social difference and sociolinguistic norms.

Sociolinguists, (social) psychologists, and psycholinguists also often differ methodologically. Sociolinguists generally obtain language data from real-world interactions, often complemented with ethnographic insight, while psycholinguists often utilize highly controlled experimental settings. Psycholinguists typically focus on perception and representation, while sociolinguists often focus on production. Yet, recent work in both areas has blurred these lines by investigating, for example, the relationship between speech production and perception and the role of local, nonlocal, and stereotype norms in perception (Clopper & Pisoni 2004; Evans & Iverson 2007; Hay, Warren, & Drager, 2006; Johnson 2006; Kendall & Fridland 2012; Kraljic, Brennan, & Samuel 2008; Niedzielski 1999; Strand & Johnson 1996).

Sumner & Samuel (2009), for instance, examined how listeners' own dialect experience affects spoken word recognition. Through several experiments with *r*-ful and *r*-less speakers from New York City and *r*-ful speakers from non-*r*-less regions (outside of NYC), they found significant differences in perceptual processing not only between non-New Yorkers and New Yorkers but also, in a long-term form priming task, between the two NYC groups, despite both groups receiving similar daily exposures to the same *r*-less variants. These results indicate that experience has consequences for language processing, and in some cases productive experience is also implicated in form processing and in differences in the underlying representation of linguistic forms. The authors further suggest that dialects should be considered not only in terms of speakers' productions but also their perceptions and representations; sociolinguists might benefit from this perspective.

With increasing knowledge about the brain and mind, sociolinguistic insights will be important for future research on language processing. In fact, neurolinguistic work has begun addressing questions at this interface. Perrachione, Chiao, and Wong (2010) examined listeners' abilities to recognize voices in samples spoken by African Americans and European Americans. The authors suggest that an own-race bias in the identification of voices appears to result from "asymmetric exposure to culturally-acquired features of spoken dialect" (52). Their interest in a cognitive model of auditory person perception builds explicitly on sociolinguistic research, such as Purnell, Idsardi, and Baugh (1999) and Thomas and Reaser (2004). These connections will certainly increase: as Kristiansen and Dirven (2008) write, "Cognitive Linguistics itself will inescapably benefit from turning its attention towards variational and interactionist linguistics" (3); in turn, sociolinguists should reach out to these areas.

Computational modeling is another promising mode of inquiry into the social processes behind language variation and change. Modeling work on areas such as sound change has existed in some form for several decades (Liljencrants & Lindblom 1972); however, recent work has begun to incorporate sociolinguistic concepts into the models (Nettle 1999) and address specific sociolinguistic research questions. For example, Baxter, Blythe, Croft, and McKane (2009) use a computational model to assess Trudgill's (2004) claims about the origins and development of New Zealand English. Baxter and colleagues argue "one cannot be certain that an intuitively plausible model actually works without a precise quantitative model" (290). Recent interest in treating language as a complex (adaptive) system—that is, where properties emerge in the system that do not appear to be properties of the individual entities in the system (Altmann, Pierrehumbert, & Motter 2009; Ellis & Larsen-Freeman 2009)—represents yet another new avenue for relating sociolinguistic work to mathematics, physics, and computation (Kretzschmar 2009).

Social network analysis (SNA; Wasserman & Faust 1994) also naturally overlaps with sociolinguistic inquiry. SNA has been incorporated into sociolinguistic research to some extent (most famously by the Milroys in their work on Belfast English; cf. Milroy 1980), but network-based approaches remain underutilized in sociolinguistic theory and methodology. SNA provides an analytic framework for quantitatively analyzing social relationships, particularly from a computational perspective; for instance, Fagyal et al. (2010) use social networks to computationally model the spread of innovations in speech communities. There is also room to expand the use of SNA in less computational areas (Dodsworth 2005).

Sociolinguistics also has close connections to corpus linguistics, with both focusing on empirical approaches to language in use (Kretzschmar 2009). But generally speaking, large-scale, spoken language corpora suitable for addressing complex sociolinguistic questions remain rare, and most sociolinguistic work is still conducted on language samples gathered via sociolinguistic field methods (Kendall 2011). Recently, research within and outside sociolinguistics has focused on generating "unconventional" corpora (Beal, Corrigan, & Moisl 2007; Kendall & Van Herk 2011). Other work seeks to make standard corpora more relevant for sociolinguistic research (Anderson 2008; Romaine 2008). Projects like the Origins of New Zealand English (ONZE; Gordon, Maclagan, & Hay 2007) and the Sociolinguistic Archive and Analysis Project (SLAAP; Kendall 2008) represent further connections between sociolinguistics and corpus linguistics. It seems likely that work across these related fields will continue to converge.

Language, Identity, and Culture

Questions of the nature of the "self," the dynamics of interpersonal interaction, and the formation of identity and culture are central to many disciplines, and an examination of language is often essential to this work. As cultural theorist and sociologist Stuart Hall notes, since discursive practice is the practice of making meaning, and "since all social practices entail meaning, all practices have a discursive aspect. So discourse enters into the influences of all social practices" (Hall 1996: 201–02). Fields within and outside linguistics have taken up the study of language, identity, and culture. Although each field formulates its own terms and theoretical stances, with varying degrees of overlap, there is a general perspective that language helps constitute and/or is constituted by identity, positionality, and social organization. Language is not considered a neutral, autonomous object that simply documents and transmits already-existing realities, nor is identity taken to be a stable, internal feature of an individual person; rather, it is a practice and resource that shapes and manifests social processes. These arguments take different forms across fields, as authors imbue them with distinct nuances, apply them to answer diverse questions, and employ various methodologies, including ethnography, interviews, linguistic mapping, and textual analysis.

The degree of interaction between scholars from these assorted fields varies, but there are some common cross-disciplinary theoretical influences. From anthropology, linguistic anthropology, linguistics, and sociolinguistics, Boas

(1966), Sapir (1949), and Whorf (1956) helped initiate a shift from the view of language as a mirror of mental processes to the suggestion that language conditions thought by constraining possible "types of observations and evaluations." Gumperz (1968) proposed the notion of "speech communities," and Hymes (1964) formulated an "ethnography of communication." These concepts helped shape the view of language as a shared practice in which individuals acquire a "repertoire of speech acts," and, through its acquisition and use, construct identity. Additionally, Labov (1966) highlighted linguistic variation within and between communities and its correlation with social stratification.

Drawing on cross-cultural examples, anthropologist Geertz (1973) argued that meaning is "stored in symbols," and that symbol systems have power to order experience. He defined culture as "webs of significance" that humankind spins and argues that anthropology is an "interpretive" science that seeks to explicate and construe meaning in social expression (5). Sociocultural psychologist Vygotsky (1986) contended that cognition and consciousness are formed through social interaction, mediated by language. From literary criticism and semiotics, Bakhtin (1981) investigated language as social practice and social force. He put forth the concepts of heteroglossia and intertextuality, arguing that all language is dialogic in nature, that all texts are in communication with one another, and that they embody and help generate competing forces within society.

Philosopher and sociologist Michel Foucault (1980) questioned "bodies of knowledge," the semiotic systems, discourses, practices, and institutionalized procedures by which we reify and reproduce our collective beliefs and attitudes, and the forces of power and control operating within these symbolic and social structures. From sociology, Bourdieu (1991) argued that acts of language generate, legitimize, and reproduce social resources, distinctions, and structures and that power is enacted and contested in the "linguistic field." From feminist theory, Butler (2006) suggests that identity is "a normative ideal rather than a descriptive feature of experience" (23). She argues that language and other symbolic acts shape identity through continual performance that "congeals" into identity, although dominant cultural constructions of identity can also be disrupted.

From these common points of ancestry, current explorations of language, identity, and culture have branched into many directions. Theories related to conceptual metaphor formulate language as central to cultural opinions and practices. Lakoff and Johnson (1980) and Lakoff (1993) argued that "root metaphors" permeate our thinking, structure our reasoning, and organize our cultural conceptual systems. Cultural psychologists Miller, Fung, and Koven (2007) discuss how narrative practices co-create identity and culture, particularly in early childhood and late adulthood: "at both ends of the life course narrative serves as a medium of both socialization . . . and innovation and transformation" (596).

Gee (1996) and other New Literacy Studies theorists take a sociocultural approach to literacy and culture, contending that meaning is culturally negotiated and that language should be considered in terms of its use in discursive practices. According to Gee (1996), "Discourses . . . are accepted as instantiations of particular identities (or 'types of people') by specific groups. . . . They are, thus, always and everywhere social" (3). The study of new literacies also explores multimodal linguistic, discursive, and symbolic practices in relation to new technological contexts and analyzes the influence of these practices on meaning construction, identity, interaction, and culture (Coiro, Knobel, Lankshear, & Leu 2008).

Scholarship from communication studies and intercultural communication also investigates language and culture as mutually constitutive. As Scollon and Scollon (2003) commented, the field of intercultural communication has moved beyond simple comparisons between cultures or individuals to explore "the co-constructive aspects of communication" (543)—or, as Philipsen (2002) noted, "the role of communication as a resource in managing discursively the individual-communal dialectic" (53). Micro- and macro-level approaches explore how "dimensions of cultural variability" (such as "power distance") may affect communication across cultures (Gudykunst & Lee 2002), and social identity is highlighted as a major influence on verbal and nonverbal accommodation practices by speakers of different groups.

Gumperz and Cook-Gumperz (1982) argued that the symbolic, discursive practices of society are terrains wherein gender, race/ethnicity, and class are "communicatively produced." Drawing on extensive field-based research, Le Page and Tabouret-Keller (1985) view language as an "act of identity" used to construct social divisions and alliances (p. 16; see also Tabouret-Keller 1997). As Bucholtz and Hall further discuss, within linguistic anthropology language is highlighted as a primary symbolic resource for (re)producing identity via the "culturally specific subject positions that speakers enact through language" (2004: 369); accordingly, they define identity as a "product of situated social action" and a "cultural effect" (376). Abundant research from linguistic anthropological perspectives investigates race, ethnicity, ideology, identity, and language (Bailey 2002; Kiesling & Paulston 2005; Scollon & Scollon 2001; Spears 1999).

From critical discourse studies, the intersection of language, race/ethnicity, ideology, and identity is also a central focus. For Fairclough (1989), power is enacted through discourse, and van Dijk (2008) argues that discourse produces, maintains, directs, and challenges power in society. Wodak and Reisigl (2003) further state that "racism, as both social practice and ideology, manifests itself discursively" (372). Much research reveals how racism emerges in culturally specific discursive contexts; some exemplars include Bonilla-Silva's (2006) sociological study of "colorblind" racism, Hill's (2008) sociolinguistic investigation of racist discourse, and Santa Ana's (1999) analysis of racist metaphors in discourses about immigration. There are also numerous studies of language, race, and ethnic identity (cf. Fishman 2001), although Anthias (2002) argues that the concept of "identity" has lost much of its heuristic utility. Instead, she advocates employing the concept of narratives of location and positionality and demonstrates this approach by examining articulations of race and ethnicity in narratives by British-born youth of Greek Cypriot background. Finally, documentary linguistics and endangered language research also overlap with sociolinguistics in their orientation to community-based field research, culture and identity-related concerns, and naturally occurring talk (Stanford & Preston 2009).

Regarding gender, extensive research on language, culture, and identity has sought to uncover "the logic of the encoding of sex differences in languages," to analyze the "oppressive implications of ordinary speech," to explain miscommunication between men and women, to explore how "gender is constructed and interacts with other identities," and to investigate "the role of language in helping establish gender identity [as] part of a broader range of processes through which membership in particular groups is activated, imposed, and sometimes contested through the use of linguistic forms…that activate stances" (Duranti 2009: 30–31). Other work explores how language is used to reproduce, naturalize, and contest gender ideologies, drawing from many disciplinary perspectives, including quantitative and qualitative traditions within sociolinguistics and linguistic anthropology (Eckert & McConnell-Ginet 2003; Holmes & Meyerhoff, 2005), cultural theory (Anzaldúa 1987), queer theory (Kulick 2005), social cognition and discursive psychology (Weatherall & Gallois 2005), textual analysis (Livia 2005), and communication studies (Thimm, Koch, & Schey 2005). Critical discourse, narrative, metaphor, and rhetorical analysis have been used to examine other gendered dimensions of processes of meaning making, such as gender bias in cell biology (Beldecos et al. 1988) and factory farm industry language used to conceal violence (Glenn 2004).

Another large body of literature has examined language, literacy, socialization, identity, and ideology. Scollon and Scollon (1981) argued that language practices and discourse patterns reflect culturally specific worldviews and "ways of knowing" and that altering one's discourse patterns may alter one's identity; for instance, Heath (1983) investigated literacy events in three communities in relation to larger sociocultural patterns and processes of socialization. Norton (1997) explored the ownership of English internationally, relating it to questions of language learning, teaching, and identity. Mithun (2004), Fill (2007), and Maffi and Woodley (2008) stressed linguistic diversity as a source of cultural heritage, a conceptual resource, and a link to biodiversity and ecological sustainability. Porter (2005) argued that invisible identity subtexts are at work in cultural discourses about sustainability.

Language and Social Stratification

In sociology, "social stratification" generally refers to the hierarchical arrangement of groups within a society and attendant processes of social inequality (Savage 2005: 250). Language is often central in considerations of prestige, status, power, and inequality, whether viewed from sociology, anthropology, or sociolinguistics. Languages and dialects are typically situated along continuums of social power and prestige (Giles 1991), which are undergirded by language ideologies—aesthetic/moral judgments about language that are often tied to sociopolitical and socioeconomic interests (Kroskrity 2004: 502–03). As sites of conflict between the norms of the elite and non-elite, standard language ideologies both contribute to and result from social stratification.

Standard language ideologies often emerge in language policies, in language planning endeavors, and in situations of language contact and endangerment (Haugen 1985; Myers-Scotton 1993; Nettle & Romaine 2002; Wright 2004). Ideologies also surround different language varieties. Within the United Kingdom, for instance, "Received Pronunciation" generally has "overt prestige" (Giles 1970). Nonstandard varieties of any language are often stigmatized, though they may have "covert prestige" (Labov 1966; Preston 1998). Speakers may, however, resist prestige labels and hold language attitudes that differ from those of the elite (Heller 2003; Rickford 1986). Speakers also variously respond to the growth of powerful languages, such as English (Crystal 2003), as seen in studies of the Jambun Aboriginal community (Schmidt 1985), the Solomon Islands (Jourdan 2008), and the Chinese Tyneside community in the United Kingdom (Li 1994).

Language use is intimately tied to the rights and privileges that social systems afford, particularly with respect to education. In rural and/or developing areas of the world, education remains limited for many women and girls (Kristof & WuDunn 2009), especially those who speak indigenous languages (Tiano 1987). In the early history of the United States, tests of "literacy" disproportionately disqualified African Americans from voting (Feagin 2000), and education was used to disrupt cultural continuity among Native Americans (Cantoni 2007). Teachers may also, consciously or not, judge students who speak nonstandard varieties as being less intelligent or unruly (Charity Hudley & Mallinson 2011; Ferguson 2001; Seligman, Tucker, & Lambert 1972). In the US context, students who speak nonstandard varieties of English score systematically lower on standardized assessments (Charity, Scarborough, & Griffin 2004). Psychologists, linguists, educational researchers, and sociologists find these differences are due to a range of social, linguistic, and economic factors often related to test design and test preparation (Charity Hudley & Mallinson 2011; Feagin 2000; Garrett 2009).

Marginalized groups also may resist educational and linguistic inequality; consider, for example, Chinese women's *Nushu* script (Liu 1997) and the coded language used by enslaved Africans brought to North America (Smitherman 1986: 48). Qualitative research from education, anthropology, linguistics, and sociology further reveals how students use linguistic performances and identity practices to express, reflect, and challenge their educational and occupational trajectories, especially those that are imposed upon them (Bettie 2003; Carter 2005; Eckert 1989; Ferguson 2001; Willis 1977).

Language ideologies are also implicated in workplace discrimination, as revealed in matched-guise studies with workers' resumes, for example, or in interview and survey-based studies of reactions by employers to workers who speak nonstandard varieties of a given language—such as, in the US context, African American English (S. L. Terrell & F. Terrell 1983) and Southern American English (Grogger 2011). Accent also can play a role in job and housing discrimination, revealed by sociolinguistic and social psychological interview, survey, and experimental studies (Baugh 2007; Lippi-Green 1997; Purnell et al. 1999). Housing discrimination affects residential segregation (Massey & Lundy 2001), a key sociological mechanism in the perpetuation of high rates of poverty, unemployment, crime, and constrained access to education for residents in the United States (Labov 2008).

Language can also affect access to health systems. Immigrants with limited language proficiency may be less likely to seek and/or receive quality care (Angel & Angel 2006; Morales, Lara, Kington, Valdez, & Escarce 2002), and doctor/patient miscommunication issues disproportionately affect racial and ethnic minorities and/or women. Research in medicine, sociology, public policy, and other fields has recently called for additional training for health providers in order to improve communication skills (Freimuth & Quinn 2004; Rao, Anderson, Inui, & Frankel 2007).

In socially stratified societies, the dynamics of social location are often linguistically constructed as well. Sociological and social psychological studies reveal that individuals routinely categorize others based on social attributes (e.g., race, gender), which can lead to stereotypes that may be used to justify discrimination (Ridgeway & Erickson 2000). Research from conversation and discourse analysis further reveals that stereotypes are often perpetuated by everyday discourse (Holtgraves 2010: 1386): for example, with respect to race and ethnicity (Bonilla-Silva 2006; Hill 2008), gender (Schulz 1975; Sutton 1995), sexual orientation (Pascoe 2007), and social class (Mallinson & Brewster 2005). Language also figures prominently in how speakers display and negotiate power through honorifics, tag questions, turn-taking, interruption, and other features (Brown & Levinson 1987; Eckert & McConnell-Ginet 2003).

Hierarchies of social stratification may also be reflected in the distribution of socially sensitive linguistic forms (Cedergren 1973; Labov 1966; Trudgill 1974). Quantitative sociolinguistic studies, which aim to derive sociologically informed models for language variation and change, generally use surveys and interviews to gather and statistically analyze data on individuals' speech patterns and their education levels, occupations, income, and so on. Early and subsequent sociolinguistic research indicates that linguistic evidence of social stratification is often transparent as well as nuanced (Mallinson 2010). Speakers may also use language to contest their real or perceived social locations. Although individuals with high social status typically use the most prestigious and the least stigmatized linguistic forms, speakers with lower status occasionally use more standard forms than expected, due to "linguistic insecurity" (Labov 1966). Speakers may also engage in hypercorrection out of a desire to use standard forms (Wolfram & Schilling-Estes 2006).

Conclusion

We have intended to help bridge gaps in disciplinary knowledge by reviewing interdisciplinary scholarship from three key zones of inquiry related to language: language, computation, and the mind; language, culture, and identity; and language and social stratification. Abundant scholarship from a variety of related fields conceptualizes language, identity, and culture as inextricably intertwined and mutually constitutive. Empirical investigations reveal how social, cultural, stylistic, ideological, and linguistic dimensions interact to produce and reproduce each other anew within specific contexts, often in relation to culturally specific subject positions. Interdisciplinary scholarship on the theme of language and social stratification reveals language to be closely implicated in the construction of identity and values and in the dynamics of allegiance and exclusion. Contributions to the study of language and social stratification have explored the power and prestige of languages and language varieties, tracked the linguistic, educational, occupational, legal, and health-related effects of social hierarchies, and revealed language to be of many intersecting symbols and practices used by speakers to construct social boundaries. Finally, the literature on language, computation, and the mind reveals that sociolinguistic interests overlap with many diverse fields. Recent years have seen variation in language and probabilistic approaches move from the periphery to the center of many linguistic and cognitive interests. Sociolinguistics can expect to continue to integrate and align with these interests through continuing advancements in technology, mathematical and computational methods, databases of available data, and knowledge of cognition.

Despite overlaps in interdisciplinary approaches to areas of sociolinguistic inquiry, the insights from various disciplines exploring similar questions must be routinely and effectively shared with researchers in other fields for interdisciplinarity to be sustained. All too often these bridges are not consistently established; Duranti (2009) bemoans "incipient separatism" growing even between the closely aligned fields of linguistic anthropology and sociolinguistics (5). As we have discussed, sociolinguists have much to borrow and gain from other fields. In return for borrowing, we also have essential insight to lend to interdisciplinary inquiry on language as a key mechanism in social, cultural, psychological, and cognitive processes.

References

Altmann, E., Pierrehumbert, J. B., & Motter, A. 2009. Beyond word frequency: Bursts, lulls, and scaling in the temporal distributions of words. *PLoS ONE* 4: e7678.

Anderson, W. 2008. Corpus linguistics in the UK: Resources for sociolinguistic research. *Language and Linguistics Compass* 2: 352–71.

Angel, J. L., & Angel, R. J. 2006. Minority group status and healthful aging: Social structure still matters. *American Journal of Public Health* 96(7): 1152–159.

Anthias, F. 2002. Where do I belong? *Ethnicities* 2: 491–514.

Anzaldúa, G. 1987. *Borderlands/La frontera: The new mestiza*. San Francisco: Aunt Lute Books.

Bailey, B. H. 2002. *Language, race, and negotiation of identity: A study of Dominican Americans*. New York: LFB Scholarly Publishing.

Bakhtin, M. M. 1981. *The dialogic imagination: Four essays*. (M. Holquist, ed., C. Emerson & M. Holquist, trans.). Austin: University of Texas Press.

Baugh, J. 2007. Linguistic contributions to the advancement of racial justice within and beyond the African diaspora. *Language and Linguistics Compass* 1: 331–49.

Baxter, G., Blythe, R., Croft, W., & McKane, J. 2009. Modeling language change: An evaluation of Trudgill's theory of the emergence of New Zealand English. *Language Variation and Change* 21: 257–96.

Beal, J., Corrigan, K., & Moisl, H. 2007. Taming digital voices and texts: Models and methods for handling unconventional synchronic corpora. In J. Beal, K. Corrigan, & H. Moisl (eds.), *Creating and digitizing language corpora*, vol. 1 1–16. Houndmills, Basingstoke: Palgrave-Macmillan.

Beldecos, A., Bailey, S., Gilbert, S., Hicks, K., Kenschaft, L., Niemczyk, N., Rosenberg, R., et al. 1988. The importance of feminist critique for contemporary cell biology. *Hypatia* 3(1): 61–76.

Bettie, J. 2003. *Women without class: Girls, race, and identity*. Berkeley: University of California Press.

Boas, F. 1966. *Race, language and culture*. New York: Free Press.

Bod, R., Hay, J., & Jannedy, S. (eds.). 2003. *Probabilistic linguistics*. Cambridge, MA: MIT Press.

Bonilla-Silva, E. 2006. *Racism without racists*. Lanham: Rowman & Littlefield.

Bourdieu, P. 1991. *Language and symbolic power*. Cambridge, MA: Harvard University Press.

Bresnan, J., & Ford, M. 2010. Predicting syntax: Processing dative constructions in American and Australian varieties of English. *Language* 86: 168–213.

Brown, P., & Levinson, S. C. 1987. *Politeness: Some universals in language use*. Cambridge: Cambridge University Press.

Bucholtz, M., & Hall, K. 2004. Language and identity. In A. Duranti (ed.), *A companion to linguistic anthropology*, 369–94. Malden, MA: Blackwell.

Butler, J. 2006. *Gender trouble: Feminism and the subversion of identity*. New York: Routledge.

Bybee, J. 2001. *Phonology and language use*. Cambridge: Cambridge University Press.

Cantoni, G. (ed.). 2007. *Stabilizing indigenous languages*. Flagstaff, AZ: Center for Excellence in Education, Northern Arizona University. Retrieved from http://jan.ucc.nau.edu/~jar/SIL/.

Carlin, A. 2002. Bibliographic boundaries and forgotten canons. In S. Herbrechter (ed.), *Cultural studies: Interdisciplinarity and translation, Critical studies*, vol. 20, 113–130. New York: Rodopi.
Carter, P. 2005. *Keepin' it real: School success beyond Black and White*. New York: Oxford University Press.
Cedergren, H. J. 1973. The interplay of social and linguistic factors in Panama. Ph.D. dissertation, Cornell University.
Chambers, J. K. 2003. *Sociolinguistic theory: Linguistic variation and its social significance*, 2nd ed. Malden, MA: Blackwell.
Charity Hudley, A. H., & Mallinson, C. 2011. *Understanding English language variation in U.S. schools*. New York: Teachers College Press.
Charity, A., Scarborough, H. S., & Griffin, D. M. 2004. Familiarity with school English in African American children and its relation to early reading achievement. *Child Development* 75(5): 1340–356.
Clopper, C., & Pisoni, D. 2004. Effects of talker variability on perceptual learning of dialects. *Language and Speech* 47: 207–38.
Coiro, J., Knobel, M., Lankshear, C ., & Leu, D. J. (eds.). 2008. *Handbook of research on new literacies*. New York: Lawrence Erlbaum Associates.
Coupland, N. 2001. Introduction: Sociolinguistic theory and social theory. In N. Coupland, S. Sarangi, & C. N. Candlin (eds.), *Sociolinguistics and social theory*, 1–26. New York: Longman.
Crystal, D. 2003. *English as a global language*. Cambridge: Cambridge University Press.
Dodsworth, R. 2005. Attribute networking: A technique for modeling social perceptions. *Journal of Sociolinguistics* 9: 225–53.
Duranti, A. (ed.). 2009. *Linguistic anthropology: A reader*, 2nd ed. Oxford: Wiley-Blackwell.
Eckert, P. 1989. *Jocks and burnouts: Social categories and identity in the high school*. New York: Teachers College Press.
Eckert, P., & McConnell-Ginet, S. 2003. *Language and gender*. Cambridge: Cambridge University Press.
Ellis, N., & Larsen-Freeman, D. 2009. *Language as a complex adaptive system*. Malden, MA: Blackwell.
Evans, B., & Iverson, P. 2007. Plasticity in vowel perception and production: A study of accent change in young adults. *The Journal of the Acoustical Society of America* 121: 3814–26.
Eysenck, H. 1967. *The biological basis of personality*. Springfield, IL: Thomas.
Fagyal, Z., Swarup, S., Escobar, A. M., Gasser, L., & Lakkaraju, K. 2010. Centers and peripheries: Network roles in language change. *Lingua* 120(8): 2061–79.
Fairclough, N. 1989. *Language and power*. New York: Longman.
Feagin, J. R. 2000. *Racist America: Roots, current realities, and future reparations*. New York: Routledge.
Ferguson, A. A. 2001. *Bad boys: Public schools in the making of black masculinity*. Ann Arbor: University of Michigan Press.
Fill, A. 2007. Language contact, culture and ecology. In M. Hellinger & A. Pauwels (eds.), *Handbook of language and communication: Diversity and change*, 177–207. Berlin: Mouton de Gruyter.
Fishman, J. A. 1991. Putting the 'socio' back into the sociolinguistic enterprise. *International Journal of the Sociology of Language* 92: 127–38.

Fishman, J. A. 1997. Bloomington, summer of 1964: The birth of American sociolinguistics. In C. Paulston & G. R. Tucker (eds.), *The early days of sociolinguistics: Memories and reflections*, 87–95. Dallas: Summer Institute of Linguistics.

Fishman, J. A. 2001. *Handbook of language and ethnic identity*. New York: Oxford University Press.

Foucault, M. 1980. *Power/knowledge: Selected interviews and other writings, 1972–1977*. (C. Gordon, ed., C. Gordon, L. Marshall, J. Mepham, & K. Soper, trans.). New York: Pantheon Books.

Foulkes, P., & Docherty, G. 2006. The social life of phonetics and phonology. *Journal of Phonetics* 34: 409–38.

Freimuth, V. S., & Quinn, S. C. 2004. The contributions of health communication to eliminating health disparities. *American Journal of Public Health* 94(12): 2053–055.

Garrett, A. J. 2009. The role of picture perception in children's performance on a picture vocabulary test. Ph.D. dissertation, University of Maryland, Baltimore County.

Gee, J. 1996. *Social linguistics and literacies: ideology in discourses*, 2nd ed. New York: Taylor & Francis.

Geertz, C. 1973. *The interpretation of cultures: Selected essays*. New York: Basic Books.

Giles, H. 1970. Evaluative reactions to accents. *Educational Review* 22(3): 211–27.

Giles, H. 1991. *Language: Contexts and consequences*. Pacific Grove, CA: Brooks/Cole.

Giles, H., Coupland, N., & Coupland, J. 1991. Accommodation theory: Communication, context, and consequence. In *Contexts of accommodation: Developments in applied sociolinguistics*, 1–68. Cambridge, UK: Cambridge University Press.

Glenn, C. B. 2004. Constructing consumables and consent: A critical analysis of factory farm industry discourse. *Journal of Communication Inquiry* 28(1): 63–81.

Goldinger, S. D. 1998. Echoes of echoes? An episodic theory of lexical access. *Psychological Review* 105: 251–78.

Gordon, E., Maclagan, M., & Hay, J. 2007. The ONZE corpus. In J. Beal, K. Corrigan, & H. Moisl (eds), *Creating and digitizing language corpora*, vol. 2, 82–104. Houndmills, Basingstoke: Palgrave-Macmillan.

Grogger, J. 2011. Speech patterns and racial wage inequality. *Journal of Human Resources 46(1)*:1–25.

Gudykunst, W. B., & Lee, C. M. 2002. Cross-cultural communication theories. In W. B. Gudykunst & B. Mody (eds.), *Handbook of international and intercultural communication*, 2nd ed., 25–50. Thousand Oaks, CA: Sage Publications.

Gumperz, J. J. (ed.). 1968. The speech community. In *International encyclopedia of the social sciences*, 381–86. New York: Macmillan.

Gumperz, J. J. (ed.). 1982. *Language and social identity*. Cambridge: Cambridge University Press.

Hall, S. 1996. The west and the rest: Discourse and power. In S. Hall, D. Held, D. Hubert, & K. Thompson (eds.), *Modernity: An introduction to modern societies*, 118–227. Oxford, UK: Blackwell.

Hambye, P., & Siroux, J. 2009. Approaching language as a social practice: Reflections on some implications for the analysis of language. *Sociolinguistic Studies* 3(2): 131–47.

Haugen, E. 1985. The language of imperialism: Unity or pluralism? In N. Wolfson & J. Manes (eds.), *Language of inequality*, 3–17. New York: Mouton.

Hay, J., Warren, P., & Drager, K. 2006. Factors influencing speech perception in the context of a merger-in-progress. *Journal of Phonetics* 34: 458–84.

Heath, S. B. 1983. *Ways with words: Language, life, and work in communities and classrooms.* Cambridge: Cambridge University Press.

Heller, M. 2003. Globalization, the new economy, and the commodification of language and identity. *Journal of Sociolinguistics* 7: 473–92.

Hill, J. H. 2008. *The everyday language of White racism.* Malden, MA: Wiley-Blackwell.

Holmes, J., & Meyerhoff, M. (eds.). 2005. *The handbook of language and gender.* Malden, MA: Blackwell.

Holtgraves, T. 2010. Social psychology and language: Words, utterances, and conversations. In *The handbook of social psychology,* 5th ed., vol. 2, 1386–422. Hoboken, NJ: John Wiley and Sons.

Horvath, B. 1998. Some 'fractious energy.' *Journal of Sociolinguistics* 2(3): 446–56.

Hymes, D. H. 1964. Introduction: Toward ethnographies of communication. In J. J. Gumperz & D. H. Hymes (eds.), *The ethnography of communication,* 1–34. Washington, DC: American Anthropologist.

Johnson, K. 1997. Speech perception without speaker normalization: An exemplar model. In K. Johnson & J. W. Mullennix (eds.), *Talker variability in speech processing,* 145–65. San Diego: Academic Press.

Johnson, K. 2006. Resonance in an exemplar-based lexicon: The emergence of social identity and phonology. *Journal of Phonetics* 34: 485–99.

Jourdan, C. 2008. Language repertoires and the middle class in urban Solomon Islands. In G. Sankoff, M. Meyerhoff, & N. Nagy (eds.), *Social lives in language—sociolinguistics and multilingual speech communities: Celebrating the work of Gillian Sankoff,* 43–67. Philadelphia: John Benjamins.

Kendall, T. 2008. On the history and future of sociolinguistic data. *Language and Linguistics Compass* 2: 332–51.

Kendall, T. 2011. Corpora from a sociolinguistic perspective (Corpora sob uma perspectiva sociolinguística). In S. Th. Gries (ed.), *Corpus studies: Future directions,* special issue of *Revista Brasileira de Linguística Aplicada* 11(2): 361–89.

Kendall, T. & Fridland, V. 2012. Variation in perception and production of mid front vowels in the U.S. Southern Vowel Shift. *Journal of Phonetics* 40(2): 289–306.

Kendall, T. & Van Herk, G. (eds.). 2011. Corpus linguistics and sociolinguistic inquiry. Special issue of *Corpus Linguistics and Linguistic Theory* 7(1).

Kiesling, S. F., & Paulston, C. B. (eds.). 2005. *Intercultural discourse and communication: The essential readings.* Malden, MA: Blackwell.

Kraljic, T., Brennan, S.E., & Samuel, A. G. 2008. Accommodating variation: Dialects, idiolects, and speech processing. *Cognition* 107: 51–81.

Kretzschmar, W. 2009. *The linguistics of speech.* Cambridge University Press.

Kristiansen, G., & Dirven, R. 2008. Introduction: Cognitive linguistics: Rationale, methods and scope. In G. Kristiansen & R. Dirven (eds.), *Cognitive sociolinguistics,* 1–20. New York: Mouton de Gruyter.

Kristof, N. D., & WuDunn, S. 2009. *Half the sky: Turning oppression into opportunity for women worldwide.* New York: Knopf.

Kroskrity, P. V. 2004. Language ideologies. In A. Duranti (ed.), *A companion to linguistic anthropology,* 496–517. Malden, MA: Blackwell.

Kulick, D. 2005. Language and desire. In J. Holmes & M. Meyerhoff (eds.), *The handbook of language and gender,* 119–41. Malden, MA: Blackwell.

Labov, W. 1966. *The social stratification of English in New York City.* Washington, DC: Center for Applied Linguistics.

Labov, W. 2008. Unendangered dialects, endangered people. In K. King, N. Schilling-Estes, L. W. Fogle, J. J. Lou, & B. Soukup (eds.), *Sustaining linguistic diversity: Endangered and minority languages and language varieties*, 219–38. Washington, DC: Georgetown University Press.

Lakoff, G. 1993. The contemporary theory of metaphor. In A. Ortony (ed.), *Metaphor and thought*, 2nd ed., 202–51. Cambridge: Cambridge University Press.

Lakoff, G., & Johnson, M. 1980. *Metaphors we live by.* Chicago: University of Chicago Press.

Le Page, R. B., & Tabouret-Keller, A. 1985. *Acts of identity: Creole-based approaches to language and ethnicity.* Cambridge: Cambridge University Press.

Lévi-Strauss, C. 1963. *Structural anthropology.* New York: Basic Books.

Li, W. 1994. *Three generations, two languages, one family: Language choice and language shift in a Chinese community in Britain.* Philadelphia: Multilingual Matters.

Liljencrants, J. & Lindblom, B. 1972. Numerical simulation of vowel quality systems: The role of perceptual contrast. *Language* 48: 839–62.

Lippi-Green, R. 1997. *English with an accent: Language, ideology, and discrimination in the United States.* London: Routledge.

Liu, F. 1997. *Nuzi (female script), Nushu (female literature), Nuge (female songs) and peasant women's de-silencing of themselves, Jiangyong County, Hunan Province, China.* Ph.D. dissertation, Syracuse University.

Livia, A. 2005. "One man in two is a woman": Linguistic approaches to gender in literary texts. In J. Holmes & M. Meyerhoff (eds.), *The handbook of language and gender*, 142–58. Malden, MA: Blackwell.

Maffi, L., & Woodley, E. 2008. *Biodiversity: Culture* (No. GEO 4). Global Environment Outlook: Environment for Development, 182–85. Nairobi: UNEP.

Mallinson, C. 2010. Social stratification. In R. Wodak, B. Johnstone, & P. Kerswill (eds.), *The Sage handbook of sociolinguistics*, 87–99. Thousand Oaks, CA: Sage.

Mallinson, C., & Brewster, Z. W. 2005. 'Blacks and bubbas': Stereotypes, ideology, and categorization processes in restaurant servers' discourse. *Discourse & Society* 16: 787–807.

Mallinson, C., & Dodsworth, R. 2009. Revisiting the need for new approaches to social class in variationist sociolinguistics. *Sociolinguistic Studies* 3: 253–78.

Massey, D. S., & Lundy, G. 2001. Use of Black English and racial discrimination in urban housing markets: New methods and findings. *Urban Affairs Review* 36(4): 452–69.

Miller, P. J., Fung, H., & Koven, M. 2007. Narrative reverberations: How participation in narrative practices co-creates persons and cultures. In S. Kitayama & D. Cohen (eds.), *Handbook of cultural psychology*, 595–614. New York: Guilford Press.

Milroy, L. 1980. *Language and social networks.* Malden, MA: Blackwell.

Mithun, M. 2004. The value of linguistic diversity: Viewing other worlds through North American Indian languages. In A. Duranti (ed.), *A companion to linguistic anthropology*, 121–40. Malden, MA: Blackwell.

Morales, L. S., Lara, M., Kington, R. S., Valdez, R. O., & Escarce, J. J. 2002. Socioeconomic, cultural, and behavioral factors affecting Hispanic health outcomes. *Journal of Health Care for the Poor and Underserved* 13(4): 477–503.

Myers-Scotton, C. 1993. Elite closure as a powerful language strategy: The African case. *International Journal of the Sociology of Language* 103(1): 149–64.

Nettle, D. 1999. Using social impact theory to simulate language change. *Lingua* 108: 95–117.

Nettle, D., & Romaine, S. 2002. *Vanishing voices: The extinction of the world's languages*. New York: Oxford University Press.

Niedzielski, N. 1999. The effect of social information on the perception of sociolinguistic variables. *Journal of Language and Social Psychology* 18: 62–85.

Norton, B. 1997. Language, identity, and the ownership of English. *TESOL Quarterly* 31: 409–29.

Ochs, E., & Schieffelin, B. 1995. The impact of language socialization on grammatical development. In P. Fletcher & B. MacWhinney (eds.), *The handbook of child language*, 73–94. Malden, MA: Blackwell.

Pascoe, C. J. 2007. *Dude, you're a fag: Masculinity and sexuality in high school*. Berkeley: University of California Press.

Pennebaker, J., & King, L. 1999. Linguistic styles: Language use as an individual difference. *Journal of Personality and Social Psychology* 77: 1296–312.

Perrachione, T. K., Chiao, J. & Wong, P. 2010. Asymmetric cultural effects on perceptual expertise underlie an own-race bias for voices. *Cognition* 114: 42–55.

Philipsen, G. 2002. Cultural communication. In W. B. Gudykunst & B. Mody (eds.), *Handbook of international and intercultural communication*, 2nd ed., 51–67. Thousand Oaks, CA: Sage Publications.

Pierrehumbert, J. B. 2001. Exemplar dynamics: Word frequency, lenition and contrast. In J. Bybee & P. Hopper (eds.), *Frequency and the emergence of linguistic structure*, 137–57. Philadelphia: John Benjamins.

Pierrehumbert, J. B. 2006. The next toolkit. *Journal of Phonetics* 34(4): 516–30.

Porter, T. B. 2005. Identity subtexts in the discursive construction of sustainability. *Electronic Journal of Radical Organization Theory* 9(1): 1–13.

Preston, D. 1998. They speak really bad English down South and in New York City. In L. Bauer & P. Trudgill (eds.), *Language myths*, 103–12. New York: Penguin Books.

Purnell, T., Idsardi, W., & Baugh, J. 1999. Perceptual and phonetic experiments on American English dialect identification. *Journal of Language and Social Psychology* 18(1): 10–30.

Rao, J. K., Anderson, L. A., Inui, T. S., & Frankel, R. M. 2007. Communication interventions make a difference in conversations between physicians and patients: A systematic review of the evidence. *Medical Care* 45(4): 340–49.

Rickford, J. R. 1986. The need for new approaches to social class analysis in sociolinguistics. *Language and Communication* 6(3): 215–21.

Ridgeway, C. L., & Erickson, K. G. 2000. Creating and spreading status beliefs. *American Journal of Sociology* 106(3): 579–615.

Romaine, S. 2008. Corpus linguistics and sociolinguistics. In A. Lüdeling & M. Kytö (eds.), *Corpus linguistics: An international handbook*, vol. 1, 96–111. New York: Mouton de Gruyter.

Santa Ana, O. 1999. 'Like an animal I was treated': Anti-immigrant metaphor in US public discourse. *Discourse & Society* 10(2): 191–224.

Sapir, E. 1949. Language. In D. Mandelbaum (ed.), *Selected writing of Edward Sapir in language, culture and personality*, 7–32. Berkeley, CA: University of California Press.

Savage, M. 2005. Class and stratification: Current problems and revival prospects. In C. J. Calhoun, C. Rojek, & B. S. Turner (eds.), *The Sage handbook of sociology*, 236–53. London: Sage Publications.

Schmidt, A. 1985. *Young people's Dyirbal: An example of language death from Australia*. New York: Cambridge University Press.

Schulz, M. R. 1975. The semantic derogation of woman. In *Language and sex: Difference and dominance*, 64–75. Rowley, MA: Newbury House.

Scollon, R., & Scollon, S. B. K. 1981. *Narrative, literacy, and face in interethnic communication*. Norwood, NJ: Ablex Pub. Corp.

Scollon, R., & Scollon, S. B. K. 2001. *Intercultural communication: A discourse approach*, 2nd ed. Malden, MA: Blackwell.

Scollon, R., & Scollon, S. W. 2003. Discourse and intercultural communication. In D. Schiffrin, D. Tannen, & H. E. Hamilton (eds.), *The handbook of discourse analysis*, 538–47. Malden, MA: Blackwell.

Seligman, C., Tucker, G., & Lambert, W. 1972. The effects of speech style and other attributes on teachers' attitudes toward pupils. *Language in Society* 1: 131–42.

Shuy, R. W. 2003. A brief history of American sociolinguistics 1949–1989. In C. B. Paulston & G. R. Tucker (eds.), *Sociolinguistics: The essential readings*, 4–16. Malden, MA: Blackwell.

Smitherman, G. 1986. *Talkin and testifyin: The language of Black America*. Detroit: Wayne State University Press.

Spears, A. K. (ed.). 1999. *Race and ideology: Language, symbolism, and popular culture*. Detroit: Wayne State University Press.

Stanford, J. N., & Preston, D. R. 2009. The lure of a distant horizon: Variation in indigenous minority languages. In J. N. Stanford & D. R. Preston (eds.), *Variation in indigenous minority languages*, 1–20. Philadelphia: John Benjamins.

Strand, E. & Johnson, K. 1996. Gradient and visual speaker normalization in the perception of fricatives. In D. Gibbon (ed.), *Natural language processing and speech technology*, 14–26. New York: Mouton de Gruyter.

Sumner, M. & Samuel, A. 2009. The effect of experience on the perception and representation of dialect variants. *Journal of Memory and Language* 60: 487–501.

Sutton, L. A. 1995. Bitches and skankly hobags: The place of women in contemporary slang. In K. Hall & M. Bucholtz (eds.), *Gender articulated: Language and the socially constructed self*, 279–96. New York: Routledge.

Tabouret-Keller, A. 1997. Language and identity. In F. Coulmas (ed.), *The handbook of sociolinguistics*, 315–26. Oxford, UK: Blackwell.

Taylor, M. C. 2010. *Crisis on campus*. New York: Knopf.

Terrell, S. L., & Terrell, F. 1983. Effects of speaking Black English upon employment opportunities. ASHA *(Journal of the American Speech and Hearing Association)* 25(6): 27–9.

Thimm, C., Koch, S. C., & Schey, S. 2005. Communicating gendered professional identity: Competence, cooperation, and conflict in the workplace. In J. Holmes & M. Meyerhoff (eds.), *The handbook of language and gender*, 528–49. Malden, MA: Blackwell.

Thomas, E. R., & Reaser, J. 2004. Delimiting perceptual cues used for the ethnic labeling of African American and European American voices. *Journal of Sociolinguistics* 8: 54–87.

Tiano, S. 1987. Gender, work, and world capitalism: Third world women's role in world development. In B. Hess & M. M. Ferree (eds.), *Analyzing gender: A handbook of social science research*, 216–43. Newbury Park, CA: Sage.

Trudgill, P. 1974. *The social differentiation of English in Norwich.* Cambridge, UK: University Press.

Trudgill, P. 2004. *New-dialect formation: The inevitability of colonial Englishes.* New York: Oxford University Press.

van Dijk, T. A. 2008. *Discourse and power.* Houndmills: Palgrave Macmillan.

Vygotsky, L. S. 1986. *Thought and language.* Edited by A. Kozulin. Cambridge, MA: MIT Press.

Wardhaugh, R. 2006. *An introduction to sociolinguistics.* Malden, MA: Blackwell.

Wasserman, S., & Faust, K. 1994. *Social network analysis: Methods and applications.* Cambridge: Cambridge University Press.

Weatherall, A., & Gallois, C. 2005. Gender and identity: Representation and social action. In J. Holmes & M. Meyerhoff (eds.), *The handbook of language and gender*, 487–508. Malden, MA: Blackwell.

Whorf, B. 1956. *Language, thought and reality: Selected writings of Benjamin Lee Whorf.* Edited by J. B. Carroll. Cambridge, MA: MIT Press.

Williams, G. 1992. *Sociolinguistics: A sociological critique.* New York: Routledge.

Willis, P. E. 1977. *Learning to labour: How working class kids get working class jobs.* Farnborough, UK: Saxon House.

Wodak, R., & Reisigl, M. 2003. Discourse and racism. In D. Schiffrin, D. Tannen, & H. E. Hamilton (eds.), *The handbook of discourse analysis*, 372–97. Oxford, UK: Blackwell.

Wolfram, W., & Schilling-Estes, N. 2006. *American English: Dialects and variation*, 2nd ed. Malden, MA: Blackwell.

Woolard, K. A. 1985. Language variation and cultural hegemony: Toward an integration of sociolinguistic and social theory. *American Ethnologist* 12: 738–48.

Wright, S. 2004. *Language policy and language planning: From nationalism to globalisation.* New York: Palgrave Macmillan.

PART II

METHODOLOGIES AND APPROACHES

CHAPTER 9

STUDIES OF THE COMMUNITY AND THE INDIVIDUAL

JAMES A. WALKER AND MIRIAM MEYERHOFF

A long-standing question of linguistics is whether language resides in the individual speaker or in the community. Despite Saussure's (1916) recognition of language as a social fact, post-Saussurean linguistics has tended to focus on individuals rather than social groups. Generative linguistics, arguably Saussure's predominant legacy, takes as its object of inquiry the knowledge of language residing in the brain of the individual speaker (cf. Chomsky's (1965) "ideal speaker-hearer in a completely homogeneous speech community"), with the language of the community seen as the intersection of the languages of the individual speakers. In contrast, the study of sociolinguistic variation and change has traditionally operated under a different set of methodological and epistemological assumptions: in general, its object of inquiry has not been the language of individual speakers but rather the extent to which groups of speakers agree or differ with regard to their linguistic behavior. At one extreme of this approach is the view that "the individual does not exist as a linguistic object" (Labov 2001: 34).

This focus has often led to the impression that the individual speaker has no place in sociolinguistics, in which studies have typically grouped individuals along different dimensions (social class, sex/gender, ethnicity) and compared the linguistic behavior across these groups. This practice has been criticized throughout the variationist enterprise, either because it gives the illusion of variability within the community by grouping speakers with different "lects" (Bickerton 1975) and/or dividing the community along externally defined measures that may not be sociolinguistically relevant.

However, within the study of sociolinguistic variation and change, two approaches have been developed that attempt to link individual speaker behavior with the study of the community. One approach makes use of *linguistic grouping*, examining the linguistic conditioning of individual speakers and looking for social correlates of the resulting groups. Such studies have demonstrated that variation persists at the level of the individual and that, given enough data per speaker, individuals can be shown to mirror the linguistic conditioning of the speech community of which they are members. Another approach is the detailed analysis of individual speakers in different social situations. Although the narrow focus of this second approach may obviate generalizations about the linguistic behavior of the speech community, it has provided important insight into the role of variation in creating and expressing social meaning.

In this chapter, we provide a synoptic overview of these two research traditions. As an illustration of the issues involved in this research, we present our analyses across groups and individuals in the English spoken on the island of Bequia (St. Vincent and the Grenadines). Two well-studied grammatical variables constitute the linguistic focus of this research: the absence of copula/auxiliary BE and existential constructions. We compare the linguistic conditioning of these features in the speech of "urban sojourners" (individuals who have left Bequia for long periods of time) with that of their stay-at-home peers. Although there are clear differences in the constraints on BE absence in three villages on Bequia, we see parallel patterns across speakers, even including the urban sojourners. In contrast, for existentials we see striking differences in rates and conditioning between some of the urban sojourners and their stay-at-home peers. The results of these studies emphasize the importance of examining both social and linguistic conditioning of variation in the study of the community and the individual.

Social Grouping

Sociolinguistic studies have traditionally relied on *social grouping* (Horvath & Sankoff 1987): that is, define social categories relevant to the sociolinguistic research question(s) (such as the speaker's sex, age-group, social class, and ethnic background), group individual speakers according to their membership in each category, and compare the linguistic behavior across groups. Wolfram and Beckett (2000: 5) identify a principle underlying this methodology, namely, that individual-speaker variation is unimportant in describing sociolinguistic variation, which they call the "homogeneity assumption." Under this assumption, data from groups of individuals can be examined together, provided that the social differences that delimit the groups are meaningful (ibid.; see also Chambers 2009: 113). Social grouping has been criticized on a number of grounds. Early in the study of linguistic variation, Bailey (1973) and Bickerton (1975) argued that grouping individuals together without examining their patterning obscured the fact that speakers might have different linguistic systems. Wolfram and Beckett (2000: 6) note the tendency in studies of linguistic variation to exclude individual speakers whose behavior is anomalous with respect to their peers. In some cases, finding an appropriate social grouping may be impossible. For example, Dorian (1994) reports a situation in Scottish Gaelic of what she calls "personal pattern variation," in which individual-speaker patterns of variation cannot be explained with reference to any kind of social grouping.

However, a closer examination of the literature on language variation and change shows a concern with the individual speaker from the earliest days of variationist analysis. In Labov's (1963) analysis of the centralization of (ay) and (aw) on Martha's Vineyard (Massachusetts), the centralization index scores were calculated for each individual speaker before the averages were compared across groups. In fact, Labov's work (1963, 1966, 2001) has tended to highlight individual speakers who are either representative of or diverge from their respective social group, such as Steve K. in New York City (Labov 1966) or Celeste S. in Philadelphia (Labov 2001). As he notes in a 2006 comment on his 1966 study of New York City:

> There are no people in most of the sociolinguistic studies that followed—just means, charts, and trends. Although I have campaigned to bring people back into the field of sociolinguistics there has been only a limited response on this front. (Labov [1966] 2006: 157)

Another area in which individual speakers have proven important is the study of language contact. For example, Rickford's (1985) study of English in the Sea Islands in South Carolina, where African Americans and white Americans have co-existed for centuries, examined the speech of two individuals, an African American woman and a white American man. Unsurprisingly, these two speakers were found to share many phonological and grammatical features characteristic of both Southern American English and African American English. However, the quantitative distributions of these features were quite different for the two speakers, demonstrating that individual speakers of linguistic varieties in contact for long periods of time can show different distributional preferences. Similarly, Wolfram and Beckett's (2000) analysis of phonological and grammatical variation in 11 elderly African Americans from Hyde County, North Carolina, found a surprising degree of heterogeneity among speakers in their convergence to white American norms. Wolfram and Beckett argue that the differences for individual speakers and individual linguistic variables are better explained by referring to aspects of "personal history, interactional relations, and attitudes and values than of conventional social divisions or even constructed social identities" (Wolfram & Becket 2000: 27).

The stability of the individual speaker's linguistic system across the lifespan (once language acquisition has been completed) is an important assumption of diachronic sociolinguistic studies, since differences among age groups are often interpreted as reflecting language change (the "apparent time" construct; cf. Bailey 2002). Real-time studies of language change tend to sample different speakers in the same community at different points in time (trend studies), though studies in which individual speakers are tracked longitudinally (panel studies) do exist, and provide insight into the assumption of individual speaker invariance across the lifespan. For example, Sankoff and Blondeau's (2007) analysis of a change in Montreal French from an apical [r] to uvular [ʀ] examined 32 individual speakers who were interviewed in 1971 and again in 1984. Although the community as a whole showed a substantial increase in uvular [ʀ], only a few of the speakers showed a substantial change, and with one exception, always in the direction of change of the entire community. In fact, they infer that "change is being implemented by people who alter their pronunciation quite rapidly, rather than a steady, incremental raising of levels across individual lifespans" (Sankoff & Blondeau 2007: 575). This conclusion provides some support for the validity of the apparent-time construct, though it does highlight the need to examine the behavior of individual speakers.

One response to the criticisms against social grouping has been to reconceptualize larger-scale groups, such as social class, into smaller-scale groupings. The Milroys' work in Belfast in the 1970s (Milroy 1987; Milroy & Milroy 1992) recast social-class distinctions in terms of the social networks that individuals engage in. Their work showed that the strength of network ties of individual speakers can act as a conservative force, resisting changes encroaching from the larger speech community, and that the types of social roles that individuals engage in are just as important as the number of ties. For example, a sex-based difference noted in one neighborhood was reversed in another neighborhood where high rates of unemployment had shifted gender roles. Similarly, Eckert and McConnell-Ginet's (1992) work on language and gender introduced the *community of practice*, defined as "an aggregate of people who come together around mutual engagement in an endeavor" (Eckert & McConnell-Ginet 1992: 464). In contrast with higher-level categories such as social class (which relate individual speakers to the means of production) and other smaller-level categories such as social network (which stress the number and nature of ties between individuals), the community of practice emphasizes the mutual engagement, joint enterprise, and shared repertoire that characterize smaller groups of individuals (Holmes & Meyerhoff 1999).

Beginning in the 1990s, some researchers questioned the very practice of grouping individual speakers into categories that may not be internally homogeneous or even salient to the speakers. Some researchers argued that sociolinguistics, as a social science, should be concerned with interrogating the stability of social categories and the manner in which language serves to create and reify social categories and hierarchies of power. This "third wave" of sociolinguistics, most strongly associated with research on language and gender (Eckert 1989), though now concerned with other categories such as sexuality (Podesva 2006) and ethnicity (Benor 2005), draws explicitly on developments in feminist theory, in which early struggles for emancipation and equal opportunity later shifted to a focus on identity and individual agency. For example, Eckert's (1989) work with high school students in Detroit showed that grouping women together simply because they are female masks important differences: differences among teenage girls were more substantial than the differences between girls and boys. Over the next decade, studies began to consider the linguistic behavior of individuals—even a single individual, in a single conversation, with a constant interlocutor (e.g., Schilling-Estes 2004). Work drawing on the methods of both discourse analysis and quantitative studies of variation was also explored (Holmes 1997). Although some third-wave sociolinguists view traditional methods of social dialectology as hopelessly outdated and some third-wave work is viewed as having lost sight of the social-group forest for the individual-speaker trees (itemizing tokens of variation), a middle road has recently taken shape, in which social-group data complement individual-speaker data, and vice versa (e.g., Eckert 2000). Thus, observations made at one level can enrich the analysis of observations at the other level (cf. Labov 2001:33), highlighting the complementarity of studies of the community and the individual.

Linguistic Grouping

While some researchers were querying the nature of social categories, others were developing an alternative approach, what Horvath and Sankoff (1987) call "linguistic grouping." Under this approach, rather than defining social groups and comparing the extent to which individuals agree with or deviate from them, research starts by examining the linguistic behavior of individual speakers and grouping speakers on the basis of similarities in their linguistic patterning (although it should be noted that researchers still have to interpret the groupings in social terms). In an instructive summary, shown in table 9.1, Guy (1980: 12) notes the four possible outcomes of examining variation between groups and between individuals in those groups. The first cell, in which variation is shared among groups and individuals, describes a situation in which a variable applies uniformly across a speech community. For example, the variation in (ing) between a velar *-ing* and an apical *-in'* exists across all varieties of English, and the evaluation of these variants (as formal/standard and

Table 9.1. Comparisons of groups and individuals

	Groups	
Individuals	Similar	Different
Similar	1. uniform variation	2. geographic or social dialects
Different	3. 'polylectal' community	4. 'free variation'

Source: Adapted from Guy (1980: 12)

informal/nonstandard) is similarly shared by all speakers. The second cell, in which variation differs between groups but is shared among individuals within those groups, describes the traditional findings of dialect differences (if the groups are geographically defined), social groups (if the groups are defined on the basis of sex, social class, or ethnicity), or language change (if the groups are defined on the basis of age). The third cell, in which different groups share variation but there are a variety of norms for individual speakers, corresponds to the situation of a "polylectal" community, like that proposed for (post)creole communities. For example, De Camp (1971) notes that, although individual speakers in Jamaica exhibit differences in their use of lexical items (*pikni* versus *child; nyam* versus *eat*), phonological features ([θ] or [t], [ð] or [d]) and grammatical features (*no ben* or *didn't*), they can nevertheless be ordered along a scale from most English-like to most creole-like, with the choice of one feature implying the presence of other features. The fourth cell, in which the variation between both groups and individuals differs, would be a situation of "free variation," or perhaps the personal pattern variation noted by Dorian (1994).

The linguistic behavior of groups and individuals can be compared either in terms of overall rates of use or the conditioning of variation by language-internal factors. The first approach has been investigated in a number of studies (e.g., Horvath & Sankoff 1987; McEntegart & Le Page 1982; Santa Ana & Parodi 1998). For example, Horvath and Sankoff (1987) use principal components analysis in a study of the vowels of Sydney, Australia, to isolate a smaller set of factors that allow them to cluster speakers into categories that they can then correlate with social characteristics. Using the number of tokens of each variant uttered by each speaker in their sample for four vowel variables, they isolate four principal component factors (plotted against each other in the four graphs shown in figure 9.1). The first factor corresponds to native-speaker status (accounting for 32 percent of the variance), differentiating those born in Sydney from those who arrived as adults. The second factor combines sex and social class (15 percent of the variance). The third factor combines age and (second-generation) ethnicity (9 percent of the variance). The fourth factor, less easily identified with social characteristics, has to do with the degree of interaction with speakers in the core speech community (8 percent of the

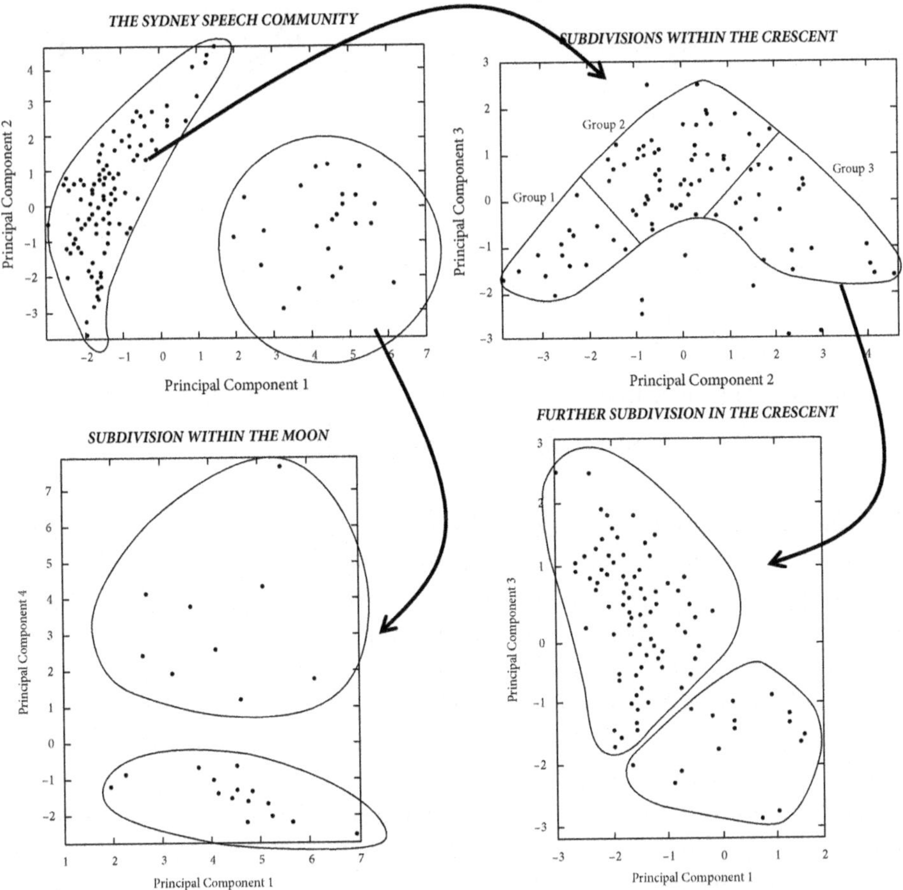

Figure 9.1. Correlations of four factors derived from principal components analysis of four vowel variables for speakers in Sydney, Australia

Source: Adapted from Horvath & Sankoff (1987)

variance). Note that, although Horvath and Sankoff allow the groupings to fall out of distributions of individual speakers' features, they must make reference to coherent and socially meaningful factors in order to interpret those groupings.

A classic use of conditioning by language-internal factors to conduct linguistic grouping is Guy's (1980) analysis of word-final (t/d)-deletion among 18 speakers from New York and Philadelphia. Deletion is conditioned at the group level by a number of factors, including the grammatical status (with monomorphemic forms showing higher rates of deletion than past-tense forms) and the preceding and following phonological context. Examining the linguistic conditioning of individual speakers, he finds first that the patterns of speakers with less data was more likely to deviate from group norms, demonstrating the need to obtain sufficient data from each speaker. If we plot the findings by individual speaker as in figure 9.2 (adapted from Guy's [1980] table 1.3), we see

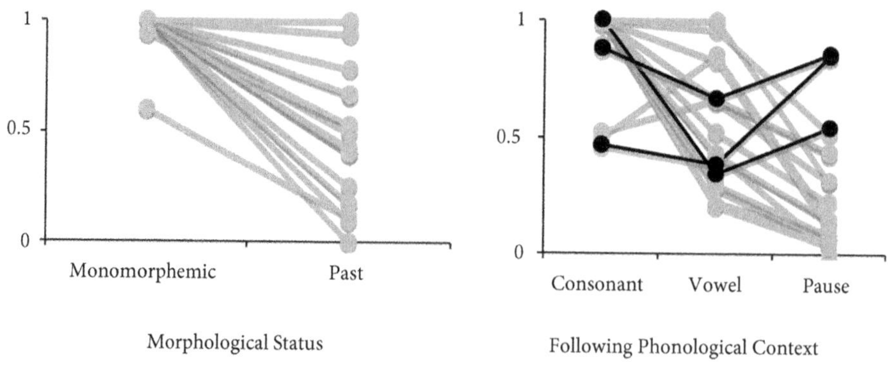

Figure 9.2. Linguistic factors contributing to (t/d)-deletion by individual speaker

Source: Adapted from Guy (1980:14)

that speakers are united in their treatment of deletion by the morphological status, with higher rates of deletion with monomorphemic forms than past-tense forms (left-hand graph) and higher rates of deletion with a following consonant than a following vowel (right-hand graph). However, as the right-hand graph shows, there are three speakers who deviate from the group norms in having high rates of deletion with a following pause. These "deviant" speakers all turn out to be from New York, suggesting that the treatment of deletion by following pause is a feature that defines a dialect difference between speech communities: in New York, a following pause is treated like a following consonant in promoting deletion; in Philadelphia, a following pause inhibits deletion. These results suggest that speakers mostly share the same linguistic constraints on (t/d)-deletion (morphological status and following consonants and vowels) (though note that one Philadelphian treats consonants and vowels equally) but that dialects may be differentiated on the basis of at least one factor (following pause).

Variation in the Community and the Individual on Bequia

In this section, we present an analysis of two well-known grammatical variables across groups and individuals in the English spoken on Bequia, an island in St. Vincent and the Grenadines with a population of about 5000 (see figure 9.3). Most of the inhabitants are the descendants of former African-origin slaves who worked the plantations after which many of the present-day villages are named, though a small percentage are descended from British who arrived in

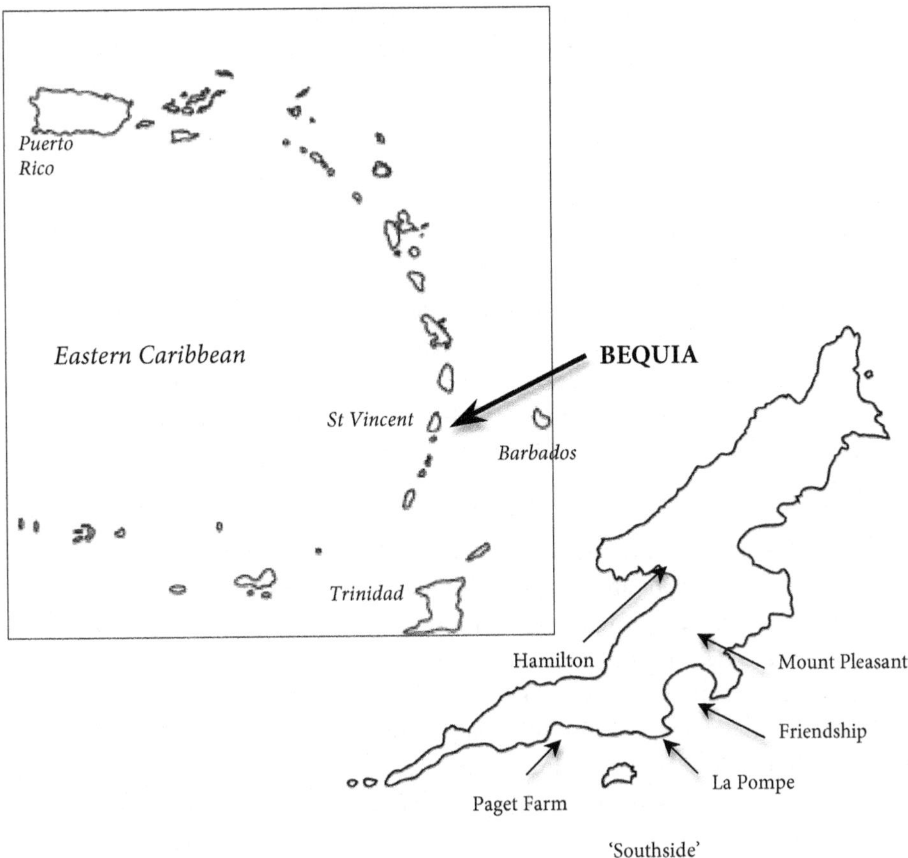

Figure 9.3. Location of Bequia in the Eastern Caribbean and research sites on Bequia.

the Caribbean in the eighteenth and nineteenth centuries. During 2003–2005, we collected data from five villages on Bequia:

- Hamilton, a former plantation and predominantly African-descent;
- Mount Pleasant, the traditional home of the British-descent population;
- La Pompe and Paget Farm, ethnically mixed fishing and whaling villages on the south side of the island; and
- Lower Bay, located at the south end of Admiralty Bay.

Although all interviewees had grown up in the village where they lived at the time of their interview, in every village there was at least one interviewee who had spent a number of years living in cities overseas (mainly London and Toronto). We call these people "urban sojourners" (Meyerhoff & Walker 2007): their residence in an overseas city before returning to Bequia exposes them to more standard varieties of English and they clearly sound more like speakers of "Standard English" than their stay-at-home peers. Contact with more standard varieties clearly adds to the linguistic resources available to the urban sojourners' stylistic repertoire, but how extensively does it impact on their linguistic system? We address this question by examining the social and linguistic conditioning across groups and individuals of two well-studied linguistic variables: BE absence and existentials.

Absence of BE

The variable absence of copula/auxiliary BE is a well-known feature of English-based creoles and African American Vernacular English (AAVE). Most attention has been focused on the effects of the grammatical category following BE, in light of Labov's (1969) finding of the hierarchy in (1) for AAVE, with decreasing BE absence from left to right:

(1) *gonna* > Verb-*ing* > adjective/locative > NP

Subsequent work separating adjectives and locatives attributed the tendency of adjectives to favor BE absence to a (prior) creole grammar in which adjectives functioned as predicates, with fluctuation in the relative ordering of adjectives and locatives reflecting decreolization (see Walker 2000 for an overview).

Despite its salience to speakers of other varieties of English, BE absence does not seem to be available to speakers on Bequia for metalinguistic comment. Although people on Bequia readily acknowledge the stylistic salience of BE absence when it is made explicit, it was never spontaneously cited in discussions of differences between villages or differences from other varieties of English.

From interviews with 18 residents of three villages (Hamilton, Mount Pleasant, and Paget Farm), we extracted a representative sample of copula contexts in present-tense finite clauses, and noted whether BE was present or absent. We coded for a number of linguistic factors (see Walker and Meyerhoff 2006 for full details), but here we focus on the following grammatical category, which was coded as *gon(na)* (2a), present participle VERB-*ing* (2b), Adjective Phrase (2c), Prepositional Phrase (2d), locative Adverb (2e) or Noun Phrase (2f).

(4) a. Yeah, I think my boy Ø gon done this year. (H5:420)
b. He Ø making speed, running. (H3:217)
c. They does go walk and bawl, days before they they're dead. (P14:274)
d. So they figure everybody is for theyself. (M303:634)
e. He Ø there in Antigua. (P19:731)
f. But her father is a Ollivierre. (P24:172)

The results for the following grammatical category are shown by village in table 9.2.[1] In all three villages there is a marked difference between auxiliary and copula functions of BE: following verbal predicates (auxiliary) massively favor absence; following nonverbal predicates (copula) disfavor absence. There is

Table 9.2. Variable-rule analysis of the linguistic constraints on BE absence in three villages on Bequia (factors favoring absence of BE are highlighted in bold)

	HAMILTON	MT. PLEASANT	PAGET FARM
	(Ø vs. F+C)	(Ø vs. C)	(Ø vs. F+C)
	(Insertion)	(Labov deletion)	(Insertion)
Total N:	1002	640	690
Input (p°):	.386	.459	.250
Following grammatical category			
gonna	.90	**.83**	.96
Verb-*ing*	**.82**	**.79**	**.84**
Adjective	**.64**	.47	**.54**
PP	.38	.53	.42
NP	.16	.12	.14
Locative adverb	.08	.53	**.54**
Subject type + preceding segment			
NP, Vowel	**.58**	.87	.50
Pronoun	**.53**	.47	.50
NP, Consonant	.43	.55	.49

also a qualitative difference between the villages in how predicate adjectives are treated: in Hamilton and Paget Farm, they are treated more like verbal predicates; in Mount Pleasant, more like nonverbal predicates. Thus, speakers in different villages on Bequia appear to have analyzed English adjectives in different ways, possibly reflecting the different settlement histories of the three villages. Since this is the most striking finding, we will take differences between individuals in this respect to be the most crucial, and indicative of fundamentally different grammars.

As we noted at the beginning of the chapter, a recurring question in sociolinguistics is whether the patterns of group variation are replicated in the performance of individuals. A particular challenge for this study is whether these patterns are replicated in the speech of the urban sojourners. To investigate this question, we undertook separate analyses of the copula for each speaker in our sample. As figure 9.4 shows, the overall rate of BE absence varies among speakers, even within a community, from highs of as much as 60 percent to lows of 8 percent. Because of the small numbers per speaker, multivariate analysis is not possible for individuals. To make interindividual comparisons, we examine the percentage of absence across different following grammatical categories. Despite these methodological adjustments, percentages with small numbers of tokens are still necessarily subject to more fluctuation between individuals than weighted probabilities are. Nonetheless, across individuals the patterns are

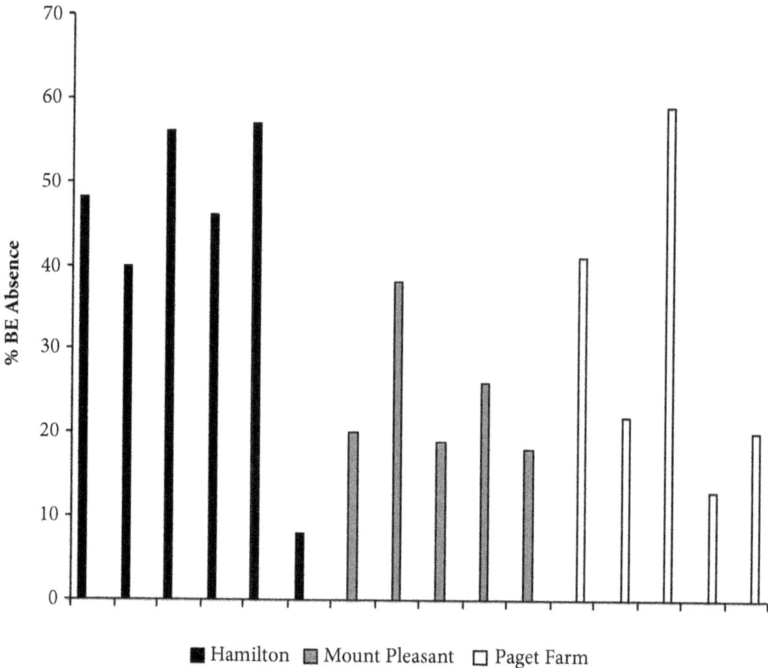

Figure 9.4. Rates of BE absence by individual speaker in Bequia.

very similar for the effect of each following grammatical category relative to all other categories.

More specifically, the rate of BE absence in the speech of each of the urban sojourners largely falls within the group norms for their stay-at-home peers. The lack of evidence for any substantial reanalysis in the urban sojourners' distribution of BE absence can be seen in figures 9.5 to 9.7, which show the patterns for all three villages,[2] with the urban sojourner in each village highlighted with a dashed line. This allows us to see how the urban sojourners are treating following adjectives, which we have argued is critical in defining each community's grammar. In Paget Farm (figure 9.5) the parallel between the urban sojourner and the average for her stay-at-home peers is extremely close; in Mount Pleasant (figure 9.6) too. In Hamilton (figure 9.7), the comparison between the urban sojourner and the rest of the community is complicated by the very small number of tokens we have for the urban sojourner with some following grammatical categories (e.g., four tokens of a following PP). In figure 9.7 we can see clearly that the urban sojourner's rate of BE absence is much lower than that of the rest of the Hamilton speakers, but even so, he clearly retains the strong preference for BE absence with a following *V-ing*, just like his stay-at-home peers.[3]

These results provide surprising evidence of the *persistence* of shared probabilistic grammars across individuals. The urban sojourners, who sound very different from their stay-at-home peers in the village, have not radically restructured their grammars.

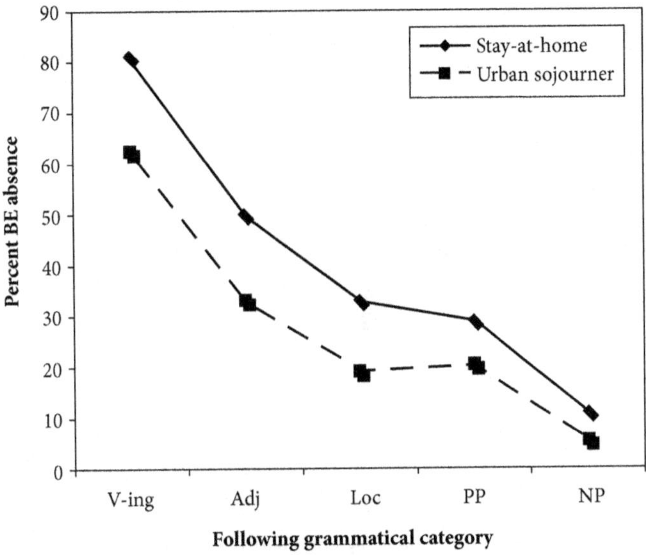

Figure 9.5. Percentage of BE absence for Paget Farm speakers: urban sojourner (*dashed*) vs. average of stay-at-home peers (*solid*).

Existentials

We contrast the foregoing analysis by turning to another well-studied variable, the choice of existential construction to introduce new or contrastive referents or information into discourse. In Bequia, existentials are variably expressed with three expletive subjects and three verbs. Expletive subject *there* occurs with the verb BE (3) as morphologically plural (3a) or singular (3b–c), as found in

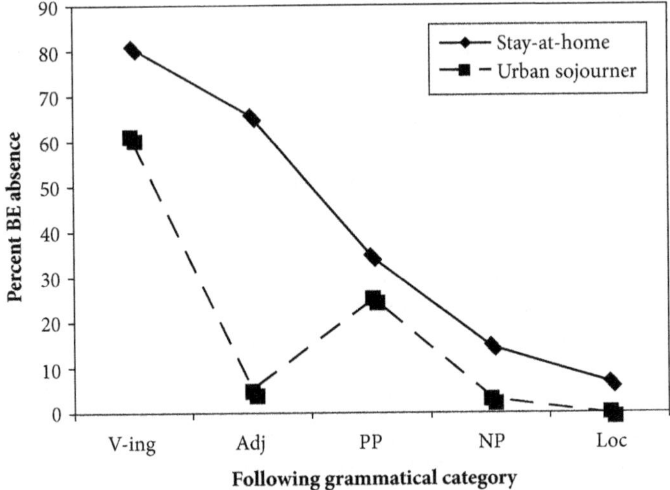

Figure 9.6. Percentage of BE absence for Hamilton speakers: urban sojourner (*dashed*) vs. average of stay-at-home peers (*solid*).

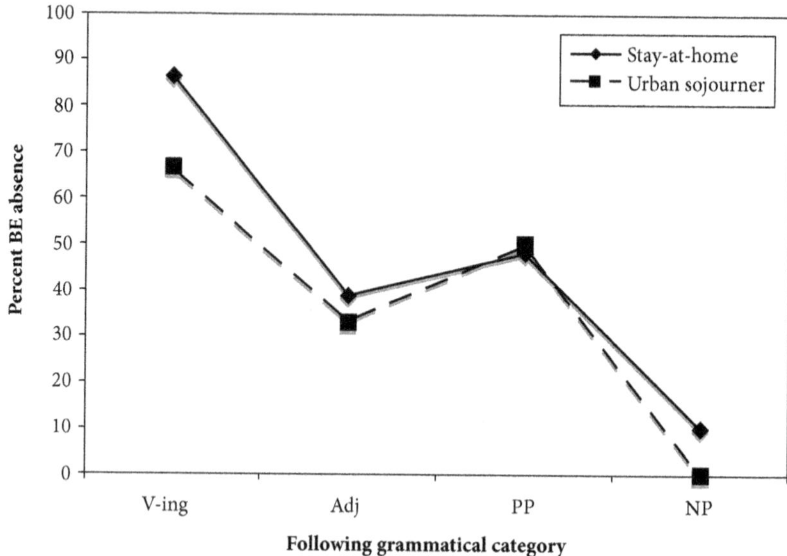

Figure 9.7. Percentage of BE absence for Mount Pleasant speakers: Urban sojourner (*dashed*) vs. average of stay-at-home peers (*solid*).

other varieties of English (see Walker 2007 for an overview). Expletive subject *it* occurs with the verb HAVE (4) (with singular or plural agreement) or GET/GOT (5), constructions that occur throughout the Caribbean. Thus, there are three primary sites of variation in existentials: the expletive subject (*there, it*), the verb (*be, get/got, have*), and agreement (singular, plural). In this analysis, we first divide the data by verb type and then examine variability in morphological agreement in the interviews of 30 individuals from four villages: Hamilton, La Pompe, Mount Pleasant, and Paget Farm.

(3) a. *There* **are** very, very few students that I can name. (L28: 351)
 b. And *there* **was** lot of fellows there who misunderstand. (L316: 1799)
 c. Well, *there*'**s** a lot of changes g- since tourists start to come in. (P14: 252)

(4) a. I would say *it* **has** some truth in it. (H2: 167)
 b. *It* **have** certain people here who giving, if you go to them for lumber. (P9: 135)

(5) a. *It* **got** fire axe all- all inside the thing you know. (H3: 1360)
 b. And open the seed and *it* **get** a white something what with it. (H16: 830)

As shown in table 9.3, the urban sojourners consistently diverge from their stay-at-home peers either in quantity or quality of the existential verb they prefer. Since *have* and *get* existentials clearly pattern alike with respect to subject type, we treat them as a single variant in subsequent analyses (Meyerhoff & Walker, under review).

Table 9.3. Overall distribution of existentials in Bequia, by village and speaker type (stay-at-home vs. urban sojourner)

	% *be* (N)	% *have* (N)	% *get* (N)	Total N
Hamilton				
stay-at-home	26 (35)	**51** (70)	23 (31)	136
urban sojourner	**99** (92)	1 (1)	0	93
La Pompe				
stay-at-home	**76** (79)	23 (24)	1 (1)	104
urban sojourner	**88** (7)	0	12 (1)	8
Paget Farm				
stay-at-home	**75** (113)	23 (34)	2 (3)	150
urban sojourner	31 (18)	**69** (41)	0	59
Mt Pleasant				
stay-at-home	30 (31)	**54** (56)	16 (16)	103
urban sojourner	**91** (32)	6 (2)	3 (1)	35
Total	407	228	53	688

BE *Existentials*

Table 9.4 shows a multivariate analysis of the factors contributing to standard agreement in BE existentials (3a).[4] For Paget Farm and La Pompe, table 9.3 showed that the overall frequency of BE existentials on Southside differs according to speaker type, with the Paget Farm urban sojourner preferring a different existential construction than their stay-at-home peers. But beneath the story of difference that these summary statistics tell, there is another story of fundamental similarity. In table 9.4, we see that if the stay-at-home speakers in these two villages use a BE existential, then they disfavor (normative) agreement (with factor weights of .42 and .32), and this is true for the urban sojourners as well (disfavoring agreement with factor weights of .20 and .14). For Hamilton, table 9.3 showed that the overall frequency of BE existentials differs according to speaker type, with the urban sojourner using vastly more BE (99 percent) than the stay-at-home peers (26 percent). As table 9.4 shows, on the occasions that the stay-at-home Hamilton speakers do use a BE existential, they favor (normative) agreement, and this is true for the urban sojourner in Hamilton too (factor weights of .63 and .75, respectively). For Mount Pleasant, table 9.3 similarly showed that the overall frequency of BE existentials differs by speaker type, with urban sojourners using BE at a much higher rate (91 percent) than their stay-at-home peers (30 percent). But in Mount Pleasant we see a slightly different pattern with respect to the constraints on the variation. Table 9.4 shows that this difference persists in speakers' preference for (normative) agreement: stay-at-home speakers disfavor agreement (.26), while the urban sojourner favors it (.78).

Table 9.4. Factors contributing to standard agreement with postverbal subjects in BE existentials in Bequia (factors favoring standard agreement are highlighted in bold)

Total N:	390
Input:	.893
Village and Speaker Type	
Mount Pleasant, urban sojourner	**.78**
Hamilton, urban sojourner	**.75**
Hamilton, stay-at-home	**.63**
Paget Farm, stay-at-home	.42
La Pompe, stay-at-home	.32
Mount Pleasant, stay-at-home	.26
Paget Farm, urban sojourner	.20
La Pompe, urban sojourner	.14
Type of Subject	
there	.53
it	.19

Factor groups not selected: sentence polarity, tense morphology.

HAVE/GET *Existentials*

Table 9.5 shows a multivariate analysis of factors contributing to the occurrence of standard agreement with HAVE/GET existentials.[5] Table 9.3 showed disagreement in three villages between urban sojourners and their stay-at-home peers in the preference for type of existential. HAVE/GET existentials are preferred by stay-at-home speakers in Hamilton and Mount Pleasant, but by the urban sojourner in Paget Farm. In La Pompe, both types of speakers agree in preferring BE existentials. Because of the small number of tokens of HAVE/GET existentials for the urban sojourners in La Pompe, Hamilton, and Mount Pleasant, we can only compare the preference for standard agreement between speaker types in Paget Farm. As table 9.5 shows, the stay-at-home speakers in La Pompe and Mount Pleasant favor agreement, while those in Hamilton disfavor agreement. In Paget Farm, despite the disagreement in preferred existential construction, the urban sojourner patterns with her stay-at-home peers in disfavoring agreement.

Discussion

Our analysis of two grammatical variables across groups and individuals in Bequia shows that the rate of BE absence in the urban sojourners largely falls

Table 9.5. Factors contributing to verbal agreement with postverbal subjects in HAVE/GET existentials in Bequia (factors favoring standard agreement highlighted in bold)

Total N:	276[a]
Input:	.840
Village and Speaker Type	
La Pompe, stay-at-home	**.82**
Mt Pleasant, stay-at-home	**.65**
Paget Farm, stay-at-home	.42
Hamilton, stay-at-home	.40
Paget Farm, urban sojourner	.34
Speaker Sex	
Male	**.66**
Female	.31

Factor groups not selected: sentence polarity, type of subject, tense morphology.

[a] The data include past and non-past existentials, though the majority (N = 178) of it HAVE tokens are past.

within the group norms for their stay-at-home peers and that the linguistic conditioning of this feature is largely parallel, suggesting that the urban sojourners have not radically restructured their grammars. We see a greater degree of divergence between urban sojourners and their stay-at-home peers in both the quantity and quality of their preferred existential variant. For some of the villages, the patterns of agreement are parallel across individuals, while in others, they are quite different.

The results of these studies provide further support for conclusions we have reached in studying other grammatical variables in Bequia, where we find divergence between villages (Daleszyńska 2012; Walker & Meyerhoff 2006; Walker & Sidnell 2011) alongside stability across (some) individuals' grammars within each village. However, the differences among speakers observed for existentials, in contrast with the uniform parallels across speakers found for BE absence, demonstrates the need to examine variables, as well as speakers, individually.

Conclusion

Sociolinguistics has tended to concentrate on community-level issues in the study of language, but this examination of the literature has shown that, although not always methodologically central, there has been a long-standing concern with the role of the individual speaker. Although most studies have relied on social grouping, the individual speaker is important in calculating group rates, in the extent to which individuals adhere to or deviate from group norms, and in the reformulation of larger-scale categories as smaller-scale structures. Moreover, as our examination of variation in the speech of urban sojourners showed, the study of individuals may be central in the application of sociolinguistic analysis to questions of language contact and language change (see also Le Page & Tabouret-Keller 1985). Even when the individual is methodologically central, as in linguistic grouping, the behavior of individual speakers (whether overall rates or linguistic conditioning) can still only be interpreted with reference to the behavior of the group.

Notes

1. Three main scenarios have been proposed for modeling the variation of BE absence: an extension of contraction (Labov deletion), independent of contraction (Straight deletion), and (non)insertion (see Walker 2000). Our statistical comparison of different models found Labov deletion to provide the best fit for Mount Pleasant and noninsertion for the other two communities (see Meyerhoff & Walker 2007; Walker & Meyerhoff 2006).
2. We exclude *gon(na)* from these figures because it almost never occurs with BE.
3. Although his preference for an overt form of BE with a following adjective is admittedly problematic for our suggestion that the treatment of adjectives might be taken as a diagnostic of adherence to the community grammar, many of the following adjectives in this speaker's interview are repetitions of *is/are weak; is/are strong* (in a discussion of homeopathy), and *that's right*.
4. The high input probability reflects the near-categorical occurrence of singular agreement (*there is, there was, there's*) in tokens with singular reference, which we retain to shore up the low number of plural tokens. Although this elevates the overall rate of singular agreement, it means that the observed effects can only be a reflection of the contribution of plural tokens.
5. As in table 9.4, the high input probability reflects categorical forms (*had, got*) included to shore up low numbers, and the effects observed can only reflect the contribution of plural tokens.

References

Bailey, C.-J. 1973. *Variation and linguistic theory*. Arlington, VA: Center for Applied Linguistics.

Bailey, G. 2002. Real and apparent time. In J. K. Chambers, P. Trudgill & N. Schilling-Estes (eds.), *The handbook of language variation and change*, 312–32. Oxford: Blackwell.

Benor, S. B. 2005. Second style acquisition: The linguistic socialization of newly Orthodox Jews. Ph.D. dissertation, Stanford University.

Bickerton, D. 1975. *Dynamics of a creole system*. Cambridge: Cambridge University Press.

Chambers, J. K. 2009. *Sociolinguistic theory*. Revised edition. Oxford: Blackwell.

Chomsky, N. 1965. *Aspects of the theory of syntax*. Cambridge, MA: MIT Press.

Daleszyńska, A. 2012. Variation in past tense marking in Bequia Creole: Apparent time change and dialect levelling. Ph.D. dissertation, University of Edinburgh.

De Camp, D. 1971. Toward a generative analysis of a post-creole speech continuum. In D. Hymes (ed.), *Pidginization and creolization of language*, 349–70. Cambridge: Cambridge University Press.

Dorian, N. C. 1994. Varieties of variation in a very small place: Social homogeneity, prestige norms, and linguistic variation. *Language* 70: 631–96.

Eckert, P. 1989. The whole woman: Sex and gender differences in variation. *Language Variation and Change* 1: 245–68.

Eckert, P. 2000. *Linguistic variation as social practice*. Oxford/Malden, MA: Blackwell.

Eckert, P., & McConnell-Ginet, S. 1992. Think practically and act locally: Language and gender as community-based practice. *Annual Review of Anthropology* 21: 461–90

Guy, G. R. 1980. Variation in the group and in the individual. In W. Labov (ed.), *Locating language in time and space*, 1–36. New York: Academic Press.

Holmes, J. 1997. Story-telling in New Zealand women's and men's talk. In R. Wodak (ed.), *Gender and discourse*, 263–93. London: Sage.

Holmes, J., & Meyerhoff, M. 1999. The community of practice: Theories and methodologies in the new language and gender research. *Language in Society* 28: 173–83.

Horvath, B., & Sankoff, D. 1987. Delimiting the Sydney speech community. *Language in Society* 16: 179–204.

Labov, W. 1963. The social motivation of a sound change. *Word* 19: 273–309.

Labov, W. (1966) 2006. *The social stratification of English in New York City*. Washington, DC: Center for Applied Linguistics, 2nd ed. Cambridge: Cambridge University Press.

Labov, W. 1969. Contract, deletion, and inherent variability of the English copula. *Language* 45: 715–62.

Labov, W. 2001. *Principles of linguistic change*. Vol. 2: *Social factors*. Oxford: Blackwell.

Le Page, R., & Tabouret-Keller, A. 1985. *Acts of identity: Creole-based approaches to language and ethnicity*. Cambridge: Cambridge University Press.

McEntegart, D., & Le Page, R. 1982. An appraisal of the statistical techniques used in the sociolinguistics of multilingual communities. In S. Romaine (ed.), *Sociolinguistic variation in speech communities*, 105–24. London: Edward Arnold.

Meyerhoff, M., & Walker, J. A. 2007. The persistence of variation in individual grammars: Copula absence in 'urban sojourners' and their stay-at-home peers, Bequia (St Vincent and the Grenadines). *Journal of Sociolinguistics* 11: 346–66.

Meyerhoff, M., & Walker, J. A. Under review. An existential question: Variation in existentials in Bequia (St Vincent and the Grenadines). *Language and Society*.

Milroy, L. 1987. *Language and social networks*. Oxford: Blackwell.

Milroy, L. & Milroy, J. 1992. Social network and social class: Toward an integrated sociolinguistic model. *Language in Society* 21: 1–26.

Podesva, R. 2006. Phonetic detail in sociolinguistic variation: Its linguistic significance and role in the construction of social meaning. Ph.D. dissertation, Stanford University.

Rickford, J. R. 1985. Ethnicity as a sociolinguistic boundary. *American Speech* 60: 99–125.

Sankoff, G., & Blondeau, H. 2007. Language change across the lifespan: /r/ in Montreal French. *Language* 83: 566–88.

Santa Ana, O., & Parodi, C. 1998. Modeling the speech community: Configuration and variable types in the Mexican Spanish setting. *Language in Society* 27: 23–51.

Saussure, F. de. 1916. *Cours de linguistique générale.* Publié par C. Bailly et A. Séchehaye avec la collaboration de A. Riedlinger. [Reprinted 1995. Paris: Payot & Rivages.]

Schilling-Estes, N. 2004. Constructing ethnicity in interaction. *Journal of Sociolinguistics* 8: 163–95.

Walker, J. A. 2000. Rephrasing the copula: Contraction and zero in early African American English. In S. Poplack (ed.), *The English history of African American English*, 35–72. Oxford: Blackwell,

Walker, J. A. 2007. "There's bears back there": Plural existentials and vernacular universals in (Quebec) English. *English World-Wide* 28: 147–66.

Walker, J. A., & Meyerhoff, M. 2006. Zero copula in the eastern Caribbean: Evidence from Bequia. *American Speech* 91: 146–63.

Walker, J. A., & Sidnell, J. 2011. Inherent variability and coexistent linguistic systems: Negation on Bequia. In L. Hinrichs & J. Farquharson (eds.), *Variation in the Caribbean: From creole continua to individual agency*, 39–55. Amsterdam: John Benjamins.

Wolfram, W., & Beckett, D. 2000. The role of the individual and group in earlier African American English. *American Speech* 75: 3–32.

CHAPTER 10

EXPERIMENTAL METHODS FOR MEASURING INTELLIGIBILITY OF CLOSELY RELATED LANGUAGE VARIETIES

CHARLOTTE GOOSKENS

THE exact number of known living languages varies from 5000 to 10,000, depending on one's definition of "language." An even larger number of dialects are spoken worldwide. Many of these languages and dialects (from now on taken together as "languages" or "varieties") are so similar that they are mutually intelligible to varying degrees, even without prior contact or formal instruction. Speakers of such different yet related languages sometimes communicate each speaking their own language. Haugen (1966) introduced the term *semicommunication* for this kind of communication. Other terms are receptive multilingualism, semibilingualism, nonconvergent discourse, asymmetric/bilingual discourse, and inherent intelligibility. Examples of observed semicommunication can be found in Zeevaert (2004).

For various reasons it may be interesting to establish the degree to which a speaker of one variety understands the speech of another closely related variety, for instance, to resolve issues that concern language planning and policies, second-language learning, and language contact. Unbiased data about distances between varieties and detailed knowledge about intelligibility can also be critical for sociolinguistic studies. Varieties that have strong social stigmas attached to them could unrightfully be deemed hard to understand (Giles & Niedzielski 1998; Wolff 1959). The relationship between attitudes and intelligibility is not a straightforward one, but advances in the field of linguistic distances and intelligibility testing provide sociolinguists with objective data to resolve conflicts that arise concerning varieties on a standard–nonstandard continuum. Knowledge about mutual intelligibility is also needed for standardization and development of new orthographies in communities where no standardized orthography exists.

To test intelligibility, a large number of tests have been developed. By means of such tests, the degree of intelligibility can be expressed in a single number, often the percentage of input that was correctly recognized by the subject. The aim of the present chapter is to give an overview of methods for measuring intelligibility of closely related languages and to discuss the advantages and disadvantages of the various methods. We focus on spoken language comprehension, but many tests can also be applied to the comprehension of written language.

Human spoken language is extremely robust, and native subjects are generally successful in getting the speaker's intentions even if the input speech is defective, for example, in cases of language or speech pathology, foreign accents, and computer speech, and even in noisy conditions. Listening to a closely related language is similar to other situations where the speech input is nonoptimal and we assume that no special mechanism is involved in decoding this kind of speech. This means that methods for investigating mutual intelligibility can be taken from other disciplines, for example, in the area of speech technology, second-language acquisition, and speech pathology.

The experimental and methodological considerations relevant for intelligibility testing have much in common with those relevant for studies in various other areas of sociolinguistics. For example, efforts must mostly be taken to control the context of speech production or speech perception as much as possible while keeping the recording or listening condition as natural as possible. A number of techniques have been developed within the area of experimental methods for the study of language variation. Often a variety of methods are used to study a phenomenon because each method has its shortcomings. Sociolinguists and dialectologists have devoted much attention to giving technical descriptions of language varieties phonetically and exploring general questions about language attitude and stereotypes. However, in recent years there has been an increasing focus on perceptual sociolinguistics (e.g., Clopper 2004; Long & Preston 2002; Preston 1999; Thomas 2002). Researchers have shown a growing interest in uncovering what linguistic and nonlinguistic features listeners react to. Methods include experimental designs using systematically manipulated speech (e.g., Fridland & Bartlett 2004) or listeners' expectations (Niedzielski 1999), as well as statistical correlations between acoustical measurements and reactions to perception experiments (e.g., Clopper & Pisoni 2004). For an overview of experimental methods for the study of language variation, see Nagy (2006).

General Methodological Considerations

This section gives an overview of methodological considerations that should be made when designing an intelligibility investigation. Factors are discussed that may influence the results and that should either be avoided or taken into consideration when interpreting the results. Topics dealt with are the test material, selection of speakers and subjects, and the characteristics of the task to be carried out by the subjects.

Test Material

To carry out an intelligibility test, recordings of the languages to be used as listening material in the test are needed. The choice of test material depends on the aim of the investigation and can vary along a number of dimensions: style (spontaneous or read, formal or informal), number of speakers involved (monologues, dialogues), linguistic entity (isolated words, sentences, texts), complexity (difficult, easy) and subject matter (daily life, science, society, technique, politics, etc.). If the intelligibility of more languages is compared, great care should be taken to keep these factors constant when collecting material for tests.

It is important that the texts represent the languages to the same extent. A way to control the material is to use translations of the same text in all the test languages. This makes it necessary to use read speech, even though it may be preferable to use spontaneous speech since this simulates a natural situation to a larger degree. A good compromise may be to use recordings of semispontaneous speech, where the material is controlled to some extent, such as in map tasks (cf. Anderson et al. 1991; Brown et al. 1984; Grønnum 2009) or picture description tasks, where speakers have to carry out some task that demands speech production in a controlled setting. However, the use of (semi)spontaneous speech makes it impossible to use the same texts and questions for the different test languages, so the results are less comparable.

When using translations, often a text in one of the test languages is translated into the other test languages. However, there is a risk that the translators may stick too closely to the original text when choosing words and expressions for the translations. To make sure that one of the test languages does not get a special status, a solution is to use translations from a language that is not one of the test languages or, alternatively, to use source texts from each of the test languages. In this way, frequent words and constructions are more likely to be represented to the same degree in all test languages. Frequent words are more easily recognized than infrequent words (Luce & Pisoni 1998).

Other word characteristics are also known to influence intelligibility and should therefore be controlled for. Words with a high neighborhood density are often more difficult to recognize than words with few competitors. A word's neighborhood density can be defined as the number of words that deviate from the target word by just one sound (Luce & Pisoni 1998). A word like *elephant* has no neighbors and is not easily mistaken for another similar word, while the word *cat* has a total of 30 neighbors, for example, *bat, kit,* and *cap* and can therefore easily be confused with another word.

Word length should also be considered. Studies have shown that longer words are better recognized than shorter words (Scharpff & Van Heuven 1988; Wiener & Miller 1946). This is attributed to the relationship between word length and the number of neighbors. Longer words have fewer neighbors than shorter words (Vitevitch & Rodriguez 2005). Furthermore, redundancy increases with word length, and this is assumed to enhance intelligibility as well.

The speech fragments selected for the intelligibility test are generally supposed to represent the language as a whole. If the sample is large enough, for example, a complete text, one may assume that it represents a random sample of the test language. However, it is important to be aware that one single unintelligible word or sound may disturb the picture so that in fact the intelligibility of the whole speech sample becomes lower. Smaller fragments (word lists, restricted sets of sentences) call for some control. For example, one can make sure that the material is phonetically and lexically balanced, that is, in accordance with the statistical distribution of the words and phonemes in the language.

When the same stimulus is presented more than once there may be a learning effect (priming). Therefore, the same stimuli should not be presented more than once to the same subject. This contradicts the fact that it is desirable to use the same stimulus material when comparing the intelligibility of more languages. The solution is to use a Latin square design where each subject hears a proportion of the stimuli in each of the test languages, and yet hears stimuli in each of the languages in equal proportions, and never hears the same stimuli twice (see table 10.1). A disadvantage is that often many groups of subjects are needed, four groups in the example in table 10.1.

Speakers

Speech understanding is affected by speaker characteristics. Some speakers are more intelligible than others, for example, because of differences in voice quality, precision of articulation, and reading ability (Hazan & Markham 2004). The sex of the speaker seems to play a role as well, female voices in general being more intelligible than male voices (Bradlow et al. 1996). Speaker

Table 10.1. Example of a Latin square design with the languages A–D, stimuli 1–4 and test versions I–IV

	Test version			
Languages	I	II	III	IV
A	1	2	3	4
B	2	3	4	1
C	3	4	1	2
D	4	1	2	3

characteristics may also vary across educational level, age, and social class. If the aim of an investigation is to compare the intelligibility of several languages, one should select speakers with similar voice characteristics and background. If the design of the experiment allows it, more than one speaker could be used per language variety, so that effects of variability between speakers will average out. If the intelligibility of only two languages is compared in a listening test one could opt for a bilingual speaker to make the stimuli. To be sure that the speaker sounds native in both languages, a voice lineup can be arranged (Schüppert, Hilton, & Gooskens accepted; Broeders, Cambier-Langeveld, & Vermeulen 2002).

Subjects

The task performance of human subjects is always somewhat noisy, or variable. Humans may be influenced by unwanted factors, such as motivation to carry out the test task and previous experience with the test language. Also, a certain relationship between attitudes and intelligibility has been found in previous research. The fact that Danes understand Swedish better than Swedes understand Danish, for example, is often explained by less positive attitudes among Swedes toward the Danish language, culture, and people than vice versa (Delsing & Lundin Åkesson 2005; Gooskens 2006). Therefore, if researchers wish to test the intelligibility of a language without the influence from attitudes, they may exclude subjects with strong positive or negative attitudes or aim to match the subject groups so that they have (approximately) the same attitudes toward the test language.

The subjects should be representative of the group of people to be tested as far as educational level, intelligence, age, gender, social class, geography, language background, and experience with the test language are concerned. In order to control for these factors it is important to select a well-defined group of subjects, for example an equal number of male and female high school pupils aged between 17 and 18 years, who are born and raised in a specific place and who have no prior experience with the test language.

To control for all the above-mentioned subject characteristics, an intelligibility test is often accompanied by a questionnaire that the subject has to fill in. Here, questions are asked about personal background (age, gender, places the subject has lived, language background of the subject and the parents of the subject, and schooling, etc.); attitude toward the test language (e.g.,"How beautiful does language X sound on a scale from 1 (beautiful) to 5 (ugly)?"); and experience with the test language (e.g., "How often do you hear/speak/read/write language X on a scale from 1 (never) to 5 (every day)?"). The answers to the questionnaires can be used to exclude certain subjects from further analysis because they do not meet all subject criteria.

Task

When designing a listening task to establish the level of intelligibility in a group of people, it is important to take into account the limitations of the task offered. The task can be either too easy or too difficult, and both situations should be avoided since they make it difficult or impossible to interpret the results.

If the task is too easy and the subjects answer all questions correctly, this will result in a ceiling effect whereby a measurement cannot take on a value higher than some limit or 'ceiling.' This will make it hard to interpret the results. There are several ways to avoid ceiling effects. The intelligibility of the speech sample can be made more difficult by manipulating the signal by means of filtering or signal-compression techniques or by adding noise. Another way to make the task more difficult is to put the subjects under time pressure, either by asking them to perform the task as quickly as possible or by giving them only a limited amount of time to answer. In addition, reaction time can be measured. This gives a more precise measurement, and even if all subjects answer all questions correctly, there may still be a difference in the time it took the subjects to correctly comprehend the various stimuli.

It is important to build a reference condition into the experiment, with native speakers listening to their own language as control group to check that the task is not too difficult. It should be kept in mind, however, that even under the most favorable circumstances, native subjects will mostly make mistakes. If the task is too difficult, the percentage of correct answers may be so low that it is difficult to interpret the results (floor effect). Furthermore, the subjects may get frustrated and decide not to finish the test. The task is for instance too difficult if it does not take the memory limitations of subjects into account. Therefore, too-complex tasks or too-long sentences should be avoided. Also the limitations of the specific subject group should be taken into account (e.g., illiteracy, hearing loss, or visual handicaps). For some groups of subjects it may be a hindrance to have to use a computer to perform the task. In reaction-time experiments it should be taken into consideration that right-handed persons generally respond faster to verbal stimuli with their right hand than with their left hand, and vice versa for left-handed persons (Rastatter & Gallaher 1982).

Methods for Measuring Intelligibility

In this section I first present methods for measuring overall intelligibility of complete spoken varieties and give examples of investigations in which these methods were used. A major division can be made between investigations in which subjects are asked how well they *think* they understand the other language (opinion testing) and investigations testing how well subjects *actually* understand the other language (functional testing). At the end of the section methods are presented for determining the role of single linguistic phenomena for intelligibility.

Intelligibility can be measured at several levels of the linguistic hierarchy, from sounds to larger entities like words, sentences, and whole texts. When testing overall intelligibility, preference may be given to the text level since this is closer to reality, where subjects are mostly confronted with whole messages. However, word level is very central, since it is the key to speech understanding. As long as the subject correctly recognizes words, he will be able to piece the speaker's message together. By testing isolated words, it becomes possible to pinpoint the role of specific sounds for intelligibility. Therefore, some tests are restricted to the word level.

Opinion Testing

An easy and efficient way to get a quick impression of the intelligibility of a language is to ask subjects to rate along scale(s) how well they think they understand the language at hand. It may provide a shortcut to functional intelligibility tests, and in addition, it provides information about people's subjective ideas about the intelligibility of languages. The results should be interpreted with some care, however, as a person's reported language behavior may not be in line with his or her actual language behavior.

Without speech samples. The simplest kind of opinion testing involves no speech fragments. An example of such an investigation is Haugen (1966). In the first large investigation on the mutual intelligibility between the three closely related Scandinavian languages, Danish, Norwegian, and Swedish, he sent questionnaires to 300 persons in each of the three countries. Three questions explored the informants' opinion concerning the level of mutual comprehension:

1. When you met an X for the first time, how well could you understand him? (not at all—with great difficulty—had to listen intently—all but a few words—understood everything)
2. Do you now understand X speech without difficulty (no—yes—fairly well)
3. When you speak with X, how well do they understand you? (same alternatives as under 1.)

An advantage of this paper-and-pencil method is that no speech material has to be selected. Furthermore, it is possible to abstract from individual speakers who may influence the results because of specific voice characteristics and speaking styles. On the other hand, it is uncertain whether respondents are actually able to judge intelligibility without speech samples. They may never or rarely have heard the language or may not remember how well they understood the speaker. The consequence may be that the respondents base their opinions on some extralinguistic factor, such as their positive or negative attitudes toward the country and its speakers, political borders, desirable answers, or the geographical distance to the place where the language is spoken.

With speech samples. An example of an investigation using speech samples to test intelligibility is Tang & Van Heuven (2007). Recordings of the same text, the fable "The North Wind and the Sun," in 15 Chinese dialects was presented to 24 subjects from each of the places where the dialects were spoken. For each dialect subjects were asked to indicate how well they believed monolingual subjects of their own dialect would understand the speaker on a scale from 0 ("They will not understand a word of the speaker") to 10 ("They will understand the other speaker perfectly"). With this approach it also is uncertain whether subjects are actually able to make the judgments on an objective linguistic basis without being influenced by nonlinguistic factors.

Functional Testing

Doubting the validity of intelligibility judgments, most researchers prefer to test actual speech comprehension. The disadvantage of this approach is that it is generally difficult to abstract away from individual speakers and test situations. In addition, an effort must be made to avoid priming effects, ceiling effects, too-heavy memory load, and other unwanted effects. These considerations often make it rather time consuming both to develop suitable tests and to carry out the tests themselves.

Content questions. In order to simulate a test situation that is as close to reality as possible, a number of investigators have tested intelligibility by means of questions about the content of a text. The intelligibility of a language variety is expressed as the mean percentage of correct answers given by the participants chosen for the task.

The questions about the texts must be formulated with great care. They should cover the content of the whole text as well as possible, and not measure the memory, general knowledge, or intelligence of the subject. Correct answers to the questions must also be well-defined. This is not always an easy task and may force the researcher to distinguish different degrees of correctness, for example,"completely correct," "partly correct," and "incorrect." A more objective solution is to use multiple-choice questions, where the subject has to choose between a limited number of possible answers. An additional advantage of this method is that the answers can be corrected rather easily, either manually or automatically by computer. A disadvantage of multiple-choice questions is that it may be difficult to find distracters that are not too easily excluded by the subjects. Furthermore, the use of multiple-choice questions is rather unnatural, since people are mostly not given several possible replies in a natural situation where intelligibility is required.

Translations. Another way of testing the intelligibility of a text is to have the subjects translate it. Intelligibility is then expressed as the percentage of correctly translated words. An advantage of this method compared to content questions is that the researcher does not have to formulate questions about the text, which, as previously noted, is sometimes a difficult task. All words in the text count to the same degree even if the subject does not completely understand the text, and general knowledge about the subject only plays a limited role.

For the researcher, it may be difficult to decide whether translations should be counted as correct or incorrect and the choice may be rather subjective. For example, a Danish person may translate Swedish *piga* 'maid' into the Danish cognate *pige* 'girl,' which has only a partly overlapping meaning. Furthermore, some subjects may have difficulty translating since for them it not a natural task to perform. The ability to translate appears to involve far more than mere intelligibility, and it may draw heavily on the subject's memory. Therefore, the text must be presented in short chunks with pauses in between during which the subject can write down the translation.

An example of a translation task is Gooskens, Beijering, & Heeringa (2008) who tested the intelligibility of "The North Wind and the Sun" in 18 Nordic language varieties among subjects from Copenhagen. The six sentences of the fable were presented sentence by sentence to the respondents with each sentence in a different variety. To avoid learning effects, the same respondents should not hear the same sentence twice, and since all sentences from the 18 varieties had to be presented, a total of 18 groups of respondents were tested. In addition to the intelligibility scores, distances between Standard Danish and each of the Nordic language varieties were measured at the lexical level and at different phonetic levels. In order to determine how well these linguistic levels can predict intelligibility, the intelligibility scores were correlated with the linguistic distances, and a number of regression analyses were carried out. The results show that for this particular set of closely related language varieties, phonetic distance is a better predictor of intelligibility ($r = -.86$) than lexical distance ($r = -.64$).

Another possibility for avoiding memory problems is to have the respondents translate a collection of isolated words that are representative for the test language, for example, a random selection or words selected from a frequency list. The correction of the translations may be even more difficult than in the case of whole texts since words may have more meanings when they are presented out of context. Furthermore, respondents often make spelling errors that might make it unclear to the researcher whether the respondent has actually understood the test word.

Kürschner, Gooskens, & Van Bezooijen (2008) tested the intelligibility of 384 frequent Swedish words among Danish subjects via the Internet. The translations were automatically categorized as right or wrong by the computer through a pattern match with expected answers. The answers that were categorized as wrong were subsequently checked manually by a Danish mother-tongue speaker. Responses that deviated from the expected responses because of a mere spelling error were counted as correct identifications. Spelling errors were objectively defined as instances where only one letter had been spelled wrong without resulting in another existing word. So, for example, the mistake in *ærende* (correct *ærinde* 'errand') is considered a spelling mistake and therefore counted as correct (only one wrong letter without resulting in another existing word), whereas *aske* (correct *æske* 'box') was not counted as correct because the mistake results in an existing word meaning 'ash'. Some Swedish words have more than one possible translation. For example, the Swedish word *brist* 'lack' can be translated into Danish *brist* or *mangel*, both meaning 'lack'. Both translations were counted as correct. In the case of homonyms, both possible translations were accepted as correct. For example, Swedish *här* can be translated correctly into Danish *hær* 'army' or her 'here'. The aim of the investigation was to determine to which degree various linguistic factors contribute to the intelligibility of Swedish words among Danes. The word intelligibility results were correlated with 11 linguistic factors. The highest correlation was found in the negative correlation between word intelligibility and phonetic distances. Also, word length, different number of syllables than in Danish, foreign sounds not present in Danish, neighborhood density, word frequency, orthography, and the absence of the prosodic phenomenon of 'stød' in Swedish had a significant influence on the level of intelligibility.

The words can be presented in a context where part of the message may be printed out with blanks for selected words only. For example, Van Bezooijen & Van den Berg (1999) played semi-spontaneous samples of various Dutch varieties to different groups of subjects from the Netherlands and Belgium. The texts were written down in Standard Dutch but the nouns were replaced by dotted lines of the same length. The subjects were asked to write the missing words on the lines while listening to the recordings. There were considerable differences in intelligibility among the tested varieties, and intelligibility depended to some extent on the geographic background of the listeners. An advantage of this test type is that it is easy to make sure that the correct translation is given. However, this approach makes it uncertain which role the (written) context plays in the interpretation of the words.

To make it easier to correct the responses, multiple-choice tests are often used in which respondents are asked to select the best possible translation from a list of choices. It is difficult to construct such a test, since the choice of distracters determines how difficult the test is, and it is often not possible to select the same distracters if more than one language is involved in the test. To solve this problem, Tang & Van Heuven (2009) determined word intelligibility by having subjects perform a semantic categorization task whereinwords had to be classified as one of ten different pre-given semantic categories, such as 'body part,' 'plant,' 'animal,' and so on. For instance, if the subject hears the word for 'apple,' she or he should categorize it as a member of the category 'fruit.' Here, the assumption is that correct categorization can only be achieved if the subject correctly recognizes the target words. Since there are as many as 10 semantic categories, the role of guessing is negligible. It is a disadvantage of this method that only words from predefined categories can be tested.

Van Heuven & Van Bezooijen (1995) provide an overview of methods for quality evaluation of synthesized speech. Here, it is mostly tested how well subjects understand synthesized speech in their own native language. I will discuss two of the translation tasks that have also been used for testing the intelligibility of natural languages. The advantage of these methods in comparison with the translation task mentioned earlier is that the test words are presented in a controlled spoken context. The results are easy to score by hand or automatically. The tests are easy to adapt to new test languages, but the number of words that can be tested in one test session is more limited than in the case of isolated words.

A set of semantically unpredictable sentences (SUS) was compiled by Benoit, Grice, & Hazan (1996). These sentences consisted of five different, common syntactic structures, and words were randomly selected from lexicons with frequent "mini-syllabic" words (smallest words available in a given category). The SUS sentences can be automatically generated using five basic syntactic structures and a number of lexicons containing the most frequently occurring short words in each language. The syntactic structures are simple and the sentence length does not exceed seven words (eight for English because of the auxiliary in questions) in order to avoid saturation of the subjects' short-term memory. The sentences have normal word order and prosody but do not permit the subject to predict the identity of content words from sentence semantics or situational context. For example, in a semantically anomalous sentence such as *He drank the wall,* the syntactic structure is correct. Subjects receive cues about syntactic category only; other than that they will not be able to make any further predictions about word identity by means of semantic or syntactic contextual cues. Since words are tested in different positions in the sentence, word segmentation is an essential feature assessed by this test. Intelligibility can be expressed as the percentage correctly translated (content) words, but the simplest and fastest way to score results is to only take into account the sentences that are entirely correctly translated. This easy-to-obtain score is strongly related to word score. Gooskens, Van Heuven, Van Bezooijen, & Pacilly (2010) presented Danish and Swedish SUS sentences to Danish and Swedish subjects in order to test the mutual intelligibility as well as the intrinsic intelligibility of the two languages.

The SPIN (Speech Perception in Noise) test is a list of sentences that test word intelligibility (Kalikow, Stevens, & Elliott 1977). The subject translates only the last word in a number of short spoken sentences. Since the position of the target word is pre-given, word segmentation problems are minimal. There are two types of materials in the SPIN test. One type presents target words that are highly predictable from the earlier context, as in *He wore his broken arm in a sling* (target underlined). The other type presents words that are not predictable from the context, as in *We could have discussed the dust.* Wang (2007) showed that the high predictability part of the SPIN test was more sensitive to differences between speaker and subject groups with different degrees of listening comprehension in English than the low predictability part. The test is easy to adapt to new test languages, but the number of words that can be tested in one test session is more limited than in the case of isolated words.

Recorded text testing. A special problem arises when a researcher wants to test the mutual intelligibility of languages that he does not master himself. For such a situation the recorded text testing (RTT) method has been developed. This method was first used in the fifties to establish the mutual intelligibility of American Indian languages (Hickerton, Turner & Hickerton 1952; Pierce 1952; Voegelin & Harris 1951). Casad (1974) & Nahhas (2006) give detailed overviews of the steps that should be taken to carry out a test with RTT. The standard method uses a short text recorded from a speaker of the speech variety to be tested. The subject hears the text, with questions in his own mother tongue about the text interspersed following the portion that contains the answer to the question. The subjects are required to answer these questions.

An alternative approach to the standard RTT question format is the RTT retelling method, which requires subjects to listen to a narrative that has been broken down into natural segments of one or two sentences each and to retell the recorded text, segment by segment, in their L1 (see Kluge 2007). In this way, the subjects do not have to answer specific comprehension questions. For each segment the number of correctly retold core elements are counted and the segment scores are added up to obtain the overall score for a given RTT text.

The main advantage of the RTT retelling method, when compared to the standard RTT question method, is that comprehension of an entire text is tested, rather than selected sections only. A second major advantage is that in many more traditional societies, retelling a story is more appropriate and less threatening than answering questions. An additional advantage is that this method does not require the design of comprehension questions and the translation of these questions into the speech varieties of the communities under investigation. The most important disadvantage is that it is very time consuming both to develop the test and to count the number of correctly retold segments.

Reaction times. In cases where the test language is very similar to the language of the subjects, an off-line intelligibility task where responses are to be given after subjects have heard test passages, may be so easy that most answers are correct, resulting in a ceiling effect. There is a need, therefore, to use more sensitive testing procedures. Reaction time is a possible response measure that might improve the sensitivity of an intelligibility test. The assumption is that the faster the subjects react, the better the intelligibility. To ensure the credibility of the experiment, the lexical decision task needs to be followed by a second meaning-identifying task.

Reaction time can be measured by means of software applications that measure temporally accurately to within a few milliseconds. The application registers when a subject performs a certain action, for example, a vocal response, pressing a button on the computer keyboard, or touching the computer screen, which makes it suitable for various groups of test subjects, including children. Response times cannot be measured precisely via the Internet, and therefore this method is not suitable for web-based experiments.

Various tasks can be used to measure overall intelligibility using reaction times. In a sentence-by-sentence listening task subjects listen to sentences and push a button whenever they are ready for hearing the next sentence (e.g., Ralston et al. 1991). Comprehension is checked afterward. In a sentence verification test (e.g., James et al. 1994), subjects decide whether or not short sentences are true statements (e.g., *Mud is dirty* and *Rockets move slowly*). Impe (2010) used a lexical decision task where the subjects had to decide as quickly as possible—by means of pushing either a yes button or a no button—whether the stimuli (200 existing and as many non-existing words in 10 Dutch language varieties) were meaningless or meaningful Dutch words.

Observations. It can be argued that by its very nature intelligibility is a quality that does not easily lend itself to quantitative measurement. It is probably possible to achieve certain pragmatic communicative goals even with a low degree of understanding. Comprehension depends on interactive cooperation, something that does not emerge in artificial test situations. Comprehension may be better in its natural context than in an artificial one because a specific setting reduces the number of possible interpretations. Börestam Uhlmann (1994) taped some thirty inter-Scandinavian arranged conversations between Danes, Norwegians, and Swedes aged 18 to 25 who were unaccustomed to the others' languages. She was first of all interested in which kind of strategies the participants used to improve mutual intelligibility, such as rephrasing, elaborate explanation, use of English, repairing and interruptions, to either clarify something or make certain that the message had been correctly understood. Her analysis of the result is mainly qualitative, but she also showed that it is possible to quantify the results by, for example, counting the number of reparations and misunderstandings. Zeevaert (2004) observed real Nordic meetings and quantitatively analyzed turn taking and length and frequency of pauses.

A disadvantage of this approach is that speakers and subjects are well able to conceal misunderstandings and to adapt their language to the conversational partner, so that it may be difficult to express exactly how well the speakers understand each other. It also demands a large effort from the researcher because he has to make a detailed analysis of the conversation.

Performance task. A way of simulating a natural communicative situation is a performance task. For example, Van Heuven & De Vries (1981) tested the intelligibility of various versions of foreign-accented speech by means of a performance task. Dutch subjects listened to recordings of Dutch accented utterances produced by a Turkish speaker who was asked to describe a number of simple actions (e.g., someone puts a spoon in a glass). The subjects were asked to perform the actions described by the speaker as quickly as possible. The mean reaction time of the correctly performed actions was the measure of intelligibility. The aim of the investigation was to investigate the role of phonic and nonphonic factors in the intelligibility of foreign-accented speech using an experimental approach. The results showed that phonic factors are more important than nonphonic factors.

The advantage of this method is that it measures intelligibility in a communicative situation. However, the fact that the subjects have to perform the described actions limits the variation in syntactic constructions and words that can be included.

Testing with the Aim of Determining the Role of Linguistic Factors

So far, methods for measuring intelligibility have been discussed that can be used to measure overall intelligibility, that is, languages as a whole. However, sometimes the aim of intelligibility testing is to assess the contribution of single linguistic phenomena to intelligibility. For example, very little is known as yet on the specific contributions of single sounds to overall intelligibility.

One approach when aiming at identifying specific factors that influence intelligibility is to do an error analysis on the test results. For example, Kürschner et al. (2008) carried out correlations and logistic regression analyses with the results of an experiment on the intelligibility of 384 Swedish words among Danes as the dependent variable, and 11 linguistic factors that have been found to contribute to L1 intelligibility in earlier studies as independent variables. In this way, they could make conclusions about the relative importance of these for intelligibility. Phonetic distance turned out to be the most important predictor of intelligibility, followed by word length.

Another way of investigating the role of specific linguistic factors is the experimental method. By keeping the effects of all factors but one constant, and systematically varying the characteristics of the latter, any difference in intelligibility must be caused by the variations in the target module. If, for example, we wish to test the hypothesis that Danish is poorly understood by Swedes due to the presence of *stød* (a voice characteristic creating phonological contrasts not present in Swedish), we can remove the *stød* from recordings of Danish. If Swedes understand the manipulated version better than the original version, *stød* must be causally related to the intelligibility of Danish.

If diagnostic testing is used to investigate the role of specific sounds, the most purposeful approach is to test the intelligibility of isolated words, since at sentence level or higher levels poor intelligibility is difficult to trace back to specific sources. If the words are presented in a sentence, the context or the situational redundancy is likely to make up for poor intelligibility.

Various diagnostic tests can be used to pinpoint linguistic factors that influence intelligibility. These factors may be found at all linguistic levels (segmental, prosodic, morphological, and syntactic). Many of the functional tests that have been discussed in the previous section may also be used for diagnostic purposes in adapted forms, and they are connected to the same advantages and disadvantages.

The results of investigations of the relative importance of various linguistic factors for intelligibility may be used to develop a model of intelligibility. As we have seen, intelligibility testing involving human subjects is often labor intensive and involves many considerations. It also yields noisy data. It would therefore be helpful to have an objective way of predicting intelligibility that would not involve actual testing. Since languages differ in many dimensions, such as sound inventories, prosody, vocabularies, morphology, and syntax, such a measure would involve linguistic distance measurements at different linguistic levels. However, we still lack information about how to weigh these dimension in order to develop a measure that can predict intelligibility. If, for example, word order differences hardly compromise the communication between speakers of two languages, while small differences between the sound systems make the mutual intelligibility difficult, then differences in phonology must be weighted much more than syntax in the computation of linguistic distance. So far, no complete model of intelligibility exists, but Gooskens et al. (2008) have shown that at an aggregate level phonetic distances measured by means of the Levenshtein algorithm (Heeringa 2004) in combination with lexical distances expressed as the percentage of noncognates (historically nonrelated words) can predict intelligibility to a large extent (.81 percent explained variance). Morphosyntax may also play a role in the intelligibility, though to a smaller degree than phonology (Hilton, Schüppert, & Gooskens 2013). A refined model may improve the predictive power, but it should be realized that nonlinguistic factors such as attitudes and previous experience may also play an important role.

Comparing Methods

In the preceding section a number of methods for measuring intelligibility were presented. Unfortunately, it is not possible to give an answer to the question of which method is best. The choice of the method to be used in an investigation depends on a large number of practical factors, such as time and funds available and the background of the subjects. Even with sufficient time and money and subjects who are able and patient enough to undergo complicated and lengthy tests, the choice of method still depends on the precise aim of the investigation.

But apart from these considerations, does it still matter which method is used? In order to shed some more light on this point, we need to know whether the same persons who achieve high scores in one test also achieve high scores in another test when all other factors are kept constant. A few researchers compared the results of different methods of measuring intelligibility. These comparisons are valuable because they give an impression of the importance of choosing a specific method. Doetjes (2007) investigated the effect of six different test types on the measurement of the intelligibility of Swedish among Danes. The same text was tested in six different test conditions: true/false questions, multiple-choice questions, open questions, word translation, summary, and short summary. The percentages of correct answers decreased from 93.0 percent for the true/false questions to 66.2 percent for the short summaries. This shows that at this point in time it is not possible to give an absolute answer to the question of how well subjects understand a language, and caution should be taken when comparing results from different investigations. When comparing various previous investigations on Swedish-Danish mutual intelligibility, for example, we see very different results, probably due to the use of different texts and tasks and the different backgrounds of the subjects. However, it is notable that Danes, for example, always have higher scores on the Swedish intelligibility tests than vice versa. This indicates that it may not be possible to express how well a language is understood in an absolute sense, but that it may be possible to compare the relative intelligibility of various languages as long as the test conditions are kept as constant as possible.

Maurud (1976) tested mutual intelligibility between the Scandinavian languages by means of word tests and content tests on the same texts. He found correlations between the test results between r = .6 and .8 for various groups of subjects. Tang & Van Heuven (2009) tested the mutual intelligibility of 15 Chinese dialects by means of functional intelligibility tests at word and sentence level and compared these with each other and with opinion scores and objective distance scores at the lexical and the phonological level. They found correlation between the opinion scores and the functional scores between r = .7 and.8. The same results were found for correlations between functional and opinion tests, on the one hand, and objective measurements, on the other hand. The authors conclude that mutual intelligibility should preferably be tested by means of functional sentence intelligibility tests. The correlation between word intelligibility and sentence intelligibility was very high (r = .9) but sentence intelligibility reflected traditional Chinese taxonomy better than word intelligibility does. So, comparisons of various tests show rather high correlations; still, a large amount of unexplained variance is left. Even though there is a large overlap, different tests measure different aspects of intelligibility.

References

Anderson, A. H., Bader, M., Bard, E. G., Boyle, E., Doherty, G., Garrod, S., Isard, S., Kowtko, J., McAllister, J., Miller, J., Sotillo, C., Thompson, H. S., & Weinhart, R. 1991. The HCRC Map Task Corpus. *Language and Speech* 34: 351–66.

Benoit, C., Grice, M., & Hazan, V. 1996. The SUS test: A method for the assessment of text-to-speech synthesis intelligibility using Semantically Unpredictable Sentences. *Speech Communication* 18: 381–92.

Börestam Uhlmann, U. 1994. *Skandinaver samtalar: språkliga och interaktionella strategier i samtal mellan danskar, norrman och svenskar.* Uppsala: Uppsala University.

Bradlow, A. R., Torretta, G. M., & Pisoni, D. B. 1996. Intelligibility of normal speech I: Global and fine-grained acoustic-phonetic talker characteristics. *Speech Communication* 20: 255–72.

Broeders, A. P. A., Cambier-Langeveld, T., & Vermeulen, J. 2002. Case report: Arranging a voice lineup in a foreign language. *The International Journal of Speech, Language and the Law* 9(1): 1350–1771.

Brown, G., Anderson, A., Shillcock, R., & Yule, G. 1984. *Teaching talk: Strategies for production and assessment.* Cambridge: Cambridge University Press.

Casad, E. H. 1974. *Dialect intelligibility testing.* Summer Institute of Linguistics Publications in Linguistics and Related Fields, 38. Norman: Summer Institute of Linguistics of the University of Oklahoma.

Clopper, C. G. 2004. Linguistic experience and the perceptual classification of dialect variation. Ph.D. dissertation, Indiana University.

Clopper, C. G., & Pisoni, D. B. 2004. Some acoustic cues for the perceptual categorization of American English regional dialects. *Journal of Phonetics* 32: 111–40.

Delsing, L-O., & Lundin Åkesson, K. 2005. *Håller språket ihop Norden? En forskningsrapport om ungdomars förståelse av danska, svenska och norska.* Copenhagen: Nordiska ministerrådet.

Doetjes, G. 2007. Understanding differences in inter-Scandinavian language understanding. In J. Ten Thije & L. Zeevaert (eds.), *Receptive multilingualism. Linguistic analyses, language policies and didactic concepts*, 217–30. Amsterdam: John Benjamins.

Fridland, V., & Bartlett, K. 2004. Do you hear what I hear? Experimental measurement of the perceptual salience of acoustically manipulated vowel variants by Southern speakers in Memphis, TN. *Language Variation and Change*, 16: 1–16.

Giles, H., & Niedzielski, N. 1998. 'Italian is beautiful, German is ugly.' In L. Bauer & P. Trudgill (eds.), *Language myths*, 85–93. London: Penguin.

Gooskens, C . 2006. Linguistic and extra-linguistic predictors of Inter-Scandinavian intelligibility. In J. Van de Weijer & B. Los (eds.), *Linguistics in the Netherlands* 23, 101–13. Amsterdam: John Benjamins.

Gooskens, C., Beijering, K., & Heeringa, W. 2008. Phonetic and lexical predictors of intelligibility. *International Journal of Humanities and Arts Computing* 2(1–2): 63–81.

Gooskens, C., Van Heuven, V. J., Van Bezooijen, R., & Pacilly, J. 2010. Is spoken Danish less intelligible than Swedish? *Speech Communication* 52: 1022–037.

Grønnum, N. 2009. A Danish phonetically annotated spontaneous speech corpus (DanPASS). *Speech Communication* 51: 594–603.
Haugen, E. 1966. Semicommunication: The language gap in Scandinavia. *Sociological Inquiry* 36: 280–97.
Hazan, V., & Markham, D. 2004. Acoustic-phonetic correlates of talker intelligibility in adults and children. *Journal of the Acoustical Society of America* 116: 3108–118.
Heeringa, W. 2004. Measuring dialect pronunciation differences using Levenshtein distance. Ph.D. dissertation, University of Groningen.
Hickerton, H., Turner, G.D., & Hickerton, N.P. 1952. Testing procedures for estimation transfer of information among Iroquois dialects and languages. *International Journal of American Linguistics* 18: 1–8.
Hilton, N. H., Gooskens, C., & Schüppert, A., 2013. The influence of non-native morphosyntax on the intelligibility of a closely related language. *Lingua*, 137, 1–18.
Impe, L. 2010. Mutual intelligibility of national and regional varieties of Dutch in the Low Countries. Ph.D. dissertation, Catholic University of Leuven.
James, C.J., Cheesman, M. F., Cornelisse, L., & Miller, L. T. 1994. Response times to sentence verification tasks (SVTS) as a measure of effort in speech perception. *Fifth Australian International Conference on Speech Science & Technology* II: 600–05.
Kalikow, D.N., Stevens, K. N., & Elliott, L. L. 1977. Development of a test of speech intelligibility in noise using sentence materials with controlled word predictability. *Journal of the Acoustical Society of America* 61: 1337–351.
Kluge, A. 2007. *RTT retelling method: An alternative approach to intelligibility testing.* SIL Electronic Working Papers, 2007–006.
Kürschner, S., Gooskens, C., & Van Bezooijen, R. 2008. Linguistic determinants of the intelligibility of Swedish words among Danes. *International Journal of Humanities and Arts Computing* 2(1–2): 83–100.
Long, D., & Preston, D. R. (eds.). 2002. *Handbook of perceptual dialectology*, vol 2. Amsterdam: John Benjamins.
Luce P. A., & Pisoni, D. B. 1998. Recognizing spoken words: The Neighborhood Activation Model. *Ear and Hearing* 19: 1–36.
Maurud, Ø. 1976. *Nabospråksforståelse i Skandinavia: en undersøkelse om gjensidig forståelse av tale- og skriftspråk i Danmark, Norge og Sverige.* Stockholm: Skandinaviskråd.
Nagy, N. 2006. Experimental methods for study of variation. In K. Brown (ed.), *Encyclopedia of language and linguistics*, 2nd ed., vol. 4, 390–94. Oxford: Elsevier.
Nahhas, R. W. 2006. *The steps of recorded text testing: A practical guide.* Chiang Mai: Payap University.
Niedzielski, N. 1999. The effect of social information on the perception of sociolinguistic variables. *Journal of Language and Social Psychology* 18(1): 62–85.
Pierce, J. E. 1952. Dialect distance testing in Algonquian. *International Journal of American Linguistics* 18: 208–18.
Preston, D. R. (ed.). 1999. *Handbook of perceptual dialectology*, vol 1. Amsterdam: John Benjamins.
Ralston, J. V., Pisoni, D. B., Lively, S. E., Greene, B. G., & Mullennix, J. W. 1991. Comprehension of synthetic speech produced by rule: Word monitoring and sentence-by-sentence listening times. *Human Factors* 33(4): 471–91.

Rastatter, M. P., & Gallaher, A. J. 1982. Reaction-times of normal subjects to monaurally presented verbal and tonal stimuli. *Neuropsychologia* 20: 465–73.

Scharpff, P. J., & Van Heuven, V. J. 1988. Effects of pause insertion on the intelligibility of low quality speech. In W. A. Ainsworth & J. N. Holmes (eds), *Proceedings of the 7th FASE/Speech-88 Symposium* (Edinburgh): 261–68.

Schüppert, A., Hilton, N. H., & Gooskens, C. Accepted. Swedish is beautiful, Danish is ugly: Investigating the link between intelligibility and language attitudes. *Linguistics*, 53(2).

Tang, C., & Van Heuven, V. J. 2007. Mutual intelligibility and similarity of Chinese dialects: Predicting judgments from objective measures. In B. Los & M. Van Koppen (eds.), *Linguistics in the Netherlands* 24: 223–34. Amsterdam: John Benjamins.

Tang, C., & Van Heuven, V. J. 2009. Mutual intelligibility of Chinese dialects experimentally tested. *Lingua* 119: 709–32.

Thomas, E. R. 2002. Sociophonetic applications of speech perception experiments. *American Speech* 77: 115–47.

Van Bezooijen, R., & Van den Berg, R. 1999. Taalvarieteiten in Nederland en Vlaanderen: hoe staat het met hun verstaanbaarheid? *Taal en Tongval* 51(s): 15–33.

Van Heuven, V. J., & De Vries, J. W. 1981. Begrijpelijkheid van buitenlanders: de rol van fonische versus niet-fonische factoren, *Forum der Letteren* 22: 309–20.

Van Heuven, V. J., & Van Bezooijen, R. 1995. Quality evaluation of synthesized speech. In W. B. Klein & K. K. Paliwal (eds.), *Speech coding and synthesis*, 707–38. Amsterdam: Elsevier Science.

Vitevitch, M. S., & Rodriguez, E. 2005. Neighborhood density effects in spoken word recognition in Spanish. *Journal of Multilingual Communication Disorders* 3: 64–73.

Voegelin, C. F., & Harris, Z. S. 1951. Methods for determining intelligibility among dialects of natural languages. *Proceedings of the American Philosophical Society* 45: 322–29.

Wang, H. 2007. *English as a lingua franca: Mutual Intelligibility of Chinese, Dutch and American speakers of English*. LOT Dissertation Series, 147. Utrecht: LOT.

Wiener, F. M., & Miller, G. A. 1946. Some characteristics of human speech. *Transmission and reception of sounds under combat conditions. Summary Technical Report of Division 17, National Defense Research Committee* (Washington, DC), 58–68.

Wolff, H. 1959. Intelligibility and inter-ethnic attitudes. *Anthropological Linguistics* 1: 34–41.

Zeevaert, L. 2004. *Interskandinavische Kommunikation. Strategien zur Etablierung von Verständigung zwischen Skandinaviern im Diskurs*. Hamburg: Kovač.

CHAPTER 11

QUANTITATIVE ANALYSIS

KYLE GORMAN AND
DANIEL EZRA JOHNSON

A sociolinguist who has gathered so much data that it has become difficult to make sense of the raw observations may turn to graphical presentation, and to *descriptive statistics,* techniques for distilling a collection of data into a few key numerical values, allowing the researcher to focus on specific, meaningful properties of the data set (see Johnson in press).

However, a sociolinguist is rarely satisfied with a mere snapshot of linguistic behavior, and desires not just to describe, but also to evaluate hypotheses about the connections between linguistic behavior, speakers, and society. The researcher begins this process by gathering data with the potential to falsify the hypotheses under consideration (e.g., Lucas, Bayley, & Valli 2001: 43). A sociolinguist who suspects that women and men in a certain speech community differ in the rate at which they realize the final consonant of a word ending in <ing> with coronal [n] rather than velar [ŋ] would collect tokens of these words in the speech of women and men, recording which variant was used. While this data, in the form of a descriptive statistic or an appropriate graph, could suggest that women differ from men in the rate at which they use these competing variants, these techniques cannot exclude the possibility that this difference is due to random fluctuations. *Inferential statistics* allow the researcher to compute the probability that a hypothesized property of the data is due to chance, and to estimate the magnitude of the hypothesized effect.

Statistical inferences may not be valid, however, if the assumptions such techniques make are inappropriate for the data. This chapter compares inferential methods for sociolinguistic data in terms of these assumptions.

The Elements of Quantitative Analysis

The sample. The data under investigation is necessarily finite. If it comes from the spontaneous speech of a speech community, a single interview makes up only a tiny fraction of any speaker's lifetime of language, and there are usually many more speakers who could have been interviewed but were not. The same concerns apply to experimental data gathering, where there are always more possible subjects to run or stimuli to present. Inferential statistics uses the finite *sample* gathered by the researcher to generate a model of the *population* of all relevant linguistic behavior in a speech community.

Hypothesis testing. Because of the variable nature of linguistic phenomena, it is always possible that the sample differs quantitatively from the population, even under careful random sampling. The sociolinguist seeks to infer whether the patterns observed in the sample are likely to generalize to the population, but the women in a sample, for instance, may not be representative of the women in the population. The possibility that a pattern, usually an observed difference, in the sample does extend to the population is called the *alternative hypothesis*, whereas the opposing view that there is no real difference to be discovered in the population is the *null hypothesis*. For example, if a sociolinguist is interested in the association between gender and speech rate, then the null hypothesis is that speech rate is constant across genders, and the alternative hypothesis is that the speech rate differs between women and men. Inferential methods provide a way to summarize the sample data as a *test statistic* (e.g., a Z-score, t-statistic, F-statistic, or chi-square statistic), then compute the probability, henceforth the p-value, that a test statistic as large or larger would have occurred under the null hypothesis (i.e., no difference in the population).

Although this threshold is arbitrary, a result where $p < 0.05$ is generally labeled *statistically significant* in the social sciences, meaning that the null hypothesis is rejected. When comparing two sample means, $p < 0.05$ indicates that a difference of such size and consistency would be observed in no more than 5 percent of samples if it were actually spurious with respect to the population.[1] In the foregoing example, the alternative hypothesis only requires that there be *some* difference between groups, but in practice it is common to use the difference estimated from the sample as a measure of the population-level difference.

This notion of statistical significance, since it is sensitive to the amount of data as much as to the magnitude of the effect, does not always mean the result should be of interest, as the label "significant" might suggest. Researchers who discover a large effect that falls short of the significance threshold may modify the alternative hypothesis for later statistical testing, or they may choose to forgo further investigation of an effect that is statistically significant but which has a vanishingly small effect on the outcomes.

Some Frequently Violated Assumptions

An inferential statistical model relies on a set of assumptions that allow the researcher, generally with help from a computer, to calculate a test statistic and *p*-value from a set of data; the responsibility of making assumptions that are appropriate for the data falls to the researcher.

The random sample. In sociolinguistic studies, the contents of the sample are shaped by convenience factors, such as speakers' willingness to be interviewed or participate in an experiment. When the presence or absence of a particular type of speaker or subject is correlated with some other factor of interest—for instance, a researcher interested in stigmatized speech may unfortunately discover that low-prestige speakers are the least likely to agree to an interview with a stranger—then the sample will not provide a good estimate of the rate at which the stigmatized variant is used in the speech community. If such information is desired, the researcher may deploy *proportional stratified sampling* (e.g., Cedergren 1973); if the population consists of middle-class speakers, who account for 25 percent of the population, and working class speakers, accounting for the remaining 75 percent, the researcher ensures that this 1:3 ratio of middle- to working-class speakers (and tokens) is also found in the sample.

The omitted variable problem. No one predictor is ever sufficient to fully determine all the variation observed in a language sample (Bayley 2002: 118). While it is in some sense impossible to include every predictor that might be relevant to the outcomes of interest, a statistical model is of little use for inferring a causal connection between predictors and outcomes if one or more important predictors have been omitted. For instance, consider a study that attempts to assess the relative influences of grammatical category and phonological context on a variable process of consonant deletion. If the researcher tests the grammatical category and phonological context separately, and finds that both are significant, it does not entail that both these predictors are independently affecting the rate of deletion.

Regression models, discussed below, are perpetually popular tools in sociolinguistics because they provide an easy way to control for this effect by specifying multiple predictors for a model. It is common to find that two predictors are both significant predictors of the outcome by themselves, but when they are combined in the same regression model, only one of the two (e.g., phonological context) is significant the other predictor (e.g., grammatical category) is said to have been suppressed (e.g., Tagliamonte & Temple 2005). Such a situation could arise if the two predictors are correlated, for example, if certain grammatical categories tend to co-occur with certain phonological contexts (e.g., Bybee 2002: 275f.), but if grammatical category itself has no additional effect on the rate of deletion.

Multicollinearity of predictors. It may however be the case that multiple predictors stand in a causal relationship with the outcome (e.g., both phonological context and grammatical category increase rate of deletion), and this must be distinguished from the above scenario. Unfortunately, carelessly including every available predictor is not a helpful for drawing this distinction. Multivariate statistical methods assume that the predictors are "orthogonal," that is, fully independent of each other. The parameters of a model that includes *multicollinear* (i.e., strongly nonorthogonal) predictors are highly unstable and greatly influenced by small fluctuations in the data. Gorman (2010) gives an example of a spurious sociolinguistic finding due to multicollinearity between measures of socioeconomic status, and demonstrates the method of residualization, one way to eliminate multicollinearity among predictors.

Independence of outcomes. Ordinary regression models make a strong assumption that once the predictors are taken into account, the outcomes themselves are mutually independent. Since it is standard, both in the field and the laboratory, to gather many data points from each speaker or subject, this assumption is frequently violated in practice. The question of whether an effect of gender in the sample is generalizable to the population is potentially of great sociolinguistic interest. To determine this fact, it is necessary to distinguish between a gender effect in the population and the presence in the sample of a few speakers who just happen to be male and furthermore are "outliers" from the rest of the sample; erroneously rejecting the null hypothesis in this latter case is known as Type I error. These two possibilities cannot easily be teased apart unless the effects of gender and speaker can be modeled simultaneously.

Insofar as speakers belonging to the same speech community may differ in the rates at which they use different variants, even after gender, age, and social status are taken into account (Guy 1980, 1991: 5), speaker identity is a strong predictor of linguistic behavior, one that is desirable to model. Yet, all tokens of a single speaker collected at a single time are also tokens of the same gender, etc.: every token from "Celeste S." also has the same value for the gender predictor ("female"), age (45), etc., and thus speaker identity fully determines these other predictors. Random effects, described later, provide a principled solution to the problems created by this nesting, without giving rise to multicollinearity.

Dichotomization and categorization. It is all too frequent that a researcher gathers observations—whether predictors or outcomes—on a continuous or integer scale, but converts these values to a few-valued (often binary) coding before performing statistical analysis. While there is occasionally a good reason to treat data that are naturally many-valued as a few-valued scale,[2] it usually increases the chance of Type II error, the error of failing to reject the null hypothesis in the case when this null hypothesis is in fact false (Cohen 1983). If a researcher posits a sound change in progress in a speech community, then a 78-year-old speaker should be less advanced with respect to this change than a 60-year-old speaker, but if these two speakers are placed together into the "60 years of age and older" bin, this trend is treated as noise rather than being credited to the alternative hypothesis of an age effect.

This example highlights another point: binning usually requires the researcher to arbitrarily choose the number and location of the cutpoint(s) between bins, and these decisions have unpredictable effects on the results that obtain. One reason this binning is so commonly seen in sociolinguistics is the "founder effect" of VARBRUL and its descendants, which require both outcomes and predictors to be categorical. However, it is incorrect to assume that VARBRUL's feature set delimits the set of possible sociolinguistic analyses, and the use of continuous predictors and/or outcomes in sociolinguistics dates back at least as far as Lennig's (1978) study of variation in the Parisian vowel system.

Another reason that some researchers are willing to bin continuous data is that the most basic use of a continuous predictor in regression assumes that the predictor and the outcome stand in a relationship that is monotonic, and more specifically, linear. A clear example of a relationship that violates this assumption is the one that holds between the use of stable sociolinguistic variables and social class, which a number of studies have found to be curvilinear, with interior social classes using the highest rates of a nonstandard variant of a stable linguistic variable (Labov 2001: 31f.). In such cases, the appropriate response to this problem, though, is not ad hoc dichotomization, but rather for the researcher to explore the relationships observed in the data (e.g., by plotting the predictor and outcome), and choosing appropriate "transformations" of the data so that the linearity assumption is satisfied.

In many cases, the hypothesis under consideration will determine an appropriate transformation. For example, the exemplar theory of lenition (e.g., Bybee 2002) predicts a relationship between the logarithm of word frequency and the rate of lenition, and thus a researcher who wishes to evaluate this hypothesis must convert word frequency to a log scale before modeling. Harrell (2001: 16–26) provides a useful discussion of transformations for regression modeling.

Summary

Inferential analysis allows for hypothesis testing, but there are many common pitfalls. The rest of the chapter outlines what we consider the best practices for analyzing the most common types of sociolinguistic data. The next two sections describe the analysis of binary and *multinomial* outcomes (categorical variables with more than two values). The following section considers methods for *continuous* outcomes, with a focus on acoustic measurements of vowels. The concluding section discusses some recent trends in the field of statistics of relevance to sociolinguists.

Methods for Binary Variables

Interpreting Cross-Tabulations

Many quantitative sociolinguistic studies compare two distinct, discrete, semantically equivalent variants in complementary distribution.

The chi-square test. In November 1962, William Labov elicited tokens of the phrase "fourth floor" from employees in three Manhattan department stores for the purpose of studying the social stratification of post-vocalic *r* realization in New York City. While this original study (Labov 2006: chapter 4), first published in 1966, does not include any inferential statistics, the cross-tabulation of the data (e.g., *r*-full vs. *r*-less tokens by store) lends itself to a simple statistical test. Consider the null hypothesis that there are no differences between the employees of the three department stores, chosen to represent the class spectrum in New York. The employees at middle-class Macy's pronounce post-vocalic *r* in 125 tokens, and do not in 211 tokens; *r* is present 37 percent of the time (= 125/336). At working-class department store S. Klein's, employees only have 21 tokens of post-vocalic *r* and 195 tokens where it is not realized, for a 10 percent rate of *r* presence. Saks, the department store representing the upper class, has a 48 percent rate of *r* presence. To compute the probability this effect is due to chance, these counts are used to compute a test statistic called Pearson's chi-square: the value obtained is 73.365. We then compute the probability of a test statistic of this size or larger being obtained for a sample of this size simply by chance using the two-tailed *chi-square distribution.* The *p*-value representing this possibility is p = 1.1e-16, indicating that there is good reason to reject the null hypothesis that there are no differences in the *r*-realization among the different department stores, and the average rates of *r* presence just calculated indicate that post-vocalic *r* is realized more often by speakers from higher social classes.

Fisher's exact test. The chi-square test is not very appropriate for small amounts of data, since it is based on an approximation that is true under the obviously false assumption of an infinite sample; the accuracy of this test is worse as the sample grows smaller. For this reason, we favor a related technique known as Fisher's exact test, which computes the "exact" (i.e., correct) *p*-value even for small data sets. As is sometimes the case, the Fisher *p*-value is somewhat smaller than the Pearson chi-square *p*-value (p = 1.4e-18), but it is always more precise. The Fisher *p*-value is often difficult to compute by hand, but since it can be computed for huge data sets by a modern computer in the blink of an eye, it should always be used rather than the chi-square test. Table 11.1 shows the results of applying the chi-square and exact test to two other contrasts in Labov's data. First, Labov feigned misunderstanding after the first "fourth floor," usually causing the speaker to repeat him- or herself, to obtain more data in a more careful speech style. Secondly, Labov recorded whether each token comes from "fourth" or "floor." These results are summarized in table 11.1; word and department store are significant predictors, but the repetition contrast is not.

Simple Logistic Regression

Because of the potential for omitted variable bias discussed above, it is preferable whenever possible to consider the relative contributions of multiple predictors in a single model. While the department-store data is relatively balanced, the *p*-values obtained from using a *univariate* method like the Fisher exact test may be inaccurate when this is not the case. *Logistic regression*, which predicts binary outcome using one or more independent predictor(s), and which will be familiar to many readers as the model underlying VARBRUL, is the appropriate model in this case.

What to include. In the logistic regression model, the outcome is either *r* or zero; the predictors, all categorical, are word ("fourth" vs. "floor"), repetition (first vs. second), and store (Saks vs. Macy's vs. S. Klein's). Modern regression software also allows the user to include what are generally called *interaction* effects, predictors that are derived from the combinations of other predictors.

Table 11.1. New York City department store (r) cross-tabulation, chi-square, and Fisher exact test

	# *r*	# zero	% *r*	*p*-value (chi-square)	*p*-value (Fisher exact)
S. Klein's	21	195	9.7	1.2e-16	1.4e-18
Macy's	125	211	37.2		
Saks	85	93	47.8		
"fourth"	87	295	22.8	1.4e-07	1.2e-07
"floor"	143	204	41.2		
first repetition	136	322	29.7	0.187	0.162
second repetition	94	177	34.7		

In this case, an interaction between word and department store allows the researcher to probe whether, in addition to any differences between "fourth" and "floor" and the different department stores, there is any difference in the difference between "fourth" and "floor" across the different department stores. For example, is "fourth" versus "floor" at Saks different from "fourth" versus "floor" at S. Klein's? There is no obvious reason to hypothesize such an interaction in this case, but it is included for the purpose of demonstration. The results from fitting this model, which reports numbers in a form that will be familiar both to users of VARBRUL and other software packages (who may know log-odds as *betas*, *coefficients*, or *estimates*) are given in table 11.2.

In this model, absence of *r* is treated as rule application, so an increase in the log-odds or the weights indicates fewer *r*'s. Just as was the case for the univariate tests mentioned earlier, there is strong support for differences between stores and the two words. The effect of repetition is approaching significance, with the second repetition being more likely to contain an overt *r* than the first, but is just short of the standard threshold of 0.05. Among the interaction terms, which taken together are nonsignificant, there is one suggestive trend: "fourth" has more *r* than "floor" at S. Klein's, but the pattern is reversed at the other two department stores.

This raises an important question: how does one decide which predictors to include and which to omit? A useful procedure, adapted from Gelman and Hill (2007: 69), is as follows. The initial model should include any predictors

Table 11.2. New York City department store (r) fixed-effects logistic regression

	log-odds	weight	*p*-value
(intercept)	0.910	0.713	8.3e-19
S. Klein's	1.304	0.787	1.2e-19
Saks	−0.875	0.294	
Macy's	−0.428	0.395	
"floor"	−0.444	0.391	
"fourth"	0.444	0.609	8.2e-09
first repetition	0.166	0.541	0.065
second repetition	−0.166	0.459	
S. Klein's and "fourth"	−0.239	0.441	0.341
S. Klein's and "floor"	0.239	0.559	
Macy's and "fourth"	0.061	0.515	
Macy's and "floor"	−0.061	0.485	
Saks and "fourth"	0.177	0.544	
Saks and "floor"	−0.177	0.441	

the experimenter has recorded and thinks might influence the outcomes. After the model is fit, the predictors are assessed in the following manner:

1. If a predictor is not statistically significant, but the estimate (or factor weight) goes in the expected direction, leave it in the model.
2. If a predictor is not statistically significant, and the estimate goes in an unexpected direction, consider removing it from the model.
3. If a predictor is statistically significant, but the estimate goes in an unexpected direction, reconsider the hypothesis and consider more data and input variables.
4. If a predictor is statistically significant, and the estimate goes in the expected direction, leave it in the model.

The resulting regression model supports the Fisher exact test observations in the sense that the same predictors are significant, but we see that the department-store p-value is now even smaller. Indeed, in the absence of multicollinearity, the p-value of a given variable usually becomes smaller when other relevant predictors are taken into account.

On stepwise techniques. This technique of allowing prior assumptions to guide variable selection, and potentially reporting non-significant effects, contrasts with the use of automated *stepwise* model selection techniques, such as is found in VARBRUL, which may be familiar to many sociolinguists but which are the target of derision by many statisticians (e.g., Harrell 2001: 56, 79f.). Step-up procedures are subject to the problem of omitted variable bias previously discussed. Step-down procedures do not suffer from this problem, as they begin with a full model (containing all the predictors), but there is no compelling reason the researcher shouldn't stop there. If a predictor actually has a small effect, it is beneficial, and if it does not, it does no harm. In contrast, the coefficients of any marginally significant predictor that are retained by stepwise methods are biased upwards in comparison.

Nesting and regression. The previous model measured a sociolinguistic variable's distribution according to department store, the grammar-internal effects of different phonological context ("fourth" vs. "floor"), and contrasts with respect to style (repetition). Since there are no more than four tokens per speaker, and 264 speakers in the sample, there is no reason to believe that some speaker outlier is driving the trend; even if some speakers in this sample do differ drastically from the rest of the population in their usage of post-vocalic *r*, one can no more detect these outliers in this data than one could reasonably assess whether a coin is or is not fair after flipping it only four times, since even a fair coin will come out all heads or all tails 12.5 percent of the time.

As mentioned above, it is generally understood that speakers may differ from each other in their overall rates of usage of different variants. What has not been as widely acknowledged is that this means when there are many tokens per speaker in the sample, that the differences between speakers must be modeled in order to satisfy the assumption of independent outcomes (see above). As already mentioned, the above fixed-effects logistic regression models do not provide any appropriate solution to the nesting between speaker and other demographic factors. One method to deal with this problem is to compute separate models by speaker, and then perform inference over the coefficients of the individual models (e.g., Gelman & Hill 2007: chapter 12; Rousseau & Sankoff 1978; Guy 1980), but this does not allow us to constrain speakers from the same speech community to behave the same with respect to grammatical constraints on variation, despite our strong bias that speakers from the same community share these constraints (Guy 1980).

Mixed-effects Regression

Mixed-effects models (Pinheiro & Bates 2000) are a recent innovation in regression which allow for, in addition to the familiar stratum of fixed-effects predictors, a set of predictors called *random effects* providing a natural solution to the nesting problem. An advantage of the mixed-effects model is that in most cases it returns more accurate *p*-values compared to a fixed-effects model that ignores nesting.

Random intercepts. The simplest type of mixed-effects model augments a standard regression with a *random intercept*, which is a predictor consisting of many levels (such as unique identifiers for the different speakers in the sample). During model fitting, the variance attributable to different levels of the random intercept is estimated, and each level of the random-effects predictor is mapped onto this normal distribution in a way that preserves the essential insight that speakers are otherwise the same. This is particularly useful for measuring the differences between speakers when a researcher is interested in social factors like gender or ethnicity in a nesting relationship with speaker identity.

Another application of random intercepts is to model word-level effects. One may have a null hypothesis that once phonological context, grammatical effects, and so on, are controlled for, there is no effect of word identity on sociophonetic variables, but there are many reports of purely lexical effects in variation (e.g., Neu 1980: 50). However, words and grammatical category may be in a nesting relationship, making word identity a good candidate for a random intercept.

An advantage of the mixed-effects model is that in many cases, it returns reduced, and more accurate, significance levels (i.e., smaller *p*-values) compared to a fixed-effects model that ignores by-subject and by-word grouping. This can be illustrated using data on the English of adolescent Polish immigrants in the United Kingdom collected by Schleef, Clark, and Meyerhoff (2011); here, the focus is a subset of their sample gathered in London. The data consists of 925 tokens of the variable (ing) from 21 speakers and representing 123 word types. This variable concerns the realization of the final consonant in word-final <ing> sequences. In addition to the velar nasal and coronal nasal articulations included here, the data also contains a third category, where the variable is realized with an oral velar stop (e.g., [iŋk]). Henceforth, this final variant is ignored, leaving 718 tokens from 21 speakers.

Despite the modest size of the data set, a fixed-effects regression identifies three significant between-word predictors (preceding phonological segment, grammatical category, and lexical frequency) and three significant between-speaker predictors (gender, English proficiency level, and friendship network), summarized in table 11.3. The fixed-effects model finds all six of these predictors highly significant. One surprising effect is that, while a higher degree of English proficiency results in a higher rate of the coronal variant, speakers with a mostly Polish friendship network are also more likely to use the coronal variant than those with a mixed or mainly English network. One might have expected that both these predictors were imperfect measures of the speaker's contact with first-language English, and thus would pattern together.

The effect of the remaining between-speaker predictor, gender, is also surprising. Whereas men generally use more of a stigmatized variant than women (Labov 2001: 264), Polish women (22 percent coronal tokens from 12 females) favor the stigmatized coronal variant more than men (9 percent coronal tokens from nine men). While this different in rate is somewhat small in absolute terms, the fixed-effects model treats gender as significant ($p = 0.015$).

The addition of random intercepts for speaker and lexical item results in somewhat different patterns of significance. All three of the between-word predictors are still found to be significant (the reported significance levels are now roughly $p = 0.001$ instead of several orders of magnitude smaller), indicating that the effects are unlikely to be due only to properties of individual words in the sample. However, as shown in table 11.3, none of the three between-speaker predictors reaches significance, and one cannot reject the null hypothesis that they have no effect on (ing).

Random slopes. Whereas the random intercepts used above adjust the model's predictions for any speaker or word, mixed-effects models can also include random slopes. These can be used, for example, to allow speakers not only to differ in the rate at which they use a variant, but also to differ in the size of the effect of between-word constraints, such as phonological context. While there may be a null hypothesis that such differences are not present in the speech community once per-speaker intercepts are properly accounted for, mixed-effects models are capable of testing this null hypothesis without elevating it to the level of a potentially dangerous assumption. Random intercepts and slopes are of particular use for modeling the results of laboratory experiments where

Table 11.3. Polish English (ing) in London fixed-effects and mixed-effects logistic regression

	Fixed-effects model		Mixed-effects model	
	log-odds	*p*-value	log-odds	*p*-value
(intercept)	−2.828	4.7e-14	−3.106	8.1e-08
lexical frequency (log)	0.978	2.0e-08	1.215	3.29e-05
noun	−0.532	6.3e-05	−0.716	0.004
verb	0.857		1.214	
gerund	0.001		0.173	
adjective	0.924		−1.204	
preposition	0.198		0.158	
discourse marker	−1.446		−0.622	
preceding apical consonant	−0.530	1.7e-05	−0.592	7.7e-04
preceding dorsal consonant	1.002		1.215	
other preceding consonant	−0.472		−0.622	
male	−0.547	1.9e-04	−0.381	0.185
female	0.547		0.381	
little English proficiency	−0.187	1.5e-06	−0.132	0.260
good English proficiency	−0.678		−0.584	
very good English proficiency	0.865		0.717	
mostly Polish friendship network	0.648	0.029	0.683	0.445
mixed friendship network	0.266		0.286	
mostly English friendship network	−0.914		−0.969	

subjects, stimuli, and conditions may all interact (e.g., Baayen, Davidson, & Bates 2008; Gorman 2009).

Summary

This section has described the application of univariate and multivariate techniques to modeling the predictors of the classic variety of sociolinguistic variable, binary outcomes in complementary distribution.

Methods for Multinomial Variables

For binary outcomes, logistic regression is the tool of choice. However, a sociolinguistic variable may be categorical, but have more than two variants in competition, as is the case with many consonantal variables. In some cases, a prior theory of the variable may make it reasonable to model these alternatives with separate binary logistic regressions. However, if the hierarchical structure of the variable is not absolutely clear, then the appropriate tool is *multinomial logistic regression*. In its most common implementation, this method does nothing more than fit multiple logistic models to the data simultaneously. However, if there is a natural ordering to the variants, and additional assumptions are reasonable, it is possible to fit a more constrained (and thus more powerful) model, *ordinal logistic regression*.

To illustrate these assumptions, we consider 8071 tokens of post-vocalic *r* gathered in Gretna, Scotland, one of the four communities investigated by the Accent and Identity on the Scottish-English Border (AISEB) project (Llamas 2010). The quality of the *r* sound was given a narrow transcription, but here we collapse the observations into three categories: taps/trills, approximants, and zero.[3] Since post-vocalic *r* is disappearing in apparent time in Gretna—moving away from a Scottish standard and toward an English one—the change can be thought of as a lenition process with a natural ordering: tap/trills > approximants > zero, and thus is a candidate for ordinal logistic regression.

To check the assumptions of a proportional odds ordinal logistic regression model, an unordered multinomial logistic regression is applied to the data. This model includes three binary external predictors: age group (older, 57–82, vs. younger, 15–27), gender (female vs. male), and social class (middle class vs. working class). The 40 Gretna speakers are a balanced sample of these external predictors, with five speakers belonging to each of the eight combinations of these three external predictors. Internal predictors relating to syllable stress, speech style, and the identity of the preceding and following segments are also included. These are *nuisance variables*, meaning that we wish to control for their effects to prevent omitted variable bias, but they are not the focus of this investigation and their effects will not be discussed. For the three external predictors, the multinomial regression produces two intercepts and six coefficients. Since each speaker in the sample produces many tokens, a mixed-effects model with a per-subject intercept would be ideal, but at the time of writing we are unaware of any software that fully supports mixed-effects multinomial models. For this reason, table 11.4 reports the log-odds, but not the potentially misleading *p*-values.

The three-valued outcome has one baseline category, here the most conservative variant: taps/trills. Each predictor is associated with two coefficients, one for approximants, and one for zeros. The first coefficient, for approximants,

Table 11.4. Gretna (r) unordered multinomial logistic regression (external effects only)

	Log-odds (approximant vs. tap/trill)	Log-odds (zero vs. tap/trill)
(intercept)	2.601	3.209
younger	0.605	1.377
older	−0.605	−1.377
male	−0.457	−0.502
female	0.457	0.502
working class	−0.024	−0.052
middle class	0.024	0.052

represents the estimated adjustment, in that environment, to the log-odds of an approximant occurring instead of a tap or trill. The coefficient for zero represents the adjustment to the log-odds of a zero occurring instead of a tap or trill.

The model output contains two intercept terms, 2.601 for approximants and 3.209 for zeros. The numbers are related to the raw proportions of the response categories—6.3 percent taps/trills, 33.3 percent approximants, and 60.3 percent zero—but adjusted to represent the mean over all the possible cells formed by the predictor variables.

The two coefficients for female gender, 0.457 for approximants and 0.502 for zeros, indicate that these two variants are approximately equally favored by females as opposed to taps/trills. A cross-tabulation shows the same fact: overall, females produced only 4.3 percent taps/trills while males produced 8.4 percent. (Note that gender has little effect on the contrast between approximants and zeros, a fact which will be important later.)

The coefficients for the younger age group, 0.605 for approximants, and 1.377 for zeros, indicate that younger speakers favor approximants over taps/trills even more than older speakers do, and that younger speakers favor zeros over taps/trills much more than older speakers do. The coefficients for social class show only a small effect in the expected direction: the middle class favors more advanced, lenited forms, while the working class preserves more traditional variants.

Some of the coefficients of this model suggest the data does not satisfy the *proportional odds* assumption of the ordinal logistic regression model. The ordinal regression divides the three-outcome variation into two cut-points: taps/trills versus {approximants, zeros} and {taps/trills, approximants} versus zeros. An ordinal model with proportional odds assumes that the predictors affect both of these cut-points identically, so there will be only one coefficient for each binary predictor, rather than *k–1* for *k* response categories, as in the unordered multinomial model.

Under proportional odds, the difference between male and female speakers must have the same effect at the two cut-points, but this is not the case here: speakers' gender has quite an effect on "first step" of lenition, from taps/trills to one of the other categories, but has little effect at the "second step," from one of the first two categories to zeros. At the first cut-point, we see 174 taps/trills versus 3894 approximants/zeros for women, and 338 taps/trills versus 3665 approximants/zeros for men. Women favor the more lenited variants by 95.7 percent to 91.6 percent, a difference of 0.725 log-odds. At the second cut-point, there are 1569 taps/trills/approximants versus 2499 zeroes for women, and 1634 taps/trills/approximants versus 2369 zeroes for men. Here, women favor the more lenited variant by 61.4 percent to 59.2 percent, a difference of only 0.094 log-odds. The proportional odds assumption does not hold with respect to gender.

For this reason, it would be inappropriate to force the Gretna post-vocalic *r* data into a proportional odds ordinal regression, although this does not indicate that the three variants are truly unordered, or that the two different stages of lenition are independent phenomena.

Ordinal logistic regression is better suited to model data on /ay/-diphthongization in Waldorf, Maryland, reported by Bowie (2001). This data set, consisting of 4038 tokens collected from 25 speakers, was originally coded with a three-way response variable: "monophthong" (9.8 percent) versus "weak glide" (12.9 percent) versus "full glide" (77.3 percent). However, the distinction was collapsed into a binary one—monophthong versus diphthong (i.e., weak and full-glide tokens)—before multivariate analysis, because the distinction between weak and full diphthongs was "not found to produce meaningful results" (342).

Bowie (2001) provides a full discussion of all the predictors analyzed, including stress, style, following phonological environment, and syntactic environment, but here, the focus is on two external predictors, age and gender. There is a clear effect of age, with younger speakers more likely to use the diphthong. Similarly, females lead in the use of the standard (diphthongal) variant. Under the hypothesis that this is an ordered process—monophthong > weak glide > full glide—then the two-way choice analyzed in Bowie (2001) is the first cut-point of an ordinal regression. The second cut-point separates monophthongs and weak diphthongs, on the one hand, from full diphthongs, on the other. We first validate the proportional odds assumption with an unordered multinomial regression model, and find that age and gender affect both steps of the diphthongization process to a similar degree, in contrast to what was observed in the Gretna sample. There are also formal tests for validating a proportional odds assumption, but Harrell (2001: 335) reports that these tests too-frequently reject the null hypothesis of proportional odds, and thus an informal approach is sufficient. We then fit an ordered multinomial model to the data; the between-speaker results are summarized in table 11.5. The results suggests that the weak/full glide distinction is indeed meaningful in this data. This is expected if monophthongization proceeds gradually, and what were

Table 11.5. Waldorf /ay/-monophthongization ordered multinomial logistic regression (external effects only)

	log-odds
Strong vs. weak glide/monophthong	1.323
Strong/weak glide vs. monophthong	2.579
male	0.336
female	−0.336
born before 1920	1.858
born 1920–1939	0.371
born 1940–1949	0.366
born 1950–1959	−0.404
born 1960–1969	−0.412
born 1970–1979	−0.954
born after 1980	−0.825

recorded as weak and full glides are not natural categories but rather a useful categorization assigned to a continuous variable, such as glide length.

If one is dealing with an ordered response and the data conforms to the proportional odds assumption, there are two main advantages to using an ordinal method. First, the coefficient estimates should be more accurate in the sense that the model will better describe the underlying population and be more useful for the prediction of future data. The second advantage to an ordinal method is that is it lowers the likelihood of Type II error (failing to reject a null hypothesis when the alternative hypothesis is true), while avoiding the problems inherent in making multiple comparisons over the results of separate binary regressions. If we have reason to believe that a multiple-variant outcome reflects an underlying ordering, then some form of ordinal modeling is desirable.

Methods for Continuous Variables

Often the variables of interest can be measured on a continuous scale, such as acoustic measures extracted from a recorded speech signal. This section compares several modern methods used to study continuous outcomes. The methods described are used here to study vowel formants in the F1 x F2 space, but such techniques apply naturally to continuous outcomes of other types.

Bigham, White-Sustaíta, and Hinrichs (2009) administered word lists to 52 Anglo-American, Mexican American, and African American speakers in Austin,

Texas; here we look at paired tokens of *bot* and *bought*, and *hod* and *hawed*. *Bot* and *hod* represent a vowel (written LOT, following Wells 1982) that is etymologically distinct from the vowel of bought and *hawed* (written THOUGHT), but these vowel classes have merged or are in the process of merging for many North American English speakers.

Simple Two-Sample Tests

These two-sample tests are univariate methods that can be used to test the null hypothesis that the two etymological classes are acoustically identical at the population level.

The t-test. The *t*-test is a class of methods for testing the null hypothesis that two subsamples have identical means. These samples can either be *paired*, in which case each observation from one subsample stands in a one-to-one relationship with an observation from the other subsample, or *unpaired*, when this does not hold. The Bigham et al. data consists strictly of minimal pairs, so it is natural to pair tokens of *hod* and *hawed*, and *bot* and *bought*, respectively. Even when the pairing requires the researcher to exclude words that are not one part of a minimal pair, Herold (1990: 73) and Johnson (2010: 108) argue that unpaired *t*-tests are a poor tool for quantifying merger, since the tests frequently result in assigning a significant effect for vowel class even to speakers who are judged by the researcher to be merged in production. This is likely caused by the omission of phonological context, which happens to be associated with vowel class membership.

Variance (equal to the standard deviation squared) is a standard measure of how far away individual values in a sample or population are from the mean. When two subsamples have the same variance, they are said to be *homoscedastic*, and heteroscedastic otherwise. For this data, the assumption of homoscedasticity is not strictly true: THOUGHT has lower variance for both F1 and F2. Heteroscedasticity between two vowel classes undergoing merger has been observed in other studies (e.g., Johnson 2010: 113, 128); this may indicate that the speaker is style-shifting towards, or away from, merger. The *unequal-variance* varieties of the *t*-test, which do not assume homoscedasticity, are the default choice for most tasks and it is this type that is used here. The results for the two formants find a difference in F1 ($p = 0.0024$) and in F2 ($p = 1.9e\text{-}05$), and inspection of the means and medians shows that LOT is lower and more front than THOUGHT.

The Wilcoxon test. The *t*-test used above does not assume the classes share the same degree of variance, but it does assume that the two classes are normally distributed. Since this assumption is often violated in practice, it is often preferable to use the family of Wilcoxon tests, especially when communicating with other fields (such as other social sciences) where the *t*-test has been replaced by this family of tests, which are free of assumptions of homoscedasticity or normally distributed data. Whereas the *t*-tests compare means, and therefore can be greatly influenced by outlying data points, the Wilcoxon tests focus on medians, for which the influence of outliers is minimal. The test used here, the *Wilcoxon signed rank* test, evaluates the null hypothesis that the paired sets of vowels have the same median formant values; the resulting p values for F1 (p = 0.002), and and F2 (p = 8.7e-05) are now somewhat smaller.

Tests with Multiple Predictors

Both the *t*-test and the Wilcoxon test found a significant difference between LOT and THOUGHT for F1 and F2. However, these univariate tests are of less use for looking at the demographic predictors of merger, since they only allow the data to be partitioned into two subsamples. In many cases, the data is unbalanced according to the various other predictors (because, for instance, it was collected from spontaneous speech), which means that a failure to control for demographic factors or grammatical factors can undermine the attempt to determine whether the two vowels are underlyingly different.

Mixed-effect regression. Linear regression is the classic technique for one or more predictors of continuous outcomes; the most basic case is not illustrated here. Linear regression also permits random effects to be included as predictors. While linear regression by default assumes homoscedasticity between binary predictors, it is also possible to allow for heteroscedasticity between, for instance, the two vowel classes.

To compute such a model over the whole sample, F1 and/or F2 values are the outcomes, and vowel-class identity and the following consonant (/t/ or /d/) are the fixed effects. To these models it is possible to add in per-speaker predictors that address the role of ethnicity, gender, and age on participation in the merger; these three are treated as fixed-effects interactions with vowel class. These interaction terms are simply the "predictor" vectors derived from the combination of vowel class and ethnicity, so that the model estimates the effect of vowel class for the whole population, but also the effect of vowel class for each ethnic group. The final components to this model are per-speaker intercepts and a random-effect interaction (or random slope) between speaker and vowel identity. The former controls for physiological differences between speakers which influence formant measures (i.e., it is a form of normalization), and the latter allows speakers to differ on their participation in the merger. Table 11.6 reports the subset of the F2 model that pertains to age and ethnicity. The column marked "estimate" reports the predicted change in F2 in Hz.

The F2 model finds a small but significant difference between the F2 of LOT and THOUGHT; for Anglo speakers, the predicted size of the contrast is approximately 70 Hz. However, there is a strong interaction between vowel class and the other two ethnicities: African American speakers have twice as large a contrast, whereas the contrast is almost completely neutralized for Mexican American speakers.

Table 11.6. Austin LOT/THOUGHT F2 heteroscedastic mixed-effects regression

	estimate	*p*-value
(intercept)	1216.47	2.2e-16
LOT	35.57	0.001
THOUGHT	−35.57	
male	−74.56	3.6e-05
female	74.56	
Anglo-American	−0.69	0.773
African American	11.21	
Mexican American	−10.52	
Anglo-American and LOT	−0.71	0.011
Anglo-American and THOUGHT	0.71	
African American and LOT	35.40	
African American and THOUGHT	−35.40	
Mexican American and LOT	−34.68	

Tests for Multivariate Outcomes

So far, F1 and F2 have been treated separately, focusing on F2's more robust separation of the vowel classes. Modeling the two formants separately makes the results difficult to interpret, since there may be some correlation between the two, especially near the bottom of the vowel space, (and of course, F2 is defined in such a way that it is always greater than F1). Just as multiple predictors are needed to deal with complex causal structures, tests for multivariate outcomes are a necessity when the outcome itself exists on more than one dimension. The designs considered in this section all convert the data into a per-speaker measure of the separation between the two vowel classes.

Euclidean distance. One way to compute a distance between two vowel classes is to compute the *Euclidean* (or Cartesian, or Pythagorean) *distance* (e.g., Gordon et al. 2004:145). This is simply the length that would be obtained by measuring the distance between two points in F1 x F2 plane with a ruler. The Euclidean distance between the points is given by the Pythagorean theorem: it is the square root of the sum of two quantities, the squared difference in mean F1 and the squared difference in mean F2. While this measure is intuitive, there are potential problems with it. First, the relative contribution of F1 and F2 to the ultimate distance measure is fixed to be equal, which may be undesirable when one of the acoustic measures has a larger range or different variance. Secondly, we have not addressed the possibility of correlations between F1 and F2; any correlative structure will be artificially inflated when they are combined in this fashion.

Multivariate analysis of variance. In a study of vowel merger, Hay, Warren, and Drager (2006) fit a type of multivariate outcome model called MANOVA to each speaker, using vowel class as the main predictor and F1 and F2 as outcomes. From these per-speaker models, Hay et al. compute a quantity called the *Pillai score* (or *trace*), which is simply the proportion of multivariate variance accounted for by the vowel class predictor. The Pillai score is near zero when no variance is accounted for by vowel class, and if all variance is due to vowel class, the Pillai score is one. This method also controls for any correlation between F1 and F2. Figure 11.1 plots the vowel-class medians of the two speakers in the Austin data with the highest, and lowest, vowel-class Pillai scores.

As can be seen, the tokens of the low Pillai score speakers are not well separated by vowel class, consistent with merger and their low score, and the speakers with the highest scores are well separated by vowel class, though these two speakers have very different acoustic targets.

Both Pillai score and Euclidean distance for the LOT-THOUGHT contrast as produced by the speakers in the *Atlas of North American English* (Labov, Ash, & Boberg 2006) is plotted in figure 11.2. The speakers are plotted by

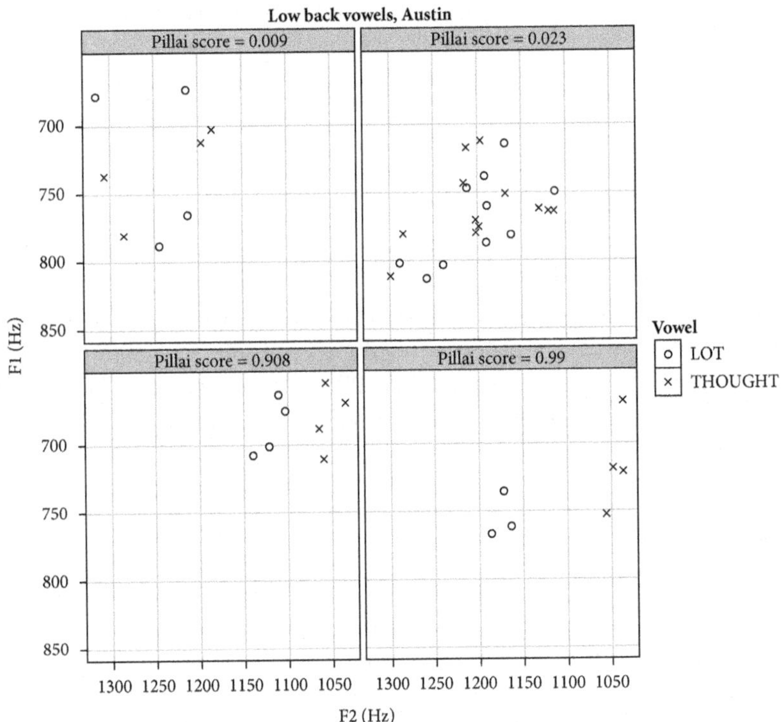

Figure 11.1. The two Austin speakers with the highest and the lowest Pillai scores for vowel class, respectively, and their vowel tokens in the F1 x F2 space

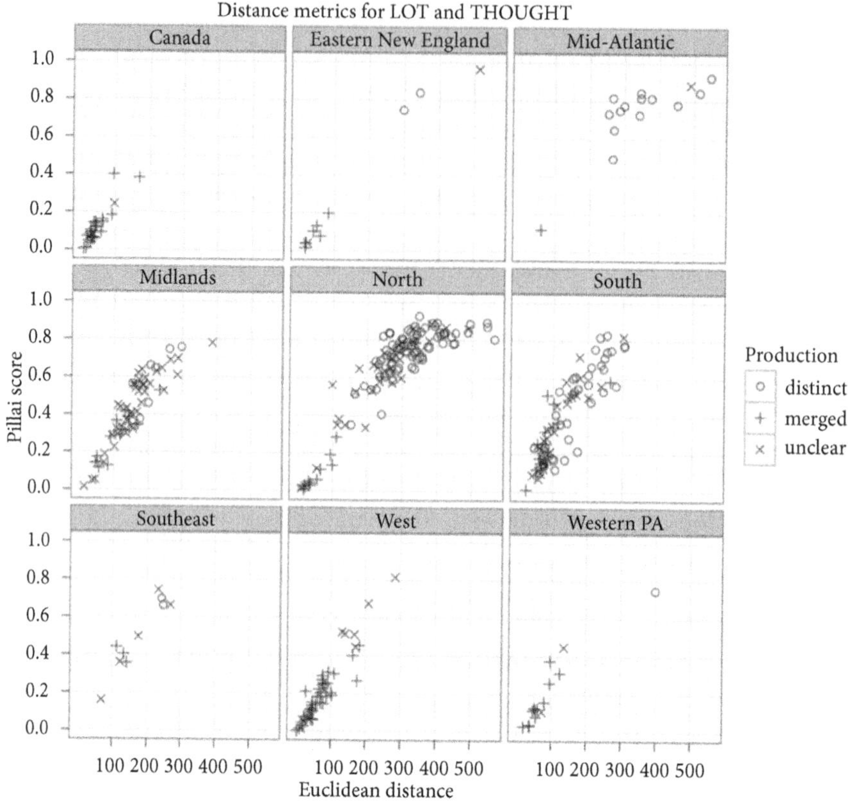

Figure 11.2. North American English LOT/THOUGHT distance by region and speaker

region (with the exception of the five speakers from New York City), and the shapes indicate the interviewers' impressionistic coding of the degree to which the speaker was perceived to be merged. As can be seen, the two measures are highly correlated in all nine regions. At least in this case, the Pillai score and Euclidean distance metrics produce results so similar that they can be used interchangeably. The one caveat is that Pillai score may not be appropriate when the number of observations per speaker is very small.

Summary

Sociolinguists can deploy a rich variety of methods in the study of continuous outcomes, including paired univariate methods with and without the assumptions of heteroscedasticity and normality (*t*-tests and Wilcoxon tests), mixed-effect linear regression, and models for correlated multivariate outcomes (MANOVA). As always, it is crucial to attend to the assumptions inherent in statistical techniques.

CONCLUSION

Having shown the effects that assumptions about the data make on the results of inferential analysis, the one assumption that remains to be considered is the *frequentist* paradigm itself.

A Bayes new world? Frequentism is the name given to the traditional approach to statistics that coalesced in the early twentieth century around the statisticians Egon Pearson, Ronald Fisher, and their collaborators, and implicitly assumed in this chapter; it stands in contrast with a second paradigm known as *Bayesianism,* after eighteenth-century minister Thomas Bayes, which has developed only in the past few decades. Whereas frequentist analysis is concerned with the probability of rejecting a null hypothesis, the Bayesian approach focuses on the change in probability of a null hypothesis before and after performing data collection and statistical testing. The following example illustrates this contrast.

Frequentism and Friday effects. A sociolinguist's data collection is very much influenced by prior knowledge about the speech community, universals of language variation, and so on. The null hypotheses that are ultimately subject to testing are generally quite likely to be false; in Bayesian terms, the prior probability of the null hypothesis is quite low, and consequently, its rejection is not a particular surprise. This logic has more interesting consequences when one considers a null hypothesis that is quite likely to be true, such as the hypothesis that New Yorkers produce the same rates of the variants of post-vocalic *r* on Fridays as during the rest of the week. If however a statistical test reports a significant Friday effect (e.g., $p = 0.03$), frequentist principles require the researcher to take this result seriously, even in the absence of a mechanistic explanation for any component of this correlation between days of the week and phonetic variation.

However, the Bayesian theory has a different take on this kind of unlikely, but significant, result. It is only rational that to reject such a strongly believed null hypothesis demands extraordinary evidence to cause us to shift our beliefs. Jeffreys (1939) describes a Bayesian method to integrate our prior beliefs about the non-existence of Friday effects with the result of the experiment. Before the experiment, the researcher must specify a prior probability of the null hypothesis. While Labov's study of New York City post-vocalic *r* discussed earlier has several replications over the last half century, none of the studies mention day-of-week effects, nor are they discussed in any sociolinguistic work of which we are aware. Given this, one might somewhat arbitrarily say that the prior probability of the null hypothesis is 0.99; that is, it is unlikely that the null hypothesis is false and there really is a Friday effect. The posterior probability (i.e., the probability that the null hypothesis is true after the statistical test) is given by dividing the *p*-value of the statistical test by the sum of the following two terms: the product of the *p*-value and the prior probability, and the product of the one minus the p-value and one minus the prior. For this example, the denominator is (0.03 x 0.99) + (0.97 x 0.01) = 0.039, and thus the posterior probability is 0.03/0.039 = 0.761. The change from the prior probability of 0.99 to the posterior of 0.7614 indicates that this single test has not deeply shaken the faith in the null hypothesis of no Friday effect. While sociolinguistics has not generally used such explicit computation of posterior probabilities, it seems unlikely a single Fridays effect study would take the field by storm, simply because of the a priori unlikeliness of such an effect. After all, events of probability 0.03 do occur by chance—3 percent of the time, to be precise—so a p-value of 0.03 should not lead to abject certainty in the veracity of the alternative hypothesis.

Proving the null. Conversely, when we apply statistical analysis under the frequentist approach and the data fails to provide strong evidence to reject a null hypothesis, it does not necessarily mean that the null hypothesis is true: the failure to reject the null hypothesis may be due to too little data or failing to control for nuisance variables, and it does not rule out the existence of some other alternative hypothesis that would result in rejection of the null. Bayesian statistical analysis tools allow the researcher to estimate the probability of the null hypothesis (e.g., Gallistel 2009). The finding of a non-effect (like Fridays) or non-interaction (for instance, between style and internal constraints on variants, as proposed by Sankoff & Labov 1979) may itself be of considerable sociolinguistic import, and only Bayesian methods are capable of identifying them.

Against a Statistical Monoculture

The collaboration between statisticians and sociolinguists in the 1970s was a fruitful one, but advances in statistics since then have been slow to diffuse into sociolinguistic practice. Mixed-effects models provide sociolinguists with an important new tool to excise the assumption that speakers or words, for instance, do not behave differently once appropriate demographic or grammatical constraints have been taken into account. While mixed-effects models provide a reasonable way to test this intuitively reasonable null hypothesis and identify when it is false, using fixed-effects models that fail to address these concerns may produce spurious inferences (Gorman 2010).

Cross-fertilization. Sociolinguists have recently availed themselves of sophisticated psycholinguistic paradigms (Loudermilk, chapter 7 this volume), and the potential for collaboration is clear. In psycholinguistics, subject and word effects have been addressed for decades (e.g., Clark 1973), and the leading *Journal of Memory and Language* recently dedicated an issue (volume 59, no. 4) to best practices in statistical analysis, which recommends mixed-effects models for these purposes. A shared statistical vocabulary will only strengthen the alliance between sociolinguists and psycholinguists (among other research communities).

Some new tools. Sociolinguists have long benefited from free software packages like VARBRUL (and descendants like GoldVarb). In the past, those who wished to use other methods (such as more-general regression models) had no choice but to pay large sums for proprietary statistical software. Sociolinguists can now avail themselves of a huge library of statistical methods using the free, cross-platform environment known as R, which has become the lingua franca for quantitative analysis of every stripe. R, of course, is capable of emulating the features of VARBRUL.[4]

There is a learning curve associated with a new statistical interface, and R is no exception. The second author is the creator of Rbrul (Johnson 2009), which provides a guided interface for regression modeling with random effects, continuous predictors and/or responses, and interactions, but this is only a stopgap measure, and researchers wishing to avail themselves of the full power of modern statistics will need the full power of modern statistical software. While this may seem daunting, it is important for sociolinguists to rise to the statistical challenges posed by their complex and meaningful data in furtherance of science.

Acknowledgment

Thanks to all those who provided the data analyzed in this chapter, especially Miriam Meyerhoff, Lynn Clark, Dominic Watt, David Bowie, Douglas Bigham, and Lars Hinrichs. We would also like to thank Douglas Bates and other members of the R-sig-ME mailing list for their wisdom.

Notes

1. In this chapter, we use p-values to report the "exact level of significance" (Gigerenzer, Krauss, & Vitouch 2004), and thus do not limit ourselves to statements like "$p < 0.05$."
2. One such case was brought to our attention by Robert Bayley. Lucas, Bayley, and Valli (2001), in a large-scale survey of variation in American Sign Language (ASL), translate the age of a signer into a three-level predictor, under the reasonable hypothesis that the true relevance of age to variation in their population is that informants of different ages encountered different administrative policies toward ASL in the classroom. Recent work by these authors and collaborators (McCaskill, Lucas, Bayley, & Hill 2011), which focuses on ASL in the African American community, groups signers into those who attended school before and after integration of the schools for Deaf children in the southern United States.

3. The models presented in this section depend on having data on the level of the observation, making it possible to control for any grammatical predictors on opposing variants. If all that is available are the percentages of variants used by each speaker, an appropriate method is *compositional data analysis* (Aitchison 2003).
4. All the analyses and graphics in this chapter were created in R. Some of the code used in this chapter is available at http://ling.upenn.edu/~kgorman/papers/handbook/.

References

Aitchison, J. 2003. *The statistical analysis of compositional data*, 2nd ed. Caldwell, NJ: Blackburn Press.

Baayen, R. H., Davidson, D., & Bates, D. 2008. Mixed-effects modeling with crossed random effects for subjects and items. *Journal of Memory and Language* 59: 390–412.

Bayley, R. 2002. The quantitative paradigm. In J. K. Chambers, P. Trudgill, & N. Schilling-Estes (eds.), *Handbook of language variation and change*, 117–41. Oxford: Blackwell.

Bigham, D., White-Sustaíta, J., & Hinrichs, L. 2009. Apparent-time low vowels among Mexican-Americans and Anglos in Austin, Texas. Paper presented at NWAV 39, University of Ottawa.

Borowsky, T. 1986. Topics in the lexical phonology of English. Ph.D. dissertation, University of Massachusetts, Amherst. Published by Garland, New York, 1991.

Bowie, D. 2001. The diphthongization of /ay/: Abandoning a southern norm in southern Maryland. *Journal of English Linguistics* 29: 329–45.

Bybee, J. 2002. Word frequency and context of use in the lexical diffusion of phonetically conditioned sound change. *Language Variation and Change* 14: 261–90.

Cedergren, H. 1973. The social dialects of Panama. Ph.D. dissertation, Cornell University.

Clark, H. 1973. The language-as-fixed-effect fallacy: A critique of language statistics in psychological research. *Journal of Verbal Learning and Verbal Behavior* 12: 335–59.

Cohen, J. 1983. The cost of dichotomization. *Applied Statistical Measurement* 7(3): 249–53.

Gallistel, R. 2009. The importance of proving the null. *Psychological Review* 116: 439–453.

Gelman, A., & Hill, J. 2007. *Data analysis using regression and multilevel/hierarchical models*. Cambridge: Cambridge University Press..

Gigerenzer, G., Krauss, S., & Vitouch, O. 2004. The null ritual: What you always wanted to know about significance testing but were afraid to ask. In D. Kaplan (ed.), *Sage handbook of quantitative methodology for the social sciences*, 391–408. Thousand Oaks, CA: Sage.

Gordon, E., Campbell, L., Hay, J., Maclagan, M., Sudbury, A., & Trudgill, P. 2004. *New Zealand English: Its origins and evolution*. Cambridge: Cambridge University Press.

Gorman, K. 2009. Hierarchical regression modeling for language research. Technical Report 09–02, Institute for Research in Cognitive Science, University of Pennsylvania. http://repository.upenn.edu/ircs_reports/202/.

Gorman, K. 2010. The consequences of multicollinearity among socioeconomic predictors of negative concord in Philadelphia. *University of Pennsylvania Working Papers in Linguistics* 16(2): 66–75.

Guy, G. R. 1980. Variation in the group and the individual: The case of final stop deletion. In W. Labov (ed.), *Locating language in space and time*, 1–35. New York: Academic Press.

Guy, G. R. 1991. Explanation in variable phonology: An exponential model of morphological constraints. *Language Variation and Change* 3: 1–22.

Harrell, F. 2001. *Regression modeling strategies: With applications to linear models, logistic regression, and survival analysis.* New York: Springer.

Hay, J., Warren, P., & Drager, K. 2006. Factors influencing speech perception in the context of a merger-in-progress. *Journal of Phonetics* 34: 458–84.

Herold, R. 1990. Mechanisms of merger: The implementation and distribution of the low back merger in Eastern Pennsylvania. Ph.D. dissertation, University of Pennsylvania.

Jeffreys, H. 1939. *Theory of probability.* Oxford: Oxford University Press.

Johnson, D. E. 2009. Getting off the GoldVarb standard: Introducing Rbrul for mixed-effects variable rule analysis. *Language and Linguistics Compass* 3: 359–83.

Johnson, D. E. 2010. *Stability and change along a dialect boundary: The low vowels southeastern New England.* Publications of the American Dialect Society 95. Durham, NC: Duke University Press.

Johnson, D. E. In press. Descriptive statistics. In R. Podesva & D. Sharma (eds.), *Research methods in linguistics.* Cambridge: Cambridge University Press.

Labov, W. 2001. *Principles of linguistic change: Social factors.* Malden, MA: Wiley-Blackwell.

Labov, W. 2006. *The social stratification of English in New York City*, 2nd ed. Cambridge: Cambridge University Press.

Labov, W., Ash, S., & Boberg, C. 2006. *The atlas of North American English: Phonetics, phonology, and sound change.* Berlin: Mouton de Gruyter.

Lennig, M. 1978. Acoustic measurements of linguistic change: The modern Paris vowel system. Ph.D. dissertation, University of Pennsylvania.

Llamas, C. 2010. Convergence and divergence across a national border. In C. Llamas & D. Watt (eds.), *Language and identities*, 227–36. Edinburgh: Edinburgh University Press.

Lucas, C., Bayley, R., Valli, C. 2001. *Sociolinguistic variation in American Sign Language.* Washington, DC: Gallaudet University Press.

McCaskill, C., Lucas, C., Bayley, R., & Hill, J. 2011. *The hidden treasure of Black ASL: Its history and structure.* Washington, DC: Gallaudet University Press.

Neu, H. 1980. Ranking of constraints on /t, d/ deletion in American English: A statistical analysis. In W. Labov (ed.), *Locating language in space and time*, 37–54. New York: Academic Press.

Pinheiro, J., & Bates, D. 2000. *Mixed-effects models in S and S-PLUS.* New York: Springer.

Rousseau, P., & Sankoff, D. 1978. Advances in variable rule methodology. In D. Sankoff (ed.), *Linguistic variation: Models and methods*, 57–69. New York: Academic Press.

Sankoff, D., & Labov, W. 19679. On the uses of variable rules. *Language and Society* 8: 189–222.

Schleef, E., Clark, L., & Meyerhoff, M. 2011. Teenagers' acquisition of variation: A comparison of locally-born and migrant teens' realisation of English (ing) in Edinburgh and London. English World-Wide 32: 206–36.

Tagliamonte, S. & Temple, R. 2005. New perspectives on an ol' variable: (t, d) in British English. Language Variation and Change 17: 281–302.

Wells, J. C. 1982. *Accents of English*. 3 volumes. New York: Cambridge University Press.

CHAPTER 12

ANALYZING QUALITATIVE DATA

MAPPING THE RESEARCH TRAJECTORY IN MULTILINGUAL CONTEXTS

JULIET LANGMAN

QUALITATIVE research methodology now has a sufficient history in multiple fields as well as with multiple epistemological approaches to allow for a consideration of the tools of inquiry and their value for understanding and explaining patterns of behavior in a complex social world. Conducting qualitative research first and foremost entails developing an understanding of the details and particularities of a social context through in-depth and often long-term analysis of the social patterns and practices that are part of the fabric of a society and the social groups within it. In the case of sociolinguistic research, qualitative research requires a focus on the details and particularities of language use in context (Ramanathan & Atkinson 1999). Qualitative approaches to sociolinguistics can rely on a range of data collection and data analysis tools and approaches, but its primary focus rests on gathering data from "unsolicited and spontaneous local social events to illuminate patterns of similarities and differences across cultures" (Spolsky 1998: 9). Research in multilingual contexts offers opportunities for in-depth analysis of language use in a wide variety of contexts, often starkly juxtaposed against one another within a particular sociopolitical context.

This chapter outlines current perspectives on conducting qualitative research in multilingual contexts. More particularly, it focuses on an understanding of the unique opportunities and challenges of conducting qualitative research in multilingual contexts in which proficiency in the various languages and multiple varieties employed in the research context is a key component of research. The researcher's knowledge of, and facility in, a variety of languages, as well as the nature of the researcher's role in multiple contexts requires serious consideration.

Using data from over 10 years of ethnographic fieldwork among members of the Hungarian minority population in Eastern Europe as one example, this chapter illustrates processes involved in qualitative research, beginning with outlining a theoretical perspective, conceptualizing a research problem, gaining access in the field, developing participant and participant-observer stances, gathering and organizing data, and finally, analyzing and verifying analyses of such data.

Historical Approaches to Qualitative Analysis of Language in Use

Parallel with the work of William Labov in quantitative sociolinguistic research, Dell Hymes and John Gumperz pioneered two approaches to conceptualizing qualitative research on language use particularly appropriate to multilingual communities (Gumperz & Hymes 1972). Gumperz (1982a, 1982b) focused on the face-to-face immediate context of interaction with the goal of understanding how each turn at talk influences subsequent turns at talk in ways that link particular conversations to broader social issues at play in multilingual contexts. Interactional sociolinguistics rests on microlevel analyses of language use that allow researchers to uncover the origins of tensions that exist between speakers of different varieties, differences that reflect broader patterns of inequality and that can lead to miscommunication. For example, Gumperz (1982a) analyzes how Indian and British participants in three short conversations had radically different perceptions of the attitudes and intentions of the Indian participants, based on the intonation patterns they used in simple questions—while the Indians intended to convey respect and deference, the British perceived their interlocutors as "surly and uncooperative" because the communicative value of rising as opposed to falling intonation patterns on simple questions are reversed for speakers of these two different English-speaking communities.

While Gumperz focused on the nature of linguistic interactions, Hymes (1973) drew insights from the field of anthropology to develop a method for understanding the intersection of culture and language. Hymes (1973, 1974) developed the ethnography of communication, which aimed at examining systematic patterns of language use in cultural contexts, with a particular focus on contexts in which issues of power and inequality occur. A focus on inequality among cultural groups has been of primary concern in the roots of the field, and is often of primary concern in the case of research in multilingual contexts. Hymes (1973) suggested that the need for the ethnography of communication derives from the necessity of linguists to consider inequality as a key concern in social science. Moreover, he argued that inequality was only considered "implicitly, falling back on a Herderian conception of the world as composed of individual language-and-culture units...because we have not thought through new ways of seeing how linguistic resources do, in fact, come organized in the world. Thus we have no accepted way of joining our understanding of inequality with our understanding of the nature of language" (58). Finding a way to explicitly link language and culture with a concern for inequality among cultural groups is a key goal of much qualitative sociolinguistic research today.

Current Approaches

Heath and Street in their recent volume on ethnography suggest the essence of qualitative research focusing on language use:

> Talking, gesturing, and waving artifacts about in locally acceptable patterns make up the glue for conversation in all human groups. But these patterns vary across languages and societies, and they change also for individuals as they mature and gain experience with different audiences, settings, and purposes. Institutions and organizations develop their own norms and genres of interactive oral and written exchange, and success in adopting these can mean the difference between membership and exclusion for individuals. The cultural patterning of interaction shapes identities and roles that then provide access and opportunities for learners. (2008: 6)

The task of researchers is thus to gather and analyze data that, at multiple levels, allows us to understand how styles of language shape and build social meanings for individuals in the societies and communities in which they live, and how, drawing on Heath and Street, language use provides "access and opportunities."

Despite differences, all current approaches focus on ways of understanding the complex relationships between social identities that individuals express through the language choices they make, and how these social identities map onto social groupings within sociopolitical entities that interpret language as a resource and therefore differentially apportion value to the varieties of language that are used. Classic studies that take multilingualism into account by drawing on in-depth analyses of language practices in context include Gal's (1979) work among Hungarians in Austria and, later, Woolard's (1997) work among bilingual youth in Catalonia, Zentella's work among Puerto Ricans in New York City (1997), as well as the range of pieces collected in Blackledge and Pavlenko

(2001), Bayley and Schecter (2003) and Pavlenko and Blackledge (2004). All these works aim to explain language choice in multilingual contexts through a careful analysis of the range of different social contexts in which such choices occur, and the types of social and political constraints that regulate the potential range of choices for particular individuals.

Three recent frameworks have extended the early work on context as it relates to language in use, namely, the community of practice (Lave & Wenger 1991; Eckert & McConnell-Ginet 1999), the ecology of language approach (Haugen 1972), and the ideology of language framework (Schieffelin, Woolard, & Kroskrity 1998). Each of these frameworks considers language and context as socially and mutually constructed and identifies discourse and identity as mediating links.

Defining Language. In defining language, the foregoing approaches favor a definition that sees language as a dynamic, communicative practice rather than a static system of signs. Kramsch suggests that language and its use are symbolic: "[1] because it mediates our existence through symbolic forms that are conventional and represent objective realities, and [2] because symbolic forms construct subjective realties such as perceptions, emotions, attitudes, and values" (Kramsch 2009: 7). That is, language is constructed in the moment, "the actualization of potential meanings produced and received by language users in multiple contexts of communication and against multiple ideological horizons" (Kramsch & von Hoene 2001: 290). Seeing language in these terms requires an approach to research that focuses on everyday, natural language use in, for example, multilingual or immigrant communities.

Defining Context. Similarly, the three above-mentioned frameworks define context as a set of concentric circles of influence on a given situation in which language is used for particular communicative purposes. Beginning with the most local context, sociolinguists are interested in understanding how the moment-to-moment actions of one speaker in a particular time and place affect both the form of what is said and the meaning that is intended, as well as the manner in which it is interpreted by others in the interaction.

The ecology of language approach calls upon researchers to pay attention to several dimensions of multilingualism at the same time: relationships among languages, among social contexts for languages, and among speakers of languages (Hornberger 2002; Hornberger & Hult 2008). As Hult (2008: 89) notes, "Central to Haugen's (1972: 325) view of the ecology of language is a two-fold focus on individual and societal dimensions of multilingualism: How do languages interact in the minds of speakers? How do languages interact in the societies where they are used (xx)?" This approach focuses to a large extent on broad questions of the distribution of languages in society (see Creese, Martin, & Hornberger 2008 for a range of studies in multilingual contexts).

The community of practice approach (Lave & Wenger 1991; Wenger 1998) has been introduced into sociolinguistic work by Eckert and McConnell-Ginet (1992; 1999) who define it as

> an aggregate of people who come together around mutual engagement in an endeavor. Ways of doing things, ways of talking, beliefs, values, power relations—in short, practices—emerge in the course of this mutual endeavor. As a social construct, a CofP is different from the traditional community, primarily because it is defined simultaneously by its membership and by the practice in which that membership engages. (1999: 246)

In multilingual contexts, the community of practice model is useful for considering issues such as those articulated by Norton and Toohey (2002)

> to develop understandings of learners as both socially constructed and constrained but also as embodied, semiotic and emotional persons who identify themselves, resist identifications, and act on their social worlds. Learners' investments in learning languages, the ways in which their identities affect their participation in second language activities, and their access to participation in the activities of their communities, must all be matters of consideration in future research. (123)

Drawing on the community of practice model, Eckert places current sociolinguistic research in its third wave. The first wave, articulated by William Labov, employed quantitative methods, while the second wave sought to combine ethnographic research methods with the quantitative, variationist tradition, with the goal of outlining the forms of speech used by speakers as identity markers, that is ways in which language choice marks membership to or alignment with particular groups.[1] The third wave of sociolinguistic research, as Eckert argues, has shifted the focus of analysis from structure to social meaning, and focuses on individuals' styles of interaction and reflects their social identities. "Third wave studies focus on the use of variation to construct personal and social styles—styles associated with social types." (Eckert under review).

Third-wave research articulates a practice approach to understanding social identities and requires a broad understanding of both identities and contexts as multiple, layered, and complex. While the tradition of sociolinguistic research does not explicitly focus on working in multilingual communities, a wealth of earlier work, together with current practice approaches allow us to consider a set of tools for data collection that allow for a multileveled analysis of the connections between forms of language and the styles and identities their use allows individuals to create in specific and layered communities.

Langman (2003) provides a concrete example of the application of the community of practice approach in the multilingual context of Eastern Slovakia, examining Hungarian minority youth. Drawing on data collected during 10 years of contact with a dance ensemble, Langman explores the nature of socialization as learning that entails the development and practice of social identity by outlining how participation in a Hungarian dance group, called the Rock Crystal Dance Ensemble provides the context for the construction of a multifaceted Hungarian identity that is, surprisingly, within the context tolerant to and supportive of practices that tie a traditional culture to a modern multicultural world. Langman argues that the identity practiced in the context of the

Rock Crystal Dance Ensemble is one that is both reflective of and resistant to dominant language ideologies of the Slovak state, seen through the contestation of the conception of the Slovak state as monolingual, and the associated concept that Hungarians in Slovakia are unwilling to learn Slovak. Key to the analysis of Rock Crystal Dance Ensemble as a core community of practice for minority youth, is the ways in which their practices, beliefs, and values shifted in ways that were intended to show a dual focus: looking back to traditional Hungarian folkways and looking forward to a multicultural society. Through careful examination of practices embedded in the community, the CoP framework allows an analysis that extends to the broader sociopolitical context.

Using a similar framework, Kalocsai (2009) examines how part-time exchange students in Hungary develop a variety of English as a lingua franca through their association with a community of practice designed to create a safe haven in a context in which students share neither a first language, nor a strong affiliation with the context of their study sojourn.

A Language Ideology Framework

The ideology of language framework (Kroskrity 2000; Schieffelin, Woolard, & Kroskrity 1998) defines language ideologies as "[r]epresentations, whether explicit or implicit, that construe the intersection of language and human beings in a social world" (Woolard 1998: 3). Language ideology, moreover can be seen as "derived from, rooted in, reflective of, or responsive to the experience or interests of a particular social position, even though ideology so often…represents itself as universally true" (Woolard 1998: 6). Language ideology, therefore, by definition is not about language alone, but rather about the link it draws between, for example, language and identity, language and aesthetics, language and power. While the content of language ideology may vary across settings, what is important for researchers is that language ideology "is the mediating link between social forms and forms of talk" (Woolard 1998: 3). Therefore, in order to understand the meaning of text we must go beyond the propositional meaning to the ideologically enriched meaning. Through an analysis of language ideology we can examine "the social-historical processes that link face-to-face communities to national and transnational spheres" (Schieffelin et al. 1998: vi).

Ideology is therefore dependent on the social world and subject to distortion dependent on how its conceptualization is employed. Primarily, ideology constitutes, "ideas, discourse, or signifying practices in the service of the struggle to acquire or maintain power" (Woolard 1998: 7). Definitions of ideology, according to Woolard, focus on four strands but can be roughly divided into those who wish to describe phenomena (neutral) and those who focus on the use and abuse of power through ideology (critical, negative).

All discourse is ideological. From the neutral perspective we can define language ideology as a set of commonsense notions about the nature of language in the world. A critical definition of language ideology, more focused on language and activism suggests that language ideologies are " 'sets of beliefs about language articulated by users as a rationalization or justification of perceived language structure and use' " (Silverstein 1979: 193 in Woolard 1998: 4).

While local practices in local contexts are negotiated, powerful external discourses are imposed. An ideology of language framework allows us to understand the relationship of "the microculture of communicative action to political economic considerations of power and social inequality, confronting macrosocial constraints on language and behavior" (Woolard & Schieffelin 1994: 72).

One strand of the language ideology research agenda, the minority approach, has an emphasis on the "multiplicity, contradiction and contentions among ideologies within particular societies" (Scheiffelin et al.: vii), thus allowing the examination of both the powerful political ideologies enacted though majority institutions, those which Kroskrity characterized as 'truly dominant' "in the sense of being widely shared throughout a community as well as being rooted in socially authoritative strata" (Woolard 1998: 16), and those of the minority groups who challenge them. In defining ideology from this perspective, distinctions between ideology defined as "subjectively explicit" versus "constructively implicit" (Woolard 1998: 6) emerge.

Like identity, ideology is performative or socially constructed; "ideology creates and acts in a social world, while it masquerades as a description of that world" (Woolard 1998; 10). Ideolog(ies), both dominant in a given social setting, as well as conflicting ideologies, underlie and influence the nature of social interactions. That is, social interaction is not natural and transparent but rather a construction, tied to a specific social historical setting (see Gal 1993).

In the specific case of Slovakia, Langman, and Lanstyák (2000) discuss minority Hungarian rejections of majority language ideologies in the context of the 1996 Slovak language law, by examining "language as ideological when/because they are also politically, morally loaded ideas about social experience, social relationships, and group membership" (Woolard 1998: 8; see also Heath 1989 and Irvine 1989). Specifically they explore powerful language ideology through an examination of the myths that underlie an ideology (*Hungarians neither want to learn nor speak Slovak*) that places Hungarian minority members in a conflictual relationship with the state.

Drawing on the discussion of a range of theoretical perspectives for carrying out research in multilingual contexts, in what follows, I articulate examples of steps in the research process.

Choosing a Site and Collecting Data

Designing a qualitative research study into the perspectives and practices of Hungarian minority youth in the newly formed Republic of Slovakia can begin with the community of practice model for identifying a research site.

In the case of my own research, such identification and development of connections took place over the course of multiple years of fieldwork in Eastern Slovakia before and after the creation of the Republic of Slovakia in 1993. My own work ultimately focused on the language and social practices of members of a particular group, as well as the connections between members of this group and others in the wider society. As with all qualitative and, more particularly, ethnographic fieldwork, the role of the researcher in the community under study must develop over time, so that the researcher can learn about the local practices and the community members can come to trust and then share personal information and their perspectives on that information with the researcher. For the example I will provide, I spent multiple months meeting group members and being introduced in turn to additional friends and family of those I initially came in contact with. In those early months, I spent my time listening and recording my thoughts on what was of interest to the members, that is, what they talked about, what they did regularly together—in short, what their shared enterprises were and what practices they engaged in routinely. Following this initial time designed to determine if the individuals under study constituted a community of practice, I began to add interviews to my observations, to focus in on particular issues related to multilingual language use. Such interviews, carried out over several years, helped to uncover how the particular ways in which these youth used language helped them to create their particular identities as minority youth in the context of a rapidly changing society.

Analyzing Data within a Language Ideology Framework

In addition to understanding the language practices of members of a group with the purpose of uncovering how multilingualism was employed as a resource for building a particular identity—that of Hungarians maintaining traditional practices (Langman 2002a, 2003)—taking a language ideology approach is a good choice for research in contexts where language is a key source of political and national tension. Central Europe in the time of the sweeping political changes in the 1990s is such a site, because language rights and issues had become primary sites of contention in many multilingual and multicultural states in the region, due to the primary link between language and nation in (re)constructions of national identity in the postcommunist era (Kontra et al. 1999).

Concretely, a language ideology approach could be conducted as follows: local language practices are viewed and interpretations of those practices are elicited in interviews with participants, these in turn are examined in the light of multiple language ideological lenses. Langman and Lanstyák (2000) conduct such an analysis, juxtaposing the myths about Hungarians and their lack of interest in learning Slovak with narratives by Hungarian minority Slovaks in which they discuss interethnic conflicts. They analyze narratives of Hungarian minority members collected as part of a survey research on the sociolinguistic situation of Hungarians in Slovakia based on data collected in 1996. The narrative analysis first examines the nature of narrative with respect to the richness of detail versus summary or rote types of narratives that represent ideologies. The analysis then examines the narratives against a set of myths about Hungarians circulating in society at the time the data were collected in 1996. A detailed analysis of narratives about interethnic conflict from the perspective of minority group members shows that at that time there was little active resistance to the myths that cast Hungarians in a negative light from the perspective of the Slovak social order. Indeed, many of the narratives outline instances that accept the myths or ideologies as true. Drawing on Barthes (1957), the paper concludes that "'it is extremely difficult to vanquish myth from the inside: for the very effort one makes in order to escape its stranglehold becomes in its turn the prey of myth: myth can always, as a last resort, signify the resistance which is brought to bear against it'" (Barthes 1957: 135, quoted in Langman & Lanstyák 2000: 69).

Transcripts of Data

A sample transcript drawn from a larger data set can be used for developing hypotheses about the influence of language practices or styles on the identities of speakers. From a sample transcript, we can also examine the effect of language ideology on the transcription and analysis process through multilayered interactions with the data. These layers of analysis can be mediated by a number of sources besides the researcher, including the assistance of "native" assistants, and the multiple ways of focusing on forms and meanings and the attitudes toward these form-meaning connections.

The example that follows draws on ethnographic interviews that form part of a larger study among Hungarian youth in Eastern Slovakia from 1993 to 1998 (see Langman 1997, 2002a). Specifically, I examine interviews with Imre, a 23-year-old, conducted during October and November 1994, where I served as the interviewer and a Hungarian university student at a university in Budapest provided transcription assistance. Embedded in the transcript are comment lines (marked with =), which I asked the transcription assistant to insert whenever he had a comment of any kind on the words they had been instructed to record *verbatim*. I had also given some instructions on how to mark pauses, hesitations, and verbal markers, as well as some discussion on how to represent the words they heard. I did not specifically tell the transcribers to use or not use standard orthography to mark differences in pronunciation or morphology (see Edwards 2001, Bucholtz 2000, Robert 1997, & Ochs 1979 on transcription as theory).

Example 1

Irme discusses Hungarian Slovak bilingualism in his hometown in Eastern Slovakia.

1	Aranyvároson már # megvan a kétnyelvűség.	in Golden, bilingualism already exists
2	itt már aktívan beszélik,	here they already actively speak
3	általába aktivan mind a két nyelvet #	as a general rule, both languages
3A	= általába(n)	
4	itt már # itt itt más a helyzet.	here the situation is already different
5	itt elmosódik nagyon az a,	here it's mixed together alot
6	nincs meg az hogy ez szlovák	it's not such that, he's Slovak
7	vagy ez magyar.	or he's Hungarian
8	van aki # no, "én szlovák vagyok" azt mondja,	there are those well, who say "I'm Slovak"
9	"én magyar vagyok"	"I'm Hungarian"
10	de a határ el van mosódva már	but the border has already been washed away
10A	= a határ már elmosódott	

In the comments provided here, the transcriber provides 'corrections' focusing on the language style in terms of morphology (3A) and syntax (10A) switching the non-standard passive voice to the use of a verbal marker indicating completion of an action.

In response to the question of whether there are problems between Slovaks and Hungarians in Golden, Imre responds:

11	hát itten olyan problémákról	well around here about such problems
12	nem lehet beszélni mint hogy #	one can't really speak, like
13	szóval úgy kifejezetten	well specifically speaking
14	hogy konkrét esetek mit én tudom	about concrete examples, I mean
14A	= mit tudom én	
15	hogy ellentétek vagy valami # nem #	like conflicts or something, no
16	igy nem lehet beszélni tényleg	one can't really talk about such things
17	semmi ilyesmiről.	nothing like that
18	előfordul hogy # az utcán tesznek	it happens that on the street they make
19	megjegyzéseket	comments
20	hogyha meghallják az embereket hogy	if they hear that people
21	magyarul beszélnek vagy valami	are speaking Hungarian or something,
22	előfordul	that happens

22A	= [!]	
23	de ezt # ritkán# no.	but that's rare. so.
24	mert mert szerintem #	but like I think
25	mer(t) nem tudom milyen ott a helyzet	but I don't know what the situation is like there
26	Komárom meg ott, azon a környékén	Komarom and in that area
27	mer(t) ott tényleg hogy # nagy kis	because there it's a fact that there is a large min-
28	szóval kisebbségben vannak a szlovákok	like the Slovaks are in the minority
29	azon a környéken az tényleg.	in that area, that's a fact
29A	= nem meri kimondani hogy ott a magyarok élnek többségben	He doesn't dare to say that the Hungarians are in the majority there

Throughout the transcripts, the transcriber provides two types of comments, language and content. The language comments come in the form of corrections without comments as well as corrections with comment on the morphophonology, syntax, and lexicon of the speaker. Comments on the content, range from drawing attention to a comment (22A) to explanations of the meaning behind the speaker's words, as in the case of the final comment on the speaker's motivation for using a particular utterance that Slovaks are in the minority in a particular area, rather than the contrasting statement that Hungarians are in the majority there (29A). This comment further assigns a reason for this use of language, namely, that the speaker is *afraid* 'to say the truth' due to degree of nationalism in Slovakia.

The language ideology framework allows two types of analysis, a bottom-up, minority analysis, as well as an analysis on the basis of the dominant ideology in Hungary on Hungarian-Slovak relations in the 1990s in Slovakia. A bottom-up analysis can cast Irme as a competent multilingual speaker, fully able to use the range of codes at his disposal to present himself as a Hungarian living in Slovakia, who is able to use and value two languages and who draws strong contrasts between life in his own community in Eastern Slovakia, where Hungarian speakers are in the minority, with life in other areas, such as in the border town of Komárom/Komarnó, where Slovaks live in the minority. (Such an analysis defines language from the perspective of the user, and points to conclusions that parallel that of Zentella [1997] on the role of bilingualism as a symbol of social identity among Nuyoricans in New York.)

A complex relationship between language and ideology can be seen from such a bottom-up approach that examines utterances from the perspective of the speaker, and in an important second step in analysis, confirms these analyses with the speaker. Here Imre is in effect drawing a map of Slovak Hungarian language use within his own community (lines 1–10), evaluating relationships between speakers in his community (lines 11–23), and comparing that with other communities within Slovakia (lines 24–29). (Later, he extends his discussion to comparisons on language use across the border into Hungary as well.)

In contrast, the transcriber, a Hungarian student in Budapest, instantiates a dominant language ideology—that is, taking as given the existence of a standard language, that spoken by educated people in Budapest, the capital of Hungary, and evaluating the speaker in light of that standard, in terms of language form (morphophonology, syntax, and lexicon that contain 'Slovakisms'). The transcriber further extends that analysis by connecting the use of particular expressions to a political stance, by pointing out that he, in contrast to the speaker, finds comments on language use remarkable (22A), and that the speaker's discourse must be interpreted in terms of fear to speak his mind about the position of Hungarians in Slovakia—that is, the transcriber is here revoicing the ideology in Hungary on the plight of Hungarians outside the borders—thereby linking the analysis to a nationalist language ideology coupled with a social justice/discrimination perspective. The interviewee and the transcriber are 'reading' the same phenomena, but interpreting them in different ways. So which analysis is correct? Is Imre a victim of poor Hungarian who is unable to express his position as a minority clearly since he lives in a nationalist and repressive society that engenders fear, or is Imre an agent of his own multiple social identities in which he uses the codes at his disposal to portray himself as a citizen of Slovakia seeking change in the direction of a more tolerant multilingual society? This small piece of text and two analytical views of its importance are insufficient to answer this question, but serve to illustrate the power of a multilayered approach to analyzing discourse in and on multilingual subjects. The concept of language ideology is that it provides "a crucial link mediating human acts and institutions" (Schieffelin, Woolard, & Kroskrity 1998: v) It is through this mediating link that local discourse and practice within a particular community of practice is tied to the society as a whole, both in terms of the influences society has on individuals and groups, and theoretically, in terms of influence of the group on society as a whole.

Lessons from the Analysis

Language learning and use in any analysis "is not the neutral and linear internalization of an artificially established standard, but an awareness that 'every individual [speaker's] multiple positionings and constructions must be seen as forms of identity and experience which frame and constitute the sexed, classed and raced human subject's life history, which give it both narrative coherence and its discursive and narrative multiplicity' " (Threadgold 1997; 7 in Kramsch & von Hoene 2001: 291). Hence, those engaging in qualitative sociolinguistic research must be aware of the local meanings of language choice, as well as the ways those meanings can be interpreted in multiple ways by speakers and those they interact with.

Extending Analyses to Multilingual Data

Historical shifts in political boundaries that lead to multilingualism can provide one lens for examining language choice and how multilingual language use can serve to express multiple identities at once by referencing concentric layers of context in terms of multiple communities of practice that individuals claim belonging to. The example of Hungarians living in East-Central Europe both inside and outside the current political borders of the Republic of Hungary can provide a rich set of examples of how to consider and analyze multilingual language use from a variety of perspectives. Take the following joke:

1. Meddig nyúl a nyúl?
2. Losoncig, utána már *zajac.*
1. How far does a rabbit stretch?
2. As far as Losonc, then it's a *rabbit.*

To understand this joke, a listener must have a wide variety of knowledge, knowledge of two languages (Hungarian and Slovak), as well as knowledge of the geographic, sociohistorical, and political contexts in which the joke may be used. Line 1 of this joke contains a Hungarian homonym: *nyúl* meaning both 'rabbit' and 'stretch.' This play on words, keys the question as humorous. Line 2, which provides the answer, contains a place name, *Losonc*, the Hungarian name for a town with the Slovak name Lučenec in the Slovak Republic. The final word *zajac* is a Slovak word that means 'rabbit.'

Interpreting a joke. At the level of the meaning of words alone, this joke is funny, because it is the first pair part of a somewhat common question–answer joke, with a variety of potential answers:

a) amíg ki nem nyúl 'until it is stretched out'
b) fülig 'to the ears'
c) a nyúl nem nyúl 'a rabbit doesn't stretch'

The answer provided here can be interpreted as funny, as it is a possible absurd answer, as Losonc is far from a number of towns in Hungary.

The interpretation of this joke, however, requires additional contextual knowledge in order to be understood in the way that it was intended when told in my presence by a young man, in a group of about 10 young people, in Budapest, at a party, during a joke-telling session. First, the young man, and five of his friends are Hungarians born in Czechoslovakia in the 1980s. At the time of the telling of the joke, in the mid-1990s, these young people have become citizens of the Slovak Republic, are proficient in both Hungarian, their native language, and Slovak, the language they have learned as a foreign language in a mother-tongue Hungarian school in Slovakia (Langman 2002b). Also present at the party are three Hungarians from Hungary and the researcher, Canadian born, who with the others shares a passion for and sustained practice of engaging in Hungarian folk dance and music. Thus, these participants belong to a large community of practice of Hungarian folk dancers, as well as belonging to smaller communities of practice tied to the dance group they are members of. Laughter at the joke occurs in three waves, first the Hungarian Slovaks, then the Hungarians, and finally the researcher, as the joke teller later in the evening unpeels the layers of meaning behind the joke.

The next layer of understanding the joke, requires an expansion of the context to the sociopolitical context of border changes and language policies in East Central Europe, with the most marked change—in the memories of these young people—coming with the redrawing of the political borders following World War I, which left a large number of Hungarian native speakers (over 500,000) in the newly created Czechoslovakia. Note that this change occurred in the lifetime of their grandparents, but was still referred to in many contexts, as if it had occurred in the last few years. These political changes resulted in a different alignment between the political border and the language border between Slovak speakers and Hungarian speakers. The joke, by mentioning *Losonc*, references the Hungarian speaking territory within modern-day Slovakia.

An additional layer to the analysis of this joke, told by this young man, in this particular context, is that *Losonc,* which is officially known as *Lučenec* in Slovak and also carries the German name, *Lizenz,* is a town whose population in 1910, prior to the Treaty of Trianon which created Czechoslovakia, was majority Hungarian (around 80 percent), and is now, majority Slovak (according to the 2001 census, approximately 80 percent.) What this young man is therefore referencing is the fact that the Hungarian language region doesn't stretch as far today as in the past, when it encompassed Losonc and rabbits were still *nyúl,* unlike today when rabbits are *zajac* in Losonc.

Underlying this joke is another layer, for which additional knowledge about the speakers and their views about bilingualism in the context of East Central Europe and more particularly Slovakia is required. Namely, the joke teller and his friends who include Imre discussed above, live in a town with fewer official speakers of Hungarian than even Losonc. But, they, as members of a Hungarian folk dance group have developed a personal identity that requires building and maintaining a Hungarian identity through a range of practices, with the Hungarian language as key. This is an identity that they feel strongly as they view themselves as minority citizens in a country where there has been wide-scale assimilation and language loss among the Hungarian population over the last century; this 'shortening of the stretch of the rabbit is a bad thing' about which the speakers have little personal control. Hence the joke, told in an ironic way. In this way, the telling of the joke may be interpreted as political.

Another layer of meaning of the joke rests in community building and references the minority and bilingual status of the speaker and his group mates—namely, they, unlike their Hungarian friends from Hungary, speak Slovak, and thus understand not only the reference to *Losonc*, but also the specific meaning of the word *zajac*. As the speaker explained to me in a retrospective interview when I asked about this joke, and several others with multilingual content, there is a feeling of community with other Slovak Hungarians that can be invoked in two seconds by the telling of this or one of many other bilingual jokes.

The analysis of the telling of this joke at this point in time could move to a further level, one that the teller of the joke also adds during the retrospective interview. This broader layer refers to the sociopolitical tensions that Hungarians in the Slovak Republic were undergoing in the mid-1990s with the creation of the Slovak Republic and the concomitant movement toward a nationalist agenda that defined Slovakia as a country with Slovak as its national language.

By combining a community of practice model with a language ideology framework, and tying it to an in-depth period of data collection and analysis, this example illustrates a number of key points important to the collection and analysis of multilingual language data. Referring back to the community of practice concept as a tool for understanding the meaning of language in use, this example shows how developing an understanding of how variations in language are used to construct, often simultaneously, multiple personal and social styles tied to social identities.

Doing Qualitative Sociolinguistic Research in Multilingual Contexts

Drawing on the foregoing theoretical and historical discussion as well as the examples, I conclude with some points to consider in designing qualitative sociolinguistic research in multilingual communities but pay particular attention to the effect of the researcher's developing multilingual proficiency on analyses of the relationship of language and identity. A key point is that all research must take account of the researcher's shifting roles in the course of fieldwork in multilingual contexts.

Constructing a Research Focus and Situating It

From the foregoing discussion of particular approaches to qualitative research, two primary questions can form the focus of current qualitative research studies in multilingual contexts:

1) What and how are identities constructed and constituted through linguistic practices?
2) How do dominant (and other) ideologies and power relations affect such constructions?

These questions can guide the development of a qualitative study. Using these questions, the researcher must next settle on a research paradigm in which to situate their work.

Choosing a Research Paradigm

What focus or angle of vision does it provide, and how does this focus compare with others? In current research, as outlined above, it is key for researchers to pinpoint definitions of language and context, and to be able to articulate how they will focus on the particularity of language data at the discourse level, as well as how they will treat the layered local to broader contexts that affect experience. Additional decisions to make on the nature of different analytic tools for arriving at an analysis of language use in context relates to the goal of providing an explanation of that language use that is satisfying to both the participants themselves, that is, one that 'rings true' as they reflect on their lived experiences, as well as from the—sometimes—more critical lens of the researcher, examining patterns of language use in one context through the lens of inequality and power. As Gee (2011) points out, in his discussion of critical discourse analysis, "we humans are very often unaware of the history of . . . interchanges, and, thus, in a deep sense, not fully aware of what we mean when we act and talk" (35), although as the example provided suggests, sometimes we are well aware of history and exploit it to express our particular identities. It is the analyst's task to look more deeply at the potential sets of meanings that words have and to place them in the context in which they are uttered.

Gathering and Transcribing Multilingual Data

At the core of research in language, is the collection of oral naturally occurring data that must be clearly and carefully contextualized. As Heath and Street (2008: 6) outline "added to the multiples of languages and literacies that ethnographers encounter in any single setting is the challenge of recording how these work hand in hand with cultural patterns" (6). What this means in terms of gathering data, is that recordings of any kind must also be carefully situated in terms of context, if their explanatory power is to be understood. Hence, multiple sources of data should support data collected through audio and video recordings: namely, field notes taken at the times of recording, together with reflections and member-checking of those notes and recordings afterwards. These can and should be further supported by collection of artifacts, interviews, and library research on the sociohistorical context.

Role of the Researcher: Reflexivity

For all qualitative research, the researcher and/or research team serves as a key actor in the research process. Hence, the first step in such research is immersion in the site. In much recent research, a debate on the notion of reflexivity, that is, who the researcher is and the types of roles and relationships the researcher has to the researched, become key questions in understanding the nature of analysis. Together with a debate on the stance of the researcher is a consideration of the role of assistants and experts in the field, who may lend support, but also steer interpretations in different directions.

The researcher's stance emerges from, among other things, her familiarity with and competence in the varieties of language used in the context of study and that will develop over time. In ethnographic approaches to qualitative research, moreover, a researcher cannot always predict in advance the types of competences needed to understand the meanings underlying the observed patterns of practice. For example, over the first year of my research among Hungarians in Slovakia, I never heard any use of Slovak within the group. However, over the course of time, the importance and place of Slovak in their lives emerged and also shifted, leading to my need to develop some proficiency in this language as well. So, part and parcel of data collection is reflections on how and what is being collected: "The . . . dynamics of our data-gathering need to be recognized and analysed rather than ignored as subjective and/or marginalized as not central to the findings" (Pini 2005: 214).

Multiple perspectives. Multiple perspectives on the meaning of language in use in any context are a given. Within multilingual communities, the power and associated interpretive perspective on the meanings of language use in context can be quite diverse and often diametrically opposed, particularly when uncovering issues of particular importance to minority group members. Untangling the local meanings of multiple perspectives on language use requires a variety of tools and techniques on the part of the researcher, one of which was illustrated with the example of drawing on the help of transcribers from the same language but not the same community of practice. Finding research assistants as well as expert consultants in multilingual contexts where language use is a contested resource is not straightforward. It leads to the need to seek a wide range of perspectives, as well as data from many sources that can be triangulated in order to connect ideologies to practices in ways that align with the research subjects' views. In terms of research assistants, the question of what constitutes a native speaker and how language is defined is a crucial part of the process of training and understanding the transcriptions and analyses of others.

CLOSING

Barbara Johnstone, in closing her *Qualitative Methods in Sociolinguistics* (2000), writes: "This book has probably raised more questions about research methods in readers' minds than it has answered. This is inevitable and intentional.

Thinking about method is something we do anew each time we plan a new project....The trick is not to learn the correct way to work, but to be able to think carefully in each new situation about the best way to work" (141). Similarly, Wheatley (2006 190) points to the joy of creativity in carrying out research: "We would seek out surprises, relishing the unpredictable when it finally decided to reveal itself. Surprise is the only route to discovery, a moment that pulsates with new learnings."

Notes

1. Note that the waves Eckert discusses do not imply a chronological sequence. Labov's (1963) study of Martha's Vineyard, for example, is classified as a second-wave study even though it predates his work on the Lower East Side of Manhattan (Labov 1966).

References

Barthes, R. 1957. Mythologies. Paris: du Seuil.

Bayley, R., & Schecter S. R. (eds.). 2003. *Language socialization in bilingual and multilingual societies.* Clevedon: Multilingual Matters.

Blackledge, A., & Pavlenko, A. 2001. Negotiation of identities in multilingual contexts. *The International Journal of Bilingualism* 5: 243–57.

Bucholtz, M. 2000. The politics of transcription. *Journal of Pragmatics* 32: 1439–465.

Creese, A., Martin, P., & Hornberger, N. (eds.) 2008. *The encyclopedia of language and education,* vol. 9: *The ecology of language.* New York: Springer.

Eckert, P. Under review. Three waves of variation study: The emergence of meaning in the study of variation. [online]. http://www.stanford.edu/~eckert/PDF/ThreeWavesofVariation.pdf. Accessed December 1, 2010.

Eckert, P., & McConnell-Ginet, S. 1992. Think practically and act locally: Language and gender as community-based practice. *Annual Review of Anthropology* 21: 461–90.

Eckert, P. and McConnell-Ginet, S. 1999. New generalizations and explanations in language and gender research, *Language in Society* 28: 185–201.

Edwards, J. 2001. The transcription of discourse. In D. Schiffrin, D. Tannen, & H. Hamilton (eds.), *The handbook of discourse analysis,* 321–48. Malden, MA: Blackwell.

Gal, S. 1979. *Language shift: Social determinants of linguistic change in bilingual Austria.* New York: Academic Press.

Gal, S. 1993. Diversity and contestation in linguistic ideologies: German speakers in Hungary. *Language in Society* 22: 337–59.

Gee, J. P. 2011. *An introduction to discourse analysis: Theory and method,* 3rd ed. New York: Routledge.

Gumperz, J. J. 1982a. *Discourse strategies.* Cambridge: Cambridge University Press.

Gumperz, J. J. (ed.). 1982b. *Language and social identity.* Cambridge: Cambridge University Press.
Gumperz, J. J., & Hymes, D. (eds.). 1972. *Directions in sociolinguistics: The ethnography of communication.* New York: Holt, Rinehart and Winston.
Haugen, E. 1972. The ecology of language. In A. Dil (ed.), *The ecology of language: Essays by Einar Haugen*, 325–39. Palo Alto, CA: Stanford University Press.
Heath, S. B. 1989. Language ideology. In *International encyclopedia of communications*, vol. 2, 393–95. New York: Oxford University Press.
Heath, S. B., & Street, B. 2008. *Ethnography. Approaches to language and literacy research.* New York: Teachers College Press.
Hornberger, N. H. 2002. Multilingual language policies and the continua of biliteracy: An ecological approach. *Language Policy* 1: 27–51.
Hornberger, N. H., & Hult, F. M. 2008. Ecological language education policy. In B. Spolsky & F. M. Hult (eds.), *Handbook of educational linguistics*, 280–96. Malden, MA: Blackwell.
Hult, F. 2008. Language ecology and linguistic landscape analysis. In E. Shohamy & D. Gorter (eds), *Linguistic landscape: Expanding the scenery*, 88–104, London: Routledge.
Hymes, D. 1973. Speech and language: On the origins and foundations of inequality among speakers. *Daedalus* 102(3): 59–85.
Hymes, D. 1974. *Foundations in sociolinguistics: An ethnographic approach.* Philadelphia: University of Pennsylvania Press.
Irvine, J. 1989. When talk isn't cheap: Language and political economy. *American Ethnologist* 16: 248–67.
Johnstone, B. 2000. *Qualitative methods in sociolinguistics.* Cambridge: Cambridge University Press.
Kalocsai, K. 2009. Erasmus exchange students: A behind-the-scenes view into an ELF community of practice. *Apples—Journal of Applied Language Studies* 3: 24–48.
Kontra, M., Phillipson, R., Skutnabb-Kangas, T., & Várady, T. (eds.). 1999. *Language: A right and a resource. Approaching linguistic human rights.* Budapest: Central European University Press.
Kramsch, C. 2009. *The multilingual subject.* Oxford: Oxford University Press.
Kramsch, C., & von Hoene, L. 2001. Foreign language study and feminist discourses of travel. In A. Pavlenko, A. Blackledge, I. Piller, & M. Teutsch-Dwyer (eds.), *Multlingualism, second language learning, and gender*, 283–306. Berlin: Mouton de Gruyter.
Kroskrity, P. (ed.). 2000. *Regimes of language: Ideologies, polities and identities.* Sante Fe, NM: School of American Research Press.
Labov, W. 1963. The social motivation of a sound change. *Word* 19: 273–309.
Labov, W. 1966. *The social stratification of English in New York City.* Washington, DC: Center for Applied Linguistics.
Langman, J. 1997. Expressing identity in a changing society: Hungarian youth in Slovakia. In L. Kürti & J. Langman (eds.), *Beyond borders: Remaking cultural identities in the new east and central Europe*, 111–31. Boulder: Westview Press.
Langman, J. 2002a. Language and identity in a Hungarian minority dance group. In I. Lanstyák & S. Simon (eds.) *Tanulmányok a Kétnyelvüségröl.* (Studies in Bilingualism), 57–70. Pozsony: Kalligram.
Langman, J. 2002b. Mother Tongue Education versus bilingual education: Shifting ideologies and policies in the Republic of Slovakia. *International Journal of the Sociology of Language* 154: 47–64.

Langman, J. 2003. Growing a (bányavirág) rock crystal on barren soil: Forming a Hungarian identity in Eastern Slovakia through joint (inter)action. In R. Bayley & S. R. Schecter (eds.) Language socialization in bilingual and multilingual societies, 182–99. Clevedon: Multilingual Matters.

Langman, J., & Lanstyák, I. 2000. Language negotiations in Slovakia: Views from the Hungarian minority. *Multilingua* 19: 55–72.

Lave, J., & Wenger, É. 1991. *Situated learning: Legitimate peripheral participation.* Cambridge: Cambridge University Press.

Norton, B., & Toohey, K. 2002. Identity and language learning. In R. Kaplan (ed.) *Handbook of applied linguistics*, 115–23. Oxford: Oxford University Press.

Ochs, E. 1979. Transcription as theory. In E. Ochs and B. Schieffelin (eds.), *Developmental pragmatics*, 43–72. New York: Academic Press.

Pavlenko, A., & Blackledge, A. (eds.). 2004. *Negotiation of identities in multilingual contexts.* Clevedon: Multilingual Matters.

Pini, B. 2005. Interviewing men: Gender and the collection and interpretation of qualitative data. *Journal of Sociology* 41: 201–216.

Roberts, C. 1997. Transcribing talk: Issues of representation. *TESOL Quarterly* 31: 167–72

Schieffelin, B., Woolard . K., & Kroskrity, P. (eds.). 1998. *Language ideologies: Practice and theory.* New York: Oxford University Press.

Silverstein, M. 1979. Language structure and linguistic ideology. In P. Clyne, R. Hanks, & C. Hofbauer (eds.), *The elements: A parasession on linguistic units and levels*, 193–247. Chicago: University of Chicago.

Spolsky, B. 1998. *Sociolinguistics.* Oxford: Oxford University Press.

Threadgold, T. 1997. *Feminist poetics, poiesis, performance, histories.* London: Routledge.

Wenger, É. 1998. *Communities of practice: Learning, meaning, and identity.* Cambridge: Cambridge University Press.

Wheatley, M, 2006. *Leadership and the new science: Discovering order in a chaotic world.* San Francisco: Berrett-Koehler Publishers.

Woolard, K. 1998. Introduction. In B. Schieffelin, K. Woolard, & P. Kroskrity (eds.), *Language ideologies: Practice and theory*, 3–47. New York: Oxford University Press.

Woolard, K. 1997. Between friends: Gender, peer group structure, and bilingualism in urban Catalonia. *Language in Society* 26: 533–60.

Woolard, K., & Schieffelin, B. 1994. Language ideology. *Annual Review of Anthropology* 23: 55–82.

Zentella, A. C. 1997. *Growing up bilingual: Puerto Rican children in New York.* Malden: MA: Blackwell.

CHAPTER 13

LONGITUDINAL STUDIES

GILLIAN SANKOFF

INTEREST in longitudinal sociolinguistic research has grown considerably over the past decade. Two earlier articles (Sankoff 2005, 2006) considered publications that had appeared through 2004, and the reader is referred to those sources for a review of many important early contributions. The current review focuses on subsequent research, which has burgeoned in the intervening years. The major reason for this surge of interest is that longitudinal research has begun to answer some of the most important questions that relate language variation and language change. What evidence can longitudinal studies provide about stability versus change? Does change from above have a different profile from change from below? How can we best understand the relationship between language change and age grading? And finally, does longitudinal sociolinguistic evidence shake accepted wisdom on the relative stability of people's grammars in adult life?

A signal contribution of sociolinguistics as of the mid-1960s was the reconciliation of the former separation between synchronic and diachronic linguistics through an understanding that change in progress can be observed synchronically. When, in a synchronic sample of the speech community, language variation relates monotonically to speaker age, two interpretations are possible. If, as linguists have generally taken to be the case, people's grammars are reasonably stable after childhood acquisition, then older speakers can be understood to have retained the grammar they first acquired. Under this assumption, if a regular increase or decrease in the frequency or other quantifiable measure of a linguistic feature (e.g., the mean formant values of a particular vowel) correlates with age, one can infer that this frequency or value prevailed in the speech community at the time individuals of any given age acquired it: the *apparent time* interpretation (Labov 1963,1972). If on the other hand older speakers have changed as they aged, *age grading*, rather than language change, is probably involved.

Longitudinal studies are crucial in resolving these ambiguities of interpretation, and real-time data has now often been used to enrich apparent time interpretations. This work includes two major strands in longitudinal sociolinguistic work that had contributed in complementary ways to understanding language change: *trend studies,* which replicate earlier research by drawing a new population directly comparable to that of the initial study, and *panel studies,* which follow as many of the individual speakers from the original study as possible across time as they age. Trend studies have proven to be the best way to find out about language change, or to confirm stability. Trend studies in contemporary sociolinguistics resemble historical research in general in that they compare observations over some span of historical time. In contrast, panel studies elucidate how maturation and the life cycle relate to the formation and development of the grammars of individual speakers as members of speech communities. Much recent sociolinguistic research has continued very profitably to use the concept of apparent time, which has become so standard, and so widely used, that it will not be possible to review the vast array of studies that feature it except when researchers have combined it with longitudinal data. One early body of work that did just that has recently been brought to the fore by Encrevé (2009), reviewing Martinet's study of the pronunciation of 400 French officers, his fellow prisoners of war in 1941. Encrevé reports that Martinet inferred change from differences across three age groups in that study, then proceeded in the 1960s to a real-time verification of phonological change.

Language Stability or Language Change?

In the early days of sociolinguistic research in the 1960s, it was difficult to relate the work to similar earlier studies. Four of the earliest modern studies in quantitative sociolinguistics, originally done in the 1960s and 1970s, have since been replicated. Cedergren (1987) found that (ch)-lenition had continued in Panamanian Spanish over the two decades since her original study. Trudgill's (1988) replication of his Norwich study revealed that three changes initially identified as change from below on the basis of an apparent time interpretation had continued over the subsequent 20 years: the *beer/bear* merger, the backing of /ɛl/, and [t] glottaling. Studying the seven morphophonological features analyzed in the Swedish city of Eskilstuna first documented by Nordberg (1972, 1985), Sundgren (2009) conducted a well-matched trend comparison 29 years later, and also reported on 13 members of the original study. Though Standard Swedish had been felt to be rapidly displacing local variants in Sweden, she found surprisingly little change toward Standard Swedish at the community level for most of the variables. This was less true, however, of women and younger speakers, and she also reported some change for the panelists across adult lifespans. In a re-study of Philadelphia vowel systems, Conn (2005) re-sampled the community to match Labov's 1970s research (Labov 2001). Conn found that the three vowels he studied had each had a different trajectory over the intervening 30 years. The fronting and raising of (aw) had reversed; women were catching up to men in raising the nucleus of (ay0) in speech production, (though centralization was still perceived as a male feature in subjective reaction tests); and (eyC), identified in the 1970s as a new and vigorous change, was continuing actively to front and raise.

Much of linguistic structure, of course, cannot be expected to be in a state of flux at any particular time, and trend studies have enabled investigators to identify stability as well as change.[1] A research project that identified phases of stability in change from below was that of Van de Velde et al. (1996) on the devoicing of Dutch fricatives by radio announcers, broadcasting between 1935 and 1993. The authors found that between 1935 and 1965, there was no devoicing of /v/ in Belgium, when it had already begun in the Netherlands. Post-1965, the Belgian announcers also began devoicing /v/ but at a rate well behind their counterparts in the Netherlands at each sample period. In their study of the *near/square* merger in New Zealand, Gordon and Maclagan (2001) recorded comparable groups of higher-, middle-, and lower-class 14-year-old children at five-year intervals between 1983 and 1998. Responses to stimulus materials including sentences, word lists, and word pairs allowed each speaker to be rated as to whether he or she did or did not display the merger. The first two periods exhibited relative stability (merged speakers inching up from 16 percent to 25 percent of the sample population, an apparent increase that was not statistically significant), followed by a big, statistically significant jump to 76 percent in 1993 that remained stable through 1998.

Other studies used earlier recordings made by dialectologists, folklorists, and others as a baseline to compare with their own recently collected recordings. Such studies, typically representing longer time spans than the sociolinguistic re-studies referred to above, also reported both stability and change. Barnfield and Buchstaller (2010) studied the trajectories of intensifiers over five decades of dialectal speech from North East England, tracing periods of stability as well as change. They documented the decline of *very*, the rise of *really* and *so*, and the brief popularity of *dead* in Tyneside English between the 1960s and 2009. Richards (2010) used recordings of 12 speakers from Leeds in 1968 and her own contemporary interviews to compare trend and apparent time analyses of four variants of the past tense of the verb *to be*. She considered not only Standard English *was* [wɒz] and *were* [wɜː] but also two intermediate variants [wə] and [wɒ], concluding that there was no evidence of change in what she describes as a conservative dialect (77). In the United States, Jose (2010) used real-time data from 20 years prior to his own research on the devoicing of final [z] in northwestern Indiana. His longitudinal data confirmed the inferences made on the basis of apparent time that indicated stability in this variable. Schilling-Estes (2005) added 1999 data from young people as a "fourth generation" in comparisons with three generations of residents of Smith Island (SI), Maryland, recorded in 1983, discovering that younger people continued to use local pronunciations of (ay) and (aw), as well as existential *it* and *weren't* (for *wasn't*). Thus the "dialect concentration" observable in apparent time in 1983 had continued through the later period. Thomas (2010) also confirmed stability on the North-Midland boundary in Ohio, using data recorded for the *Dictionary of American Regional English (DARE)* project from 1967 to 1969 for 22 speakers born between 1890 and 1907. These individuals were compared with his own interviews (1999–2008) of 42 speakers born between 1970 and 1994. The analysis revealed that the nineteenth-century settlement patterns separating northern from southern Ohio continue to define the dialect boundary today. Thomas concluded that "vowel variants seem to mark the boundary more distinctly than they did in the past" (419).

Studies from the United States, Canada, and New Zealand have made profitable use of recordings of speakers born in the nineteenth century. McCarthy (2010) used *DARE* interviews with six Chicago speakers born between 1891 and 1919 to investigate the early stages of the Northern Cities Shift. In a confirmation of apparent time inferences, she concluded that the fronting of /æ/ 'cat' and of /ah~o/ 'cot' were the two earliest stages of the shift. Raising of /æ/ was clearly a later development, since it was observed only for three speakers born between 1909 and 1919. Further, she found that (uw)-fronting, described in the *Atlas of North American English* (*ANAE*) of Labov et al. (2006) as a recent change in most US dialect areas, was absent from all six of the nineteenth- and early twentieth-century speakers, but well in evidence from a speaker born in 1937.

The Origins of New Zealand English (ONZE) project grew out of Gordon's ambitious program of archiving and analyzing thousands of recordings made in the 1940s by the New Zealand Broadcasting Service, including interviews with people born as early as 1851. Fully aware of the care needed in interpreting apparent time data, Gordon et al. (2004) showed conclusively that the New Zealand Chain Shift was initiated by the raising of the TRAP and DRESS vowels and followed by the backing of the KIT class.[2]

Another project that used early data is based on the Récits du Français québécois d'Autrefois (RFQ), a corpus of Québécois French speakers born between 1846 and 1895, recorded in the 1940s and 1950s (Poplack & St-Amand 2007). This data was used in a trend comparison with contemporary sociolinguistic data from the Ottawa-Hull area, documenting a substantial increase in the use of the periphrastic future at the expense of the synthetic future over the past century (Poplack & Dion 2009). The RFQ was also used by Blondeau (2003) in comparison with data from Montréal in 1971 to show that the transition from *nous* to *on* to express the first person plural was of greater historical depth than had previously been understood and to demonstrate both continuity and change in the constraints on the alternation between *nous* and *nous-autres*. In another study of morphosyntactic variation, Malvar (2003) investigated the competition among four different variants used to express the future in Portuguese across five centuries. Using plays as the closest approximation to spoken language from the sixteenth to the nineteenth century, she compared twentieth-century plays with speech recorded in sociolinguistic interviews, finding that the rise of periphrastic futures with *ir* 'to go' + infinitive was almost as robustly represented in plays as in spontaneous speech (see also Poplack & Malvar 2007).

Several studies have explored the rapid diffusion of innovative quotatives among younger speakers. Tagliamonte and D'Arcy (2004) studied the spread of quotative *be like* in a sample of young people in Toronto between the ages of 10 and 19, comparing the results with those of an earlier study. Buchstaller et al. (2010) traced the rise and fall of quotative *be all*, which originated in California in the early 1980s and expanded through 1994 and 1995, subsequently declining in favor of *be like*. They first dated the rise of *all* to the early 1980s on the basis of apparent time inference: the difference between high school and college students in a spoken corpus from the early 1990s. This was confirmed in real time with data from another California spoken corpus from the early 2000s, as well as from year-by-year data from internet newsgroups. Whereas the studies discussed above analyzed only recorded speech, this project illustrated the benefits of using the written material that is increasingly available in online corpora.

As is clear from the wide range of studies reviewed above, inferences from apparent time in past research have received massive confirmation from real time data in studies of change from below, especially those involving adult speakers. The picture becomes even more complicated, however, in two other situations: that of change from above (to be dealt with in the next section) and when considering adolescent speakers. In the case of stable variation, the use of non-standard variants, such as negative concord or [th]/[dh] (Labov 2001), often peaks among adolescents such that the inclusion of adolescents creates a spike in the age distribution. In these cases of stable variation, age grading is clearly involved. Further, Labov's (2007) model of the incrementation of change accounted for an adolescent peak in phonological change in progress, a pattern also observed by Tagliamonte and D'Arcy (2009) for a number of morphosyntactic changes in English. A similar pattern (an adolescent peak) is thus observed not only for stable variables, but also in synchronic data in the case of change from below, involving adolescent incrementation followed by maintenance of the rate of use or value of the innovative variant achieved by late adolescence. Thus change from below apparently does not involve age grading, but simply the crest of a wave of change reaching a high water mark when successive cohorts of speakers attain a state of stabilization (Labov's model takes an age of 17 as the best estimate available from previous research). The result of two different processes yielding superficially similar age-related patterns makes all the more crucial the use of real time data.[3]

Change from Above or Change from Below? Different Profiles?

Change from above was initially defined as change above the level of awareness on the part of speech community members (Labov 1966:128). In practice, this almost always involves features originating outside the local speech community, and thus the results of dialect contact are an important strand in studies of change from above.[4]

Processes of leveling and convergence occurring in many European countries during the twentieth century involved changes in local dialects due to contact with national standards or regional varieties (e.g., Auer et al. 2005; Gerritsen 1999) or koineization due to population movements (Kerswill & Williams 2005), where change from above has been involved. Although the data in these studies is spatial, there has been a longstanding interest in the temporal interpretation of spatial relations. Tagliamonte (2003) used data from three UK towns to infer temporal relations: a sequence of stages in the change from 'have' to 'have got' in British English which, in each location, is also a strong effect in apparent time.[5]

Relatively little research on dialect contact has been based on trend or panel studies. Two exceptions, both retrospective trend studies of change from above, are Hernandez-Campoy et al. (2003) and Cornips and Corrigan (2005). Hernandez-Campoy et al. examined the influence of seven standard Castilian Spanish phonological features on Murcian Spanish from 1975 to 2000, studying politicians versus lower- and middle-class men in radio interviews. Standard variants increased for both speaker groups, with politicians in the lead. In research on Dutch reflexives in Limburg, Cornips and Corrigan compared results from the Willems questionnaire of 1885 with questionnaires similarly designed in 1994 and 1995. This remarkable trend study spanning 110 years suggests "a convergence of dialects in this region between 1885 and 1994... [such that]...the reflexive instrumental construction implies...the reflexive adjunct middle, [which implies] the reflexive impersonal middle" (121).

Prestigious changes originating outside of local communities may operate on a national level. Non-rhotic dialects, traditionally found in the American South and New England (and among African Americans elsewhere) have been steadily giving way to rhoticity (Labov in press). Nguyen (2006) documented this change in her real-time trend study that compared 12 African Americans recorded in Detroit in 1966 with 12 recorded between 1998 and 2003. Nguyen also identified stability in (ay) monophthongization, and a change toward glottal stop and zero variants of syllable-final (d), this latter showing a profile more typical of change from below.

Whether a particular dataset evidences change from above or from below is not always easy to interpret. Labov (2007) proposed that changes internal to a community are passed on across age cohorts growing up in that community by processes of transmission, whereas changes from outside are introduced by diffusion, usually to adult speakers (children normally lack the extra-local contacts required). Yet we have seen that the spread of quotative *be like* involves diffusion to adolescent speakers. Johnson (2009) studied the boundary of the *caught/cot* merger in eastern Massachusetts, which had been stable for at least three adult generations. Johnson attributed its sudden spread westward among school-age children to the immigration of families from Boston in numbers large enough to trigger the merger. In some cases, a change from below in one region may be found in another region where diffusion via adult speakers, rather than transmission, seems more likely (cf. the account in ANAE of Northern Cities Shift features in the St. Louis corridor south of Chicago). The presence of the Canadian Shift in St. Johns, Newfoundland may stem from a similar process. Hollett (2006) compared four St. Johns middle-class women in their mid-40s in 2003 with two groups of women in their early 20s: one group recorded in the same year and one in 1980. Because the 40-year-olds in 2004 were more advanced in the shift than either of the other groups, Hollett argued that they must have changed as adults. Her 'change from above' interpretation was bolstered by her description of features originating in mainland Canada as prestigious.

Whereas trend studies can confirm a state of change or stability in the language, panel studies offer the possibility of better understanding whether and how individual speakers experience change, to be reviewed in the next section.

Lifespan Change? The Evidence from Panel Studies

Given the difficulty and expense of tracking and re-studying any group of people, few panel studies have involved substantial numbers of speakers. The smaller the sample, the less dependable are any generalizations we can make to the larger speech community. We can, however, learn a good deal about age grading and lifespan trajectories from even the study of one individual, as has long been understood in diary-style studies of L1 and L2 acquisition.[6] In some cases, studies of one or a handful of individuals can be set against a backdrop of what is already known about change. So for example, Harrington's longitudinal research (2006; 2007) based on the Christmas broadcasts of Queen Elizabeth II spanning the 50 years between 1952 and 2002, indicated gradual change in two of her vowels (/u/ as in *who'd* and /æ/ as in *had*) that provided "evidence for phonetic adaptation in the Christmas broadcasts towards a more modern, less aristocratic form of RP" (2007: 127) on the part of Queen Elizabeth.

Elliott (2000) studied rhoticity in the film speech of 202 male and female actors in American films from 1932 to 1980. Professional actors of course are probably among the most adept at altering their speech patterns, and rhoticity was conditioned by stylistic factors, the type of role being played (e.g., "good girl" vs. "bad girl"), and others. Nevertheless, rhoticity was conditioned principally by the dialect origins of the actors (rhotic vs. non-rhotic dialects) and the decade. In the 1930s, the heyday of non-rhotic prestige in the United States, actors from non-rhotic dialect backgrounds had a non-rhotic rate of 83 percent. Even those from rhotic backgrounds achieved a rate of 52 percent. Rates for both groups declined regularly: by the 1970s, when rhoticity had become the general American norm, non-rhoticity in films had decreased to 2 percent for native rhotic, and 18 percent for native non-rhotic actors. The sample contained only some of the same actors across the decades, so on the whole, decreased non-rhoticity is best understood as a community level trend. However, longitudinal results from some individual actors reflected the overall decline.

In research on short (a) in Danish, Gregersen et al. (2009) studied 43 subjects in Copenhagen and Næstved, a smaller regional center, recorded 20 years after initial interviews in the 1980s, when panelists were between 25 and 40. The alternation between [æ], the standard, and [ɛ], is described as "a Copenhagen (specifically a Copenhagen working class) shibboleth" (78). Whereas three-fourths of the subjects retained the same distribution of the two variants, one-fourth changed over a period well past the critical age. Three Copenhagen speakers with [æ] variants of 80 percent to 90 percent at Time 1 had increased [æ] to 100 percent by Time 2. Three others showed a decrease, with the result that in Copenhagen, the rate remained stable for the group as a whole (less than 10 percent [ɛ] overall). In Næstved, a highly significant decrease in [ɛ] from 20 percent to 12 percent brought this community into line with the Copenhagen pattern. Heightened awareness of [ɛ] appears to have produced an "earlier peak" (78) in Copenhagen, and the subsequent decline in the smaller town was captured during the study period.

Bowie (2005) studied the vowels of five church elders (ages 47–94) in Utah, born between 1873 and 1900, measured acoustically from recordings of their preaching at 20-year intervals. He reported some instability for three of the 13 vowels analyzed: the *fill-fell* merger (three of five speakers stably conservative); short (a) raising before nasals (two of five speakers stably conservative), and the fronting of long (u), for which only one speaker was stably conservative. Of only eight instances where a particular speaker showed instability, his change was in the direction of ongoing community changes in five cases.

Three studies of the transition from adolescence to adulthood were Wagner (2008), DeDecker (2006) and Woolard (2011). Wagner's research was designed to distinguish age effects in stable variables from those involved in change. Female Philadelphia high school juniors and seniors were re-interviewed a year later. For the highest SES group, nonstandard variants of stable variables (dh) and (ing) registered a significant decrease, concomitant with attenuation of neighborhood contacts and engagement with new college friends. For the other subjects, the rate of nonstandard variants remained high, not showing this adolescent peak. Wagner's study suggested that both age grading and adult participation in (or withdrawal from) community language change are more likely in cases of stable stereotypical features. DeDecker recorded four young Canadian women in their last year of high school and again three years later as university students. Immersion in new, metropolitan social networks where the Canadian Shift was more advanced resulted in increased participation in a key feature of the Canadian Shift, the retraction of short (a), for three of the four. Similarly, Wagner's middle-class subjects matched their age mates at the crest of the wave for newer, less salient changes from below in Philadelphia, for example, the lowering of short (e). Woolard re-contacted a group of bilingual (Spanish/Catalan) speakers she had first observed as high school students in Barcelona some 20 years earlier, finding that their fluency in Catalan had increased substantially as they matured into adults, concomitant with the life changes that freed them from the pressures of adolescent peer groups. All three studies showed the importance of the transition to adulthood as crucial in altering previous linguistic patterns.

Blondeau et al. (2002) followed 12 Montréal French speakers from 1971, when most were in their early twenties, through 1984 and 1995 in a panel study of two changes from above: the innovative [ʀ] and the standard form of tonic plural pronouns (the replacement of the vernacular *nous-autres* [lit. 'we-others'], and so on, by the analogous forms minus *autres*). Individual trajectories showed a much greater adoption of the phonetic change than of the morphological change, with the expected strong social class differences (overall stability among working-class speakers).

Two important studies on Brazilian Portuguese followed the same 16 speakers across two decades, focusing on subject-verb agreement and on noun phrase internal number and gender agreement (Naro & Scherre 2002, 2003). In the early 1980s (T1), six of eight speakers age 18 or younger were still students and thus had had further education by the time of the second interview in the early 2000s (T2). The other eight speakers ranged between age 30 and 60 at T1, and none subsequently received further education. Eight speakers, including five of the six with further education, used substantially more subject-verb agreement at T2. Results for internal NP agreement were similar: probabilities of using agreement at T2 for all six of those with further education increased more than 0.2 (on a scale from 0 to 1). For both variables, change occurred for all speakers whose T1 age was 16 or under (the three 18-year olds were split). Of the eight speakers over age 16, none changed significantly on internal NP agreement, and only two significantly increased subject-verb agreement. As part of the standard language taught in schools, increased agreement is clearly a change from above. This is also an ongoing change in the speech community, with rising educational levels in Brazil in the last decades of the twentieth century. It is difficult to disentangle age effects (greater malleability of adolescent speakers) from the effects of education in this case, but both factors were probably at work. The changes observed in these studies for the adolescents still in school at T1 are likely to remain part of their grammars long after T2, and indeed, for the rest of their lives.

Overall, the panel studies indicate that, in a situation of change, a majority of older speakers retain their earlier-acquired patterns, but a minority may change somewhat, generally in the direction of a change active among younger speakers in their community. My earlier summary of this conclusion is as follows:

> [P]eople as they age register lesser differences from their earlier selves than does the community over the same time interval...This means first, that it must be younger speakers who are in the vanguard of change. Those adult speakers who change are (a) in the minority; (b) concentrated in the younger age cohorts of adults and (c) make less significant advances than the community as a whole. (Sankoff 2006)

It seemed at that time that the only type of change typical of adult speakers was a change in the direction of ongoing change in the community, under the influence of younger speakers. However, other research by Blondeau contradicted that assumption. Blondeau's (2006) panel study of 12 individuals recorded in sociolinguistic interviews in 1971, 1984, and 1995 in Montréal French dealt with a change with known historical directionality: the inflected or synthetic future (SF; e.g., *je ferai* 'I will do') has progressively given way to the periphrastic future (PF; e.g., *je vais faire* 'I'm going to do'). Surprisingly, the average rate of SF, 14 percent in 1971 (mean speaker age of 23), had increased to 23 percent in 1984, remaining stable in later adulthood: 22 percent in 1995. Blondeau clearly identified this counter-historical lifespan change as age grading.

Suzanne Wagner and I continued this research in a larger panel study over the crucial years Blondeau had isolated (1971–1984), using all available data from the same corpus. Examining all 60 speakers who were interviewed in both years, we confirmed Blondeau's results, and closely examined their social correlates. Retrograde change was more common among speakers who made the transition to adulthood during the 11-year interval between the two samples. As a conservative feature characteristic of written language, it was also more prevalent among speakers of higher socio-professional status (Wagner & Sankoff 2011). In addition to adult stability and adult lifespan change in the direction of community change, it is clear that a third trajectory type needs attention: adult retrograde change, probably more typical of late-stage changes where the conservative form has become salient (Sankoff in preparation).

The panel studies reviewed so far have tracked adults, or adolescents on the way to adulthood. In the latter case, we expect to see the adolescent peak followed by relative stability for stable variables and to see incrementation by successive cohorts, again followed by relative stability, for variables involved in change. These patterns are less likely to occur in panel studies of young children or early adolescents, whose linguistic systems are more malleable and whose life courses expose them progressively to quite different linguistic input.

Carter (2007) documented a change between primary school and middle school for a Mexican immigrant student in North Carolina. In a white-majority primary school at age 10, her English included a high front allophone of short (a) prenasally, similar to that of her classmates; in a middle school under the influence of other Latinos at age 13, her short (a) no longer featured this nasal allophone.

A long-term longitudinal project on language and school achievement conducted since 1990 under the aegis of the Frank Porter Graham Child Development Institute in Chapel Hill, North Carolina, allowed Van Hofwegen and Wolfram (2010) to track 32 African American children across six stages: in preschool (at age 48 months) and then in grades 1, 4, 6, 8, and 10. At each stage, they calculated a "dialect density measure" (DDM) by combining the frequencies of 29 morphosyntactic and three phonological features—most of them specific to African American Vernacular English (AAVE)—to assess "vernacularity." The DDM across the six periods showed that vernacular features were high among preschoolers, followed by a considerable dip in grades 1 and 4. As of grade 6, two subsequent patterns emerged for 26 of the children: six children's DDM scores continued rising across grades 6, 8 and 10 (the "curvilinear," or "U-shaped pattern"); for the majority (22 others), scores peaked in grade 6, then fell slightly in grade 8 and more steeply in grade 10 (the "roller coaster" pattern). Results for four individual features reported on separately are particularly interesting because previous literature has generally characterized the first three as stable and the last as a more recent development. The first feature (the [in] variant of (ing)) is both stable and non-specific to AAVE. Its "roller coaster" pattern for these speakers as they aged closely matched that of the second variable (absence of third singular (-s)), which seems to confirm an age-grading interpretation for both of these stable variables, peaking in the sixth and eighth grades. The third stable variable, copula absence, also dipped as the children entered school, with a stable leveling off (rather than a subsequent falloff) after the grade 4 rise. The preschoolers' very high vernacular rates for these three variables probably reflected their primary language learning at home. In contrast, the fourth variable (invariant *be*) was very little used by the youngest children, with a sudden big increase in grade 6. Since evidence from elsewhere (e.g., Cukor-Avila & Bailey 2011) suggests that the spread of invariant *be* is relatively recent, the grade 8 peak in this case was perhaps less likely to indicate age grading than to represent ongoing change in the speech community.

Van Hofwegen and Wolfram's study is unique not only in dealing with the transition from early childhood to adolescence but also because the patterns for most of the variables indicate age grading rather than change in progress. Age grading as a concept seems more naturally applicable to life stages, matching transitions that are culturally or institutionally prescribed. But the changes documented in most of the panel studies of adults do not necessarily line up with life stages.

What can we learn about change in adult grammars from the panel studies reviewed here? Not all of them explicitly discussed change from above versus change from below, but in fact, only a couple appear to involve change from below. Wagner's evidence is moot on the vowel changes from below, probably since a one-year interval is insufficient to register ongoing, community-internal change. Upwardly mobile speakers withdrew somewhat from the more salient stable variables and older dialect-internal changes that had become local stereotypes. The very gradual movement of two of Queen Elizabeth's vowels shows that older speakers can readjust their vowel systems, as do the three elders for whom Bowie documented vowel changes, but studies of only a few individuals do not tell us how common such behavior may be in adult speakers in general. Bowie found stability across 88 percent of the vowel contexts examined, and the majority of Queen Elizabeth's vowels were also stable. These two cases also importantly have in common that the data were drawn from formal public speaking and that the changes involved were in the direction of ongoing change in the wider society. The cases analyzed by Naro and Scherre (2003), Blondeau (2003), and Wagner and Sankoff (2011) all involved changes from above.

Combined Trend and Panel Studies

Panel studies can tell us whether and to what extent individuals change, but individual change is not language change. Relatively little research has combined both trend (or, as a substitute, apparent time) and panel components.

Cukor-Avila (2002) combined apparent time interpretation with a panel study of quotatives among African Americans in the rural hamlet of Springville, Texas. Eight speakers born prior to 1966 used only three tokens of *be like* (N > 1800), whereas the five speakers born between 1978 and 1982 ranged up to 19 percent *be like* (14, table 2). Her inference of local historical change was enriched by a panel study of three younger speakers, ages 9 to 19. The adoption of *be like* by these young women resulted from their expanded social networks in a larger neighboring town during adolescence. Cukor-Avila and Bailey (2011) provided similar results in analyzing the increased use of invariant *be* across adolescence for the same young women.

Sankoff & Blondeau (2007) studied the change (from above) from apical to posterior /r/ in Montréal French. The panel component compared recordings of the same 32 speakers in 1971 and 1984; the trend component compared two sets of 32 speakers (a different set from each of the same years). Each set was matched for age, sex, and social class. The trend comparison showed substantial community change: the mean rate of posterior /r/ for older speakers in 1971 was 34 percent; their 1984 counterparts registered 75 percent. For younger speakers, the analogous figures were 69 percent and 93 percent (574, table 13). The panel as a group registered a more modest change in the same direction, but the 32 individuals were quite variable: in 1971, 10 had already adopted the innovative posterior variant; by 1984, nine of the remaining 22 had done so—41 percent of that pool of possible adoptees (573).

MacKenzie and Sankoff (2009) studied the diphthongization of long vowels in Montréal French, a previously identified change from below (Cedergren et al 1981). A trend comparison matched six speakers age 15 to 27 in 1971 by age, sex, and social class with an analogous sample from 1984. Comparisons based on normalized F1 and F2 measurements revealed lowering and backing of front vowel nuclei (/iː/ *sourire* 'smile'; /yː/ *sûr* 'sure'; /ɛː/ *père* 'father'; /œː/ *peur* 'fear'), and decreased diphthongization. Back vowel nuclei (/uː/ *cour* 'yard'; /oː/ *chose* 'thing'; /ɔː/ *alors* 'so'; /ɑː/ *art* 'art') were stable, but glides reduced to again yield decreased diphthongization. A six-member panel sample matched the community only in part. Though for a majority, most vowels were either stable or changed in the same direction as the community, stability in vowel diphthongization was clearly not the dominant trend for all six panelists. We concluded that inter-speaker variation, coupled with social-class-based differences indicated the need for an expanded panel sample.

Zilles (2005) presented data from five Brazilian cities on the alternation between the conservative first person plural pronoun *nos* and innovative *a gente* (literally 'people'), conducting a trend and panel comparison in the southern city of Porto Alegre. The trend sample of twenty 1970s speakers and sixteen 1990s speakers, all with at least secondary education, indicated a significant increase from 56 percent to 72 percent use of *a gente*. Zilles identified this as a change from below because it was led by women and presented a curvilinear social class pattern. In a panel comparison of 13 speakers recorded at both periods, 11 were stable, and two (both women in their seventies at the time of the second recording) significantly reduced their use of *a gente*—a retrograde lifespan change.

In Conclusion: Two Important Questions

Of the many general issues that are illuminated by the longitudinal studies reviewed here, only two will be brought to the fore in conclusion. These relate to how the longitudinal research illuminates (1) the issue of change, post-L1 acquisition, in speakers' grammars and (2) the utility of the concept of apparent time.

Panel studies reveal considerable differences in the usage patterns of children and adolescents growing up. Some of these differences relate to age grading, caused by young people's participation in different social circles as they mature. And some are surely evidence also of grammatical malleability through adolescence and even young adulthood. Panel studies of adults, however, are quite different. Adult lifespan change is heavily weighted toward young adults, and it generally involves features that are closer to conscious awareness: change from above, or stable sociolinguistic variables, or internal, community-generated features that have become stereotypes for community members. As with L2 acquisition in adulthood, interindividual variability is usual, as is the partial and piecemeal adoption typical of diffusion. With the exception of the retrograde pattern observed in Wagner and Sankoff (2011) and Zilles (2005), the adult lifespan changes reviewed here have involved a minority of speakers changing in the direction of the community, or of standard or supra-local influences. This is also true in studies by Sundgren (2002), Kurki (2004), and Nahkola & Saanilahti (2004). The default for adults is apparently stability.[7]

Lastly, what of apparent time? If a minority of adult speakers experience lifespan change in the direction of ongoing community change, a strict application of apparent time underestimates the rate of change. If 20 percent of 50-year-olds have participated in a community change during their adult lives, this means that 40 years ago, these people used the innovative variant less than they do now and so have changed more over that time span. The apparently uncommon reverse case (retrograde lifespan change) would imply an overestimation of the rate of change. Nevertheless, sociolinguists have never slavishly applied apparent time to calculate rates of change, and the construct continues to be extremely helpful, especially when used (as it generally is) in conjunction with the best available historical evidence.

It should also be pointed out that real-time re-studies cannot "contradict" apparent time inferences that, by their nature, provide a window only on the past. In the interim, a previous change may have reached completion, or even reversed itself. Working in a field whose core is change and variation, sociolinguists will surely continue to use the entire arsenal of tools available to them, and longitudinal studies will continue to enrich our analyses of the processes we seek to understand.

Acknowledgment

I am grateful to Bill Labov and Suzanne Evans Wagner for helpful discussion of many of the issues raised in this review; their contributions have saved me from several egregious errors and omissions. Any such that remain are my entire responsibility. I also thank the editors for their patience and encouragement.

Notes

1. Hermann (1929) discovered one completed change among the seven previously identified by Gauchat (1905) in Charmey. The relative rarity of such documentation probably stems in part from scholars' tendency to target features they already have reason to believe are changing. This practice may lead to a somewhat misleading picture of greater instability in language than actually exists.
2. A selection of recent publications, including many dealing with morphological and other features, is available on the ONZE website: http://www.lacl.canterbury.ac.nz/onze/.
3. Since most well-known cases of stable sociolinguistic variation have been confirmed historically, the curvilinear pattern of an adolescent peak would not be misinterpreted as change. Nevertheless, the rare studies that show a convergence of results from apparent and real time in cases of stability (e.g., Jose 2010) provide ratification for the reliability of apparent time inferences.
4. Of course, contact can also lead to changes well below the level of speakers' awareness.
5. This paper does not discuss whether the change is from above or from below. Tagliamonte comments (p.c.) that it has the earmarks of originally having been a change from below that was widely diffused later on as a change from above.
6. Acquisition studies fall outside of the scope of this review.
7. Working from a different angle, this conclusion was also reached by Meyerhoff and Walker (2007) in demonstrating that long-term 'urban sojourners' from the Caribbean island of Bequia have retained native grammatical constraints on copula variation despite considerable adult exposure to other dialects.

References

Auer, P., Hinskens, F., & Kerswill, P. (eds.), 2005. *Dialect change: Convergence and divergence in European languages.* Cambridge: Cambridge University Press.

Barnfield, K., & Buchstaller, I. 2010. Intensifiers on Tyneside: Longitudinal developments and new trends. *English World-Wide* 31(3): 252–87.

Blondeau, H. 2003. The old *nous* and the new *nous*: A comparison of 19th and 20th century spoken Quebec French. *University of Pennsylvania Working Papers in Linguistics* 9(2):1–14.

Blondeau, H. 2006. La trajectoire de l'emploi du futur chez une cohorte de Montréalais francophones entre 1971 et 1995. *Canadian Journal of Applied Linguistics* 9: 73–98.

Blondeau, H., Sankoff, G., & Charity, A. 2002. Parcours individuels dans deux changements linguistiques en cours en français montréalais. *Revue québécoise de linguistique* 31: 13–38.

Bowie, D. 2005. Language change over the lifespan: A test of the apparent time construct. *University of Pennsylvania Working Papers in Linguistics* 11(2): 45–58.

Buchstaller, I., Rickford, J., Traugott, E., Wasow, T., & Zwicky, A. 2010. The sociolinguistics of a short-lived innovation: Tracing the development of quotative *all* across spoken and internet newsgroup data. *Language Variation and Change* 22:191–219.

Carter, P. 2007. Phonetic variation and speaker agency: Mexicana identity in a North Carolina middle school. *University of Pennsylvania Working Papers in Linguistics* 13(2): 1–14.

Cedergren, H. 1987. The spread of language change: Verifying inferences of linguistic diffusion, In P.H. Lowenberg (ed.), *Language spread and language policy: Issues, implications and case studies*, 45–60. Georgetown: Georgetown University Press.

Cedergren, H., Clermont, J., & Côté, F. 1981. Le facteur temps et deux diphtongues du français montréalais. In D. Sankoff & H. Cedergren (eds.), *Variation Omnibus*, 169–76. Alberta: Linguistic Research.

Conn, J. C. 2005. Of "moice" and men: The evolution of a male-led sound change. Ph.D. dissertation, University of Pennsylvania.

Cornips, L., & Corrigan, K. 2005. Convergence and divergence in grammar. In P. Auer, F. Hinskens, & P. Kerswill (eds.), *Dialect change: Convergence and divergence in European languages*, 96–134. Cambridge: Cambridge University Press.

Cukor-Avila, P. 2002. She say, She go, She be like: Verbs of quotation over time in African American Vernacular English. *American Speech* 77: 3–31.

Cukor-Avila, P., & Bailey, G. 2011. The interaction of transmission and diffusion in the spread of linguistic forms. *University of Pennsylvania Working Papers in Linguistics* 17(2): 1–9.

DeDecker, P. 2006. A real-time investigation of social and phonetic changes in post-adolescence. *University of Pennsylvania Working Papers in Linguistics* 12(2): 65–76.

Elliott, N. 2000. A sociolinguistic study of rhoticity in American film speech from the 1930s to the 1970s. Ph.D. dissertation, University of Indiana.

Encrevé, P. 2009. Méthodes en linguistique synchronique: Conférence pour l'ouverture du centenaire de la naissance d'Andre Martinet. *La Linguistique* 45: 37–57.

Gauchat, L. 1905. L'unité phonétique dans le patois d'un commune. In *Aus Romanischen Sprachen und Literaturen: Festgabe für Heinrich Morf*, 175–232. Halle, Germany: Max Niemeyer Verlag.

Gerritsen, M. 1999. Divergence of dialects in a linguistic laboratory near the Belgian-Dutch-German border: Similar dialects under the influence of different standard languages. *Language Variation and Change* 11: 43–65.

Gordon, E., Campbell, L., Hay, J., Maclagan, M., Sudbury, A., & Trudgill, P. 2004. *New Zealand English: Its origins and evolution*. Cambridge: Cambridge University Press.

Gordon, E., & Maclagan, M. 2001. Capturing a sound change: A real time study over 15 years of the NEAR/SQUARE diphthong merger in New Zealand English. *Australian Journal of Linguistics* 21: 215–38.

Gregersen, F., Maegaard, M., & Pharao, N. 2009. The long and short of (ae)-variation in Danish: A panel study of short (ae)-variants in Danish in real time. *Acta Linguistica Hafniensia* 41: 64–82.

Harrington, J. 2006. An acoustic analysis of 'happy-tensing' in the Queen's Christmas broadcasts. *Journal of Phonetics* 34: 439–57.

Harrington, J. 2007. Evidence for a relationship between synchronic variability and diachronic change in the Queen's annual Christmas broadcasts. In J. Cole & J. Hualde (eds.), *Laboratory Phonology 9*, 125–43. Berlin: Mouton de Gruyter.

Hermann, E. 1929. Lautveränderungen in der individualsprache einer Mundart. *Nachrichten der Gesellschaft der Wissenschaften zu Göttingen*. Phl.-his. Kll., 11: 195–214.

Hernandez-Campoy, J. M., & Jimenez-Cano, J. M. 2003. Broadcasting Standardisation: An analysis of the linguistic normalisation process in Murcian Spanish. *Journal of Sociolinguistics* 7: 321–47.

Hollett, P. 2006. Investigating St. John's English: Real- and apparent-time perspectives. *The Canadian Journal of Linguistics* 51: 143–60.

Johnson, D. E . 2009. *Stability and change across a dialect boundary: the low vowels of southeastern New England*. Publication of the American Dialect Society 95. Durham, NC: Duke University Press.

Jose, B. 2010. The apparent-time construct and stable variation: Final /z/ devoicing in northwestern Indiana. *Journal of Sociolinguistics* 14(1): 34–59.

Kerswill, P., & Williams, A. 2005. New towns and koineization: Linguistic and social correlates. *Linguistics* 43:1023–048.

Kurki, T. 2004. Applying the apparent-time method and the real-time method on Finnish. In B.-L. Gunnarsson et al. (eds.), *Language Variation in Europe: Papers from the Second International Conference on Language Variation in Europe (ICLaVE)* 2, pages 241–52. Uppsala University, Sweden.

Labov, W. 1963. The social motivation of a sound change. *Word* 19: 273–309. Revised as Ch.1 of W. Labov, 1972. *Sociolinguistic patterns*. Philadelphia: University of Pennsylvania Press, 1–42.

Labov, W. 1966. *The social stratification of English in New York City*. Washington DC: Center for Applied Linguistics.

Labov, W. 2001. *Principles of Linguistic Change, vol. 2: Social factors*. Oxford: Blackwell.

Labov, W. 2006. *The social stratification of English in New York City*, 2nd ed. Cambridge: Cambridge University Press.

Labov, W. 2007. Transmission and diffusion. *Language* 83: 344–87.

Labov, W. (in press). *Dialect diversity in North America: The politics of language change:* Charlotteville: University of Virginia Press.

Labov, W., Ash, S., & Boberg, C. 2006. *The atlas of North American English: Phonology and sound change*. Berlin: Mouton de Gruyter.

MacKenzie, L., & Sankoff, G. 2009. A quantitative analysis of diphthongization in Montreal French. *University of Pennsylvania Working Papers in Linguistics* 15(2): 90–99.

Malvar, E. 2003. Future temporal reference in Brazilian Portuguese: Past and present. Ph.D. dissertation, University of Ottawa.

McCarthy, C. 2010. The Northern Cities Shift in real time: Evidence from Chicago. *University of Pennsylvania Working Papers in Linguistics* 15(2): 101–10.

Meyerhoff, M., & Walker, J. A. 2007. The persistence of variation in individual grammars: Copula absence in 'urban sojourners' and their stay-at-home peers, Bequia (St Vincent and the Grenadines). *Journal of Sociolinguistics* 11: 346–66.

Nahkola, K., & Saanilahti, M. 2004. Mapping language changes in real time: A panel study on Finnish. *Language Variation and Change* 16: 75–92.

Naro, A. J., & Scherre, M. 2002. *The individual and the community in real-time linguistic change: Social dimensions*. Paper presented at NWAV31, Stanford University.

Naro, A. J., & Scherre, M. 2003. Estabilidade e mudança lingüística em tempo real: A concordância de número. In M. De Paiva & M. E. Duarte (eds.), *Mudança Lingüística em tempo real*, 47–62. Rio de Janeiro: Capa.

Nguyen, J. G. 2006. Real-time changes in social stratification: Status and gender in trajectories of change for AAE variables. *University of Pennsylvania Working Papers in Linguistics* 12(2):159–71.

Nordberg, B. 1972. Böjningen av neutrala substantiv i Eskilstunaspråket (The inflection of neuter nouns in the urban dialect of Eskilstuna). *Nysvenska studier* 51(1971): 117–227.

Nordberg, B. 1985. Det mångskiftande språket. Om variation i nusvenskan (The variable language. On variation in modern Swedish). *Ord och Stil. Språkvårdssamfundets skrifter 14*. Malmö, Sweden.

Poplack, S., & Dion, N. 2009. Prescription vs. praxis: The evolution of future temporal reference in French. *Language* 85: 557–87.

Poplack, S., & Malvar, E. 2007. Elucidating the transition period in linguistic change: The expression of the future in Brazilian Portuguese. *Probus* 19: 121–69.

Poplack, S., & St-Amand, A. 2007. A real-time window on 17th century vernacular French: the Récits du français québécois d'autrefois. *Language in Society* 36: 707–34.

Richards, H. 2010. Preterite *be:* A new perspective? *English World-Wide* 31: 62–81.

Sankoff, G. 2005. Cross-sectional and longitudinal studies in sociolinguistics. In A. Ulrich, N. Dittmar, K. J. Mattheier, & P. Trudgill (eds.), *An International Handbook of the Science of Language and Society,* vol. 2, 2nd ed., 1003–013. Berlin: Mouton de Gruyter.

Sankoff, G. 2006. Age: Apparent time and real time. In K. Brown (ed.), *Encyclopedia of Language and Linguistics*, 110–16. Boston: Elsevier.

Sankoff, G. (in preparation). Language change across the lifespan: The three trajectory types. Paper delivered to the Linguistic Society of America, January 2013.

Sankoff, G., & Blondeau, H. 2007. Language change across the lifespan: /r/ in Montreal French. *Language* 83: 560–88.

Schilling-Estes, N. 2005. Language change in apparent and real time: The community and the individual. *University of Pennsylvania Working Papers in Linguistics* 10(2): 219–32.

Sundgren, E. 2002. Aterbesok i eskilstuna: en undersokning av morfologisk variation och forandring i nutida talsprak (Eskilstuna revisited: An investigation of morphological variation and change in present-day spoken Swedish). Ph.D. dissertation, Uppsala University.

Sundgren, E. 2009. The varying influence of social and linguistic factors on language stability and change: the case of Eskilstuna. *Language Variation and Change* 21: 97–133.

Tagliamonte, S. A. 2003. Every place has a different toll: Determinants of grammatical variation in cross-variety perspective. In G. Rhodenberg & B. Mondorf (eds.), *Determinants of grammatical variation in English*, 531–54. Berlin: Mouton de Gruyter.

Tagliamonte, S. A., & D'Arcy, A. 2004. He's like, she's like: The quotative system in Canadian youth. *Journal of Sociolinguistics* 8: 493–514.

Tagliamonte, S. A., & D'Arcy, A. 2009. Peaks beyond phonology: Adolescence, incrementation, and language change. *Language* 85: 58–108.

Thomas, E. R. 2010. A longitudinal analysis of the durability of the Northern-Midland dialect boundary in Ohio. *American Speech* 85: 375–430.

Trudgill, P. 1988. Norwich revisited: Recent linguistic changes in an English urban dialect. *English World-Wide* 9: 33–49.

Van de Velde, H., Gerritsen, M., & van Hout, R. 1996. The devoicing of fricatives in Standard Dutch: A real-time study based on radio recordings. *Language Variation and Change* 8: 149–75.

Van Hofwegen, J., & Wolfram, W. 2010. Coming of age in African American English: A longitudinal study. *Journal of Sociolinguistics* 14: 427–55.

Wagner, S. E. 2008. Language change and stabilization in the transition from adolescence to adulthood. Ph.D. dissertation, University of Pennsylvania.

Wagner, S. E., & Sankoff, G. 2011. Age grading in the Montréal French inflected future. *Language Variation and Change* 23(3): 275–313.

Woolard, K. 2011. Is there linguistic life after high school? Longitudinal changes in the bilingual repertoire in metropolitan Catalonia. *Language in Society* 40(5): 617–48.

Zilles, A. M. S. 2005. The development of a new pronoun: The linguistic and social embedding of *a gente* in Brazilian Portuguese. *Language Variation and Change* 17: 19–53.

CHAPTER 14

METHODS FOR STUDYING SIGN LANGUAGES

CEIL LUCAS

IN March of 2008, a research team flew from Washington, DC, to Houston, Texas, to collect filmed data to collect data for a project on Black ASL (McCaskill et al. 2011). This trip naturally entailed detailed logistics, not the least of which involved recruiting members of the Houston black Deaf community to participate in the filming. The team had two contact people in Houston, members of the community who contacted other members to recruit them for a session during which they would be videotaped in free conversation and in an interview, a session for which they would be paid and offered lunch. As the time approached for the team to fly to Houston, it appeared that a good number had agreed to come to the session. However, upon arrival in Houston, the contact people informed the team that a leader of the Dallas Deaf community had found out about the taping session and had warned as many people as she could to not cooperate with the contact people. In the view that she shared widely, "those Gallaudet University researchers" were coming to Houston to steal the language of the community and to make money off of the Deaf community. The team did end up with some excellent free conversations and interviews, so the trip was certainly not wasted, but the warning by the Dallas leader also managed to keep a number of potential participants away. One of the project co-directors was subsequently able to contact the Dallas leader and explain to her at length and face-to-face via video phone the purpose and value of the project, and she was able to gain an understanding of what the team was doing. But it was of course too late for that particular data collection session.

This anecdote serves as a clear example of the kinds of methodological issues that can arise when collecting sociolinguistic data in Deaf communities. Many of these issues are, of course, not unique to Deaf communities—researchers who work in spoken language communities encounter many of the same issues. This chapter will discuss methods for sociolinguistic studies in sign language communities and will touch on four main topics: (1) data collection, (2) defining variables and constraints, (3) data reduction, and (4) dissemination of the findings.[1]

Collecting Data

Selection of Subjects

A major component of data collection, of course, is the selection of the subjects. Sociolinguistic studies seek to determine the correlation between language variation and speaker—in this case, signer—characteristics, including age, gender, ethnicity, region, and socioeconomic status. Although some characteristics like gender, age, and ethnicity might be common to all studies of linguistic variation, many of these characteristics need to be articulated more fully when they are put into research practice in a particular community. This is particularly true for studies of linguistic variation in Deaf communities. Notions like socioeconomic status or even age cannot be simply borrowed whole from studies of variation in spoken language communities. The differences in social characteristics when applied to Deaf communities are of two types. The first type includes characteristics, like age and region that may have a different meaning when the history of Deaf communities is taken into account. The second type includes characteristics that are unique to Deaf communities, like language background.

For deaf people, regional background, or where they were born, may be less important than where they attended school (especially if it was a residential school), or where their language models acquired ASL. Age as a characteristic may have different effects on linguistic variation because of the differences in language policies in schools and programs for deaf children that have existed since 1817. Some differences in language use may be the result of changes in educational policies, like the shift from oralism to Total Communication or from Total Communication to a bilingual-bicultural approach.[2] These language policies have affected not only which language is used in the classroom but also teacher hiring practices that supported hiring either deaf teachers who know the sign language in question or hearing teachers who cannot sign. These language policies have affected deaf children's access to appropriate language models, and this access may have varied across time to such an extent that it has affected the kind of variation that we see in sign languages today.

One strong example of this differential access concerns the black Deaf community in the United States. Following the Civil War, 17 states and the Kendall School in the District of Columbia established separate schools for black deaf children or opened "departments" on the campus of schools for white children (i.e., separate buildings). Even though deaf education started propitiously in 1817 at the American School for the Deaf in Hartford, Connecticut, with ASL as the medium of instruction, by 1880, oralism was firmly established in the schools for white deaf children, with many deaf teachers being fired. However, the policy of oralism was not extended evenly to the schools for black deaf children, and the use of sign language as the medium of instruction was widely allowed. In addition, some schools for black deaf children had white, deaf, ASL-signing teachers, providing the children with ASL input. Then, following the Supreme Court's 1954 decision in *Brown v. Board of Education*, black and white deaf children slowly began to attend school together (but some states, like Louisiana, managed to delay integration until 1978!), and the practice of mainstreaming began to take over education at residential schools, so deaf children increasingly had more contact with their hearing peers. All of this helps explain the variation in Black ASL that McCaskill et al. (2011) have found: for example, noticeably less mouthing in older signers, since they had less direct exposure to oralism and hearing peers who spoke English.

This discussion illustrates clearly that the selection of subjects for sociolinguistic studies of sign languages must take into account the meaning of age, ethnicity, and region in Deaf communities, in order for the resulting analyses to be meaningful. Furthermore, large studies of sociolinguistic variation in ASL (Lucas et al. 2001) and other sign languages such as Auslan (Schembri et al. 2009) have clearly shown the importance of whether a subject comes from a Deaf family in which the sign language is used or from a non-signing family, be it hearing or deaf. For example, Lucas et al. (2001) demonstrated that subjects from Deaf families were more likely to use the standard "citation" forms of signs, such as signs like KNOW produced at the forehead as opposed to lower locations.

Contact People

Central to the selection of subjects are contact people. The approach to participants in Lucas et al. (2001) and McCaskill et al. (2011), for example, was guided by the work of Labov (1972a, 1972b, 1984) and Milroy (1987). Groups were assembled in each area by a contact person, a Deaf individual living in the area with a good knowledge of the community. These contact people were similar to the "brokers" described by Milroy, individuals who "have contacts with large numbers of individuals" in the community (1987: 70). It was the responsibility of the contact people to identify persons suitable for the study—in the case of the 2001 and 2011 studies, fluent lifelong users of ASL who had lived in the community for at least 10 years.

As we saw in the opening section, community members can be decidedly reluctant about participating in a study and may outright refuse to do so. This is not at all unique to Deaf communities. As Wolfram (chapter 37, this volume) explains, "community members may have underlying questions and concerns about sociolinguists' motivations in working in their community. What are they really doing in their community? Why are they so obsessed with the minutia of language? Do they have an underlying sociopolitical agenda in terms of language?" He goes on to say that "we need to enter the community fully understanding and appreciating the legitimacy of the community's practical cautions and concerns about the motives of sociolinguistic researchers." Feagin (2002: 26) observes that "skin color, class affiliation, speech, or education may all set the investigator apart."

There are particular concerns in Deaf communities, directly tied to the history of Deaf education and to how research on sign languages has taken place. Oralism, the belief that spoken language is inherently superior to sign language, played an important role in Deaf education. Even though Deaf education in the United States began in 1817 with sign language as the medium of instruction, by 1880, the oral method of instruction was well established in the white schools (Lane et al. 1996). As Burch and Joyner (2007: 21) note, "the rise of oralism motivated schools across the country to replace deaf teachers with hearing instructors who would speak to students rather than sign with them." In the mid-1970s, in light of low reading levels among deaf students, the transition was made to the simultaneous use of speaking and signing, on the theory that deaf students could thus see English being produced on the mouth and hands, to help them in their learning of English. Specific manual codes for English (MCEs) were devised such as Signing Exact English (SEE; Gustason, Pfetzing, & Zawolkow 1972), which purported to represent the syntax, morphology, and lexicon of spoken English. As Ramsey (1989: 123) states, "The developers built the requisite MCE lexicon by borrowing ASL signs, modifying ASL signs with handshape features from the manual alphabet, and inventing signs specifically to represent English derivational and inflectional morphemes." She goes on to observe that "the materials used to construct SEE 2 are highly valued linguistic resources in the Deaf community: ASL lexical items and the medium of signing itself. These resources are being used to promote the linguistic values of another community" (143), that is, the teachers and parents and educational administrators who see MCEs as an answer for teaching deaf children.

At the same time that MCEs were being devised, research on the structure and use of sign languages was underway in many places, with many members of the Deaf community serving as informants and sign models for hearing researchers. Not infrequently, this research was published with only a brief mention, if any, of these informants and models, naturally leading to resentment. Singleton, Jones, and Hanumantha (2012) conducted a focus-group study with members of the Deaf community and researchers and reported that two main issues emerged: lack of trust and confidentiality. The lack of trust has to do in part with feelings of tokenism on the part of Deaf researchers, "feelings of being exploited and that they had not received adequate credit for their contributions to the work" (21). Resentment can also arise concerning the ownership of the research findings, and "some resented the academic superiority of English over ASL in the publication world and the fact that published materials are predominantly in English" (23). Issues that have arisen in doing research in Deaf communities have also been explored by Baker-Shenk and Kyle (1990) and Harris, Holmes, and Mertens (2009). Harris et al. (2009: 114) state, "it is critical that researchers attempt to determine the ways in which Sig Language [*sic*] community members feel and think about the world and give these the recognition they deserve." Based on Osborne and McPhee's (2000) indigenous terms of reference, they propose six principles to be considered when sign language communities are studied, principles that center on openly involving and empowering the members of the community. The fact that community members have most often not been involved and empowered has led to caution and, often, reluctance by community members to cooperate with researchers, a reluctance that the contact people have to mediate.

The Observer's Paradox

Another factor that shapes data collection is the sensitivity of signers to the audiological status and ethnicity of the audience. The amount of attention language users pay to their language production has been addressed by sociolinguists starting with Labov (1972a), who discussed what he referred to as "Observer's Paradox"; that is, our interest is in the language signers and speakers use when they are not being observed, but to obtain the kind of data that we need for analysis, we need to record signers' (or speakers') production in situations that often lead to self-consciousness. The problem is particularly acute in sign linguistics because on video, there is no way that signers can be completely anonymous. In addition, as scholars who have discussed the influence of audience design on language use have shown (see, e.g., Bell 1984, 2001; Giles 1973, 2001; Giles & Powesland 1975), speakers and signers often adjust their language use to accommodate to what they perceive as the preference of their interlocutors.

In sign linguistics, Lucas and Valli (1992) demonstrated that ASL users are very sensitive to an interviewer's audiological status and ethnicity, that is, hearing or deaf, black or white. This sensitivity may be manifested by rapid switching from ASL to Signed English (a manual code for English) or Contact Signing (an outcome of the contact between ASL and English characterized by core features from both languages and continuous mouthing). As explained by Giles's Accommodation Theory (1973), many Deaf people will adjust their signing to bring it closer to what they perceive to be the preference of their interlocutor.

Issues of the lack of anonymity need to be clearly and carefully handled during the consent process, so that subjects consent (or do not) to having their images shown as part of conference presentations or in publications. As Singleton et al. (2012: 4) state, there may be a "need to translate informed consent documents into the native language of the host community (i.e., videos using American Sign Language) to ensure that Deaf participants, who may have limited English proficiency, are offered accessible information regarding their rights as research participants." To avoid codeswitching caused by the interviewer, researchers need to be very mindful of the audiological status and ethnicity of the interviewer. One instance from the Black ASL project illustrates this quite starkly: the Black ASL team interviewed an elderly signer. The team consisted of four black Deaf researchers and one white hearing researcher. At the end of the interview, the elderly signer wanted to know who everyone was. She knew that the interviewer was deaf and confirmed, one by one, that the other three were also deaf. The hearing white researcher then introduced herself, and because she is hearing, the elderly signer who had been signing for 90 minutes with no voice turned on her voice, speaking English for the remaining 30 minutes that the team was in her house. The hearing white researcher had stayed out of sight during the interview. Had she been present, the chances are good that the data would be quite different.

Of course, the actual tools used can include interviews, structured elicitation, questionnaires, as well as free conversation sessions. The first three must be designed with the issues discussed here in mind: for example, who is doing the interviewing and the elicitation? Are questionnaires written in English entirely accessible to all deaf ASL users or does the researcher need to go over the questionnaire with the subject? Recent advances in communication technology have directly affected the collection of sign language data. For example, researchers can now administer survey questions virtually, and subjects can respond to them virtually; that is, subjects can see the researchers asking them the questions in sign language on a computer and can respond to the researchers in sign language on the same computer. Researchers no longer have to recruit subjects to come to a physical location for data collection. This has naturally led to adjustments in the traditional signed consent form and to considerations of the effects of providing virtual responses on the nature of the resulting data. In addition, there now exists a whole new source of publicly available data, in the form of YouTube and vlogs (video logs) for example, also raising issues of permission and a wide variety of uncontrolled data collection settings. Finally, the video relay service is now being used widely for interpreting, wherein a Deaf person and an sign interpreter can actually see each other. An interpreter may be interpreting for a Deaf person from anywhere in the country, not just in his or her immediate area, and issues of how to handle lexical variation have frequently arisen and are being researched (Palmer, Reynolds, & Minor 2012).

Defining Variables and Linguistic Constraints

Variables

There are a number of phonological and morphosyntactic features of sign languages that behave variably. We see phonological variation in the handshape, location, palm orientation and movement of a sign. Some two-handed signs may be produced with one hand. In terms of syntactic variation, most sign languages are pro-drop languages and hence show variability in their use of subject pronouns. Variability is also seen in WH and negative elements, in the use of constructed dialogue and constructed action, and in the size of the signing space. There is, of course, also widespread lexical variation. The challenge is to identify which variable features of sign languages can be identified and analyzed as sociolinguistic variables. As seen with Hoopes (1998) and his study of pinky extension, one part of the challenge can be *confirming* a variable. The pinky can easily be extended as a part of signing, and the issue was to determine if this extension constituted a sociolinguistic variable. Hoopes focused on signs such as TOLERATE and WONDER and demonstrated that pinky extension tended to co-occur with prosodic features of emphatic stress, and that it tended to occur with lexemes used repeatedly within a discourse topic, before pauses and with lexemes lengthened to almost twice their usual duration.

Another example of confirming a variable can be found in the Black ASL project. During the process of writing the grant proposal to obtain funding for the project, the researchers viewed tapes of interviews done with black signers and noticed that the signers used a lot of repetition of lexical items, clauses, or whole sentences. This use of repetition was added to the list of features that might distinguish Black ASL as a separate variety of ASL and later analysis showed that it was indeed one such feature.

Sometimes the challenge can be in *identifying* a variable. An example comes from studies of Tactile ASL (TASL), the signing used by deaf-blind people in the United States,[3] specifically those with the genetic condition Usher's syndrome I. Individuals with this syndrome are born deaf and later, usually in their teen years, start losing vision in varying degrees due to retinitis pigmentosa. Crucially, most deaf-blind people in this category grow up using ASL and are fluent signers by the time they begin to lose their sight. A variety of ASL has emerged in this community that accommodates the loss of sight at all linguistic levels: phonological, morphological, syntactic, and discourse. One of the consequences of the loss of sight is that deaf-blind people no longer have access to the numerous ASL grammatical and discourse markers produced on a signer's face. Remarkably, these non-manual (facial) markers are produced on the hands in Tactile ASL. For example, the raised eyebrows required for yes/no questions or the nodding required for back- channeling are produced manually (see Collins & Petronio [1998] and Collins [2004] for fuller accounts). As mentioned, features of Tactile ASL are manifested at every level of the language and there is a vigorous community of deaf-blind signers who use Tactile ASL. Tactile ASL qualifies as a clear example of a variety of ASL but arriving at this conclusion required identifying the features that would make this so and clearly distinguishing them from the features of "visual" ASL.

Confirming and identifying variables can happen with reference to earlier studies. For example, studies done in the 1970s had shown that two-handed signs could become one-handed (Woodward & DeSantis 1977), that signs could be lowered and moved to a more central signing space (Woodward, Erting, & Oliver 1976; Frishberg 1975) and that signs such as DEAF could experience metathesis (Liddell & Johnson 1989). Confirming and identifying can also happen through observation, as in the case of repetition described earlier. And it can happen via informed intuition. This was the case in the Black ASL project (McCaskill et al. 2011) with the incorporation of features of spoken African American English into ASL signing. It simply stood to reason that younger black signers who had attended integrated educational programs would incorporate such features into their signing and in fact, they do. Expressions such as "girl, please" and "my bad" find their way into ASL, as does slapping five in agreement during the course of a conversation.

The Envelope of Variation

A related issue has to do with defining the *envelope of variation*, that is, deciding which instances of a particular phenomenon will be included or excluded from an analysis and why. A sociolinguistic variable may be defined as two ways of saying or signing the same thing, with the distribution of different forms influenced by linguistic and social factors (Labov 1972b). For example, an ASL user may sign DEAF from ear to chin or from chin to ear. However, the meaning of the concept DEAF does not change. And, as Bayley, Lucas, and Rose (2000) have shown, signers' choices among the different forms of DEAF are affected by the grammatical class to which the sign belongs, as well as by a number of social factors, including the region where the signer lives and age. Turning to an example from variation between one-handed and two-handed versions of the same sign, it is clear that DEER signed with two hands and DEER signed with one hand refer to the same creature.

Before we begin coding examples, then, we first need to decide which signs to include in the envelope of variation and which signs to exclude. We can consider the case of two-handed signs that can be signed one-handed. The task is complicated to a certain extent by the fact that ASL contains different types of two-handed signs. Signs of Type 1 can be produced with only one articulator. Examples include: DEER, DON'T KNOW, FINISH, HORSE, NOW, PONDER, SICK, TIRED, and WANT. Signs of Type 2 may be divided into two subtypes. Type 2a signs cannot usually be produced with only one hand. Examples include CAN'T, CHEESE, CHURCH, SOCKS, STAR, and WORK. Signs that can be designated as Type 2b can be produced with a substitute base or produced one-handed in very particular discourse situations. Examples include RIGHT, PAPER, SCHOOL, and SHOES. In an earlier study of handedness (Lucas et al. 2007) and in the Black ASL study (McCaskill et al. 2011), we coded only signs that can be produced with two hands or one hand unremarkably. Signs in Type 2a and 2b were excluded as being outside the "envelope of variation" or subject to constraints that have nothing to do with linguistic variation, such as the presence or absence of a convenient substitute base. Similarly, in Lucas et al. (2001), signs with a 1 handshape that depict verbs (also widely referred to as *classifier predicates*) were excluded, since the handshape in those signs is semantically motivated.

Table 14.1 provides a summary of variables looked at in studies of ASL, Black ASL, Australian and New Zealand Sign Languages (Auslan, NZSL), and Italian Sign Language (LIS), along with the number of tokens of each variable were included.

Table 14.1. Summary of variables in different sign languages

Language	Variable	Number of tokens
American Sign Language (ASL)	1 handshape	5195
	location	2862
	DEAF	1618
	Pro-drop	429
	2 hand—> 1 hand	2258
Black ASL	2 hand—> 1 hand	818 (+2258 earlier study)
	location	877 (+2862 earlier study)
	size of signing space	2247
	clausal or phrasal repetition	172
	mouthing	221
	Constructed dialogue/ constructed action	1021
Auslan/New Zealand Sign Language (NZSL)	location	2667 Auslan, 2096 NZSL
	PRO-DROP	977 Auslan, 2145 NZSL
Italian Sign Language (LIS)	WH elements	1400 annotated, 646 coded

Sources: For ASL, Lucas et al. (2001); Lucas & Bayley (2010); for Black ASL, McCaskill et al. (2011); for Auslan/NZSL, McKee et al. (2011), Schembri et al. (2009); for LIS, Geraci & Bayley (2011).

Linguistic Constraints

Recall that internal constraints on variation are linguistic features that may play some role in the occurrence of variation. Wolfram (pers. comm. 1994) has stated that the internal constraints on variables may be compositional, sequential, functional, or having to do with structural incorporation. Compositional constraints are those that have to do with the linguistic nature of the variable itself. Battison, Markowicz, and Woodward (1975), for example, stated that thumb extension in such signs as FUNNY and CUTE had to do with how many other fingers were extended and whether there was internal movement in the sign. In the signs FUNNY and CUTE, the fingers oscillate. Sequential constraints are features in the immediate linguistic environment surrounding the variable, such as the handshape or palm orientation of the sign immediately preceding or following the variable sign. Functional constraints relate to the role that the sign's grammatical category plays in variation, while the constraint of structural incorporation concerns the syntactic environment of a variable. Finally, there may be pragmatic constraints on variation, as Hoopes (1998) found for pinky extension.

Earlier studies of sign language phonology (Liddell & Johnson 1989) claimed that variation such as the lowering of signs, such as KNOW or the metathesis observed in the sign DEAF, had constraints of a sequential nature, as in spoken languages, such that DEAF followed by a sign on the forehead might be signed chin to ear while DEAF followed by a sign on the torso might be signed ear to chin. However, the results of Lucas et al. (2001) and Hoopes (1998) demonstrate that the analysis of internal constraints on variation in sign languages needs to be done carefully because the identification of such constraints is not always completely straightforward. For example, further examination of DEAF, signs like KNOW, and 1-handshape signs has shown that the grammatical category of the target sign may have a significant role in explaining the variation. For all three variables—DEAF, signs like KNOW, and 1-handshape signs—grammatical category is at least as important in explaining the variation as sequential features, such as the preceding or following sign. For example, when DEAF is a predicate ('I am deaf'), it tends to be signed ear to chin. Adjectives ('deaf cat') and nouns ('Deaf [people] know that') use both ear to chin and chin to ear forms, while compound signs (DEAF^WORLD, DEAF^CULTURE) tend to favor the contact-cheek form of DEAF.

The main question is: why do grammatical and prosodic constraints seem to have a more important role than the features of the preceding and following signs in conditioning phonological variation in ASL? The first answer is simply that, as in spoken languages, phonological variation in ASL is not constrained exclusively by phonological factors. The focus heretofore may have been on features of the preceding and following signs, but large quantitative studies such as the one undertaken by Lucas et al. (2001) show that grammatical factors must also be considered.

A second answer concerns differences between spoken and sign languages. Having established that sign languages are indeed "real" languages, research on all aspects of sign language structure has begun to show some fundamental and most likely modality-related differences between spoken and sign languages. Of greatest relevance to the present discussion are the basic differences in how morphology functions and how these differences manifest themselves in variation. In many of the spoken languages in which phonological variation has been extensively explored, morphology is a "boundary phenomenon;" that is, meaningful segments are added to the beginning or end of other units in the language in the form of plural markers, person and tense markers, derivational affixes, and so forth. These units are essentially added to an existing phonological environment. It stands to reason that when variation occurs, a good place to look for the cause of this variation is the immediate environment to which units have been added (i.e., the preceding and following segments). In fact, many studies of spoken language variation have demonstrated the key role of the immediate phonological environment in governing variation.

However, morphology in sign languages is by and large not a boundary phenomenon, in that there exist very few sequential affixes. Morphological distinctions are accomplished by altering one or more features in the articulatory bundle that makes up a segment, or by altering the movement path of the sign. For example, segments are not usually added to other segments to provide information about person or aspect. Rather, the location feature of a segment (e.g., near or away from the signer) indicates person, and movement between locations indicates the subject and object of the verb in question. Similarly, a particular movement path may indicate continuative or inceptive aspect. As Emmorey (1999: 173) states with regard to aspect marking in ASL:

> In many spoken languages, morphologically complex words are formed by adding prefixes or suffixes to a word stem. In ASL and other signed languages, complex forms are most often created by nesting a sign stem within dynamic movement contours and planes in space…, ASL has many verbal inflections that convey temporal information about the action denoted by the verb, for example, whether the action was habitual, iterative, continual. Generally, these distinctions are marked by different movement patterns over- laid onto a sign stem. This type of morphological encoding contrasts with the primarily linear affixation found in spoken languages. For spoken languages, simultaneous affixation processes such as template morphology (e.g. in Semitic languages), infixation, or reduplication are relatively rare. Signed languages, by contrast, prefer nonconcatenative processes such as reduplication; and prefixation and suffixation are rare. Sign languages' preference for simultaneously producing affixes and stems may have its origins in the visual-manual modality.

The results of Lucas et al. (2001) indicate that these fundamental differences manifest themselves in the variable components of the language. That is, the immediate phonological environment turns out not to play the major role in governing phonological variables, in part because the variables themselves are not affixes. The grammatical category to which the variable in question belongs is consistently the first-order linguistic constraint. (In this regard, see also Brentari 2002.)

This finding has important implications for our understanding of variation in spoken and signed languages. As the modality differences between spoken and signed languages manifest themselves in the basic phonological, morphological, and syntactic components of the language, so they also seem to appear in the patterns of linguistic variation. As the phonological and morphological processes go, so, apparently, goes variation.

Data Reduction

Once the data has been collected, decisions need to be made about how and to what extent it will be reduced. The central issue is how to record in a useful way manual-visual languages that do not have written forms.[4] As seen in some of the examples in this chapter, one very common approach is to *gloss* signs using the written language with which the sign language is in contact—written English for ASL and Auslan, written Italian for Italian Sign Language (LIS), and so forth. So a gloss for the English word *table* would be TABLE; a gloss for the Italian word *casa* 'house' would be CASA. Glosses are not limited to single lexical items; sentences and whole texts can be glossed. Glosses can be very basic, with just the signs indicated, or they can be very complex, with indications of non-manual signals, indexing, repetition, and other features. Issues arise, of course, concerning the generalizability of glosses; that is, can the glosses developed by one researcher be understood and of use to another researcher? Given lexical variation, which sign for the gloss WATCH (verb) will a signer envision—a V handshape with the palm down or a C handshape at the mouth? Seeing the gloss for WALK, will a signer envision a V handshape appearing iconically like "legs," or two B handshapes alternating in movement, palm down? And how much of this detail should be included with the gloss?

Sign language researchers naturally want to refer to the actual signing event, and this is now possible with software such as the EUDICO Linguistic Annotator (ELAN) annotation system developed at the Max Planck Institute. This allows for a video clip being glossed to appear on the screen, and it also allows for numerous levels—"tiers"—of information to be coded. One tier can be a basic gloss and other tiers can have non-manual information, separate coding for each hand, occurrences of gestures, instances of constructed action and constructed dialogue, and so forth.

Other analyses require detailed *phonetic notation*. The first such system was introduced in 1965 by William Stokoe in his *Dictionary of American Sign*

Language (with Casterline & Croneberg), in which he presented signs according to their handshape (tabula, "tab"), location (designator, "dez") and movement (signation, "sig"). This was the first sign dictionary to present signs not by the alphabetical order of the English word to which they correspond but by their handshapes, locations, and movements. For example, the first sign in the dictionary is the sign for 'boss' or 'person in charge,' produced with an A handshape. One significant shortcoming of Stokoe's system was that he did not recognize the easily demonstrable sequentiality in the production of the parts of signs, sequentiality of handshapes, locations, movements, palm orientations, and non-manual signals. Liddell and Johnson (1989; Johnson & Liddell 2011) introduced their Movement-Hold model, which represented signs as sequences of movement segments and hold segments, parallel to sequences of consonants and vowels in spoken languages, with the features of handshape, location, palm orientation, and non-manual signals as an articulatory bundle contained in each segment. Their system has evolved over the years and is used for very close analysis of sign phonetics and phonology.

Finally, there are some situations in which a *translation* from a sign language to a written language might be needed. These are situations where a broad comparison of meaning might be required, and would be of use in research on sign interpretation or in representations of the data in which the point is to convey a general meaning. For example, the interviews in the Black ASL project (McCaskill et al. 2011) revealed some striking perceptions about the differences between black signing and white signing. Subjects were simply asked if they noticed differences between black signing and white signing, and as part of their responses, a number of them expressed the view that "white signing is better than black signing" because "white signing is more advanced, more complex." White signing is, of course, *not* more advanced or complex than black signing—in fact, one of the major findings of the project is that, because of social and geographic isolation, black signing uses more traditional, standard forms—and these perceptions are clearly a reflection of the oppression and inferior education that black deaf students had to endure. The most powerful way to present this information, particularly to hearing, non-signing audiences, is with the stark translation, "white signing is better than black signing."

Dissemination of the Findings

We come finally to the issue of disseminating the research findings. There are, of course, the usual avenues in scholarly journals and books. For conference presentations and workshops, a distinction must be made between dissemination to hearing, non-signing audiences and signing audiences that may include both deaf and hearing people.

Hearing, Non-Signing Audiences

One issue has to do with the relevance of sign language studies for spoken language linguists. In the 50 years since research on sign languages has been undertaken, research findings have informed spoken language studies in significant ways in the areas of gesture (Taub et al. 2008), the structure and use of metaphor (Taub 2001), bilingualism and language contact (Lucas & Valli 1992), first and second language acquisition (Chen Pichler 2010, 2012; Petitto 2000), variation, and the emergence of varieties of language (Lucas et al. 2001; McCaskill et al. 2011). Making the relevance of sign language studies for spoken language linguists and the sign language–spoken language connections clear is a challenge faced by sign language researchers. Meeting this challenge is accomplished by a steadily increasing presence of sign language researchers at scholarly conferences and in scholarly journals that traditionally focus on spoken languages, and by increasing collaborations of spoken language and sign language researchers working on the same topic with the shared goal of understanding how human language works, be it spoken or signed.

However, since presentations about sign languages usually involve either live demonstrations of signs or filmed examples, and also deaf presenters with interpreters, it is quite common for hearing non-signers to conclude that, since a presentation is about sign language, "I can skip this one, because I don't sign." The challenge for sign language researchers is to think about how captions, voice-over, slow motion, and careful explanation can be used effectively to make the information fully accessible and of interest to a hearing, non-signing audience. Researchers also need to think about the starting point: how much does the audience already know about sign languages and research on sign languages and how much of a foundation needs to be provided?

Signing Audiences

A signing audience is one whose members may be both deaf and hearing, as most hearing researchers who work on sign languages sign and can follow lectures in sign language. While some deaf members of a signing audience may be trained linguists, many others may be community members from many different walks of life who attend a conference because they are interested in what is being said about their language. As mentioned earlier, sign languages are highly valued cultural resources, and tension can arise when the scientific terms and academic style being used to describe them are incomprehensible to community members: "what are you saying about my language?" Researchers are challenged to handle this tension. This challenge relates directly to Wolfram's (see chapter 37, this volume) observation that the right nontechnical level for presenting one's findings needs to be found. He goes on to say that "there is often a tension between the specialized expertise of the linguist and the community perspective on language." It may happen that the findings being presented are emotionally difficult for an audience to receive. For example, for reasons clearly having to do with oppression and segregation, a number of participants in the Black ASL study, when asked if there are differences between black signing and white signing, immediately responded that "white signing is better, more advanced." One might expect this response from older signers, but it was the response of younger signers, as well. Many in the audience at a meeting of the National Black Deaf Advocates (NBDA) where these findings were presented were shocked and saddened to see signers give these responses, surprised that the younger signers still had these perceptions. And it was the challenge of the researchers presenting these findings to handle these reactions very carefully. Related challenges have to do with whether hearing presenters choose to speak or sign. They may choose to speak if their signing skills are not good enough for a formal presentation; they may choose to sign to clearly establish their connection to the community. If they choose to speak, as Singleton et al. (2012: 19) point out, this may also "raise the possibility of misanalysis of linguistic data and [question] the researcher's ability to run the study effectively and objectively when they possess limited sign proficiency."

Giving Back to the Community

One final issue related to dissemination has to do with giving back to the community. Wolfram (chapter 37, this volume) describes Labov's Principle of Error Correction (1982: 172) and Principle of Debt Incurred (1982: 173), along with his own Principle of Linguistic Gratuity (1993: 227), stating that Labov's two principles "focus on the obligation of linguists to expose misunderstandings and misinterpretations about language" (chapter 37, this volume) and to use their knowledge for the benefit of the community being studied, while Wolfram's urges researchers to "pursue positive ways in which they can return linguistic favors to the community" (Wolfram 1993: 227).

Giving back to the community is of course an issue in sign language research. Some of this giving back can be said to be of a "global" nature, while some of it is of a more "local" nature. Stokoe's (1960) pioneering work, which clearly demonstrated that sign languages are full-fledged linguistic systems that are structurally independent from the spoken languages with which they come in contact, and all of the work that followed on the structure and use of sign languages has constituted the giving back of a "global" nature; this legitimization of sign languages as "real" languages has made possible the use of sign languages as the media of instruction in the education of deaf children. This has meant that many deaf children all over the world now have unfettered access to academic content through the visual sign languages that they understand, as opposed to through oral systems or systems which combine speaking and signing (Johnson, Liddell, & Erting 1989). It has led to the recognition of sign languages as official languages in many countries, which in turn has meant that deaf people can participate in the social and legal systems of their countries by means of interpreters. Sociolinguistic research on bilingualism and language contact, variation, language planning and language policy, and language attitudes pertaining to sign languages has reinforced the status of sign languages as "real" languages and has revealed both parallels and differences with spoken languages.

Giving back of a "local" nature has involved sharing the research findings in an accessible way, as in the book and DVD entitled *What's your sign for PIZZA?* (Lucas, Bayley, & Valli 2003), which provides an introduction to variation in ASL for a popular audience, and of which copies were provided to the communities that participated in the original study. This giving back had Wolfram and Schilling-Estes's (1997) model for the Ocracoke community specifically in mind; their book was produced for a popular audience and royalties go to the historical society of the island. The royalties for *PIZZA* are donated to a scholarship fund for deaf students. A similar book-DVD package (McCaskill et al. 2011) has been prepared for the Black ASL project. And giving back locally also includes numerous free workshops for community groups about projects, interpreter-training programs, and the incorporation of project findings into course curricula. Finally, deaf undergraduate and graduate students serve as research assistants on sociolinguistic research projects and thus receive a direct introduction to the world of sign language research. Many of these students go on to earn advanced degrees and become teachers themselves.

I come back, then, to where I started, to the Texas Deaf community leader who so powerfully expressed her concerns and influenced the data collection process. Her concerns are not merely imagined. With this chapter, I hope to have illustrated the kinds of issues that arise with data collection, identification of variables and constraints, data reduction, and dissemination in the sociolinguistic study of sign languages.

Notes

1. Portions of this paper are adapted from Hoopes et al. (2001); Lucas, Bayley, and Valli (2001); and Lucas and Bayley (2010).
2. Oralism is a method that involves teaching deaf children solely through speech, to the total exclusion of any signing; Total Communication (Denton 1976) was a philosophy supporting the use of both speech and signing, most often simultaneously.
3. Tactile signing is not limited to the United States; see, for example, Mesch (2000) on tactile signing in Sweden.

4. Attempts have been made to develop writing systems for sign languages; see, for example, www.signwri.

References

Baker-Shenk, C., & Kyle, J. 1990. Research with Deaf people: Issues and conflicts. *Disability, Handicap and Society* 5: 65–75.

Battison, R., Markowicz, H., & Woodward, J. 1975. A good rule of thumb: Variable phonology in American Sign Language. In R. W. Fasold & R. W. Shuy (eds.), *Analyzing variation in language*, 291–302. Washington, DC: Georgetown University Press.

Bayley, R., Lucas, C., & Rose, M. 2000. Variation in American Sign Language: The case of DEAF. *Journal of Sociolinguistics* 4: 81–107.

Bell, A. 1984. Language style as audience design. *Language in Society* 13: 145–204.

Bell, A. 2001. Back in style: Reworking audience design. In P. Eckert & J. R. Rickford (eds.), *Style and sociolinguistic variation*, 139–69. Cambridge: Cambridge University Press.

Brentari, D. 2002. Modality differences in sign language phonology and morphophonemics. In R. Meier, D. Quinto-Pozos, & K. Cormier (eds.), *Modality in language and linguistic theory*, 35–64. Cambridge: Cambridge University Press.

Burch, S., & Joyner, H. 2007. *Unspeakable: The story of Junius Wilson*. Chapel Hill: University of North Carolina Press.

Chen Pichler, D. 2010. Sources of handshape error in first-time signers of ASL. D. J. Napoli & G. Mathur (eds.), *Deaf around the world*, 96–121. Oxford: Oxford University Press.

Chen Pichler, D. 2012. Language acquisition. In R. Pfau, B. Woll, & M. Steinbach (eds.), *Handbook of linguistics and communication science: Sign language*, 646–86. Berlin: Mouton de Gruyter.

Collins, S. C. 2004. Adverbial morphemes in Tactile American Sign Language. Ph.D. dissertation, The Union Institute.

Collins, S. C., & Petronio, K. 1998. What happens in Tactile ASL? In C. Lucas (ed.), *Pinky extension and eye gaze: Language use in Deaf communities*, 18–37. Washington, DC: Gallaudet University Press.

Denton, D. 1976. The philosophy of total communication. Supplement to the *British Deaf News*. Carlisle, UK: The British Deaf Association.

Emmorey, K. 1999. The confluence of space and language in signed languages. In P. Bloom, M. A. Peterson, L. Nodel, & M. F. Garrett (eds.), *Language and space*, 171–209. Cambridge, MA: MIT Press.

Feagin, C. 2002. Entering the community: Fieldwork. In J. K. Chambers, P. Trudgill, & N. Schilling-Estes (eds.), *The handbook of language variation and change*, 20–39. Oxford: Blackwell.

Frishberg. N. 1975. Arbitrariness and iconicity: Historical change in American Sign Language. *Language* 51: 696–719.

Geraci, C., & Bayley, R. 2011. Chi, cosa, dove, perché e quando: la distribuzione dei segni wh- in LIS. In A. Cardinaletti, C. Cecchetto, & C. Donati (eds.), *Grammatica, lessico e deimensioni di variazione nella LIS*, 127-44. Milan: FrancoAngeli.

Giles, H. 1973. Accent mobility: A model and some data. *Anthropological Linguistics* 15: 87–105.

Giles, H. 2001. Couplandia and beyond. In P. Eckert & J. R. Rickford (eds.), *Style and sociolinguistic variation*, 211–19. Cambridge: Cambridge University Press.

Giles, H., & Powesland., P. F 1975. *Speech style and social evaluation*. London: Academic Press.

Gustason, J., Pfetzing, D., & Zawolkow, E. (eds.). 1972. *Signing exact English*. Los Alamitos, CA: Modern Signs Press.

Harris, R., Holmes, H., & Mertens, D. 2009. Research Ethics in Sign Language Communities. *Sign Language Studies* 9: 104–31.

Hoopes, R. 1998. A preliminary examination of pinky extension: Suggestions regarding its occurrence, constraints and function. In C. Lucas (ed.), *Pinky extension and eye gaze: Language use in Deaf communities*, 3–17. Washington, DC: Gallaudet University Press.

Hoopes, R., Rose, M., Bayley, R., Lucas, C., Wulf, A., Petronio, K., & Collins, S. 2001. Analyzing variation in sign languages: Theoretical and methodological issues. In V. Dively et al. (eds.), *Signed languages: Discoveries from international research*, 135–62. Washington, DC: Gallaudet University Press.

Johnson, R., Liddell, S., & Erting, C. 1989. Unlocking the curriculum: Principles for achieving access in Deaf education. Gallaudet Research Institute Working Paper 89–3. Washington, DC: Gallaudet University.

Johnson, R., & Liddell, S. 2011. Toward a phonetic representation of signs, 1: Sequentiality and contrast. *Sign Language Studies* 11: 241–73.

Labov, W. 1972a. *Sociolinguistic patterns*. Philadelphia: University of Pennsylvania Press.

Labov, W. 1972b. *Language in the inner city*. Philadelphia: University of Pennsylvania Press.

Labov, W. 1982. Objectivity and commitment in linguistic science. *Language in Society* 11: 165–201.

Labov, W . 1984. Field methods of the Project on Language Change and Variation. In J. Baugh & J. Sherzer (eds.), *Language in use: Readings in sociolinguistics*, 28–53. Englewood Cliffs, NJ: Prentice-Hall.

Lane, H., Hoffmeister, R., & Bahan, B. 1996. *A journey into the DEAF^WORLD*. San Diego: DawnSign Press.

Liddell, S., & Johnson, R. 1989. American Sign Language: The phonological base. *Sign Language Studies* 64: 195–278.

Lucas, C., & Bayley, R. 2010. Variation in American Sign Language. In D. Brentari (ed.), *Sign languages*, 451–75. Cambridge: Cambridge University Press.

Lucas, C., Bayley, R., & Valli, C. 2001. *Sociolinguistic variation in American Sign Language*. Washington, DC: Gallaudet University Press.

Lucas, C., Bayley, R., & Valli, C. 2003. *What's your sign for PIZZA? An introduction to variation in ASL*. (with DVD). Washington, DC: Gallaudet University Press.

Lucas, C., Goeke, A., Briesacher, R., & Bayley, R. 2007. Phonological variation in ASL: 2 hands or 1? Paper presented at NWAV 36, University of Pennsylvania, Philadelphia, October.

Lucas, C., & Valli, C. 1992. *Language contact in the American Deaf community*. San Diego: Academic Press.

McCaskill, C., Lucas, C., Bayley, R., & Hill, J. 2011. *The hidden treasure of Black ASL: Its history and structure*. (with DVD). Washington, DC: Gallaudet University Press.

McKee, R., Schembri, A., McKee, D., & Johnston, T. 2011. Variable 'subject' presence in Australian Sign Language and New Zealand Sign Language. *Language Variation and Change* 23: 375–98.

Mesch, J. 2000. Tactile Swedish Sign Language: Turn-taking in signed conversations of people who are deaf and blind. In M. Metzger (ed.), *Bilingualism and identity in Deaf communities*, 187–203. Washington, DC: Gallaudet University Press.

Milroy, L. 1987. *Observing and analyzing natural language*. Oxford: Blackwell.

Osborn, R. & McPhee, R. 2000. Indigenous terms of reference (ITR). Presented at the 6th UNESCO-ACEID International Conference on Education, Bangkok, December 12–15.

Palmer, J., Reynolds, W., & Minor, R. 2012. "You want *what* on your PIZZA?!": Videophone and video relay service as potential forces on lexical standardization of American Sign Language. *Sign Language Studies* 12(3): 371–97.

Petitto, L. A. 2000. On the biological foundations of human language. In K. Emmorey & H. Lane (eds.), *The signs of language revisited: An anthology in honor of Ursula Bellugi and Edward Klima*, 447–71. Mahwah, NJ: Lawrence Erlbaum.

Ramsey, C. 1989. Language planning in Deaf education. In C. Lucas (ed.), *The sociolinguistics of the Deaf community*, 123–46. San Diego: Academic Press.

Schembri, A., McKee, D., McKee, R., Pivac, S., & Johnston, T. 2009. Phonological variation and change in Australian and New Zealand Sign Languages: The location variable. *Language Variation and Change* 21: 193–231.

Singleton, J., Jones, G., & Hanumantha, S. 2012. Deaf friendly research? Toward ethical practice in research involving Deaf participants. *DSDJ: Deaf Studies Digital Journal* 3. http://dsdj.gallaudet.edu/index.php?view=entry&issue=4&entry_id=123. Accessed 8/8/2012.

Stokoe, W. 1960. *Sign language structure: An outline of visual communication systems of the American Deaf.* Studies in Linguistics: Occasional Paper 8. Buffalo, NY: University of Buffalo, Linguistics Department.

Stokoe, W., Casterline, D., & Croneberg, C. 1965. *A dictionary of American Sign Language*. Silver Spring, MD: Linstok Press.

Taub, S. 2001. *Language from the body*. Cambridge: Cambridge University Press.

Taub, S., Galvan, D., & Piñar, P. 2008. The role of gesture in crossmodal typological studies. *Cognitive Linguistics* 20: 71–92.

Wolfram, W. 1993. Ethical considerations in language awareness programs. *Issues in Applied Linguistics* 4: 225–55.

Wolfram, W., & Schilling-Estes, N. 1997. *Hoi toide on the Outer Banks*. Chapel Hill: University of North Carolina Press.

Woodward, J., Erting, C., & Oliver, S. 1976. Facing and hand(l)ing variation in American Sign Language. *Sign Language Studies* 10: 43–52.

Woodward, J., & DeSantis, S. 1977. Two to one it happens: Dynamic phonology in two sign languages. *Sign Language Studies* 17: 329–46.

PART III

BILINGUALISM AND LANGUAGE CONTACT

CHAPTER 15

PIDGINS AND CREOLES

ERIC RUSSELL WEBB

It is hardly difficult to make the case for the inclusion of pidgins and creoles in volume dedicated to sociolinguistics. Emerging in contact environments, these languages are and have been profoundly influenced by sociolinguistic forces and offer compelling evidence of the extent to which extra-grammatical factors contribute to the shape of language. This chapter pursues two interleaved questions. What is the interest of these languages to contemporary sociolinguistics? And how can the adoption of a sociolinguistic posture better address the distinction between creoles and non-creoles? The first question is inevitable given the scope of this volume, whereas the second may appear out of place. Such inquiry is perhaps unavoidable in a chapter dedicated to a group of languages that cannot be readily distinguished from others.

Background to Pidgins and Creoles

Pidgin and creole languages are found throughout the world, with relatively greater concentrations in the Caribbean basin, the Indian Ocean, the coast of Western and Central Africa, and Oceania. In most literature, pidgins and creoles are grouped according to respective lexifiers from which the bulk of their vocabulary derives. According to Holm (2000), English lexifier pidgins

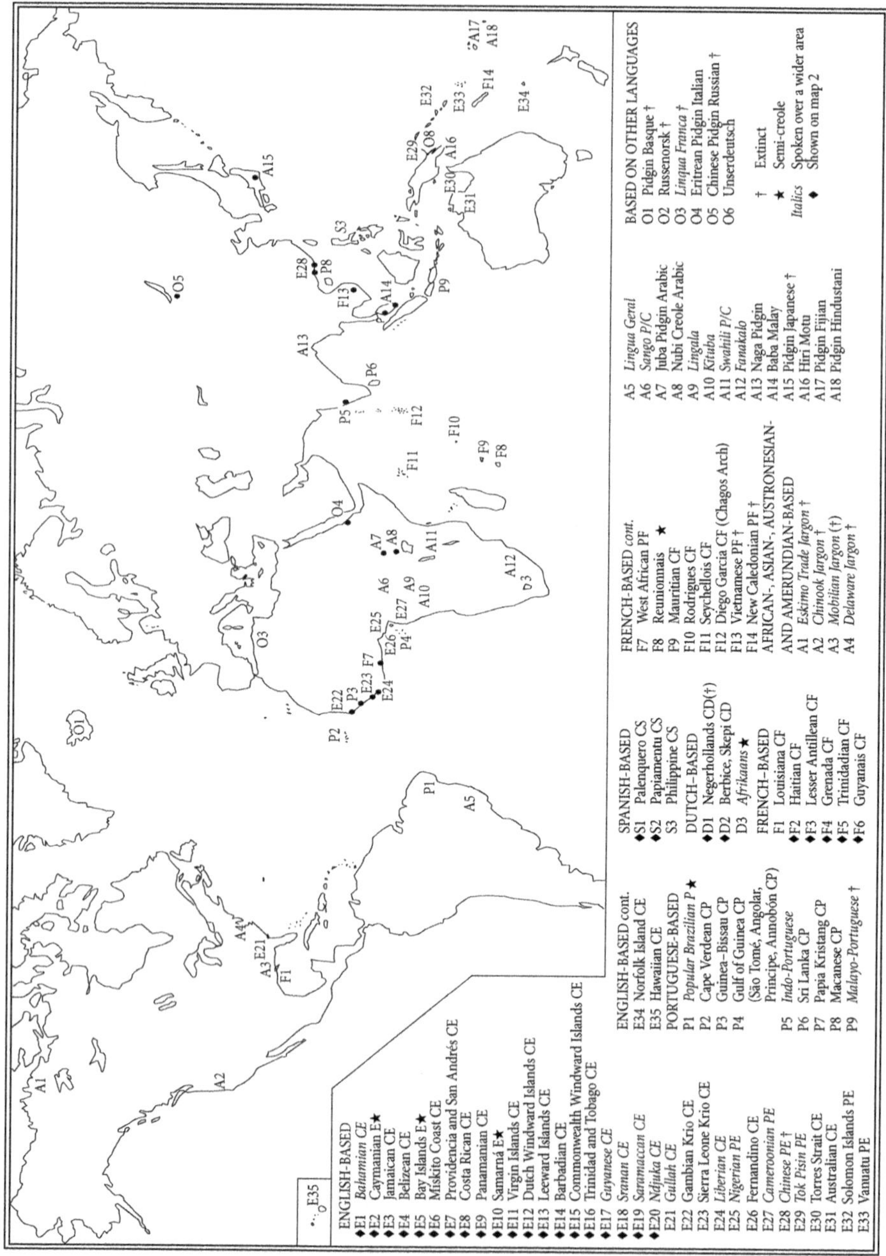

Figure 15.1a Geographic distribution of creoles and pidgins

and creoles are the most numerous at 38; French lexifier pidgins and creoles are numbered at 15; Portuguese counts for nine; Spanish three; and Dutch a further three. Holm groups an additional 18 languages as African, Asian, Austronesian. and Amerindian based (see figure 15.1a and b for the geographic distribution of pidgins and creoles).

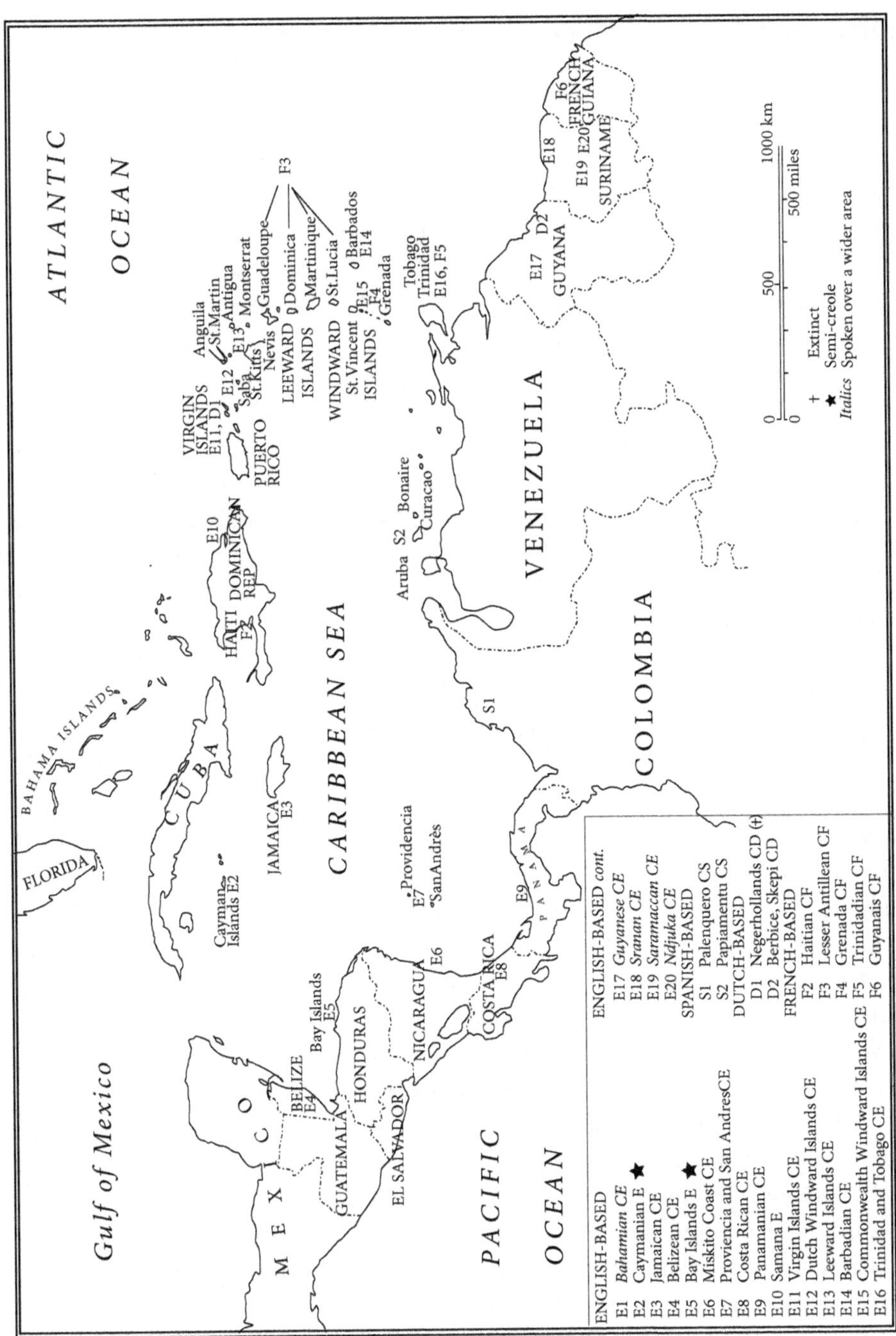

Figure 15.1b Caribbean creoles and pidgins

It is noteworthy that not all pidgins and creoles emerged within polities colonized by or associated with their respective lexifiers. For example, Negerhollands, a now defunct Dutch lexifier creole, was spoken on islands under centuries-long ownership of Denmark and the United States, while St. Lucian is spoken by a population long ruled by the United Kingdom.

Distinguishing between Contact Languages

Whereas it is relatively easy to group languages according to their lexifier, distinguishing between pidgins and creoles is far from straightforward. Generally speaking, pidgins do not constitute the first language (L1) of any speech community and are often used in few functional domains, for example, trade. One widely held view is that there are no native pidgin speech communities, only communities in which pidgins are used (Romaine 1988; Thomason & Kaufmann 1988; Winford 2002; cf. Bakker 1995; Sankoff & Lebarge 1980). This truism masks a good deal of variability, however.

In some instances, contact is limited and the use of any vernacular confined to a handful of contexts. For example, Russenorsk was used in between Russian traders and Norwegian fishermen along the Kola peninsula. Its restricted use was closely associated with seasonal commerce and, unsurprisingly, it showed lexical and grammatical restriction, as well as relative variability (Lunden 1978). Other pidgins emerge from a broader mingling of communities and are used in wider domains. A noteworthy example of this is Nigerian Pidgin English, which serves as a supra-territorial language in Nigeria and is employed in a variety of situations, having a relatively richer lexicon and less variable grammar (Berry 1971; Faraclas 1996).

The most widely accepted distinction between pidgin and creole stems from the latter's status as the first language (L1) of a speech community. By extension, creoles are susceptible to be used in broader communicative domains, importantly including the home, and are transmitted to subsequent generations in the same manner as "non-creole" vernaculars. Many creoles plausibly emerged from pidgins that were used as second languages for intercommunity communication. Louisiana Creole French, for example, likely evolved from a stable pidgin. At a first stage of development, it appears that slaves lived in relative demographic parity and proximity to lexifier speakers. Only after a period of destabilization involving the forced separation of collocutors and importations of additional slaves did this supplant speakers' original languages (Klingler 2003).

In other situations, creoles plausibly emerged in the absence of a stabilized pidgin, a process known as abrupt creolization (Thomason & Kaufmann 1988: 148–160). For example, from the very beginning of French colonization of Mauritius, economic development lead to the importation of indentured and enslaved laborers from Western and Eastern Africa, the Indian subcontinent, and Madagascar who rapidly constituted a demographic majority. Under such conditions, which ultimately lead to the emergence of Mauritian Creole, the development and use of a pidgin was likely to have been transient and the survival of erstwhile L1s even more tenuous (Baker 1972).

This tidy divide between pidgin and creole belies a great deal of murkiness. One example of the fluid nature of contact languages can be seen in the example of Tok Pisin, which serves as an official language of Papua New Guinea and is spoken by some 6 to 7 million people, of whom perhaps 1 to 2 million acquire it as an L1 (Smith 2002). For this reason, Tok Pisin is often referred to as an expanded pidgin. A distinct question is raised by semi-creolized or partially restructured languages (Holm 2004), the most widely studied example of which is Afrikaans. Like pidgins and creoles, Afrikaans emerged in contact, but is relatively more similar to Dutch (its lexifier) than are other vernaculars and its status is widely disputed (Markey 1982; Reinecke 1937; cf. Kotzé 2001).

Pidgin and Creole Formation

The issue of creole emergence or formation (how contact vernaculars come to be and the manner by which they attain their surface form) is a primary concern of creolists. A recurring theme in early literature is the centrality of a Portuguese-lexifier pidgin used in the Atlantic slave trade (Schuchardt 1882 et seq.; Thompson 1961; Whinnom 1965). Most contemporary authors ascribe creole emergence to a plurality of factors. While the mono- versus polygenetic debate has largely dissipated, the polemic concerning the ultimate source of creole distinctiveness is far from resolved. Here, discussion has largely concretized around two poles of thought: universalism and substratism. The former are predicated by an assumption of innate features of Universal Grammar (UG), the latter look principally to the influence of substrates.

Universalists, most notably Bickerton (1984), assert that creole can be characterized by their relative proximity to UG. Accordingly, when confronted by highly variable, relatively impoverished input in L1 acquisition, children in creolizing environments defaulted to innately specified parameters. This proposition is largely rejected by substratists, who situate the locus of creole specificity in properties of substrate languages and the transfer of L1 properties into an emerging L2 (Siegel 2007; Sprouse 2006). This is, indeed, among the most long-standing analytical postures vis-à-vis pidgins and creoles (see e.g., Hall 1966). One of the most influential contemporary articulations of substratism is seen in Lefebvre (1998 et seq.), whose Relexification Hypothesis integrates principles gleaned from research into second language acquisition. Others bridge the universalist-substratist gap, for example, Myers-Scotton (2001), who argues that the motivation for structure in creole formation comes from innate architecture of language manifested via transfer.

More pertinent to the present discussion are the contexts in which pidgins and creoles emerged. Chaudenson (1992) distinguishes between two settings, which he refers to as *sociétés d'habitation* and *sociétés de plantation*. The former characterize small holder farmsteads that were often the first establishments of colonial power. Here, populations of slaves, indentured servants, and European settlers coexisted in relative demographic parity and stability. In many instances, ethnolinguistic ties were preserved among the enslaved populations. As in the early colonial period in Louisiana described by Klingler (2003), for example, pidgins emerged as intercommunity languages, much as trade languages emerge in other contact situations.

The *société de plantation* is relatively distinct. On these vast agricultural estates, large numbers of enslaved peoples worked in grueling conditions for distant masters, coming into little or no contact with lexifier speakers. Mortality and turnover were atrociously high: in the most extreme cases, for example, on Saint Domingue, it is estimated that 60 percent to 65 percent of slaves perished during their first year of service and few survived beyond a decade after arrival (Fick 1990). The commensurate lack of cohesion and stability among the enslaved population is thought to have promoted rapid creole emergence. A related socio-demographic profile is seen in maroon societies, for example, among the Ndyuka of Surinam and French Guyana. This English lexifier creole emerged among escaped slaves who settled in isolated regions and appears to have preserved more structural elements of substrate origin (Huttar & Huttar 1994).

Importantly, it cannot be argued that original creole speakers had no access to sociolinguistic structures; rather, these were superseded or rendered irrelevant by particular conditions. Even in so-called radical creolizing contexts, social networks inevitably emerged. However, these, like the language that emerged from social upheaval, cannot be characterized as modified versions of a structure imposed from above or transferred *in toto* from below; rather, the social and sociolinguistic structures that emerged in contact environments were unique to these times, places and peoples.

This assertion highlights the effects of contact on acquisition and transmission, thus on innovation and emergence. However, the context in which creole formation plays out is distinct vis-à-vis other contact profiles. For example, numerous studies have traced the expansion of bilingualism and language shift among immigrants (Bohn & Munro 2007) and the connections between creole formation and language acquisition have been increasingly called into question in recent decades (Steele & Brousseau 2006; Véronique 1994). Largely ignored in this discussion are issues surrounding acquisition and transmission in what might be best termed a sociolinguistic vacuum, where even the most immediate social structures (family, tribe, etc.) are undermined by larger circumstances. Creole formation is, in essence, an extreme case of naturalistic language acquisition; any contact between substrate/L1 speakers and lexifier/L2 speakers was sporadic, indirect, and plausibly mediated by interlanguage (Plag 2008 et seq.; Winford 2002 et seq.; Russell Webb 2010).

This is not to say that pidgin and creole formation is linear or leads to invariant outcomes. For example, in the transition from pidgin to creole, as well as in the initial or radical emergence of a creole, inter-speaker and intra-community variability was likely the norm. While variation is part and parcel of all language use, it is also commonly accepted that variation is constrained and shaped by use (Beckner et al. 2009). In a context in which a new variety emerges, there must be some degree of dialect leveling. Factors that may inform the understanding of particular outcomes include the frequency of one or another variant, co-occurring variables and their significance, the weight or prestige of different variants (i.e., the values attributed to their speakers), and other usage-based or -derived effects. This observation, and the need for more and richer research, speaks directly to sociolinguists.

Pidgins and Creoles Today

The contemporary situation of pidgins and creoles offers fertile ground for sociolinguistic inquiry, especially as it concerns the notion of speech community. Regarding pidgins, the question is raised as to whether a community can comprise speakers who use a language restrictively or occasionally, or whether usage must be more habitual and widespread? And what of the overlap between languages within a community, for example, in the case of Nigerian Pidgin English, where speakers putatively hold several identities? Concerning creoles, the notion of speech community is far from categorical, as well, especially given many speakers' plural self-identifications. In the French Antilles, for example, an individual or group may adhere to one or more distinct linguistic communities: creole, French, and/or regional French speaking (Hazaël-Massieux 2004).

A number of commonalities are nevertheless observed across contexts. These include status, planning and policy, education and politics, and the development of standard orthographies and grammars. Functional and statutory concerns readily intersect in pidgin- and, especially, creole-speech communities, as seen in efforts to preserve and promote those languages that are considered autochthonous (typically in the face of a lexifier or other dominant language), and decisions pertaining to the place of creoles in education and administration.

With few exceptions, pidgins and creoles have long existed in positions of inequality, especially vis-à-vis their respective lexifiers or languages associated with authority. The perception in many societies is often that pidgins and creoles are inferior to or represent defective forms of "real languages," a point of view reinforced by *de jure* and *de facto* statuses. Of the 77 extant pidgins, creoles, and semi-creoles listed in Holm (2000), only eight enjoy *de jure* official recognition: Afrikaans, Birman, Haitian, Hiri Motu, Papiamentu, Seychellois, Swahili, and Tok Pisin. A further 14 are recognized in some manner, either as national language (e.g., Jamaican) or as a community or regional language used in restricted domains (e.g., Sranan in Suriname, Chavacano in the Philippines). The vast majority of pidgins enjoy no recognition, perhaps because these do not "belong" to any community in the same manner as do creoles.

Several creoles are sanctioned in all or nearly all domains. A noteworthy example is Papiamento, which enjoys de jure recognition and is increasingly used in education and government on Curaçao. In other environments, for example, in the French Antilles, efforts to promote creoles are hampered by acquiescence to French, the official and undisputedly vehicular language. As these islands constitute an integral part of the French Republic, French remains the sole official language in most formal education, interaction with local and national institutions, and public media, as in other allophonic regions (e.g., Alsace, Brittany, Corsica).

Other creoles enjoy no statutory recognition. This is the case for Louisiana Creole French, spoken by some 60,000 to 80,000 in the southwestern corner of that state, as well as by dwindling numbers in isolated pockets of the Mississippi delta (Neumann 1985). French and, to a lesser extent, Cajun are promoted by the Council for the Development of French in Louisiana, established by the state legislature; Louisiana Creole French has been included in recent promotional efforts, but only as a "form of French spoken in Louisiana," and not as an independent entity. A more striking example of statutory invisibility is seen in the case of Hawaiian Creole English, not to be confused with Hawaiian (a Polynesian language, itself under pressure from English). The latter is co-official with English for state government and benefits from certain protections, whereas recognition of the former is patently absent.

It is not surprising that pidgin- and creole-speaking communities are typically characterized by the simultaneous presence of multiple languages and their asymmetric functional distribution. Creoles are frequently excluded from high functions, reflecting their statutorily inequality. At the same time, the traditional definition of pidgin, that is, as a language facilitating communication between language groups and as the L1 of none, precludes its wider functionality, although this need not exclude it from certain high functions, notably national government. The intersection of functional and statutory issues is especially interesting as this concerns language policy and planning in creolophone communities. Decolonization and efforts to increase literacy in many societies have given rise to vehicularization and instrumentalization, most notably through standardization. A widely studied example of this is Haiti, where creole promotion has been relatively successful (Spears & Berotte Joseph 2010).

The murkiness surrounding creole speech communities is compounded by the existence of linguistic strata and their asymmetrical distribution. Traditionally, these are referred to as acrolectal, mesolectal, and basilectal forms, referring to their relative structural distinction vis-à-vis a lexifier. First described by Schuchardt, the movement away from creole-specific forms and structures to those more closely resembling an erstwhile lexifier has been widely observed, especially in contexts where creole and lexifier coalesce, a process referred to as a creole "life-cycle" (DeCamp 1971; Rickford 1987). The inevitability of this cycle, as well as the causalities behind this has been questioned in recent decades. Numerous authors have reexamined the presumption of innovation in decreolization, noting that in some cases, acrolectal forms of a creole are attested from a very early period and that the presence of these may be confused with change resulting in the adoption of lexifier-like forms (Chaudenson 2000; Valdman 1991; Winford 1997). Accordingly, relevant data are vestiges of creole formation and not necessarily the product of recent change. In a similar vein, Schwegler (2000) suggests that certain instances of decreolization might best understood as *debasilectification*: the abandonment of basilectal forms in favor of those more closely aligned with a lexifier. From this point of view, change constitutes a type of dialect leveling, in this instance favoring forms more closely aligned with the prestigious language. While it may be the case that speakers avoid basilectal forms in favor of acrolectal ones, this is not a priori a grammatical change, but a sociolinguistic one, similar to other instances of shift.

Creoles versus Non-Creoles: Typology, Particularity, Exceptionalism

Any linguistically savvy observer of pidgins and creoles is struck by two grammatical characteristics of these languages: the degree to which they represent a restructuring of their respective adstrates; and their structural resemblance, irrespective of geographic or sociocultural context and linguistic antecedence. The recurrence of synthetic structures, the avoidance of analytical morphology, the presence of TMA (Tense, Mood, Aspect) markers, and the lack of distinctive tone are but a few widely cited commonalities (see Holm 2000).

Given the above, it is unsurprising that accounting for cross-creole similarity has been one of—if not *the*—core pursuit of creolistics since its emergence in second half of the twentieth century. Within this subdiscipline, two poles of thought have emerged. One, which considers pidgins and creoles as typologically distinct, has received prominent attention in McWhorter (1998 et seq.). He proposes that creoles be defined synchronically according to a prototype motivated by synchronic features that, according to the author, "are known to arise only over time," such as inflectional affixation, the loss of contrastive tone, and semantic drift (2000: 86). More recently, this position has been taken up with a view to empirical grounding in Bakker et al. (2011). They make the case for typology based on constellations or clusters, using computer modeling to demonstrate the relative relatedness of creoles, their similarity regardless of adstrate, and their simplicity versus structurally similar non-creoles (see also Parkvall 2008; Plag 2011).

The possibility of typological classification has been denied, at times vociferously, by many. Perhaps the most important body of scholarship advocating the abandonment of structural considerations is seen in the work of Mufwene (2000, 2001). He adopts an ecological posture that situates questions of creole formation within the wider domains of language change, acquisition, and transmission. This is echoed in Ansalado and Matthews, who view creole exceptionalism as "a set of sociohistorically-rooted dogmas, with foundations in (neo) colonial power relations, not a scientific conclusion based on robust empirical evidence" (2007: 14). Winford (1997) surveys some of the more long-standing questions in the field and advocates the abandonment of different *-izations* (pidgin-, koiné-, creoli-), arguing that creole formation involves the same processes seen in other types of contact situations (see also Winford 2005, 2008). Similarly, DeGraff (1999, 2001) provides a useful introduction to the state of affairs with regard to creole formation and language change. Other notable opponents of a creole typology include those who attribute creole formation to substrate transfer and/or second language acquisition effects. Here, the proposition that creoles are relexified versions of various substrates implicationally denies any coherent typology.

Rather than argue for a given typological classification or against the possibility typology, it may be asserted that creole particularity (the terms "exceptionalism" and "typology" are avoided here) can be only motivated by socio-historical facts and that any creole distinction from non-creole should be considered emergent and epiphenomenal, rather than inevitable and intrinsic. The remainder of this chapter is given to this argument, largely ignoring questions concerning pidgins.

Particularity

At first blush, creole typology might appear self-evident, if only because a vast and compelling literature has referred to these languages as a cohesive group—a tradition that has, undoubtedly and in turn fueled a discursive bias among linguists and non-linguists alike. Broadly speaking, it is possible to distinguish between structural and ontological motivations for a creole–non-creole divide, the first of these having received relatively more attention in the literature (perhaps due to a disciplinary preference for formal, parametric typologies).

The essence of the structural argument rests on the possibility that there is a feature or combination of features that allow for the definition of "what makes a creole." If these are understood as necessary and sufficient to the delimitation of a class, all attempts fall short. For example, the features of the Creole Prototype elaborated in McWhorter (2005) do not exclude non-creole languages, as seen in the examples of diachronic change and synchronic structure cited by the author, and are not inevitable, that is, are not found in all creoles. The selection of features and their inclusion in empirical counts or statistical analyses also skirts the edge of circuitousness. Even the best of computational algorithms can only attend to the input and constraints imposed upon it: if these input are limited to a number of features that are already deemed "creole-like" and if computation is founded upon the presence or absence of such features, it should come as little surprise that such features are more frequently found in "creole" languages.

Viewed from a substratist perspective (e.g., Lefebvre 1998), the recurrence of certain features is hardly surprising and does little to motivate their particularity as anything but innovative offspring of other, "non-creole" languages, both sub- and superstrate. Relexification is also variable, with some creoles being relatively more (e.g., Ndyuka) and some being relatively less (e.g., Bajan) structurally distinct from their respective adstrates. It is worth noting that relexification is hardly unique to creoles, even if it is perhaps seen in its most extreme form in these languages. The process by which a source lexical item is reanalyzed and adapted is seen in other contact situations.

While Bakker et al. (2011) do not claim that all features are present in all creoles and deny a parametric typology, focusing rather on clusters and notions of simplicity, their claims are not beyond scrutiny. That creoles can be defined as simplified languages, that is, as less structurally complex than non-creoles, is far from innovative. This proposition has its roots in a long-standing linguistic tradition, much of it predicated by perceived inferiority, and is hardly anachronistic, as seen in recent publications (e.g., Bickerton 1995; McWhorter 2005). Other approaches couch views of simplicity, at times avoiding this term, in theory-specific understandings of markedness (e.g., Uffmann 2003). Summarily, each of these approaches has in common a view that creole distinctiveness can be motivated by structural parameters not seen or having a lesser effect in non-creoles. For proponents of simplicity, this rests on ad hoc understandings of structural density, that is, that certain forms and structures are more complex (or simpler) than others; for proponents of markedness, this relies upon a theoretical *prise de position.*

Both approaches are built upon inherently problematic foundations. Simplicity depends upon a formalistic leap of faith, providing that complexity and simplicity are intrinsic characteristics, rather than perceived and therefore relative values. For example, while it may appear that the lack of overt morphological marking seen in many creoles is inherently simple, especially as compared to the diversity of morphology in the worlds' languages (let alone in many lexifiers), it can hardly be stated that creoles do not or cannot attain the same functional ends by other means. That a language like French marks tense and aspect with (inter alia) verbal inflections, whereas a language like Haitian marks these with separate morphemes, says nothing about the overall structural density of one or the other language (Arends 2001; Lefebvre 2001). Rather, this is a straightforward observation that speakers of distinct languages accomplish the same goals by different means. Even if viewed under the narrow optic of inflectional morphology, simplicity is poorly grounded, the concept of what constitutes inflection being more a product of the observer than a characteristic of the observed. Likewise, the notion that less marked forms are seen more frequently in creoles is both deterministic—as it relies upon a theory-specific understanding of markedness, one that is agnostic with regard to typology or exceptionalism—and, even if this is accepted, conflates markedness and simplicity (Russell Webb 2009).

The essence of the ontological argument is that creoles are developmentally unique due to their emergence, specifically their passage from reduced language or pidgin to a full-fledged L1 of a community. This theme is seen under different titles, often evoking notions of creoles as being a type of fossilized and/

or developed interlanguage (see notably Plag 2008 et seq.). It is proposed that creoles are the byproduct of a particular type of language acquisition, one which did not benefit from close proximity between L1 and L2 speakers, and one in which speakers were forced to default to universal operating parameters when confronted by nonnative input. Analyses of particular data sets have proven to be amenable to this approach, built upon substratist/transfer understandings, also drawing upon universal tendencies in acquisition (Siegel 2003; Singler 1996). However compelling this may be for analysis of creole formation, it is difficult to see how this can motivate creole typology, let alone exceptionalism, as there is no assertion that the ontological forces at play are unique to creoles. Rather, the reverse logic is implicated: these forces are at play, albeit to different extents, in all contact situations, even when a creole is not the ultimate result. Any explanation as to why these forces should shape language development to the degree or manner they do in one, but not another context must look to sociolinguistic—and not linguistic—factors.

The ontological definition of creoles faces additional problems, especially the observation that not all pidgins lead to creoles and not all creoles emerge from pidginization. As noted above, some pidgins have not undergone creolization (e.g., Chinese Pidgin English, Vietnamese Pidgin French), and some creoles emerged absent a period of pidginization (e.g., Ndyuka, Sranan). The view that creoles can be defined ontologically simply pushes back the goal line, as it requires that pidgins be clearly defined and delimited from non-pidgins and that the particular type of interlanguage or contact-induced variety that leads to or underlies a creole be distinguished from others. This is troubling as it concerns distinction between pidgins and other contact vernaculars, as well as among interlanguages that lead to creoles and those that do not. While many pidgins may indeed be the L1 of no one, the same can be said of linguae francae (e.g., global English at present, Latin in medieval Europe). Likewise, pidgin structural restriction and reduction is hardly an exclusive property of these, and is seen in other trade languages, jargons, and intercommunity vernaculars. Finally, there are numerous examples of contact varieties resembling interlanguages that are not, at least commonly, subsumed under the title of pidgin or creole (e.g., Meisel 1975).

Against Exceptionalism, for Emergent Particularity

Similarity is not tantamount to typology, traditionally understood as motivated by one or more characteristics that are both necessary and sufficient to delimit a class. For example, the SVO typology necessarily includes the syntactic order subject—verb—object; it is concurrently sufficient that a language display this structure for it to be typologically subsumed. A typology is inclusive and exclusive, as it establishes a bidirectional implication: if a language is SVO, it is not SOV; if a language is SOV, it is not SVO. Particularity, on the other hand, can be understood as a reliance on inevitability and unidirectional implication, for example, that if a language *L* is to be subsumed under within the particularity *P*, it is inevitable that *L* includes the feature *f*, but it is not inevitable that other languages exclude *f*. Particularity can only include, but cannot exclude. Apparently trivial, this is an important caveat to any attempt to answer the question, "why creoles are creoles" or, at least, why the creole—non-creole divide appears tenable.

A structural or structurally oriented approach may attain descriptive adequacy, but does not attain—nor does it pretend at—explanatory adequacy to particularity, that is, it describes a state of affairs but does not hypothesize as to why that state of affairs exists. In order to explain featural constellations or clusters, the conditions that render these outcomes more or less probable must be clarified, especially as these pertain to the transmission and acquisition of language. In other words, it cannot be the case that there is an explanation for creole particularity lying in the structure itself, unless one accepts a strong UG approach, along the lines of Bickerton (1984), which places any explanatory burden outside of creolistics in any event. Likewise, it cannot be processing itself that distinguishes creole from non-creole. Rather, explanation of particularity depends on extra-linguistic factors that framed the emergence of innovative grammatical competence and resulting performances, perhaps in a pseudo-inevitable manner, leading to the emergence of featural clusters or constellations.

At the same time, it is impossible to promote a view that creoles are exceptional, if by this they are to be understood as an exclusive grouping. Even within the structural constellations of Bakker et al. (2011), several features are present in only a handful of creoles and others are not exclusive to these languages. Creoles are thus hardly exceptional, although they display tendencies (of varying strength) toward a given structure or set of features. It bears reemphasis that the recurrence and clustering of these structures or features is perhaps adequate to describe the outward characteristics of a group, but offers no explanation as to why such characteristics should be more or less probable at any point in time, nor does it explain how such characteristics would have been likely or unlikely to emerge in a given environment, predicated by given linguistic input, and with given sociolinguistic forces in play. The question remains as to not simply why creoles *appear* to be different than non-creoles, but why the emergence of certain features and structures was *inevitable or highly probable* in some contexts and was *improbable or unexpected* in others. This requires a motivation for and grounding of particularity.

Two possibilities can be identified within and beyond creolistic literature in this regard. The first, and least tenable, looks to society; the second, somewhat paradoxically, is founded on a reconciliation of the pro- and anti-typological stances reviewed above, asking specifically what combination of circumstances would implicate the emergence of languages that tend to—but do not inevitably—display certain features. In so doing, it situates the locus of particularity in diachrony and extra-grammaticality, notably in sociolinguistics.

One possible motivation for creole particularity is premised on language mythology, that is the beliefs about language that are shared by a speech community. Here, it is possible to assert that creoles are creoles, because they are referred to as such. As unsophisticated as this may appear, such rationales are far from uncommon within linguistics. Most readers are undoubtedly familiar with this logic, providing for instance that Caucasian languages are "languages spoken in the Caucuses," interlanguages consist of "language knowledge that is neither L1 nor target-like," and that official languages are "those that have been denoted as official." While tautological, mythology does attain a reasonable degree of descriptive power, if only because of the inevitability of its conclusions and the facility of its aims.

A more plausible approach to particularity looks not to the surface structure of creoles, but to the conditions in which these emerged and the links between transmission and acquisition, on the one hand, and the results of these processes, on the other. Increasingly, scholarship has admitted the importance of social factors in the creolistic debate. Mufwene (2000) situates creole emergence within the larger framework of language change. He considers language a complex adaptive system influenced by the social components active in societies in which contact occurs and novel linguistic forms emerge (see also Le Page & Tabouret-Keller 1985; Mühlhäusler 1997; Beckner et al. 2009). The success or failure of a particular feature will be determined by how it responds to the context-specific needs of its users. Those that are ecologically successful will be transmitted; those that are not will disappear. Thus, any understanding of why a given feature emerges or recurs, either in a specific speech community or across speech communities, must look to the larger ecology in which these communities exist: importantly, this requires an understanding of sociolinguistic facts and factors. Broadly speaking, the ecology of emerging creoles implicates four particularities: settings, participants, the contact profile, and use. Each of these factors is reviewed with the goal of establishing a discursive and analytical framework that may move the ball forward, even if the disciplinary match is far from decided here.

The sociopolitical and sociocultural settings in which participants in creole formation found themselves undoubtedly contributed to language use. These include demographic disparities, economic deprivations, and political policies noted in creolizing societies that were removed from larger populations. Focusing on the Caribbean basin, Faraclas et al. (2007) conclude that there is a strong "correlation between political economy . . . and the extent and nature of influences from African substrate languages on the speech varieties that developed under colonialism" (258). Furthermore, creolizing environments were relatively and variably cut off from adstrate influence, be this lexifier or substrates, in physical, socioeconomic, or sociocultural terms. In so-called normal situations of language contact, speakers maintain and even reinforce the social networks that influence their language use and contribute to their language identity. While many contact situations are predicated on violence and upheaval, these rarely affect an entire society to the extent seen in creole formation, especially as this concerns the massive movement of enslaved people, their (at times purposeful) isolation from collocutors, and their forced integration within harsh living conditions. Other factors include extreme physical hardships and high rates of mortality in many creolizing environments, which served to obviate prior social networks and reinforce those emerging within the nascent creolophone society.

The type of language contact engendered within these settings and the ways in which speech communities coalesced undoubtedly contributed to creole ecological particularity. Here, contact among initial creole participants can be characterized as proximal, durative, and multifaceted. While it may not be the case that substrate speakers were often—or ever—in direct contact with the lexifier, they were plausibly in close, sustained contact with lexifier-derived interlanguages and were required to use these in several functional domains, if only because they could not rely on their respective L1s for broader communicative needs. Language contact in creole emergence does not target, or targets only superficially, a lexifier; rather, contact involves a nascent creole, a highly variable code used by a population primarily composed of slaves and disenfranchised individuals and not, with few exceptions, of lexifier speakers.

This observation highlights a third factor active in creolizing ecologies: the relationship between different participant subgroups and adstrate speech communities. If it is accepted that creoles emerge among adults, it must also be accepted that participants in creole formation were not on equal footing. Lexifier speakers were held at a relative and often insurmountable distance from substrate speakers, at times being completely separated from them. These communities existed in highly stratified relationships one to another and were demographically skewed, such that substrate speakers of varying backgrounds, who collectively constituted a majority, could not call upon a vehicular language other than the lexifier-like interlanguage for inter- and intra-community communications. This is notably the case in the case of spontaneous or radical creoles, but similar situations also emerged in other creole environments over time, often predated by a stable pidgin.

A fourth factor contributing to the creolizing ecology evokes the manners in which these languages were used, as well as the ways in which an emerging contact-induced vernacular was or was expected to be used. Creoles and pidgins-turned-creoles supplanted all other adstrates to become the L1 of a speech community, even if at times other languages continued to be used in functionally restricted domains. These were not, or were not ultimately, simple trade jargons or vehicular codes for intercommunity communication: they became, at times rapidly, *the* language of a speech community. Thus, their use was universal, at least within the context of a creolophone community.

The ecology in which creoles emerged is a combination of peculiar circumstances that, taken individually, do not lead inevitably or probabilistically to creole formation and to the featural constellations that are putatively the result of this process. No one factor is sufficient to motivate particularity; rather, this requires a concomitance of factors and an overlapping of effects. For example, a setting involving the clear economic delimitation of speech communities, if overlain with durative, proximal language contact does not a priori lead to the emergence of creoles, but more likely to diglossia. Likewise, demographic particularities (population disparities, stratification) and proximal, durative language contact often preceed language shift and, perhaps, language death, but not the emergence of a third language. At the same time, the interleaved particularities deriving from participant profiles and particular setting may facilitate societal bilingualism, but not necessarily the development of a new language. The concomitance of these three factors might render the emergence of a pidgin more probable, wherein the factor requiring the use of a contact-induced variety as the L1 of a community is overlain to provide for the set of ecological conditions necessary for a creole to emerge. This is schematized in figure 15.2.

Following this approach, no grammatical feature or set of features is parametrically necessary and sufficient for distinguishing creoles from non-creoles. Furthermore, any evidence for their clustering, that is, any structural similarity or set of shared surface features, cannot be viewed as anything but diachronic

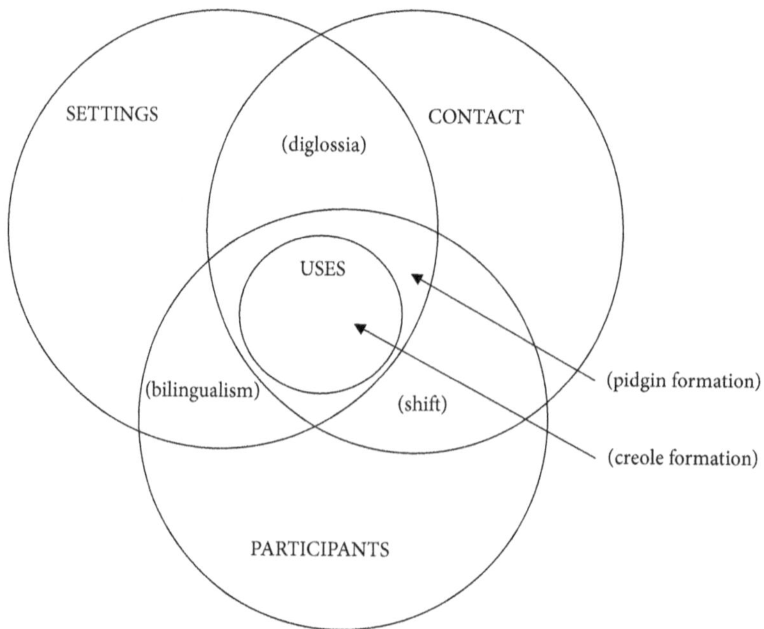

Figure 15.2. Schematization of social factors and the ecology of creole formation

residue of the situations in which creoles arose. While it is beyond the scope of the present work (and, perhaps, beyond the current capabilities of the field) to fully address these factors, it is entirely possible to formulate a set of hypotheses pertaining to the relative probability or improbability by which a given form or structure would emerge. This requires a close understanding of the grammatical input from adstrates, as well as the adoption of a theoretical stance vis-à-vis universal principles and parameters governing the perception, cognition, processing, and actuation of language, as well as the relative effect of these on participants in a given sociolinguistic environment. In essence, it requires investigation into language as a complex adaptive system in the highly peculiar circumstances in which creole formation took place, with primary focus given to the mechanisms underlying adaptation and change, rather than to the results of this.

In this regard, the approach to creole particularity advocated here does not hark to a traditionally defined linguistic typology, but to an emergent particularity. It is founded not upon formal structure, but on the sociolinguistic constraints that would render the emergence of a structure more (or less) probable. This stance is, of course, hardly innovative. For example, Kihm (2011) provides that what makes creoles special is not essential, but is the result of historical connections, what he terms a "virtual *Sprachbund*." It is argued that this constitutes as more powerful and more effective means of describing how creoles are distinct from non-creoles, hinting at an explanation of why they appear to be so.

References

Ansalado, U., & Matthews, S. 2007. Deconstructing creoles: The rationale. In U. Ansalado, S. Mattews, & L. Lim (eds.), *Deconstructing creole*, 1–18. Amsterdam: John Benjamins.

Arends, J. 2001. Simple grammars, complex languages. *Linguistic Typology* 5: 180–82.

Baker, P. 1972. *Kreol: A description of Mauritian Creole*. London: Hurst.

Bakker, P. 1995. Pidgins. In J. Arends, P. Muysken, & N. Smith (ed.), *Pidgins and creoles: An introduction*, 25–39. Amsterdam: John Benjamins.

Bakker, P, Daval-Markussen, A., Parkvall, M., & Plag, I. 2011. Creoles are typologically distinct from non-creoles. *Journal of Pidgin and Creole Languages* 26: 5–42.

Beckner, C, Blythe, R., Bybee, H., Christianen M. H., Croft, W., Ellis, N. C., Holland, J., Ke, J., Larsen-Freeman, D., & Schoenemann, T. 2009. Language as a complex adaptive system: Position paper. *Language Learning* 59: 1–26.

Berry, J. 1971. Pidgins and creoles in Africa. In T. A. Sebeok (ed.), *Linguistics in Sub-Saharan Africa*, 510–36. The Hague: Mouton

Bickerton, D. 1984. The language bioprogram hypothesis. *Behavioral and Brain Sciences* 7: 173–221.

Bickerton, D. 1995. *Language and human behavior.* Seattle: University of Washington Press.

Bohn, O-S., & Munro, M. J. 2007. *Language experience in second language speech learning: In honor of James Emil Flege.* Amsterdam: John Benjamins.

Chaudenson, R. 1992. *Des îles, des hommes, des langues.* Paris: L'Harmattan.
Chaudenson, R. 2000. Créolisation du francais et francisation du créole. In I. Neumann-Holzschuh & E. W. Schneider (eds.), *Degrees of restructuring in creole languages,* 361–81. Amsterdam: John Benjamins.
DeCamp, D. 1971. The study of pidgin and creole languages. In D. Hymes (ed.), *Pidginization and creolization of languages,* 13–42. Cambridge: Cambridge University Press.
DeGraff, M. 1999. *Language creation and language change.* Cambridge, MA: MIT Press.
DeGraff, M. 2001. On the origin of creoles: A Cartisian critique of Neo-Darwinian linguistics. *Linguistic Typology* 5: 213–310.
Faraclas, N. 1996. *Nigerian English.* London: Routledge.
Faraclas, N., Walicek, D. E., Alleyne, M., Geigel, W., & Ortiz, L. 2007. The complexity that really matters: The role of political economy in creole genesis. In U. Ansalado, S. Mattews, & L. Lim (eds.), *Deconstructing creole,* 227–64. Amsterdam: John Benjamins.
Fick, C. E. 1990. *The making of Haiti: The Saint Domingue revolution from below.* Knoxville: University of Tennessee Press.
Hall, R. A. 1966. *Pidgin and creole languages.* Ithaca, NY: Cornell University Press.
Hazaël-Massieux, M-C. 2004. Le créole de Guadeloupe. In C. Feuillard (ed.), *Créoles—Langages et politiques linguistiques: Actes du XXVIe Colloque International de Linguistique Fonctionnelle,* 3–12. Bern: Peter Lang.
Holm, J. 2000. *An introduction to pidgins and creoles.* Cambridge: Cambridge University Press.
Holm, J. 2004. *Languages in contact: The partial restructuring of vernaculars.* Cambridge: Cambridge University Press.
Huttar, G. L., & Huttar, M. L. 1994. *Ndyuka.* London: Routledge.
Kihm, Alain. 2011. Pidgin-creoles as a scattered sprachbund. *Journal of Pidgin & Creole Languages* 26: 43–88.
Klingler, T. A. 2003. *If I could turn my tongue like that: The creole language of Pointe Coupee Parish, Louisiana.* Baton Rouge: Louisiana State University Press.
Kotzé, E. F. 2001. Adjectival inflection in Afrikaans diachronics: An argument against the validity of creolization checklists. *Journal of Germanic Linguistics* 13:381–91.
Le Page, R. B., & Tabouret-Keller, A. 1985. *Acts of identity: Creole-based approaches to language and ethnicity.* Cambridge: Cambridge University Press.
Lefebvre, C. 1998. *Creole genesis and the acquisition of grammar.* Cambridge: Cambridge University Press.
Lefebvre, C. 2001. What you see is not always what you get: Apparent simplicity and hidden complexity in creole languages. *Linguistic Typology* 5: 186–213.
Lunden, S. S. 1978. Tracing the ancestry of Russenorsk. *Slavia Orientalis* 27: 213–17.
Markey, T. L. 1982. Afrikaans: Creole or non-creole? *Zeitschrift für Dialektologie und Linguistik* 49:169–207.
McWhorter, J. H. 1998. Identifying the creole prototype: Vindicating a typological class. *Language* 74: 788–818.
McWhorter, J. H. 2005. *Defining creole.* Oxford: Oxford University Press.
Meisel, J. M. 1975. Ausländerdeutsch und Deutsch ausländischer Arbeiter: zur möglichen Entstehung eines Pidgin in der BRD. *Zeitschrift für Literaturwissenschaft und Linguistik* 51: 9–53.
Mufwene, S. S. 2000. Creolization is a social, not a structural, process. In I. Neumann-Holzschuh & E. W. Schneider (eds.), *Degrees of restructuring in creole languages,* 65–84. Amsterdam: John Benjamins.

Mufwene, S. S. 2001. *The ecology of language evolution*. Cambridge: Cambridge University Press.

Mühlhäusler, P. 1997. Language ecology: Contact without conflict. In M. Pütz (ed.), *Language choices: Conditions, constraints, and consequences*, 3–15. Amsterdam: John Benjamins.

Myers-Scotton, C. 2001. Implications of abstract grammatical structure: Two targets in creole formation. *Journal of Pidgin and Creole Languages* 16: 217–73.

Neumann, I. 1985. *Le créole à Breaux Bridge, Louisiane. Etude morphosyntaxique, texts, vocabulaire*. Hamburg: Helmut Buske.

Parkvall, M. 2008. The simplicity of creoles in a cross-linguistic perspective. In M. Miestamo, K. Sinnemäki & F. Karlsson (eds.), *Language complexity: Typology, contact, change*, 265–85. Amsterdam: John Benjamins.

Plag, I. 2008. Creoles as interlanguages: Inflectional morphology. *Journal of Pidgin and Creole Languages* 23: 109–30.

Plag, I. 2011. Creolization and admixture: Typology, feature pools, and second language acquisition. *Journal of Pidgin and Creole Languages* 26: 89–110.

Reineke, J. 1937. *Marginal Languages: a sociological survey of the creole languages and trade jargons*. Ph.D. dissertation, Yale University.

Rickford, J. R. 1987. *Dimensions of a creole continuum: History, texts, and linguistic analysis of Guyanese Creole*. Palo Alto, CA: Stanford University Press.

Romaine, S. 1988. *Pidgin and creole languages*. London: Longman.

Russell Webb, E. 2009. Neither simpler nor more complex: Optimality and Creoles. In N. Faraclas & T. B. Klein (eds.), *Simplicity and complexity in creoles and pidgins*, 67–80. London: Battlebridge.

Russell Webb, E. 2010. Creole phonological restructuring: The role of perception in contact-induced change. *Journal of Pidgin and Creole Languages* 25: 263–88.

Sankoff, G., & Lebarge, S. 1980. The acquisition of native speakers by a language. In G. Sankoff (ed.), *The social life of language*, 195–209. Philadelphia: University of Pennsylvania Press.

Schuchardt, H. 1882. *Kreolische Studien*. Vienna: Carl Gerold.

Schwegler, A. 2000.The myth of decreolization: The anomalous case of Palenquero. In I. Neumann-Holzschuh & E. W. Schneider (eds.), *Degrees of restructuring in creole languages*, 409–36. Amsterdam: John Benjamins.

Siegel, J. 2003. Substrate influence in creoles and the role of transfer in second language acquisition. *Studies in Second Language Acquisition* 25: 185–209.

Siegel, J. 2007. Transmission and transfer. In U. Ansalado, S. Mattews & L. Lim (eds.), *Deconstructing creole*, 167–201. Amsterdam: John Benjamins.

Singler, J. V. 1996. Theories of creole genesis, sociohistorical considerations, and the evaluation of evidence: The case of Haitian Creole and the relexification hypothesis. *Journal of Pidgin and Creole Languages* 11: 185–230.

Smith, G. P. 2002. *Growing up with Tok Pisin: Contact, creolization, and change in Papua New Guinea's national language*. London: Battlebridge.

Spears, A. K., & Berotte Joseph, C. 2010. *The Haitian Creole language: History, structure, use, and education*. Lanham, MD: Lexington.

Sprouse, R. 2006. Full transfer and relexification: Second language acquisition and creole genesis. In C. Lefebre, L. White, & C. Jourdan (eds.), *L2 acquisition and creole genesis*, 169–81. Amsterdam: John Benjamins.

Steele, J., & Brousseau, A-M. 2006. Parallels in process: Comparing Haitian Creole and French learner phonologies. In C. Lefebvre, L. White, & C. Jourdan (eds.), *L2 acquisition and creole genesis*, 331–52. Amsterdam: John Benjamins.

Thomason, S. G., & Kaufmann, T. 1988. *Languages in contact, creolization and genetic linguistics*. Berkeley: University of California Press.

Thompson, R.W. 1961. A note on some possible affinities between the creole dialects of the Old World and those of the New. *Creole Language Studies* 2: 107–13

Uffmann, C. 2003. Markedness, faithfulness and creolization: The retention of the unmarked. In I. Plag (ed.), *The phonology and morphology of creole languages*, 3–23. Tübingen: Niemayer.

Valdman, A. 1991. Decreolization or dialect contact in Haiti. In F. Byrne & T. Huebner (eds.), *Development and structures of creole languages*, 75–88. Amsterdam: John Benjamins.

Véronique, D. 1994. Naturalistic adult acquisition of French as L2 and French-based creole genesis compared: Insights into creolization and language change? In D. Adone & I. Plag (eds.), *Creolization and language change*, 117–37. Tübingen: Niemayer.

Whinnom, K. 1965. The origin of the European-based creoles and pidgins. *Orbis* 14: 509–27.

Winford, D. 1997. Reexamining Caribbean English creole continua. *World Englishes* 16: 233–79.

Winford, D. 2002. Creoles in the context of contact linguistics. In G. Gilbert (ed.), *Pidgin and creole linguistics in the twenty-first century*, 287–354. New York: Peter Lang.

Winford, D. 2005. Contact-induced changes: Classification and processes. *Diachronica* 22: 373–427.

Winford, D. 2008. Processes of creole formation and related contact-induced language change. *Journal of Language Contact Thema* 2:124–45.

CHAPTER 16

LANGUAGE MAINTENANCE AND SHIFT

KIM POTOWSKI

THE intergenerational transmission of a language from parents to children, and the subsequent use of that language in society, is common throughout the world. It only becomes remarkable when it is threatened—that is, when shift to another language is a possibility. Language shift is the replacement of one language by another as the primary means of communication and socialization within a community. There are many factors that contribute to language shift, and there can be multiple causalities, such that separating these factors into neat categories is not possible. Broadly speaking, language shift is a phenomenon that must be understood at both the individual level and the group level, because it is through individuals' speech behavior that a language is either maintained or lost in a family and in broader society.

Before discussing language shift, we should briefly explore situations in which shift does *not* occur. Multiple languages share geopolitical space for a number of reasons, including immigration (voluntary and involuntary), conquest, and other historical developments involving the migration of people and borders. In most multilingual nations, there is one dominant language used in wider society, and non-dominant languages can coexist with it in a state of relatively stable multilingualism in one of several fashions. There can be monolingual individuals of different languages, such as monolingual French speakers and monolingual German speakers coexisting in Switzerland, or monolingual English speakers and monolingual French speakers in Quebec, Canada. This is often referred to as societal bilingualism with individual monolingualism. Alternatively, there can be a number of bilingual individuals, such as individuals bilingual in Hindi and English in India, in Catalan and Castilian in Spain, in Guaraní and Spanish in Paraguay, or in Swahili and Hausa, English, and/or Yoruba in Nigeria. This situation is usually called societal combined with individual bilingualism. In other nations, however, and typically as a result of immigration, bilingualism is temporary and individual rather than stable and societal, with the following pattern emerging. Adolescent and adult immigrants arrive as fluent speakers of their home language; their children raised in the new country become bilingual in the home language and the dominant language; and their children (the grandchildren of the original immigrants) are monolingual in the societally dominant language, perhaps with minimal receptive skills in the heritage language. This pattern has been widely attested in immigrant contexts around the world.

In an effort to understand the factors that contribute to language shift and those that seem to militate against it, this chapter explores several immigrant and non-immigrant contexts around the world, with particular focus on the United States. The principal factors—which will be divided into individual, family, community, and broader societal factors—are often interdependent. Space restrictions will permit only a sampling of cases of language shift around the world, some which represent immigrant contexts and others involving non-immigrant contexts. I also return quite frequently to the basic tenet emphasized by Fishman (1991) that language maintenance must involve intergenerational transmission of the language; that is, it must be passed on from parents to children over successive generations. If intergenerational transmission of a language ceases, it can be said that the speakers have shifted to another language.

Individual Factors

At its most basic level, language shift is an individual phenomenon because it involves the language behaviors of individual speakers. One primarily individual factor is proficiency in the minority language. If a person does not acquire a certain level of proficiency in a language, it will be difficult, if not impossible, to use it in socially significant ways, and it will be a challenge to pass that language on to children. There are many factors involved in developing proficiency in two languages from birth, including the input received, requirements to use a particular language with certain interlocutors, level of cognitive development and, in later years, relationships between language and identity. *Bilingual first language acquisition* (De Houwer 2009) is a situation in which a child hears two languages from birth and often (but not always) develops proficiency in both languages. Some children of immigrants are examples of bilingual first-language acquisition, but many other children of immigrants are actually monolingual in their parents' language until they begin school; it is *their* children, the grandchildren of the original immigrants, who often end up barely proficient in the minority language. Along with attrition (the loss of previously acquired forms), incomplete acquisition, or complete acquisition of a contact variety, another common phenomenon among bilinguals is code-switching, which some see as a sign of language shift, but others consider a sign of maintenance (see Li, chapter 18, this volume).

Another principally individual[1] factor are attitudes toward the minority language. Gibbons and Ramirez (2004) found that, among 106 Spanish-speaking teenagers in Sydney, Australia, there was a strong and direct connection between positive beliefs in favor of bilingualism and greater Spanish proficiency. In spite of this connection, however, positive attitudes are not enough for language maintenance to occur. Among Spanish-speakers in the United States, for example, it has frequently been reported that speakers hold positive attitudes toward Spanish, but almost all of them clearly shift to English by the third generation (Attinasi 1985; Potowski 2004; Zentella 1997). Some exceptions to Spanish language shift in the United States will be explored in a separate section.

In a case involving a very different set of attitudes, Kuncha and Bathula (2004) found that more than half of the Telugu-speaking mothers and children in New Zealand felt it was a "waste of time" to learn Telugu; they were shifting to English after an average of just two years. So, although positive attitudes are not enough to guarantee language maintenance, negative attitudes lead to rapid shift.

Immigrants abandon their heritage languages for a variety of reasons including peer pressure, lack of opportunity to use the language, or fear that it will interfere with their ability to learn English or get ahead in mainstream society. As noted by Tse (2001: 33), "[w]hereas knowing [the majority language] may bring prestige and acceptance, speaking another language—especially a low-status language—can do the opposite" by causing shame for being different or attracting xenophobic reactions in others. Despite these negative affiliations, loss of the heritage language can have serious negative consequences. It can create feelings of linguistic insecurity and identity loss. Zhou and Bankston (2000) argue that loss of heritage language and identity leads some students to engage in delinquent behavior at school in the quest for a new identity. Particularly devastating is the weakening of the family, as parental authority is often diminished when parents and children cannot communicate with each other, and elders can no longer transmit family and ethnic values (Rodriguez 1982; Tse 2001: 52). We now turn to studies on the role of the family in language maintenance.

The Role of the Family

Fishman (1991) proposed a scale to measure the degree of shift in a community, called the Graded Intergeneration Disruption Scale (GIDS). The eight stages of this scale are presented in table 16.1—note that "Xish" refers to any particular language. Stage 8 represents situations in which a language is no longer spoken in a community, and Stage 1 is rather robust use of a language. According to Fishman, only when Stage 6 is stable—when the language is being passed on in the home—is there a chance of long-term survival of that language. He argues that without intergenerational transmission, the efforts of schools, churches, and communities are largely symbolic and not likely to reverse shift, and that it is very difficult to move up the scale into stronger positions. Thus, even if the education system and government provide support for the home language, this will be valuable only if family adults use the language with children and continually foster acquisition and use of that language.

This brings us to a closer inspection of the role of parents in language maintenance. Parents are often the individuals who have the earliest influence on the language their children acquire. Pauwels (2005) and others suggest that the most successful pattern for minority language transmission is one in which each parent uses a different language with the children, often referred to as the "one parent, one language" model. However, other research has noted that a minority language is more likely to be acquired by children if both parents speak it, rather than in "mixed" or linguistically exogamous marriages (Zentella 1997; see Piller 2002 for descriptions of bilingual couples). For example, De Houwer

Table 16.1 Fishman's (1991) Graded Intergeneration Disruption Scale

Stage 8: Most vestigial users of Xish are socially isolated old folks and Xish needs to be reassembled from their speech and taught to demographically unconcentrated adults.
Stage 7: Most users of Xish are a socially integrated and ethnolinguistically active population, but they are beyond childbearing age.
Stage 6: The attainment of intergenerationl informal oralcy and its demographic concentration and institutional reinforcement.
Stage 5: Xish literacy in the home, school and community, but without taking on extra-communal reinforcement of such literacy.
Stage 4: Xish in lower education that meets the requirements of compulsory education laws.
State 3: Use of Xish in the lower work sphere (outside of the Xish neighborhood/ community) involving interaction between Xmen and Ymen.
Stage 2: Xish in lower governmental services and mass media but not in the higher spheres of either.
Stage 1: Some use of Xish in higher level educational, occupational, governmental and media efforts, but without the additional safety provided by political independence.

(2009: 112) cites several studies indicating that a greater percentage of children ended up bilingual when both parents used both languages with the children, citing the amount of support that each language receives in the home as the decisive factor. Consider an example of Arabic speakers in France. Assuming that both parents speak French, the majority language, their children will more likely end up proficient in Arabic if both parents speak to them in Arabic than if the "one parent, one language" model is followed.

Moving from parents to families, Pauwels (2005) notes that much work on immigrant languages in Australia documents the important role of the family as a site of language maintenance. In particular, her review documents the challenges faced by immigrant families in passing the minority language to their Australian-born children. The six patterns she cites as typical in Australia are in fact very common in the United States as well (see table 16.2): the presence of grandparents, overseas visitors from the home country, and visits to the home country have a very positive effect on home language use.

Other research has shown that multigenerational households with grandparents and other older relatives present contribute to language maintenance (including Sofu 2009). However, without access to minority language classes or activities—when young people's contact with the language is limited to the family—there is a very heavy burden on families, particularly on nuclear families with limited access to a network of relatives.

There are gendered aspects to family language use as well. For example, Kamada (1997) completed a case study of 10 families living in Japan in which one parent was Japanese and the other was a speaker of either Chinese or English. The children with minority-language-speaking mothers ended up becoming more proficient bilinguals than those with minority-language-speaking fathers. Several minority-language-speaking fathers "had tried, with some success in the early stages, to instill the [minority language in] their children, but later gave

Table 16.2. Common minority language use patterns among children

(1) Use of the minority language is primarily for communication with parents and grandparents.
(2) Seldom use the minority language with siblings or peers. Exceptions: recently arrived youth or during trips abroad.
(3) Decrease in willingness to use the minority language with interlocutors who know the dominant language.
(4) Willingness to use the minority language decreases with age, particularly upon entry into the school system (age 5) and again in adolescence.
(5) The more minority language exposure in the home, the more likely it will be used. Ultimate proficiency depends on factors including input, output, personality, family support, etc.

Source: Pauwels (2005)

up after realizing the difficulty of the task and requirement of total dedication" (1997: 53). In cases where the minority-language-speaking mother chose not to speak the minority language, it was not acquired by the children. Similarly, Okita's (2002) portrayal of 28 families living in Britain (Japanese mothers and British fathers) details the difficulties of the mothers in transmitting and sustaining the minority language. Overall, it was not easy or natural for the mothers to use Japanese in the ways suggested by bilingual childrearing books, and the responsibility for nurturing the children's bilingualism fell upon the mothers more than the fathers. Mothers cited the draining requirements of time, energy, and money necessary to teach their children to read and write in Japanese, which needed to be balanced with concerns for children's English development, homework assistance, housework, and attending to their other children, their husbands, and themselves. Okita calls this language maintenance another type of "invisible work," much like housework and kin-keeping, and highlights that "[l]anguage use in intermarried families is deeply intertwined with the experience of childrearing. . . . [and is] impossible to separate from interpersonal, family, and societal contexts" (232).

Zentella (1997) underscores the *economic* difficulties faced by many Puerto Rican families in New York, who simply could not afford to place Spanish maintenance high on their list of priorities. This, coupled with the fact that most community members felt that one could be legitimately Puerto Rican without speaking Spanish, meant that there were relatively few community pressures to develop Spanish proficiency, and in fact there were several young boys in the network who were English monolinguals. Phinney et al. (2001) point out that, although knowledge of an ethnic language is significantly less by the third and fourth generation, members of some groups maintain a strong ethnic identity independent of language usage. Thus, other factors besides language are often sufficient to successfully create a sense of oneself as an ethnic group member.

Similarly to Pauwels (2005), Sofu (2009) argues that the family is one of the most important factors in the shift or maintenance of a community language. Studying three Arabic-speaking families in southern Turkey, he found that shift among the second generation was related to contact with monolingual Turkish-speaking families and increased job mobility. Language maintenance was supported most especially by the presence of Arabic-speaking grandparents in the home. However, it was also shown that members of the third generation "seem to be more language conscious and see the maintenance of their language as a way to preserve their cultural identity" (256).

Returning briefly to the concept of linguistic exogamy, Romaine (1995) notes that where a mixed language community exists, the loss rate of the minority language is highest. She cites findings in Wales that there are almost as many marriages where only one spouse speaks Welsh as there are where both speak Welsh (and, following the gender patterns cited earlier, data show that *mothers* in such mixed marriages have a better chance of passing Welsh on to their children). Although the inability of minorities to maintain the home as an intact domain for the use of their language is usually decisive in language shift, Romaine notes that "this is generally symptomatic of a more far-reaching disruption of domain distribution and pattern of transmission" (42). Thus, when the home no longer becomes a protected domain for the minority language (as in Stage 6 of Fishman's GIDS), it is usually the case that other domains are not protected, either.

Parental attitudes were examined by Pérez-Leroux, Cuza, and Thomas (2011) among Spanish-speaking families in Toronto, Canada. Two findings are of note here. First, more of the recently arrived families had a neutral stance toward Spanish maintenance than the long-time resident families, most likely because the recent arrivals place more instrumental value on mastery of English, while, only after attaining success in the new society, do they permit themselves the luxury of maintaining Spanish. Second, highly positive parental attitudes were correlated with higher degrees of parental language initiations in Spanish and with the degree of Spanish exposure offered to the children outside the home, which in turn were correlated with higher levels of Spanish proficiency among the children. However, in El Paso, Texas, Velázquez (2009) found that even when parents held positive attitudes toward Spanish, this did not always result in the considerable investment of time and resources required to foster Spanish development among their children. In those households in which the mother perceived a bilingual identity as desirable for her children's future, however, the children were expected to speak Spanish at home and generally experienced greater opportunities to use Spanish, again highlighting a gendered aspect to language use in families.

Community Factors

The broad definition of *community* used here includes neighborhoods, schools and peers, social networks, and participation in local religious institutions. Usually one of the first factors cited in language maintenance is the *concentration* of speakers who live in the immediate neighborhood, with the assumption that greater concentration equals better the chances for language maintenance (Portes & Rumbaut 1996: 229). For example, Alba et al. (2002) found that a third-generation Cuban child living in Miami, where over half of the population is Spanish speaking, was 20 times more likely to be proficient in Spanish than a child living in an area where just 5 percent of the population spoke Spanish. Sofu (2009) also found that lack of a strong Arabic-speaking presence in various Turkish neighborhoods played a role in Arabic language loss. Noting that there are relatively few speakers of non-English language in the United States who are more than two generations removed from their family's immigrant origins, Fishman (2006: 407) points out two exceptions. Yiddish-speaking Hasidic Jews in New York and Pennsylvania Dutch–speaking Amish and Old Order Mennonite communities live in a kind of self-imposed isolation (which also results in demographic concentration) that has permitted intergenerational transmission of their languages well beyond the third generation, yet has not stopped them from acquiring English. Navajo and Spanish in the Southwest United States may also constitute exceptions to the general pattern of shift to English by the third generation.

There are cases in which speakers of a minority language live close to a country in which that language is spoken regularly throughout society. Romaine (1995) points out that closer distance to such a border can influence language maintenance. For example, Francophones in northern Vermont, New Hampshire, and Maine tend to retain French more than those living inland in Maine and Rhode Island. Bills, Hudson, & Hernández-Chávez (2000) also found that distance from the Mexican border was correlated with integration into mainstream Anglophone society and less census–reported use of Spanish.

Contact with monolingual speakers can be established through immigration as well. For example, it has been posited by researchers in the United States (Leone & Cisneros 1983; Lynch 2000) that the continued influx of new Latino immigrant populations "revitalizes" the Spanish of resident populations. This idea of revitalization implies that there is contact between the more-established generations of Latinos and the new arrivals. However, several researchers (Mendoza-Denton 1999, Rivera Mills 2000; Gorman & Potowski 2009) have shown that second- and third-generation Latinos in the United States in fact reject newly arrived Spanish-speaking immigrants as neighbors, friends, and schoolmates for a variety of social reasons. Thus, the large rates of immigration from Spanish-speaking countries may bolster the presence of Spanish in the United States but not necessarily contribute to its long-term maintenance, as understood by Fishman (1991), through intergenerational transmission. A possible scenario of immigration contributing to intergenerational transmission would be if a second- or third-generation bilingual married a first-generation monolingual speaker, and the couple decided to speak their shared minority language to their children.

The home and parents are the primary site for language transmission. Another primary institution, where many youth spend a third of their waking hours, is school. Although some studies suggest that the formal teaching of a language is unlikely to have much effect on the spoken language (Li, Milroy, & Ching 1992: 148), other work suggests that bilingual students attending a dual immersion school where 50 percent to 80 percent of the school day is taught in Spanish may show higher levels of accuracy and overall proficiency in Spanish than students attending an all-English school (Montrul & Potowski 2007). Valdés (2011) argues that because third-generation immigrants have less exposure to the minority language both at home and within the community, the direct involvement of educational institutions is essential if they are to have the opportunity to develop their competence in the minority language. While schooling in a minority language may contribute in some degree to its maintenance, we must recall Fishman's (1991) emphasis that school and community efforts are largely symbolic in the absence of home-based intergenerational transmission. Valdés (2011) also details the challenges of developing a minority language among third-generation youth given the pervasive presence of English in their daily lives and the lesser prestige attributed to Spanish, which results in the difficult task of defining their identity in a society in which dual cultural and ethnic membership is often not viewed favorably.

Many ethnic communities have established Saturday schools seeking to promote linguistic and cultural knowledge. Chinen and Tucker (2005) found that adolescents enrolled in a Saturday Japanese-heritage school in California exhibited positive gains in ethnic identity and self-assessed Japanese proficiency. However, Zhang, and Slaughter-DeFoe (2009) found that while a group of Chinese parents in Philadelphia valued Chinese as a resource, their children failed to see the relevance of learning Chinese and often resisted parents' efforts to develop their heritage language skills. The authors suggested that American mainstream schools work together with immigrant parents and community heritage language schools to incorporate children's home languages in the official school curriculum and create a supportive environment.

Concurrent with the beginning of formal schooling, the primary influence on children often shifts from parents to peers. In a 19-year ethnographic study in the United States of the home French use of his three children, Caldas (2006) documents that the children spoke spontaneous French in the home up until the age of approximately 10. During their adolescent years, the children spoke absolutely no French around the dinner table when the family lived in monolingual English-speaking Louisiana. But during their summers in monolingual French-speaking Quebec, they spoke only French at the dinner table. For the children, the dominant language outside the home became the dominant language inside the home, regardless of which language the parents spoke. Caldas provides ample documentation that parents and schools had little influence on his children's language-use patterns. In fact, when the parents noticed that none of the students at the French immersion school in Louisiana actually spoke French with each other, they "began to soberly assess the limits of a school language immersion program, especially when it came up against adolescence in America." (Caldas 2006: 6). The author concluded that societal immersion with friends—that is, being surrounded by monolingual peers in Quebec—was the key factor to developing his children's French fluency, adding that "even if tremendous effort is exerted to preserve a minority language, if that language is not cherished by the adolescent's peer group, he or she will likely not speak the language—even in the home" (Caldas 2006: 163).

In Chicago, the amount of Spanish that Latino youth reported speaking on average each day was almost equal to the amount they spoke with their friends, which among the third generation averaged around 20 percent (Potowski 2004).

They used much higher percentages of Spanish with their parents and other older relatives, but these interlocutors did not raise the averages for overall daily average Spanish. This suggests that adolescents and young adults spend a great bulk of their time interacting with same-age peers in the societally dominant language. Very importantly, they often find their future mates from within peer groups, with whom they often have children and either continue or more frequently discontinue intergenerational transmission of the heritage language.

The importance of peers among adolescents brings us to the value of the social network as a heuristic for understanding language maintenance and shift. As Li, Milroy, and Ching (1992) note, an analysis of social networks can reveal factors that help explain why some groups maintain or shift away from a minority language. They note that close-knit networks help to maintain community languages, and that these networks form not only in small rural communities but also in modern cities. They found that variations in language choice patterns in Tynsdale, United Kingdom, could not be explained entirely by age and generation. Social networks were more relevant in understanding language use: Those individuals with greater numbers of ties with Chinese speakers in their exchange networks used more Chinese. Based on these findings, the authors propose that internal social organization of the community, persistence of pre-emigration social networks, and strategies developed by the community for maintaining these networks all contribute to language maintenance.

In a study that combines parental and peer influences, Phinney et al. (2001) attempted to construct a model of the influences on ethnic identity among adolescents in Armenian, Vietnamese, and Mexican families in the United States. Across all groups, parental cultural maintenance predicted adolescent ethnic language proficiency. That is, behaviors reported by parents to promote cultural maintenance, such as talking about the history of the ethnic group and "encouraging children to learn and practice cultural traditions and values" (144) were correlated with their children's self-reported proficiency in the heritage language. Among the Armenian youth, interacting with Armenian peers was directly correlated with proficiency in Armenian; this relationship did not obtain for the other two groups.

We frequently find that the *local community* views and influences the minority community, often in negative ways. For example, Guardado (2011) documents the intense pressures to assimilate to English exerted by school and the broader society on a Guatemalan family in Vancouver, Canada. In contrast, Walker (2011) in New Zealand highlights the ways in which local community clubs and other organizations provide support for families to engage in cultural practices that promote the use of Spanish and allow second-generation immigrants to construct a Latino identity. Hamp (1978) notes that Albanians maintain their language better in Italy than in Greece because of cultural ideology. In Italy, a "localist" attitude prevails in which each region values its own dialect, whereas Greece is said to exert more pressure on a normative standard. In addition, the degree of linguistic similarity between the majority and minority language may facilitate or hinder shift. Clyne (1991) speculates that, in Australia, Dutch speakers retain more Dutch because of its similarity with English, while Maltese-speakers shift away from Maltese. Pérez-Leroux, Cuza, and Thomason (2011) noted that the families they interviewed had generally favorable views toward Spanish and toward bilingualism in general, which they argued matched the overall stance of the Toronto community, where languages and diverse ethnic backgrounds are accepted as the norm, and there is an abundance of multilingual media; street signs; language services in government, education, and commercial establishments; and community support for ethnic celebrations.

Finally, religion often plays an important role in language maintenance. The examples cited earlier of Yiddish-speaking Hasidic Jews in New York and Dutch-speaking Amish and Old Order Mennonites in Pennsylvania both utilize their minority language for religious purposes. Some Arabic-speaking families in the United States participate in religious after school and Saturday/Sunday programs held in mosques, although such programs are considered not viable by many secular and non-Muslim Arabic-speaking families in the community.

Romaine (2011) argues that today there are increased possibilities for maintaining heritage languages—and to construct more transnational identities—due to greater opportunities to travel to the countries of origin, access to online media, and computer-mediated communication with friends and relatives in the countries of origin. However, these advantages are often overshadowed by negative pressures, not only from local communities as just described above, but also from broader mainstream society. We turn our attention now to these broader factors.

Broader Societal Factors Affecting Language Shift

Societies can exhibit different attitudes toward language minorities based on current events. For example, anti-German legislation and negative sentiment during and after the two world wars damaged the use and transmission of German in the United States (Ludanyi 2010). Fishman (2006: 410) contends that the increase in the proportion of Americans who claimed a mother tongue other than English on the 1970 Census was due to the ethnic movements of the mid-1960s and the resultant visible displays of ethnic pride, including in the media (ethnic radio, television, and newspapers) and community schools. However, after 1979, concerns about slower U.S. economic growth compared to Asia led to a negative ethnolinguistic climate, resulting in English-only laws and tremendous pressure on parents and communities to "constantly justify themselves, in the face of a wall of doubt and disbelief, for simply doing what is normal all over the world, namely, making sure that their children are following in the ethnolinguistic and ethnocultural footsteps of their parents and grandparents" (2006: 414).

In Australia, Martin (2011) documents that although official language policy has evolved, the low status of languages other than English and assimilationist pressure on immigrant families have remained the same, particularly in the context of the schools. He observes that while Australian teachers no longer advise parents to speak only English to their children, the overall negative linguistic social climate (what Schiffman [1996] calls "linguistic culture") clearly has affected immigrants' language choices. In spite of the tremendous pressure of the wider society, Fishman maintains that "local circumstances and efforts are frequently the ultimate determiners of local successes or failure" (2006: 414).

Other broad societal influences are not related to world politics but rather to cultural mores that change over time. Studying third-generation Arabic-speakers living in Turkey, Sofu (2009) found that the first generation lived in the first half of the twentieth century, when men were tradesmen, farmers, and artisans and women were housewives. Members of this generation felt they had to hide their Arabic identity and transmitted this sentiment to their children, restricting use of Arabic to the home only. In the second generation, people were exposed to Turkish through schooling, and the men held other-than-manual-labor jobs and were thus exposed to speakers of Turkish. The third generation has had exposure to Arabic television as well as more-varied labor roles for women, and express pride in their Arabic identity.

Case Study: Spanish in the United States

The United States, a nation that has been a major immigrant destination since its inception, has been referred to as a melting pot. A more current metaphor is that of a "salad" in which each ingredient retains its primary characteristics. However, linguistically the melting pot metaphor is still valid. When examining 35 different nations in the world, in no other country was the rate of mother tongue shift toward monolingualism in the national dominant language as fast as in the United States (Lieberson, Dalto, & Johnston 1975). Even the most recently arrived groups exhibit patterns of language use that suggest that the adoption of English is well underway. Veltman (2000), for example, found that after zero to five years in the United States, 20 percent of immigrants aged 0 to 14 at the time of arrival had already adopted English as their preferred, usual language. After five additional years, the number rose to 40 percent. In addition, he found that younger people today are more likely to adopt English than their older peers did when they were young.

Adopting English as a preferred language in the United States does not necessarily mean that the family language is abandoned, although that is often the case. In 2006, Rumbaut, Massey, and Bean (2006) found that the "life expectancy" of five languages in southern California (Spanish, Tagalog, Chinese, Vietnamese, and Korean) was no more than two generations. That is, Spanish can be expected to begin to die out with the children of immigrants, and not be spoken well or at all by the grandchildren of immigrants—while the Asian languages die out even faster, often not being spoken well by the children of immigrants. An examination of the 12 most commonly spoken non-English language in the United States as well as Native American languages (Potowski 2010) indicates that speakers of immigrant languages are shifting to English and that only continued immigration is sustaining the non-English languages.

With 37 million speakers, Spanish in the United States is an illustrative case to consider; if any immigrant language were to survive here, it should be Spanish. Since approximately 40 percent of the US Hispanic population was born in Latin America, the nation's increasing number of Latinos is due in part to new immigration from Spanish-speaking countries. However, members of the second and third generations constitute the other 60 percent of US Latinos, and most of these individuals have learned English. Overall 51 percent of US Hispanics claimed to speak English "very well" (United States Census 2000).

The majority of Spanish maintenance research in the United States has taken place in the Southwest, New York, and Miami. Floyd's (1985) review of eight Southwest language-use surveys published between 1970 and 1984 found evidence of a process of language shift from Spanish to English, particularly among younger speakers. More recent studies in the Southwest have also found evidence of Spanish loss and shift to English (e.g., Rivera-Mills 2000). Silva-Corvalán's (1994) data indicate that third-generation Spanish speakers in Los Angeles have considerably reduced Spanish verbal systems, which undoubtedly has important effects on language transmission and change.

New York and Miami have also seen a good deal of Spanish maintenance research. Among Puerto Ricans in New York City, Zentella (1997) and Pedraza (1985) found a definite shift to English, but one that was accompanied by domains in which Spanish was preferred (such as child rearing) and, somewhat paradoxically, there was a high degree of loyalty to Spanish and a concept of Latino identity that did not require Spanish proficiency. García et. al. (1988) found that Dominicans in two New York neighborhoods reported using significant amounts of Spanish (between 84 percent and 98 percent) with siblings and parents, and only slightly less (between 66 percent and 72 percent) with children and friends. The middle-class group used more English in public than the working-class group, which the authors attributed to the need for linguistic minorities to "respond to the language surround in which they are immersed" (1988: 508). In addition, speakers of stigmatized varieties of Spanish may prefer to abandon Spanish in favor of English. Another sign of shift in that study was that Puerto Ricans and Cubans used considerably less Spanish with children and friends than with parents. However, publications about Spanish maintenance in New York appear slightly more optimistic than those in the Southwest, probably due to the recency of Hispanic immigration on the East coast.

In Miami, Lynch's (2000) observations that Spanish use is robust among Cuban Americans are countered by evidence that English is replacing Spanish to a significant degree (García & Díaz 1992; Portes & Schauffler 1996; Zurer Pearson & McGee 1993). Contrary to the correlation between higher social class and English use found by García et. al. (1988) in New York, Lambert and Taylor (1996) found that middle-class Cubans maintain Spanish to a greater degree than working-class Cubans, who were shifting to English in an attempt to gain economic stability. Portes and Schauffler (1996) found that higher socioeconomic levels in Miami correlated in some ways with Spanish retention and in other ways with a shift to English. They also found that "even among youths educated in bilingual schools at the core of an ethnic enclave, linguistic assimilation is proceeding with remarkable speed" (21–22) and that

> [t]heir hopes of communicating with their children and grandchildren in their native language likely will be disappointed. . . . Only where immigrant groups concentrate physically, thus sustaining an economic and cultural presence . . . will their languages survive past the first generation. In the absence of policies promoting bilingualism, even these enclaves will be engulfed . . . in the course of 2–3 generations. (28)

Similarly, García and Otheguy (1988) claim that in Cuban American communities, only demographic growth appears favorable to Spanish maintenance, while sociocultural, economic, ideological, and political factors are leading to a shift to English. Discrepancies among these studies point to the difficulty of assigning either/or values to a phenomenon as complex as language shift. They may also reflect methodological differences. For example, studies that interpret census data may be problematic because when respondents claim to "speak Spanish in the home," there are no details on the quantity of that Spanish use. Self-reports of language use may be reliable and lead to more accurate interpretations than census data, but they will not be infallible. Interviews and long-term ethnographic observation (e.g., Zentella 1997) are likely to provide more reliable measures of language shift, although they are more time consuming, tend to use smaller sample sizes, and are not free from some degree of researcher bias.

Relatively few studies have been done on Spanish use in the Midwest, despite the fact that the 81 percent growth of the Latino population between 1990 and 2000 (Census 2000) was the largest reported for all US geographic areas. In Minneapolis–St. Paul, second-generation respondents reported much less Spanish use than first-generation respondents (Leone & Cisneros 1983). In a small Iowa town (González & Wherritt 1990), respondents reported 90 percent Spanish use with their parents, under 80 percent with siblings, and 60 percent with their children. Attinasi (1985) compared self-reports of language use and attitudes among Latinos in Northwest Indiana (immediately outside the metropolitan Chicago area) and in New York. He found evidence of "a stage of bilingualism with greater fluency in English" (1985: 54) that included very positive attitudes toward bilingual education and cultural allegiance to the Spanish language. However, shift to English was further along in Northwest Indiana than in New York, and the low Spanish use and proficiency reported in Northwest Indiana led the author to conclude that it was unlikely that Spanish would be transmitted to future generations. And in Chicago, the third largest Spanish-speaking city in the nation after New York and Los Angeles, Potowski (2004) found the same thing that has been found everywhere else in the country: a clear and steady decline in Spanish use from first- to second- to third-generation speakers.

In general, then, Spanish is not being transmitted intergenerationally in the United States; speakers are shifting to English equally or perhaps more rapidly than in past generations. It is really the large influx of new immigrants that creates the impression of ethnolinguistic vitality. Villa and Rivera-Mills (2009) did find some receptive Spanish comprehension among seventh-generation individuals in the Southwest, who they proposed might play a role in reversing language shift by relearning Spanish and transitioning to maintenance bilingualism. However, it is unclear how likely this phenomenon is to occur.

Conclusions

Many of the world's 6000 to 7000 languages are being lost—by some estimates, up to half of them—mostly due to the spread of a few dominant languages that many speakers are shifting to. Thus, it is not only situations of immigration that give rise to language shift. Fishman (1991) proposes that minority languages, to the extent that they belong to minority *groups*, would benefit greatly from group-based legal protection, similar to the Americans with Disabilities Act, as well as a more proactive stance by community members toward their preservation. It is important to realize that *who* speaks a language is often more important than *how many* people speak it, although a large minority group often has better luck maintaining its language because of increased mobilization in support of its language.

Fishman's insistence on the importance of intergenerational language transmission in language maintenance, along with understanding how such transmission is socioculturally constructed and results from a combination of social, economic, and political experiences (Fishman 2006: 408), as well as the fragility of certain languages in the worldwide "ecology" (Romaine, chapter 38, this volume) underscore the precariousness of minority languages, the likelihood of shift, and the challenges to maintenance.

Notes

1. While attitudes are held by individuals, an individual's attitudes are strongly shaped by those of the local society, making it difficult to separate the individual from the social.

References

Alba, R., Logan, J., Lutz, A., & Stults, B. 2002. Only English by the third generation? Loss and preservation of the mother tongue among the grandchildren of contemporary immigrants. *Demography* 39(3): 467–84.

Attinasi, J. 1985. Hispanic attitudes in Northwestern Indiana and New York. In L.Elías-Olivares, E. Leone, R. Cisneros, & J. Gutierrez (eds.), *Spanish language use and public life in the USA*, 527–80. Berlin: Mouton.

Bills, G., Hudson, A., & Hernández-Chávez, E. 2000. Spanish home language use and English proficiency as differential measures of language maintenance and shift. *Southwest Journal of Linguistics* 19(1): 11–27.

Caldas, S. 2006. *Raising bilingual-biliterate children in monolingual cultures*. Clevedon, UK: Multilingual Matters.

Chinen, K., & Tucker, G. R. 2005. Heritage language development: Understanding the roles of ethnic identity and Saturday school participation. *Heritage Language Journal* 3(1): 27–59.

Clyne, M. 1991. German and Dutch in Australia. In S. Romaine (ed.), *Language in Australia*, 241–48. Cambridge: Cambridge University Press.

De Houwer, A. 2009. *Bilingual first language acquisition*. Clevedon, UK: Multilingual Matters.

Fishman, J. 1991. *Reversing language shift: Theory and practice of assistance to threatened languages*. Clevedon, UK: Multilingual Matters.

Fishman, J. 2006. Language maintenance, language shift, and reversing language shift. In T. Bhatia & W. Ritchie (eds.), *The handbook of bilingualism*, 406–36. Oxford: Blackwell.

Floyd, MaryBeth . 1985. Spanish in the Southwest: Language maintenance or shift? In L. Elías-Olivares, E. Leone, R. Cisneros, & J. Gutierrez (eds.), *Spanish language use and public life in the USA*, 13–25. Berlin: Mouton.

García, O., Evangelista, I., Martínez, M., Disla, C. & Paulino, B. 1988. Spanish language use and attitudes: A study of two New York City communities. *Language in Society* 17: 475–511.

García, O., & Otheguy, R. 1988. The language situation of Cuban Americans. In S. McKay & S. Wong (eds.), *Language diversity: Problem or resource?* 166–92. New York: Harper and Row.

García, R., & Díaz, C. 1992. The status and use of Spanish and English among Hispanic youth in Dade County (Miami) Florida: A sociolinguistic study, 1989–1991. *Language and Education* 6: 13–32.

Gibbons, J., & Ramirez, E. 2004. Different beliefs: Beliefs and the maintenance of a minority language. *Journal of Language and Social Psychology* 23: 99–117.

González, N., & Wheritt, I. 1990. Spanish language use in West Liberty, Iowa. In J. Bergen (ed.), *Spanish in the United States: Sociolinguistic Issues*, 67–78. Washington, DC: Georgetown University Press.

Gorman, L., & Potowski, K. 2009. Language contact between second/third and first generation Spanish-speaking adolescents. Paper presented at the 22nd Conference on Spanish in the U.S., Miami, FL.

Guardado, M. 2011. Language and literacy socialization as resistance in Western Canada. In K. Potowski & J. Rothman (eds.), *Child bilinguals: Spanish in English-speaking societies*, 177–98. Amsterdam: John Benjamins.

Hamp, E. P. 1978. Problems of multilingualism in small linguistic communities. In J. E. Alatis (ed.), *International dimensions of bilingual education*, 155–65. Washington, DC: Georgetown Univesity Press.

Kamada, L. 1997. Bilingual family case Studies, vol. 2. Monographs on Bilingualism No. 5. Japan Association for Language Teaching, Tokyo.

Kuncha, R. & Bathula, H. 2004. The role of attitudes in language shift and language maintenance in a new immigrant community: A case study. Working Paper #1, April 2004. AIS St. Helen's Centre for Research in International Education.

Lambert, W., & Taylor, D. 1996. Language in the lives of ethnic minorities: Cuban American families in Miami. *Applied Linguistics* 17: 476–500.

Leone, E., & Cisneros, R. 1983. Mexican-American language communities in the Twin Cities: An example of contact and recontact. In L. Elías-Olivares (ed.), *Spanish in the U.S. setting: Beyond the Southwest*, 181–209. Rosslyn, VA: National Clearinghouse for Bilingual Education.

Li, W ., Milroy, L., & Ching, P.S. 1992. A two-step sociolinguistic analysis of code-switching and language choice. *International Journal of Applied Linguistics* 2(1): 63–86.

Lieberson, S., Dalto, G., & Johnston, M. E. 1975. The course of mother-tongue diversity in nations. *American Journal of Sociology* 81: 34–61.

Ludanyi, R. 2010. German in the USA. In K. Potowski (ed.), *Language diversity in the USA*, 146–63. New York: Cambridge University Press.

Lynch, A. 2000. Spanish-speaking Miami in sociolinguistic perspective: Bilingualism, recontact, and language maintenance among the Cuban-origin population. In A. Roca (ed.), *Research on Spanish in the U.S.*, 271–83. Somerville, MA: Cascadilla Press.

Martin, D. 2011. Reactions to the overt display of Spanish language maintenance in Australia. In K. Potowski & J. Rothman (eds.), *Child bilinguals: Spanish in English-speaking societies*, 283–307. Amsterdam: John Benjamins.

Mendoza-Denton. N. 1999. Fighting words: Latina girls, gangs, and language attitudes. In D. L. Galindo & M. D. Gonzales (eds.) *Speaking Chicana: Voice, power, and identity*, 39–56. Tucson: University of Arizona Press.

Montrul, S., & Potowski, K. 2007. Command of gender agreement in school-age Spanish bilingual children. *International Journal of Bilingualism* 11: 301–28.

Okita, T. 2002. *Invisible work: Bilingualism, language choice and childrearing in intermarried families*. Amsterdam: John Benjamins.

Pauwels, A. 2005. Maintaining the community language in Australia: Challenges and roles for families. *International Journal of Bilingual Education and Bilingualism* 8: 124–31.

Pedraza, P. 1985. Language maintenance among New York Puerto Ricans. In L. Elías-Olivares, E. Leone, R. Cisneros, & J. Gutiérrez (eds.), *Spanish language and public life in the United States*, 59–71. New York: Mouton de Gruyter.

Pérez-Leroux, A. T., Cuza, A., & Thomas, D. 2011 From parental attitudes to input conditions: Spanish-English bilingual development in Toronto. In K. Potowski & J. Rothman (eds.), *Child bilinguals: Spanish in English-speaking societies*, 149–76. Amsterdam: John Benjamins.

Phinney, J., Romero, I. Nava, M., & Huang, D. 2001. The role of language, parents, and peers in ethnic identity among adolescents in immigrant families. *Journal of Youth and Adolescence* 30: 135–53.

Piller, I. 2002. *Bilingual couples talk: The discursive construction of hybridity.* Amsterdam: John Benjamins.

Portes, A., & Rumbaut, R. 1996. *Immigrant America: A portrait.* Berkeley: University of California Press.

Portes, A., & Schauffler, R. 1996. Language and the second generation: Bilingualism yesterday and today. In A. Portes (ed.), *The new second generation*, 8–29. New York: Russell Sage.

Potowski, K. 2004. Spanish language shift in Chicago. *Southwest Journal of Linguistics* 23(1): 87–116.

Potowski, K. (ed.) 2010. *Language diversity in the USA*. New York: Cambridge University Press.

Rivera-Mills, S. 2000. Intraethnic attitudes among Hispanics in a northern California community. In A. Roca (ed.) *Research on Spanish in the United States: Linguistic issues and challenges*, 377–89. Somerville, MA: Cascadilla Press.

Rodriguez, R. 1982. *Hunger of memory: The education of Richard Rodriguez.* New York: Bantam.

Romaine, S. 1995. *Bilingualism*, 2nd ed. Oxford: Blackwell.

Romaine, S. 2011. Identity and multilingualism. In K. Potowski & J. Rothman (eds.), *Child bilinguals: Spanish in English-speaking societies*, 7–30. Amsterdam: John Benjamins.

Rumbaut, R., Massey, D., & Bean, F. 2006. Linguistic life expectancies: Immigrant language retention in Southern California. *Population and Development Review* 32(3): 447–60

Schiffman, H. 1996. *Linguistic culture and language policy.* New York: Routledge.

Silva-Corvalán, C. 1994. *Language contact and change: Spanish in Los Angeles.* Oxford: Clarendon Press.

Sofu, H. 2009. Language shift or maintenance within three generations: Examples from three Turkish-Arabic-speaking families. *International Journal of Multilingualism* 6(3): 246–57.

Tse, L. 2001. *Why don't they learn English? Separating fact from fallacy in the U.S. language debate.* New York: Teachers College Press.

United States Census 2000. http://www.census.gov/main/www/cen2000.html.

Valdés, G. 2011. The challenge of maintaining Spanish-English bilingualism in American schools. In K. Potowski & J. Rothman (eds.), *Child bilinguals: Spanish in English-speaking societies.* Amsterdam: John Benjamins.

Velazquez, I. 2009. Intergenerational Spanish transmission in El Paso, Texas: Parental perceptions of cost/benefit. *Spanish in Context* 6(1): 69–84.

Veltman, C. 2000. The American linguistic mosaic: Understanding languages shift in the United States. In S. McKay & S. Wong (eds.), *New immigrants in the United States*, 58–93. Cambridge: Cambridge University Press.

Villa, D., & Rivera-Mills, S. 2009. An integrated multi-generational model for language maintenance and shift: The case of Spanish in the Southwest. *Spanish in Context* 6: 26–42.

Walker, U. 2011. The role of community in preserving Spanish in New Zealand. In K. Potowski & J. Rothman (eds.), *Child bilinguals: Spanish in English-speaking societies*, 331–54. Amsterdam: John Benjamins.

Zentella, A.C. 1997. *Growing up bilingual: Puerto Rican children in New York*. Malden, MA: Blackwell.

Zhang, D., & Slaughter-DeFoe, D. 2009. Language attitudes and heritage language maintenance among Chinese immigrant families in the USA. *Language, Culture and Curriculum* 22(2): 77–93.

Zhou, M., & Bankston, C. L. III. 2000. *Straddling different social worlds: The experience of Vietnamese refugee children in the United States*. New York: ERIC Clearinghouse on Urban Education, Institute for Urban and Minority Education, Teachers College, Columbia University.

Zurer Pearson, B., & McGee, A. 1993. Language choice in Hispanic-background junior high school students in Miami: A 1988 update. In A. Roca & J. Lipski (eds.), *Spanish in the United States: Linguistic contact and diversity*, 91–102. New York: Mouton de Gruyter.

CHAPTER 17

SOCIOLINGUISTICS AND SECOND LANGUAGE ACQUISITION

MARTIN HOWARD, RAYMOND MOUGEON, AND JEAN-MARC DEWAELE

DESPITE the development since the 1970s of second language acquisition (SLA) and sociolinguistics as strands within applied linguistics, the study of the acquisition of sociolinguistic and sociopragmatic variation has only been consolidated as a new wave of study within SLA research during just over the last decade. While the focus on sociolinguistic and sociopragmatic variation is therefore relatively new, linguistic variation had nonetheless been and continues to be an important issue that SLA research has grappled with. By linguistic variation, we understand the learner's variable use of two or more L2 forms to express the same functional value, where one or all forms are non-native. In so doing, L2 learners do not use or underuse the appropriate form in context, such that there is a form-function mismatch in their interlanguage. Such variation is highly characteristic of L2 development, evident from a very early stage, such that the challenge for the learner is to overcome such variation by increasingly engaging in appropriate form-function relations. Such variation is exemplified in the following case of the expression of negation in English:

"don't go" versus "no go"

In contrast to such non-native-like variation that Dewaele and Mougeon (2002) and Rehner (2005) label type I variation, type II variation is concerned with the learner's ability to use native-speaker sociolinguistic and sociopragmatic variants, as exemplified in the following cases of the variable realization of /ng/ and /n/ and variable t/d deletion in English:

"I'm going out" versus "I'm goin' out"
"I don't follow" versus "I don'(t) follow"

This chapter focuses on type II variation, and it aims to present an overview of the research findings that illuminate the challenge to the learner of developing sociolinguistic and sociopragmatic competence in the L2. While the application of sociolinguistic variationist methods to the study of type II variation has been relatively recent in SLA research, such methods have also been fruitfully used by some SLA researchers in relation to type I variation. For example, learner, or interlanguage, variation in invariable contexts has been explored using sociolinguistic variationist methods in studies such as Adamson (1989), Bayley (1996), and Young (1991). These studies point to the relative systematicity underlying such variation, although the issue of systematic versus non-systematic variation in learner language remains a much-debated one. Moreover, in earlier SLA research, the issue of linguistic variation was explored primarily in relation to stylistic factors, such as attention and monitoring and the role of the learner's interlocutor (e.g., Tarone 1988).

Beyond such work on type I variation, the more recent study of type II variation has developed following the initial impetus provided by Adamson and Regan (1991), and has been consolidated by a range of studies in different learning contexts: a classroom environment, a naturalistic environment, an immersion setting, and a study-abroad context. In each context, the focus has predominantly been on L2 French, although in a naturalistic context studies of L2 English are also available. Concerning naturalistic studies, one can mention a large-scale project on L2 French acquisition among Anglophone adult learners in Montreal (e.g., Blondeau et al. 2002), and projects on L2 English acquisition by adult immigrant learners in the United States (Adamson & Regan 1991; Bayley 1996; Major 2004). In the case of classroom learners, university students of French have been the focus of study in Dewaele's project on Flemish-speaking learners in a Belgian context, and multilingual learners in the UK (Dewaele 1992, 2002, 2004a, 2004b). In their respective longitudinal projects concerned with the relative impact of long-term naturalistic input on sociolinguistic development in comparison with classroom exposure, Howard (2010) and Regan (1996) have focused on Irish university learners in a study-abroad context. Barron (2003) provides a similar longitudinal study of Irish learners' sociopragmatic development during a year-long stay in Germany. Mougeon and his collaborators, Rehner and Nadasdi, have examined extensively the learning of variation by adolescent learners in a Canadian French immersion setting (for an overview, see Mougeon et al. 2002, 2004, 2010). Their work is complemented by a more recent project by Françoise Mougeon and Rehner in a university setting on the long-term impact of classroom immersion in the case of former immersion learners (Mougeon & Rehner 2009; Rehner 2010, 2011).

While the spectrum of languages investigated is somewhat restricted, thanks to their investigation of a range of sociolinguistic variables across various learning contexts, the projects referred to provide significant insights into the L2 acquisition of sociolinguistic variation. In the following, we will present an overview of the main findings from this body of work.

Sociolinguistic Development in the L2

Level of Use of (In)formal and Vernacular Sociolinguistic Variants

Since existing studies generally focus on advanced L2 learners, it remains unclear whether sociolinguistic variation is evidenced in less advanced learners. However, since the research that we have to hand points to the underuse of informal sociolinguistic variants even in advanced learners relative to their frequency in native-speaker discourse, it may be the case that sociolinguistic variation only emerges following stability in the learner's grammatical development. In this regard, Adamson and Regan (1991) posit that the learner's development of morphosyntactic features over time is a prerequisite to their variable use in sociolinguistic terms. When such variation does emerge, findings across studies point to considerable overuse of formal variants by classroom learners, even after many years of classroom L2 exposure, be it in the foreign-language classroom or in an immersion setting, with concomitant underuse of informal variants relative to native-speaker frequency of use. For example, such underuse has been observed in relation to a number of classic grammatical variables in French, such as use versus non-use of the negative particle "ne" (Dewaele 1992, 2004a; Dewaele & Regan 2002; Regan 1996; Rehner & Mougeon 1999), use of the first-person plural subject form "on" in relation to "nous" ["we"] (Dewaele 2002a; Rehner et al. 2003), use of the periphrastic future verb form as opposed to the inflected form (Howard 2010; Nadasdi et al. 2003; Regan et al. 2009), as well as some socio-phonological variables such as /l/ deletion versus retention (Howard et al. 2006; Mougeon et al. 2010; Thomas 2004), schwa deletion versus retention (Uritescu et al. 2004) and variable liaison realization (Howard 2006, 2010; Thomas 2004). Indeed, on some of these variables, some studies have found that classroom learners do not realize the informal variant at all (see, e.g., Regan's 1996 study of "ne" deletion, as well as Howard et al.'s and Mougeon et al.'s studies of /l/ deletion).

If informal variants are underused, research has also shown that vernacular variants are minimally used, if at all. In contrast to informal variants, vernacular variants are deemed erroneous according to standard prescriptive norms, are socially stigmatized in native-speaker discourse, and are usually associated with speakers from lower social strata. Examples include use of some slang vocabulary, as well as some grammatical features. For instance, in their study of Canadian French immersion learners, Mougeon et al. (2010) report the absence of vernacular variants such as "ça fait que" ["so"] in the expression of consequence and the future time form, "m'as" ["going to"], while the first-person plural subject pronoun form, "nous-autres on" ["we"], as well as "rien que" ["only"] for the marking of restriction are also found to be highly infrequent. The only vernacular-like variants used with some frequency in their learner corpus are forms that may in fact be residual developmental features, for example, "avoir" ["to have"] used as an auxiliary to mark perfectivity on "être" ["to be"] verbs (Knaus & Nadasdi 2001; Mougeon et al. 2010).

Given such underuse, and even non-use in some cases, of informal and vernacular sociolinguistic variants, in contrast with the overuse of formal variants by classroom learners, the question arises as to what role the linguistic input plays in the acquisition of sociolinguistic variation. On this count, the availability of studies across a range of learning contexts allows a number of important insights.

The Role of Learning Context in L2 Sociolinguistic Development

In contrast to a classroom context, studies of learners in a naturalistic environment, as well as comparative studies of learners in both learning contexts, generally point to the highly positive impact of naturalistic exposure on L2 sociolinguistic development. For example, in a naturalistic environment, Blondeau et al.'s (2002) work on adult Anglophone learners of French in Montreal points to levels of use of some informal variants that approach native-speaker levels, in particular in the case of use of the first-person plural subject pronoun "on" and the "ne" deletion in the marking of negation. A highly positive effect for native-speaker contact is observed, such that those learners who report high levels of contact increasingly approach native-speaker levels of use on other variants such as /l/ deletion and subject-doubling. Although approaching to a lesser degree native-speaker levels of usage, the highly positive effect for native-speaker contact is also reported in the case of a number of local variants specific to Quebecois French, such as realization of affricative /t/ and /d/ and use of composed subject pronoun forms such as "eux-autres" ["they"]. In the case of L2 English, Bayley (1996) arrived at similar findings. Focusing on t/d deletion among Chinese adult learners, he reports higher levels of deletion among those speakers evidencing high degrees of social integration compared to speakers with lower degrees of integration.

Research on classroom learners who have spent time in a naturalistic context also points to the highly beneficial role of such naturalistic exposure. For example, whereas the learners in Regan's (1996) longitudinal study of Irish university learners of French minimally engaged in "ne" deletion prior to a year-long stay in the target-language community, they significantly increased their levels of deletion during that time. Indeed, in a follow-up study, Regan (2005) shows that they continued to maintain their deletion rates a full year later, following their return to their home university. Such a finding is further confirmed by Howard (2010) in a similar longitudinal study looking at a range of variables in French including the use versus non-use of "ne," "nous"/"on" variation, variable marking of futurity, and /l/ deletion.

Beyond French, some studies also exist of L2 German and L2 Japanese. In the former case, Barron (2003) tracks the socio-pragmatic development evidenced by Irish university learners spending a year in Germany. She focuses specifically on their use of various pragmatic devices in the expression of requests, offers and refusals. While the learners demonstrated progress throughout the study in the direction of native-speaker norms, the author notes that movement in the direction of those norms, as opposed to actually reaching them, best characterized the learners' socio-pragmatic development during the year-long study. In the case of L2 Japanese, Marriott (1995) explores socio-pragmatic development among adolescent Australian learners spending a sojourn in Japan. The positive impact of such naturalistic exposure is noted, although development is limited in some regard with respect to the learners' selection and use of an appropriate honorific style. Dewaele (2010) showed that the effect of context of acquisition of a language (instructed, naturalistic, or mixed) continues to exert a significant effect on multilinguals' later use of that language to swear or to express strong emotions. Languages that had been learned exclusively in a formal context were less likely to be used to express emotions, which could be interpreted as a lack of socio-pragmatic competence, or confidence.

While such work integrates a comparative dimension concerning the relative impact of naturalistic exposure in relation to classroom exposure, other studies have also illuminated the role of naturalistic L2 contact in the case of immersion learners. For example, Mougeon et al. (2010) report a positive effect of such contact among their Canadian French immersion learners. In particular, they found that, primarily, those learners enjoying longer stays in a naturalistic context, along with learners who accessed spoken French media outside the classroom and who had resided with French families, engaged in increased use of informal sociolinguistic variants relative to those learners who had received minimal or no exposure to native French outside the classroom. Indeed, generally, the longer the stay, the more beneficial the impact. The effect emerges across a range of mildly marked variants that are frequent in native-speaker discourse, namely "ne" deletion (Rehner & Mougeon 1999), use of the adverb of restriction, "juste" ["only"] (Mougeon & Rehner 2001), use of "on" as a first-person plural subject pronoun (Rehner et al. 2003), discourse markers (Rehner 2005), and schwa deletion (Uritescu et al. 2004). The authors also report a positive effect for naturalistic exposure on the acquisition of "difficult" variants, such as third-person plural forms of irregular verbs in the present, as well as use of the notionally specialized preposition "chez" ["at"/"to"] to indicate location at and motion to one's dwelling.

That highly positive effect for naturalistic exposure further emerges in a number of recent studies based on Françoise Mougeon's spoken-French corpus of former Canadian French immersion learners pursuing their studies in a bilingual university setting, allowing them extensive access to naturalistic input through their fellow students as well as through some courses taught in the target language. The corpus is complemented by a further corpus of spoken French elicited from university learners who followed a "core French" program during their schooling prior to pursuing their studies at the same bilingual university. Recent studies emanating from the project (Mougeon & Rehner 2009; Rehner 2010, 2011) concerning the learners' use of lexical variables as well as "ne" deletion suggest an important effect for access to such naturalistic input. "[T]he university learners from former French immersion programs are outperforming their university core French and high school French immersion counterparts in terms of their frequency of use of less-formal variants, their range of informal variants used, and their ability to make individualized lexical choices in the face of lexical priming" (Rehner 2011: 256).

In his study of Flemish-speaking university learners of French in Belgium, Dewaele reports a similar beneficial impact for informal register exposure outside the classroom, even if this exposure is not in the target-language community. Such exposure can take the form of informal contact with native-speaker friends, as well as access to various audio-visual media such as reading, watching TV, and listening to the radio. For example, in the author's study of "ne" deletion (Dewaele & Regan 2002), deletion rates were found to correlate with the learners' informal French usage and audio-visual exposure outside the classroom, while length of classroom instruction had no effect. Frequency of use and exposure were also found to have an effect in Dewaele's (2004d) study of the variable use of pronouns of address in French, with informal "tu" ["you"] being more frequent among those who used French more frequently outside the classroom, although such use did not diminish the learners' perception of the difficulty underlying the variation between pronouns of address, as reflected in a subsequent questionnaire study (Dewaele & Planchenault 2006). Dewaele's (2002) study of the variable use of the subject pronouns "on" and "nous" to express the first-person plural form also reveals an effect for frequency of extracurricular language use, with the informal "on" form being more frequent among those who used their French regularly outside school. Finally, a similar effect emerged in the author's study of lexical variation in relation to colloquial vocabulary usage (Dewaele 2004c).

Notwithstanding the significant impact of naturalistic exposure on both immersion and non-immersion classroom learners' sociolinguistic development, the findings suggest that such exposure is not enough to bring about native-speaker levels of frequency of use of informal sociolinguistic variants. In relation to native-speaker levels, learners enjoying extensive naturalistic exposure are found to continue to underuse such variants, while overusing their formal variant equivalents (Regan 1996; Mougeon et al. 2004, 2010).

Apart from illuminating the effect of naturalistic exposure on classroom learners, the availability of studies of similar variables in an educational context as well as in an immersion context allows insight into the impact of the type of educational input. On this count, immersion learners seem to perform better than their non-immersion classroom counterparts, whereby immersion learners demonstrate higher levels of frequency of use of informal variants compared to non-immersion classroom learners. For example, a comparison of rates of "ne" deletion investigated in data using similar elicitation methods in Rehner and Mougeon's (1999) and Regan's (1996) respective studies suggests that immersion learners engage in "ne" deletion to a higher level than university learners. Similar evidence is provided in the case of variable marking of futurity, as presented in Regan et al. (2009) and Nadasdi et al. (2003). In turn, however, the same studies suggest that the effect for study abroad is more positive than for the immersion context, such that study abroad learners seem to outperform immersion learners. The impact of study abroad, however, is not as great as long-term naturalistic exposure, with naturalistic learners generally demonstrating the highest levels of use of informal variants, approaching native-speaker norms. In sum, the effect for educational versus naturalistic exposure on L2 acquisition of informal variants can be summarized as follows:

Naturalistic context > study abroad > immersion > regular classroom

The more limited impact of classroom exposure, be it in an immersion or non-immersion classroom, may reflect the more reduced frequency of use of informal variants in educational input. Mougeon et al. (2010) provide a rare insight into such input, by examining the frequency of use of informal variants in teacher discourse, as well as in classroom materials, primarily manuals and textbooks. Their findings show that formal variants overwhelmingly prevail even in the representations of informal speech written by the manuals' authors (e.g., a conversation at home), such that classroom learners are in fact minimally exposed to informal variants.

While our review of the findings on L2 sociolinguistic development has so far been solely concerned with level of use in relation to the impact of learning context, studies have also been concerned with the learner's acquisition of the native-speaker patterns of variation. These patterns concern the (extra)linguistic and stylistic factors that constrain use of the variables in native-speaker discourse, such as linguistic factors defining the linguistic context in which the variable occurs, classic sociobiographical characteristics such as gender and social class, and speech style. Since the learners are generally young adults or adolescent L2 speakers, the factor of age has not been widely investigated, and even when it has, no effect has been found. For example, in his work on "ne" deletion, variable "on"/"nous" usage, and variable use of pronouns of address, Dewaele (2002, 2004a, b, & d) finds no significant differences in frequency of usage across adult learners in different age brackets. In the following, we will consider the acquisition of native speech patterns by L2 learners.

The L2 Acquisition of Native Speech Patterns

Linguistic Factors

Variationist studies of the same variants in L2 speaker and native-speaker discourse allow insight into whether similar (extra)linguistic and stylistic factors constrain use of those variants in both speaker populations. On this count, L2 studies across a range of sociolinguistic variants have shown that L2 learners are sensitive to those factors in native-speaker discourse, such that they by no means make random use of a variant irrespective of the linguistic and social context. For example, the acquisition of the linguistic constraints underlying native-speaker use of a number of variants has been observed in L2 French, such as in the case of "ne" deletion (Regan 1996), /l/ deletion (Howard et al. 2006), variable use of "nous"/"on" (Rehner et al. 2003), schwa deletion (Uritescu et al. 2004), the variable use of the adverbs of restriction "seulement" and "juste" ["only"] (Mougeon et al. 2010), and the variable use of the prepositions of location and motion, "chez"/"à la maison" ["at the house of"] (Mougeon et al. 2010). Moreover, studies within a study-abroad context have shown that following study abroad, the constraint ordering evidenced by classroom learners increasingly approaches that found in the native speaker (Regan 1996). In the case of some variants, however, non-acquisition or partial acquisition of the linguistic constraints have also been observed, such as in the case of the variable use of future time forms in French (Nadasdi et al. 2003) and "ne" deletion (Rehner & Mougeon 1999). Learners have also been found to display constraints that are particular to them, such as in the case of adverbs of restriction in French, which they sometimes use left of the verb (Mougeon & Rehner 2001).

Social and Stylistic Factors

Gender. With regard to social and stylistic factors, it is interesting to observe that L2 learners are also sensitive to the patterns underlying these factors in native-speaker discourse. For example, in the case of gender, previous studies of a range of variants indicate that female L2 speakers are found to use the formal variant more than their male counterparts, while male L2 speakers use the informal variant more than their female counterparts. In so doing, both sexes seem to be attempting to express their respective gender identities by distinguishing their level of use of each variant from that of their opposite sex, just as native speakers do. On this count, Regan (2010) suggests that L2 speakers are actively seeking to sound native-like by applying and approaching native-speaker gender patterns in their speech. She draws in particular on a study of adult immigrant learners in a naturalistic context (Adamson & Regan 1991). Major's (2004) study of a number of socio-phonological variants in L2 English among immigrant learners in the United States further corroborates Regan's findings. Major's study suggests that L2 speakers are particularly sensitive to gender variation in native-speaker speech, and try to replicate such gender patterns in their own speech.

An association between male speakers and informal variants also emerges in the case of five variants as part of Mougeon et al.'s (2010) study of Canadian French immersion learners, namely "ne" deletion, use of the adverbs of restriction "seulement" and "juste," "nous"/"on" variation, variable use of the auxiliary verbs "avoir" and "être" in the expression of past time through the *passé composé*, and the variable use of verb morphology for the expression of futurity. The finding is also reported for the latter variable in a study presented in Regan et al. (2009) on Irish university learners. Mougeon et al. (2004) explain such an effect for gender in terms of a possible influence of educational input, whereby the minimal use of informal variants in such input may alert the learners to their very status as informal variants. The authors similarly invoke the educational input to explain their failure to identify an effect for gender on use of four other variants that they studied, suggesting that they are simply not frequent enough in the educational input, or are treated invariably in that input. The variants concern lexical variation underlying use of "habiter" and "emploi" in the expression of the concepts of "dwell" and "work," third-person plural forms of irregular verbs in the present tense, and use of first-person singular periphrastic verb forms in future time contexts. In contrast, Dewaele (2004a, 2004d) fails to find an effect for gender in his study of "ne" deletion and of the variable use of pronouns of address among British university learners, pointing to an important difference between Dewaele's university classroom learners and Mougeon et al.'s adolescent immersion learners.

Social class. In the case of social class, findings are generally restricted to those in a Canadian French immersion setting, as detailed in Mougeon et al. (2010). The findings available indicate that L2 classroom learners reflect native-speaker social class patterns, whereby middle class speakers make greater use of formal variants than their lower class counterparts. In turn, the latter make greater use of informal variants than middle class speakers. However, as we mentioned previously, use of vernacular variants, defined as stigmatized variants restricted in use to a specific social grouping, are generally lacking among all speakers, irrespective of social class. Interestingly, the variants for which an effect for social class is reported in Mougeon et al.'s work are generally similar to those where an effect for gender is also observed.

Style and modality. Apart from social and linguistic factors, the other factor type concerns the effect of speech style on L2 sociolinguistic variation. In the case of many of those variants investigated in L2 French, stylistic constraints are evident in native-speaker discourse. Formal variants are found to be more frequent in a formal style than in an informal one, and similarly, informal variants are more frequent in an informal style than in a formal one (see, e.g., Armstrong 2000). In contrast, however, such stylistic constraints have not been widely observed in the case of the L2 speaker, a notable exception being Regan's (1996) study of "ne" deletion among Irish university learners. The failure to observe any effect for style has been reported, for example, in Dewaele and Regan's (2002) study of "ne" deletion among Flemish learners of French, where minimal differences are found in deletion rates between a formal and informal situation. Such lack of stylistic differentiation suggests incomplete mastery of the variant. Rehner and Mougeon (1999) report a similar finding for the same variant, as do Uritescu et al. (2004) in a study of schwa deletion in French.

In the case of L2 English, Major's (2004) study of a number of socio-phonological variants particularly highlights the difficulty surrounding the acquisition of stylistic constraints underlying choice of variant. Finding that his adult immigrant learners evidenced gender variation but not stylistic variation on the same variants, the author suggests that stylistic constraints are acquired later compared to gender patterns.

A related factor is that of modality, which has been minimally investigated, the vast majority of studies focusing solely on the spoken language. Dewaele's (2002) study of "nous"/"on" variation is one of the few studies that compares spoken and written media. The author, however, fails to find significant differences in use of the variable between both media, suggesting limited stylistic awareness on the learners' part concerning this variable. While such comparative studies of sociolinguistic variation across spoken and written media are few, van Compernolle and William's (2009) work provides complementary insights in the case of their studies of a number of variables in computer-mediated communication.

Beyond such classic sociolinguistic factors of style, social class, and gender, a number of other factors have also been investigated in L2 speech, such as personality and other related psycholinguistic factors, as well as factors surrounding the defining characteristics of the variants themselves. We consider these in the following section.

Other Factors Impacting L2 Sociolinguistic Development

Personality and sociopsychological factors. Within SLA research on inter-learner variation, a range of sociobiographical factors has been investigated to illuminate that variation. Apart from the sociolinguistic factors that we have already discussed, they include learner characteristics such as personality, motivation and attitudes, and intelligence and aptitude. While these latter factors have not received attention in the literature on sociolinguistic development, one factor, namely personality, has been specifically explored in Dewaele's work. As Dewaele (2004a) outlines, learner personality arises out of a range of psychological traits, such as learner anxiety, risk-taking, and degree of extraversion. Such personality differences in terms of the extraversion/introversion distinction are explained for example by differences in arousal levels in the autonomous nervous system in relation to external stimuli such as the communicative situation, as well as in relation to internal factors to do with cognition. Introverts are seen as over-aroused, in contrast to the extravert's propensity for under-arousal. Extraverts thus tend to be more fluent in stressful oral interactions. A complementary explanation of personality differences concerns differences in cognitive control, whereby introverts may be more cautious in their behavior, giving rise to greater self-monitoring compared to extravert learners. In contrast, the latters' less cautious approach may give rise to more impulsive behavior in spite of the sociopsychological costs of inappropriate language usage.

Such personality differences might suggest that the introvert learner engages in far less use of informal language forms compared to the extravert speaker for fear of inappropriate use that may cause offence. In contrast, as a risk taker, who is both less inhibited and less anxious, the extravert may make relatively greater use of informal sociolinguistic variants. Dewaele's work illuminates such a hypothesis across a number of sociolinguistic variants in L2 French, based on two corpora collected among Flemish and British university learners. The hypothesis is generally supported. For example, in the case of colloquial vocabulary, extraverts use such vocabulary more frequently than both introvert and ambivert learners, who show no differences (Dewaele 2004c). In a study of "ne" deletion (Dewaele 2004a; Dewaele & Regan 2002), a similar difference is observed, although the correlation is only marginally positive.

Exogenous factors: Dyad effects and interlocutor characteristics. The effect of the learner's interlocutor on use of sociolinguistic variables has been examined in terms of the effect of gender differences, the speaker's age, and whether the interlocutor is a native or non-native speaker. Dewaele's (2004a) study of "ne" deletion among his British university learners of French reveals no effect for the gender composition of the dyad, while age only has a marginal effect. However, the interlocutor's (non)native status does play a role, with deletion rates being higher when he or she is speaking with a native speaker. Given the unequal size of the subsamples used in the comparison, as well as the use of multiple t-tests on the same sample, the author notes, however, the need for caution in interpreting the results.

In a further study of the variable use of pronouns of address in L2 French, Dewaele (2004d) reports no effect for the interlocutor's gender in the spoken data, although a questionnaire of self-reported usage reveals a gender effect where females are addressed with the more familiar "tu" more than male interlocutors. A strong effect for age emerged in both the spoken and self-reported data, with greater use of the more formal "vous" ["you"] observed when the interlocutor was older than the learner-speaker. The interlocutor's status as a stranger or acquaintance was also found to play a role, similar to the effect of this factor in native-speaker French.

Characteristics and status of the sociolinguistic variants. This issue concerns the defining linguistic characteristics of the variants themselves in terms of the relative ease or difficulty surrounding their realization, as well as their relative status in the process of native-speaker language change. Unlike the issue of the socio-stylistic characteristics of the variants, the first issue relates to the structural makeup of the variants themselves. In this regard, some variants can be seen as structurally more complex than others, giving rise to potential learning difficulties. An example concerns the pragmatic use of the conditional, a synthetic form in L2 French, for the expression of polite requests. Swain and Lapkin (1990) find that such use of the conditional is infrequent among their Canadian French immersion learners, which the authors explain in terms of an effect of the structural complexity of the conditional form in French. A similar explanation is offered by Nadasdi et al. (2003) concerning the more frequent use of the analytic form of the periphrastic future in French as opposed to its synthetic equivalent, the inflected future.

Apart from considering the structural characteristics of the variants, we can also consider whether there is an effect for their relative frequency in native-speaker discourse, reflecting differences in the relative degree to which they are advanced in the process of language change. That is to say, native-speaker studies clearly indicate that some variants are much newer relative to long-established variants that are more advanced in the process of language change. The differences between variants mean that some are much more frequent in native-speaker input than others (for an overview, see Armstrong 2000; Armstrong & Pooley 2010). Thanks to the study of a range of variants in L2 French, it is possible to consider how such frequency differences may be perceived by the learner. For example, long-established variants that are now quite advanced in the process of language change concern "ne" deletion and use of "on," in contrast with relatively less advanced variants such as the expression of futurity through the periphrastic form as well as /l/ deletion. On this count, Regan et al. (2009) suggest that their Irish university learners' less frequent use of the latter variants in contrast with their more frequent use of the former ones reflects an effect for the status of the variants in the process of language change in native-speaker French. In particular, it seems that learners are sensitive to differences in the relative frequencies of occurrence of the variants in the input, such that they reflect to some degree those frequency differences in their own speech.

The effect of the learner's L1. The effect of the learner's L1 has been explored in the case of the acquisition of some L2 sociolinguistic variants that have a formally similar counterpart in the L1. For example, Mougeon et al.'s (2004, 2010) work on L2 French demonstrates positive transfer of some variants from other Romance languages, notably Italian and Spanish, although an effect for L1 English is also observed in the case of use of the adverb of restriction "juste." The Romance-specific variants concern "ne" deletion, use of the subject pronoun "nous," use of the discourse marker "alors" ["so"], use of the adverb of restriction "seulement," and use of the lexical item "travail" ["work," used as a noun]. Beyond such findings in an immersion education context, Blondeau et al. (2002) also report an effect for L1 transfer in a naturalistic environment.

The effect of the learner's L1 can be further seen in the more frequent use of some variants compared to others. For example, while /l/ deletion in French is minimally observed across Anglophone learners in an educational setting, another French socio-phonological variant, namely schwa deletion is much more frequent. Mougeon et al. (2004) explain such a difference in terms of a possible effect for L1 English that allows the deletion of mid-vowels, similar to the phenomenon of schwa deletion in French. In contrast, /l/ deletion is not a permissible word-final phenomenon in English. A similar explanation can be offered to explain the more frequent use of the subject pronoun "on" and use of the periphrastic future compared to other structurally different variants such as the variable expression of negation in L2 French.

Concluding Discussion

As a relatively new strand of SLA research, the study of sociolinguistic variation has provided a range of insights into the development of L2 sociolinguistic competence. Those insights relate to use of a range of sociolinguistic variants by learners in different learning contexts, as well as to the range of factors, be they linguistic, stylistic, social, psychological or sociobiographical that impinge on their usage. Notwithstanding the significant insights that existing research has brought to the field, there is now a need for the field to turn its attention to a number of issues that remain unanswered.

A first issue concerns the need for studies of a wider range of L2s to test the validity of the findings presented, which have, in the main, focused on L2

French. Just how those findings might be true of other L2s remains unclear. Rather unusually, very little research has been carried out on the acquisition of sociolinguistic variation in L2 English, although there are some notable exceptions such as Adamson's (1989), Bayley's (1996), Major's (2004) and Li's (2010) respective work. There is also a clear gap in the literature for studies of other Romance L2s where research would complement the extensive findings available for French. Geeslin and Gudmestad's (2010) study of the range and frequency of variants occurring in L2 Spanish is a welcome addition to the literature. Beyond Indo-European languages, studies of typologically different languages, such as Chinese and Japanese, would provide further insights by illuminating the challenge posed to the learner of acquiring highly complex sociolinguistic variants, such as the honorific system characterizing Japanese. Some important studies do exist in this regard, such as Iwasaki's (2008) and Marriott's (1995) studies of Anglophone learners in Japan. There is, however, much scope to complement their findings to provide a more comprehensive picture of the L2 learner's sociolinguistic development across a range of learner cohorts and variants in such Asiatic languages.

Indeed, not only do we need studies of a wider range of L2s, but we also need studies involving learners with a wider range of L1s. To date, the research has mainly involved Anglophone learners in a classroom context, although Dewaele's work on Flemish learners is an exception. While some studies in an English naturalistic context have included non-Indo-European speakers, such as Adamson and Regan (1991), Bayley (1996), and Major (2004), comparative studies involving different ethnic groups would be a welcome means of exploring the issue of ethnicity as a factor in L2 sociolinguistic development.

A further issue concerns the need for studies that focus on the specificity of the acquisition process underlying the development of L2 sociolinguistic competence. The current literature primarily focuses on the sociolinguistic product, whereby findings are mainly based on studies of the learner's sociolinguistic repertoire at a particular moment in time, and the features of that repertoire are correlated with various factors, as we outlined, as a means of explaining differences between learners. In the case of the limited number of longitudinal studies that do exist, findings are generally based on a comparison between two data collection times, which allows the changes in the learners' use of different sociolinguistic variants to be identified (see Howard 2010; Regan 1996). However, we need much more work on the developmental process underlying those changes. For example, what are the factors that motivate learners in a naturalistic context to increasingly use an informal variant, and in turn, to decrease their use of a formal variant? And why are some learners more motivated to do so than others? Since the studies report considerable individual variation, we need to enhance our understanding of such variation. While current research demonstrates the effect of a range of sociobiographical and psychological factors, issues underpinning the emergence of sociolinguistic variation in relation to the construction of learner identity and input engagement in both educational and naturalistic contexts are potential areas worthy of fruitful investigation. On these counts, interesting issues to explore concern, for example, the relationship between the learner's use of particular variants, and the sociolinguistic identity she or he wishes to portray in the L2. For example, if learners acquire native-speaker patterns of sociolinguistic variation, such as gender patterns, to what extent are those gender patterns a specific and conscious attempt to 'do' gender in the L2, by expressing and creating a sense of gendered identity in the same way as the native-speaker might?

On such issues of identity construction and input engagement, Kinginger's (2008) work in a study abroad context constitutes a pivotal example of the ethnolinguistic insights to be gained from the researcher's pursuit of the L2 learner in a naturalistic environment. Drawing on sociocultural theory (see Lantolf 2000), Kinginger's work uses longitudinal data from diary entries and ethnolinguistic interviews to demonstrate the variable engagement that L2 learners evidence in relation to L2 and native-speaker contact in a naturalistic environment. Indeed, one of the crucial findings to emerge from Kinginger's work concerns the importance of identity and attitudes in that process of L2 engagement, whereby some learners report withdrawing from opportunities for L2 engagement. In so doing, they outline their rejection of L2 norms of behavior on the basis of L1 attitudes and negative L2 experiences, as well as maintaining L1 norms of identity. In contrast, others engage to a greater degree with the L2 through native-speaker interactions to assume L2 sociolinguistic norms as a means of positively identifying with native-speaker peers.

Kinginger's work goes some way to demonstrate the benefits of such an ethnolinguistic approach by evidencing some factors that impact the process of sociolinguistic development from time *x* to time *y*. However, those insights could now be neatly complemented by more work in relation to the issue of meta-awareness in sociolinguistic development. For example, it is unclear to what extent learners consciously notice sociolinguistic norms in their adoption of such norms—what are the moments of insight that encourage learners to decrease their use of formal variants in favor of informal ones? And to what extent do learners actively experiment with use of those informal variants, before enthusiastically engaging in their robust usage? From this point of view, apart from the ethnolinguistic approach we have referred to, we also need investigations of learners' meta-awareness of their use of sociolinguistic variation and the implications of such use. For example, in his analysis of "ne" deletion among British university learners, Dewaele (2004a) signals that it is unclear whether his learners are genuinely consciously aware of how they vary in their use of this variant, in the way a native speaker might be. Thus, an interesting study might aim to tap into the learners' meta-awareness of why they sometimes use a variant, and sometimes do not, in relation to specific examples of their sociolinguistic realizations in the L2. It would be equally interesting to investigate the reactions of native speakers to the use of informal variants by L2 learners/users. It seems that what is considered appropriate in the mouth of a native speaker might be judged inappropriate when uttered by an L2 user (Dewaele 2008). Given that previous studies have generally failed to find evidence of stylistic constraints, one can legitimately ask to what extent learners are genuinely aware of the sociolinguistic implications of their use of specific variants. In other words, it is unclear whether oftentimes such usage is not simply an automatic reflex, as opposed to a creative attempt, however conscious, to use a specific sociolinguistic variant because of its appropriateness in context. Indeed, evidence for use of informal sociolinguistic variants as an automatic reflex can be seen in Regan (1996) where she shows that a large proportion of her learners' tokens of "ne" deletion is based on lexicalized chunks. Such chunks allow the learner to sound native-like, without necessarily evidencing creative realization of the informal variant in other linguistic contexts.

Related to the issue of meta-awareness is that of the role of meta-knowledge. In this regard, we have few studies of the detail of the learner's declarative knowledge in the sociolinguistic realm, and how such knowledge relates to real time production in the L2. For example, most of the studies carried out so far are based on production data. Exceptions concern studies such as Kinginger (2008), which includes meta-awareness tasks before and after study abroad, as well as some studies that tap into the learner's awareness of factors underlying use of sociolinguistic norms, such as Coveney (1998) and Dewaele and Planchenault (2006). Indeed, such studies of the relationship between meta-awareness and sociolinguistic usage are the exception rather than the norm. There is therefore much scope to enhance our understanding of how such meta-awareness feeds into sociolinguistic usage, especially in an educational context where there is the opportunity to actively develop such awareness, be it implicitly or explicitly. From this point of view, more experimental approaches to the study of the development of sociolinguistic competence are called for, as a means of exploring how different types of educational input may impact differentially such development. While we have to hand research in both an immersion and non-immersion classroom, it remains unclear how the differential pedagogical treatment of sociolinguistic variation in an educational context may lead to differential outcomes. Such an experimental approach is exemplified in Lyster's (1994) study of the impact of teaching sociolinguistic norms through explicit methods in the classroom, where he finds that such norms can be taught, leading to very positive sociolinguistic outcomes for the learner.

And finally, a remaining direction for the study of sociolinguistic variation concerns the need to widen the pool of learners in relation to proficiency levels. Most of the research to date has focused on advanced learners, reflecting the fact that sociolinguistic variation seems to be acquired reasonably late, and that more proficient learners make greater use of informal variants. However, some studies that have included less advanced learners in a naturalistic environment suggest that such learners can also acquire sociolinguistic variation. For example, Marriott's (1995) study of Australian learners at different levels of proficiency spending a sojourn in Japan suggests that even beginner learners are sensitized to and engage in such variation. Studies that track the emergence of sociolinguistic variation in less advanced learners would now complement the findings for more advanced learners by illuminating just how advanced one needs to be in order to engage in sociolinguistic variation. At the other end of the acquisition continuum, studies of near-native speakers would also allow us to identify the limits of the acquisition of sociolinguistic variation. Much of the current research on advanced learners suggests that that acquisition is incomplete, especially since the learners still under- and overuse the variants in relation to native-speaker norms, as well as generally failing to engage in the stylistic variation characteristic of the native speaker's use of similar variants. Thus, an interesting question for the future will be to focus on how the learner may come to evidence native-speaker norms, if at all.

As a burgeoning area of SLA research, such questions suggest that future studies within the SLA wave of sociolinguistic research promise to be as rich as past studies in the fruitful insights they will bring.

Acknowledgment

Martin Howard's contribution to this chapter was greatly facilitated through a Canadian Government Faculty Research Award, which is gratefully acknowledged.

References

Adamson, H. D. 1989. *Variation theory and second language acquisition*. Washington DC: Georgetown University Press.

Adamson, H. D., & Regan, V. 1991. The acquisition of community speech norms by Asian immigrants learning English as a second language. *Studies in Second Language Acquisition* 13: 1–22.

Armstrong, N. 2000. *Social and stylistic variation in spoken French*. Amsterdam: John Benjamins.

Armstrong, N., & Pooley, T. 2010. *Social and linguistic change in European French*. London: Palgrave Macmillan.

Barron, A. 2003. *Acquisition in interlanguage pragmatics: Learning how to do things with words*. Amsterdam: John Benjamins.

Bayley, R. 1996. Competing constraints on variation in the speech of adult Chinese learners of English. In R. Bayley & D. Preston (eds.), *Second language acquisition and linguistic variation*, 97–120. Amsterdam: John Benjamins.

Blondeau, H., Nagy, N., Sankoff, G., & Thibault, P. 2002. La couleur locale du français des Anglo-Montréalais. *Acquisition et Interaction en Langue Étrangère* 17: 76–100.

Coveney, A. 1998. Awareness of linguistic constraints on 'ne' omission. *Journal of French Language Studies* 8: 159–87.

Dewaele, J-M. 1992. L'omission du 'ne' dans deux styles oraux d'interlangue française. *Interface. Journal of Applied Linguistics* 7: 3–17.

Dewaele, J-M. 2002. Using socio-stylistic variants in advanced French interlanguage: the case of 'nous'/'on.' *Eurosla Yearbook* 2: 205–26.

Dewaele, J-M. 2004a. Retention or omission of the 'ne' in advanced French interlanguage: The variable effect of extralinguistic factors. *Journal of Sociolinguistics* 8: 433–50.

Dewaele, J-M. 2004b. The acquisition of sociolinguistic competence in French as a second language: An overview. *Journal of French Language Studies* 14: 301–19.

Dewaele, J-M. 2004c. Colloquial vocabulary in the speech of native and non-native speakers: The effects of proficiency and personality. In P. Bogaards & B. Laufer (eds.), *Learning vocabulary in a second language: Selection, acquisition and testing*, 127–53. Amsterdam: John Benjamins.

Dewaele, J-M. 2004d. 'Vous' or 'tu'? Native and non-native speakers of French on a sociolinguistic tightrope. *International Review of Applied Linguistics* 42: 383–402.

Dewaele, J-M. 2008. Appropriateness in foreign language acquisition and use: Some theoretical, methodological and ethical considerations. *International Review of Applied Linguistics* 46: 235–55.

Dewaele, J-M. 2010. *Emotions in multiple languages*. Basingstoke: Palgrave Macmillan.

Dewaele, J-M., & Mougeon, R. 2002. *L'acquisition de la variation par les apprenants du français langue seconde*. Special issue of *Acquisition et Interaction en Langue Etrangère*, v. 17.

Dewaele, J-M., & Planchenault, G. 2006. 'Dites-moi tu'?! La perception de la difficulté du système des pronoms d'adresse en français. In M. Faraco (ed.), *Regards croisés sur la classe de langue: pratiques, méthodes et théories*, 153–71. Aix-en-Provence: Publications de l'Université de Provence.

Dewaele, J-M., & Regan, V. 2002. Matriser la norme sociolinguistique en interlangue française: le cas de l'omission variable de 'ne.' *Journal of French Language Studies* 12: 123–48.

Geeslin, K., & Gudmestad, A. 2010. An exploration of the range and frequency of occurrence of forms in potentially variable structures in second-language Spanish. *Studies in Second Language Acquisition* 32: 433–63.

Howard, M. 2006. Variation in advanced French interlanguage: A comparison of three (socio)linguistic variables. *Canadian Modern Language Review* 62: 379–400.

Howard, M. 2010. S'approprier les normes sociolinguistiques en langue étrangère—quel rôle pour l'enseignement? In O. Bertrand & I. Schaffner (eds.), *Quel français enseigner? La Question de la norme dans l'enseignement / l'apprentissage*, 283–96. Paris: Editions de l'Ecole Polytechnique.

Howard, M., Lemée, I., & Regan, V. 2006. The L2 acquisition of a socio-phonetic variable: The case of /l/ deletion in French. *Journal of French Language Studies* 16: 1–24.

Iwasaki, N. 2008. Style shifts among Japanese learners before and after study abroad in Japan: Becoming active social agents in Japanese. *Applied Linguistics* 31: 45–71.

Kinginger, C. 2008. *Language learning during study abroad: Case studies of Americans in France*. Oxford: Wiley-Blackwell.

Knaus, V., & Nadasdi, T. 2001. 'Être ou ne pas être' in immersion French. *Journal of French Language Studies* 5: 286–306.

Lantolf, J. 2000. *Sociocultural theory and second language learning*. Oxford: Oxford University Press.

Li, X. 2010. Sociolinguistic variation in the speech of learners of Chinese as a second language. *Language Learning* 60: 366–408.

Lyster, R. 1994. The effect of functional-analytic teaching on aspects of French immersion students' sociolinguistic competence. *Applied Linguistics* 15: 263–87.

Major, R. 2004. Gender and stylistic variation in second language phonology. *Language Variation and Change* 16: 169–88.

Marriott, H. 1995. The acquisition of politeness patterns by exchange students in Japan. In B. Freed (ed.), *Second language acquisition in a study abroad context*, 198–224. Amsterdam: John Benjamins.

Mougeon, F., & Rehner, K. 2009. From grade school to university: The variable use of 'on'/'nous' by university FSL students. *Canadian Modern Language Review* 66: 269–97.

Mougeon, R., Nadasdi, T., & Rehner, K. 2002. Etat de la recherche sur l'appropriation de la variation par les apprenants avancés du FL2 ou FLE. *Acquisition et Interaction en Langue Étrangère* 17: 7–30.

Mougeon, R., Nadasdi, T., & Rehner, K. 2004. The learning of spoken French variation by immersion students from Toronto. *Journal of Sociolinguistics* 8: 408–32.

Mougeon, R., Nadasdi, T., & Rehner, K. 2010. *The sociolinguistic competence of immersion students*. Bristol: Multilingual Matters.

Mougeon, R., & Rehner, K. 2001. Variation in the spoken French of Ontario French immersion students: The case of 'juste' vs 'seulement' vs 'rien que.' *Modern Language Journal* 85: 398–415.

Nadasdi, T., Mougeon, R., & Rehner, K. 2003. Emploi du 'futur' dans le français parlé d'élèves d'immersion. *Journal of French Language Studies* 13: 195–219.

Regan, V. 1996. Variation in French interlanguage: A longitudinal study of sociolinguistic competence. In R. Bayley & D. Preston (eds.), *Second language acquisition and linguistic variation*, 177–201. Amsterdam: John Benjamins.

Regan, V. 2005. From speech community back to classroom: What variation analysis can tell us about the role of context in the acquisition of French as a foreign language. In J-M. Dewaele (ed.), *Focus on French as a foreign language: Multidisciplinary perspectives*, 191–209. Clevedon: Multilingual Matters.

Regan, V. 2010. Sociolinguistic competence, variation patterns and identity construction in L2 and multilingual speakers. *Eurosla Yearbook* 10: 21–37.

Regan, V., Howard, M., & Lemée, I. 2009. *The acquisition of sociolinguistic competence in a study abroad context*. Bristol: Multilingual Matters.

Rehner, K. 2005. *Developing aspects of second language discourse competence*. Munich: Lincom Europa.

Rehner, K. 2010. The use/non-use of 'ne' in the spoken French of university-level FSL learners in the Canadian context. *Journal of French Language Studies* 20: 289–311.

Rehner, K. 2011. The sociolinguistic competence of former immersion students at the post-secondary level: The case of lexical variation. *International Journal of Bilingualism and Bilingual Education* 14: 243–59.

Rehner, K., & Mougeon, R. 1999. Variation in the spoken French of immersion students: To 'ne' or not to 'ne,' that is the sociolinguistic question. *Canadian Modern Language Review* 56: 124–54.

Rehner, K., Mougeon, R., & Nadasdi, T. 2003. The learning of sociolinguistic variation by advanced FSL learners: The case of 'nous' versus 'on' in immersion French. *Studies in Second Language Acquisition* 25: 127–56.

Swain, M., & Lapkin, S. 1990. Aspects of the sociolinguistic performance of early and late French immersion students. In R. Scarcella, S. Anderson, & S. Krashen (eds.), *Developing communicative competence in a second language*, 41–54. New York: Newbury House.

Tarone, E. 1988. *Variation in interlanguage*. London: Arnold.

Thomas, A. 2004. Phonetic norm versus usage in advanced French as a second language. *International Review of Applied Linguistics* 42: 365–82.

Uritescu, D., Mougeon, R., Rehner, K., & Nadasdi, T. 2004. Acquisition of the internal and external constraints of variable schwa deletion by French immersion students. *International Review of Applied Linguistics* 42: 349–64.

van Compernolle, R., & Williams, L. 2009. Learner versus non-learner patterns of stylistic variation in synchronous computer-mediated French. *Studies in Second Language Acquisition* 31: 471–500.

Young, R. 1991. *Variation in interlanguage morphology*. New York: Peter Lang.

CHAPTER 18

CODESWITCHING

LI WEI

IMAGINE meeting someone at a party for the very first time. How do you tell if the person is bilingual or not? Here are some possibilities:

1. You ask the person directly whether she is bilingual.
2. The person introduces herself as bilingual.
3. Someone else introduces her as bilingual.
4. You hear the person speaking two or more languages with other people.

It is only in no. 4 that you have evidence to confirm that the person is, in fact, bilingual. Psycholinguists such as Grosjean (1998) maintain that bilinguals operate between monolingual modes and a bilingual mode. What this means is that bilinguals can behave as if they were monolingual by using only one of the languages they know. It is only when they are using more than one language in the same episode of interaction that we say that they are in a bilingual mode,that is, being bilingual. *Codeswitching* is often used as a cover term to describe a range of linguistic behavior that involves the use of more than one language or language variety in the same interaction. Linguists of different persuasions have investigated various aspects of codeswitching. This chapter focuses on some of the key issues of codeswitching that sociolinguists have investigated. It begins with a discussion of the terminological and methodological issues, with an analysis of a variety of examples. Such a discussion is necessary because there is considerable confusion and controversy over what distinguishes codeswitching from other language contact phenomena. This is followed by a review of the studies on the motivations and structural patterns of codeswitching. An alternative approach to codeswitching that views it as a creative performance rather than simply a combination of linguistic structures is then presented.

Codeswitching and Other Types of Bilingual Speech Production: Terminological and Methodological Issues

It is almost a cliché now to say that bilingualism is the norm of today's world. The vast majority of the world's population is indeed bilingual or multilingual. Yet there are huge individual variations in terms of the motivation and process of acquiring different languages and the experience of using them. Such variations result in very different types of bilingual language users; some use different languages in different contexts (e.g., one language at home with family and a different one at work); others speak a highly mixed code and never separate their languages; still others are highly proficient in a particular language but only use it in a specific setting (e.g., professional translators or interpreters).

Bilingual speech production takes places in many different forms, ranging from implicit influence of one language on the speech production in another language, to frequent alternation between different languages. Here are some examples:

1. "It's absolutely scandalistic." (referring to a news story)
2. "Can you open the light?"
3. "lam:a fəlik bjɪʒe" (referring to a cartoon character) (Khattab 2009: 152) (Arabic. '*when Flick comes*', with *Flick* pronounced with an epenthetic vowel, as in Arabic)
4. Girl 1: ¿Dónde estás?
   (Spanish. '*Where are you?*')
   Girl 2: *Upstairs.*
   Girl 1: ¿Dónde?
   (Spanish. '*Where?*')
   Girl 2: En mi habitación.
   (Spanish. '*In the bedroom.*')
5. Mother: *Nei sik muyt-ye a?*
   (Cantonese. '*What do you want to eat?*')
   Son: (1.0) Just apples.
   Mother: Just /n/ just apples? *Dimgai m sik yogurt a?*
   (Cantonese. '*Why not have some yogurt?*')
6. "There was a guy, you know, *que* ['that'] he *se montó* ['got up']. He started playing with *congas*, you know, and *se montó y empezóa brincar* ['got up and started to jump'] and all that shit." (Winford, 2003: 105)
7. *Ngaw wei* solve *di* problem

(Cantonese. 'I will; that/those. *I will solve that problem.*')

8. *Tu peux* me pick-up-er?
   (French: 'You can. *Can you pick me up?*') (Gardner-Chloros, 2009: 97)
9. I'm LAVing PANDELCAGEs.
   (Danish. 'Make, pancake. *I'm making pancakes.*') (Petersen, 1988)
10. *I have* cha de/*-ed* chulai
    (*de*—Chinese case marker. 'I have checked.')
11. *Traditional* de, *simplified*/de (*de*—Chinese case marker)
12. *She asked me*, 'nei *ha* m *ha-ppy* la?' *So I told her*, 'ho m *happy* la'.
    (Cantonese. 'You NEG. PART. Very PART. *Are you happy or not? Very unhappy.*')
13. *Sho* shenme *ping*!
    (Mandarin. 'What. *What shopping!*')[1]

Example 1 illustrates what might be called *interference* of Italian in an otherwise English utterance. It was produced by a native speaker of English working in Italy who also speaks fluent Italian. The word "scandalistic" sounds English and would be acceptable in English in terms of phono-morphological structure. But it is not an English word, and is clearly influenced by the Italian word "scandalistico." One can detect a switch from English to Italian in the speaker's mind when the word was produced. Yet the output is neither Italian nor English.

Example 2 was produced by Chinese-English bilinguals. It sounds non-native and could be regarded as a learner error, or *transfer*. It is triggered by a mismatch between two collocations: *kai deng* (literally 'open light') in Chinese and 'switch on light' in English. The Chinese verb *kai* is in fact a polysemic word and can be used with a variety of objects, such as *kai men* 'open the door', *kai hui* 'have a meeting', *kai che* 'drive a car', *kai huo* 'fire' (v.), and *kai yan* 'start a show'. However, on its own, it is often translated as 'open,' which seems to be the meaning that gets generalized to other usages by Chinese-English bilinguals. As in example 1, the speaker seems to be thinking of one language yet producing another. Psycholinguists would argue that the English production has gone through a Chinese filter, a mental translation process.

Example 3 is taken from Khattab (2009) and produced by a seven-year-old English-Arabic bilingual boy (Mazen). The boy can speak perfectly well monolingually in either language and with a native-like accent. But when he speaks to his bilingual parents, as in the present case, he often adapts his English with a degree of foreign accent. Khattab describes Mazen's production of the word *flick* as an example of phonetic codeswitching and a case of what she calls *overcompensation* "by breaking the initial cluster and producing a high tense vowel in the second syllable" (152).

Examples 4 and 5 are instances of some of the most frequently occurring types of codeswitching. In a given episode of interaction, the speakers may choose to use different languages in consecutive turns, as in the first two turns of 4 and 5. This would be inter-turn and inter-speaker codeswitching. When one of the speakers changes her choice of language in a subsequent turn, as Girl 2 does in her second turn in 4, we have an example of inter-turn but intra-speaker codeswitching, that is, same speaker codeswitching in different turns. In comparison, the Mother in her second turn in five switches from English to Cantonese within the same turn. This is an example of intra-turn and intra-speaker codeswitching. The motivations for the different kinds of codeswitching illustrated in these two example are likely to be rather different. We will return to that topic in the next section.

Examples 6 and 7 contain instances of both *inter-clausal* and *intra-clausal* codeswitching. *Inter-clausal* codeswitching is sometimes also called *inter-sentential*, as some people use the notion of *sentence* in their analysis of bilingual speech. However, this can cause confusion because *inter-clausal* codeswitching can occur within what technically may be described as a sentence. Indeed, some people use the term *intra-sentential* codeswitching to refer to instances of *inter-clausal* codeswitching. In the meantime, *intra-clausal* codeswitching can take many different and complex forms, as 6 and 7 as well as 8 and 9 show.

In the case of example 8, the speaker is trying to resolve a conflict in the pronoun object placement between French and English by giving the phrasal verb *to pick up* a French infinitive ending *-er*. Gardner-Chloros suggests that "[t]his sounds more 'grammatical' in French than if she had used the bare form" (97) and shows the speaker's awareness and creativity to overcome potential difficulties. Example 9 is a classic case of what has been termed *morphological codeswitching*, in that Danish words are given English morphological markers.

Examples 10 and 11 also contain examples of morphological codeswitching. However, in both cases, the marking is ambiguous. In Chinese, the completion of an action can be marked by *de*, which, as it happens, sounds very similar to the English present perfect maker *-ed*. While the English auxiliary *have* may suggest that it is *-ed* that the speaker produced, the Chinese intensifier *chulai* ('done') suggests that it could be *de* as well. Such double marking is by no means rare in bilingual speech, where the speaker produces compromised structures, leaving the interpretation to the hearer. Example 11 involves a Chinese marker that has the same phonological form but this time marking an adjective. We can be sure that the *de* after *traditional* is definitely Chinese, but the one after *simplify* is ambiguous.

Examples 12 and 13 could also be considered as morphological codeswitching. They involve splitting two-syllable English words and inserting a Chinese element in between. The speakers are evidently following a commonly occurring Chinese discourse strategy, which is to insert elements into the so-called splittable words, standard two-syllable words that involve syntactic relations of various kinds (Siewierska, Xu, & Xiao 2010). For example, the Chinese word *shuijiao* 'sleep' can be made into *shui lan jiao* 'have a lazy sleep'; and *bangmang* 'help', into *bang da mang* 'offer a big help'. In the present examples, Chinese elements are inserted in unsplittable English words.

There is much controversy as to whether some or all of these examples should be described as instances of codeswitching. Indeed, on what ground can we distinguish codeswitching from other language contact phenomena that involve mixing elements from different languages, such as lexical or syntactic borrowing, linguistic convergence, pidginization, and creolization? Moreover, should alternation between different dialects, registers, and styles of the same language be regarded as codeswitching as well? The term *codeswitching* seems to imply two things: (1) it can be linguistic code of various kinds. Indeed, some have suggested that the underlying mechanisms for codeswitching between different languages and style shifting in the same language are very similar (Milroy & Gordon 2003: chapter 8); and (2) the speaker can switch backward and forward between different codes. This second point has led some researchers to argue that in codeswitching the speaker must know the equivalents in different languages or language varieties and has a choice of which code to use in the given context. It is further suggested that codeswitching usually takes the form of overt, unintegrated elements from different languages or language varieties, thus differentiating it from *borrowing*, which is usually integrated into the recipient linguistic system.

Muysken (2000) offers a typology of codeswitching, namely. (1) insertion, (2) alternation, and (3) congruent lexicalization, each inviting a particular structural analysis. In the insertional type of codeswitching, one language will determine the overall structure into which constituents from another language are inserted. Example 7 is of the insertional type. Various grammatical models exist to account for the different roles played by the different languages (e.g., Myers-Scotton 1997). In alternation, on the other hand, different languages occur alternately, each with its own structure, with the switch point being located at a major syntactic boundary. Examples 5 and 6 are examples of alternation, as is the title of Poplack's (1980) famous article "Sometimes I'll Start a Sentence in the Spanish Y TERMINO EN ESPAÑOL." At exactly which point in the exchange an alternation takes place seems to be governed by both grammatical constraints (e.g., Poplack 1980) and interactional principles (Auer 1984; Li Wei 2005). In the third type, congruent lexicalization, the grammatical structure is shared by the contributing languages, and a succession of single lexical items from different languages are selected seemingly randomly, as in example 14 from Bolle (1994: 75, cited in Muysken 2000): 139):

14. Dutch-Sranan
    wan heri *gedeelte* de ondro *beheer* fu *gewapende machten*
    one *wholepart* COP under *control* of *armed force*
    'One whole part is under control of the armed forces'

This type of codeswitching tends to occur between typologically similar languages, especially where there is no tradition of overt language separation and where the contributing varieties have roughly equal prestige.

A very different way of defining codeswitching is proposed by Poplack (2004). Following the variationist sociolinguistic principles, Poplack first establishes, on quantitative grounds, that "lone other-language items are by far the most important—in some cases, virtually the only!—component of mixed discourse," and "multiword other-language fragments, other than tags and other frozen forms, while frequent in some communities, is in the aggregate relatively rare" (590). She then sets out to compare the lone other language items with their counterparts in both the donor and recipient languages. "If the rate and distribution of morphological marking and/or syntactic positioning of the lone other-language items show quantitative parallels to those of their counterparts in the recipient language, while at the same time differing from relevant patterns in the donor language" (591), the lone other-language items should be considered as *borrowing*. In borrowing, only the grammar of the recipient language is operative. On the other hand, if the lone other-language items "pattern with their counterparts in the monolingual donor language, while at the same time differing from the patterns of the unmixed recipient language" (591), they are examples of codeswitching.

Once these two broad types of bilingual phenomena are distinguished, we can compare the sociolinguistic norms of the communities in which they occur. Poplack (2004) identifies four community norms of combining languages intra-sententially: (1) smooth codeswitching at equivalence sites; for example, the New York Puerto Rican community, where there is a widespread high degree of Spanish-English bilingualism; (2) flagged codeswitching, as in the Ottawa-Hull region of Canada, where French-English bilinguals prefer to flag any use of codeswitching for specific rhetorical purposes; (3) constituent insertion, for instance, the insertion of a French NP in an Arabic utterance by Moroccan Arabic-French bilinguals; and (4) nonce borrowing, which Poplack maintains is the most prevalent type of codeswitching in a wide variety of communities worldwide.

Poplack's typology enables not only a more careful distinction among the various linguistic manifestations of language contact, but also a systematic examination of the key factors influencing the use of codeswitching over and above the grammatical constraints that affect the location of the switch in the sentence. According to Poplack, one recurrent and overriding factor is bilingual ability. Poplack argues that "those with greater proficiency in both languages not only switch more, they switch more intra-sententially, and at a wider variety of permissible CS sites." (2004: 594). Those who are less proficient in one of the languages, however, also engage in codeswitching, but tend to do so at sites and for types that require little or even no productive knowledge of the donor language, such as tags, routines or frozen phrases. To be sure, Poplack is not suggesting that language proficiency is in any way causative of codeswitching. Research evidence confirms that speakers who engage in the most complex type of intra-sentential codeswitching tend to be the most proficient in all the contributing languages. Another recurrent factor that Poplack argues to be influential in the community patterns of codeswitching is prestige. However, "the contribution of the prestige factor varies from community to community and may act to promote or inhibit codeswitching" (2004: 494).

Motivations: Why Do Bilinguals Codeswitch?

The typologies of codeswitching proposed by Muysken and Poplack raise the issue of what motivates codeswitching. Why can't bilinguals speak one language only (OLON) or one language at a time (OLAT). After all, the OLON and OLAT ideologies are prevalent in many situations, especially in situations that involve young children (e.g., Li Wei & Wu 2009). Community norms, as Poplack has described, are clearly a factor: in some communities, codeswitching is the normal discourse mode and most speakers are bilingual and switch frequently between languages. But in other communities, codeswitching is used in specific contexts and conveys special communicative meanings.

There are many myths surrounding the reasons bilinguals engage in codeswitching. To those who have little personal experience with codeswitching, it is sometimes seen as a sign of lack of mental control or confusion. Young children, therefore, are often discouraged from codeswitching, even though their parents and other adults they regularly interact with are habitual codeswitchers. Even distinguished scholars sometimes claim that bilinguals codeswitch simply because they have word-finding difficulties. Yet exiting research evidence all points to the fact that codeswitching requires a high level of cognitive control, involving neural networks known as the executive system in the brain, as well as a good knowledge of the grammatical systems of the different languages involved. Uncontrolled codeswitching has been observed only in a handful of patients who have suffered specific brain damage. John Gumperz was among the first to distinguish between factors that are external to the speaker from those internal to the speaker that trigger codeswitching. He called the former *situational* and the latter *metaphorical* (see Blom & Gumperz 1972; Gumperz 1982).

The external or situational factors for codeswitching may include the setting of the interaction, the participants, and the relationships among the participants, as well as the topic of the exchange. In situational codeswitching, the change of language usually corresponds to changes in the situation; for example, in Sauris, Italy, speakers use a localized German dialect at home, but speak Friulian, an Italian dialect, in semi-public setting such as the local bar, and standard Italian at school and church. Similarly, an adult Berber-speaking Moroccan in the Netherlands speaks Berber wither another Berber-speaking Moroccan, but changes to Moroccan Arabic when speaking to a non-Berber Moroccan. As Blom and Gumperz (1972: 425) commented, "the notion of situational switching assumes a direct relationship between language and social situation." Subsequently, it is possible to formulate predictive models of codeswitching at the community level. More recently, sociolinguists have spent a considerable amount of time analyzing the history of language contact as well as linguistic ideologies of the communities under investigation to argue that sociocultural values, power relations, and identity are all factors that can motivate codeswitching of specific kinds (e.g., studies in Heller 2009).

The internal factors, in comparison, are mainly to do with the speaker's intention to convey specific communicative effects through codeswitching, and they tend to do so when there is no change of the participants, the setting, or the topic. Codeswitching is therefore used as a 'metaphor.' Gumperz (1982: 75–84) identifies a number of communicative functions of metaphorical codeswitching, including quotation, addressee specification, interjection, reiteration, message qualification, and personalization versus objectivization. Other functions can easily be identified and added to this list.

Myers-Scotton (e.g., 1993) tried to bring the external and external factors together in an integrated model of the social motivations of codeswitching, namely, the Markedness model, which has been recast as a rational choice model. Working with Swahili, English, and a variety of East African languages used in Kenya, Myers-Scotton argues that bilinguals have an innate theory of socially relevant markedness and indexicality of the different languages and language varieties. This theory enables them to make rational choices in social interaction by calculating the costs and benefits of their actions. The centerpiece of the Markedness model is a "negotiation principle" that directs speakers to choose the form of their conversational contribution such that it symbolizes the set of rights and obligations that they wish to be in force between the participants for the present exchange. Bilingual speakers can make unmarked choices in cases where situational factors change during the course of a conversation, or marked choices when they wish to dis-identify with the unmarked rights and obligations set for the interaction and negotiate a change in the social distance between the participants.

Myers-Scotton argues that the bilingual speaker's innate knowledge of the markedness and indexicality of the various linguistic codes provides not only a normative framework for them to make choices but also limits the interpretations of codeswitching, that is, participants interpret each other's moves with reference to the rights and obligations set. One problem with such an approach is that the meaning of codeswitching is the accumulation of the associations between linguistic varieties and conventionalized conversational exchanges. Linguistic codes come to index a particular rights and obligations set because they are regularly used in a particular interaction type. Codeswitching itself does not seem to be constitutive or creative, as interaction merely consists of the reproduction or reification of preexisting meanings. There has been considerable debate over the question how much of the meaning of codeswitching is "brought along" and how much of it is "brought about" in interaction (Li Wei 1989). The markedness theory of codeswitching emphasizes the "brought along" meaning. The languages involved in codeswitching have distinctive social, symbolic values, which simply have to be indexed in the interaction in order to become, or to remain, relevant. The alternative is to focus on the emergent character of meaning of codeswithing in interaction: meaning emerges as a consequence of bilingual participants' contextualization work. It is 'brought about' by the speakers through the very act of codeswitching.

Patterns and Structures: How Do Bilinguals Codeswitch?

Another common myth of codeswitching is that it is a random behavior. This has turned to be a rather difficult myth to dispel. Linguists with a particular interest in structural patterns of codeswitching have tried to develop various models to account for the mixed-code constructions that they have observed with various language combinations. But the predictive power of the models remains weak, as outliers and counterexamples are frequently cited. Nevertheless, the majority of researchers agree that in most cases codeswitching is well-formed and conforms to the grammatical structures of the contributing languages. The disagreement is over the question of whether there are universal grammatical constraints that operate in all language combinations. What lies at the heart of the disagreement seems to be the issue of whether codeswitching should be regarded as part of the speaker's linguistic *competence* or *performance*. There is a particular prejudice in formal linguistics that languages should be treated as mental objects, or I-language, and that the theoretical models of language should therefore be about the mentally represented linguistic knowledge, that is, competence. Performance, or E-Language, on the other hand, encompasses different kinds of language use or behavioral patterns shared by a community. It is not regarded as useful in the study of innate linguistic knowledge, even though it may seem sensible, intuitive, and useful in other areas of study (Chomsky 1986). Linguists approaching codeswitching from a competence perspective tend to argue that codeswitching patterns can be and should be accounted for within the general, and primarily generative, frameworks without evoking any codeswitching-specific mechanisms (e.g., MacSwan 1999). Yet, even those linguists who insist on codeswitching-specific constraints often appeal to the notion of competence. Myers-Scotton, for example, described her Matrix Language Frame model as a "bilingual language competence model" (1993, 2002; Myers-Scotton & Jake 1995). Poplack, who herself has contributed a great deal to the identification of structural patterns of codeswitching, suggests, "The patterning of CS within a community is a historical development over time, but the actual structural form it takes is arbitrary" (Poplack 2004: 594).

One point that seems to have often been missed in the search for the patterns and structures of codeswitching is that it is essentially an interactional strategy that bilingual speakers deploy, either to respond to other participants' moves or to indicate their own specific communicative intents. The sequential organization of codeswitching in talk-in-interaction therefore should be given priority over other structural considerations. Indeed, from the speakers' point of view, the immediate interactional task is to find what they would regard as the most appropriate language to use for their speaking turns. The intricacies of the grammatical structural juxtaposition, important as they may be, are only secondary considerations and may in any case depend heavily on the speaker's proficiencies in the different languages as well as sociolinguistic considerations. Using the analytic framework provided by Conversation Analysis (CA), Auer (e.g., 1984) identified a number of sequential patterns of language choice in bilingual conversation. The first pattern looks like this:

Pattern Ia:...A1 A2 A1 A2 // B1 B2 B1 B2...

Here a language-of-interaction (variably called base, matrix, or unmarked language) A has been established; at a certain point, the Speaker 1 switches to language B. This new language choice is accepted by Speaker 2 as the new language-of-interaction, so that beyond the switching point, only B is used. The pattern is usually considered to be the prototypical case of conversational codeswitching. A variant of this pattern would be when codeswitching occurs within a single speaker's turn:

Pattern Ib:...A1 A2 A1 A2 A1 // B1 B2 B1 B2...

A different pattern of language choice that Auer identifies can be schematized as follows:

Pattern IIa:...A1 B2 A1 B2 A1 B2 A1 B2...

In this pattern, Speaker 1 consistently uses one language, but Speaker 2 consistently uses another language. Such patterns of language choice are not normally sustainable in spontaneous conversation. After a short run of divergent language choices, one participant usually accepts the other's language, and the exchange continues with an agreed language as the language-of-interaction. The resulting pattern looks like this:

Pattern IIb:...A1 B2 A1 B2 A1 // A2 A1 A2 A1...

In all these patterns, the change of language is accompanied by a change of speakership. It is frequently observed, however, that bilingual speakers keep language choice open by switching between languages within a turn, as many of the examples cited earlier show. The recipient of a turn that contains two languages may continue in this mode, giving rise to Pattern IIIa, or choose the language he or she thinks is appropriate or preferred, leading to Pattern IIIb.

Pattern IIIa:...AB1 AB2 AB1 AB2...
Pattern IIIb:...AB1 // A2 A1 A2...

Finally, codeswitching may occur in the middle of a speaker's turn without affecting language choice for the interaction at all. Such momentary crossovers into the other language usually occur because a word, a phrase or another structure in language B is inserted into a language A frame. The insertion has a predictable end. Schematically, this pattern is represented as follows:

Pattern IV:...A1 [B1] A1...

For those who are interested in both the structural patterning as well as the meaning of codeswitching, the CA approach has at least two advantages. First, it gives priority to what Auer calls the *sequential implicativeness* of language choices in conversation, that is, the effect of a participant's choice of language at a particular point in the conversation on subsequent language choices by the same and other participants. Second, it "limits the external analyst's interpretational leeway because it relates his or her interpretation back to the members' mutual understanding of their utterances as manifest in their behaviour" (Auer 1984: 6). Given that codeswitching can be, and indeed has been, described and interpreted in so many different ways, how do analysts show that their descriptions and interpretations are relevant to the participants themselves in an ongoing interaction? There is a tendency in codeswitching research to attribute macrosocietal value to individual instances of switching and to assume that speakers intend such meaning to be understood by their co-interactants. Analysts who adopt the CA approach argue that while codeswitching is indeed a socially significant behavior, their task is to try to show how their analyses are demonstratively relevant to the participants. The notion of "procedural consequentiality" is crucial in the CA approach to codeswitching. It involves demonstrating whether and how extra-linguistic context has determinate consequences for conversational interaction. It also relates to the balance of social and conversational structures. Those who adopt the CA approach to codeswitching argue that one must not assume that, in any given conversation, speakers switch languages in order to "index" speaker identity, attitudes, power relations, formality, and so on; rather, one must be able to demonstrate how such things as identity, attitudes, and relationship are presented, understood, accepted, rejected, or changed in the process of interaction. These points imply an important shift of analytic focus. While there are clear links between the motivations (why) and the patterns and structures (how) of codeswitching, any interpretation of the *why* questions must come after fully examining the *how* questions, that is, the ways in which the participants locally constitute the phenomena. In Auer's words, one needs to look for the procedures

> used by participants in actual interaction, i.e. that they are supposed to be interactionally relevant and 'real', not just a scientific construct designed to 'fit the data'. So there is an analytic interest in members' methods (or procedures), as opposed to an interest in external procedures derived from a scientific theory. In short, our purpose is to analyse *members' procedures to arrive at local interpretations of language alternation.* (Auer, 1984: 3; original italics)

From Codeswitching to Translanguaging: Toward a Poetics of Multilingual Interaction

Taking codeswitching seriously as a conversational activity, as the conversation analysts do, also means to look at codeswitching, not simply as a juxtaposition of different grammatical and structural elements, but also as an expressive act, a creative performance. At the same time that we focus on the details, such as phonetic and morphological integration, sequential organization, co-occurrence of pauses, loudness, and other paralinguistic features (structural concerns), we must also give greater attention to context and the consequentiality of the performative, the act of codeswitching. As anthropological linguists such as Hymes, Bauman, and Sherzer demonstrate in what they call *ethno-poetics*, each performance is keyed, and relies on a performer's assumption of responsibility for the emergent event. Ethno-poetics as a performance theory is an analysis of the rich convergence of the performer, the situation and setting, the audience, and the wider society. It recognizes that the symbolic forms have their primary existence in the action of people and their roots in social and cultural life. It also recognizes that not all performances are equal. Full performance involves a level of competence that produces artistry or creativity, though measures of competency are to be discovered in each situation and with awareness of local measures of creativity. Less than full performance, on the other hand, may give us clues as to the performer's individual capacity, their sociocultural background and position, as well as their relationships with and the culture of the social group and the audience (see further Hymes 1981; Bauman 1984; Sherzer 2002; also Bauman & Briggs 1990).

From the perspective of performance theory, codeswitching is a creative and critical act that multilingual language users perform in specific social contexts for specific purposes. As part of a large research project on the multilingual practices of minority ethnic children in complementary schools in four urban centers in Britain, I have studied the British-Chinese children's codeswitching behavior in the classroom, a specific setting with different actors playing specified roles. Complementary schools are voluntary, community organizations primarily aimed at literacy teaching to the British-born generations of young multilingual children. They run at weekends, and most of them have an implicit OLON or OLAT policy, usually the minority ethnic language. Elsewhere, I have raised the question (Li Wei & Wu 2008, 2009) about the implications of such policies. To me, OLON and OLAT policies are another form of the monolingual ideology. In any case, maintaining a strict 'no English' policy in the complementary schools is almost an impossibility in practice due to the frequent and habitual codeswitching by both the teachers and the pupils.

Using Vivian Cook's notion of *multicompetence* (e.g., 1991, 1992), I have examined the structural, cognitive, and sociocultural dimensions of codeswitching in an integrated way, and focused on the children's creativity and criticality that manifest in their multilingual practices. I define creativity as the ability to choose between following and flouting the rules and norms of behavior, including the use of language, and to push and break boundaries between the old and the new, the conventional and the original, and the acceptable and the challenging. An important prerequisite for linguistic creativity is knowledge of the linguistic system. For the multilingual, it is crucial to consider that knowledge in a holistic way, not just as one of the languages in the multilingual language user's linguistic repertoire, which would be only a subsystem for the user. A holistic conceptualization of the knowledge of the multilingual language user would need to account for all the languages she knows, as well as knowledge of the norms for use of the languages in context and of how the different languages may interact in producing well-formed, contextually appropriate mixed-code utterances. The knowledge of appropriate use of multilingual resources in context also provides the foundation for criticality—the ability to use evidence appropriately, systematically, and insightfully to inform considered views of cultural, social, and linguistic phenomena; question and problematize received wisdom; and express views adequately through reasoned responses to situations. The two concepts—creativity and criticality—are intrinsically linked: one cannot push or break boundaries, that is, be creative, without being critical; and the best expression of one's criticality is one's creativity (see, further, Li Wei 2011a and b).

Example 15 is taken from a recording of a Mandarin session in a London Chinese school. The school was set up as a Cantonese school. The majority of children in this school are Cantonese-English bilinguals. But since 2001, Mandarin is also offered to all children. One of the tensions in the Chinese complementary school classrooms is between the traditional way of teaching and what is appropriate for this particular group of Chinese pupils. In the example, the teacher asked the class to make sentences with the Chinese adverb 就 (*jiu*). This is a particular complex word, as it has several meanings, including *at once, as early as, just about, really, simply, exactly,* and so on, and can be used with various functions. G1 responded to the teacher and made a sentence with the target word. The teacher asked the class whether or not G1 got the sentence right. This is a typical teaching method in Chinese classrooms where the teacher asks the pupils to point out each other's mistakes and correct them collectively. In written examinations, "correcting mistakes" is often used as a method of assessing the learner's linguistic knowledge. However, as we can see in the example, the pupils think that this kind of pedagogical activity is picking on people, not just the language errors. There seems to be two kinds of cultural expectations and practices at work here.

15. (G1: girl in class; T: teacher; B1 and B2: boys in class)

G1: 他就想睡觉。(*ta jiu xiang shuijiao.*)
He really/just wants to sleep.
T: Good. Is there any mistake in what she said?
..... (no response from pupils)
T: (To B1) XXX, what do you think?
B1: *M ji la?*
NEG. know PART.
Don't know.
T: (To B2) XX, 你呢? (*ni ne?*)
You PART.
How about you?
B2: 我也(*wo ye*) *mu ji.*
I also
I also don't know/am a hen.
All laughed loudly.
T: Stop it. 安静。(*anjing*). Be quiet.
Silence.
B1: Can we do something else?
T: 先说完了这个。(*xian shuo wanle zheige.*)
Let's finish talking about this first.
B2: Why 总要挑人家错啊? *(zongyao tiao renjia cuo a?)*
always pick other people mistake PART.
Why do we always pick on other's mistakes?

When the class did not respond to her initial question, the teacher specified B1 and asked him to say whether he thought G1 had produced a correct sentence using the target word. B1 responded in Cantonese as he is a Cantonese L1 speaker, and he knew that the teacher also understood Cantonese. His response consists of a typical Cantonese negation marker *m*, a verb *ji* (know), and an utterance particle *la*. I have spelled these out in Roman letters, as the pronunciation here is a crucial factor. When the teacher turned to B2 and asked for his opinion, B2 made a pun by simply adding a vowel to the Cantonese negation maker. However, *mu* in Mandarin means '*female*', and *ji* in Mandarin means '*chicken*'. By changing the pronunciation from *m ji* to *muji*, B2 made the phrase into *I am also a hen*. Cantonese-Mandarin bilinguals would understand the pun easily, and the whole class laughed. G2 thus gained some popularity in the classroom context. When the teacher tried to stop him from making fun of the activity, both boys, B1 and B2, protested and asked the teacher to change the activity to something different. B2's direct question to the teacher challenges the pedagogical practice.

There is another even subtler, but perhaps more important, point of the two boys' responses to the teacher in this example. Let us remind ourselves that this is a Mandarin session to a group of children, most of whom are Cantonese-English bilinguals. They are learning Mandarin as an additional language. Mandarin is being actively promoted in the Chinese community in Britain as a new Chinese lingua franca to connect with mainland China and is fast gaining currency, at least in formal settings. Official visits by the Chinese embassy staff to the local Chinese community organizations are always conducted in Mandarin and cultural events such as Chinese New Year celebrations are increasingly done in Mandarin as well. Mandarin has also replaced Cantonese in much of the Chinese satellite television and other entertainment media in Europe. Even Cantonese-speaking parents often encourage their children to learn Mandarin at the Chinese school. However, enthusiasm for Mandarin is not universal in the Chinese diasporas. There are groups who feel a stronger affinity to Hong Kong and nostalgia for the pre-1997 life in the former British colony. They see the spread of Mandarin another example of the increasing power and influence of the Chinese government in Beijing. Even among people who are not directly linked to Hong Kong, there are those who see the spread of Mandarin as a threat to the Cantonese cultural heritage. Recent reports from Guangdong province of mainland China of public protests against the testing of Mandarin proficiency for people who wish to hold public offices and the increasing use of Mandarin in the media are examples of the popular unease. What we do not know is how the British-born generations of Chinese children and young people feel about the elevated status of Mandarin vis-à-vis Cantonese. While we cannot be absolutely sure why in the present example B1 chose to respond to the teacher in Cantonese, his choice of language, and B2's making fun of it, certainly has the effect of undermining the purpose of the class, which is to teach Mandarin. When we presented the case to the head-teacher of the school and asked if she thought the pupils were resisting Mandarin, she gave a very interesting answer. She told us that when the school first decided to teach Mandarin to the children on a voluntary basis in an extended period following the normal standard hours for Cantonese, thereby allowing the children to decide for themselves whether they wanted to stay an extra hour for Mandarin, the take-up rate was very low, around 20 percent. So the school decided to incorporate Mandarin into the main teaching hours and made it compulsory to all. The head teacher claimed that this has been a success and that the school has been held as an example of excellence in promoting Mandarin by the UK Association for the Promotion of Chinese Education, which is the main national advocate for Mandarin teaching. The examples we have seen here in the pupils' actual responses in the classroom may show a different side of the story.

Let us turn now to an example of codeswitching that involves different modalities. As was said earlier, a particular focus of the complementary schools for minority ethnic children in Britain is on literacy teaching, that is, literacy in the heritage language, not English. However, all the children are literate in English; some may have learned other languages and writing systems too. As far as the Chinese complementary schools are concerned, most of the teachers believe that teaching the children to read and write Chinese characters is their most important task. Most of the classroom time is spent on getting the children to read the Chinese characters and a considerable amount of writing is also done in the classroom.

Most of the Chinese characters are either pictographs and ideographs or a combination of the two. In order to teach the characters, the teacher sometimes draws pictures showing the origins of pictographs or analyzes and explains the meanings of the ideographs. Many Chinese pupils are fascinated by the stories behind some of the characters. However, it is traditional for the Chinese teachers to insist on good handwriting, by which they often mean following a strict order of the strokes and balancing the sizes of the different component parts. They also tend to ask the pupils to copy the characters repeatedly. It is very common for a teacher at the Chinese school to ask the pupils to copy any new character 50 to 100 times, and collective correction of mistakes in character writing is a common activity in class. The pupils in the schools that I studied were unhappy with the teaching method, even though they were keen to learn about the characters. In Example 16 below, which was recorded in a Mandarin school in Newcastle, the pupils are making fun of the task by deliberately writing the wrong characters.

16. (T: teacher; B1: boy in class)

T: 候车室的候有没有一个小竖 (*houcheshi de hou youmei you yige xiao shu*)?
The word 'wait' in waiting room, does it have a small downward stroke or not?
(No response from the pupils)

The teacher wrote on the white board: 侯车室 (*houcheshi*—waiting room)

T: 这个侯对不对 (*zhege hou dui bu dui*)?
This wait, is it correct?

B1: Don't know. 对，不对 (*dui, budui*) 。
Correct, not correct.

T: 你上来写一下。 写对的。(*ni shanglai xie yixia xie dui de*)
You come up and write one. Write the correct one.

B1 went to the white board and wrote 猴 (monkey). Everybody laughed.
The teacher put a cross over it and said, 认真点(*renzhen dian*—Be serious.)
and wrote the correct character 候.

In this example, the teacher was trying to draw the pupils' attention to the details of a specific character. She deliberately wrote the wrong character, without the small downward stroke in the middle, and asked the class whether it was correct or not. The teacher's question 对不对 (*dui bu dui* — 'correct or not') is of a unique syntactic structure in Chinese, A not A. B1 knows exactly what the teacher is asking and how the structure works. He first responded in English "Don't know." He then switched to Chinese and copied the teacher's phrase, except that he added a very short pause after the first 对(*dui*—correct), making it sound as if he was hesitating. The response then became "Correct. Not correct." meaning "I'm not sure whether it is correct or not." When the teacher asked him to come up to the whiteboard and write the correct character, he wrote the character for monkey, which has the target character for 'wait' in it, but has an additional radical on the left meaning 'animal.' What it shows is that B1 knew exactly how to write the correct character. He took the opportunity to make fun of the exercise and made the class laugh.

The highly creative nature of the multilingual practices as seen in these examples calls for an alternative conceptualization and terminology to the existing ones of codeswitching. What the children in our examples are doing is *translanguaging*, both going between different linguistic codes and structures and going beyond them (Li Wei 2011a). It includes the full range of linguistic performances of multilingual language users for purposes that transcend the combination of structures, the alternation between systems; the transmission of information; and the representation of values, identities and relationships (see, further, Li Wei, 2011a). Translanguaging provides a clear example of multicompetence as well of what Kramsch (2006) calls 'symbolic competence'—"the ability not only to approximate or appropriate for oneself someone else's language, but to shape the very context in which the language is learned and used" (Kramsch and Whiteside 2008: 664). As Kramsch and Whiteside argue, a multilingual *sens pratique* multiplies the possibilities of meaning offered by the various codes in presence. They point out that

> [i]n today's global and migratory world, distinction might not come so much from the ownership of one social or linguistic patrimony (e.g. Mexican or Chinese culture, English language) as much as it comes from the ability to play a game of distinction on the margins of established patrimonies (Kramsch and Whiteside, 2008: 664).

To many bilingual speakers, codeswitching is a routine, rapid, and unremarkable linguistic behavior. Yet there is a widespread perception that such behavior is somehow out of the ordinary, abnormal, or deviant. Baetens Beardsmore (2003) talks about the fears of bilingualism—parental ("What have I done to my child?"), cultural ("Will bilingualism lead to cultural alienation?"), educational ("Does bilingualism hinder academic progress?") and politico-ideological ("Is bilingualism a threat to society and the nation-state?"). Many, if not all, of these fears are also of codeswitching. There is a pervasive belief in society, bilingual and monolingual alike, that languages are best kept separate, discreet, and pure; mixing and switching between languages is seen as interference or trespassing that will have a detrimental effect on both individual language users and the communities they live in. While considerable progress has been made in understanding what motivates bilingual speakers to engage in codeswitching and the complex nature of the structural configuration of codeswitching in interaction, more work is clearly needed in order to dispel the many myths and fears that still surround this defining bilingual behavior. For any future work, the different dimensions of codeswitching—the structural, the cognitive, and the social—ought to be examined as an integrated whole. Codeswitching is a highly dynamic and creative behavior that requires analytic approaches that transcend traditional disciplinary boundaries. But above all, it cannot be regarded as a disembodied superorganic object. It needs to be studied in situ, that is, in the interactional, linguistic, historical, and ideological contexts.

Notes

1. Example 1 was given to me by Rosemary Wilson; examples 10 and 11 were given by Agnes He, and 13 by Hongyin Tao. The other unattributed examples are taken from my fieldwork with Chinese-English bilinguals.

References

Auer, P. 1984. *Bilingual conversation*. Amsterdam: John Benjamins.

Baetens Beardsmore, H. 2003. Who's afraid of bilingualism? In J.-M. Dewaele, A. Housen, & Li Wei (eds), *Bilingualism: Beyond basic principles*, 10–27. Clevedon: Multilingual Matters.

Bauman, R. 1984. *Verbal art as performance*. Long Grove, IL: Waveland Press.

Bauman, R., & Briggs, C. L. 1990. Poetics and performance as critical perspectives on language and social life. *Annual Review of Anthropology* 19: 59–88.

Blom, J.-P., & Gumperz, J. J. 1972. Social meaning in lingusitic structure: Codeswitching in Norway. In J. J. Gumperz & D. Hymes (eds.), *Directions in sociolinguistics*, 407–34. New York: Holt, Rinehart and Winston.

Bolle, J. 1994. *Sanan Tongo-Nederlands: Code-wisseling in ontlenig.* MA thesis, University of Amsterdam.

Chomsky, N. 1986. *Knowledge of language*. New York: Praeger.

Cook, V. 1991. The poverty-of-the-stimulus argument and multi-competence. *Second Language Research* 7: 103–17

Cook, V. 1992. Evidence for multicompetence. *Language Learning* 42: 557–91

Gardner-Chloros, P. 2009. *Code-switching.* Cambridge: Cambridge University Press

Grosjean, F. 1998. Studying bilinguals: Methodological and conceptual issues. *Bilingualism: Language and Cognition* 1: 131–49

Gumperz, J. J. 1982. *Discourse strategies*. Cambridge: Cambridge University Press.

Heller, M. (ed.). 2009. *Bilingualism: A social approach*. Basingtoke, UK: Palgrave Macmillan.

Hymes, D. 1981. *In vain I tried to tell you: Essays in Native American ethnopoetics.* Philadelphia: University of Pennsylvania Press

Khattab, G. 2009. Phonetic accommodation in children's code-switching. In B. E. Bullock & A. J. Toribio (eds.), *The Cambridge handbook of linguistic code-switching*, 142–59. Cambridge: Cambridge University Press

Kramsch, C. 2006, From communicative competence to symbolic competence. *Modern Language Journal* 90: 249–52.

Kramsch, C., & Whiteside, A. 2008. Language ecology in multilingual settings: Towards a theory of symbolic competence. *Applied Linguistics* 29: 645–71.

Li, W. 1989. The 'why' and 'how' questions in the analysis of conversational code-switching. In P. Auer (ed.), *Code-switching in conversation: Language, interaction, and identity*, 156–79. London: Routledge.

Li, W. 2005. How can you tell? Toward a common sense explanation of conversational codeswitching. *Journal of Pragmatics* 37(3): 375–89.

Li, W. 2011a. Moment analysis and translanguaging space. *Journal of Pragmatics* 43: 1222–235.

Li, W. 2011b. Multilinguality, multimodality and multicompetence: Code- and mode-switching by minority ethnic children in complementary schools. *Modern Language Journal* 95(3): 370-94

Li, W., & Wu, C.-J. 2008, Code-switching: ideologies and practices. In A. He & Y. Xiao, (eds.), *Chinese as a heritage language: Fostering rooted world citizenry*, 225–38. Honolulu: National Foreign Language Resource Center and University of Hawai'i Press.

Li, W., & Wu, C.-J. 2009. Polite Chinese children revisited: Creativity and the use of codeswitching in the Chinese complementary school classroom. *International Journal of Bilingual Education and Bilingualism* 12: 193–211.

MacSwan, J. 1999. *A minimalist approach to intrasentential code switching*. New York: Garland.

Milroy, L, & Gordon, M. 2003. *Sociolinguistics: Methods and interpretation*. Oxford: Blackwell.

Muysken, P. 2000. *Bilingual speech: A typology of code-mixing*. Cambridge: Cambridge University Press.

Myers-Scotton, C. 1993. *Social motivations for codeswitching: Evidence from Africa*. Oxford: Oxford University Press.

Myers-Scotton, C. 1997. *Duelling languages: Grammatical structure in codeswitching*, 2nd ed. with added Afterword. Oxford: Oxford University Press.

Myers-Scotton, C. 2002. *Contact linguistics: Bilingual encounters and grammatical outcomes*. Oxford: Oxford University Press.

Myers-Scotton, C., & Jake, J. 1995. Matching lemmas in a bilingual language competence and production model: Evidence from intrasentential code-switching. *Linguistics* 33: 981–1024.

Petersen, J. 1988. Word-internal code-switching constraints in a bilingual child's grammar. *Linguistics* 26: 479–93.

Poplack, S. 1980. Sometimes I'll start a sentence in Spanish Y TERMINO EN ESPAÑOL: Toward a typology of code-switching. *Linguistics* 18: 581–618.

Poplack, S. 2004. Code-switching. In U. Ammon, N. Dittmar, K. J. Mattheier, & P. Trudgill (eds), *Soziolinguistik: An international handbook of the science of language and socieity*, 2nd ed., 589–96. Berlin: Walter de Gruyter.

Sherzer, J. 2002. *Speech play and verbal art*. Austin: University of Texas Press

Siewierska, Anna, Xu, Jiajin, & Xiao, Richard. 2010. Bang-le yi ge da mang (offered a big helping hand): A corpus study of the splittable compounds in spoken and written Chinese. *Language Sciences* 32(4): 464–87

Winford, D. 2003. *An introduction to contact linguistics*. Oxford: Blackwell.

CHAPTER 19

SIGN LANGUAGE CONTACT

DAVID QUINTO-POZOS AND ROBERT ADAM

LANGUAGE contact is the norm in Deaf communities, and Deaf people are typically multilingual.[1] They use signed, written, and, in some cases, spoken languages for daily communication, which means that aspects of the spoken and/or written languages of the larger communities are in constant interaction with the signed languages.[2] In some cases, the contact has resulted in spoken language structures that have become incorporated into the sign languages—having been modified over time to conform to the linguistic processes of signed languages. However, in other cases the contact may not be influencing structural changes to either language. These points about contact are true whether an interaction occurs between deaf and hearing signers or solely among deaf signers. Language contact has played a very important role in the creation and evolution of signed languages, and it surfaces in the daily interactions between their users.

In some cases, contact phenomena in Deaf communities may not be attributable to ambient spoken and/or written languages but rather stem from the use of two (or more) signed languages. This type of scenario is especially true in international border areas and in transnational gatherings of Deaf people, although such contact might also occur within a single country when communities of Deaf signers who use different signed languages interact. Two different signed languages can also coexist within a single city (e.g., Langue de Signes Québécoise and American Sign Language in Montreal, Canada) or within a country (Yucatec Maya Sign Language and Mexican Sign Language in Mexico; Johnson 1991).

The prevalence of language contact within Deaf communities throughout the world provides a rich web of linguistic phenomena to be investigated. If one considers the contact that results from users of two different signed languages interacting, various comparisons can be made to contact that occurs across two or more spoken languages. The term *unimodal contact*, or that which comes about because of two languages within the same modality (whether the modality be visual-gestural or auditory-oral) can be used to characterize such contact. However, if one considers the contact that results from interaction between a signed and a spoken or written language, the term *bimodal* (or even *multimodal*) *contact* is more appropriate. It should be noted that even in cases where unimodal contact occurs between two signed languages, the bimodal or multimodal contact phenomena surface as well.

We suggest that particular aspects of the visual-gestural modality contribute to the list of attested language contact phenomena in unique ways and thus create a list of outcomes that do not typically characterize spoken language contact situations. However, it is also true that multimodal contact—especially contact involving visual-gestural language, provides supporting examples for attesting to the types of language contact phenomena that have been described for spoken languages.

Language Contact as a Function of Language Modality

This chapter is organized by common outcomes of language contact that occur based on languages and communication systems within and across communication modalities (sign, speech, and writing). It may be the case that the categories of contact outcomes that we propose are not mutually exclusive (i.e., an example of contact that is described in one classification could also appear within another, related category).[3] The reader will also notice that, at least with respect to sign-speech contact and sign-writing contact, the effects of contact on each language are clearly not equal. It is most often the case that the spoken and written languages have an influence on the structure and daily use of signed languages, though the reverse is infrequently so.

Sign-Speech Contact

Sign-speech contact seems to have generated the most scholarly interest throughout the years. We begin by highlighting some older works that have influenced the field for decades and include more recent studies that have allowed us to push the boundaries of what we know about signed language contact.

Influence from spoken language grammar on the signed language. Various analyses of contact between a signed and a spoken language have focused on the ways in which signed languages seem to take on characteristics of spoken language grammar. Early on, specific cases of such contact were thought to result in a signed pidgin (Woodward 1973b) and cases of diglossia within sign[4] (Stokoe 1970; Woodward 1973a).

In the case of American Sign Language (ASL), the pidgin analysis was adopted by many people (perhaps more by lay people than by linguists), which resulted in common use of the term Pidgin Signed English, or PSE. That label was used for years, even though the initial analysis was not without debate. Woodward (1973b) was an early proponent of the pidgin analysis, and he noted that PSE is characterized by "reduction and mixture of grammatical structures of both languages as well as some new structures that are common to neither of the languages" (40). Among the structures referred to by Woodward were articles, plural markers, and the copula—none of which are common to both English and ASL.

However, over the years various authors have pointed out that, in several ways, PSE does not seem to resemble spoken language pidgins. Cokely (1983) argued in favor of an analysis that considered interactions between deaf and hearing signers as instances of foreigner talk, judgments of proficiency, and ASL learners' attempts to master the target language. Fischer (1996) pointed out that the alleged pidgin, PSE, is the opposite of what is typically found in spoken language pidgins since its vocabulary comes from the substrate (ASL), whereas its grammar comes from the superstrate (English). We revisit the idea of pidgin creation through contact in our discussion of International Sign.

Later work agued in favor of a different analysis of the contact between English and ASL. Lucas and Valli (1992) suggested that the term *contact signing* was a more appropriate label for varieties of sign language that combine features of ASL and English and exhibit significant individual variation in terms of the occurrence of features. They also pointed out that, despite the individual variation, some linguistic features from ASL and English seldom occur in contact signing, such as ASL nonmanual syntactic markers that occur with topicalization and various bound morphemes from English (e.g., plural *-s*, third-person singular *-s*, possessive *'s*, past tense *-ed*, or comparative *-er*).

Influence from spoken words on the signed language: Mouthings. Another characteristic of contact between a signed and a spoken language is the signer's voiceless articulation of spoken words while producing signs. In such cases, the signer articulates aspects of the *visual* signal that is perceived when looking at the mouth of the spoken language user.[5] Sometimes the visual signal seems to capture aspects of the entire spoken word, whereas at other times there are only parts of that word visible (e.g., the onset of the word or certain syllables with other part of the spoken word not represented in the visual signal).

Mouthings tend to occur most often when signers are manually articulating nouns, open-class items, and morphologically simpler signs (see Crasborn et al. 2008). These mouthings differ from *mouth gestures*, which are often used for adjectival or adverbial functions, are indigenous to a sign language, and do not usually reflect contact with a spoken language.

Several authors have addressed the phenomenon of mouthings with data from various signed and spoken languages (ASL/English: Davis 1989; Swiss German Sign Language (GSL)/German: Boyes Braem 2001; New Zealand Sign Language [NZSL] and Maori-influenced English: McKee et al. 2007; Chinese Sign Language/Chinese: Yang 2008; Ajello et al. 2001 for Italian Sign Language/Italian; see Ann 2001 for other examples). For many authors this type of contact reflects instances of borrowing, and the mouthings are often viewed as integrated into the morpho-syntactic structures of signed languages (see Crasborn et al. 2008 for references). Whereas, another point of view is that the mouthings, while still coming about because of language contact, are examples of code mixing and not integrated into the linguistic structure of the signed language (see e.g., Ebbinghaus & Hessmann 2001; Hohenberger & Happ 2001).

Signed languages also exist within regions where more than one spoken language is used regularly, and that can result in mouthings that reflect contact with either or both of the spoken languages. Quinto-Pozos (2002, 2008) reports that in a transnational border region where English and Spanish are used regularly mouthings of Spanish words can accompany ASL signs and mouthings of English words can accompany Mexican Sign Language (LSM) signs. In one example from the border data, the Spanish word *igual* ('same') appeared as a mouthing while the signer simultaneously signed the ASL sign SAME.

Vocabulary creation through contact. Some vocabulary items in signed languages appear to be borrowed from spoken and written language words. For example, Johnston and Schembri (2007) note that, in Auslan, compounds such as SPORT+CAR are created through contact with English. In some cases, the English-influenced compound coexists with a sign that is indigenous to the signed language, such as the loan translation BREAK-DOWN and the native sign BREAKDOWN, the latter of which was not borrowed from English. For the most part, the semantics of the spoken language are used in the borrowed form. Brentari and Padden (2001) discuss similar examples in ASL such as DEAD+LINE and BABY+SIT. Some compounds contain fingerspelled components such as SUGAR + F-R-E-E. In all of these cases, lexical items from the ambient spoken language have influenced the signs (and sign-fingerspelling combinations) that are used in the sign language.

The unique mixing of languages across modalities: Code-blending. Various studies have reported on the use of features of a spoken and a signed language simultaneously. In most cases, the studies of this phenomenon have focused on the language use of hearing individuals who are fluent in a signed and a spoken language, but the phenomenon could also appear in the language use of deaf individuals who choose to use speech in addition to sign—such as with their hearing children. The language users are often referred to as *bimodal bilinguals*[6] (Bishop & Hicks 2008; Emmorey, Borinstein, & Thompson 2005; Emmorey, Borinstein, Thompson, & Gollan 2008), and the language mixing has been termed *code-blending* because of the simultaneous expression of features of both languages.

An example of code-blending is shown in (1), which is taken from Emmorey et al. (2005: 668). In that example, the signs and English words are produced simultaneously.

(1)	English:	An old woman seem her bird she protect.
	ASL:	A-N OLD WOMAN SEEM POSS BIRD.PRO PROTECT
	Translation:	'There's this old woman, and it seems it's her bird. She protects it.'

The word order of the signs/words in (1) do not follow conventional English grammar, but they are more ASL-like in structure. In some instances, aspects of one language are not represented, which means that the interlocutor must understand both languages to fully understand a message. This phenomenon is also frequently referred to as "Coda Talk" (Bishop & Hicks 2008) by some authors.

Code-blending has been claimed to differ from signing while speaking, or what is often referred to as Simultaneous Communication or SimCom. Essentially, SimCom is claimed to commonly result in speech dysfluencies because of the "dual-task properties" of this type of communication that are unlike natural bilingual communication. (Emmorey et al. 2005:670). Emmorey and colleagues suggest that code-blending is a natural type of language use by those bilinguals who acquire a signed and a spoken language as children.

Some analyses have examined variation within the types of language mixing that are produced by bimodal bilinguals (Baker and van den Bogaerde 2008; Bishop & Hicks 2008; van den Bogaerde & Baker 2005). In such analyses, the researchers examine code-blended segments in order to determine a *base language*, a designation based on the meaning generated by each language. For example, Baker and van den Bogaerde report on variation in code-blending strategies in Dutch and Sign Language of the Netherlands (NGT) in families with Deaf and hearing members. The researchers noted that code-blends were found both in mothers' input to their children and in the children's output. The segment in (2), taken from Baker and van den Bogaerde (2008: 7) demonstrates a mother's output where Dutch is designated as the base language because of its greater contribution to the overall meaning of the sentence.

(2) signed: VALLEN
fall
spoken: die gaat vallen
that goes fall
translation: That [doll] is going to fall

Sign-Writing Contact

Signed languages contain many examples of contact with the written words of ambient spoken languages. Many people consider the contact to result in "borrowing," though the borrowing is characteristically different than spoken language borrowing. In particular, the contact in question reflects influence from the orthography of spoken languages—the actual letters of the spoken language words.

Fingerspelling. Manual systems for representing entire words of written language are commonly known as *fingerspelling*, and it is the case that many (if not most) sign languages possess fingerspelling systems. Some of the systems are articulated with one hand (e.g., French Sign Language and LSM) and others require the use of two hands for production (e.g., British Sign Language and Czech Sign Language, see Sutton-Spence 2003). In these systems, certain handshapes, movements, (and locations, for two-handed fingerspelling) represent letters of the written alphabet.

Various researchers have highlighted ways in which fingerspelling can adapt to the natural processes of a signed language. In an early work on the linguistic processes that act on fingerspelling, Battison (1978) addressed the manner in which some fingerspelled words become lexicalized over time. For example, the fingerspelled letters J-O-B were the source material for a sign that developed in ASL (often transcribed as #JOB) with the same meaning and only some features of the original fingerspelled item. Only the handshapes that represent the first and last letters of the word are visible in the lexicalized form, and the B-handshape changes orientation so that the palm faces toward the signer at completion of the sign.

Similar types of lexicalization processes can occur in sign languages that utilize a two-handed system, such as British Sign Language (BSL). As with one-handed systems, BSL fingerspelling can demonstrate processes of nativization (Cormier et al. 2008: 3; Kyle and Woll 1985; Sutton-Spence 1994, 1998), where a fingerspelled event is considered a lexical sign.

Fingerspelling has also been considered within a model that divides elements of signed languages into native and nonnative items (Brentari and Padden 2001; Padden 1998). In that analysis fingerspelling is viewed as a nonnative subset of the lexicon, a part that is "borrowed" from English through contact though the nonnative items can undergo processes that allow them to appear more ASL-like (i.e., native-like), a suggestion that was also made earlier

(Battison 1978). In some cases, the fingerspelled items can form compounds with ASL signs, as was mentioned earlier.

As evidence that contact phenomena can becoming nativized within a language, a recent study has shown that the cognitive processing of fingerspelling has become incorporated into a signed language to the extent that it is processed like other aspects of sign for deaf language users—rather than as written language, which it represents (Waters et. al. 2007).

Other works have suggested that fingerspelling can be viewed as code switching between ASL and written English (Kuntze 2000), and it can also be considered a form of borrowing (Miller 2001).

Initialized signs and abbreviations as examples of borrowing. Whereas fingerspelling is characteristically sequential (i.e., the letters of written words are depicted in a particular order, one after another), initialized signs are just like other signs of signed languages—with simultaneity being one of the primary forces driving linguistic structure.

In sign languages with one-handed fingerspelling systems, initialized signs are those whose handshape(s) correspond to the manual representations of letters of the written alphabet (see Padden 1998 for a discussion of such signs and various examples from ASL). For example, the ASL sign WATER is articulated with an ASL W-handshape, and the ASL sign TEAM is produced with an ASL T-handshape. In some cases, there are initialized and non-initialized variants of signs in ASL—the latter of which might be more semantically general in nature. For example, in the case of the two-handed sign TEAM, there are non-initialized variants (produced with other handshapes) that contain the same movement and place of articulation values, but different handshapes. So, the signs CLASS and GROUP are also initialized, though there is a general sign for the concept of 'group' that is articulated with the ASL clawed-5 handshape. However, in the case of some initialized signs (e.g., WATER; see figure 19.1), there exist no non-initialized variants in current ASL.

Figure 19.1. American Sign Language lexical item WATER

Padden (1998) also writes about abbreviation signs in ASL, or those that also demonstrate some influence from letters of English words. Examples of such signs in ASL are WORKSHOP, FEEDBACK, and WITHDRAW. Such signs are like the initialized signs just described, yet they display the manual handshapes that correspond with two letters of the written word rather than just the initial letter of the word. So, for WORKSHOP, the letters "W" and "S" are found within the handshapes that make up the sign, though the movement, place of articulation, and orientation values adhere to indigenous phonological constraints of word formation for the language.

Initialization of signs in languages with two-handed fingerspelling systems is also possible, but it is perhaps less common. The reason for this difference is that the one-handed systems usually support the identification of the alphabetic item with solely a handshape (in most cases), and that allows for the movement and place of articulation parameters to either mirror non-initialized variants or else to engage in their own sanctioned combinations in order to create a sign. Since two-handed systems require place of articulation values (and also movements, in some cases), there are fewer parameters that are free for sign formation. However, some authors (Cormier et al. 2008; Sutton-Spence 1994; Sutton-Spence & Woll 1999) have described particular signs in two-handed systems as *single manual letter signs* (SMLS), which are signs that are produced by articulating the fingerspelled letter that corresponds with a letter (usually the first, as in initialized signs in one-handed systems) of a semantically equivalent written word from the ambient spoken language. See figure 19.2 for an example of a SMLS with the BSL sign for FATHER. These signs generally allow for limited movements from the non-dominant hand and are usually articulated in neutral space (Cormier et al. 2008).

We have noted that initialized signs of signed languages represent contact between the signed and the written version of the spoken language. Certainly, initialized signs attest to long-standing contact between signed languages and

Figure 19.2. British Sign Language and Auslan lexical item FATHER

the ambient spoken/written languages of their communities. Much of this contact begins early in the history of a signed language, with the establishment of schools for deaf children and teaching methods that focus on the learning of spoken and/or written language.

Initialized signs exist in many sign languages. For example, they have been attested for LSM, which represents contact between LSM and Spanish (Guerra Currie, 1999), Thai Sign Language, for contact with Thai (Nonaka 2004), and Quebec Sign Language, which reflects contact with French (Machabée 1995). Johnston and Schembri (2007) also report that some initialized signs in Australian Sign Language, a language with a two-handed fingerspelling system, are actually produced as one-handed signs because of contact with Irish Sign Language (ISL)–initialized signs. The ISL fingerspelling system is one-handed. For an example of the ISL sign for GARDEN, see figure 19.3.

Borrowings from electronic communication. Electronic communication has also become a source of borrowings into signed language from written language. Schneider et. al (2011) report this phenomenon for ASL and English. They found that internet messaging and short messaging service (SMS), which are replete with abbreviations and acronyms, have become so widespread that some abbreviations such as LOL ('laugh out loud') and WTF ('what the fuck') have likely become a part of the ASL lexicon along with items that have presumably been part of ASL (and English) vocabulary for a longer period of time. Among those later signs are ASAP ('as soon as possible') and FYI ('for your information'). Schneider et al. also found age- and gender-based variation in their sample that was taken from surveys. This work highlights the important role of electronic communication in the modern evolution of language.

Tracing written forms during sign discourse. At least one other phenomenon is noteworthy with respect to the influence of written forms of spoken language on signed languages: the tracing of written forms—either in the palm of the hand or in the air—by the signer within signed language discourse. Older

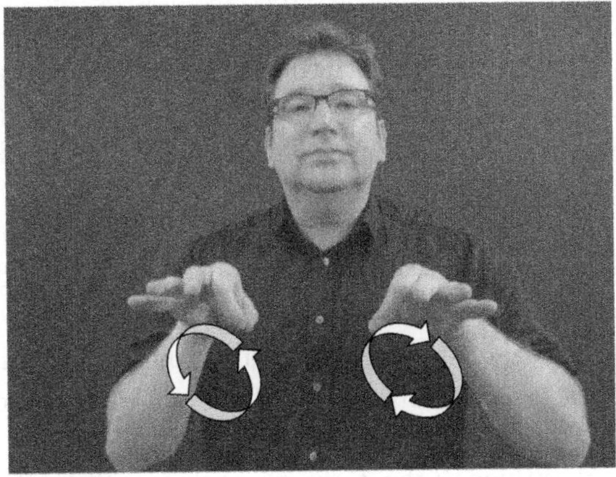

Figure 19.3. Irish Sign Language lexical item GARDEN

signers of NZSL have been described as using this strategy (Forman, 2003, though also see Dugdale, Kennedy, McKee, & McKee 2003 for noteworthy commentary on Forman's writings). In such cases, the signer normally uses an index finger to trace the shape of the written alphabetic letter or logographic character that is being referenced. This tracing alternates with signs and other aspects of the signed language. However, there often also exist signs that represent certain logographic characters. Yang (2008) provides an example of a Chinese Sign Language user tracing a character sign within the palm of his hand during sign discourse.

Influence of the signed language on written language.[7] Plaza-Pust (2008) provides a detailed account of literacy development for deaf children who sign DGS and are learning written German. She argues that the variation and errors that are demonstrated by the children in their written German is representative of L2 acquisition of literacy—rather than from primary contact with DGS. However, the author also notes some types of influence that DGS seems to be exerting on the children's written German. As one example, various written German sentences produced by the children did not contain overt verbs, a feature of DGS (and other sign languages), which can use other means to create predication.

(3) Taken from Plaza-Pust (2008: 122)

Written German:	der	Junge	Angst
English:	the	boy	fear
Translation:	'The boy is frightened'		

Sign-Sign Contact and Other Forms of Visual-Gestural communication

Lucas and Valli (1992) suggested that there are likely various possible outcomes of contact between two signed languages: lexical borrowing, foreigner talk, interference, and the creation of pidgins, creoles, and mixed systems. Some of these have been attested in the literature. Additionally, Quinto-Pozos (2007) proposed that certain inherent characteristics of signed languages likely influence the language contact phenomena that ensue. In particular, he suggested that the prevalence of visual iconicity and the utilization of gestural resources create language contact phenomena that are unique to signed language. Additionally, the interlingual structure similarity of sign languages likely has salient effects on contact between signed languages, as well. In this section we provide details about the claim that gestural resources play an important role in contact within the visual-gestural modality. See Quinto-Pozos (2007) for discussions of iconicity and the claim that sign languages share some structural features that likely influence the form of contact within the visual-gestural modality.

Codeswitching. Codeswitching has been attested in the contact between two sign languages.[8] In particular, Quinto-Pozos (2002, 2009) provide evidence that U.S.-Mexico border signers of LSM and ASL engage in *reiterative codeswitching*, the sequential use of synonymous signs for the purposes of reiteration—much like certain switches described in spoken languages. One example (taken from Quinto-Pozos 2009: 230) can be found in (4).

(4) point: middle finger (for listing) TOMATO **TOMATE (LSM sign)** ADD-INGREDIENTS MIX gesture: "thumbs-up"
'(...and then you take) tomatoes and you add them to the other ingredients and mix everything together. It's great.'

Nonreiterative examples of codeswitching between two sign languages have also been attested (Nonaka 2004; Quinto-Pozos 2009). Nonaka describes instances of codeswitching between Ban Khor Sign Language and Thai Sign Language, with a focus on inventories of color terms that are not similar across the two languages. The codeswitching, then, is done out of necessity—when a particular item does not exist within one language.

Quinto-Pozos points out that there are various issues that must be considering when analyzing data from two sign languages. In particular, some items may be articulated similarly in both sign languages, and that makes it difficult to determine which language is being produced. Examples are various types of points, so-called classifier constructions, commonly used gestures, and enactments that involve upper body parts (known in the literature as *construction action*; see Quinto-Pozos & Mehta 2010 for a discussion of constructed action patterns). When such meaningful devices exist within the sign stream, it is not clear how to label a particular utterance (e.g., a so-called classifier construction from Language A or Language B, an emblem from the ambient hearing community versus a sign, or the use of constructed action versus a language-specific lexical item).

Adam (2012) examined contact between dialects of BSL (Auslan and BSL) and dialects of ISL (Australian Irish Sign Language and Irish Sign Language) using Muysken's (2000) typology of code-mixing. Muysken's (2000) typology categorizes code-mixing into three processes: insertion—where a lexical item or a phrase is inserted into a sentence; alternation—where codes are switched at utterance boundaries; and congruent lexicalization—where the two languages share similar grammatical structures and language nodes are shared between the two codes, but at the lexical level there are items from the different languages. Examples of all three types of code mixing were found in the data by Adam (2012) and the initial analysis showed that congruent lexicalization was the most common form of code mixing although subsequent re-analysis shows that insertion was the most common form.

Performance of bilinguals on experimental language switching tasks (e.g., picture naming) can be informative with respect to cognitive processes that assist with the management of multiple languages. Several works suggest assymetries with regard to language switching, and it appears that there are more costs for a second language (L2) learner to switch *into* their native language as opposed to switching *from* their native language into their second language (Costa & Santesteban, 2004; Meuter & Allport, 1999). In an experimental study which examined codeswitching by individuals bilingual in BSL and ISL in (by means of a switch task using picture stimuli in different colors to cue switching) Adam (2012) found there was also a cost for switching between sign languages in terms of longer response latency, comparable to that reported for spoken language bilingualism.

The code switching that some deaf users of ASL and Cued Speech engage in has also been viewed as a form of contact between ASL and English. In this manual system for representing spoken language, consonant and vowel sounds are represented by the hands, and, in theory, any spoken language can be cued. Hauser (2000) describes the signing of a 10-year-old girl who is fluent in both ASL and Cued English and gives examples of how she code-switches between the two forms of manual communication.

Linguistic interference. Interference is another possible outcome of contact between two sign languages, and this phenomenon can be described as the surfacing of the articulatory norms of one sign language in the production of another. Some instances of inteference may be evident in the phonological parameters of sign formation. Lucas and Valli (1992: 35) refer to this type of interference as follows: "It might be precisely the lack of phonological integration that might signal interference—for example, the involuntary use of a handshape, location, palm orientation, movement, or facial expression from one sign language in the discourse of the other." Interference may also be evident at other levels of language structure, such as the morphology or syntax of one or both of the signed languages.

Interference is also discussed in Quinto-Pozos (2002, 2008). The analyses focus primarily on the phonological parameter of handshape and the LSM and ASL non-manual signals that are used for *wh*-question formation. The data indicate that signers, like users of spoken language, exhibit features of interference when they articulate items from their nonnative language. For example, a signer who grew up in Mexico signing LSM might sign ASL FAMILY with an LSM F handshape rather than an ASL F handshape. The two handshapes are similar, but they differ in the contact between thumb and index finger and also in the degree to which the non-selected fingers (i.e., the middle and ring fingers and the pinky) are spread outward.

Lexical borrowing across sign languages. Several studies that have compared lexical items across sign languages generally agree that sign languages are lexically more similar to each other than spoken languages are (e.g., see Guerra Currie et al. 2002). While this may not be a result of contact between sign languages, some researchers have investigated the likelihood of historical contact (e.g., Davis 2007, 2010; McKee & Kennedy 2000). Higher degrees of lexical similarity clearly hold even for languages that are unrelated and whose users live in very disparate parts of the world. As a result, these works raise questions about the role of visual iconicity in the development of sign languages and in the comparison of sign lexicons. See Quinto-Pozos (2007) for a discussion of the role of iconicity with respect to lexical similarity across sign languages.

Some authors have also examined current lexicons of different languages in order to test theories of historical contact. In a comparison of the sign languages of the United Kingdom, Australia, New Zealand, and the United States, McKee and Kennedy (2000) have demonstrated that ASL is very different, at least lexically, from the varieties that have connections to nineteenth-century British Sign Language. This is true in spite of the claim that ASL may have been influenced somewhat by BSL of the late eighteenth and early nineteenth centuries (Groce 1985). In addition, Davis (2007, 2010) investigates signs used by Native Americans during the beginnings and early development of ASL (1880s and early 1900s). His analysis proposes that the signs of the Native Americans exhibit sufficient similarity to suggest that a single system, Plains Indians Sign Language (PSL) influenced the beginnings of ASL through borrowings.

Discussions of signed languages in Asia and Africa have also appeared in literature descriptions of lexical borrowing across signed languages. Sasaki (2007) addresses lexical contact between Japanese Sign Language (NS, or Nihon Syuwa) and Taiwan Sign Language (TSL). Historical accounts of the development of TSL cite NS as one of the sign languages that influenced the development of TSL (Ann et al. 2007). Schmaling (2001) suggests that ASL in contact with Hausa Sign Language (HSL) in northern Nigeria has resulted in the appearance of some ASL forms in HSL (e.g., loan signs and the use of the manual alphabet for the creation of initialized signs).

Borrowing of gestures from the ambient hearing community. Signers take advantage of commonly used non-linguistic gestures from the ambient hearing communities. Some of those gestures may become part of the lexicon or grammar of the sign languages as evidenced, in part, by changes in their articulation vis-à-vis the manner in which hearing people use those gestures. However, Deaf signers also articulate gestures that, at least on the surface, do not appear to differ from some of those that hearing people use in conjunction with speech. As with iconic devices, such gestural resources—some of which may display language-like properties and others that pattern in non-linguistic ways—present challenges for the researcher of signed language contact. One challenge for some analyses (e.g., a syntactic account of codeswitching) is to determine whether a meaningful form is, in some cases, a sign or a non-linguistic gesture.

Various authors have suggested ways in which the gestures—both manual and non-manual—of hearing people can now be considered as part of a sign language. For example, Janzen and Shaffer (2002) maintain that some hand gestures have been grammaticalized as modals in ASL and that some facial gestures (specifically brow raise) have been incorporated as non-manual signals that provide syntactic information (e.g., topic markers). McClave (2001) has also proposed that non-manual signals (e.g., head shifts for direct quotes) in ASL have been influenced by the gestures of hearing people. Casey (2003) has shown that directional gestures and torso movements of non-signers are similar to verb directionality and torso movement for role shift in signed language. She suggests that directionality in ASL (and other sign languages) originated from non-linguistic gestures, but first- versus non-first-person distinctions have been grammaticalized; thus not all of the directional gestures can be considered purely gestural.

Other works have addressed the roles of other gestures within the signed stream. Pietrosemoli (2001) writes about the emblems (or "cultural signs," in her terminology; see McNeill 1992 for a discussion of categories of gesture) that hearing Venezuelans commonly use and that signers of Venezuelan Sign Language (LSV) also produce. She reports that the emblematic signs appear to reflect a code-switching of emblems with linguistic items or a borrowing of the emblems into LSV. In addition, Quinto-Pozos (2002) noted that emblematic gestures alternate with lexical signs of LSM and ASL in the discourse of deaf signers who live along the United States–Mexico border.

Pidgin creation: International Sign and so-called Foreigner Talk. In terms of the creation of mixed systems as a result of contact, it is vital to include discussion of *International Sign*, a "type of signing used when deaf signers communicate across mutually unintelligible language boundaries" (Supalla and Webb 1995: 334). Segments of the international Deaf Community are highly mobile and regularly attend international and regional events (e.g., meetings of the World Federation of the Deaf Congress and the Deaflympics Games) that occur throughout parts of the world. Deaf individuals who interact with each other in these types of international gatherings use International Sign for communication. As a result, International Sign may function as a type of "foreigner talk." There do not appear to be native users of International Sign, which is employed only for restricted purposes. Based on these social phenomena, some may wonder if International Sign resembles spoken language pidgins, though various structural patterns of International Sign suggest otherwise.

In terms of grammatical devices, various researchers claim that International Sign is structurally more complex than spoken language pidgins are (McKee & Napier 2002; Rosenstock 2004; Supalla & Webb 1995). Supalla and Webb discuss the rule-governed nature of the syntactic structure of International Sign and various features of its vocabulary. In particular, they claim that verb agreement, word order, and negation in International Sign are systematic and rule governed. They also report that verbs are frequently inflected in complex ways. The word order of International Sign is usually SVO, but it can also be described in terms of other regular structures. With regard to negation, Supalla and Webb (1995: 346–47) claim that a signer of International Sign appears to use "a limited number of negative devices similar in structure and form to those used in full signed languages." Rosenstock (2004) reports that International Sign contains highly iconic signs, as well as more arbitrary ones that may be loans from full sign languages. By describing a number of grammatical and otherwise communicative devices used in International Sign, Rosenstock shows that International

Sign contains an "extremely complex grammatical system with a rather limited lexicon" (212). This is possibly due to the great similarity of the grammatical and morphological structures of the languages in contact—to the extent that International Sign has been suggested to possibly represent a koine (Supalla & Webb 1995).

Regarding lexical matters, International Sign does not have its own lexicon like a full-fledged sign language (Allsop, Woll, & Brauti 1995), though there do exist a core set of signs that are commonly recognized as conventional within International Sign. A signer who is using International Sign normally incorporates a myriad of meaningful devices within their signing (e.g., signs from their own native sign language, signs from another sign language, signs recognized as conventional in International Sign, mimetic enactments, or so-called classifiers). The lexicon of conventional signs is also "highly situational, shifting from event to event according to the participants' multilingual ability in various national sign languages" (Murray 2009: 947). As can be noted, signers of International Sign "combine a relatively rich and structured grammar with a severely impoverished lexicon" (Allsop et al. 1995: 197).

Language attrition and Language death. Yoel (2007) reported on an unfortunate outcome of language contact—the decline in use of an immigrant community's language due to replacement of that language by the host country's language. She focused on the attrition of Russian Sign Language (RSL) in several individuals who immigrated to Israel and subsequently learned Israeli Sign Language. Whereas, some of the signs of RSL were remembered and correctly articulated by the immigrants years after arriving in Israel, there were multiple examples in Yoel's data of incorrectly articulated RSL signs or else signs that were fully forgotten.

Language death has also been suggested, albeit minimally, to result from contact between sign languages. Much of this contact is a result of the work of foreign missionaries, foreign instructors, and even deaf people from those countries who have learned ASL and other Western sign languages and returned to their own country. Woodward (2000) claims that indigenous sign languages of Southeast Asia seem to be dying out and are apparently being replaced by signed languages influenced by ASL or French Sign Language (LSF).

Yoel (2009) reports on the rapid decline in the use of Maritime Sign Language (MSL), what is used by elderly Deaf people in Canada's Maritime Provinces. The majority of Deaf Canadians use ASL, though there is also a population of Langue de Signes Québécoise (LSQ) in the province of Quebec. Yoel suggests that there are fewer than 100 users of MSL, and contact with ASL may be at the heart of the decline. MSL is reported to have its roots in BSL, but contact with ASL has resulted in the addition of many lexical items from that language. Unfortunately, her analysis suggests that MSL is "moribund; it is beyond revival and survival. It will die out within its last remaining users" (iii).

Likewise, Nonaka (2004), in her account of indigenous sign languages of Thailand, writes of the need to remember sign languages in discussions of language endangerment and in language preservation efforts. Nonaka discusses indigenous varieties of sign language in Thailand, such as Ban Khor Sign Language and those referred to as Old Bangkok and Old Chiangmai sign varieties. Whereas the national sign language, Thai Sign Language, seems to be thriving, according to Nonaka, the future of the indigenous varieties is uncertain. It is clear that language contact can result not only in the creation of new varieties but also in the drastic alteration or destruction of others.

Concluding Remarks

Most work on signed language contact has focused on the interaction of signed and spoken and/or written languages. This multi-modal contact may be due to the fact that signed languages most often exist within larger communities where spoken and written languages are used daily. These oral and written modalities of language exert much linguistic (and cultural) influence on signed languages. This has been true as long as deaf children have been educated and guided through the acquisition of literacy. This has also been true because of the interactions between deaf and hearing users of signed languages. Deaf people and signed languages do not exist in a vacuum; they are surrounded by many non-native signers and languages (both spoken and written) that are structured differently. We suggest that the fact that Deaf signers are multi-modal bilinguals/multilinguals creates a fertile landscape for the creation of contact phenomena.

There are also cases of signed languages coming into contact with each other—either in transnational border communities or through international travel experiences. Such cases of unimodal contact are particularly interesting because they allow the investigator of language contact an opportunity to examine how language contact may have unique characteristics if considered solely within the visual-gestural modality (see Quinto-Pozos [2007] for discussions of common characteristics of such contact).

It has been suggested that Deaf learners of a spoken/written language demonstrate learning strategies consistent with a L2 learner of a spoken/written language (Plaza-Pust 2008). Additionally, the multilingual development that most Deaf individuals experience likely leads to very specific language mixing. As Plaza-Pust (2008: 127) notes, "This is an important conclusion given the myths that surround the acquisition of a written language by deaf students." Language mixing and contact are the norm in Deaf communities.

The study of contact in the visual-gestural modality is fascinating. It can tell us much about natural language structure, the influence of society on language, and the role of modality on language. By considering the ways in which bimodal bilinguals/multilinguals shape their languages, the general study of the human language capacity is taken to another level.

Acknowledgment

The support of the Economic and Social Research Council (ESRC) is gratefully acknowledged. Robert Adam was supported by the ESRC Deafness Cognition and Language Research Centre (DCAL) Grant RES-620-28-0002.

Notes

1. We use the convention "Deaf" to refer to signed language users who are also part of a cultural minority. The non-capitalized "deaf" is used to refer solely to audiological status or in cases where linguistic and cultural status is not being highlighted.
2. Following Wilcox and Wilcox (1997), we use the term "sign language" to refer to specific languages (e.g., Mexican Sign Language) and "signed language(s)" to refer more generally to visual-gestural language(s).
3. Also see Quinto-Pozos (2007) and Adam (in press) for detailed accounts of linguistic loci for signed language contact.
4. Tervoort (1973: 378) also argued that for diglossia to be present, the High and Low forms had to be varieties of the same language. Since ASL and English are two different languages, he suggested that language use could be better characterized as a form of bilingualism.
5. In many cases, Deaf and hard-of-hearing people, like those with typical hearing, are also users of spoken language. This likely depends on various factors such as the level of hearing that a deaf or hard of hearing person possesses as well as whether or not they participated in and benefited from speech-language therapy services.
6. Although not generally the practice, the term bimodal bilingual could, in theory, also be used to refer to Deaf ASL signers who often engage in reading and writing English. However, many Deaf people use signed, written, and spoken language for communication, which would suggest that the term *multimodal* may also be appropriate.
7. There also exists the possibility of influence of signed language on spoken language, though it is much less common. One possible example of such influence was recently offered by Bencie Woll in an online discussion of contact phenomena in sign languages (SLLING listserve, Woll 2010). Woll suggested that the term "hearing" in English, which can be used to refer to a person who can hear (usually as an adjective) may represent a loan translation or calque from a sign language

(e.g., British Sign Language) to English. Presumably, this sense of the word has been influenced greatly by the Deaf community and users of signed language.
8. See Quinto-Pozos (2007, 2009) for reviews of codeswitching phenomena in signed languages.

REFERENCES

Adam, R. 2012. Language contact and borrowing. In R. Pfau, M. Steinbach, & B. Woll (eds.), *Sign language: An international handbook*, 841–62. Berlin: Mouton de Gruyter.

Adam, Robert. (2012). Unimodal bilingualism in the Deaf community: Contact between dialects of BSL and ISL in Australia and the United Kingdom. Ph.D. dissertation, University College London.

Ajello, R., Mazzoni, L., & Nicolai, F. 2001. Linguistic gestures: Mouthing in Italian Sign Language (LIS). In P. Boyes Braem & R. Sutton-Spence (eds.), *The hands are the head of the mouth: The mouth as articulator in sign language*, 231–46. Hamburg: Signum.

Allsop, L., Woll, B., & Brauti, J. M., 1995. International sign: The creation of an international deaf community and sign language. In H. F. Bos & G. M. Schermer (eds.), *Sign Language Research 1994: Proceedings of the Fourth European Congress on Sign Language Research, Munich, September 1–3, 1994*. Hamburg: Signum.

Ann, J. 2001. Bilingualism and language contact. In C. Lucas (ed.), *The sociolinguistics of sign language*, 33–60. New York: Cambridge University Press.

Ann, J., Smith, W.H., & Yu, C. 2007. The sign language of mainland China at the Ch'iying School in Taiwan. In D. Quinto-Pozos (ed.), *Sign language contact*, 235–58. Washington, DC: Gallaudet University Press.

Baker A. E., & van den Bogaerde, B. 2008. Codemixing in signs and words in input to and output from children. In C. Plaza-Pust & E. Morales-Lopéz (eds.), *Sign bilingualism: Language development, interaction, and maintenance in sign language contact situations*, 1–27. Amsterdam: John Benjamins.

Battison, R. 1978. *Lexical borrowing in American Sign Language*. Silver Spring, MD: Linstok.

Bishop, M., & Hicks, S. 2008. Coda talk: Bimodal discourse among hearing, native signers. In M. Bishop & S. Hicks (eds.), *Hearing, mother father Deaf: Hearing people in Deaf families*, 54–96, Washington DC: Gallaudet University Press,

Bogaerde, B. van den, & Baker, A. 2005. Code mixing in mother-child interaction in deaf families. *Sign Language and Linguistics* 8: 155–78.

Boyes Braem, P. 2001. Functions of the mouthing component in the signing of deaf early and late learners of Swiss German Sign Language. In D. Brentari (ed.), *Foreign vocabulary in sign languages: A cross-linguistic investigation of word formation*, 1–47. Mahwah, NJ: Lawrence Erlbaum.

Brentari, D., & Padden, C. A. 2001. Native and foreign vocabulary in American Sign Language: A lexicon with multiple origins. In D. Brentari (ed.), *Foreign vocabulary in sign languages: A cross-linguistic investigation of word formation*, 87–119. Mahwah, NJ: Lawrence Erlbaum.

Casey, S. 2003. "Agreement" in gestures and signed languages: The use of directionality to indicate referents involved in actions. Ph.D. dissertation, University of California, San Diego.

Cokely, D. 1983. When is a pidgin not a pidgin? *Sign Language Studies* 38: 1–24.

Cormier, K., Tyrone, M., & Schembri, A. 2008. One hand or two? Nativisation of fingerspelling in ASL and BANZSL. *Sign Language and Linguistics* 11: 3–44.

Costa, A., & Santesteban, M. (2004). Lexical access in bilingual speech production: Evidence from language switching in highly proficient bilinguals and l2 learners. *Journal of Memory and Language* 50(4): 491–511.

Crasborn, O., van der Kooij, E., Waters, D., Woll, B., & Mesch, J. 2008. Frequency distribution and spreading of different types of mouth actions in three sign languages. *Sign Language and Linguistics* 11: 45–67.

Davis, J. 1989. Distinguishing language contact phenomena in ASL interpretation. In C. Lucas (ed.), *The sociolinguistics of the Deaf community*, 85–102. San Diego: Academic Press.

Davis, J. 2007. North American Indian signed language varieties: A comparative historical linguistic assessment. In D. Quinto-Pozos (ed.), *Sign languages in contact*, 85–122. Washington, DC: Gallaudet University Press.

Davis, J. 2010. *Hand talk: Sign language among Indian nations of North America.* Cambridge: Cambridge University Press.

Dugdale, P., Kennedy, G., McKee, D., & McKee, R. 2003. Aerial spelling and NZSL: A response to Forman (2003). *Journal of Deaf Studies and Deaf Education* 8: 494–97.

Ebbinghaus, H., & Hessmann, J. 2001. Sign language as multidimensional communication: Why manual signs, mouthings, and mouth gestures are three different things. In P. Boyes Braem & R. Sutton-Spence (eds.), *The hands are the head of the mouth: The mouth as articulator in sign language*, 133–51. Hamburg: Signum.

Emmorey, K., Borinstein, H., & Thompson, R. 2005. Bimodal bilingualism: Code-blending between spoken English and American Sign Language. In J. Cohen, K. T. McAlister, K. Rolstad, & J. MacSwan (eds.), *ISB4: Proceedings of the 4th International Symposium on Bilingualism*, 663–73. Somerville, MA: Cascadilla Press.

Emmorey, K., Borinstein, H., Thompson, R., & Gollan, T. 2008. Bimodal bilingualism. *Bilingualism: Language and Cognition* 11: 43–61.

Fischer, S. 1996. By the numbers: Language-internal evidence for creolization. *International Review of Sign Linguistics* 1: 1–22.

Forman, W. 2003. The ABCs of New Zealand Sign Language: Aerial spelling. *Journal of Deaf Studies and Deaf Education* 8: 92–96.

Groce, N. E. 1985. *Everyone here spoke sign language.* Cambridge, MA: Harvard University Press.

Guerra Currie, A.-M. 1999. A Mexican Sign Language lexicon: Internal and cross-linguistic similarities and variation. Ph.D. dissertation, University of Texas, Austin.

Guerra Currie, A.-M. P., Meier, R. P., & Walters, K. 2002. A cross-linguistic examination of the lexicons of four sign languages. In R. P. Meier, K. Cormier, & D. Quinto-Pozos (eds.), *Modality and structure in signed and spoken languages*, 224–36. New York: Cambridge University Press.

Hauser, P. C. 2000. An analysis of codeswitching: American Sign Language and cued English. In M. Metzger (ed.), *Bilingualism and identity in Deaf communities*, 43–78. Washington, DC: Gallaudet University Press.

Hohenberger, A., & Happ, D. 2001. The linguistic primacy of signs and mouth gestures over mouthing: Evidence from language production in German Sign Language

(DGS). In P. Boyes Braem & R. Sutton-Spence (eds.), *The hands are the head of the mouth: The mouth as articulator in sign language*, 159–89. Hamburg: Signum.

Janzen, T., & Shaffer, B. 2002. Gesture as the substrate in the process of ASL grammaticization. In R. P. Meier, K. Cormier, & D. Quinto-Pozos (eds.), *Modality and structure in signed and spoken languages*, 199–223. New York: Cambridge University Press.

Johnson, R. 1991. Sign language, culture, and community in a traditional Yucatec Maya village. *Sign Language Studies* 73: 461–74.

Johnston, T., & Schembri, A. 2007. *Australian Sign Language (Auslan): An introduction to sign language linguistics*. Cambridge: Cambridge University Press.

Kuntze, M. 2000. Codeswitching in ASL and written English language contact. In K. Emmorey & H. Lane (eds.), *The signs of language revisited: An anthology to honor Ursula Bellugi and Edward Klima*, 287–302. Mahwah, NJ: Lawrence Erlbaum.

Kyle, J., & Woll, B. 1985. *Sign language: The study of Deaf people and their language*. New York: Cambridge University Press.

Lucas, C., & Valli, C., 1992. *Language contact in the American Deaf community*. San Diego: Academic Press.

Machabée, D., 1995. Description and status of initialized signs in Quebec Sign Language, In C. Lucas (ed.) *Sociolinguistics in Deaf communities*, 29-61. Washington D.C.: Gallaudet University Press.

McClave, E. Z. 2001. The relationship between spontaneous gestures of the hearing and American Sign Language. *Gesture* 11: 51–72.

McKee, D., & Kennedy, G. 2000. Lexical comparison of signs from American, Australian, British, and New Zealand sign languages. In K. Emmorey & H. Lane (eds.), *The signs of language revisited: An anthology to honor Ursula Bellugi and Edward Klima*, 49–76. Mahwah, NJ: Lawrence Erlbaum.

McKee, R., & J. Napier. 2002. Interpreting into International Sign Pidgin. *Sign Language and Linguistics* 51: 27–54.

McKee, R.L., McKee, D., Smiler, K., & Pointon, K. 2007. Māori signs: The construction of indigenous Deaf identity in New Zealand Sign Language. In D. Quinto-Pozos (ed.), *Sign languages in contact*, 31–81. Washington, DC: Gallaudet University Press.

McNeill, D. 1992. *Hand and mind*. Chicago: University of Chicago Press.

Meuter, R., & Allport, A. (1999). Bilingual language-switching in naming: Asymmetrical costs of language selection. *Journal of Memory and Language* 40: 25–40.

Miller, C. 2001. The adaptation of loan words in Quebec Sign Language: Multiple sources, multiple processes. In D. Brentari (ed.), *Foreign vocabulary in sign language: A cross-linguistic investigation of word formation*, 139–73. Mahwah, NJ: Lawrence Erlbaum.

Murray, J. 2009. Sign Languages. In A. Iriye & P. Y. Saunier (eds.), *The Palgrave dictionary of transnational history*, 947–48. Basingstoke, UK: Palgrave Macmillan.

Muysken, P. 2000. *Bilingual speech: A typology of code-mixing*. Cambridge: Cambridge University Press.

Nonaka, A. M. 2004. The forgotten endangered languages: Lessons on the importance of remembering from Thailand's Ban Khor Sign Language. *Language in Society* 33: 737–67.

Padden, C. 1998. The ASL lexicon. *Sign Language and Linguistics* 1: 39–60.

Pietrosemoli, L. 2001. Politeness in Venezuelan Sign Language. In V. Dively, M. Metzger, S. Taub, & A. M. Baer (eds.), *Signed Languages: Discoveries from international research*, 163–79. Washington, DC: Gallaudet University Press.

Plaza-Pust, C. 2008. Why variation matters. In C. Plaza-Pust & E. Morales-Lopéz (eds.), *Sign bilingualism: Language development, interaction, and maintenance in sign language contact situations*, 73–135. Amsterdam: John Benjamins.

Quinto-Pozos, D. 2002. Contact between Mexican Sign Language and American Sign Language in two Texas border areas. Ph.D. dissertation, University of Texas at Austin.

Quinto-Pozos, D. 2007. Outlining considerations for the study of sign language contact. In D. Quinto-Pozos (ed.), *Sign languages in contact*, 1–28. Washington DC: Gallaudet University Press.

Quinto-Pozos, D. 2008. Sign language contact and interference: ASL and LSM. *Language in Society* 37: 161–89.

Quinto-Pozos, D. 2009. Code-switching between sign languages. In B. Bullock & J. Toribio (eds.), *The handbook of code-switching*, 221–37. Cambridge: Cambridge University Press.

Quinto-Pozos, D., & Mehta, S. 2010. Register variation in mimetic gestural complements to signed language. *Journal of Pragmatics* 42: 557–84.

Rosenstock, R. 2004. An investigation of international sign: Analyzing structure and comprehension. Ph.D. dissertation, Gallaudet University.

Sasaki, D. 2007. Comparing lexicons of Japanese Sign Language and Taiwan Sign Language: A preliminary study focusing on the differences in the handshape parameter. In D. Quinto-Pozos (ed.), *Sign languages in contact*, 123–50. Washington, DC: Gallaudet University Press.

Schmaling, C. 2001. ASL in northern Nigeria: Will Hausa Sign Language survive? In V. Dively, M. Metzger, S. Taub, & A. M. Baer (eds.), *Signed languages: Discoveries from international research*. 180–193. Washington, DC: Gallaudet University Press.

Schneider, E., Kozak, L. Viola, & Santiago, R. 2011. The effects of electronic communication on American Sign Language. Georgetown University Roundtable on Languages and Linguistics (GURT) 2011.

Stokoe, W. 1970. Sign language diglossia. *Studies in Linguistics* 21: 27–41.

Supalla, T., & Webb, R. 1995. The grammar of International Sign: A new look at pidgin languages. In K. Emmorey & J. Reilly (eds.), *Language, gesture, and space*, 333–52. Mahwah, NJ: Lawrence Erlbaum.

Sutton-Spence, R. 1994. The role of the manual alphabet and fingerspelling in British Sign Language. Ph.D. dissertation, University of Bristol.

Sutton-Spence, R. 1998. English verb loans in BSL. In Lucas, C. (ed.), *Pinky extension and eye gaze: Language use in Deaf communities*, 41–58. Washington DC: Gallaudet University Press.

Sutton-Spence, R. 2003. British manual alphabets in the education of Deaf people since the 17th century. In L. Monaghan, C. Schmaling, K. Nakamura, & G. T. Turner (eds.). *Many ways to be Deaf: International variation in Deaf communities*, 25–48. Washington, DC: Gallaudet University Press.

Sutton-Spence, R., & Woll, B. 1999. *The linguistics of British Sign Language: An introduction*. Cambridge: Cambridge University Press.

Tervoort, B. 1973 Could there be a human sign language? *Semiotica* 9: 347–82.

Waters, D., Campbell, R., Capek, C. M., Woll, B., David, A. S., McGuire, P. K., Brammer, M. J., & MacSweeney, M. 2007. Fingerspelling, signed language, text and picture processing in deaf native signers: The role of the mid-fusiform gyrus. *Neuroimage* 35: 1287–302.

Wilcox, S., & Wilcox, P. 1997. *Learning to see. Teaching American Sign Language as a second language.* Washington DC: Gallaudet University Press.

Woll, B., b.woll@ucl.ac.uk, (2010). *SLLING-L Digest—18 Aug 2010 (#2010–41).* [email] Message to Rannveig Sverris (rannsve@hi.is). Sent Thursday 18 July 2010, 02:20. Available at: http://listserv.linguistlist.org/cgi-bin/wa?A0=SLLING-L [Accessed 29 August 2010].

Woodward, J. 1973a. Implicational lects on the deaf diglossic continuum. Ph.D. dissertation, Georgetown University.

Woodward, J. 1973b. Some characteristics of Pidgin Sign English. *Sign Language Studies* 3: 39–46.

Woodward, J. 2000. Sign languages and sign language families in Thailand and Viet Nam. In K. Emmorey & H. Lane (eds.), *The signs of language revisited: An anthology to honor Ursula Bellugi and Edward Klima*, 23–47. Mahwah, NJ: Lawrence Erlbaum.

Yang, Jun Hui. 2008. Sign language and oral/written language in deaf education in China. In C. Plaza-Pust & E. Morales-López (eds.), *Sign bilingualism: Language development, interaction, and maintenance in sign language contact situations*, 297–331. Amsterdam: John Benjamins.

Yoel, J. 2007. Evidence for first-language attrition of Russian Sign Language among immigrants to Israel. In D. Quinto Pozos (ed.), *Sign languages in contact*, 153–91. Washington DC: Gallaudet University Press.

Yoel, J. 2009. Canada's Maritime Sign Language. Ph.D. dissertation, University of Manitoba.

PART IV

VARIATION

CHAPTER 20

SOCIOPHONETICS

MACIEJ BARANOWSKI

THE term *sociophonetics* refers to the interface of sociolinguistics and phonetics, and specifically to the use of modern phonetic methods in the quantitative analysis of language variation and change. Although its definition can be quite broad, including any sociolinguistic study involving sounds analyzed impressionistically, it usually implies the use of instrumental techniques. It remains to be seen whether sociophonetics develops into a separate discipline, with its own questions and standards of proof, or whether it continues to mark a methodological approach within variationist sociolinguistics. This chapter takes the more modest view of sociophonetics as a tool contributing to our understanding of the nature of language variation and change. Assuming a basic knowledge of acoustic phonetics, it focuses on sociophonetic methodology, with particular attention paid to the practice of acoustic vowel analysis.

The foundations of what is referred to as sociophonetics today were laid by Labov, Yeager, and Steiner (hereafter, LYS; 1972) in their seminal study of variation and change in American English vowels; the term *sociophonetics* has until recently been largely associated with acoustic vowel analysis. Although it is now broader and includes the instrumental analysis of other types of speech sounds, the acoustic analysis of vowel variation and change remains its central focus. For the first few decades following LYS, acoustic studies of vowel variation were conducted almost exclusively in the United States, first at the University of Pennsylvania, for example, Hindle (1980), Labov (1991, 1994), Ash (1996), Fought (1999), and then elsewhere, for example, Fridland (2001), Thomas (2001). The last decade has seen a rapid growth of acoustic vowel studies, both of North American English, for example, Baranowski (2007), Boberg (2008), Yaeger-Dror and Thomas (2010), and of other varieties of English, for example,

Australian English (Cox 1999), Singapore English (Deterding 2003), English English (Kerswill, Torgersen, & Fox 2008), Brunei English (Sharbawi 2006), and New Zealand English (Maclagan & Hay 2007). The *Atlas of North American English* (hereafter ANAE) by Labov, Ash, and Boberg (2006) deserves special mention as the most comprehensive and arguably most important sociophonetic study of vowel variation and change since LYS.

Most sociophonetic studies of vowels have investigated variation and changes in the position of vowels in phonetic space, measured in terms of differences in F1 and F2 (and occasionally F3, for example, Bowie 2008), over time and across different dialects or social groups. These include studies of vowel shifts mentioned above, and studies of vowel mergers (e.g., Baranowski 2013; Johnson 2010; Eberhardt 2008) and near mergers (e.g., Di Paolo & Faber 1990; Labov, Karen, & Miller 1991). Vowel duration has been studied as a factor in chain shifts (e.g., Jacewicz, Fox, & Salmons 2006; Labov & Baranowski 2006; Langstrof 2009) and mergers (Di Paolo 1992), in regional variation in American English (Jacewicz, Fox, & Salmons 2007; Tauberer & Evanini 2009) and in studies of the Scottish Vowel Length Rule (e.g., Scobbie, Hewlett, & Turk 1999).

Selection of Tokens for Analysis

The minimum number of tokens required depends on the research questions of the study and on the number of speakers involved. In studies investigating vowels, the first question to consider is whether the complete vowel systems of the informants are to be studied or whether the focus is on one or two vowels. The latter includes studies of the movement of a particular vowel in phonetic space, for example, Fabricius's (2002) study of the tensing of word-final /i/, as in *city*, *happy*, or investigations of the phonemic status of two vowels, such as studies of the *cot-caught* merger in North American English (e.g., Johnson 2010; Nycz 2011). Such studies often involve the measurement of a large number of tokens per speaker of just one or two vowel phonemes. Large numbers of tokens of a phoneme are particularly desirable when there are lexical effects at play. When there is some indication that the same phoneme may behave differently in different words depending on their frequency (Bybee 2002), for instance, then the vowel should be measured in as many different words as are available in the recording.

Many other studies, however, investigate the complete vowel systems of the informants, for example, LYS, ANAE, Baranowski (2007), Dinkin (2009), and Thomas (2001); they include the measurement of all vowel phonemes in all phonological environments relevant in a given dialect. One major advantage of this approach is that changes to a particular phoneme are often part of a larger change involving other vowels in the same subsystem. In other words, the vowel we are interested in may be affected by changes to other vowels and it itself may affect other vowels as well; looking at the whole vowel system may allow us to gain a better understanding of the mechanisms of these changes. This is seen most clearly in chain shifts, such as the Northern Cities Shift (ANAE; Gordon 2001) or the Southern Shift (ANAE; Fridland 2001; Labov 1994), where one cannot fully understand a change in one vowel without looking at changes in the rest of the system.

Another case in point is the *cot-caught* merger mentioned above. It is often part of a larger change, co-occurring with a shift in the position of other vowels, that is, the backing of /æ/ and the backing and lowering of /e/ and /ɪ/. It is a feature of Canadian English known as the Canadian Shift (see Boberg 2005), but similar developments have recently been found in sociophonetic studies of California (Eckert 2004), Charleston, South Carolina (Baranowski 2013), and Illinois (Bigham 2009). This insight would have been lost if the focus had been exclusively on the two low back vowels.

An intermediate approach is, while focusing on a particular phoneme, to include the formant measurements of a few other vowels occupying the most peripheral positions in acoustic space which are known to be stable in the speech community, that is, are not undergoing change. These vowels, for example, the highest and frontest and the lowest or most retracted, are treated as anchor points which can be used to study the relative position of other vowels and their change in apparent time. This approach was successfully adopted by Fought (1999) in her study of /uw/-fronting in Chicano English, where the vowel of *seat* and the vowel of *cot* and *father* (merged in the dialect) were used as anchor points. Fought took the ratio of the speakers' mean F2 of /uw/ to the mean F2 of the two anchor vowels as the measure of the extent of the fronting.

The difficulty here is knowing whether the vowels used as anchor points are actually stable in the community. Therefore it is best to obtain measurements of the complete vowel system for at least a selection of speakers, those representing the oldest and the youngest generations, even if the focus of the study is on one or two phonemes. Naturally, for a study of a speech community whose vowel system has not been studied systematically before, looking at the complete vowel system is the best option.

In order to measure the complete vowel systems of our informants, we first need to identify all the vowel phonemes, that is, all the relevant word classes. For British English dialects, the word classes identified by Wells (1982) can be used. Chapter 2 of the ANAE provides a list of word classes relevant to the study of American English dialects. Each of them should be assigned a unique code used in the logging of the measurements and in statistical analyses. It is best not to use phonetic symbols, as those may not be read by statistical software. The ANAE, for example, adopts the numerical codes used in the Plotnik program (Labov 2011), with a single digit identifying short vowels and double-digit codes identifying long vowels.

Normally only vowels in fully stressed syllables in mono- or disyllabic words should be selected for analysis. They should not be preceded by obstruent-liquid clusters, as those have a lowering and backing effect on the position of vowel nuclei. Therefore, for example, it is not a good idea to use the words representing Wells's (1982) lexical sets, such as *dress, trap, strut*, or *fleece*; other words representing those classes, ones without initial clusters, should be used instead. The point is not necessarily to exclude tokens with initial clusters from the study entirely, as there may be good reasons for looking at them, but to be sure to exclude them from the calculation of the vowel's mean formant values. Similarly, vowels preceded by glides, as in *weed* or *you*, are best avoided, as it is difficult to determine reliably where the consonants ends and the vowel begins in such tokens. Words with initial /h/, as in *hat* or *hit*, are the best because of the minimal effect of /h/ on the following vowel; they should be the first candidates for wordlist items.

A related requirement in selecting tokens for analysis is that they should occur in different phonological environments. Our view of the acoustic position of a vowel might be skewed if, for instance, all our tokens should have coronal onsets. One well-known case of strong allophonic differentiation in English is the influence of the preceding consonant on the extent of the fronting of /uw/: after coronals, as in *two* or *do*, /uw/ tends to be more fronted than after non-coronal consonants, as in *move* or *hoot* (ANAE: ch. 12; Fridland & Bartlett 2006). Therefore tokens of /uw/ in both environments should be measured.

Following liquids and nasals require special attention. In rhotic dialects of English, the influence of a following /r/ on the preceding vowel is so strong that such vowels form a separate sub-system and as such should be analyzed separately from tokens of the same vowel in non-rhotic environments. The influence of a following lateral is often quite strong as well. For example, in most dialects of English the fronting of back upgliding vowels /uw/, as in *too* and *food*, and /ow/, as in *go* and *boat*, is markedly less advanced when the vowel is followed by /l/, as in *tool, fool*, and *goal* and *pole*, respectively. Therefore tokens with a following /l/ should be analyzed separately, that is, they should not be included in the calculation of the mean formant values of a vowel. Similarly, tokens with following nasals may need to be analyzed separately because of the strong effect of nasals on the quality of a preceding vowel, which can lead to marked allophonic differentiation between nasal and non-nasal tokens, for example, in short-*a*, as in *ban* and *sad*, in many dialects of American English (ANAE: ch. 13.2). The influence of a following nasal can also lead to the loss of phonemic distinctions between vowels, as in the *pin-pen* merger (ANAE: 67; Baranowski 2013; Brown 1990). In the *cot-caught* merger, tokens followed by nasals and laterals tend to be higher and more retracted than when followed by other consonants, therefore they should be analyzed separately.

Finally, for those vowels which can occur in either checked or free position, for example, /ow/, as in *go* and *goat*, respectively, that is, for phonologically long vowels, both should be represented in the measurements and should be coded separately. In free position, /ow/ (*go*) tends to show more advanced fronting than in checked position (*goat*) (Labov 1994; Baranowski 2008). In Philadelphia, the nucleus of /ey/ in free position, as in *pay*, is quite open, aligning itself with the South, whereas in checked position, as in *pace*, it is being raised, a reversal of a previous lowering trend (Labov 2001; Conn 2005). Without tokens measured in both positions, coded separately, it would have been difficult to spot such differentiation. This also suggests that the coding needs to go beyond the words representing Wells's (1982) lexical sets, where FACE stands for both *pay* and *pace*, and GOAT includes *goat* and *go*.

Assuming that checked and free vowels are coded separately, the minimum number of tokens required for analysis in each category ranges from ten to fifteen. This way, the complete vowel system of a speaker of American English can be captured with the measurement of 300 to 400 tokens. Whilst more tokens can be measured if we are particularly interested a phoneme undergoing a change or if there are lexical effects at play, it is probably not a good idea to include more than three or four tokens of the same word.

Selection of the Points of Measurement

The number of points of formant measurement in the vowel can vary from a single point in the nucleus (with another at the glide) to a measurement at regular intervals, for example, every 10 milliseconds, throughout the duration of the vowel. The choice is determined by the research questions of the study. Vowel trajectories, for example, are best studied with multiple points. They may reveal important differences between regions or social groups, as found in the studies of vowel diphthongization and shifting in the South (Feagin 1996; Koops 2010; Yaeger-Dror & Thomas 2010). Detailed investigations of vowel trajectories can also improve our understanding of the mechanisms of vowel mergers, such as the *cot-caught* merger (Di Paolo 1992; Majors 2005) or the *pin-pen* merger (Scanlon & Wassink 2010).

However, while multiple measurement points can give us a wealth of information about the trajectory of a vowel, they make comparing large numbers of tokens and speakers difficult. In order to illuminate the mechanisms of language variation and change, we often need to compare speakers representing different generations and social groups. A single point of measurement in the vowel nucleus (and another at the glide) has proved to be effective at distinguishing social groups and dialect regions and identifying leaders of linguistic change. This is the approach adopted in the ANAE, which had been pioneered in LYS and has been used in numerous sociophonetic studies of vowels since, for example, Baranowski (2007), Boberg (2008), Conn (2005), Dinkin (2009), Labov (1994, 2001, 2010).

The main difficulty in this approach is deciding where in the vowel that point should be, given that the formant measurements taken at that point should best represent our overall impression of the quality of the vowel. There are two main approaches to this problem. One is to select a point after some specified amount of time from the beginning of the vowel, in order to avoid the transition from the preceding consonant. All tokens are then normally measured at the same point in time, for example, 50 milliseconds. More commonly, the point is identified as a proportion of the duration of the vowel. Evanini (2009) tested a number of different percentage points, comparing the resulting measurements with the ANAE measurements (selected individually for each token) using the same tokens, and concluded that whilst for monophthongs the 50 percent point is usually fine, the best point for diphthongs is earlier, at around 30 percent of the vowel duration.

The other approach is to try to select a point in time that is the best indication of the central tendency of the nucleus of the vowel, that is, its most important perceptual cue, which may be different for different phonemes (ANAE: 38). This is usually a point of inflection where the tongue has reached an extreme position in the nucleus before it starts moving into the glide. For short monophthongal vowels and for long upgliding vowels, this usually coincides with the lowest position of the tongue, indicated by a maximum F1 and a steady state, before it moves up again for the production of the glide or consonantal transition; the F2 is taken at the same point in time. The central tendency of ingliding vowels does not coincide with a steady state in F1 but rather with a movement towards and then away from the front or back periphery of the system. This point of inflection appears to be the best indication of the vowel's target, as in, for example, short-*a* before nasals, as in *ban* and *Sam*, in American English, or the short front vowels /ɪ/ and /e/, as in *sit* and *set*, respectively, which are tense and ingliding in Southern Shift systems (ANAE: Ch. 11; Feagin 1996). In such cases, the point of measurement is at the maximum F2, indicating the maximum peripheral displacement of the tongue, with F1 measured at the same point. For ingliding vowels at the back of the vowel space, as in the long-o vowel (*caught, off*) in New York City or Philadelphia (Labov 1994, 2006a) the maximum displacement of the tongue towards the periphery of the system is indicated by a minimum F2, which is where the formant measurement is taken for such vowels. The is the approach taken in the ANAE and in many other large-scale studies of vowel variation and change, for example, Baranowski (2013), Boberg (2008), and Dinkin (2009).

This method of selecting the point of measurement, individually for each token, while ultimately more accurate and therefore better for the purposes of investigating the often subtle differences found between speakers in studies of sound change in progress, is fairly time consuming, as it requires the visual and auditory inspection of each token. It is also less amenable to automated formant measurement, where a Praat script (Boersma & Weenink 2011) can take measurements at some predefined point in time for each vowel token automatically. There is ongoing work on improving the accuracy of automatic formant measurement for the purposes of studying vowel variation and change. William Labov's current project at the University of Pennsylvania (Labov & Rosenfelder 2010, 2011) has had promising results in this area; it provides automatic formant and duration measurement for a few thousand tokens per interview in a matter of seconds. The system requires that the complete interview be transcribed beforehand, so that the vowel tokens in the sound file can be automatically aligned with the transcript using the Penn Phonetics Lab Forced Aligner (Yuan & Liberman 2008); the formant measurements are then taken automatically at the 30 percent point. Although more work is needed—high vowels do not yet reach the level of accuracy obtained for non-high vowels—and the need for a complete transcript is a potential resource issue, this is the direction in which the field is moving, particularly for studies involving large numbers of tokens. However, for smaller sociophonetic projects, with a limited number of speakers and tokens, selecting the point of measurement individually for each token may still be the best approach.

Logging and Plotting of Measurements

Once the point of measurement is selected, the values obtained are logged in a text file, together with the appropriate vowel code, along with additional coding, for example, for style, which is then imported for plotting and statistical analyses. The logging of the measurements, even when the measurement point is selected individually for each token, can be automated with the help of a Praat script. (See the Praat User List at http://uk.groups.yahoo.com/group/praat-users/ for advice on Praat scripting.) Alternatively, Bartek Plichta's (2011) Akustyk package helps automate the analysis of formant frequencies, bandwidths, amplitudes, voicing parameters, duration, intensity, nasalization, and voice quality.

Before the measurements can be analyzed statistically, a critical next step is correcting gross errors and identifying outliers through the visual inspection of the vowel plots for each speaker. Gross errors are often due to the miscoding of a token as belonging to the wrong vowel class; such tokens can be easily spotted on a vowel plot because they usually occupy an unexpected position on the F1-F2 plane. There may also be tokens coded correctly that are clearly separated from the other tokens of the same phoneme. It is important to listen to those tokens and re-measure them if necessary. For example, if a vowel that looks to be much fronter than the other tokens of the same phoneme does *not* sound fronter than the other tokens, then this is most likely a measurement error, due to the influence of the surrounding consonants. If, however, it does sound different from the other tokens, then it is a genuine outlier that should not be discarded, as it may be an advanced token pointing in the direction of a sound change in progress; see Labov, Baranowski, and Dinkin (2010) for a discussion of how to identify outliers and of their role in the perception of sound change.

The most commonly used tool for plotting vowels on an F1-F2 chart is the Plotnik program developed by William Labov (2011); the vowel plots in the ANAE were produced with Plotnik. It is much more than a plotting system—for many researchers, it is an indispensible analytical tool. It is used to display complete vowel systems or selected subsystems, for example, back upgling vowels, short vowels, and the like, or selected phonemes or tokens. Plotnik automates the coding of tokens for their phonological environment on the basis of the spelling of the word, so that we can quickly display or highlight vowels with, for example, following nasals or liquids, or voiceless consonants; the selection criteria can also include style and stress. It calculates and displays mean values (excluding tokens before nasals and laterals) and standard deviations for all or selected vowels, and calculates T-tests of statistical significance between the mean positions of any two vowels. Tokens can be labeled automatically and connections between nuclei and glides can be plotted.

Normalization

Because young children, women, and men have different vocal tract lengths, and consequently different formant values for the same vowel phonemes, their formant measurements cannot be directly compared unless they are adjusted through normalization. The main goal of vowel normalization in sociophonetic studies is to eliminate variation due to the physical differences between speakers while preserving dialectal or sociolinguistic differences present in the speech community.

There are two main approaches to vowel normalization: vowel-intrinsic and vowel-extrinsic. Vowel-intrinsic methods use information obtained for a single vowel, such as fundamental frequency and formant values, without relying on information about the speaker's other vowels. For example, the method proposed by Syrdal and Gopal (1986) computes differences between Bark-converted F0, F1, F2 and F3 to model the degree of vowel advancement and height. One major advantage of vowel-intrinsic methods is that they do not require the measurement of the complete vowel system of a speaker. In addition, since they do not refer to the other vowels in the system, they work better in comparing language and dialects with different vowel inventories. Their main drawback, however, is that they rely heavily on F3, whose accurate measurement can be problematic. For some voices and in poor-quality recordings, a given setting of the expected number of formants may work well for F1 and F2 but not for F3; this is a particular problem for automatic formant measurement. These methods are also affected by rhoticized vowels, where F3 is lowered.

Vowel-extrinsic normalization methods use information on the formants of other vowels (usually F1 and F2) of the same speaker. They tend to be work better than vowel-intrinsic methods for the purposes of studying vowel variation and change, but they are most effective when the speaker's complete vowel system has been measured. The two most commonly used methods are those devised by Lobanov (1971) and Nearey (1977), where the formant values of a token are adjusted through an algorithm using a grand mean of the formant values of all vowel tokens; Lobanov based on z-scores, Nearey based on log-means. In a more recent method by Watt & Fabricius (2002), the centroid value used in the calculation of normalized values is based on the F1 and F2 means of the most peripheral vowels in a speaker's system: one for high front, one for high back, and one for the bottom region of the vowel space. One potential problem with this method is that it assumes a triangular shape of the vowel system, with one vowel at the bottom periphery of the system, whereas many vowel systems, at least in American English, show a butterfly-like pattern, with two low groups of vowels. Although a number of comparisons between the different normalization approaches have been made (Fabricius, Watt, & Johnson 2009; see also Labov 2006b), none of these methods can be said to be better than the others in all respects. Nearey is probably the most commonly used method in studies of American English vowels; a modified version is used in the ANAE and is implemented in the Plotnik program.

The NORM website (Thomas and Kendall 2007) provides a tool for normalizing formant measurements using different methods, including the three mentioned above, and discusses their advantages and disadvantages; see also Thomas (2011) for an accessible discussion of the differences between different normalization methods.

Consonants

The study of consonantal variation has played a central role in sociolinguistics from its beginning, with many of the early studies exploring consonantal variables, for example, rhoticity and TH-stopping in New York City (Labov 2006a [1966]), T-glottalling in Norwich (Trudgill 1974) and Glasgow (Macaulay 1977), and lenition of /tʃ/ to /ʃ/ and /r/-spirantization in Panama City (Cedergren 1973), and consonantal variables in AAVE (Wolfram 1969). In fact, the bulk of variationist sociolinguistics dealing with sounds has involved the study of consonantal variation and change. This is particularly true of the United Kingdom, where the consonants have been affected by a number of changes, such as the glottalization of voiceless stops, TH-fronting, or the retreat of H-dropping (Williams & Kerswill 1999). Variationist studies of consonants in North America have focused on stable variation in the obstruents, for example, in Philadelphia (Labov 1994, 2001), and have explored variation and change in the liquids, for example, the decline of r-lessness in the South (Feagin 1990) and New England (Nagy & Irwin 2010), the change from alveolar to dorsal /r/ in Montreal French (Sankoff & Blondeau 2007), and /l/-vocalization (Ash 1982).

The vast majority of consonantal sociolinguistic studies conducted to date, including the ones mentioned earlier, have used impressionistic measurement methods. This is because in many cases, impressionistic analysis has proved sufficient and less time consuming than instrumental analysis. Another reason is that clear-cut correlates of auditory impressions in the acoustic domain have often proved hard to find. On the other hand, auditory analysis is more subjective and tends to impose binary categorization on what may actually be phonetically gradient phenomena. Foulkes and Docherty (2006) stress that the use of instrumental methods, in addition to auditory analysis, can provide us with important new detail, unavailable through impressionistic measurement.

This approach is illustrated by their seminal work on the voicing and glottalization of voiceless stops in Newcastle and Derby (Docherty & Foulkes 1999), where acoustic displays of the speech signal were used to determine the presence or absence of an oral gesture, the presence and timing of voicing and creaky voice, the presence of a release burst, and the presence and type of stop frication. The acoustic measurements were critical in distinguishing between a number of different glottalized variants of /t/ present in Tyneside, each showing social correlations, which would have been difficult to detect impressionistically. Similarly, in Straw and Patrick's (2007) study of glottal variation in /t/ in the speech of Barbadians in Ipswich, the visual inspection of spectrograms and waveforms of every token was used to determine the presence or absence of a glottal occlusion, the duration of the gap, and the presence and location of laryngealization; see Thomas (2011) for hands-on guidance on using acoustic methods in the analysis of t-glottaling. Instrumental methods have also benefited studies of variation and change in Voice Onset Time, for example, in the English of the Shetland Islands (Scobbie 2006), and investigations of substrate effects on the voicing of final consonants, for example, in Wisconsin English (Purnell, Salmons, & Tepeli 2005).

Liquids show a particularly high level of variation, both within and across languages. One well-known case is the variation between clear and dark /l/ in English, with clear /l/s tending to be produced in syllable onsets and dark /l/s in syllable rimes. There is regional variation in both the distribution of the two variants and degree of /l/ darkening. Some dialects have been described as preferring one of the variants in both positions; for example, Welsh English and many dialects of Irish English have traditionally been reported to use clear /l/ in all positions, whereas Lancashire English, most dialects of Scottish English, New Zealand English, or American English tend to use dark /l/ in all positions (Wells 1982).

Although Sproat and Fujimura (1993), using acoustic and X-ray microbeam data, concluded that l-darkening is a purely gradient process, with the two variants forming a single phonological entity, Yuan and Liberman's (2009) large-scale study measuring l-darkening through forced alignment suggests that there are indeed two distinct categories. F2 and the difference between F2 and F1 appear to be the most important acoustic correlates of the difference between clear and dark /l/: clear /l/ shows higher F2 values than those seen in dark /l/. Carter and Local (2007) used differences in F2 in their investigation of regional variation in the distribution and degree of /l/-darkening in Newcastle-upon-Tyne and Leeds. Similarly, Recasens and Espinosa (2005) used F2 and the difference between F2 and F1 as a measure of /l/ darkening in Catalan.

Another source of sociolinguistic variation in the liquids is /l/-vocalization. It is found across the English-speaking world, for example, in many urban varieties of British English (Wells 1982; Foulkes & Docherty 1999), Glasgow (Stuart-Smith, Timmins, & Tweedie 2006), Philadelphia (Ash 1982), and Australian English and New Zealand English (Horvath & Horvath 2001). As opposed to /l/ darkening or velarization, /l/ vocalization has proved a much bigger challenge to study acoustically, as the acoustic picture of a vocalized /l/ is almost identical to that of [w] or [o]. Although F3 has a lower amplitude (it is fainter in the spectrogram) in dark /l/ in comparison with a vocalized /l/ (Thomas 2011), in practice it is difficult to distinguish between the two reliably. The search for a robust acoustic correlate of /l/ vocalization continues, with promising attempts such as Dodsworth, Plichta and Durian (2006) using formant amplitude differences between /l/ and the preceding vowel, though the effectiveness of their method has yet to be replicated.

Articulatory methods have substantially improved our understanding of variation in /l/ production. They include X-ray microbeam mentioned above, electropalatography (Scobbie & Pouplier 2010), and ultrasound tongue imaging (UTI; Gick et al. 2006). UTI holds particular promise as it is safer and less intrusive than the other methods, and it offers better coverage of the tongue.

The study of rhotics can also benefit from modern instrumental techniques. The term *rhotics* subsumes quite a diverse group of sounds, all spelt as "r" (see Van de Velde & van Hout 2001). There is the well-known effect of a lowered F3 in approximant variants of /r/, so F3 can be used as a measure of the degree of rhoticity in most dialects of English (though see Heselwood 2009). While there may be some lowering of F3 during apical trills, this is not the case in vernacular Scottish English accents, where F3 is normally flat (Stuart-Smith 2007). Uvular variants of /r/ show some raising, rather than lowering, of F3, with a lowered F2 (Thomas 2011). Another variant that shows no lowering of F3 is labiodental /r/ found in British English (Foulkes & Docherty 2000). This suggests that acoustic techniques by themselves are not sufficient for a full understanding of the production of different rhotics, and should be supplemented with articulatory methods. Indeed, considerable progress has been made in recent years in uncovering the details of /r/ variation thanks to the use of UTI, for example, in the study of /r/ in Glasgow by Lawson, Scobbie, and Stuart-Smith (2011).

Beyond Segments

Suprasegmentals have received limited attention in variationist studies in comparison with consonants and, especially, vowels. The areas that have been explored sociophonetically include variation in speech rate, rhythm, and intonation. There has been recent work on dialectal differences in speech rates, for example, between New Zealand English and American English (Robb, Maclagan, & Chen 2004), Dutch spoken in the Netherlands and in Belgium (Verhoeven, De Pauw, & Kloots 2004), or dialects of American English (Jacewicz et al. 2009). Kendall (2009) looks at variation, both individual and across speakers, in speech rate and silent pause duration in four ethnicities in North Carolina, Ohio, Texas, Washington, DC, and Newfoundland.

In the area of prosodic rhythm, sociophonetic studies have looked at substrate effects by measuring and comparing rhythm in English, a strongly stress-timed language, with varieties of English influenced by languages closer to the syllable-timed end of the rhythm spectrum. Low, Grabe, and Nolan (2000) established much of the current methodology of measuring rhythm and tested their formulas for the normalized Pairwise Variability Index by comparing rhythm in British and Singaporean English. Thomas and Carter (2006) compare the rhythm of African Americans born in the mid-nineteenth century with the speech of European American Southerners born in that period and with Southerners of both ethnicities born in the twentieth century. White and Mattys (2007) compare Standard Southern British English with Welsh, Shetland, and Orkney English, where substrate influences have resulted in more syllable-timed characteristics. Similar comparisons have been made for other languages, for example, Arabic dialects (Ghazali, Hamdi, and Barkat (2002)), and Parisian French of European and North-African origin (Fagyal 2010).

Sociolinguistic studies of intonation have focused on dialectal variation. They tend to be studies of single dialects, whose goal was not to look at inter-speaker variation, e.g. Manchester (Cruttenden 2001) and Belfast (Wells and Peppe 1996), though a number of studies have looked at inter-speaker variation in one dialect, for example, London English (Peppé, Maxim, & Wells 2000). There have also recently been a number of projects comparing different dialects, for example, the Intonational Variation in English project (Grabe 2004), exploring intonational variation in nine dialects of English spoken in the British Isles, based on different speakers controlled for dialect, age, peer group, and gender.

One prosodic feature that has attracted particular attention from sociolinguists is the rising intonation at the end of statements, referred to as uptalk or the High Rising Terminal, found particularly in Australian English (Guy et al. 1986), New Zealand English (Warren 2005), and American English (Liberman 2008). This is also one of the areas where gender differences in prosody have been explored; another is variation in F0 range and in average F0 as affected by gender and sexual identity (Podesva 2007).

Sociophonetic studies of voice quality remain a much under-researched area deserving more attention from sociolinguists. The few variationists studies that have been conducted suggest that voice quality may show correlations with social factors (Esling 1978) and may play a role in sound change. Stuart-Smith (1999), for example, found in her Glasgow study that tongue settings and other voice quality parameters were significantly correlated with age, social class, and gender. Phonation differences have been found to play a role in maintaining a distinction between tense and lax /u/ before /l/ (*fool-full*, etc.) in Utah English, where the two vowels overlapped in F1-F2; the measure used (Voice Quality Index) was the difference between the amplitudes of F0 and F1 (Di Paolo & Faber 1990). Finally, there is a growing body of research investigating correlations between the use of voice quality features such as falsetto, breathy voice, or creaky voice, and gender identity (Henton & Bladon 1988; Podesva 2007; Yuasa 2010).

Perception Studies

Although sociophonetic research has largely focused on the production side of linguistic variation, studies of speech perception have played an increasingly important role in illuminating both the mechanisms of sound change in progress and the construction of the social meaning of variation (see Drager 2010; Thomas 2002). There is a sizeable body of research exploring the connection between phonetic variables and the social characteristics of the speakers as attributed to them by listeners. One group of studies deal with the identification of speakers' dialect, that is, how accurate listeners are and what phonetic cues they rely on in their perception of different dialect regions (e.g., Clopper & Pisoni 2004; Preston 1999). Other studies explore the phonetic cues involved in the identification of speakers' ethnicity (Graff, Labov, & Harris 1986; Purnell, Idsardi, & Baugh 1999; Preston & Niedzielski 2010), sexuality (e.g., Levon 2006), and children's gender (Foulkes et al. 2010).

There is also a growing body of experimental work exploring the perception of stable sociolinguistic variation. In a series of matched-guise experiments, Campbell-Kibler (e.g., 2007) looks at the social evaluation of the (ING) variable, finding interaction between the social characteristics attributed to speakers on the basis of the phonetic realization of the variable and different social contexts, including other linguistic cues, in which the variants occur. Labov et al. (2011) test listeners' sensitivity to differences in the frequencies of (ING) variants used in the same context through matched-guise experiments using a technique of magnitude estimation (Bard, Robertson, & Sorace 1996); they draw inferences on the window of temporal resolution of the sociolinguistic monitor, its sensitivity, and the pattern of attenuation over time.

There have been a number of studies exploring the perception of sound change in progress. Labov et al. (1991) studied listeners' ability to discriminate between the vowels in the Philadelphia near-merger of /e/ and /ʌ/ before intervocalic /r/ (*ferry-furry*, etc.) using unsynthesized tokens; a follow-up study used a series of tokens re-synthesized along the *ferry-furry* continuum (Labov 2006b). Similarly, Di Paolo and Faber (1990) investigated the perception of the near merger of lax and tense vowels before /l/ in Utah English. Labov and Baranowski (2006) manipulated the duration of /e/, as in *sex*, and /o/, as in *socks*, overlapping in F1-F2 space due to the Northern Cities Shift, to test the role of duration in category identification. Labov et al. (2010) studied the role of outliers in the perception of vowel shifts in Philadelphia by using tokens of the vowel in *bad* resynthesized along the front diagonal and registering listeners' impressions of the quality of the vowel through magnitude estimation (Bard et al. 1996). Plichta and Rakerd (2010) tested the perception of the fronting of the vowel of *hot* and *sock* involved in the Northern Cities Shift by using resynthesized tokens with varying F2 values; see Plichta's Akustyk package for a vowel synthesis tool with multimedia tutorials.

In addition, a number of studies have looked at the role of active sound changes in the perception and comprehension of dialects. Labov and Ash (1997; Labov 2010: ch. 4) conducted gating experiments with spontaneous speech tokens to test the ability of listeners from Philadelphia, Chicago, and Birmingham, Alabama, to identify advanced tokens of the sound changes characterizing each of the areas, that is, Philadelphia sound changes, the Northern Cities Shift, and the Southern Shift, respectively; they concluded that the changes can lead to miscomprehension by both outsiders and members of the same speech community. Preston (2010) tested the comprehension of single-word tokens containing vowels involved in the Northern Cities Shift by listeners affected by the shift, and Fridland, Bartlett, and Kreuz (2004) explored the perceptual salience of the Southern Shift and back vowel fronting by using resynthesized tokens with shifted formant values.

Another recent line of research explores the influence of stereotypes and speakers' social characteristics on the perception of their speech. Niedzielski (1999) played tokens of /aw/, as in *house* and *about*, produced by a Detroit speaker to listeners from the same area and asked them to match their impressions of the quality of the vowel to a series of resynthesized tokens. Those listeners who had been told that the speaker was from Canada perceived the vowel to be higher than those who had been told she was from Michigan, who in turn perceived the Michigan-labeled vowel to be lower than it actually was, suggesting that dialect stereotypes affected their perceptions. Similarly, in an experiment using video guises, Plichta (2001) demonstrated that the ethnicity attributed to speakers can affect the evaluation of their speech.

Hay, Warren, and Drager (2006) showed that the perception of the distinction between the vowels in *near* and *square*, which have been undergoing a merger in New Zealand English led by low-status groups, depended on the age and socioeconomic status attributed to the speakers on the basis of photographs showing the same speakers in different guises. Similarly, Koops, Gentry, and Pantos (2008) used eye tracking to show that the perception of the *pin-pen* merger in Houston is affected by the perceived age of the speaker. These results bear upon the question of the direction and incrementation of linguistic change, suggesting that children may use correlations between speakers' social characteristics, such as age and social class, and the degree of the advancement of a change in progress (which may be below the level of conscious awareness) in the construction of a vector pointing them in the direction of the change.

The last decade has seen a dramatic rise in the popularity of the term *sociophonetics*. This is at least partly due to its convenience in that it denotes both an area within sociolinguistics dealing with speech sounds and a methodological approach involving the use of modern instrumental techniques; at the same time it differs from lab-based phonetic studies in its focus on naturally occurring speech and greater emphasis on the representativeness of the speaker sample. However, the research questions, at least for now, are essentially those of variationist sociolinguistics, centering on the mechanisms of linguistic change and on the social evaluation of variation, that is, the way social information is stored and processed. Although the use of sociophonetic methods has grown tremendously in the last decade or so, it remains to be seen whether sociophonetics develops into an independent discipline. While some sociophoneticians have suggested that their results disprove traditional architectures of grammar and models of linguistic change (e.g., Foulkes & Docherty 2006), this claim remains controversial (cf. Labov 2006b). In any case, one of the biggest challenges in this area of research will be to ascertain whether newly discovered correlations between fine phonetic detail and social characteristics of speakers (or between fine phonetic detail and social meanings in the "indexical field" (Eckert 2008)) are more than correlations: in short, to determine to what extent the socio-indexicality of variation is cognitively real and under cognitive control.

References

Ash, S. 1982. The vocalization of /l/ in Philadelphia. University of Pennsylvania dissertation.

Ash, S. 1996. Freedom of movement: /uw/-fronting in the Midwest. In J. Arnold, R. Blake, B. Davidson, S. Schwenter, & J. Solomon (eds). *Sociolinguistic variation: Data, theory, and analysis: Selected papers from NWAV 23 at Stanford*, 3–23. Stanford, CA: CSLI.

Baranowski, M. 2007. *Phonological variation and change in the dialect of Charleston, South Carolina*. Durham, NC: Duke University Press.

Baranowski, M. 2008. The fronting of the back upgliding vowels in Charleston, South Carolina. *Language Variation and Change* 20: 527–51

Baranowski, M. 2013. On the role of social factors in the loss of phonemic distinctions. *English Language and Linguistics* 17/2: 271–295.

Bard, E., Robertson, D., & Sorace, A. 1996. Magnitude estimation of linguistic acceptability. Language 72: 1–31.

Bigham, D. S. 2009. Correlation of the low-back vowel merger and TRAP-retraction. *University of Pennsylvania Working Papers in Linguistics* 15(2): Article 4.

Boberg, C. 2005. The Canadian Shift in Montreal. *Language Variation and Change* 17: 133–54.

Boberg, C. 2008. Regional phonetic differentiation in Standard Canadian English. *Journal of English Linguistics* 36: 129–54.

Boersma, P., & Weenink, D. 2011. Praat: doing phonetics by computer. [software]. Ver. 5.2.38. Retrieved 6 September 2011 from http://www.praat.org/.

Bowie, D. 2008. Acoustic characteristics of Utah's *card-cord* merger. *American Speech* 83: 35–61.

Brown, V. R. 1990. Phonetic constraints on the merger of /ɪ/ and /ɛ/ before nasals in North Carolina and Tennessee. *SECOL Review* 14: 87–100.

Bybee, J. 2002. Word frequency and context of use in the lexical diffusion of phonetically conditioned sound change. *Language Variation and Change* 14: 261–90.

Campbell-Kibler, K. 2007. Accent, (ING), and the social logic of listener perceptions. *American Speech* 82: 32–64.

Carter, P., & Local, J. 2007. F2 variation in Newcastle and Leeds English liquid system. *Journal of the International Phonetics Association* 37: 183–99.

Cedergren, H. 1973. The interplay of social and linguistic factors in Panama. Ph.D. dissertation, Cornell University.

Clopper, C. G., & Pisoni, D. B. 2004. Some acoustic cues for the perceptual categorization of American English regional dialects. *Journal of Phonetics* 32: 111–40.

Conn, J. 2005. Of "moice" and men: The evolution of a male-led sound change. Ph.D. dissertation, University of Pennsylvania.

Cox, F. 1999. Vowel change in Australian English. *Phonetica* 56: 1–27.

Cruttenden, A. 2001. Mancunian intonation and intonational representation. *Phonetica* 58: 53–80.

Deterding, D. 2003. An instrumental study of the monophthong vowels of Singapore English. *English World-Wide* 24: 1–16.

Di Paolo, M. 1992. Hypercorrection in response to the apparent merger of (ɔ) and (ɑ) in Utah English. *Language and Communication* 12: 267–92.

Di Paolo, M., & Faber, A. 1990. Phonation differences and the phonetic content of the tense-lax contrast in Utah English. *Language Variation and Change* 2: 155–204.

Dinkin, A. 2009. Dialect boundaries and phonological change in upstate New York. Ph.D. dissertation, University of Pennsylvania.

Docherty, G. J., & Foulkes, P. 1999. Derby and Newcastle: Instrumental phonetics and variationist studies. In P. Foulkes & G. J. Docherty (eds.), *Urban voices: Accent studies in the British Isles*, 47–71. London: Arnold.

Dodsworth, R., Plichta, B., & Durian, D. 2006. An acoustic study of Columbus /l/ vocalization. Paper presented at NWAV 35, Columbus, OH.

Drager, K. 2010. Sociophonetic variation in speech perception. *Language and Linguistics Compass* 4: 473–80.

Eberhardt, M. 2008. The low-back merger in the Steel City: African American English in Pittsburgh. *American Speech* 83: 284–311.

Eckert, P. 2004. California Vowels. http://www.stanford.edu/~eckert/vowels.html.

Eckert, P. 2008. Variation and the indexical field. *Journal of Sociolinguistics* 12(4): 453–76

Esling, J. 1978. The identification of features of voice quality in social groups. *Journal of the International Phonetic Association* 8: 18-23.

Evanini, K. 2009. The permeability of dialect boundaries: A case study of the region surrounding Erie, Pennsylvania. Ph.D. dissertation, University of Pennsylvania.

Fabricius, A. 2002. Weak vowels in modern RP: An acoustic study of happy-tensing and kit/schwa shift. *Language Variation and Change* 14: 211–37.

Fabricius, A. H., Watt, D., and Johnson, D. E. 2009. A comparison of three speaker-intrinsic vowel formant frequency normalization algorithms for sociophonetics. *Language Variation and Change* 21: 413–35.

Fagyal, Z. 2010. Rhythm types and the speech of working-class youth in a banlieue of Paris: The role of vowel elision and devoicing. In D. R. Preston & N. Niedzielski (eds.) *A reader in sociophonetics*, Part I, 91–132. Berlin: Mouton de Gruyter.

Feagin, C. 1990. The dynamics of a sound change in Southern States English: From r-less to r-ful in three generations. In J. Edmondson, C. Feagin, P. Mülhäusler (eds.). *Development and diversity: Linguistic variation across time and/space,* 129–46. Arlington: SIL/University of Texas.

Feagin, C. 1996. Peaks and glides in Southern States short-*a*. In G. R. Guy, C. Feagin, D. Schiffrin, & J. Baugh (eds.), *Towards a social science of language: Papers in honor of William Labov,* 135–60. Amsterdam: John Benjamins.

Fought, C. 1999. A majority sound change in a minority community: /u/-fronting in Chicano English. *Journal of Sociolinguistics* 3: 5–23

Foulkes, P., & Docherty, G. J. (eds.). 1999. *Urban voices: Accent studies in the British Isles*. London: Arnold.

Foulkes, P., & Docherty, G. J. 2000. Another chapter in the story of /r/: 'Labiodental' variants in British English. *Journal of Sociolinguistics* 4: 30–59

Foulkes, P., & Docherty, G. J. 2006. The social life of phonetics and phonology. *Journal of Phonetics* 34: 409–38.

Foulkes, P., Docherty, G. J., Khattab, G., & Yaeger-Dror, M. 2010. Sound judgements: Perception of indexical features in children's speech. In D. R. Preston & N. Niedzielski . *A reader in sociophonetics*, Part I, 327–56. Berlin: Mouton de Gruyter.

Fridland, V. 2001. Social factors in the Southern Shift: Gender, age and class. *Journal of Sociolinguistics* 5: 233–53.

Fridland, V., & Bartlett, K. 2006. The social and linguistic conditioning of back vowel fronting across ethnic groups in Memphis, Tennessee. *English Language and Linguistics* 10: 1–22.

Fridland, V., Bartlett, K., & Kreuz, R. 2004. Do you hear what I hear? Experimental measurement of the perceptual salience of acoustically manipulated vowel variants by Southern speakers in Memphis, TN. *Language Variation and Change* 16: 1–16.

Ghazali, S., Hamdi, R., & Barkat, M. 2002. Speech rhythm variation in Arabic dialects. In Bernard Bel & I. Marlin (eds.), *Proceedings of the Speech Prosody 2002 conference,* 127–32. Aix-en-Provence: Laboratoire Parole et Langage.

Gick B., Campbell, F., Oh, S., & Tamburri-Watt, L. 2006. Toward universals in the gestural organization of syllables: A cross-linguistic study of liquids. *Journal of Phonetics* 34: 49–72

Gordon, M. 2001. *Small-town values, big-city vowels: A study of the Northern Cities Shift in Michigan*. Durham, NC: Duke University Press

Grabe, E. 2004. Intonational variation in urban dialects of English spoken in the British Isles. In P. Gilles & J. Peters (eds.) *Regional variation in intonation*, 9–31. Tübingen: Niemeyer Verlag.

Graff, D., Labov, W., & Harris, W. A. 1986. Testing listeners' reactions to phonological markers of ethnic identity: A new method for sociolinguistic research. In D. Sankoff (ed.), *Diversity and diachrony*, 45–58. Amsterdam: John Benjamins.

Guy, G., Horvath, B., Vonwiller, J., Daisley, E. & Rogers, I. 1986. An intonation change in progress in Australian English. *Language in Society* 15: 23–52

Hay, J., Warren, P., & Drager, K. 2006. Factors influencing speech perception in the context of a merger-in-progress. *Journal of Phonetics* 34: 458–84.

Henton, C., & Bladon, A. 1988. Creak as a sociophonetic marker. In L. Hyman & C. N. Li (eds.) *Language, speech, and mind*, 3–29. London: Routledge.

Heselwood, B. 2009. Rhoticity without F3: Lowpass filtering, F1-F2 relations and the perceptions of rhoticity in 'NORTH-FORCE', 'START' and 'NURSE' words. *Leeds Working Papers in Linguistics and Phonetics* 14: 49–64

Hindle, D. 1980. The social and structural conditioning of phonetic variation. Ph.D. dissertation, University of Pennsylvania.

Horvath B., & Horvath R. J. 2001. A multilocality study of a sound change in progress: The case of /l/ vocalisation in New Zealand and Australian English. *Language Variation and Change* 13: 37–57.

Jacewicz, E., Fox, R. A., O'Neill, C., & Salmons, J. 2009. Articulation rate across dialect, age, and gender. *Language Variation and Change* 21: 233–56.

Jacewicz, E., Fox, R. A., & Salmons, J. 2006. Prosodic prominence effects on vowels in chain shifts. *Language Variation and Change* 18: 285–316.

Jacewicz, E., Fox, R. A., & Salmons, J. 2007. Vowel duration in three American English dialects. *American Speech* 82: 367–85.

Johnson, D. E. 2010. *Stability and change along a dialect boundary: The low vowels of southeastern New England*. Durham, NC: Duke University Press.

Kendall, T. S. 2009. Speech rate, pause, and linguistic variation: An examination through the sociolinguistic archive and analysis project. Ph.D. dissertation, Duke University.

Kerswill, P., Torgersen, E., & Fox, S. 2008. Reversing 'drift': Innovation and diffusion in the London diphthong system. *Language Variation and Change* 20:451–91.

Koops, C. 2010. /u/-fronting is not monolithic: Two types of fronted /u/ in Houston Anglos. *University of Pennsylvania Working Papers in Linguistics* 16/2: Article 14.

Koops, C., Gentry, E., & Pantos, A. 2008. The effect of perceived speaker age on the perception of PIN and PEN vowels in Houston, Texas. *University of Pennsylvania Working Papers in Linguistics* 14: 91–101.

Labov, W. 1994. *Principles of linguistic change*, vol. 1: *Internal factors*. Oxford: Blackwell.

Labov, W. 2001. *Principles of linguistic change*, vol. 2: *Social factors*. Oxford: Blackwell.

Labov, W. 2006a. *The social stratification of English in New York City*, 2nd ed. Cambridge: Cambridge University Press.

Labov, W. 2006b. A sociolinguistic perspective on sociophonetic research. *Journal of Phonetics* 34:500–15.

Labov, W. 2010. *Principles of linguistic change*, vol. 3: *Cognitive and cultural factors*. Oxford: Blackwell.

Labov, W. 2011. *Plotnik 10*. [Software] http://www.ling.upenn.edu/~wlabov/Plotnik.html.

Labov, W., & Ash, S. 1997. Understanding Birmingham. In C. Bernstein, T. Nunnally, & R. Sabino (eds.), *Language variety in the South revisited*, 508–73. Tuscaloosa: Alabama University Press.

Labov, W., Ash, S., & Boberg, C. 2006. *The atlas of North American English: Phonetics, phonology, and sound Change*. Berlin: Mouton de Gruyter.

Labov, W., Ash, S., Ravindranath, M., Weldon, T., Baranowski, M., & Nagy, N. 2011. Properties of the sociolinguistic monitor. *Journal of Sociolinguistics* 15: 431–63.

Labov, W., & Baranowski, M. 2006. 50 msec. *Language Variation and Change* 18: 1–18.

Labov, W., Baranowski, M., & Dinkin, A. 2010. The effect of outliers on the perception of sound change. *Language Variation and Change* 22: 175–90.

Labov, W., Karen, M., & Miller, C. 1991. Near mergers and the suspension of phonemic contrast. *Language Variation and Change* 3: 33–74.

Labov, W., & Rosenfelder, I. 2010. PLOTNIK/PRAAT Interaction and Automatic Vowel Analysis. Workshop at NWAV 39.

Labov, W., & Rosenfelder, I. 2011. The Philadelphia Neighborhood Corpus.

Labov, W., Yaeger, M., & Steiner, R. 1972. *A quantitative study of sound change in progress*. Vol. 1. Report on National Science Foundation Contract NSF-GS-3287. Philadelphia, U.S. Regional Survey.

Langstrof, C. 2009. On the role of vowel duration in the New Zealand English front vowel shift. *Language Variation and Change* 21: 437–53.

Lawson, E., Scobbie, J. M., & Stuart-Smith, J. 2011. The social stratification of tongue shape for postvocalic /r/ in Scottish English. *Journal of Sociolinguistics* 15: 256–68.

Levon, E. 2006. Hearing "gay": Prosody, interpretation, and the affective judgments of men's speech. *American Speech* 81: 56–78.

Liberman, M. 2008. "The phonetics of uptalk." Language Log post, available at: http://languagelog.ldc.upenn.edu/nll/?p=586. Accessed July 7, 2011.

Lobanov, B.M. 1971. Classification of Russian vowels spoken by different listeners. *Journal of the Acoustic Society of America* 49(2B): 606–08

Low, E. L., Grabe, E., & Nolan, F. 2000. Quantitative characterizations of speech rhythm: Syllable-timing in Singapore English. *Language and Speech* 43: 377–401.

Macaulay, R. K. S., 1977. *Language, social class and education: A Glasgow study*. Edinburgh: Edinburgh University Press.

Maclagan, M., & Hay, J. 2007. Getting fed up with our feet: Contrast maintenance and the New Zealand English "short" front vowel shift. *Language Variation and Change* 19: 1–25.

Majors, T. 2005. Low back vowel merger in Missouri speech: Acoustic description and explanation. *American Speech* 80: 165–79.

Nagy, N., and Irwin, P. 2010. Boston (r): Neighbo(r)s nea(r) and fa(r). *Language Variation and Change* 22: 241–78

Nearey, T. M. 1977. Phonetic feature systems for vowels. Ph.D. dissertation, University of Connecticut.

Niedzielski, N. 1999. The effect of social information on the perception of sociolinguistic variables. *Journal of Language and Social Psychology* 18: 62–85.

Nycz, J. R. 2011. Second dialect acquisition: Implications for theories of phonological representation. Ph.D. dissertation, New York University.

Peppé, S., Maxim, J., & Wells, B. 2000. Prosodic variation in southern British English. *Language and Speech* 43: 309–34.

Plichta, B. 2001. Hearing faces: The effects of ethnicity on speech perception. Paper presented at NWAV 30, Raleigh, NC.

Plichta, B. 2011. *Akustyk 1.8.3: A free Praat plug-in for sociolinguistics.* [software]. http://bartus.org/akustyk/.

Plichta, B., & Rakerd, B. 2010. Perceptions of /a/-fronting across two Michigan dialects. In D. R. Preston & N. Niedzielski (eds.) *A reader in sociophonetics*, Part I, 223–39. Berlin: Mouton de Gruyter.

Podesva R. 2007. Phonation type as a stylistic variable: The use of falsetto in constructing a persona. *Journal of Sociolinguistics* 11: 478–504

Preston, D. R. (ed.) 1999. *Handbook of perceptual dialectology*, vol. 1. Philadelphia: John Benjamins.

Preston, D. R. 2010. Belle's body just caught the fit gnat: The perception of Northern Cities Shifted Vowels by local speakers. In D. R. Preston & N. Niedzielski (eds.), *A reader in sociophonetics*, Part I. 241–52. Berlin: Mouton de Gruyter.

Preston, D. R. & Niedzielski, N. (eds.). 2010. *A reader in sociophonetics*, Part I. Berlin: Mouton de Gruyter.

Purnell, T., Idsardi, W., & Baugh, J. 1999. Perceptual and phonetic experiments on American English dialect identification. *Journal of Language and Social Psychology* 18: 10–30.

Purnell, T., Salmons, J., Tepeli, D. 2005. German substrate effects in Wisconsin English: Evidence for final fortition. *American Speech* 80: 135–64.

Recasens, D., & Espinosa, A. 2005. Articulatory, positional and coarticulatory characteristics for clear /l/ and dark /l/: evidence from two Catalan dialects. *Journal of the International Phonetic Association* 35: 1–25.

Robb, M. P., Maclagan, M. A., & Chen, Y. 2004. Speaking rates of American and New Zealand varieties of English. *Clinical Linguistics & Phonetics* 18: 1–15

Sankoff, G., & Blondeau, H. 2007. Language change across the lifespan: /r/ in Montreal French. *Language* 83: 560–88.

Scanlon, M., & Wassink, A.B. 2010. Using Acoustic Trajectory Information in Studies of Merger. *University of Pennsylvania Working Papers in Linguistics* 16/2, Article 19.

Scobbie, J. M. 2006. Flexibility in the face of incompatible English VOT systems. In L. Goldstein, D. H. Whalen, & C. T. Best (eds.), *Laboratory phonology 8*, 367–92. Berlin: Mouton de Gruyter.

Scobbie, J. M., Hewlett, N., & Turk, A. E. 1999. Standard English in Edinburgh and Glasgow: The Scottish vowel length rule revealed. In P. Foulkes and G. J. Docherty, *Urban voices, Accent studies in the British Isles*, 230–45. London: Arnold.

Scobbie, J. M. & Pouplier, M. 2010. The role of syllable structure in external sandhi: An EPG study of vocalization and retraction in word-final English /l/. *Journal of Phonetics* 38: 240–59

Sharbawi, S. H. 2006. The vowels of Brunei English: An acoustic investigation. English World-Wide 27: 247–64.

Sproat, R., & Fujimura, O. 1993. Allophonic variation in English /l/ and its implications for phonetic implementation. *Journal of Phonetics* 21: 291–311.

Straw, M., & Patrick, P. L. 2007. Dialect acquisition of glottal variation in /t/: Barbadians in Ipswich. *Language Sciences* 29: 385–407.

Stuart-Smith, J. 1999. Glasgow: Accent and voice quality. In P. Foulkes and G.J. Docherty, *Urban voices: Accent studies in the British Isles*, 203–22. London: Arnold.

Stuart-Smith, J. 2007. A sociophonetic investigation of postvocalic /r/ in Glaswegian adolescents. In J. Trouvain and W.J. Barry (eds.) *Proceedings of the 16th International Congress of Phonetic Sciences: ICPhS XVI*, 1449–452. Saarbrucken.

Stuart-Smith, J., Timmin, C., & Tweedie, F. 2006. Conservation and innovation in a traditional dialect: L-vocalization in Glaswegian. *English World-Wide* 27: 71–87.

Syrdal, A. K., & Gopal, H. S. 1986. A perceptual model of vowel recognition based on the auditory representation of American English vowels. *Journal of the Acoustical Society of America* 79:1086–100

Tauberer, J., & Evanini, K. 2009. Intrinsic vowel duration and the post-vocalic voicing effect: Some evidence from dialects of North American English. *Proceedings of Interspeech 2009*. Brighton, UK: International Speech Communication Association, 2211–214.

Thomas, E. R. 2001. *An acoustic analysis of vowel variation in New World English*. Durham, NC: Duke University Press.

Thomas, E. R. 2002. Sociophonetic approaches of speech perception experiments. *American Speech* 77: 115–47.

Thomas, E. R. 2011. *Sociophonetics: An introduction*. New York: Palgrave Macmillan.

Thomas, E. R., & Carter, P. M. 2006. Rhythm and African American English. *English World-Wide* 27: 331–55.

Thomas, E. R., & Kendall, T. 2007. NORM: The vowel normalization and plotting suite. http://ncslaap.lib.ncsu.edu/tools/norm/.

Trudgill, P. 1974. *The social differentiation of English in Norwich*. Cambridge: Cambridge University Press.

Van de Velde, H., & van Hout, R. (eds.). 2001. *'r-atics: Sociolinguistic, phonetic and phonological characteristics of /r/*. Brussels: Etudes & Travaux, ILVP.

Verhoeven, J., De Pauw, G., & Kloots, H. 2004. Speech rate in a pluricentric language: A comparison between Dutch in Belgium and the Netherlands. *Language and Speech* 47: 297–308

Warren, P. 2005. Patterns of late rising in New Zealand English: Intonational variation or intonational change? *Language Variation and Change* 17:209–30.

Watt, D., & Fabricius, A. 2002. Evaluation of a technique for improving the mapping of multiple speakers' vowel spaces in the F1 ~ F2 plane. *Leeds Working Papers in Linguistics and Phonetics* 9: 159–73.

Wells, B., & Peppe, S. 1996. Ending up in Ulster: Prosody and turn-taking in English dialects. In E. Couper-Kuhlen & M. Selting . *Prosody in conversation: Interactional studies*, 101–30. Cambridge: Cambridge University Press.

Wells, J. C. 1982. *Accents of English*. Cambridge: Cambridge University Press.

White, L., & Mattys, S. L. 2007. Rhythmic typology and variation in first and second languages. In P. Prieto, J. Mascaró, & M. J. Solé (eds.), *Segmental and prosodic issues in Romance phonology*, 237–57. Amsterdam: John Benjamins.

Williams, A., & Kerswill, P. 1999. Dialect levelling: Change and continuity in Milton Keynes, Reading and Hull. In P. Foulkes & G. J. Docherty (eds.), *Urban voices: Accent studies in the British Isles*, 141–62. London: Arnold.

Wolfram, W. 1969. *A sociolinguistic description of Detroit Negro Speech*. Washington, DC: Center for Applied Linguistics.

Yaeger-Dror, M., & Thomas, E.R. (eds.). 2010. *African American English speakers and their participation in local sound changes: A comparative study*. Publication of the American Dialect Society 94. Durham, NC: Duke University Press.

Yuan, J., & Liberman, M. 2008. Speaker identification on the SCOTUS corpus. *Proceedings of Acoustics '08*, Paris: Société Française d'Acoustique, 5687–690; software available at: http://www.ling.upenn.edu/phonetics/p2fa/.

Yuan, J., & Liberman, M. 2009. Investigating /l/ variation in English through Forced Alignment. *Proceedings of Interspeech 2009*. Brighton, UK: International Speech Communication Association, 2215–218.

Yuasa, I. P. 2010. Creaky voice: A new feminine voice quality for young urban-oriented upwardly mobile America in women? *American Speech* 85: 315–37.

CHAPTER 21

PHONOLOGY AND SOCIOLINGUISTICS

NAOMI NAGY

SINCE the 1960s, there has been a transition in the target of linguistic description, from intuitive representations of the "ideal speaker/listener" (Chomsky 1965) to naturalistic data whose gradience is quantified. The transition is captured by Pierrehumbert:

> [L]anguage exhibits variability at all levels of representation, from phonetics to phonology and syntax, right through to pragmatics. Thus the issue is how variation fits into our scientific understanding of language.... [V]ariation penetrates further into the core of the theory than generally supposed, and that variation should be exploited rather than disregarded in investigating language. (1994: 233–234)

Related to this are changing views in how human memory, and cognition more generally, work. The present chapter surveys effects of these two developments on the fields of phonology and sociolinguistics, focusing on examples that bring their domains closer. We see resulting developments in more accurate descriptions and robust theoretical models. This chapter reviews instances in which data organized by variationists have served to further develop Lexical Phonology (LP), Optimality Theory (OT), and Exemplar Theory (ET). This transition requires reexamining certain fundamental assumptions of traditional models of generative phonology. We will consider ways in which these developments have influenced sociolinguistic research design and interpretation, particularly regarding which gradient aspects are relevant to social perception and categorization. One goal of this chapter is to provide the groundwork for a unified linguistic model to be developed by collaboration across sociolinguistics, phonology, and other fields. This will allow us to better understand language within the broader context of cognition, to take into account linguistic and non-linguistic factors in an integrated fashion, and to develop formal models of observed patterns.

Phonology and Sociolinguistics: Their Divided Past

The programs of study outlined for many linguistics departments, the tables of contents of textbooks introducing the field of linguistics, and general linguistics conference programs suggest that the fields of phonology and sociolinguistics are separate. Separate faculty, different course requirements, stand-alone chapters, and parallel competing sessions exist for these fields, with little suggestion of any connection between them. Early differences between the two fields may be summarized as follows.

The goals of early mainstream American Generative Phonology were to develop a formal theory of how phonological knowledge is represented, to account for the commonalities of language, as well as the variability observed across languages, within a single formal model. Other modules of grammar were considered only to the extent that they interacted with the phonological system. A guiding principle in developing these theories was that "redundancies and variation are extracted from the signal and code and discarded rather than stored in memory" (Bybee 2010: 14–15).

The goals of traditional variationist sociolinguistics were to understand which parts of grammar are variable and what factors correlate with the variation and to understand the connections between synchronic and diachronic variation. Sociolinguists sought to understand how language change starts, progresses, and finishes (Weinreich et al. 1968). Early quantitative work examined both phonology (cf. Labov 1963, 1972) and morphosyntax (cf. Sankoff 1980). Another difference is that while formal theoreticians "have typically focused on standard varieties, [...] variationists have normally dealt with nonstandard varieties" (Mufwene 1994: 208).

There were also contrasts among some of the crucial assumptions in the two fields. Traditional Generative Phonology assumed that language universals could be observed in synchronic patterns, while sociolinguistics considered the links between diachrony and synchrony. In phonology, language units have traditionally been qualitatively distinguished and categorically distinct. The rules or constraints affecting them are categorical. Rule exceptions and variability are problematic. In contrast, sociolinguistic operations (rules or constraints) have always been probabilistic. Variation is inherent to the system (Labov 1972:

274). Multiple types of contexts, linguistic, social, and stylistic, are considered in analyzing sociolinguistic variation, while the linguistic context has privileged status in phonology.

What constituted data in the two fields also differed. In phonology, transcriptions of sounds and intuitions concerning phonological patterns were traditionally based on impressions. When the target of research was a non-native language, the phonologist generally relied on the original fieldworker's impressionistic transcriptions, assumptions about the phonemic status of the sounds being transcribed, and so forth. A single observed utterance could serve as evidence or be dismissed as a "speech error" or a "slip of the tongue" and not contribute to the model. Sociolinguistic data come from recording a variety of speakers representing a community, focusing on "natural conversation," as well as word lists and speakers' comments about their attitudes to the community and/or language.

This leads to another importance difference: in traditional Generative Phonology, the goal was to model competence, and variability was considered "just" a matter of performance. Sociolinguists take performance, constituted as multiple tokens found in actual utterances, as the target of analysis, with a preference for those utterances that occur in more naturalistic contexts rather than elicitations. Both fields seek patterns within the variability: categorical patterns in phonology and probabilistic patterns in sociolinguistics. In phonology, these are traditionally organized as phonemes, sets of surface forms that alternate categorically according to phonological context. In sociolinguistics, the unit is the variable, a set of surface forms that alternate stochastically according to linguistic and social context.

The difference is underscored by differing approaches to frequency: type-based frequencies are traditionally exploited in phonology while token-based frequencies are calculated in variationist sociolinguistics. Type frequencies are how frequently a phoneme occurs in the dictionary of a language. Token frequency is how frequently a phoneme occurs in a particular corpus of speech or text. "Type frequencies [give] information about the structure of a language, whereas token frequency reveals patterns of usage" (Hume & Mailhot 2011: 97–98). Different predictions are made by type versus token frequency statistics (see Munson 2000).

The different types of data implicate differences in methodology. Sociolinguistics began with smaller corpora than are common now: Labov's famous department store study uses four tokens from each of 264 speakers (1972: 50), and while his Martha's Vineyard study analyzed 5000 tokens of two diphthongs, acoustic analysis was reported for only 86 (14–16). Corpora are increasing in size as technology improves for the organization, processing, and storage of larger data sets. From these corpora are culled multiple examples of the variable under examination. Increasingly larger data sets are being deployed to allow for simultaneous analysis of a greater number of variables. Examples of this expanded approach include Raymond et al.'s (2006) study of some 7000 word-internal alveolar stop tokens. They found effects for the linguistic factors of word class (function vs. content word), length, and predictability; syllable position; prominence; preceding and following context; and the speaker-related factors of age, speech rate, and fluency. Similarly, Nagy and Irwin's (2010) study of more than 11,000 tokens of (r) in Eastern New England examined effects of seven linguistic factors and six social factors.

Because of the range of factors that can be examined, sociolinguistics suffers a lower degree of cross-linguistic comparability. Phonology, in contrast, seeks to identify common and/or differing patterns across languages, and refines its formal models to predict such patterns. However, there is no agreement about how many examples constitute a sufficient base on which to build a model. Indeed in phonology there is often an abstraction away from actual utterances toward an assumed underlying form of the "ideal speaker-hearer." The contrast in approaches is seen in table 21.1, which compares the number of articles that focus on single languages with those that focus on more than one language, in three representative journals:

Chronological trends in these tallies show the fields diverging in this regard: only phonology focuses increasingly on multilingual articles. The languages most often studied (in the same sample) also varies tellingly (see table 21.2).

Phonology and Sociolinguistics Have Acquired Overlaps

In spite of these different starting points, cross-disciplinary approaches arose as each field expanded. A concrete example involves fast speech rules. Subsequent to the establishment of Lexical Phonology (Kiparsky 1982), phonological rules have been proposed that apply within certain stylistic contexts. These rules apply post-lexically and are therefore exceptionless, applying whenever the context of application is met. We can see quantitative variationist approaches as expanding from a small set of explicitly defined, non-overlapping styles, in which a lenition rule categorically either does or does not apply, to a broad

Table 21.1. Language-specific vs. articles analyzing more than one language in three major journals

	Language Variation and Change	*Journal of Sociolinguistics*	*Phonology*
Years surveyed	1989–2007	1997–2008	1990–95, 2005–10
No. of language-specific articles	100	181	41
% articles to analyze >1 language	11%	28%	39%

Table 21.2. Languages examined in three major journals

Journal	English	Asian	African	Romance	Other
Language Variation and Change	53%	8%	4%	25%	10%
Journal of Sociolinguistics	62%	7%	3%	11%	17%
Phonology	17%	15%	22%	<1%	46%

range of overlapping definitions of contexts, each with an associated probability of rule application. These probabilistic distributions of stylistic variants mirror the probabilities associated with the rule application in different sectors of the community (Bell 1984), rounding out the sociolinguist's more nuanced understanding of language variation. This example highlights an important development in phonology that has contributed to the overlap of the two fields: the distinction between lexical and post-lexical rules and models that allow different types of factors to influence different types of rules (e.g., stylistic differences may influence only post-lexical rules).

Later phonological approaches emphasize a need to understand the nature of phonological rules rather than just to stipulate them. Two examples are Grounded Phonology (Archangeli & Pulleyblank 1994), wherein phonological rules and representations are phonetically motivated, and Lab Phonology (cf. Kingston & Beckman 1990), in which phonetic measures are integrated with theoretic accounts. Functional Phonology (Boersma 1998) similarly draws on connections between articulation and perception, as do Hume and Johnson (2001) and Steriade (2009). Interest grew in incorporating probabilistic factors relating to the frequency of phonological and lexical units into phonological accounts (Bod et al. 2003; Boersma & Hayes 2001; Frisch 1996; Hume 2004; Munson 2000; Pierrehumbert 2001a, 2001b; studies summarized in Bybee 2010: 20). Organizing these effects into constraint-based approaches, which focus on the aggregate effects of different rules, has been integral to this expansion. Boersma and Hayes's (2001) approach has been the most explicit regarding the incorporation of frequency effects into the phonological model by establishing probability weights that rank each constraint and change according to the frequency with which certain tokens (favored by that constraint) are encountered during the learning process.

There has been increased interest in accounting for language variation and change in formal models of phonology. For example, Guy (1991) introduced a modification of LP (Kiparsky 1982) to allow probabilistic cyclical rules: a model to predict the stochastic distribution of reduced consonant clusters. Guy and Boberg (1997) introduced the Optional Contrast Principle to further account for the distribution in the same variable, focusing on the role of similarity between adjacent segments.

Anttila (1997) proposed that variation exists where the grammar does not fully determine the output, in particular where certain constraints are not ranked with respect to each other. Nagy and Reynolds (1997: 37) presented Floating Constraints, whereby some particular constraint within a single grammar may be represented as falling anywhere within a designated range in the ranking hierarchy. Thus, two constraints that are unranked with respect to each other "float" around each other, each out-ranking the other half the time (by chance). In a model of post-tonic deletion in Faetar, this model accounts for the stochastic distribution of forms in a sample of over 600 tokens. The data suggest a gradual change in the Floating Constraint's range over time, given different distributions for older versus younger speakers. Reynolds (1994) showed that Floating Constraints account for quantitative data in other languages. Nagy and Heap (1997) further pursued this model, in morphology, showing how Floating Constraints account for the variable presence of subject pronouns in samples of Faetar and Francoprovençal from different time periods.

Zubritskaya (1997: 1) proposed a model of subsegmental phonology within OT that diverged from standard Autosegmental Phonology both in its limited use of representational distinctions and in the form of the grammar to which the representations are submitted. Capitalizing on the concept of phonological units that are invisible to parsing in certain contexts, such as floating features, she demonstrated that a model that derives the variety of surface phenomena from a single underlying representation can correctly classify the full range of Russian consonant cluster behavior in her sample.

Zubritskaya's (1994) work highlights the conflict noted in the Pierrehumbert quote cited earlier. She convincingly demonstrates the danger of proposing different (invariant) competing grammars to account for variation by showing the "unwieldy" number of grammars needed to account for "a rather trivial sound change (simple loss of assimilation)" (346–347). This echoes Pierrehumbert's (1994) generalization that, while competing grammars might be a valid account for variation between two (or a few more) discrete outcomes, they cannot account for gradient or continuous effects, as these would require "an entire continuum of grammars" (245). This number increases exponentially as we consider the simultaneous variation that occurs across the large number of variables in actual speech production.

Twenty-First-Century Rapprochement

In the past 10 years, the expansion of both fields into the same territory has made it more difficult to conceive of them as distinct fields. In contrast to the areas of increasing overlap surveyed here, research programs in each field that do not engage with the other field still exist. A key example is Substance Free Phonology, which espouses the view that "phonology consists of a set of formal properties, (e.g., organization into syllables and feet, feature spreading processes) that are modality independent and thus not based on phonetic substance" (Hale & Reiss 2000: 3). Similarly, one need not look far to find sociolinguistic analyses that do not engage with phonological theory. This section highlights advances that *do* produce greater overlap.

Following on from the earlier developments in stochastic OT (at which point Anttila [2002: 212] remarked that "it is not the business of grammatical theory to explain the effects of sex, age, style, register and social class"), Bernard et al. (2007) account for inter-speaker variation in forms of post-vocalic (r) in Boston English. They show that implicational hierarchies among constraints restrict the amount and type of variation to be expected in a grammar.

Boersma and Hayes (2001: 45) introduced an important element to stochastic OT approaches: illustrations of learnability of stochastic patterns. In their model, an algorithm directly perturbs constraint rankings in response to stochastic language data. The algorithm is error driven: it changes the ranking of the constraints only when the input data conflict with its current ranking. It assumes a continuous scale of constraint strictness, rather than discretely ranked constraints, and some noise in the model allows for the production of variable outputs when constraints are ranked close to each other.

Cutillas Espinosa (2004) gives another approach to quantifying the frequency of different forms. It differs from Boersma and Hayes's approach in proposing that each speaker has three discrete grammars rather than a grammar continuum. Each grammar is a set of constraints associated with different probabilities. Grammar 1 is the standard, prestigious variety and Grammar 3 is the local vernacular (or "native") grammar; the model requires the speaker to have access to both of these. Grammar 2 is an individual's "extremely dynamic" grammar, which is designed to convey "different sorts of social and personal meaning" (172). Grammar 2 seems to be as many different settings of the constraints' probabilities as needed to account for the contexts examined.

More constrained means of selecting optimal candidates have since appeared. Coetzee and Pater (2011) provide a concise summary of alternatives and illustrate that a Maximum Entropy Harmonic Grammar model can create an extremely good match to empirical data for consonant cluster simplification patterns.

The preceding studies bring important elements of phonological theory together with accountability to the variable patterns in naturally occurring speech. While the domain of inquiry for phonology has expanded, there is still a focus on synchronic phonological systems and the quest for universal grammar. In contrast, recent sociolinguistics seeks to understand change in a more principled way, developing constraints that account for the unidirectionality of changes and establishing driving forces for linguistic change. Among these are renewed interest in longstanding claims, such as:

- Garde's Principle: "mergers cannot be reversed by linguistic means";
- Herzog's Corollary to this: "mergers expand at the expense of distinctions";
- maximal dispersion (in acoustic space) of the phonemes of a linguistic system (noted by Martinet 1955: 62); and
- principles of chain shifting, such as the direction of shift of vowels along the interior versus peripheral zones of the vowel space (Labov 1994, 2010).

These allow for better understanding, in a phonemic context, of the sound patterns found in large-scale studies such as the *Atlas of North American English* (Labov et al. 2005) and *The World Atlas of Language Structures* (Haspelmath et al. 2005).

An understanding of the differing behaviors of children versus adults in dialect acquisition also better organizes our understanding of the types of changes to expect in different contexts. These are explicitly contrasted to account for the diffusion versus transmission of patterns of vowel shifts and mergers in Labov (2007); for short (a) patterns in New York (Dinkin 2008); and for the diffusion of (r) (the variable surfacing of coda /ɹ/ from Boston into New Hampshire) in contrast to its faithful inter-generational transmission within Boston (Nagy & Irwin 2010).

This brings us to the social side of sociolinguistics. First examined in Labov (1963), analysis of speakers' orientation or attitude has become more complete. Examples include

- interspeaker differences in life-span trajectories of use of the phonological variable (R) in Montreal French (Sankoff & Blondeau 2007);
- the use and interpretation of quotative *be like* in Britain versus the United States (Buchstaller 2006; Dailey-O'Cain 2000);
- quantification of ethnic orientation in studies of English and heritage language usage in Toronto (Hoffman & Walker 2010; Nagy 2011);
- divergence from metropolitan norms in New England (Nagy 2001; Nagy & Irwin 2010; Wood 2010);
- perception of acoustic patterns influenced by orientation (Johnson 2006; Niedzielski 1999, 2002) and social context (Dodsworth 2008); and
- folk linguistics, a subfield in which laypeople's beliefs about language inform linguistic research (Preston & Niedzielski 2009).

Exemplar models can unify such approaches with those that examine the effects of linguistic context by postulating a unified means of acquiring and organizing relevant information of many types, including phonological and social context. Bybee explains,

> Exemplar representations are rich memory representations; they contain, at least potentially, all the information a language user can perceive in a

> linguistic experience. This information consists of phonetic detail, including redundant and variable features, the lexical items and constructions used, the meaning, inferences made from this meaning and from the context, and properties of the social, physical and linguistic context. (2010: 14)

This contrasts with earlier approaches in which memory limitations were assumed to require that particular tokens of language use could not be part of permanent memory representations. As Bybee noted, "beliefs about memory limitations fuelled the search for ever simpler types of representation" (15).

Exemplar Theory (ET; Bybee 1994, 2010; Johnson 1997; Pisoni 1997) is a model of the structure of language in which each token is modeled as a constellation of factors. Every encountered token is stored in memory as an exemplar. Category structure is gradient within and across categories, and exemplars are weighted with respect to their contribution to category structure. Abstraction is implied in both acquisition and categorization of the exemplars. Each token's constellation has some features in common with every other token's. ET models the relations among factors by different strengths of connections between elements. There is no a priori assumption of which types of factors, or links between them, are most important. ET captures the trajectory of experience as tokens are accumulated through exposure to language: exposure to different sets of tokens by different speakers accounts for inter-speaker differences.

ET, with this concept of the interconnectedness of different forms according to various sorts of similarities (phonetic, semantic, social context, etc.), allows for the incorporation of the concept of indexicality: that linguistic forms acquire layers of association to certain groups of speakers (Kiesling 2010; Silverstein 2003). The connections between this approach and Labov's (1972) *indicator, marker,* and *stereotype* division of linguistic variables are neatly explained in Johnstone and Kiesling (2008), using the Pittsburgh English variable (au) to illustrate. This concept has been developed in work by Eckert (2008), Mendoza-Denton (2004) and Podesva (2007). This body of work shows important developments since Lambert and colleagues' development of matched guise studies. There we see evidence of listeners making judgments about speakers depending on which guise or variety the speaker uses (e.g., local vernacular vs. standard; Lambert et al. 1960, 1966). A crucial development in the link between sociolinguistic interest in attitude and the modeling of phonological variation was a series of matched guise studies (e.g., Campbell-Kibler 2009; Labov et al. 2011) where one phonological variable was manipulated while the rest of the recording was held constant. These show that speakers respond (with differing attitude judgments) to particular sounds rather than to the overall dialect or accent. These studies also showed that a single variable, in these cases (ing) or (r), can index a range of social information for different listeners, justifying a model in which variation along numerous linguistic and social dimensions is simultaneously incorporated.

Foulkes (2010) notes that "exemplar theory makes broad predictions about the order of indexical learning, based on (i) the overall contribution of indexical factors to the input, and (ii) the transparency of phonetic cues to the indexed category" (20). His list of predictions include a chronological sequence for the acquisition of indexical knowledge: first about the maternal voice, then other familiar individuals, then sex and age distinctions and child-directed speech, and later to less familiar individuals and dialects. He calls directly for increased collaboration between the fields of lab phonology and "adjacent fields such as language acquisition, anthropology, dialectology, sociolinguistics, bilingualism, and conversation analysis" (32), to improve our understanding of their intersections.

The role of lexical factors, such as frequency, in accounting for sociolinguistic variation as well as in phonological models constitutes another overlap between the fields. This has been seen since Phillips (1984) noted that "changes affecting the most frequent words first typically involve either vowel reduction and eventual deletion or assimilation," that is, lenition (322). Supporting this claim, Abramowicz (2007) and Dinkin (2008) show the relevance of lexical frequency to lenition but not other types of changes. Abramowicz examined (ing), finding that it was not a lenition pattern and not subject to lexical frequency effects. Dinkin contrasted short vowel centralization, a form of lenition that exhibits frequency effects, to other non-lenition patterns, such as fronting of diphthongs, which show no frequency effects. Guy (2007), Guy et al. (2008), and Coetzee and Pater (2011) illustrate that (certain) high-frequency words behave differently from lower-frequency words. Hay and Maclagan (2010) show that contexts, both phonological and social, in which reduction of intrusive (r) occurs more frequently also undergo more drastic acoustic reduction.

Through these progressions, the two fields have come to share more assumptions: phonological knowledge is now believed (by some theorists) to contain more than just categorical information, bringing it closer to the starting position of sociolinguistics, and sociolinguistics is making efforts to develop universal generalizations about sound patterns, bringing it closer to the starting position of phonology. Methods have evolved as well, often in parallel. Both fields have increased use of perception experiments, rather than relying just on production data (cf. Campbell-Kibler 2009 and Hay & Warren 2002 on the sociolinguistic side; and Boersma 1998; Flemming 2002, 2005; Hume 2004; Mielke 2003, 2005; articles collected in Hume & Johnson 2001 and Hayes, Kirchner, & Steriade 2004; and Liljencrants & Lindblom 1972 and Ohala 1993).

Larger corpora and the computational tools to manage them are being increasingly used in both fields as well. Some examples in phonology include Hayes and Cziráky Londe's (2006) analysis of Hungarian vowel harmony that used data automatically harvested via Internet searches, the UCLA Phonetic Segmental Inventory Database (UPSID) developed by Maddieson and Precoda (Reetz 2006), and Mielke's (2007) searchable database of sound patterns in 500 languages. A large-scale perception study is being conducted by Stuart-Smith (2005) and her colleagues to learn about effects of television pronunciations on adolescents.

To summarize, there are a number of crossover contexts in which researchers from one domain use insights from the other. Advances include an understanding of how sounds pattern within and across languages, insight into which patterns tend to occur systematically across languages and which do not, an enriched view of the linguistic factors (phonetic, morphologic, syntactic, etc.) that influence sound patterns, and new formal mechanisms to express generalizations. Contributions from sociolinguistics include an understanding of the range of non-linguistic factors that can influence sound patterns, an analytical approach that starts by treating all factors, linguistic and non-linguistic, as equal in terms of their potential predictive power, stochastic (vs. categorical) models of effects, and an appreciation for the role of experience as a factor influencing language shape and usage.

These changes have led to questioning some crucial assumptions in both fields. The categorical nature of phonological phenomena is challenged by findings reported in Hay and Maclagan (2010) and Pierrehumbert (2003a, esp. fig. 7B, and 2003b). Gradient information is shown to be relevant to social perception and categorization in work by Docherty and Foulkes (2005) for Tyneside variants of (t); Docherty and Foulkes (2001) for (r); and Currie Hall (2008) for the relationship between categoricity and allophony in Canadian Raising. Probabilistic information has been incorporated into phonological models (e.g., OT, discussed earlier). Probabilistic information has also been incorporated in work such as Jurafsky et al.'s (1998) study of phonetic reduction of function words, Raymond et al.'s (2006) study of word-internal alveolar stop reduction, and ET analyses, such as Hay and Maclagan's (2010) study of intrusive (r) in New Zealand English.

The existence of distinct underlying versus surface representations, and how to map between them, is reconceived in both constraint-based approaches like OT (Prince & Smolensky 1993), in which different surface forms are evaluated by a set of constraints rather than being produced by derivation from an underlying form, and in ET. Cole and Hualde (1998) critique approaches that depend on underlying representations, using arguments based in phonology (lack of ability to encode contrast), psycholinguistics (lack of ability to account for lexical retrieval experimental data), and historical linguistics (inaccurate predictions about language change). However, everything that was developed in traditional generative phonology need not be eliminated: Pierrehumbert (2003b) suggests a "form of scaffolding of abstract labels erected over the exemplar base, with connections retained to map between the two layers of representation." The transition from entirely lexical to partially abstract information during the acquisition process is explored in Docherty et al. (2006) and Beckman et al. (2007).

Major reconceptions that involve the entire field of linguistics, not just phonology, include: the very existence of the innateness of aspects of language (Mielke 2006 and 2008 question the innateness of phonological features), the concomitant possibility that universals do not in fact exist (Evans & Levinson 2009) and the primacy of synchronic explanation (Blevins 2004). This latter corresponds to an increase in the use of real-time studies in sociolinguistics, which provide evidence about how language actually changes rather than relying on assumptions that inter- and intra-speaker variability reflect diachronic variation. Such studies include Bailey et al. (1991), which illustrates the mirror images of linguistic patterning (lexical and phonological) in Texas English that come from a comparison of speakers of different ages to data collected at different time points. More recently, real-time studies of phonological change in Montreal (R) have identified life-span changes which suggest that our apparent time estimates underrepresent real time change (Sankoff & Blondeau 2007).

Methods Have Gotten More Similar Too

In sociolinguistics, databases of large corpora are used. Some important sources are the Linguistic Data Consortium (1992), which houses thousands of audio, video, and text files of many languages in many contexts; the International Corpus of English (ICE) project, consisting of one million words from each of about 20 regional varieties of spoken and written English produced post-1989 (Nelson 2010); the Sociolinguistic Archive and Analysis Project at North Carolina State University, "an interactive web-based archive of sociolinguistic recordings," which integrates playback, annotation, acoustic analysis, and corpus analysis (Kendall 2007, 2008) and the Newcastle Electronic Corpus of Tyneside English (Corrigan 2007).

Another important advance is the development of time-aligned transcription systems, such as ELAN (Max Planck Institute 2008). These allow for transcriptions in which each annotation is time-linked to a segment of the recording of the original speech event (Kendall 2007). Thus, one can search the text, which may be more broadly transcribed, and retrieve any necessary phonetic detail from the recording. This alleviates the need for pre-hoc decisions about the size of the units of analysis, the amount of context that is relevant, and the type and degree of phonetic detail. The resulting analysis can be more accountable to the original data rather than necessarily reflecting assumptions made prior to analysis (Nagy 2011).

Statistical methods have been part of sociolinguistics since its start. They are increasingly used in phonological studies as well, with probabilistic distributions, rather than just categorical ones, serving as evidence for formal theories. Some examples include statistics derived from the UPSID database and work showing gradient effects of the Obligatory Contour Principle in a variety of languages by Mester (1988), Frisch and Zawaydeh (2001), and Guy (1991).

These innovations illustrate how understanding what structures can undergo change or vary synchronically, and what types of change and variation are possible, improves theoretical models by restricting the types of possible changes (synchronic and diachronic) that should be modeled.

Phonology and Sociolinguistics in the Future: A Unified Approach

We have seen that both phonology and sociolinguistics have broadened in several ways, focusing just on the changes that give the two fields more in common. The domains of inquiry now overlap substantially in terms of what counts as relevant conditioning factors. Many tools and concepts from one field have been adapted in the other. The common core goals are now to understand language within the broader context of human cognition by taking into account both linguistic and non-linguistic factors and to develop a formal model to accurately predict observed patterns. There is a drive to understand the interaction of different types of factors to interpret (as opposed to just report) the data. There has been some success in finding a meeting ground between elegant formal theories and messy data from real speakers.

What remains to be developed is an integrated model that can simultaneously account for the effects of these many types of factors and integrate them into a cognitive model, as proposed by Hume and Nagy (2008). The goal is to develop a formal mechanism for expressing relations among linguistic elements, among the factors influencing the elements, and the interactions among the elements and factors. The relevant factors include at least

- the person's existing phonological system, including information about prosodic structure, sound and feature categories, relations among sounds (allophonic, contrastive), and so on;
- perceptual factors: quality of the acoustic/auditory cues to the identification of sounds influenced by acoustic/auditory similarity;
- production factors: the amount of precision required to produce a given sound or sequence of sounds, influenced by factors such as the complexity of the articulation and the similarity among sounds in a sequence;
- contextual probability: the probability that a linguistic element (feature, sound, contrast, morpheme, word, syllable, etc.) will occur in a particular context, as a function of frequency (type or token) and predictability (including transitional probabilities between sequences of elements);
- lexical factors such as word probability and neighborhood effects;
- cognitive factors such as attention paid to speech, saliency, generalization, and expectation; and
- social factors: the amount of social value accorded a particular sound or sequence and its associations to identity or group membership.

To this model phonology can contribute an understanding of how sounds pattern within and across languages, insight into which patterns tend to occur with systematicity across languages and which ones do not, an enriched view of the linguistic factors that influence sound patterns, and formal mechanisms to express generalizations about language across languages. An example of this sort of contribution is Currie Hall et al.'s (forthcoming) study of contrast enhancement and epenthesis (see also Hume & Mailhot in press, a study of phonologization which considers the effects of entropy and information content).

Sociolinguistics can contribute an understanding of the range of non-linguistic factors that influence sound patterns, an analytic approach that starts by treating all factors, linguistic and non-linguistic, as of equal potential to predict patterns, a conception of what types of rules are expected to be categorical, how to work with probabilistic distributions, and an appreciation for the role of experience or usage as factors dynamically influencing language's shape. Additionally, it possesses models that allow for interaction among factors. This is important in cases where, for example, phonological factors have a greater effect in one morphological class than another or where certain social factors behave differently in different sectors of society. An appealing model for this purpose is ET.

Research by many scholars, working on many languages and variables in many communities, provides an inventory of effects of various factors. This sets the stage for work toward a generalized predictive theory of the contributions of such factors. Many questions remain to be addressed, however. These include:

- Which factors interact, and why?
- Under what conditions do factors interact?
- What constrains interactions?
- How are factors weighted with respect to one another? To what extent are weightings predictable?

This sort of work necessitates collaboration among researchers from different fields. Phonologists can't do it alone, nor can sociolinguistics.

Acknowledgement

This chapter is based primarily on a paper prepared and delivered with Beth Hume at the 2008 Annual Meeting of the LSA. I am grateful to the participants in that panel and especially to Beth for constructive discussion of these issues, as well as to others, too numerous to list, who provided helpful views on the co-development of the two fields examined here.

References

Abramowicz, L. 2007. Sociolinguistics meets Exemplar Theory: Frequency and recency effects in (ing). *University of Pennsylvania Working Papers in Linguistics* 13(2): 27–38.

Anttila, A. 1997. Deriving variation from grammar. In F. Hinskens, R. van Hout, & L. Wetzels (eds.), *Variation, change and phonological Theory*, 35–68. Amsterdam: John Benjamins.

Anttila, A. 2002. Variation and phonological theory. In J. K. Chambers, P. Trudgill, & N. Schilling-Estes (eds.), *The handbook of language variation and change*, 206–43. Oxford: Blackwell.

Archangeli, D., & Pulleyblank, D. 1994. *Grounded phonology*. Cambridge, MA: MIT Press.

Bailey, G., Wikle, T., Tillery, J., & Sand, L. 1991. The apparent time construct. *Language Variation and Change* 3(3): 241–65.

Beckman, M., Munson, B., & Edwards, J. 2007. Vocabulary growth and developmental expansion of types of phonological knowledge. In J. Cole & J. Hualde (eds.), *Laboratory phonology* 9, 241–64. Berlin: Mouton de Gruyter.

Bell, A. 1984. Language style as audience design. *Language in Society* 13: 145–204.

Bernard, E., Andrus, C., & Anttila, A. 2007. Linking-r in Eastern Massachusetts and Optimality Theory. Paper presented at NWAV 37, Philadelphia, PA.

Blevins, J. 2004. *Evolutionary phonology: The emergence of sound patterns*. New York: Cambridge University Press.

Bod, R., Hay, J., & Jannedy, S. (eds.). 2003. *Probabilistic linguistics*. Cambridge, MA: MIT Press.

Boersma, P. 1998. *Functional Phonology. Formalizing the interactions between articulatory and perceptual drives*. The Hague: Holland Academic Graphics.

Boersma, P., & Hayes, B. 2001. Empirical tests of the Gradual Learning Algorithm. *Linguistic Inquiry* 32: 45–86.

Buchstaller, I. 2006. Social stereotypes, personality traits and regional perceptions displaced: Attitudes towards the "new" quotatives in the UK. *Journal of Sociolinguistics* 10: 362–81.

Bybee, J. 1994. A view of phonology from a cognitive and functional perspective. *Cognitive Linguistics* 5: 285–305.

Bybee, J. 2010. *Language, usage and cognition*. New York: Cambridge University Press.

Campbell-Kibler, K. 2009. The nature of sociolinguistic perception. *Language Variation and Change* 21: 135–56.

Chomsky, N. 1965. *Aspects of the theory of syntax*. Cambridge, MA: MIT Press.

Coetzee, A., & Pater, J. 2011. The place of variation in phonological theory. In J. Goldsmith, J. Riggle, & A. Yu (eds.), *Handbook of phonological theory*, 2nd ed., 401–434. Oxford: Wiley-Blackwell.

Cole, J., & Hualde, J. 1998. The object of lexical acquisition: A UR-free model. In M. C. Gruber, D. Higgins, K.S. Olson, & T. Wysocki (eds.), *Proceedings of the 34th Regional Meeting of the Chicago Linguistic Society* 34(2): 447–58.

Corrigan, K. 2007. *Newcastle Electronic Corpus of Tyneside English*. http://research.ncl.ac.uk/necte. Accessed March 30, 2011.

Currie Hall, K. 2008. Phonological relationships: Beyond contrast and allophony. Poster presented at the 11th Conference on Laboratory Phonology, Wellington, New Zealand.

Currie Hall, K., Wedel, A., & Ussishkin, A. 2011. Entropy as an organizing principle of phonology. *Theoretical Linguistics*. Information-Theoretic Approaches to Lingusitics, Boulder, CO. http://www.ling.osu.edu/~kchall/Hall_Wedel_Ussishkin.pdf, Accessed August 7, 2012.

Cutillas Espinosa, J. 2004. Meaningful variability: A sociolinguistically-grounded approach to variation in Optimality Theory. *International Journal of English Studies* 4(2): 165–84.

Dailey-O'Cain, J. 2000. The sociolinguistic distribution and attitudes towards focuser like and quotative like. *Journal of Sociolinguistics* 4: 60–80.

Dinkin, A. 2008. The real effect of word frequency on phonetic variation. *University of Pennsylvania Working Papers in Linguistics* 14(1): 97–106.

Docherty, G., & Foulkes, P. 2001. Variation in (r) production: instrumental perspectives. In H. Van de Velde & R. van Hout (eds.), *'R-atics: Sociolinguistic, phonetic and phonological characteristics of /r/. Etudes & Travaux* 4: 173–84.

Docherty, G., & Foulkes, P. 2005. Glottal variants of (t) in the Tyneside variety of English: An acoustic profiling study. In W. Hardcastle & J. Mackenzie Beck (eds.), *A figure of speech: A Festschrift for John Laver,* 173–99. London: Lawrence Erlbaum.

Docherty, G., Foulkes, P., Tillotson, J., & Watt, D. 2006. On the scope of phonological learning: Issues arising from socially structured variation. In L. Goldstein, D. Whalen, & C. Best (eds.), *Laboratory phonology 8,* 393–421. Berlin: Mouton de Gruyter.

Dodsworth, R. 2008. Sociological consciousness as a component of linguistic variation. *Journal of Sociolinguistics* 12: 34–57.

Eckert, P. 2008. Variation and the indexical field. *Journal of Sociolinguistics* 12(4): 453–76.

Evans, N., & Levinson, S. 2009. *The myth of language universals: Language diversity and its importance for cognitive science.* New York: Cambridge University Press.

Flemming, E. 2002. *Auditory representations in phonology.* New York: Routledge.

Flemming, E. 2005. Speech perception and phonological contrast. In D. Pisoni & R. Remez (eds.), *The handbook of speech perception,* 156–81. Oxford: Blackwell.

Foulkes, P. 2010. Exploring social-indexical knowledge: A long past but a short history. *Laboratory Phonology* 1: 5–39.

Frisch, S. 1996. Frequency and similarity in phonology. Ph.D. dissertation, Northwestern University.

Frisch, S., & Zawaydeh, B. 2001. The psychological reality of OCP-Place in Arabic. *Language* 77(1): 91–106.

Guy, G. 1991. Explanation in variable phonology: An exponential model of morphological constraints. *Language Variation and Change* 3(1): 1–22.

Guy, G. 2007. Variation and phonological theory. In R. Bayley & C. Lucas (eds.), *Sociolinguistic variation: Theories, methods, and applications,* 5–23. New York: Cambridge University Press.

Guy, G., & Boberg, C. 1997. Inherent variability and the OCP. *Language Variation and Change* 9(2): 149–64.

Guy, G., Hay, J., & Walker, A. 2008. Phonological, lexical, and frequency factors in coronal stop deletion in early New Zealand English. Paper presented at the 11th Conference on Laboratory Phonology, Wellington, New Zealand.

Hale, M., & Reiss, C. 2000. Phonology as cognition. In N. Burton-Roberts, P. Carr, & G. Docherty (eds.), *Phonological Knowledge: Conceptual and Empirical Foundations,* 161–84. Oxford: Oxford University Press.

Haspelmath, M., Dryer, M., Gil, D., & Comrie, B. 2005. *The world atlas of language structures.* Oxford: Oxford University Press.

Hay, J., & Maclagan, M. 2010. Social and phonetic conditioners on the frequency and degree of 'intrusive /r/' in New Zealand English. In D. Preston & N. Niedzielski . (eds.), *A reader in sociophonetics,* 41–70. New York: Mouton de Gruyter.

Hay, J., & Warren, P. 2002. Experiments on /r/-intrusion. *Wellington Working Papers in Linguistics* 14: 47–58.

Hayes, B., & Cziráky Londe, Z. 2006. Stochastic phonological knowledge: the case of Hungarian vowel harmony and computational power. *Phonology* 23(1): 59–104.

Hayes, B., Kirchner, R., & Steriade, D. (eds.). 2004. *Phonetically based phonology*. New York: Cambridge University Press.

Hoffman, M., & Walker, J. 2010. Ethnolects and the city: Ethnic orientation and linguistic variation in Toronto English. *Language Variation and Change* 22(1): 37–67.

Hume, E. 2004. The indeterminacy/attestation model of metathesis. *Language* 80(2): 203–37.

Hume, E. 2011. Markedness. In M. van Oostendorp, C. Ewen, E. Hume, & K. Rice (eds.), *Companion to phonology*, 79–106. Oxford: Wiley-Blackwell.

Hume, E., & Mailhot, F. In press. The role of entropy and surprisal in phonologization and language change. In A. Yu, (ed.), *Origins of sound patterns: Approaches to phonologization*. Oxford University Press.

Hume, E., & Johnson, K. 2001. *The role of speech perception in phonology*. New York: Academic Press.

Hume, E., & Nagy, N. 2008. Sociolinguistics and linguistic theories: Giving and taking—phonology. Linguistic Society of America Plenary Symposium. Chicago.

Johnson, K. 1997. Speech perception without speaker normalization: An exemplar model. In K. Johnson & J. Mullennix (eds.), *Talker variability in speech processing*, 145–65. San Diego: Academic Press.

Johnson, K. 2006. Resonance in an exemplar-based lexicon: The emergence of social identity and phonology. *Journal of Phonetics* 34: 485–99.

Johnstone, B., & Kiesling, S.F. 2008. Indexicality and experience: Exploring the meanings of /aw/-monophthongization in Pittsburgh. *Journal of Sociolinguistics* 12(1): 5–33.

Jurafsky, D., Bell, A., Fosler-Lussier, E., Girand, C., & Raymond, W.D. 1998. Reduction of English function words in Switchboard. In *Proceedings of the International Conference on Spoken Language Processing* 7: 3111–114.

Kendall, T. 2007. Enhancing sociolinguistic data collections: The North Carolina Sociolinguistic Archive and Analysis Project. *University of Pennsylvania Working Papers in Linguistics* 13(2): 15–26.

Kendall, T. 2008. On the history and future of sociolinguistic data. *Language and Linguistics Compass* 2: 332–51.

Kiesling, S. F. 2010. *Sociolinguistic variation and change*. Edinburgh: University of Edinburgh Press.

Kingston, J., & Beckman, M. (eds.). 1990. *Papers in laboratory phonology I: Between the grammar and physics of speech*. Cambridge: Cambridge University Press.

Kiparsky, P. 1982. Lexical phonology and morphology. In I. Yang (ed.), *Linguistics in the morning calm*, 3–91. Seoul: Hanshin Publishing.

Labov, W. 1963. The social motivation of a sound change. *Word* 19: 273–309.

Labov, W. 1972. *Sociolinguistic patterns*. Philadelphia: University of Pennsylvania Press.

Labov, W. 1994. *Principles of linguistic change*, vol. 1: *Internal factors*. Oxford: Blackwell.

Labov, W. 2007. Transmission and diffusion. *Language* 83: 344–87.

Labov, W. 2010. *Principles of linguistic change*, vol. 3: *Cognitive and cultural factors*. Oxford: Wiley-Blackwell.

Labov, W., Ash, S., & Boberg, C. 2005. *Atlas of North American English*. Berlin: Mouton de Gruyter.

Labov, W., Ash, S., Ravindranath M., Weldon, T., Baranowski, M., & Nagy, N. 2011. Properties of the sociolinguistic monitor. *Journal of Sociolinguistics* 15(4): 431–64.

Lambert, W. E., Frankel, H., & Tucker, R.A. 1966. Judging personality through speech: A French-Canadian example. *Journal of Communication* 16: 304–21.

Lambert, W. E., Gardner, R.C., & Fillenbaum, S. 1960. Evaluational reactions to spoken language. *Journal of Abnormal and Social Psychology* 60: 44–51.

Liljencrants, J., & Lindblom, B. 1972. Numerical simulation of vowel quality systems: The role of perceptual contrast. *Language* 48: 839–62.

Linguistic Data Consortium. 1992. http://www.ldc.upenn.edu. Accessed July 30, 2010.

Martinet, A. 1955. *Economie des changements phonétiques: Traité de phonologie diachronique.* Berne: A. Francke AAG Verlag.

Max Planck Institute. 2008. ELAN is a professional tool for the creation of complex annotations on video and audio resources. http://tla.mpi.nl/tools/tla-tools/elan/ Accessed October 1, 2012.

Mendoza-Denton, N. 2004. Language and identity. In J. K. Chambers, P. Trudgill, & N. Schilling-Estes (eds.), *Handbook of language variation and change,* 475–99. Oxford: Blackwell.

Mester, A. 1988. Dependent tier ordering and the OCP. In H. van der Hulst & N. Smith (eds.), *Features, segmental structure, and harmony processes, 127–44.* Foris: Dordrecht.

Mielke, J. 2003. The interplay of speech perception and phonology: Experimental evidence from Turkish. *Phonetica* 60(3): 208–29.

Mielke, J. 2005. Ambivalence and ambiguity in laterals and nasals. *Phonology* 22(2): 169–203.

Mielke, J. 2006. Moving beyond innate features: A unified account of natural and unnatural classes. In L. Bateman & C. Ussery (eds.), *Proceedings of NELS* 35. 435–50.

Mielke, J. 2007. *P-base.* http://aix1.uottawa.ca/~jmielke/pbase/. Accessed August 1, 2010.

Mielke, J. 2008. *The emergence of distinctive features.* Oxford: Oxford University Press.

Mufwene, S. 1994. Theoretical linguistics and variation analysis: Strange bedfellows? In K. Beals, J. Denton, R. Knippen, L. Melnar, H. Suzuki, & E. Zeinfeld (eds.), *Papers from the 30th Regional Meeting of the Chicago Linguistic Society: The Parasession on Variation in Linguistic Theory,* 202–31.

Munson, B. 2000. Phonological pattern frequency and speech production in children and adults. Ph.D. dissertation, Ohio State University.

Nagy, N. 2001. 'Live free or die' as a linguistic principle. *American Speech* 76(1): 30–41.

Nagy, N. 2011. A multilingual corpus to explore variation in language contact situations. *Rassegna Italiana di Linguistica Applicata.* 43(1-2): 65–84.

Nagy, N., & Heap, D. 1997. Subject pronoun variation in Faetar and Francoprovençal. *Papers in Sociolinguistics. NWAVE-26 à l'Université Laval,* 291–300. Québec: Nota bene.

Nagy, N., & Irwin, P. 2010. Boston (r): Neighbo(r)s nea(r) and fa(r). *Language Variation and Change* 22: 241–78.

Nagy, N., & Reynolds, W. 1997. Optimality theory and variable word-final deletion in Faetar. *Language Variation and Change* 9: 37–56.

Nelson, G. 2010. *International Corpus of English.* http://ice-corpora.net/ice/. Accessed July 9, 2010.

Niedzielski, N. 1999. The effect of social information on the perception of sociolinguistic variables. *Journal of Language and Social Psychology* 18(1): 62–85.

Niedzielski, N. 2002. Attitudes toward Midwestern American English. In D. Long & D. Preston (eds.), *Handbook of perceptual dialectology,* 323–29. Amsterdam: John Benjamins.

Ohala, J. 1993. The perceptual basis of some sound patterns. In D. Connell & A. Arvaniti (eds.), *Papers in laboratory phonology IV: Phonology and phonetic evidence,* 87–94. New York: Cambridge University Press.

Phillips, B. 1984. Word frequency and the actuation of sound change. *Language* 60: 320–432.

Pierrehumbert, J. 1994. Knowledge of variation. In K. Beals, J. Denton, R. Knippen, L. Melnar, H. Suzuki, & E. Zeinfeld (eds.), *Papers from the 30th Regional Meeting of the Chicago Linguistic Society: The Parasession on Variation in Linguistic Theory,* 232–56.

Pierrehumbert, J. 2001a. Exemplar dynamics: Word frequency, lenition, and contrast. In J. Bybee & P. Hopper (eds.), *Frequency effects and the emergence of lexical structure,* 137–57. Amsterdam: John Benjamins.

Pierrehumbert, J. 2001b. Stochastic phonology. *Glot International* 5(6): 195–207.

Pierrehumbert, J. 2003a. Phonetic diversity, statistical learning, and acquisition of phonology. *Language and Speech* 46: 115–54.

Pierrehumbert, J. 2003b. Probabilistic phonology: Discrimination and robustness. In R. Bod, J. Hay, & S. Jannedy (eds.), *Probabilistic linguistics,* 177–228. Cambridge, MA: MIT Press.

Pisoni, D. 1997. Some thoughts on "normalization" in speech perception. In K. Johnson & J. Mullennix (eds.), *Talker variability in speech processing,* 9–32. San Diego: Academic Press.

Podesva, R. 2007. Phonation type as a stylistic variable: The use of falsetto in constructing a persona. *Journal of Sociolinguistics* 11: 478–504.

Preston, D., & Niedzielski, N. 2009. Folk linguistics. In N. Coupland & A. Jaworski (eds), *The new sociolinguistics reader,* 356–73. Basingstoke, England: Palgrave/Macmillan.

Prince, A., & Smolensky, P. 1993. *Optimality theory: Constraint interaction in generative grammar.* New Brunswick: NJ: Rutgers University Center for Cognitive Science. Technical Report 2.

Raymond, W., Dautricourt, R., & Hume, E. 2006. Word-medial /t,d/ deletion in spontaneous speech: Modeling the effects of extra-linguistic, lexical, and phonological factors. *Language Variation and Change* 18(1): 55–97.

Reetz, H. 2006. *UCLA Phonological Segment Inventory Database.* http://web.phonetik.uni-frankfurt.de/upsid.html. Accessed July 9, 2010.

Reynolds, W. 1994. Variation and phonological theory. Ph.D. dissertation, University of Pennsylvania.

Sankoff, G. 1980. *The social life of language.* Philadelphia: University of Pennsylvania Press.

Sankoff, G., & Blondeau, H. 2007. Language change across the lifespan: /r/ in Montreal French. *Language* 83(3): 560–88.

Silverstein, M. 2003. Indexical order and the dialectics of social life. *Language and Communication* 23: 193–229.

Steriade, D. 2009. The phonology of perceptibility effects: The P-map and its consequences for constraint organization. In S. Inkelas & K. Hanson (eds.), *The nature of the word,* 151–80. Cambridge, MA: MIT Press.

Stuart-Smith, J. 2005. Accent change: Is television a contributory factor in accent change in adolescents? Economic and Social Research Council Award

R000239757. http://www.gla.ac.uk/schools/critical/research/fundedresearchprojects/accentchange. Accessed August 7, 2012.

Weinreich, U., Labov, W., & Herzog, M. 1968. Empirical foundations for a theory of language change. In W.P. Lehmann & Y. Malkiel (eds.), *Directions for historical linguistics: A symposium*, 95–188. Austin: University of Texas Press.

Wood, J. 2010. Short-a in Northern New England. *Journal of English Linguistics* 20: 1–31.

Zubritskaya, E. 1994. Sound change in Optimality Theory and constraint tie. In K. Beals, J. Denton, R. Knippen, L. Melnar, H. Suzuki, & E. Zeinfeld (eds.), *Papers from the 30th Regional Meeting of the Chicago Linguistic Society: The Parasession on variation in linguistic theory*, 335–49.

Zubritskaya, E. 1997. Mechanism of sound change in Optimality Theory. *Language Variation and Change* 9(1): 121–48.

CHAPTER 22

MORPHOSYNTACTIC VARIATION

RUTH KING

SINCE Labov's studies of copula variation (1969) and negative concord (1972) in African American English, morphosyntactic variation has figured in the sociolinguistic tradition of finely grained quantitative analysis of data from large linguistic corpora, involving a wide array of languages past and present. Some of this work has focused on functional, some on formal accounts of variation. The latter is the focus here.

This chapter first reviews early methodological and theoretical debates regarding the nature of variation above the level of phonology. These debates include whether or not the notion of the linguistic variable can be legitimately extended to morphosyntactic variation; the nature of the relationship between quantitative data and the statistical results based on them and linguistic competence; and what role, if any, linguistic introspection should play. The extent to which these issues have been resolved, have been transformed, or still figure in the literature, is discussed.

The bulk of the chapter is concerned with current trends in modeling morphosyntactic variation, or, put differently, with the emerging field of sociosyntax (Cornips & Corrigan 2005). There are two main responses to the question of where morphosyntactic variation comes from. One perspective involves the postulation of multiple grammars, most prominently in Kroch's Competing Grammars model (Kroch 1989, 1994, 2000). The other general perspective relies on the Minimalist operations of feature interpretation and feature checking (latterly feature valuation) to build optionality into the grammar, an approach associated with David Adger and a number of others (Adger & Smith 2005;

Adger 2006; King 2005; Nevins & Parrott 2010), which either integrates or is largely compatible with the theory of Distributed Morphology (Embick & Noyer 2007; Halle & Marantz 1993).

Early Controversies

Where Does the Sociolinguistic Variable Stop?

The sociolinguistic variable is typically exemplified with cases of phonetic and phonological variation, for example, English in(g), French (r), or Spanish final (s), where different variants may be considered "alternate ways of saying the same thing" (Labov 1972: 188).[1] Lavandera (1978), in the article that provides the subtitle for this section, challenged the idea that the sociolinguistic variable construct should be applied to variation above the level of phonology. She criticizes the fact that in some studies the variable context is reduced to a small proportion of actual tokens of the forms in question, as in Sankoff and Laberge's (1977) study of auxiliary alternation in French. She notes that for Sankoff and Laberge, copular uses of *avoir–être* do not "count" nor do tokens involving incompleted actions, where *être* is the only auxiliary possible. Thus the variable is reduced to "the one context in which they [i.e., the variants] seem not to introduce any difference in meaning and where they vary according to social and lexical constraints" (178). Lavandera also argues that in other cases, so-called variants of a sociolinguistic variable, such as active-passive alternation in English (Weiner & Labov 1977,1983), do not in fact share the same referential or truth value nor do they vary in social meaning. Such cases are not on a par with phonological variables and lead her to question the extension of the sociolinguistic variable to morphosyntax.[2]

Some 30 years later, the delimiting of the variable context, as in the French auxiliary example, is standard to variationist work. With regard to active-passive alternation (for which status as a sociolinguistic variable was also criticized by Cheshire [1987] and Romaine [1982]), Adger and Trousdale (2007: 269–270) remind us that the early variable rule framework was closely related to transformational grammar of the same period, wherein both active and passive surface structures were in fact derived from the same underlying structure, a position no longer held. Rather, as they note, "semantic interpretation was eventually concluded to be read off the output of transformations, rather than the input... [T]he semantic component can [thus] be sensitive to the different structures provided by the grammar, and it becomes a moot question as to whether two structures have the same meaning."

In much recent variationist work, the criterion of having the same referential value has been replaced, some might say relaxed, to having the same grammatical function. Schwenter and Torres-Cacoullos (2008: 10–11) make a strong argument for the latter criterion. In language change, they argue, particular variants may retain earlier functions as they grammaticalize: "Grammaticalization's retention hypothesis offers fresh insight into the polyvalence in linguistic form-function relationships: there is variation in function—a single form covers a range of meanings—as well as (the more familiar) variation in form—different forms serve the same grammatical function...functional polyvalence makes the semantic equivalence issue moot for grammaticalizing variants: we cannot circumscribe the variable context by grammatical function narrowly, since a single form may cover a range of meanings along a grammaticalization path." In their study of the rise of the present perfect in Peninsular Spanish, Schwenter and Torres-Cacoullos found usage of this variant to range from resultative at the early stage of the process to perfective at the other end: in order to capture change in progress, they argue, the variable context needs to be defined as broadly as possible. This position is also supported by non-functionalist studies of morphosyntactic change, such as King, Martineau, and Mougeon's (2011) study of the rise and ultimate domination of first-person plural *on* in French.

The Theoretical Status of Variable Rules

Variable rules were introduced in Labov (1969), with the first statistical program VARBRUL developed shortly thereafter by David Sankoff (Cedergren & Sankoff 1974).[3] Sankoff and Cedergren's original article was entitled "Variable Rules: Performance as a Statistical Reflection of Competence," building on Labov's argument that speakers possess variable constraints on usage as part of their mental grammars. They present the mathematical background for probabilistic rules and explain how "the notion of competence must be strengthened to include representation of systematic covariation between elements of language, even when this covariation cannot be described in categorical (zero-one) terms" (352). However, the concept of the variable rule was subject to a range of criticism in the late 1970s and in the 1980s, which is documented by Fasold (1991). As Fasold noted some 20 years ago, no one actually writes Labovian-style variable rules any more, and the actual status of the tables of factor weights and constraint orderings that we do find in variationist research is often under-articulated. In contrast, in variationist phonology, particularly with the rise of formal constraints-based theoretical models such as Optimality Theory, there has been a rich tradition of theoretical debate concerning probabilistic constraints for some time, as in the work of Gregory Guy and his associates (e.g., Guy 1997). Over the last decade, however, there has been a turn to theoretical (re)engagement with probabilistic grammars, as in Bender's (2001) HPSG-based analysis of copula deletion in African American

Vernacular English (AAVE), which includes probabilistic social weightings, and Bresnan, Deo, and Sharma's (2007) analysis of *be* and *'nt* variation in the *Survey of English Dialects* within the framework of Stochastic Optimality Theory. As we see below, current formal approaches to morphosyntactic variation engage with the question of whether probabilities should be built into the grammar, though there would appear to be a consensus that variant choice rather than use (i.e., social and other extragrammatical weightings), should be included such models.

The Role of Introspection

Linguistic introspection has played a limited role in sociolinguistics. Although Labov (1972: 192–199) does discuss experiments involving speakers' grammaticality judgements (on the interaction of negation with use and interpretation of the quantifier *any*), data from language use is privileged in variationist research. This, of course, presents a challenge for research in morphosyntax, given the fact that particular grammatical structures may be infrequently occurring: for example, Henry (2005: 1609) found only three tokens for the *after* perfect in a 720,000 word corpus for Belfast English, although speaker intuitions indicated it to be commonly accepted (and, indeed, it is a well-known feature of Hiberno English generally). In research that seeks to investigate idiolectal variation in this particular dialect, Henry (2005) relies on data from native speakers well known to the investigator, for whom she assembles a corpus of grammaticality judgements. She argues that "native speakers are themselves the experts on their own language varieties and it is in working with them, rather than 'studying' their output in corpus form, or looking at their responses to fixed questionnaires, that their underlying grammars can best be discovered" (1617). However, Henry's approach has come under methodological criticism for not allowing for gradient judgments and for lack of quantitative analysis (Parrott 2007b: 429). More general criticism of (sole) reliance on native-speaker grammaticality judgments is that it is often difficult to tease out what sort of knowledge the speaker is drawing on. Is knowledge of the dialect in question entirely separate from knowledge of more prestigious varieties (cf. Adger & Trousdale 2007: 265)? Is it the grammar in the narrow sense of the term, rather than other cognitive systems, which is at issue (Embick 2008:73)? In actual fact, most research on morphosyntactic variation, at least from a formal perspective, is probably not so cut and dried as to completely reject or to depend mainly on introspective data: for instance, Auger (1994) supplements data from the 1971 and 1984 sociolinguistic corpora for Montreal French with native speaker judgments, while King (2000) and Adger and Smith (2010) do the same for Acadian French and Scottish English, respectively. It is also worth noting the considerable recent literature in linguistics on this topic (for discussion, see Gervain & Zemplén 2005).

The Grammar Competition Model

The Constant Rate Effect

An important breakthrough in the study of morphosyntactic variation and change was Kroch's establishment of the Constant Rate Effect. Contrary to the widely held view that change spreads at different rates across different contexts (a view typically based on the comparison of raw frequencies), Kroch showed that the actual rate of change, measured on a logistic scale,[4] is constant. Perhaps the best-known illustration of the Constant Rate Effect is Kroch's account of the rise of periphrastic *do* in English. On the basis of data from Ellegård (1953) for the time period 1425–1600, Kroch showed that even though some constructions—seven different types were compared—displayed a higher overall rate of use of the innovating variant at particular points in time, they followed the classic S-curve of change, indicating that the increase in use across time was the same in all contexts. Kroch (1989: 199) argues that "[c]ontexts change together because they are merely surface manifestations of a single underlying change in grammar. Differences in frequency of use of a new form across contexts reflect functional and stylistic factors, which are constant across time and independent of grammar."[5] The single change underlying the rise of periphrastic *do* is taken to be the loss of V to T movement: English went from a positive to a negative setting for this parameter as main verbs ceased to raise to T. The fact that Ellegård's texts do not show categorical evidence for either setting of the V to T movement parameter would reflect grammar competition: for a considerable period of time two grammars, one with a positive setting for V to T movement (the old grammar) and one with a negative setting (the innovating grammar), were available to speakers. Since parameters are generally agreed to be set for one and only one value in a particular grammar, Kroch's postulation of multiple grammars makes variation in texts compatible with formal syntactic theory, as is discussed in the next section.[6]

A number of other studies across a range of languages have shown the Constant Rate Effect to be operative. For example, in the same 1989 article, Kroch shows that three constructions taken to be reflexes of the loss of Verb Second in Middle French—the loss of subject-auxiliary inversion, the loss of null subjects and the rise of Left Dislocation—all occur at the same rate during the period 1400 to 1700. Since Kroch's foundational work, the CRE has also been shown to be operative in cases of change in a number of languages: Kroch (1989) for Portuguese; Santorini (1992) for Yiddish; Taylor (1994) for Classical Greek; Pintzuk (1991) for Old English; and Kroch and Taylor (1997, 2000) and Kroch, Taylor, and Ringe (2000) for Middle English. These researchers have shown the same constant rate of change across constructions, reflexes of single syntactic processes.[7]

Competing Grammars

The idea that cases of variation are not contained within a single grammar, is linked to the notion of blocking effects. Kroch (1994: 180) asserts that "syntactic heads [such as Tense] behave like morphological formatives generally in being subject to the well-known Blocking Effect (Aronoff 1976), which excludes morphological doublets, and more generally, it seems, any coexisting formatives that are not functionally differentiated in a kind of global economy constraint on the storage of linguistic items." Kroch makes the case that doublets such as *dived-dove* arose in situations of language contact and dialect mixture: in this particular case, northern English dialects would have had regularized past tense forms due to contact with Scandinavian languages, caused by widespread immigration of Scandinavian speakers in the north and northeast of England during the later Old English period. Preference for regularized forms is argued to be part of second language acquisition by adults. Kroch suggests that grammars do not in fact exhibit doublets in the morphology or in the syntax, but rather they "are always the reflections of unstable competition between mutually exclusive grammatical options" (181). Since system-internal optionality is not allowed in such a model, competition between two grammars would ensue until one option wins out.[8]

Kroch and his associates' account of the loss of Verb Second in English (Kroch, Taylor, & Ringe 2000; Kroch & Taylor 2000) exemplifies the Competing Grammars model. On the basis of data from the Penn-Helsinki Corpus of Middle English, they argue that during the Middle English period there existed existed two dialects of English—a northern one and a southern one, which both had Verb Second but which differed in one crucial respect: in both dialects, topicalized structures with lexical subjects exhibited the order XP—V—S; however, in the southern dialect, topicalized structures with pronominal subjects exhibited the order XP—pro—V, that is, with the order of the verb and subject pronoun inverted. The data in 1, cited by Kroch and Taylor, are taken from Pintzuk's (1991) study of Old English word order (i.e., the source of the Middle English southern dialect pattern):

1 a & of heom twam is eall manncynn cumen (Whom 6.52)
and of them two is all mankind come
b Ælc yfel he mæg don (Whom 4.62)
each evil he can do

It is suggested that V2 was in the process of being lost at the dialect boundary, the Midlands, by the fourteenth century: Midlands speakers would have interpreted southern XP—pro—V as a violation of V2 order, leading them to conclude that their interlocutors spoke a mixed V2, non-V2 variety. Dialect accommodation on the part of the Midland speakers would then have provided the route by which they started to produce some "non-V2" usage themselves, changing the Primary Linguistic Data to which language learners were exposed.

While there is textual evidence that some southerners (notably Chaucer) picked up the northern pattern, a non-V2 grammar won out in the north and subsequently spread to the south.

Criticisms of the Model

There have been two types of criticism of Competing Grammars. One concerns a perceived lack of textual and sociohistorical evidence in support of the model. For instance, Roberts (2006) suggests that the data made available by studies of the OV to VO change in the history of English, a change that has been analyzed in terms of competing grammars by Pintzuk (e.g., 2002), do not show evidence of manipulation of high and low registers in a single text, manipulation that would be expected if the two varieties were in a classic diglossic relationship. Roberts also notes that the data do not show evidence of all the possible word orders that intrasentential codeswitching would make available, another theoretical possibility for such a model. In an otherwise favorable review, van Kemenade (2007) suggests that the type of north-south dialect contact and spread argued to be responsible for the loss of V2 in English has never actually been established. She notes that this type of relevant sociohistorical research has been conducted for small Dutch cities in the sixteenth and seventeenth centuries (Goss & Howell 2006) and, I might add, for Paris (Lodge 2004), but not for fifteenth-century London. One reply to such criticisms regarding gaps in the data is that they apply to diachronic studies in general, not just to the Competing Grammars model.

Other criticisms of the model revolve around the claim that it is overly powerful. Koopman and van der Wurff (2000: 279) argue that it is a "brute force" mechanism, leading to, as Harris and Campbell (1995: 86) put it, the postulation of "a plethora of grammars." Biberauer and Richards (2004) argue that "[g]iven n binary parameters, we must potentially allow for 2^n competing grammars, a computational nightmare," a sentiment echoed by Nevins and Parrott (2010: 1139). Kroch's response to this line of reasoning is that not all examples of, for instance, register variation should necessarily be given a Competing Grammars analysis: rather, as with any theoretical approach to variation,

> the linguist will have in practice [the problem of] distinguishing grammar competition, peripheral constructions, and E-language effects from the core object of study. When we reach the point where the linguist has as good a theoretical grasp on Universal Grammar as the language learner has an unconscious one, grammar competition will be as easily recognizable to the former as it already is to the latter. (1994: 184)

In his evaluation of Competing Grammars, Roberts (2006) gives a number of criteria for the evaluation of implementations of this model: that they provide the best linguistic analysis of the data, that grammars that are purported to be syntactically distinct should be distinct on other linguistic levels, that the different grammars be socially or contextually distinct, and that change from grammar competition to a single grammar should coincide with change in social value.

On a different note, Embick (2008) points to a particular advantage that the Competing Grammars model has over probabilistic grammar models: since the former does not encode usage probabilities, it does not have to deal with those cases of variation in which choice is socially constrained. A probabilistic approach would go against the basic assumption of modularity found in most formal models of grammar, that is, that grammar and use are modularily distinct. A response to the problem posed for probabilistic grammars is presented in Adger's recent work, discussed in the next section.

Recent Generative Approaches

As Hudson (2007: 683) notes, as recently as 1998, Wilson and Henry (2) could assert that "[t]here have been few real attempts to marry these seemingly divergent positions [i.e., variationist sociolinguistics and generative theory]." Since that time there have been a number of workshops, conferences, articles, and book-length volumes devoted to the topic, and it is fair to say that this type of work is now flourishing. A 2005 paper by David Adger and Jennifer Smith provided considerable impetus for this new research activity; I will describe that paper here before turning to more recent theorizing and ensuing debates.

Adger and Smith analyze variation in agreement marking in the vernacular spoken in the small fishing community of Buckie, in northern Scotland. Specifically, they study alternation between *was* and *were* in all plural contexts—full lexical subjects, first- and second-person pronouns—except that of the third-person plural pronoun *they*, where *were* is categorical, a pattern found in northern dialects generally.[9] The type of variation that occurs is illustrated in (2), with second-person subjects (p. 156, data from Smith's sociolinguistic corpus for Buckie);

2 a He says, 'I thocht you were a diver or somethin'
  b 'Aye, I thocht you was a scuba diver'

The relevant Buckie English paradigm is given in table 22.1. I ignore the treatment of variability with lexical subjects here as it would require an excursion into the featural systems of DPs.

In Kroch's system, *was-were* would have to be treated as doublets, subject to blocking effects, and Buckie speakers bidialectal (see Adger & Smith's fn. 8, 174). In contrast, Adger and Smith build optionality into the grammar by exploiting particular mechanisms which are part of Minimalist syntax,

Table 22.1. Copular verb paradigm for Buckie English

	Number	
Person	Singular	Plural
1st	was	was/were
2nd	was/were	was/were
3rd	was	were

specifically feature interpretation and checking (the latter recast as feature valuation in later work[10]). A long-held generative assumption is that lexical items are bundles of phonological, semantic, and syntactic features. A more recent, Minimalist assumption (Chomsky 1995) is that there are two kinds of features, interpretable, that is, those that come with a semantic interpretation, like the feature [present] on a verb and uninterpretable, that is, those that don't have a semantic interpretation, like agreement marking on a verb. Uninterpretable features must be checked and assigned a value by a matching interpretable feature. In a sentence like *They sing*, a head T[ense] bears an interpretable [tense:pres] feature and two uninterpretable features, [*u*case:nom] and [*u*num:pl]. Pronouns bear interpretable person and number features: for person, first and second person is distinguished from third person by the specification [pers:+] for first- and second persons and [pers:-] for third person, that is, third person lacks a positive specification for person. Thus Adger and Smith assume that [pers:1] and [pers:2] are the two possible feature specifications for person. In the example *They sing*, a checking relationship, called Agree, obtains between T and the pronoun and all of the uninterpretable features are checked and valued. A crucial point for the analysis below is that, while only interpretable features can affect meaning, both types of features can affect phonological form.

In order to derive combinations like *we were*, T would agree with the pronominal subject as follows:[11]

3 T[tense:past, *u*case:nom, *u*num:, *u*pers:]...pronoun [num:pl, pers:1, *u*case:] →
T[tense:past, ~~ucase~~:nom, ~~unum~~:pl:, ~~upers~~:1]...pronoun [num:pl, pers:1, *u*case:nom]

Similarly, the spell-out of *she was* would involve (4):

4 T[tense:past, *u*case:nom, *u*num:, *u*pers:]...pronoun [gen:fem, num:sg, pers:-, *u*case:] →
T[tense:past, ~~ucase~~:nom, ~~unum~~:sg:, ~~upers~~:-]...pronoun [gen:fem, pers:-, *u*case:nom]

Following Adger and Smith (2005:166), "variation will arise if there is another lexical item that can combine with the same pronominals to give the same output of interpretable features, but that has a different featural content in terms of interpretable features." In this case, they label this item *be* T2. T2 is unspecified for uninterpretable number features ([T2 [tense:past, *u*case:nom,*u*pers]).

5 [be T[tense:past, ~~ucase~~:nom, ~~unum~~:pl:, ~~upers~~:1]] spells out as *were*
6 [be T2[tense:past, ~~ucase~~:nom, ~~upers~~:1]] spells out as *was*
7 [be T2 [[tense:past, ~~ucase~~:nom, ~~upers~~:-]] cannot spell out

What prevents the non-occurring *they was*? T2 can only spell out when it has a non-third-person number specification, since it lacks a number feature. Variation, then, boils down to whether or not functional heads have an extra interpretable feature.

Adger and Smith thus provide a concrete answer to the question of how morphosyntactic variation may be represented in a grammar. As a number of subsequent writers have noted, Adger and Smith's model (see fn. 3, 174) closely resembles Distributed Morphology: most obviously, it relies on late insertion of morphological features (in comparison to an early Minimalist approach whereby lexical items would enter the Numeration (and undergo Merge and Agree) fully specified for morphophonological features). Other work from the same period (indeed other researchers who present rather similar proposals, such as King 2005 and Parrott 2007a) fully embraces a Distributed Morphology approach (Halle & Marantz 1993; Embick & Noyer 2007) to cases of variable agreement. Distributed Morphology is a formal framework within Minimalism in which formal features are manipulated in the syntactic component of the grammar: Vocabulary Items (the actual sound and meaning correspondences) are only inserted at PF. Morphology is not limited to the Lexicon, but phenomena that are morphological in nature are distributed throughout the grammar. We will not dwell on these different implementations of optionality here, since the discussion takes another turn fairly quickly, to the relationship between optionality and probabilistic grammars, to be discussed below.

Combinatorial Variability

Adger's (2006) paper builds on the work presented in the preceding section. He argues that grammars contain an evaluation metric that chooses the optimal set of uninterpretable feature specifications for lexical items, an operation which captures both patterns of variability and categoriality in the grammar. Further, such a metric can predict particular probability distributions of forms. Adger exemplifies the Combinatorial Variability model with the variable discussed in the preceding section, *was/were* variation in Buckie English.

Table 22.2. The Buckie paradigm

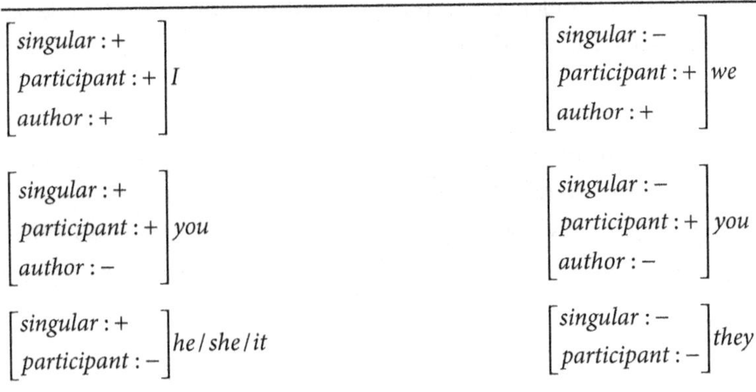

[*singular*:+, *participant*:+, *author*:+] *I*	[*singular*:–, *participant*:+, *author*:+] *we*
[*singular*:+, *participant*:+, *author*:–] *you*	[*singular*:–, *participant*:+, *author*:–] *you*
[*singular*:+, *participant*:–] *he/she/it*	[*singular*:–, *participant*:–] *they*

Returning to the set of uninterpretable features necessary to derive the correct outputs for the Buckie data, Adger (drawing on Halle 1997 and Harley & Ritter 2002) assumes that the following features are associated with (English) pronouns: [singular:+/-], [author:+/-] and [participant:+/-], displayed in the Buckie paradigm in table 22.2 (taken from Adger 2006: 520).

From the six lexical items (i.e., feature bundles) generated, the evaluation metric leads the learner of Buckie Engish to reduce optionality, synonymy, and the actual size of the lexicon to the following:[12]

8 (a) [*u*singular:+] was
  (b) [*u*singular:-] were
  (c) [*u*participant:+] was
  (d) [*u*author:-] were
  (e) [*u*author:+] was

To see the metric in operation, consider the second-person singular, where both *you was* and *you were* are possible: [singular:+, participant:+, author:-]. The evaluation metric predicts this order of forms: (a) *was*; (c) *was*; (d) *were*. The uneven distribution of forms is predicted to be as follows: if a choice of variant is made x times, then the surface form of the variant will be *was* 0.66x times and *were* 0.33x times. This prediction is borne out, in fact, as 69 percent of second-person singular tokens found in the corpus were for *was*; thus, the combinatorial properties of the system makes the correct prediction in terms of frequency of distribution.[13]

It must be borne in mind that Buckie *was/were* variation is a long-term pattern of variation, holding across generations with little or no social differentiation (Adger 2006: 525) so the quantitative patterns regarding *was/were* usage are largely unperturbed by social phenomena. The model aggregates all of the data for the variable (a decision justified on the grounds that large amounts of data are needed to run the algorithm), and variation arising from differing performance on the basis of social factors is not computed. Adger (2006: 527; see as well Adger 2007) is clear that the model is not intended to incorporate social information: "In my model, the input probabilities for the set of lexical items that constitute variants are all equal, but I agree with Bender [see above] that certain social and psychological factors may very well alter these input probabilities. I disagree that there is any need to build these social factors into the linguistic information on input probabilities, however." Adger and Smith (2010) extend the model to several other cases of variation in Buckie English and suggest that it provides superior modeling of the variation than do other formal analyses of the same or similar phenomena, as well as analyses involving surface, construction-based constraints.

Variation and Impoverishment Theory

While Adger locates variation in the feature specification of lexical items, in a 2010 article Nevins and Parrott focus on postsyntactic morphological rules. They provide an approach to cases of what they term paradigmatic syncretism, such as *was-were* leveling, within a Distributed Morphology model that makes crucial use of Impoverishment rules, that is, markedness-induced deletion rules that operate during the postsyntactic morphological computation to the PF interface to produce loss of otherwise-expected 'rich' morphological distinctions. One of the cases they consider is the Buckie example discussed above, to which we return here.

First I introduce the relevant theoretical background. Vocabulary Insertion must obey the Subset Principle (Halle 1997, among others).

9 The Subset Principle for Vocabulary Insertion
The Subset Clause: A phonological exponent realizes a morpheme in a terminal string if the item matches all or a subset of the grammatical features specified in the terminal morpheme. Insertion does not take place if the Vocabulary Item contains features not present in the morpheme.
The Maximal Subset Clause: Where several Vocabulary items meet the conditions for insertion, the item matching the greatest number of features specified in the terminal morpheme must be chosen.

A suppletion mechanism called Fusion will combine the features of the adjoined terminals BE and T[φ + past] to produce the following Vocabulary item for (Standard) English past tense BE:

10 Vocabulary of [BE φ + past]

[-pl]	↔	was
elsewhere	↔	were

In keeping with the crosslinguistic literature on markedness, Nevins and Parrott assume that the positive value of all three phi features (±participant, ±author and ±plural) are marked.

In their account of *was*-leveling with pronominal subjects in Buckie English, Nevins and Parrott propose that past tense BE contains two homophonous items for *were* and an elsewhere (i.e., default) item for *was*.[14] They follow Adger and Smith's set of combinatorial phi-features for English, with the exception that number is [± plural] rather than [± singular], as the notation in 10 shows. Recall that in this variety, *were* is categorical in the third-person plural while there is variation in the first- and second-person pronouns, pronouns that share a marked feature [+participant]. Because Buckie levels to *was*, it is assumed to be the default form:

11 Vocabulary of [BE φ + past], Buckie

[+part −auth]	↔	were
[+pl]	↔	were
elsewhere	↔	was

Nevins and Parrott (2010: 1146) propose a variable Impoverishment rule that deletes all of T's phi features when T has a [+participant] feature: "This allows variable insertion of the elsewhere exponent *was*...[this rule] will not apply when T's participant feature has a negative value." They argue that an advantage of their model over Adger's model is that it identifies the actual source of leveling through its markedness component: they note, for example, that in the present tense, *am* could never be inserted as a result of Impoverishment because it is the most specified member of the paradigm. Adger's model, they suggest, could potentially generate a wide range of patterns, including *am*-leveling.

On the other hand, Nevins and Parrott acknowledge that Adger's approach does allow the modeling of frequency in the proportion of variants, as we have seen above. Nevins and Parrott (2010: 1156) state that their own model is in fact compatible with the Labovian probabilistic variable rule model, but leave it, as they say, "an open question whether it is necessary or desirable to capture usage frequencies over community-level dialects within a formal model of an individual's grammar." Like Adger (2007) and Embick (2008), at this point at least, they maintain a strictly modular view of grammar.

Conclusions

The approaches to morphosyntactic variation developed in the past decade present, like the Competing Grammars model, a welcome *rapprochement* between formal theory and variationist linguistics. It is important to keep in mind, though, that some of the methodological problems raised by the 1970s research have not disappeared: the newer approaches require relatively high levels of frequency of variants, something that clearly obtains for the variable agreement phenomena that have provided recent case studies. Like the Competing Grammars model, the focus of most recent theorizing is on how to capture variation within the grammar, in essence the same focus as in the early days of variationist sociolinguistics. In current generative-inspired research on morphosyntactic variation, though, a line is generally drawn between grammar and use. That said, the extension of the object of study to morphosyntactic variation would now appear to be uncontroversial.

Acknowledgment

The initial impetus for this paper was an invitation from Karin Corrigan and Leonie Cornips to contribute to their 2005 volume on "reconciling the biological and the social," for which I analyzed variable agreement phenomena in Acadian French within a Distributed Morphology framework. This work in turn led me on an excursion into general issues in modeling morphosyntactic variation. Thanks to Karin and Leonie, and to the present volume's editors Robert Bayley and Richard Cameron for their comments and encouragement. All errors are my own. This research has been funded by Standard Research Grants from the Social Sciences and Humanities Research Council of Canada.

Notes

1. Note, though, that Labov (1972: 188) does illustrate this definition with some examples of syntactic variation, including "syntactic options such as *Who is he talking to?* vs. *To whom is he talking?* or *It's easy for him to talk* vs. *For him to talk is easy.*" See as well Labov's (1978) reply to Lavandera's general criticisms.
2. In recent work in qualitative sociolinguistics, the idea of "one form, one social meaning" even for phonological variables is questioned, on the grounds that it assumes a direct, indexical relationship between linguistic form and social group membership, regarded as overly simplistic. See Coupland (2007: 18–24) for a discussion of social meaning and indexicality, along with Eckert (2011) for an outline of "third wave" variationist research.
3. An offshoot of the original program, GoldVarb (Sankoff, Tagliamonte & Smith 2005), is today standard to much variationist analysis, although some attractive alternatives, such as R-Varb (Paolillo 2002) and RBrul (Johnson 2009) are also current. See Gorman and Johnson, in chapter 11, this volume.
4. See Kroch (1989) for equations for calculating the logistic and related technical details.
5. As Pintzuk, Tsoulas, & Warner (2000: 15, following on Kroch 1989) note, the Constant Rate Effect raises a problem for functional accounts of language change,

as from such a perspective one would expect the rate of change to differ across contexts in terms of their functional potential.

6. I present the argument here in the "classic" sense of Principles and Parameters at the time of Kroch's writing. The nature and status of parameters within the Minimalist Program is a matter of much current theoretical debate (see Newmeyer 2005; Roberts & Holmberg 2005; Boeckx 2010, among others).
7. Note that this concentration on particular European languages is necessitated by the fact that the Constant Rate Effect can only be tested on languages for which there is a rich historical record: large amounts of data spread across two or three centuries which exhibit examples with the change having taken place and examples of it not having taken place.
8. Embick (2008) recasts Kroch's proposal in terms of Distributed Morphology: in a grammar with *dove*, DIVE would be a listed Vocabulary Item whereas in a grammar with *dived*, DIVE would not be listed. See Embick for technical details.
9. The article also deals with a second case of variation, involving negative declaratives, which I leave aside since much of the relevant new literature deals with agreement phenomena.
10. Within the (early) Minimalist Program (see Chomsky 1995), case is viewed as a "pure" uninterpretable feature, i.e., it does not get matched with an interpretable case feature in some minimal domain. Thus [*u*case:] on the pronoun is checked by *u*case:nom on the Tense head in the example here, even though both are uninterpretable features. However, in *Derivation by Phase*, Chomsky (2001) moves from the notion of feature checking to feature valuation, motivated by the traditional idea that structural case is derived. Under this approach, arguments would enter the derivation with an unvalued case feature. An agreement operation would then value the phi-features of the Case assigner (in this instance, T(ense) and it would also value the Case feature of the nominal argument appropriate to the type of Case assigner (in this instance, nominative).
11. For simplicity of explanation, I leave aside all other aspects of the derivation, except to note that the pronominal subject will be Merged in the specifier position of VP while the copula will be Merged to the left of vP. Movement processes will eventually position the subject to the left of T and the copula in T (see Adger & Smith for details).
12. The evaluation metric is as follows: Seek Maximal Generalization by (a) generating all n-feature LIs, where n = 1; (b) mapping them to form, so that a successful mapping is made which the LI always matches—essentially reduces multiple exponence (Reject Optionality); (c) delete any spurious LIs (i.e., delete each n-feature LI and check if coverage is reduced; if it is, reinstate, if not continue)—essentially reduces synonymy (Reject Synonymy); and (d) Recursing over n = n + 1, with the proviso that if a form has been successfully analyzed in the n-1th step, LIs capturing it in the nth step will be rejected (Minimize Lexicon; Adger & Smith 2010: 1111).
13. Note that Adger suggests that social/external factors are responsible for the variation between the predicted 66 percent and the actual 69 percent *was* occurrence in the corpus.
14. Recall that Adger (2006: 521) proposes two different Vocabulary Items for *were*, one the invariable [*u*author:-] *were* (*they were*) and another to allow for [*u*singular:-] *were* (since *you were* is a possible form). Note as well that Nevins and Parrott

ignore *was*-leveling with full lexical subjects here since they present an additional complication (see Adger & Smith 2005).

References

Adger, D. 2006. Combinatorial variability. *Journal of Linguistics* 42: 503–30.

Adger, D. 2007. Variability and modularity: A response to Hudson. *Journal of Linguistics* 43: 695–700.

Adger, D., & Smith, J. 2005. Variation and the minimalist program. In L. Cornips & K. Corrigan (eds.), *Syntax and variation: Reconciling the biological and the social*, 149–78. Amsterdam: John Benjamins.

Adger, D., & Smith, J. 2010. Variation in agreement: A lexical feature-based approach. *Lingua* 120: 1109–134.

Adger, D., & Trousdale, G. 2007. Variation in English syntax: Theoretical implications. *English Language and Linguistics* 11(2): 261–78.

Aronoff, M. 1976. *Word formation in generative grammar.* Cambridge: MIT Press.

Auger, J. 1994. Pronominal clitics in Quebec colloquial French: A morphological analysis. Ph.D. dissertation, University of Pennsylvania.

Bender, E. 2001. Syntactic variation and linguistic competence. Ph.D. dissertation, Stanford University.

Biberauer, T., & Richards, M. 2004. True optionality: When the grammar doesn't mind. Handout from Minimalist Theorizing Workshop, Indiana University, June 6, 2004.

Boeckx, C. 2010. What principles and parameters got wrong. http://ling.auf.net/lingbuzz/001118.

Bresnan, J., Deo, D., & Sharma, D. 2007. Typology in variation: A probabilistic approach to be and n't in the Survey of English Dialects. *English Language and Linguistics* 11: 301–46.

Cedergren, H., & Sankoff, D. 1974. Variable rules as a statistical reflection of competence. *Language* 50: 333–35.

Cheshire, J. 1987. Syntactic variation, the linguistic variable, and sociolinguistic theory. *Linguistics* 25: 257–82.

Chomsky, N. 1995. *The minimalist program.* Cambridge, MA: MIT Press.

Chomsky, N. 2001. Derivation by phase. In M. Kenstowitz (ed.), *Ken Hale: A life in language*, 1–52. Cambridge, MA: MIT Press.

Cornips, L. & Corrigan, K. (eds.). 2005. *Syntax and variation: Reconciling the biological and the social.* Amsterdam: John Benjamins.

Coupland, N. 2007. *Style: Language variation and identity.* Cambridge: Cambridge University Press.

Eckert, P. 2011. Where does the social stop? In F. Gregersen, J. K. Parrott, & P. Quist (eds.), *Language variation—European perspectives 2 (iCLaVE 5) V*, 13–30. Amsterdam: John Benjamins.

Ellegård, A. 1953. *The auxiliary* Do: *The establishment and regulation of its use in English.* Stockholm: Almqvist and Wiksell.

Embick, D. 2008. Variation and morphosyntactic theory: Competition fractionated. *Language and Linguistic Compass* 2: 59–78.

Embick, D., & Noyer, R. 2007. Distributed morphology and the syntax/morphology interface. In G. Ramchand & C. Reiss (eds.), *Oxford handbook of linguistic interfaces*, 289–324. Oxford University Press.
Fasold, R. 1991. On the quiet demise of variable rules. *American Speech* 66: 3–21.
Gervain, J., & G. Zemplén. 2005. Focus raising: A paradigmatic example of the treatment of syntactic variation. In L. Cornips & K. Corrigan (eds.), *Syntax and variation: Reconciling the biological and the social*, 123–48. Amsterdam: John Benjamins.
Goss, E. L., & Howell, R. B. 2006. Social and structural factors in the development of Dutch urban vernaculars in the early modern period. In T. D. Cravens (ed.), Variation and reconstruction, 59–88. Amsterdam: John Benjamins.
Guy, G. 1997. Violable is variable: Optimality theory and linguistic variation. *Language Variation and Change* 9: 333–47.
Halle, M. 1997. Distributed morphology: Impoverishment and fission. *MIT Working Papers in Linguistics* 30: 425–49.
Halle, M., & Marantz, A. 1993. Distributed morphology and the pieces of inflection. In K. Hale & J. Keyser (eds.), *The view from Building* 20, 111–76. Cambridge, MA: MIT Press.
Harley, H., & Ritter E. 2002. Person and number in pronouns: A feature-geometric analysis. *Language* 78: 482–526.
Harris, A., & Campbell, E. 1995. *Historical syntax in cross-linguistic perspective.* Cambridge: Cambridge University Press.
Henry Alison. 2005. Non-standard dialects and linguistic data. *Lingua* 115: 1599–617.
Holmberg, A. & I. Roberts. 2005. Introduction: Parameters in minimalist theory. In T. Biberauer, A. Holmberg, I. Roberts & M. Sheehan (eds.), *Parametric variation: Null subjects in minimalist theory*, 1–57. Cambridge: Cambridge University Press.
Hudson, R. 2007. Inherent variability and minimalism: Comments on Adger's 'Combinatorial variability'. *Journal of Linguistics* 43: 683–94.
Johnson, D. E. 2009. Getting off the GoldVarb standard: Introducing Rbrul for mixed-effects variable rule analysis. *Language and Linguistics Compass* 3: 359–83.
King, R. 2000. *The lexical basis of grammatical borrowing.* Amsterdam & Philadelphia: John Benjamins.
King, R. 2005. Morphosyntactic variation and theory: Subject verb agreement in Newfoundland French. In L. Cornips & K. Corrigan (eds.), *Syntax and variation: Reconciling the biological and the social*, 198–229. Amsterdam: John Benjamins.
King, R., Martineau, F., & Mougeon, R. 2011. The interplay of internal and external factors in grammatical change: First person plural pronouns in French. *Language* 87: 470–509.
Koopman, W., & van der Wurff, W. 2000. Two word order patterns in the history of English: Stability, variation and change. In R. Sornicola, E. Poppe, & A. Shisha-Halevy (eds.), 259–83. *Stability, variation and change of word-urder patterns over time.* Amsterdam: John Benjamins.
Kroch, A. 1989. Reflexes of grammar in patterns of language change. *Language Variation and Change* 1: 199–244.
Kroch, A. 1994. Morphosyntactic variation. In K. Beals (ed.), *Proceedings of the Thirtieth Annual Meeting of the Chicago Linguistic Society*, vol. 2, 180–201. Chicago: Chicago Linguistics Society.
Kroch, A. 2000. Syntactic change. In M. Baltin & C. Collins (eds.), *The handbook of contemporary syntactic theory*, 629–739. Oxford: Blackwell.

Kroch, A., & Taylor, A. 1997. Verb movement in Old and Middle English: Dialect variation and language contact. In A. van Kemenade & N. Vincent (eds.), *Parameters of morphosyntactic xhange*, 297–325. Cambridge: Cambridge University Press.

Kroch, A., & Taylor, A. 2000. Verb-complement order in Middle English. In S. Pintzuk, G. Tsoulas, & A. Warner (eds.), *Diachronic syntax: Models and mechanisms*, 132–63. Oxford: Oxford University Press.

Kroch, A., & Taylor, A., & Ringe, D. 2000. The Middle English verb-second constraint: A case study in language contact and language change. In S. Herring, L. Schoesler, & P. van Reenen (eds.), *Textual parameters in older language*, 353–91. Amsterdam: John Benjamins.

Labov, W. 1969. Contraction, deletion, and inherent variability of the English copula. *Language* 45:715–62.

Labov, W. 1972. *Language in the inner city*. Philadelphia: University of Pennsylvania Press.

Labov, W. 1978. Where does the sociolinguistic variable stop? A reply to B. Lavandera *Texas Working Papers in Sociolinguistics* 4. Austin: Southwest Education Development Laboratory.

Lavandera, B. 1978. Where does the sociolinguistic variable stop? *Language in Society* 7: 171–82.

Lodge, A. 2004. *A sociolinguistic history of Parisian French*. Cambridge: Cambridge University Press.

Nevins, A., & Parrott, J. K. 2010. Variable rules meet Impoverishment theory: Patterns of agreement leveling in English varieties. *Lingua* 120: 1135–159.

Newmeyer, F. 2005. *Possible and probable languages: A generative perspective on linguistic typology*. Oxford: Oxford University Press.

Paolillo, J. 2002. *Analyzing linguistic variation: Statistical models and methods*. Stanford, CA: CSLI Publications.

Parrott, J. K. 2007. Distributed morphological mechanisms of Labovian variation in syntax. Ph.D. dissertation, University of Pennsylvania.

Parrott, J. K. 2007. Review of Cornips and Corrigan, *Syntax and variation: Reconciling the biological with the social. English Language and Linguistics* 11: 425–35.

Pintzuk, S. 1991. Phrase structures in competition: Variation and change in Old English word order. Ph.D. dissertation, University of Pennsylvania.

Pintzuk, S. 2002. Verb-object order in Old English: Variation as grammatical competition. In D. Lightfoot (ed.), *Syntactic effects of morphological change*, 276–99. Oxford: Oxford University Press.

Pintzuk, S., Tsoulas, G., & Warner, A. 2000. Syntactic change: Theory and method. In S. Pintzuk, G. Tsoulas, & A. Warner (eds.), *Diachronic syntax: Models and mechanisms*, 1–32. Oxford: Oxford University Press.

Roberts, I. 2006. *Diachronic syntax*. Oxford: Oxford University Press.

Romaine, S. 1980. On the problem of syntactic variation: A reply to Beatriz Lavandera and William Labov. *Texas Working Papers in Sociolinguistics* 82. Austin: Southwest Educational Development Laboratory.

Sankoff, D., & S. Laberge. 1977. The linguistic market and the statistical explanation of variability. In D. Sankoff (ed.), *Linguistic variation: Models and methods*, 239–50. New York: Academic Press.

Sankoff, D., Tagliamonte, S., & Smith, E. 2005. Goldvarb X. A multivariate analysis application. http://individual.utoronto.ca/tagliamonte/goldvarb.htm.

Santorini, B. 1992. Variation and change in Yiddish subordinate clause word order. *Natural Language and Linguistic Theory* 10: 596–640.

Schwenter, S., & Torres-Cacoullos, R. 2008. Defaults and indeterminacy in temporal grammaticalization: the 'perfect' road to perfective. *Language Variation and Change* 20: 1–37.

Taylor, A. 1994. The change from SOV to SVO in Ancient Greek. *Language Variation and Change* 6: 1–37.

Van Kemenade, A. 2007. Formal syntax and language change. *Diachronica* 24: 155–69.

Weiner, J. E., & Labov, W. 1983. Constraints on the agentless passive. *Journal of Linguistics* 19: 29–58.

Wilson, J., & Henry, A. 1998. Parameter setting within a socially realistic sociolinguistics. *Language in Society* 27: 1–21.

CHAPTER 23

PRAGMATICS AND VARIATIONIST SOCIOLINGUISTICS

RICHARD CAMERON AND SCOTT SCHWENTER

Pragmatics begins in the semiotics of Morris (1938) and semantics of Carnap ([1942] 1961). Both set forth an agenda for pragmatics relative to semantics and syntax. Differing slightly from Morris, Carnap (9) proposed that pragmatic research necessarily referred to "the speaker" whereas semantic and syntactic research would not. If pragmatics invokes "the speaker," one senses relevance for sociolinguists. Definitions of pragmatics as "the study of language use" (Verschueren 1999: 1) also presuppose common ground. Yet, as Ariel (2008) and Levinson (1983) would argue, delimiting pragmatics relative to sociolinguistics, psycholinguistics, semantics, or syntax is not a mere turf dispute. It is crucial to theories of meaning. However, such boundary disputes have proven useful in work that mines the pragmatic-semantics-syntax interfaces by exploring conjunction, quantification, transitivity, reference, presupposition, focus, prosody, and information structure (Horn 2006; López 2009; Van Valin 2008; Ward and Birner 1998).

Pragmatics is also prefigured in the research of linguists like Firth (1935), Harris (1952), Mathesius (1928), and Mitchell (1957); the philosophers Bar-Hillel (1954), Peirce (Hartshorne & Weiss 1932), Schutz (1967), and Strawson (1950); the anthropologist Malinowski (1923); the psychologist Bartlett (1932); and the sociologists Garfinkel (1964) and Goffman (1955). As noted by Huang (2007: 4), and perhaps owing to this diversity of origins, two schools of pragmatics have emerged: Anglo-American and European-Continental. Our focus will fall mostly within the Anglo-American approach.

The Anglo-American school is heavily influenced by Grice (1957, 1968, 1975). Much research targets problems of deixis, anaphora, mutual knowledge, negation, implicature, presupposition, speech acts, and related aspects of discourse. A perennial topic is the role of inference and tacit assumptions in speech planning and interpretation. Sperber and Wilson (2002) identify this as the central issue. Why? Nearly all of what we say to one another under-determines the range of meanings that we intend. Thus, as we interact, we infer, and we expect others will infer, meanings above and beyond what is said. In order to do this, we rely on tacit assumptions that facilitate our inferences of one another's intentions. This issue is also referenced by distinctions of sentence versus utterance or word/sentence meaning versus speaker meaning. Such distinctions, in turn, point to a model of how communication is achieved.

Often called the Inferential Model (Schiffrin 1994), briefly, it works like this: as a speaker communicates, she develops a theory of the listener's mind (Baron-Cohen 1995). Think of this as an updateable mental model of what the listener is currently attending to, knows or could know, believes or could believe, as well as who the listener is relative to the speaker's face interests in context. As interaction proceeds, the speaker strategically selects from sets of linguistic resources, obeying discourse- and listener-based constraints among others (Prince 1992), so as to best produce intended responses in the listener. Thus, the speaker deliberately chooses not only what to say but how. One additional intended response is that the listener recognize the speaker's intentions to produce these responses and that this recognition serve as a reason for responding. Linguistic form, then, provides a blueprint for the listener who actively crafts understandings of what the speaker says and why. Speakers emerge as rational message designers, seeking intersubjectivity via coherent discourse. How and why speakers and listeners collaborate to do this is what pragmatics is about. Many of these topics stem from Grice as well as Austin (1962) and Searle (1969). Goffman (1955) also identified social motivations for collaboration. For updates of the Gricean agenda, consider Horn (1984), Levinson (2000), and Sperber and Wilson (1995).

Because communication entails acts of language use that require, minimally, two people for their achievement, we see how communication is intrinsically social. Owing to the inferential nature of communication, there always exists the risk of miscommunication and subsequent social consequences. Given the overlap with sociolinguistics, one might expect interaction between researchers. In practice, we find that variationists have explored ideas and analysis from pragmatics, yet little evidence exists of researchers in pragmatics taking into account the findings of variationists who work from a pragmatic perspective. This may result from widespread inattention to statistical analysis in the Anglo-American school of pragmatics. By a pragmatic perspective among variationists, we mean quite narrowly those researchers who focus on morphological or syntactic variation and critically engage in pragmatic agendas.

Recently, an important approach called Variational Pragmatics (Barron and Schneider 2009) has emerged. Despite its name, this framework does not necessarily take into consideration linguistic variables, that is, the oft-cited "two (or more) ways of saying the same thing," in the Labovian sense. Rather, Variational Pragmatics investigates how particular speech acts, routines, or even broader notions such as politeness, are realized across varieties of the same language. This is similar to quantitative research into cross-cultural Speech Act realizations in Applied Linguistics (Yu 2005). This approach does not preclude variationist methodology, since a particular pragmatic routine could be realized by two or more variant strategies. However, the focus of Variational Pragmatics is not on the variant forms and their internal linguistic conditioning, but rather on the macro-social processes and cultural values associated with speaker strategies for carrying out pragmatic routines in natural discourse.

In the overall plan of a variationist project, one may identify five stages. First, we identify a variable and its variants. Second, we identify those contexts in which variation does and does not occur while simultaneously generating initial hunches or hypotheses about what types of constraints/correlations may provide the bases for statistical patterning. Theory-driven falsifiable predictions may be formulated. Third, we code the data and analyze. This may involve a recycling back through the first two steps. Fourth, we do the statistical runs and generate results. Fifth, we interpret the results, sometimes in light of a guiding prediction, sometimes via ex-post facto interpretation.

In this chapter, we will identify how pragmatics may inform definitions of the sociolinguistic variable, provide a basis for generating hypotheses about constraints, and contribute to useful debates about where variation may or may not occur. In turn, we will show how variationist research may provide empirically based tests of pragmatic hypotheses, contribute to discussions of meaning-in-use, and also identify facts of language use that challenge key ideas in the field of pragmatics, such as the speaker as rational message designer.

Pragmatics and Meaningful Variation

How might pragmatics be relevant to the study of sociolinguistic variation? Return to the five stages of a variationist project. See stages one and two: identifying the variable and the envelope of variation. When defining the envelope of variation, we seek to identify where variation between the variants of a variable does not occur so as to identify the contexts where variation does occur. In the process, we necessarily rely on grammaticality and felicity judgments about where variants of a linguistic variable could *potentially* occur, even if they do not occur in a given data set. This research strategy, not unlike those pursued in Formal Pragmatics (Kadmon 2001), follows from Labov's (1972: 72) Principle of Accountability.

Some of the reasoning here stems from the once furious debate initiated by Lavandera (1978). In question form, that debate is this: can we extend the tool of the sociolinguistic variable beyond phonology into morphology or syntax? When responding, it is useful to distinguish between linguistic and social meaning. Phonological variants do not have meaning beyond the social or stylistic. Yes, the two voiced bilabial stops in English, /p/ and /b/, do distinguish one word from another as in 'pit' and 'bit'. However, variationists do not investigate phonemic contrasts per se, though they would in cases of phonemic mergers or splits. Instead, we statistically analyze allophonic alternations, as may happen with, for example, multi-syllabic English words ending in *–ing*. Consider 'running' and 'runnin'. Whether a speaker produces a velar or an alveolar nasal in words like this is immaterial to their semantic meaning. Thus, the two pronunciations would count as two ways of saying the same thing. This may not be the case for morphology or syntax where the choice of, say, an active or a passive sentence structure in a given discourse may convey distinct meanings, informational statuses, or differing speaker intentions. If so, actives and passives would not be considered variants of the same variable because they are not two ways of saying the same thing in the sense of 'running' versus 'runnin.'

By the way, *-ing* is actually a morphological variable subject to constraints from within multiple levels of the grammar (Hazen 2008).

Now, at least since Dines (1980: 15), variationist research beyond phonology has evoked some notion of a "common function in discourse" when identifying the variants of a syntactic variable. Function is a pragmatic notion closely related to speaker intention. Indeed, in Walker's (2010) work, he speaks of two ways of determining the variable context: one based on form, the other on function. In studies of phonology, form-based analyses prevail. But, for research into morphological or syntactic variation, function-based approaches are increasingly favored (Buchstaller 2006). In practice, this amounts to studying sociolinguistic variables in which the variants may differ in meaning and thus count as what Guy et. al (1986: 28) once termed "meaningful variation." In turn, variationists have used quantitative methods to identify what the meanings of the variants of these variables may actually be. We have moved beyond Lavandera's critique.

Consider the future tense in Spanish. One could identify the variants of the variable strictly on the basis of form and examine, thereby, two variants: the synthetic future (*cantaré* 'I will sing') and the periphrastic future (*voy a cantar* 'I am going to sing'). One may do this for diachronic reasons because the periphrastic future is the newer form and has intruded on some contexts of use previously occupied by the synthetic form. As a consequence, the synthetic form has moved into the domain of epistemic modality in much of the

Spanish-speaking world (Aaron 2010). While a form-based approach can provide interesting findings, a function-based approach would cover the total meaning space of future expression by including any future-oriented uses of the simple present (e.g., *Mañana canto* 'Tomorrow I sing') and possibly also of the present progressive (*Mañana estoy cantando* 'Tomorrow I am singing'). There are, of course, good reasons for choosing either of these strategies, depending on the goals of the research. However, only in the second case can it be said that the Labovian Principle of Accountability is being met to the fullest extent.

The function-based approach also introduces an important implication. Given that syntactic forms occur as elements within speech acts, and given that speech acts are nearly always multi-functional, it can be difficult to discern exactly which function a given syntactic variant has in discourse. Thus, there is no guarantee that a noncontroversial definition of the function will emerge. Nonetheless, the journey is worth the trip.

Pragmatics, Constraints, and Debating the Envelope of Variation

Aside from exploring the variable and envelope of variation in stage two of a variationist project, we also generate hypotheses about what types of constraints might result in genuine statistical patterning. Research in pragmatics may inform both what constraints we decide to investigate and how we identify where those constraints exist within the grammar. For instance, based on Harris's (1952: 1) definition of discourse analysis as the study of structure "beyond the limits of a single sentence," Cameron (1998) investigated constraints on direct quotation strategies both within and beyond the level of the sentence. Within the sentence, constraints included clause type, person and number, and the presence of adverbials, among others. Constraints beyond the sentence included reference relationships between the subjects of the reporting sentence and the preceding sentence as well as repetitions of quotation strategies across sequences of adjacent direct quotations. Termed Switch Reference and Perseveration respectively, we return to these constraints further on.

On the other hand, findings from variationist research, expressed either in quantitative results or as arguments about the envelope of variation, may elicit qualitative responses informed by pragmatic research. To illustrate, here we use commutation tests and felicity judgments in a debate on the role of contrast as a "don't count" case in research into Spanish subject expression.

Spanish is a null subject language that variably permits subject pronouns (or SPPs) and null subjects in subject position. For instance, one may say "Yo trabajo" (I work) or "Ø trabajo" (Ø work). Variation between these two options has been explained intuitively with pragmatic sounding terms. Among these, one often finds "contrast" or "emphasis" as partial motivations for why Spanish speakers employ an SPP even though the verb morphology or discourse context make clear who the referent of the sentential subject is.

When considering the use/non-use of SPPs in contrastive contexts, there has typically been a sequential focus on adjacent sentential utterances, whether explicitly conjoined or not, which are necessarily switch in reference with respect to their subjects (Cameron 1995). Switch reference means that the subject Y of a given sentence is different from the subject X of a preceding sentence. Thus, all instances of contrast are also instances of switch reference, but not all instances of switch reference are instances of contrast. Contrastive contexts therefore represent a small subset of cases of switch reference.

Among this group of contrastive contexts, there are examples where SPPs are clearly obligatory, and, as a result, must be considered "don't count" cases for variationist analysis. For example, no variation between overt and null subject appears possible in (1), where the subject pronoun *nosotros* 'we' in A's second utterance is obligatory. Without the pronoun, the sentence would be unacceptable in this discourse context. Following practice in the variationist literature on SPPs, we indicate the unacceptability of the null subject option with a star. Note, however, that it is not ungrammaticality *per se* that is at issue here, but rather pragmatic infelicity. The null subject sentence *Ø lo tenemos el viernes* '(We) have it on Friday' is perfectly grammatical in any dialect of Spanish as an isolated sentence, but in the context of (1) it is not, since it is in contrast with the last sentential subject *vosotros* 'you (pl.)':

(1) From Esgueva and Cantarero (1981: 309):
Inf. A: ¿Vosotros [lo] tenéis el lunes?
'You (PL) have [it] on Monday?'
Inf. B: El lunes. Un día, un día estratégico, además.
'Monday. A day, a strategic day, besides.'
Inf. A: Bueno, **(nosotros / *Ø)** lo tenemos el viernes.
'OK, we have it on Friday.'

Why are SPPs like *nosotros,* considered obligatory in contexts like (1)? One answer is that there is a contrast between what is predicated of the switch reference subjects (*vosotros* (you) vs. *nosotros* (we)). Moreover, this predicated material "in contrast belong[s] to the same semantic field" (Silva-Corvalán 1982: 114). The material contrasted in this way in (1) are the days of the week *lunes* 'Monday' and *viernes* 'Friday'.

Along with this characterization of a contrastive context, it is important to point out a guiding yet often unstated assumption. The contrast between subjects in contrastive contexts in Spanish cannot be expressed by the inflectional verbal morphology alone. As noted by Haverkate for Spanish (1976: 1196): "el sujeto realizado únicamente por la desinencia verbal nunca encierra información contrastiva" ('the subject marked only by the verbal inflection never carries contrastive information'). Thus, in an example like (1) above, the contrasting content basically boils down to what is represented in pseudo-algebraic form in (2):

(2) x tener el lunes (x to have Monday)
y tener el viernes (y to have Friday)
x≠y, el lunes ≠ el viernes (Monday ≠ Friday)

While it is true that the removal of *nosotros* in (1) would result in oddity, what has *not* been noticed is that the obligatoriness of the SPP in (1) above fades away when an adverbial, which can indirectly express the contrast between one subject and another, is inserted into the sentence. Compare (1) with a modified version of this same example in (3), where a null subject, indicated by Ø, could occur instead of the SPP. The slash between the overt SPP *nosotros* and the null subject indicates that either is possible:

(3) Inf. A: ¿Vosotros [lo] tenéis el lunes?
'You (PL) have [it] on Monday?'
Inf. B: El lunes. Un día, un día estratégico, además.
'Monday. A day, a strategic day, besides.'
Inf. A: Bueno, aquí (**Nosotros /Ø**) lo tenemos el viernes.
'OK, here we/ Ø have it on Friday.'

The contrast in (3) between what is said by A and B does not necessarily have to be expressed through overt SPPs that are switch in reference. The locative adverb *aquí* 'here', in conjunction with the first-person plural morphology on the verb, is sufficient to license the contrasting predications made by A and B. The SPP could also occur in (3) in combination with *aquí*, but the relevant point is that the SPP is not obligatory once the adverb is inserted. Thus, the adverb appears to have the capacity to express the contrastive interpretation that would otherwise require the presence of the SPP.

It would seem that the possibility of a null subject in examples like (3) would be sufficient to contradict the claim that SPPs are obligatory in contrastive contexts. However, Silva-Corvalán (2003: 853) has criticized these kinds of counterexamples, first presented in Schwenter (2002): "estos ejemplos no constituyen excepciones a la regla de 'la doble oposición' (i.e. sujeto y predicado), pues el sujeto no es el foco de contraste y por tanto su expresión deja de ser obligada. El foco de contraste es claramente el adverbio o la frase adverbial."[1] Silva-Corvalán provides (4) as another example (2003: 854):

(4) Ellos hablan inglés en la casa, pero en la nuestra (**Nosotros / Ø**) hablamos español.
'They speak English at home, but in our [house] we /Ø speak Spanish.'

Thus, for Silva-Corvalán, the optionality of the SPP *nosotros* in (4) stems from the fact that the "focus of contrast" is the adverbials (or their implicated content): *en la casa* 'in their house' and *en la nuestra* 'in our [house]'; the subjects, therefore, are not the "focus of contrast" in this example. However, if this analysis is correct, the prediction that follows would be that *any* case of contrast between adverbials will license a null subject. That this prediction is incorrect can be demonstrated by another example where different adverbials constitute the focus of contrast:

(5) Nosotros siempre hablamos inglés, pero en ocasiones **(Ellos / *Ø)** hablan español.
'We always speak English, but on occasions they /*Ø speak Spanish.'

In keeping with Silva-Corvalán's position, (5) should be acceptable with either an overt SPP or a null subject, as a result of the focal contrast holding between the temporal adverbials *siempre* 'always' and *en ocasiones* 'on occasions.' But this sentence is clearly ungrammatical without the SPP *ellos* 'they' or a 3pl. lexical NP subject.

Why is (5) unacceptable with a null subject, but the null subject in (4) is fine? We believe the answer to be because the adverbial *en la nuestra* 'in our [house]' in example (4) can be construed as referring, via metonymic inference (Nunberg 1995), to the referent of the subject of the sentence in which this adverbial appears, namely *nosotros* 'we'. The morphology of the verb indicates the subject referent (i.e. first-person plural) and the referent of the possessor in the adverbial phrase can be associated with that subject referent, thereby providing a tonic constituent to index the subject referent, in addition to the atonic verbal person/number inflection. By contrast, in (5) no associative inferencing process can be realized, since the temporal adverbial *en ocasiones* 'on occasions' cannot be interpreted as indirectly referring to the referent of the subject of the verb *hablan* 'they speak'.

More crucially, to claim that the adverb or the adverbial phrase is the focus of contrast in examples like (4) or (5) suggests that contrast is construed directly between competing linguistic forms. Contrast as a pragmatic category is not interpreted in this way; rather, it is interpreted between the *discourse referents* that such forms refer to, whether more directly, as in the case of pronouns, or more indirectly, as in the case of some adverbials. Once this understanding of "focus of contrast" is made the relevant one, differences between otherwise similar examples like (4) and (5) can be accounted for straightforwardly.

Modifications similar to those carried out on (1) above can be made to other so-called "don't count" examples in the literature, that is, examples where it is assumed that the SPP must be expressed to preserve grammaticality/felicity. For instance, (6) is Bayley and Pease-Álvarez's (1997: 356) example of a "contrastive context" where the pronoun is assumed to be obligatorily overt:

(6) Cindy toma café con leche pero **yo** /*Ø prefiero café negro.
'Cindy drinks coffee with milk but **I** /*Ø prefer black coffee.'

Indeed, (6) would be infelicitous without the SPP *yo* 'I', due to the contrasting predications and switch-reference subjects. But notice how the option of a null subject in (6) becomes fully acceptable once a potentially contrastive adverbial like *por mi parte* 'in my case' is added, as in (7):

(7) Cindy toma café con leche, pero por mi parte **(yo / Ø)** prefiero café negro.
'Cindy drinks coffee with milk but in my case I / Ø prefer black coffee.'

In both (4) and (7), the lexical content of the adverbials indirectly expresses the identity of the subject via the possessive determiners *nuestra* 'our' and *mi* 'my'. The person/number features of these forms are associated with the first-person verb morphology of the following verb in order to achieve the intended reference. But recall that there is no restriction such that only adverbials that are overtly morphologically marked for person/number can carry out indirect subject reference.

(8) Ella siempre quiere ir al cine. **Yo / *Ø** preferiría estar en casa.
'She always wants to go to the movies. I / *Ø would prefer to stay home.'

(9) Ella siempre quiere ir al cine. Honestamente, **(yo / Ø)** preferiría estar en casa.
'She always wants to go to the movies. Honestly, I / Ø would prefer to stay home.

Why would the null subject option be possible in (9), which only differs from (8) by virtue of the adverb *honestamente* 'honestly'? Because this adverb, in this syntactic position (but not necessarily in others), must be identified as indexing specifically the viewpoint of the speaker. The subject of *preferiría* 'I would prefer' is first-person singular, that is, co-referential with the speaker in (9), and therefore the adverb is compatible with the corresponding person/number features of the subject referent. Thus, it seems that all that is actually required is an adverbial that can be identified, via indirect reference, with the referent of the subject of the second clause. Corroborating evidence for this analysis is that *honestamente* cannot co-occur with a null subject in the following example:

(10) Ella siempre quiere ir al cine. Honestamente, **(ellos / *Ø)** preferirían estar en casa.
'She always wants to go to the movies. Honestly, they would prefer to stay at home.

In (10), the third-person-plural subject referent of *preferirían* in the second sentence *cannot* be co-referential with the (referent of the) speaker, which is first-person singular. As a result, an appropriate SPP such as *ellos* (or a third-person-plural lexical subject) must be overtly expressed.

Variationist Sociolinguistics, Meanings in Use, and Hypothesis Testing

Even if different yet related morphosyntactic expressions are presumed to convey different meanings, we can still define a variable context in order to apply the Principle of Accountability—account for occurrences as well as non-occurrences of a variant expression. This allows us to submit the data to multivariate analysis, as a heuristic tool for establishing the contexts of use of these expressions. By so identifying the contexts which favor one variant or another, we may also contribute to identifying the meanings associated with the variants.

With intransitive motion verbs in Spanish, a reflexive clitic pronoun occurs with some verbs. This is called middle marker *SE*. Maldonado (1999) has argued that *SE* serves to selectively focus a listener's attention on an individual's experience of physical motion and the change this entails. It does so by highlighting a point in space rather than the entire trajectory of motion. From this, *SE* in turn also develops as a marker of counter-expectation. For example, we might interpret *se*-marked *bajar* 'go down' in (11a) as indicating an event viewed as contrary to expectations or conventions—going down to dine alone on one's wedding night. *SE* has also been interpreted as an expression of subject involvement, in concentrating attention on the subject via double mention (the clitic pronoun as well as the person suffix; García [1975: 158–161]), as perhaps illustrated in (12).

(11) mi mujer no tenía ganas de cenar, cuando llegamos; pero yo dije, pues, mira pues yo sí, así que (a) *ME bajo* a cenar solo y (b) *bajé* a cenar ¡je, je! al comedor, a pesar de recién casado. (Esgueva and Cantarero 1981: 232)
[on their wedding night] my wife didn't feel like dinner when we arrived [at the
hotel]; but I said, well, look I do, so (a) I SE **go down** to eat alone and (b) I Ø
went down to eat, ha ha, in the dining room, in spite of just getting married.'

(12) tuvo que poner unas bombillas en un techo muy alto y no SE subía. *ME* tuve que subir yo, lo cual, demuestra lo de la mujer. (Esgueva & Cantarero 1981: 189)
'he had to put some light bulbs on a very high ceiling and he wouldn't SE go up. I
had to SE **go up**, which goes to show about women.'

But as (11b) indicates, the *se*-marked and the non-*se*-marked form may appear in near-identical contexts. Rather than attributing different meanings based on cherry-picked examples, variationists employ quantitative reasoning.

Patterns of co-occurrence with features of the linguistic and extra-linguistic environments in which choices among variant expressions occur provide a replicable way to define the differences among these expressions (Poplack & Tagliamonte 1996). Contextual features, including those associated with pragmatics, are operationalized as factors or constraints, to test hypotheses about what motivates variant choice.

How can we operationalize speaker expectations and involvement? For *se*-marking on intransitive motion verbs *bajar* 'go down' and *subir* 'go up' Torres Cacoullos and Schwenter (2008) made the following predictions. First, if *SE* focuses on the source or end point rather than trajectory of motion, it should be favored by locative expressions with the prepositions *a* 'to', *de* 'from,' or *en* 'on', as in (13), rather than with other prepositions, such as *por* 'by, along' (14), or in the absence of locative prepositions. Second, counter-expectation is more likely to be overtly indicated on past situations, which are actual specific events, than on present situations, which are largely habitual and thus predictable. And third, if *SE* expresses a greater degree of subject involvement, it should be favored with first- and second-person subjects (example (12)), which "exhibit subjectivity," since their meaning is based on the speaker's point of view (Traugott & Dasher 2002: 22).

(13) *SE baja* de la cama (COREC, ALUD023A)
'She SE *gets off* of the bed'

(14) *hemos bajado* por la, por la Costa [...] Brava hasta Barcelona. (Esgueva and Cantarero 1981: 147)
'we Ø *went down* along the Costa Brava until Barcelona'

Table 23.1 shows that, as predicted, *bajarse* and *subirse* are favored when an *a, de,* or *en* locative co-occurs, when the event is in the past, and when the subject is the speaker or the interlocutor. These contextual features are compatible with a focus on the change of state of the experiencer of the motion event and the expression of counter-expectation and subject involvement.

However, the data also reveal a number of constructions, from fixed expressions with particular lexical items (e.g., *subirse a la cabeza* 'get intoxicated', literally: 'go up to one's head') to more schematic structures with open slots, with strong tendencies to appear with or without *SE*. For example, *subir/bajar* 'go up/down' + STAIRS is overwhelmingly non-*se*-marked, whereas *subirse a* 'climb' + TREE is. It turns out that entering and exiting a vehicle (e.g., auto, bus, metro), conventionally referred to with *subir* and *bajar*, makes up about one-fifth of the data. This factor has the highest weight in table 23.1: the tendency is to use *SE* in the *subir/bajar* 'enter-exit' + VEHICLE construction. In fact, cross-tabulations show that co-occurring *a, de, en* locatives, even though they are more frequent in the vehicle context, have no effect in this highly favorable construction. Furthermore, the strong tendency to use *SE* with vehicles appears to override pragmatic considerations of counter-expectation. For example, in (15), we have a non-specific subject and a routine event.

Table 23.1. Variable-rule analysis of factors contributing to choice of *se*-marked *bajar-subir* N = 646

Construction		N
Enter-exit vehicle	.78	125
Other uses	.42	521
Co-occurring locative preposition		
a 'to', *de* 'from', *en* 'on'	.67	172
Other or none	.43	439
Subject		
First and second person	.58	204
Third and non-specific	.46	415
Tense		
Past	.55	208
Non-past	.47	309

Input:.17 (overall rate of *se* = 21%). Also significant: medium; non-significant: clause type, dialect, verb type.

Source: Adapted from Torres Cacoullos & Schwenter (2008: 1462)

(15) cada vez que un ciudadano de Madrid SE *sube* en el autobús, en cercanías
o en el Metro, eh—el Estado le da 20 pesetas (COREC, APOL023A)
'each time a citizen of Madrid SE *gets on* the bus, on the local train or on the metro, the State gives them 20 pesetas'

Thus, research in pragmatics will benefit from considering conventionalized form-meaning pairings (constructions), which may constrain speaker choices beyond pragmatic considerations. Another kind of effect that may override pragmatics is structural perseveration, which we illustrate with Spanish subject expression in the next section.

Variationist Sociolinguistics, Rationality, and Perseveration

The model of the rational speaker within the Inferential Model of communication is akin to what Simon (1979: 500) and Pollock (2002) call the "classical model." A classically rational speaker selects a linguistic option in keeping with some measure of utility. This enables "calculations to optimize rewards" as Myers-Scotton and Bolonyai (2001: 2) phrase it in their rational choice model of codeswitching. Thus, the fully rational speaker evaluates, ranks, and then selects the best option for the intention at hand. This entails deliberation and computation, knowledge of the options and of the problem to be solved by selecting an option, and the ability to forecast the consequences of each option prior to actual use. Yet, beginning with Simon's concept of "bounded rationality" (1957: 196–206), classical rationality has repeatedly been critiqued in the decision sciences (Gigerenzer and Selten 2001).

Bounded rationality refers to the limits of our ability to act rationally. It entails at least two key processes: search and satisficing. Search involves acts of deliberation and option evaluation. Satisficing is the act of selecting an option prior to completing a full search in the absence of a clear forecast of the consequences. If choice occurs prior to full evaluation, cognitive heuristics and processes may be involved, some of which may operate like Gricean maxims, others not (Piatelli-Palmarini 1994). For instance, from psycholinguistics we know that speakers are subject to automatic processes that occur "without intention and conscious awareness" (Levelt 1989: 20). These processes also systematically contribute to the construction of linguistic form, that blueprint of speaker intentions. Therefore, not all linguistic form introduced into discourse can be a function of speaker intentions and rational calculations. To borrow from Goffman's (1963: 14) discussion of "expressive" communication, some of this linguistic blueprint is "uncalculated, spontaneous, and involuntary."

Evidence for this emerges in controlled experiments of psycholinguists and in spontaneous speech studied by sociolinguists (Bock, Dell, Chang, & Onishi 2007; Travis 2007). In both fields, systematic effects are reported for what researchers identify as priming or persistence or perseverance or perseveration. Following on the terminology for speech error types of Dell, Burger, and Svec (1997: 124), we use "perseveration" as a cover term. The different terms all point to one discovery. Speakers repeat forms or structures. Some repetitions in discourse are clearly intended. However, as Bock and Griffin (2000: 177) observe, others are "unintentional and pragmatically unmotivated." Within these statistically demonstrable repetitions, the presence of one form or structure correlates to subsequently higher frequencies of the same forms or structures relative to other options. In her work on syntactic perseveration, the psycholinguist Bock (1986) provided related insight.

> An utterance takes the grammatical form that it does because the procedures controlling its syntax are more activated than the procedures for an alternative form, with the higher level of activation being an automatic consequence of the prior production of the same form. (379)

When this happens, by definition, rationality is not the cause. However, it is clear that the grammatical forms of a speaker's utterance at one point may systematically influence what this same speaker says next. And yet, what the speaker says next still displays sensitivity to discourse- and listener-based constraints along with those of phonology, morphology, and syntax. For example, in the work of Cameron and Flores (2004), we showed how perseveration intersects with Switch Reference, a central constraint in variationist treatments of the alternation of null and pronominal sentential subjects in Spanish. As noted before, Switch Reference is a relation of same or different reference that holds between a targeted subject NP, where the variation occurs, and the preceding subject NP called the trigger. The target is the first [+human] subject of a tensed verb to occur immediately after the preceding trigger subject. The target subject NP is analyzed as switch or same in reference with respect to the preceding trigger.

With this working model, we can show how Switch Reference statistically constrains pronominal expression in interview data from 10 speakers from San Juan, Puerto Rico, and ten from Madrid, Spain (see table 23.2). In this data set, we focused only on singular subjects because in earlier work, Cameron (1994) assumed that the perseverative effect would not occur in plural subjects given the relative infrequency of plural subject pronouns. However, see Flores-Ferrán (2002) for perseverative effects on plural subjects as well (see table 23.2).

In both dialects, the effects of Switch Reference are the same. When there is a switch in reference, pronominal subjects are favored, and, conversely, null subjects are disfavored. When trigger and target subjects are the same in reference, there is a disfavoring of pronouns and, conversely, a favoring of null subjects.

Using Switch Reference as analytic frame, we turn to the presence of perseveration. We do this by intersecting each category of reference, switch and same, with two factors defined in terms of the lexical status of the trigger. We may identify a trigger as either a subject pronoun or a null subject. By classifying the trigger according to lexical status, we create an Overt Context, with a pronominal trigger, and a Null Context, with a null trigger. By comparing the relative probabilities of pronominal subjects in the target of these two contexts, we statistically illustrate the pattern of perseveration whereby a pronominal trigger relatively favors a pronominal target. In contrast, a null trigger relatively favors a following null target (see table 23.3).

In both dialects, there is a clear difference in the probabilities of pronominal expression in the target of an Overt Context compared to the Null Context. In the switch reference context, the weights indicate that when the trigger is a pronoun, there is a stronger tendency to express pronouns in the target than when the trigger is a null subject. In San Juan, compare the value of .74 (in the Overt Context) relative to the value of .66 (in the Null Context). In Madrid, compare the value of .75 (in the Overt Context) relative to the value of .68 (in the Null Context). In the same reference contexts, we find the same ranking of constraints. In San Juan, compare the value of .48 (in the Overt Context) relative to the value of .28 (in the Null Context). In Madrid, compare the value of .50 (in the Overt Context) relative to the value of .33 (in the Null Context).

Table 23.2. VARBRUL weights for switch reference San Juan vs. Madrid (singular subjects only: probability of pronoun in target NP)

	San Juan	Madrid
Switch	.65	.66
Same	.35	.35

Source: Adpated from Cameron and Flores Ferrán (2004: 47–48)

Observe that the degree of difference is greater in the context of sameness of reference than in a switch of reference. This indicates that the different referential contexts constrain the output of the perseverative effect on subject pronoun expression. Cameron and Flores (2004: 62) provide an account for these differing degrees of perseveration within the framework of Spreading-Activation Theory, a psycholinguistic theory of language production based on speech errors (Dell 1986). Bock, et.al. (2007: 439) also pursue connections between perseveration and implicit learning. Therefore, the study of these unintentional repetitions across discourse apparently has implications not only for pragmatics but also for research into language learning.

At the outset, we noted the five stages of a variationist project. In the fifth stage, the results of statistical analysis are interpreted in light of a guiding prediction or via ex-post facto interpretation. In pragmatics, a primary source of interpretation is the Gricean agenda. Yet, we find it difficult to account for the perseverative patterns reported here and elsewhere within this agenda. The problem may be the assumption of classically rational behavior. The online discourse behaviors of perseveration are not rational, though they are orderly.

Table 23.3. Null and pronominal triggers cross-tabulated with switch reference in San Juan and Madrid (singular subjects only: probability of pronoun in target NP)

	San Juan	Madrid
Trigger type	Target	Target
Trigger is switch in reference		
Overt context	.74	.75
Null context	.66	.68
Trigger is same in reference		
Overt context	.48	.50
Null context	.28	.33

Source: Adpated from Cameron and Flores Ferrán (2004: 47–48)

Nonetheless, if the goal of pragmatics is to account for how and why speakers and listeners communicate, and if a persistent aspect of speaker behavior involves perseveration of linguistic form, then research in pragmatics would benefit from engaging with these findings. Discourse modeling research in computational linguistics already does so (Jurafsky & Martin 2008: 78, 358, 421).

Another approach to discourse modeling that could, perhaps, incorporate findings of perseveration is Mayol and Clark's (2010) use of Game Theory to analyze alternations of null and pronominal anaphora in Catalan. Game theory, like work on bounded rationality, focuses on decision making. Decision makers are conceived of as interdependent communicating rational agents with agendas to pursue in an uncertain world. In this approach, linguistic choice is modeled as probabilistic. A key instrument is a game tree. A game tree is a directed graph model of the sequence of acts that make up the game and of the sets of choices for each act. Also included are the factors that probabilistically affect choice as well as the payoffs of choice. Including perseverative tendencies of speakers within game trees may add greater precision to predictions of choice. Applications of game theory to theories of meaning, as in Parikh (2006), may also entice those in formal pragmatics to explore statistical analysis.

Conclusion

Early on, we noted the asymmetrical relationship between the fields of Pragmatics and Variationist Sociolinguistics. Of course, the reasons for this are many. We mentioned the lack of statistical analysis in much of Pragmatics. Other reasons may actually be visible in Harris's (1952) writing on Discourse Analysis, which foreshadows some of contemporary Pragmatics. Harris argued for two analytic approaches to discourse. We could extend descriptive linguistics into sequences of language use beyond the sentence, or we could analyze discourse by (1) "correlating 'culture' and language (i.e. non-linguistic and linguistic behavior)." But, he then dismissed such correlations as (2) "beyond the scope of linguistics." In the meantime, Mitchell (1957) was doing exactly what Harris dismissed by investigating (31) "the language of buying and selling" in Cyrenaica, Libya. There, he pursued correlations between social facts, the act sequences of buying and selling, and (33) "verbal behavior as part of the job at hand." Much of this prefigures work in Speech Act theory. We admire both Harris and Mitchell. We further suggest that both fields, Pragmatics and Variationist Sociolinguistics, would benefit from more mutual engagement, just as Harris and Mitchell could have benefited from sharing a beer. Here, we have illustrated a few examples of how that engagement may proceed.

Acknowledgment

We thank Rena Torres Cacoullos for her important contributions to the section "Variationist Sociolinguistics, Meanings in Use, and Hypothesis Testing" and for feedback on the entire article.

Notes

1. Translation: 'These examples do not constitute exceptions to the "double opposition" (i.e., subject and predicate) rule, since the subject is not the focus of contrast and therefore its overt expression is no longer obligatory. The focus of contrast is clearly the adverb or the adverbial phrase.'

References

Aaron, J. 2010. Pushing the envelope: Looking beyond the variable context. *Language Variation and Change* 22: 1–36.

Ariel, M. 2008. *Pragmatics and grammar.* Cambridge: Cambridge University Press.

Austin, J. L. 1962. *How to do things with words*, 2nd edition. Cambridge, MA: Harvard University Press.

Bar-Hillel, Y. 1954. Indexical expressions. *Mind* 63: 359–79.

Baron-Cohen, S. 1995. *Mindblindness: An essay on autism and theory of mind.* Cambridge, MA: MIT Press.

Barron, A., & Schneider, K. 2009. Variational pragmatics: Studying the impact of social factors on language use in interaction. *Intercultural Pragmatics* 6: 425–42.

Bartlett, F. C. 1932. *Remembering: A study in experimental and social psychology.* New York: Macmillan.

Bayley, R., & Pease-Álvarez, L. 1997. Null pronoun variation in Mexican-descent children's narrative discourse. *Language Variation and Change* 9: 349–71.

Bock, K. 1986. Syntactic persistence in language production. *Cognitive Psychology* 18: 355–87.

Bock, K., Dell, G., Chang, F., & Onishi, K. 2007. Persistent structural priming from language comprehension to language production. *Cognition* 104: 437–58.

Bock, K., & Griffin, Z. 2000. The persistence of structural priming: Transient activation or implicit learning. *Journal of Experimental Psychology: General.* 129: 177–92.

Buchstaller, I. 2006. Diagnostics of age-graded linguistic behavior: The case of the quotative system. *Journal of Sociolinguistics* 10: 3–30.

Cameron, R. 1994. Switch reference, verb class, and priming in a variable syntax. In K.Beals. et. al. (eds.), *Papers from the 30th regional meeting of the Chicago Linguistic Society: Volume 2: The parasession on variation in linguistic theory*, 27–45. Chicago: Chicago Linguistic Society.

Cameron, R. 1995. The scope and limits of switch reference as a constraint on pronominal subject expression. *Hispanic Linguistics* 6/7: 1–27.
Cameron, R. 1998. A variable syntax of speech, gesture, and sound effect: Direct quotations in Spanish. *Language Variation and Change* 10: 43–83.
Cameron, R., & Flores Ferrán, N. 2004. Perseveration of subject expression across regional dialects of Spanish. *Spanish in Context* 1: 41–65.
Carnap, R. (1942) 1961. *Introduction to semantics and formalization of logic.* Cambridge, MA: Harvard University Press.
COREC n.d. = Corpus de Referencia de la Lengua Española Contemporánea: Corpus Oral Peninsular, director Francisco Marcos Marín. Available at: www.lllf.uam.es/~fmarcos/informes/corpus/corpusix.html.
Dell, G. 1986. A spreading-activation theory of retrieval in sentence production. *Psychological Review* 93: 283–321.
Dell, G., Burger, L., & Svec. W. 1997. Language production and serial order: A functional analysis and a model. *Psychological Review* 104: 123–47.
Dines, E. 1980. Variation in discourse: "And stuff like that." *Language in Society* 9: 13–31.
Esgueva, M., & Cantarero, M. (eds.). 1981. *El habla de la ciudad de Madrid: Materiales para su estudio.* Madrid: Consejo Superior de Investigaciones Científicas, Instituto Miguel de Cervantes.
Firth, J. R. 1935. The technique of semantics. *Transactions of the Philological Society,* 36–72.
Flores Ferrán, N. 2002. *Subject personal pronouns in Spanish narratives of Puerto Ricans in New York City: A sociolinguistic perspective.* Munich: Lincom-Europa.
García, E. 1975. *The role of theory in linguistic analysis: The Spanish pronoun system.* Amsterdam: North-Holland.
Garfinkel, H. 1964. Studies of the routine grounds of everyday activities. *Social Problems* 11: 225–50.
Gigerenzer, G. & Selten, R. (eds.). 2001. *Bounded rationality: The adaptive toolbox.* Cambridge, MA: MIT Press.
Goffman, E. 1955. On face-work: An analysis of ritual elements in social interaction. *Psychiatry: Journal for the Study of Interpersonal Processes* 18: 213–31.
Goffman, E. 1963. *Behavior in public places.* London: Collier-Macmillan.
Grice, H. P. 1957. Meaning. *Philosophical Review* 67: 377–88.
Grice, H. P. 1968. Utterer's meaning, sentence-meaning, and word-meaning. *Foundations of Language* 4: 1–18.
Grice, H. P. 1975. Logic and conversation. In P. Cole & J. Morgan (eds.), *Syntax and semantics.* Vol. 3: *Speech acts,* 41–58. New York: Academic Press.
Grice, H. P. 1957. Meaning. *Philosophical Review.* 67: 377–88.
Guy, G., Horvath, B. Vonwiller, J., Daisley, E., & Rogers, I. 1986. An intonational change in progress in Australian English. *Language in Society* 15: 23–52.
Harris, Z. 1952. Discourse analysis. *Language* 28: 1–30.
Hartshorne, C., & Weiss, P. (eds.) 1932. *Collected papers of Charles Sanders Peirce,* vol. 2: *Elements of logic.* Cambridge, MA: Harvard University Press.
Haverkate, H. 1976. Estructura y función del sujeto en el español moderno. *Actas du XIIIe Congrès International de Linguistique et Philologie Romanes,* I, 1191–197. Quebec: Université Laval.
Hazen, K. 2008. (ing): A vernacular baseline for English in Appalachia. *American Speech.* 83: 116–40.

Horn, L. 1984. Toward a new taxonomy for pragmatic inference: Q-based and R-based implicature. In D. Schiffrin (ed.), *Meaning, form, and use in context: Linguistic applications*, 11–42. Washington, DC: Georgetown University Press.
Horn, L. 2006. The border wars: A neo-Gricean perspective. In K. von Heusinger & K. Turner (eds.), *Where semantics meets pragmatics*, 21–48. Amsterdam: Elsevier.
Huang, Y. 2007. *Pragmatics*. Oxford: Oxford University Press.
Jurafsky, D., & Martin, J. 2008. *Speech and language processing: An introduction to natural language processing, computational linguistics, and speech recognition*, 2nd ed. Upper Saddle River, NJ: Pearson-Prentice Hall.
Kadmon, N. 2001. *Formal pragmatics: Semantics, pragmatics, presupposition, and focus*. Oxford: Wiley-Blackwell.
Labov, W. (1972). *Sociolinguistic patterns*. Philadelphia: University of Pennsylvania Press.
Lavandera, B. 1978. Where does the sociolinguistic variable stop? *Language in Society* 7: 171–82.
Levelt, W. 1989. *Speaking: From intention to articulation*. Cambridge, MA: MIT Press.
Levinson, S. 1983. *Pragmatics*. Cambridge: Cambridge University Press.
Levinson, S. 2000. *Presumptive meanings: The theory of generalized conversational implicature*. Cambridge: Cambridge, MA: MIT Press.
López. L. 2009 *A derivational syntax for information structure*. Oxford: Oxford University Press.
Maldonado, R. 1999. *A media voz: problemas conceptuales del clítico se*. Universidad Nacional Autónoma de México.
Malinowski, B. 1923. The problem of meaning in primitive languages. C. K. Ogden & I. A. Richards (eds.), *The meaning of meaning*, 296–336. New York: Harcourt Brace Jovanovich.
Mathesius, V. 1928. On linguistic characterology with illustrations from Modern English. *Actes du Premier Congrès International de Linguistes à La Haye*, 56–63. Reprinted in J. Vachek (ed.). 1964. *A Prague school reader in linguistics*, 59–67. Bloomington: Indiana University Press.
Mayol, L., & Clark, R. 2010. Pronouns in Catalan: Games of partial information and the use of linguistic resources. *Journal of Pragmatics* 42: 781–99.
Mitchell, T. F. 1957. The language of buying and selling in Cyrenaica: A situational statement. *Hespéris* 44: 31–71.
Morris, C. W. 1938. *Foundations of the theory of signs*. Chicago: University of Chicago Press.
Myers-Scotton, C., & Bolonyai, A. 2001. Calculating speakers: Codeswitching in a rational choice model. *Language and Society* 30: 1–28.
Nunberg, G. 1995. Transfers of meaning. *Journal of Semantics* 12: 109–33.
Parikh, P. 2006. Radical semantics: A new theory of meaning. *Journal of Philosophical Logic* 35: 349–91.
Piatelli-Palmarini, M. 1994. *Inevitable illusions: How mistakes of reason rule our minds*. New York: John Wiley & Sons.
Pollock, J. 2002. Rational choice and action omnipotence. *Philosophical Review* 111: 1–23.
Poplack, S. & Tagliamonte, S. 1996. Nothing in context: Variation, grammaticization and past time marking in Nigerian Pidgin English. In P. Baker & A. Syea (eds.), *Changing meanings, changing functions*, 71–94. Westminster, UK: Battlebridge Press.

Prince, E. 1992. The ZPG letter: Subjects, definiteness, and information-status. In W. Mann & S. Thompson (eds.), *Discourse description: Diverse linguistic analyses of a fund-raising* text, 295–326. Amsterdam: John Benjamins.

Schiffrin, D. 1994. *Approaches to discourse.* Cambridge, MA: Blackwell.

Schutz, A. 1967. *The phenomenology of the social world.* Evanston, IL: Northwestern University Press.

Schwenter, S. A. 2002. The notion of contrast in the study of Spanish subject personal pronouns. Paper given at the Workshop on Subject Pronoun Expression in Spanish, CUNY Graduate Center.

Searle, J. 1969. *Speech acts: An essay in the philosophy of language.* Cambridge: Cambridge University Press.

Silva-Corvalán, C. 1982. Subject expression and placement in Mexican-American Spanish. Spanish in the United States: Sociolinguistic aspects. In J. Amastae & L. Elías-Olivares (eds.), 93–120. Cambridge,UK: Cambridge University Press.

Silva-Corvalán, C. 2003. Otra mirada a la expresión del sujeto como variable sintáctica. In F. Moreno Fernández et al. (eds.), *Lengua, variación y contexto: Estudios dedicados a Humberto López Morales,* 849–60. Madrid: Arco/Libros.

Simon, H. 1957. *Models of man: Social and rational: Mathematical essays on rational human behavior in a social setting.* New York: John Wiley & Sons.

Simon, H. 1979. Rational decision making in business organizations. *American Economic Review* 69: 493–513.

Sperber, D. & Wilson, D. 2002. Pragmatics, modularity and mind-reading. *Mind and Language* 17: 3–23.

Sperber, D., & Wilson, D. 1995. *Relevance: Communication and cognition,* 2nd ed. Oxford: Blackwell.

Strawson, P. F. 1950. On referring. *Mind* 59: 320–44.

Torres Cacoullos, R., &. Schwenter, S. 2008. Constructions and pragmatics: Variable middle marking in Spanish subir(se) 'go up' and bajar(se) 'go down'. *Journal of Pragmatics* 40: 1455–477.

Traugott, E., & Dasher, R. 2002. *Regularity in semantic change.* Cambridge: Cambridge University Press.

Travis, C. 2007. Genre effects on subject expression in Spanish: Priming in narrative and conversation. *Language Variation and Change* 19: 101–35.

Van Valin, R. (ed). 2008. *Investigations of the syntax-semantics-pragmatics interface.* Amsterdam: John Benjamins.

Verschueren, J. 1999. *Understanding pragmatics.* London: Arnold.

Walker, J. A. 2010. *Variation in linguistic systems.* London: Routledge.

Ward, G., & Birner, B. 1998. *Information status and noncanonical word order in English.* Amsterdam: John Benjamins.

Yu, M-C. 2005. Sociolinguistic competence in the complimenting act of native Chinese and American English speakers: A mirror of cultural value. *Language and Speech* 48: 91–119.

CHAPTER 24

VARIATION AND CHANGE

ALEXANDRA D'ARCY

Variation ... and then Change

Natural language—regardless of medium—is characterized by structured heterogeneity (Weinreich et al. 1968: 100). This is evident in the deterministic alternations that form the core of introductory linguistics textbooks. The reason is straightforward: It is precisely the systematic and rule-governed structure of these emic-etic relationships that drives the scientific approach to language. But variation is also evident in less conventionally reified aspects of language, in the "noise" introduced "out there" in the social world of actual language use. This kind of heterogeneity has long been recognized as a characteristic of synchronic production, but where once ignored for pragmatic reasons (see Romaine 1982: 10), probabilistic variation is now understood as the natural state of language and, by extension, the natural state of linguistic structure itself. As summarized by Foulkes (2006: 654), variation is not "a nuisance" but "a universal and functional design feature of language."

Nowhere is this more manifest than in language change. Living language changes constantly, meaning that structure cannot be fixed. It must be fluid, capable of accommodating this perpetual state of flux. The continuous nature of change inevitably leads to differences across speakers in terms of the way in which some structural category or meaning is realized. But variation is not limited to inter-speaker applicability. It is normal for an individual to not only produce alternate realizations but to do so for a wide range of features. Some of these features may be involved in change, and others may not. But what variationist research has clearly established is that while much heterogeneity in language is not predictable in an absolute sense, very little of it is random or meaningless. A complex matrix of language-internal (linguistic) and language-external (social) factors constrains variation and change in natural language.

At the same time, even though linguistic structure is inherently heterogeneous and is constantly changing, variation and change do not in fact have equal status. Variation can be quite stable. Its presence does not automatically entail that a change is occurring. In contrast, change ipso facto entails variation (see Weinreich et al. 1968: 188). That change involves a period of oscillation between conservative and innovative forms is the foundational element in the development of an empirical theory of language change. *A* does not become *B*; rather, *A* and *B* alternate for a period and the frequency of one (or more) competing variants increases, spreading in both linguistic and social space. For this reason, change is often formalized as in (1):

$$(1)\ \{A\} \quad \rightarrow \quad \begin{Bmatrix} A \\ B \end{Bmatrix} \quad \rightarrow \quad \{B\}$$

This formalization elegantly reflects the central role of variation. However, while change is regular in many respects, it is rarely so tidy and conclusive. Change may well involve a binary competition, with one (innovative) variant ultimately ousting another (conservative) variant. But it is more often the case that multiple (discrete) forms alternate or that gradient shifts progress through acoustic space. More crucially though, change is not deterministic, and yet this is precisely what (1), in its replacive characterization of change, would seem to suggest. There is no requirement that—once initiated—a change must progress to completion (where "completion" is the wholesale loss of an earlier form; see, too, Labov 2001: 75). A change may begin and simply fail to advance, receding before it has the opportunity to accelerate and spread through linguistic and social structure (Labov 2001: 462). Alternatively, it may progress to a certain point and then reverse, as was the case for analytic comparatives in English (Kytö & Romaine 1997). It is also possible that a change may reach an equilibrium in which the alternants remain in a state of stable variation, such as the case of [n] ~ [ŋ] variation in the pronunciation of the English *-ing* suffix. It is also possible for older forms to become entrenched in particular contexts and constructions. This is precisely what appears to be occurring with English *shall*. Once the primary marker of English future temporal reference, its use is now highly restricted, virtually non-existent outside first-person interrogatives and formal speech (Poplack & Tagliamonte 1999: 321, n.4). In other words, rather than obsolescing across the board, *shall* has become highly specialized. With respect to sound change, numerous examples of both lexical and geographic exceptions illustrate the great frequency with which innovations "fail" to diffuse in full (e.g., Chambers & Trudgill 1980).

Determining the circumstances, linguistic and social, that lead to each scenario is part of the variationist enterprise. The questions raised in this endeavor are complex: Why does a particular change take place when and where it does (and not at some other time or in some other place)? Why does it proceed as it does (and not in some other fashion)? Why does it proceed at all? How does a change come to be embedded in linguistic and social structure? What can the lack of change (i.e., stable variation) tell us? The ultimate concern of variationist sociolinguistics, then, is the evolution of linguistic systems and the mechanisms that operate on them.

One feature that offers particularly good insight into these issues is quotative *be like*, exemplifed in (2), a relatively recent and robust change that has affected varieties of English worldwide. It is also an intensively studied phenomenon, forming the basis of a wide range of empirically grounded research efforts.

(2) a. I saw her face and I *was like* 'Who's that? She looks familiar.' (Toronto, Canada)
b. She looks at me and I'*m like* 'Yeah? What?' and she'*s like* 'I know you, aye?' (Christchurch, New Zealand)
c. I'*m like* '[scared face]' but it's exhilarating! (St. John's, Newfoundland)

Over the course of this chapter I illustrate the types of theoretical issues that *be like* has been used to explore. I begin, however, with a discussion of the quantitative paradigm and the analytical assumptions underlying variationist work on direct quotation.

The Quotative System and the Variationist Paradigm

Quotative *be like* is an ideal vehicle for observing language change in action. Not only is it a recent innovation, but it is also diffusing with extreme rapidity in linguistic, social, and geographic space. Since its earliest mentions in the literature (Butters 1982; Schourup 1982), research interest in this form has grown steadily. Beginning with Blyth, Recktenwald, and Wang (1990), Romaine and Lange (1991), and Ferrara and Bell (1995), much of this work has focused on American English varieties, but empirical evidence is increasingly being provided from geographic locales as diverse as Australia (Winter 2002), Scotland (Macaulay 2001), and Malta (Bonnici 2010). But *be like* it is not unique to English. Analogous forms are currently on the rise in languages such as French, Swedish, Norwegian, German, and Hebrew (e.g., Kotsinas 1994; Fleischman

1998; Golato 2000; Hasund 2003; Maschler 2009), and a parallel construction has also been discussed for Hittite (Joseph 1981). This is a particularly important point, because such similar cross-linguistic developments suggest that general functional mechanisms are at play.

However, while *be like* may draw our attention, no individual linguistic item can be the sole focus of variationist analysis. This is because one of the key foundational concepts of the Labovian quantitative framework, and that which sets it apart from other quantitative approaches, is the Principle of Accountability (Labov 1966, 1972). Under this principle, variationist analysis considers where the variant of interest occurs as well as where it could have but did not. For this reason no select subset of variants can be the focus either. The variationist conceptualization of accountability thus foregrounds the importance of context: we can neither assess nor ascertain how a particular variant functions without considering the whole of the variable system in which it operates.

Let us consider what this entails in the case of quotative *be like*. As a verb of direct quotation, its function is to introduce "constructed dialogue" (Tannen 1986). A host of other verbs also performs this function, though only a handful recurs with any degree of regularity in spontaneous speech: *say*, *think*, *go* and the null form, Ø. That said, it is clear that *say* and *think*, for example, do not do the same job: the former (virtually always) introduces speech while the latter (always) introduces thought. In contrast, *be like* is remarkably versatile: It is not pragmatically restricted to either speech or thought encoding. As a consequence, if we are to understand how *be like* (or any other form, for that matter) functions within the system of direct quotation, we cannot limit the analysis to just one type of quoted content. We have to consider everything. In other words, the point of the exercise is to contrast the uses of individual forms with those of others within the broader context of direct quotation more generally (see also Tagliamonte & Hudson 1999: 155).

A further consideration relates to the development of grammatical forms: A number of works suggest that *be like* is a case of grammaticalization in progress (Romaine & Lange 1991; Tagliamonte & Hudson 1999; Tagliamonte & D'Arcy 2004). This process results in the layering of various forms as well as the persistence of older functions alongside newer ones (Hopper 1991). To track the ongoing development of *be like* as a quotative verb of English, it is again critical to include all contexts to which it may or may not be expanding. This necessarily requires examining the system as a whole.

What Can We Learn from *Be Like*?

Labov once described *be like* as "one of the most striking and dramatic linguistic changes of the past three decades" (pers. comm. 2000). He argued that *be like* offered a perhaps unprecedented opportunity to study "rapid language change in progress on a large scale in order to address the general questions on the mechanism, the causation, and the consequences of change" (see Cukor-Avila 2002: 21). With the benefit of hindsight, it is clear that *be like* has indeed proven a robust heuristic in the ongoing effort to hone an empirical theory of language change. It belongs to that set of features upon which variationists have come to rely to answer questions that are central to the discipline, features like (t,d) and (ng) (e.g., Guy 1980; Labov 1989). However, while (t,d) and (ng) are stable, vernacular universals, *be like* has proven instrumental for very different reasons. In the next section I provide an overview of the insights enabled by this innovation, with an eye on the "general questions" referenced above by Labov.

The Mechanism of Change

The mechanism of change refers to the way in which a change proceeds in social and linguistic structure. Though attitudinal factors are part of this complex (Dailey-O'Cain 2000; Buchstaller 2006b), they will not be addressed here. The focus will be on the status of *be like* as a change and what that entails for our understanding of types of change, for the incrementation of change, and for the constraints on variation as a change progresses.

Be like: Change in progress versus age grading. In the early stages of its development, much of the scholarly debate concerning *be like* centered on the question of age grading. This was a necessary discussion, since apparent time data alone are insufficient for disentangling the association of a linguistic feature with a particular life stage (i.e., age grading) from change in progress. With a feature such as *be like*, which has a high degree of social awareness and which, as a result, is amenable to conscious manipulation, age grading is a distinct possibility (see, e.g., Milroy & Gordon 2003: 36*f*). It was argued that the popularity of *be like* was linked to its trendy status in adolescent culture, an argument bolstered by the recurrent finding that adolescents were its most frequent users. But of course, this same type of pattern is predicted for change in progress: It is adolescents who will exhibit the highest frequencies of use of incoming forms, a trajectory that becomes increasingly exaggerated with higher rates of change. Thus, the sudden popularity of *be like* and its concomitant association with adolescents created an analytical conundrum.

Variationists called for three kinds of evidence to shed light on the situation: longitudinal studies, real-time comparisons, and data from older speakers. When such evidence was considered, it became apparent that *be like* was not only an incoming form but also one that was quickly becoming entrenched in the quotative system (Cukor-Avila 2002; Buchstaller 2006a; Tagliamonte & D'Arcy 2007). It also became apparent, however, that *be like* did not represent the "normal" type of linguistic change in which incremental shifts in the frequency of a form are observed from one age cohort to the next. This kind of generational change results in a monotonic age distribution such as that visible for *be like* among speakers aged 17 and older in figure 24.1, where frequency and age exhibit a linear correspondence. Labov argues that monotonicity derives from the assumption that once speakers become "linguistic adults," their individual vernaculars stabilize (Labov 2001: 463).

This assumption is in fact the basic premise underlying apparent time, though it is an assumption that *be like* (among other features) has forced us to reconsider. Individuals continue to advance their use of *be like* well into adulthood; the system remains amenable to shifts in frequencies. For example, in 1995, Ontarioans aged 18 to 27 quoted with *be like* at a rate of 13 percent overall. Seven years later, in 2002, that same cohort evinced significantly higher rates of *be like* usage: 31 percent among 30- to 34-year-olds (speakers who were in their mid to late twenties in 1995). Among 25- to 29-year-olds (speakers who were in their late teens and early twenties in 1995), the rate was even higher, 58 percent (Tagliamonte & D'Arcy 2007). Buchstaller (2006a) reports the same pattern for American English. Thus, *be like* is not only an incoming innovation, but it is also subject to life-span change, a historical (rather than cyclic) pattern in which individual speakers change linguistic practice alongside the rest of the community (Sankoff 2005).

The incrementation of change. Once established as change in progress, *be like* raised questions about the way in which successive age cohorts continued to advance it beyond the level of the previous one, in the same direction. *Be like* has progressed with remarkable speed: The S-curve—an established template for diachronic change[1]—is visible in figure 24.1. The trajectory for *be like* is also notable for the peak it evinces among speakers aged 17 to 19. It is now understood that this peak is predicted "as a general requirement of change in progress" (Labov 2001: 455); *be like* has contributed to this understanding, extending

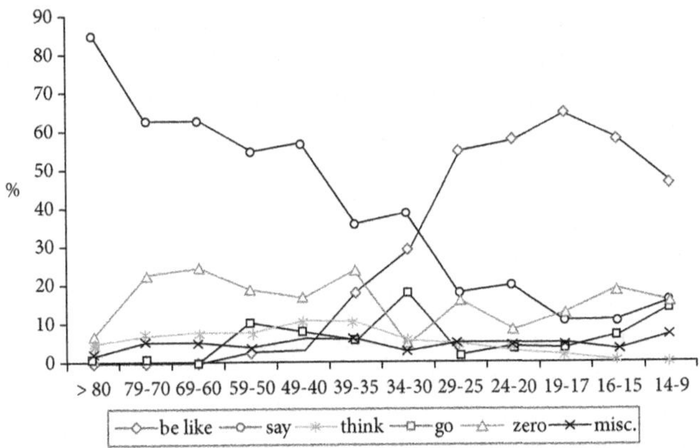

Figure 24.1. Overall distribution of quotative verbs across apparent time, c.2002

Source: Tagliamonte & D'Arcy (2007: 205, fig. 2)

the prediction from sound change to discourse-pragmatics (Tagliamonte & D'Arcy 2009).

The adolescent peak has long been a recurrent finding in studies of language variation and change (e.g., Cedergren 1973, 1988), but it remained an anomaly until formalized by Labov (2001). The original expectation was that the apparent time trajectory of a change in progress would continue upward as age groups became younger and younger. This was not the case. Instead, when younger adolescents and preadolescents were sampled, the curve consistently shifted downward for these age groups. The peak therefore required a principled explanation; it was too regular for ad hoc interpretation. Labov (2001) drew on a range of fields, incorporating empirical findings and theoretical apparatus from historical linguistics, language and dialect acquisition, and variationist sociolinguistics to develop an approximation of the basic model for the incrementation of change. The key assumptions of this model are

1. the rate of change proceeds logistically (slowly at first, speeds up at mid-point, subsequently tails off);
2. participation in change entails *vernacular re-organization* (literally, the changing of the vernacular away from the model provided by the primary caretaker to one approximating that of the older peer group);
3. vernacular re-organization begins around age 4 and continues until approximately the age of 17, when the vernacular stabilizes.

The logistic function (assumption (1)) is ultimately additive: the progress of a change at any point is determined by the sum of the increments for each year that change has been ongoing. The size of the increments, however, is mediated by the rate of change: faster rates, found at the midcourse of a change, produce larger increments, and slower rates, found in the initial and terminal stages, produce smaller increments. Given vernacular re-organization (assumption (2)) and its requisite cessation (assumption (3)), the appearance of a peak is purely mathematical. Each subsequent cohort surpasses the level of the previous one: they started out with a higher value and progressed further.

Quotative *be like* has diffused quickly (i.e., at an elevated rate). If the model holds predictive power, a prominent peak should be evident. Figure 24.2, based on the data from figure 24.1, displays a scatter plot for just *be like*. Individuals are indicated by their sex, male as (m) and female as (f). A line has been fit across these data to track the overall distribution of *be like* across apparent time. The correlation between the frequency of *be like* and speaker age was assessed using a Spearman rank correlation test. In this test, correlation coefficients (*rho*) vary between 1 and –1, and the closer the *rho* is to 1 or –1, the stronger the correlation is between the factors being tested. In figure 24.2, the correlation value between age and *be like* is strong, negative and highly significant: –5599834, $p < 0.0001$. This means that as age decreases, the frequency of *be like* increases significantly.

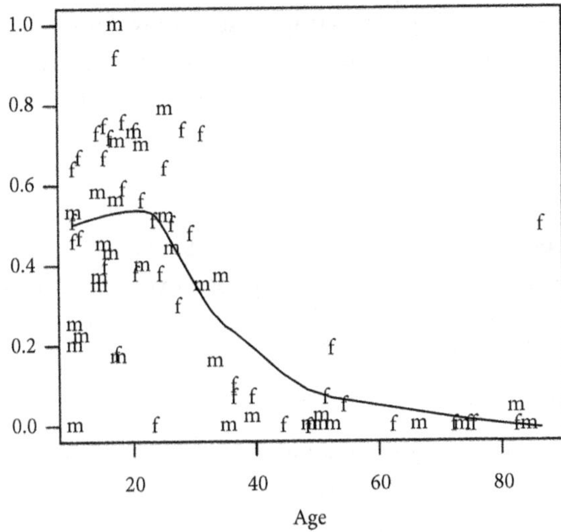

Figure 24.2. Scatter plot showing the distribution of *be like* across apparent time, c.2002. The y-axis displays frequency; the x-axis displays speaker age.

Source: Tagliamonte & D'Arcy (2009: 84, fig. 7a)

Nonetheless, the relationship between *be like* and speaker age is not linear in figure 24.2: It is more frequent among speakers in their early 20s and is less frequent among older *and* younger speakers. As summarized in table 24.1, if the sample is configured in line with Labov's (2001) age divisions, the frequency differences that create the peak in figures 24.1 and 24.2 are highly significant. The peak is not due to chance fluctuation in the data set. It is a bona fide characteristic of the progression of this change across apparent time.

Be like has thus contributed to our understanding of the mechanics driving linguistic change. The adolescent peak is a general requirement of synchronic change. This association of high frequencies with the late teen years, however, was part of the reason for the age grading debate in the early stages of the development of be *like*. The situation was exacerbated by the speed at which this form was progressing, which resulted in usage rates that were significantly higher among late teens than they were among other, contiguous age groups.

Table 24.1 Significance tests for adjacent age groups

age groups	*p* value (nonpaired Wilcoxan test)
< 13 vs. 13–16	0.0075
13–16 vs. 17–29	0.0001
17–29 vs. 30–39	0.0001

Source: Tagliamonte & D'Arcy (2009: 87, table 6)

Constraints on variation. To paraphrase Labov (2001: 84), sociolinguistic variables are in the grammar, constrained by the grammar, and cannot be described apart from the grammar. One of the most fundamental understandings that research on language on variation and change has contributed to linguistic science is that heterogeneity is structured. In the case of *be like*, two constraints in particular have featured regularly in the literature: grammatical person and content of the quote (Tagliamonte & D'Arcy 2004, 2007). In probabilistic terms, first-person subjects favor *be like* over third-person subjects, and inner thoughts and attitudes favor *be like* over direct speech. The examples in (3) illustrate these contexts.

(3) a. quoted attitude:
She'll walk in the room and *be like* 'What up, I'm Stacy and like cater to me 'cause I'm awesome.' (Victoria, Canada)
b. first person:
I *was like* 'Yeah, we went to Oscar's and had a really good time.' (York, England)
c. first person inner thought/attitude:
We *were like* 'Oh you stupid girl.' (Christchurch, New Zealand)

Once the directions of effect are established for constraints on variation, these probabilistic hierarchies become diagnostics for probing further into the mechanisms of change. Researchers have therefore used *be like* to investigate the operation of the constraints on variation as this form progresses in social space, temporal space, and geographic space. The focus of this section will be the first two of these considerations; I return to the question of geography below.

Be like is a fairly recent innovation. In the early 1980s it was incipient (e.g., Butters 1982; Tannen 1986). This means that it occurred at low rates and would have had little in the way of social correlates. It also means that speakers who were in their 30s around the year 2000 would likely constitute the first generation of native users, since they were teenagers during the initial stages in the diffusion of *be like* (Tagliamonte & D'Arcy 2007: 204). In figure 24.1, this group captures a critical phase in the frequency of *be like* across apparent time, dividing cohorts with little or no instances of *be like* (ages 40 and over) from those for which it is a majority form (ages 29 and under). If the speakers from figure 24.1 are viewed in terms of developmental stages, as in table 24.2, a number of insights can be gained from the way in which the variable grammar operates both within groups and across groups.

In addition to grammatical person and content of the quote, two further constraints are included in Table 24.2: Tense/temporal reference and speaker sex. The present tense has long been associated with *be like* (e.g., Blyth et al. 1990: 218). However, in speech direct quotation tends to be embedded in narrative sequences. An important feature of English narrative is the Historical Present (HP), the use of present tense morphology to refer to past time events. Although a number of functions have been attested for the HP (e.g., Schiffrin

Table 24.2 Developmental trajectory for *be like*

Constraints	Stage 1 (30-year-olds)	Stage 2 (20-year-olds)	Stage 3 (17–19 years)
Content of quote	thought strongly favors	leveling trend visible but thought favors	leveling trend visible but thought favors
Grammatical person	1st persons favor	1st persons favor	1st persons favor
Tense and temporal reference	present tense favors	HP breaks away	HP highly favors
Speaker sex	weak sex effect; men favor	weak sex effect; women favor	women favor; men strongly disfavor

Source: Adapted from Tagliamonte & D'Arcy (2007: 209, fig. 3)

1981; Wolfson 1981, 1982), the concern here is the correlation between morphology (tense) and temporal reference. Speaker sex is pertinent since women tend to lead linguistic change (Labov 1990), and men tend to retreat from or resist an incoming form once an association with women is established (Labov 2001: 306ff.). Sex differences are most marked during the upswing of the S-curve, when the rate of change is at its maximum.

All of the constraints in table 24.2 significantly constrain the use of *be like* in all stages, and, with just one exception (i.e., the effect of sex among 30-year-olds), the directions of effect are also consistent across all stages. This suggests that the variable grammar is stable within and across the population of speakers who use *be like.*

At the same time, subtle shifts take place in apparent time. In the first stage, *be like* is strongly correlated with quoted thought, and while this effect perseveres in the second and third stages, its strength is attenuated. In contrast, the sex effect becomes more robust between the second and third stages. Moreover, the direction of effect reverses between the first and second stages: Women come to favor *be like,* and then men become disassociated from it. Finally, there is tense/temporal reference. In all stages, *be like* is strongly disfavored with past tense. The effect of present tense, however, reverses in apparent time. Stage 1: *be like* is favored for present tense, regardless of temporal reference. Stage 2: temporal reference begins to disentangle present tense contexts. The HP favors *be like* but regular present tense has an intermediate effect, neither favoring nor disfavoring. Stage 3: only the HP is a favoring context. At this stage, *be like* is heavily disfavored for regular present tense in addition to past tense.

These results are informative on two levels, particularly when interpreted in the context of ongoing change (the frequency of *be like* is significantly different from one stage to the next). From the perspective of the community, incrementation is accompanied by subtle shifts in the operation of the variable grammar. These shifts occur in both social and linguistic structure. In this instance then, generational change entails both frequency and constraints on variation.

From the perspective of the individual, however, changes in frequency are not accompanied by grammatical or social restructuring. That is, since discernable stages are apparent in table 24.2, lifespan change does not appear to affect the operation of the constraints on variation: They remain intact, regardless of (possible) shifts in frequency post-vernacular stabilization.

The Causation of Change

One of the more fundamental questions with which variationists grapple concerns the causes of change (Weinreich et al. 1968). What gives rise to a particular form, at a particular time, in a particular place? *Be like* is fully entrenched in the grammar of English, constrained by and within the system of direct quotation. Since its inception, it has functioned to introduce first-person inner thought. That the constraints on its use shift over time, however, indicates that at least part of the variable grammar was emergent: It was not fully established from the outset.

A common aspect of linguistic change is that as the frequency of an incoming form increases, that of an older one decreases. This appears to be the case in figure 24.1, where *be like* and *say* display a relationship of complementarity. As *be like* increases, *say* decreases. However, *say* is a verb of speech. While it can introduce quoted thought, it rarely does so. Ultimately, *say* is probabilistically predicted for contexts where *be like* is not: past tense, third-person speech (Tagliamonte & D'Arcy 2007: 210). Conclusion: *be like* is not a lexical replacement for *say*. It is an innovation in every sense of the word. The reason behind this innovation seems to be, at least in part, that the way in which English speakers use direct quotation has changed. In particular, self-revelation has become fashionable, arguably because it creates listener involvement by heightening the sense of drama (Tannen 1989).

Figure 24.3 traces the proportion of direct quotation that encoded thought over a 120-year period. For speakers born in the second half of the nineteenth century, quotation was used almost exclusively to report speech. By the turn of the twentieth century, a shift was underway: Speakers were beginning to quote their inner thought processes and attitudes. Very quickly, internal states emerged as "dramatic reenactments of personal experience" (Ferrara & Bell 1995: 283). This trend is not unique to New Zealand, where these particular data were gathered; apparent time evidence from England, Canada and the United States (Tagliamonte & D'Arcy 2007; Buchstaller & D'Arcy 2009) suggest that it is a characteristic of (native) English more generally.

The verb *think* is traditionally that used to introduce internal states, a fact that is reflected in Figure 24.3 by the identical frequency values of *think* and quoted thought among all speakers up to those born in the 1940s. At that point, the trajectories diverge. The rate of quoted thought continues to increase but the rate of *think* tails off. This is the precise point at which *be like* entered the

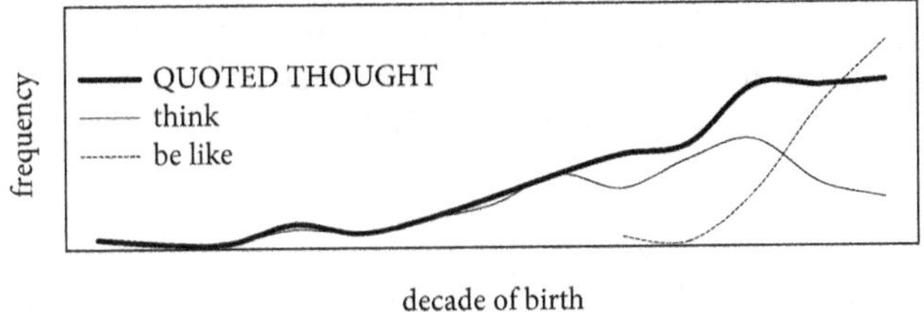

Figure 24.3. Quoted thought across time in New Zealand English

Source: D'Arcy (2012, fig. 3)

repertoire. The question is, what may have motivated the development of a new form? This is particularly intriguing given that the coexistence of *think* and *be like* appears to introduce a redundancy in the system: Both are used to introduce first-person thought.

Given our understanding of the constraints on variation, however, there are other factors to explore which can help shed light on this apparent overlap in function. As discussed above, one of these is tense/temporal reference. *Be like* is strongly favored in HP contexts. *Think*, on the other hand, is not. In fact, in these data *think* almost categorically fails to encode the HP; instead it is favored for past tense. A further effect concerns the use of voicing effects (i.e., mimesis), whereby a speaker may affect a different accent, pitch, intonational pattern, and so on, for dramatic effect (see Buchstaller & D'Arcy 2009: 297). Again *think* and *be like* pattern in opposition: *think* favors quotes rendered in the speaker's normal talking voice, but *be like* favors mimesis. In short, the domains of *think* and *be like* do not fully overlap; each does different work within the system. The net effect is that, while both *think* and *be like* introduce first-person thought, they introduce different types of first-person thought. For *think*, it is past tense and non-mimetic; for *be like*, it is HP and mimetic. In other words, causation in this instance derives from the development of a new niche in the grammar for constructed dialogue: *be like* emerged as a narrative present marker (Tagliamonte & D'Arcy 2007).[2]

The Consequences of Change

One of the strongest assumptions about *be like*, both in ideological and in sociolinguistic terms, is that it has spread across varieties of English from an American epicenter (see Romaine & Lange 1991: 248). There is also an assumption that it has been propelled along this trajectory by the media, as a discourse-pragmatic example of Milroy's (2007) "off the shelf" changes (i.e., features that are culturally constructed and widely accessible, regardless of a speaker's primary social networks). Regardless of the medium behind the global spread of linguistic forms, when changes diffuse across inter-varietal lines, a number of outcomes are possible: wholesale adoption, outright rejection, or interaction between the local system and the innovative feature (Britain 2002). In the case of *be like*, it is clear that this form does not impose itself on an existent system but rather is integrated into it in ways that cohere with the system's prevailing, and preexisting, overall configuration (Buchstaller & D'Arcy 2009: 317–21).

In this sense, the consequences of change are not universal. As *be like* is indigenized by local speakers, the outcomes have the potential to vary along a number of dimensions: social, functional, probabilistic. We can ask, therefore, which constraints on *be like* are subject to reorganization and which remain intact? Buchstaller and D'Arcy (2009) explored these questions by considering the patterning of *be like* in three varieties of English: American, English, and New Zealand. Their analysis indicated that from a functional perspective, three constraints operate uniformly: *be like* is consistently favored for first-person, mimetic thought. The effect of tense, on the other hand, is particularized to variety and is dependent on (1) existent systemic demands and (2) competition with quotative *go*. Thus, in American English, *be like* is favored with present tense morphology; in New Zealand English it is favored for the HP, while in English English the HP is the only context in which *be like* is disfavored (*go* encodes the HP).

These findings can be summarized as such: The constraints that are significant in the (putative) donor variety are also significant in the receptor varieties. However, one constraint is reorganized, and, though not discussed here, the extent to which each constraint "matters" also differs along local lines (see Buchstaller & D'Arcy 2009:314*f*). Thus, the content of the quote as either thought or speech exerts differential effects across varieties in that it accounts for more of the variation in New Zealand, for example, than it does in the United States. What we can conclude from these types of findings is that as *be like* is incorporated into the quotative repertoire, new and localized balances are created. In other words, global patternings cannot be explained without looking at the specificities of local systems.

There Is Still More to Learn: E.g., the Outer Circle

Despite the range of research questions that have been addressed using *be like* as a diagnostic, work on variation and change in the English quotative system has focused almost exclusively on varieties from the Inner Circle.[3] These varieties constitute the traditional bases of English, where English is the primary and native language of most speakers: the United Kingdom, the United States, (Anglophone) Canada, (Anglophone) South Africa, Australia, and New

Zealand. However, we may also look to varieties with other kinds of ecologies, where English is either non-native and/or it exists in multilingual societies. In particular, the Outer Circle—where for historical reasons English plays a key role in institutional life (often as an official, legal, or educational language)—presents a prime opportunity to examine the grass-roots forces that act on globalizing features such as *be like*.

Consistent with the aims of the variationist paradigm, however, it is first necessary to situate *be like* within the system of direct quotation for any individual variety. Table 24.3 presents the overall distributions of verbs of direct quotation in five Outer Circle varieties: Hong Kong, India, Philippines, Singapore, and Kenya (South Africa). The data come from the International Corpus of English (ICE; see Greenbaum 1996).

It is immediately clear that the repertoires of these varieties are distinct from what is reported for contemporary Inner Circle varieties. For one, the rates of quoted speech are extremely high overall. In this respect, the ICE data resemble the quotative system of late nineteenth- and early twentieth-century Inner Circle English (see figure 24.3 above, from D'Arcy 2012; also Buchstaller 2011): It is highly circumscribed to the reporting of speech. Following from this observation, *say* is consistently the most frequent quotative overall in these data, while *think* is in all cases a minority form, consistently (among) the least frequent of all the verbs used. Thus, the elevated rates of inner state reporting that are found in contemporaneous Inner Circle varieties simply do not manifest in these Outer Circle ICE materials.

Moreover, these repertoires are more constrained than those of the Inner Circle in that fewer verbs function to introduce direct quotation. The choices are restricted to the forms that appear in table 24.3. These repertoires are also notable with respect to *be like*: it never occurs in ICE India and in the other corpora it is highly infrequent. At the same time, *ask* and *tell* consistently

Table 24.3. Overall distributions of quotative verbs in five Outer Circle International Corpus of English (ICE) corpora

Hong Kong		India		Philippines		Singapore		Kenya	
(N = 213)		(N = 156)		(N = 339)		(N = 494)		(N = 126)	
Say	61.0	*say*	65.4	*say*	39.2	*say*	65.8	*say*	41.3
Ø	13.1	*tell*	10.9	Ø	20.6	Ø	14.2	*tell*	23.8
Ask	7.5	*ask*	7.1	*be like*	11.2	*ask*	5.7	Ø	11.9
tell	6.1	Ø	7.1	*go*	8.3	*tell*	4.5	*be like*	7.9
be like	4.7	*think*	3.4	*ask*	6.8	*be like*	3.6	*ask*	7.1
think	3.8			*tell*	6.5	*think*	2.2	*think*	2.4
				think	1.2	*go*	1.4	*go*	0.8
88% speech		94% speech		86% speech		91% speech		86% speech	

appear among the top four contenders. They never rank this high in North American, British or Southern Hemisphere Englishes, where it is extremely rare for these verbs to introduce direct quotations. Their primary function in the Inner Circle is to introduce indirect quotation.

To that end, another notable characteristic of the Outer Circle data is the tendency for quotatives to collocate with the complementizer 'that,' even when introducing direct quotation. This is exemplified by the examples in (4), where it is clear from a number of cues (contextual, pragmatic, discursive, referential) that the quoted material constitutes an overt re-creation rather than an indirect reporting of what was said.

(4) a. After the movie I just *said* that 'Oh Frank I cannot walk.' (Hong Kong; S1A041;169:1)
b. And then like he *said* that 'Oh you have to do like French Revolution.' (Hong Kong; S1A098;43:1)
c. There was one chap in Jubilee who *said* that 'I can't do anything about uh this guy.' (India; S1A083;141:1)
d. Never a husband *says* that 'I'll make a cup of tea okay, you sit. I'll make a cup of tea.' (India; S1A087;126:1)
e. So Kabuwe Abuwe *told* us that 'If it is for wedding I am not going to contribute.' (Kenya; S1A016K)

This is not a marginal phenomenon. In ICE India, for example, the complementizer occurs with 11 percent of direct quotes (N = 156). In ICE Hong Kong, the figure rises to 16 percent overall (N = 213). Thus, this construction cannot simply reflect a second language error, but must constitute a more systematic aspect of direct quotation in these varieties.

The nearly categorical tendency to report speech rather than other types of content, the restricted repertoire, and the ability to collocate 'that' with verbs of direct quotation suggest that the ecology of quotation functions distinctly in Outer Circle Englishes than it does in Inner Circle varieties. Since it is clear that *be like* is subject to system-specific pressures in receptor varieties, we may wonder how this innovation functions when it spreads to non-native speakers, who use English in a range of functional and institutional domains and for whom norms of use are emergent (as opposed to being dependent on those of the Inner Circle).

Figure 24.4 displays the distributional patterns for the "classic factors" of grammatical person and content of the quote (Tagliamonte and D'Arcy 2007: 203) in ICE Hong Kong, Philippines, Singapore and Kenya. In this figure, the darker bar for each constraint represents the probabilistically favored context in Inner Circle Englishes: first person and thought, respectively. The lighter bar represents the probabilistically disfavored context in the Inner Circle: third person and speech. If these two factor groups pattern similarly to native Englishes, then the darker bars should consistently show higher frequency effects than the lighter ones. This is precisely the case in Hong Kong: The distributional pattern indicates that *be like* introduces first person thought. This, however,

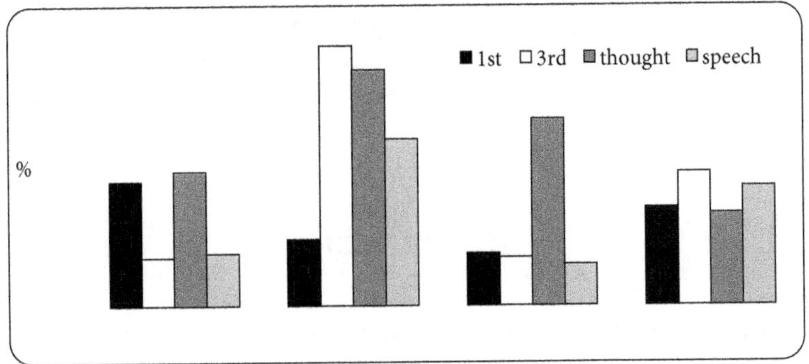

Figure 24.4. Constraint effects on *be like* in four Outer Circle varieties

is the only Outer Circle variety in figure 24.4 for which this is the case. In ICE Philippines, *be like* introduces not first-person thought but third-person thought. In ICE Singapore, it simply introduces thought (there is no person effect), and in the Kenyan data, *be like* introduces third-person speech. In other words, it patterns in direct opposition to the Inner Circle norms.

Conclusion

Labov maintains that "the language has not in effect changed unless the change is accepted as part of the language by other speakers" (1994: 45, fn.2; also Weinreich et al. 1968: 187), and it may seem that this chapter has focused quite squarely on *change*, perhaps to the detriment of *variation*. In choosing to frame the discussion in light of *be like*, a new, robust, and versatile feature of the English quotative system, that may be an inevitable consequence of our ideological association of *be like* with innovation. However, what makes *be like* such a useful and powerful heuristic for testing theories of language change is, in fact, variation and the constraints that operate upon it. It is the operation of the variable grammar across speakers, time, and space that enable us to address the mechanism, the causation, and the consequences of change. Living language is no static entity. It is ineradicably subject to variation. At times this variation leads to change, and at others it is stable. At all times, however, it is structured.

Notes

1. For an alternate view, see Denison 2003.
2. A persistent hypothesis about the function of *be like* is that of hedge: because it lacks the directness of *say* and *think*, it allows plausible deniability on the part

of the speaker. As far as I am aware, however, this possibility has never been examined empirically.
3. On the Three Circles of English, see Kachru (1985, 1992).

References

Blyth, C., Recktenwald, S., & Wang, J. 1990. I'm like, 'Say what?!'. A new quotative in American oral narrative. *American Speech* 65(3): 215–27.

Bonnici, L. M. 2010. Variation in Maltese English: The interplay of the local and the global in an emerging postcolonial variety. Ph.D. dissertation, University of California, Davis.

Britain, D. 2002. Space and spatial diffusion. In J. K . Chambers, P. Trudgill, & N. Schilling-Estes (eds.), *The handbook of language variation and change,* 603–37. Oxford: Blackwell.

Buchstaller, I. 2006a. Diagnostics of age-graded linguistic behaviour: The case of the quotative system. *Journal of Sociolinguistics* 10(1): 3–30.

Buchstaller, I. 2006b. Social stereotypes, personality traits and regional perception displaced: Attitudes towards the 'new' quotatives in the U.K. *Journal of Sociolinguistics* 10(3): 362–81.

Buchstaller, I. 2011. Quotations across the generations. *Corpus Linguistics and Linguistic Theory* 7(1): 59–92.

Buchstaller, I., & D'Arcy, A. 2009. Localized globalization: A multi-local, multivariate analysis of quotative *be like. Journal of Sociolinguistics* 13(3): 291–331.

Butters, R. R. 1982. Editor's note [on 'be like']. *American Speech* 57(2): 149.

Cedergren, H. J. 1973. The interplay of social and linguistic factors in Panama. Ph.D. dissertation, Cornell University.

Cedergren, H. J. 1988. The spread of language change: Verifying inferences of linguistic diffusion. In P. Lowenberg (ed.), *Language spread and language policy: Issues, implications, and case studies,* 45–60. Washington, DC: Georgetown University Press.

Chambers, J. K., & Trudgill, P. 1980. *Dialectology.* Cambridge: Cambridge University Press.

Cukor-Avila, P. 2002. *She say, she go, she be like*: Verbs of quotation over time in African American Vernacular English. *American Speech* 77(1): 3–31.

Dailey-O'Cain, J. 2000. The sociolinguistic distribution and attitudes towards focuser *like* and quotative *like. Journal of Sociolinguistics* 4(1): 60–80.

D'Arcy, A. 2012. The diachrony of quotation: Evidence from New Zealand English. *Language Variation and Change* 24(3).

Denison, D. 2003. Log(ist)ic and simplistic S-curves. In R. Hickey (ed.), *Motives for language change,* 54–70. Cambridge: Cambridge University Press.

Ferrara, K., & Bell, B. 1995. Sociolinguistic variation and discourse function of constructed dialogue introducers: The case of *be + like. American Speech* 70(3): 265–90.

Fleischman, S. 1998. Des jumeaux de discours. *La Linguistique* 34(2): 31–47.

Foulkes, P. 2006. Phonological variation: A global perspective. In B. Aarts & A. M. S. McMahon (eds.), *The handbook of English linguistics,* 625–69. Oxford: Blackwell.

Golato, A. 2000. An innovative German quotative for reporting on embodied actions: *ich under so/und er so* 'and I'm like/and he's like'. *Journal of Pragmatics* 32: 29–54.

Greenbaum, S. (ed.). 1996. *Comparing English worldwide: The International Corpus of English*. Oxford: Clarendon Press.

Guy, G. 1980. Variation in the group and the individual: The case of final stop deletion. In W. Labov (ed.), *Locating language in time and space*, 1–36. New York: Academic Press.

Hasund, I. K. 2003. The discourse markers *like* in English and *liksom* in Norwegian teenage language: A corpus-based, cross-linguistic study. Unpublished doctoral dissertation. University of Bergen and Agder University College.

Hopper, P. 1991. On some principles of grammaticalization. In E. Traugott & B. Heine (eds.), *Approaches to grammaticalization*, 17–35. Amsterdam/Philadelphia: John Benjamins.

Joseph, B. D. 1981 [1982]. Hittite *iwar, wa(r)* and Sanskrit *iva*. *Zeitschrift für vergleichende Sprachforschung* 95: 93–98.

Kachru, B. 1985. Standards, codification and sociolinguistic realism: The English language in the Outer Circle. In R. Quirk & H.G. Widdowson (eds.), *English in the world: Teaching and learning the language and literatures*, 11–30. Cambridge: Cambridge University Press.

Kachru, B. 1992. Teaching world Englishes. In B. Kachru (ed.), *The other tongue: English across cultures*, 2nd ed., 355–66. Urbana-Champaign: University of Illinois Press.

Kotsinas, U-B. 1994. *Ungdomsspråk*. Uppsala: Hallgren & Fallgren.

Kytö, M., & Romaine, S. 1997. Competing forms of adjective comparison in Modern English: What could be *more quicker* and *easier* and *more effective*? In T. Nevalainen & L. Kahlas-Tarkka (eds.), *To explain the present: Studies in the changing English language in honour of Matti Rissanen*, 329–52. Helsinki: Société Néophilologique.

Labov, W. 1966. *The social stratification of English in New York City*. Washington, DC: Center for Applied Linguistics.

Labov, W. 1972. *Sociolinguistic patterns*. Philadelphia: University of Pennsylvania Press.

Labov, W. 1989. The child as linguistic historian. *Language Variation and Change* 1: 85–97.

Labov, W. 1990. The intersection of sex and social class in the course of linguistic change. *Language Variation and Change* 2: 205–54.

Labov, W. 1994. *Principles of linguistic change*, vol. 1. *Internal factors*. Malden, MA: Blackwell.

Labov, W. 2001. *Principles of linguistic change*, vol. 2. *Social factors*. Malden, MA: Blackwell.

Macaulay, R. 2001. You're like 'Why not?' The quotative expressions of Glasgow adolescents. *Journal of Sociolinguistics* 5: 3–21.

Maschler, Y. 2009. *Metalanguage in interaction: Hebrew discourse markers*. Amsterdam: John Benjamins.

Milroy, L. 2007. Off the shelf or under the counter? On the social dynamics of sound changes. In C. M. Cain & G. Russom (eds.), *Studies in the history of the English language III*, 149–72. Berlin / New York: Mouton de Gruyter.

Milroy, L., & Gordon, M. 2003. *Sociolinguistics: Method and interpretation*. Malden, MA: Wiley-Blackwell.

Poplack, S., & Tagliamonte, S. 1999. The grammaticalization of *going* to in (African American) English. *Language Variation and Change* 11(3): 315–42.
Romaine, S. 1982. *Socio-historical linguistics: Its status and methodology*. Cambridge: Cambridge University Press.
Romaine, S., & Lange, D. 1991. The use of *like* as a marker of reported speech and thought: A case of grammaticalization in progress. *American Speech* 66: 227–79.
Sankoff, G. 2005. Cross-sectional and longitudinal studies in sociolinguistics. In U. Ammon, N. Dittmar, K. J. Mattheier, & P. Trudgill (eds.), *An international handbook of the science of language and society*, vol. 2, 1003–013. Berlin: Mouton de Gruyter.
Schiffrin, D. 1981. Tense variations in narration. *Language* 57(1): 45–62.
Schourup, L.C. 1982. Common discourse particles in English conversation. Ph.D. dissertation, Ohio State University. [Published, New York: Garland, 1985.]
Tagliamonte, S. A., & D'Arcy, A. 2004. *He's like, she's like*: The quotative system in Canadian youth. *Journal of Sociolinguistics* 8(4): 493–514.
Tagliamonte, S. A., & D'Arcy, A. 2007. Frequency and variation in the community grammar: Tracking a new change through the generations. *Language Variation and Change* 19: 199–217.
Tagliamonte, S. A., & D'Arcy, A. 2009. Peaks beyond phonology: Adolescence, incrementation, and language change. *Language* 85(1): 58–108.
Tagliamonte, S. A., & Hudson, R. 1999. *Be like* et al. beyond America: The quotative system in British and Canadian youth. *Journal of Sociolinguistics* 3(2): 147–72.
Tannen, D. 1986. Introducing constructed dialogue in Greek and American conversational and literary narrative. In F. Coulmas (ed.), *Direct and indirect speech*, 311–32. Amsterdam: de Gruyter.
Tannen, D. 1989. *Talking voices: Repetition, dialogue and imagery in conversational discourse*. Cambridge: Cambridge University Press.
Weinreich, U., Labov, W., & Herzog, M. 1968. Empirical foundations for a theory of language change. In W.P. Lehmann & Y. Malkiel (eds.), *Directions for historical linguistics. A symposium*, 95–195. Austin: University of Texas Press.
Winter, J. 2002. Discourse quotatives in Australian English: Adolescents performing voices. *Australian Journal of Linguistics* 22(1): 5–21.
Wolfson, N. 1981. The conversational historical present alternation. *Language* 55: 168–82.
Wolfson, N. 1982. *CHP: The conversational historical present in American English narrative*. Dordrecht, The Netherlands: Foris.

CHAPTER 25

SOCIOLINGUISTIC VARIATION AND CHANGE IN SIGN LANGUAGES

ADAM SCHEMBRI AND TREVOR JOHNSTON

In this chapter, we describe sociolinguistic variation and change in sign languages, the natural language of deaf communities. It has been a long-standing observation that there is considerable variation in the use of most well documented sign languages (e.g., Stokoe, Casterline, & Croneberg 1965). Work over the last two decades has shown that factors that drive sociolinguistic variation and change in both spoken and signed language communities are broadly similar. Social factors include, for example, a signer's age group, region of origin, gender, ethnicity, and socioeconomic status (Lucas, Bayley, & Valli 2001). Linguistic factors include phonological processes such as assimilation and reduction (Schembri et al. 2009), and grammaticalization (Johnston & Schembri 2010).

Some factors involved in sociolinguistic variation in sign languages, however, are distinctive. For example, phonological variation includes features, such as whether a sign is produced with one or two hands, that have no direct parallel in spoken language phonology. In addition, deaf signing communities are invariably minority communities embedded within larger majority communities whose languages are in another entirely different modality and which may have written systems and extensive written literatures, unlike sign languages. Some of the linguistic outcomes of this contact situation (such as the use of individual signs for letters to spell out written words on the hands, known as *fingerspelling*) are unique to such communities (Lucas & Valli 1992). This picture is further complicated by patterns of language transmission that see many deaf individuals acquiring sign languages as first languages at a much later age than hearing individuals (Emmorey 2002).

In the following sections, we examine and exemplify sociolinguistic variation in signed languages at the levels of phonology, lexicon, and grammar.

Linguistic Variables in Signed Languages

Variation in signed languages may be found at all levels of structural organization. As in spoken languages, variation may occur in all sublexical features of signs, including handshape (e.g., an extended index finger or flat-hand configuration in the sign PRO-1 in American Sign Language) and hand location (e.g., the handshape in the sign KNOW can be produced on the forehead or cheek in Australian Sign Language), as we shall see. Lexical variation also occurs: regional varieties of Australian Sign Language (Auslan) vary in their use of signs for colors, such as BLUE, GREEN, and WHITE (Johnston & Schembri 2007). With regard to grammatical variation, we will see that American Sign Language (ASL) and Auslan both exhibit variable expression of subject/agent roles. Although we do not cover stylistic variation in this chapter, this includes, for example, the fact that conversations in British Sign Language (BSL) appear to differ in structure from narratives: turn taking may occur in conversations, with a range of visual cues used to determine whose turn it is to sign (Coates & Sutton-Spence 2001). In narratives, however, usually the storyteller speaks with minimal interruptions, using a structured sequence of sentences that describe events in the order in which they occur.

Phonological Variation and Change

Earlier studies conducted into phonological variation in ASL include an investigation by Woodward and DeSantis (1977) into two-handed versus one-handed forms of ASL signs such as COW (see figure 25.1). They found that white signers using significantly more of the newer one-handed variants of these signs when compared to black signers. They also found that Southern signers used more two-handed variants than non-Southerners, and that older signers used more than younger signers. Recent work specifically on the the variety of ASL used by Southern African American signers, using a much larger sample of 96 participants, has confirmed the earlier findings. Results from this work indicate

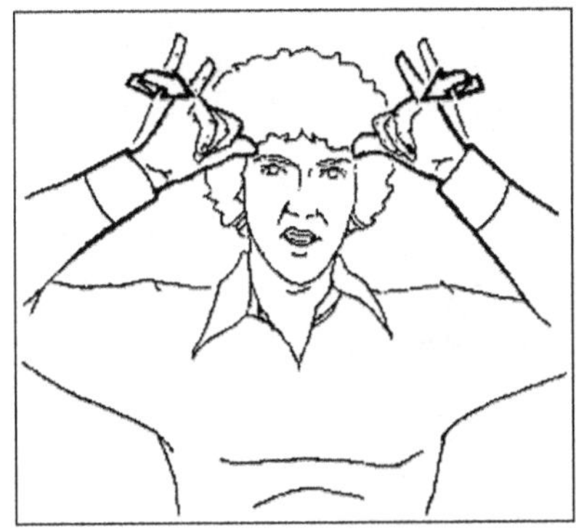
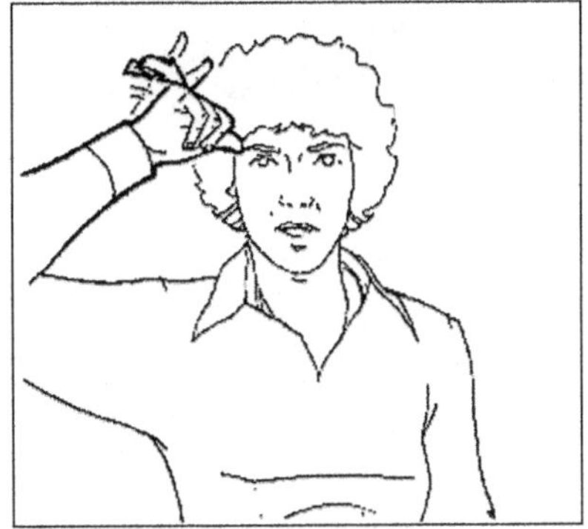

Figure 25.1. Two-handed and one-handed variants of the ASL sign COW (Baker & Cokely 1980). Reprinted with permission from Gallaudet University Press.

that younger black signers are significantly less likely to use the traditional two-handed signs than older black individuals. In addition, the handedness of the following and preceding sign was an important factor, with two-handed forms more likely when this was also a feature of signs in the phonological environment of the target sign (McCaskill, Lucas, Bayley, & Hill 2011).

Frishberg (1975) compared lexical signs listed in the 1965 dictionary of ASL with the same signs in publications that documented older varieties of ASL and French Sign Language (to which ASL is related historically). In particular, she found that many newer forms of signs involved changes from two-handed variants to one-handed forms (e.g., the sign COW in figure 25.1), from less to more symmetrical variants (e.g., the sign LAST), and/or moved from more peripheral locations in the signing space to more centralized places of articulation (e.g., the sign FEEL). Similar findings for BSL were reported in Woll (1987), such as the movement of signs from higher to lower locations (e.g., the sign PERHAPS from the head to in front of the body as shown in figure 25.2), as well as a tendency for two-handed signs to become one-handed. Both Frishberg (1975) and Woll (1987) remarked that diachronic changes in ASL and BSL were related to synchronic phonological variation.

Many research projects into sociolinguistic variation in ASL have tended to draw on data from small numbers of participants, and sometimes from only a single participant (e.g., Hoopes 1998). In the 1990s, the first large-scale studies of phonological variation in ASL were undertaken by Ceil Lucas and her colleagues (Lucas, Bayley, & Valli 2001). These investigations drew on a representative sample of the American deaf population and employed multivariate analyses of the data using Varbrul software. The dataset for this major study consisted of videotaped conversations, interviews, and lexical sign elicitation sessions collected from 207 deaf native and early learner signers of ASL in seven sites across the United States: Staunton, Virginia; Frederick, Maryland; Boston, Massachusetts; Olathe, Kansas; New Orleans, Louisiana; Fremont, California; and Bellingham, Washington. The participants included a mix of

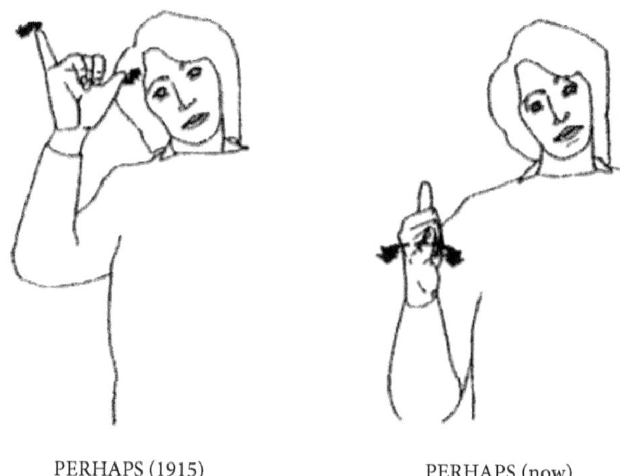

Figure 25.2. Historical change in the BSL sign PERHAPS (Kyle & Woll 1985). Reprinted with permission from Cambridge University Press.

men and women, both white and African American, from three different age groups (15–25, 26–52, and 55 years and over). The sample also included signers from both working-class and middle-class backgrounds.

The first study in the ASL project investigated variation in the sign DEAF. This sign has a number of phonological variants, but three were the focus of the study (see figure 25.3): the citation form in which the 1 handshape contacts the ear and then moves down to contact the chin, and two non-citation forms

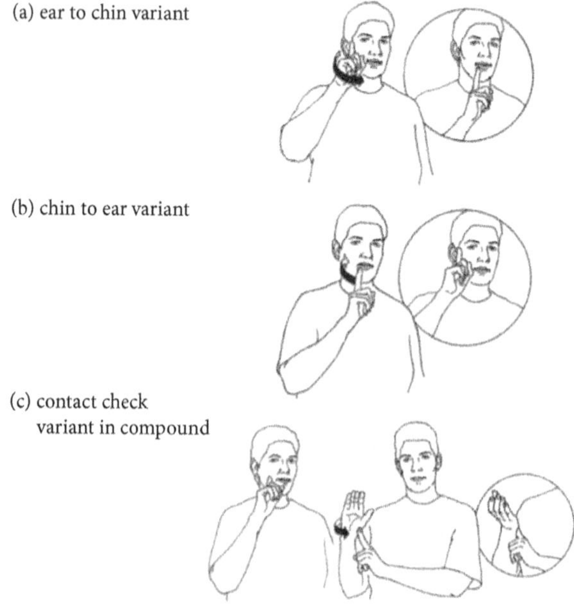

Figure 25.3. Phonological variation in the ASL sign DEAF (Lucas et al. 2001). Reprinted with permission from Cambridge University Press.

that consist of either a reversed movement of the hand from chin to ear or a reduced form in which the handshape simply contacts the cheek. Results from the multivariate analysis of 1618 examples showed that the factors that conditioned such phonological variation were mostly linguistic and social in nature. First, Lucas et al. (2001) reported that signers were less likely to use a citation form in nominal compounds, such as DEAF^CULTURE, but more likely to do so when DEAF was part of a predicate, as in PRO-3 DEAF 'She is deaf.' Second, social factors such as region and age were important. Signers in southern states tended to use non-citation forms of DEAF more than twice as often as signers in Boston. Despite this, older signers in Boston were found to be consistently more likely to use the citation form than younger signers.

Lucas and her colleagues next explored variation in ASL signs produced in citation form with the 1 handshape, such as lexical signs BLACK, together with functors such as BUT. This class of signs exhibit variation in hand configuration. Lucas et al. (2001) found that this variation may be relatively minor, with some bending of the index finger of the 1 handshape, or thumb extension. In some cases, however, the assimilation may be more marked, with the thumb and other fingers also extended. Analysis of the 5356 examples in the ASL dataset using Varbrul showed that, while assimilation effects due to the surrounding phonological environment were important, grammatical function was the strongest influence (as was also true of the sign DEAF). Signers are more likely to choose non-citation handshapes for wh-signs and pronouns (particularly PRO-1); whereas other lexical and function signs are more often realized in citation form. Interestingly, work on variation in the 1 handshape in a large-scale sociolinguistic investigation into BSL based on 2110 tokens from 210 participants in seven cities across the United Kingdom reported similar results (Fenlon, Schembri, Rentelis & Cormier, in press), although phonological environment was the most important constraint in BSL, and lexical frequency was found to be an additional important factor. Social factors were also important in the ASL data (but less so in the BSL study), with signers in California, Kansas/Missouri, Louisiana, and Massachusetts favoring the citation form, while those in Maryland, Virginia, and Washington state all disfavored it.

Lucas and her team also investigated location variation in a class of ASL signs represented by KNOW. In their citation form, these signs are produced on or near the signer's forehead, but often may be produced at locations lower than this, either on other parts of the signer's body (such as near the cheek) or in the space in front of the signer's chest. Again, Varbrul analysis of 2594 ASL examples in their dataset showed that grammatical function was the strongest linguistic factor, with nouns, verbs, and adjectives (e.g., FATHER, UNDERSTAND, DIZZY) appearing more often in citation forms, while prepositions (e.g., FOR) and interrogative signs (e.g., WHY) favored lowered variants. Phonological environment was also important, with preceding signs made on or near the body having a significant influence on whether or not the target sign appeared as a lowered variant. The results also indicated that younger signers, men, and non-native signers all favored lowered variants when compared to older signers, women, and native signers. Regional and ethnic differences also emerged, with African American deaf people and those from Virginia and Washington state tending to use more citation forms than whites and signers from the five other regions.

Similar patterns of variation and change emerged in a study of NZSL numeral signs (McKee, McKee & Major 2011) in which it was noted that variants consistently favored by the younger generation for numerals SIX to TEN utilize only the dominant hand, whereas older signers are more likely to use a two-handed system for these numerals (e.g., signing FIVE on the non-dominant hand simultaneously with TWO on the dominant hand for 'seven,' similar to the number gestures sometimes used by hearing people).

The NZSL numerals data comes from a major NZSL sociolinguistic project that, like the related Auslan variation project that preceded it, replicated the work of Lucas and colleagues in these two closely related southern hemisphere sign language varieties. The Auslan and NZSL sociolinguistic variation projects also investigated phonological variation, focusing specifically on variation in the location parameter in a class of signs that includes THINK, NAME, and CLEVER, which, like the similar class of signs in ASL studied by Lucas et al. (2001), could be produced at locations lower than the forehead place of articulation seen in their citation forms (see figure 25.4).

Schembri et al. (2009) reported that variation in the use of the location parameter in these signs reflects both linguistic and social factors, as has also been reported for ASL. Like the American study, the Auslan results provided evidence that the lowering of this class of signs reflects a language change in progress in the Australian deaf community, led by younger people and individuals from the larger urban centers. This geolinguistic pattern of language change (i.e., from larger to smaller population centers) is, as shown elsewhere in this volume, quite common cross-linguistically (Labov 1990). The NZSL study found evidence of similar regional differences in the use of lowered variants, but age was not a significant factor in their dataset.

Furthermore, the results indicated that some of the particular factors at work, and the kinds of influence that they have on location variation, appear

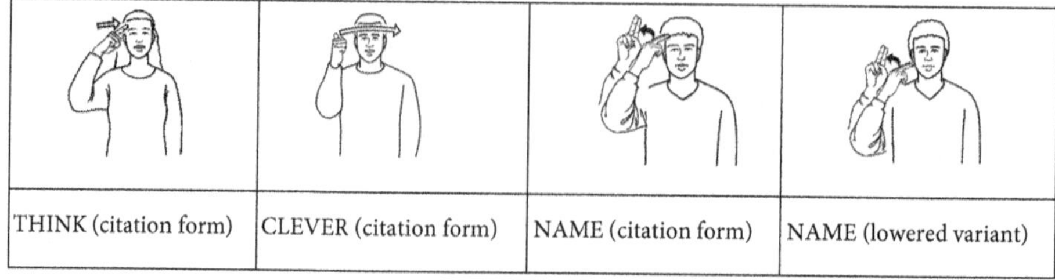

Figure 25.4. Three Auslan/NZSL forehead location signs and one lowered variant. (Johnston & Schembri, 2007). Reprinted with permission from Cambridge University Press.

to differ in Auslan and NZSL when compared to ASL. First, the Auslan and NZSL studies suggested relatively more influence on location variation from the immediate phonological environment (i.e., from the preceding and following segment) than is reported for ASL. Second, the Auslan and NZSL data suggested that location variation in this class of signs is an example of language change led by deaf women, not by deaf men as in ASL (Lucas et al. 2001). This is typical of a change from below (Labov 1990). Third, the Australian and New Zealand researchers showed that grammatical function interacts with lexical frequency in conditioning location variation (i.e., they found that high frequency verbs were lowered more often than any other class of signs), a factor not considered in the ASL study.

Lexical Variation and Change

Lexical variation presents the clearest examples of sociolinguistic variation in many sign languages, with lexical choices often systematically associated with signers of a particular age, gender, region, ethnicity, or educational background (Schembri et al., 2010).

Region

Regional lexical variation has been noted in a wide range of signed languages, such as Brazilian Sign Language (Campos 1994), South African Sign Language (Penn 1992), and Indo-Pakistani Sign Language (Zeshan 2000). Even signed varieties that are used across relatively small geographical areas, such as those in the Flemish-speaking areas of Belgium (Vanhecke & De Weerdet 2004) and in The Netherlands (Schermer 2004), can have multiple distinctive regional variants: Sign Language of The Netherlands has five regional dialects, with significant lexical differences between all regions but particularly between the south and the rest of the country.

In our discussion that follows, we largely draw on data from sociolinguistic studies of ASL, Auslan, NZSL, BSL and new data from a large-scale study into Italian Sign Language (LIS). The reason is that what is of more importance and interest than actual examples is that the phenomenon stems from similar sociolinguistic factors in different signing communities, and manifests itself in very similar ways.

Take, for example, the two main regional varieties of Auslan—the northern dialect and the southern dialect. Most noticeably, these two dialects differ in the signs traditionally used for numbers, colors, days of the week, and some other concepts (Johnston 1998). Indeed, the core set of vocabulary in certain semantic areas (e.g., color signs) is actually different for every basic term in these dialects (see figure 25.5).

Figure 25.5. Color signs in the northern (*top*) and southern (*bottom*) dialects of Auslan (Johnston & Schembri, 2007). Reprinted with permission from Cambridge University Press.

In NZSL, there is similar evidence of regional variation in the lexicon (see Kennedy et al. 1997), associated with three main concentrations of deaf population in North (Auckland), Central (Wellington) and Southern (Christchurch) cities.

Regional lexical variation in BSL is well known in the British deaf community (Sutton-Spence, Woll, & Allsop 1990). For example, Manchester signers traditionally use a unique system of signs for numbers, but the number system varies in other regions as well. Work on the large-scale BSL study mentioned earlier has revealed that the use of traditional regional number signs appear, however, to be diminishing. Data on the signs ONE through TWENTY elicited from 249 participants in eight cities across the United Kingdom (London, Bristol, Cardiff, Birmingham, Manchester, Newcastle, Glasgow, and Belfast) indicates that younger signers (aged 16–39 years) used significantly fewer traditional signs than signers in the oldest age group (60 or over). Those educated in local schools rather than in schools outside their region were also more likely to use traditional number signs, as were deaf individuals who had deaf parents. Furthermore, like the studies of ASL, two-handed versus one-handed variation was also significant, with older signers, women and deaf individuals with deaf parents all significantly favoring the use of two-handed variants (Stamp et al. accepted).

Ceil Lucas and her colleagues collected lexical data for 34 stimulus items from 207 signers in their study (Lucas et al. 2001). They carefully distinguished between distinct lexical variants with identical meanings and phonological variants of the same lexical item. Thus, in ASL, there are different lexical variants for PIZZA, none of which share handshape, movement, or location features. With the sign BANANA, however, one lexical variant has a number of phonological variants that vary in the handshape on the dominant hand. The researchers found that there was an average of seven lexical variants for each sign, and that signers from Massachusetts and Kansas/Missouri had the largest number of unique variants.

These examples of lexical variation in Western signed languages are likely due to the fact that residential deaf schools were set up independently from each other in different parts of those countries during the nineteenth and twentieth centuries. When many of these schools were established in the United Kingdom, for example, there was no single, centralized training program for educators of deaf children who wished to use sign language in the classroom; thus the signs used within each school (by the teachers and by the students) must have varied from school to school. Furthermore, in some schools, signed communication was forbidden during the latter part of the nineteenth and for much of the twentieth century, leading to the creation of new signs by deaf children (because few language models were available) while using their signed communication outside the classroom. Because sign languages must be used face to face, and because opportunities for travel were few, each variant tended to be passed down from one generation to the next without spreading to other areas. In a 1980 survey (Kyle & Allsop 1982), for example, 40 percent of people surveyed in the Bristol deaf community claimed that they had never met a deaf person from farther than 125 miles away. As a result, around half of the individuals said they could not understand the varieties of BSL used in distant parts of the United Kingdom.

In their lexical variation study of ASL, Lucas and her colleagues found that of the 34 target items they studied, 27 included a variant that appeared in the data from all seven sites across the United States. Lucas et al. (2001) suggested that shared lexical forms exist alongside regional variants due to historical patterns of transmission of ASL across the country. The residential schools in each of the seven sites studied in the project all had direct or indirect links with the first school, the American School for the Deaf in Hartford, Connecticut. In the past, this school trained its deaf graduates as teachers who then were sent out across the United States to establish new schools, leading to the spreading of a standardized variety of ASL across the country and into much of Canada.

Increased travel and regular signing on broadcast television in the United Kingdom, however, means that British deaf people are now exposed to many more lexical variants of BSL than they once were. It appears that this is the reason deaf people increasingly report much less trouble communicating with those from distant regions of the United Kingdom (Woll 1994). Indeed, it is possible that this greater mixing of the variants may lead to dialect leveling, as results from the BSL number sign study mentioned earlier suggest (Stamp et al. accepted).

Age

The vast majority of deaf people have non-signing, hearing parents, and the age at which they acquire signed languages thus may be very late and tends to involve peer-to-peer transmission rather than parent-to-child. This can result in considerable differences across generations. An early study of the Bristol and Cardiff communities showed that the BSL color signs BROWN, GREEN,

PURPLE, and YELLOW and numbers HUNDRED and THOUSAND used by older deaf people were not used by younger deaf people from hearing families in Bristol (Woll 1983).

Sutton-Spence, Woll, and Allsop (1990) conducted a major investigation of sociolinguistic variation in fingerspelling in BSL, using a corpus of 19,450 fingerspelled items collected from 485 interviews with BSL signers on the deaf television program *See Hear.* They analyzed the use of the British manual alphabet in relation to social factors, such as gender, region and age. There were no effects due to gender on the use of fingerspelling, but age was a significant factor. Sutton-Spence and her colleagues found that over 80 percent of all clauses included a fingerspelled element in the data from those aged 45 years or older. In comparison, fingerspelling was used in fewer than 40 percent of clauses in the data from participants aged under 45. Region was also an important variable: the most use of fingerspelling was found in the signing of individuals from Scotland, Northern Ireland, Wales, and central England, with the least use by signers from the south-western region of England. Data from signers in northern England and in the southeast included moderate amounts of fingerspelling.

A much smaller study of fingerspelling use in Auslan by Schembri and Johnston (2007) found that that deaf signers aged 51 years or over made more frequent use of the manual alphabet than those aged 50 or younger. This was particularly true of those aged 71 years or older. In a short paper on the use of fingerspelling by deaf senior citizens in Baltimore, Kelly (1991) suggested that older ASL signers appeared to make greater use of the manual alphabet than younger signers.

In ASL, Auslan, and BSL, these age-related differences in fingerspelling usage undoubtedly reflect the educational experiences of older deaf people, many of whom were instructed using educational approaches that emphasized the use of fingerspelling over signing. Language attitudes may also play a role here, with older people possibly also retaining relatively stronger negative attitudes toward sign language use, although this has not yet been the focus of any specific empirical study. Language change is important here, too, as many older signers appear to prefer the use of traditionally fingerspelled items rather than the "new signs" used by younger people. For example, signs such as TRUCK, SOCCER, AND COFFEE were used by younger signers in the Schembri and Johnston (2007) dataset, whereas only older individuals fingerspelled T-R-U-C-K, S-O-C-C-E-R, and C-O-F-F-E-E.

The lexical variation study in ASL conducted by Lucas and her colleagues showed that there were lexical variants for 24 of the 34 stimulus items that were unique to each age group. Older signers produced unique forms for PERFUME, SNOW, and SOON, for example, and did not use the same signs as younger signers for DOG and PIZZA. They specifically investigated evidence of language change in two sets of signs. First, they looked in detail at DEER, RABBIT, SNOW and TOMATO because claims had been made in earlier work that phonological change was underway in these signs with DEER changing from two-handed to one-handed, RABBIT moving down from a head to hands location, and SNOW and TOMATO undergoing reduction and deletion of segments. Second, they were interested in the signs AFRICA and JAPAN because new, more "politically correct" variants of these signs had recently emerged as a result of the perception that the older variants reflected stereotypes about the physical appearance of people from these parts of the world. The picture that emerged from their analysis was complex, however, with some evidence that language change was taking place for RABBIT, SNOW, TOMATO, JAPAN, and AFRICA only in some regions and in some social groups: no signers in Maryland used the head variant of RABBIT any longer, for example, and no younger signers from California, Maryland, and Virginia used the old form of AFRICA (see figure 25.6), and there was no evidence of change in DEER at all.

As in the BSL study, variation in the NZSL numeral signs ONE to TWENTY is also systematically conditioned by social characteristics, especially age (McKee, McKee & Major 2011). The NZSL sociolinguistic variation project drew on a corpus of NZSL generated by 138 deaf people in conversations and interviews; the sample is balanced for region (Auckland, Palmerston North/Wellington, and Christchurch), gender, and age group. All participants acquired NZSL before the age of 12 years, and the majority of these before the age of seven. Multivariate analysis of this data revealed that age has the strongest effect on variation in the number system, followed by region and gender. With respect to region, signers from Auckland (the largest urban center) are slightly more likely to favor less common variants forms than those from the Wellington and Christchurch, who are more likely to favor the more standard signs. Overall, men are slightly more likely than women to favor less common forms, although gender has the weakest effect of the three social factors.

Variation in numeral usage reveals diachronic change in NZSL, and increasing standardization in this subset of the lexicon: all 15- to 29-year-olds produced the same forms for numerals ONE to TWENTY, except for numbers NINE, ELEVEN, TWELVE, and NINETEEN, which exhibited minor variation. Signers over 30 years of age, and especially above 45 years, exhibited more in-group variation (using a greater range of lexical variants), reflecting the fact that they were not exposed to a conventional signed lexicon at school. For certain numbers, such as EIGHT, the change is complete, in that none of the youngest age group use older forms of this numeral, shown in figure 25.7 as A, C, and D. In other

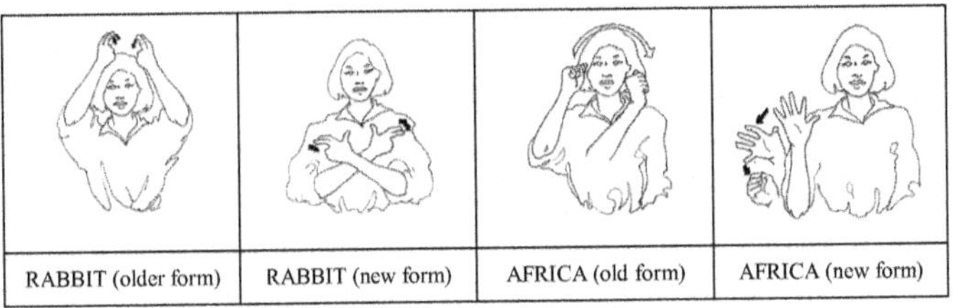

Figure 25.6. Lexical variation due to age in ASL (Lucas, Bayley, Reed, & Wulf, 2001). Reprinted with permission from Duke University Press.

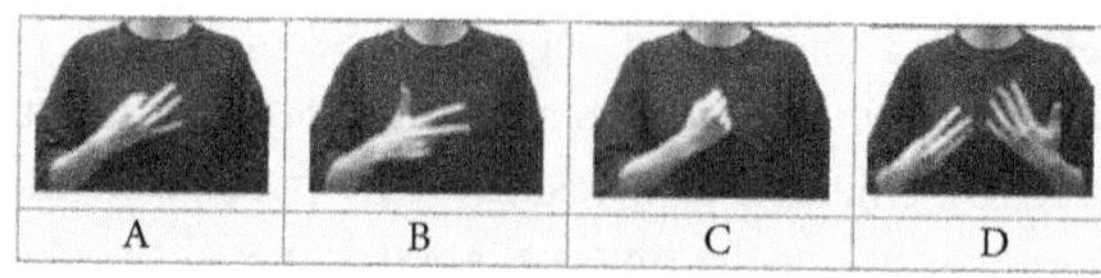

Figure 25.7. Variation due to age in NZSL EIGHT (McKee, McKee, & Major, 2011). Reprinted with permission from Gallaudet University Press.

cases, alternate variants still coexist, or in some cases, a change is apparently in progress toward a standard form.

Work on LIS, like the NZSL and BSL findings, also indicates language change in process, with traditional regional variants giving way to more standardized forms. In a preliminary report drawing on data for eight lexical items (BIRTHDAY, CHEESE, COFFEE, GOOD, HOUSE, INTELLIGENT, SEE, UNDERSTAND) from 95 participants in six cities, Geraci et al. (2011) show that older signers strongly favor regional variants for these signs, while younger signers disfavor them. Moreover, signers in the north and south of the country favor the regional forms, while those from the central regions of Italy disfavor them (Rome and other central cities are in fact the sources of these emerging standard variants).

Gender and Sexuality

There have not yet been any empirical studies demonstrating systematic lexical variation due to gender in any of the sign languages discussed above. A number of studies have suggested that gender may influence lexical variation in ASL, however. Lucas et al. (2001) report that only eight of the 34 stimulus items they studied did not show variants unique to either men or women, building on earlier findings by Mansfield (1993).

Quite significant lexical variation based on gender has been the focus of research into Irish Sign Language (ISL). For over a century, the Irish deaf community maintained distinct vocabularies associated with the different traditions of sign language use in the single-sex residential deaf schools in Dublin: St. Mary's School for Deaf Girls and St. Joseph's School for Deaf Boys. Using a set of 153 stimuli, Le Master and Dywer (1991) reported that 106 of the items were distinct, although 63 percent of these were related in some way. The male and female signs for GREEN, for example, differ in handshape, location and movement, whereas the men's and women's signs for APPLE and DAUGHTER share hand configuration (see figure 25.8). Although these lexical differences have lessened in contemporary ISL, Leeson and Grehan (2004) suggest that such gender differences do in fact continue in the language.

Gender differences in the use of fingerspelling in ASL have been reported by Mulrooney (2002). Drawing on a dataset of 1327 fingerspelled tokens collected

Figure 25.8. Examples of lexical variation in ISL due to gender. Reprinted with permission from Barbara LeMaster.

from interviews with eight signers, she found evidence in her dataset that men were more likely to produce non-citation forms (e.g., one-handed fingerspelling produced outside the usual ipsilateral area near the shoulder and/or with some of the manual letters deleted) than women.

A number of other aspects of language use have been reported to vary according to gender. For example, Coates and Sutton-Spence (2001) suggested that female BSL signers used different styles of conversational interaction than males. In their dataset, deaf women tended to set up a collaborative conversational floor in which multiple conversations could take place simultaneously, while males signers generally took control of the floor one at a time and used fewer supportive back-channeling strategies.

Studies conducted by Rudner and Butowsky (1981) and by Kleinfield and Warner (1997) compared American gay and heterosexual signers' knowledge of ASL signs related to gay sexuality and lifestyle. Both studies reported straight and gay individuals differing in their sign usage and in their judgements of commonly used signs related to sexuality. Kleinfeld and Warner found, for example, that the reduced fingerspelled variant of the sign GAY appeared to be most acceptable to gay and lesbian signers, possibly because this English borrowing had fewer negative associations with it then other signs.

Ethnicity and Religion

Research has established the existence of a distinct African American variety of ASL (Aramburo 1989). Like the gender differences in ISL, the emergence of this lexical variation reflects the historical context of American deaf education, with specific schools having been established for African American deaf children in some southern states during the period of segregation in the nineteenth and twentieth century. Work by Aramburo (1989) indicated that African American ASL signers had unique lexical variants, such as FLIRT, SCHOOL (shown in figure 25.9) and BOSS. Further supporting evidence for lexical variation was found in the sociolinguistic variation study conducted by Ceil Lucas and her colleagues: of the 34 stimuli, only six did not have uniquely African American variants.

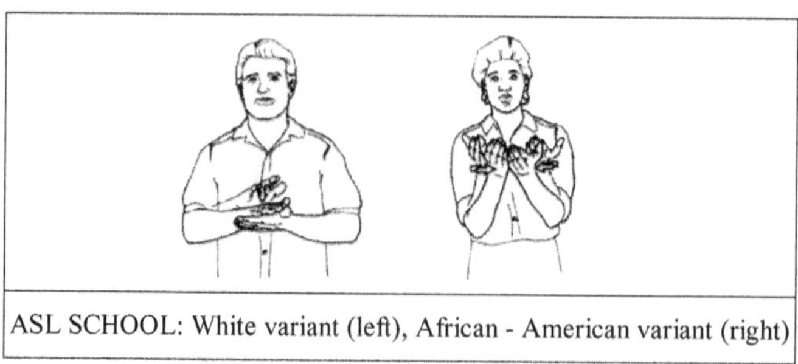

ASL SCHOOL: White variant (left), African - American variant (right)

Figure 25.9. Example of lexical variation due to ethnicity in ASL (Valli et al., 2005). Reprinted with permission from Gallaudet University Press.

Results from Black ASL Project indicate that a number of other differences can be identified in addition to use of specific lexical variants (McCaskill et al. 2011). For example, findings suggest that, compared to white signers, black signers produce fewer lowered variants of signs in the class of signs including KNOW. A study drawing on narratives elicited from 24 signers (12 black, 12 white) tested the claim that black signers use a larger signing space than white signers (something often remarked upon in the Amerian deaf community), and found that this did appear to be the case, at least for older signers (Hill, McCaskill, Lucas, & Bayley 2009).

Generally, there are few documented lexical variants in the sign varieties used by various ethnic groups in the United Kingdom and Australia, partly because the education of deaf children in these countries has, for the most part, never been segregated by ethnicity. Many deaf people in the United Kingdom from minority ethnic backgrounds are, however, increasingly forming social groupings that combine their deaf and ethnic identity (e.g., social groups formed by deaf people with south Asian backgrounds in London) and thus we might expect some sociolinguistic variation reflecting these identities to be developing, but this has not yet been the focus of any research. This is true of the Jewish Deaf Association, for example, many of whose members were educated in a separate Jewish deaf school that existed in London from 1866 to 1965 (Jackson 1990; Weinberg 1992). A book of BSL signs used to represent key elements of Judaism was published in 2003 (Jewish Deaf Association, 2003). More work on this issue has been undertaken for NZSL. NZSL exists in contact with both the dominant host language of English and Māori as the spoken language of the indigenous people of New Zealand. There is no empirical evidence that Māori signers' use of NZSL varies systematically from that of non-Māori deaf people, whose social networks and domains of NZSL use substantially overlap. Contact between hearing speakers of Māori and the Māori deaf community over the last decade has led to the coinage of signs and translations of Māori concepts that are in the process of becoming established 'borrowings' into NZSL—used for both referential purposes and to construct Māori deaf ethnic identity. These borrowings (locally referred to as 'Māori signs', see figure 25.10), such

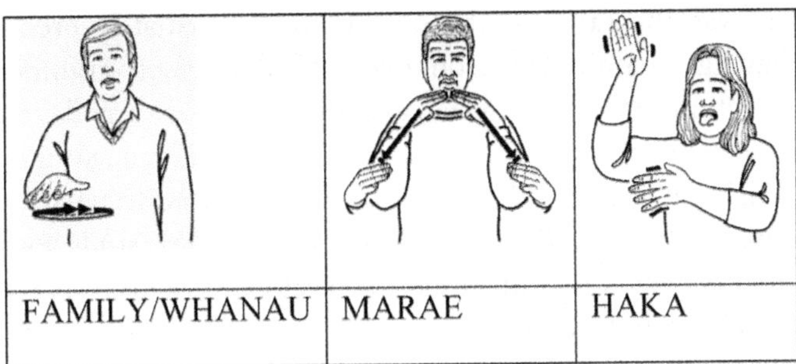

Figure 25.10. Examples of Maori signs in NZSL (Kennedy et al., 1997). Reprinted with permission from University of Auckland Press/Bridget Williams Books.

as WHANAU (extended family), MARAE (meeting place), and HAKA (a Māori dance ritual), are constructed by several processes: semantic extension of existing NZSL signs by mouthing Māori equivalents (e.g., WHANAU which is also a widely used sign meaning 'family'), loan translations of Māori word forms, and coining of neologisms (e.g., MARAE and HAKA) (McKee et al. 2007).

As it also true of New Zealand, separate schools for Catholic deaf children were established in Britain and Australia. All of these institutions employed ISL as the language of instruction until the 1950s. As a result, an older generation of signers in some regions of the United Kingdom and Australia make some use of ISL signs and the Irish manual alphabet, particularly when in the company of those who share their educational background.

Grammatical Variation

There has been little research into morphosyntactic variation and change in sign languages, although differences in grammatical skills in native (i.e., the minority with deaf signing parents) and non-native signers (i.e., the majority with non-signing hearing parents) have been reported several times in the literature (e.g., Boudreault & Mayberry 2006).

As part of the sociolinguistic variation in ASL, Auslan, and NZSL projects described earlier, variation in the presence of subject/actor noun phrases was investigated in narratives (e.g., Lucas et al. 2001). Like other signed languages, both ASL and Auslan exhibit significant variation in the expression of subject. The ASL study drew on a dataset of 429 clauses containing only plain verbs, whereas the Auslan study used a larger corpus of 976 clauses. Both datasets were collected from spontaneous narratives produced by 19 deaf signers from ASL, and 20 from Auslan. The overall results were remarkably similar. Schembri and Johnston (reported in McKee et al. 2011) found that almost two thirds (63 percent) of clauses had no overt subject noun phrase, almost identical to the figure in ASL (65 percent). Factors that conditioned an increased tendency to omit subject arguments in both Auslan and ASL included the use of a subject that identified a referent that was the same as the one in the immediately preceding clause; the subject having a non-first-person referent (first-person arguments strongly favored the retention of overt subjects); and the absence of any degree of English influence in the clause (English not being a pro-drop language like Auslan and ASL). These linguistic factors are similar to those reported to be at work in other pro-drop languages such as Spanish. In addition, the ASL study found evidence for social factors playing a role in variable subject expression. In particular, it was found that women and older signers (i.e., over 55 years of age) favored overt subjects, whereas men and younger signers (i.e., aged 15–54) did not. It may be that women and older signers produce more pronouns than men and younger signers because of a perception that the use of more English-like structures represents a prestige variety of signed communication (certainly this pattern with gender variation is characteristic of many spoken languages, see Labov 1990). Unlike ASL, however, multivariate statistical analysis of the Auslan data suggested that social factors such as the signer's age and gender were not significant.

A similar, larger study on variable subject/actor expression was carried out for NZSL (McKee et al. 2011). Using 2145 clauses from conversational and narrative data produced by 33 signers, it was also found that co-reference was an important factor, but, unlike ASL and Auslan, person was not. The data also suggest that subject drop occurred more often in the conversational data than in the narrative data. They found interesting patterns of age differences, with older signers (65 years and over) avoiding subject drop, while signers in the middle age group (40–64 years old) favored it, and signers in the youngest group (15–39 years old) neither favored nor disfavored subject drop. Lastly, ethnicity was a significant factor, with non-Māori signers favoring drop when compared to Māori deaf people.

Recently, preliminary results from a studying investigating the position of wh-signs in clauses in LIS has been reported (Geraci et al. 2010). The LIS project involved filming 180 participants in three age groups from 10 cities and towns distributed across Italy: Turin, Milan, Brescia, Bologna in the north; Florence and Rome in the central region; and Bari, Catanzaro, Ragusa, and Salerno in the south. The data analyzed thus far involved 401 clauses in which the wh-sign either precedes or follows the predicate. Wh-signs after the predicate were favored for direct rather than indirect questions, and by urban signers versus rural signers. Wh-signs before the predicate were favored by older signers compared to signers in middle and younger age groups. The researchers suggested that this provides evidence that wh-sign position in LIS is at an advanced stage of language change in which wh-signs after the predicate represents an emerging standard construction.

Conclusion

In this chapter, we have explored some of the research conducted in the past few decades on sociolinguistic variation in deaf communities, with a particular focus on ASL, BSL, Auslan, NZSL, and LIS. We have shown how, just as the 'first wave' of work on spoken language communities did (Eckert 2012), variation is often not random, but is conditioned by linguistic and social factors. Although our understanding has grown significantly in the last decade, much work remains to be done. The major sociolinguistic studies of sign languages to date have covered a number of different regions in each country, but have not yet examined any particular region's deaf community to the same depth that is common in ethnographic studies of spoken language variation and change. Moreover, many regions were not included in these studies (no rural sites were visited in the United Kingdom, for example). Other sociolinguistic variables need to be investigated (e.g., the mouthing of English words while signing BSL), and stylistic factors need to be more fully explored. The influence of immigrant communities, and the impact of the many late learners and hearing and deaf second-language users on established signed languages is also important. Such work could contribute to studies in which the social meaning of sign language language variation and change, and its relationship to the construction of identity, could be explored. Pursuing such research questions will increase our knowledge about the sociolinguistics of signed languages, as well as broaden our understanding of variation in language general.

Acknowledgment

Some of the material related to BSL was adapted from material co-written with Kearsy Cormier and Bencie Woll; and some of the NZSL material, with Rachel McKee and David McKee (see Schembri, Cormier, McKee, McKee, Johnston, & Woll 2010). A longer version of this chapter will appear in *Sign Language: An International Handbook*, edited by Roland Pfau, Markus Steinbach, and Bencie Woll, published by Walter de Gruyter.

References

Aramburo, A. 1989. Sociolinguistic aspects of the Black Deaf community. In C. Lucas (ed.), *The sociolinguistics of the Deaf community*, 103–21. San Diego: Academic Press.

Baker, C., & Cokely, D. 1980. *American Sign Language: A teacher's resource text on grammar and culture*. Washington DC: Gallaudet University Press.

Boudreault, P., & Mayberry, R. 2006. Grammatical processing in American Sign Language: Age of first language acquisition effects in relation to syntactic structure. *Language and Cognitive Processes* 21: 608–35.

Campos de Abreu, A. 1994. The deaf social life in Brazil. In C. Erting (ed.), *The Deaf way*, 114–16. Washington DC: Gallaudet University Press.

Coates, J., & Sutton-Spence, R. 2001. Turn-taking patterns in deaf conversation. *Journal of Sociolinguistics* 5: 507–29.

Eckert, P. (accepted, 2012). Three waves of variation study: The emergence of meaning in the study of sociolinguistic variation. *Annual Review of Anthropology*, 41.

Emmorey, K. D. 2002. *Language, cognition, and the brain: Insights from sign language research*. Mahwah, NJ: Lawrence Erlbaum.

Fenlon, J., Schembri, A., Rentelis, R., & Cormier, K. in press. Variation in handshape and orientation in British Sign Language: The case of the '1' hand configuration. *Language and Communciation*.

Frishberg, N. 1975. Arbitrariness and iconicity: Historical change in American Sign Language. *Language* 51: 696–719.

Geraci, C., Battaglia, K., Cardinaletti, A., Ceccheto, C., Donati, C., Guidice, S., et al. 2011. The LIS Corpus Project: A discussion of sociolinguistic variation in the lexicon. *Sign Language Studies*, 11(4): 528-574.

Geraci, C., Cardinaletti, A., Cecchetoo, C., & Donati, C. 2010. *Linguistic issues in building a corpus for LIS (Italian Sign Language)*. Paper presented at the Tenth International Conference on Theoretical Issues in Sign Language Research, September 30–October 2, Purdue University.

Hill, J., McCaskill, C., Lucas, C., & Bayley, R. 2009. *Signing outside the box: The size of the signing space in black ASL*. Paper presented at the Conference on New Ways of Analyzing Variation 38, October 22–25, University of Ottawa.

Hoopes, R. 1998. A preliminary examination of pinky extension: Suggestions regarding its occurrence, constraints, and function. In C. Lucas (ed.), *Pinky extension and eye gaze: Language use in Deaf communities*, 3–17. Washington, DC: Gallaudet University Press.

Jackson, P. W. 1990. *Britain's deaf heritage*. Edinburgh: Pentland.

Jewish Deaf Association. 2003. *Sign language in Judaism*. London: Jewish Deaf Association.

Johnston, T. (ed.). 1998. *Signs of Australia: A new dictionary of Auslan*. Sydney: North Rocks Press.

Johnston, T., & Schembri, A. 2007. *Australian Sign Language (Auslan): An introduction to sign language linguistics*. Cambridge: Cambridge University Press.

Johnston, T., & Schembri, A. 2010. Variation, lexicalization and grammaticalization in signed languages. *Langage et Société* 131: 5–17.

Kelly, A. B. 1991. Fingerspelling use among the deaf senior citizens of Baltimore. In E. A. Winston (eds.), *Communication forum 1991*, 90–98. Washington, DC: Gallaudet University School of Communication.

Kennedy, G., Arnold, R., Dugdale, P., Fahey, S., & Moskovitz, D. (eds.). 1997. *A dictionary of New Zealand Sign Language*. Auckland: Auckland University Press with Bridget Williams Books.

Kleinfeld, M. S., & Warner, N. 1997. Lexical variation in the deaf community relating to gay, lesbian, and bisexual signs. In A. Livia & K. Hall (eds.), *Queerly phrased: Language, gender, and sexuality, 58–84*. New York: Oxford University Press.

Kyle, J., & Allsop, L. (1982). *Deaf people and the community*. Bristol: University of Bristol, Centre for Deaf Studies.

Kyle, J., & Woll, B. 1985. *Sign language: the study of deaf people and their language*. Cambridge: Cambridge University Press.

Labov, W. 1990. The intersection of sex and social class in the course of language change. *Language Variation and Change* 2: 205–54.
Le Master, B., & Dwyer, J. P. 1991. Knowing and using female and male signs in Dublin. *Sign Language Studies* 73: 361–69.
Leeson, L., & Grehan, C. 2004. To the lexicon and beyond: The effect of gender on variation in Irish Sign Language. In M. V. Herreweghe & M. Vermeerbergen (eds.), *To the lexicon and beyond: Sociolinguistics in European deaf communities*, 39–73. Washington DC: Gallaudet University Press.
Lucas, C., & Valli, C. 1992. *Language contact in the American Deaf community*. San Diego: Academic Press.
Lucas, C., Bayley, R., & Valli, C. 2001. *Sociolinguistic variation in American Sign Language*. Washington, DC: Gallaudet University Press.
Lucas, C., Bayley, R., Reed, R., & Wulf, A. 2001. Lexical variation in African American and white signing. *American Speech* 76(4): 339-360.
Mansfield, D. 1993. Gender differences in ASL: A sociolinguistic study of sign choices by deaf native signers. In E. Winston (ed.), *Communication forum*, 86–98. Washington DC: Gallaudet University Press.
McCaskill, C., Lucas, C., Bayley, R., & Hill, J. 2011. The hidden treasure of Black ASL: Its history and structure. Washington, DC: Gallaudet University Press.
McKee, D., McKee, R., & Major, G. 2011. Numeral variation in New Zealand Sign Language. *Sign Language Studies* 11(5): 72-97.
McKee, R., McKee, D., Smiler, K., & Pointon, K. 2007. Maori signs: The construction of indigenous deaf identity in New Zealand Sign Language. In D. Quinto-Pozos (ed.), *Sign languages in contact*, 31–80. Washington DC: Gallaudet Unviersity Press.
McKee, R., Schembri, A., McKee, D., & Johnston, T. (2011). Variable subject expression in Australian Sign Language and New Zealand Sign Language. *Language Variation and Change* 23(3): 375-398.
Mulrooney, K. 2002. Variation in ASL fingerspelling. In C. Lucas (ed.), *Turn-taking fingerspelling, and contact in signed languages*, 3–26. Washington, DC: Gallaudet University Press.
Penn, C. (ed.). 1992. *Dictionary of southern African signs for communicating with the deaf*. Pretoria, South Africa: Human Science Research Council.
Rudner, W. A., & Butowsky, R. 1981. Signs used in the deaf gay community. *Sign Language Studies* 30: 36–38.
Schembri, A., & Johnston, T. 2007. Sociolinguistic variation in the use of fingerspelling in Australian Sign Language (Auslan): A pilot study. *Sign Language Studies* 7: 319–47.
Schembri, A., Cormier, K., Johnston, T., McKee, D., McKee, R., & Woll, B. 2010. Sociolinguistic variation in British, Australian and New Zealand sign languages. In D. Brentari (Ed.), *Sign languages*, 479–501. Cambridge: Cambridge University Press.
Schembri, A., McKee, D., McKee, R., Pivac, S., Johnston, T., & Goswell, D. 2009. Phonological variation and change in Australian and New Zealand sign languages: The location variable. *Language Variation and Change* 21: 193–231.
Schermer, T. 2004. Lexical variation in The Netherlands. In M.V. Herreweghe & M. Vermeerbergen (eds.), *To the lexicon and beyond: Sociolinguistics in European deaf communities*, 91–110. Washington DC: Gallaudet University Press.

Stamp, R., Schembri, A., Fenlon, J., & Rentelis, R. accepted. Variation and change in British Sign Language number signs. *Journal of Sociolinguistics.*

Stokoe, W. C., Casterline, D. C., & Croneberg, C. G. 1965. *A dictionary of American Sign Language on linguistic principles.* Washington, DC: Gallaudet College Press.

Sutton-Spence, R., Woll, B., & Allsop, L. 1990. Variation and recent change in fingerspelling in British Sign Language. *Language Variation and Change* 2: 313–30.

Valli, C., Lucas, C., & Mulrooney, K. J. 2005. *Linguistics of American Sign Language: A resource text for ASL users.* Washington, DC: Gallaudet University Press.

Vanhecke, E., & Weerdt, K. d. 2004. Regional variation in Flemish Sign Language. In M. V. Herreweghe & M. Vermeerbergen (eds.), *To the lexicon and beyond: Sociolinguistics in European deaf communities,* 27–38. Washington DC: Gallaudet University Press.

Weinberg, J. 1992. *The history of the Residential School for Jewish Deaf Children.* London: Reunion of the Jewish Deaf School Committee.

Woll, B. 1983. *Historical change in British Sign Language.* Unpublished manuscript, Deaf Studies Unit, University of Bristol, Bristol.

Woll, B. 1987. Historical and comparative aspects of BSL. In J. G. Kyle (ed.), *Sign and school,* 12–34. Clevedon: Multilingual Matters.

Woll, B. 1994. The influence of television on the deaf community in Britain. In I. Ahlgren, B. Bergman, & M. Brennan (eds.), *Perspectives on sign language usage: Papers from the Fifth International Symposium on Sign Language Research,* 293–301. Durham, UK: International Sign Linguistics Association.

Woodward, J. C., & DeSantis, S. 1977. Two to one it happens: Dynamic phonology in two sign languages. *Sign Language Studies* 17: 329–46

Zeshan, U. 2000. *Sign language in Indo-Pakistan: a description of a signed language.* Amsterdam: John Benjamins.

PART V

LANGUAGE POLICY, LANGUAGE IDEOLOGY, AND LANGUAGE ATTITUDES

CHAPTER 26

LANGUAGE POLICY, IDEOLOGY, AND ATTITUDES IN ENGLISH-DOMINANT COUNTRIES

THOMAS RICENTO

MANY subfields within sociolinguistics have been influenced by developments in linguistics and social theory over the past half century. This has certainly been the case in the field of language policy and planning (LPP), which has incorporated new ways of thinking about language, society, and cognition, as evidenced by the published research in journals and books. In the earliest stage of LPP as a scholarly field, sociolinguists used their skills in descriptive linguistics for language planning activities in newly independent countries in Africa and Asia, usually with the goal of "standardizing" and elaborating local languages within a paradigm of stable diglossia with a colonial European language, such as English, French, Portuguese, Dutch, or Italian. The motivation underlying much of this work reflected long-held, often implicit, views that modernization required a common national language to improve efficiency, develop nationalistic attitudes, and promote economic development. The approach taken by scholars (early practitioners of what came to be known as LPP) was claimed to be non-political, technical in nature, interested in solving "problems," and pragmatic, that is, results oriented. In general, the Western-influenced approaches to LPP in the developing world did not achieve the hoped for results, both in terms of language modernization or socioeconomic development. In fact, "newly independent states found themselves in some ways more dependent on their former colonial masters than they had been during the colonial era" (Ricento 2000: 200). Critical and postmodern theories began to influence the ways in which scholars analyzed the relations between language policies and social inequalities. Changing views about the nature of language, along with the ubiquity and "naturalness" of bi- and multilingualism documented in developing nations (and increasingly in "developed" nations), have led to paradigmatic changes in the field of language policy and planning (Ricento 2006). In this chapter, I consider the ways in which views on the nature of language, language ideologies, and language and identity have fundamentally altered the research agendas and foci in the field of LPP over the past several decades. Following this brief assessment, I will consider how these newer ways of understanding language in society have been applied to English-speaking countries, particularly with reference to North America.

Language

Although in much of the published research in LPP, agreement on what "language" means or refers to is assumed, such assumptions need to be critically examined. Chomsky's (1969) autonomous linguistics represents one end of a continuum whereby language was conceived as a highly articulated and innate faculty of the brain that needed only the input of human language to "grow" into the particular named "language" the child was exposed to from birth, for example, English, French, Japanese, and so on. Chomsky analogized the growth of language to the growth of organs or limbs in that in both cases, the "program" for "growth" into the adult form is specific, predictable, and with very particular outcomes. His methodology stipulated a homogeneous speech community in which the ideal hearer/speaker would acquire his or her language x. While Chomsky's theory of language and language acquisition was groundbreaking, revolutionizing the field of linguistics, it also tended to reify monolingualism and monoculturalism (even if this was an unintended consequence of the Chomskyean model) as intrinsic and normal characteristics of humans and human society. The construct of a homogeneous speech community ignored the fact that speech communities are more typically heterogeneous (culturally) and heteroglossic (linguistically), and growing up with more than one language is far from uncommon. The theory of language as an autonomous system and the "normal" speaker as possessing intact and separate "languages" was consonant with idea of the nation-state as a bounded entity unified in large measure by the sharing of a common "national" language. The fact that transformational grammar claimed to be a "descriptive" science, that is, based on how people actually *use* language, has been shown to be inaccurate, as the grammatical intuitions of generative linguists tended to be based on the standard, *prescriptive* variety that they had acquired and used (Taylor 1997).

At the other end of the continuum of theories about language is the claim that named languages are constructs and that the "science" of linguistics, therefore, is based on a myth (Harris 1990: 45). Makoni and Pennycook (2007) argue that in order to deal with the damaging legacy of colonialism in Africa and elsewhere, we must "disinvent" language. They cite the work of Harris (1981) who has argued that "linguistics…has profoundly misconstrued language through its myths about autonomy, systematicity and the rule-bound nature of language, privileging supposedly expert scientific linguistic knowledge over everyday understandings of language" (in Makoni and Pennycook 2007: 18–19). Hopper (1998: 157–8) argues "there is no natural fixed structure to language. Rather, speakers borrow heavily from their previous experiences of communication in similar circumstances, on similar topics, and with similar interlocutors. Systematicity, in this view, is an illusion produced by the partial settling or *sedimentation* of frequently used forms into temporary subsystems." Empirical research on the language repertoires of individuals living in heteroglossic communities, such as New York City (e.g., Zentella 1997), has shown that complex patterns of language mixing and codeswitching are not unusual, and do not comport with commonsense (or some theoretical) views about "normal" linguistic competence. In fact, such "ways of doing language," rather than aberrations from the "norm," are in fact widely attested throughout the world. Makoni and Pennycook (2007: 21) go so far as to argue that "all languages are creoles, and that the slave and colonial history of creoles should serve as a model on which other languages are assessed. In other words, it is what is seen as marginal or exceptional that should be used to frame our understandings of language."

Once we begin to think about language, and especially "standard" languages, as constructs "posited as separate entities at a particular moment in European philosophical and political thought" (Makoni and Pennycook 2007: 21), it becomes much easier to understand how LPP evolved as a normative and descriptive activity of "counting," "codifying," and "standardizing" languages as "things," possessed by "native speakers" who had "mother tongues" and who might speak "other (named) languages." Historical linguistic research demonstrated the relationships among Indo-European languages; however, it wasn"t until the development of nation-states in the eighteenth century that the quasi-mythological notion that a common, named language is a necessary, if not sufficient, requirement for national identity gained traction, and this has continued to influence how people think and talk about language/s. The naming and invention of what were, in fact, heteroglossic (and usually locally unnamed) varieties of spoken language in colonized territories in Africa, the Americas, Asia, and Australasia and the ascription of shared cultural origins among disparate ethnolinguistic areas in what today is called Europe, was one of the signal legacies of the modernist project of the European empires (see Willinsky 1998).

Ideology

Ideology is defined by van Dijk (1998: 8) as "the shared framework(s) of social beliefs that organize and coordinate the social interpretations and practices of groups and their members." All groups and societies have ideologies; as Silverstein (1992: 315) notes: "[T]here is no possible *absolutely* pre-ideological, i.e., zero-order, social semiotic." When frameworks of social beliefs are widely shared in societies, or by groups in society, they tend to be viewed as natural, normal, and commonsense, while alternative frameworks that run counter to widely shared beliefs tend to be viewed as deviant, abnormal, and irrational. For example, many readers of this chapter will find the assertion that named languages (as opposed to *language*) are constructs and that "there is no natural fixed structure to language" to be contrary to their "commonsense" beliefs about language, beliefs that are based on their socialization into particular speech communities and, especially, as a result of many years of formal schooling in which they learned about the "rules" of language, "parts of speech," "good grammar," and so on. In fact, for many people born and raised in monolingual homes and educated in monolingual schools, it is not at all surprising that they would consider multilingual competence, language mixing and codeswitching, hybridity, and bidialectalism as "different," even "abnormal," perhaps "uneducated," and possibly incompatible with modernity and upward socioeconomic mobility. As we will see, there is evidence that such views, in fact, are widespread in the United States and Canada, and to varying degrees in the United Kingdom, Australia, and New Zealand, and that they inform attitudes and policies about language-in-education, the role of minority languages in the public sphere, and even linguistic requisites for citizenship and social acceptance.

English Monolingualism and Standard Language Ideology

Although English is not designated as the official language of the United States, the United Kingdom, or Australia (it is an official language in Canada and New Zealand), the ideology of English monolingualism makes such a designation superfluous. As Wiley and Lukes (1996: 519) note: "The ideology of monolingualism sees language diversity as largely a consequence of immigration. In other words, language diversity is viewed as imported." A related concept is what Silverstein (1996) refers to as the "monoglot" ideology, which rests on the belief "that a society is *in effect* monolingual...coupled with a denial of practices that point toward factual multilingualism and linguistic diversity" (cited in Blommaert 2006: 243–44). Blommaert (2006: 244–45) goes on to describe the effects of the monoglot ideology: (1) it informs practical language regimes in education and other crucial spheres of public life; (2) it produces and regulates identities; and (3) it has had a tremendous impact on scholarship. If we focus on the situation in the United States, historical research demonstrates that although many languages were spoken in North America prior to the establishment of the United States, the number increasing over time as a result of immigration, the association of English with national (American) identity became solidified during and after the United States' involvement in the war in Europe beginning in 1914 (Ricento 2003; Wiley 1998). This period witnessed the first Americanization movement, the goal of which was to "Americanize" the large number of European immigrants who arrived in the period between 1880 and 1910 (Ricento 2003). A principal means of achieving Americanization was through massive education programs that sought to teach American values, ways of thinking, ways of living, and especially the national language, English. Hyphenated Americans (e.g., Italian-Americans, Irish-Americans, German-Americans) were not considered 100 percent or "true" Americans; the teaching, learning, and even use of non-English immigrant languages was considered by many to be un-American and a sign of resistance to social integration. One hundred years later, it can be argued that matters have not changed significantly. To become American one had to think (in English) like an American, as demonstrated in these excerpts from the Bulletin *Americanization* of January 1, 1919:

> All Americans must be taught to read and write and think in one language. This is a primary condition to that growth which all nations expect of us and which we demand of ourselves.
>
> Do you know what a 100 percent American means? Many of us have the wrong idea in thinking that he is a person born or naturalized in our country. No, that is not enough. He is a person who believes in American ideas and ideals. You of foreign birth need not forget the teachings of your old home. Just translate them into the thoughts of America.

The effects of the ideology of English monolingualism on attitudes toward "other" languages is manifested in many ways. For example, even though Spanish pre-dates the arrival of English on the North American continent, it has typically been taught as a "foreign" language in schools and in recent decades efforts (many successful) have been made to outlaw or restrict bilingual English/Spanish education, restrict or rescind bilingual voting ballots, and to reduce or eliminate bilingual services in the public sector. This is occurring at the same time that Spanish is widely used in daily life in cities such as Miami and in many towns in Texas, Arizona, New Mexico, and California, especially near the Mexican border. Perhaps most telling has been the concerted effort over the past 30 years to declare English the official language of the United States (Ricento 1998a), largely in reaction to increased immigration from Latin America that has positioned Spanish as the most widely spoken language in the United States after English.

Another ideology described by Wiley and Lukes (1996) is the *standard language ideology*, which elevates a particular variety of a named language spoken by the dominant social group to a (H)igh status while diminishing other varieties to a (L)ow status. This variety, based on prescriptive norms of the written language, is believed to be more "correct," "logical" and "efficient" in communicative terms than other varieties, many of which are identified as being "nonstandard," "illegitimate," "ignorant," or just plain "bad." The standard language is, in effect, "*the* language" (English, French, Japanese, etc.) idealized in dictionaries and grammar books (which never reflect actual usage in any systematic way), which follows from the ideology of what a language is, or ought to be (described earlier). The named/standard language is something imposed through a process whereby the social and political elite in a state or territory codify their variety of speech in written form, and make it the "standard" against which all other ways of speaking and writing are judged. Over time, it is learned through schooling and becomes the de facto norm. Persons speaking other stigmatized ("nonstandard") varieties tend to be viewed as having deficiencies in intelligence, morality, and/or character and are often less successful in achieving upward social mobility, which generally requires proficiency in the standard "national" language. This has certainly been the case in the English-dominant countries in which speakers of nonstandard varieties of English, such as African American English, Chicano English, Maori-influenced English, Aboriginal and Native American varieties of English, and certainly the millions of speakers of regional and socioeconomically indexed varieties of English in the United Kingdom, such as Cornish, Yorkshire, Cockney, and so on, have faced discrimination because of the language variety they grew up with. Other factors and ideologies certainly have played a role in limiting opportunities of speakers of nonstandard varieties, including discrimination based on perceived or ascribed categories of race, ethnicity, and national origin, but findings in sociolinguistic research using Likert, Matched Guise, and the Semantic Differential techniques, along with ethnographic studies in multilingual communities, clearly demonstrate that negative judgments are often linked to perceptions of "foreign" accents and "nonstandard" language forms, irrespective of a person"s physical appearance (Preston 2009; Baker 2006).

"Language-as-Resource"

Ideologies about language(s) are part of academic theorizing no less than they are attributes of the "objects," that is, texts, discourses, and societies studied by academics. As such, academic constructs will not be immune from the ideological formations present in their societies. Ruiz (1984) posits three approaches to language planning that can be found in the literature of language planning: "language-as-problem," "language-as-right," and "language-as-resource." He argues that the language-as-resource approach has advantages over the other two:

> [I]t can have a direct impact on enhancing the language status of subordinate languages; it can help to ease tensions between majority and minority communities; it can serve as a more consistent way of viewing the role of non-English languages in US society; and it highlights the importance of cooperative language planning. (1984: 25–26)

He notes that such an approach is not without its problems, but that a "fuller development of a resources-oriented approach to language planning could help to reshape attitudes about language and language groups" (27). The idea that languages are resources appears, at first blush, to be a big improvement over the idea that languages are problems, especially for those who, in principle, support language diversity. However, the way in which this approach has been taken up in academic theorizing reveals how the language-as-resource metaphor is embedded within economic and, ultimately, nationalist discourses that tend to represent language(s) as commodities with primarily economic and political qualities and values. For example, Brecht and Rivers (2002) compare language planning to natural resource management. Spolsky (2009) claims that language managers control choices about language learning and use, analogous to business models of resource allocation. Ricento (2005a) found that the language-as-resource metaphor was prominent in texts published on various websites of organizations that strongly support the teaching and learning of Heritage languages in the United States. Using the methodology of Critical Discourse Analysis (CDA), Ricento found in the texts examined that languages were systematically conceptualized as commodities, de-linked to people or communities, with economic and military/security benefits as the primary reason they should be "cultivated," "conserved," and "developed." The needs, interests, and aspirations of minority language communities themselves (let alone any intrinsic value of language diversity) are either not mentioned or are at the very bottom of the list of reasons Americans should support the learning of Heritage languages. If we position these texts within the broader sociohistorical context of languages in America, we can better understand why supporters might focus on a calculated *strategic* approach in promoting Heritage languages since the maintenance and teaching of minority/immigrant languages in the United States has generally been frowned upon, even outlawed in some states, throughout the twentieth century. By metaphorizing languages as commodities whose value lies in their utilitarian benefit in strengthening American security (especially salient in the wake of the attacks of September 11, 2001, and the ongoing shortage of linguistically competent security personnel) and promoting international trade, this discourse does not contradict the prevalent (but implicit) ideology of English monolingualism as "normal" and "desirable," since in the documents analyzed, the learning of English is nearly *always* mentioned as being more important, that is, preceding, the learning (or maintaining) of Heritage (still characterized as *foreign*) languages. Ricento (2005a) argues that one of the reasons the campaign to significantly expand the capacity of foreign language learning has been unsuccessful, especially in "strategically important" languages such as Arabic, Mandarin, Farsi, Urdu, and Pashto, is because the use of non-English languages in public (and even private) space has historically been stigmatized as a sign of "foreignness" and being "unAmerican"; therefore, immigrant speakers of these languages in the United States, Canada, and other English-dominant countries tend to assimilate quickly into the "English monolingualism," "English Only" expected cultural norm, leaving their "heritage" languages behind, or reserved for special purposes. The recent attempts to reinvigorate interest in the learning and use of these languages in the United States is, therefore, hampered by a more powerful ideological (but by now "commonsense") framework that links the use of foreign languages with negative characteristics and motivations, including lack of patriotism, divided loyalties, and an unwillingness to "assimilate". Thus, the ideology of English monolingualism, and English as *the* marker of national (American) identity, actually work *against* the (purported) "national interest" in developing "foreign" language resources and functional bilingualism at a time when there actually *is* a need to increase the supply of competent speakers of other languages, at least in terms of declared state interests in matters of national security and international trade.

Language Attitudes and Language Policy in Canada

The language situation in Canada shares characteristics with other English-dominant countries, while differing in important ways. Few countries have Canada's unique combination of a high percentage of immigrants, substate nationalism (Quebec), and aboriginal people (Kymlicka 2004). None of the other English-dominant countries share all three of these features. Canada's model of multiculturalism within a bilingual framework has come about as a compromise, largely as a response to social and political tensions that began soon after the British Conquest of 1760. The history of language policy development in Canada is invoked by academics and activists in the United States and elsewhere as being either exemplary or a failure, depending on the orientations, values, and ideologies of the commentator. What is certainly true is that language matters have been front and center in Canadian politics, especially since the inception of the "quiet revolution" in the 1960s, and there is no indication that this will change for the foreseeable future.

Of the five English-dominant countries, only Canada (officially bilingual: English and French) and New Zealand (officially trilingual: English, Maori, New Zealand Sign Language) have declared at least one language to be official at the federal level. However, in Canada, outside of the Province of Quebec, where nearly 86 percent of the population speak French and about 80 percent claim it as their mother tongue, English is the dominant language (only one Province, New Brunswick, is officially bilingual, although 67 percent of the population there speaks English as their first language, while Quebec has but one official language: French). Only about 17 percent of Canadians claimed to be bilingual English-French speakers in 2007 (Statistics Canada 2007), reflecting a stable trend (about 13 percent claimed English-French bilingualism in 1971). Thus, while Canada recognizes two official languages, most Canadians with French or English mother tongues are effectively monolingual (see table 26.1), although Francophones are far more likely to be bilingual than Anglophones (41 percent vs. 9 percent). And while 20 percent of the population claim neither French nor English as their mother tongue, less than 2 percent of the population claim they speak neither French nor English. These figures demonstrate that the "English fact" in North America continues to put pressure on French and that speakers of immigrant languages—especially outside of Quebec—acquire English as their customary language in schooling and the workplace.

However, the data on English-French bilingualism is quite misleading and obscures the percentage of people whose bilingualism is in an official language and another non-official language (or languages). Based on the census data in table 26.1, if we add to the 17.4% of the population who are French-English bilinguals the 12% who speak 'other' languages (in addition to French or English), we find that nearly 30% of Canadians enumerated in the census are at least fluently bilingual, a very substantial portion of the national population. And if we look more closely at cities like Montreal, Ottawa, Toronto, and Vancouver, we will find much higher levels of bilingualism and trilingualism than are indicated by aggregate national figures. Jedwab (2007) notes that in the 2006 Census, 18.3% of the Montreal population (or about 660,000 people) claim to be trilingual (an increase of about 2% from the 2001 census data). Even more interesting is the fact that among persons in Montreal whose mother tongue is neither English nor French (i.e., allophones), constituting about 50.2% of the Montreal population, it is a fair assumption that they are trilingual to varying degrees. In addition, according to Jedwab (2007), 94,000 Montrealers report knowledge of four languages, representing nearly 3% of the metropolitan

Table 26.1. Canada's official languages

	Number	Percentage (%)
Total population by mother tongue*	31,241,030	100.0
English	18,055,685	57.8
French	6,892,230	22.1
Non-official languages	6,293,110	20.1
Total population by knowledge of official languages	31,241,030	100.0
English only	21,129,945	67.6
French only	4,141,850	13.3
English and French	5,448,850	17.4
Neither English nor French	520,385	1.7
Total population by first official language spoken*	31,241,030	100.0
English	23,363,060	74.8
French	7,370,355	23.6
Neither English nor French	507,620	1.6
Total population by language spoken most often at home*	31,241,030	100.0
English	20,840,565	66.7
French	6,690,130	21.4
Non-official languages	3,710,335	11.9

*After distribution of multiple responses.
Source: Statistics Canada. 2007. Profile of Language, Immigration, Citizenship, Mobility and Migration for Canada, Provinces, Territories and Federal Electoral Districts (2003 Representation Order), 2006 Census. Statistics Canada Catalogue no. 94-577-X2006007. Ottawa.

region's population. In Canada, 2 million persons report knowledge of three languages, constituting 6.4% of the population. Yet, these facts about Montreal's and Canada's trilinguals are invisible in the Census data in which Provincial aggregate data minimize the fact of vibrant multilingualism in major urban centers, such as in Montreal.

Canadian Official Multiculturalism

Although French achieved co-equal status with English at the federal level as a result of the Official Languages Act of 1969, non-official languages received little attention. In recognition of this oversight, the first federal multiculturalism policy was announced by Prime Minister Pierre Trudeau in 1971. Berry

(1998: 84–85) identified four elements stipulated in the policy: (1) the policy aims to avoid assimilation, and to promote "own group maintenance and development;" (2) the policy seeks to improve intergroup harmony by promoting "other group acceptance and tolerance;" (3) "intergroup contact and sharing" is required to lead to group acceptance; and (4) in order for cultural groups to attain full participation, a common language must be learned, that is, English and/or French.

After seventeen years, a Multiculturalism Act was passed in 1988. Unlike the original policy of 1971, the 1988 act focused mostly on the importance of the rights of aboriginal peoples, the equality of all Canadians, and equality of opportunity, regardless of race, national or ethnic origin, and color; freedom from discrimination based on culture, religion, or language; and the diversity of Canadians as a fundamental characteristic of Canadian society. There was no mention of support for group maintenance and development necessary to avoid assimilation. These changes reflected a continuous and strong opposition from both French (Quebec) nationalists, who saw official multiculturalism as a strategy to undermine Canadian biculturalism (French/English) and the historical contribution of French Canadians by reducing their status to "just one of the ethnic groups" (Kymlicka 2004: 162), and from English-speaking assimilationists who considered the Multiculturalism Act to be divisive and impractical; they argued that immigrants should completely sever any ties to their countries of origin and embrace a Canadian identity and way of living:

> The waves of immigrants that arrived on the prairies early in the 20th century were quickly cut off from the old country. That doesn't happen to today's immigrants; many maintain intimate links to their homelands...Only Canada, through its policy of official multiculturalism, actually encourages newcomers to cling to their original identities rather than fully embrace the identity of their new home. (Stoffman 2002: 42–43)

One in five English-speaking Canadians was born in another country (Statistics Canada 2006), compared to 11.8 percent in the United States who were born in another country. Recent polls suggest that the vast majority of Canadians (74 percent) support the federal policy of multiculturalism (Dasko 2004). However, a survey conducted in 1991 revealed that while Canadians generally support multiculturalism, they do not support governmental funding of policies and programs intended to support ethnic (i.e., allophone or indigenous) communities (Garcea 2004). Another interesting finding suggests that economic factors play a role in shaping attitudes toward multiculturalism. In the early 1990s, when the economy was in recession and the unemployment rate high, polls indicated that Canadians were less likely to accept multiculturalism (54 percent approval rate) than in 2002 (74 percent approval rate) when the economy picked up (Dasko 2004: 131). Younger and more educated people tend to be more appreciative of linguistic and cultural diversity, but a significant percentage believes that the multiculturalism policy gives too much power to ethnic groups. One in three university-educated Canadians under the age of 35 believes that aboriginal people have too much power, while one in seven considers that immigrants have too much power (Bibby 2004).

As in the United States, policy regarding Heritage languages (the term itself is fraught with implications of something old, with sentimental value) in Canada is largely symbolic; it symbolizes the self-ascribed belief that Canada is a mosaic of cultures and languages. The federal government does not directly fund heritage language classes. According to official policy, the government's position is that the multiculturalism policy "aims to preserve and enhance the use of other languages, while strengthening the status and use of official languages" (Multiculturalism and Citizenship Canada 1991: 20). According to the Annual Report on the Operation of the Canadian Multiculturalism Act (Canadian Heritage 2006–2007), the Multicultural Program of the Department of Canadian Heritage funds initiatives in four activity areas: support to civil society, research and policy development, support to public institutions, and public education and promotion. The stated goal of the Multiculturalism Program is to "support the removal of barriers related to race, ethnicity, cultural support or religious background that would prevent full participation in Canadian society" (Canadian Heritage 2006–2007: 9). No mention is made of support for minority languages in particular. The fragile truce that has existed for 40 years between Anglophone and Francophone Canada cannot, apparently, withstand the expansion of language rights to other groups.

Although important political goals have been achieved through the establishment of official bilingualism in Canada, namely, avoiding the fragmenting of the country into English-speaking Canada and an independent and French-speaking Quebec, the formalizing and implementation of language policy is primarily the responsibility of provinces and territories. This is also the situation in the United States, where education policies are devised and implemented at the state and local levels. Thus, even though the Canadian federal government may encourage ethnic groups to celebrate their cultures and languages by providing Multiculturalism grants to groups and associations in various provinces, it provides no funding for the teaching and learning of non-official languages. The federal funding that is provided is directed to support the teaching of one of the official minority languages in geographical areas where the other one is dominant. However, in about half of the Canadian provinces heritage language courses are offered after school hours or on Saturday (Early 2008). Some provinces offer fully bilingual programs in English and a heritage language. Alberta, Manitoba, and Saskatchewan collaborated to develop the Common Curriculum Framework for Bilingual Programming in International Languages, Kindergarten to grade 12 along with the Common Curriculum Framework for International Languages, Kindergarten to grade 12 (Ricento and Cervatiuc 2010: 34). In the province of Alberta, which is 90 percent Anglophone, all K-12 students are expected to be able to communicate in two languages, and in Calgary (Alberta), there are bilingual programs in English-Spanish, English-German, and English-Mandarin, in addition to Japanese language and culture courses and highly regarded French immersion and FSL (French as a second language) programs. Internationalizing the curriculum and developing linguistically competent graduates are aspirations that, at least, recognize the widespread monolingualism of native-born Canadians even if the political climate works against funding such programs. The teaching of heritage and international languages has been vehemently contested in some areas, including the metropolitan Toronto area, based on the belief that teaching languages other than the official ones (French and English) will promote cultural division and hinder immigrants' integration into Canadian mainstream society (Cummins & Danesi 1990).

Language, Identity, and Language Policies

The preceding sections highlight some of the ways that attitudes about languages are often based on deeply held values that are often linked to emotions and "commonsense" beliefs about "us" and the "other" in society. In immigrant countries, such as the United States, Canada, and Australia (and increasingly in the United Kingdom and New Zealand), "otherness" may be based on perceived differences in ethnicity, race, culture, and language. In the end, the construct of ethnicity (like race) is a concept (i.e., linguistically coded) because humans pay attention to the way people look, talk, and behave and note how "their" group differs from the "other" groups they come in contact with. Ricento (2005b: 896), notes that "Glynn Williams (1999) argues that in American sociology, ethnicity became a dichotomized construct of the normative/standard group—a unitary citizenry speaking a common language (us)—and non-normative/nonstandard groups—including those speaking other languages—(them). This naturalizing of a sociological construct (ethnicity) informs the widely held popular view promoted by Western scholarship that 'reasonable' (modern) people should naturally become part of the culture of the state (or transnational world) and speak 'its' language, whereas 'irrational' (traditional) people will tend to cling to their 'ethnic language and culture.'"

The connections between language and identity have been explored by interactional sociolinguists (e.g., Gumperz 1982; Heller 1995), who show that both the choice of language (code) and the use of the code in particular ways signal "social relationships based on shared or unshared group membership" (Heller, 1982: 5). Language is one, often very important, aspect of a person's identity, and the degree to which it is an essential or non-essential element depends on many factors, both personal and societal (May 2001). For example, research in the United States indicates that language is an important component of the collective identification of Latinos (Garcia-Bedolla 2005). Sears et al.

(1999) found that second- and third-generation Latinos progressively lose ties to their heritage language (Spanish) at the same time they are assimilating to mainstream US culture (as occurred with previous immigrants from Europe). Pita and Utakis (2002) examine the economic, political, social, cultural, and linguistic dimensions of the transnational Dominican community in New York City. They argue that in order to function effectively in their lives, members of this community require enriched bilingual bicultural programs in order to promote parallel development so that students can succeed in either country.

Language is mutable, that is, a person may learn other languages in addition to the one they first acquired, and may even decide to identify to greater or lesser degrees with a group to which they might "naturally" not belong, based on physical or cultural characteristics alone (Rampton 1995). Identity through language is also contingent and pragmatic; Hall (2002: 97), in a study of a Punjabi community in Leeds, England, found that "the use of Punjabi as a reified political symbol is contrasted with Sikh teenagers' patterns of Punjabi language use.... As they move through the social worlds that make up their everyday lives, Sikh teens actively construct linguistic practices that make use of a mixture of linguistic forms and styles in relation to influences, expectations, and interests that are situational and shifting. Sikh teens assess and reassess the value of Punjabi as they participate in different types of social interaction, media consumption, and cultural events." Pennycook (2007) examines the ways in which English has been taken up, transformed, interpreted, and embedded in cultural forms throughout the world. His focus is on hip-hop, an idiom that originated in the United States but that has now been taken up and localized throughout the world. Just as a named language can no longer be thought of as a discrete, bounded system "belonging" to a group or nation, identity is better understood as performed through language—but not isomorphic with one code—and contingent, not an invariant trait.

However, as Pennycook (2007:113) notes, while to "use English" may mean many things, "to have a command of English sufficient to rap in the language may, in some contexts, imply a very particular class background." Indeed, one's ability to *chose* which language(s) to learn is constrained by factors such as social class, access to free (or private) education, gender, and occupation, among other variables. That is, one may be motivated to acquire English in North America, for example, and have the desire to assimilate into the mainstream English-speaking society, and yet be unsuccessful in achieving those goals. Norton (2000: 5) uses the term identity "to reference how a person understands his or her relationship to the world, how that relationship is constructed across time and space, and how the person understands possibilities for the future." Norton uses the term *investment* to characterize the complex motives and desires that language learners may have vis-à-vis a target language. Based on a study of five female immigrants in Canada, Norton (2000: 10) argues that "if learners invest in a second language, they do so with the understanding that they will acquire a wider range of symbolic and material resources, which will in turn increase the value of their cultural capital." In order to understand why some immigrants, circumstantial bilinguals, and speakers of nonstandard varieties "fail" to acquire, or use, the dominant national language we must consider the social aspect of language learning, and especially the ways in which differences in power may impede integration even when an individual desperately wishes to assimilate or be accepted in society. Further, barriers that limit access to acquisition of cultural capital, such as poverty, lack of educational opportunities, and dead-end jobs can negatively affect a person's desire to invest in acquiring the dominant language.

Understanding the reasons and motivations that inform decisions about the language(s) a person uses, or does not use, is important for research and theory-building in the field of second language acquisition. However, the ideologies of English monolingualism, standard language, the monoglot society, and even "language-as-resource" continue to influence the politics of language. The expectation that immigrants should "assimilate" or "integrate" linguistically and socially is not sensitive to the complex motives, desires, and actual language behavior of immigrants and speakers of nonstandard varieties. Hence, especially in the United States and Canada, because of the *perception* that the use of multiple languages in public and private life *must* lead to conflict and social instability, there has been a concerted and continuing effort to declare English the official language of the United States, to restrict or ban bilingual (mostly English/Spanish) programs in public schools, to reduce or eliminate bilingual ballots, and to essentially limit all foreign language materials and services except in certain federal departments and agencies, such as the State Department, Department of Defense, and in the areas of trade and commerce. The "facts" of multilingualism in the United States are viewed by significant portions of the country as a threat to their conception of American national identity, and a way to deal with the "problem" is to restrict domains for other languages while "sending a message" about the importance of English. Schmidt, Sr. (2006: 97) notes: "Because the central issues in language policy conflict revolve around competing attempts to socially construct group and individual identities, disputed questions of *meaning* and *significance* abound in the politics of language." Schmidt, Sr. argues that "identity politics" is at the core of movements that seek to restrict the use of other languages while enhancing the status of English, as has been occurring in the United States, especially during the past 30 years (see Schmidt Sr. 2006).

Conclusions

It is virtually impossible to talk about language, and languages, apart from the worlds they inhabit. Although languages can be studied, analyzed, taught, and even cease to be spoken, they are never not embedded in all aspects of social life.

Hence, in order to understand how languages gain or lose status, speakers, and power, researchers in Language Policy and Planning must avail themselves of a broad range of perspectives from core social science disciplines, including ethnography, geography, historiography, linguistics, political science, psychology, and sociology. With the advent of the state system beginning in the eighteenth century extending to the present day, governments have sanctioned particular language varieties as national languages, even though most territorial states are multilingual and multicultural. This means that non-dominant/minority language groups incorporated within the territory of the state have had to deal with their minority status over long periods of time, often leading to conflicts and uncomfortable accommodation with dominant language groups. However, people do not stay in one place, and, as Blommaert (2010: 6) notes, "Movement of people across space is...never a move across empty spaces. The spaces are always someone's space, and they are filled with norms, expectations, conceptions of what counts as proper and normal (indexical) language use and what does not count as such." Those who move from a place in which their language is dominant to a place in which it is not dominant, or even recognized, will find their identity and status challenged in unexpected ways (Blommaert 2008). Globalization and migration create unprecedented challenges in many domains of language policy and planning. Should everyone have the option to be educated in their "mother" tongue, have access to public services in the language(s) they speak and write, and enjoy the right to use their native language in the workplace? When such rights have been asserted or even granted by governmental authorities, as occurred in the United States with congressional passage of the Bilingual Education Act of 1968, activists opposed to bilingualism or multilingualism have been quick to challenge them, with varying results (Ricento 1998b). In the end, these are all questions best responded to in terms of *degree* of recognition and accommodation rather than whether there should be recognition at all. However, in the case of the United States, false perceptions fuel emotional responses to non-existent problems. For example, the claim that Latinos are failing to assimilate to English (Huntington 2004) is directly contradicted by empirical research on patterns of language retention. Rumbaut, et al. (2006: 458), relying on data from two published studies and a survey they conducted themselves in Southern California during 2001–2004, conclude that "under current conditions...the ability to speak Spanish very well can be expected to disappear sometime between the second and third generation for all Latin American groups in Southern California." They also found that "the average Asian language can be expected to die out at or near the second generation" (ibid). To account for such a wide discrepancy between the apparent facts and widely held misperceptions, it is necessary to consider the influence, and effects, of deeply held beliefs about language and identity that are resistant to contrary evidence. These beliefs are operationalized in political movements and policy positions that may, ironically, undermine the political and economic interests of the state. This strongly suggests that attitudes toward language(s) are fundamentally tied to identities, and hence *emotions*, despite loud protestations from those who seek to fortify the national language that they are only doing so out of concern for others' (perhaps not as wise or perceptive as they) best interests, "others," it turns out, whose motivations and desires are probably not understood or appreciated by "guardians of the national language."

References

Baker, C. 2006. Psycho-sociological analysis in language policy. In T. Ricento (ed.), *An introduction to language policy: Theory and method*, 210–28. Malden, MA: Blackwell.

Berry, J. 1998. Official multiculturalism. In J. Edwards (ed.), *Languages in Canada*, 84–101. Cambridge: Cambridge University Press.

Bibby, R. 2004. Beyond the prosaic mosaic: Canadian inter-group attitudes, 1975–2000. In M. Zachariah, A. Sheppard, & L. Barratt (eds.), *Canadian multiculturalism: Dreams, realities, expectations*, 221–40. Edmonton, AB: Canadian Multicultural Education Foundation.

Blommaert, J. 2006. Language policy and national identity. In T. Ricento (ed.), *An introduction to language policy: Theory and method*, 238–54. Malden, MA: Blackwell.

Blommaert, J. 2008. *Grassroots literacy: Writing, identity and voice in Central Africa*. New York: Routledge.

Blommaert, J. 2010. *The sociolinguistics of globalization*. Cambridge: Cambridge University Press.

Brecht, R., & Rivers, W. 2002. The language crisis in the United States: Language, national security and the federal role. In S. Baker (ed.), *Language policy: Lessons from global models*, 76–90. Monterey, CA: Monterey Institute of International Studies.

Canadian Heritage. 2006–2007. Promoting Integration. Annual report of the Canadian Multiculturalism Act 2006–2007. Quebec: Canadian Heritage.

Chomsky, N. 1969. *Aspects of the theory of syntax*. Cambridge, MA: The MIT Press.

Cummins, J., & Danesi, M. 1990. *Heritage languages: The development and denial of Canada's linguistic resources*. Toronto: Our Schools/Our Selves and Garamond Press.

Dasko, D. 2004. Multiculturalism by Canadian numbers. In M. Zachariah, A. Sheppard, & L. Barratt (eds.), *Canadian multiculturalism: Dreams, realities, expectations*, 129–34. Edmonton, AB: Canadian Multicultural Education Foundation.

Early, M. 2008. Second and foreign language learning in Canada. In N. Hornberger & Nelleke Van Deusen-Scholl (eds.), *Encyclopedia of language and education*, vol. 4, *Second and foreign language education*, 197–208. New York: Springer.

Garcea, J. 2004. Reflections on institutional responses to multiculturalism in light of terrorism. In M. Zachariah, A. Sheppard, & L. Barratt (eds.), *Canadian multiculturalism: Dreams, realities, expectations*, 141–50. Edmonton, AB: Canadian Multicultural Education Foundation.

Garcia-Bedolla, L. 2005. *Fluid borders: Latino power, identity, and politics in Los Angeles*. Berkeley: University of California Press.

Gumperz, J. J. 1982. *Discourse strategies*. Cambridge: Cambridge University Press.

Hall, K. 2002. Asserting "needs" and claiming "rights": The cultural politics of community language education in England. *Journal of Language, Identity,and Education* 1(2): 97–119.

Harris, R. 1981. *The language myth*. London: Duckworth.

Harris, R. 1990. On redefining linguistics. In H. Davis & T. Taylor (eds.), *Redefining linguistics*, 18–52. London: Routledge.

Heller, M. 1982. *Language, ethnicity, and politics in Quebec*. Unpublished doctoral dissertation, University of California, Berkeley.

Heller, M. 1995. Language choice, social institutions, and symbolic domination. *Language in Society* 24(3): 373–405.

Hopper, P. 1998. Emergent grammar. In M. Tomasello (ed.), *The new psychology of language*, 155–75. Mahwah, NJ: Lawrence Erlbaum.

Huntington, S. 2004. *Who are we? The challenges to America's national identity*. New York: Simon & Schuster.

Jedwab, J. 2007. Canada's changing language realities and the challenge ofbilingualism (Part I). Available online at [http://www.acs-aec.ca/pdf/polls/11998891657623.pdf].

Kymlicka, W. 2004. Canadian multiculturalism in historical and comparative perspective. In M. Zachariah, A. Sheppard, & L. Barratt (eds.), *Canadian multiculturalism: Dreams, realities, expectations*, 157–72. Edmonton, AB: Canadian Multicultural Education Foundation.

Makoni, S., & Pennycook, A. 2007. Disinventing and reconstituting languages. In S. Makoni & A. Pennycook (eds.), *Disinventing and reconstituting languages*, 1–41. Clevedon, UK: Multilingual Matters.

May, S. 2001. *Language and minority rights: Ethnicity, nationalism, and the politics of language*. London: Longman.

Multiculturalism and Citizenship Canada. 1991. Multiculturalism: What is it really about? Canada: Government Publications.

Norton, B. 2000. *Identity and language learning: Gender, ethnicity, and educational change*. Edinburgh Gate: Pearson Education.

Pennycook, A. 2007. *Global Englishes and transcultural flows*. London: Routledge.

Pita, M. D., & Utakis, S. 2002. Educational policy for the transnational Dominican community. *Journal of Language, Identity, and Education* 1(4): 317–28.

Preston, D. 2009. Linguistic profiling: The linguistic point of view. In M. R. Salaberry (ed.), *Language allegiances and bilingualism in the US*, 53–79. Clevedon, UK: Multilingual Matters.

Rampton, B. 1995. *Crossing: Language and ethnicity among adolescents*. London: Longman.

Ricento, T. 1998a. Partitioning by language: Whose rights are threatened? In T. Ricento (ed.), *Language and politics in the United States and Canada: Myths and realities*, 317–30. Mahwah, NJ: Lawrence Erlbaum.

Ricento, T. 1998b. National language policy in the United States. In T. Ricento (ed.), *Language and politics in the United States and Canada: Myths and realities*, 85–112. Mahwah, NJ: Lawrence Erlbaum.

Ricento, T. 2000. Historical and theoretical perspectives in language policy and planning. *Journal of Sociolinguistics* 4(2): 196–213.

Ricento, T. 2003. The discursive construction of Americanism. *Discourse & Society* 14(5): 611–37.

Ricento, T. 2005a. Problems with the 'language-as-resource' discourse in the promotion of heritage languages in the U.S.A. *Journal of Sociolinguistics* 9(3): 348–68.

Ricento, T. 2005b. Considerations of identity in L2 learning. In E. Hinkel (ed.), *Handbook of research in second language learning and teaching*, 895–910. Mahwah, NJ: Lawrence Erlbaum.

Ricento, T. (ed.) 2006. *An introduction to language policy: Theory and method.* Malden, MA: Blackwell.

Ricento, T., & Cervatiuc, A. 2010. Language minority rights and educational policy in Canada. In J. Petrovic (ed.), *International perspectives on bilingual education: Policy, practice, and controversy*, 21–42. Charlotte, NC: Information Age Publishing, Inc.

Ruiz, R. 1984. Orientations in language planning. *NABE Journal* 8(2): 15–34.

Rumbaut, R. G., Massey, D. S., & Bean, F. D. 2006. Linguistic life expectancies: Immigrant language retention in Southern California. *Population and Development Review* 32(3): 447–60.

Schmidt Sr., R. 2006. Political theory and language policy. In T. Ricento (ed.), *An introduction to language policy: Theory and method*, 95–110. Malden, MA: Blackwell.

Sears, D., Citron, J., Chelden, S., & van Laar, C. 1999. Cultural diversity and multi-cultural politics: Is ethnic balkanization psychologically inevitable? In D. Prentice & D. Miller (eds.), *Cultural divides: Understanding and overcoming group conflict*, 35–79. New York: Russell Sage Foundation.

Silverstein, M. 1992. The uses and utility of ideology: Some reflections. *Pragmatics* 2(3): 311–23.

Silverstein, M. 1996. Monoglot "standard" in America: Standardization and metaphors of linguistic hegemony. In D. Brenneis & R. Macaulay (eds.), *The matrix of language: Contemporary linguistic anthropology*, 284–306. Boulder, CO: Westview Press.

Spolsky, B. 2009. *Language management.* Cambridge: Cambridge University Press.

Statistics Canada. 2006. Immigration in Canada: A portrait of the foreign-born population, 2006 Census. Retrieved April 23, 2008 from http://www12.statcan.ca/english/census06/analysis/immcit/index.cfm.

Statistics Canada. 2007. and migration for Canada, Provinces, Territories and Federal Electoral Districts, 2006 Census. Statistics Canada Catalogue no. 94-577-X2006007. Ottawa.

Stoffman, D. 2002. *Who gets in?* Toronto: Macfarlane, Walter & Ross.

Taylor, T. J. (ed.) 1997. *Theorizing language: Analysis, normativity, rhetoric, history.* Amsterdam: Pergamon.

van Dijk, T. A. 1998. *Ideology: A multidisciplinary approach.* London: Sage.

Wiley, T. G. 1998. The imposition of World War I era English-only policies and the fate of German in North America. In T. Ricento (ed.), *Language and politics in the United States and Canada: Myths and realities*, 211–41. Mahwah, NJ: Lawrence Erlbaum.

Wiley, T. G., & Lukes, M. 1996. English-only and standard English ideologies in the U.S. *TESOL Quarterly* 30(3): 511–35.

Williams, G. 1999. Sociology. In J.A. Fishman (ed.), *Handbook of language and ethnic identity*, 164–80. Oxford, UK: Oxford University Press.
Willinsky, J. 1998. *Learning to divide the world: Education at empire's end.* Minneapolis: University of Minnesota Press.
Zentella, A.C. 1997. *Growing up bilingual: Puerto Rican children in New York.* Malden MA: Blackwell.

CHAPTER 27

ENGLISH IN LANGUAGE POLICIES AND IDEOLOGIES IN AFRICA

CHALLENGES AND PROSPECTS FOR VERNACULARIZATION

NKONKO M. KAMWANGAMALU

THIS chapter discusses the impact of English on language policy and ideologies in Africa, with a focus on vernacularization. Following Cobarrubias (1983), I define *vernacularization* as the use of an indigenous African language in the higher domains, such as the educational system. Vernacularization has been at the heart of the debate around the medium of instruction in African education for half a century. This debate is rooted in the unrealized expectations in postcolonial Africa that in retaining former colonial languages as official languages, they would bring about national unity, develop into viable media of national communication, and spread as lingua franca and perhaps eventually as first languages by replacing local languages, as was the case for Spanish and Portuguese in large parts of Latin America (Heine 1990: 176). To remedy this situation, the literature has highlighted the cognitive advantages of an education through the medium of an indigenous language vis-à-vis a former colonial language, and has called for vernacularization to play a greater role in

African education (UNESCO 1995). What seems to have received relatively little attention in this ongoing debate, however, is how vernacularization can succeed against more hegemonic language ideologies such as linguistic internationalization, globalization, and what Blaut (1993) has termed "the colonizer's model of the world," as defined in the abstract. To cite a more recent example, consider the UNESCO-sponsored monograph titled *Why and How Africa Should Invest in African Languages and Multilingual Education* (Quane & Glanz 2010). In this monograph, the authors offer ten recommendations aimed at promoting the use of African languages in education. However, like previous studies (UNESCO 1995), the proposed recommendations speak only to the cognitive advantages of an education through the medium of indigenous languages, but they hardly link an education in the indigenous African languages with economic returns or payoffs, nor do they treat the African languages themselves as potential cash cows.

In this chapter I take up the issue of the relationship between African languages and the economy by addressing vernacularization against the aforementioned language ideologies from the perspective of theoretical approaches to the spread of English (Fishman, Conrad, & Rubal-Lopez 1996; Phillipson 1992), on the one hand, and recent developments in the economics of language (Grin 1996), on the other. I first summarize postcolonial language-in-education policies in Africa, and the role of English and other former colonial languages in those policies. Next, I discuss theoretical approaches to the spread of English in Africa to provide the background against which the ideologies that inform the spread of English, to be discussed in the subsequent section, can be understood better. I argue that for vernacularization to succeed in Africa, especially in the era of globalization, African languages must be assigned an economic value at least in the local linguistic market place. In the last section of the chapter I suggest some of the ways in which that value could be assigned, drawing on recent theoretical developments in language economics as well as on successful case studies of vernacularization informed by language economics in various parts of the world.

Colonial and Postcolonial Language Policies in Africa: Match or Mismatch?

Colonial language policies in Africa were informed by the ideology of the nation-state, which was popular in Europe at the time European powers conquered and divided up the African continent among themselves at the Berlin Conference of 1884–1885. Inspired by the ideology of the nation-state, which by definition requires unitary symbols, among them one nation, one language, one culture, one belief system, and so on, the colonial authorities designed language policies that embraced monolingualism in a European language as the norm; treated the diversity of African languages as a problem and a threat to social order; and considered the African languages themselves as inadequate for advanced learning and socioeconomic development. As Wardhaugh (1987) remarks with respect to French colonial language policy in Africa and elsewhere, just as the Breton and Basque were despised in the hexagon, all the indigenous languages of the colonies were treated with the same contempt. Since French was assumed to be the language of civilization, a local elite had to be educated in French and civilized through that language to act as the link between the colonial masters and their subjects. The French believed, as Pierre Alexander (1972) observes, that by offering French to Africans, France was offering the Africans everything that was best in culture, in the whole of mankind: the French culture itself. Comparing the attitudes of the French and the English toward the indigenous African languages, Haugen (1983:11) puts it bluntly: "The English were tolerant of native tongues but unwilling to accept their speakers as equals. The French were willing to receive natives of all colors into the French community provided they gave up their identity and learned French." Whitehead (1995) provides a similar account of British colonial language policy in Africa. He refers to a certain British official named Sir Rivers-Smith, who was director of education in what was then Tanganyika, now Tanzania, and notes that this official could not even contemplate using an African language in education. For Sir Rivers-Smith, use of the vernacular could isolate a tribe from commercial intercourse: "To limit a native to a knowledge of his tribal dialects is to burden him with an economic handicap under which he will always be at a disadvantage when compared with others who, on account of geographical distribution or by means of education, are able to hold intercourse with Europeans or Asiatics" (Whitehead 1995: 8).

The assumed functional or formal inadequacy of the indigenous African languages and therefore, of indigenous mind or civilization was often alleged to justify European tutelage (Gillian 1984: 68). It is ironic that the colonial authorities, be they French, Portuguese, English or Spanish, who took pride in and associated their vernaculars with economic development and progress, could not bring themselves to see the languages spoken by their subjects in the same light. Instead, they associated the indigenous languages with economic and technological stagnation and backwardness. The African elites to whom power passed when colonialism ended adopted not only the colonial language policies they inherited from the metropole but also the negative attitudes that the colonial masters had toward the indigenous languages. As Fishman (1996: 5) remarks, "although the lowering of one flag and the raising of another may indicate the end of colonial status, these acts do not necessarily indicate the end of imperialist privilege in neo-colonial disguise." The essentialist sanction of European languages as the only appropriate languages of schooling has marginalized and precluded the development of African vernaculars. Consequently, as the late Adegbija (1994: 11) remarks sarcastically, in postcolonial Africa "European languages have everything they require to make it, whereas the indigenous languages have everything to make them go hang." With the advent of the global spread of English, which is discussed in the next section, the hope is fading especially in sub-Saharan Africa that African languages will ever be developed to empower their speakers to participate in the socioeconomic development of the continent.

Theoretical Approaches to the Spread and Hegemony of English

In his introduction to Gillian Sankoff's book, *The Social Life of Language*, Dell Hymes writes a little over a quarter of a century ago about the hegemony of European languages: "A new world that had thousands of distinct languages in 1492 is now dominated by English, French, Portuguese, and Spanish over most of its terrain" (1980: xii). Today, that New World is almost exclusively dominated by one language, English, as is evident from its unprecedented penetration into major political and economic institutions on virtually every continent of the globe (Tollefson 1991:82). But why does English spread? Two competing theories offer to explain this unprecedented phenomenon of the spread of English: the *Anglo-American Conspiracy Theory* (Phillipson 1992), and the *Grassroots Theory* (Fishman et al. 1996).

The Conspiracy Theory

The key argument advanced by the adherents of the Conspiracy Theory is that the spread of English has been engineered by powerful British and American interests through systematic and often semi-secret language policies (Phillipson 1992). On this view, Tollefson (1991: 82) notes that English spreads as a result of the economic and military power of English-speaking countries and the expansion of the integrated economic market which they have dominated. Consequently, what the spread of English does is to squeeze other languages into less and less central roles, eroding their functions until eventually they are marginalized to the private and the home and finally lost (Davies 2003). In this regard, Phillipson (2010) notes that the transplantation and export of languages is sometimes referred to as language spread. The term, he says, "is misleading since it can be interpreted as signifying an agent-less process, as though languages, like living organisms, expand and contract according to nature's laws" (2010: 3). Quoting an English-language entrepreneur who said, "Once we used to send gunboats and diplomats abroad; now we are sending English teachers," Phillipson argues that the spread of English around the world is the result of "linguistic imperialism." He defines *linguistic imperialism* as "ideologies, structures and practices which are used to legitimate, effectuate and reproduce an unequal division of power and resources (both material and non-material) between groups which are defined on the basis of language (on the basis of their mother tongues)" (Skutnabb-Kangas & Cummins 1988: 13). Along these lines, it is noted that linguistic imperialism has the following features, among others:

- It is *structural*: more material resources and infrastructure are accorded to the dominant language than to others.
- It is *ideological*: beliefs, attitudes, and imagery glorify the dominant language, stigmatize others, and rationalize the linguistic hierarchy.
- The dominance is *hegemonic*: it is internalized and naturalized as being normal.
- In essence it is about *exploitation*, injustice, inequality, and hierarchy, that privileges those able to use the dominant language.
- This exploitation entails *unequal rights* for speakers of different languages.
- Language use is often *subtractive*, proficiency in the imperial language and in learning it in education involving its consolidation at the expense of other languages.

Against this background, Phillipson (2007) takes exception to arguments that reduce linguistic imperialism to a conspiracy theory(Spolsky 2004), noting that the latter concept is theoretically inadequate and often serves to deflect attention from underlying foreign policy goals and the realities of how dominance and inequality are maintained and legitimated. Therefore, Phillipson argues that "ignoring the interlocking of the promotion of English with wider political and economic activities amounts to a *conspiracy of silence*" (Phillipson 2007: 377). Phillipson's theory of linguistic imperialism, dealing as it does with issues in language, domination and power, finds company in the works of scholars in critical linguistics (Pennycook 1998; Tollefson 2006), as well as in the works of scholars who are interested in language issues in postcolonial settings, such as Fanon (1963), Ngugi wa Thiong'o (1986), and others. Anticipating Phillipson's theory, Fanon (1963) remarks that the continuing use of European languages in postcolonial settings betrays the hidden hand of former colonial masters who are determined to maintain their economic, cultural, and political dominance over their former colonies (Chew 1999). Like France Fanon, Ngugi wa Thiong'o (1986) has also reacted negatively to linguistic imperialism, which he experienced firsthand as a schoolchild, by writing some of his literary works in his native language, Kikuyu. He recalls the time when the indigenous African languages were banned from the school-ground, and what happened when the ban was violated: "The culprits were given corporal punishment . . . or were made to carry a metal plate around the neck with the inscriptions such as 'I am stupid, I am a donkey'" (1986: 11), because they used their indigenous languages within the school compound.

The Grassroots Theory

The Grassroots Theory is proposed in a collection of essays titled *Post-Imperial English*, edited by Fishman, Conrad, and Rubal-Lopez (1996). This theory, which finds support in subsequent essays by, for instance, Chew (1999), Ager (2001), and others, is based on empirical investigations of English in 20 different settings, ranging from the European Union to Nigeria, Sudan, and Cuba. The main argument of the Grassroots Theory is that the spread of English in the world today is not the product of British and American conspiracy, "despite the attempts of some commentators to see devious British or American plots at work"(Ager 1999: 98–115). Rather, the language spreads because, for many different reasons, individuals opt for English rather than alternative languages. In this regard, Lionel Wee (2003: 211), in his paper on the spread of English in Singapore explains that English spreads because of its linguistic instrumentalism, which he describes as a view of language that justifies its existence in a community in terms of its usefulness in achieving specific utilitarian goals, such as access to economic development or social mobility. Ager (2001: 119) concurs, arguing that historical factors aside, currently the motivation that individuals and communities demonstrate for English is economic and pragmatic. He cites Laitin (1997: 288) who says rather crudely that "[p]eople are willing to pay high personal costs to learn English, [but] they have to be bribed to learn French or German. The microeconomic handwriting is on the wall." On a rather less crude note, Chew (1999: 37) says that "the relentless demand for English needs to be understood in terms of the empowering role of English, which is evident in the employment opportunities the language can bestow on its users . . . and the access it provides both to knowledge and to markets."

Irrespective of the theory one embraces, whether the Conspiracy Theory or the Grassroots Theory, the fact remains that English is spreading like wildfire in virtually all countries around the globe, including countries that have no colonial ties to Britain or the United States, such as Rwanda, South Korea, Japan, Germany, and China, to name a few. It is not a coincidence that Bamgbose (2003), for instance, refers to English as a recurring decimal, for the language seems to turn up everywhere. Besides the views expressed by the adherents of the Grassroots Theory, in Africa the hegemony of English over local languages can be explained in terms of the language ideologies discussed in the following section, including the colonizer's model, internationalization and globalization. This is because these ideologies cast English and other colonial languages as the languages for socioeconomic development and upward social mobility, but they view the indigenous languages as a mere token for cultural preservation.

English in Colonial and Postcolonial Language Policies and Ideologies in Africa

Language ideologies, or what Woolard and Schieffelin (1994: 55) refer to as "cultural conceptions of the nature, structure and use of language," are ingrained, unquestionable beliefs that people have about language (Wolfram & Schilling-Estes 2006: 35) and that influence their linguistic choices in various domains. As these beliefs continue to hold sway, they assume ever-greater force, regardless of their accuracy or correspondence to present realities (McGroarty 2010). In this regard, Blommaert (1999: 10–11) remarks that the more a linguistic ideology is taken up in any setting, the more likely it is to undergo normalization, a hegemonic pattern in which the ideological claims are perceived as normal ways of thinking and acting. At their core, language ideologies represent the perception of language and discourse that is constructed in the interest of a specific social or cultural group; that is, they are rooted in the socioeconomic power and vested interests of dominant groups and serve to sustain relations of domination and inequality (Thompson 1984). Essentially, as Dyers and Abongdia (2010) note pointedly, language ideologies are reflected in actual language practice—how people talk, what they say about language and their actual language choices, and their sociopolitical positioning with regard to different languages. Thus, the language ideologies to be discussed here form an essential frame of reference in terms of which individuals and groups in Africa evaluate their linguistic choices especially in the higher domains, such as education in particular.

English, Colonialism, and the Colonizer's Model of the World

Blaut (1993) raises the following question in his discussion of language policy and literacy practices in the Western Hemisphere and their implications for language policies in developing nations: how is the rise and subsequent linguistic dominance of the West to be explained? He theorizes that this question can be addressed from the perspective of what he calls *the colonizer's model of the world*, also known as Eurocentric Diffusionism (Blaut 1993: 10). This is a Western-based paradigm once used to justify colonialism and the repression of indigenous peoples, and one according to which "all good things, including dominant languages, develop first in the West, and are then '*diffused*' to the periphery, based on Western models" (Wiley 2006: 143). This ideology views language planning as "a form of social engineering that can be used to advance higher levels of educational achievement through mass literacy in 'underdeveloped' countries" (Blaut 2000: 9). Other major premises of the colonizer's model include the following: (a) most human communities are *uninventive*; (b) a minority of human communities, places, or cultures are *inventive*; and (c) these remain the world's *permanent* geographical centers of cultural change and progress. In addition to these permanent centers, the world also has permanent peripheries: the former represent an *Inside*, while the latter (i.e., permanent peripheries) represent an *Outside*. *Inside* leads, *Outside* lags; *Inside* innovates, *Outside* imitates (Blaut 1993: 1). In order for developing nations to progress and modernize, then, they must receive knowledge and techniques that are diffused from the permanent centers, the *Inside* (Wiley 2006: 142). Blaut rejects all of the premises of the colonizer's model. He argues forcefully that European colonialism not only initiated the development of Europe and the underdevelopment of non-Europe in 1492, but that ever since, the wealth obtained from non-Europe through colonialism in its many forms, including linguistic neocolonialism, has been a necessary and very important basis for the continued development of Europe at the expense of non-Europe (Blaut 1993: 10).

The "colonizer's model of the world" approach to language planning and policy, based as it is on the rationalist model since it uses the nation-state as its quintessential goal, was transplanted into the territories that Europe colonized in Africa and possibly elsewhere. It continues to inform language-policy decision making in postcolonial societies, and in Africa in particular, as is evident from the two related ideologies, internationalization and globalization, discussed in the next and subsequent section, respectively.

English and Internationalization: Neocolonialism in Disguise?

As a result of the colonizer's model, African countries have adopted the ideology of internationalization that the metropole passed down onto the elite when colonialism ended. Internationalization entails the choice of an international language such as English, French, Portuguese, or Spanish as the official language of the state. I argue that internationalization is an exercise in neocolonialism, for it carries on with the mission of linguistic marginalization of the indigenous languages in favor of the former colonial language, much as was the case in the colonial era. The mission, which is carried out by African elites, entails limiting the use of African languages in education to the first three years of primary school, and requires proficiency in the former colonial language for access to resources and advanced education.

In Africa, the choice of internationalization has resulted in language hierarchization. This is captured in a language policy proposal that Laitin (1992) describes as the " 3 ± 1 language outcome." By this formula, Laitin is referring to the number of languages a citizen needs to know if he or she is to have a wide set of mobility opportunities within his or her country. These languages would include an international language, that is, a European language, which will be used in domains such as higher education and trade and serve as a gateway to the outside world; a language for national integration, such as Swahili in Tanzania or Hindi in India, which will be the medium of instruction in later years of primary education; and a national or regional language, which will be the medium of instruction in early years of primary education. It is observed that those citizens whose mother tongue is the same as the national language will need to learn only two languages, hence the 3 – 1 outcome; while those whose vernacular is not will need to learn four, hence the 3 + 1 outcome.

What Laitin does not say, though, is that the 3 ± 1 language planning outcome is a recipe for the status quo. Commenting on Laitin's framework, Fardon and Furniss (1994) observe pointedly that the originality of Laitin's interpretation of language policies in Africa lies in demonstrating that radical departure from this pattern is highly unlikely, unless there is a radical change against the inherited language policies and especially against social forces such as the elite who, understandably, have a vested interest in maintaining the status quo. The merit of Laitin's 3 ± 1 language outcomes lies in what he calls the *private subversion of the public good*, that is, the practice by language policy makers of agreeing with language policy publicly but subverting it privately (Laitin 1992: 43, 1993: 233) by ensuring that their own children attend English-medium schools where vernacularization is not allowed. As a result, the ideology of internationalization through the medium of English reigns supreme over vernacularization, much as it did in the colonial era. Internationalization has now morphed into a much more hegemonic ideology, namely, globalization.

English and Globalization: Morphed Internationalization?

Hegemonic language practices in Africa, which in the main favor the ideology of internationalization over vernacularization, are a legacy of colonial traditions, one of which is the imposition of the European colonial languages as emblems of socioeconomic status and political power. As a result of the emergence of English as a global language, the ideology of internationalization is now competing with a more hegemonic ideology, globalization, especially in non-English speaking countries in Africa and elsewhere. Mufwene and Vigouroux (2008) view globalization in terms of the interconnectedness of different parts of the world due to better networks of communication and transportation, both of which have facilitated worldwide exchanges of goods and movements of people. Other writers view globalization as the interaction of economic, social, political, cultural, and technological factors, and as resulting in growing economic development, shifting power relationships, and reduced social variation and greater contact (Heller 2003).

One key feature of globalization is inequality among peoples that often goes hand in hand with regional disparities and geographical inequities (Vigouroux 2008). Approached from this perspective, I view globalization as *morphed internationalization*, that is, it is an extension of the old project of neocolonization that until recently was carried out through the ideology of internationalization. The only difference between globalization and internationalization is that the former functions universally through the medium of one language, English, the global commodity; while the latter (internationalization) operates—regionally—through the medium of a former colonial language, either Spanish, Portuguese, or French.

In Africa and other postcolonial settings, the impact of globalization on vernacularization has yet to be fully investigated. It suffices to say, however, that globalization has made the implementation of vernacularization in African education a distant dream. African elites have not succeeded in their veiled attempt to implement vernacularization in education against the forces of internationalization. It is unlikely, therefore, that they will succeed in implementing vernacularization against a more powerful ideology like globalization. Globalization is so powerful that it can threaten an already established national language, as Song (2011) reports with respect to the tension between English and the Korean language in South Korea due to the proposal that English be accorded the status of official language. Globalization can also bring down an already established official language, as it has in a dramatic fashion in Rwanda, where English has literally replaced French as the official language of the state. Some facts about Rwanda are noteworthy to appreciate this dramatic change in the country's language policy. Rwanda is a monolingual country where, according to Rosendal (2009), as high as 99.4 percent of the population speak Kinyarwanda as first/home language, and approximately 90 percent speak only Kinyarwanda. Put differently, only about 10 percent of Rwanda's population is bilingual in Kinyarwanda and French, the language of the former colonial power Belgium. However, evoking globalization rather than the genocide of 1994, which it alleges occurred with the complicity of France, Rwanda has, in a veiled retribution against France, replaced French with English as the country's sole official language. Not only has Rwanda replaced French with English, the country has also left the Francophony, an organization of postcolonial French-speaking countries, and has joined the East African Union, an organization that uses English as the language of business because its member states, Kenya, Tanzania, and Uganda, are former British colonies. Globalization, or *morphed internationalization*, provides a convenient excuse for the continued failure to not only implement vernacularization but, as Song (2011) puts it, to resolve the many social issues related to the exclusive use of former colonial languages in education in postcolonial settings.

The language situation in Rwanda—where the case for vernacularization could be made convincingly since Rwanda does not have a so-called multilingualism problem—takes me back to the central question of this chapter: How can vernacularization succeed against more powerful ideologies such as those described in this chapter? The answer to this question, I argue, lies in moving the debate around vernacularization away from current research paradigms—where the focus is on a critical analysis of colonial and postcolonial language policies—and re-conceptualize the discourse of vernacularization through the prism of recent theoretical developments in the field of language economics. In the next section I suggest that for vernacularization to succeed, the indigenous languages must be assigned an economic value, that is, they must be viewed as a commodity in the acquisition of which language consumers would have a keen interest to invest.

Indigenous African Languages and Language Economics

Language economics seeks to explain how linguistic and economic variables influence one another. In Africa, and arguably elsewhere, economic variables tend to inform parents' choice of the medium of instruction for their children, irrespective of the loyalty they might have for their own indigenous languages. Although Le Page and Tabouret-Keller (1985) remind us that languages, in this case the indigenous African languages, remain a marker of individual or group identity, Sankoff (1980), however, raises the question under what circumstances does the identity function become inverted in such a way that a particular group becomes alienated from its own language and begins to regard it as inferior to some other language? Sankoff explains that these tend to be circumstances in which access to a particular language works to create and maintain real differences in power and wealth. In this regard, scholars interested in the economics of language maintain that, on a given linguistic market, some languages and language-related products, such as accents, are valued more highly than others (Grin 2001). The market value of a linguistic product such as the vernacular is an index of the functional appreciation of the language by the relevant community, and is determined in relation to other languages in the planetary economy (Coulmas 1992: 77–85).

Against this background, I offer the following suggestions to inform language-policy decisions on vernacularization in the African context: First, official African languages need to undergo what Kamwangamalu (1997) refers to as "vernacular education cleansing," that is, they need to be rid of the stigma with which they have been associated since the colonial era, when they were seen as unsuitable for advanced learning and knowledge acquisition. The cleansing of that stigma, however, cannot be done by simply signing a legislation making the indigenous African languages officially equal to a former colonial language such as English. Rather, the indigenous languages need to be revalorized with the view to inducing potential users to adopt them, whether adoption is viewed as awareness or positive evaluation (Cooper 1989). Second, there is the need to vest official African languages with some of the privileges and material gains that are currently associated only with English and other former colonial languages. For that to happen, however, and this is the third suggestion, a certified knowledge, that is, school-acquired knowledge of official African languages should become one of the criteria for access to employment, much as is currently the case for English and other former colonial languages in the African continent. The literature provides several case studies of successful vernacularization that support the suggestions made here and in previous studies on this topic (e.g., Kamwangamalu 1997, 2004). Some such case studies include, for instance, Afrikaans in South Africa, Mandarin Chinese in Singapore and Australia, the Basque language in Spain, official regional languages in India, Maori in New Zealand, Welsh in Wales, and Nepali in Nepal, to name but a few.

With respect to South Africa, the question is, how did Afrikaans manage to shed its image as a kitchen language and become the language of upward social mobility in that country? The oppressive nature of apartheid language-in-education policies to promote Afrikaans against the indigenous languages is well documented (N. Alexander 1997), and I am not by any means advocating such policies. Instead, I would like to highlight the relationship between Afrikaans and the economy, as reported in Malherbe (1977). Malherbe acknowledges that Afrikaans benefited both from the language loyalty of its speakers and the political and material support it received from the state. However, other factors, such as incentives in the form of monetary rewards, tend to be overlooked in the discourse about the success of Afrikaans. In this regard, Malherbe (1977: 112) points out that Afrikaans was promoted through the offering of incentives and rewards to the top achievers in the language. He notes that to encourage pupils to become bilingual in English and Afrikaans, the governments of Tranvaal and Natal awarded monetary grants—bilingual bonuses or merit grants—as inducements. Attached to these grants was the condition that such pupils had, on completion of high school, to go to a training college in order to become teachers.

With respect to Singapore, the country has a multilingual language policy that requires that, in addition to English, all Singaporeans learn their ethnic mother tongue; that is, Chinese children learn Mandarin, the Malays learn Malay, and the Indians learn Tamil or any other Indian languages offered by the school. The literature (Gupta 1997; Tan & Rubdy 2008) indicates, however, that Tamil and Malay parents encourage their children to learn Chinese instead of Tamil and Malay so that they will be prepared to compete in the labor market, where Chinese is increasingly becoming the language of the future. A similar attraction to Chinese is noted among immigrant children in Australia. Gopinath (2008) reports that most immigrant children invariably opt to learn Chinese over any other international language, for they are aware of the material benefits that can accrue to them as a result of their knowledge of the Chinese language. Gopinath also refers to efforts to promote regional official languages in the Indian subcontinent. In particular, he notes that regional governments promote India's indigenous official languages against the hegemony of English by requiring them as the languages for local government administration, funding the development of technical dictionaries, and standardizing software for word processing (Gopinath 2008: 58).

In a similar study, Giri (2010) provides an account of why speakers of Sino-Tibetan languages in Nepal are attracted to Nepali rather than to their own indigenous languages as the medium of instruction. She remarks that, in Nepal, Nepali and English are status symbols and tools in the hands of the ruling elites, who use them to create linguistic hegemony within the polity. As a result, speakers of Sino-Tibetan languages choose Nepali as their second language because their own indigenous languages "do not have the same value in employment, business, media and education as English or Nepali" (Giri 2010: 93).

Along these lines, Kamwangamalu (2010: 13–14) highlights successful case studies of vernacularization as reported in Fishman (2006), Le Page (1997), Edwards (2004), and Ferguson (2006). For instance, Fishman (2006) points to the success of the *Basquecization* activities in Spain, that is, activities intended to promote the Basque language in that country. He explains that Basquecization activities were successful because participation in these activities yielded certification at various levels of competence, entitling their bearers to qualify for promotions, raises, job tenure, and other perquisites of success in the workplace (Fishman 2006). In a related comment on the Spanish Basque, Le Page (1997: 16) draws attention to the considerable political will exerted to ensure the success of policies favoring the use of the Basque language alongside Spanish, not only in education, but also in every domain, and to the availability of financial resources to implement those policies.

Like Fishman and Le Page, Vivian Edwards (2004) asserts that although language is part of our cultural capital, its market value is variable. She points to the case of Welsh and Maori, noting that the official status of these languages has generated a range of employment prospects for minority language speakers in education, the media, and government. A similar comment on Welsh can be found in Ferguson (2006), who provides a comparative study of Welsh and Breton, showing that the revival of Welsh and the continuing decline of Breton are mostly due to different sociopolitical and economic factors. Ferguson notes further that within the United Kingdom itself, Welsh speakers in Wales are working hard to make sure that their language is not quashed by English, by encouraging its use and passing laws requiring public agencies to provide services in both English and Welsh. Before I conclude this section on the economic value of vernacular languages, I would like to mention the case of vernacularization in European countries such as Denmark, the Netherlands, and Sweden, for these countries are often held up as models of successful language learning: They are successful, as Davies (2003) points out, because they succeed in acquiring the foreign language, English, and becoming proficient in it while at the same time not losing their first language: Danish, Swedish, Dutch, and so on. What needs explaining, however, is how and why the first language is maintained. The first language is maintained because it is, like English and unlike an indigenous African language, kept economically viable that is, it provides access to employment, economic resources, and upward social mobility.

Essentially, all the cases of successful vernacularization highlighted in the foregoing discussion have one thing in common: the languages involved, Afrikaans, Chinese, Welsh, Nepali, Maori, Basque, and Hindi are viewed by both their speakers and potential users as a commodity that has an economic value, at least in the local linguistic market place. As Tollefson (1991) aptly observes, only when a language achieves a full range of functions, and no stigma is attached to its use, has it arrived. For the African vernaculars "to arrive," the masses need to know what an education through the medium of an African language would do for them in terms of upward social mobility. Would such an education, for instance, be as rewarding as, say, English-, French-, or Portuguese-medium education? Put differently, promoting an indigenous African language in a domain such as education entails communicating the benefits that the language carries and persuading its speakers to adopt it as the medium of instruction. On this view, Dominguez (1998) observes that the fact that access/promotion to certain jobs requires a language qualification has very visible economic component. It follows that the African masses would not support vernacular-medium education, even if it were made available, unless that education were given a real cachet in the broader political and economic context. It is not surprising, then, that Africa is arguably the only continent in the world where the majority of school-age children receive an education through the medium of a language that is not their own. What distinguishes an education through the medium of a former colonial language such as English vis-à-vis an education through the medium of an indigenous African language is that the former is an education with a difference: it is enabling and empowering rather than disabling and disempowering; it ensures its consumers upward social mobility, allows them access to employment and economic resources, and facilitates their participation in the socioeconomic and political development of the state.

Conclusion

Vernacularization—or its denial—is as important as any other aspects, political and economic planning among them, which have perennially been the main concern of virtually all African states. I have argued that for vernacularization to succeed it must be associated with an economic value, at least in the local linguistic marketplace. This argument entails both an enhanced role in education for African languages and democratization of access to former colonial languages. I have suggested ways in which African languages can be assigned an economic value, drawing on language economics as well as on successful case studies of vernacularization informed by language economics in various parts of the world. In the absence of that economic value, market forces will continue to drive schools to provide the education that the people, not the politicians, in theory, want (Vorhies 1992). For former British and American colonies, and for countries with no colonial ties to Britain or the United States but where English has displaced another former colonial language, as is the case in Rwanda, that education is most likely to be provided through the medium of English, the global commodity. This will result in the further marginalization and exclusion of African languages and the majority of their speakers from participation in the social, political, and economic development of the continent. If we accept the view, after Brock-Utne (2000), that if Africa is to develop economically and encourage mass participation in this process the secret lies with its languages; and if we also accept the view, by Nettle and Romaine (2000: 172), that true development of a political, economic, or social nature cannot take place unless there is also development of a linguistic nature, then African languages must become a commodity in the academic acquisition of which individuals have a good reason to invest. Unless the indigenous African languages are perceived to facilitate access to the wider society and economic advancement, the attraction of English as opposed to the African languages will continue to be overwhelming. It follows that hegemonic language ideologies such as internationalization, globalization, and the colonizer's model of the world will continue to inform Africa's language-in-education policies, thus making vernacularization in Africa a distant dream for current and future generations.

References

Adegbija, E. 1994. *Language attitude in sub-Saharan Africa: A sociolinguistic overview.* Clevedon: Multilingual Matters.

Ager, D. 1999. *Identiy, insecurity and image. France and language.* Clevedon: Multilingual Matters.

Ager, D. 2001. *Motivation in language planning and language policy.* Clevedon: Multilingual Matters.

Alexander, N. 1997. Language policy and planning in the new South Africa. *African Sociological Review* 1: 82–98.

Alexander, P. 1972. *Languages and language in Black Africa.* Evanston, IL: Northwestern University Press.

Bamgbose, A. 2003. A recurring decimal: English in language policy and planning. *World Englishes* 22: 419–31.

Blaut, J. M. 1993. *The colonizer's model of the world: Geographical diffusionism and Eurocentric history.* New York: Guilford.

Blaut, J. M. 2000. *Eight Eurocentric historians.* New York: Guilford.

Blommaert, J. 1999. The debate is open. In J. Blommaert (ed.), *Language ideological debates*, 1–38. Berlin: Mouton de Gruyter

Brock-Utne, B. 2000. *Whose education for all? The recolonization of the African mind.* New York: Falmer Press.

Chew, P. C.-L. 1999. Linguistic imperialism, globalism, and the English language. *AILA Review* 13: 37–47.

Cobarrubias, J. 1983. Ethical issues in status planning. In J. Cobarrubias & J. A. Fishman (eds.), *Progress in language planning*, 41–86. The Hague: Mouton.

Cooper, R. 1989. *Language planning and social change.* Cambridge: Cambridge University Press.

Coulmas, F. 1992. *Language and the economy.* Oxford: Blackwell.

Davies, A. 2003. *The native speaker: Myth and reality.* Clevedon: Multilingual Matters.

Dominguez, F. 1998. Toward a language-marketing model. *International Journal of the Sociology of Language* 134: 1–13.

Dyers, C., & Abongdia, J.-F. 2010. An exploration of the relationship between language attitudes and ideologies in a study of Francophone students of English in Cameroon. *Journal of Multilingual and Multicultural Development* 31: 119–34.

Edwards, V. 2004. *Multilingualism in the English-speaking world.* Malden, MA: Blackwell.

Fanon, F. 1963. *The wretched of the earth.* New York: Grove

Fardon, R., & Furniss, G. (eds.). 1994. *African languages, development and the state.* London: Routledge

Ferguson, G. 2006. *Language planning in education.* Edinburgh: Edinburgh University Press.

Fishman, J. A. 1996. Introduction: Some empirical and theoretical issues. In J. A. Fishman, A. Conrad, & A. Rubal-Lopez (eds.), *Post Imperial English: Status change in former British and American colonies, 1940–1990*, 3–12. New York: Mouton.

Fishman, J. A. 2006. Language policy and language shift. In T. Ricento (ed.), *An introduction to language policy: Theory and method*, 311–28. Malden, MA: Blackwell.

Fishman, J. A., Cooper, R.L., & Rubal-Lopez, A. (eds.). 1996. *Post-imperial English: Status change in former British and American colonies, 1940–1990.* New York: Mouton.

Gillian, A.M. 1984. Language and 'development' in Papua New Guinea. *Dialectal Anthropology* 8: 303–18.

Giri, R. A. 2010. Cultural anarchism: the consequences of privileging languages in Nepal. *Journal of Multilingual and Multicultural Development* 31: 87–100.

Gopinath, C. 2008. *Globalization: A multildimensional system.* Los Angeles: Sage.

Grin, F. 1996. Economic approaches to language and language planning: An introduction. *International Journal of the Sociology of Language* 121: 1–6.

Grin, F. 2001. English as economic value. *World Englishes* 20: 65–78

Gupta, A. 1997. When mother tongue education is *not* preferred. *Journal of Multilingual and Multicultural Development* 18: 496–506.

Haugen, E. 1983. The implementation of corpus planning: Theory and practice. In J. Cobarrubias & J. Fishman (eds), *Progress in language planning: International perspectives*, 269–89. Berlin: Mouton.

Heine, B. 1990. Language policy in Africa. In B. Weinstein (ed.), *Language policy and political development*, 167–84. Norwood, NJ: Ablex.

Heller, M. 2003. Globalization, the new economy, and the commodification of language and identity. *Journal of Sociolinguistics* 7: 473–92.

Hymes, D. 1980. Foreword. In G. Sankoff, *The social life of language*, ix-xv. Philadelphia: University of Pennsylvania Press.

Kamwangamalu, N. M. 1997. Multilingualism and education policy in post-apartheid South Africa. *Language Problems & Language Planning* 21: 234–53.

Kamwangamalu, N. M. 2004. Language policy/language economics interface and mother tongue education in post-apartheid South Africa. *Language Problems and Language Planning* 28: 131–46.

Kamwangamalu, N. M. 2010. Vernacularization, globalization, and language economics in non-English-speaking countries in Africa. *Language Problems and Language Planning* 31: 1–23.

Laitin, D. D. 1992. *Language repertoires and state construction in Africa*. Cambridge: Cambridge University Press

Laitin, D. D. 1993. The game theory of language regime. *International Political Science Review* 14: 227–39.

Laitin, D. D. 1997. The cultural identities of a European state. *Politics and Society* 25: 277–302.

Le Page, R. B. 1997. Introduction. In A. Tabouret-Keller, R. Le Page, P. Gardner-Chloros, & G. Varro (eds.), *Vernacular literacy: A re-evaluation*, 1–20. Oxford: Clarendon Press.

Le Page, R., & Tabouret-Keller, Andree. 1985. *Acts of identity: Creole-based approaches to language and ethnicity*. Cambridge: Cambridge University Press.

Malherbe, E. G. 1977. *Education in South Africa*, vol. 2: *1923–75*. Cape Town: Juta.

McGroarty, M. 2010, Language and ideology. In N. Hornberger & S. McKay (eds.), *Sociolinguitics and language education*, 3–39. Clevedon: Multilingual Matters.

Mufwene, S., & Vigouroux, C. 2008. Colonization, globalization and language vitality in Africa: An introduction. In C. Vigouroux & S. Mufwene (eds), *Globalization and language vitality*, 1–31. New York: Continuum.

Nettle, D., & Romaine, S. 2000. *Vanishing voices: The extinction of the world's languages*. Oxford: Oxford University Press.

Pennycook, A. 1998. *English and the discourses of colonialism*. London: Routledge.

Phillipson, R. 1992. *Linguistic imperialism*. Oxford: Oxford University Press

Phillipson, R. 2007. Linguistic imperialism: A conspiracy, or a conspiracy of silence? *Language Policy* 6: 377–83.

Phillipson, R. 2010. Colonialism and neocolonialism and language policy and planning. Manuscript. Copenhagen School of Business.

Quane, A., & Glanz, C. 2010. *Why and how Africa should invest in African languages and multilingual sducation*. Hamburg: UNESCO Institute for Lifelong Learning. [www.unesco.org/uil].

Rosendal, T. 2009. Linguistic markets in Rwanda: Language use in advertisements and on signs. *Journal of Multilingual and Multicultural Development* 30: 19–39.

Sankoff, Gillian. 1980. *The social life of language*. Philadelphia: University of Pennsylvania Press.

Skutnabb-Kangas, T., & Cummins, J. (eds). 1988. *Minority education: From shame to struggle*. Clevedon: Multilingual Matters.

Song, J. J. 2011. English as an official language in South Korea: Global English or social malady. *Language Problems and Language Planning* 35: 1–18.

Spolsky, B. 2004. *Language policy*. New York: Cambridge University Press.

Tan, P., & Rubdy, R. (eds.). 2008. *Language as commodity: Global structures, Local marketplaces.* London: Continuum.

Thompson, J. 1984. *Studies in the theory of ideology.* Berkeley: University of California Press.

Tollefson, J. W. 1991. *Planning language, planning inequality.* London: Longman.

Tollefson, J. W., & Tsui, Amy B. (eds.). 2004. *Medium of instruction policies: Which agenda? Whose agenda?* Mahwah, NJ: Lawrence Erlbaum.

Tollefson, J. W. 2006. Critical theory in language policy. In T. Ricento (ed.), *An introduction to language policy: Theory and method,* 42–59. Oxford: Blackwell.

UNESCO. 1995. *The use of vernacular languages in education.* Paris: UNESCO.

Vigouroux, C. 2008. From Africa to Africa: Globalization, migration and language vitality. In C. Vigouroux & S. Mufwene (eds.), *Globalization and language vitality: Perspectives from Africa,* 229–54. New York: Continuum.

Vorhies, F. 1992. A market-based approach to the education industry. In R McGregor & Anne McGregor (eds.), *Education alternatives,* 479–93. Cape Town, South Africa: Juta.

Wardhaugh, R. 1987. *Languages in competition: Dominance, diversity, and decline.* Oxford: Blackwell.

Wa Thiong'o, N. 1986. *Decolonizing the mind: The politics of language in African literature.* London: James Currey.

Wee, L. 2003. Linguistic instrumentalism in Singapore. *Journal of Multilingual and Multicultural Development* 24: 211–24

Whitehead, C. 1995. The medium of instruction in British colonial education: A case of cultural imperialism or enlightened paternalism. *History of Education* 24: 1–15.

Wiley, T. 2006. The lessons of historical investigation: Implications for the study of language policy and planning. In T. Ricento (ed.), An introduction to language policy: Theory and practice, 135-52. Malden: Blackwell.

Wolfram, W., & Schilling-Estes, N. 2006. *American English: Dialect sand variation,* 2nd ed. Malden, MA: Blackwell.

Woolard, K. A., & Schieffelin, B. B. 1994. Language ideology. *Annual Review of Anthropology* 23: 55–82.

CHAPTER 28

LANGUAGE POLICY AND IDEOLOGY

GREATER CHINA

QING ZHANG

THIS chapter discusses language policies in the People's Republic of China (PRC), including the Hong Kong Special Administrative Region (HKSAR, since 1997), and Taiwan. The term "Greater China" in the title of this chapter refers to the aforementioned three territories. Contemporary language policies in the region are driven by the needs for, and play a vital role in, building a unified modern nation-state (Chen 1999; Hsiau 1997; Zhou & Ross 2004). Language policy is shown to be informed and shaped by (language) ideologies and attitudes, as well as by sociohistorical, geopolitical, and economic considerations. All three territories have witnessed drastic socioeconomic and political change since the last two decades of the twentieth century. Such transformations have undoubtedly left their impact on the languages and language policies.

THE PEOPLE'S REPUBLIC OF CHINA

Demographic and Language Information

The population of the PRC is approximately 1.347 billion; about 91.51 percent are Han Chinese, and 8.49 percent are ethnic minorities (National Bureau of

Statistics 2011). Chinese is well known as the language with the largest number of speakers, over 1.3 billion, the majority of whom are in the PRC and Taiwan. What is commonly known as "Chinese" is not a monolithic linguistic entity but consists of multiple *fangyan*, or groups of regional varieties, or regionalects (DeFrancis 1984) or topolects (Mair 1991). Hence, what is known as "the Chinese language" is a sociopolitical construct that masks linguistic differences among the regionalects, likened to those among Romance languages in Europe (e.g., DeFrancis 1984). Linguists often classify the regional varieties into seven or eight groups. They are (in decreasing number of speakers) *Beifanghua* or *Guanhua* (Mandarin); *Wu*; *Yue* (Cantonese); *Xiang*; *Min* (further divided into Southern Min and Northern Min by some linguists); *Kejia* or Hakka; and *Gan* (ibid.). The non-Mandarin varieties are also referred to as Southern varieties. The number of languages in China ranges from the official number of 80, to 120 in Sun (1999, cited in Bradley 2005), to 292 in *Ethnologue* (Lewis 2009).

Historical Background: Language Policy from the Late Nineteenth Century to 1949

The historical roots of contemporary language policy in PRC and Taiwan lie in the second half of the nineteenth and early twentieth centuries, a time often considered a humiliating period when China was defeated repeatedly by foreign powers in the Opium Wars (1840–1842, 1856–1860) and the first Sino-Japanese War (1894–1895), which resulted in the concession of Hong Kong to the British Empire in 1842, and Taiwan to Japan in 1895. These defeats prompted a widely perceived urgent need to modernize the country. Language was identified as a key target for reform so that a modernized and unified language could serve as a tool for building a modern and unified country (DeFrancis 1950; Chen 1999).

Earlier Chinese language reformers, many of whom studied in Japan, were inspired by the successful language reform carried out in Meiji Japan (1868–1912), where the establishment of a unified national language with a spoken standard language and a modern written language based on the spoken vernacular was achieved in a relatively short period of time (Chen 1999). Influential Chinese intellectuals in the late nineteenth century saw the need to promote *guoyu* 'national language' as the unified standard language of China and initiated what was known as the National Language Movement (ibid.). The earlier efforts in language reform and language policy focused on three areas. First, the establishment and promotion of a unified spoken standard that serves as a lingua franca among mutually unintelligible regional varieties; second, the development of a modern written language that is closer to the daily vernacular; third, the reform of the traditional ideographic script (ibid.). Language reform was guided by a Herderian ideology "one language, one nation" in which linguistic unification was to bring about national unity (e.g., DeFrancis 1950).

Significant progress in the first two areas was achieved in the first half of the twentieth century under the Nationalist government established in 1912. In 1913, the Committee for the Unification of Pronunciation was established under the Ministry of Education (MOE; Chen 1999). Numerous phonetic schemes were developed to facilitate the annotation and standardization of a unified spoken language. In 1918, a system called *Zhuyin Zimu*, or Phonetic Symbols, was approved by the MOE. This system uses symbols or simple forms derived from traditional Chinese characters (Chen 1999). It was later revised and referred to as the *Guoyin Zimu* 'National Phonetic Symbols (NPS)' and promulgated by the MOE in 1930 (Tsao 2008a). It played an important role in the promotion of *guoyu* during the early decades of its promulgation in the mainland and later in Taiwan. In 1928, the MOE authorized the first roman-alphabet-based system, called *Guoyu Luomazi*, designed by linguists including Chao Yuen Ren. This system, also known as the second form of NPS (NPS2) was later revised and used as one of the three popular phonetic schemes in Taiwan (Tsao 2008a). After years of debate over which variety should serve as the basis for the spoken national language, Beijing dialect won out. The new standard pronunciation was defined as "the speech of natives of Peking who have received a middle-school education" (DeFrancis 1950: 76). In 1932, a new *Vocabulary of National Pronunciation for Everyday Use* replaced the old *Dictionary of National Pronunciation*. The pronunciation of characters in Beijing Mandarin was transcribed using the new *Guoyu Luomazi* (Chen 1999; DeFrancis 1950).

The most significant achievement was in the second area, the development of a modern written language that is closer to the daily vernacular. *Wenyuan* 'classical literary Chinese', the most prestigious form of written Chinese up to the beginning of the twentieth century, was replaced by *baihua* 'vernacular-based literary Chinese.' In 1920, the MOE stipulated that all primary school textbooks should be written in *baihua* instead of *wenyan*. Furthermore, the use of *baihua* was widely promoted in the print media, including journals, newspapers, and literary works (Chen 1999). By the 1930s, *baihua* was established as the basis for the standard written language for all purposes and occasions (Chen 1999). Little progress was made on the simplification of the logographic script in the first half of the twentieth century. In 1935, the MOE published a list of 324 simplified characters, but it was aborted the following year due to opposition from conservatives in the government and the outbreak of the second Sino-Japanese War (1937–1945; Chen 1999; Zhao 2008).

In summary, prior to 1949 the language policy approach of the Nationalist government can be characterized as "non-interventionist" (Zhao & Baldauf 2008: 43). Such a stance was changed to a top-down approach both in the PRC under the Chinese Communist Party (CCP) and in Taiwan under the Kuomintang (KMT) government after it was defeated by the CCP in 1949.

Language Policy in the PRC since 1949

Unifying the spoken language and reforming the writing system have remained the focus of language policy since the establishment of the PRC in 1949, with the latter encompassing character simplification and the development of a phonetic alphabet. Language policy continues to serve as a means to build a unified, modern Chinese state (e.g., Zhou & Sun 2004). Compared with the non-interventionist stance toward language issues under the KMT, the new PRC under the leadership of the CCP adopted a top-down approach to language reform and policy with extensive involvement of state organizations and top party-government leaders (Zhao & Baldauf 2008). Language reform was carried out on an unprecedented scale (Zhou 2003). The (changing) political agenda and ideologies of the CCP exerted tremendous influence on language reform and policies (Blachford 2004; Zhao 2008).

Language reform as one of the top national priorities of the newly established PRC can be seen in the establishment of the *Zhongguo Wenzi Gaige Xiehui* 'Chinese Script Reform Association' in October 1949, immediately following the declaration of the founding of the PRC. The new government saw the urgent need of script reform to combat illiteracy and build a socialist new China. The Committee was renamed in 1955 as the *Zhongguo Wenzi Gaige Weiyuanhui* 'Committee for Chinese Script Reform' directly under the State Council. In October 1955 the Committee and the MOE convened two conferences in Beijing that were of historical significance. The agenda of language reform was set at the *Quanguo Wenzi Gaige Huiyi* 'National Conference on Script Reform.' The main tasks included the simplification of the Chinese character, promulgation of a spoken standard Chinese, called *Putonghua* (PTH), and the development of a phonetic alphabet (Chen 1999). At the *Xiandai Hanyu Guifanhua Xueshu Huiyi* 'Symposium on the Standardization of Modern Chinese', the resolution on the official definition of PTH was passed (Rohsenow 2004: 23). The *Zhongyang Tuiguang Putonghua Gongzuo Weiyuanhui* 'Central Working Committee for the Promotion of Putonghua' was also established in January 1956 to coordinate the nationwide campaign. In February 1956, the State Council issued 'Directives concerning the promotion of *Putonghua*' (*Guowuyuan guanyu tuiguang Putonghua de zhishi*) in which PTH was officially defined as

> the standard form of Modern Chinese with the Beijing phonological system as its norm of pronunciation, Northern Mandarin as its base dialect, and the exemplary works of modern *baihua* [vernacular literary language] literature as its grammatical norms. (Guojia Yuyan Wenzi 1996: 12, translation adapted from Chen 1999: 24)

Efforts in simplification of characters were also carried out in the early 1950s. Traditional characters were not only seen as a great barrier to mass literacy but also a means to sustain the privilege and power of the former ruling classes (Zhao & Baldauf 2008). In 1956, the First Scheme of Simplified Chinese Characters was published, consisting of 515 simplified characters and 54 simplified *pianpiang*, or basic character components. The average number of strokes of characters was reduced by about half from 16 to eight per character (Chen 1999: 157). In 1964, a comprehensive list of 2236 simplified characters, entitled the General List of Simplified Characters (*Jianhuazi Zongbiao*), was published (Zhao 2008). This list reduced the average number of strokes of the most commonly used 2000 characters from 11.2 to 9.8 (Chen 1999: 157). The General List was republished in 1986 with minor changes. It serves as the standard for all publications in mainland China, "except for special purposes or in such specialized areas as classic studies" (ibid.: 155). Research has shown that the simplified script facilitates acquisition of literacy by adult and children (Chen 1999).

The government continued the effort to develop a phonetic script. In 1958, *Hanyu Pinyin Fang'an* 'Scheme for the Phonetic Alphabet of Chinese' was approved by the National People's Congress and officially published in 1964 (Rohsenow 2004). *Pinyin* serves as a sound annotation tool that provides the standard pronunciation for Chinese characters. It is promoted as an auxiliary system that is not intended to replace the existing logographic Chinese script (Chen 1999). *Pinyin* has become indispensable in facilitating character learning, the teaching of PTH, and the teaching of Chinese as a foreign language.

Language reform made great strides in the first decade following the establishment of the PRC. However, language planning work was interrupted in the next two decades by continuous political campaigns, particularly, the disastrous Great Leap Forward (1958–1960) and the ten-year Cultural Revolution (1966–1976; Rohsenow 2004). It was also during the Cultural Revolution that the Second Scheme of Simplified Chinese Character was developed and published in 1977. It was met with widespread opposition from both the public and scholars and was withdrawn after six months.

After the Cultural Revolution, China embarked on economic reform and globalization. Language issues continue to figure prominently in the country's development, national unity, and national identity. There have been accelerated government efforts in language standardization and regularization, specifically the promotion of PTH and standard Chinese characters. PTH received constitutional support for the first time in 1982 in the revised version of the Constitution of the PRC . Under Article 19, it is stipulated that PTH is to be promoted nationwide. In 1986, the Second National Conference on Script Reform was convened by the newly organized State Language Commission (formerly the Committee on Script Reform) and the MOE in Beijing. Promotion of PTH was made the top priority of language and script work in the new era (Rohsenow 2004: 31). The goals to be achieved by the end of the twentieth century laid out in the conference included:

(1) Putonshua to become the language of instruction in all schools nationwide;
(2) Putonghua to become the working language of government at all levels;
(3) Putonghua to be the language used in radio and television broadcasting, and in cinemas and theatres;
(4) Putonghua to become the common language used among speakers of various local dialects. (Rohsenow 2004: 31)

As Chen (1999) and Rohsenow (2004) observe, the fact that these goals were almost exactly the same as those laid out at the First National Conference 30 years earlier indicates that not much progress was made in the promotion of PTH as a national standard spoken language. Since the conference, the government has promoted PTH more vigorously, and numerous laws and regulations on language use have been issued over the past 25 years to consolidate the status of PTH as the national standard language and lingua franca.

The most important language legislation during this period is *Guojia Tongyong Yuyan Wenzi Fa* 'Law of the National Commonly Used Language and Script of the PRC,' commonly known as the National Common Language Law, which was passed by the National People's Congress on October 31, 2000, and came into effect on January 1, 2001. The Law affirms the legal status of the national commonly used language in its spoken form, PTH, and the written, the standard simplified character script (Article 2). Language as a sociopolitical tool for nation-building is reiterated in Article 5:

> The use of the national common language and script shall be conducive to maintaining national sovereignty and dignity, be conducive to national integrity and unity, and be conducive to the construction of socialist material and spiritual civilization. (translation adapted from Rohsenow 2004: 41)

The law stipulates that PTH and the standard Chinese characters should be the language used for government business, in schools and other educational organizations, in publications in Chinese, in radio and television broadcasting, and as the language of service in the public sector (Articles 9, 10, 11, 12, 13). It specifies for the first time four public occasions where dialects may be used (Article 16) and situations where traditional complex characters may be used (Article 17). The Law (in Article 19) also states that the PTH proficiency of broadcasters; program hosts; film, television, and stage actors; teachers; and government employees should meet specific levels as determined by the state through taking the Putonghua Proficiency Test (*Putonghua Shuiping Ceshi*). In addition, as one of the measures to implement the Common Language Law, the State Council is instructed to issue Standards for the Grading System of Putonghua Proficiency Test or *Putonghua Shuiping Ceshi Dengji Biaozhun* (Article 24). Thus, Articles 19 and 24 pave the way for proficiency in PTH to become a gatekeeping mechanism for access to job opportunities in certain areas of social mobility.

The Putonghua Proficiency Test (*Putonghua Shuiping Ceshi*; PSC hereafter), given support in the Common Language Law, is another crucial measure to implement the standard language policy in the key domains of education, the media, and government. Developed in the early 1990s, it was implemented in 1994 and applied to people in the above-mentioned three areas, including teachers in primary and secondary schools and in teachers' colleges; radio and television broadcasters and program hosts; professional actors in film, television drama, and theater (PSC 1994); and civil servants (PSC 1999). The test specifies three proficiency levels (each further split into Grade A and Grade B) based on error rates of lower than 8 percent (Level 1), 20 percent (Level 2), and 40 percent (Level 3). Passing examinees receive a Certificate of Putonghua Proficiency Level. It was recommended that a system of *chi zheng shang gang* 'holding the Certificate to take a position' be gradually implemented starting in 1995 (PSC 1994). A comprehensive official guide to the PSC, *Putonghua Shuiping Ceshi Shishi Gangyao* 'Outline for the Implementation of the PSC', was published in 2004 (State Language Commission 2004).

The implementation of the PSC ended a period of no government requirement of knowledge of the spoken standard language for positions in the state sector. It not only serves as a heavy-handed measure to reinforce PTH in education, broadcasting media, and government offices, but also safeguards that the Beijing Mandarin sound system is the standard of pronunciation. For example, a Level 1 Grade A proficiency (with an error rate lower than 3 percent), which is required of all national and provincial-level radio and television broadcasters and program hosts (PSC 1997), means that the speaker demonstrates a very high level of standard pronunciation, conforming strictly to the norms of Beijing Mandarin phonology, including the correct usage of *qing sheng* 'neutral tone' (especially in lexically weak-stress syllables) and *er-hua* 'rhotacization of the syllable rhyme.' These two features are native to Beijing Mandarin speakers and mainly shared among Northern Mandarin varieties. Hence, testing the correct production of neutral tone and rhotacization puts the speakers of southern and non-Mandarin varieties at a disadvantage, as they have to devote extra effort to learning the prescribed usage of these two features. Since its implementation in 1994, more than 35 million person-times have taken the test (State Language Commission 2010).

Another key measure to promulgate PTH nationwide is the "National *Putonghua* Promotion Publicity Week" (NPPPW) that takes place in the third week of every September, first launched in 1998. Prior to each NPPPW, an official Notice of the NPPPW is issued, specifying the theme and objectives of the promotion week, laying out guiding principles, and suggesting activities and slogans to be used. The Notices and speeches by top government officials during the week provide important information about (changes in) language policy. Key domains for the promotion of PTH are designated with different roles in the nationwide campaign in which "schools serve as the base, Party and government organizations as the leader, radio and television news media as the example, and public service sector as the window to lead the entire country in the promotion and popularization of PTH" (e.g., NPPPW 1999). While Notices for NPPPW from 1998 to 2004 identified "large-to-medium-sized cities as the center" of promotion activities, in the latest Notice, it is explicitly stated that the focus of PTH promotion work is to be shifted from the city to rural areas and minority nationality regions (NPPPW 2011). Increasing government involvement in PTH promotion is also demonstrated by the number of government organizations that jointly issue the annual Notice. The relation between PTH and the Chinese national identity and unity is reiterated in the latest Notice, which also identifies the promotion of PTH as a "core national interest" (NPPPW 2011).

Minority Language Policy in the PRC

China's minority language policy serves as a key instrument to establish national unity and to integrate its 55 minority nationalities into a unitary multinational Chinese state (Dwyer 2005; Zhou 2003). The Constitution guarantees equality among all nationalities, the freedom of all nationalities to use and develop their own languages and scripts. However, since the establishment of the PRC, policies on minority languages have vacillated between accommodation to repressive assimilation. The huge swings in policy are the result of changing Party political ideologies and agendas at different times (Blachford 2004; Zhou 2003).

Zhou (2003: 42–98) identifies three periods in the PRC's minority language policy. The first pluralistic stage was from 1949 to 1957, "during which accommodation was the rule and the CCP promoted the use and development of minority languages and scripts in minority communities" (Zhou 2003: 37). Minority language policy in the early 1950s was part of a broader endeavor to consolidate the CCP's control of China and to fend off domestic and international adversaries so that the new country could embark on social and economic development. This led to an accommodationist approach to minority languages that tolerates diversity and supports minority language development (cf. Blachford 2004; Dreyer 2003a). The articles on minority language use stipulated in the 1954 Constitution reflect such an approach. During this period, academic work on minority identification and the survey and documentation of minority languages were also carried out (Zhou 2003).

The first period of tolerance and accommodation came to an end with the launching of the Great Leap Forward in 1958. The political campaign aimed to accelerate the pace of socialist reform. Under the Party's political agenda, minority language policy and language development work were again recruited in the country's rush to communism. The Great Leap Forward and the Cultural Revolution constitute the second period of minority language policy, "the Chinese monopolistic stage (1958–1977), when the CCP pushed assimilation, promoted Chinese in minority communities at the expense of minority languages and scripts" (Zhou 2003: 37). During this period, ethnic nationalism, linguistic and cultural diversity were considered impediments to socialism and national unity, and linguistic assimilation served as a shortcut to national convergence.

The emphasis on national convergence and integration of minority nationalities into the Han Chinese nation also impacted policy and practice on minority language work. One measure to achieve national convergence through linguistic convergence was to use Roman alphabet, and specifically, Chinese

Pinyin as the basis for the creation and reform of minority language writing systems. The goal of such a move was to bring the newly created Roman alphabet writing systems as close as possible to Pinyin, which in effect was to bring minority languages closer to PTH (Zhou 2003; Q. Zhou 2004). For example, in Xinjiang, Pinyin replaced the traditional Arabic-based Uygur and Kazak writing systems (Blachford 2004). Research on minority languages that emphasized linguistic differentiation—either among minority languages or between Chinese and minority languages—was criticized for threatening ethnic and national unity (Zhou 2003; Q. Zhou 2004). Work on minority language development and reform was interrupted during the Cultural Revolution and forced assimilation was particularly intensified during this period (Zhou 2003). Chinese-only in education and government service was widely practiced in minority communities. The use of minority languages in public domains became severely limited (Zhou 2003). All such integrationist practices that impinged on minority rights were done while the 1954 Constitution was still in effect, which attests to M. Zhou's (2004) observation that the CCP's policies prior to the 1980s often lacked due respect for the Constitution.

The repressive period ended with the downfall of the Gang-of-Four in 1976. Since the implementation of the policy of economic reform and the opening up to the outside world in the late 1970s and early 1980s, minority language policy entered "the second pluralistic stage (1978-present [2002]), which saw the return of accommodationism in the CCP minorities policy, and a return to the promotion of both Chinese and minority languages and scripts in minority communities" (Zhou 2003: 37). This shift in language policy came with a more general liberalization of government and Party policies under the leadership of Deng Xiaoping (Dreyer 2003a). The minority rights, including language rights, enshrined in the 1954 Constitution were restored in the 1982 Constitution (as discussed earlier). The rights to use minority language in government (Article 21), schools (Article 37), and courts of law (Article 47) are reaffirmed in the "Law on Regional Autonomy for Minority Nationalities in the PRC," adopted in 1984 and revised in 2001. Bilingual education has been the general policy in minority schools since the 1980s. The Common Language Law, with its scope restricted to PTH and the Chinese script, represents careful consideration of the sociolinguistic complexities of minority languages and a respect for constitutionally guaranteed minority language rights (Rohsenow 2004).[1] The Common Language Law also reaffirms minority nationalities' "freedom to use and develop their own languages and scripts" (Article 8) in addition to the promulgation of PTH across the country.

As has been shown, the current policies on minority languages stipulated in national and local laws and regulations adhere to the constitutional principle of use and development of minority languages and other language rights. However, as M. Zhou (2004) and others have pointed out, there is always a large gap between the ideals enshrined in the Constitution and other language laws and the local realities of minority languages (Bulag 2003; Blachford 2004;

Dwyer 2005). In addition to ineffective and inconsistent policy implementation at the local levels (e.g., Blachford 2004), major factors contributing to such discrepancy, as evidenced in the previous discussion on the "Chinese monopolistic stage (1958–1977)", are the Party's policies and political agenda, which may contradict and override language rights protected by the laws (M. Zhou 2004; Blachford 2004). Another barrier to the realization of the ideals is an entrenched ideology of Han superiority that treats ethnic minorities as "backward" and "low quality" or *suzhi di*, who need to be brought up to speed with the Han civilization and whose languages are not adequate to meet the needs of modernization, particularly modern technology and science (Dwyer 2005; Harrell 1993). Such an ideology is not only shared among members of the majority group but also influences minority leaders, many of whom are "the most assimilated members of their nationality" (Bradley 2005: 8). The belief in Han superiority manifests itself in discriminatory attitudes toward minority languages and peoples (Bulag 2003; Blum 2004) and (covert) assimilationist policy practices (Dwyer 2005), as well as "in the ethnological theory that guides the process of nationality work" (Harrell 1993: 112).

Another related factor is the contradiction between an overt, tolerant, accommodationist policy and a covert, long-term monist assimilationist policy, initiated in the early 1990s, that seeks to integrate the ethnic minority groups into the Chinese nation, or *Zhonghua Minzu* (Bulag 2003; Zhou 2003). Dwyer's (2005) analysis of language policy and identity politics in the Xinjiang Uyghur Autonomous Region shows that a multilingual and multicultural policy orientation in the 1980s has been curtailed and replaced by a policy that favors monolingualism and monoculturalism to assimilate the major ethic group, the Uyghurs, into the Chinese nation. Minority and Chinese schools began to be merged in the mid 1990s under the claimed goal to raise education outcomes, but it has been shown to be ineffective and to reproduce inequality between Han and Uyghur students (Tsung & Cruickshank 2009). According to Dwyer (2005), this demonstrably counterproductive policy shift has fueled the rise of Uyghur nationalism and separatist movements.

After six decades of rigorous promotion of PTH at the expense of minority languages, varieties of PTH have become the first and second languages of more than half of the ethnic minority people in China (Zhou 2003: 27). According to Bradley (2007), as many as 85 minority languages are endangered in China. Minority language shift and loss are likely to become escalated with increasing migration to areas of better economic opportunity, where Chinese varieties are required for socioeconomic advancement. Recent government policy statements emphasize the importance of the maintenance and revitalization of endangered minority languages (e.g., State Ethnic Affairs Commission 2010). At the same time, these policy statements, such as the "Eleventh Five-Year" Plan of State Language and Script Work (for years 2006–2010; Ministry of Education 2007) and the "Outline of the state mid-to-long-term reform and development plan for the enterprise of language and script (2010–2020)" (Jiao 2011), all emphasize the guiding principle of building a harmonious social linguistic life and unity of dominance (*zhuti xing*) and diversity (*duoyang xing*). Such policy statements demonstrate again that the PRC's language policy is guided by the CCP's current political agenda, which is to build a harmonious socialist society. The principle on the one hand recognizes linguistic diversity in terms of regional varieties and minority languages as the reality of sociolinguistic life in China and promotes a harmonious relationship between the national standard language and other language varieties. On the other hand and more importantly, it guarantees the absolute dominant status (*zhuti diwei*) of PTH and the standard simplified Chinese script.

Hong Kong Special Administrative Region

Demographic and Language Information

The Hong Kong Special Administrative Region (HKSAR) has a population of approximately seven million (National Bureau of Statistics 2011), 95 percent of whom are ethnic Chinese (Census and Statistics Department 2006: 7). Hong Kong became a British colony in 1842 and was returned to the PRC in 1997. Under the principle of "One Country, Two Systems," the Basic Law of the HKSAR guarantees the region a high degree of autonomy (Basic Law 1990, Article 2), and that "the socialist system and policies shall not be practised in the HKSAR, and the previous capitalist system and way of life shall remain unchanged for 50 years" (Basic Law 1990, Article 5).

English was the de facto and de jure official language under much of the British rule until 1974 when the Official Languages Ordinance was adopted, giving Chinese co-official status with English (Johnson 1994). However, Chinese was not granted equal status in all domains of use, particularly in higher levels of administration, the legislature, and the judiciary. It was not until the Official Languages (Amendment) Ordinance in 1987 that Chinese was given equal status as a working official language in addition to its statutory status (Chen 2001a). The official status of Chinese is reaffirmed in Article 9 of the Basic Law, which states: "In addition to the Chinese language, English may also be used as an official language by the executive authorities, legislature and judiciary of the Hong Kong Special Administrative Region." The term "Chinese" is not explicitly defined in all three of the above legal documents. In practice, "Chinese" in the context of Hong Kong refers to Modern Standard Chinese (using traditional complex Chinese character script) as written form and Hong Kong Cantonese as the spoken form (Johnson 1994).

According to the results of the 2006 By-Census (Census and Statistics Department 2006: 7), Cantonese is the language most commonly used at home for 91 percent of the population aged five and over. The other two major languages are English and PTH. Forty-five percent of the population reported that they were able to speak English either as the usual language (2.8 percent) or another language (41.9 percent), and 40.2 percent claimed to be able to speak PTH either as the usual language (0.9 percent) or another language (39.2 percent)

Language Policy prior to 1997

Language policy in Hong Kong under much of British colonial rule is often characterized as *laissez-faire* and focused primarily on language-in-education policy (e.g., Evans 2000; Hopkins 2006; Poon 2000). As numerous scholars have pointed out, the *laissez-faire* approach during the colonial period is largely a myth that disguises the ideological motivations of policy decisions that ultimately served the British colonial governance (Pennycook 2002), perpetuated the symbolic dominance of English (Lin 1996) and produced a steady supply of local English speakers who act as "intermediaries" (Pennycook 1998: 112) or "linguistic middle men" (Luke & Richards 1982: 54) between the colonial government and the local masses.

During the first hundred years of British rule, Hong Kong's educational system was organized into two streams, English-medium (originally called Anglo-Chinese) and Chinese-medium. In the 1950s, a reasonable balance existed in the dual-stream system, wherein the majority of primary schools used Chinese as the medium of instruction, and there was a comparable number of English- and Chinese-medium secondary schools (Evans 2000: 186). Despite repeated recommendations on Chinese or "mother tongue" as the medium of instruction (MOI) at the secondary level by experts on educational grounds, the government did not make any policy changes citing parental preference for English medium instruction (EMI) and the economic value of English in international communication as justifications (Tsui 2008). The result is that the number of English-medium secondary schools soared at the expense of Chinese-medium schools such that by the end of the colonial rule, 94 percent of secondary schools were English medium, whereas only 6 percent were Chinese medium. The Chinese stream remained dominant at the primary level (Tsui 2008; Evans 2000).

The *laissez-faire* policy began to change as Hong Kong was approaching the transfer of sovereignty. In 1990 the Education Commission Report No. 4 proposed a new language-in-education policy, often referred to as the "streaming policy." The Report recommended that mother tongue, i.e., Chinese, be used as the MOI in secondary schools, and that mixed-code should be reduced in favor of the consistent use of either Chinese or English (Tsui 2008). A timetable was also proposed in the Report, specifying that the full implementation of the policy would start in the 1998–1999 school year, by which time schools would be given firm guidance on their MOI (ibid.). The new policy started to operate in 1994 when students were streamed into three types of schools—Chinese-medium, English-medium, and two-medium—based on assessment of their language ability in Primary 6 (Poon 2000). Despite the government's insistence that the policy was based on educational grounds and for the benefit of students, the strategic timing of the policy, with its full implementation starting in 1998, led some researchers to conclude that it was politically motivated as part of the colonial government's "noble retreat" (Tsui 2008: 441) and "a gesture to appease China" (Poon 2010: 40). The streaming policy reflects the government's long-held negative attitude toward code-mixing and codeswitching in teaching and learning (Hopkins 2006; Lin 1996). What underlies such an attitude is an ideology of monolingualism and linguistic purism (Li 1998; Lin 2006). Poon's (2000) study of the implementation of the streaming policy in four schools found a big gap between policy and practice. The implementation of the policy was largely ineffective, and the use of mixed codes was prevalent in the majority of nominally English-medium schools.

Language Policy since 1997

Soon after the return of Hong Kong to the PRC, in September 1997, the Education Department issued the "Medium of Instruction Guidance for Secondary Schools" advising all public secondary schools use the Chinese medium of instruction (CMI) starting in the 1998–1999 school year. Only schools meeting the three criteria, concerning student ability, teacher capability, and support strategies and programs (Education Department 1997, paragraph 2.4) are exempted and allowed to use English as medium of instruction. Under this mandatory CMI policy, 114, or 27 percent, of public secondary schools (out of 421) were eventually granted permission to adopt EMI (Poon 2010; Tsui 2008). The Guidance in effect abolished the streaming policy, and with it, schools' autonomy in the choice of MOI, and initiated a mandatory Chinese MOI policy (Poon 2010).

The streaming policy and the strict implementation of the mandatory Chinese MOI in 1998 drew fierce criticism from the community, including (primarily Chinese-medium) schools, students, parents, and teachers (Tsui 2008). Such a policy is considered socially divisive and reproduces the symbolic dominance of English, elitism, and social injustice by denying the majority of students access to the language (Hopkins 2006; Sun 2002). As Lin's (1996) powerful analysis has shown, over a period of one and a half centuries of British colonialism, English has become a form of dominant linguistic capital in a "universally recognized, unified and legitimized" linguistic market in Hong Kong (1996: 54). Hence possession of this symbolic capital provides access to better socioeconomic opportunities and social advancement in Hong

Kong. The symbolic value and dominance of English has historically contributed to the dominance of English-medium schools at the secondary and tertiary levels and a widely shared belief that English is the most useful and valuable language.

In 2009, the Education Bureau issued Circular No. 6, "Fine-tuning the Medium of Instruction for Secondary Schools," which laid out a fine-tuned framework for MOI arrangements to be implemented in the 2010–2011 school year. The framework gave schools more freedom and flexibility in adopting the appropriate MOI for non-language subjects. This document officially marked the end of the streaming policy, including abolishing classifying schools into CMI and EMI schools, and a shift away from the compulsory CMI policy (Education Bureau 2009, paragraph 5; Poon 2010).

As mentioned earlier, the ideology of linguistic purism underlies the government's aggressive stance toward code-mixing and codeswitching in education. According to Li (1998), such an ideology also contributes to a widely shared perception of declining language standards, particularly English standards. The perceived declining language standards prompt what Poon (2010) refers to as language enhancement policies aiming to ensure and enhance the language standards of students, teachers, and employees in various sectors beyond education. For example, a Native English Teachers Scheme was launched in 1998 to support the employment of one native English teacher for each secondary school (Poon 2010). Such a policy of "insert[ing] more 'real' English into Hong Kong secondary school environment" (Hopkins 2006: 281) is an example of what Pennycook terms "colonial continuities" that reproduce "the inherent superiority of the native speaker" (1998: 194).

A language enhancement policy that extends beyond education is the biliterate/trilingual policy. "Biliterate" refers to the ability in written Chinese and English, and "trilingual" refers to the ability in Cantonese, PTH, and spoken English. The first official announcement of the policy was in the 1999 Policy Address delivered by Tung Chi Hwa, the first Chief Executive of the HKSAR (Zhang & Yang 2004: 114). Although billions of Hong Kong dollars have been spent to promote English, Chinese, and Putonghua (Poon 2010), and although biliteracy and trilingualism are reiterated in numerous policy statements, more emphasis seems to be placed on the promotion of English (Zhang & Yang 2004).

In addition to the promotion of PTH under the biliterate/trilingual policy, other measures have been developed to promote the national language since 1997. It became a required subject in the school curriculum in 1998, and an elective subject in the Hong Kong Certificate of Education Examination in 2000. However, Zhang and Yang (2004) report that in terms of teaching hours as specified by the Curriculum Development Council, PTH is allocated one-third of the teaching time as that of English in primary school.

After more than 150 years of British rule, Hong Kong has changed from a society of what Luke & Richards (1982) characterize as "societal bilinguialism" and "diglossia without bilingualism" (Fishman 1967) to one characterized by Li (1999) as polyglossia with individual bilingualism. With Cantonese as the language of an overwhelming majority of the population, sociolinguistic surveys conducted by researchers at the University of Hong Kong in 1983, 1993, and 2003 show a steady increase of people who claim to be Cantonese-English-PTH trilinguals, from 17 percent in 1983 to 63 percent in 2003 (Bacon-Shone & Bolton 2008). Lai's (2005) recent survey of language attitudes among 1048 secondary school students shows that Cantonese remains the most salient marker of a Hong Kong identity. English has shifted from a colonizer's language that indexes an elitist distinction (Luke & Richards 1982; Pierson, Fu, & Lee 1980) and a threat to the ethnolinguistic identity of a Hong Konger (Pierson, Fu, & Lee 1980) to an international language of wider communication (Axler Yang, and Stevens 1998; Pennington & Yue 1994) and carrying a smaller share of the semiotic freight of a Hong Kong identity (Lai 2005). English being ranked the highest on the instrumental orientation indicates the persistent symbolic dominance of English as the most valuable linguistic capital to access better socioeconomic opportunities. PTH was ranked the lowest in both integrative and instrumental value. Lai's (2010) survey of students from different socioeconomic classes confirms the earlier attitude patterns. Although working-class students display a slightly more positive attitude toward PTH and despite government policy, it is far from becoming valuable symbolic capital in the linguistic market in Hong Kong.

Taiwan

Demographic and Language Information

Taiwan has a population of about 23 million, of which 95 percent are Han Chinese, and approximately 504,500 belong to the 14 officially recognized indigenous groups or *yuanzhu min*. Three large groups constitute the Han people: the Holo (Hok-lo), or *Minnan ren* 'Southern Min people,' account for about 70 percent and the Hakka about 20 percent of the Han population. The remainder are immigrants from Mainland China who arrived in 1949, also known as the "Mainlanders" (Government Information Office 2010). The official language of Taiwan is Mandarin, or *Guoyu* 'national language'. Although today's Taiwan *Guoyu* can be traced back to the Beijing Mandarin-based *Guoyu* established in the early twentieth century in Mainland China, it has developed phonological, lexical, and syntactic features that are distinctive from Beijing Mandarin as a result of contact with southern Chinese varieties, particularly Southern Min (Cheng 1985; Kubler 1985). The indigenous languages in Taiwan are classified as Formosan languages, belonging to the Proto-Austronesian language family. The other major language varieties include, Southern Min, commonly known as *Taiyu* or Taiwanese, Hakka, and other Chinese varieties that are the native varieties of the "Mainlanders" and their descendants (Government Information Office 2010). The traditional complex Chinese character script is the official written script. There are three Roman phonetic alphabets currently in use, namely, the Second Form of National Phonetic Symbols (or NPS2), the Tong-yong Phonetic Scheme, and *Hanyu Pinyin*, the official Chinese phonetic alphabet used in the PRC (Tsao 2008a: 269).

Historical Background: Language Policy Prior to 1945

Prior to the concession of Taiwan to Japan in 1895, language policies in Taiwan during the Dutch and Spanish colonial rule in the seventeenth century were largely pragmatic and tolerant. Under the rule of Qing Dynasty from 1683 to 1895, the government's efforts to promote Mandarin since the 1790s largely failed due to lack of enthusiasm and local support (Chen 1999). Classical Chinese was taught in schools with local languages as the MOI (Scott & Tiun 2007).

The concession of Taiwan to Japan in 1895 as a result of China's defeat in the first Sino-Japanese War marked the beginning of a half century of assimilationist language policies (1895–1945). Japanese was imposed on Taiwan and other overseas colonies of the Empire not as a foreign language but as the national language to assimilate Taiwanese as the subjects of the Japanese Emperor (Gottlieb 2008). Policies became increasingly oppressive during the later half of the Japanese colonial rule. In addition to the closing down of Chinese schools, in 1937 Chinese was prohibited in all public domains, including schools, government offices, and newspapers, and Taiwanese was banned in 1939 (Chen 2001b; Tsao 2008a). An "only-Japanese-speaking-families" campaign was launched in 1938 to force the local languages out of the family domain (Tsao 2008a). By the end of the Japanese rule, Taiwan had become a highly Japanized, bilingual diglossic society in which more than half of the population spoke Japanese as their first or second language and Japanese became the high language in education, government, and other formal occasions (Huang 2000; Chen 2001b).

Language Policy since 1945

After the restoration of Chinese sovereignty over Taiwan, language policy in Taiwan under the KMT government from 1945 to late 1990s was guided by a Herderian ideology in which "the KMT state, the Chinese nation, the Chinese culture, and Mandarin are identified with one another" (Hsiau 1997: 312; Sandel 2003). Language policy served as a powerful tool to integrate Taiwan into the Chinese nation and to establish national unity (e.g., Dreyer 2003b; Tsao 2008a).

"Mandarin-only" (1945–1987). After the restoration of Chinese sovereignty over Taiwan in 1945, the KMT government implemented a top-down assimilationist language policy to propagate *guoyu* and to integrate Taiwan into the Chinese nation. This Chinese nation was the Republic of China, which the KMT government hoped to reestablish on the mainland after its retreat to Taiwan in 1949 (Hsiau 1997). The language policy under the KMT from 1945 to the late 1990s was thus guided by a "Chinaisation" ideology that promoted Mandarin monolingualism with the suppression of local and indigenous languages (Hsiau 1997; Scott & Tiun 2007). In 1946, the *Taiwan Sheng Guoyu Tuixing Weiyuanhui* 'Taiwan Provincial Committee for the Promotion of Guoyu' was established under the Department of Education of the Provincial Government of Taiwan and served as the main government agency for the design and implementation of language policy (Tsao 2008a). A Guoyu Promotion Institute was established at the city and county level across the island to implement the policies developed by the Committee (Chen 2001b).

After a brief period of a relatively tolerance toward non-Mandarin languages, more stringent polices were implemented, beginning with the launching of *Jiang Guoyu Yundong* 'Speaking *Guoyu* Movement' in 1956 (Chen 2001b). Mandarin then became the medium of instruction in schools. Children were punished if caught speaking dialects in schools, a practice similar to that of the colonial period (Chen 2001b; Tsao 2008a). In 1965, all civil servants were required to speak Mandarin when conducting government business. *Guoyu* was also designated as the language of the courts (Hsiau 1997). The Radio and Television Law implemented after 1976 specified the ratio of the use of *guoyu*, no less than 55 percent for radio and no less than 70 percent for television. It also decreed that "the use of dialects should decrease year by year" (Hsiau 1997: 308; cf. Tsao 2008a). Mandarin monolingualism became iconic of Chinese nationalism and ethnic harmony. The use of non-Mandarin languages and multilingualism were considered a threat to national unity. Resistance to the spread of Mandarin was considered suspect of communist intention and separatism (Chen 2001b; Hsiau 1997). To establish the symbolic dominance of *guoyu*, local and indigenous languages, particularly Southern Min, perceived as the most powerful threat to Mandarin, were also stigmatized in the media (Hsiau 1997). Through metapragmatic typification in television shows, Taiwanese was linked to images displaying such disparaging characteristics as backwardness, vulgarity, crudeness, ignorance, aging, and low socioeconomic status. In contrast, Mandarin was elevated as a marker of modernity, refinement, literacy, urbanity, and high socioeconomic status (Hsiau 1997; Dreyer 2003b). In addition to the promotion of *guoyu*, the KMT government also promoted Chinese culture by suppressing local culture as part of "Chinaising" the island (Dreyer 2003b; Scott & Tiun 2007). For example, students learned more about the history of China and the ethnic groups on the Mainland than about the history of Taiwan and the indigenous Austronesian peoples (Dreyer 2003b)

"Mandarin-Plus" (1987 to present). Relaxation of the oppressive "Mandarin-only" language policy began with the lifting of the Martial Law in 1987. Fundamental changes in language policy have taken place since then as part of a broader societal transformation to liberalization and democratization (Chen 2006; Tsao 2008b.). The "Mandarin-only" policy began to give way to a "Mandarin-plus" policy in the early 1990s, ushering in the period of indigenization, Taiwanization, and de-Chinaization (Chen 2006; Scott & Tiun 2007). Mandarin remains the official language, but policies that restricted the use of local and indigenous languages have been replaced by measures to promote their use (Scott & Tiun 2007). Indigenization led to the Mother Tongues Movement, which resulted in policy changes, including the revision of the Broadcast Bill in 1993 to allow the use of native languages, and "the local-languages education" or mother-tongue education policy. The latter, implemented since 2001, requires primary school children to study at least one local language at school for at least one hour per week (Chen 2006; Scott & Tiun 2007; Tsao 2008b).

Democratization led to the establishment of oppositional parties in the late 1980s, and languages have been used as an important tool to rally support in political campaigns (Hsiau 1997; Liao 2008; Tse 2000; Wei 2008). *Taiyu* became the "language of election" in the late 1980s (Hsiau 1997: 309). Tse (2000) observes that during the 1996 presidential election, candidates from the KMT and Democratic Progressive Party (DPP) used languages, including Mandarin, Southern Min, and Hakka, to win voter support and get their messages across, rather than to mark ethnic boundaries. This served as evidence that a supra-ethnic identity, the "New Taiwanese," is emerging in Taiwan "as language gradually loses its saliency as an external criterion for characterizing ethnicity" (Tse 2000: 162). Wei's (2008) analysis of the campaign speeches of President Chen Shuibian in 2001, who became the first elected president from the opposition DPP in 2000, showed Chen's strategic switching between Mandarin and *Taiyu* to perform a variety of functions. Her study also indicates that the rise of the political power of DPP, whose (founding) members are strong advocates of a Taiwanese identity and of Taiwan's independence, has played a crucial role in revalorizing Southern Min as the language of the people (Wei 2008). Liao's (2008) study of the perception of two Taiwan Mandarin varieties, Taipei-accented Mandarin and Taichung-accented Mandarin, provides further evidence of the impact of the changing political dynamics on language ideology and the indexical meanings of accents. The former is commonly perceived as a more standard accent; the latter, as a vernacular accent. The strongest correlation was found between accent and political orientation, that is, someone with a Taipei accent was perceived to orient toward "pan-blue," or the KMT, whereas a Taichung accent indicated a "pan-green," or DPP orientation. Furthermore, a Taipei accent was also highly correlated with a high education level, speaking English, high income, and high social class. In contrast, someone with a heavy vernacular accent was perceived to have low education, non-English speaking but speaking Taiwanese, low income, and low social class. Su's (2008) investigation of discourses on *qizhi* 'refined disposition' also finds that a standard Mandarin accent indexes *qizhi,* whereas Taiwanese and Taiwanese-accented Mandarin are associated with poor *qizhi*. Unlike Taiwanese, which is positively valued as being linguistically pure and structurally more sophisticated than Mandarin, Taiwanese-accented Mandarin is particularly stigmatized as a deviant and hybrid variety.

Simultaneous with the promotion of indigenization is the emphasis on internationalization to enhance Taiwan's competitiveness in the global market. In 2001, the same year that mother-tongue education began, English education policy was revised to allow the teaching of English starting in the fifth grade (Chen 2006; Tsao 2008b). The policy was revised again in 2005 to start the teaching of English in the third grade (Chen 2006). Scott and Tiun (2007) observe that English is given more emphasis than mother-tongue education.

The simultaneous emphasis on indigenization and internationalization in Taiwan's current language policy reflects a shift from a monolingual assimilationist approach to one that encourages linguistic pluralism and multiculturalism. However, the dominance of a heavy-handed monolingual policy, first under Japanese colonization and then under the KMT government has led to language shift and loss in indigenous communities. Among the Chinese varieties, Hakka is undergoing the most rapid loss (Taiwan Yearbook 2005, cited in Scott & Tiun 2007). The most recent large-scale survey, reported in Chen (2010), based on 2139 questionnaires from 11 locales found that about 98 percent of the people surveyed reported to be able to speak Mandarin fluently. However, only about 50 percent of Hakka descendants and aborigines can speak their native language. Mandarin was also found to dominate all of the integrative and most of the instrumental values, such as being a tool for communication in Taiwan and expressing authority. English was rated as having greater instrumental values than Mandarin in expressing global views, social status, and social upward mobility (Chen 2010; see also Lan 2003). These findings indicate that, despite revalorization of major local languages as a result of political liberalization, the Taiwan linguistic market is still dominated by Mandarin and that local languages are losing out on the alternative/vernacular linguistic market in which they "have to share with Mandarin as linguistic capital" (Sandel 2003: 54).

Conclusion

The foregoing discussion of language policies in the three regions illustrates how language policy is shaped by a combination of endogenous and exogenous forces as well as historical, political, and socioeconomic factors. Language policy almost always serves as a tool for some larger project(s) of the government, be it nation building or enforcing social control over the masses, as in the case of colonial Hong Kong. The cases discussed here also demonstrate the role that ideology plays in the formation of language policy. A Herderian ideology of one language, one nation underpins language policies in both Mainland China and Taiwan, and linguistic purism is most explicitly stated in some of the policy documents on MOI in Hong Kong. Finally, similar to other regions in the world, discrepancies are found between policy and practice (e.g., Spolsky 2004), with respect to the implementation of the policy on the ground as well as the linguistic practices of people in situ.

Notes

1. The original proposal, with the title "*Zhonghua Renmin Gongheguo Yuyan Wenzi Fa*" ('The Language and Script Law of the PRC'), would have granted the law a broader scope to be applicable to all languages in the country (Rohsenow 2004: 35).

References

Axler, M., Yang, A. & Stevens, T. 1998. Current language attitudes of Hong Kong Chinese adolescents and young adults. In M. C. Pennington (ed.), *Language in Hong Kong at century's end*, 391–418. Hong Kong: Hong Kong University Press.

Bacon-Shone, J. H., & Bolton, K. 2008. Bilingualism and multilingualism in the HKSAR: Language surveys and Hong Kong's changing linguistic profile. In K. Bolton & H. Yang (eds.), *Language and society in Hong Kong*, 25–51. Hong Kong: Open University Press.

Basic Law. 1990. The Basic Law of the Hong Kong Special Administrative Region of the People's Republic of China. http://www.basiclaw.gov.hk/en/basiclawtext/images/basiclaw_full_text.pdf. Accessed June 3, 2010.

Blachford, D. R. 2004. Language spread versus language maintenance: Policy making and implementation process. In M. Zhou & H. Sun (eds.), *Language policy in the People's Republic of China: Theory and practice since 1949*, 99–122. Boston: Kluwer Academic.

Blum, S. 2004. Good to hear: Using the trope of standard to find one's way in a sea of linguistic diversity. In M. Zhou & H. Sun (Eds.), *Language policy in the People's Republic of China: Theory and practice since 1949*, 123–41. Boston: Kluwer Academic.

Bourdieu, P. 1991. *Language and symbolic power*. Translated by G. Raymond & M. Adamson. Cambridge, MA: Harvard University Press.

Bradley, D. 2005. Introduction: Language policy and language endangerment in China. *International Journal of the Sociology of Language* 173: 1–21.

Bradley, D. 2007. East and Southeast Asia. In C. Moseley (ed.), *Encyclopedia of the world's endangered languages*, 349–424. London: Routledge.

Bulag, U. E. 2003. Mongolian ethnicity and linguistic anxiety in China. *American Anthropologist* 105: 753–63.

Census and Statistics Department. 2006. 2006 Population By-Census Summary Results. http://www.bycensus2006.gov.hk/FileManager/EN/Content_962/06bc_summary_results.pdf. Accessed November 27, 2010.

Chen, P. 1999. *Modern Chinese: History and sociolinguistics.* Cambridge: Cambridge University Press.

Chen, P. 2001a. Language policy in Hong Kong during the colonial period before July 1, 1997. In P. Chen & N. Gottlieb (eds.), *Language planning and language policy: East Asian perspectives*, 95–110. Richmond: Curzon.

Chen, P. 2001b. Policy on the selection and implementation of a standard language as a source of conflict in Taiwan. In P. Chen & N. Gottlieb (eds.), *Language planning and language policy: East Asian perspectives*, 111–28. Richmond: Curzon.

Chen, S.-C. 2006. Simultaneous promotion of indigenization and internationalization: New language-in-education policy in Taiwan. *Language and Education* 20(4): 322–37.

Chen, S.-C. 2010. Multilingualism in Taiwan. *International Journal of the Sociology of Language* 205: 79–104.

Cheng, R. L. 1985. A comparison of Taiwanese, Taiwan Mandarin, and Peking Mandarin. *Language* 61 (2): 352–77.

DeFrancis, J. 1950. *Nationalism and language reform in China.* Princeton, NJ: Princeton University Press.

DeFrancis, J. 1984. *The Chinese language: Fact and fantasy.* Honolulu: University of Hawaii Press.

Dreyer, J. T. 2003a. The evolution of language policies in China. In M. E. Brown & S. Ganguly (eds.), *Fighting words: Language policy and ethnic relations in Asia*, 353–84. Cambridge, MA: MIT Press.

Dreyer, J. T. 2003b. The evolution of language policies and national identity in Taiwan. In M. E. Brown & S. Ganguly (eds.), *Fighting words: Language policy and ethnic relations in Asia*, 385–409. Cambridge, MA: MIT Press.

Dwyer, A. M. 2005. *The Xinjiang conflict: Uyghur identity, language policy, and political discourse.* Washington, DC: East-West Center Washington.

Education Bureau. 2009. Fine-tuning the Medium of Instruction for Secondary Schools. http://www.edb.gov.hk/FileManager/EN/Content_7372/edbc09006e.pdf. Accessed November 27, 2010.

Education Department. 1997. Guidance for Secondary School. http://www.edb.gov.hk/index.aspx?nodeID=1905&langno=1. Accessed November 27, 2010.

Evans, S. 2000. Hong Kong's new English language policy in education. *World Englishes* 19(2): 85–204.

Fishman, J. A. 1967. Bilingualism with and without diglossia; diglossia with and without bilingualism. *Journal of Social Issues* 23(2): 29–38.

Gottlieb, N. 2008. Japan: Language policy and planning in transition. *Current Issues in Language Planning* 9: 1–68.

Government Information Office. 2010. Taiwan Yearbook 2010. http://www.gio.gov.tw/taiwan-website/5-gp/yearbook/. Accessed July 8, 2011.

Guojia Yuyan Wenzi. 1996. Guowuyuan guanyu tuiguang Putonghua de zhishi (1956–02–06) (State Council directives concerning the promotion of Puthonghua [02-06-1956]). In *Guojia Yuyan Wenzi Zhengce Fagui Huibian* (1949–1995) *'Collection of national policies and laws on language and script'*, 11–6. Beijing, China: Yuwen Chubanshe.

Harrell, S. 1993. Linguistics and hegemony in China. *International Journal of the Sociology of Language* 103: 97–114.

Hopkins, M. 2006. Policies without planning? The medium of instruction issue in Hong Kong. *Language and Education* 20(4): 270–86.

Hsiau, A. 1997. Language ideology in Taiwan: The KMT's language policy, the Tai-yu Language Movement, and ethnic politics. *Journal of Multilingual and Multicultural Development* 18(4): 302–15.

Huang, S. 2000. Language, identity, and conflict: A Taiwanese study. *International Journal of the Sociology of Language* 143: 139–49.

Jiao, X. 2011. Zunzhong yuyanwenzi fazhan guilü goujian hexie yuyan shenghuo: Yuyan wenzi guihua gangyao peixun huiyi juxing (Respect the developmental rules of language and collectively construct a harmonious linguistic life: Training meeting for Guidelines of Language Planning). http://www.moe.gov.cn/publicfiles/business/htmlfiles/moe/moe_1485/201105/119463.html. Accessed July 15, 2011.

Johnson, R. K. 1994. Language policy and planning in Hong Kong. *Annual Review of Applied Linguistics* 14(1): 177–99.

Kubler, C. C. 1985. The influence of southern Min on the Mandarin of Taiwan. *Anthropological Linguistics* 27 (2): 156–76.

Lai, M. L. 2005. Language attitudes of the first postcolonial generation. *Language in Society* 34: 363–88.

Lai, M. L. 2010. Social class and language attitudes in Hong Kong. *International Multilingual Research Journal* 4(2): 83–106.

Lan, P.-C. 2003. "They have more money but I speak better English!" Transnational encounters between Filipina domestics and Taiwanese employers. *Identities: Global Studies in Culture and Power* 10(2): 133–61.

Lewis, M. P. (ed.). 2009. *Ethnologue: Languages of the world*, 16th edition. Dallas, TX: SIL International. Online version: http://www.ethnologue.com/.

Li, D. C. S. 1998. The plight of the purist. In M. C. Pennington (ed.), *Language in Hong Kong at century's end*, 161–90. Hong Kong: Hong Kong University Press.

Li, D. C. S. 1999. The function and status of English in Hong Kong: A post-1997 update. *English World-Wide* 20(1): 67–110.

Liao, S. 2008. A perceptual dialect study of Taiwan Mandarin: Language attitudes in the era of political battle. In M. K. M. Chan & H. Kang (eds.), *Proceedings of the 20th North American Conference on Chinese Linguistics (NACCL-20)*, vol. 1, 391–408. Columbus: The Ohio State University.

Lin, A. M. Y. 1996. Bilingualism or linguistic segregation? Symbolic domination, resistance and code switching in Hong Kong schools. *Linguistics and Education* 8(1): 49–84.

Lin, A. M. Y. 2006. Beyond linguistic purism in language-in-education policy and practice: Exploring bilingual pedagogies in a Hong Kong science classroom. *Language and Education* 20(4): 287–305.

Luke, K. K., & Richards, J. C. 1982. English in Hong Kong: Functions and status. *English World-Wide* 3(1): 47–64.

Mair, V. H.1991. What is a Chinese "dialect/topolect"? Reflections on some key Sino-English linguistic terms. *Sino-Platonic Papers* 29: 1–31.

Ministry of Education. 2007. *Guojia yuyan wenzi gongzuo "shi-yi wu" guihua* (The Eleventh Five-Year Plan for language and script work). http://www.moe.edu.cn/publicfiles/business/htmlfiles/moe/moe_800/201001/xxgk_78577.html, Accessed August 7, 2010.

National Bureau of Statistics. 2011. *2010 nian diliuci quanguo renkou pucha zhuyao shuju gongbao* (2010 The Sixth National Census Main Data Public Report). http://www.stats.gov.cn/tjgb/rkpcgb/qgrkpcgb/t20110428_402722232.htm. Accessed July 15, 2011.

NPPPW. 1999. *Guanyu kaizhan di er jie quanguo tuiguang Putonghua xuanchuan zhou huodong de tongzhi* (Notice for the Second National Putonghua Promotion Publicity Week). http://www.hbe.gov.cn/content.php?id=1268. Accessed August 7, 2010.

NPPPW. 2011. *Guanyu kaizhan di shisi jie quanguo tuiguang Putonghua xuanchuan zhou huodong de tongzhi* (Notice for the Fourteenth National Putonghua Promotion Publicity Week). http://www.moe.gov.cn/publicfiles/business/htmlfiles/moe/s3135/201108/xxgk_123847.html. Accessed July 15, 2011.

Pennington, M. C., & Yue, F. 1994. English and Chinese in Hong Kong: Pre-1997 language attitudes. *World Englishes* 13: 1–20.

Pennycook, A. 1998. *English and the discourses of colonialism*. New York: Routledge.

Pennycook, A. 2002. Mother tongues, governmentality, and protectionism. *International Journal of the Sociology of Language* 154: 11–28.

Pierson, D. H., Fu, S. G., & Lee, S. Y. 1980. An analysis of the relationship between language attitudes and English attainment of secondary school students in Hong Kong. *Language Learning* 30: 289–316.

Poon, A. Y. K. 2000. *Medium of instruction in Hong Kong: Policy and practice*. Lanham, MD: University Press of America.

Poon, A. Y. K. 2010. Language use, and language policy and planning in Hong Kong. *Current Issues in Language Planning* 11(1): 1–66.

PSC. 1994. *Guojia yuwei, guajia jiaowei, guangbo dianying dianshi bu guanyu kaizhan Putonghua shuiping ceshi gongzuo de jueding* (State Language Commission, Ministry of Education, State Administration of Radio Film and Television Decision on Work of Putonghua Proficiency Test). http://202.205.177.9/edoas/website18/level3.jsp?tablename=687&infoid=5154. Accessed August 7, 2010.

PSC. 1997. *Guanyu Putonghua shuiping ceshi guanli gongzuo de ruogan guiding (shixing)* (Some regulations for the administration of the Putonghua Proficiency Test [trial]). http://www.china-language.gov.cn/8/2007_6_20/1_8_2605_0_1182323779390.html. Accessed August 7, 2010.

PSC. 1999. *Guanyu kaizhan guojia gongwuyuan Putonghua peixun de tongzhi* (Notice for the Putonghua training for civil servants). http://202.205.177.9/edoas/website18/50/info5150.htm. Accessed August 7, 2010.

Rohsenow, J. S. 2004. Fifty years of script and written language reform in the P.R.C.: The genesis of the language law of 2001. In M. Zhou & H. Sun (eds.), *Language policy in the People's Republic of China: Theory and practice since 1949*, 21–43. Boston: Kluwer Academic.

Sandel, T. L. 2003. Linguistic Capital in Taiwan: The KMT's Mandarin language policy and its perceived impact on language practices of bilingual Mandarin and Tai-gi Speakers. *Language in Society* 32: 523–51.

Scott, M, & Tiun, H. 2007. Mandrin-only to Mandarin-plus: Taiwan. *Language Policy* 6: 53–72.

Spolsky, Bernard. 2004. *Language policy*. Cambridge: Cambridge University Press.

State Ethnic Affairs Commission of the PRC. 2010. *Guojia minwei guanyu zuohao shaoshu minzu yuyan wenzi guanli gongzuo de yijian* (State Ethnic Affairs Commission Opinion on the work on national minority languages and scripts). http://www.seac.gov.cn/art/2010/6/18/art_142_103787.html. Accessed July 15, 2011.

State Language Commission. 2004. *Putonghua shuiping ceshi shishi gangyao (Implementation Outline for the Putonghua Proficiency Test)*. Beijing: Commercial Press.

State Language Commission. 2010. *Language Situation in China: 2010*. Beijing: Commercial Press. http://www.moe.gov.cn/publicfiles/business/htmlfiles/moe/s5586/201105/119487.html. Accessed July 15, 2011.

Su, H.-Y. 2008. What does it mean to be a girl with *qizhi*? Refinement, gender and language ideologies in contemporary Taiwan. *Journal of Sociolinguistics* 12(3): 334–58.

Sun, C. F. 2002. Hong Kong's language policy in the postcolonial age: Social justice and globalization In M. K. Chan & A. Y. So (eds.), *Crisis and transformation in China's Hong Kong*, 283–306. Armonk, NY: M. E. Sharpe.

Tsao, F.-F. 2008a. The language planning situation in Taiwan. In R. B. Kaplan & R. B. Baldauf Jr. (eds.), *Language planning and policy in Asia, Vol. 1: Japan, Nepal and Taiwan*, 237–84. Bristol: Multilingual Matters.

Tsao, F.-F. 2008b. The language planning situation in Taiwan: An update. In R. B. Kaplan & R. B. Baldauf Jr. (eds.), *Language planning and policy in Asia*, vol. 1: *Japan, Nepal and Taiwan*, 285–300. Bristol: Multilingual Matters.

Tse, J. K.-P. 2000. Language and a rising new identity in Taiwan. *International Journal of the Sociology of Language* 143: 151–64.

Tsui, A. B. M. 2008. Medium of instruction in Hong Kong: One country, two systems, whose language? In M. Bolton & H. Yang (eds.), *Language and Society in Hong Kong*, 428–52. Hong Kong: Open University of Hong Kong Press.

Tsung, L. T. H., & Cruickshank, K. 2009. Mother tongue and bilingual minority education in China. *International Journal of Bilingual Education and Bilingualism* 12(5): 549–63.

Wei, J. W. 2008. *Language choice and identity politics in Taiwan*. Lanham: Lexington Books.

Zhang, B., & Yang, R. 2004. Putonghua education and language policy in postcolonial Hong Kong. In M. Zhou & H. Sun (eds.), *Language policy in the People's Republic of China: Theory and practice since 1949*, 143–61. Boston: Kluwer..

Zhao, S., & Baldauf, R. B. Jr. 2008. *Planning Chinese characters: Reaction, evolution or revolution?* Dordrecht: Springer.

Zhao, S. 2008. Chinese Character modernisation in the digital era: A historical perspective. In R. B. Kaplan & R. B. Baldauf (eds.), *Language planning and policy in Asia*, 38–101. Buffalo, NY: Multilingual Matters.

Zhou, M. 2003. *Multilingualism in China: The politics of writing reforms for minority languages 1949–2002*. Berlin / New York: Mouton de Gruyter.

Zhou, M. 2004. Minority language policy in China: Equality in theory and inequality in practice. In M. Zhou & H. Sun (eds.), *Language policy in the People's Republic of China: Theory and practice since 1949*, 71–95. Boston: Kluwer..

Zhou, M, & Sun, H. (eds.). 2004. *Language policy in the People's Republic of China: Theory and practice since 1949*. Boston: Kluwer.

Zhou, M., & Ross, H. A. 2004. Introduction: The context of the theory and practice of China's language policy. In M. Zhou & H. Sun (eds.), *Language policy in the People's Republic of China: Theory and practice since 1949*, 1–18. Boston: Kluwer..

Zhou, Q. 2004. The creation of writing systems and nation establishment: The case of China in the 1950s. In M. Zhou & H. Sun (eds.), *Language policy in the People's Republic of China: Theory and practice since 1949*, 55–70. Boston: Kluwer..

CHAPTER 29

LANGUAGE POLICIES AND POLITICS IN SOUTH ASIA

VINEETA CHAND

In South Asia (SA), feelings toward linguistic diversity—as realized through national language policies and in actual national language management practices—are highly diverse. The negotiation of and diachronic changes in language policies vis-à-vis functional and ideological goals—visible through language attitudes, overt and covert language policies and diachronic changes in language competencies—offer a lens for understanding language management and value. This chapter explores socioeconomic, political, religious ethno-cultural, and national positions toward language management that underlie diachronic changes in SA nations' language policies and linguistic ideologies.

South Asian Demographics

South Asia (figure 29.1) is one of the most linguistically diverse and socially complex areas of the world (Sarangi 2009). It is home to 1.47 billion people—approximately 21 percent of the world's population, speaking 10.7 percent of living languages (Lewis 2009)—a multitude of scripts (Daniels 2008), and five language families: Indo-European, Dravidian, Tibeto-Burman, Austro-Asiatic,

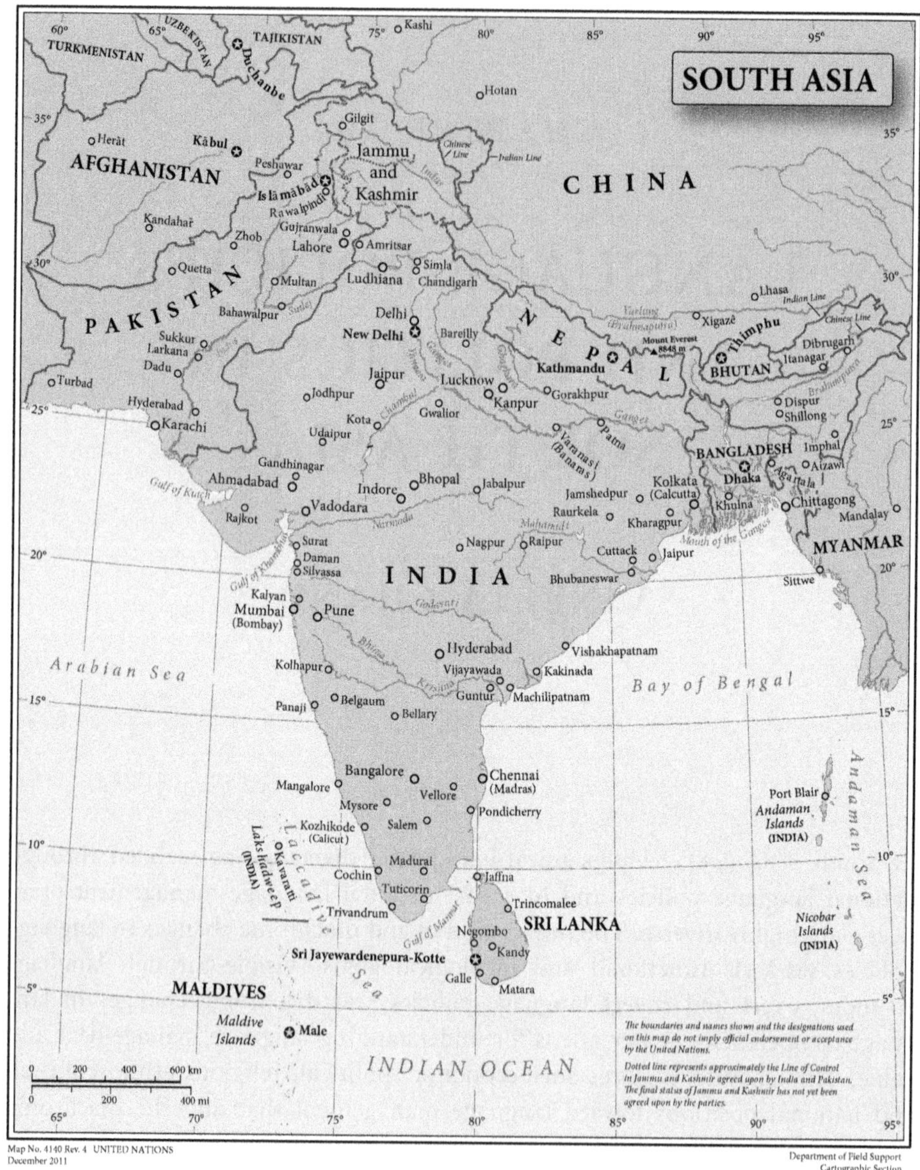

Figure 29.1. Contemporary South Asia.

Source: United Nations (2011)

and Great Andamanese (although Jero, with seven speakers remaining, may be the only indicator of a possible sixth SA language family [Abbi 2009]), in addition to several linguistic isolates. SA has a prolonged history of multilingualism and multiliteracy, and social groups have diachronically changing linkages with a range of codes and scripts. Past surveys are complicated by non-neutral assessments of codes as languages versus dialects, variation in census data collection, and diachronic sociopolitical changes (Singh 2006). Further, while any

Figure 29.2. The growth of the Mughal Empire in India

Source: Pearcy & Dickson (1996)

single SA country's language policy history cannot be covered here (indeed, several monographs are devoted to this topic, e.g., Brass 1974; Rahman 1996b; Sarangi 2009), SA language management and language-in-education policies are continuously contested and evolving.

India, Pakistan, and Bangladesh

India, Pakistan and Bangladesh have a shared history of non-indigenous rule that can be separated into three consecutive periods—the Mughal rule, colonialism under the East India Company (EIC) and then directly through the British Empire (the British Raj), and independence as nation-states—the latter two most salient to understanding contemporary language management.

Transition from the Mughal Empire

The Muslim Mughal Empire (1483–1774; figure 29.2) created the first centralized SA government, demonstrated more linguistic and religious tolerance than subsequent non-indigenous rulers, and had lasting religious and cultural impact. During the Mughal period, while Persian was already an established language for literature and culture, it became the "dominant vehicle of Islamic culture in India" (Rahman 2002: 123) and the language of courts and edicts. The Mughal framework of governing through a foreign language and script largely continued with the British: indigenous elites thus maintained domain-specific bi/multilingualism and literacy (Rahman 2002). However, under the British Raj the political power—and value—of Persian was gradually usurped by English, courts began using indigenous vernacular languages (vernaculars hereafter), and Persian was largely replaced in religious and cultural spaces by Urdu, for Muslims, and Hindi, for Hindus.

British India

The East India Company (EIC) ruled key areas in the SA subcontinent (with progressive regional expansion) from 1757 through 1858, when, following the 1857 Indian Rebellion, the British crown assumed direct administration. In the latter period, two approaches to language management and education (Orientalist and Anglicist) were pursued, reflecting different socioeconomic goals and beliefs about SA.

Orientalist Colonial Period (1774–1835). The Orientalists respected Indian classical literature, encouraged British officers to learn vernaculars and envisioned transmitting Western knowledge to Indians through vernacular-based translations (Mohanty 2002). Their governance supported vernacular-based education and local cultures, in contrast with subsequent colonial language management.

Anglicist Colonial Period (1835–1947). The Anglicists believed that Persian, if maintained in any form, would evoke memories of localized leadership, could become a tool for dissidence, and hence, must be disempowered. The larger Anglicist position toward SA language management is (in)famously represented by Macaulay, who, in 1835, issued his Minute on English education. He advocated creating, through English-medium education, "a class of persons Indian in blood and colour, but English in tastes, in opinions, in morals and in intellect" who would endorse the "intrinsic superiority of the Western literature" over Indian and Arabian literature (Macaulay [1920] 1965). English was established in higher education, vernaculars in lower education (Mohanty 2002), and English replaced Persian in official government domains. Collectively, these policies were intended to signify the end of the Muslim ascendancy, appeal to the local masses (who did not speak Persian), and reduce the power of non-English speaking local elites (Devotta 2001; Rahman 2002).

Partition (1947)

Mobilization for the British to "quit India" began in the late 1800s. The pre-Partition interim government, comprised dominantly of northern elites, represented several cultures, religions and languages, and debates over the national language(s) were highly contentious. The majority shared a general agreement that national unity would best be encouraged by officially sanctioning Hindi, Urdu, and/or Hindustani as the national language(s), while minority groups, with allegiances split across several south Indian languages, unsuccessfully advocated for a south Indian language or English (Austin 2009). English was disfavored because of its colonial links but considered because it was entrenched in government administration, and it would not favor one vernacular (and linguistic community) over another. While Hindi and Urdu were—and are—closely related, their development diverged through script (Devanagiri vs. Perso-Arabic) and vocabulary (drawing on Sanskrit and English vs. Persian and Arabic). The choice between these two—or Hindustani, an amalgamated lingua franca used in north Indian bazaars but not considered a robust linguistic system—brought religion to the forefront of the language debate (Ahmad 2008).

Both Jarwarhalal Nehru, India's first prime minister, and M. K. Gandhi, a leader in the peaceful protest against British rule, felt that an indigenous language, namely, Hindi or Hindustani, would best empower and unite Indians. However, none of the languages under serious discussion—including English—were spoken by a majority of the Indian people: any language would be a compromise, yet not choosing a single language was seen as a significant hindrance to developing a strong national identity. Debate was further complicated by fears of linguistic and/or political marginalization based on new territorial lines, for example, northern Muslims were against linguistic and territory decisions that would disenfranchise Muslims, having already lost power in the transition from Persian to English. Disagreements on these and other topics eventually led to the contentious Partition of India into two nation-states: India, as a secular, multilingual, and pluralistic country, and Pakistan, comprising two non-contiguous territories (East Pakistan and West Pakistan), as an Islamic nation. When the Partition of India was announced on August 15, 1947, exact borders were not presented. The borders, when revealed, divided several seemingly contiguous areas and stranded many in the "wrong" country, resulting in violent riots and a massive emigration of 12.5 million people across national borders.

India

India (population 1.134 billion, 65 percent literacy) is home to 450-plus languages (Lewis 2009). Sociolinguistic research includes attention to language-in-education (e.g., Ramanathan 2005); minority language endangerment, shift, and revitalization (e.g., Abbi 2009; Jalaluddin 1983); the development of English bilingualism (e.g., Kachru 1986b; Sahgal 1991); language attitudes and the iconization of languages and scripts (e.g., Ahmad 2008); areal (socio)linguistics (e.g., Emeneau [1956]1980); and linguistic changes linked to politico-ideological alignments (e.g., Chand 2011; Mukherjee 1989). While a significant body of Indian research espouses prescriptive and/or harmonious interpretations that contribute to the analytic creation of Indian homogeneity and nationalism (Aggarwal 1997), language management debates continue today.

The 1950 Constitution attempted to reconcile several issues: (1) India's linguistic diversity and myriad of language loyalties, (2) English's established role in government, and (3) the lack of an indigenous language established and rich enough in vocabulary and/or fluent speakers to fulfill the cultural and instrumental role of India's national language. It established Hindi as the official language, with 15 vernaculars designated as Scheduled (officially sanctioned and funded) languages of government. Indian states were constitutionally authorized to establish their own state-based official language(s), resulting in an array of officially sanctioned languages and scripts. Meanwhile, English was authorized for official purposes for a 15-year development period, after which Hindi would fully replace English (Article 343, Constitution of India 2007).

The 15-year Hindi development plan established the Three Language Formula for multilingual education (TLF, enacted 1964–66), which would encourage "unity in diversity" by promoting several lingua francas and ensuring more widespread Hindi fluency over time (LaDousa 2005). However, in 1952, Potti Sriramulu, a south Indian politician who was fasting in support of the creation of an independent Telugu linguistic state, died. The ensuing riots forced the federal government to recognize (1) the cultural and emotional value attached to a multitude of indigenous languages and (2) the divisive power Hindi wielded in the south, contrasting with state-imagined unification ideologies (Mitchell 2009). The planned transition to Hindi was abandoned and, within four days, the Telugu linguistic state of Andhra (eventually, Andhra Pradesh) was created (Mitchell 2009). This also led to the States Reorganization Act (1956) that attempted to redraw state boundaries based on language boundaries, and the 1967 Official Languages Act, empowering English as a perpetual "associate-official" language.

State linguistic reorganization also involved transitioning several northeastern tribal territories into states (i.e., Nagaland, Meghalaya, Arunachal Pradesh, Mizoram, Manipur, and Tripura; Aggarwal 1992), resulting in the elevation to Scheduled status of several northeastern regional languages (e.g., Assamese, Bodo, Dogri, Kashmiri, Manipuri). Concurrently, India's territory expanded to consolidate protectorates like the then independent kingdoms of Sikkim and of Jammu and Kashmir, along with British-annexed Assam. Strategically and ideologically valuable as international borders, each protectorate underwent political instability, internal civil strife, and rapidly changing demographics through in-migration preceding their establishment as Indian states (Mazumdar 2005).

Sociopolitically, while southern pre- and immediately post-Partition linguistic movements are distinguishable from recent movements as rooted in linguistic discrimination versus linguistic (sometimes dialectic) difference as a justification for increased power (Mitchell 2009), contemporary northern language struggles are still rooted in linguistic and socioeconomic discrimination against minority ethnic groups. Contemporary separatist movements by, for example, Muslim Assamese, Sikh Punjabis, and Muslim Kashmiri groups, are tied to current and historic issues of ethnolinguistic, religious, political, and socioeconomic marginalization (Baruah 2009; Tremblay 2009; Van Dyke 2009). In northern Hindi and Hindu-dominant areas, urban lower-middle-class and forward-looking castes are practically and ideologically threatened by rural mobalization, increased financial and educational allocations for traditionally disadvantaged groups, and Muslim economic empowerment through wage remittance from relatives working in Gulf states (LaDousa 2005). Here, a progressive Sanskritization of Hindi is emerging alongside Hindu nationalistic ideologies that ignore south Indians (and their languages) and are positioned against English-speaking elites, the only community with access to quality English education (LaDousa 2005).

The TLF, state linguistic reorganization, and state autonomy to decide official languages and scripts suggest a federal awareness of the ideological and practical difficulty of rallying all Indians under the banner of Hindi, despite continued endorsement of this plan in the northern Hindi belt. Educationally, southern states have not included Hindi as one of their three languages (LaDousa 2005). Largely unchallenged at the federal level, this suggests that Hindi nationalistic ideologies are actively contested, and differences between actual TLF policy and on-the-ground implementation are used to appease proponents of minority ethnolinguistic empowerment. Indian language management continues to negotiate increasing sociopolitical and ethnolinguistic fractures with homogenizing nationalistic movements.

East Pakistan and West Pakistan

Pakistan, originally comprised of two non-contiguous land areas, established Urdu as the national language, imagining it as a unifying Islamic symbol. However, Urdu was only spoken in West Pakistan by a minority—it was virtually unknown in East Pakistan. To promote this Muslim-unification-through-Urdu ideology, Urdu was privileged in government, and Urdu fluency was required for government *salariat* 'civil service' jobs (Rahman 1996b). However, with no knowledge of and limited access to Urdu, East Pakistanis were marginalized (Devotta 2001). Ironically, the central government presented itself as for self-determination in Kashmir (which, they hoped, would join Pakistan), while against such in East Pakistan (Devotta 2001). The government emphasis on industrialization and modernization in West Pakistan—in contrast to its singular emphasis on Islamic training in East Pakistan—further isolated and angered East Pakistanis eager to reap the socioeconomic benefits they expected from a unified state (Devotta 2001). These inequities pushed East Pakistanis to differentiate themselves, and the Bengali language was a readily available tool for identification (Devotta 2001). As language became a pressure point, Pakistan acceded to East Pakistani linguistic needs, in 1956 making Bengali a co-national language, along with Urdu. However, discrimination continued, culminating in the secessionist War of 1971 and the creation of the independent nation-state of Bangladesh.

Pakistan. Contemporary Pakistan (population 158 million, 26 percent literacy) is home to 50-plus languages, 6 dominant: Punjabi, 44 percent; Pashto, 15 percent; Sindhi, 14 percent; Siraiki, 10 percent; Urdu, 7.6 percent; and Baloochi 3.5 percent (Lewis 2009). Urdu is still the national language, despite its continued minority mother-tongue population. While Pakistani linguistics is largely philological in nature, language management research has examined minority ethno-nationalism (Ghufran 2009; Khan 2009; Rahman 1996a), the relationship between literacy, gender, and localized identity development (Zubair 2007), and the competing roles of ethnolinguistic and national identity on language attitudes and competencies (e.g., Rahman 1996b; Rahman 2006).

Language management is contentious in part because of the limited number of people who command Urdu, the growing value of English, inequities in resource distribution, and increased ethno-nationalism by minority communities. Pakistan is balancing a desire for national unity through a lingua franca to promote sociopolitical stabilization with their agreement, in principle, with the mother-tongue approach to primary education (Rahman 2002). Urdu is not taught across Pakistan, and Urdu's federally perceived unification and religious value are disputed and negotiated in various ways. For example, the Sindh region, which advocated autonomy pre-Partition, resulting in a separate Sindh province in 1931, underwent massive demographic changes during Partition. The historically rural, impoverished Sindhi-speaking majority was challenged by an influx of city-dwelling, educated, Urdu-speaking Mujahirs who fled India (Rahman 1996a). The two communities have each acted against changing language policies with linguistic protests over purported favoritism. Both Muslim, they use language as a means to highlight their respective identities and cultures, and to advocate for power (Rahman 1996a).

Language is not always the initial spark for discord: socioeconomic and political disenfranchisement has also provoked separatism based on ethno-nationalistic, religious, and regional alignments in the Northwest Frontier Province (NWFP) and Baloochistan states. In the NWFP, a pre-Partition movement toward Pushtun ethno-nationalism—through a political merger with Afghanistan or the creation of an independent nation of Pushtunistan—contrasts with a contemporary rise in Taliban insurgency rooted in an Islamic ideology distinct from mainstream Pakistani Islamic ideology, cuts across ethnolinguistic boundaries, and, while including a Pushtun majority, also includes other ethnolinguistic and religious groups, for example, Punjabis (Ghufran 2009). Contemporary NWFP ideological alignments are provoked by their growing marginalization, and specifically to the state of Punjab's increased power and influence based on the inequitable allocation of national resources and services. Educationally, this is linked to a rise in Islamic schools, *madrassas*, favoring Islamic training through Pashto, Urdu, and Arabic medium schooling (Rahman

2002), which itself challenges the federally imagined correlation between Urdu and Islam.

The Baloochi situation is also based on anti-Punjabi sentiment, here in response to the Punjabi-dominated military and state-sponsored disenfranchisements. Baloochistan is the most ethnically and linguistically diverse state, with no majority group. Originally valued by the British as a buffer against the Russian empire, the federal government perpetuates this ideology, and has offered limited economic and infrastructure development. The continued economic marginalization (benefiting local Punjabi-dominated military garrisons, national coffers, and other Pakistani states at the expense of the Baloochis) and the increasing usurpation of Baloochi land and natural resources have led to secular ethno-nationalist sentiment and calls for Baloochi autonomy and/or independence (Khan 2009). The increasing secular-based civil strife since 2000 is undermined by state-encouraged religious education: "[d]espite a ban on madrassas . . . as part of Pakistan's contribution to the U.S. 'War on Terror,' the Pakistani federal government . . . continued to support their establishment" (Khan 2009: 1083). These Persian, Urdu, and Arabic-based religious schools promote the "Talibanization" of Baloochistan, and serve as justification for the continued military presence and authoritarian rule. Significantly, one Baloochi nationalist demand is for Baloochi as a medium of instruction (Khan 2009). The central government has offered a halfhearted response, only encouraging Baloochi-medium schooling in rural areas, leading to further linguistic "ghettoizing" (Rahman 2002). It is unclear how Baloochi is currently being operationalized as a sociolinguistic identity: speaking Baloochi ideologically rejects Pakistani hegemony, yet does not provide sociopolitical power, and this largely holds true for other Pakistani ethnic minority languages.

Conflicts between Westernized English-educated historic elites, indigenous "anti-English," Urdu-educated, proto-elite urban nationalists and periphery minority language proponents over medium of instruction in education illuminates an additional component of Pakistani language management conflict (Rahman 1997). These controversies are but one component of larger struggles between center and periphery, and between Pakistani nationalists and historic elites. With multiple parties vying for power, the inconsistent implementation of federal mandates, and both veiled and direct resistance (Rahman 1997), these disputes, often associated with but not always centrally based on language, are unlikely to be resolved easily.

Bangladesh. Bangladesh (population 153 million, 42 percent literacy), has 42 living languages (Lewis 2009) and is 89.5 percent Muslim (Bangladesh Census 2001). Surprisingly, no additional linguistic data is available from otherwise thorough census data. Sociolinguistic research on Bangladesh is sparse, focusing on the independence struggle, while minority language sociolinguistics (e.g., Brightbill et al. 2007) and analyses of the motivations for codeswitching (Banu & Sussex 2001) are also salient to understanding Bangladeshi language management.

The Bengali majority in Bangladesh have variously rallied behind region, religion and language in negotiations for power, autonomy and representation. Pre-Partition, the majority Muslim population aligned to create Pakistan in response to the Hindu swath of India. They then abandoned religion to instead identify as distinct from West Pakistan in language and culture in response to political and economic marginalization (Devotta 2001). Despite having fought a violent war (over 1 million killed) for independence, Bangladesh has been less responsive—both before and after independence—to its approximately 2 percent, approximately 632,000-strong ethnolinguistic minority population, which includes at least 49 distinct groups (Panday & Jamil 2008). In a classic case, the Chittagong Hill Tract (CHT; regionally encompassing approximately 10 percent of Bangladesh, with several non-Bengali-speaking and non-Muslim communities), was autonomous under the British Raj, but lost this status with the 1963 Pakistani constitution. CHT communities have experienced discrimination and marginalization through, for example, land appropriation, the 1962 forced relocation of 100,000 minorities during the flooding to create the Kaptai Hydro-Electric Dam, and the 1963 government-sponsored migration of majority communities into erstwhile minority CHT areas, for example, the "Bangalisation" of the region (Panday & Jamil 2008, 2009). Subsequent revolts were quelled with the 1997 CHT Peace Accord, which promised a revival in cultural (but not specifically linguistic) identity (Panday & Jamil 2008). The continued dispute—compounded by government indifference toward enforcing the Accord, and despite international media and NGO claims of genocide (Panday & Jamil 2009)—suggests that the forcible assimilation of non-Bengali-speaking, non-Muslim indigenous communities is preferred, despite striking similarities between this scenario and the earlier Bangladeshi independence movement.

Sri Lanka

Sri Lanka (population ~20 million, 91.1 percent literacy) has 7 living languages: majority groups of 15.5 million Sinhalese and 3.7 million Tamil contrast with approximately 0.8 million native English, Indo Portuguese, Sri Lankan Creole Malay, Sri Lankan Sign Language, and Veddah users. The two majority indigenous groups (northern Ceylon Tamil-speaking Hindus and southern Sinhalese-speaking Buddhists) are locally considered different ethnicities and distinguished through "languages, scripts, religions, social organization, territorial concentration and sense of collective history" (Kearney 1978: 526). There is also a shrinking minority population of Indian Tamils who are immigrants and descendants of immigrants from south India who originally arrived during the nineteenth century as indentured laborers. Demographically, an 82 percent Sinhalese majority dominates several numeric minorities (4 percent, Ceylon Tamil; 5.1 percent, Indian Tamil; 7.9 percent, Sri Lanka Moor; 0.2 percent, Burgher; 0.3 percent, Malay; and 0.2 percent Other; Census of Sri Lanka 2001; Lewis 2009). These ethnic groups demonstrate unequal need and value for multilingualism and specific languages: few Sinhala-speaking Sinhalese are bilingual in Tamil (4 percent) and English (13.2 percent), while bilingualism is more common in minority ethnolinguistic groups with histories of disenfranchisement. Tamil mother tongue Ceylon Tamils, Indian Tamils, and Sri Lankan Moors have much higher Sinhala and English bilingualism (64.6 percent and 24.1 percent, 50.8 percent and 8.7 percent, 60.9 percent and 20.6 percent, respectively; Census of Sri Lanka 2001; McGilvray 1998).

Sociolinguistic research—albeit limited—has linked language policy and sociolinguistic identity to civil strife, while studies problematizing English medium education (e.g., Canagarajah 2006) and documentation of language shift in minority populations (e.g., Bhatt & Mahboob 2008) also exist. Meanwhile, Sri Lanka's history—as a colony and then an independent nation marred by an extended civil war—is tumultuous and salient for understanding local language management.

Colonial Period (1796–1948)

As a crown colony administered by the EIC and the British Raj, Sri Lanka (then Ceylon) was separate from British India despite intermittent long-term contact with southern populations. During the British Raj, English-medium schooling created a feeding pool for both Ceylon Tamil and Sinhalese English-speaking elite to enter civil-service administration—offices of relative power. English, as a second language/literacy, did not dissolve existing ethno-religious-linguistic alignments, and instead was perceived as an imported, *additional* language, while the British, through a Christian proselytizing agenda, unintentionally encouraged local religious identity formation (Devotta 2001). Significant for contextualizing later struggles, pre- and post-independence Sinhalese nationalists believe that Ceylon Tamils were unfairly privileged by the British (Tambiah 1986).

Independent Sri Lanka (1948–present)

Despite some expectations that Sri Lanka would be incorporated into India, it achieved its own independence after Partition, in 1948. Further, while in the colonial-period elite Ceylon Tamils and Sinhalese were united in some movements and enjoyed special privileges (Kearney 1978), and the pre-independence language plan called for a gradual shift from English to Tamil and Sinhalese as co-official languages, Sri Lanka's extended civil war (1983–2009) can be traced back to British-implemented, unequal legislative representation. The immediate post-independence period saw a resurgence in Sinhalese Buddhist nationalism and a steady escalation of Tamil marginalization through one-upmanship in Sinhalese nationalist government policies on several fronts, including language (Sriskandarajah 2005; Tambiah 1986). Based on territorial and demographic distribution, the Sinhalese majority was used to establish the 1956 Official Languages Act (a.k.a the Sinhalese Only Act), legislating Sinhalese as Sri Lanka's sole national language and eliminating English and Tamil as examination and government languages. The language management and value debate shifted from targeting multicultural English-educated elites into an ethnic conflict where Sinhalese represented a powerful majority, approximately 70 percent (Kearney 1978).

"Although the Sinhala conception of nationalism critically related Buddhism to the polity . . . language has nevertheless been a more important issue than religion in the Sinhalese-Tamil conflicts" (Tambiah 1986: 73). Reflecting this, the 1956 law forced non-Sinhalese civil servants to resign. While creating positions for Sinhalese speakers, this move denied Ceylon Tamils any practical or ideological power within the newly formed nation. While some argue that this was part of a larger attempt to reverse colonial discrimination against the Sinhalese, disparities in income, education, and employment were minimal between Sinhalese and Tamil, compared with within-group inequalities (Sriskandarajah 2005). Regardless, given the essentialist Sinhalese language policies and government-sponsored movement of Sinhalese people into northern Tamil areas (interpreted by Tamil leaders as further disenfranchising Tamils), language was the lightning rod for empowering Sinhalese at the expense of Tamils. This scenario culminated in the 1976 Tamil demand for a separate state (Kearney 1978).

Civil War (1983–2009). Beginning with the 1983 riots, the Liberation Tigers of Tamil Eelam (LTTE) waged an intermittent war against the Sri Lankan government that ended with the 2009 LTTE decimation. However, it is argued that language gradually lost significance within the struggle: in 1958 Sri Lanka authorized Tamil for public government correspondence in the Northern and Eastern Provinces, the 1978 Constitution granted Tamil national language status, and Tamil was established as co-official language (with Sinhalese and English) in 1987 (Thirumalai 2002).

Post Civil War (2009–present). Early Sinhalese-favoring language policies were a catalyst for divisiveness and disenfranchisement and language remains a fundamental issue. Current mandates for a bilingual government (Sinhalese and Tamil) encourage—through training and additional pay (and, contrarily, a pay freeze for remaining monolingual)—civil servants toward Sinhalese/Tamil bilingualism within five years of appointment (Dissanayake 2007). Meanwhile, English is officially recognized as a link language and continues to have an ideologically privileged status. Through much of Sri Lanka's postcolonial history, the instrumental value of Tamil has decreased through language policies favoring Sinhalese though it has maintained high covert prestige, given the extended civil war, and its cultural value as an index of Tamil identity. While both the political situation and dominant language management ideologies continue to evolve—with the civil war ceasefire and recent decrees making Sinhalese-Tamil multilingualism socio-economically profitable—the ultimate success of this bilingual approach to language management and language education and how indigenous languages will stand up to the international socioeconomic value of English remain to be seen.

Small States: The Maldives, Bhutan, Nepal

Beyond significant differences from larger SA counterparts in governance, foreign policy interests, internal homogeneity, historic backdrop, and contemporary sociopolitical situations and aspirations, a proportional comparison of population, land area, economic prosperity and stability locates the Maldives, Bhutan, and Nepal as "small" SA states (Misra 2004b). Nepal and Bhutan are isolated, landlocked mountainous territories with continuous histories as independent kingdoms. The Maldives, an archipelago trading stop in the Indian Ocean, has an extended Islamic history and currently depends heavily on tourism, as a tropical island. Facing different challenges as developing, third-world nations, their contemporary sociopolitical—and linguistic—situations are quite divergent.

The Maldives

The Maldives (population 359,000, 96 percent literacy) is home to an ostensibly culturally, religiously, and ethnolinguistically homogeneous population of Muslims who speak Maldivan (Dhievhi), the officially sanctioned language (Lewis 2009). Physically and ideologically isolated from the rest of SA (Misra 2004a), sociopolitically the Maldives had, until 2008, an extended period of authoritarian rule (no political parties existed: the president was elected six times, spanning 30 years, via a single yes/no referendum offering no alternative candidates) with media closely governed and granted only limited criticism of the state (Misra 2004b). While 2008 marked the first democratic election, it's not certain how this change and subsequent sociopolitical turbulence may affect the climate for sociolinguistic research. There is no sociolinguistic (or really, any linguistic) research on the Maldives, unsurprising given the extended authoritarian rule and uncertain contemporary political climate.

Future research would help to verify Maldivian monolingualism and understand how ideologies challenging national policy are expressed, how Dhievhi has developed in similar or divergent ways from Sinhalese (a close cousin) given the heavy Maldivian Islamic influence (e.g., the Islamicization of English in Pakistan, cf. Mahboob 2009), examine how language practices and policy frameworks may relate to political changes and to document how Maldivian language management develops in light of continued land erosion and ecological destruction and subsequent potential increases in outside influence.

Bhutan

Bhutan's small population (~650,000, ~50 percent literacy) and 24-plus languages (including Nepali, but excluding English [Lewis 2009]) suggest rich linguistic diversity ripe for examination. The national language is Dzongkha, while regional lingua francas exist (i.e., in the east, Tshangla, in the south, Nepali, and across the country, English [van Driem 1994]). Dzongkha, the only indigenous language with a literary history—if it can be considered as having an independent literary history, given that the written form of Dzongkha is Classical Tibetan (Chöke), a precursor to contemporary Dzongkha (Hyslop & Tshering 2009; Simoni 2003)—has been the language of the court, military, government administration, and educated elite for centuries. Dzongkha continues to be standardized and modernized, with progressive vernacularization of the written form undertaken under the auspices of the Dzongkha Development Commission, which also supports linguistic surveys of grammar and lexicon (Simoni 2003).

In writing, a domain-specific diglossia and written/oral divide pervades: written Chöke is used in formal legal domains, while spoken Dzongkha is used in homes, media and traditional arts (van Driem 1994). However, the case is arguably more complex: most educated elite (often educated in India, given the lack of Bhutanese higher education) are literate in English but only semiliterate in Dzongkha, yet legal documents must be issued in Dzongkha. Drafts tend to be produced in English, while specialists, with the help of classical Tibetan dictionaries for translating modern English legal words with no Dzongkha equivalent, produce Dzongkha-based publications. These, in turn, are beyond the grasp of lawmakers, given their limited written Dzongkha proficiency, and the transmutations involved in converting modern legalese into a language lacking such concepts (Simoni 2003).

Education has transitioned from written Chöke (used for centuries within monastic education, continuing with the advent of formalized education in the mid-1950s) with Hindi as the "ancillary" oral medium (mid-1950s–1964, due to the availability of Hindi materials from India) to English as the ancillary medium (1964–1971) to modern Dzongkha (1971 onward), while Nepali was used for a brief period in southern regions (van Driem 1994). It is unclear how non- or minority Dzongkha speakers negotiate gaps between home and school languages, and what proficiencies and literacies students emerge with.

While little (socio)linguistic research exists, language management issues in Bhutan can be gleaned from documented sociopolitical processes. Bhutan is perhaps best known for its ideology promoting Gross National Happiness as a measure of national success (Simoni 2003). However, despite the positive image portrayed in popular media—and some (socio)linguistic research—suggesting a humane and peaceful Buddhist kingdom nestled between India and China, common Bhutanese people enjoy limited individual rights, and minorities are actively disenfranchised through programs that enforce traditional Buddhist Drukpa culture, imagined by the government as the sole true Bhutanese identity.

Bhutan's current sociopolitical ideology of "one nation, one people" (established in 1961) with its official sanctioning of the Drukpa culture, religion, dress, and Dzongkha as the sole national language, is tied to its history as a small kingdom wishing to retain independence in the face of continued Chinese and Indian expansion. Its boundaries have been challenged and reduced (e.g., China's 1959 takeover of Tibet also appropriated some contested Tibetan/ Bhutanese land), while the recent history of nearby Sikkim is iconic of how SA kingdoms can loose their independence (Kharat 2004). Sikkim was part of the EIC empire and then a protectorate of India, while a British colonial policy of reducing Tibetan influence encouraged large-scale immigration of ethnic Nepalese. With indigenous Sikkimese a minority, this led to the Indian 1975 invasion and Sikkim's subsequent inclusion as an Indian state (Evans 2010; Wangchuk 2004).

Envisioning indigenous homogeneity as a prerequisite for continued independence, Bhutan has expelled over 100,000 Lhotshampas, a borderland Nepali-speaking Hindu population that migrated from India and Nepal (1865–1930) and consider themselves "Nepali-speaking Bhutanese" (Evans 2010). Distinct from indigenous northern Bhutanese, who are Tibeto-Burman-language-speaking Buddhists with different cultural practices (Evans 2010: 27), the Lhotshampas were discriminated against through unequal taxation, restricted employment opportunities, violence (e.g., the pervasive and actual fear of losing six inches—i.e., being beheaded—by state police), and derision of their language, religion, and culture (Evans 2010). This culminated in the 1985 passage of restrictive citizenship laws requiring Dzongkha fluency and proof of pre-1958 residency and the 1989 reaffirmation of the one nation, one people law enforcing Drukpa linguistic and cultural assimilation. Language in particular became a tool within the country's increasing hostility toward non-Drukpa communities: in 1989 Nepali was removed from the curriculum in southern schools, and Nepali textbooks were reportedly burned (Hutt 2003, cited in Evans 2010), followed by the 1991 (and onward) forcible expulsion of non-Drukpas. The government coerced Lhotshampas to fill out Dzongkha-based forms (which they could not read), which were actually "voluntary migration forms" then used to justify their expulsion (Evans 2010). Ironically, one survey of a Nepal-based refugee camp demonstrated that over 99 percent of exiles held "incontrovertible evidence of Bhutanese origin and nationality" (Association of Human Rights Activists 2000, cited in Evans 2010). This forced migration has been labeled a cultural/ethnic cleansing by international press (Misra 2004a: fn. 6), and serves as a powerful counterpoint to more common portrayals of Bhutan's "accommodating and hospitable attitude" (e.g., van Driem 1994) toward sociolinguistic and cultural diversity.

Beyond Bhutan's management of the Lhotshampas, its official linguistic and cultural policies also affect indigenous Bhutanese and Tibetan refugees. Since 1959 the latter have largely been "migrated" to India based in part on their alleged stronger allegiance to the Dalai Lama over the Bhutanese constitutional monarchy (Kharat 2004). The remaining Tibetan minority (~1200) is not insular, and has linguistically assimilated across two generations to Dzongkha, while some also reportedly speak additional indigenous languages (van Driem 1994). In contrast, southern Nepali-speaking Bhutanese have avoided assimilation to a larger degree, for several possible reasons: earlier Nepali-based schooling in southern Bhutan is likely to percolate into current adult competencies, and the ongoing tension between the state and Nepali-speaking Bhutanese may encourage Nepali as indexing community identity and a rallying point for expanded rights. There is other evidence of linguistic shift, for example, the previously undocumented Tasha-Sili community is hypothesized to have recently shifted from an unknown, low-prestige, indigenous language to Tasha-Sili (which is either a dialect of Dzongkha or a separate language borrowing from Dzongkha lexicon and phonology, but divergent in morphosyntax [Hyslop & Tshering 2009]). The Tasha-Sili scenario highlights what may in fact be a more common, yet thus far undocumented, sociolinguistic process in Bhutan: language shift and dialect creation based on modern sociopolitics.

Bhutanese sociolinguistic future. Given that no script development is underway for minority languages, the increased valorization of Dzongkha and English (and, arguably, Hindi) vis-à-vis indigenous oral languages lacking a script is likely to provoke language shift and language loss in minority and socioeconomically impoverished communities (Hyslop & Tshering 2009). Further, it is unclear how or whether minority communities contest or conform to national language policies, what linguistic and social processes these might involve, and how Hindi and English competencies holding higher SA and global value, respectively, may change over time and whether they will subsume or be subsumed by Bhutan's one nation, one people ideology.

Nepal

Nepal (population 27 million, 54 percent literacy) is a multilingual and pluralistic nation with 104-plus living languages from four language families (Lewis

2009), at least six scripts (Dahal 2000), and a distinct Nepali Sign Language (Hoffmann-Dilloway 2008). Nine mother tongues represent over 75 percent of the population (Giri 2010), and no minority linguistic community holds a demographic advantage (Bhattarai 2004). Language management research has focused on socioeconomic, regional, and linguistic center/periphery issues (e.g., Dahal 2000; Giri 2010), language-in-education policy and implementation (e.g., Shrestha & Van den Hoek 1995; Yadav 1992), minority ethnolinguistic issues (e.g., O'Neill 1994; Turin 1997; Webster 1997), and structural variation reflecting sociopolitical and ideological positions (e.g., Hoffmann-Dilloway 2008; Upadhyay 2009).

Nepali (also known as Nepalese) has held a special role in national unification through three recent sociopolitical periods and continuing today. For much of Nepal's contemporary history, language policy favoring Nepali has obscured or erased linguistic diversity, with implications for the current sociopolitical and economic crises. Nepal is the leading contender to be the first failed SA nation: its economy is among the lowest in the world—in line with some sub-Saharan African nations—and sociopolitical stability is marred by a prolonged civil war and extensive government corruption (Misra 2004b). Yet, it receives the highest per-head foreign aid of any nation worldwide, has attracted hordes of NGOs and INGOs, and boasts the most robust sociolinguistic literature of any of small SA nation.

Nepal has never been under outside colonial rule; however, indigenous rule has not necessarily led to more protection for Nepalese pluralism. The Gorkha Empire (1722–1846) and the following Rama Empire (1846–1950) protected Nepali and encouraged its standardization and modernization. The 1951 introduction of a multiparty democracy continued this agenda, ensuring that Nepali retained power in government and non-government elite domains. Following this, minority linguistic communities attempted to use language as a tool for greater socioeconomic mobility. However, in 1957 all languages but Nepali were removed from the education system. Three years later, 1960 saw the dissolution of the democracy, replaced by the Panchayat Monarchy, which viewed language diversity as a threat to national stability. The Panchayat Monarchy introduced linguistic nationalism through the one nation, one political system agenda, framing Nepali as a vehicle of unification, or "Nepalization" of the masses. The revised 1962 constitution also did not address linguistic freedom, and it made Nepali the sole national language. In the period from 1962–1989, Nepali developed and expanded as a medium of instruction, used in parliament, the court system, and media (Dahal 2000).

While there were no significant language movements during the Panchayat period, from 1981 to 1991 there was a sharp drop in census-reported Nepali speakers, coinciding with an upswing in other vernacular identifications (Upadhyay 2009). Mass uprisings in 1990 led to the re-creation of Nepal as a pluralistic democracy that acknowledged the multilinguistic and multiethnic nature of Nepal. The 1990 constitution recognized Nepali (in Devanagari script) as the national language, while it permitted (yet did not fund) developing indigenous languages, cultures, and scripts and establishing primary schools in various mother tongues. Following this, Radio Nepal started broadcasting in other languages (e.g., Hindi, English, Newari, Magar, Tamang), and Nepal TV produced vernacular-medium made-for-TV films. Despite protests, no widespread or systematic minority language planning or development occurred, given the lack of tangible financial and government political support. Also salient to minority language development success were educators themselves, who were hostile to minority vernaculars (especially those lacking a script; Giri 2010). Meanwhile, middle-class and elite populations continued to use language to subtly and blatantly devalue minority linguistic communities (Giri 2010).

Minority linguistic-diversity movements were then stalled by political turmoil. In 1996 the Communist Party of Nepal (Maoist) attempted to replace the royal parliamentary Panchayat system, provoking civil war, which was further complicated by the massacre of most of the royal Nepali family in 2001, the 2005 dissolution of government by the late king's brother, and the 2006 re-creation of Nepal as a secular federal republic. All of these political movements have involved civil violence and protests, and Nepal currently lacks a comprehensive and integrated language policy (Giri 2009). Indeed, it also lacks a constitution (following multiple extensions of the 2007 Interim Constitution—originally written as a stopgap during the political transition, and establishing the Constitutional Assembly as a body charged with writing a new permanent constitution—the Constitutional Assembly was dissolved May 28, 2012, by Prime Minister Baburam Bhattarai with no constitutional documents produced, while no subsequent extensions of the Interim Constitution have been issued [Jha 2012]). This limits projections for Nepal's future language management. English, while not mentioned in any constitution thus far, has evolved into the language of higher education, science, technology, public administration, and diplomatic relations, increasing its instrumental value, especially given the preponderance of NGOs using English. Despite political uncertainty, Nepali and English are privileged by the elite, perpetuate class divisions, and are linked to language shift in lower socioeconomic strata aspiring toward economic and social mobility (Giri 2010).

Discussion

India was the first SA nation to enact comprehensive language policies as a modern independent nation-state and put considerable early emphasis on using one language to unite its diverse population. The idea of a single official language continues to hold sway across SA as an imagined aspect of unification. However, this exploration of SA language management demonstrates that prior and continuing SA language mandates have been equally unsuccessful at implementing this ideology. Each nation's respective approaches to and success with language management are distinguished by unique, contextualized histories, negotiations with and management of different demographics, values for language and future aspirations.

Acknowledgment

This chapter is dedicated to Shibu, whose personal experiences with Bhutan and Nepal challenged the rosy and limited sociolinguistic data available. Her stories reminded me that a lack of sociolinguistic research may also be significant to understanding local language management and policing.

References

Abbi, A. 2009. Vanishing diversities and submerging identities: An Indian case. In A. Sarangi (ed.), *Language and politics in India*, 299–311. New Delhi: Oxford University Press.

Aggarwal, K. S. 1992. To include or not to include: An attempt to study the language conflict in Manipur. *Language Problems & Language Planning* 16(1): 21–37.

Aggarwal, K. S. 1997. What's Indian about Indian plurilingualism? *Language Problems & Language Planning* 21(1): 35–50.

Ahmad, R. 2008. Scripting a new identity: The battle for Devanagari in nineteenth century India. *Journal of Pragmatics* 40: 1163–183.

Austin, G. 2009. Language and the constitution: The half-hearted compromise. In A. Sarangi (ed.), *Language and politics in India*, 41–92. New Delhi: Oxford University Press.

Banu, R., & Sussex, R. 2001. Code-switching in Bangladesh. *English Today* 17(2): 51–61.

Baruah, S. 2009. Separatist militants and contentious politics in Assam, India: The limits of counterinsurgency. *Asian Survey* 49(6): 951–74.

Bhatt, R. M., & Mahboob, A. 2008. Minority languages and their status. In B. Kachru, Y. Kachru, & S. N. Sridhar (eds.), *Language in South Asia*, 121–31. Cambridge: Cambridge University Press.

Bhattarai, H. P. 2004. Cultural diversity and pluralism in Nepal: Emerging issues and the search for a new paradigm. *Contributions to Nepalese Studies* 31(2): 293–340.

Brass, P. R. 1974. *Language, religion and politics in North India*. London: Oxford University Press.

Brightbill, J., Kim, A., & Kim, S. 2007. The War-Jaintia in Bangladesh: A sociolinguistic survey. SIL Electronic Survey Report 2007–13. http://www.sil.org/silesr/2007/silesr2007-013.pdf. Accessed August 15, 2010.

Canagarajah, A. S. 2006. Negotiating the local in English as a lingua franca. *Annual Review of Anthropology* 26: 197–218.

Chand, V. 2011. Elite positionings toward Hindi: Language policies, political stances and language competence in India. *Journal of Sociolinguistics* 15: 1–30.

Dahal, R. K. 2000. Language politics in Nepal. *Contributions to Nepalese Studies* 27(2): 155–90.

Daniels, P. T. 2008. Writing systems of major and minor languages. In B. Kachru, Y. Kachru, & S. N. Sridhar (eds.), *Language in South Asia,* 285–308. Cambridge: Cambridge University Press.

Democratic Socialist Republic of Sri Lanka. 2001. Census of Sri Lanka. Department of Census and Statistics. http://www.statistics.gov.lk/home.asp. Accessed August 15, 2010.

Devotta, N. 2001. The utilisation of religio-linguistic identities by the Sinhalese and Bengalis: Towards a general explanation. *Commonwealth & Comparative Politics* 39: 66–95.

Dissanayake, D. 2007. Implementation of Official Language Policy. Ministry of Public Administration and Home Affairs. Colombo: Public Administration Circular 07/2007. http://www.languagescom.gov.lk/Annex%20%28X%29%20B.pdf. Accessed August 15, 2010.

Emeneau, M. B. (1956) 1980. India as a Linguistic Area. In A. S. Dil (ed.), *Language and linguistic area: Essays by Murray B. Emeneau,* 105–25. Palo Alto, CA: Stanford University Press.

Evans, R. 2010. The perils of being a borderland people: On the Lhotshampas of Bhutan. *Contemporary South Asia* 18: 25–42.

Ghufran, N. 2009. Pushtun ethnonationalism and the Taliban insurgency in the North West Frontier Province of Pakistan. *Asian Survey* 49: 1092–114.

Giri, R. A. 2009. English in Nepalese Education: An analysis of theoretical and contextual issues for the development of its policy guidelines. PhD Dissertation, Faculty of Education, Monash University.

Giri, R. A. 2010. Cultural anarchism: The consequences of privileging languages in Nepal. *Journal of Multilingual and Multicultural Development* 31: 87–100.

Government of India. 2008. The Constitution of India. By the Ministry of Law and Justice (Legislative Department). http://lawmin.nic.in/coi/coiason29july08.pdf. Accessed August 15, 2010.

Hoffmann-Dilloway, E. 2008. Metasemiotic regimentation in the standardization of Nepali Sign Language. *Journal of Linguistic Anthropology* 18(2): 192–213.

Hutt, M. 1993. Refugees from Shangri-La. *Index on Censorship* 22: 9–14.

Hyslop, G., & Tshering, K. 2009. The Tasha-Sili language of Bhutan: A case study in language shift and Bhutanese pre-history. In H. Elnazarov & N. Ostler (eds.), *Proceedings of the Foundation for Endangered Languages (FEL XIII): Endangered languages and history,* 101–08. Foundation for Endangered Languages: Bath, UK..

Jalaluddin, A. K. 1983. Problems of transition of rural Indian society from oral to written tradition through adult education. *Journal of Pragmatics* 7: 517–31.

Jha, P. 2012. Nepal's CA fails to write constitution. In *The Hindu,* http://www.thehindu.com/news/international/article3463109.ece. Accessed August 8, 2012.

Kachru, B. B. 1986b. *The alchemy of English: The spread, functions and models of non-native Englishes.* Oxford: Pergamon Press.

Kearney, R. N. 1978. Language and the rise of Tamil separatism in Sri Lanka. *Asian Survey* 18(5): 521–34.

Khan, A. 2009. Renewed ethnonationalist insurgency in Balochistan, Pakistan. *Asian Survey* 49(6): 1071–091.

Kharat, R. 2004. Bhutan's security scenario. *Contemporary South Asia* 13(2): 171–85.

LaDousa, C. 2005. Disparate markets: Language, nation, and education in North India. *American Ethnologist* 33(3): 460–78.

Lewis, M. P. (ed.) 2009. *Ethnologue: Languages of the World*. 16th edition. Dallas, TX: SIL International.

Macaulay, T. B. (1920) 1965. Minute on Education by the Hon'ble T. B. Macaulay, dated the 2nd February 1835. National Archives of India. Calcutta: Superintendent, Government Printing, 107–17. http://www.columbia.edu/itc/mealac/pritchett/00generallinks/macaulay/txt_minute_education_1835.html. Accessed August 15, 2010.

Mahboob, A. 2009. English as an Islamic language: A case study of Pakistani English. *World Englishes* 28(2): 175–89.

Mazumdar, A. 2005. Bhutan's military action against Indian insurgents. *Contemporary South Asia* 45(4): 566–80.

McGilvray, D. 1998. Arabs, Moors, and Muslims: Sri Lankan Muslim Ethnicity in Regional Perspective. *Contributions to Indian Sociology* 32(2): 433–83.

Misra, A. 2004a. An introduction to the 'small' and 'micro' states of South Asia. *Contemporary South Asia* 13(2): 127–31.

Misra, A. 2004b. Theorising 'small' and 'micro' state behaviour using the Maldives, Bhutan and Nepal. *Contemporary South Asia* 13(2): 133–48.

Mitchell, L. 2009. *Language, emotion and politics in South India: The Making of a Mother Tongue*. Bloomington: Indiana University Press.

Mohanty, P. 2002. British language policy in 19th century India and the Oriya language movement. *Language Policy* 1: 53–73.

Mukherjee, A. 1989. Some sociopsychological correlates of linguistic assimilation: The case of the Bengalis in Delhi. *International Journal of the Sociology of Language* 75: 27–45.

O'Neill, T. 1994. Peoples and polity: Ethnography, ethnicity and identity in Nepal. *Contributions to Nepalese studies* 21(1): 45–72.

Panday, P. K., & Jamil, I. 2008. The Elusive Peace Accord in the Chittagong Hill Tracts of Bangladesh and the continuous agonies of the Indigenous People. *Journal of Contemporary and Commonwealth Politics* 46(4): 464–89.

Panday, P. K., & Jamil, I. 2009. Conflicts in the Chittagong Hill Tracts of Bangladesh: An unimplemented accord and continued violence. *Asian Survey* 49(6): 1052–70.

Pearcy, T., & Dickson, M. 1996. Mughal Empire in India, 16th century. *World Civilizations*. New York: W.W. Norton.

People's Republic of Bangladesh. 2001. Census. Bureau of Statistics. http://www.bbs.gov.bd/. Accessed August 28, 2010.

Rahman, T. 1996a. The Sindhi language movement and the politics of Sindh. *Ethnic Studies Report* XIV(1): 99–116.

Rahman, T. 1996b. *Language and politics in Pakistan*. Karachi: Oxford University Press.

Rahman, T. 1997. The medium of instruction controversy in Pakistan. *Journal of Multilingual and Multicultural Development* 18(2): 145–54.

Rahman, T. 2002. *Language, ideology and power: Language-learning among the Muslims of Pakistan and North India*. Oxford: Oxford University Press.

Rahman, T. 2006. Language policy, multilingualism and language vitality in Pakistan. In A. Saxena & L. Borin (eds.), *Lesser-known languages of South Asia: Status and policies, case studies and applications of information technology*, 175, 73–106. Berlin / New York: Mouton de Gruyter.

Ramanathan, V. 2005. *The English vernacular divide: Postcolonial language politics and practice*. Clevedon: Multilingual Matters.

Sahgal, A. 1991. Patterns of language use in a bilingual setting in India. In J. Cheshire (ed.), *English around the world: Sociolinguistic perspectives*, 209–307. Cambridge: Cambridge University Press.

Sarangi, A. (ed.) 2009. *Language and politics in India* (Themes in politics). New Delhi: Oxford University Press.

Shrestha, B. G., & Van den Hoek, B. 1995. Education in the mother tongue: The case of Nepalbhasa (Newari). *Contributions to Nepalese Studies* 22(1): 73–86.

Simoni, A. 2003. A language for rules, another for symbols: Linguistic pluralism and the interpretation of statutes in the kingdom of Bhutan. *Journal of Bhutan Studies* 8: 29–53.

Singh, U. N. 2006. The *new* Linguistic Survey of India. *South Asian Languages Analysis (SALA) 26* (Kannada University and Central Institute of Indian Studies).

Sriskandarajah, D. 2005. Socio-economic inequality and ethno-political conflict: Some observations from Sri Lanka. *Contemporary South Asia* 14(3): 341–56.

Tambiah, S. J. 1986. *Sri Lanka: Ethnic fratricide and the dismantling of democracy*. Chicago and London: University of Chicago Press.

Thirumalai, M. S. 2002. Sri Lanka's Language Policy: A brief introduction. *Language in India* 1(9). http://www.languageinindia.com/jan2002/srilanka1.html. Accessed August 15, 2010.

Tremblay, R. C. 2009. Kashmir's secessionist movement resurfaces. *Asian Survey* 49(6): 924–50.

Turin, M. 1997. Too many stars and not enough sky: Language and ethnicity among the Thakali of Nepal. *Contributions to Nepalese studies* 24(2): 187–99.

United Nations. 2011. South Asia Political Map No. 4140 Rev. 4. Department of Field Support, Cartographic Section. http://www.un.org/Depts/Cartographic/map/profile/Souteast-Asia.pdf. Accessed August 8, 2012.

Upadhyay, S. R. 2009. The sociolinguistic variation of grammatical gender agreement in Nepali. *Journal of Pragmatics* 41: 564–85.

van Driem, George. 1994. Language policy in Bhutan. In Aris, M., and Hutt, M. (eds.), *Bhutan: Aspects of culture and development*. Kiscadale Asia Research Series No. 5. Gartmore, Scotland: Paul Strachen–Kiscadale Ltd.

Van Dyke, V. 2009. The Khalistan movement in Punjab, India, and the post-militancy era: Structural change and new political compulsions. *Asian Survey* 49(6): 975–97.

Wangchuk, T. 2004. The middle path to democracy in the kingdom of Bhutan. *Asian Survey* 44(6): 836–55.

Webster, J. D. 1997. Indicators of bilingual proficiency in Nepali among Tibeto-Burman peoples of Nepal. *Contributions to Nepalese Studies* 24(2): 233–62.

Yadav, R. 1992. The use of the mother tongue in primary education: The Nepalese context. *Contributions to Nepalese Studies* 19(2): 177–90.

Zubair, S. 2007. Silent birds: Metaphorical constructions of literacy and gender identity in women's talk. *Discourse Studies* 9(6): 766–83.

CHAPTER 30

LANGUAGE POLICY AND IDEOLOGY IN LATIN AMERICA

RAINER ENRIQUE HAMEL

To approach language policies in Latin America entails investigating how different peoples, emerging nations, ethnolinguistic groups, or other social aggregates use the differences between languages and varieties of languages to (1) construct their group identities, (2) distinguish themselves from the "others," and (3) build power structures. One strand of research focuses on the construction of Spanish and Portuguese as independent national languages, a process related to nation building after Independence at the beginning of the nineteenth century that extended well into the twentieth century. However, most language policy research belongs to a second strand: the relation of Spanish and Portuguese as colonial and national languages to indigenous and immigrant languages. A third topic area, which has received less attention, involves policies toward the teaching and values of foreign languages, which overlaps with the focus on some European immigrant languages, such as English, French, German, and Italian.

The most significant areas where language politics become salient and language policies intervene are in the domains of societal multilingualism. Two different types of linguistic communities in Latin America have created their own domains of bilingual communication, including bilingual education: indigenous and immigrant communities. Both communities exist as bilingual enclaves in socio-historic formations of nation-state building processes. These processes are oriented by European models of linguistic and cultural homogeneity that seek to assimilate those who are different. In most Latin American countries, the dominant language ideology expects their citizens to be monolingual speakers of the national language and, in the middle and upper classes, to have some command of a foreign language. Those who speak *other mother tongues* arouse suspicions about their national loyalty, even if they are equally proficient in the country's language. Foreign languages are welcome as long as they do not possess a territorial base, which often assigns a conflicting status to languages like Italian or German.

Areas and traditions that practice natural plurilingualism are excluded or hidden from public recognition and its discourses. Among them are indigenous areas in the rain forest that exhibit extraordinary linguistic diversity where people naturally speak four languages or more. Similarly, both indigenous urban multilingualism, which has increased over the past decades due to migration into the big cities, and existing immigrant language enclaves are basically kept invisible in the constructed image of modern states and their metropolises.

In sum, instances of societal multilingualism are viewed as an exception in Latin America, even more so in the "imagined community" of the nation than in communicative practice. Any stable bilingual community—indigenous or immigrant—faces adverse sociolinguistic conditions and will have to develop specific ideological, cultural and linguistic justifications for the preservation of its bilingual domains.

Fundamental contradictions often persist between the states' overt language policies and planning, and the impulses and orientations of vigorous societal forces. During colonial and early republican times, the state pressure for assimilation and the eradication of indigenous languages was resisted in regions of massive indigenous population or isolated areas. Conversely, modern governmental policies that foster diversity and enrichment perspectives today meet strong resistance both from mainstream society and from indigenous teachers and parents who sometimes oppose bilingual education because they deeply internalized the dominant ideology of monolingualism (Hamel 2008a, 2008b).

To interpret the complex field of language policies in Latin America requires a conceptual framework broader than the traditional models of language policy, planning, or management which typically reduce their object to overt state interventions designed to change the "natural" course of language development. Rather, language policies will be understood in this framework as sociohistorical processes that change language constellations (i.e., whole systems of communication) where state institutions and other social forces intervene. Such a process implies a transformation of discursive and linguistic structures and uses (e.g., standardization, diffusion, shift, or revitalization). More fundamentally, it also entails a change in the language ideologies and a change in the relationships that speakers maintain with the prevailing language constellations in shared territories as part of overall power relations (see Hamel 2008c, 2010 for a broader discussion).

Within this historical perspective, we can identify three ideological orientations to language and cultural politics in Latin America that correspond to historical phases but survive at the same time as competing positions today (see figure 30.1).

Figure 30.1. Ideological orientations in language and cultural policy

Colonialism developed *monoculturalism* and *monolingualism* as the dominant position that was reinforced by the nascent republics after Independence. This orientation denied the indigenous populations the right to exist as distinct ethnic peoples, for example, in nineteenth-century Argentina and Chile, or it erased its presence and visibility, as happened in Brazil after the early colonial period. This ideology has been challenged since the beginning of the twentieth century by a competing orientation that I want to frame as *multiculturalism* and *multilingualism*. These orientations acknowledge the existence of ethnic minorities but define diversity negatively as a problem ("the Indian problem"). The cultural and linguistic expressions of indigenous and other minorities are recognized both as a problem *and* as a right, and their existence is seen as a barrier to national unity (see Ruiz 1984 for a different conceptualization). *Pluriculturalism* and *plurilingualism* represent a third orientation based on an enrichment perspective. This vision shares with multiculturalism a similar recognition of factual diversity but differs in its valuation. Diversity is considered an asset and potential cultural capital for the nation as a whole. It is grounded in a cultural base theory as laid down in the theoretical foundations of intercultural education (Monsonyi & Rengifo 1983).

All three orientations are still present and compete in contemporary society. Multilingualism is probably hegemonic but is losing force in many countries. The fundamental question today is how to move from a multilingual and multicultural orientation that recognizes diversity but regards it as a problem to a plurilingual and pluricultural enrichment perspective within the broader context of societal transformations in Latin America.

In this chapter I focus primarily on language policies in the domains of bi- and multilingualism and the associated language ideologies that contrast mono- and multilingual with plurilingual orientations. Since education is no doubt the single most salient arena of these controversies, I will concentrate on the ways in which language policies and ideologies intervene in the educational systems and options in Latin America. First, I will outline the history and some general characteristics of the indigenous and the immigrant educational settings with regard to the macrolevel of policy and the microlevel of curriculum. I will then look at some basic differences as well as shared problems and solutions in order to develop an integrated interpretation of language and education policy in Latin America. Next, I will explore what solutions different countries and regions offer to the challenges of globalization, from new foreign language policies and primary education bilingual programs to South American integration based on massive bilingualism of the main state languages.

Indigenous Language Policy and Education in Latin America

I will not engage here in the debate about language classification and competing typologies. My data stem from the most recent authoritative sociolinguistic atlas (Sichra 2009) and from an up-to-date survey on indigenous education in Latin America (López 2009). In 2009 slightly less than 30 million indigenous citizens, speaking well over 500 languages, lived in Latin America. An extreme diversity of numbers, demographic density, linguistic and sociolinguistic differentiation, and degrees of assimilation characterize their present ways of life. Taking into account this heterogeneity, it is possible to distinguish three main groupings among Amerindian peoples.

Over 80 percent of the indigenous population is concentrated in two macro-ethnoses located in the areas where highly differentiated societies existed before the European conquest. One occupies the *Mesoamerican plateau* containing central and southeast Mexico, Guatemala, and Belize. Some 80 languages are spoken by this ethnic family, modern Náhuatl (1.4 million speakers) and modern Mayan languages (6.2 million speakers) being the most important ones. The other macro-ethnos is located in the *Andean area,* which stretches from the south of Columbia to the north of Chile, including Argentina (north), Bolivia, Chile (north), Colombia (south), Ecuador, and Peru. Here two languages, Quechua (12 million speakers) and Aymara (3 million speakers) are dominant.

The second grouping is subdivided into more than 300 languages whose speakers are scattered over the whole of the Latin American territory. Their main areas of residence are located in Central America (except Guatemala and Belize), the Caribbean coast of South America, the Amazonian basin, and the extreme south of the continent. Different from the first, this ensemble of Amerindian micro-ethnoses is characterized by low demographic density, high linguistic diversity, and a wide variety of stages on the continuum of assimilation that range from still fairly isolated hunter and collector societies to almost fully assimilated groups.

The third and relatively new grouping is growing fast at the expense of the other two: it comprises the urban indigenous population of several million that share the living conditions of the urban sub-proletariat dwelling in the huge shantytowns that surround Latin American big cities.

From the beginning of the Conquest in 1492, two colonialist strategies—assimilation versus subordinate preservation of indigenous peoples—developed and materialized in education and the teaching of Spanish or Portuguese. These continue today. The first strategy aimed at linguistic and cultural assimilation through direct imposition of the national language, leading to submersion or fast transitional programs. The second strategy involved transitional and some exceptional maintenance programs. In most cases, diverse bilingual methods were introduced, where the Indian languages played a subordinate role as languages of instruction and initial alphabetization.

Today, the debate about indigenous education centers around two fundamental issues. On the macro-political and anthropological level, a powerful alternative to assimilation has emerged that strives for the transformation of the existing nation states into plurilingual and pluricultural polities who should approach existing diversity from an enrichment perspective. This orientation proposes that autochthonous First Nations, African descent, and European heritage participate as three distinct roots in the forging of a new type of nation and of Latin American integration that should reconcile national unity with the preservation of cultural and linguistic diversity.

The second issue refers to the micro-political dimension of curriculum and the cultural, pedagogical, and linguistic organization of the schools. In view of previous failures with submersion and fast transitional programs, a number of new modalities have emerged since the 1970s. In most countries, bilingual and bicultural programs designed to help preserve and foster indigenous languages gave way to the new concept of "intercultural bilingual education" (IBE) in the early 1990s except in Colombia, which preserves its definition of "ethno-education" (see table 30.1).

Content matters and competencies from indigenous funds of knowledge, as well as from national programs, should be integrated into a culturally and pedagogically appropriate curriculum, giving priority to the indigenous content and worldviews to redress historical imbalance. First, children should know and appropriate their own culture in order to build a solid base of competencies, values and ethnic identity (the intracultural component). They should then proceed to learn content matters from the national and global societies in order to integrate knowledge and competencies from several sources without diluting them (the intercultural component).

Under the label of "intercultural education for all," a relationship of mutual understanding and respect should involve the countries' whole school population. Mainstream students are supposed to learn about indigenous cultures right from the start and are expected to develop positive values toward diversity through a process of knowing, recognizing, and valorizing the other cultures (Gallardo et al. 2005). In areas of high indigenous population density, these students should learn one of the indigenous languages of the region in

Table 30.1. Indigenous peoples, population, and languages in Latin America

Country and date of latest national census	Total national population	Indigenous peoples	Indigenous population		Indigenous languages	Political status of indigenous languages
			#	%		
Argentina (2001)	36,260,160	30	600,329	1.6	15	Languages of education
Belize (2000)	232,111	4	38,562	16.6	4	----------
Bolivia (2001)	8,090,732	36	5,358,107	66.2	33	Co-official with Spanish
Brazil (2000)	169,872,856	241	734,127	0.4	186	Languages of education
Chile (2002)	15,116,435	9	692,192	4.6	6	Languages of education
Colombia (2005)	41,468,384	83	1,392,623	3.3	65	Co-official with Spanish
Costa Rica (2000)	3,810,179	8	65,548	1.7	7	----------
Ecuador (2001)	12,156,608	12	830,418	6.8	12	Official regional use
El Salvador (2007)	5,744,113	3	13,310	0.2	1	---------
French Guyana (1999)	201,996	6	3,900	1.9	6	Languages of education
Guatemala (2002)	11,237,196	24	4,487,026	39.9	24	National languages
Guyana (2001)	751,223	9	68,819	9.1	9	Languages of education
Honduras (2001)	6,076,885	7	440,313	7.2	6	Languages of education
Mexico (2010)	112,322,757	67	6,695,228	6.0	64	National languages
Nicaragua (2005)	5,142,098	9	292,244	5.7	6	Of official regional use
Panama (2000)	2,839,177	8	285,231	10.0	8	Languages of education
Paraguay (2002)	5,163,198	20	108,308	2.0	20	Guarani as co-official
Peru (2008)	28,220,764	43	3,919,314	13.9	43	Of official regional use
Surinam (2006)	436,935	5	6,601	1,5	5	---------

Country and date of latest national census	Total national population	Indigenous peoples	Indigenous population		Indigenous languages	Political status of indigenous languages
			#	%		
Uruguay (2004)	3,241,003	0	115,118	3.5	0	- - - - - - - - -
Venezuela (2001)	23,054,210	37	534,816	2.3	37	Co-official with Spanish
Latin America	479,754,341	661	29,491,090	6.1%	557	

Source: Adapted and updated from López (2009: 3)

Bolivia, Mexico, and some other countries (Albó & Anaya 2004; López 2005, 2009; Schmelkes 2006).

A more radical discourse has emerged since the end of the twentieth century, especially in Bolivia and Ecuador, which proposes *decolonization* of society and education to overcome the historical submission of indigenous culture and exclusion of its funds of knowledge. It demands the recognition of equal status for both worldviews and of epistemic rights for indigenous peoples, that is, the right to produce authoritative knowledge and the power to propose it (Quijano 2000).

Which curriculum and pedagogical approach and what functional language distribution will be able to integrate overall cultural and linguistic aims with academic achievement and empowerment in the context of prevailing asymmetric power relations?

The officially adopted intercultural, bilingual model establishes the right to mother-tongue literacy and content teaching, plus Spanish or Portuguese as a second language for students who have an indigenous language as their first language (L1). The indigenous languages should be taught as second language (L2), where the European language is the students' stronger language (Albó 2002). No doubt such a curriculum would be more appropriate, both from a pedagogical and psycholinguistic perspective, and from the standpoint of the official goals of language maintenance and cultural development. However, historical discrimination and a pervasive diglossic ideology deeply rooted in both mainstream and indigenous teachers' and parents' attitudes raise high barriers against implementation. Although proposals based on research about the common underlying proficiency and the transfer hypothesis were introduced since the 1980s (Hamel 1988: López 1995, 2005), they could overcome resistance only in exceptional cases. Especially in the Andean and the Mesoamerican macro-areas, cultural and language maintenance education does not yet constitute a solid, well-organized, and accepted educational practice. The most widespread modality still is transitional "Castillanization," which teaches literacy and content areas in Spanish and makes use of indigenous languages as the initial medium of instruction where necessary (Hamel 2008b). By and large, indigenous education still contributes more to ongoing language shift and loss than to maintenance and revitalization.

In contrast to official and mainstream education, an increasing number of experimental school projects and other local initiatives have engaged in new ways of improving indigenous education since the 1980s. They establish novel relations between academic achievement and bilingual language use. Most experimental projects claim as their goal the maintenance or revitalization of Indian cultures and languages. Paradoxically, they comply much more appropriately with the new laws of educational and linguistic rights, as well as with the official IBE programs, than does de facto mainstream indigenous education. Notwithstanding this, they are regarded as marginal or experimental both inside and outside the system.

From Immigrant to Elite Bilingual Education

The history of European and, to a lesser extent, Middle East and Asian immigration to Latin America is well documented. I will limit my analysis to linguistic groups other than speakers of Spanish and Portuguese. Argentina, Brazil, Chile, Paraguay, and Uruguay absorbed about 90 percent of the European immigration to Latin America. During the period of massive immigration (1875–1930), Spaniards and Italians represented the largest immigrant groups in most countries, followed by the British, Germans, Polish, Yugoslavians (mainly Croatians), and French. Throughout that time, about 1.5 million Italians migrated to Argentina; and 1.5 million to Brazil. More than 100,000 British citizens (mainly Welsh and Irish) and about 120,000 Germans settled in Argentina, 250,000 Germans in Brazil, and 200,000 in Chile (see Baily & Miguez 2003). For 1990, estimates establish some 500,000 German speakers and almost 12 million citizens of German decent in Brazil, 300,000 speakers and one million descendants for Argentina, and 20,000 speakers out of 200,000 descendants for Chile.

In Argentina, rapid and pacific assimilation in the cities and the construction of a national identity based on Argentine Spanish monolingualism was largely due to the integrative force of Argentina's impressive socioeconomic development and to the high academic level of public education (Axelrud 1999). Lower-class Italians and Poles assimilated more rapidly than middle-class British, French, or Germans. In rural areas, in contrast, European migrants formed large enclave communities that preserved their ethnolinguistic loyalty into the second half of the twentieth century.

In all Latin American countries, mainly the British (English, Welsh, and Irish), as well as French-, and German-speaking settlers, founded their own schools and other social institutions to preserve their languages, traditions, and endogamic kinship relations. Most of these schools went through three historical phases, and some of them reached a fourth stage. They were founded as monolingual community or heritage language schools in the nineteenth century or early twentieth century to provide the children of the settlers with appropriate education, especially in rural areas where no other schooling was available. Teaching was conducted entirely in the immigrant language in most cases, and students from outside the community were rarely admitted.

In a second phase, settlers brought over teachers from their heritage countries, and the national language was introduced almost as a foreign language to provide the language skills necessary in dealing with the external society. Content matters were usually taught entirely in the immigrant language to foster language maintenance. In their third phase, immigrant schools gradually weakened their character of being enclave and ethnic community schools and joined the group of national elite schools, opening their doors to the children of the countries' economic and power elites. Although many alumni became leading public personalities over time, those schools with formal support from their countries of origin never lost their ambiguous status of being considered both national *and* foreign. Due to shrinking numbers of immigrants and ongoing language shift, education in these schools gradually became bilingual. Two convergent processes triggered significant changes in curriculum and language policy. As the immigrant schools became attractive to the national elites, they had to offer a curriculum that could satisfy the educational needs of their new customers. At the same time, general education laws promulgated during the last quarter of the nineteenth century established requirements for private institutions that sought state recognition and certification. The increasingly nationalist governments wanted to establish a new power relationship by extending their control over those schools, to cultivate patriotism among their students and thus contribute to the assimilation of the immigrant communities.

Permanent negotiations and the attempt to conciliate sometimes divergent orientations led to a wide array of bilingual curricula. Today, some schools teach the national syllabus as the core curriculum and the foreign language area as an extracurricular program. In most cases, a dual system of parallel curricula developed in each language, each with its own faculty and management. The schools have to hire teachers with quite different qualifications for each language and content area (Banfi & Day 2004). Very often, the requirements of each system increase the study load and unnecessarily double certain content matters taught in both languages. Many schools established segregated tracks, separating the descendents of immigrants as native speakers from students who learn the immigrant language as a foreign language.

In sum, many of the private bilingual schools basically combine two types of approaches. The bilingual immigrant students are exposed to a strong component of L1 literacy development and content teaching, whereas the monolingual national-language group is often schooled in immersion or strong L2 programs in the foreign language at entrance level. These syllabuses integrate the advantages of L1 development in one case and immersion in the immigrant/foreign language in the other as a means of developing highly proficient bilingualism within an enrichment perspective. Once an advanced threshold level of proficiency in both languages is achieved, the two cohorts can be integrated in a number of content areas that may be taught in either language.

In a fourth phase, those schools associated with prestigious and internationally powerful language communities developed into "global language schools" (Banfi & Day 2004) during the second half of the twentieth century. The era of globalization that began in the 1970s, which imposed a drastic reduction of state expenditures, severely affected public education and damaged a long history of outstanding quality and humanistic tradition in public education in the more developed countries. The decline in public education increased the relevance of international bilingual schools as part of the small group of elite institutes that offer modern, international technology and curriculum together with class segregation and the promise of molding the future leaders of business and politics at national and international level. Only those former heritage schools that were able to keep pace with the dynamics of swift globalization could compete with other top private schools for the offspring of the economic and political elite. In the neoliberal era, high-quality education has become an expensive commodity.

The transition from dual-language schools still rooted in their immigrant communities to modern, elite schools with strong links to global educational development is still under way (de Mejía 2008). A central asset when competing with other private elite schools is the global language schools' intensive plurilingual programs that are offered to students right from the start, with exchange and study-abroad opportunities in industrialized countries and improved studying and job opportunities for graduates. International degrees like the renowned International Baccalaureate add a cutting edge to the value of these institutions. Schools representing international languages in decline, such as French, German, or Japanese, offer English as a strong third language and advertise themselves as trilingual schools.

Elite bilingual schools share a model of enrichment plurilingualism as a societal perspective and additive bi- or multilingualism as an individual goal. None of the languages involved is under threat or stigmatized as inadequate for advanced content teaching or communication. And students are systematically encouraged, awarded, and recognized for the bi- or trilingual competence they develop in the world's "good" languages.

In the process of gradually integrating their communities into the host country's society, immigrant bilingual schools became a significant force for national development, in some cases providing models for the design of the public school system. At the same time, their development occasionally led to conflict and constant negotiation with national educational authorities. Both aspects—diverse educational cultures and programs as well as integration and reciprocal transfer—have shaped their identities and roles. The fact that plurilingualism was established as a visible and positive trademark in a domain of social prestige helped to introduce an enrichment perspective and to mitigate Latin American policies of building homogeneous and monolingual nation states.

Differences and Similarities in Indigenous and Elite Bilingual Education: Integration and Conflicting Orientations

The two systems under review certainly have little in common in terms of their socioeconomic context. They are located at the polar extremes of rich and poor. In most studies of educational outcomes, these differences are identified as basic determinants of achievement gaps. Whereas *immersion* education typically produces high achievement in elite schools, *submersion* leads to poor results in indigenous education. These striking disparities can be explained in terms of social-class differences and their consequences for overall quality, additive versus subtractive orientations, and the prestige attached to the languages involved.

Despite fundamental differences in a range of aspects, however, a number of sociolinguistic and curricular phenomena related to the languages involved in each system allow for cautious comparison. I will focus on a variety of challenges that could be subsumed under the heading of *integration*. Both systems exhibit problems of integration on various levels: (1) the internal integration of curriculum and school communities; (2) the national integration or indeed segregation from the country's political and cultural context; and (3) the integration into a global community of education and other international networks.

Elite Bilingual Schools

One significant challenge that affects most elite bilingual schools is internal integration, that is, how to incorporate languages, content matters, teaching methods into a well-structured curriculum. From the beginning, students often have to struggle with the implementation of two national curricula and separate teaching faculty who frequently are not fully bilingual and know little about the "other" language and curriculum. Such segregation runs counter to any pedagogical teaching strategy of integrating content and language learning. This also casts doubt on the soundness of an orientation toward additive bilingualism and enrichment biculturalism and it limits national integration of elite bilingual education (EBE) schools.

Conversely, global integration emerges as a decisive force in an era of national disintegration and internationalization. In fact, EBE in Latin America increasingly incorporates its members into the emerging global arena, creating new de-territorialized "third cultures." International networks encompass global management customs, the international community of science and technology, fashion, music, and other fields of culture, with their own discourses and language uses.

Although at first sight national and international integration may appear to be mutually exclusive targets, a pluralistic orientation of cultural and linguistic enrichment and intercultural learning could point to ways in which both objectives reinforce each other. In terms of language choice, they could open up a truly global arena where English plays a significant role, but plurilingualism is the main goal. Several languages could be included in their programs in flexible combinations.

Indigenous Education

Problems and challenges of integration emerge for indigenous education as well, though in different ways. Most countries in Latin America possess a national curriculum that engages in a complex relationship with the curriculum needs and practices of IBE for indigenous populations. Education and language planning for such programs pose problems that can be traced to similar levels of internal, external, or national and international integration.

As a consequence of structural tensions between the national curriculum and local needs, a number of contradictions arise for the internal integration of the intercultural and bilingual component of IBE. Content matters and competencies from indigenous funds of knowledge and world views, as well as from national programs, have to be integrated in a culturally and pedagogically adequate fashion. To design the appropriate curriculum, indigenous funds of knowledge need to be identified, recovered from oblivion and fragmentation, and systematized to serve as the pedagogical input for the indigenous part of the curriculum. The successful integration of such an intercultural curriculum presents significant challenges for curriculum design (Hamel 2009; López 2009). It has to avoid imbalance, unsuitable misrepresentation of indigenous knowledge funds via "Western" systematization and dichotomized juxtaposition. As we have seen, the role and the functional integration of the two languages and strategies for their teaching in diverse sociolinguistic conditions posit similar, yet unsolved, problems.

Similarly, the external or national integration of IBE still presents a number of unsolved challenges. To attend the specific local needs, an appropriate IBE curriculum requires a substantial degree of independence from the national curriculum, which is matter of conflict and negotiation. Some countries like Brazil, Colombia, or Venezuela allow advanced autonomy on the basis of a minimal common core, whereas countries like Mexico or Argentina impose the national curriculum with only slight adaptations.

Contrary to traditional stereotypes, indigenous communities participate actively in the process of globalization in various ways. International migration has become the hope of survival for millions of Indians throughout Latin America. Many migrants reinforce their ethnic identity and language use in their host countries in Latin America, the United States, or Europe, where they build up lively transnational, often trilingual communities and strengthen their ethnic citizenship. Their experiences abroad by themselves constitute powerful processes of education, learning, and reorientation for adults and children. Schools in both the home nations and the host countries reveal considerable difficulties and resistance when adapting to the new circumstances and needs of migrants, in general. They are even less prepared to deal with indigenous migration.

Increasingly, indigenous communities in Mexico demand multilingual education, including English, since they know that their destiny will take them northward across the border. Although educational authorities oppose such demands as disruptive, the migrants themselves show the pathways for innovation when they creatively integrate their own languages plus Spanish and English into a powerful communicative repertoire.

From Nationalist Ideologies to Plurilingual Policies in the Era of Globalization: Immigrant versus Foreign Languages, Regional versus Global Integration

Since independence, foreign-language policies in most Latin American countries have developed in close relationship to the construction of a homogenous nation-state, as I explained earlier. They reflected generalized interest in Europe and the influence of the main immigrant groups. Foreign-language learning was limited to the small elite that had access to secondary and tertiary education.

The most prestigious European languages offered in public education coincide with the presence of immigrant groups of French, English, Italian, and German origins. However, the official reasoning behind teaching these languages has usually been of an instrumental nature, without reference to these immigrant groups, since the general policy supported monolingualism in Spanish or Portuguese. Teaching French was justified given France's cultural weight; English, for its commercial importance; Italian, as the language of law and music; and German, representing philosophy and natural sciences. This ideological distinction between public and private spheres to substantiate language policy reflects a language policy and language ideology divergence that preserves its relevance today. The learning of foreign languages is shaped as a competence that does not relate to any territorial base and represents no threat to the national identity, unity, and loyalty of the nation's citizens as long as it is nobody's first language. The same language, however, when cultivated as the mother tongue and language of identity in immigrant communities, triggers stridently different attitudes and easily arouses deep-seated fears of national disintegration, as is evidenced during the period of immigrant language repression in Brazil between 1935 and 1955.

Regional Integration through Widespread Bilingualism

Since the 1990s, language policy in South America has been challenged by conflicting orientations between global integration via English and regional integration through massive Spanish-Portuguese bilingualism. The language policy of Mercosur (The Common Market of the Southern Cone) is a unique attempt at cultural and geolinguistic integration in the whole region, which reverses long-standing traditions and posits new alternatives for plurilingualism (Hamel 2003). At the beginning of the 1990s, four countries—Argentina, Brazil, Paraguay, and Uruguay—joined in a Common Market that should integrate not only their economies but also their peoples and cultures. Portuguese and Spanish were declared the Market's official languages.

Following independence, Argentina and Uruguay developed nationalistic policies that considered Brazil a military and economic menace. Therefore, Portuguese was excluded from learning at school and beyond. On the Brazilian side, the same military doctrine prevailed; Spanish, however, has always been present among the Brazilian elite, but it has played a fairly insignificant role as a foreign language compared to English and French. With the emergence of Mercosur, an integrationist enthusiasm broke out that tore down the historical barriers. All of a sudden, everyone wanted to learn the "other" language on both sides of the linguistic border. A common language policy evolved that pushed for a regional integration based on massive Portuguese-Spanish bilingualism which should be developed as early as possible in public education (Barrios 1996).

This language orientation was contested, however, by more pro-US sectors that favored English over the regional languages in education. Local language policy experts (Barrios 1996; Arnoux & Bein 1997) suggest that a direct confrontation between the two regional languages and English should be avoided. The official languages of Mercosur should be defined as *languages of integration and participation*, not as *foreign* languages, a conceptual distinction that separates them from English and other foreign languages. To create a new regional identity, a new communication system based on massive receptive bilingualism is encouraged, which ought to allow extensive interaction within the Common Market. The interesting difference with international language communities such as the English-speaking Commonwealth or the Francophonie is that, in the case of Mercosur, integration should not be constructed around *one* hegemonic language but on the basis of a bilingual system of communication and identity building grounded in two languages that have at the same time national, regional, and international status.

The language-policy debate is still not settled at the time of this writing. By 2012, the four member states had established similar regulations obliging each state to offer the "other" language in secondary education without yet making it compulsory. A globalizing influence intervenes through Spain's imperial policy to aggressively conquer the Spanish language teaching market in Brazil (and in the United States) through its Instituto Cervantes, attempting to push out Brazil's Hispanic neighbors as the natural language teaching providers and to subordinate Brazilian academia and Spanish teaching faculty (del Valle & Villa 2007).

Global Orientations: From Limited Plurilingualism to English Only?

In Latin America, the salient foreign language well into the twentieth century was French, followed by English, Italian, and German (Bein 1999; Bertolotti 2003). In many cases, two different European languages were taught throughout secondary school. Given traditionally strong "multilingualism-as-a-problem" orientations in countries with a high percentage of indigenous population, foreign-language learning played a minor role in public education. Mexico, with two thousand miles of borderline with the United States, has until recently developed strikingly little interest and investment in English-language teaching in public education. The comparatively weak position of English in Mexico (Cifuentes et al. 1994) questions simplistic views of linguistic imperialism and language dominance and can only be interpreted as a covert language policy based on Mexican nationalism and deep-seated mistrust of the United States, rooted in Mexican-American history. Beyond specific reasons, as in the Mexican case, habitually low levels of achievement in foreign-language acquisition in many Latin American countries reflect nationalist and ethnocentric traditions shared with European colonial empires. In the past, advanced foreign-language instruction was to a large extent relegated to private education.

Over the twentieth century, the historical dominance of French and a plurilingual foreign-language policy gave way to the rise of English as the first, and increasingly only, foreign language considered in public education. Although smaller in numbers of learners, other foreign languages still maintain a significant role in elite bilingual schools and in European-language institutions. A new and rapidly growing player in the field is the Chinese Confucius Institute, with some 20 institutions in Latin America in 2009.

Spanish-English Bilingualism in Primary Education

A growing number of countries try to overcome their deficient foreign-language policy and identify integration into the globalizing process with English teaching. Among them, Colombia and Mexico developed programs to introduce a compulsory foreign language in primary education, which is usually English.

In 2004, Colombia launched the Programa Nacional de Bilingüismo, an ambitious plan to transform Colombia into a bilingual country by 2019. One foreign language, which is de facto English, is introduced in primary education. Students should reach a B1 level (threshold or pre-intermediate) by grade 11 as defined in the Common European Framework of Reference for Languages (CEFRL). In 2012, implementation was still under way in public education. Following initial research (de Mejía & Montes Rodríguez 2008), the program met a number of obstacles, including resistance by teachers, student, and parent communities, especially in lower-class public schools, who argue reduced perspectives of actually using English (de Mejía 2012).

To define what is meant by bilingualism and bilingual education is still an issue in Colombia. The international, elite, bilingual schools, which "use both Spanish and a foreign language as media of teaching and learning" (de Mejía & Montes Rodríguez 2008: 112) no doubt qualify as bilingual schools. A second group of national institutions offers a strong foreign-language component but does not teach content matters in both languages. The two types of schools, of which Colombia has about one hundred, all belong to the private sector. It remains a topic of debate whether bilingualism and bilingual education should be defined by extramural social use of both languages, by content and language-integrated learning or the standards achieved in the second or foreign language. Here and in other contexts, such as the United States, we observe an extension of the term "bilingual education" to contexts that were traditionally labeled as foreign-language teaching. No doubt the line between the two types of language education is blurred today. The main challenge of Colombia's ambitious program will certainly be to achieve the envisaged standards in English in the public school system, given the lack of trained teachers, the traditionally low levels of proficiency obtained, the lack of motivation, and even significant resistance to the national program. Here again, we come upon a case where an explicit top-down language policy launched by the government encounters resistance from a largely implicit language policy inherent in the language orientations felt by local communities. A much more diversified, locally grounded language policy that works bottom up is called for, as claimed by Hornberger (1997) and others.

The Mexican government launched an educational reform for its basic education (pre-primary to grade 9) in 2008 (Secretaría de Educación Pública 2010). As a major innovation, it introduces the teaching of "an additional language" in primary education that should continue in secondary schools. In practice "additional language" means English for the general system, where it should be taught from pre-primary grade 3 through the sixth grade of primary (1—6) and three grades of secondary school (7—9), for an average of 100 hours per year (SEP 2010). A B1 level should be attained by the end of ninth grade. In the subsystem of indigenous education, the local indigenous language is to be taught from pre-primary to the seventh grade (first grade of secondary education) for the same amount of time. Neither system envisages systematic content and language integrated learning.

Although implementation is still in its beginnings, a series of conceptual and structural problems are already in sight, of which I will identify only three. Lack of integration of the "additional language" into the curriculum will very likely cause problems in both systems. English will be taught from P3 through the whole period of literacy acquisition. It is difficult to envisage how a foreign language could be taught simultaneously without any integration of content matters and the coordinated development of cognitive academic language proficiency in both languages. This lack of integration becomes even worse in indigenous education, where the national curriculum will develop alongside a specific, non-integrated subject called "indigenous language." Such an approach implies, first, that the students' indigenous language has so far not had any curricular place and function in their education. Second, it contradicts existing legal dispositions that establish for indigenous children the linguistic right to have access to education and content matters *through* their language as well as through Spanish. Third and perhaps inadvertently, the language policy behind the new curriculum puts English to compete with the indigenous languages in primary and secondary education. Given the fact that schools from both systems exist side by side in many indigenous and mixed areas, the differentiated additional language teaching is bound to cause conflicts, especially in indigenous areas where up to 50 percent of the economically active population, including their families, face the prospect of migration to the United States. Those who might most urgently need at least basic skills in English to survive abroad will be excluded from English at school. Most likely, pressure will build up to trade indigenous language teaching for English in the indigenous system, a consequence that would further debilitate and pervert intercultural bilingual education.

Plurilingual Education as a Touchstone for Pluricultural States

When we analyse the language policies concerning the different types of societal multilingualism and bilingual education in Latin America, we realize that the common issue that allows for an integrated interpretation is the relationship between the allophone communities, the state, and the dominant society. Conservative nationalist forces still consider multilingualism to be a problem, although certain rights are recognized, and the assimilation of minorities is still their overall goal. For them, ethnolinguistic minorities constitute a threat since their loyalty to the state is questioned. Many of the minorities' members have internalized this hegemonic ideology and exhibit defensive attitudes regarding the legitimacy of their languages. Here, a new language policy needs to be developed to transform the relationship that the dominant *and* the subordinate actors maintain vis-à-vis the prevailing language constellation.

Bilingual communities and their educational institutions at the two poles of societal stratification may contribute significantly to this transformation in their own ways. They can join their voices with those in growing sectors in most Latin American societies who increasingly understand and appreciate diversity as an asset for societal enrichment and the broadening of democracy. In particular, they can demonstrate how the funds of knowledge stemming from their heritage languages and cultures—indigenous or immigrant—make significant contributions and enrich the dominant societies. The undeniable educational leadership of elite bilingual schools in developing enrichment plurilingualism can help to further erode the unsustainable ideologies of mono- or multilingualism. And the unquestionable legitimacy of indigenous claims to be recognized as peoples and to have their linguistic and educational rights respected converges with a growing awareness of indigenous cultural enrichment for the nations. This process may work toward the same goal from a different societal pole.

There can be little doubt that IBE for indigenous peoples will only succeed if pressure to assimilate is removed as a result of significant changes in Latin American societies to embrace a pluricultural enrichment orientation. Such a transition to a pluricultural and plurilingual value system could open new ways of looking at immigrant and global bilingual schools in which heritage language knowledge may be equally considered a valuable resource for the nation as a whole. Furthermore, new light could be shed on the prospect of massive foreign-language learning in public education. Language and education policies for majorities and minorities can no longer be dismissed as marginal components of state policy. They have become a touchstone for appraising the quality of democracy, pluricultural commitment, and the construction of modern states in Latin America and elsewhere in the world.

References

Albó, X. 2002. *Educando en la diferencia. Hacia unas políticas interculturales y lingüísticas para el sistema educativo.* La Paz: Ministerio de Educación, UNICEF & CIPCA.

Albó, X., & Anaya, A. 2004. *Niños alegres, libres, expresivos: La audacia de la educación intercultural bilingüe en Bolivia.* La Paz: CIPCA & UNICEF.

Arnoux, E., & Bein, R. 1997. Problemas político-lingüísticos en la Argentina contemporánea. *Quo Vadis Romania? Zeitschrift für eine aktuelle Romanistik* 3: 50–65.

Axelrud, B. C. (1999). Alcances y proyecciones de la integración regional en Argentina. *Políticas Lingüísticas para América Latina. Actas del Congreso Internacional 1997,* 59–72. Buenos Aires: UBA.

Baily, S., & Míguez, E. J. (eds.) 2003. *Mass migration to modern Latin America.* Wilmington, DE: Scholarly Resources Inc.

Banfi, C., & Day, R. 2004. The evolution of bilingual schools in Argentina. *International Journal of Bilingual Education and Bilingualism* 7: 398–411.

Barrios, G. 1996. Planificación lingüística e integración regional: El Uruguay y la zona de frontera. In A. M. Trinidade & L. E. Behares (eds.), *Fronteiras, educação, inegração,* 83–110. Santa María: Pallotti.

Bein, R. 1999. El plurilingüismo como realidad lingüística, como representación sociolingüística y como estrategia glotopolítica. In E. Arnoux & R. Bein (eds.), *Prácticas y representaciones del lenguaje,* 191–216. Buenos Aires: Eudeba.

Bertolotti, V. (ed.) 2003. *Relevamiento de la enseñanza de lenguas romances en el Cono Sur.* Montevideo: Unión Latina.

Cifuentes B., Hidalgo, M., & Flores Farfán, J. A. 1994. The position of English in Mexico 1940–1993. In J. Fishman (ed.), *English World-Wide,* 113–38. Berlin: Walter de Gruyter.

de Mejía, A-M. 2008. Enrichment bilingual education in South America. In J. Cummins & N. H. Hornberger (eds.), *Encyclopedia of language education,* vol. 5, *Bilingual education,* 323–31. New York: Springer.

de Mejía, A. M. (2012) English language as intruder: The effects of English language education in Colombia and South America: A critical perspective. In V. Rapatahana & P. Bunce (eds.), *English language as hydra: Its impacts on non-English language cultures (Linguistic Diversity and Language Rights).* Clevedon, UK: Multilingual Matters.

de Mejía, A-M., & Montes Rodríguez, M. E. 2008. Points of contact of separate paths: A vision of bilingual education in Colombia. In C. Hélot & A-M. de Mejía (eds.), *Forging multilingual spaces. Integrated perspectives on majority and minority bilingual education,* 109–39. Clevedon: Multilingual Matters.

del Valle, J., & Villa, L. 2007. La lengua como recurso económico: Español S. A. y sus operaciones en Brasil. In J. del Valle (ed.), *La lengua, ¿patria común? Ideas e ideologías del español,* 97–142. Madrid: Iberoamericana,

Gallardo, A. et al. 2005. *Ideas centrales que orientan la elaboración de los programas de la asignatura de lengua y cultura indígena para la educación secundaria.* México: CGEIB.

Hamel, R. E. 1988. Determinantes sociolingüísticas de la educación indígena bilingüe. *Signos. Anuario de Humanidades* UAM-I: 319–76.

Hamel, R. E. 2003. Regional blocs as a barrier against English hegemony? The language policy of Mercosur in South America. In J. Maurais & M. A. Morris, (eds.). *Languages in a globalising World,* 111–42. Cambridge: Cambridge University Press.

Hamel, R. E. 2008a. Indigenous language policy and education in Mexico. In S. May & N. H. Hornberger (eds.), *Encyclopedia of Language and Education,* vol. 1, *Language policy and political issues in education.* 301–13. New York: Springer.

Hamel, R. E. 2008b. Bilingual education for indigenous communities. In J. Cummins & N. H. Hornberger (eds.), *Encyclopedia of language and education, vol. 5, Bilingual education.* 301–13. New York: Springer.

Hamel, R. E. 2008c. Plurilingual Latin America: Indigenous languages, immigrant languages, foreign languages: Towards an integrated policy of language and education. In C. Hélot, & A-M. de Mejía (eds.), *Forging multilingual spaces: Integrated perspectives on majority and minority bilingual education,* 58–108. Clevedon: Multilingual Matters.

Hamel, R. E. 2009. La noción de calidad desde las variables de equidad, diversidad y participación en la educación bilingüe intercultural. *Revista Guatemalteca de Educación* 1(1): 177–230.

Hamel, R. E. 2010. L'aménagement linguistique et la globalisation des langues du monde. *Télescope* 16(3): 1–21.

Hornberger, N.H. (ed.). 1997. *Indigenous literacies in the Americas: Language planning from the bottom up.* Berlin: Mouton de Gruyter.

López, L. E. 1995. La eficacia y validez de lo obvio: lecciones aprendidas desde la evaluación de procesos educativos bilingües. *Revista Paraguaya de Sociología* 34 (99): 27–62.

López, L. E. 2005. *De resquicios a boquerones. La EIB en Bolivia.* La Paz: GTZ, UNICEF & Plural Editores.

López, L. E. 2009. Reaching the unreached: Indigenous intercultural bilingual education in Latin America. Commission Background Study for EFA Global Monitoring Report 2009. UNESCO. http://unesdoc.unesco.org/images/0018/001866/186620e.pdf. Accessed 2011-03-30.

Monsonyi, E. E., & Rengifo, F. 1983. Fundamentos teóricos y programáticos de la educación intercultural bilingüe. In N. J. Rodríguez, E. Masferrer K., & R. Vargas Vega (eds.), *Educación, etnias y descolonización en América Latina,* 209–30. México: UNESCO & III.

Quijano, Aníbal 2000. Colonialidad del poder, eurocentrismo y América Latina. In E. Lander (ed.), *La colonialidad del saber: Eurocentrismo y ciencias sociales. Perspectivas latinoamericanas,* 201–45. Caracas: CLACSO.

Ruiz, R. 1984. Orientations in language planning. *NABE Journal* 8(2): 15–34.

Schmelkes, S. 2006. La interculturalidad en la educación básica. *Revista PRELAC* 3: 120–27.

Secretaría de Educación Pública. 2010. Curricular foundations: Preschool, elementary school, secondary school. Mexico: Secretaría de Educación Pública.

Sichra, I. (ed.). 2009. *Atlas sociolingüístico de pueblos indígenas en América Latina.* Cochabamba: PROEIB Andes, UNICEF & AECID.

CHAPTER 31

LANGUAGE POLICY, IDEOLOGY, AND ATTITUDES

KEY ISSUES IN WESTERN EUROPE

FRANÇOIS GRIN

ALTHOUGH Europe may be seen as less linguistically diverse than other continents (Skutnabb-Kangas 2000), it remains a part of the world where language issues have high saliency in scientific research, political debate, and media coverage.

Let us start by circumscribing the terrain addressed in this chapter. A list of the languages used in Europe depends on three sets of criteria. First, what counts as "Western" Europe and, more precisely, how far east does it extend? Secondly, what are the languages taken into account? Do we mean actors' mother tongue only, or should Europe's linguistic diversity be taken to include their foreign language skills? In either case, how should we deal with more complex situations, for example, when a person's main language is not the first language acquired as a child? Thirdly, do "languages used in Western Europe" mean any language at all, including those used by recent immigrants or even tourists visiting from other parts of the world, or do we mean the languages considered autochthonous to Western Europeand then, what is a proper basis for defining "autochthony"?

For the purposes of this chapter, let us define Western Europe as a set comprising the 27 member states of the European Union, plus Iceland, Norway and

Switzerland, and Europe's five "micro-states" (Andorra, Liechtenstein, Monaco, San Marino, and the Vatican). Because Pavlenko's entry in this *Handbook* (chapter 32) is specifically devoted to ex-Soviet republics (including Estonia, Latvia, and Lithuania), when discussing these countries, I will do so only with respect to the first of the three issues examined in this chapter, namely, language management in the institutions of the European Union. For those countries of the erstwhile "Eastern block" (Poland, the Czech Republic, Slovakia, Hungary, Slovenia, Romania, and Bulgaria) that are now part of the European Union, I shall do the same. For the same reason, the constituent parts of the former Yugoslavia (Croatia, Bosnia-Herzegovina, Serbia, Montenegro, Macedonia, and newly born Kosovo), with the exception of Slovenia as a European Union member state, will not be considered in this entry.

For our purposes, the core of Europe's linguistic diversity is residents' respective mother tongues. The concept of "mother tongue," or native language, is admittedly not fully satisfactory, but it remains widely used, and censuses as well as quantitative surveys consistently indicate that the overwhelming majority of respondents have no problem indicating their mother tongue. Even persons raised in more than one language usually find it quite easy to identify two mother tongues or more, without casting doubt on the very notion of mother tongue or even of identifiable "languages." This notion is what logically enables us to identify, by contrast, second- and foreign language learning as a language policy issue.

Finally, owing to contemporary migration flows, the scope of European multilingualism has markedly expanded. Across Western Europe, permanent residents include migrants speaking hundreds of languages that were previously absent from its linguistic landscape. Many immigrant languages (such as Turkish in Germany or Arabic in France) are now firmly part of Western Europe's linguistic makeup, raising associated policy issues.

Western Europe's linguistic diversity is a fluid reality where official national languages, autochthonous regional or minority languages, and immigrant languages meet, mix, and sometimes compete. In addition to the 23 official languages of the 27-member European Union, some 60 languages are described as regional or minority languages, yielding a total of 83. However, some of them, like Welsh, are spoken in one particular region only and counted only once, while others, like German in southern Demark and eastern Belgium, are used in more than one minority context, and may also be used as a national or official language in other states and hence be counted several times. Excluding double or treble counting, the total number of *different* autochthonous languages in Western Europe, including the 23 EU languages, its minority languages, as well as national and minority languages used in non-EU member states[1] can be estimated at somewhere between 55 and 60, including Yiddish and Romani as non-territorial languages (this total, however, does not include sign languages). As to the number of immigrant languages, there is no basis for producing a reliable estimate covering Western Europe as a whole.

Needless to say, the panoply of specific language policy issues that arise in various parts of Western Europe is endless. They also mesh with more general issues in different ways, and it would be illusory to try to account for them all here.[2] Therefore, this chapter emphasizes issues that are generally relevant across Western Europe. These are

- the management of communication in supra-, inter- or multinational structures, in particular the European Union;
- the protection and promotion of regional or minority languages;
- the linguistic dimensions of immigration and migrant integration.

These issues give rise to complex challenges, and one section is devoted to each. I shall attempt to characterize each of them by discussing distinct, sometimes opposing ways to address them, highlighting the ideological choices that underpin potentially conflicting approaches. The concluding section proposes an integrative assessment, before venturing suggestions regarding suitable policy responses to meet these challenges.

Communication in Multilingual Settings: Combining Efficiency and Fairness in the European Union

What is now the European Union (hereafter EU) emerged in the late 1950s as a six-member club of states with four official languages, namely Dutch, French, German, and Italian. The often-quoted "Regulation 1" of 1958 established the basic principle of equal treatment of the member states' official languages.[3] With successive waves of enlargement, most recently on January 1, 2007, the EU is now a supranational organization with a population of 500 million and 23 "official EU languages,"[4] in compliance with Article 55 of the Lisbon Treaty,[5] which came into force on December 1, 2009. EU legal provisions concerning languages, as well as their implications, are complex, and can only be sketched briefly here (Volman 2012). Article 314 of the Treaty states that all language versions of the Treaty are authentic; citizens have the right to use any of the Treaty languages to petition the European institutions (Article 20) and are entitled to a reply in the same language (Article 24). Changes in the rules governing the languages of the Union require unanimity of the Council (Article 342). This set of provisions reflects the commitment enshrined in Article 3, which stipulates that the Union "shall respect [Europe's] rich linguistic diversity."[6] Note that although this formulation amounts to a recognition of linguistic diversity as a core value of the Union, it is considerably more vague—and less binding—than a core *principle*, such as the free movement of goods, services, capital, and labor (Nic Shuibhne 2004).

A distinction must be made between two levels: first, the use of languages by EU institutions themselves, itself broken up into two parts, namely, internal operations versus communication between these institutions and the citizens of member states (or, more loosely, "European citizens"); secondly, the general linguistic landscape of Europe and the role of different languages across domains. Ultimately, these two levels cannot be considered in isolation from one another, which is why our discussion, which starts with the first level, will progressively broaden to encompass the second.

The touchstone of the EU's unique language regime is the concept of the "state languages" of member states, which are recognized as the 23 "official EU languages."[7] If all these languages must indeed be used, and considering that individual actors' language skills cannot be expected to encompass more than a couple of languages in addition to their respective mother tongues, the system must rely on other strategies, first and foremost translation and interpreting (hereafter T&I). In any *N*-language context, this implies $N \times (N\text{-}1)$ T&I directions, that is, 506 in the case of the EU. Ideally, a civil servant working for some EU institution at the Brussels headquarters should, for example, be able to draft an internal memo in any language she chooses (because it will be translated into the other 22), and receive her colleagues' comments in the language of her choice, because irrespective of the language used by these colleagues when drafting their comments, these would have been translated into the other 22 languages.

Actual practice, however, is much less multilingual. Full multilingualism is indeed guaranteed for most (though not all) communications between the EU and citizens[8]; and one major EU institution, the European Parliament, largely ensures that translation and interpretation are provided out of and into all the 23 languages, often using relay languages, a technique that partly circumvents the lack of translators and interpreters for unusual language pairs. But other EU institutions operate with a significantly less multilingual regime. For example, the European Commission conducts its internal business in a subset of three languages—in principle, English, German, and French, which have been labeled "languages of procedure" (Krämer 2010). In reality, however, English is by far the language most frequently used (Phillipson 2003; Volman, 2012); already in 2006, and considering the entirety of the texts (external as well as internal) sent to the Commission's translation services, English accounted for 72 percent of the original drafts (vs. 14 percent for French, 2.8 percent for German, and 10.8 percent for other languages; see Krämer 2010: 99; see also Gazzola 2006a: 43–56).

The EU's language regime inspires a large body of scientific commentary (e.g., Castiglione & Longman 2007; Arzoz 2008), and the frequently noted discrepancy between lofty multilingual ideals and the more mundane reality often raises criticism (e.g., Phillipson 2003, 2010; Ammon 2006). It has also given rise to a flurry of official documents (resolutions of the European Council; conclusions of the Presidency of the Union; reports to, resolutions by, and recommendations of the European Parliament; reports to and policy documents by the

Commission) whose recurring motifs are the reaffirmation of the equal status of the languages of the Union and of their importance to Europe's identity, as well as the need to promote multilingualism through language learning (see Hanf, Malacek, & Muir 2010 or Volman 2012 for recent overviews).

This stream of discourse is in itself revealing of the complexity of the problems at hand and of the extent of disagreement over how to manage efficient and fair communication in this multilingual setting. Most observers concur that it is difficult to design and run a language regime abstracting from the sociolinguistic realities experienced by citizens. Hence, the problem is not confined to working out an appropriate language regime for EU institutions (encompassing both internal and external communication), but to develop a sustainable approach to the management of multilingualism for the EU as a whole, including a vision of how Europeans should communicate with each other. This is why discussing language regimes for EU institutions leads us to turn to the broader question of managing multilingualism in the EU through appropriate policies. This connection is reflected in official discourse too, as can be seen in policy documents emanating from the European Commission (e.g., 2003, 2005), which frequently address foreign-language learning, a generally consensual issue.[9]

However, even relatively non-contentious proposals about the virtues of foreign language learning (not least because of the advantages this yields on the labor market) fall short of a clear political stand on the extent of societal multilingualism aimed at, let alone of an integrated language policy that would help to achieve this goal. This is particularly evident when discourse drifts toward language teaching techniques: even the most carefully documented considerations on *how* best to teach languages simply do not answer the questions of *what* languages should be taught and *why*, which require a policy analysis approach.

With respect to the persisting challenges of managing multilingualism, several strategies have been put forward, each of them harking back, explicitly or not, to a certain ideological stance regarding linguistic diversity. These strategies should not be seen as discrete and necessarily incompatible; they are related to each other in various ways and reflect a more complex intellectual geography. Four of them will be discussed here.

The "Panarchic" Model

This label (borrowed from Pool 1992; see also Pool 1996), denotes the fullest extent of multilingualism. As we have seen, this ideal is maintained in parts of EU operations. It rests on the dual justification of democratic participation (if the European Parliament, for example, is to be a fully democratic body, it must be possible for citizens to be elected independently of their language skills, and in any event, given the EU's competence in adopting legislation affecting all citizens, they are entitled to be informed about it in their own language) and of respect for Europe's linguistic and cultural heritage. It also embodies the principle of equal dignity of the member states. Yet this regime, because it entails a considerable effort in T&I,[10] is often criticized as unduly expensive, although the per-capita cost of the current regime (which admittedly falls short of panarchic multilingualism across EU institutions), is relatively modest: it can be estimated at some € 2.3 per year in 2006–2007 (Gazzola 2006b), an amount which is very likely to be well below the average citizen's willingness to pay (WTP) for multilingualism. The panarchic approach is also criticized by some on the grounds that it prevents the emergence of a unified political debate; they appear to assume, in line with John Stuart Mill ([1861] 1991: 428), that "among a people without fellow-feeling, especially if they read and speak different languages, the united public opinion, necessary to the working of representative government, cannot exist."

Oligarchic Regimes

These regimes, in which a subset of M languages out of N (where $1 < M < N$) is selected for EU business, come in many different forms. As noted above, one such regime, using three languages, is already implemented by the Commission for its internal business. Oligarchic regimes reduce the number of T&I directions required (e.g., in a three-language regime, no more than six directions, or three pairs, are needed). Oligarchic regimes are sometimes perceived as "natural," in the sense that they reflect, even if not strictly, the relative demolinguistic importance of different languages, since most oligarchies typically privilege the larger languages. This type of regime can take account of existing foreign language skills and open the way to an approach in terms of "disenfranchisement": the idea is to prioritize languages spoken either as a mother tongue or as a foreign language, thereby "disenfranchising" fewer people (Ginsburgh & Weber 2005). The problem of any oligarchic design, however, is precisely that it remains undemocratic because it offers unequal access to common affairs, and places an unfair language-learning burden on some citizens, but not on others who are lucky enough to be native speakers of one of the languages in the oligarchy. Some commentators have suggested that the countries whose language is among the official ones should pay out compensating subsidies to the others. However, even proponents of compensatory payments concede that they would be politically unlikely or even impracticable (van Parijs 2007).

"English Only"

Some commentators (e.g., van Parijs 2011) propose a radical solution and advocate the adoption of English as the only common language of European institutions, arguing that it already is the most widely known foreign language among European citizens, since 38 percent of them claim to be able to hold a conversation in it (European Commission 2006: 12). Arguments of economy are often put forward to this effect (Jones 2000). Yet there are a number of weaknesses in the "English-only" approach even from a cost-benefit perspective. The first is that it ignores the considerable language-learning burden that it places on all nonnative speakers of English, that is, some 85 percent of the population of the EU (even more if non-EU countries of Western Europe are taken into account). Adopting a common language does not reduce costs: it merely shifts them. The second is that despite sustained investment in English as a foreign language, only a small minority of learners achieves a level of fluency in it that gives them a degree of confidence comparable to what they have in their mother tongue. Closer examination of figures from the 2005 Eurobarometer (European Commission 2006) reveals that only 7% of EU citizens report having a "very good" level of English as a foreign language; 17%, a "good" level; and 11%, a "basic" level. Fluency in English simply cannot be considered a universal "basic skill," and all but the most fluent nonnative speakers remain at a notable disadvantage. Using only English also gives rise, in the aggregate, to considerable financial transfers to native speakers of English who are, by comparison, largely exempted from the need to learn foreign languages. The value of these transfers can be evaluated at billions of Euros annually (Grin 2005). It is hardly surprising that the British government has decided to lower the amount of foreign-language teaching that schools are required to offer, which saves time and financial resources that can be invested elsewhere, while communicational costs are borne by non-Anglophones. The suggestion that Europe should use one language only arguably implies considerable intangible, symbolic effects as well, and these may, in turn, carry financial implications that favor English speakers. These effects stem, in particular, from a privileged position in the areas of culture and science (Durand 2002; Ammon & Carli 2007).

In order to deflect some of this criticism, some applied linguists are arguing that English, when used as a lingua franca, is no longer "owned" by native speakers of the language, and is being appropriated and changed by nonnative users. This process allegedly deprives native speakers of their privilege, because nonstandard forms are spreading (Jenkins 2007).[11] The "English as a lingua franca" (ELF) approach, however, is not tenable as a policy solution for several reasons. Quite apart from its logical inconsistency (in particular the recurring ambiguity over whether ELF is a language *different* form English, or a way of using a language that ultimately *is* English), let us first observe that the actual departures from native-speaker standard, as listed by ELF specialists, though linguistically intriguing, turn out to be rather anecdotal (the most frequently quoted example being nonnative speakers' tendency to drop the final "s" in the third person singular of conjugated verbs; see e.g., Seidlhofer et al. 2006). Then of course, learners of the language across the world do not ask to be taught "ELF": demand is for instruction in standard English. The immediate consequence is that the use of nonnative forms by nonnative speakers changes nothing to the status of English as an internationally dominant language and to the unequal distribution of language-learning effort that linguistic hegemony implies (Phillipson, 2006).[12] Obviously, these efficiency and fairness problems have nothing to do with the English language as such. The real issues have to do with power, and they would be similar if the internationally hegemonic language were Italian, Finnish, or Efik.

Esperanto

Despite an image of quaintness, Esperanto remains among the approaches put forward as a solution to the challenges of European multilingualism. Esperanto is a language designed in the late nineteenth century to be as easy to learn as possible and thus provide a means of communication accessible to all, while at the same time providing all the expressive resources offered by "natural" languages. Fiedler (2010: 12) points out that Esperanto "is the only system (among about 1000) that has managed the successful transition from a mere project to a genuine language" (see also Blanke 2000). Esperanto presents two main advantages: the amount of time needed to acquire it is estimated to be six to nine times less than for other foreign languages, depending on the L1-L2 pairs considered; and because it is virtually nobody's native language, it eschews the fairness issues that arise in the case of English—or any other "natural" language when used as an international language. Although Esperanto vocabulary is heavily Indo-European, its syntax is not, and tests indicate that native speakers of Indo-European languages are not, when learning it, at a significant advantage over, say, speakers of languages of the Sino-Tibetan group (Parkvall 2010.). Given the relative absence of consistent arguments against the adoption of Esperanto, the fact that it has never spread more widely may be explained by psychological resistance (Piron 1994), the complex dynamics of a "take-off point" (Pool 1991), or by the fact that it could pose a serious threat to the interests of the dominant languages (Gobbo 2009). In any event, these negative perceptions prevent "constructed" languages from being regarded, at least for now, as the solution to the challenges of multilingual communication in Europe.

Several additional strategies have been put forward as possible elements fitting into some of the broader approaches above. Three of them should be mentioned here.

The first is *intercomprehension*, or "receptive competence" (ten Thije & Zeevaert 2007; Conti & Grin 2008). Intercomprehension banks on the existence of strong similarities in vocabulary, morphology, and syntax between related languages (e.g., among Romance languages). With specifically designed pedagogical methods (whose development has often been supported by the European Commission, e.g., *EuRom4*; see Blanche-Benveniste 1995) and comparatively little learning effort, speakers of one language can read and understand texts in related languages, without aiming at speaking or writing them. A systematic implementation of intercomprehension could, therefore, allow for highly multilingual practices, because users could more frequently express themselves, orally or in writing, in their first language and be understood by their interlocutors, all this with lower T&I costs.

Another concept is that of *personal adoptive language*, or PAL, put forward by a group of intellectuals invited to draft a report on multilingualism for the European Commission (Maalouf 2008). A PAL is a language other than one's "language of identity" *and* one's "language of international communication" (meaning, in general, English). Learners would be encouraged to develop high-level competence in their PAL and in-depth knowledge of the associated culture. A PAL-based approach to foreign language education goes beyond the "1 + 2" model, because its emphasis on a close, almost intimate connection with another language and culture expresses a deep multilingual *ethos*, and firmly establishes the latter at the heart of citizens' human and social capital.

Finally, mention must be made of the considerable investment being made in computer-assisted or automatic translation (reviewed, e.g., in Arnold et al. 2008). The development of language technologies lowers the cost of translation, and thus makes multilingualism a more cost-effective solution, mainly by generating rough translations that save translator time, it being understood that professional human intervention remains necessary whenever a high-quality text in the target language is needed.

Well beyond mere communication, the quest for an efficient and fair solution to the challenges of European multilingualism also raises issues related to identity, culture, and geopolitical balance. This quest is far from over. At this stage, it seems likely that the most promising avenues are to be found by *combining* some the approaches just discussed, a perspective that we return to in the closing section.

Protecting and Promoting Regional or Minority Languages

A traditional issue confronting European multilingualism is that of the place of regional or minority languages (hereafter, RMLs), also called "lesser-used languages" (Sanguin 1993; Hogan-Brun & Wolff 2003). Europe numbers an estimated 50 million users of RMLs, including some countries' official languages spoken in another state as a minority language, like Swedish in Finland, Slovene in Austria, or Hungarian in Romania, in addition to "unique" RMLs like Breton or Welsh.

The underlying concept of "minority" refers to established definitions such as Capotorti's ([1979] 1991), which specifically apply to "citizens" of a state who have a "longstanding association" with it. This leaves out immigrant groups discussed in the following section. RML situations are very varied, and the common challenge confronting RMLs and their speakers is not necessarily political recognition, for example through the granting of some form of autonomy (although this may be relevant too), but the long-term maintenance of their language, as reflected in the number of speakers, the frequency with which it is used, and the range of domains in which it can be used. This is why it is relevant to focus on the protection and promotion of RMLs.

The extent of recognition of RMLs in Europe and the range of language rights currently enjoyed by their speakers has regularly increased over the past quarter century (CIEMEN 2001; EBLUL 2003). This required overcoming major political and cultural hurdles. One is nation-states' widespread inclination to view minorities as a threat to their geopolitical integrity; this hostility usually extends to the minorities' languages too. The history of countries like France, the United Kingdom, or Spain is notorious for the repression to which speakers of Breton, Welsh, and Basque—to quote but a few examples—have been subjected over decades or even centuries. The other obstacle was the trauma of the Second World War, during which ethnicity was so horrendously distorted and exploited by fascism that for years following the end of the war, the very notion of any ethno-cultural trait serving as a basis for defining groups was studiously avoided. For decades, the focus was almost exclusively placed on *human* rights and the latter's universality, pointedly avoiding any reference to minorities (e.g., in the Universal Declaration of Human Rights). The reassertion of local and regional languages and cultures was a gradual process, which eventually engendered the concept of *linguistic human rights* (Skutnabb-Kangas & Phillipson 1994).

In parallel, minority rights and language rights were spelled out in various legal instruments (see de Varennes 1996; Henrard 2000; Dunbar 2001; Ruiz-Vieytez 2006; Ruiz-Vieytez, & Dunbar 2007; Vizi, 2012). The most directly relevant here is the *European Charter for Regional or Minority Languages* (hereafter, the Charter), which was opened for signature in 1992 and came into force in 1998.[13] The Charter was developed in the context of the (currently) 47-member Council of Europe (as distinct from the EU); however, it has been embraced by the EU, which requires new members to sign and ratify the Charter.

The Charter is an original instrument whose provisions are formulated with reference to RMLs themselves rather than groups of users, and which abstains from mentioning "rights." Its focus is on the maintenance of small, often threatened languages as part of Europe's identity and cultural heritage. The Charter lists 68 concrete undertakings in the areas of education, judicial authorities, administrative authorities and public services, media, cultural activities and facilities, economic and social life, and transfrontier exchanges. For each language listed in the ratification instrument, contracting states must pick at least 35 of these 68 measures in such a way as to cover these seven areas, and specify the languages to which these provisions will apply as well as the part of the national territory on which they will be implemented. They must also agree to submit to an elaborate system of periodical reporting and monitoring, meant to ensure that the commitments they enter when ratifying the Charter are followed by effective action. The Charter, therefore, is a considerably more targeted instrument than other (much more classical) international treaties addressing the situation of minorities, like the *Framework Convention for the Protection of Persons Belonging to National Minorities.* By spelling out explicit measures, the Charter connects policy decisions with policy outcomes, thus lending itself to evaluation in the perspective of policy analysis.

The political and institutional context is, therefore, more favorable to RMLs now than it has been for most of the past two hundred years, since the rise of the model of the unified nation-state. RML communities no longer have to rely entirely on the goodwill of national governments in which members of a linguistic majority usually hold the balance of power. The inclusion in the Lisbon Treaty of the *European Charter of Fundamental Rights*, which explicitly prohibits discrimination on the grounds of language and/or membership of a minority, and which is binding upon EU member states, provides stronger legal safeguards for RMLs than at any time in history. The European Parliament has also been quite consistent in supporting RMLs, as reflected in a series of communications and resolutions adopted since the late 1970s (these, however, are not binding upon member states).

Although these framework conditions are indisputably better than they used to be, the actual fortunes of RMLs are uneven. Even in the most favorable contexts, the dynamics of language maintenance and shift are complex (Fishman 1991). They can be influenced through language policy, but the conditions for long-term maintenance are demanding, since they seem to require the co-presence of three conditions (Grin & Vaillancourt 1999; Grin 2003a): these are the *capacity* to use a language, which means it must be taught at school, ideally all the way through tertiary education; *opportunities* to use it, which implies its presence across domains, from public services to the media and economic activity; and of course people's *desire* to use it, which requires that the RML and its users are no longer subjected to ridicule, marginalization or even outright oppression, but on the contrary, that using an RML can be a source of pride and a tool for self-accomplishment.

Obviously, the prospects for individual languages are extremely different. Catalan, for example, enjoys a status and a range of use comparable to that of many national majority languages; even smaller languages like Welsh or Basque are stronger than they have been for decades or more; and the situation of RMLs used as a majority language in a neighboring state (like Danish in northern Germany or Slovene in the Austrian state of Carinthia) tends to be more secure, despite occasional tensions (as in the case, for example, of Hungarian in Slovakia). The future of other RMLs, however, remains a source of concern, particularly for those that have suffered long-term attrition and extensive domain loss, like Breton, Romansch, or Scottish Gaelic. The challenge of designing and implementing effective, cost-effective and democratic policies to ensure their vitality in the long run is undiminished.

Language in Migrant Integration Policies

Whereas Europe had long been a provider of migrants to other continents, it is now attracting them, and most countries in Western Europe (as defined earlier) register net population increases from migration.[14] Of the various issues discussed here, migration probably is, owing to its complexity, the one where the construction of social reality is most difficult to disentangle from discourse about it. The fact of migration, together with the associated discourse, explains why the notion of "multiculturalism" has, over the past 20 years, gained such a high profile in research, political debate, and the media (Inglis, 1996). Its importance is such that when talking about the management of diversity, many commentators turn out to be thinking mainly about migration-induced issues (Wieviorka 1998; Wieviorka & Ohana 2001).

In fact, European discourses about various manifestations of diversity remain somewhat disconnected from one another, although an increasing number of linkages are made in the linguistic human rights literature (Skutnabb-Kangas & Phillipson 1994; Kontra et al. 1999), as well as in some policy analysis approaches to diversity management (Grin 2003b). This situation may be contrasted with that of North America, where the debate on diversity management, particularly in political theory, has generally been more integrated (see e.g., Taylor 1994; Kymlicka & Patten 2003; Biles et al. 2008).

Actual debates surrounding migration are highly idiosyncratic, in the sense that they reflect local conditions which differ from one country to the next, whether in terms of political landscape, regulations regarding citizenship, or the social, cultural and linguistic make-up of the immigrant population. A crucial feature of contemporary migration is that it is no longer confined to impoverished groups fitting the traditional image of the huddled masses; in many Western European countries, migration flows are increasingly made up of highly trained professionals. Another significant change is that owing to the development of information and communication technologies and to the drop in the cost of international travel, the cost of maintaining contact with one's country of origin has declined in real terms, fundamentally altering the linguistic and cultural implications of migrating.

Much of the discussion on migration revolves around issues of cultural difference (including its religious components, with a strong focus on Islam) rather than language. Discussion on the linguistic dimensions involved mainly focuses on two issues: the acquisition, by immigrants, of the language of the country of residence; and the maintenance by immigrants of skills in their languages of origin. Perhaps paradoxically, given the highly complex nature of migration, there is a relative degree of consensus on how language policy should deal with these two issues.

The acquisition of the local language by immigrants is widely regarded as an incontrovertible necessity, for both social integration and economic advancement. Research in this field is country-specific, but available evidence confirms that language skills are key determinants of migrants' successful participation in social and political life (Extra 2008), and that lack of such skills generally entails a penalty on the labor market (e.g., Dustmann and van Soest 2002; Esser 2006). The question, however, quickly becomes political, because the sticky point is the extent to which the acquisition of citizenship (along with the rights that it carries) should be made legally conditional on the achievement of a certain level of competence in the receiving country's official language(s), or at least on some explicit, formalized commitment by the applicant that she will endeavor to acquire the language(s). There again, the approach to this question is country-specific; the general trend across Western Europe seems to be one toward making language requirements on immigrants binding and more explicit.

There is, however, one exception to this trend, which cuts right to the heart of the ideological debates on the handling of linguistic diversity. It has to do with the requirements placed on highly skilled professionals, such as diplomats or non-diplomatic officers working for international organizations, as well as professionals working abroad in the private sector—in short, the people usually called "expats," as distinct from "migrants." Expats appear to remain, at this time, almost entirely exempted from the rising requirements faced by "lower-end" migrants. Although legal status in the host country (e.g., in the form of the type of residency permit held) may be used as a basis for a differentiated approach, the frontier between the two categories of situations is often fuzzy, raising questions of equality of treatment: why should a Kurdish-speaking worker (who may have had little access to a formal education, let alone foreign-language instruction), now employed by a cleaning company in Frankfurt but intending to retire to his country of origin, be required to speak German, while an Indian financial analyst working at the Frankfurt branch of a multinational bank can get by on, or away with, English only? The reconfiguration of migration flows is forcing Western European societies to confront issues of language that had been assumed away until now.

The maintenance by migrants of skills in their "heritage language" (hereafter, HL) used to be regarded as proof of migrants' failure to "assimilate." However, the very notion of "assimilation" has generally been replaced, in Western European countries, by one of "integration," leaving more space for expressions of diversity, including competence in one's HL. For the past ten years, however, discussion has progressed one step further: not only are HL skills considered compatible (despite a few dissenting voices, such as Esser 2006) with the acquisition of the local language, but they are sometimes also seen as a potential asset. The latter notion can be approached at two levels. First, recent research indicates that immigrant children do better at school, in terms of both general cognitive development and learning of the local language, if they also develop literacy in the HL they speak at home (Cummins 2003; García 2008). Second, HLs may be regarded as financially profitable elements of human capital: evidence to this effect is still limited (Grin, Sfreddo, & Vaillancourt 2010), but as globalization deepens, the likelihood that HL skills provide economic advantage is likely to increase.[15] This suggests that HLs will strengthen their position as elements of Western Europe's linguistic landscape.

Assessment and Perspectives

Language issues in Western Europe are currently in a state of flux and may evolve in very different directions, making any prognosis risky. While it is tempting to think in terms of binary oppositions, the ideological terrain is not quite so simple: for example, the concerns of advocates of RMLs and of immigrants' language rights may or may not coincide; the defense of multilingualism may turn out to mean quite different things, depending on whether it is approached in terms of human capital with measurable financial returns, or in terms of the aggregate value (including symbolic components) of more or less diverse linguistic environments. Ideological differences in the approaches to what constitutes a desirable linguistic environment often crystallize in policy (Bourdieu et al. 2001; Ost 2009). Let us briefly review two issues related to the educational sphere, which has particular importance because education remains the main vehicle for language policy.

The contents, extent, and organization of *foreign-language teaching* raise two types of questions. Some have to do with *what* languages should be taught, to whom, up to what level of competence, and for what reasons; others have to do with *how* they should be taught. The first set of questions is obviously the most politically delicate, since it directly harks back to the societal choices Europeans have to make: how multilingual do they want their linguistic environment to be? Can choices in this respect be made more discerningly, possibly by giving differentiated answers for different tiers of this linguistic environment? The second set of questions is related to the efficiency of language education, which is itself the object of a considerable literature (see e.g., Beacco & Byram 2003), in which the advantages of bilingual education, including for majority language children, are ever more generally acknowledged (Baetens Beardsmore 1993; Baker 2001; Dewaele et al. 2003).

Language use in *higher education* probably is one of the most contentious issues nowadays. There is sharpening opposition between those advocating a broader role for English as "the" language of science (encompassing, in their view, research across disciplines, but also teaching across tiers of the university system), and whose position is usually put forward in blogs and newspapers' op-ed columns, and those who insist that tertiary education, whether for reasons of efficiency or for reasons of fairness, must take place through different languages (Carli & Ammon 2007). This ties in with geopolitically major issues related to the international ranking of countries' scientific performance (Sandelin & Sarafoglou 2004; Gazzola 2012). At this time, university authorities across Europe appear to be tempted by the former view, mostly because they see offering tuition in English as an easy way to attract foreign students, who typically pay higher fees. There is, however, no lack of dissenting voices, stressing that the stampede toward English in non-English-speaking countries can have a detrimental effect on the quality of teaching (Usunier 2010) and research (Lévy-Leblond 1996). The distributional, or fairness-related impacts of linguistic hegemony (no matter which language finds itself in the position of hegemon) are relatively straightforward, and could justify compensating transfers. Its allocative, or efficiency-related impacts are more conjectural, and hinge on two types of effects: the role of language in communicational effectiveness and the possible contribution of multilingualism to creativity and innovation. Research into these links may be seen as a priority, in order for the political debate to continue on a more informed basis.

Having taken stock, in this chapter, of the main language-related issues confronting contemporary Western Europe, let us in closing try to sum it up in terms of fundamental societal choices. Most of the questions currently being debated ultimately boil down to the following: first, what kind of linguistic environment do Europeans wish to live in? Do they want what has been called here "deep multilingualism" or a mere veneer of linguistic diversity on an increasingly uniform environment? Secondly, what are the policy measures that may nudge a complex reality toward the type of environment desired?

It may not be possible to answer the former question in the absolute, but a less ambitious approach may be considered, in which citizens are asked to compare more or less multilingual options, and to state what they prefer, and for what reasons. On this basis, language policy choices, instead of being inspired by superficial, often clichéd views, may be guided by a more sober assessment of what citizens want.

As to the latter question, it appears unlikely that any simple, unidimensional language policy can suffice to meet all the challenges confronting Europe today—efficient and fair communication in multilingual contexts, the preservation of the more threatened components of linguistic diversity, and the management of the linguistic implications of contemporary migration. Unless one advocates a linguistically uniform world, it is probably more reasonable for Europe to invest in the design of *complex language policies* (Grin, Sfreddo, & Vaillancourt 2010), in which several strategies are combined and complement each other: effective foreign-language teaching, some reliance on lingua franca models using English but also leaving space for more cost-effective and non-discriminatory alternatives like Esperanto, support for intercomprehension, and a widespread, along with a targeted use of translation and interpretation backed up by sophisticated language technologies. The implementation of complex language policies also requires states to coordinate their action, because linguistic environments are interdependent systems—just like environmental quality can only be ensured if appropriate measures are adopted internationally.

Complex language policies raise major conceptual challenges, and significant progress will also need to be made in data gathering and the monitoring, through well-designed indicator systems, of sociolinguistic realities. At the same time, the entire process must be held to impeccable standards of democracy—a notion which is keeping not only with the political ideals that Europe likes to pride itself on, but also with the principles of proper policy analysis, whose function is not to dictate choices, but to help citizens make them in a more informed way.

Acknowledgment

The author thanks Richard Cameron, Michele Gazzola, and Till Burckhardt for helpful comments and research assistance. The usual disclaimer applies.

Notes

1. Icelandic and Norwegian, but also Romansch in Switzerland, Catalan in Andorra, and even Latin in the Vatican.
2. Language issues in Europe are the object of an abundant literature, which it would be impossible to review here (e.g., Coulmas 1991; Calvet 1993; Labrie 1993; Ó Riagáin & Harrington 1996; Council of Europe 2000; Schena & Soliman 2002; Iannàccaro & Dell'Aquila 2002; Phillipson 2003; Gazzola 2006a, 2006b; Castiglione & Longman 2007; Arzoz 2008; Lauridsen & Toudic 2008; Hanf, Malacek, & Muir 2010, etc.). For a recent review of national-level language policies, see e.g., DGLFLF (2007) or Stickel (2009).
3. http://eur-lex.europa.eu/LexUriServ/site/en/consleg/1958/R/01958R0001–20070101-en.pdf. Accessed August 11, 2012.
4. Bulgarian, Czech, Danish, Dutch, English, Estonian, Finnish, French, German, Greek, Hungarian, Irish, Italian, Latvian, Lithuanian, Maltese, Polish, Portuguese, Romanian, Slovak, Slovene, Spanish, and Swedish; on terminology, see also note 8.
5. http://eur-lex.europa.eu/JOHtml.do?uri=OJ:C:2007:306:SOM:EN:HTML. Accessed August 11, 2012.

6. Article 22 of the Charter of Fundamental Rights, which is linked to the Treaty, contains similar wording; it applies to the implementation of EU law by member states and its transposition to national legislation.
7. "Official languages" are "languages used for legal and public administration purposes within a specified area of a country or reaching over the whole state [. . .]" (European Commission, 2006: 5). Thus, the concept of "official EU languages" does not include regional or minority languages, or the languages used by immigrants, called "non-indigenous languages" (ibid.).
8. Exceptions concern, for example, the activities related to EU programs for research and development. The language of the calls to tender, applications, financial reporting, scientific reports, and the associated administrative correspondence is overwhelmingly English, with occasional use of French, and barely any use of any other language.
9. Even then, consensus is not complete. The official line recommends what is known as the "1 + 2" or even "1 +> 2" model, according to which every European should, in addition to her mother tongue, learn two foreign languages (or more than two, hence the "bigger than" (>) sign preceding the "2"). However, it is easily shown (e.g., Grin 2006) that learning two out of 23 languages will generally fail to guarantee full intercommunication between participants in a group, as soon as the size of the group exceeds a few persons, *unless* one of the two foreign languages learned happens to be the same for everybody. Hence, foreign-language learning is bound to converge on a very narrow selection of languages, and, in practice, mainly one. This, in turn, makes the learning of a second foreign language redundant for communication purposes. It follows that the "1 +> 2 model" not only represents a truncated form of multilingualism: it is also sociolinguistically unsustainable, unless a set of accompanying measures aimed at ensuring "deep" multilingualism is also implemented.
10. The EU's translation and interpreting services are the largest in the world. For example, the European Commission alone employs some 1750 translators and some 850 interpreters (40% of the latter working free-lance; see Krämer, 2010: 100).
11. Some commentators (e.g., Nerrière, 2004) speak of "Globish," arguing that the English-based *koinê* used in much international communication no longer qualifies as proper English.
12. Native speakers of English can take courses where they learn to speak their native language "exolingually," that is, with nonnative interlocutors in mind. This may require them, for example, to avoid colloquialisms or arcane cultural references. Such courses, however, typically take a few hours, a far cry from the thousands of hours of learning and practice required for a nonnative speaker of English to achieve some degree of fluency in the language.
13. http://conventions.coe.int/treaty/en/Treaties/Html/148.htm. Accessed August 11, 2011. The Charter has been signed by 33 and ratified by 25 countries.
14. OECD population statistics and vital statistics. http://oberon.sourceoecd.org/vl=34828405/cl=34/nw=1/rpsv/dotstat.htm. Accessed Aug. 11, 2012.
15. The economic value of HLs was first identified as a policy issue in Australia in the 1970s (see Lo Bianco 1988).

References

Ammon, U. 2006. Language conflicts in the European Union: On finding a politically acceptable and practical solution for EU institutions that satisfies diverging interests. *International Journal of Applied Linguistics* 16: 319–38.

Arnold, D., Balkan, L., Meijer, S., Humphreys, R.L., & Sadler, L. 2008. *Machine translation: An introductory guide.* http://www.essex.ac.uk/linguistics/external/clmt/MTbook/. Accessed August 11, 2012.

Arzoz, X. (ed.). 2008. *Respecting linguistic diversity in the European Union.* Amsterdam: John Benjamins.

Baetens Beardsmore, H. 1993. *European models of bilingual education.* Clevedon, UK: Multilingual Matters.

Baker, Colin. 2001. *Foundations of bilingual education and bilingualism.* Clevedon, UK: Multilingual Matters.

Beacco, M., & Byram, M. 2003. *Guide for the development of language education policies in Europe. From linguistic diversity to plurilingual education.* Strasbourg: Coucil of Europe. http://www.coe.int/t/dg4/Linguistic/Source/FullGuide_En.pdf. Accessed September 2, 2010.

Biles, J., Burstein, M., & Frideres, J. (eds.). 2008. *Immigration and integration in Canada in the twenty-first century.* Montreal & Kingston: McGill-Queen's University Press.

Blanche-Benveniste, C. (ed.). 1995. *EUROM4. Méthode d'apprentissage simultané de quatre langues romanes: portugais, espagnol, italien, français.* Florence: Nuova Italia.

Blanke, D. 2000. Vom Entwurf zur Sprache. *Journal of Applied Linguistics* 15: 37–89

Bourdieu, P., De Swaan, A., Hagège, C., Fumaroli, M., & Wallerstein, I. 2001. Quelles langues pour une Europe démocratique? *Raisons politiques* 2: 41–64.

Calvet, L.-J. 1993. *L'Europe et ses langues.* Paris: Plon.

Capotorti, F. 1991. *Study on the rights of persons belonging to ethnic, religious and linguistic minorities* (UN Doc E/CN.4/Sub.2/384/Add.1–7). Geneva: United Nations Center for Human Rights.

Carli, A., & Ammon, U. (eds.). 2007. *Linguistic inequality in scientific communication today,* Theme issue 20 of the *AILA Review.*

Castiglione, D., & Longman, C. (eds.). 2007. *The language question in Europe and diverse societies: Political, legal and social perspectives.* Oxford: Hart Publishing.

CIEMEN. 2001. *Les nouvelles législations linguistiques dans l'Union européenne.* Barcelona: Editorial Mediterrània.

Conti, V., & Grin, F. (eds.). 2008. *S'entendre entre langues voisines: vers l'intercompréhension.* Geneva: Georg.

Coulmas, F. (ed.). 1991. *A language policy for the European community: Prospects and quandaries.* Berlin: Mouton de Gruyter.

Council of Europe. 2000. *Linguistic diversity for democratic citizenship in Europe.* Strasbourg: Council of Europe Publishing.

Cummins, J. 2003. *Bilingual children's mother tongue: Why is it important for education?* http://www.iteachilearn.com/cummins/mother.htm. Accessed September 2, 2010.

Délégation générale à la langue française et aux langues de France (DGLFLF). 2007. *Les politiques des langues en Europe.* Paris: Ministère de la culture.

de Varennes, F. 1996. *Language, minorities, and human rights*. The Hague: Martinus Nijhoff.

Dewaele, J.-M., Housen, A., & Wei, L. (eds.). 2003. *Bilingualism: Beyond basic principles*. Clevedon, UK: Multilingual Matters.

Dunbar, R. 2001. Minority language rights in international law. *International & Comparative Law Quarterly* 50, Part 1: 90–121.

Durand, C.-X. 2002. *La mise en place des monopoles du savoir*. Paris: L'Harmattan.

Dustmann, C., & van Soest, A. 2002. Language fluency and the earnings of immigrants. *Industrial Labor Relations Review* 55: 473–92.

Esser, H. 2006. *Migration, Sprache und Integration*. Berlin: Arbeitsstelle interkulturelle Konflikte und gesellschaftliche Integration, Wissenschaftszentrum Berlin für Sozialforschung.

European Bureau for Lesser Used Languages (EBLUL). 2003. *Vade-Mecum. A guide to international documents on lesser-used languages in Europe*. Brussels: EBLUL.

European Commission. 2003. *Promoting language learning and linguistic diversity: An action plan 2004–2006*. http://ec.europa.eu/education/doc/official/keydoc/actlang/act_lang_en.pdf. Accessed August 30, 2010.

European Commission. 2005. *A new framework strategy for multilingualism*. http://ec.europa.eu/education/policies/lang/doc/com596_en.pdf. Accessed August 11, 2012.

European Commission. 2006. *Europeans and their languages* (Eurobarometer Report), http://ec.europa.eu/education/languages/pdf/doc631_en.pdf. Accessed August 11, 2012.

Extra, Guus. 2008. Immigrant languages in continental Europe: Comparative perspectives. In U. Ammon & H. Haarmann (eds.), *Wieser encyclopedia: Western European languages*, 489–518. Klagenfurt: Wieser.

Fiedler, S. 2010. Approaches to fair linguistic communication. *European Journal of Language Policy* 2: 1–22.

Fishman, J. A. 1991. *Reversing language shift. Theoretical and empirical foundations of assistance to threatened languages*. Clevedon, UK: Multilingual Matters.

García, O. 2008. *Bilingual education in the 21st century: A global perspective*. Malden, MA: Wiley-Blackwell.

Gazzola, M. 2006a. La gestione del multilinguismo nell'Unione europea. In A. Carli (ed.), *Le sfide della politica linguistica di oggi*, 17–116. Milan: FrancoAngeli.

Gazzola, M. 2006b. Managing multilingualism in the European Union: Language policy evaluation for the European Parliament. *Language Policy* 5: 393–417.

Gazzola, M. 2012. The linguistic implications of academic performance indicators. *International Journal of the Sociology of Language* 216: 131–156.

Ginsburgh, V., & Weber, S. 2005. Language disenfranchisement in the European Union. *Journal of Common Market Studies* 43: 273–86.

Gobbo, F. 2009. *Fondamenti di interlinguistica ed esperantologia*. Milano: Raffaelo Cortina Editore.

Grin, F. 2003a. *Language policy evaluation and the European Charter for Regional or Minority Languages*. Basingstoke: Palgrave Macmillan.

Grin, F. 2003b. Diversity as paradigm, analytical device, and policy goal. In W. Kymlicka & A. Patten (eds.), *Language rights and political theory*, 169–88. Oxford: Oxford University Press.

Grin, F. 2005. *L'enseignement des langues étrangères comme politique publique*. Report to the Haut Conseil de l'évaluation de l'école. Paris: Ministère de l'éducation nationale. http://lesrapports.ladocumentationfrancaise.fr/BRP/054000678/0000.pdf. Accessed August 30, 2010.

Grin, F. 2006. Peut-on faire confiance au modèle '1+2'? Une évaluation critique des scénarios de communication dans l'Europe multilingue, *Revista de Llengua i Dret* 45: 217–31.

Grin, F., Sfreddo, C., & Vaillancourt, F. 2010: *The economics of the multilingual workplace.* New York: Routledge.

Grin, F., & Vaillancourt, F. 1999: *The cost-effectiveness of minority language policies: Case studies on Wales, Ireland, and the Basque Country.* Flensburg: European Centre for Minority Issues.

Hanf, D. Malacek, K., & Muir, E. (eds.). 2010: *Langues et construction européenne.* Brussels: Peter Lang.

Henrard, K. 2000. *Devising an adequate system of minority protection.* The Hague: Martinus Nijhoff.

Hogan-Brun, G., & Wolff, S. (eds.). 2003. *Minority languages in Europe: Framework, status, prospects.* Basingstoke: Palgrave Macmillan.

Iannàcaro, G. and Dell'Aquila, V. 2002. *Modelli europei di pianificazione linguistica.* Vich/Vigo di Fassa: Istitut Cultural Ladin.

Inglis, C. 1996. *Multiculturalism: New policy responses to diversity. UNESCO MOST Policy Papers 4.* http://www.unesco.org/most/pp4.htm. Accessed August 11, 2012.

Jenkins, J. 2007. *English as a lingua franca: Attitude and identity.* Oxford: Oxford University Press.

Jones, E. 2000: The case of a shared world language. In M. Casson and A. Godley (eds.), *Cultural factors in economic growth,* 210–35. Berlin: Springer.

Kontra, M. Phillipson, R. Skutnabb-Kangas, T., & Várady, T. (eds.), 1999. *Language: A right and a resource: Approaching linguistic human rights.* Budapest: Central European University Press.

Krämer, L. 2010: Le régime linguistique de la Commission européenne. In Hanf, Dominique, Malacek, Klaus, & Muir, Elise (eds.), *Langues et construction européenne,* 97–108. Brussels: Peter Lang.

Kymlicka, W., & Patten, A. (eds.). 2003. *Language rights and political theory.* Oxford: Oxford University Press.

Labrie, N. 1993. *La construction linguistique de la Communauté européenne.* Paris: Honoré Champion.

Lauridsen, K.M., & Toudic, Daniel (eds.). 2008. *Languages at work in Europe.* Göttingen: V&R Unipress.

Lévy-Leblond, J.-M. 1996. *La pierre de touche (la science à l'épreuve).* Paris: Gallimard.

Lo Bianco, J. 1988: Some economic implications of taking languages seriously. In R. J. Holton (ed.), *Immigration, Multiculturalism and economic development,* 83–95. Bedford Park: University of Southern Australia.

Maalouf, A. et al. 2008. *A rewarding challenge: How the multiplicity of languages could strengthen Europe.* http://ec.europa.eu/education/languages/pdf/doc1646_en.pdf. Accessed August 11, 2012.

Mill, J. S. 1991 [1861]. Considerations on representative government. In *On liberty and other essays,* 203–467. Oxford: Oxford University Press.

Nerrière, J.-P. 2004. Le globish. *Panoramiques* 69: 39–49.

Nic Shuibhne, N. 2004. Case comment on Kik v Office for Harmonisation in the Internal Market. *Common Market Law Review* 41: 1093–111.

Ó Riagáin, P., & Harrington, S. (eds.). 1996. *A language strategy for Europe: Retrospect and prospect.* Dublin: Bord na Gaeilge.

Ost, F. 2009. *Traduire. Défense et illustration du multilinguisme.* Paris: Fayard.

Parkvall, M. 2010. How European is Esperanto? *Language Problems and Language Planning* 34: 63–79.

Phillipson, R. 2003. *English-only Europe?* New York: Routledge.

Phillipson, R. 2006. Figuring out the Englishisation of Europe. In C. Leung & J. Jenkins (eds.), *Reconfiguring Europe: The contribution of applied linguistics*, 65–86. London: Equinox.

Phillipson, R. 2010. *Linguistic imperialism continued*. New York: Routledge.

Piron, C. 1994. *Le défi des langues. Du gâchis au bon sens*. Paris: L'Harmattan.

Pool, J. 1991. The world language problem. *Rationality and Society* 3: 21–31.

Pool, J. 1992. Multilingualism versus language policy: Alternative models for the EC. *Language and Society Papers, Linguistic Decisions Series*, No. LD20, Interdisciplinary Research Committee on Language and Society, University of Washington, Seattle.

Pool, J. 1996. Optimal language regimes for the European Union. *International Journal of the Sociology of Language* 21: 159–79.

Ruiz-Vieytez, E. 2006. *Minorías, inmigración y democracia en Europa*. Valencia: Tirant Lo Blanch.

Ruiz-Vieytez, E., & Dunbar, R. (eds.). 2007. *Human rights and diversity: New challenges for plural societies*. Bilbao: University of Deusto.

Sandelin, B., & Sarafoglou, N. 2004. Language and scientific publication statistics. *Language Problems & Language Planning* 28: 1–10.

Sanguin, A.-L. (ed.). 1993. *Les minorités ethniques en Europe*. Paris: L'Harmattan.

Schena, L., & Soliman, L.T. (eds.). 2002. *Prospettive linguistiche della nuova Europa*. Milan: Egea.

Seidlhofer, B., Breiteneder, A., & Pitzl, M.-L. 2006. English as a *lingua franca* in Europe: Challenges for applied linguistics. *Review of Applied Linguistics* 26: 3–34.

Skutnabb-Kangas, T. 2000. *Linguistic genocide in education or worldwide diversity and human rights*. Mahwah, NJ: Lawrence Erlbaum.

Skutnabb-Kangas, T., & Phillipson, R. (eds.), in collaboration with Rannut, M. 1994. *Linguistic human rights: Overcoming linguistic discrimination*. Berlin: Mouton de Gruyter.

Stickel, G. (ed.). 2009. *National and European language policies*. Frankfurt: Peter Lang.

Taylor, C. 1994. *Multiculturalism and the politics of recognition*. Princeton: Princeton University Press.

ten Thije, J., & Zeevaert, L. 2007. *Receptive multilingualism*. Amsterdam: John Benjamins.

Vizi, B. 2012. Minority Languages and Multilingualism in Europe and in the European Union. In Marácz, László & Rosello, Mireille (eds.), *Multilingual Europe, Multilingual Europeans*, 135–157. Amsterdam: Rodopi.

Volman, Y. 2012. The Lisbon Treaty and Linguistic Diversity: Policy and Practice in the European Institutions. In Marácz, László & Rosello, Mireille (eds.), *Multilingual Europe, Multilingual Europeans*, 37–56. Amsterdam: Rodopi.

Usunier, J.-C. 2010. Un plurilinguisme pragmatique face au mythe de l'anglais *lingua franca* de l'enseignement supérieur. In *Les enjeux du plurilinguisme pour la construction et la circulation des savoirs*, 37–48. Bern: Schweizerische Akademie der Geistes und Sozialwissenschaften.

van Parijs, P. 2007. Tackling the Anglophones' free ride: Fair linguistic cooperation with a global lingua franca. In U. Ammon & A. Carli (eds.). *Linguistic inequality in scientific communication today*, 72–86. Theme issue No. 20 of *AILA Review*.

van Parijs, P. 2011. *Linguistic justice for Europe and for the world*. Oxford: Oxford University Press.

Wieviorka, M. 1998. Is multiculturalism the solution?, *Ethnic and Racial Studies* 21: 881–910.

Wieviorka, M., & Ohana, J. 2001. *La différence culturelle. Une reformulation des débats*. Paris: Balland.

CHAPTER 32

LANGUAGE MANAGEMENT IN THE RUSSIAN EMPIRE, SOVIET UNION, AND POST-SOVIET COUNTRIES

ANETA PAVLENKO

This chapter examines four aspects of language management—nativization, linguistic assimilation, de-russification, and bilingual education—on the multilingual territory first occupied by the Russian Empire, then by the USSR, and then by the successor states. The rationale for this diachronic approach is twofold. The three settings are interrelated: post-Soviet developments cannot be fully understood outside of their historic context, just as the full impact of Soviet language policies can only be established through the post-Soviet lens. The historic overview also has comparative value: the nativization in the successor states can be productively compared with that of the early Soviet years, just as Soviet approaches to bilingual education can be traced all the way to the Russian Empire. In addition, sociolinguists generally lack familiarity with Russian and Soviet language management. Experts on Russian and Soviet language and nationality policies have traditionally resided in departments of history, political science, and Russian studies. As a result, the bulk of the research has appeared in journals such as *American Political Science Review*, *Soviet Studies*, *Russian Review*, and *Slavic Review*. This chapter draws on this literature alongside sociolinguistic publications. The focus of the discussion is on the territories occupied by the fourteen successor states and on their titular languages; the processes taking place in the Russian Federation are sufficiently different to merit a separate review.

Language Management in the Russian Empire (1721–1917)

Language management in the Russian Empire is commonly imagined as a coherent russification policy that aimed to erase linguistic and national differences. Yet historiographic studies show that the Russian government had no unified language and nationality policy: its strategies varied across territories and time periods, and were mediated by political, ethnic and religious concerns (Dowler 2001; Pavlenko 2011a; Suny 2001; Thaden 1981; Thaden & Thaden 1984; Weeks, 1996). The history of Russian language management can be divided into four periods: (1) autonomy (1721–1830), (2) selective russification (1830–1863), (3) expanding russification (1863–1905), and (4) retrenchment of russification (1905–1917).

1721–1830. The date of Russia's official transformation into an empire, 1721, is selected here as a starting point because prior to the eighteenth century the Tsardom of Russia had no language policy—Peter I was the first to articulate policies that ensured the autonomy of German as the language of administration and education in the Baltic provinces (Belikov & Krysin 2001). The territories of Finland and Poland enjoyed similar autonomy, while the non-autonomous territory of left-bank Ukraine experienced administrative russification, initiated by Catherine II (for incorporation dates, see table 32.1). The government also encouraged the provision of Russian-language education but the number of Russian schools was negligible and they could not compete with the well-developed system of education in German (Baltic provinces), Swedish (Finland), and Polish (Western provinces, contemporary Belarus, Lithuania, and right-bank Ukraine; Thaden & Thaden 1984).

1830–1863. During the second period, associated with the reign of Nicholas I (1825–1855) and following the Polish uprising of 1830, the government made more concerted efforts to "liberate" the Western provinces from seditious Polish influence and replaced Polish with Russian as the language of administration and instruction in state-supported schools (Thaden 1981; Weeks 1996). Similar policies were applied in the Caucasus, where Russian replaced Georgian in the

Table 32.1. Successor states: history of incorporation into the Russian Empire and the USSR

Current country name	Historic names*	Russian Empire: dates of incorporation	USSR: dates of incorporation
Armenia	Khanate of Erivan	1828 Treaty of Turkmanchay	1922 Transcaucasian SFSR 1936 Armenian SSR
Azerbaijan	Khanate of Nakhichevan Khanate of Talysh	1818 Treaty of Gulistan 1828 Treaty of Turkmanchay	1922 Transcaucasian SFSR 1936 Azerbaijanian SSR
Belarus	Western provinces	1654 annexation of Smolensk 1667 Treaty of Andrusovo 1772–1795 partitions of Poland	1919 Belorussian SSR 1921 Treaty of Riga partition 1922 Belorussian SSR 1924–6 transfer of additional territories from Russia 1940 annexation of Western Belorussia
Estonia	Estland Livland	1710 annexation 1721 Treaty of Nystad	1939–40 annexation 1940 Estonian SSR 1944 re-annexation, reestablishment of Estonian SSR
Finland	Grand Duchy of Finland	1809 Treaty of Frederikshavn	
Georgia	Kingdom of Kartli-Kakheti Kingdom of Imereti Abkhazia Svaneti Mingrelia	1783 Treaty of Georgievsk 1801 annexation 1809–11 annexation 1818 Treaty of Gulistan 1857 annexation	1922 Transcaucasian SFSR 1936 Georgian SSR
Kazakhstan	Kazakh Khanate Khanate of Kokand Turkestan	1822–4 incorporation of Middle and Small Hordes 1845–8 incorporation of Inner and Great Hordes	1918 Turkestan ASSR 1920 Kirgiz ASSR 1925 Kazakh ASSR 1936 Kazakh SSR
Kyrgyzstan	Khanate of Kokand	1855–63 annexation of Northern territories 1876 annexation of Southern territories	1918 Turkestan ASSR 1924 Karakirgiz Autonomous Region 1925 Kirgiz ASSR 1936 Kirgiz SSR
Latvia	Livland Latgale Kurland	1710 annexation of Livland 1721 Treaty of Nystad 1772 partition of Poland (Latgale) 1795 partition of Poland (Kurland)	1939–40 annexation 1940 Latvian SSR 1944 re-annexation, reestablishment of Latvian SSR

Continued

Table 32.1. (*Continued*)

Current country name	Historic names*	Russian Empire: dates of incorporation	USSR: dates of incorporation
Lithuania	Western provinces Lithuania	1772–1795 partitions of Poland	1939–40 annexation 1940 Lithuanian SSR 1944 re-annexation, reestablishment of Lithuanian SSR
Moldova	Bessarabia	1812 Treaty of Bucharest	1922 part of Ukrainian SSR 1924 Moldavian ASSR 1939–40 annexation of Bessarabia and Northern Bukovina 1940 Moldavian SSR 1944 re-annexation and reestablishment of Moldavian SSR
Poland	Polish-Lithuanian Commonwealth Congress Poland	1772–1795 partitions of Poland 1815 Congress of Vienna	
Tajikistan	Khanate of Kokand Emirate of Bukhara Turkestan	1866–76 annexation	1918 Turkestan ASSR 1924 Tajik ASSR in Uzbek SSR 1929 Tajik SSR
Turkmenistan	Khanate of Khiva Emirate of Bukhara Turkestan	1868–1887 annexation	1918 Turkestan ASSR 1924 Turkmen SSR
Ukraine	Western provinces Left-bank Ukraine (Little Russia) Right-bank Ukraine Crimea	1654 Treaty of Pereyaslav 1667 Treaty of Andrusovo 1772–1795 partitions of Poland 1782	1919 Ukrainian SSR 1922 Ukrainian SSR 1924 transfer of territories to RSFSR 1939 annexation of Western Ukraine 1944 re-annexation of Western Ukraine 1954 transfer of Crimea from Russia to Ukraine
Uzbekistan	Khanate of Kokand Emirate of Bukhara Khanate of Khiva	1865–1873 annexation	1918 Turkestan ASSR Bukharan People's Soviet Republic Khorezmi People's Soviet Republic 1924 Uzbek SSR

*In most cases there is no direct correspondence between the borders of the territory under the Russian Empire and the current country borders—over the three centuries, many borders had shifted repeatedly due to wars, partitions, and the efforts of Russian and Soviet administrators.

state schools (Hewitt 1985). Baltic provinces, Congress Poland, and Finland retained their autonomy, and Baltic provinces also developed Latvian- and Estonian-language elementary education for local peasants. Russian began making inroads as a subject but levels of Russian proficiency remained low (Thaden 1981; Thaden & Thaden 1984).

1863–1905. The third period began with ascension of Alexander II, whose reforms aimed to modernize the empire and to unify it through gradual russification. In Congress Poland, following the 1863 rebellion, Russian replaced Polish as the language of administration (1868), secondary education (mid-1860s), higher education (1869), court proceedings (1875), and primary education (1885) (Thaden 1981; Thaden & Thaden 1984; Weeks 1996). In the Western provinces, in an attempt to limit Polish influence suspected to be behind local nationalist movements, the authorities restricted the use of written Ukrainian, Belorussian, and Lithuanian (in Latin script) (Saunders 1995; Snyder 2003; Spires 2001; Weeks 2001). In the case of Ukrainian, for instance, the state banned the publication of scientific and instructional books (1863), state-sponsored instruction (1864), and import of Ukrainian books from abroad (1876). These measures aimed to prevent Ukrainian intelligentsia from establishing primary education in Ukrainian and from using it to transmit separatist ideas (Saunders 1995; Weeks 1996).

The administration of Alexander III, troubled by the influence of Baltic German elites, began enforcing Russian in the Baltic provinces: in administration and court proceedings (1889) and primary (late 1880s), secondary (1887–1892) and higher education (1889–1895) (Thaden 1981). Brief attempts to russify Finland made in 1890s were met with organized resistance and did not go very far (Thaden 1981). Non-Christian non-Russians (*inorodtsy*) continued to receive primary education in their native languages. The 1870 decree sanctioned transitional bilingual education for these learners that began in the pupils' native languages (often transcribed in Cyrillic) and then shifted to Russian, with the native language used as an aid and studied as a subject. This approach, developed by a turkologist Il'minskii, was widely applied in bilingual schools in the Volga region, Siberia, and Central Asia (Akiner 1997; Belikov & Krysin 2001; Dowler 1995, 2001; Edgar 2004; Fierman 1985).

1905–1917. After the 1905 revolution, the government adopted a more tolerant policy of linguistic accommodation, allowing for limited native language education among other non-Russians and for publications in a variety of languages, including the previously banned Ukrainian and Belorussian (Dowler 2001; Thaden 1981; Weeks 1996).

Together, the studies to date show that the term "russification" does not have a unitary meaning and may refer to: (a) administrative russification, that is, centralization of administrative practices and introduction of Russian legal norms; (b) religious russification, that is, conversion to Orthodox Christianity; (c) linguistic russification, that is, intentional spread of Russian as a second language (L2) through its use in administration, education, and the army (*obrusevanie*); and also (d) voluntary integration (*obrusenie*) (Suny 2001; Thaden 1981).

With regard to linguistic russification, the studies to date converge on three conclusions. First, they show that russification as a goal was mediated by political, economic, religious, and ethnic concerns and did not apply equally to all populations. The only people viewed as full-fledged members of the Russian nation were Orthodox Slavs: *Malorossy* (Little Russians, a contemporary term for Ukrainians) and *Belorusy* (White Russians or Belorussians). They were commonly perceived as dialect-speaking Russians—similar to Bavarians in Germany or Neapolitans in Italy—who had been forcibly separated from Great Russians by Poles. The adoption of russification measures with regard to these populations was facilitated by the fact that Belorussia and Ukraine did not have powerful elites who could maintain social order and lobby the imperial government for rights and privileges. In contrast, Baltic provinces, Finland, and Congress Poland, populated by Catholics and Lutherans, did not experience russification pressures until the second half, and sometimes the very end, of the nineteenth century, which is commonly explained by the high regard of the Russian administration for the efficiency of the local institutions and the loyalty of the Baltic German and Swedish (although not Polish) elites (Thaden 1981; Thaden & Thaden 1984). The subsequent russification is best understood as an attempt to subjugate local elites, rather than to convert locals into Russians, an enterprise viewed as impossible in the case of Poles (Weeks 1996). The assimilation of non-Christian ethnics was considered premature—they had to be converted to Christianity first and were, therefore, allowed to have primary education in their native languages (Dowler 1995, 2001).

Secondly, studies to date show that the implementation of russification policies was significantly hampered by the vast geography of Russia, the inadequacies of its bureaucratic machine, the scarcity of competent officials, the dearth of qualified teachers, and insufficient funding, in particular for schooling (Dowler 2001; Weeks 1996). Even when implemented, tsarist decrees were often ignored or circumvented, and sometimes they simply did not have the desired effect (Spires 2001). The ban on Ukrainian and Belorussian publications, for instance, directly affected only literate people who constituted a negligible segment of the population. Among Ukrainians, according to the 1897 Census, 91 percent were peasants (as were 98 percent of Belorussians), only 18.9 percent over the age of 10 were literate (as compared with 96.2 percent of Estonians), and only 0.36 percent progressed beyond primary school (Saunders 1995; Snyder 2003).

To account for the undeniable, if limited, success of russification, we need to consider not only top-down policies but also bottom-up integration processes. In the Russian Empire, as later in the USSR, russification (*obrusenie*) was often the result of social incentives and migration. Promotion in the imperial service offered an effective assimilation inducement for many upwardly mobile ethnic elites; Germans were particularly favored by the regime: their participation in the imperial government was vastly disproportionate to their small number and many attained high rank in the military, civil, and diplomatic service (Belikov & Krysin 2001; Saunders 1995; Snyder 2003; Thaden 1981; Weeks 1996).

Educational opportunities also attracted non-Christians, and in particular Jews, who did not have access to the social promotion ladder. Migration flows also facilitated russification: Russians settling in Siberia, Far East, Ukraine, Northern Caucasus, Kazakhstan, and Central Asia spread their language among the local populations, while non-Russians—oftentimes peasants in search of land—settling in the same areas were likely to use Russian as a lingua franca.

To sum up, for most of its history Russian language management was a laissez-faire affaire: "the prerevolutionary Russian government had neither the means nor even the desire to extirpate all non-Russian languages" (Weeks 2001: 96). Consistent russification began only in the second half of the nineteenth century and commonly "stopped with the elites" (Suny 2001: 41), while peasants, nomads, and members of other social strata retained their linguistic, cultural, religious, and tribal identities. In Central Asia and Transcaucasia, Russian never got beyond the main urban centers (Akiner 1997; Dowler 2001; Fierman 1985; Hewitt 1985). The russification measures also elicited the opposite of the desired outcome: instead of increasing the loyalty of the empire's subjects, they reinforced Polish national aspirations and inspired other nationalist movements (Pavlenko, 2011a; Snyder 2003; Thaden 1981; Weeks 2001).

Language Management in the USSR (1917–1991)

In the tumultuous years following the dissolution of the Russian Empire and the Bolshevik takeover, Estonia, Finland, Latvia, Lithuania, and Poland formed independent nation-states, while other imperial constituencies became the founding Soviet republics (table 32.1). Based on the key education reforms, the history of Soviet language management can be divided into four periods: (1) nativization (1918–1938); (2) introduction of Russian as L2 (1938–1958); (3) bilingual education (1958–1978); and (4) russification (1978–1988).

1918–1938. The first period of Soviet language planning, known as nativization (*korenizatsia*), involved the most complex and vast undertaking in the history of multilingual management: a development of institutional structures and educational establishments in more than a hundred languages, many of which existed only as oral vernaculars spoken by largely illiterate populations. Lenin and his followers opposed the idea of an obligatory state language and aimed to create a progressive state that "not only passively tolerated but actively institutionalized the existence of multiple nations and nationalities as fundamental constituents of the state and its citizenry" (Brubaker 1996: 23). Yet the Soviets did not inherit many nations in the modern sense of the word. To organize the population into stable, and economically and administratively viable, territorial and political units, Soviet nationality planners drew and redrew borders (see also table 32.1), formed new national territories (e.g., Turkmenistan), increased others (e.g., Belorussia), dissolved some ethnic groups (e.g., making Sarts into Uzbeks), reinforced boundaries between fluid identity categories (e.g., Uzbek/Tajik, Kazakh/Kirgiz), and created new languages and ethnicities (e.g., Moldavian/Moldavians) (Edgar 2004; Hirsch 2005; Martin 2001; Slezkine 1994). This approach reified and naturalized national categories and embedded them into the very fabric of Soviet life, with important consequences for the future.

Starting with a 1918 decree "On National Minority Schools" that required provision of instruction in local languages, Soviet language management involved systematic efforts to codify more than 40 languages, to standardize established languages, to transfer written languages from the Arabic script (associated with Islam) or Cyrillic (associated with russification) to the Latin alphabet (associated with internationalization and modernity), to translate world literature into local languages, to replace Russian-medium schools with native-language schools, to open schools in all native languages of Soviet populations, to eradicate illiteracy by teaching local populations to read and write—and sometimes even speak—in "their own" languages, to make local administrations and courts function in local languages, to train and appoint local cadres familiar with local languages and customs, and to encourage incoming officials to learn local languages (Akiner 1997; Alpatov 2000; Ewing 2006; Grenoble 2003; Kreindler 1982; Lewis 1972; Liber 1991; Pool 1978; Slezkine 1994; J. Smith 1997).

The results of these efforts included a dramatic rise in literacy levels (to 81.2 percent by 1939) and establishment of a compulsory primary education system in more than 70 languages (by 1938) and of secondary and higher education in several titular and minority languages (Ewing 2006; Grenoble 2003; Kreindler 1982; Simon 1991). Great successes were achieved in Armenia, Georgia, and Ukraine, in contrast, in Central Asia advances were complicated by interethnic strife, poverty, Islamic resistance, illiteracy, and scarcity of loyal local cadres and qualified Russian teachers (Edgar 2004; Fierman 1985; J. Smith 1997; M. Smith 1998).

1938–1958. By mid-1930s, the administration realized that "presiding over 192 languages and potentially 192 bureaucracies was not a very good idea after all" (Slezkine 1994: 445). The ensuing shift in language management had taken a three-prongued approach that involved status and acquisition planning (Russian) and corpus planning (local languages). In the area of status planning, Russian began to take over administrative functions previously fulfilled by minority languages, such as Chuvash (Alpatov 2000). In the area of acquisition planning, a 1938 decree "On the Obligatory Study of Russian Language in National Republic and Regional Schools" stressed the need for a common language and made Russian language and literature obligatory subjects in all non-Russian-medium schools. While some schools already offered Russian, the decree centralized the curriculum, increased the number of hours dedicated to

Russian, and made textbook publication and teacher training a priority (Blitstein 2001). In the area of corpus planning, several languages were transferred from the Latin to Cyrillic alphabet, to facilitate the study of Russian (Clement 2008; Hatcher 2008). Linguists also began to base grammars of the newly codified languages on Russian and to ensure that Russian was the main source of neologisms (Akiner 1997; Alpatov 2000; Grenoble 2003; Pool 1978). World War II disrupted the schooling efforts and after the war the education system had to be restored before it could be expanded. The authorities also extended Soviet-style education to the territories annexed as a result of the 1939 Molotov-Ribbentrop pact: Estonia, Latvia, Lithuania, Romanian Bessarabia and Northern Bukovina (divided between Moldavia and Ukraine), Finnish Karelia (joined to Russia) and Eastern Poland (subsequently Vilnius, the capital of Lithuania, Western Belorussia, and Western Ukraine) (Dunstan 1997; Snyder 2003).

This period is marked by achievement of near-universal literacy (98.5 percent by 1959), establishment of a general seven-year education (80 percent of students by 1958), the consolidation and expansion of titular languages, and the spread of L2 Russian facilitated by education, mass radio, and mass migrations, induced by war, urbanization, collectivization and industrialization (Deineko 1964; Lewis 1972; Simon 1991; M. Smith 1998). At the same time, titular children continued to be educated in titular-medium schools, in many of which the teaching of Russian was in dire straits due to teacher and textbook shortages and, in Central Asia, extremely low quality of instruction (Blitstein 2001; Dunstan 1997; Fierman 1985; M. Smith 1998).

1958–1978. The 1958 law "On Strengthening the Link between School and Life" abrogated Stalin's 1938 decree and gave parents the right to choose the primary language of instruction for their children and their secondary language. This law is frequently treated as a russification tool, but in actuality its implementation and impact varied across republics. A comparison of enrollments in 1955–1956 with those in 1980–1981 in table 32.2 shows that in the next two decades the enrollment in Russian-medium schools tripled in Belorussia and almost doubled in Ukraine, coinciding with language shift among the titulars (table 32.3). Significant increases were also experienced in Estonia and Latvia—these increases, however, reflected the in-migration of Russian-speakers. The increases in Armenia, Georgia, Lithuania, and Moldova were minor (between 1.1 percent and 3.9 percent), while in Azerbaijan, Kazakhstan, Kirgizia, Tajikistan, Turkmenistan, and Uzbekistan the enrollments increased in titular-medium schools. Furthermore, in most republics the second language remained mandatory: titular-medium schools continued to offer compulsory Russian classes and Russian-medium schools compulsory titular language instruction (Lipset 1967; Simon 1991). Minority language schooling, on the other hand, experienced further decrease in the number of languages used as the medium of instruction; at the same time the availability of non-Russian languages as subjects had increased and so did the highest grade level at which they were offered (Alpatov 2000; Anderson & Silver 1984, 1990; Lipset 1967).

Table 32.2. Student distribution by language of instruction in (day) secondary schools in Soviet republics and successor states

Republics/ Successor states	1955–1956*	1980–1981	1988–1989	1990–1991	1995–1996	2003–2004
Armenia						
Titular language	91.0%*	79.8%	80.5%	86.9%	98.4%	98.3%
Russian	9.0%	11.8%	15.1%		1.4%	1.7%
Minority languages		8.4%	4.4%		0.2%	
Azerbaijan					1996–1997	2005–2006
Titular language	77.0%*	83.4%	79.5%	86.1%	92.7%	93.0%
Russian	23.0%	14.2%	18.5%		7.1%	6.9%
Minority languages		2.4%	2.0%		0.2%	0.1%
Belorussia/Belarus						
Titular language	78.5%	35.0%	20.8%	20.8%	34.8%	24.5%
Russian	21.5%	65.0%	79.2%	79.2%	65.2%	74.2%
Minority languages						1.3%
Estonia						
Titular language	78.0%	67.5%	63.5%	63.2%	67.7%	75.0%
Russian	22.0%	32.5%	36.5%	36.8%	32.3%	24.1%
Minority languages						0.9%
Georgia						
Titular language	80.0%*	67.6%	66.6%		83.0%	86.4%
Russian	20.0%	21.1%	23.6%		6.6%	5.0%
Minority languages		11.3%	9.8%		10.4%	8.6%
Kazakhstan						
Titular language	34.0%*	33.0%	30.2%	32.4%	44.7%	54.9%
Russian	66.0%	64.2%	67.4%	65.1%	52.2%	40.8%
Minority languages		2.8%	2.4%	2.5%	3.1%	4.3%
Kirgizia/Kyrgyzstan						
Titular language	51.0%*	52.7%	52.4%	55.7%		62.1%
Russian	49.0%	34.0%	35.7%			23.8%
Minority languages		13.3%	11.9%			14.1%
Latvia						
Titular language	67.0%	55.9%	52.4%		60.4%	70.4%
Russian	33.0%	44.1%	47.6%		39.3%	29.2%
Minority languages					0.3%	0.4%
Lithuania						
Titular language	89.0%*	84.6%	82.2%	81.6%	86.0%	90.8%
Russian	11.0%	12.8%	15.8%	15.2%	10.6%	5.5%
Minority languages (Polish)		2.6%	2.0%	3.2%	3.4%	3.7%

Republics/ Successor states	1955–1956*	1980–1981	1988–1989	1990–1991	1995–1996	2003–2004
Moldavia/Moldova						
Titular language	67.0%*	63.1%	59.1%	60.2%	75.0%	79.3%
Russian	33.0%	36.9%	40.9%	39.8%	24.7%	20.6%
Minority languages					0.3%	0.1%
Tajikistan						2004–5
Titular language	84.0%*	64.4%	66.0%	67.2%	73.3%	73.7%
Russian	16.0%	10.0%	9.7%		1.2%	2.2%
Minority languages		25.6%	24.3%		25.5%	24.1%
Turkmenistan						
Titular language	79.0%*	78.0%	76.9%	76.6%		
Russian	21.0%	15.2%	16.0%			
Minority languages		6.8%	7.1%			
Ukraine						
Titular language	72.8%	54.6%	47.5%	47.9%	58.0%	74.9%
Russian	26.3%	44.5%	51.8%		41.0%	24.1%
Minority languages	0.9%	0.9%	0.7%		1.0%	
Uzbekistan						
Titular language	80.0%*	77.7%	76.8%	78.1%		
Russian	20.0%	13.6%	15.0%	12.2%		
Minority languages		8.7%	8.2%	9.7%		

*Data combine titular and minority schools. Belorussia, Estonia, and Latvia did not offer minority schooling in 1955–1956.

Sources: CIS Committee for Statistics (1995), Demoscope Weekly (www.demoscope.ru), Kul'turnoe Stroitel'stvo SSSR (Cultural development in the USSR). (1956) Moscow: Gosudarstvennoe statisticheskoe izdatel'stvo, 186–87; Landau & Kellner-Heinkele, 2001), Ryan (1990).

1978–1988. The last period of Soviet language management is marked by concerns about continuously low levels of Russian competence, in particular in Central Asia: the 1970 Census revealed that only 37.1 percent of non-Russians were fluent in L2 Russian (see also table 32.3). The 1978 decree "On Measures for Further Improving the Study and Teaching of the Russian Language in the Union Republics" signaled an expansion of russification efforts, which included increases in the number of hours devoted to Russian, earlier starting dates for Russian study in titular-medium schools, creation of new pedagogical materials and special enriched and intensive programs, and introduction of Russian lessons in non-Russian kindergartens. In the next decade, these efforts increased enrollment in Russian-medium schools everywhere but Tajikistan (table 32.2).

Table 32.3. Language maintenance and russification among the titulars in the Soviet republics and successor states*

Countries	1926	1939	1959	1970**	1979	1989	1995–2004
Armenia							
Titulars in the population	84.6%	82.8%	88.0%	88.6%	89.7%	93.3%	97.8%
Titular L1				99.8%		99.6%	
Russian L1			0.7%	0.2%	0.6%	0.3%	
Russian L2				23.3%	34.2%	44.3%	
Azerbaijan							**1999**
Titulars in the population	63.3%	58.4%	67.5%	73.8%	78.1%	82.7%	90.6%
Titular L1				98.9%		99.1%	99.7%
Russian L1			0.8%	0.7%	1.0%	0.4%	0.04%
Russian L2				14.9%	27.9%	31.7%	
Belarus							**1999**
Titulars in the population	80.6%	82.9%	81.1%	81.0%	79.4%	77.9%	81.2%
Titular L1			93.2%	90.1%	83.5%	80.2%	
Russian L1			6.8%	9.8%	16.5%	19.7%	
Russian L2				52.3%	62.9%	60.4%	
Estonia		**1934**					**2000**
Titulars in the population		88.1%	74.6%	68.2%	64.7%	61.5%	67.9%
Titular L1				99.2%	99.0%	98.9%	97.9%
Russian L1			0.7%	0.7%	1.0%	1.0%	
Russian L2				27.5%	23.1%	33.6%	68.2%
Georgia							**2002**
Titulars in the population	67.6%	61.4%	64.3%	66.8%	68.8%	70.1%	83.8%
Titular L1				99.4%	99.5%	99.7%	
Russian L1			0.4%	0.4%	0.5%	0.2%	
Russian L2				20.1%	25.5%	31.8%	
Kazakhstan							**1999**
Titulars in the population	57.1%	37.8%	30.0%	32.6%	36.0%	39.7%	53.4%
Titular L1			98.4%	98.9%	97.5%	98.6%	99.4%
Russian L1			0.8%	1.1%	1.4%	1.4%	
Russian L2				41.6%	50.6%	62.8%	75.0%
Kyrgyzstan							**1999**
Titulars in the population	66.8%	51.7%	40.5%	43.8%	47.9%	52.4%	64.9%
Titular L1			98.7%	99.7%	97.9%	99.5%	
Russian L1			0.2%	0.2%	0.4%	0.3%	
Russian L2				19.8%	28.5%	36.9%	

Countries	1926	1939	1959	1970**	1979	1989	1995–2004
Latvia	**1925**	**1935**					**2000**
Titulars in the population	73.4%	77.0%	62.0%	56.8%	53.7%	52.0%	57.7%
Titular L1			98.4%	98.1%	97.8%	97.4%	95.7%
Russian L1			1.5%	1.8%	2.2%	2.6%	3.5%
Russian L2				45.3%	58.3%	65.7%	75.8%
Lithuania							**2001**
Titulars in the population	84.2%		79.3%	80.1%	80.0%	79.6%	83.5%
Titulars L1				99.5%	99.7%	99.6%	96.7%
Russian L1			0.1%	0.2%	0.2%	0.3%	0.3%
Russian L2				34.8%	52.2%	37.4%	
Moldova							**2004**
Titulars in the population	30.1%		65.4%	64.6%	63.9%	64.5%	75.8%
Titular L1			98.2%	97.7%	96.5%	95.4%	78.4%
Russian L1			1.3%	2.0%	3.3%	4.3%	2.5%
Russian L2				33.9%	46.2%	53.3%	
Tajikistan							**2000**
Titulars in the population	74.6%	59.5%	53.1%	56.2%	58.8%	62.3%	79.9%
Titular L1			98.1%	99.4%	97.8%	99.2%	
Russian L1			0.4%	0.4%	0.5%	0.5%	
Russian L2				16.6%	29.6%	30.0%	
Turkmenistan							**1995**
Titulars in the population	73.8%	59.2%	60.9%	65.6%	68.4%	72.0%	77.0%
Titular L1			98.9%	99.3%	98.7%	99.2%	
Russian L1			0.5%	0.7%	0.7%	0.7%	
Russian L2				14.8%	24.2%	27.5%	22.2%
Ukraine							**2001**
Titulars in the population	80.1%	76.5%	76.8%	74.9%	73.6%	72.7%	77.8%
Titular L1	94.1%		93.5%	91.4%	89.1%	87.7%	85.2%
Russian L1	5.5%		6.5%	8.6%	10.9%	12.2%	14.8%
Russian L2				35.8%	51.8%	59.5%	
Uzbekistan							**1995**
Titulars in the population	65.9%	65.1%	62.2%	65.5%	68.7%	71.4%	75.8%
Titular L1			98.4%	98.9%	98.8%	98.7%	
Russian L1			0.3%	0.3%	0.4%	0.4%	
Russian L2				13.1%	52.9%	22.3%	

*Possible minor discrepancies between the data reported here and in other sources stem from the fact that some scholars use all-Union statistics on titular populations which include titulars living outside of the titular republics. The data reported here is limited to titulars residing in "their own" republics and successor states.

**The question about a second language was not asked prior to the 1970 Soviet Census

Sources of Soviet Census data: www.demoscope.ru; Goskomstat SSSR.

At the same time, the russification pressures set off protests in the Union republics (Raun 1985), and in between 1988 and 1990 led to adoption of laws strengthening the status of titular languages (Grenoble 2003; Simon 1991).

Together, studies of Soviet language management show that, contrary to the popular image, Soviet russification did not involve systematic replacement of *all* languages with Russian. As pointed out by Brubaker (1996), if the Soviet government were intent on "nation-destroying," it would have abolished national republics and made Russian the sole language of instruction. Instead, the USSR had pursued a dual course supporting the spread of Russian and the maintenance of titular and some minority languages (Anderson & Silver 1984; Blitstein 2001; Pool 1978; Silver 1978; Slezkine 1994; M. Smith 1998). As seen in table 32.2, in the last Soviet school years, in 11 of the republics most pupils were still enrolled in titular-medium schools.

The studies also reveal that Soviet language management was guided by a four-tiered hierarchy, based on the political status of respective languages: (1) Russian occupied the top place as a de facto state language; (2) it was followed by titular languages which served as de facto or, in Transcaucasia, de jure state languages, used in republican administration, media, and secondary and higher education; (3) the third place was occupied by languages of autonomous republics and regions—by the 1970s and 1980s their use as a medium of instruction had significantly decreased but they continued to be widely studied as subjects; (4) the last place was occupied by languages of autonomous districts and indigenous languages without any territorial rights (and often with small populations)—these languages received limited use in publishing and media and appeared in education only as subjects (Alpatov 2000; Anderson & Silver 1984, 1990; Grenoble 2003; Silver 1978; M. Smith 1998). This hierarchy provides a useful context for understanding the decline in minority language schooling, which cannot be fully explained by decisions from the center. In some cases, the decline was also precipitated by assimilationist tendencies by republican governments: for instance, in Georgia, the authorities transferred Abkhazian and Ossetian to Georgian script and closed native-language schools (1944–1953) (Grenoble 2003; Hewitt 1989). In other cases, local authorities simply did not see value in allocating resources to schooling in local languages, and yet in others it was parents who favored Russian-medium schools as a way to higher education and social advancement (Belikov & Krysin 2001; Blitstein 2001; Hewitt 1989; Kreindler 1982; Pool 1978).

Insofar as russification is concerned, the data available to date warrant the following conclusions. On the one hand, unlike the Russian Empire, the USSR succeeded in implementing administrative russification and in spreading the knowledge of Russian as L2. On the other hand, similar to imperial Russia, Soviet authorities achieved this outcome not only through top-down policies but also through social inducements: the adoption of L2 Russian was a pragmatic choice, particularly pronounced in language contact zones, created by mass migration, urbanization and industrialization (Silver 1978). The media played an important role in this process by using Russian to create a common multiethnic cultural space.

At the same time, the spread of L2 Russian was still limited: in 1989, only 47.5 percent of non-Russians declared L2 Russian competence (Goskomstat SSSR 1991). Undoubtedly, Census data are not entirely trustworthy. Data from Central Asia may over-represent the L2 Russian competence, with the 1979 spike in Uzbekistan a particularly egregious example of over-reporting by republican authorities to please the center (Akiner 1997). In turn, data from the Baltic republics may under-represent this competence. Post-Soviet census data in table 32.3 reveal an increase in levels of L2 Russian competence among the titulars in Estonia and Latvia. Given the political situation in both countries, this increase is best seen as a more realistic assessment than that in 1989, rather than as an actual improvement. Despite these inconsistencies, scholars concur that the spread of Russian as L2 was limited by the support of titular and minority languages, nationalist resistance, settlement and occupation patterns, lack of Russian teachers and, among rural populations, inefficient Russian instruction, low levels of contact with Russian speakers, and the actual lack of need for Russian (Alpatov 2000; Anderson & Silver 1990; Fierman 1985; Grenoble 2003; Pool 1978; Raun 1985; Silver 1976, 1978). The shift to L1 Russian was even less successful: after three decades of russification efforts, the total number of non-Russians with L1 Russian rose from 10.2 million (10.8 percent) in 1959 to 18.7 million (13.3 percent) in 1989 (Anderson & Silver 1990; see also table 32.3).

To sum up, Soviet language management efforts led to high levels of monolingualism among native speakers of Russian, high levels of native language maintenance and bilingualism among the titulars, and language shift among minority language speakers. Furthermore, just as in the Russian Empire, at the end Soviet language planning had an effect opposite to the one intended: the intensification of russification efforts fueled national resistance movements, while titular language support provided these movements with languages to rally around.

Language Management in Post-Soviet Countries (1991–2012)

In 1991, the fourteen successor states had common goals—to distance themselves from the Russian Federation and the Soviet past and to build legitimate nation-states. These goals were reflected in their language planning objectives: (a) to ensure that administration, education, and the media function predominantly in the titular language; (b) to remove Russian from the public space, (c) to de-russify the titular language corpus; (d) to replace Soviet-era place names with titular names; (e) to spread the knowledge of the titular language among those who did not know it; and (f) to increase levels of competence in English as an alternative to the former lingua franca Russian.

In the past two decades, these language planning efforts have been examined in several types of studies: (a) cross-country surveys (e.g., Iatsenko et al. 2008; Lebedeva 1995; Savoskul 2001); (b) surveys within single countries (e.g., Besters-Dilger 2009; Smagulova 2008); (c) ethnographic studies (e.g., Bilaniuk 2005; Brown 2007; Ciscel 2007; Korth 2005; Laitin 1998; Silova 2006); and (d) analyses of language and education policies (e.g., Landau & Kellner-Heinkele 2001; Pavlenko 2008a, 2008b). Together with post-Soviet census data and the Council of Europe (COE) country reports, these studies allow us to start putting together a coherent picture of post-Soviet language management. Based on the relative success of nativization, the successor states can be divided into four groups: (1) countries where nativization has been successfully completed; (2) countries where nativization has been successful but Russian retains importance; (3) countries where nativization has been successful among the titulars but not among minorities; (4) countries that retained some form of titular-Russian bilingualism. In what follows, I will discuss each group in turn, highlighting factors that mediate the outcomes of language planning efforts.

Mission Accomplished: Armenia, Lithuania, and Turkmenistan

Very different at first glance, Armenia, Lithuania, and Turkmenistan had three characteristics in common in 1991: strong national movements, fully developed languages (although Turkmen required further standardization), and titular populations with high levels of titular language loyalty who, throughout the Soviet era, continued to send their children to titular-medium schools (tables 32.2 and 32.3). These characteristics, however, do not differentiate them from Azerbaijan, Estonia, Georgia, and Latvia, where language development, titular language loyalty and national consciousness were just as high. What distinguished Armenia and Lithuania was the high proportion of titulars in the population (table 32.3) and a high level of titular language competence among the non-titulars: 37.5 percent of Russians in Lithuania and 33.8 percent in Armenia were fluent in titular languages, as compared to 14.4 percent in Azerbaijan, 15 percent in Estonia, 22.3 percent in Latvia, and 23.7 percent in Georgia (Goskomstat SSSR 1991).

Turkmenistan, in contrast, was more ethnically diverse and its Russian community had low levels of titular language competence (2.5 percent); there, nativization was facilitated by forceful governmental policies and low levels of Russian competence among the titulars (27.5 percent) (Goskomstat SSSR 1991). Under the autocratic president Niyazov, the authorities quickly completed script transition from Cyrillic to Latin (1993–1996) and by 2000 transformed the state structures, secondary and higher education, the media, and the semiotic landscape into Turkmen-only spaces (Abdurasulov 2007; Clement 2008; Landau & Kellner-Heinkele 2001; Permanov et al. 2010). Russian-medium schools were closed or turned into bilingual schools, which in 2001–2002 were converted into Turkmen-medium schools, with some Russian classes (Shustov 2009). In the informational space, the government banned Russian TV channels (mid-1990s), the import of Russian periodicals (2002), and Russian radio (2004) (Abdurasulov 2007). These measures, combined with employment and social promotion policies that marginalized non-Turkmen, led to significant out-migration of Russian speakers which further facilitated de-russification (Landau & Kellner-Heinkele 2001). After Niyazov's demise in 2006, his successor Berdymukhamedov reversed many of his policies and reintroduced Russian as a second language in kindergarten, school, and college curricula, raising the levels of Russian competence and enabling Turkmen students to study in Russia (Permanov et al., 2010).

Armenia also closed its Russian-medium schools (1993) and removed Russian from the titular curriculum. While some closings were prompted by out-migration, there was also an inverse relationship, with Russian-speaking migrants pointing to school closings among the reasons for their departure (Lebedeva 1995; Savoskul 2001). At present, only one state school, in the old believer village of Fioletovo, functions fully in Russian, while 35 more have Russian sections (Report on Armenia 2008). During the presidency of Kocharian (1998–2008), the state attitude toward Russian had changed and steps were made to retain Russian as part of Armenians' multilingual repertoires, including re-introduction of Russian as an obligatory foreign language in Armenian schools and creation of intensive Russian programs.

In Lithuania, the authorities reduced the number of Russian-medium schools and adopted language legislation that requires state language examinations for citizenship, secondary school graduation, and employment in the public and semipublic sector. At present, Lithuanian minority schools function in a bilingual mode, with part of the curriculum taught in Lithuanian (Bulajeva & Hogan-Brun 2008). In their Opinion on Lithuania (2003), COE experts expressed concerns about the lack of clear legal framework regarding minority language instruction, minority language broadcasts, and use of place names.

Overall, the three countries have been successful in establishing titular languages across all domains and relegating Russian to the dual role of a foreign language and a minority language (see also table 32.2). The key difference between them is in the role Russian plays for the titulars. At present in Armenia and Turkmenistan, the goal of language education is trilingual competence in the titular language, Russian (an obligatory foreign language), and another foreign language (Report on Armenia 2008; Permanov et al 2010). In Lithuania, the goal is multilingual competence in Lithuanian and an array of foreign languages, of which English is frequently selected first and Russian second (Bulajeva & Hogan-Brun 2008).

These differences are shaped by political and economic factors. Armenia has a long history of political conflicts with its Muslim neighbors, Azerbaijan and Turkey, and depends on Russia for military support. Russia is also home to a large Armenian diaspora and the main direction for its labor migration. Turkmenistan, oriented toward Turkey and the Islamic world, is reestablishing a relationship with Russia (Permanov et al 2010). In contrast, Lithuania is a member of the European Union (EU) and its orientation is toward Western Europe.

Russian as a Resource: Azerbaijan, Moldova, Uzbekistan, Tajikistan

In 1991, Azerbaijan, Moldova, Uzbekistan, and Tajikistan also had strong national movements, titulars with high levels of levels of titular language loyalty and competence, and small Russian communities (Fierman 2009; see also tables 32.2 and 32.3). The transition to independence plunged Tajikistan into civil war, while Azerbaijan, Moldova, and Uzbekistan began de-russification efforts, including the shift from Cyrillic to Latin script (Hatcher 2008; Landau & Kellner-Heinkele 2001; Savoskul 2001).

In Moldova, the authorities removed Russian from the titular curriculum, closed many Russian preschools and turned some Russian-medium schools into Moldovan-medium schools or, in the cities, moved them from the center to the periphery (Savoskul 2001). These radical reforms antagonized part of the population and led to a civil war and secession of Transnistria, which adopted three official languages: Moldovan (in Cyrillic), Russian, and Ukrainian. In the aftermath of the civil war, the political—albeit not economic—situation in the country had stabilized; subsequent attempts to upgrade the status of Russian have been unsuccessful but the identity of the state language as Moldovan or Romanian remains unresolved (Ciscel 2007, 2008). Secondary and higher education in Moldova functions in Moldovan/Romanian, and, for minorities, in Russian, with other languages taught as subjects. In Transnistria education is offered in the three official languages with the predominance of Russian.

In Azerbaijan, nativization has also been successful (Fierman 2009; Hatcher 2008; Landau & Kellner-Heinkele 2001) but Russian remains an important resource, as seen, for example, in the fact that in 2002, the country's first COE report was submitted in Russian. Azerbaijan is also among the few successor states that preserved its Russian school network: in the year 2005–2006, the country had 18 Russian-medium and 335 bilingual schools (Report on Azerbaijan 2007). Higher education functions in Azerbaijanian, Russian, English, and Turkish, and the de-russification efforts focused on the media, where access to Russian TV channels has been restricted (Iatsenko et al. 2008).

In Uzbekistan, the Uzbek script reform initiated in 1993 has not yet been finalized—its completion dates have been postponed first till 2005 and then till

2010, while the two scripts continue to co-exist (Sharifov 2007). The deadline for transfer to Uzbek as the sole language of administration was also extended, because state sector employees were used to rely on Russian, while Uzbek required further terminological development (Radnitz 2006). Russian also continues to be obligatory in Uzbek-medium schools. Higher education functions in Uzbek, Russian, Karakalpak, and English, with Russian remaining the language of professional literature, in particular in science and technology, as well as the preferred medium for the use of the internet (Landau & Kellner-Heinkele 2001; Nazaryan 2007; Radnitz 2006).

Tajikistan began the transition to Tajik as a state language (in Cyrillic) only in the mid-1990s, after the cessation of the civil war (Landau & Kellner-Heinkele 2001). Since Russian was officially recognized as a language of interethnic communication, documents continued to be produced in Tajik and Russian, with Tajik becoming a single language of administration only in 2010. Russian, however, still has a role to play. In 2004, Russian instruction again became obligatory in Tajik- and Uzbek-medium schools; higher education is offered in Tajik, Russian, and Uzbek; and dissertations, since 2005, once again have to be written in Russian (Nagzibekova 2008).

Studies to date show that while the functions of Russian have been significantly reduced in all four countries, it remains an important resource for administration, interethnic communication, academic cooperation, and information access. The shift to English as a lingua franca proved difficult to accomplish due to the lack of resources and qualified teachers: in Uzbekistan, for instance, most texts in use are Soviet-era textbooks that teach English through the medium of Russian (Hasanova 2007; Nazaryan 2007). Russian also constitutes an important linguistic resource for labor migrants to Russia, the majority of whom come from Moldova, Tajikistan, and Uzbekistan (Iatsenko et al. 2008; Laruelle 2007).

Resistance to Assimilation: Estonia, Georgia, Latvia

The titulars in Estonia, Georgia, and Latvia also had fully developed languages, high levels of national consciousness and titular language loyalty, and, in Estonia and Georgia, relatively low levels of Russian competence (tables 32.2 and 32.3). Politically, the three countries were oriented away from Russia and toward the West. It is not surprising then that all three had embarked on intensive de-russification efforts and successfully accomplished the de-russification and nativization of administration, linguistic landscape, and higher education. These language management efforts, however, have been hampered by low levels of titular language competence among the non-titulars who constitute large proportions of respective populations.

In Estonia and Latvia, the non-titulars are predominantly L1 Russian speakers who were sent by the Soviet authorities to industrialize the region

(Rannut 2008; Schmid 2008). In 1989, they constituted 42.5 percent of the population in Latvia and 32.5 percent in Estonia (Goskomstat SSSR 1991). The new governments did not perceive these communities as potential nation-state constituencies—Russian was declared a "foreign language" and titular languages were positioned as the only means of integration. To encourage Russian speakers to assimilate or emigrate, they adopted stringent *ius sanguinis* citizenship laws that offered automatic citizenship only to citizens or descendants of citizens of the inter-war republics. The descendants of those who settled there after the 1940 Soviet annexation had to apply for naturalization and pass a titular language test and a history and civics test. New language laws also imposed occupational restrictions and outlined a transition to titular-only education at all levels.

During the EU accession negotiations, European organizations sharply criticized Baltic language legislation and pressured Estonia and Latvia to amend citizenship, language, and education laws in order to protect minority rights (Jurado 2003; Rannut 2008; Schmid 2008). While several modifications were incorporated, COE observers are still dissatisfied with the slow rate of naturalization, high number of stateless residents, and the low levels of economic, social, and educational integration of minority language speakers (ECRI Report on Estonia 2010; ECRI Report on Latvia 2008; Opinion on Estonia 2006). In education, the key reason for the lack of integration is the perpetuation of the ethnically (self-)segregated school system inherited from the Soviet era. While Latvian authorities did want Russian-speakers to acquire Latvian competence, they did not want them to come en masse to Latvian schools; instead, integration was envisioned as latvianization of Russian schools (Björklund 2004; Silova 2006). Since 2004, 60 percent of the subjects in Russian-medium schools are taught in Latvian and 40 percent in Russian (Silova 2006; Schmid 2008). In Estonia, a similar transitional bilingual education model was adopted in 2007 starting with tenth grade (www.hm.ee).

In Georgia, the main challenge involves compactly settled Armenian and Azerbaijanian communities with low levels of Georgian competence. To this day, Russian may be used in communication between these communities and the state authorities because Armenians and Azerbaijanis may be more fluent in Russian than in Georgian, while Georgian authorities are much more likely to understand Russian than Armenian or Azerbaijanian (ICG 2006; Opinion on Georgia 2009). Language is also one of the points of contention between Georgia and secessionist Abkhazia and South Ossetia that resist the imposition of Georgian and favor native- and Russian-medium schooling (Hewitt 1989; Opinion on Georgia 2009). To increase titular-language competence, Georgian authorities have adopted a transitional bilingual education approach, similar to that in the Baltic countries: in the year 2010–2011, minority-medium schools began teaching social science subjects in Georgian (Opinion on Georgia 2009).

Several factors explain low levels of linguistic assimilation in the three countries. Demographically, the non-titulars are compactly settled and have no everyday need for the titular language nor the opportunity to practice it (ICG 2006; Laitin 1998; Rannut 2008; Siiner 2006). Aware of their second class status, minorities may also have low motivation for titular language study: in Georgia, for instance, educational and employment opportunities for minorities are so constrained that even those with excellent Georgian-language skills have little chance of social advancement (ICG 2006; Opinion on Georgia 2009). In Latvia, on the other hand, Russian-speakers, locked out of the state sector, created a thriving private sector, where the knowledge of Latvian is unnecessary (Commercio 2004). In educational settings, the learning of titular languages is hampered by insufficient resources, the lack of workable curricula, inadequate teacher preparation, shortages of bilingual textbooks, and, in adult education, inaccessibility of free instruction (ECRI Report on Estonia 2010; ECRI Report on Latvia 2008; Opinion on Estonia 2006; Opinion on Georgia 2009; Rannut 2008; Silova 2006).

Bilingualism: Belarus, Kazakhstan, Kyrgyzstan, and Ukraine

In addition to Latvia and Estonia, in 1991 four other states had large proportions of L1 Russian speakers: Kazakhstan (47.4 percent), Ukraine (33.2 percent), Belarus (32.3 percent), and Kyrgyzstan (25.6 percent) (Goskomstat SSSR 1991). Unlike Latvia and Estonia, these countries settled on a bilingual compromise.

Several factors explain the different approaches adopted in Estonia and Latvia on the one hand and Belarus, Kazakhstan, Kyrgyzstan, and Ukraine on the other, but two are central. The first is political orientation of the countries in question: Estonia and Latvia were oriented toward the West and the EU and wanted to sever the relationship with Russia, while Belarus, Kazakhstan, Kyrgyzstan, and Ukraine aimed to preserve political and economic ties with the Russian government. The second key factor is the russification of the titulars. In 1988–1989, Belarus, Kazakhstan, and Ukraine were the only republics where the majority of the students were enrolled in Russian-medium schools (table 32.2). Belarusians and Ukrainians also led the shift to Russian as L1 (table 32.3). Kazakhs and Kyrgyz favored titular languages in their census responses but for many it was a symbolic choice: in both countries, urban titulars favored Russian and often displayed low levels of titular language competence (Korth 2005; Landau & Kellner-Heinkele 2001; Smagulova 2008). Titular languages, in all four countries, were associated with the rural sphere and Russian with urbanization and modernity (Bilaniuk & Melnyk 2008; Giger & Sloboda 2008; Fierman 2009; Laitin 1998; Orusbaev et al. 2008).

The most spectacular failure of the de-russification process occurred in Belarus, where a popular vote in the 1995 national referendum made Russian the second state language. This vote showed that the extent of russification among Belarusians has been underrepresented in the Soviet Census data. The 1999 Belarusian Census revealed that Russian was the main language of 62.8 percent of ethnic Belarusians (www.belstat.gov.by) (see also Brown 2005). At present, Russian functions as the de facto main language in Belarus across all domains, from media to education, while Belarusian plays a symbolic function indexing the nation in official documents and public spaces (Brown 2005, 2007; Giger & Sloboda 2008). From a historic standpoint this outcome is not surprising: previous waves of Belorussian national revival were equally weak. The nineteenth century national movement lacked an urban base and support from abroad (Snyder 2003; Thaden & Thaden 1984), while belorussification of the 1920s was directly opposed by many russified Belorussians who saw the Belorussian republic as an artificial Soviet creation that cultivated a nonexistent titular nation (Hirsch 2005: 149–155).

Kazakhstan and Kyrgyzstan had stronger national movements but their titular languages had to be standardized and modernized before taking on a full range of functions. The two governments also wanted to prevent further out-migration of Russians who played important roles in the countries' economic infrastructure (Landau & Kellner-Heinkele 2001). To help negotiate the transitional period and to preserve political and economic stability, the authorities upgraded the status of Russian to that of official language (1995 in Kazakhstan, 2000 in Kyrgyzstan) and preserved the Cyrillic script in the titular languages. At the same time, both governments still aim to transfer all the paperwork to titular languages, but the process has been slowed down by internal resistance and low titular literacy skills among state employees (Fierman 2009; Orusbaev et al. 2008; Smagulova 2008). The goal of language education in Kazakhstan and Kyrgyzstan is trilingual competence in the titular language, Russian, and English. Secondary education is offered in the titular language and Russian and in a range of minority languages, with obligatory study of the titular languages in Russian-medium schools and Russian in titular-medium schools (Diatlenko 2010; Fierman 2006; Korth 2005; Orusbaev et al. 2008; Smagulova 2008). Higher education functions in Russian and the titular languages, with opportunities also available in some minority languages, English, and in Kyrgyzstan Turkish. Russian continues to dominate academic work, the media, and the internet (Orusbaev et al. 2008; Smagulova 2008; Uffelmann 2011). In the 2009 Census, 94.9% of adult Kyrgyz reported Russian as their second language (Diatlenko 2010).

Ukraine so far has preserved a single state language, but in August of 2012 the Ukrainian government passed a language law that enables adoption of Russian as a regional language by individual cities and regions. As in the other three countries, Soviet censuses under-represented the degree of russification of Ukrainians because many titulars indicated Ukrainian as their native language yet spoke Russian on the daily basis (Besters-Dilger 2009; Bilaniuk 2005; Kulyk 2010; Pavlenko, 2011b). The shift to L1 Russian has continued in the post-Soviet era (table 32.3), suggesting that, similar to Belarus, russification in Ukraine is a bottom-up process. Unlike Belarus, however, Ukraine also has a strong nationalist movement, centered in Western Ukraine and supported by the Ukrainian diaspora. As a result, the country is split along linguistic lines, with Ukrainian-dominant West favoring the idea of monolingual Ukraine, and Russian-speaking East and South pushing for a bilingual solution (Besters-Dilger 2009; Bilaniuk 2005; Bilaniuk & Melnyk 2008; Kulyk 2010). In the past two decades, the authorities have succeeded in making Ukrainian the main language of the administration, documentation, and education. This spread, however, has been achieved through legislative measures that were often less than democratic: in some contexts, for instance, the authorities determined the numbers of schools operating in particular languages on the basis of the ethnic composition of the population, ignoring the preferences of Russophone Ukrainians, and in others, most notably in the capital Kyiv, Russian-medium schools were transformed into Ukrainian-medium schools without any recourse to demographics or parental preferences (Pavlenko, 2011b). Protests were also elicited by laws that required the dubbing of Russian-language movies and TV shows (Besters-Dilger 2009).

At present, the linguistic situation in Belarus satisfies the majority of the population, but supporters of Belarusian language revival bemoan the demise of the language (Giger & Sloboda 2008). In contrast, in Kazakhstan, Kyrgyzstan, and Ukraine the uneasy compromise does not fully satisfy either side: supporters of full nativization perceive the continuous presence of Russian as a threat, while Russian-speakers are concerned about the reduction in the sphere of Russian use (in particular in the media), and decreasing numbers of Russian-language schools (Besters-Dilger 2009; Bilaniuk & Melnyk 2008; Diatlenko 2010; Pavlenko, 2011b; Orusbaev et al. 2008; Smagulova 2008). It remains to be seen how future governments will maintain the balance between these conflicting sets of demands.

Conclusions

Many observers have commented on the irony of the fact that the titular elites who most vocally protested the Soviet imposition of Russian have come to appreciate the need for a unifying state language and did not hesitate to adopt the same—and sometimes much harsher—measures to enforce titular languages (e.g., Björklund 2004). The studies to date show, however, that a lingua franca is not easy to eliminate. After the intense derussification of the 1990s, the sphere of Russian use in most successor states has narrowed yet the language did not go away nor was it replaced by English. Rather, Russian assumed a place alongside English as the lingua franca of the geopolitical region, as seen in the presidential websites and other official, business, and tourist-oriented sites of the successor states. The 2000s also witnessed a change of course in several countries, with Armenia, Tajikistan, Turkmenistan, and Uzbekistan reintroducing Russian in secondary school curricula, colleges, and, in Turkmenistan, even kindergartens (Nagzibekova 2008; Permanov et al. 2010). Yet the supply does not satisfy the demand – survey respondents in Armenia, Georgia, Kyrgyzstan, Moldova, and Tajikistan stated that Russian should be offered more widely in their countries (Iatsenko et al., 2008).

Behind this change is Russia's spectacular economic recovery in the late 1990s, a combined result of economic reforms and the rising world oil prices. The resurgence as a geopolitical power allowed Russia to reestablish its economic and political influence on parts of the former federation: in 2008, leading destinations for Russian foreign investments in the CIS were Belarus (58%), Ukraine (23.4%), Kazakhstan (7.4%), Armenia (4.3%), and Kyrgyzstan (3.8%) (Pavlenko in press). Russia is also the main labor market of the region, with remittances from labor migrants constituting a large proportion of the GDP of Tajikistan, Moldova, Georgia, Armenia, and Kyrgyzstan, the same countries whose survey respondents expressed the greatest desire for expanded Russian-language offerings. The new economic opportunities have led to revalorization and commodification of Russian as a useful tool in the new regional economy.

At the end, the juxtaposition of Russian, Soviet, and post-Soviet language management leaves us with a question regarding the relationship between states and their citizens: were Russian imperial authorities correct in assuming that it is only the citizens who are responsible for learning the languages of their states? Or did the early Soviet planners have it right when positing that states—and in particular new states—are also responsible for learning the languages of the citizens they inherited?

References

Abdurasulov, A. 2007. Russkie v Turkmenii: Razrushaia chary Rukhnamy [Russians in Turkmenistan: Destroying the spell of "Rukhnama"]. BBC News, August 3, 2007. http://news.bbc.co.uk/hi/russian/in_depth/newsid_6929000/6929162.stm. Accessed 7.23.10.

Akiner, Sh. 1997. Survey of the lexical influence of Russian on modern Uzbek (1870–1990). *Slavonic and East European Review* 75: 1–35.

Alpatov, V. 2000. *150 iazykov i politika: 1917–2000* [150 languages and politics: 1917–2000] Moscow: KRAFT + IV RAN.

Anderson, B., & Silver, B. 1984. Equality, efficiency, and politics in Soviet bilingual education policy, 1934–1980. *The American Political Science Review* 78(4): 1019–039.

Anderson, B., & Silver, B. 1990. Some factors in the linguistic and ethnic russification of Soviet nationalities: Is everyone becoming Russian? In L. Hajda, &

M. Beissinger (eds.), *The nationalities factor in Soviet politics and society*, 95–130. Boulder: Westview Press.

Belikov, V., & Krysin, L. 2001. *Sotsiolingvistika* [Sociolinguistics]. Moscow: Russian State University of the Humanities.

Besters-Dilger, J. (ed.). 2009. *Language policy and language situation in Ukraine: Analysis and recommendations*. Frankfurt: Peter Lang.

Bilaniuk, L. 2005. *Contested tongues: Language politics and cultural correction in Ukraine*. Ithaca, NY: Cornell University Press.

Bilaniuk, L., & Melnyk, S. 2008. A tense and shifting balance: Bilingualism and education in Ukraine. *International Journal of Bilingual Education and Bilingualism* 11: 340–72.

Björklund, F. 2004. Ethnic politics and the Soviet legacy in Latvian post-Communist education: The place of language. *Nationalism and Ethnic Politics* 10: 105–34.

Blitstein, P. 2001. Nation-building or russification? Obligatory Russian instruction in the Soviet non-Russian school, 1938–1953. In R. Suny & T. Martin (eds.), *A state of nations: Empire and nation-making in the age of Lenin and Stalin*, 253–74. New York: Oxford University Press.

Brown, A. 2005. Language and identity in Belarus. *Language Policy* 4: 311–32.

Brown, A. 2007. Status language planning in Belarus: An examination of written discourse in public spaces. *Language Policy* 6: 281–301.

Brubaker, R. 1996. *Nationalism reframed: Nationhood and the national question in the New Europe*. Cambridge: Cambridge University Press.

Bulajeva, T., & Hogan-Brun, G. 2008. Language and education orientations in Lithuania: A cross-Baltic perspective post-EU accession. *International Journal of Bilingual Education and Bilingualism* 11: 396–422.

CIS Committee for Statistics. 1995. *The statistical handbook of social and economic indicators for the former Soviet Union*. New York: Norman Ross Publishing.

Ciscel, M. 2007. *The language of the Moldovans: Romania, Russia, and identity in an ex-Soviet republic*. Lanham: Lexington Books.

Ciscel, M. 2008. Uneasy compromise: Language and education in Moldova. *International Journal of Bilingual Education and Bilingualism* 11: 373–95.

Clement, V. 2008. Emblems of independence: Script choice in post-Soviet Turkmenistan. *International Journal of the Sociology of Language* 192: 171–85.

Commercio, M. 2004. Exit in the Near Abroad: The Russian minorities in Latvia and Kyrgyzstan. *Problems of Post-Communism* 51(6): 23–32.

Deineko, M. 1964. *Public education in the USSR*. Moscow: Progress.

Diatlenko, P. 2010. Russkii iazyk v Kirgizstane: sovremennoe polozhenie, trendy i pespektivy (Russian language in Kyrgyzstan: Current status, trends and prospective). In Mustajoki, A., Protassova, E., & N. Vakhtin (eds.) *Instrumentarium of linguistics: sociolinguistic approaches to non-standard Russian*, 211–26. Helsinki: Slavica Helsingiensia.

Dowler, W. 1995. The politics of language in non-Russian elementary schools in the Eastern Empire, 1865–1914. *Russian Review* 54: 516–38.

Dowler, W. 2001. *Classroom and empire: The politics of schooling Russia's eastern nationalities, 1860–1917*. Montreal: McGill-Queen's University Press.

Dunstan, J. 1997. *Soviet schooling in the Second World War*. Macmillan Press.

Edgar, A. 2004. *Tribal nation: The making of Soviet Turkmenistan*. Princeton: Princeton University Press.

European Commission against Racism and Intolerance (ECRI). 2008. *Third report on Latvia.* Strasbourg: Council of Europe.

European Commission against Racism and Intolerance (ECRI). 2010. *ECRI Report on Estonia.* Strasbourg: Council of Europe.

Ewing, Th. 2006. Ethnicity at school: 'Non-Russian' education in the Soviet Union during the 1930s. *History of Education* 4: 499–519.

Fierman, W. 1985. Language development in Soviet Uzbekistan. In I. Kreindler (ed.), *Sociolinguistic perspectives on Soviet national languages: Their past, present, and future,* 205–33. Berlin: Mouton De Gruyter.

Fierman, W. 2006. Language and education in post-Soviet Kazakhstan: Kazakh-medium instruction in urban schools. *Russian Review* 65: 98–116.

Fierman, W. 2009. Language vitality and paths to revival: Contrasting cases of Azerbaijani and Kazakh. *International Journal of the Sociology of Language* 198: 75–104.

Giger, M., & Sloboda, M. 2008. Language management and language problems in Belarus: Education and beyond. *International Journal of Bilingual Education and Bilingualism* 11: 315–39.

Goskomstat SSSR [Государственный комитет СССР по статистике]. 1991. *Национальный состав населения СССР (по данным Всесоюзной переписи населения 1989 г.).* (USSR population, based on the 1989 Soviet Census data). Moscow: Finansy i Statistika.

Grenoble, L. 2003. *Language policy in the Soviet Union.* Dordrecht: Kluwer.

Hasanova, D. 2007. Teaching and learning English in Uzbekistan. *English Today* 23(1): 3–9.

Hatcher, L. 2008. Script change in Azerbaijan: Acts of identity. *International Journal of the Sociology of Language* 192: 105–16.

Hewitt, G. 1985. Georgian: A noble past, a secure future. In I. Kreindler (ed.), *Sociolinguistic perspectives on Soviet national languages: Their past, present, and future,* 163–79. Berlin: Mouton De Gruyter.

Hewitt, G. 1989. Aspects of language planning in Georgia (Georgian and Abkhaz). In M. Kirkwood (ed.), *Language planning in the Soviet Union,* 123–44. London: Macmillan

Hirsch, F. 2005. *Empire of nations: Ethnographic knowledge and the making of the Soviet Union.* Ithaca, NY: Cornell University Press.

Iatsenko, E., Kozievskaya, E., & Gavrilov, K. (eds.). 2008. *Russkii iazyk v novykh nezavisimykh gosudarstvakh: Rezul'taty kompleksnogo issledovania* (Russian language in the new independent states: Results of a comprehensive study). Moscow: Fond Nasledie Evrazii.

International Crisis Group (ICG). 2006. Georgia's Armenian and Azeri minorities. *Europe Report,* 178, November 2006, Tbilisi/Brussels. http://www.crisisgroup.org.

Jurado, E. 2003. Complying with European standards of minority education: Estonia's relations with the European Union, OSCE, and Council of Europe. *Journal of Baltic Studies* 34: 399–431.

Korth, B. 2005. *Language attitudes towards Kyrgyz and Russian: Discourse, education, and policy in post-Soviet Kyrgyzstan.* Bern: Peter Lang.

Kreindler, I. 1982. The changing status of Russian in the Soviet Union. *International Journal ofthe Sociology of Language* 33: 7–39.

Kulyk, V. (ed.). 2010. Languages and language ideologies in Ukraine: Special issue. *International Journal of the Sociology of Language,* 201.

Laitin, D. 1998. *Identity in formation: The Russian-speaking populations in the Near Abroad*. Ithaca, NY: Cornell University Press.

Landau, J., & Kellner-Heinkele, B. 2001. *Politics of language in the ex-Soviet Muslim states: Azerbayjan, Uzbekistan, Kazakhstan, Kyrgyzstan, Turkmenistan and Tajikistan*. Ann Arbor: University of Michigan Press.

Laruelle, M. 2007. Central Asian labor migrants in Russia: The "diasporization" of the Central Asian states? *China and Eurasia Forum Quarterly* 5(3): 101–19.

Lebedeva, N. 1995. *Novaia russkaia diaspora: Sotsial'no-psikhologicheskii analiz* [New Russian diaspora: Socio-psychological analysis]. Moscow: Russian Academy of Sciences.

Lewis, G. 1972. *Multilingualism in the Soviet Union*. The Hague: Mouton.

Liber, G. 1991. *Korenizatsia*: Restructuring Soviet nationality policy in the 1920s. *Ethnic and Racial Studies* 14(1): 15–23.

Lipset, H. 1967. The status of national minority languages in Soviet education. *Soviet Studies* 19(2): 181–89.

Martin, T. 2001. *The affirmative action empire: Nations and nationalism in the Soviet Union, 1923–1939*. Ithaca, NY: Cornell University Press.

Nagzibekova, M. 2008. Language and education policies in Tajikistan. *International Journal of Bilingual Education and Bilingualism* 11: 501–08.

Nazaryan. 2007. Iazykovaia situatsia v Uzbekistane: Real'nost' i perspektivy [Language situation in Uzbekistan: Reality and future trends]. http://www.mapryal.org/content/russkii-yazyk-v-mire.

Opinion on Estonia. 2006. *Advisory committee on the Framework Convention for the protection of national minorities: Second opinion on Estonia*. Strasbourg: Council of Europe.

Opinion on Georgia. 2009. *Advisory committee on the Framework Convention for the protection of national minorities: Opinion on Georgia*. Strasbourg: Council of Europe.

Opinion on Lithuania. 2003. *Advisory committee on the Framework Convention for the protection of national minorities: Opinion on Lithuania*. Strasbourg: Council of Europe.

Orusbaev, A., Mustajoki, A., & Protassova, E. 2008. Multilingualism, Russian language, and education in Kyrgyzstan. *International Journal of Bilingual Education and Bilingualism* 11: 476–500.

Pavlenko, A. (ed.). 2008a. Multilingualism in post-Soviet countries. Special issue. *International Journal of Bilingual Education and Bilingualism*, no. 3–4.

Pavlenko, A. 2008b. Multilingualism in post-Soviet countries: Language revival, language removal, and sociolinguistic theory. *International Journal of Bilingual Education and Bilingualism* 11: 275–314.

Pavlenko, A. 2011a. Linguistic russification in the Russian Empire: Peasants into Russians? *Russian Linguistics* 35: 331–50.

Pavlenko, A. 2011b. Language rights versus speakers' rights: On the applicability of Western language rights approaches in Eastern European contexts. *Language Policy* 10: 37–58.

Pavlenko, A. In press. Commodification of Russian in post-1991 Europe. *Globalisierung, Migration, Fremdsprachenunterricht*, ed. by Marcus Bär, Andreas Bonnet, Helene Decke-Cornill, Andreas Grünewald, and Adelheid Hu. Baltmannsweiler: Schneider Hohengehren.

Permanov, S., Protassova, E. & A. Golubeva. 2010. O russkom iazyke v Turkmenistane (On Russian in Turkmenistan). In A. Mustajoki, E. Protassova, & N. Vakhtin (eds.), *Instrumentarium of linguistics: sociolinguistic approaches to non-standard Russian*, 239–251. Helsinki: Slavica Helsingiensia.

Pool, J. 1978. Soviet language planning: Goals, results, options. In J. Azrael (ed.) *Soviet nationality policies and practices*, 223–49. New York: Praeger.

Radnitz, S. 2006. Weighing the political and economic motivations for migration in post-Soviet space: The case of Uzbekistan. *Europe-Asia Studies* 58: 653–77.

Rannut, M. 2008. Estonianization efforts post-independence. *International Journal of Bilingual Education and Bilingualism* 11: 423–39.

Raun, T. 1985. Language development and policy in Estonia. In I. Kreindler (ed.), *Sociolinguistic perspectives on Soviet national languages: Their past, present, and future*, 13–35. Berlin: Mouton De Gruyter.

Report on Armenia. 2008. *European Charter for Regional or Minority Languages: Second periodical report*. Strasbourg: CoE.

Report on Azerbaijan. 2007. *Second report submitted by Azerbaijan pursuant to article 25, paragraph 1, of the Framework Convention for the protection of national minorities*. Strasbourg: CoE.

Ryan, M. 1990. *Contemporary Soviet society: A statistical handbook*. Brookfield, VT: Edward Elgar.

Saunders, D. 1995. Russia's Ukrainian policy (1847–1905): A demographic approach. *European History Quarterly* 25: 181–208.

Savoskul, S. 2001. *Russkie novogo zarubezhia: Vybor sud'by* [Russians in the new abroad: The choice of destiny]. Moscow: Nauka.

Schmid, C. 2008. Ethnicity and language tensions in Latvia. *Language Policy* 7: 3–19.

Sharifov, O. 2007. The Uzbek language exists in two graphic forms simultaneously and neither seems capable of ousting the other. http://enews.ferghana.ru/article.php?id=1954.

Shustov, A. 2009. Russkie shkoly vytesniaiutsia turetskimi: O sostoianii russkogo obrazovania v gosudarstvakh Central'noi Azii [Russian schools are being displaced by Turkish ones: On the state of Russian education in Central Asian states]. http://www.stoletie.ru/geopolitika/russkije_shkoly_vytesnajutsa_tureckimi_2009-12-11.htm.

Siiner, M. 2006. Planning language practice: A sociolinguistic analysis of language policy in post-Communist Estonia. *Language Policy* 5: 161–86.

Silova, I. 2006. *From sites of occupation to symbols of multiculturalism: Reconceptualizing minority education in post-Soviet Latvia*. Greenwich, CT: Information Age Publishing.

Silver, B. 1976. Bilingualism and maintenance of the mother tongue in Soviet Central Asia. *Slavic Review* 35: 406–24.

Silver, B. 1978. Language policy and the linguistic russification of Soviet nationalities. In J. Azrael (ed.), *Soviet nationality policies and practices*, 250–306. New York: Praeger.

Simon, G. 1991. *Nationalism and policy toward the nationalities in the Soviet Union: From totalitarian dictatorship to post-Stalinist society*. Translated from German by K. Forster & O. Forster. Boulder, CO: Westview Press.

Slezkine, Y. 1994. The USSR as a communal apartment, or how a socialist state promoted ethnic particularism. *Slavic Review* 53: 414–52.

Smagulova, J. 2008. Language policies of kazakhization and their influence on language attitudes and use. *International Journal of Bilingual Education and Bilingualism* 11: 440–75.

Smith, J. 1997. The education of national minorities: The early Soviet experience. *Slavonic and East European Review* 75: 281–307.

Smith, M. 1998. *Language and power in the creation of the USSR, 1917–1953*. Berlin: Mouton De Gruyter.

Snyder, T. 2003. *The reconstruction of nations: Poland, Ukraine, Lithuania, Belarus, 1569– 1999*. New Haven: Yale University Press.

Spires, S. 2001. Language shift in Lithuania, 1850–1900: A reinterpretation. *Journal of Baltic Studies* 32: 44–61.

Suny, R. 2001. The empire strikes out: Imperial Russia, "national" identity, and theories of empire. In R. Suny & T. Martin (eds.) *A state of nations: Empire and nation-making in the age of Lenin and Stalin*, 23–66. New York: Oxford University Press.

Thaden, E. (ed.). 1981. *Russification in the Baltic provinces and Finland, 1855–1914*. Princeton, NJ: Princeton University Press.

Thaden, E., & Thaden, M. 1984. *Russia's Western borderlands, 1710–1870*. Princeton, NJ: Princeton University Press.

Weeks, Th. 1996. *Nation and state in late imperial Russia: Nationalism and russification on the Western frontier, 1863–1914*. De Kalb: Northern Illinois University Press.

Weeks, Th. 2001. Russification and the Lithuanians, 1863–1905. *Slavic Review* 60: 96–114.

CHAPTER 33

LANGUAGE IDEOLOGIES, POLICIES, AND ATTITUDES TOWARD SIGNED LANGUAGES

JOSEPH HILL

POLICIES and attitudes about signed languages have been driven by ideologies concerning the fundamental nature of signed languages and their suitability for use by humans, that is, (1) whether humans should be allowed to communicate with their hands as opposed to their voices and what it means if they do; (2) what it means when humans cannot hear; and (3) what the implication of deafness is to society. These ideologies parallel those concerning the suitability of nonstandard and unwritten varieties of spoken languages but are unique in that they concern the basic issue of language modality, which is an information-encoded form of sensory perception that is used in a communication exchange. Spoken languages are of the aural-oral modality, the predominant form of communication in the world, whereas signed languages are of the visual-kinetic modality, which is typically associated with deafness. According to people who subscribe to the medical model of deafness, deafness is conventionally seen as a physical impairment that severely affects one's life, but there is the cultural model of deafness, which attributes a positive meaning to deafness (Lane 2002; Lane, Hoffmeister, & Bahan 1996). The cultural model reflects Deaf[1] people as a linguistic and cultural minority whose primary language is a signed language. Notwithstanding, deafness has historically been seen as a medical problem requiring remediation. As a result, the medical model is much more prevalent than the cultural model. The medical model creates a conditional existence of the signed languages of Deaf people, meaning that if deafness were to be completely cured, signed languages would lose their usefulness and Deaf cultures, which are intimately intertwined with signed languages, would be drastically affected.

This chapter describes how ideologies about signed languages have come about and what policies and attitudes have resulted. Language ideologies have governed the formal recognition of signed language at local, national, and international levels, such as that of the United Nations (Monaghan 2003; Reagan 2010). This chapter discusses three major areas in the study of attitudes toward signed languages: (1) attitudes versus structural reality; (2) the social factors and educational policies that have contributed to language attitudes; (3) the impact of language attitudes on identity and educational policies.

Most of the examples used for the three major areas are from ASL and English. The struggles to dismantle the misconceptions about the language status and linguistic structure of ASL, to have ASL legally recognized as a natural language of the Deaf, and to institute ASL as a language of instruction for deaf and hard-of-hearing children are more or less paralleled by the struggles in other countries with their respective signed languages (Reagan 2010). As background, the chapter first provides a discussion of language attitudes, language status, and the historical context of attitudes about ASL and English.

Language Attitudes and Language Status

Language Attitudes

Attitude is very much part of every aspect of life and society in regard to any entity or a collection of entities, real or imagined, as an object of evaluation. Attitudes are not always held on the conscious level of awareness, nor are they always visibly or, at least, publicly expressed. Attitude is defined as "a psychological tendency that is expressed by evaluating a particular entity with some degree of favor or disfavor" (Eagly & Chaiken 1993: 1). A particular entity that is under attitudinal evaluation is an "attitude object" (Eagly & Chaiken 2007: 583). Attitude objects may be conceptual (e.g., ideology, belief, or knowledge) or tangible (e.g., a house, a car, a person, or an animal), and the objects may be individual (e.g., the current US president, or a reality TV star) or collective (e.g., college students or the US Congress; Eagly & Chaiken 2007: 583). Attitudes are generally formed and expressed in one or more types of evaluative responses to attitude objects: affective, cognitive, and behavioral. An *affective* type has to do with feelings toward attitude objects; a *cognitive* type deals with knowledge and belief about attitude objects; and a *behavioral* type focuses on reactions toward attitude objects.

In this chapter the attitude objects are languages, so the scope on attitudes has been narrowed to language attitudes, which encompass affective, cognitive, and behavioral types of evaluative responses toward particular language varieties, based on stereotypical perceptions of social groups who use those varieties (Campbell-Kibler 2006, 2009; Garrett 2010; Preston 2002). Responses to language varieties, which are attitude objects, are based on two perceptions: a sensory perception of linguistic items and a stereotypical perception of a social group that uses these items. Linguistic items can be found on different linguistic levels, from phonology (in the specific sense) to discourse (in the broadest sense). For example: on the phonological level, a community produces a vowel in a word differently from another community (i.e., vowels /ɛ/ and /I/ in pin); on the lexical level, how two mutually intelligible linguistic communities use different words to refer to same objects (i.e., soda/pop/coke, sofa/couch/davenport); and on the grammatical and discourse levels, how a community has a sentential construction that is different from that in another community that produces the same meaning (i.e., "She **is usually** home at 7"/"She **be** home at 7"); see Green (2002) on the meaning of *be* in African American English.

Linguistic items usually evoke a stereotypical image of a social group that uses the items. For example, the grammatical construction of "She be home at 7" is a typical and acceptable construction in African American English (AAE), but it is not typical or acceptable in Standard American English. This is where a stereotypical perception of a social group comes into play. Variants of a linguistic item are forms that are perceived to constitute a particular linguistic community, and the variants are used by members of a social group to identify speakers who are socially similar or different; in other words, the variants carry social meaning for people to implicitly perceive and inform each other of their social characteristics (Campbell-Kibler 2009; Garrett 2010). Social meaning may elicit different evaluative responses to a person's language and, in a social context, influence the social standing of members of a linguistic community. Attitudes toward language varieties are generally influenced by the process of language standardization (Garrett 2010:7).

When one language variety is deemed "standard," that impacts (usually devalues) the status of other language varieties and of the social groups using those language varieties in a particular context (Garrett 2010: 7). Everyone in the society, regardless of social status, consciously or unconsciously "subscribe[s] to the ideology of the standard language" (Milroy 2001: 535) because of a belief in correctness. Even with people's awareness of a standard language or language variety, "standard" is relative, based on perceptions of standardness in different geographical regions, as it is with all languages and varieties, for example, *r* deletion in the eastern New England dialect (i.e., /ka/ instead of /kar/ for 'car') is perceived as standard in New England English, and the presence of *r* in the southeastern US region is perceived as standard as well (Wolfram 1991: 8). The sentences, "they go to the **beach**," "they go to the **shore**," and "they go to the **ocean**," are also judged to be part of Standard English, depending on where the sentences are used (Wolfram 1991: 8).

Language Status

Language status is determined by majority recognition, extent of language use, social capital of the language users, and other favorable sociocultural and socioeconomic conditions, and status clearly influences the perceptions of the language or language variety. Attitude studies of languages (e.g., English, French, Hawaiian, and Spanish), and language varieties (e.g., Standard English, Standard Mexican Spanish), whose language status is well established are likely to differ from studies of languages and language varieties whose language status is still in question (e.g., pidgins, creoles, and sign languages). In the former case, speakers of one language may question the prestige of another language but not the belief in its status as a "real language." Indeed, prestige is acquired through the process of standardization in a given society in a given time, and it is most often associated with a social group with weighty influence in the society (Milroy 2001).

As discussed by Potowski (chapter 16, this volume), if schools in United States have to decide about whether to use Spanish as the medium of instruction in all classes, it is likely that the decision is never based on the perception that Spanish, which has been recognized as a language with the large number of users and a rich cultural history, might not be a real language. However, the decision could be based on the social and political capital of Spanish. English is already the language of the majority and there has been a troubled relationship with the presence of Spanish in the United States because of economic and political pressures. Attitude studies of languages with well-established language status could have clear results relating to people's attitudes toward the languages under study.

ASL is in an interesting position because it is often unrecognized as a language by the US majority (and is stigmatized in some places). However, it is recognized as a language by most people who are involved in or with the American Deaf community, where it enjoys prestige. With the history of suppression and misconceptions of ASL, the language status of ASL is still largely uncertain in United States and in part of the American Deaf community. In addition to the skepticism about the ASL's status a language, different forms of manually coded English (MCE), an English-based visual communication system of signs, were introduced in the place of ASL as a medium of instruction for deaf and hard-of-hearing children. That introduction has resulted in a contact variety of ASL (Lucas & Valli 1992). However, the standardization of ASL is ongoing via dictionaries, textbooks, curricula, and language-proficiency assessments, and ASL has been gaining recognition in some places. For example, a few states, such as Alabama, Maine, Colorado, and Rhode Island, have legislatively recognized ASL as a natural and legitimate language of the Deaf community, while some states and the District of Columbia, rather than recognize ASL as a fully developed language of the Deaf community, *only* legislate ASL for two purposes: as a foreign language that can (or in some cases, *may*) be studied and accepted for school and universitiy credit, and as a communication accommodation, with the provision of ASL interpreters (Reagan 2011). The double status of ASL (prestigious and stigmatized) may lead to a wide range of judgments about what linguistic features constitute ASL (as opposed to the contact variety and MCE) and of its legitimate status as a language.

Historical Context for Attitudes about ASL and English

Before the 1860s, deaf schools in America used manual-based instruction, meaning that the instructors signed in their teaching. Although the schools were concerned about students' reading and writing abilities in the majority language, deaf students' oral communication skills were not greatly emphasized (Baynton 1996; Lane et al. 1996). In fact, instructors were more concerned about the content that deaf students received than their development of oral and aural communication. Signing was an accessible mode of communication that was suitable for the education of deaf students; but for oralists, signing was not a perfect solution. During 1860s, a movement for oralism (i.e., the method of educating deaf children through the exclusive use of speech and lip reading) started gaining momentum in deaf schools. What motivated the oralist movement was the popularity of Darwin's evolutionary theory. Communication was one of the characteristics used to distinguish the civilized from the primitive (Baynton 1996). In the eyes of the oralists, speech was the highly evolved form of communication and signing was viewed as an animalistic communication system (Baynton 1996). Oralists believed that to appear as normal as possible, deaf children must speak like civilized people and avoid signing completely.

In 1880, a conference was held in Milan, Italy, at which delegates of French, Italian, and American deaf schools debated the mode of communication in deaf education (Baynton 1996). American delegates had reservations about the effectiveness of instructing deaf students through oral communication, but most delegates were impassioned about the need to restore deaf children to mainstream society by banning signed language from schools and encouraging students to use the spoken language of their respective countries, so they could pass as hearing. At the close of the conference, a majority supported oral education, and deaf schools in America and Europe underwent major changes that affected not only Deaf students, but also Deaf instructors, the future generation of Deaf graduates, the livelihood of the Deaf community, and ultimately, life in the Deaf culture. This was the beginning of the worldwide oralism underpinned by an ideology that viewed deafness as a pathological mark that could be mitigated by the exclusive use of speech, combined with the view that sign language was an impediment to deaf children's assimilation to society (Baynton 1996). Normality is a main concern, so such ideology has been a main determinant of the language policies regarding a communication method for deaf children.

The exclusive oral practice in American deaf education continued well past the middle of the twentieth century, when questions were raised about the benefits of teaching deaf students through oral-only instruction (Lane et al. 1996) and linguistic studies (e.g., Stokoe 1960) confirmed the status of ASL as a natural language. Expectations for deaf students' acquisition of the majority spoken language and academic development had not been met, and some educators realized that the students needed to communicate visually to learn well. But after a long period of repeated attempts to supplant ASL and to circulate misconceptions about the language development of deaf children, it was difficult to embrace ASL as a natural medium of instruction (Lane et al. 1996). The common misconceptions were (and still are) that ASL is a broken English, that it is a gestural system with a flexible or nonexistent grammar, that it is is too conceptual to be a language, that it does not have abstract forms, that it is not a language because it has no written form, and that it is a crutch for deaf children and hampers their development in written English (Lane et al. 1996; Markowicz 1980; Schein & Stewart 1995). These misconceptions feed the skepticism about the linguistic status of ASL, and this is not helped by the fact that ASL is a minority language in the country. The effectiveness of ASL as the medium of instruction is still hotly debated, especially when it comes to teaching English. Since deaf and hard-of-hearing students attend US schools where English is the language of majority, the students are expected to develop good literacy skills in English, and the skepticism about the status of ASL may be one cause for the invention of MCE.

I now turn to the three major areas in attitudes toward sign languages.

Attitudes versus structural reality. Since the introduction of English-based sign systems, these sign systems and ASL have coexisted in some places, a situation that eventually led to a contact signing system with different combinations of features and forms. But some members of the Deaf community are particularly averse to English-based sign systems for historical, linguistic, and cultural reasons. With this aversion as a motivation, there have been attempts to standardize ASL to preserve its features through dictionaries, ASL proficiency exams, ASL teaching materials, training and organizations, and ASL courses. This is parallel to standard languages, such as English, which are "codified in dictionaries and grammar books, for example, and spread through educational systems" (Garrett 2010: 7).

As with spoken language, linguistic items and features can be on different linguistic levels, from phonological (e.g., a P handshape and a 5 handshape in the sign PARENT) to syntactic (e.g., ASL and English word order) to discourse (e.g., the use of eye gaze in signing). Difference between ASL and English-based signing systems is contrastive on most linguistic levels, but when it comes to a contact variety possessing features and items from ASL and English-based signing systems, the distinction is less clear, and variation in contact signing is largely based on individuals. Consider a simple example of contact signing: a signer produces linguistic items with obvious ASL features on all linguistic levels except for the syntactic level, on which some phrases produced are in English word order, and the lexical level, where only four English-based signs—AND, BUT, THEN, and BECAUSE— are used. These are used instead of a body shift that is a translation equivalent to the conjunction "and," the ASL sign UNDERSTAND, an ASL rhetorical question to convey a conjunction "but," an ASL conditional or body shift for "then," and a rhetorical question WHY for "because," respectively. These English-based signs are strongly discouraged by in the American Sign Language Teachers Association (ASLTA) teacher-certification evaluation application and the ASL language-proficiency evaluation instruction (ASLTA 2010; Newell & Caccamise 2008). Aside from the perception of linguistic items, we need to consider a stereotypical image of a social group evoked by the perception of linguistic items. In the American Deaf community there is a general perception that standard ASL is being carried by Deaf persons in Deaf generational lineage or by people who attended a special school for the deaf where ASL was the norm for deaf and hard of hearing students, as opposed to deaf people who were reared by hearing parents or schooled in a mainstream educational setting where English was a primary medium of instruction.

In the American Deaf community there is a general understanding that the stereotypical social identity of an interlocutor influences a signer's choice of signing based on what the signer imagines the interlocutor's communication preference to be. For example, Deaf signers use ASL with each other but, consciously or unconsciously, switch to contact signing or Signed English when a hearing signer joins their conversation. When the hearing signer leaves, Deaf signers will revert to ASL. However, Lucas and Valli (1992), who have investigated the switch between signing varieties based on the social identities (Deaf or hearing) of the interlocutors, have shown that social identity is not a significant factor in the change of signing styles between interlocutors, meaning that some Deaf signers will use ASL with a hearing person, and some Deaf signers will use contact signing, and even MCE signing, with other Deaf signers. Other factors that influence signing choices with an interlocutor include the formality of the setting, familiarity with the interlocutor, and pride in one's membership to a social group (Lucas & Valli 1992: 63–64).

Not only did Lucas and Valli (1992) examine the signers' choice of signing type in various situations, they also looked at how the signing was perceived.

Lucas and Valli used a panel of ASL language professionals as experts to judge a total of 20 clips of different signers as "ASL" and "not ASL." The experts were unanimous in their judgments, rating five clips as "ASL" and the rest as "not ASL." The same clips were tested on Deaf "naïve" judges who had no linguistic training. Their judgments did not always agree with those of the experts. The difference in results led Lucas and Valli to explore possible correlations with the judges' social characteristics. For example, for one clip, all the expert judges agreed that it was "not ASL." However, 37 percent of the white naïve judges judged the clip as "ASL," and 82 percent of black naïve judges judged it as "ASL" (70). The discrepancy in judgment between the white and black naïve judges could be related to the salience of linguistic structures in their perception. For instance, a signer in the clip used contact signing with English word order but also used key ASL features such as eye gaze, referential spaces, and body shift (100). The saliency of these key ASL features in the black judges' perception despite the obvious presence of English could account for the discrepancy in the results.

Hill (2011), based on Lucas and Valli (1992), reports on four studies that analyze attitudes toward variations in signing, ranging from ASL to Signed English (hereafter referred to collectively as "signing types"), and the extent of influence of the signing types on the attitudes from the perception of linguistic items and social characteristics. The studies are as follows: (1) the perception of signing types, (2) the effects of social information on signing perception, (3) the evaluation of signing, and (4) the description of signing. The participants involved differed by race (black and white), age (young and old), and age of ASL acquisition (native and non-native). Studies 1 and 2 had 60 short (10–15 second) videoclips of signing, sorted into four signing types: *Strong ASL* (19 videoclips), *Mostly ASL* (16), *Mixed* (15), and *Not ASL* (10). Based on the results of a pilot study, the signing types were organized in the consecutive order of the productive presence of ASL based on the Deaf experts' ratings "ASL," "Between," and "Not ASL." For example, a videoclip that received mostly "ASL" ratings would be labeled as *Strong ASL*, and a videoclip that received mostly "Not ASL" ratings would be labeled as *Not ASL*; the sorting of *Mostly ASL* and *Mixed* was based on the mixed ratings of "ASL," "Between," and "Not ASL," with the number of ASL ratings as a lead indicator in the difference between *Mostly ASL* and *Mixed*.

Study 1 required the participants to indicate their choice of "ASL" or "Not ASL" for each of the 60 videoclips. While the participants might be aware of the difference in the signing produced in the videoclips, they were not aware of the classification of the signing types. The findings of study 1 were that all participants were similar in their systematic separation of the signing types by the collective ratings of "ASL." Even Strong ASL and Mostly ASL were significantly different from each other based on the ratings of "ASL" and "Not ASL." But three social groups of the participants (native younger black, nonnative older black, nonnative older white) differed from the rest of the social groups based on the ratings for *Non-ASL* videoclips. The former groups perceived the videoclips as a mixture of ASL and English, whereas the latter groups perceived it as closer to English.

Study 2 was similar to study 1 except that it introduced social information with the intention of influencing the participants' perception of the signing types. This study followed the method of the influence of a social characteristic on language perception (e.g., Niedzielski 1999; Williams et al. 1971). Six pieces of social information were used in the study: "Deaf family," "Hearing family," "Deaf school," "Hearing school," "College," and "High school." The culturally Deaf-related information, such as "Deaf family" and "Deaf school," was a common assumption about a native ASL signer whereas the non-culturally deaf-related information, such as "Hearing family" and "Hearing school," was a common assumption about a deaf person who was not fluent in ASL. The school information was related to educational status, which was a factor for some deaf people who assumed that English-based signing was a sign of high educational status and that ASL signing was a sign of a low educational status. The findings of study 2 were that "Hearing family" and "Hearing school" caused a significant drop in "ASL" ratings, whereas "Deaf family" and "Deaf school" had no effect, and "High school" produced a small drop in the "ASL" ratings whereas "College" produced no effect. However, the conclusion of the study must be treated with caution because there were outliers that might have had a considerable influence on the results, and a greater number of videos was needed to generate a stronger effect.

Study 3 and 4 used eight videoclips, which were different from and longer (1 minute) than the previous set of videoclips used in studies 1 and 2. The objective of study 3 was to gather the attitudinal evaluations of the signing types (i.e., ASL, Mixed, and Signed English) by employing an indirect method. The participants were to indicate their agreement, disagreement, or neutrality (henceforth called "evaluative responses") with the statements related to the signing based on aesthetic, purity, and fluidity and to the signers in the videoclips based on leadership, Deaf and Hearing identities, education, and intelligence. The evaluative responses were in conjunction with the signing types that the participants determined earlier. The findings were that of the eight videoclips that were judged to be "ASL," the relative frequency of agreement responses was higher on every statement except the Hearing identity statement, which had a considerable proportion of disagreement responses; of the videoclips that were judged to be "Mixed," the relative frequencies of the evaluative responses were mixed as well on the purity, aesthetic, and leadership statements but were similar to those of ASL on the rest of the statements; and of the videoclips that were judged to be "Signed English," the significantly large proportions of disagreement responses were on the purity, aesthetic, leadership, and Deaf identity statements and a large proportion of agreement responses on the Hearing identity, but the rest of the statements were similar to those of ASL.

Study 4 drew from a smaller pool of the participants for interviews to describe the linguistic items of the signing types in their own words. The purpose of the study was to see what linguistic items led them to determine the signing types (ASL, Mixed, or Signed English) after viewing the videoclips and their views of the items. Of the videoclips they judged to be ASL, the participants generally made positive comments about the linguistic items that were found to be consistent with the ideological standard of ASL, for example, non-manual signals involving eyes, face, head, and body; classifiers; vernacular signs; lesser extent of English word order; and lack of initialized signs (the modified handshapes in ASL signs to correspond with the initial letter of words or morphemes). However, there were a few negative comments regarding ASL as having no word order, lacking in classifiers and non-manual signals, and even indicating one's inferior socioeconomic status (i.e., "vocational" and "grass roots," which is defined by Jacobs 1989 and Padden & Humphries 2005 as a group of less educated members of the Deaf community). As for Mixed and Signed English, the comments became increasingly negative when the signing was more like English, for example, lack of non-manual signals, lack of classifiers, more initialized signs, and heavy English word order. The important thing to note here is that with the eight videoclips, some clips were "ASL" to some participants but were "Mixed" or even "Signed English" to the other participants. Even with the noticeable improvement in the positive attitude toward ASL, the language status of ASL is mixed to this day.

Social factors and educational policies that have contributed to language attitudes. English is a dominant language in the United States, viewed as a standard language with an overt prestige unmatched by other languages in the country. The status of English also has a tremendous effect on perceptions of the status and linguistic structure of ASL in the American Deaf community because of the ideology of deafness as pathological and sign language as a mark of failure to integrate (Baynton 1996).

In the history of deaf education in America, there was great pressure to remove ASL as a medium of instruction and replace it with oral English language (Baynton 1996; Lane et al 1996). Years later when that failed in some places, there was an agreement to use signed communication in classroom with deaf and hard-of-hearing students, but only a visual communication method based on English. Even though ASL was still used, however surreptitiously, the general avoidance or suppression of ASL by educators and administrators sent a message to deaf and hard-of-hearing students that English was better than ASL and that using English in the written and oral forms was the way for them to succeed in American society. For a long time, deaf and hard-of-hearing children and adults internalized negative thinking about ASL, until William Stokoe (1960) demonstrated that ASL was a valid linguistic system that could be analyzed in the same way as any other language.

The discovery did not result in an immediate widespread acceptance of ASL as a valid language by the Deaf community due to internalized oppression and conflicting emotions and opinions about ASL. But as time passed and with an increasing number of research studies on ASL and more ASL course offerings and the rippling effect on the America Deaf community of the Deaf President Now (DPN) movement in 1988,[2] the respect for ASL had been gaining within the American Deaf community. Now ASL is one of the most popular foreign languages taught in schools, colleges, and universities (Padden & Humphries 2005; Rosen 2010); ASL teaching materials have been produced; evaluations of the ASL skills of deaf, hard-of-hearing, and hearing signers have been developed; professional and academic organizations focus on teaching, education, and the linguistics of ASL. ASL has arrived at an interesting destination in America as being perceived as a standard language with prestige (acquired through the standardization with dictionaries, textbooks, classes, and language proficiency evaluation) in the American Deaf community while at the same time remaining a stigmatized language in the mainstream. However, not all deaf and hard-of-hearing individuals use or even view ASL the same way.

A very small percentage of deaf and hard-of-hearing Americans was born to deaf or hard-of-hearing parents whose communication preference might be signing, oral, or both (Mitchell & Karchmer 2004, 2005). A large proportion of the deaf population acquired signing systems (ASL, contact signing, English-based signing, cued speech) in formal education settings. A considerable number of deaf and hard-of-hearing people who have attended deaf schools (which have been long considered active centers for the transmission and maintenance of ASL) acquired ASL or signing in some form in youth (Lane et al. 1996). The rest of the population has been mainstreamed in restricted or inclusive settings in public or private schools, with a variety of communication methods made available by educators and administrators, including English-based systems (Karchmer & Mitchell 2003). With the declining number of enrollments in deaf schools, that translates into the increasing number of deaf and hard-of-hearing students whose exposure to ASL is wholly dependent on the kinds of educational settings available to them, parents' wishes, and the presence of a deaf community in town (Lane et al. 1996; Mitchell & Karchmer 2006). In some places and groups in America, English is still seen as the way to be successful, and it is suggested that ASL, based on the number of misconceptions (i.e., that it is broken English, grammarless, and impediment to English skills development), is a secondary communication method or something to be avoided. With the additional factors of the onset of deafness and age of ASL acquisition as well as social diversity in terms of race (see McCaskill et al. 2011), ethnicity, and socioeconomic status, the picture of perceived status of ASL and English is complicated in terms of prestige, identities associated with signing, the purity of ASL, and the extent of English influence in the signing of deaf and hard-of-hearing people.

Other signed languages in the world endure the same kind of complications: issues about language status, contention as a medium of instruction with the manual sign codes based on their respective spoken languages, changes in deaf education, and social diversity in the deaf communities (Reagan 2010).

The impact of language attitudes on identity and educational policy. Attitudes toward signing varieties are tied to the perceptions of social identities related to deafness and signing abilities. The social identities in the American Deaf community are as follows: *Deaf* as a person with an entrenched cultural identity and a carrier of ASL; *hard-of-hearing* as a person with residual hearing and speech capacity and possible signing proficiency in whatever mode, whether ASL, contact signing, or MCE; *oral deaf* as a person with little or no hearing but with a strong preference for oral communication over signing for daily use; *late-deafened* as a person who possessed normal hearing and speech abilities before losing them as a result of medical conditions, for example, an illness, a genetic predisposition, or an accident; and *hearing* as a person with normal hearing and speech abilities who is in contact with a deaf community in whatever role (see Jacobs 1989; Kannapell 1994; Stone & Stirling 1994; and Leigh 2009 for further discussion on various identities in the Deaf community). Although the identities listed above are presented in a simple manner, they are not as clean and fixed as they appear. Throughout the world, deaf identities and the notion of Deaf culture may not be the same in all deaf communities because "the nature of deaf and Deaf identity in a given community depends on the forms of community and language," and with respect to forms, "the form any sign language takes is intertwined with the nature of the community that uses it" (Monaghan 2003: 20). Leigh (2009) covers the complexity and gradience of identities related to auditory and communication abilities in a given context in terms of space, time, and community.

Notwithstanding the complexity of deaf identities, the use of ASL is one qualifying property (i.e., shared language) signaling a membership of the American Deaf community (Kannapell 1994) along with other properties that underpin a Deaf identity, such as a collective name, sense of community, shared and distinct values and customs, knowledge of the culture, history, social structures, and arts (Leigh 2009). Even Deaf children are aware of the importance of social identities relating to language use and socialize with children whose language is most like their own. According to Johnson and Erting (1989), Deaf children who were proficient in ASL communicated and associated with each other more often than did Deaf children who were less proficient in ASL. The researchers noted that "both the form of the language and the content of the conversational interactions are important in the socialization of deaf children" (83). Children develop a social identity through interactions based on language use and form, and their interactions form their language attitudes that lead them to favor a group that uses the language form most like theirs. To sum up, the use of ASL, contact signing, or MCE is a signal carrying social meaning from which others infer one's membership to social groups in the American Deaf community.

Before the 1960s, 80 percent of deaf and hard-of-hearing students attended deaf residential schools. Since the advent of mainstreaming, the number of deaf schools has been decreasing, and more deaf and hard-of-hearing students attend mainstream programs. The implication of the student demographics for communication exposure is that, because the MCE systems or English-style signing are the norm in mainstream programs, more deaf and hard-of-hearing students have been exposed to them since the creation of the systems. Deaf schools typically use ASL for deaf and hard-of-hearing students although some instructors might use MCE or contact signing. MCE systems are typically more often used in mainstream settings, because it is easy for hearing instructors to learn and to use them with speech and they are believed to be useful tools in exposing deaf and hard of hearing students to English. For example, Ward Trotter (1989) found even though the deaf-education teachers in training were hypothesized to be idealistic and flexible in terms of educational methods, they still expressed a general preference to Signed English over ASL as a medium of instruction. But in the past few decades, the number of ASL-English bilingual/bicultural education programs has been on the rise with the intent of teaching ASL and English equally in the sense of language status and separately in the sense of language production, but the programs face ongoing challenges: the rise of cochlear implants and the closing of deaf schools (Padden & Humphries 2005; Reagan 2010).

A cochlear implant is a surgically implanted prosthetic device that reduces natural sounds into electrical signals, which are then transmitted via electrodes inside the cochlear. The cochlear implant was invented in 1957, but the major breakthrough occurred in the 1970s when the number of deaf patients receiving the implants started to grow (Eisen 2009). Like conventional hearing aids, cochlear implants were created with the goal of correcting deafness by providing a sense of hearing to people with hearing loss (Padden & Humphries 2005; Reagan 2010). This goal is based on the medical model that renders deafness as a problem and considers deaf people to be impaired in the aural and oral communication mode, never mind that a sign language can be used normally to facilitate the language development and socialization of the deaf and hard-of-hearing individuals. Unlike conventional hearing aids, which can be worn temporarily behind the ear or inside the ear canal, surgery is needed to implant the cochlear device behind the ear in order to stimulate the cochlea. Depending on the recommendation of the medical professional, a recipient can receive one or two cochlear implants to gain a perception of hearing. Since cochlear implants are electrical devices, they transmit electrical signals, not natural sounds, and there are limits to the perception and quality of sounds. As with all surgeries, the cochlear implant surgery has its risks, which range from minimal (e.g., scarring) to severe (e.g., infection or paralysis).

The advance of cochlear implants has been perceived as a threat to the Deaf communities in the world because of the intention behind the creation of the implants (Lane et al. 1996; Padden & Humphries 2005; Reagan 2010). To medical professionals, cochlear implants are merely devices that provide a perception of hearing; to Deaf communities, they are another means of sign language suppression that will lead to the eradication of Deaf culture. The debate centers on the appropriateness of deaf children receiving cochlear implants when there is a natural medium—sign language—that they can use to acquire language and social skills (Lane et al. 1996). Some Deaf people are completely opposed to cochlear implants; however, others are open to the idea of combining cochlear implants and sign language to maximize the benefits of language acquisition in speech and sign modalities (Padden & Humphries 2005). Despite this compromise, some medical professionals have argued that sign language is not necessary, and some have gone as far as saying that sign language impedes the development of language, evoking the same rhetoric used in 1880 by the proponents of oralism who claimed that signing impeded speech.

In addition to the increase in the number of cochlear implanted deaf children, the number of deaf children attending mainstream school programs instead of deaf schools has been increasing and that enlarges the social distance between the children, making them less likely to be exposed to signed language. Mitchell and Karchmer (2006) report that, based on the Gallaudet Research Institute's (GRI) 2002–2003 Annual Survey of Deaf and Hard of Hearing Children and Youth statistics, 80 percent of the participating schools serving deaf and hard-of-hearing students in a mainstream setting have three or fewer deaf and hard of hearing students, accounting for 40 percent of 40,282 deaf and hard-of-hearing students reported in the Annual Survey (Mitchell & Karchmer 2006; Gallaudet Research Institute 2003). In addition, almost one of every five deaf and hard of hearing students in mainstreaming is the only such student in a school (Mitchell & Karchmer 2006:99).

Conclusion

Even in the United States, American Sign Language does not get the recognition as a language in every region and the attempt to suppress sign language is still operative. The focus of the chapter has been on ASL, but this is a world-wide issue for many countries with histories of opposition to the use of signed languages that parallel the history of the United States.

For example, in May 2011, a major controversy erupted in Italy about the official recognition of the signed language used by Italian Deaf people (Searls 2011; Nassisi 2010; La protesta 2011; LIS Subito! n.d.). Since the 1980s, the signed language has been recognized in the Italian Deaf community as *Lingua dei Segni Italiana* (LIS) or "Italian Sign Language," but recognition has not been achieved outside of the Deaf community. Community leaders had been working to achieve the official recognition of LIS to affirm its language status and its necessity for Deaf people's access to education, employment, and services.

Recognition had nearly been acheived the Italian Senate approved the bill in recognizing LIS. However the bill needed approval from the Chamber of Deputies to pass (La protesta 2011). In May 2011, the House of Deputies amended the bill to designate what they considered the accurate name for the signed language: *Linguaggio Mimico-Gestuale* (LMG; Searls 2011). The English translation of the name is "language of mime and gesture" with the meaning of *linguaggio* as "a particular communication activity" (e.g., baby talk or technical jargon) rather than "a full-fledged linguistic system," which in Italian would be *lingua*. The former name had reflected and affirmed the linguistic status of the signed language, but the new name disavowed the status. The Parliament was willing to pass the bill with the new name but the Deaf community soundly rejected it and called for keeping the former name, which reflected the actual nature of LIS (LIS Subito! n.d.). Despite the intervention by the leaders of the Italian Deaf community and academics and researchers in LIS- and Deaf-related fields, the call for retaining the former name went unheard and instead, the Parliament, with the support of medical professionals, drafted a new bill that required speech and hearing interventions for deaf children, including the use of cochlear implants, in order to ensure their proper educational and language developments (LIS Subito! n.d.). This is the reality for the Deaf communities in Italy, America, and many other countries whose signed languages are largely ignored, viewed as impediments, or used as communication support systems instead of languages in their own right. This view is an outgrowth of an ideology held by individuals and institutions that signing is a visual representation of deafness, which is the problem in society and the belief that deaf people with deafness need to be restored to full citizenship by using the aural/oral mode of communication.

Communities of signed language users in the world may be small in comparison to some populations of spoken language users and the issues of modality, physical ability, education, and culture may be special to the communities of deaf and hard-of-hearing members. Even with the differences, the study of signed languages in the area of language ideologies, policies, and attitudes is just as important as the study of spoken languages because the former can offer insights and understanding in the investigation of language ideologies, policies, and attitudes that may not be otherwise achieved in the study of spoken languages.

Notes

1. The term "Deaf" with the uppercase *D* is used to describe communities of sign language users with various degrees of hearing loss who subscribe to cultural values, beliefs, and behaviors relating to deafness. The term "deaf" with the

lower-case *d* describes deafness as physical deficiency in the context of medical viewpoint.

2. The Deaf President Now movement took place at Gallaudet University in 1988. Students, faculty and staff joined together with members of the Deaf community to successfully demand that the world's only university dedicated to the education of Deaf and hard of hearing students be led by a Deaf president. On March 13, 1988, Dr. I. King Jordan was named as the university's first Deaf president. For further information see: http://www.gallaudet.edu/about_gallaudet/history_of_the_university/dpn_home.html.

References

ASLTA. 2010. The American Sign Language Teachers Association (ASLTA): Procedures & Materials for Provisional Certification. [online]. www.aslta.org.

Baynton, D. C. 1996. *Forbidden signs: American culture and the campaign against sign language*. Chicago: University of Chicago Press.

Campbell-Kibler, K. 2006. *Listener perceptions of sociolinguistic variables: The case of (ing)*. Ph.D. dissertation. Stanford University.

Campbell-Kibler, K. 2009. The nature of sociolinguistic perception. *Variation and Change* 21: 135–56.

Eagly, A., & Chaiken, S. 1993. *The psychology of attitudes*. Orlando, FL: Harcourt Brace Javanovich.

Eagly, A., & Chaiken, S. 2007. The advantages of an inclusive definition of attitude. *Social Cognition* 25: 582–602.

Eisen, M.D. 2009. The history of cochlear implants. In J. K. Niparko (ed), *Cochlear implants: principles & practices*, 2nd ed., 89–94. Philadelphia: Lippincott Williams & Wilkins.

Gallaudet Research Institute. 2003. *Regional and national summary report of data from the 2002–2003 annual survey of deaf and hard of hearing children and youth*. Washington, DC.

Garrett, P. 2010. *Attitudes to language*. Cambridge: Cambridge University Press.

Green, L. J. 2002. *African American English: A linguistic introduction*. Cambridge: Cambridge University Press.

Hill, J. 2011. *Language attitudes in the American Deaf community*. Ph.D. dissertation. Gallaudet University.

Jacobs, L.M. 1989. *A Deaf adult speaks out*. Washington, DC: Gallaudet University Press.

Johnson, R. E., & Erting, C. 1989. Ethnicity and socialization in a classroom for Deaf children. In C. Lucas (ed.), *The sociolinguistics of the Deaf community*, 41–83. San Diego: Academic Press.

Kannapell, B. 1994. Deaf identity: An American perspective. In C. Erting, R. C. Johnson, D. L. Smith, & B. D. Snider (eds.), *The Deaf way: perspectives from the international conference on Deaf culture*, 44–48. Washington, DC: Gallaudet University Press.

Karchmer, M. A., & Mitchell, R. E. 2003. Demographic and achievement characteristics of deaf and hard-of-hearing students. In M. Marschark & P. E.

Spencer (eds.), *Oxford handbook of Deaf studies, language, and education*, 21–37. Oxford: Oxford University Press.

La protesta dei sordomuti, la lingua dei segni deve avere la stessa dignità di quelle parlate. 2011. *La Repubblica*, May 30, 2011. [online]. http://www.repubblica.it/solidarieta/volontariato/2011/05/30/news/la_protesta_dei_sordomuti_la_lingua_dei_segni_deve_avere_la_stessa_dignit_di_quelle_parlate-16977846/index.html.

Lane, H. L. 2002. Do Deaf people have a disability? *Sign Language Studies* 2: 356–79.

Lane, H., Hoffmeister, R., & Bahan, B. 1996. *A journey into the DEAF-WORLD*. San Diego: Dawn Sign Press.

Leigh, I. 2009. *A lens on Deaf identities*. Oxford: Oxford University Press.

LIS Subito! (n.d.) Retrieved September 13, 2011 from Movimento Lingua dei Segni Italiana Subito! http://www.lissubito.com/.

Lucas, C., & Valli, C. 1992. *Language contact in the American Deaf community*. San Diego: Academic Press.

Markowicz, H. 1980. Myths about American Sign Language. In H. Lane & F. Grosjean (eds.), *Recent perspectives on American Sign Language*, 1–6. Hillsdale, NJ: Lawrence Erlbaum.

McCaskill, C, Lucas, C., Bayley, R., & Hill, J. 2011. *The hidden treasure of Black ASL: Its history and structure*. Washington, DC: Gallaudet University Press.

Milroy, J. 2001. Language ideologies and the consequences of standardization. *Journal of Sociolinguistics* 5: 530–55.

Mitchell, R. E., & Karchmer, M. A. 2004. When parents are deaf versus hard of hearing: Patterns of sign use and school placement of deaf and hard-of-hearing children. *Journal of Deaf Studies and Deaf Education* 9: 133–52.

Mitchell, R. E., & Karchmer, M. A. 2005. Parent hearing status and signing among deaf and hard of hearing students. *Sign Language Studies* 5: 231–44.

Mitchell, R. E., & Karchmer, M.A. 2006. Demographics of deaf education: More students in more places. *American Annals of the Deaf* 151(2): 95–104.

Monaghan, L. 2003. A world's eye view: Deaf cultures in global perspective. In L. Monaghan, C. Schmaling, K. Nakamura, & G. H. Turner (eds.), *Many ways to be Deaf: International variation in Deaf communities*, 1–24. Washington, DC: Gallaudet University Press.

Nassisi, S. 2010. Lingua dei segni, ancora ritardi la legge è ferma in commissione. *La Repubblica*, 27 Decemeber 2010. [online]. http://www.repubblica.it/solidarieta/volontariato/2010/12/27/news/lingua_dei_segni_ancora_ritardi_la_legge_ferma_in_commissione-10633842/index.html.

Newell, W., & Caccamise, F. 2008. Section 10: Connection American Sign Language (ASL) instruction and the sign language proficiency interview (SLPI). [online]. http://www.ntid.rit.edu/slpi.

Niedzielski, N. 1999. The effect of social information on the perception of sociolinguistic variables. *Journal of Language and Social Psychology* 18:62–85.

Padden, C. & Humphries, T. 2005. *Inside Deaf culture*. Cambridge, MA: Harvard University Press.

Preston, D. R. 2002. Language with an attitude. In J. K. Chambers, P. Trudgill, & N. Schilling-Estes (eds.), *The handbook of language variation and change*, 40–66. Oxford: Blackwell.

Reagan, T. G. 2010. *Language policy and planning for sign languages*. Washington, DC: Gallaudet University Press.

Reagan, T. G. (2011) Ideological barriers to American Sign Language: Unpacking linguistic resistance. *Sign Language Studies* 11(4): 606–36.
Rosen, R. 2010. American Sign Language curricula: A review. *Sign Language Studies* 10:348–81.
Schein, J.D., & Stewart, D.A. 1995. *Language in motion: Exploring the nature of sign.* Washington, DC: Gallaudet University Press.
Searls, D.B. 2011. A commentary on the recent controversy to recognize Lingua dei Segni Italiana. E-letter, 1 June 2011. [online]. http://www.discoveringdeafworlds.org/component/k2/item/4-when-your-voice-is-no-longer-your-own-a-commentary-on-the-recent-controversy-to-recognize-lingua-dei-segni-italiana.html.
Stokoe, W. 1960. *Sign language structure: An outline of visual communication systems of the American Deaf.* Studies in Linguistics: Occasional Paper 8. Buffalo, NY: University of Buffalo, Linguistics Department.
Stone, R., & Stirling, L. O. 1994. Developing and defining an identity: Deaf children of deaf and hearing parents. In C. Erting, R. C. Johnson, D. L. Smith, & B. D. Snider (eds.), *The Deaf Way: Perspectives from the International Conference on Deaf Culture,* 48–54. Washington, DC: Gallaudet University Press.
Ward Trotter, J. 1989. An examination of language attitudes of teachers of the deaf. In C. Lucas (ed.), *The sociolinguistics of the Deaf community,* 211–28. San Diego, CA: Academic Press.
Williams, F., Whitehead, J. L., & Miller, L. M. 1971. Ethnic stereotyping and judgments of children's speech. *Speech Monographs* 38:166–70.
Wolfram, W. 1991. *Dialects and American English.* Englewood Cliffs, NJ: Prentice Hall.

PART VI

SOCIOLINGUISTICS, THE PROFESSIONS, AND THE PUBLIC INTEREST

CHAPTER 34

LANGUAGE AND LAW

GREGORY MATOESIAN

SINCE the groundbreaking works of Atkinson and Drew (1979) and O'Barr (1981) the field of language and law has developed at a brisk and productive pace to become a dynamic fixture on the sociolinguistic landscape. From trials to jury deliberations, from credit card disclosures to law school socialization, from police interviews to citizen's emergency calls, language is the central vehicle through which the business of law is transacted (Hobbs 2008). Rather than being the passive vehicle for the imposition of legal variables, language constitutes the interactional medium through which evidence, precedent, and identity are forged into legal relevance, anchoring the infrastructure of legal decision making and integrating social context into the fabric of legal conduct. In this chapter I focus on the complex yet elusive relationship between language, law, and sociocultural context.

In the case of language and law, we can trace a historical relationship to ancient Rome, where lawyers were referred to as "orators," (Friedman 1977: 21), while in medieval England barristers were called "storytellers" (from the Latin "narrators," Simpson 1988: 149), both terms highlighting the legal value placed on verbal skills. Modern linguists define the law as a "law of words" (Tiersma 1999: 4) and an "overwhelmingly linguistic institution" (Gibbons 2003: 1), one that not only includes formal jurisprudence but also police-citizen encounters, classrooms and criminal justice interviews. In fact, the title of the first major textbook on language and law, *Just Words* (Conley and O'Barr 2005), symbolizes the systemic relationship between linguistic and legal institutions.

While practical interest in legal discourse emanates from a centuries-old quest for the holy grail of legal argument, systematic research on the relationship between legal discourse and sociocultural organization is a relatively recent subfield that crisscrosses linguistic and social sciences. In the first attempt to integrate social structure with linguistic variables, O'Barr (1981) employed mock witness-jury experiments to demonstrate how variation in linguistic forms like hypercorrection, hedges, empty adjectives, and politeness correlated with attitudinal outcomes such as convincingness, trustworthiness, persuasiveness, and competence. Individuals who were low in socioeconomic status used more powerless forms (e.g., hedges) while higher status speakers employed more powerful forms and thus scored higher on attitudinal outcome measurements, reproducing social inequalities in the process.

Since then we have witnessed a surge of research that integrates language, culture, and social identity across a range of legal contexts, most notably centered on how social power is embodied in and reproduced through legal discourse. As Mertz (2003) observes, the crowning achievement of the language and law field—its cutting edge contribution to not only sociolinguistics but law and social science more generally—has been its ability to develop sophisticated formulations of how social power functions in the situated details of linguistic interaction. I share this deep commitment to analyzing micro forms of sociolegal conduct while grounding analysis in the broader historical circumstances and cultural contexts that shape and are shaped by sociolinguistic processes of legal interaction.

In this chapter I discuss the sociocultural dimensions of language and law, paying particular attention to the role of power in legal discourse, and offer the following outline. Because studies of language and law typically cross artificial disciplinary boundaries to reveal the semiotic resources participants bring to bear on the joint construction of legal realities and institutional identities, section one discusses the major contributing approaches to the sociocultural analysis of language and law: Conversation Analysis (CA), linguistic anthropology and, to a lesser extent, Critical Discourse Analysis (CDA). I address the conceptual and methodological tools these fields provide for the study of language, law, and power, the ongoing debate they generate and, conversely, the contribution of language and law studies to studies of language use more generally. For clarity and consistency of exposition, I use data from trial examination as illustrations. The second section covers substantive studies from what has been referred to as the *language and power school of legal anthropology*: law school socialization, police-citizen interaction, courtrooms, bilingual encounters, and cross-cultural misunderstandings in legal interviews and translation. In the final section, I suggest a new direction for the study of language and law, one that may provide a deeper understanding of language, law and sociocultural context.

Theoretical Disciplines

Conversation Analysis

CA, a microsociological perspective that derives from the work of Goffman and Garfinkel, imposes a strict methodological discipline governing acceptable data and analysis. Avoiding premature coding schemes, abstract theorizing, and ideal types it adopts a data-driven approach that focuses on talk produced by and relevant to the participants at specific moments in the interaction. Unlike survey or interview data (or memories, recollections, and experiments) that uses language as an unexplicated resource to gain access to some topic, it considers naturally occurring data—data preserved and inspected through transcripts of audio and/or audio-video recordings—as a topic worthy of study in its own right. A rigorously empirical form of inquiry preoccupied with scientific replication, it analyzes sequential structures of talk, like turn taking, as the joint accomplishment of conversational participants.

A major conceptual development from CA influenced the study of language and law. According to Sacks et al (1974), turn-taking systems exist along a linear array of speech exchange systems based on degree of preallocation of turns and turn types, from natural conversation on the one hand to debates, on the other, with courtrooms, medical consultations, news interviews, therapy sessions, classrooms, and other speech events nestled in between. The notion of speech exchange system provides the basis for a comparative analysis of institutional forms—how these vary from the base line of natural conversation on the one hand and other institutional forms on the other.

In the first comprehensive study of institutional variation from a CA perspective, Atkinson and Drew (1979) noted that courtroom language operates in a distinct speech exchange system with differential participation rights based on institutional identities. In contrast to the "local" grounding of everyday conversation, courtroom discourse possesses a system of turn and turn-type preallocation in which attorneys ask questions while witnesses answer, a discursive division of labor visible not only through aggregate patterns but also in participant orientation to deviant cases or violations of institutional protocol. In the process, the institution of law is *talked into being* (Drew & Heritage 1992), as the following example (Matoesian 2008) illustrates:

Extract 1 (A=Attorney / W=Witness)

001 A: You knew that you were going to be asked questions
002 . . .
003 (1.1)
004 W: Yes.
005 (7.3)

006 W: ((*slight head tilt forward and back at 7.0*))
007 W: ((*lip smack/alveolar click and head movement forward toward microphone with thinking face display at 7.3*))
008 W: I would like to complete my answer on uh:: the question (.)
009 about (.) saying that Senat[or Kennedy was watching.
010 [((gaze moves to DA))
011 (0.9)
012 W: ((*raised and sustained eyebrow flash with mouth open-close co-occurring with three microvertical head nods*))
013 (3.3)
014 A: Uh::: (.) which question are you answering now:: miss::://
015 W: You had asked me uh::: (.) yesterday (0.5) n'you also asked me
016 this morning (0.5) **about** my statement to the police

Notice first that W waits till a lengthy pause in the A's talk before *requesting* permission to complete a statement from the prior day's questioning. She does not merely produce the statement but formally requests permission, maintaining institutional and discursive identities of attorney/questioner and witness/answerer in the process. Second, after A fails to respond (notice the 0.9 second pause in line 11), she produces a series of visual increments consisting of a raised eyebrow flash and three micro head nods in an escalating attempt to elicit an answer while withholding continuation of her statement (still maintaining institutional arrangements). Third, when A starts to talk, after a lengthy 3.3 second pause, his response is prefaced with two further delay components, the first a prolongation on utterance initial *Uh:::*, the second a short micropause—both marking violations of institutional protocol through perturbations in delivery of his turn-in-progress. Last, when he finally responds he does so not with an answer but with a question that reformulates her request as an answer to some prior question (line 014), thus maintaining the discursive division of labor in which attorneys ask questions while witnesses answer them. In this short exchange, we can see the interactive dynamics between participants, how both shape the organization of deviant turn incursion, mark it as a departure from institutional structure and, in so doing, contextualize the relevance of law in the unfolding talk.

The legal institution may be talked into being through explicit metapragmatic structure when, for example, the judge or attorney constrains the witness's verbal contribution.

Extract 2 **(Judge)**
001 A: So you were aware of the meaning of this song, "Going to go downtown,"
002 and in the colloquial... "Gonna go and get me some ass"
003 is that correct?
004 W: . . . Can I ask you a question?
005 J: No.

Extract 3 below illustrates a similar case in point. In everyday conversation, simultaneous talk is locally managed or resolved by the participants on a moment-by-moment basis. In courtroom interaction, however, there is a techno-legal constraint that *may* serve to minimize simultaneous talk.

Extract 3 (Court Reporter).

001 A: What's the it?
002 W: Patricia Bowman's account...
003 is a damnable lie
004 [
005 A: So you're saying that she's a liar=
006 CR: =...I can't- can't report over (( ))
007 (1.2)
008 J: Missuz Lasch (.) there's been no objection from Mr. Black
009 but there is one from Mr. Crane...And Mr. Crane speak up
010 if you can't report.

Here, we can see that the one-party-at-a-time rule, minimizing and resolving simultaneous talk, may function in and through the institutional demands that the court reporter capture the proceedings for the record, and violations of that institutional requirement (the simultaneous talk in lines 3–5) may be resolved by judicial authority.

In extract 4 below we can see another instance in which the legal order shapes the organization of question and answer sequences, one that departs significantly from both everyday conversation and other institutional contexts, one that captures a unique institutional signature of legal language. Unlike other linguistic contexts, questions in the courtroom do not automatically inherit answers in next turn. Objection sequences—the objection-opportunity space following each question—suspend, and may even terminate the relevance of an answer entirely. They demonstrate how legal context is not only oriented to by participants but is also relevant for the evidential organization of trial discourse—not question/answer but an *objection-mediated question/answer system*.

Extract 4

001 A: What about Detective Rigolo? She saw Ms. Bownman...were you
002 aware that she also saw her in a distraught mood?
003 A: Objection...Assumes facts not in evidence...
005 J: OK, members of the jury, questions by lawyers are not evidence and I
006 need to confer with the attorneys...

In sum: the notion of speech exchange system represents a fertile contribution to the study of language and law because it captures structural aspects of legal discourse in a systematic model, a rich analytic stimulus for generating a cumulative body of replicable research findings. If attorneys control the turn-taking system and turn types embedded in it, then they control the use of questions; and if they control questions, then they may shape topics, ideologies, and presuppositions to their advantage during the proceedings. Still, while the notion of speech exchange system appears posed as the conceptual platform for systematic analysis of power and sociolegal epistemology based on asymmetrical distribution of discursive options, CA has been reluctant to bestow such transcendental attributes upon the data. I will explain why shortly.

Linguistic Anthropology

Linguistic anthropological approaches to discourse operate with different methodologies, concepts, and assumptions about data, meaning, and context. These differences possess important implications for research.

Gumperz's (1982) work in interactional sociolinguistics (IS) shows how the sequential structures of CA constitute only one of the indexical practices that ground conversational inference and shape meaning. His concept of contextualization cues brings into analytic prominence the integration of nonrepresentational signs or tacit signaling devices such as bodily conduct intonation; stress; pitch register; tempo; and paralinguistic and stylistic devices that participants employ to co-construct context, perform identity, and frame interactional meaning. They channel conversational inferences necessary for the successful coordination of social interaction.

Broader than the local context characteristic of CA, contextualization conventions are mediated by cultural variables like age, class, race, gender and ethnicity, and such diversity among social groups produces differential expectations that shape the production and reception of contextualization cues. Although lack of interactional synchrony often appears, on the surface, as cross-cultural "misunderstanding," it may also reflect ideological processes that naturalize deeply engraved forms of domination. Erickson and Schultz's (1982) micro-ethnography *The Counselor as Gatekeeper* represents a perfect case in point. They discuss how different cultural expectations about contextualization conventions mediate the gatekeeping interview and shape the co-construction of social identity, generating significant outcomes for the reproduction of social inequality. Methodologically, this study demonstrates how interactional sociolinguistic approaches are ethnographically rooted in the cultural experiences of participants, not just sequential marking.

Silverstein's (1993) ideas on metapragmatics, linguistic ideologies, and intertextuality have exerted a strong influence in studies of language and law. He integrates language with sociocultural context through the concept of linguistic ideology—folk rationalizations or beliefs about language use.

Linguistic ideologies create novel and emergent ensembles of context in meticulously orchestrated real-time linguistic interaction, transforming language into a vehicle of emotional expression and encoding culture through a medley of semiotic resources like iconicity, stance, and indexicality. To illustrate, a crucial feature of law involves the historical circulation of language in the form of reported speech. From first-year law school classes studying precedent in contract law to opening statements in a trial, from written intake interviews of battered women seeking restraining orders to criminal confessions, reported speech constitutes the evidential and precedential infrastructure of law. This intertextual grounding occurs as speakers extract speech from its historical setting, position it in a new speech event and naturalize or authorize it as the same.

Silverstein draws on work by Goffman (1981) on participation and footing and by Bakhtin (1981) and Voloshinov (1973) on voicing in dialogue. Goffman introduced footing to illustrate speakers' relationship to their utterances, decomposing participant roles into more discriminating categories. The animator verbally or physically produces the words; the author composes them; and the principal authorizes the production of those words as the responsible party. In a similar vein, Bakhtin and Voloshinov demonstrated that reported speech was not a mere replication of historical discourse but constructed speech in which the speaker inserts his or her voice as a discursive strategy. With these (grossly simplified) points in mind, consider the following extract from an opening statement in a criminal trial.

Extract 5

001	A:	She ca:::lls Ann Mercer and says
002		"I've been raped come and pick me up."

In line 2 the attorney uses a direct quote attributed to the victim in a rape trial. Grammatical features such as tense, person, contracted auxiliary and quotative verb index an image of authentic wording—an ideology of meaning as reference—from the victim's historical speech. Moreover, the quote occurs without any prosodic or paralinguistic marking, suggesting an oddly stoic way to talk about the unsettling sweep of events that had just transpired at the defendant's residence. By projecting a reflexive relationship among verbal style, legal identity, and affective stance, he tacitly evaluates the victim's speech and fosters the impression that lack of emotion is inconsistent with the claim of just having been raped (see Wilce 2009). As Silverstein notes, this is how the linguistic ideology of reference and folk beliefs about ownership of the quote—literalized in grammatical and prosodic structure—not only frame our interpretation of language but also shape legal identity and evidence by naturalizing denotational text over strategic meaning in the historical circulation of utterances.[1] By appearing as the mere animator of the victim's words while projecting her as the author and principal, A conceals his voice in the quote to generate a powerful emotional inconsistency: a linguistic ideology of inconsistency. The inconsistency is not merely a logical juxtaposition of contradictory facts but is also a strategic logic of power in the naturalization of gender identity and the authorization of meaning. As this happens, we can witness an integration of language use with sociocultural context in the mobilization of meaning.

Both Gumperz's interactional sociolinguistics and Silverstein's semiotic anthropology overlap with CA in a preference to study (1) real-time interaction, (2) meaning as a linguistic co-construction between participants and, most importantly, (3) social identity, not as a passive, a priori attribute of individual personality, but as a contextually situated and interactionally emergent performance. And each analytic preference has played a pivotal role in the study of language and law. But their contextual diversity in concepts like power and intertextuality departs significantly from CA.

Critical Discourse Analysis

While most linguistic anthropological approaches to discourse operate with bottom-up analyses in which culture, identity, and power emerge in real-time interaction, CDA is much more explicit regarding political orientation and the relevance of institutional context; its primary goal is integration of language and critical social theory, especially social power. Focusing on semantio-grammatical meanings of political, educational, racial, and capitalist texts as well as on mass media images, CDA invokes a top-down approach to language and hidden forms of domination in a post-Marxian quest for political emancipation from oppressive social structures. Wodak (1995: 204) sums up this position when she notes that CDA studies "opaque as well as transparent relationships of domination, discrimination, power and control as manifested in language."

The Language, Law, and Power Debate

And it is this politically motivated approach to language use—the a priori imposition of power and ideology in discourse—that forms the axis for the most crucial debate in the field of language and law: the politics of legal language in the reproduction of sociolegal domination (Travers 2006).

CA argues that exogenous variables in the form of social structure and power must be *demonstrably* relevant to the participants—rather than the analysts—of interaction and procedurally consequential for communicative practice. This is not to say, a priori, that power and social structure are irrelevant to the interaction order, but imposition of institutional or political context must reflect participant orientations and possess organizational consequences at precisely designated spatial-temporal environments (as we saw in extracts 1–4). A priori contextualizations of power, identity, or social structure violate the integrity of the interaction order and erase participant's orientations to the organization of social action. Moreover, when social power frames discourse from "on high" it becomes a self-fulfilling prophecy as research selects relevant data to support the analyst's a priori contextualizations—setting about the task of finding confirming instances of power or social structure—rather than consider participant-relevant contexts.

Because the legal institution is talked into being, CA takes a dynamic view of context and identity as incrementally developed and contingently renewed on a moment-by-moment basis. Legal context and identity are inherently transformable in the sequential rhythms of talk, as Schegloff (1988) demonstrated in his classic study of the George W. Bush–Dan Rather affair (what started out as a news interview transformed into an everyday argument). Such an improvisational view of institutional interaction offers a corrective to the reification of culture, power, and identity in which discourse is "read off" of transcendent structures—a tempting analytic strategy in legal settings because of the pre-allocation of turns and turn types. CA directs this poignant critique not only at CDA and linguistic anthropology but at power-driven approaches in the study of language and law. To see the importance of this critique, consider the following.

Extract 6

A: And you don't have any idea how she got those bruises?
W: . . . while Patty Bowman was with me she did not get those
bruises. If you're asking me how somebody might get bruises
who's on a blood thinner I can give you any number of different
reasons. She may have gotten them dancing (0.7) She may
have gotten them chasing around a child (.) She may have gotten
gotten them taking pantyhose off in the car…

According to CA, power-driven approaches assume that institutional identities reflect asymmetrical distributions of power; those who question have more power than those who answer. However, power grounded in real-time discursive interaction constitutes a negotiated process involving multiple contexts, not a single context predetermined by institutional structure. In extract 6 (from Matoesian 2001), A produces an inference that the defendant caused the victim's bruises after a sexual assault. After denying the accusation, W poses an *if*-conditional attributed to A, which he then proceeds to answer in hypothetical detail. However, A never asked the recalibrated question in line 3. In this extract, W recalibrates questioner and answer roles, reconfigures them into novel forms of institutional participation (in which W transforms his legal identity from witness/defendant to medical expert offering hypothetical opinion through the repetition of modal perfects) and projects his own question to which an answer can arguably be heard, creating a subtle yet telling shift in topic. Just because attorneys inhabit the institutionally endowed role of asking questions does not mean that witnesses only answer. While the attorney asks questions, witnesses may (1) provide answers, (2) project "virtual" questions that displace the attorney's question, (3) recontextualize answers that align with their virtual question—fostering the impression that their *response is a reply to the attorney's question*—and, in so doing, (4) index legal identity. Answers are not passive discursive objects but strategic and interactive resources participants deploy to calibrate and recalibrate participation roles. That institutional practices and legal identities mirror structural arrangements ignores their interactionally emergent and contextually situated logic.

But if the legal institution is merely talked into being as CA claims, capable of being reshaped in each indexically situated utterance, then what explanatory power does the concept of speech exchange system possess? If the institution is talked into being then how can any institutional setting import transcendental structure into discourse above and beyond each unfolding utterance? Of course, analysts can impose such order but then we get back to the problem of reifying structure. On the other hand, if institutional structures are contingently enacted in each successive utterance then is the notion of speech exchange system in general and courtroom systems in particular redundant in an explanatory sense?[2]

Participant orientation presents us with a much more contentious matter. How strict should we interpret this restriction on analysis? Although CA portrays participant orientations as empirically transparent, this is not necessarily the case. By way of analogy (yet, of course, in a quite different analytic context), Berlin, Breedlove, and Raven (1968) found the unique beginner category in some folk taxonomies was not overtly lexicalized or linguistically marked yet still functioned as a perceptually salient category. At the same time, Berlin and Kay (1969) discovered that human perceptual discriminatory ability could not be inferred by the mere presence or absence of a particular color term.

By the same token, why assume that sociocultural categories must be sequentially marked to make analytic claims about participant's orientations? Even in the case of discursive marking, the interpretation is open to dispute because participants may orient to different levels of sociocultural context. Additionally, the analyst's interpretation of participant's interpretation will always be in issue and, according to some linguistic anthropologists (Blommaert, 2005), CA ignores this crucial entextualization issue.

A useful way of addressing the issue would be to consider a classic CA example from Drew (1992) in his study of a defense attorney's cross-examination of a rape victim.

Extract 7 (from Drew 1992)

23	A:	Well you kne:w at that ti:me. that the
24		defendant was. in:terested (.) in you
25		did'n you?
26		(1.3)
27	W:	He: asked me how I'(d) bin: en
28		(1.1)
29		J- just stuff like that
30	A:	Just asked yuh how (0.5) yud bi:n (0.3)
31		but he kissed yuh goodnigh:t (0.5) izzat righ:t

In Drew's analysis, A questions W about the defendant's "interest" and uses her alternative description in lines 27–29 as the basis for the formally marked contrast in lines 30 and 31. In the process, he assembles an inconsistency in the victim's version to suggest a degree of intimacy and interest.

However, why does W dispute A's question with an alternative characterization? Why not just say, hypothetically: "Yes I knew he was interested in me" or "I was interested in him"? Is it possible that terms like "interest" and "intimacy" possess sociocultural meanings not embedded on the surface of the question-answer sequence? While such questions go beyond CA's restrictions on analysis, do they reach beyond participants' orientations? W knows that any "interest" the defendant has in her or she in him will be interpreted, not from some generic sense of interest, but from an ideological framework of sexual interest: the way men are interested in women. W's understanding of interest will be erased and displaced by a "reciprocal" sexual interest that applies "co-equally" to both him and her. This is a sociocultural form of domination rooted in the participant's orientation but at a different level than Drew's analysis, a context that arrogates the female perspective on sexual preference as it simultaneously projects the male standard of sexuality and sexual access (impersonal sex) as normatively transparent. And she displays an orientation to the relevance of intimacy and interest in this sociocultural context at this specific moment. The inconsistency stems from the fact that W consents not to sex but to dominational standards of sexuality and sexual access, and her position in the linguistic double-bind motivates the contrasting version. Agreeing to even the most innocent form of flirtation or "intimacy" means sexual consent; on the other hand, to deny or even minimize such "interest" creates what Drew sees as a logical inconsistency.

Here, we can gain a more symbolic understanding of a participant's orientation by observing how the co-construction of linguistic meaning indexes sociocultural context and aligns sociolegal power at precise moments in the interaction. But to do so we must address the following: what do intimacy, interest, and consent mean and whose account counts? We have to show not only the participant's orientation to the interaction order but relevant sociocultural contexts and how they mutually elaborate one another.

In this instance, an argument can be made that inconsistency is not merely a natural juxtaposition of contradictory facts of evidence or legal rationality but also a thoroughly contingent microculture of linguistic logic.

This is not a critique of CA but a limitation of analytical scope. CA can analyze the institution marked through sequential practices but not how it embeds ideological or power-driven contextualizations. Moreover, there is no a priori reason to assume that all studies of power assume a political stance or ignore participant's orientations. In this regard, Drew's data reveals legal language as not only an indexically situated co-construction but also a socially reproduced instrument of legal hegemony.

CA makes metaphysical assumptions about the ontological supremacy and analytic priority of natural conversation as the interactional infrastructure from which institutional language ostensibly derives. That sequential analysis is autonomous, indigenous, and not justified by reference to external reality is a deep leitmotif of CA. That institutional discourse derives from natural conversation is merely an essentialistic aspect of the general theory. This forms the basis for comparative analyses of institutional talk and informs the claim that legal language involves reductions and transformations of everyday conversation (Drew & Heritage 1992).

In terms of comparative analysis, the question about the supremacy of natural conversation over institutional forms is problematic. It is not addressed as an empirical matter; rather it is an a priori assumption that CA makes about the nature of language, meaning, and analysis (Briggs 1997). That natural conversation stands in a position of analytic and empirical priority over legal language ignores how law contributes to the adversarial culture of talk and limits our ability to examine single cases in detail to see the indexical emergence of sociocultural context.[3] For students of language and law, a more useful approach envisions legal language as a structurally anchored *and* emergent activity designed to manage institutionally specific tasks, inferences, and identities in legal context. Legal language is not merely a constraint (or derivation or subsidiary of natural talk) but a sociocultural resource participants bring to bear on the interactive co-construction of legal reality.

In this regard consider the continuation of extract 1.

Extract 8

001 W: *I would like to complete that answer for the jury please.*
002 (0.9)
003 A: *You mean* this is an answer that I asked you yesterday you
004 now after thinking about it overnight want to complete the
005 ah::: answer//
006 W: Ah::: No. I didn't have the opportunity to *answer your*
007 *question yesterday ((staccato delivery))*
008 A: I'm sorry I thought you had uh:: completed your answer.
009 If you want to say something to the jury that you've had
010 time to think about (.) // please go ((lower volume))
011 W: No- it- >*I haven't had time to think about it.*
012 *I would have said the same thing yesterday when*
013 *you asked me.*< ((*Sped up, stress & +volume*))
.
.
022 I had asked her (.) uh few questions (1.7) Uh:::
023 she repeated (2.5) th- that *he was watching, he was watching*
024 (2.8) I (.) then, in return, asked her (.) who was watching. (0.8)
025 [*Was Senator Kennedy watching*?
026 [((eyebrow flash))

Comparative studies that collect detached taxonomies of reported speech, for example, would miss the interactive processes of sociolegal power in the above extract. Notice how A enacts evidential authority to shape the epistemological criteria for gauging the truth of utterances; utterances that are planned beforehand are evidentially and epistemologically "contaminated" and constitute inferior forms of legal knowledge (lines 3–5 and 8–10). Just as important,

W's interruptive and prosodically marked "defensiveness" in lines 11–13 interacts with A's metapragmatic structuring to draw disparaging attention to the authenticity of her forthcoming direct quotes. When the quotes materialize in lines 23 and 25, they appear rehearsed, overly formal—shaped by A's metapragmatic structuring in concert with W's prior denials. Notice, in particular, that the parenthetical in line 24 and the highly animated eyebrow flash co-occurring with the quote in line 26 help foster this theatrical self-presentation.[4]

Two final issues: first, reported speech not only inheres in the grammatical, sequential and paralinguistic properties of an isolated speaker's narrative or utterance (or even in the immediate sequential environment) to project onto extralinguistic reality; it is contingently grounded in the broader constellation of metapragmatic power and epistemic gestalt in which it is interactively encrusted. Only by looking at the interaction order and sociocultural context simultaneously and in-depth can we envision the reflexive relationship between them. Of course, we need comparative studies to specify the species-specific sequential structures of legal discourse. But if, on the other hand, our aim is to analyze the sociocultural resources participants bring to bear on the constitution of legal realities then research can proceed with or without comparative institutional analysis. And, second, this example delivers on the promissory note stated in my introduction: that the study of legal discourse not only draws on sociolinguistic disciplines for analytic inspiration but makes distinct contributions to sociolinguistic inquiry.

The Language and Power School of Legal Anthropology

And it is this reflexive relationship that lays the sociocultural foundation for studying language and law. Travers (2006) christened the *language and power school of legal anthropology* (or LPS) in reference to a loose coalition of research that draws its inspiration from the work of Conley and O'Barr on language, law, and power. For Conley and O'Barr (2005: 129) "language is the essential mechanism through which the power of law is realized, exercised, reproduced and occasionally challenged and subverted." Rather than being the institutional site for the realization of social justice and equality, legal discourse also serves to legitimate legal-rational domination and impede social-legal change. The LPS incorporates ideas from CA, linguistic anthropology, and CDA to integrate sociocultural context with the fine-grained details of legal language. Power is not a mere reflex of asymmetrically structures but reproduced through communicative practice. The substantive studies described below integrate these two dimensions of social life.

Courts

Conley and O'Barr's (1990) study of cultural variation in legal practice and evidence initiated the language and power school tradition. Studying small claims courts, they found two types of ideological narratives in the constitution of legal identity and culture. Lawyers, business owners, and the highly educated bring a rule orientation to court that emphasizes formal legal rationality a la Weber, a formal logic in which particular cases are subsumed under the auspices of universal and impersonal laws like legal responsibility. They possess the cultural capital that resonates with judicial ideology and tend to prevail in verbal disputes. Lay litigants—the poor, minorities, and women—bring a relational orientation to court that emphasizes substantive legal rationality a la Weber, personal, emotionally-laden stories that invoke values, justice, and social need. Their low levels of cultural capital translate into negative experiences in court.

More recent studies on the role of ideology in court by Philips, Hirsch, and Richland stand in line of descent from Conley & O'Barr while also drawing heavily on Silverstein's ideas on linguistic ideology. Philips (1998) examines intertextual variation when judges take guilty pleas from defendants in Arizona state courts and how stylistic features of language such as variation in question form index a complex interpenetration of legal, political, and cultural ideologies. Hirsch (1998) analyzes the discursive production and reproduction of gender in Swahili Muslim courts. She relates linguistic ideologies that prescribe proper linguistic behavior in terms of complaining and gossiping about marital discord to grammatical, stylistic, and phonological features of courtroom discourse and their effects on case outcome. In a study of Hopi tribal courts, Richland (2008) studies how linguistic ideologies construct, contest, and negotiate tradition as a form of sociolegal power. He shows judges and tribal elders engaging in a discursive clash over control of legal evidence based on cultural ideas of sameness and difference, which in turn, constitutes control over knowledge, power, and authority in the Hopi legal order.

Each of the above studies illuminates the intertextual dynamics of ideology, not as a theoretical structure arbitrarily imposed by the analyst, but as an interactively emergent process that materializes in linguistic and discursive form to play a powerful role in the sociocultural process of constructing legal identity.

Atkinson and Drew's (1979) classic study *Order in Court* provided the analytic direction for CA-inspired studies of legal language. According to Atkinson and Drew, language in court operates within the surface syntax of question-answer sequences, mirroring the legal-linguistic ideology that only answers from witnesses, not questions from attorneys, constitute evidence. This means that attorneys must map illocutionary acts and other activity types onto question form to generate accusations, comments, and inconsistencies. Moreover, since witnesses rarely agree with accusations and other face-threatening acts in cross-examination, attorneys have to orchestrate inferences through a progressive elicitation of facts and get witnesses to agree with them, an interactive process that often yields an progressive series of questions.[5]

Cotterill, Ehrlich, and Matoesian draw on Atkinson and Drew's insights but integrate CA with IS and CDA to analyze how questions function as negotiated forms of control. The key issue for the LPS in this regard is: how do the "facts" relate to sociolegal power and sociocultural inferences? In the Kennedy Smith rape trial, the defense attorney created inferences about the victim's moral character and sexual history by referring to her ex-boyfriend as "*your daughter's father,*" even though such history is formally prohibited by rape shield statutes. Similarly, in the O. J. Simpson trial (Cotterill 2003) the prosecuting attorney referred to the defendant as an "abusive husband" whose violent pattern escalated to the murder of his wife while the defense characterized those same events as "isolated incidents" of ordinary family disputes. Ehrlich (2001) investigated the questioning power of defense attorneys as they frame legal representations of sexual assault to create cultural inferences that the victim did not resist to the utmost.

Each study illuminates the negotiation of accusations, blame, and responsibility in the co-construction of legal realities. But, departing from strict CA canon, the LPS *adds* how questioners generally, though not invariably, wield power to frame topics and exploit ideological hegemonies during the course of questioning. Not only is the institution talked into being, so is power.

Any discussion of language in court would be incomplete without brief mention of the most important development in contemporary law in the United States—the role of expert evidence in criminal and civil cases. As Carr (2010: 17) mentions: "The anthropology of expertise focuses on what people do rather than what they possess." Rather than view expertise as a static legal identity authorized by judicial ruling, the LPS sees expert identity—and the evidential authority bestowed upon it—as a dynamic process enacted in performance. While lay witnesses can testify only to their personal observations, experts may provide opinions and explanations based on their special skills, training, education and qualifications. As we saw in extract 6, while not a formally or legally tendered expert, the witness in a trial indexed expert identity through poetic repetition of modal perfects and technical terms in the medical register (*blood thinner*)—sociocultural context woven deeply into grammatical and discursive form—to cast doubt on the nature of the victim's injuries after the attorney "opened the door" by asking for his explanation on the causes of the victim's injury. In his study of the Rodney King trial, Goodwin (1994) illustrated how a defense expert played a crucial role in the acquittal of four officers charged with police brutality through the use of coding schemes, highlighting, and manipulation of physical artifacts. And Cotterill's (2003) comparison of expert and lay witnesses showed how the former correlated with longer-turn length, more interruptions, and topic shifts in relation to questioning attorneys, recalibrating the institutionally endowed power asymmetry between them.

Law School, Restraining Orders, and Bilingual Translation

In *The Language of Law School,* Mertz describes how legal expertise and the reproduction of law occurs in law school classrooms, where students train to "think like lawyers." For Mertz, professional "thinking" emerges through discursive socialization rituals of learning to read, write, and talk like a professional, learning new ideologies of language that bleach social, emotional and moral contexts to reach an epistemologically privileged sanctum of legal truth and facticity, cloaking "the impact of social power" and reproducing "social inequalities through law" (Mertz 2007: 217).

In *Latinas, Narratives of Domestic Abuse,* Trinch (2003) analyzes intertextual and bilingual forms of linguistic control in the protective order interview for battered women. The protective order interview represents the final link in an interinstitutional and intertextual chain of speech events where the victim tells her story to a variety of criminal justice gatekeepers, who in turn, translate and distort her intercultural experience of abuse into institutionally privileged genres.

Berk-Seligson (2009) and Eades (2008) also deal with the impact of bilingualism, intercultural communication and translation in the legal system. Berk-Seligson analyzed police interrogations of immigrant Latino suspects with limited English proficiency. Police interrogators and police interpreters (with limited Spanish proficiency) use coercive interrogations to obtain false confessions from suspects. While forensic psychology and legal research have examined eyewitness error, withholding evidence, lack of competent counsel, police and prosecutor misconduct, her study discovered that language proficiency and subtle shifts in footing play a major role in obtaining false confessions. As with other LPS studies, she focuses on language and institutional power: the asymmetrical relationship between police and suspects. Studying Australian hearings, Eades demonstrated how attorneys strategically exploited cultural differences between Standard English and Aborigine English to generate unflattering inferences about the credibility of Aborigine witnesses. Minorities are not only linguistically vulnerable but legally disadvantaged too.

In summary, the language and power school of legal anthropology views law as a natural site for exploring the negotiation of power in the sociolegal life of language. But, as mentioned to in the introduction, there is an undeveloped component of language that must be included in the study of legal discourse.

Conclusion: A Direction for Future Research

In the movie *The Devil's Advocate,* Al Pacino's character, Satan, refers to the law as the "ultimate backstage pass" and lawyers as the "new priesthood," along with a thoroughly unveiled allusion about their (and his) power in society. To continue with the Goffmanian analogy, I would add that it constitutes the penultimate front stage ritual, a linguistic performance that permeates our modern and postmodern condition from the most intimate aspects of social life to the most impersonal contracts, accelerating the globalization of rationality and channeling the powerful conflicts associated with it.

But while the new "priests" (like the old priests) are indeed powerful, they perform their sociolegal rituals with quite a bit more than just verbal and/or written modes of language. In closing this chapter I would like to offer both a critique of, and new direction for, the sociolinguistic study of law by expanding the orthodox conception of language currently employed in the field.

Language and law studies operate with a limited verbal bias that ignores how discourse functions as a multimodal resource in the construction of institutional identity and management of legal interaction. Ironically, while the scholarly study of gesture and other forms of bodily conduct originated with the study of legal oratory (Kendon 2004: 20), contemporary investigations of legal discourse focus exclusively on verbal or written language. Recent advances by McNeill (1992) and Kendon (2004), however, reveal that speakers integrate temporally synchronized and semantically linked co-speech gestures (or idiosyncratic hand movements) into the stream of utterance construction to configure emergent ensembles of meaning. Working from a CA perspective, Goodwin (1981) and Heath & Hindsmarsh (2002) demonstrate that interlocutors integrate gesture, gaze, posture, technological devices and material artifacts into the unfolding stream of talk to manage turn taking and other sequential activities. As we saw briefly in extracts 1 and 8, legal discourse functions as a multimodal and interactive field of joint action that contextualizes participation, grounds epistemic stance and constructs culture in the management of turn taking and identity and enables attorneys to make metapragmatic evaluations otherwise suppressed in linguistic form alone (Matoesian 2005, 2008). Bodily conduct is not mere affective embellishment of verbal or written modes but contributes its own distinct strands of discursive relevance in the semiotic integration of utterance construction and situated meaning. If language is multimodal, then it follows that the study of legal language needs to incorporate a more comprehensive view of language: language as the improvisational integration of verbal and visual modes in the contextualization of sociolegal action. Ignoring this other half of the language equation leaves us with an incomplete understanding of the "new priesthood" and the sociocultural dynamics embodied in it.

Notes

1. In a brilliant overview of the topic, James Wilce (2009) shows that emotion or affect is not a personal or psychic experience but a strategic interactional and semiotic resource in the co-construction of meaning; even lack of emotion, as in the above extract, displays emotion. Following Silverstein, he argues the notion of

emotion as an inner psychic experience is a linguistic ideology or folk belief about the role of language and culture in everyday experience.

2. Even deviant case analysis, valuable as it is, fails to comprehend this dilemma. The deviant case is merely another contingent and spatiotemporal discursive object that marks the institution only at that moment. Why assume that it possesses transcendent patterning beyond its indexical moment of production?
3. As Tannen (1999) notes we live in an argument culture, and since the law has existed for over two thousand years, as Tiersma (1999) mentions, it is entirely plausible that natural conversation incorporates various dimensions of our legal culture, especially in the West.
4. The highly animated "eyebrow flash" (raised eyebrows) signals a sense of surprise. While there is no verbal frame for the quote, making it appear as free direct speech, her facial expression functions as a multimodal framing device that marks *Was Senator Kennedy watching* as a quote.
5. Because of syntactic and evidential constraints, attorneys cannot produce direct assessments, statements, or accusations (like "give me a break" or "you're lying"). Thus language in court constitutes a richly inferential environment in which ambiguity and indirection are built into the structure of questioning. On the flip side of that observation, answers, just like questions, perform any number of actions other than just answering, as we saw in extract 6.

References

Atkinson, J. M., & Drew, P. 1979. *Order in court.* New York: MacMillian.

Bakhtin, M. 1981. *The dialogic imagination.* Austin: University of Texas Press.

Berk-Seligson, S. 2009. *Coerced confessions.* Berlin: Mouton de Gruyter.

Berlin, B., Breedlove, D., & Raven, P. 1968. Covert categories and folk taxonomies. *American Anthropologist* 70: 290–99.

Berlin, B., & Kay, P. 1969. *Basic color terms.* Berkeley: University of California Press.

Blommaert, J. 2005. *Discourse.* New York: Cambridge University Press.

Briggs, C. 1997. From the ideal, the ordinary, and the orderly to conflict and violence in pragmatics research. *Pragmatics* 7(4): 451–59.

Carr, E. S. 2010. Enactments of expertise. *Annual review of Anthropology* 39: 17–32.

Conley, J., & O'Barr, W. 1990. *Rules versus relationships.* Chicago: University of Chicago Press.

Conley, J. ,& O'Barr, W. 2005. *Just words,* 2nd ed. Chicago: University of Chicago Press.

Cotterill, J. 2003. *Language and power in court.* New York: Palgrave Macmillan.

Drew, P. 1992. Contested evidence in courtroom cross-examination: The case of a trial for rape. In P. Drew & J. Heritage (eds.), *Talk at work: Interaction in institutional settings,* 470–520. Cambridge Cambridge University Press.

Drew, P., & Heritage, J. 1992. Analyzing talk at work: An introduction. In P. Drew & J. Heritage (eds.), *Talk at work: Interaction in institutional settings,* 3–65. Cambridge: Cambridge University Press.

Eades, D. 2008. *Courtroom talk and neocolonial control.* New York: Mouton.

Ehrlich, S. 2001. *Representing rape.* New York: Routledge.

Erickson, F., & Shultz, J. 1982. *The counselor as gatekeeper.* New York: Academic Press.

Friedman, L. 1977. *Law and society*. Englewood Cliffs: Prentice-Hall.
Gibbons, J. 2003. *Forensic linguistics*. Oxford: Blackwell.
Goffman, E. 1981. *Forms of talk*. Philadelphia: University of Pennsylvania Press.
Goodwin, C. 1981. *Conversational organization*. New York: Academic Press.
Goodwin, C. 1994. Professional vision. *American Anthropologist* 96(3): 606–33.
Gumperz, J. 1982. *Discourse strategies*. New York: Cambridge University Press.
Heath, C., & Hindmarsh, J. 2002. Analyzing interaction. In T. May (ed.), *Qualitative research in action*, 99–121. London: Sage.
Hirsch, S. 1998. *Pronouncing and persevering: Gender and the discourses of disputing in an African Islamic court*. Chicago: University of Chicago Press.
Hobbs, P. 2008. Discourse in the law. In W. Donsbach (ed.), *The international encyclopedia of communication*, vol. 4, 239–40. Oxford: Wiley-Blackwell.
Kendon, A. 2004. *Gesture*. New York: Cambridge University Press.
Matoesian, G. 2001. *Law and the language of identity*. Oxford: Oxford University Press.
Matoesian, G. 2005. Nailing down an answer. *Discourse Studies* 7: 733–59.
Matoesian, G. 2008. You might win the battle but lose the war: Multimodal, interactive, and extralinguistic aspects of witness resistance. *Journal of English Linguistics* 3: 195–219.
McNeill, D. 1992. *Hand and mind*. Chicago: University of Chicago Press.
Mertz, E. 2003. Review of G. Matoesian, *Law and the language of identity*. *American Ethnologist* 30: 632–34.
Mertz, E. 2007. *The language of law school*. New York: Oxford University Press.
O'Barr, W. 1981. *Linguistic evidence*. New York: Academic Press.
Philips, S. 1998. *Language in the ideology of judges*. New York: Oxford University Press.
Richland, J. 2008. *Arguing with tradition: The language of law in Hopi tribal court*. Chicago: University of Chicago Press.
Sacks, H., Schegloff, E., & Jefferson, G. 1974. A simplest systematics for the organization of turn-taking for conversation. *Language* 50: 696–735.
Schegloff, E. 1988. From interview to confrontation. *Research on Language and Social Interaction* 22: 215–40.
Silverstein, M. 1993. Metapragmatic discourse and metapragmatic function. In J. A. Lucy (ed.), *Reflexive language: Reported speech and metapragmatics*, 33–58. Cambridge: Cambridge University Press.
Simpson, A. 1988. *Invitation to law*. Oxford: Blackwell.
Tannen, D. 1999. *The argument culture*. New York: Ballantine.
Tiersma, P. 1999. *Legal language*. Chicago: University of Chicago Press.
Trinch, S. 2003. *Latinas narratives of domestic abuse*. Amsterdam: John Benjamins.
Travers, M. 2006. Understanding talk in legal settings. *Law and Social Inquiry* 31(2): 447–65.
Voloshinov, V. 1973. *Marxism and the philosophy of language*. Cambridge, MA: Harvard University Press.
Wilce, J. 2009. *Language and emotion*. New York: Cambridge University Press.
Wodak, R. 1995. Critical linguistics and critical discourse analysis. In J. Verschueren, J.-O. Östman, J. Blommaert, & C. Bulcaen (eds), *Handbook of pragmatics*, 204–10. Amsterdam: John Benjamins.

CHAPTER 35

OUR STORIES, OURSELVES

CAN THE CULTURE OF A LARGE MEDICAL SCHOOL BE CHANGED WITHOUT OPEN HEART SURGERY?

RICHARD M. FRANKEL

> In the early 1980s I was a third-year medical student working in the ER when a family (grandmother, uncle, and 10-year-old girl) came in badly burned in a house fire...The girl was in arrest and, despite all our efforts, died. The grandmother was alive but critically burned. The smell of charred flesh was overpowering. I was sent to ask the mother for an autopsy. Instead of beginning by informing her of the death I began with, "Sorry to bother you at this time but..." and then asked if we could do an autopsy. She screamed and collapsed, hysterical at my feet. I was aghast, guilty, stunned, felt inadequate to make any appropriate response. (spoken tearfully) I still feel awful about it to this today.

The story above was told recently by a senior physician at an American College of Physicians workshop on delivering bad news to patients. After telling it, the physician shared the fact that this was the first time he had ever told the story since the incident occurred some 25 years earlier. It would be comforting if this story and its silent history was unusual or an isolated example of the ways in which physicians were trained two to three decades ago, but this is not the case. I have heard hundreds of such stories, especially from mid- to late career physicians recalling challenges in their medical school or residency training. The stories share several common features. They almost always involve strong residual, and many times unexpressed, emotions such as sorrow, anger, or regret over events that occurred years to decades earlier. As well, the narrators universally felt isolated and alone with the knowledge and feelings of what happened. Help or support is reported as having been minimal or actively discouraged. Finally, there is a strong desire to spare young physicians the distress the narrator went through in his or her training. Taken together, the narratives offer a glimpse into the organizational culture and norms that dominated medical education during the mid- to late twentieth century.

Times have changed, and many educational reforms such as duty hour restrictions, the requirement in all graduate medical education that trainees exhibit competence in such core skills as communication and team work, and undergraduate medical school curricula that stress the importance of full disclosure of medical mistakes, have had a positive effect on education and institutional culture. Despite these positive developments there is still a widespread public perception that physicians lack the core skills of empathy and compassion necessary for "caring" for patients (Glass 1996; Stein, Nagy, & Jacobs 1998). The challenge for medical education and educators is how to create a culture of caring, competence, and community that will be carried forward into the professional lives and behaviors of graduates and practicing physicians.

Sociolinguistics as a field of scholarship has done much to add to our knowledge about discourse and social interaction, for example, how narratives are constructed and used by individuals and in organizations, language as performance, the effect(s) of context on language use, and the role of speech performance in such diverse fields as medicine, the law, education, and aviation (Cicourel 1983; Linde 2000; Mehan 1979; Mishler 1984, 1990; Tannen & Wallat 1983; Thornborrow & Coates 2005). While findings from these studies have created a rich empirical basis for understanding how language is used in everyday life, implementing these findings in large-scale change processes has been more promise than product.

My goals in this chapter are to (1) combine traditional approaches to analyzing narratives with strategies for *using* them to change organizational culture; (2) introduce the concepts of emergent design and appreciative inquiry as a framework for uncovering and disseminating an organization's core narrative, and (3) describe several innovative organization-level activities that used emergent design and appreciative inquiry narratives to change the culture of a large medical school.

In the Beginning...

Indiana University School of Medicine (IUSM) is currently the largest medical school in North America. With an entering class of 330 students per year, 1000 medical residents, a full-time faculty of 1200, and nine regional centers in which training occurs, it is a large and very complex organization. In late 2002, prior to the start of our culture change project, the school was saddled with several chronic problems: space was at a premium and budgets were tight, often causing conflict and distress; there was a feeling of anomie (just being a number in a very large machine) that pervaded the campus. In addition, students were quite dissatisfied with the quality of their education and the responsiveness of the administration to their concerns. This was reflected in distressingly low scores on the American Association of Medical College's (AAMC) graduation questionnaire, sent to all graduating senior students after their Dean's letter had been written and there was no possibility of reprisals. Compared with students from all other medical schools, IUSM was well below the national average in terms of quality of educational experience and students' perceptions of the administration's responsiveness to their concerns. This, despite the fact that IUSM students scored well on national exams—higher when matched with equivalent controls from other medical schools. Finally, the school had seen declining applications for admission for the past ten years.

In January of 2003, the Relationship Centered Care Initiative (RCCI) was launched with an audacious goal: to change the culture of the school and reverse some of the negative trends it had been experiencing over the prvious decade. Relationship-centered care (RCC) is an expanded form of patient-centered care, which focuses on including the values, attitudes, and preferences of patients as they seek and receive care. RCC also stresses the importance of affect and emotion, the personhood of both the physician and patient as a prerequisite for establishing genuine relationships, and the importance of reciprocal influence in relationships. RCC principles are also applicable to understanding organizational behavior. In contrast to thinking about an organization as bricks and mortar, a relationship-centered approach views organizations as composed at any given moment of a number of ongoing conversations and relationships (Suchman 1998). Changes in the nature of the conversations that make up the organizational narrative represent changes in the organization itself. Thus, the goal of the RCCI was to introduce new ways in which conversations and narratives in the organization might occur.

First Steps

A guiding concept throughout the RCCI was the use of "emergent design," basically, finding our way from opportunity to opportunity. Theoretically, emergent design stems from the idea in adult education that intrinsic motivation rather than controlling or dictating others' actions and learning is the most effective way of bringing about change (Stacey 1996). Using emergent design, our initial action was form a discovery team (DT) to uncover the organizational narrative of IUSM at its best and communicate the results back to the organization.

With the help of a thought partner, the associate dean for medical education, the RCCI leadership team approached 12 faculty members who were thought to be interested in culture change. The project was explained at a kick-off meeting and all agreed to participate and to interview other faculty members using appreciative inquiry (AI) as a framework. AI is an organizational-change approach that was developed by David Cooperrider, a professor in the business school at Case Western University (Cooperrider 2001). It has been used widely in the business community to shift organizations from a critical stance to quality (weed out poor performers, punish those responsible for errors, find and fix problems) to an appreciative stance (finding out what works well in an organization and asking how to get more of it, describing what it's like when people in the organization are at their best, sharing and learning from mistakes).

In the first six months of the project, the DT conducted 80 appreciative interviews with fellow faculty members. To ensure comparability a script was developed and each interviewer read the script to the respondent. The script read as follows:

> People do their best work when they are doing things that they find personally meaningful, and when they feel that their work makes a difference. During your time at IUSM, there have no doubt been highs points and lows, peaks and valleys. For now, I'd invite you think of a time that stands out for you as being particularly meaningful; a time that brought out the best of who you are, in which you felt connected to your values and your sense of calling and purpose:
>
> - Please tell the story of that time.
> - Without worrying about being modest, please tell me what was it about you—your unique qualities, gifts or capacities; decisions you made; or actions you took—that contributed to this experience?
> - What did others contribute?
> - What aspects of the context or situation contributed (setting, time, background circumstances, etc.)?

After the responses were collected an analysis team used an iterative consensus-building process to conduct a sociolinguistic analysis of the 80 narratives. Details of this process are reported elsewhere (Suchman, Williamson, Litzelman, Frankel, Mossbarger, & Inui 2004). Four themes were identified: believing in the capacity of all people to learn and grow, the importance of connectedness, the importance of passion, and the wonderment of medicine. The organizational narrative that emerged from the thematic analysis suggested that when those who made up the school of medicine were at their best, they embodied many of the qualities that seemed to be lacking in the AAMC exit questionnaire and other data about the school. Our assumption was that if we could use the results of our analysis to change conversations among faculty, staff, and students from what was missing to what we were like when we were at our best, it would create a natural pathway for the community to realize its positive potential.

After analyzing the narratives, the RCCI leadership team hosted a series of six "Town Hall Meetings" to share the results with the community at large. An open invitation went out to all faculty staff and students via *Scope*, the school's weekly electronic newsletter (http://scope.medicine.iu.edu/). The hour-long sessions were typically attended by the dean and executive associate deans and between 40 and 50 participants. Selected stories collected by the DT were retold, either by the faculty member who had conducted the interview or the individual who had been interviewed. Following the reading of the DT narratives, there was an "open mike" period in which those who felt moved were invited to tell their own appreciative stories and/or join the DT. Within 18 months of the project's inception the DT had grown from 12 to 175 active members. The following narrative illustrates the types of stories that were told at the Town Hall meetings.

Discovery Interview with an IUSM Faculty Member

> I had a patient who had cancer and eventually lost both kidneys, got on dialysis, and had a stroke. An Indiana farmer, he had been an extremely independent man who was now very dependent…He was miserable. Then he had a heart attack and was placed in the ICU. Once out, he said he never wanted to return…and didn't want any more therapy. I had a junior student, Chris, who got very close to this patient. While I was out of town the patient died. Chris took it hard. He had worked with the patient and his family, mainly his daughter, to help them understand their options…I called the daughter, thinking she might be upset that I was out of town when her father died, but she was fine. A very religious woman, she told me that her family had wondered a long time why God had allowed her dad to suffer so much and for so long, but now she knew why. She said her dad went through all that and died to make Chris a better doctor.

RCCI Takes on a Life of Its Own

As word began to spread about the RCCI, a number of "hot spot groups" with energy for culture change emerged. By its conclusion, every major committee, the senior administration, faculty, students, residents, and staff had initiated projects associated with the RCCI. Three initiatives, in particular, one by students, one for students, and one for the community at large illustrate the power of narrative to create culture change. Other initiatives are described in a series of publications about the RCCI (Cottingham et al. 2008; Inui et al. 2006; Inui et al. 2008; Litzelman & Cottingham 2007).

Taking Root

Shortly after the Town Hall meetings began, several students approached the DT interested in collecting appreciative stories from their fellow students. Using the same guidelines as the faculty, the students conducted 200 appreciative interviews which they edited down into a booklet containing 20 that were emblematic of their most positive experiences at the school. They entitled the booklet, "Taking Root and Becoming a Physician at Indiana University School of Medicine." In thinking about how best to disseminate their work, the students came up with the idea of putting a copy of the booklet into the pocket of the white coats the incoming matriculants don on their first day of meical school in a special ceremony that includes families, faculty, and friends. In so doing, the students reasoned, new matriculants would receive a powerful message about the community, its aspirations, and what it is like when it is at its best. Collecting new appreciative stories to share as a gift with incoming students has become a "tradition" at the School and has been carried on by the students for the last six years (see figure 35.1 for a photo of the appreciative story booklets).

Strategic Teaching and Evaluation of Professionalism (STEP)

Professionalism is a core competency that physicians are expected to evidence in their clinical and social behavior. It is an area of medicine that is often difficult to teach didactically because it is so complex and context dependent. During the RCCI, faculty on the leadership team received a small STEP grant from the American Medical Association. After reviewing many different approaches they concluded that using narrative was the most efficient and effective way to teach this important competency. What ensued was an educational experience built around students' professionalism narratives.

The program, which occurs during the students' third-year medicine rotation, uses a password protected secure website, where each student posts a weekly narrative about an experience (either positive or negative) that "taught you something about professionalism." At the end of each four-week rotation, all the narratives that have been posted are stripped of names or other identifiers and merged into a single document. The students meet with a faculty facilitator in a small group and spend the first part of the session reading through

Figure 35.1. Student narrative publications 2004–2010

a xeroxed copy of all the de-identified narratives that they and their classmates on the rotation have posted. The faculty preceptor invites the students to be on the lookout for the narratives that stand out for them. The selected narratives are read out loud to the group and a discussion of the professionalism issues involved ensues. Guiding questions posed by the facilitator to the group include: What was it about this story that caught your attention? Why did this happen? Have any of the rest of you seen something like this? What did it make you think? How did you feel in the moment? Now? What were the choices in this situation? Would you make the same choices? If not, why not? What would you do? What would you actually say? What are the risks? Below is a sample narrative chosen by a small group to discuss.

> My team had a patient who needed to be rushed to the cath lab to be intubated.... When nothing was said to the patient about where we were going or what we were doing she became anxious, started gagging and tried to pull the tube out. At this point, I could not take any more. I stepped past the cardiologist, held her hand, called her by name and told her where she was and what was happening... Without saying a word, the cardiologist again took the probe and started to push it in her mouth unsuccessfully. Next, he put a plastic syringe between her teeth to wedge her mouth open

> but was unsuccessful. Again, I stepped in and told her to try to relax and this time it advanced successfully. The next day, I was told she had died over night.... I know this was an urgent situation but I don't think it would've taken much to explain what was happening and for the cardiologist to talk to her before putting the probe in her mouth. I hope I never get used to seeing someone suffer without asking myself what I can do to help.

During the discussion of this narrative many students commented that the writer, one of their classmates, had acted very professionally in her attempt to humanize a difficult situation without provoking the cardiologist and causing more distress. At the same time, there were a few students who felt as though the narrator was out of line and should not have intervened. One of those who felt the student was not acting properly said to the group, "The narrator acted improperly because it was the cardiologist, after all, who had the 'big picture' in mind." Several students disagreed, stating that it was actually the medical student who saw the big picture and as a result acted to comfort the patient. The faculty facilitator suggested that issues of professionalism are often context dependent and are a matter of one's values, beliefs, and perspective. The students all agreed that this particular narrative was helpful in changing their conversation from defending right and wrong to expressing differing opinions in a respectful manner.

In addition to their impact on the groups of students who generated and reflected on them, each month's narratives were added, with permission, to a data base with the proviso that none would be used for research or educational purposes until after the students had graduated from IUSM. Since its inception in 2004, close to 1500 narratives have been collected, analyzed, and shared as part of the RCCI. Some of the uses to which the narratives have been put beyond the small, group sessions are schematized below in figure 35.2. These include use of the stories for a one-day intersession on professionalism for third-year students (MS3s), house staff orientation, DOM (department of medicine) grand rounds, research collaboration with the National Board of Medical Examiners, other courses and clerkships (such as OB/GYN and surgery), presentations at national meetings and workshops, hospital staff physician meetings, faculty development, and in scholarly publications (Karnieli-Miller et al. 2010). The cost of the program is approximately $3000 per year.

Mindfulness and Medicine

As the number and types of stories that were collected, analyzed, and used in the various venues in which RCCI was active increased it became apparent that there was a need and opportunity to create organization-wide dialog by calling attention to events and incidents that affected the entire community. To that end, a group from the leadership team created a column in the school's electronic newsletter, Scope, called "Mindfulness and Medicine" (M&M). The idea behind M&M was to harvest from the many stories that were being collected those that could be articulated briefly (in one or two paragraphs) and would have potentially high impact for community dialog. In addition to the story itself, we also sought commentary from a community member who could interpret and put the story in the larger organizational context.

Below is the inaugural column as it appeared in Scope.

> M&M: Mindfulness in Medicine
>
> The following story was shared an MSIII at a vertical mentoring meeting:
>
> A student reports: A surgery resident was to begin a procedure and have the patient ready for the attending when he arrived. When he didn't arrive on time, the resident told those assembled that he would wait since he had never done this procedure before and was uncomfortable starting it without supervision. When the attending arrived, he publicly "bawled out" the resident. After he had calmed down and reflected for a bit, the attending said that the resident had, in fact, made the right decision and apologized for making a scene. He admitted that his strong reactions were due to his own discomfort and embarrassment at being late. The attending's admission of responsibility left a positive impression on the student and was seen was a model of "conducting oneself professionally."

Publication of this story also included a commentary by the newly appointed chairman of the department of surgery.

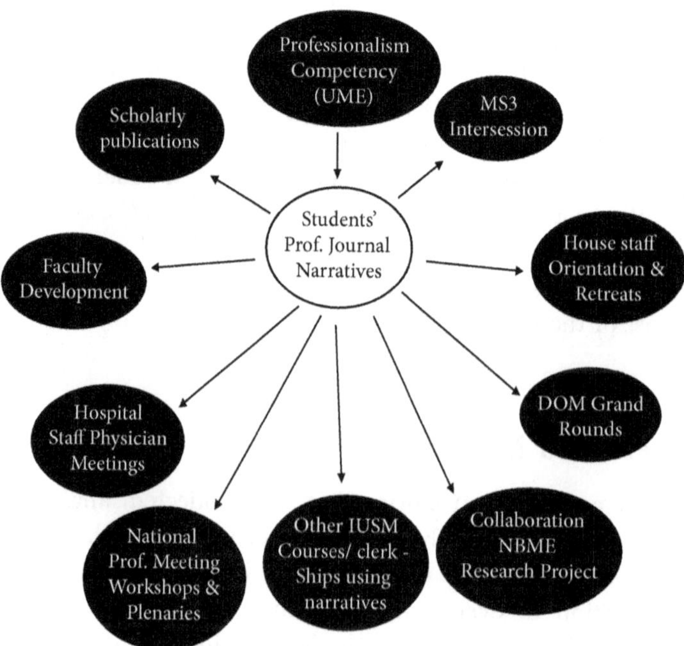

Figure 35.2. Impact of student professionalism narratives at Indiana University School of Medicine

Commentary: Chair of Surgery

Unfortunately, the event described here happens far too commonly on the surgical service... Upon discovering that the resident had not made progress to help him "catch up," his frustration led to a public display of displeasure. Regrettably, many surgeons have learned such behavior having seen it modeled by their own teachers.

I am sure that the attending realized within minutes that the resident had done the right thing and that it was the attending's reaction that was inappropriate. Rather than try to save face and continue to show "command" of the situation, he made the effort to publicly apologize for his error and affirm that the resident had made the right decision.

It is important for surgeons to remember that there is no one, resident, scrub nurse, anesthesia team member or other, who is not trying to do his or her best... This incident shows that we surgeons are learning to better deal with frustrating situations. It is my hope that my surgical colleagues will continue to maintain this progress in the future.

M&M columns have appeared in Scope for the past five years and the editors have received very positive feedback from faculty staff and trainees about the effect of the column in raising awareness of issues relevant to the community. Some of the issues raised in M&M create ongoing opportunities for reflection and change. For example, a recent column featured a picture of a poster advertising a lecture by a visiting professor of Indian extraction that had been defaced. The incident was brought to light by a student who had seen someone writing on the poster but didn't realize it was defamatory until several minutes later when she walked by it. As a result, she was unable to positively identify who the culprit was. The poster as it appeared in *Scope* is reproduced in figure 35.3.

The commentary that followed a short description of the incident was written by a third year medical student.

Response: Diversity of opinion is important in any organization, but promoting an atmosphere characterized by respect—a safe and trustworthy place for the exchange of ideas—is a cornerstone of academia. How does it make you, the reader, feel to see this kind of deliberate defamation? What does this incident, and our reaction to it, say about the writer, about us individually, and about our educational community? An incident such as this provides a valuable opportunity for our entire community to reflect on who we want to be and lessons to be learned. We can learn that it is important to encourage diversity of opinion through face-to-face conversations and academic discussion; not in defacing or defaming another's integrity anonymously or surreptitiously. We can resolve that stereotyping, especially of those who are "different" in language, culture or ethnicity has no place in our institution. We can value integrity... and reflect on the kind of medical school we most want to create, rededicating ourselves to building a community of trust and tolerance.

In essence, M&M allowed the RCCI to use narratives as a way of creating community dialog across the entire organization and to connect the dots,

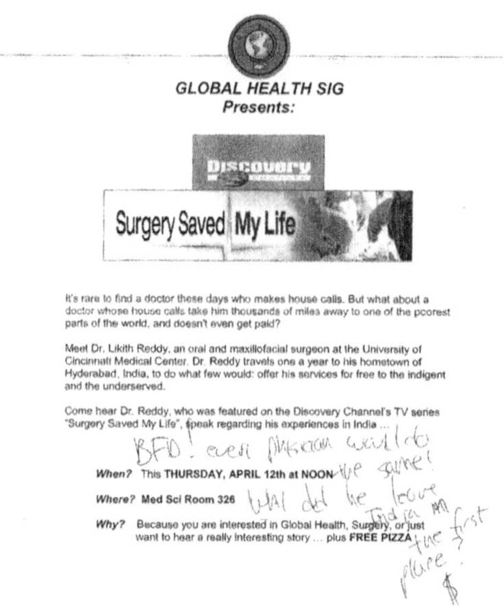

Figure 35.3. Photo of defaced poster published in *Mindfulness and Medicine*

as it were, between narrative-based conversations that were going on in town hall meetings, individual teaching sessions, clinical departments and scholarly activities. All were in the service of changing the culture of the school.

Evidence of Change

I began this chapter by noting that when the RCCI began, IUSM was facing some significant challenges and a culture marked by anomie, student dissatisfaction, and a perception that the school's administration was insensitive to student concerns. Recall also that the RCCI was based on emergent design, an attempt to focus on positive aspects of our culture and ongoing sociolinguistic analysis of narratives collected in a variety of venues across the organization. Six years later, many RCCI groups are active and new initiatives have sprung up where there is energy and enthusiasm. Although the initiative did not specifically target problems that were extant in 2003, we have noted changes in several outcomes that speak to a change in culture.

For example, we have compared the rates of student satisfaction with the overall quality of fmedical education prior to and during the RCCI (figure 35.4). Prior to its initiation satisfaction was well below the national average based on AAMC exit questionnaire data. By its second year, notable improvements in satisfaction were seen and this continued throughout the rest of the project.

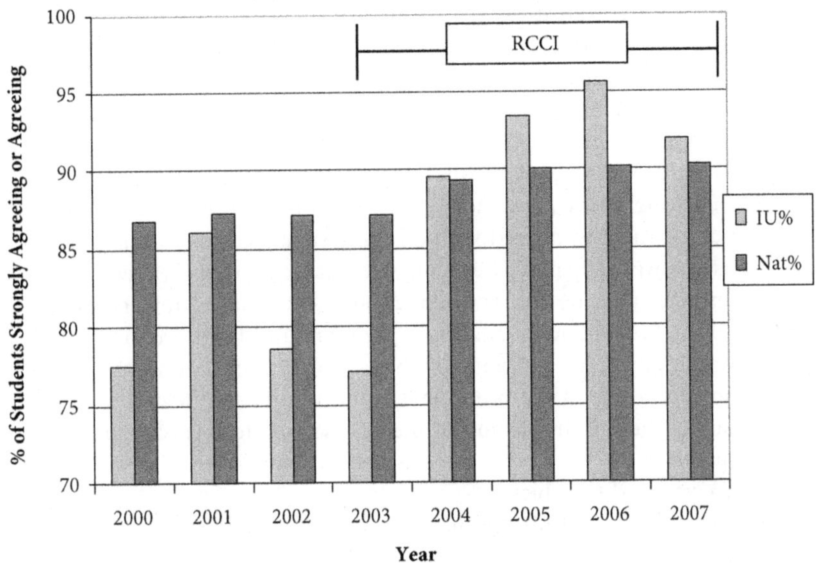

Figure 35.4. Overall satisfaction with quality of education

Similarly, when one looks at the AAMC exit data for responsiveness of administration to student concerns one sees a similar pattern of improvement beginning in the second year of the initiative and continuing forward. Figure 35.5 summarizes this data.

The change in student perceptions of administration's responsiveness to their concerns is useful and heartening in the aggregate. It also parallels our experience at ground level. The letter below, from a first year student, addressed to the executive associate dean for education, tells the story from a more holistic perspective.

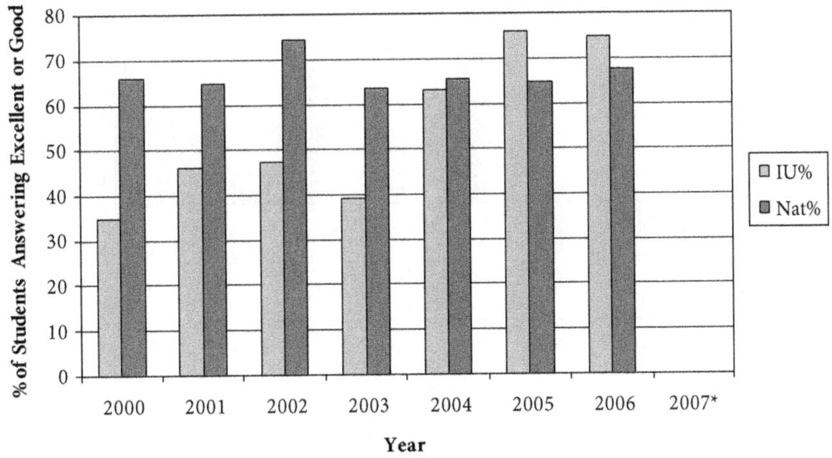

Figure 35.5. Responsiveness of administration to student concerns

Unsolicited Student Narrative

Dear Dean Lambert,*

I am sending this e-mail from the hospital where my mom had breast surgery less than two hours ago. I am sitting with her and she is doing fine…I was frustrated and really needed a second opinion in addition to my mom's surgeon. Wondering what to do, I remembered that you are a surgeon. Looking at my admission letter signed by you, I read the titles that you carry and I wondered with all the responsibilities you have, if you could even answer my email. I e-mailed you at 9:25 am on Friday, and in only 44 minutes at 10:09 am, you replied my e-mail, called my cell phone, and called my home. You arranged for my mom and I not only to meet with the right physician, but with the best. That was exactly what I needed, the opinion from one of the prominent authorities in the field. You have already taught me my first lesson in medical school: to respect, care and love my patients.

Thank you and God bless

August 5, 2008 *Not his real name.

Finally, figure 35.6 provides data on rates of application to IUSM from 2000 through 2007. Again, one can see that prior to the beginning of the RCCI rates of application were in decline. During this same time period, the average medical school applicant pool in the US grew by 3 percent, to 5 percent per year. From 2003 to 2007 applications to IUSM jumped 100 percent. Members of the admissions committee, including myself, reported that when applicants asked why they were applying to IUSM, many replied that they had heard about the competency curriculum and the RCCI and were interested in coming to a medical school that promoted values they aspired to.

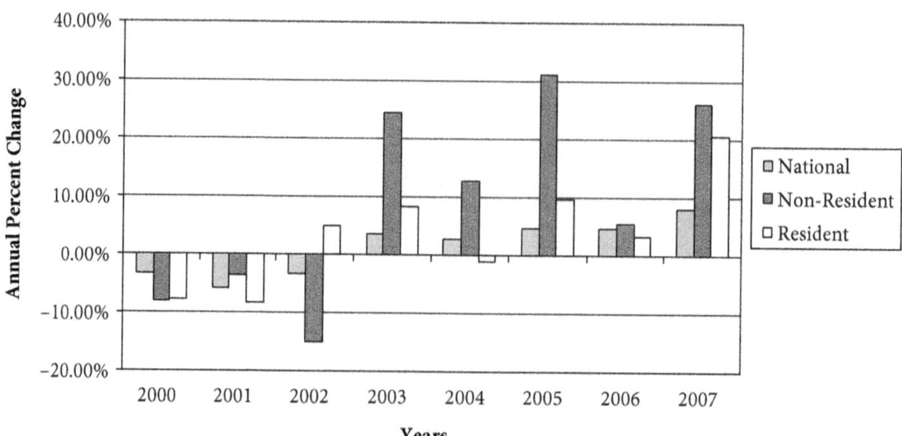

Figure 35.6. Percentage change in number of applications to all US medical schools and to IUSM from Indiana residents and nonresidents

Conclusion

The point of departure for this chapter has been combining traditional sociolinguistic analysis of narratives with large-scale organizational change strategies. It is interesting to note overlapping concepts in these two streams of scholarship. For example, a core concept in AI (which is decidedly non-linguistic in its origins) is that words create reality and change the way people think and act (Cooperrider, Whitney, & Stavros 2007). The selfsame assertion can be found in the Sapir-Whorf hypothesis, which argues that reality is built upon the language (speech) habits of a community and that this predisposes its members to particular choices of interpretation and thought (Whorf 1940). Our assumption in starting the RCCI was that if we could change the nature of the conversations that were going on in our organization, ipso facto we would change the organization. The outcome data that we have collected suggest that we are on the right path.

Using AI, focusing on who we are when we're at our best, led us to discover that our strength lay in qualities such as personal growth, connectedness, passion, and wonder, all of which turned out to be where people's energy for change and improvement were. In addition, we learned that we could use narratives at every level of the organization to change the nature of its members' conversations. Finally, by encouraging others to lead according to *their* hopes, dreams and energy; not our prescriptions or pedagogy, we learned that letting go of control and investing in relationships paid rich dividends in terms of the attractiveness of the RCCI to others and its effects in changing the culture of our school. It has been rich, rewarding and inspiring work, as I hope this chapter has made clear.

References

Cooperrider, D., Whitney, D., & Stavros, J. 2007. *Appreciative inquiry handbook*, 2nd ed. San Francisco: Berrett-Koehler.

Cooperrider, D. L. 2001. *Appreciative inquiry: An emerging direction of organization development*. Champaign, IL: Stipes.

Cottingham, A. H., Suchman, A. L., Litzelman, D. K., Frankel, R. M., Mossbarger, D. L., Williamson, P. R., Baldwin, D. C. Jr., & Inui, T. S. 2008. Enhancing the informal curriculum of a medical school: A case study in organizational culture change. *Journal of General Internal Medicine* 23: 715–22.

Glass, R. M. 1996. The patient-physician relationship. JAMA focuses on the center of medicine. *Journal of the American Medical Association* 275: 147–48.

Inui, T. S., Cottingham, A. H., Frankel, R. M., Litzelman, D. K., Mossbarger, D. Suchman, Vu, T.R., & Williamson, P. 2006. Educating for professionalism at Indiana University School of Medicine: Feet on the ground and fresh eyes. In D. Wear & J. M. Aultman (eds.), *Professionalism in medicine: Critical perspectives* 165–84. New York: Springer.

Inui, T.S., Cottingham, A. H., Frankel, R. M., Litzelman, D. K., Suchman, A. L., & Williamson. 2008, P. Supporting teaching and learning of professionalism—Changing the educational environment and students' "navigational skills." In R. L. Cruess, S. R. Cruess, & Y. Steinert (eds.), *Teaching medical professionalism,* 108–23. New York: Cambridge University Press.

Karnieli-Miller, O., Taylor, A. C., Cottingham, A. H., Inui, T. S., Vu, T.R., & Frankel, R. M. 2010. Exploring the meaning of respect in medical student education: An analysis of student narratives. *Journal of General Internal Medicine* 25: 1309–304.

Linde, C. 2000. The acquisition of a speaker by a story: How history becomes memory and identity. *Ethos* 28: 608–32.

Litzelman, D. K., & Cottingham, A. H. 2007. The new formal competency-based curriculum and informal curriculum at Indiana University School of Medicine: Overview and five-year analysis. *Academic Medicine* 82: 410–21.

Mehan, H. 1979. *Learning lessons: Social organization in the classroom.* Cambridge, MA: Harvard University Press.

Mishler, E. G. 1984. *The discourse of medicine: Dialectics of medical interviews.* Norwood, NJ: Ablex.

Mishler, E. G. 1990. Validation in inquiry-guided research: The role of exemplars in narrative studies. *Harvard Educational Review* 60: 414–42.

Stacey, R. 1996. *Complexity and creativity in organizations.* San Francisco: Berrett-Koehler.

Stein, T. S., Nagy, V. T., & Jacobs, L. 1998. Caring for patients one conversation at a time: Musings from the interregional clinician patient communication leadership group. *Permanente Journal* 2: 62–68.

Suchman, A. L. 1998. Control and relation: Two foundational values and their consequences. In A. L. Suchman, R. J. Botelho, & P. Hinton-Walker (eds.), *Partnerships in healthcare: Transforming relational Process,* 9–18. Rochester: University of Rochester Press.

Suchman, A. L., Williamson, P., Litzelman, D. K., Frankel, R. M., Mossbarger, D. L., & Inui. T. S. 2004. Towards an informal curriculum that teaches professionalism: Transforming the social environment of a medical school. *Journal of General Internal Medicine* 19: 501–04.

Tannen, D., & Wallat, C. 1983. Doctor/mother/child communication: Linguistic analysis of a pediatric interaction. In S.Fisher & A. D. Todd (eds.), *The social organization of doctor-patient communication,* 203–19. Washington: Center for Applied Linguistics.

Thornborrow, J., & Coates, J. 2005. *The sociolinguistics of narrative.* Amsterdam: John Benjamins.

Whorf, B. L. 1940. Science and linguistics. *Technology Review* 42: 229–31.

CHAPTER 36

SOCIOLINGUISTIC STUDIES OF SIGNED LANGUAGE INTERPRETING

MELANIE METZGER AND CYNTHIA ROY

SOCIOLINGUISTIC processes are inherent in the practice of interpretation. Interpreters, within seconds, receive, interpret, and reconstruct utterances between two languages, using their linguistic, social and cultural, or sociolinguistic knowledge to create a successful, communicative exchange. Interpreting simultaneously constitutes intentional sociolinguistic analyses by interpreters, and reflects the tacit, sociolinguistic knowledge of interpreters engaged in the task. Despite the fact that investigations of interpreting span many disciplines, sociolinguistic approaches and methodologies are well suited to interpreting studies, precisely because interpreting involves such a complex array of language and social behavior. Richards (1953, cited in Cokely 1985) declared interpreting to be "probably the most complex type of event produced in the evolution of the cosmos" (250). While that might be hyperbole, scholars in a variety of disciplines agree that interpretation is indeed an intricate and multifaceted process (Anderson 1976; Brislin 1976; Nida 1964; Shuy 1987; Wadensjö 1992).

Eugene Nida, a respected linguist and translation scholar, was the first to urge the application of the perspectives and methodologies of sociolinguistics to translation/interpretation issues. He believed that sociolinguistics offered a way to systematically analyze the communicative whole of texts, including information outside the text itself, stating that "only a sociolinguistic approach to translation is ultimately valid" (1976: 77). In this sense, not only is the sociolinguistic context a relevant aspect of interpretation as a profession, but also the larger sociolinguistic context in which interpreters work. Each interpreted interaction undertaken by a professional interpreter is situated within communities that harbor their own unique multilingual, bilingual, and language contact phenomenon; within a setting that represents a snapshot of what may be a long history of language policies and planning; and in a social environment beset with language attitudes about one or both of the languages involved.

While much of the early research and discussion of interpreting focused on information-processing models of interpretation, the dynamic nature of interpreted interaction and the convergence of sociology, anthropology, and linguistic approaches soon led researchers to sociolinguistic studies of interpreting. These studies have followed a variety of methodological approaches within sociolinguistics, as well as described different aspects of interpretation. Since the earliest studies of signed language interpretation in the 1970s, a growing body of research from a variety of disciplines has contributed to our understanding of interpretation as an interdisciplinary activity (Metzger 2006).

In this chapter, we will describe some major and minor sociolinguistic studies of interpretation with the underlying assumption that interpretation itself constitutes a sociolinguistic activity from the moment an assignment is accepted, including the products and processes inherent to the task, reflecting variously issues of bilingualism or multilingualism, language contact, variation, language policy and planning, language attitudes, and of course, discourse analysis.

Contextualizing Sociolinguistic Studies of Interpretation

In 1964, when the American professional association of signed language interpreters was established as the Registry of Interpreters for the Deaf (RID), the members of this association, acknowledging a growing need for more interpreters, pushed for educational programs, which in turn motivated and encouraged research (Per-Lee 1981). Interpreting is both a cognitive activity as well as a sociolinguistic activity, and much of the research in both spoken and signed languages began with a focus on the cognitive process that could be explored experimentally. Researchers were fascinated by the idea of a bilingual who could listen to a message in one language and then, with the slightest of delays, simultaneously transfer the message into a different language, turning to information-processing models for insight into how interpreters manage this task. These studies focused on input, manipulation and segmentation of information, and strategies to cope with information overload, seeking to describe cognitive stages or test the number and type of errors committed by interpreters (Treisman 1965; Gerver 1974; Moser 1978).

While there are several American studies on signed language interpreting from the 1970s and early 1980s (Brasel 1976; Colton 1982; Hurwitz 1980), it was not until the mid-1980s that sociolinguistic studies first made their appearance. While many of the first studies were experimental, the emerging field of sociolinguistics and its exploration of how people spoke in a natural setting pushed researchers toward data that was authentic and produced in a setting where the participants were involved in a real activity, such as giving a lecture. Researchers began to move away from concerns of error, correctness, and source-text /target-text comparisons and to focus on the multiparty interaction with the interpreter as coordinator and negotiator of meanings (Wadensjö 1998).

Toward a Sociolinguistic Model

The first signed language interpreting dissertation to be called a sociolinguistic study was by Cokely (1985), which, while focusing on "miscue analysis" recognized that sociolinguistic factors influence interpreter choices. Cokely's dissertation, "Towards a sociolinguistic model of the interpreting process: A focus on ASL and English" and later book, *Interpretation: A sociolinguistic model* (1992), analyzes the performance of six interpreters at a conference and identifies a taxonomy of interpreter miscues that include omissions, substitutions, additions, intrusions, and anomalies. These miscues point to cognitive stages of information-processing from which Cokely designed a seven-stage model of the interpreting process, from the moment an interpreter receives an incoming message from a speaker of one language to the production of the final message in the target language.

Cokely's greatest nod toward sociolinguistic methodology was in terms of data collection: he filmed interpreters as they worked, interpreting from English to American Sign Language (ASL) at a conference on interpreter education. He transcribed four speeches and their simultaneous interpretations into ASL, and then sampled 20 percent of the taped time, or the final minute of each five-minute segment. While attention centered on single lexical items and syntactic or semantic equivalence, Cokely also pointed out anomalies, inappropriate translations according to social and cultural norms. His work began to bridge the previous focus on cognitive processing to a new sociolinguistic focus.

The next major sociolinguistic studies of interpretation applied methodological approaches and theoretical frameworks developed within sociolinguistics, ranging from conversational analysis, to frames and schemas, to codeswitching and code-mixing, and discourse analysis, among others.

Interpreting as a Discourse Process

The next major sociolinguistic study was conducted by Roy (1989, 2000) whose approach comes from interactional sociolinguistics, specifically following in the steps of Gumperz (1982) and Tannen (1984). Roy's study focused on the turn exchanges of an interpreted interaction between a college professor and a graduate student. Up to this point, investigations into interpreting had either been experiments or films of interpreters as they worked in large, public settings. But signed language interpreters do the bulk of their work in face-to-face, private meetings with three participants: two primary speakers and an interpreter. This study was the first to film the kind of interaction interpreters engage in on a daily basis.

A professor-student interaction was filmed, transcribed and, then, combining structural perspectives from Conversation Analysis with Tannen's (1984) use of sociolinguistic playback interviews to determine participant perspectives, the interaction among all three participants was analyzed. Roy's findings focused on both the structure of the turn taking (Sacks, Schegloff, & Jefferson 1974) in the three-way conversation, and on the participants' intentions and interpretations about the turns that were taken (Bennett 1981, Tannen 1984). Her findings revealed that speakers take turns with the interpreter, the interpreter takes turns, and that this activity demonstrates that the interpreter, rather than being a neutral conveyor of messages, is an active participant who can potentially influence the direction and outcome of the event. At that time, the ideology of the field was that interpreters should make it seem as if speakers are talking directly to each other, and to act as a mechanical conduit and simply pass messages back and forth. Roy's work demonstrated that, although many turns are exchanged through the interpreter smoothly, there are also turns that are problematic, and interpreters are in a position to manage and direct the interaction. Roy's findings have been supported by Sanheim (2003), who replicated her study in an examination of turn taking in an interpreted medical encounter.

Where Roy demonstrated that interpreters are active in the communicative process via turn taking, Metzger (1995, 1999) pursued the question of interpreter influence in interactions further and in much greater detail, combining several approaches of sociolinguistics. As she explained, the paradox of interpreting is that, while the goal of interpreters is to provide access to an interaction of which they are not a part, they are, in fact, physically and interactionally present (1999: 21–24). Thus, the question should be, what is the interpreter's influence on interactive discourse?

Metzger examined two videotaped, medical interviews, one a mock, student-interpreted interview; and the other, a real-life, professionally interpreted, pediatric interview. Using frame and schema theories (Tannen 1979; Tannen & Wallat 1993; Schiffrin 1994), Metzger identified four frames in both interactions, and was able to show that while the participants shared similar schemas for the medical encounters, they did not share similar schemas for the interpreted encounter. This mismatch had an impact on the interaction and the interpreters produced self-generated utterances, which manifested in a variety of ways (such as explanations, repetitions, responses to questions, and others), whether interpreters were relaying messages or managing the interaction. These findings complement Roy's findings of the active participation of an interpreter in one encounter and mirror Wadensjö's (1992) findings in spoken language interpretation, and they lead to a more complex picture of the question about interpreter neutrality. Metzger demonstrated, for example, that if interpreters do not generate contributions, a myriad of interactional problems can ensue, while interpreter behavior becomes even more marked. Her study was expanded in Metzger, Fleetwood, and Collins (2004) by applying her findings to additional discourse genres and modes. Specifically, a comparison of an interpretation of a graduate seminar course and an interpretation of a panel of Deaf Blind people being interviewed about the Deaf Blind community with the original medical data revealed that interpreter-generated contributions are common regardless of setting or mode, but that variation can exist within the interpreter-generated contributions.

Metzger's study models and exemplifies the ways in which sociolinguistics is extraordinarily suited for this complex study of human interaction. The act of interpreting is a search for meaning in what is uttered or signed in a context, including the linguistic, social, and cultural knowledge that participants use to make sense of what they hear or see. This is the focus of sociolinguistic studies and of interpreting, in both a theoretical sense and a practical sense.

The major impact of the Roy and Metzger studies was to greatly expand sociolinguistic approaches in studying all aspects of the interpretation activity in both spoken and signed language interpreting, and, primarily, aim at analyzing the discourse of interpreters in the workplace. Since these two studies, studies of interpreted discourse with similar results have followed. For example, Sanheim (2003) extends Roy's work on turn taking by applying her taxonomy to a medical interpreted encounter and supports Roy's findings regarding turns taken by the interpreter. Additionally, Mather (2005) assesses and identifies turn-taking regulators used by teachers and interpreters in mainstream classrooms. Her study expands the examination of interpretation and turn-taking through analysis of the multiparty interaction inherent in classrooms. Belangér (2004) focused on interpreter-mediated encounters between LSQ (Langue des signes québécoise; the sign language used by Deaf people of francophone families in Québec) and spoken French in Canada. Using symbolic interactionism as a framework, Bélanger's (2004) study confirmed the findings of Roy and Metzger as to the extent of the interpreter's participation in interaction, and explored the patterns of communicative behavior, demonstrating that while six different configurations were possible, it could be construed as two different levels: a primary exchange and collateral exchanges. Findings suggest that collateral exchanges arise as needed by participant face-work and may or may not include the interpreter.

Studies focusing on other sociolinguistic aspects of discourse include politeness, prosody, marking topic boundaries, and use of constructed action and dialogue. Roush (2007) addresses the stereotype that Deaf ASL-users are direct or blunt, through analysis of two speech/social activities of requests and refusals. He finds that these particular speech acts lend themselves to indirect ways of speaking in ASL and suggests that interpreters should develop "a macro level understanding of the politeness dynamics within each language community" to expand their role as politeness mediators (145). Nicodemus (2009) examines prosodic markers as interpreters produce them. She finds that interpreters make both systematic and stylistic use of prosodic markers and produce multiple prosodic markers at utterance boundaries—seven or more markers were produced within a two-second interval and one-third of the markers were sequential rather than simultaneous. These findings impact not only discourse structure and cohesion, but also issues of equivalence.

Winston and Monikowski (2003) analyze interpreters' marking of topic boundaries in an analysis of commercially produced interpreting and transliterating models. Their primary focus was prosodic features (Winston 2000), in particular, pausing which indicated major topic segments that were produced by three different interpreters who were producing both an interpretation (a freer rendition) and a transliteration (a more literal rendition) of the same English source text. A major finding was that all three interpreters, while interpreting, produced "extralinguistic" pauses; that is, they stopped signing and clasp their hands in front of their lower body. This study incorporates the discourse-based analysis of topics in discourse, but by virtue of its focus on both free and literal interpretation, also addresses issues related to variation, as will be discussed below.

In another study steeped in both variation and discourse, Armstrong (2003) examines the use of constructed action and constructed dialogue by interpreters. This study examined the work of four interpreters, two of whom were native users of ASL, and two who were second language users. In the English texts, the interpreters who were also native signers created and produced 16 or more instances of constructed action and dialogue, whereas the interpreters who were second language users may have attempted to create action and dialogue but were not successful. Moreover, in 8 out of 16 examples of native signers, the action and dialogue sequences appear in the same place.

Napier's (2001) dissertation is a study of omissions in interpreted target texts from a university lecture source, typically examined as a kind of error associated with cognitive processing, but, in this study, she does so from a discourse-based, interactional perspective in which the omissions are categorized based on how aware the interpreter is of them and how intentional the omissions are. Napier finds that interpreters make intentional omissions that are strategically designed to support the quality of their target productions, in addition to other types of omissions. Moreover, her study demonstrated that sociolinguistic factors, such as the context of situation, familiarity with the discourse environment, knowledge of the topic, and familiarity with the Deaf and non-Deaf participants affected the rate and types of omission occurrences.

It is clear from the studies reported in this section that discourse analysis provides a variety of methods and theoretical perspectives that support the examination of interpretation. Discourse-based analyses of interpretation have focused on a variety of discourse-based features or strategies, including turn taking, politeness, topic, constructed action and dialogue, and analysis of interpretation as an interactional, social encounter, including studies of the interpreter-generated contributions and the role of omissions from an interactional perspective. Despite this rich variety, meaningful examination of interpretation is not limited to a discourse perspective.

Bilingualism, Multilingualism, and Language Contact

Sociolinguistics devotes much attention to people who come into contact with more than one language, whether it be due to the type of interaction across language communities resulting in language contact phenomena or the knowledge of and use of two or more languages by an individual or community. Signed language interpreters, be they Deaf or hearing, native signers or second language signers, professional or lay interpreters, by nature of the interpreting task, constitute bilingualism or multilingualism and language contact. This section will discuss some sociolinguistic studies that focus on interpreting from this sociolinguistic perspective.

In such a study of interpreters, one issue pertains to interpreters working around geographical and/or political boundaries. Ramsey and Peña (2010) interview each other "to document issues in *la interpretación en la frontera* (border interpreting) as well as our respective histories as participants in border life." (5). Specifically, sociocultural issues are addressed by Ramsey and Peña as they examine the convergence of physical and cultural borders within quadrilingual interpreters interpreting between Mexican Sign Language, ASL, Spanish and English around the Mexico-United States border. The variability that sign language interpreters who work in the border zone encounter includes understanding the linguistic variation of Mexican Deaf people, who typically have a limited exposure to schooling, if any, as well as a limited exposure to Mexican Sign Language or Spanish. Moreover, they must apply their own multicultural and multilingual life experiences to master ways to explain social and cultural traditions and expectations within American, Mexican, and Deaf cultures.

Martinez (2007) examines the complicated, multilingual process of codeswitching by Filipino interpreters when interpreting from Filipino Sign Language to Filipino, English, or another of the numerous languages spoken in the Phillipines. Surprisingly, the interpretations revealed consistent and ongoing codeswitching between Filipino and English for both monolingual and bilingual hearers. While the study offered no reasons as to why, it was clear that the interpreters needed to know not only Filipino and English, but other possible languages of the archipelago. Because these studies address issues of bilingualism and multilingualism as they pertain to interpretation, they touch on the unavoidable issue of language contact. Numerous studies of signed language interpretation examine the language contact question from different angles. Language contact, that is, codeswitching, code-mixing, and lexical borrowing between English and ASL, exists within the scope of interpretation, as it requires that two languages be in contact in one social encounter. Understanding the effect of language contact in interpretations into ASL or other signed languages is vital in judgments of acceptability and accuracy in interpreting.

Davis (1990) filmed four interpreters as they interpreted a faculty lecture at Gallaudet University for a campus audience. He then transcribed and analyzed their target-language output in ASL. The questions he asked were about how codeswitching, code-mixing, and borrowing were manifested and the nature and structure of these phenomenon including the understanding that the situation, topic, and audience were also impacting linguistic decisions made by the interpreters. Because ASL is not only conveyed by signs, but also has oral, facial, and spatial channels for linguistic output, interpreters can visually represent English by lip movements or by fingerspelling English words.

In this study and in later work (cf. Davis 2003), Davis found that the ASL-English interpreters could move from ASL mouth movements to forming English words on their lips, a sequence performed sequentially that is also a form of codeswitching. When the interpreters were using both facial and manual components of ASL, they could simultaneously represent English with lip movements, a form of code-mixing. And finally, they could borrow from English using lip movements and fingerspelling and then restructure to conform to the manner in which ASL uses lip movement (reducing the enunciation of a word) and fingerspelling (becoming a sign). The uses of these strategies patterned similarly across all four interpreters, regardless of their native or nonnative fluency in ASL, and were strategies that allowed interpreters to elucidate and disambiguate interpreted messages. This study is a major contribution to the understanding of bilingual behaviors in language contact situations and how that impacts the linguistic choices interpreters make.

Regarding interpretation and Deaf communities, language contact also results in a form of contact signing[1] (Lucas & Valli 1992). Where interpreters are concerned, this issue can be examined as described above in the study conducted by Davis. However, in the American Deaf community, as is true in many communities that constitute a linguistic minority, language policies also enter into the experience of bilingual and multilingual people's lives.

For the American Deaf Community this has taken the form of inventions of coding systems that connect English words to ASL signs for use in education. Although this extends beyond the scope of this section (and this chapter), it is worth noting that interpreters interpret with adults who are products of an educational system; interpreters must by necessity be prepared to interpret with deaf adults who may either have grown up signing a code for English and prefer English-like signing,[2] or who might, as ASL-English bilinguals, prefer to themselves interpret the meaning of a spoken source text rather than have access to only an ASL translation. Studies of interpretations that seek to find various ways of saying the same thing, as translations from spoken English into ASL or English-like signing, are discussed below.

Variation

Variation as a sociolinguistic area of study examines the systematic choices made by members of a language community in keeping with linguistic and social factors and reflecting the social organization of the community as well as grammatical constraints (see Bayley, this volume; Lucas, Bayley, Valli, Rose, & Wulf, 2001). In this section we examine studies of interpretation as the target text varies between ASL, contact signing or even some coded form of English. These studies focus on a variety of aspects, including the occurrence of grammatical and prosodic behaviors on the face and the use of space[3] in target interpretations that are intended to be an English-like variety of signing, or contact signing.

In a seminal case study, Winston (1989) investigated the discourse strategies of a more "literal" interpretation, "transliteration," in a classroom lecture. Her study was not only the first of its kind, but was also chosen by the national association of signed language interpreters to represent the standards for judging this kind of interpreting. Winston found in her case study that the interpreter used a number of features not anticipated in an English-like variety of interpreted target text, such as the use of spatial features found in ASL, and sections in which the source English was rearranged into a more "ASL-like" English for the signed target. One example of this occurred when the interpreter reinterpreted passive structures into English active structures before signing an English-like variety. Thus, the interpreter maintained her goal of interpreting into an English-like variety of signing, but also adhered to the principle of making her target interpretation clear in the signed mode. Prior to this study the expectation was generally held that literal interpretation or transliteration would simply code English words into signs and string them together in English word order. This study provides clear evidence of an interpreter's tacit understanding of the different language varieties with which she works, which warrants more research on both varieties of signing and on the nature of interpretation and the preparation those who work as professional interpreters.

In another study of interpreters working in a mainstream educational program[4] in which interpreters were asked to sign "English" or some form of sign-coded English, rather than ASL as a part of their daily professional work, Sofinski (2003) analyzed the occurrence of grammatical features that appear on the face used by interpreters in signed language transliteration. This study, like Winston (1989), finds that interpreters do incorporate ASL-like elements in their English-like signing varieties while at work. Sofinski, like Winston, also focused on transliteration; however, in a discourse-based study of how interpreters mark topic boundaries in both interpretation and transliteration, Winston and Monikowski (2003) examine variation between ASL interpreted and transliterated target texts from the same spoken English source text as presented by the same professional interpreting model. This study provides a rare glimpse of the interpreter's different ways of saying the same thing in two variations of signing and while engaged in the more free or more literal ends of the interpreting continuum.

Collins (1993, 2004) has examined Tactile ASL[5] (TASL) and Deaf Blind interpretation.[6] In his study of adverbial markers in TASL, he makes clear that TASL and ASL variation exists. Haas, Fleetwood, and Ernst (1995), and Metzger, Fleetwood, and Collins (2004) examine TASL conversation regulators and Deaf Blind interpretation (respectively) as issues related to variation in interpretation. Perhaps the study of TASL even more than the study of English-like signing varieties offer an informative glimpse into the tacit understanding of language variation held by interpreters, and the manner in which variation is manifested in their work.

In addition to the study of literal interpreting and of TASL interpreting, some studies examine two or more interpreters and compare their ways of saying the same thing (as controlled by a source text). For example, Tray (2005) conducts an examination of innuendo in ASL by comparing a native signer's rendition versus a nonnative signer's interpretation of innuendo within an English source text. Using a script, *Princess Plays with Wood,* both native signers and interpreters choose strategies that displayed the literal meaning, yet also conveyed the sexual innuendo behind both words and sentences. Similarly, Santiago and Barrick (2007) also examine how interpreters deal with translating source language idioms into ASL by comparing the different choices interpreters exhibited when conveying the same idioms. Overall the interpreters tended to render plain language target texts while native signers used more figurative language

Variation issues pertain to interpretation in numerous ways. Variation within a single interpreter as they translate a source text into varieties of sign is but one example discussed above. Analyzing the ways in which a variety of interpreters translate a single source text provides another example of how interpreting studies address the question of variation. Finally, examination of varieties of ASL, including contact sign, English-like signing, and Tactile ASL as they appear in the work of interpreters also reflects aspects of the sociolinguistic nature of interpretation.

Language Policy and Planning

According to Reagan (2010), language policy and planning is an area of sociolinguistic inquiry relevant to both spoken and signed language communities, focusing on such relevant aspects of social and education as language status, reform, and revitalization. Language policy and planning pertains to signed language interpretation in numerous ways, beginning with interpreters working with deaf youth, as in medical and educational settings, and subsequently with these youth throughout their lives and into adulthood, using the language or variety that language planners and policy makers may have imposed upon them. Further, language policies are often directly aimed at interpreters themselves. This could take the form of regulating whether or not interpreters hold professional credentials and qualifications. It could also take the form of stipulating which settings and in what capacity interpreters may or may not provide services. It could even take the form of stipulating interpreters' work environment resulting in the potential for occupational hazards for interpreters, and therefore, on the availability of interpreters for deaf and hearing community members.

LaBue (1998) conducted the first major, in-depth study on the impact of learning through an interpreter. Around the United States, Deaf students are in classrooms where social and academic information is presented in spoken English, requiring the use of a sign language interpreter. Learning academic content in this manner raises complex linguistic and educational issues about how deaf students learn, or fail to learn. LaBue's study included filming ten class lectures and discussions, observation and field notes, and interviews with the teacher, students, and the interpreter. From transcripts and live data a sociolinguistic analysis of the context and linguistic form of one teacher's spoken, literacy-related instructional discourse, and an interpreter's rendition of that discourse was performed.

The interpreter in this study was herself a teacher of deaf students and had no training as an interpreter. This, unfortunately, is a situation that holds true in public schools all over the United States. Consequently, she did not lag behind the teacher's talk enough and often created ungrammatical and incomprehensible renditions of the teacher's talk. She failed to create discourse markers and other cohesive devices, such as repetition and pronominal use, so that tracking topic changes and shifts was difficult, if not impossible. Because no one prepared the teacher for having deaf students in class, the turn taking was governed by auditory cues, and deaf students were excluded from participation cues that might have allowed their participation in classroom discussions. Moreover, this affected the teacher's evaluation of the deaf students; for example, she described one of the students as "immature" rather than recognizing the student might be performing as a second language learner of English. Additional studies of interpreters working in educational settings focus on a variety of language and policy-related topics, including not only the interpreter's role in a classroom (see also Harrington 2005), but also the impact of coded sign systems on language learning (cf. Winston 2004; Stack 2004), the impact of learning in a mediated (interpreted) learning situation versus direct instruction on sociocultural development of students (Schick 2004), and on the lack of educational preparation for educational interpreters and the impact of that on both interpreters and students (see Langer 2004; Schick 2004; Winston 2004)

Although further from the nature of language use itself, policies related to communication, language, and to the provision of and care of interpreters' health all represent policy and planning issues that have an impact on the lives of a linguistic community. Madden (2005) explores the prevalence of chronic occupational physical injury among Australian Sign Language interpreters due to the stress created by constant demand and the lack of recognition of their professional rights.

Finally, as language professionals making on-the-job decisions as they work, interpreters themselves are often faced with situated encounters in which they make individual decisions of a possibly small-scale policy and planning nature. In a recent turn in sociolinguistic studies (McKee and Awheto 2010), researchers are collaborating with practitioners as they reflect upon their work—the continuous struggle to make appropriate choices for communicative success in multilingual, multicultural settings. These retrospections are tape-recorded interviews/discussions between the authors soon after the event. They treat the tape transcript as data that they analyze to explore how the practitioners contributed to producing the event from various positions as an interpreter. They focus on themes such as co-constructing the event, language challenges, the importance of social identity, and responsibilities invoked by the interpreter's cultural allegiance.

These issues can manifest themselves in any interpreting situation, ranging from those involving deaf children to those involving trilingual interpreters working with indigenous Deaf people. For example, Locker-McKee and Awheto show

> how the interpreter, from her own cultural position as a trilingual Māori woman, responds to the sociocultural dimensions of the event in negotiating her role. Her macro-level awareness of peoples' intentions, identities, and varying cultural schemas for the event determine the way in which she mediates interaction, often motivating her to take participant positions that depart from the 'normative' interpreter role. (2010: 87)

Together, they examined how the interpreter negotiated her position as an interpreter in a trilingual situation involving hearing, Deaf, Māori, and Pākehā[7] participants with disparate cultural schemas and discourse repertoires. Their analysis of Awheto's explanations of her actions and behaviors highlighted her highly visible position and her multiple footings as the interaction unfolded. The interpreter's concern for protecting the integrity of the cultural norms of all the participants was moving. Thus, at times, she positioned herself as a mediator, "encouraging each party to make their perspectives more explicit to the other, in order to mitigate potential social damage within and beyond the event" (2010: 113).

This case reinforces that it is impossible to neutralize the impact of an interpreter's personal cultural orientation and identity on the way in which she negotiates her roles in a given interaction. The interpreter's decisions in mediating communication in this situation were clearly shaped by her own enculturation, her ethnic alliance with, and social network knowledge of, other participants, and were promoted by her tri-cultural perception of the gap between parties in knowing how to construct this particular event together.

Whether examining an interpreter's choices at work, the regulations or expectations that impact upon an interpreter's physical well-being while at work, or policies that affect the communities with whom interpreters work, language policy and planning play an integral and daily role in the professional lives of signed language interpreters.

Language Attitudes

Interpretation is by its very nature, a language-centered social activity. Attitudes about language are difficult to separate from attitudes about interpreters themselves. Several studies examine this phenomenon.

Forestal (2005) investigates the shifting attitudes of Deaf leaders toward signed language interpreters. Forestal notes how older leaders think of interpreters as their friends in exchanges, whereas Deaf individuals who attended mainstream schools possessed different feelings about interpreting. Napier and Rohan (2007) investigate interpreting from the perspective of deaf consumers in Australia to explore their agenda for quality interpreting services. They found that general satisfaction levels are high among Deaf consumers, even though they seem to have little choice about who will interpret. For these consumers, the key factors for working with interpreters include understanding the consumer and the context, professionalism, and attitude.

Also attitudes of interpreters themselves, be they hearing or deaf, signers as L1 or L2, are reflected in the language choices that they make while at work.

For example Stone (2010) finds in his study of Deaf interpreters working in public media such as television, that Deaf interpreters and hearing interpreters have a qualitatively different product as a result, in part, of different attitudes about what constitutes discourse, its meaning, and the translation thereof.

Stone concentrated his research in the United Kingdom. Specifically, he examined the rendering of English broadcast television news into British Sign Language (BSL) by both Deaf and hearing T/Is. Segments of the data feature simultaneous Deaf and hearing in-vision T/I broadcasts. Recording these broadcasts produced a controlled product that enabled direct comparison of the Deaf and hearing T/Is. Close analysis of these examples revealed to Stone that Deaf T/Is not only employ a Deaf translation norm, they also take labors to shape their BSL text into a stand-alone product rather than a translation.

Language attitudes can also be reflected in the attitudes that consumers may hold regarding interpreters. Studies of these attitudes have focused on those of deaf students (see, e.g., Kurz and Langer 2004), Deaf leaders (Forestal 2005), and even on the attitudes of Deaf consumers regarding the nature of the service, such as whether it is an interpretation or a more literal transliteration (see, e.g., Livingston, Singer, & Abramson 1995).

Language attitude research has taken many forms in the sociolinguistic examination of language users, be they mono-, bi-, or multilingual. The varying practices of interpreters (such as Deaf or hearing interpreters, native signing versus nonnative signing interpreters, and so forth) reflect language attitudes held by interpreters who work as language professionals as well as the attitudes of the consumers of interpretation. It is worth noting that, similarly, the language attitudes of interpreters as embodied in their interpretations undoubtedly also inform the attitudes held by consumers of interpreting about the interpreters with whom they work.

Interpreting as a Sociolinguistic Activity

In this chapter we have attempted to demonstrate that, by its very nature, interpreting is a sociolinguistic activity. We have provided evidence by selecting studies from a growing body of interpreting research that sociolinguistic concerns relating to discourse analysis, bilingualism, multilingualism, and language contact, language variation, language policy and planning, and language attitudes all constitute aspects of the processes and products of signed language interpretation. It is worth noting that many sociolinguistic studies of interpretation do not fit neatly into one or another subfield of sociolinguistics. For example, Napier's (2003) study of omissions applies a discourse perspective, yet also represents a study of variation in the target interpretations of a number of professional interpreters. Similarly, many studies addressing these topics have been undertaken by researchers from outside the sociolinguistic sphere. For example, Schick and Williams (2004) describe a large-scale study of the competencies held by educational interpreters and make an excellent case regarding language policy and planning involving both practitioner qualifications and those in education affecting student outcomes, yet their work is not necessarily steeped in sociolinguistic-inspired methodology. In short, sociolinguistic concerns are such an integral part of interpretation that relevant sociolinguistic areas are being studied by a variety of researchers from diverse and interdisciplinary backgrounds. Just as the study of sociolinguistic issues as they pertain to interpreting have a great potential to impact interpreting practice and pedagogy, the study of interpreters and interpretation has much potential to contribute to our understanding of sociolinguistics and the sociolinguistics of deaf communities.

Notes

1. Contact signing is a variety of ASL that incorporates features of both ASL and English, and tends to portray a more English-like meaning.
2. English-like signing is another name for contact sign.
3. Signers make use of the physical space in front of their bodies to indicate locations, directions, and other features of the language.
4. In mainstream programs Deaf students attend a public school with the services of an interpreter for classroom instruction.
5. Tactile ASL is a variety of ASL used by Deaf-Blind persons in which one interlocutor signs while the other interlocutor puts one hand over one of the signing hand of the other.
6. Deaf-Blind interpreting involves people who are both deaf and blind and thus must have someone who can communicate using Tactile ASL (TASL) in which everything must be communicated via touch.
7. Māori people are indigenous New Zealanders, and Pākehā people are non-Māori New Zealanders of European ancestry.

References

Anderson, R. B. W. 1976. Perspectives on the role of an interpreter. In R. Brislin (ed.), *Translation: applications and research*, 208–28. New York: Gardner Press.

Armstrong, J. 2003. An investigation of constructed action and constructed dialogue in an ASL interpreted lecture. M.A. thesis. Ball State University.

Bélanger, D. C. 2004. Interactional patterns in dialogue-interpreting. *Journal of Interpretation*: 5–18.

Bennett, A. 1981. Interruptions and the interpretation of conversation. *Discourse Processes* 4: 171–88.

Brasel, B. 1976. The effects of fatigue on the competence of interpreters for the deaf. In H. Murphy (ed.), *Selected readings in the integration of Deaf students at CSUN*, 19–22. Center on Deafness, California State University, Northridge.

Brislin, R. (ed.) 1976. *Translation: Applications and research*. New York: Gardner Press.

Collins, S. 1993. Deaf-Blind Interpreting: The Structure of ASL and the Interpreting Process. In E.A. Winston (ed.), *Communication Forum 1993*, School of Communication Student Forum 2: 20–36. Washington, DC: Gallaudet University School of Communication.

Collins, S. 2004. Adverbial morphemes in Tactile American Sign Language. Ph.D. dissertation, The Union Institute and University.

Cokely, D. R. 1985. Towards a sociolinguistic model of the interpreting process: Focus on ASL and English. Ph.D. dissertation, Georgetown University.

Cokely, D. 1992. *Interpretation: A sociolinguistic model*. Burtonsville, MD: Linstok Press.

Colton, P. 1982. A study of the validity and reliability of the Comprehensive Skills Certification Evaluation for sign language interpreters: A report to the profession. *RID Interpreting Journal* 1(2): 16–37.

Davis, J. 1990. Linguistic transference and interference: Interpreting between English and ASL. In C. Lucas (ed.), *Sign language research: Theoretical issues*, 308–21. Washington, DC: Gallaudet University Press.

Davis, J. 2003. Cross-linguistic strategies used by interpreters. *Journal of Interpretation* 95–128.

Forestal, L. 2005. Attitudes of Deaf leaders toward signed language interpreters and interpreting. In M. Metzger & E. Fleetwood (eds.), *Attitudes, innuendo, and regulators: Challenges of interpretation*, 71–91. Washington, DC: Gallaudet University Press.

Gerver, D. 1974. Simultaneous listening and speaking and retention of prose. *Quarterly Journal of Experimental Psychology* 26: 337–42.

Gumperz, J. J. 1982. *Discourse strategies*. Cambridge: Cambridge University Press.

Haas, C., Fleetwood, E. & Ernst, M. 1995. An analysis of ASL variation within DeafBlind interaction: Question forms, backchanneling, and turn-taking. In L. Byers, J. Chaiken, and M. Mueller (eds.), *Gallaudet University Communication Forum 1995*, 103–140. Washington, DC: Gallaudet University School of Communication.

Harrington, F. 2005. A study of the complex nature of interpreting with Deaf students in higher education. In M. Metzger & E. Fleetwood (eds.), *Attitudes, innuendo, and regulators: Challenges of interpretation*, 162–86. Washington, DC: Gallaudet University Press.

Hurwitz, A. 1980. Interpreter effectiveness in reverse interpreting Pidgin Sign English and American Sign Language. In F. Caccamise (ed.), *A century of Deaf awareness in a decade of interpreting awareness*, 157–87. Silver Spring, MD: RID Publications.

Kurz, K. B., & Langer, E. C. 2004. Student perspectives on educational interpreting: Twenty Deaf and hard-of-hearing students offer insights and suggestions. In E. Winston (ed.), *Educational interpreting: How it can succeed*, 9–47. Washington, DC: Gallaudet University Press.

LaBue, M. 1998. Interpreted education: A study of Deaf students' access to the form and content of literacy instruction in a mainstreamed high school English class. Ph.D. dissertation, Harvard University.

Langer, E. 2004. Perspectives on educational interpreting from educational anthropology and an internet discussion group. In E. A. Winston (ed.), *Educational interpreting: How can it succeed,* 91–112. Washington, DC: Gallaudet University Press.

Livingston, S., Singer, B., & Abramson, T. 1995. A study to determine the effectiveness of two different kinds of interpreting. E. A. Winston (ed.), *Mapping our course: A collaborative venture. Proceedings of the Tenth National Convention of the Conference of Interpreter Trainers,* 175–97. CIT Publications.

Lucas, C., Bayley, R., Valli, C., Rose, M., & Wulf, A. 2001. Sociolinguistic variation. In C. Lucas (Ed.), *The sociolinguistics of sign languages,* 61–111. Cambridge: Cambridge University Press.

Lucas, C., & Valli, C. 1992. *Language contact in the American Deaf community.* San Diego: Academic Press.

Madden, M. 2005. The prevalence of occupational overuse syndrome in signed language interpreters in Australia: What a pain! In M. Metzger & E. Fleetwood (eds.), *Attitudes, innuendo, and regulators: Challenges of interpretation,* 3–70. Washington, DC: Gallaudet University Press.

Martinez, L. 2007. Initial observations on code-switching in the voice interpretation of two Filipino interpreters. In M. Metzger & E. Fleetwood (eds.), *Translation, sociolinguistic, and consumer issues in interpreting,* 71–102. Washington, DC: Gallaudet University Press.

Mather, S. 2005. Ethnographic research on the use of visually based regulators for teachers and interpreters. In M. Metzger & E. Fleetwood (eds.), *Attitudes, innuendo, and regulators: Challenges of interpretation,* 136–61. Washington, DC: Gallaudet University Press.

McKee, R. L. & S. Awheto. 2010. Constructing roles in a Māori Deaf trilingual context. In R.L. Mckee & J. Davis (eds.), *Interpreting in multilingual, multicultural contexts,* 85–118. Washington, DC: Gallaudet University Press.

McKee, R. L., & J. Davis. 2010. *Interpreting in multilingual, multicultural contexts.* Washington, DC: Gallaudet University Press.

Metzger, M. 1995. The paradox of neutrality: A comparison of interpreters' goals with the reality of interactive discourse. Ph.D. dissertation, Georgetown University.

Metzger, M. 1999. *Sign language interpreting. Deconstructing the myth of neutrality.* Washington, DC: Gallaudet University Press.

Metzger, M. 2006. Salient studies of signed language interpreting in the context of community interpreting scholarship. *Linguistica antverpiensia* 5: 263–91.

Metzger, M., Fleetwood, E., & Collins, S. 2004. Discourse genre and linguistic mode: Interpreter influences in visual and tactile interaction. *Sign Language Studies* 4: 118–37.

Moser, B. 1978. Simultaneous interpretation: A hypothetical model and its practical application. In D. Gerver & H. Sinako (eds.), *Language interpretation and communication,* 353–68. New York: Plenum Press.

Napier, J. 2001. *Linguistic coping strategies of sign language interpreters.* Ph.D. dissertation, Macquarie University.

Napier, J. 2002. *Sign language interpreting: Linguistic coping strategies.* Coleford, UK: Douglas McLean.

Napier, J. 2003. A sociolinguistic analysis of the occurrence and types of omissions produced by Australian Sign Language-English interpreters. In M. Metzger, S. Collins, V. Dively & R. Shaw (eds.), *From topic boundaries to omission: New research on interpretation*, 99–153. Washington, DC: Gallaudet University Press.

Napier, J., & Rohan, M. 2007. An invitation to dance: Deaf consumers' perceptions of signed language interpreters and interpreting. In M. Metzger & E. Fleetwood (eds.), *Translation, sociolinguistic, and consumer issues in interpreting*, 159–203. Washington, DC: Gallaudet University Press.

Nicodemus, B. 2009. *Prosodic markers and utterance boundaries in American Sign Language interpretation*. Washington, DC: Gallaudet University Press.

Nida, E. 1964. *Toward a science of translating*. Leiden: Brill Publishing.

Nida, E. 1976. A framework for the analysis and the evaluation of theories of translation. In R. Brislin (ed.), *Translation: Applications and research*, 47–91. New York: Gardner Press.

Per-Lee, M. 1981. *Interpreter research: Target for the eighties*. Washington, DC: Gallaudet College, National Academy.

Ramsey, C., & Peña, S. 2010. Sign language interpreting at the border of the two Californias. In R. Locker McKee & J. Davis (eds.) *Interpreting in multilingual, multicultural contexts*, 3–27. Washington, DC: Gallaudet University Press.

Reagan, T. 2010. *Language policy and planning for sign languages*. Washington, DC: Gallaudet University Press.

Roush, D. 2007. Indirectness strategies in American Sign Language requests and refusals: Deconstructing the Deaf-as-direct stereotype. In M. Metzger & E. Fleetwood (eds.), *Translation, sociolinguistic, and consumer issues in interpreting*, 103–57. Washington, DC: Gallaudet University Press.

Roy, C. 2000. *Interpreting as a discourse process*. New York: Oxford University Press.

Roy, C. B. 1989. *A sociolinguistic analysis of the interpreter's role in the turn exchanges of an interpreted event*. Ph.D. dissertation, Georgetown University.

Sacks, H., Schegloff, E., & Jefferson, G. 1974. A simplest systematics for the organization of turn-taking in conversation. *Language* 50: 696–735.

Sanheim, L. 2003. Turn exchange in an interpreted medical encounter. In M. Metzger, S. Collins, V. Dively, & R. Shaw (eds.), *From topic boundaries to omission: New research on interpretation*, 27–54. Washington, DC: Gallaudet University Press.

Santiago, R., & Barrick, L. 2007. Handling and incorporation of idioms in interpretation. In M. Metzger & E. Fleetwood (eds.), *Translation, sociolinguistic, and consumer issues in interpreting*, 3–44. Washington, DC: Gallaudet University Press.

Schick, B. 2004. How might learning through an educational interpreter influence cognitive development? In E. Winston (ed.), *Educational interpreting: How it can succeed*, 73–87. Washington, DC: Gallaudet University Press.

Schick, B., & Williams, K. 2004. The educational interpreter performances assessment: Current structure and practices. In E. Winston (ed.), *Educational interpreting: How it can succeed*, 186–205. Washington, DC: Gallaudet University Press.

Schiffrin, D. 1994. *Approaches to discourse*. Malden, MA: Blackwell.

Shuy, R. 1987. A sociolingustic view of interpreter education. In M.McIntire (ed.), *New dimensions in interpreter education: Curriculum and instruction*. In M. McIntire (ed.), *Proceedings from the Sixth National Conference of Interpreter Trainers*, 1–8. Silver Spring, MD: RID Publications.

Sofinski, B. 2003. Adverbials, constructed dialogue, and use of space, Oh my!: Nonmanual elements used in sign language transliteration. In M. Metzger,

S. Collins, V. Dively, & R. Shaw (eds.), *From topic boundaries to omission: New research on interpretation*, 154–86. Washington, DC: Gallaudet University Press.

Stack, K. 2004. Language accessibility in a transliterated education: English signing systems. In E. Winston (ed.), *Educational interpreting: How it can succeed*, 61–72. Washington, DC: Gallaudet University Press.

Stone, C. 2010. *Toward a Deaf translation norm*. Washington, DC: Gallaudet University Press.

Tannen, D. 1979. What's in a frame? Surface evidence for underlying expectations. In R. Freedle (ed.), *New Directions in Discourse Processing*, 137–81. Norwood, NJ: Ablex.

Tannen, D. 1984. *Conversational style: Analyzing talk among friends*. Norwood, NJ: Ablex.

Tannen, D., & Wallat, C. 1993. Interactive frames and knowledge schemas in interaction: Examples from a medical examination/interview. In D. Tannen (ed.), *Framing in discourse*, 57–76. New York: Oxford University Press.

Tray, S. 2005. What are you suggesting? Interpreting innuendo between ASL and English. In M. Metzger & E. Fleetwood (eds.), *Attitudes, innuendo, and regulators: Challenges of interpretation*, 95–135. Washington, DC: Gallaudet University Press.

Treisman, A. 1965. The effects of redundancy and familiarity on translation and repeating back a foreign language and a native language. *British Journal of Psychology* 56: 369–79.

Wadensjö, C. 1992. *Interpreting as interaction: On dialogue interpreting in In immigration hearings and medical examinations*. Ph.D. dissertation, Linköping University.

Wadensjö, C. 1998. *Interpreting as interaction*. London: Longman.

Winston, E. A. 1989. Transliteration: What's the message? In C. Lucas (ed.), *Sociolinguistics of the Deaf community*, 147–64. New York: Academic Press.

Winston, E.A. 2000. It just doesn't look like ASL! Defining, recognizing, and teaching prosody in ASL. In *CIT at 21: Celebrating excellence, celebrating partnership. Proceedings of the 13th National Convention of CIT*, 103–16. Silver Spring, MD: RID Publications.

Winston, E. A., & Monikowski, C. 2003. Marking topic boundaries in signed interpretation and transliteration. In M.Metzger, S. Collins, V. Dively, & R. Shaw (eds.), *From topic boundaries to omission: New research on interpretation*, 187–227. Washington, DC: Gallaudet University Press.

Winston, E. A. 2004. Interpretability and accessibility of mainstream classrooms. In E. A. Winston (ed.), *Educational interpreting: How it can succeed*, 132–67. Washington, DC: Gallaudet University Press.

CHAPTER 37

LANGUAGE AWARENESS IN COMMUNITY PERSPECTIVE

OBLIGATION AND OPPORTUNITY

WALT WOLFRAM

COMMUNITY-based research is at the core of sociolinguistics, and practically all sociolinguistic researchers work with speech communities of some type. These communities may be based on a variety of social and demographic factors, such as geography, ethnicity, sociohistorical background, economic, and political factors—or, more typically, embedded combinations of these factors. The community of Harkers Island located off the coast of Carolina, for example, is defined initially by its geography as an island community, but it is also defined by its genealogical legacy and social organization. At the same time, this island is subsumed under the regional umbrella of the Outer Banks that includes other islands such as Ocracoke (Wolfram & Schilling-Estes 1997) and Roanoke Island (Carpenter 2005), which, in turn, may be united with coastal mainland residents of Eastern North Carolina (*Downeasters*) as opposed to North Carolinians to the west and other Southerners. The awareness of regional and social place is hierarchical in that people identify strongly with their local neighborhood, their immediate community of residency, the regional areas and the state in which their community is located, and an overarching region, such as the South (Reed 1993, 2003). In the final analysis, there are many levels of local, regional, and cultural affiliations that might be included in the definition of speech community (Patrick 2002), and sociolinguistic researchers may have opportunities to work with communities on multiple levels of these embedded and hierarchical notions of community.

Community-Researcher Relationships

Admittedly, the focus of sociolinguists on language variation and change is typically viewed as an oddity in most communities. While community members may readily recognize language differences, they are much more likely to be attuned to economic, social, and political issues, thinking that sociolinguistic obsession with language is strange if not unnatural. Accordingly, community members may have underlying questions and concerns about sociolinguists' motivations in working with their community. What are they really doing in their community? Why are they so obsessed with the minutia of language? Do they have an underlying sociopolitical agenda in terms of language? These are legitimate questions and concerns, and the reality is that most sociolinguists do, in fact, have vested academic interests and an underlying ideological agenda. Sociolinguists, for example, typically promote an agenda of social and educational change that is at odds with mainstream language ideology, namely, the belief that Standard English is inherently "better" than vernacular varieties and should be promoted to the exclusion of vernacular varieties. Community members can hardly be faulted for being cautious about these academics who have entered their community with their strange views of language. We need to enter the community fully understanding and appreciating the legitimacy of the community's practical cautions and concerns about the motives of sociolinguistic researchers. As we initiate the collaborative process, we need to be proactive in explaining ourselves and our practical rationale in terms that the community can understand.

As sociolinguists collect their data from communities, they can assume a number of relationships and roles in relation to the community. Cameron, Frazer, Harvey, Rampton, and Richardson (1992) define several different kinds of research based on relationships between researchers and those they are researching, including ETHICAL RESEARCH, ADVOCACY RESEARCH and EMPOWERING RESEARCH. Ethical research assumes that there is minimal inconvenience to participants and that the subjects are adequately acknowledged for their contributions. Advocacy-based research is characterized by a "commitment on the part of the researcher not just to do research on subjects but research *on* and *for* subjects" (Cameron et al. 1992: 14), whereas empowering research is research *on*, *for*, and *with* the community in light of the fact that "subjects have their own agendas and research should try to address them." However sociolinguists may define their relationship, it seems that there is an increasing sense of obligation in the social sciences for researchers to give back to the communities from which they collect their data. As Rickford (1999: 315) notes:

> The fundamental rationale for getting involved in application, advocacy, and empowerment is that we owe it to the people whose data fuel our theories and descriptions; but these are good things to do even if we don't deal directly with native speakers and communities, and enacting them may help us to respond to the interests of our students and to the needs of our field.

The obligation of sociolinguists to give back to research communities can be summarized in Labov's PRINCIPLE OF ERROR CORRECTION (1982: 172) and PRINCIPLE OF DEBT INCURRED (Labov 1982: 173), as well as Wolfram's PRINCIPLE OF LINGUISTIC GRATUITY (1993: 227). Labov's principles are primarily reactive in that they focus on the obligation of linguists to expose misunderstandings and misinterpretations about language "to the attention of the widest possible audience" (Labov 1982: 172) and to "use knowledge based on data for the benefit of the community, when it has need for it" (Labov 1982: 173), whereas Wolfram's gratuity principle is more proactive in urging researchers to "pursue positive ways in which they can return linguistic favors to the community" (Wolfram 1993: 227).

Linguistic Knowledge and the Community

There are a variety of ways and levels on which sociolinguists can work with community members to ensure that language variation is documented and described. They can also work with them to raise the level of consciousness within and outside the community about the past, current, and future state of the language variation and to engage representative community agents and institutions in an effort to explicate the role of language in community life. On a national level, some sociolinguists have been at the forefront of public debates in advocating the linguistic legitimacy of vernacular dialects (Labov 1972; Rickford & Rickford 2000; Baugh 1999, 2001), applying Labov's (1982) principles of error correction and debt incurred. Many of these efforts have involved more general ethnic or regional notions of language, for example, African American English or Appalachian English. While engagement in national debates about language is obviously an essential dimension of promoting language awareness—and one that has involved sociolinguists since the earliest difference versus deficit debates of the 1960s—it is also important to work with local communities where we carry out our active research program. The need for language awareness in a variety of contexts is obviously critical, and different kinds of obligations and opportunities attend to these varied levels of language awareness. For example, reacting to a national news story about an educational or sociopolitical issue involving African American English or Appalachian English involves a very different kind of opportunity for sociolinguistic awareness than working on a collaborative activity with a local, community-based project involving a community of a couple of hundred people. Both entail obligation and opportunity, but the collaborative relationship with the "community" involves very different levels of interaction and personal engagement. In the following discussion, our primary focus is on working with locally situated communities where we have actually interacted with participants in community-based studies.

The cornerstone of language awareness is founded in Cameron et al.'s (1992: 24) declaration that "if knowledge is worth having, it is worth sharing." At first glance, this statement seems relatively straightforward and uncontroversial, but it raises a number of significant questions about content, format, and methods of knowledge sharing. What are sociolinguists obligated to share with community members about their research and how is that most effectively disseminated? What kinds of collaborative opportunities exist for sociolinguists and communities to raise consciousness about language and enhance appreciation for language diversity in general and the language of the local community in particular? In the following sections, we address some of these issues based upon several decades of experience working with local communities in engagement and in programmatic development related to language awareness. Under the rubric of the North Carolina Language and Life Project (NCLLP), established at North Carolina State University in the early 1990s (Wolfram 2007), we have attempted to unite research and engagement under an explicit set of NCLLP goals: (1) to gather basic research information about language varieties in order to understand the nature of language variation and change; (2) to document language varieties in North Carolina and beyond as they reflect the varied cultural traditions of their residents; (3) to provide information about language differences for public and educational interests; and (4) to use research material for the improvement of educational programs about language and culture (Wolfram 2007: 159). Under this approach, research and engagement, including community collaboration, are intrinsically linked in a synergistic relationship. In addition, we strongly endorse the "scholarship of engagement" in which the study of engagement activities is considered to be a research goal in its own right. Reaser's study of the effectiveness of a pilot dialect awareness curriculum in a school setting (2006) and Sweetland's research on the measurable effects of a dialect awareness program on writing achievement (2006), for example, are outstanding examples of the scholarship of engagement that make this type research no different from any other research inquiry.

Levels of Knowledge

I recently visited the fieldwork site of one of the pioneering studies in sociolinguistics, a community known to practically all students of sociolinguistics. Out of curiosity, I asked some longtime residents of the community if they had ever heard of this study. Not one person indicated any knowledge of the study or the language situation to which I was alluding, although, when informed about the study, they found my summary of the findings fascinating. Further inquiry indicated that even community members with a vested or official interest in historical documentation and preservation in the community were also completely unaware of the language situation even though it fell well within the purview of their cultural and historical interests. The experience reminded me of both the obligation and the opportunity to inform communities about the findings from our sociolinguistic studies, and the apparent ease with which these responsibilities can be overlooked. Though there may be some researchers who feel that we have no obligation to the communities that serve as the basis for our scientific inquiry, most sociolinguists have a sense of social responsibility to their research communities. In fact, there is a well-established tradition of engagement and extension within sociolinguistics that has extended from its modern inception a half century ago to the present.

There are obviously different levels of knowledge about sociolinguistic research that might be shared but, at the very least, some community representatives and agents should be aware of the study and its goals. It is not enough to restrict sharing our study with the study participants; sociolinguists need to be proactive in disseminating information not only to study participants but to others in the community. The first time we ever visited Ocracoke Island two decades ago, we arranged to meet with the president of the Ocracoke Preservation Society, the principal of the school, and informal community leaders to describe our proposed study. In these meetings we presented our research study in nontechnical terms and offered to work with the community in a way that might help residents understand the linguistic situation and celebrate the linguistic heritage of the island. We offered to talk to civic groups and to classes in the school about dialects in general and our study on the island in particular, and to work collaboratively on projects of general interest to the community and students. Happily, they took us up on the initial offer, and two decades later, the community is well aware of the status of its dialect through programs and activities that include a language curriculum developed for Grade 8 students that has now been taught every year for the last 20 years, the construction of a permanent exhibit on dialect in the museum operated by Ocracoke Preservation Society, two video documentaries that run on loops in different rooms of the museum, two CD collections of oral history narratives rendered in the vernacular dialect, and a popular book (Wolfram & Schilling-Estes 1997) that sells in local gift shops, convenience stores, and tourist information centers.

Though the response of this community might seem exceptional, practically all of the communities where we have conducted studies over the past couple of decades have worked with us collaboratively in some way to inform the community about it language and culture.

Given the relatively complex and technical nature of most sociolinguistic analyses, what aspects of our research do we share and how do we share them? At the very least, the community should know about the general nature of the study and how it relates to possible community interests. They further deserve to be apprised of its progress and the general findings of the study, though this information naturally has to be disseminated in nontechnical ways that are sensitive to the concerns of the community. It is essential that community members not be overwhelmed with technical details and sociolinguistic jargon. Accordingly, researchers need to pay careful attention to communicate information in a way that is accessible to lay audiences, a formidable challenge for most sociolinguists. Although we have offered copies of our academic studies to community members on various occasions, to be honest, we have found little to no interest in the technical details of these studies. As one community leader commented when I gave her a reprint of a published article I had written on a particular linguistic structure of the vernacular dialect, "I can't believe you wrote 30 pages on single linguistic structure, Walt. You need to get a life."

In presenting information about local dialects, we need to recognize that there is often a natural tension between the specialized expertise of the linguist and the community perspective on language. Vernacular language norms within the community may stand in opposition to those of mainstream, Standard English varieties, leading to an ideological conflict (e.g. Lippi-Green 2012; Preston 1997; Wolfram & Schilling-Estes 2006). In most cases, communities do not want socially disfavored linguistic traits of their speech highlighted in the representation of their language. At the same time, linguistic experts need to carefully format their presentations in such a way that erroneous impressions, negative stereotypes, and linguistic myths are not perpetuated by community members. The effects of linguistic subordination are pervasive, and just about all vernacular-speaking, non-mainstream communities suffer from a collective perception of linguistic inferiority aligned with mainstream language ideologies.

Despite attempts to define our relationship with community members as partners and friends, our essential relationship in these communities is still framed by our role as university-based language experts, and this specialized language expertise sets up an asymmetrical hierarchical relationship when it comes to language matters—no matter how comfortable and egalitarian our relationships with community members may be in other areas. Native community members may be intriguing as speakers, storytellers, and interpreters of local traditions, but they cannot be expected to share the linguist's approach to language differences and description.

On the other hand, residents have expertise in local traditions and livelihood that far exceeds the knowledge of linguists in these areas, and it is important for researchers to acknowledge this. Acknowledging disparate areas of expertise for local participants and sociolinguists helps keep us humble and assists in establishing an egalitarian working relationship in our collaboration. As one local fisher said to me after watching me fail to tie an appropriate knot to secure a boat, "Walt, you're the dumbest smart guy I've ever seen." Sociolinguists cannot be proud; we need to genuinely recognize and acknowledge our many areas of incompetency in local culture and customs as part of our working relationship with communities.

There is no fail-safe strategy for overcoming the tradition of linguistic subordination in collaborative projects, but our experience has taught us that the most effective approach appears to be "flying under the ideological radar." We have found that positively framed presentations of language variation hold a greater likelihood of being received than those that directly confront language ideologies considered to be unassailable. This is the approach we have taken in our presentations to community residents, our presentation format in video documentaries (e.g., Hutcheson 2001, 2004, 2005; Cullinan 2011), and our approach in our curriculum on dialects (Reaser & Wolfram 2007). Though we naturally cannot avoid controversial language issues when community members raise them, we do not explicitly raise them ourselves. And when raised, we attempt to frame our responses in a positive historical and cultural perspective rather than direct confrontation.

Associating linguistic issues with positive historical and cultural images while avoiding red-flag labels and hot-button controversies can foster the positive reception of potentially controversial linguistic ideas. As noted in Wolfram (2010), for example, a TV documentary we produced on North Carolina language varieties (Hutcheson 2005) used strategic sequencing, positive narrative framing, visual historical landmark associations, and upbeat local music to introduce the topic of African American English (AAE), the most controversial dialect in the United States. AAE was intentionally introduced following the presentation of two regional varieties of English (Outer Banks and Appalachian) and two other sociocultural language varieties (Cherokee and Lumbee English). The synergistic effect of the visual images, the music, and the narrative set a highly positive image of place, setting, and language that apparently was effective, as we have never encountered a single complaint or received a negative comment about our presentation of AAE in that presentation. Instead, we have received only positive comments on our portrait of the linguistic landscape of the Tar Heel state, and the DVD was used as an incentive giveaway item for donor contributions to the public TV station. As one viewer observed, "They ought to give you a copy of *Voices of North Carolina* as part of your welcome packet to the state because it is so informative." This experience demonstrated that it is indeed possible to counter controversial language issues with positive framing that avoids the direct discussion of red-flag issues.

VENUES OF OUTREACH AND ENGAGEMENT

There are, of course, a wide range of activities and programs that might qualify as outreach and engagement, from opportunistic-based, teachable moments that spontaneously arise from current news events, to specific programs for formal education. We limit ourselves in this discussion to programmatic efforts that we have personally engaged in over the past several decades, happily acknowledging the efforts of others who have engaged in similar or varied kinds of activities (e.g., Lucas, Bayley, & Valli 2003; Nunnally 2011; Hazen 2005). These include dialect dictionaries, documentary films and DVDs, museum exhibits, audio CDs, books and booklets for popular audiences, and a middle school dialect curriculum for formal public education.

The compilation of a modest dialect dictionary (e.g., Locklear, Wolfram, Schilling-Estes, & Dannenberg 1999; Schilling-Estes, Estes, & Premilovac 2002) can be one of the most collaborative activities because the lexicon is one of the most accessible and transparent levels of language differences. Community residents are often aware of some of the lexical differences associated with their community or region, and assume native-speaker knowledge—and ownership—of their referential meaning and use, so that a genuinely collaborative and equal partnership can take place. It can further engage local residents meaningfully in the collection of data and in some aspects of the compilation process, and can be produced as an ongoing project within a relatively short time frame. In fact, we have found local community members to become more engaged proactively in this activity than in any other language-related project we have conducted. Local residents and visitors have found these dialect dictionaries to be of considerable interest, and the one domain of language study that allows community members unequivocally to assert proprietary language knowledge (Wolfram 1998).

Video documentaries produced with and on behalf of local communities are becoming an increasingly realistic option for outreach and engagement. Productions by the NCLLP have ranged from special TV programs that have aired nationally, regionally, or on the state affiliate of the Public Broadcasting Service ([PBS]; e.g., *Indian by Birth: The Lumbee Dialect* [Hutcheson 2001]; *Mountain Talk* [Hutcheson 2004]; *Voices of North Carolina* [Hutcheson 2005]; and *The Queen Family: Appalachian Tradition and Back Porch Music* [Hutcheson 2006]) to those produced primarily for community organizations (e.g., *The Ocracoke Brogue* [Blanton & Waters 1996]; and *Hyde County Talk: The Language and Land of Hyde County, NC* (*Hyde Talk: The Language and Land of Hyde County* [Torbert 2002]), though these are not mutually exclusive. The majority of our documentaries have focused on language (e.g., Blanton & Waters 1996; Hutcheson 2001, 2004, 2005), but our collaboration has sometimes extended to topics considerably beyond language as a natural extension of partnerships with communities that have goals and agendas different from our sociolinguistic ones (e.g., Grimes & Rowe 2004; Hutcheson 2006; Rowe

& Grimes 2007). Video projects have, in fact, ranged from short promotional features about a community (e.g., *Celebrating Princeville* [Hutcheson 2003]) to the celebration of people and events that are important to community members (e.g., *Celebrating Muzel Bryant* [Grimes 2004]). Fortunately, the current video editing software available at most universities makes these types of projects quite feasible for students and faculty to produce at modest expense.The audio CD is another popular venue for collaborative engagement with communities. For example, in collaboration with a local Ocracoke historian, we have produced a compact disc and an accompanying booklet, *Ocracoke Speaks* (Childs, Wolfram, & Cloud 2000) in which we compiled stories and anecdotes from different speakers, and Mallinson, Childs, and Cox (2006) produced a CD and accompanying booklet to document and preserve local traditions, stories, and history for Texana, a unique African American community nestled in the Smoky Mountains of Appalachia, and projects that merge oral history and sociolinguistics are becoming more popular (Hutcheson 2004, 2006; Kretzschmar, Childs, Anderson, & Lanehart 2004) and highly affordable with current editing software.

The community-based museum exhibit is a particularly productive venue for collaboration since it typically involves the donation of artifacts, images, and other memorabilia from the community. Such exhibits provide a presentation format of local culture and history for visitors at the same time that they celebrate the local community life and language. With the cooperation of community-based preservation societies and museums, we have now constructed several permanent exhibits that highlight language diversity (Gruendler & Wolfram 1997, 2001), as well as limited-time exhibits on history, culture, and prominent citizens in the community. For example, an exhibit titled *Freedom's Voice: Celebrating the Black Experience on the Outer Banks* (Vaughn & Grimes 2006) includes many poster images, a documentary, interactive audiovisuals, and artifacts and panels that highlight African Americans' involvement in the history of coastal North Carolina. In an important sense, this exhibition combines history and culture through language in narrating the story of the "other lost colony" on Roanoke Island.

There are also outreach and engagement activities related to popular writing, ranging from popular trade books (Rickford & Rickford 2000; Tannen 1990, 2006; Wolfram & Schilling-Estes 1997; Wolfram & Ward 2006; Wolfram & Reaser forthcoming) and articles, to collaborative community-based dialect dictionaries as noted previously. Trade books may also provide a venue for collaborative engagement. The book, *Fine in the World: Lumbee Language in Time and Place* (Wolfram, Dannenberg, Knick, & Oxendine 2002), is distributed through the Museum of the Native American Resource Center in Robeson County, the homeland of the Lumbee, and two of the authors are from the community. The book is also distributed widely among teachers throughout Robeson County schools in an effort to educate them and their students about the role of dialect in Lumbee life. A more recent popular book on language and dialect, *Talkin' Tar Heel: Voices of North Carolina* (Wolfram & Reaser forthcoming) foucses on an entire state, seizing on the state pride of residents of North Carolina.

One of our most ambitious outreach programs in public education involves the development of formal curricular materials on language diversity in the public schools. Unfortunately, formal education about dialect variation is still a relatively novel and, in most cases, controversial idea. Though we have taught school-based dialect awareness programs since the early 1990s (Wolfram, Adger, & Detwyler 1992) and an annual program on Ocracoke for the past two decades (Wolfram, Schilling-Estes, & Hazen 1994; Reaser & Wolfram 2007), school-based programs have still not progressed from a pilot stage (Reaser 2006; Sweetland 2006). Our pilot program is a middle-school curriculum in social studies that connects with language arts (Reaser & Wolfram 2007), but similar units might be designed for other levels of K-12 education as well. Such curricula are based on humanistic, scientific, and social science rationales, and engage students on a number of different participatory levels. In the process, students and teachers learn about dialect study as a kind of scientific inquiry and as a type of social science research. The examination of dialect differences offers great potential for students to investigate the interrelation between linguistic and social diversity, including diversity grounded in geography, history, and cultural beliefs and practices. There are a number of creative ways in which students can examine how language and culture go hand-in-hand as they address language diversity.

One of the greatest advantages of a curriculum on dialects is its potential for tapping the linguistic resources of students' indigenous communities. In addition to classroom lessons, students learn by going into the community to collect current dialect data. In most cases, the speech characteristics of the local community should make dialects come alive in a way that is unmatched by textbook knowledge. Educational models that treat the local community as a resource to be tapped rather than as a liability to be overcome have been shown to be quite effective in other areas of language arts education (Robertson & Bloome 1997), and there is no reason why this model cannot be applied to the study of dialects. The program naturally fits in with North Carolina's standard course of study for eighth grade social studies (www.ncpublicschools.org/curriculum/socialstudiesa/scos/2003-04/050eighthgrade) that includes the curricular themes of "culture and diversity," "historic perspectives," and "geographical relationships" as they relate to North Carolina. In addition, the dialect awareness curriculum helps fulfill social studies competency goals, such as "Describe the roles and contributions of diverse groups, such as American Indians, African Americans, European immigrants, landed gentry, tradesmen, and small farmers to everyday life in colonial North Carolina" (Competency Goal 1.07) or "Assess the importance of regional diversity on the development of economic, social, and political institutions in North Carolina" (Competency Goal 8.04). In aligning materials with competency goals, it is essential to seek ways to help teachers accomplish the goals they have for their students both in terms of the standard course of study and in terms of more abstract goals, such as teaching students to be better writers (Sweetland 2006).

A further consideration in targeting the social studies curriculum is the fact that it tends to have more flexibility in terms of innovative materials than language arts, which is traditionally constrained by year-end standardized performance testing. The subject of language diversity may naturally merge with language arts, and even science, at points where the focus is on language analysis as a type of scientific inquiry. Students are not the only ones who profit from the study of dialect diversity. Teachers also find that some of their stereotypes about languages are challenged and that they become more knowledgeable and enlightened about language diversity in the process of teaching the curriculum (Reaser 2006).

The venues for outreach and engagement highlighted in this section are meant to be illustrative rather than exhaustive, and may be complemented by a number of other activities. Lectures and workshops on dialect variation in different communities are relatively common, including presentations for preservation and historical societies as well as for other special interest groups. Workshops on dialects for teachers and school children and special presentations at museums and historical societies have also been conducted, including many requested by the community. These activities may involve key community members and local institutions such as civic organizations and governing councils in an effort to raise awareness about local dialect history and customs. In some communities, this work may be highly collaborative and visible on a public level, with strong public support from community agencies.

The Collaborative Relationship

The nature of the collaborative relationship between sociolinguistic researchers and the community is always complicated. Sociolinguists and community members bring different socialized backgrounds, diverse areas of interest and expertise, variant understandings of language and other behavioral phenomena, and varied goals and concerns that may even be in conflict. Nonetheless, there is great potential for working together on projects that are of mutual benefit to community members and sociolinguists.

It is reasonable to involve community participants during at least three stages in the process—in the initial conceptualization of the project, during the active production of the activity, and in the final stage before the program or product is released. Engagement in the initial collaborative conceptualization allows us to define a project together and to share in the initial decision about its goals, nature, and structure. It also gives the community a vested interest in the project from the onset. Linguists have to be open at this point to significant reconceptualization based on community interests, or even to abandoning the original project for an alternative one. In fact, in one media project, initial discussion with community representatives resulted in the production of a documentary on the historical development of the community (Grimes & Rowe 2004; Rowe & Grimes 2007) rather than a language-based feature on the local, rural variety of African American English. Enabling the town's residents to promote this interest in the formulation of the project and throughout our production actually led to a more synergistic research effort for our sociolinguistic team, but of course, the negotiations also led us away from a sociolinguistic documentary *per se*. If we are serious about working with communities, then they must also have a stake in decision making about the nature of the project itself, though we of course run the risk that communities may move us away from our vested interest in the presentation of language variation.

The selection of participants to represent a community is an important one, but it also can be highly sensitive. In small communities, local leaders have to participate, but it is also important not to limit selection to only those community members who have roles as external agents for the community (see Briggs 1986) or represent local power hierarchies. It is also important to consult with community members who have little or no vested political interest within the community and represent a bottom-up perspective of the community to complement the top-down vantage point that is often the default relationship when working with communities

Both local organizations and individuals apart from these organizations need to be engaged. Historical and preservation societies often play a significant role in the small, rural communities where we do a lot of our current engagement, and several of our most active, ongoing partnerships have taken place under the auspices of these community agencies. Unlike their largely invisible, institutional counterparts in most metropolitan areas, these organizations are often ascribed local status and civic prominence. Accordingly, some of our most supportive and productive collaborative experiences have taken place with preservation societies, historical societies, and museums, such as the Ocracoke Historical Society, the Outer Banks History Center, and the Museum of the Native American Resource Center. These organizations often share with us a value about cultural and historical legacy that can extend to language and dialect. The perception that culture, history, and language are inseparable is a common theme voiced in interviews with residents in language communities and serves as one of our focal points for establishing collaborative projects. In fact, the link between language and social and regional place is arguably the biggest sociolinguistic enticement we offer these organizations. For example, many Lumbee Indians of North Carolina, whose authentic Native American identity is constantly under scrutiny from groups that range from the federal government to European American and African American cohort groups, express pride over the fact that they are uniquely identifiable through their dialect of English (Wolfram et al. 2002).

One of the sensitive dimensions of community engagement relates to the establishment of credibility, both in terms of the local community and in terms of outsiders, two groups whose standards may not always overlap. How do we ensure that the presentation will be received in the spirit it was intended and be embraced by community members? Though there are no guarantees of acceptance, we have adopted several strategies that seem to offer the potential for mutual support. First, we often involve recognized community leaders and personalities. Though hardly foolproof, it seems most appropriate to be respectful of social hierarchies within the community. For projects requiring narration, such as a documentary, we typically select a local, recognized leader for this position. In a strategic decision to provide credibility for the presentation of our documentary, *Voices of North Carolina*, we enlisted William C. Friday, arguably the most highly respected public figure in North Carolina, to narrate the documentary. For the documentary film, *Indian by Birth: The Lumbee Language*, we selected a respected Lumbee historian, teacher, and community leader. Tapping into local institutions and organizations is another way of promoting the community connection. The use of local performers, musicians, and artists, along with highlighting noteworthy community traditions and landmarks, also helps frame programs as symbolically collaborative and centered within the community.

In working with local organizations and people it must be recognized that even the smallest community is not free of internal political conflict. While taking a public, neutral stance towards internal community conflict, there are factions that have to be accommodated in the participatory process. In one film production and museum exhibit, for example, we had to confront rival tribal groups within the Lumbee community who were in litigation about the right to represent the Lumbee tribe at the time of our production. In this instance, we simply asked members from both groups to serve on our advisory panel to ensure that both factions were represented in the selection of spokespeople for the tribe. Political sensitivity, compromise, and diplomacy are attributes that must be present throughout the community engagement, even as we appear to be politically neutral and naïve about intra-community politics in navigating a path of least resistance in representing the widest range of community interests. In several instances, we found that our triangulation with different factions in a common-goal, community-presentation project actually seemed to sublimate and mitigate some long-standing conflict.

As noted above, it is not enough to consult with community members in the conceptualization of the project; it is also necessary to involve them as the product is being shaped. This does not mean micromanaging the project, but it should involve critiques of the process and the emerging product while there is still ample time for significant feedback. For example, in producing an oral history CD for the local community and for external distribution, we consulted with community agents at several points in the rough cuts, and then before the final production was finally burned. While this is hardly standard procedure for most audiovisual productions, collaborative projects with communities require a somewhat different participatory model that ensures their involvement throughout the process.

Finally, we usually share our penultimate version of the production to a number of different groups, including community members, linguistic students, non-linguistic students and other focus groups that represent general public audiences. Often, the director, producer, and researcher will have specific questions about the representation of the community in particular scenes that only the community can address. For example, in our portrayal of the Cherokee language in our documentary *Voices of North Carolina,* there is an interview in which the interviewee mocks the beautiful names (e.g., "Floating Eagle Feather," "Princess Pale Moon," etc.) appropriated by Cherokees in the commodification of Indianess for tourists. We were unsure if this reference might be offensive to some people within the community so we asked several Cherokee leaders their feelings about it. Somewhat surprisingly—at least to us—the leaders were adamant in their insistence about keeping this clip in the final version of the documentary, alleviating our concern about its potential offensiveness. Up to the very end of the final edit—and sometimes beyond—there is a need to remain actively engaged with community members in collaborative projects of this type.

Collaborative projects must routinely expect unforeseen obstacles that simply cannot be anticipated, ranging from glitches in technology to unexpected reactions and behaviors by community members. These issues seem inevitable and must be considered inherent within the collaborative process. Furthermore, some of the issues severely test the notion of collaboration. As reported in Wolfram et al. (2008), our ventures have not been immune to disappointing failures in the collaborative process as well as some outstanding successes. Collaboration among linguists, community members, and producers is, in fact, an ongoing process of negotiation and compromise that is both process and product. Linguists and producers need to be sensitive to criticism and input from different interest groups throughout the process of the development of a project, remembering why the projects were undertaken in the first place. Criticism of our projects needs to be taken seriously but not personally, and linguists cannot afford to be defensive about the investment of professional expertise, creativity, energy, resources, and good intentions. We further need to be flexible in the evolution of a project and realize that the final product may sometimes end up a faint resemblance of the original idea. And the ultimate shape of our project should reflect as much concern for this process as the final product.

One of the enduring questions about researcher-community collaborations is the question of need and profit. Do communities really want and need our seemingly invasive collaboration? Who really profits from our participation in the community? In some of our projects, for example, we have been careful to invest financially in the community and have shared revenues from our projects, but generally, the potential profit is more in terms of the symbolic capital of gaining an understanding of language variation as a symbol of cultural heritage that is is heightened through our involvement. But we need to ask if this is a shared goal derived from the partnership or simply an imposition of our sociolinguistic and sociopolitical agenda on the community? We have, of course, profited in terms of our research reputations, professional advancement, and even in our recognition for proactive involvement with local vernacular-speaking communities (Rickford 1997: 184). Given that we stand to profit in our profession from such partnerships, it is hard to claim that we have no profit motive. Even if we took the position that favors to communities should be limited to activities unrelated to language, such as volunteering in community activities, our motives for offering such services might be suspect.

Conclusion

It is apparent that there are many issues that need to be considered in advocating researcher-community partnerships and the implementation of the linguistic gratuity principle. Our discussion is neither comprehensive nor complete, and these reflections are offered simply as a starting point for examining the full implications of sharing knowledge and expertise with host research communities in the name of linguistic gratuity. Though relationships of empowerment may seem to be an ideal goal (Cameron et al. 1992), they are also an elusive ideal given the differential status of language researchers and community members and prevailing language ideologies in society with respect to non-mainstream varieties of language. Relationships are always a dynamic negotiation, and our collaboration never really has an end point if we are faithful to our obligation. More than four decades after we conducted research into AAE in Detroit (Wolfram 1969), we are still obligated to work with and for the community to share knowledge and understanding about the nature of AAE and its implications for society and education.

Notwithstanding these realistic issues and concerns, the notion of returning linguistic favors in some form seems to be an appropriate activity when we have mined—if not exploited—so many of the speech community's linguistic resources to our advantage. Perhaps more importantly, the return of linguistic favors should not be viewed as a special commitment or ancillary role to our mission as sociolinguists. This responsibility should be as part and parcel of our professional life as sociolinguists—in a way that is parallel to our assumption of social responsibility for the welfare of society as ordinary citizens. Though language may be studied rigorously as a science and/or social science, it should not be detached from its everyday role in society. As the pioneering, theoretical linguistic, Ferdinand de Saussure, put it a century ago:

> Of what use is linguistics?...In the lives of individuals and of society, Language is a factor of greater importance than any other. For the study of language to remain solely the business of a handful of specialists would be a quite unacceptable state of affairs. In practice, the study of language is in some degree or other the concern of everyone. (Saussure [1916] 1986: 7)

Though we may feel obligated to return favors because of our commitment to the people and to the communities whose data fuel our theories and descriptions, collaborative linguistic engagement is a good thing to do even if we don't deal directly with native speakers and communities. Socially responsibility about language issues should be assumed as linguistic and sociolinguistic citizens, and should not be viewed as a separate mission or calling. It should be inherent within our overarching professional obligation, along with our commitment to mentor our students, undertake peer reviews, support professional organizations, and be responsible citizens in our departments and universities. In assuming this responsibility, we respond to the needs of our field and the well being of society.

Acknowledgment

I gratefully acknowledge funding from NSF Grants ESI-0652343, ESI-0354711, and SBR-9616333 for the documentary productions discussed here, as well as the Friday Endowment and the College of Humanities Extension and Engagement Program at North Carolina State University. Some of the material in this article is based on Wolfram, Reaser, and Vaughn (2008) and Wolfram (2010).

References

Baugh, J. 1999. *Out of the mouths of slaves: African American language and educational malpractice.* Austin: University of Texas Press.

Baugh, J. (2000). *Beyond Ebonics: Linguistic pride and racial prejudice.* Oxford: Oxford University Press.

Blanton, P., & Waters, K., producers (1996) *The Ocracoke Brogue.* Raleigh: North Carolina Language and Life Project.

Briggs, C. L. 1986. *Learning how to ask: A sociolinguistic appraisal of the role of the interview in social science research.* Cambridge: Cambridge University Press.

Cameron, D., Fraser, E., Harvey, P., Rampton, M. B. H., & Richardson, K. 1992. *Researching language: Issues of power and method.* New York: Routledge.

Carpenter, J. 2005. The invisible community of the lost colony: African American speech on Roanoke Island. *American Speech* 80: 227–55.

Childs, B., Wolfram, W. & Cloud, M. 2000. *Ocracoke Speaks: The Distinct Sounds of the Hoi Toide Brogue.* Raleigh: North Carolina Language and Life Project.

Cullinan, D., producer. 2011. *Spanish voices.* Raleigh: North Carolina Language and Life Project.

Grimes, D., producer 2004. *Celebrating Muzel Bryant.* Raleigh: North Carolina Language and Life Project.

Grimes, D., & Rowe, R., producers. (2004). *Princeville remembers the flood.* Raleigh: North Carolina Language and Life Project.

Gruendler, S., & Wolfram, W. 1997. The Ocracoke Brogue. An exhibit at the Ocracoke Preservation Society. Ocracoke: North Carolina Language and Life Project.

Gruendler, S., & Wolfram, W. 2001. Lumbee Language. An exhibit at the Museum of the Native American Resource Center. Pembroke: North Carolina Language and Life Project.

Hazen, K. 2005. The West Virginia dialect project. http://www.as.wvu.edu/dialect/index.html.

Hutcheson, N., producer. 2001. *Indian by birth: The Lumbee dialect.* Raleigh: North Carolina Language and Life Project.

Hutcheson, N., producer. 2003. *Celebrating Princeville.* Raleigh: North Carolina Language and Life Project.

Hutcheson, N., producer. 2004. *Mountain talk.* Raleigh: North Carolina Language and Life Project.

Hutcheson, N., producer. 2004. *An unclouded day: Stories and songs of the Southern Appalachian Mountains.* Raleigh: North Carolina Language and Life Project.

Hutcheson, N., producer. 2005. *Voices of North Carolina.* Raleigh: North Carolina Language and Life Project.

Hutcheson, N., producer. 2006. *The Queen family: Appalachian tradition and back porch music.* Raleigh: North Carolina Language and Life Project.

Kretzschmar, W., Childs, B., Anderson, B., & Lanehart, S. 2004. *Roswell voices.* Roswell: Roswell Folk and Heritage Bureau.

Labov, W. 1972. *Language in the inner city: Studies in the Black English vernacular.* Philadelphia: University of Pennsylvania Press.

Labov, W. 1982. Objectivity and commitment in linguistic science. *Language in Society* 11: 165–201.

Lippi-Green, R. 1997. *English with an accent: Language, ideology, and discrimination in the United States.* New York: Routledge.

Locklear, H. A., Wolfram, W., Schilling-Estes, N., & Dannenberg, C. 1999. *A dialect dictionary of Lumbee English.* Raleigh: North Carolina Language and Life Project.

Lucas, C., Bayley, R., & Valli, C. 2003. *What's Your Sign for PIZZA? An Introduction to Variation in ASL.* (book and DVD). Washington, DC: Gallaudet University Press.

Mallinson, C., Childs, B., & Cox, Z. 2006. *Voices of Texana.* Texana: Texana Committee on Community History and Preservation.

Nunnally, T. E. (ed). 2011. *Speaking of Alabama: Language history, diversity, and change.* Tuscaloosa: University of Alabama Press.

Patrick, P. L. 2002. The speech community. In J. K. Chambers, P. Trudgill, & N. Schilling-Estes (eds), *The handbook of language variation and change*, 573–97. Malden, MA: Blackwell.

Preston, D. 1997. The South: The touchstone. C. Bernstein, T. Nunnally, & R. Sabino (eds), *Language variety in the South revisited*. University, AL: University of Alabama Press, 311–51.

Reaser, J. 2006. The effect of dialect awareness on adolescent knowledge and attitudes. Ph.D. dissertation, Duke University.

Reaser, J., & Wolfram, W. 2007. *Voices of North Carolina: Language and life from the Atlantic to the Appalachians*. Raleigh: North Carolina Language and Life Project.

Reed, J. S. 1993. *Surveying the South*. Columbia: University of Missouri Press.

Reed, J. S. 2003. *Minding the South*. Columbia: University of Missouri Press.

Rickford, J. R. 1997. Unequal partnership: Sociolinguistics and the African American speech community. *Language in Society* 26: 161–98.

Rickford, J. R. (1999). *African American English: Features, evolution, and educational implications*. Malden, MA: Blackwell.

Rickford, J. R., & Rickford, R. J. 2000. *Spoken soul: The story of Black English*. New York: John Wiley & Sons.

Robertson, A. E., & Bloome, D. (eds.). 1997. *Students as researchers of culture and language in their own communities*. Cresskill: Hampton Press.

Rowe, R., & Grimes, A., producers. 2007. *This side of the river: Self-determination and survival in Princeville, NC*. Raleigh: North Carolina Language and Life Project.

Saussure, F. De. (1916) 1986. *Cours de linguistique génerale*. Paris: Payot. End. Ed. Course in general linguistics. Translated by R. Harris. LaSalle, Il: Open Court.

Schilling-Estes, N., Estes. C. & Premilovac, A. 2002. Smith Island voices: A collection of stories, memories, and slices of life from Smith Island, Maryland, in the late 20th and early 21st centuries. CD. Crownsville, MD: Maryland Historical Trust.

Sweetland, J. 2006. *Teaching writing in the African American classroom: A sociolinguistic approach*. Ph.D. dissertation, Stanford University.

Torbert, B. producer. 2002. *Hyde talk: The language and land of Hyde County, NC*. Raleigh: North Carolina Language and Life Project.

Vaughn, C., & Grimes, D. 2006. *Freedom's Voice: Celebrating the Black Experience on the Outer Banks*. An exhibit at the Outer Banks History Center. Roanoke Island: North Carolina Language and Life Project and the Outer Banks History Center.

Wolfram, W. 1969. *A sociolinguistic description of Detroit Negro speech*. Washington, DC: Center for Applied Linguistics.

Wolfram, W. 1993. Ethical considerations in language awareness programs. *Issues in Applied Linguistics* 4: 225–525.

Wolfram, W. 1998. Scrutinizing linguistic gratuity: A view from the field. *Journal of Sociolinguistics* 2: 271–79.

Wolfram, W. 2007. Sociolinguistic myths in the study of African American English. *Language and Linguistics Compass* 2: 292–313.

Wolfram, W. 2010. Collaborative issues in language variation documentaries. *Language and Linguistics Compass* 4: 293–303.

Wolfram, W., Dannenberg, C., Knick, S., & Oxendine, L. 2002. *Fine in the world: Lumbee language in time and place*. Raleigh: North Carolina State Humanities Extension/Publications.

Wolfram, W., Adger, C., & Detwyler, J. 1992. *All about dialects: Instructor's manual*. Washington, DC: Center for Applied Linguistics.

Wolfram, W., & Reaser, J. forthcoming. *Talkin' Tar Heel: Voices of North Carolina*. Chapel Hill: University of North Carolina Press.

Wolfram, W., Reaser, J., & Vaughn, C. 2008. Operationalizing linguistic gratuity: From principle to practice. *Language and Linguistics Compass* 3: 1109–134.

Wolfram, W., & Schilling-Estes, N. 1997. *Hoi toide on the Outer Banks: The story of the Ocracoke nrogue.* Chapel Hill: University of North Carolina Press.

Wolfram, W., & Schilling-Estes, N. 2006. *American English: Dialects and variation.* 2nd edition. Malden, MA: Blackwell.

Wolfram, W., Schilling-Estes, N., & Hazen, K. 1994. *Dialects and the Ocracoke Brogue.* A dialect curriculum for eighth-graders in Ocracoke, NC. Raleigh: The North Carolina Language and Life Project.

Tannen, D. 2006. *You're wearing that? Understanding mothers and daughters in conversation.* New York: Random House.

Wolfram, W., & Ward, B. (eds.). 2006. *American voices: How dialects differ from coast to coast.* Malden, MA: Blackwell.

CHAPTER 38

LINGUISTIC AND ECOLOGICAL DIVERSITY

SUZANNE ROMAINE

GLOBAL linguistic diversity is rapidly declining. According to some projections, 50 percent to 90 percent of the world's 6900 or more languages may soon become extinct (Nettle & Romaine 2000). Crystal (2000: 19) believes that one language may vanish every two weeks. At the same time, the world is experiencing a substantial decline in biodiversity, with annual losses of plant and animal species estimated at 1000 or more times greater than historic background rates (Millennium Ecosystem Assessment 2005). The ultimate cause of all extinctions is environmental change. As Wilson (1998: 328) contends with respect to the disappearance of species, "the outright elimination of habitat...is the leading cause of extinction. But the introduction of aggressive exotic species...come[s] close behind in destructiveness." Much of the globe is now covered with a few species of Eurasian origin, such as wheat, barley, cattle, rice (Crosby 1994). These monocultures are rapidly replacing a profusion of endemic diversity. The situation for languages is strikingly similar, but the spreading varieties are large languages like English, Spanish, and Chinese, and the like. We are crossing a threshold of irreversible loss of species and languages into a fundamentally changed and less diverse world. Although the precise details of the direct and indirect causes of these parallel declines in linguistic diversity and biodiversity are extremely complex, both species and languages are in danger of becoming extinct in the same places, with languages at even greater risk than species (Sutherland 2003). Both kinds of diversity are heavily concentrated through the tropics and tail off towards the poles, with approximately three-fourths of the world's languages occupying about one-fourth of the earth's land area. This striking overlap leads Nettle & Romaine (2000) to use the term "biolinguistic diversity" to refer to the rich spectrum of life encompassing all the earth's species of plants and animals along with human cultures and their languages. Recognizing the intimate connections between language and culture, others use terms such as "biocultural diversity" (see Pretty et al. 2009; Maffi 2001, 2005; Skutnabb-Kangas, Maffi, & Harmon 2003; Loh & Harmon 2005), "ethnosphere" (Davis 2001) or "logosphere" (Krauss 2007a) in a similar encompassing fashion.

The reasons for this remarkable overlap are presently not well understood and likely vary from place to place, but both biodiversity and linguistic diversity clearly face common threats. Language shift and death are responses to pressures of various kinds on communities. Communities can thrive and transmit their languages only where their members have a decent environment to live in and a sustainable economic system. In a rapidly globalizing world with a handful of very large languages and many thousands of small ones, maintenance of linguistic diversity is inextricably linked to the survival of small communities, whose subsistence lifestyles depend on healthy ecosystems and access to land. Without such resources these groups find it hard to maintain their ways of life and their cultural identities on which the continued transmission and vitality of their languages depends. Above all, however, the parallel extinction crises in species and languages means that as the world is becoming less biologically diverse, at the same time it is becoming culturally and linguistically less diverse as well. Documenting and analyzing the geographic co-occurrence of these two kinds of diversity provides critical first steps in addressing the loss of human and non-human variety on earth in a more systematic and integrated fashion. After outlining the current state of linguistic diversity and language endangerment, this chapter will examine the nature of the geographic interface between linguistic and ecological diversity, in order to explain why the extinction of languages is part of the larger picture of near total collapse of the worldwide ecosystem, and why languages are vital parts of complex local ecologies that must be supported if global biodiversity is to be maintained. In view of the strong relationship between areas of potential endangerment for species and for languages and their associated cultures, integrated strategies need to be developed to ensure the survival of both human diversity and biological diversity on our rapidly globalizing planet.

The Current State of Linguistic Diversity and Language Endangerment

No one knows exactly how many languages or cultures there are in the world, either historically or currently, but most assessments rely on the Ethnologue data compiled by the Summer Institute of Linguistics, cataloguing all the known languages of the world; in practice, this includes a total of 6909 languages spoken by 5.9 billion people (Lewis 2009). This does not include dialects because there are no clear criteria for defining the boundaries between languages and dialects (see Wolfram & Schilling-Estes 1998 for discussion of dialect endangerment). As recently as 500 years ago there may have been some 12,000 to 14,000 cultural groups. More than half of this cultural diversity has possibly been lost (Sponsel 2000; Price 1990). Meanwhile, perhaps half the known languages in the world have disappeared over this same time period, and up to 90 percent of the world's currently spoken 6909 languages may vanish over the next 100 years, most of them unwritten and undocumented. (Krauss 1992; Harrison 2007; Nettle & Romaine 2000; UNESCO 2001). The crucial role language plays in the acquisition, accumulation, maintenance, and transmission of human knowledge means that the prospect of language extinction on such a large scale raises critical issues about the survival of humanity's rich and diverse intellectual heritage. A recent statement by UNEP (United Nations Environment Program) not only acknowledges that the concept of biodiversity also incorporates human cultural diversity, but also recognizes that both kinds of diversity can be affected by the same drivers, with resulting impacts on ecosystems. The conservation of biodiversity and sustainable development are therefore inextricably linked (UNEP 2007: 160–61).

For most of the many millennia of human history, the world was close to linguistic equilibrium, with the number of languages lost roughly equaling the new ones created. The reason this balance persisted so long is that there were no massive, enduring differences between the expansionary potential of different peoples of the kind that might cause the spread of a single, dominant language. Over the past 10,000 years, however, various events have punctured this equilibrium forever. Firstly, the invention and spread of agriculture; the rise of colonialism; later, the Industrial Revolution; and today, the spread of mass media, globalization of economies, and so forth, have created the global village phenomenon. These forces have propelled a few languages—all Eurasian in origin—to spread over the last few centuries. Now all but a handful of hunter-gatherer societies live outside their local ecosystems. The world's remaining small bands are found only in ecosystems unsuited for agriculture or pastoralism, typically in rainforests (e.g., Pygmies of the Congo river basin, the Andaman Islands, and scattered groups in the Amazon, South Indian forests, the Malay Peninsula, Borneo, the Philippines, and New Guinea), deserts (Kalahari, Australia, Great Basin), and arctic/antarctic areas (northeast Siberia, arctic North America, Tierra del Fuego).

The spread of large languages in modern times has rendered the global distribution of linguistic diversity strikingly uneven and resulted in marked disparities in the size of populations speaking the world's languages. Figure 38.1 shows that over 80 percent (N = 5640) of the world's languages are found in just 20 countries including some of the richest in the world (United States, Canada,

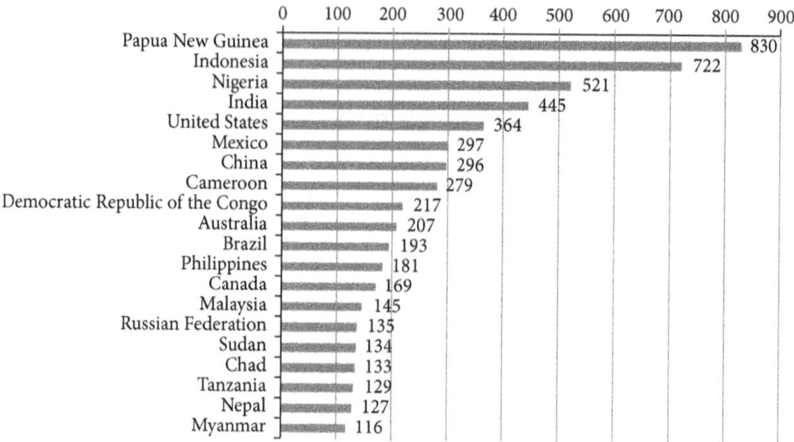

Figure 38.1 Twenty countries with highest number of languages

Source: Based on data from Lewis (2009)

and Australia) as well as some of the poorest (Chad, Democratic Republic of the Congo, and Nigeria). Figure 38.2 shows that only nine languages have more than one hundred million speakers; altogether they are spoken by about 50 percent of the world's population. These include Chinese (1.23 billion speakers), Spanish (329 million), English (328 million), Arabic (221 million), Hindi (182 million), Bengali (181 million), Portuguese (178 million), Russian (144 million), and Japanese (122 million). The spread of these languages would be even more extensive if figures for second language speakers were included. These very large languages are all spoken in more than one country, such as English, for instance, with large groups of speakers in the United Kingdom, United States, New Zealand, Canada, Australia, and South Africa. Although English is not the largest language in the world, it is one of a small handful of what may be called global languages in terms of geographic spread and number of users worldwide. With estimates of the number of nonnative speakers of English ranging from 470 million to more than a billion, nonnative users now greatly outnumber native speakers (Crystal 2003).

At the other end of the size spectrum are ca. 548 languages with fewer than 99 speakers, comprising nearly one-tenth of the world's languages. If all languages were equal in size, they would have around 860,000 speakers. According to the Ethnologue, however, the median size for a language is actually only about 7500 speakers. Only 389 (or nearly 6 percent) of the world's languages have at least one million speakers and account for 94 percent of the world's population. The remaining 94 percent are spoken by only 6 percent of the world's people (Lewis 2009).

As large language communities continue to expand, others contract. Over the last five hundred years, small languages nearly everywhere have come under intense threat as the world's tribes are dying out or being assimilated

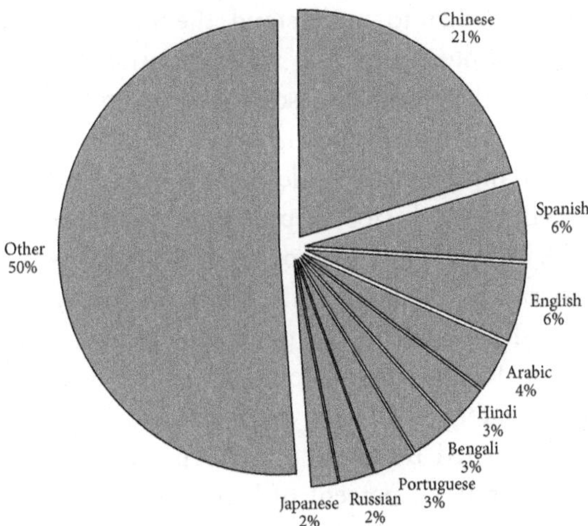

Figure 38.2. Languages with 100 million or more speakers as a proportion of world population

Source: Based on data from Lewis (2009)

into modern nation-states. People do not normally give up their languages or cultures willingly, but continue to transmit them, albeit in changed form over time. The disappearance of a language and its related culture almost always forms part of a wider process of social, cultural, and political displacement. Not coincidentally, the vast majority of today's threatened languages and cultures are found among socially and politically marginalized and/or subordinated national and ethnic minority groups. Estimates of the number of such groups range from 5000 to 8000 and include among them the world's indigenous peoples, who make up about 4 percent of the world population but speak up to 60 percent of its languages (Nettle & Romaine 2000: ix). The fate of most of the world's linguistic diversity, and by implication its cultural diversity, therefore lies in the hands of a small number of people most vulnerable to pressures of globalization.

Because a large part of any language is culture specific, people feel that an important part of their traditional culture and identity is also lost when that language disappears. Most languages are unwritten, leaving much of the world's so-called traditional ecological knowledge to be passed down orally and potentially only a generation away from extinction. The traditional inhabitants of Marovo Lagoon (Solomon Islands), for instance, have names for at least 500 plants, 70 birds, 350 fish, 100 marine shells; some 50 distinct terms for forest types, land topography, and freshwater systems; and more than 70 separate terms for reef types and underwater and coastal topography (Hviding 2006: 79). The disappearance of hundreds of species along with their names and related knowledge of their habitat and behavior represents a huge loss to science at precisely the time when we need most urgently to manage local ecosystems more effectively.

More research is needed to understand the impact of various factors in supporting language maintenance. The wide variation in projected extinction rates for languages found in both the scholarly and popular literature reflects inadequate information for many languages as well as lack of consensus on criteria for assessing endangerment (Nettle and Romaine 2000; Landweer 2000; UNESCO 2001; UNESCO Ad Hoc Expert Group on Endangered Languages 2003; Krauss 2007b). Nevertheless, the pulse of a language quite obviously lies in the youngest generation. Languages are clearly at risk when they are no longer transmitted naturally to children by parents or other caretakers. At the same time, however, lack of documentation for most of the world's languages means that few data exist on intergenerational transmission. UNESCO (2001) suggests that languages being learned by fewer than 30 percent of the younger generation may be at risk; overall, 50 percent of languages may be in various degrees of endangerment. Although linguists have been applying the Red Book/List approach to languages for the past decade or so, there is still no system of language ranking in terms of risk that can claim the broad attention and authority enjoyed by the IUCN (International Union for Conservation of Nature) Red List for species. Martí et al. (2005) surveyed the state of 725 languages by questionnaire, finding just over half (53 percent) being transmitted; overall, 42 percent are in danger. Other estimates can be gleaned from census and other data as well as from fieldworkers' reports. Norris and Jantzen (2002) assessed the continuity of Aboriginal languages using Canadian census statistics from 1981 to 1996, finding that the proportion of children with an Aboriginal mother tongue is well below UNESCO's (2001) suggested minimum of 30 percent. Only about 20 out of 50 languages are at or above this threshold. A few small languages with fewer than 10,000 speakers (Attikamek, Montagnais, Dene) and the three largest languages (Inuktitut, Ojibway, Cree) emerge as the strongest languages by this measure, with over 70 percent of children having them as home languages. Over the past 100 years nearly 10 have become extinct, and at least a dozen more are on the brink of extinction (Task Force on Aboriginal Languages and Cultures 2005). The situation for native American languages in the United States is equally alarming. Of an estimated 300 languages spoken when Columbus arrived in the New World in 1492, possibly only Navajo and a few others such as Yupik in Alaska will survive in the long term as community languages. In California none of the remaining indigenous languages is spoken natively by anyone under the age of 60 and only five have more than about 10 speakers.

The Australian continent is a linguistic graveyard, with only about 55,000 speakers remaining of what were once as many as 250 indigenous languages. From 1800 to 1996 there has been a decrease of 90 percent in the number of indigenous languages spoken fluently and regularly by all age groups as well as a decrease in the percentage of people speaking an Aboriginal language from 100 percent to 13 percent (McConvell & Thieberger 2001, 2006). Most Aboriginal languages in Canada, the United States, and Australia cannot draw on official support or rely on institutions, such as the schools, to produce new users.

The domains in which a language is used may also tell us something about its long-term viability. Fewer than 4 percent of the world's languages have any kind of official status in the countries where they are spoken. A very small handful of dominant languages prevail as languages of government and education. English, for example, is the dominant de facto or official language in over 98 countries; French has official or co-official status in 54. Fewer than 10 percent of the world's languages are used in education. The fact that most languages are unwritten, not recognized officially, restricted to local community and home functions, and spoken by very small groups of people reflects the balance of power in the global linguistic marketplace. In so far as status offers a degree of protection against endangerment, the only languages that may be considered safe are the small handful of politically dominant languages of modern nation-states (Romaine 2007).

Language shift may be thought of as a loss of speakers and domains of use, both of which are critical to the survival of a language. The possibility of impending shift appears when a language once used throughout a community for everything becomes restricted in use as another language intrudes on its territory. Usage declines in domains where the language was once secure, for example, in church, the workplace, schools, and, most importantly, the home, as growing numbers of parents fail to transmit the language to their children. In the absence of systematic and reliable data on intergenerational transmission, Nettle and Romaine (2000) relied on size as a proxy for degree of endangerment to assess risk both globally and in specific regions. Even so, estimates for the number of languages at risk vary in relation to number of speakers considered necessary for a language to be viable. If Krauss (1992) is right in thinking that only languages with over 100,000 speakers are safe, then up to 90 percent of the world's languages may be at risk. All our estimates are guesses, but even if the viability threshold is set at the lower level of 10,000 speakers, over 50 percent (N = 3688) of all languages may already be endangered, as indicated in table 38.1. Just over a quarter of all languages (N = 1779) are spoken by fewer than 1000 speakers. The Ethnologue also designates 473 languages as nearly extinct because they are spoken by only a few elderly speakers. Table 38.1 also shows that the number of languages at risk by size varies considerably by continent. Languages in Australia, the Pacific, and the Americas are mostly very small, almost all with fewer than 100,000 speakers. Africa, Asia, and Europe, by contrast, have some very large languages and a fair number of medium-sized ones (100,000 to 1 million speakers). Such languages are probably safer, in the short term at least.

Although size does not tell the whole story, it may be the best surrogate at the moment for vulnerability to the kinds of pressures leading to language extinction. A large language such as Quechua with millions of speakers in several South American countries can be endangered in locations where external pressures are great, while a very small language like Icelandic with fewer than 300,000 could be perfectly safe as long as the community is functional

Table 38.1 Number of languages by continent having fewer than 10,000 and 1000 speakers

Continent	Fewer than 10,0000	Fewer than 1000	A few elderly speakers
Africa	651	140	46
Americas	831	503	182
Asia	769	249	84
Europe	48	16	9
Pacific	1389	871	152
Total	3688	1779	473

Source: Based on data from Lewis (2009)

and the environment stable. Nevertheless, small languages can disappear much faster than large ones, and forces have now been unleashed in the world that small communities find very difficult to resist, while larger groups may have the resources to do so.

Linguistic Diversity in Biodiversity Hotspots

Although previous research has revealed that biological and linguistic diversity often occur in the same places, this work has been largely based on data sets with limited geographic precision, with researchers looking mainly at total numbers of languages and species per country or region (e.g., Harmon 1996; Nettle & Romaine 2000; Oviedo, Maffi, & Larsen 2000; Skutnabb-Kangas, Maffi, & Harmon 2003; Loh & Harmon 2005). However, languages, like species, do not always observe geopolitical boundaries. GIS (global information systems) mapping has become an increasingly important tool for understanding a range of social, economic, linguistic, and environmental problems. Gorenflo et al. (forthcoming) relied on greatly improved data showing the geographic extent of more than 6900 spoken languages, compiled by Global Mapping International (2006) in GIS format, to analyze linguistic diversity in 39 regions independently identified by Conservation International, one of the largest conservation organizations, as areas containing exceptionally high biodiversity (Myers et al. 2000; Mittermeier et al. 2004). Conservation International identified 34 hotspots characterized by exceptionally high occurrences of endemic species (i.e., those found nowhere else) defined according to the IUCN Red List and by loss of at least 70 percent of their natural habitat. These hotspots make up only about 2.3 percent of the earth's terrestrial surface, but contain more than 50 percent of the world's vascular plant species, and at least 42 percent of terrestrial vertebrate species as endemics. The five high-biodiversity wilderness areas, also rich in endemic species, are large regions (minimally 10,000 square kilometers) with relatively little human impact that have lost 30 percent or less of their natural habitat. Making up about 6.1 percent of the terrestrial area of the planet, the remaining habitat in these five high-biodiversity wilderness areas contains 17 percent of the world's vascular plants and 8 percent of terrestrial vertebrates as endemics.

A total of 3174 languages (nearly half of those on earth) are currently spoken in the 34 biodiversity hotspots. Hotspots with particularly high linguistic diversity include the East Melanesian Islands (some 1600 islands lying northeast and east of New Guinea, including the Bismarck and Admiralty Islands, the Solomon Islands, and the islands of Vanuatu), Guinean Forests of West Africa (comprising all the lowland forests of West Africa from Guinea and Sierra Leone eastward to the Sanaga River in Cameroon), Indo-Burma (beginning in eastern Bangladesh and extending across north-eastern India, south of the Bramaputra River, to encompass nearly all of Myanmar; part of southern and western Yunnan Province in China; all of the Lao People's Democratic Republic, Cambodia and Vietnam; the vast majority of Thailand; and a small part of Peninsular Malaysia), Mesoamerica (comprising Guatemala, Belize, El Salvador, Honduras, Nicaragua, and Costa Rica, as well as a third of Mexico and nearly two-thirds of Panama), and Wallacea (the central islands of Indonesia east of Java, Bali, and Borneo, and west of the province of New Guinea, and all of Timor Leste). Each of these hotspots contains more than 250 indigenous languages. Some 1616 different languages are spoken in the five high-biodiversity wilderness areas. The New Guinea Wilderness Area (comprising the island of New Guinea and outlying islands), with 958 languages, has the highest linguistic diversity. The next most diverse wilderness area linguistically is Amazonia (the world's largest intact tropical forest spanning nine South American countries), containing 281 languages.

A total of 2185 of the languages spoken in the 34 biodiversity hotspots are endemic to individual regions. Four hotspots—Indo-Burma, Wallacea, East Melanesian Islands, and Sundaland (covering the western half of the Indo-Malayan archipelago including Borneo and Sumatra)—have particularly high linguistic endemism, each with 240 or more languages unique to their respective regions. The New Guinea Wilderness Area again contains the greatest number of endemic languages, totaling 953, while Amazonia contains 213. These results are broadly in agreement with those of other studies relying on data sets organized by countries or other geographical areas. Regions of high biodiversity (variously defined), such as Meso-America, Western Africa, the Himalayas, South Asia, and the Pacific, tend to be areas of high cultural and linguistic diversity. Loh and Harmon (2005), for instance, identified three core areas of global biocultural diversity: Central Africa, Indo-Malaysia/Melanesia, and the Amazon Basin.

Gorenflo et al. (forthcoming) also considered two thresholds to identify potentially endangered languages co-occurring with the hotpots and high-biodiversity wilderness areas: those with 10,000 or fewer speakers (figure 38.3), and those with 1000 or fewer speakers (figure 38.4). Looking specifically at the speaker base of languages occurring in hotspots, 48 percent (N = 1524) of the 3174 languages are spoken by 10,000 or fewer people, and 18 percent (N = 57) are spoken by fewer than 1000. In the five high-biodiversity wilderness areas, 76 percent (N = 1235) of the 1616 languages are spoken by 10,000 or fewer speakers, while 42 percent (N = 683) are spoken by 1000 or fewer. These small language groups are potentially at great risk. Overall, the results of this analysis indicate that nearly 4800 of the more than 6900 languages currently spoken on earth are found in regions containing high biodiversity. This means that nearly 70 percent of the world's languages are spoken in roughly 24 percent of the earth's terrestrial surface (26 percent if we exclude Antarctica).

Sutherland's (2003) comparison of projected extinction rates for languages with those for various species, including fish (5 percent), plants (8 percent), birds (11 percent), and mammals (18 percent), indicate that even with his admittedly conservative estimate of 30 percent for languages, languages are overall at greater risk than species. Moreover, the high degree of endemism among languages with small numbers of speakers means that the risk to rare and unique

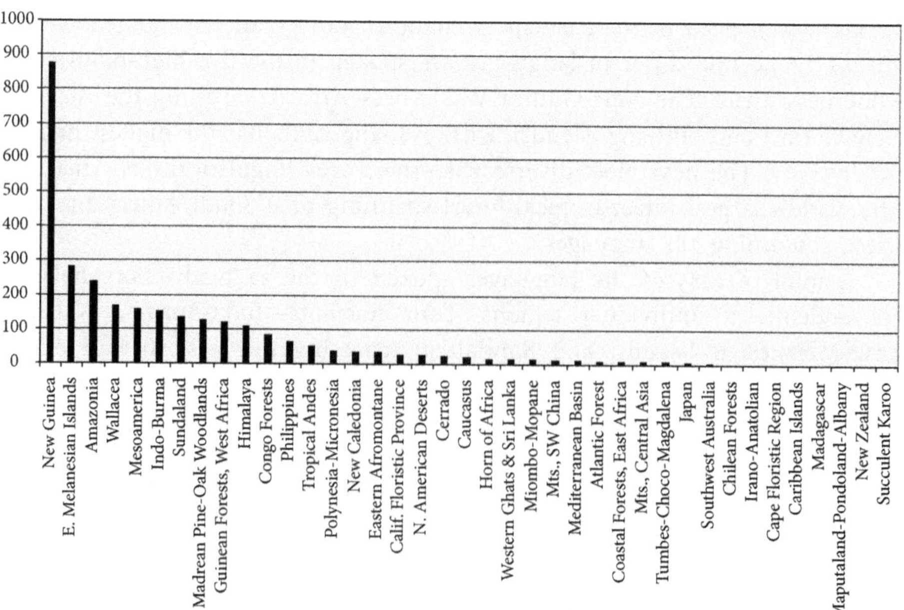

Figure 38.3 Number of languages spoken by fewer than 10,000 speakers in high biodiversity regions

Source: Data based on Gorenflo et al. (forthcoming)

languages is greater than the risk to more common ones. The African continent, for instance, contains 2110 languages (about one-third of the world's total), but relatively few (ca. 20) genetically distinct families. Most belong to the Bantu group and are structurally similar. If some horrific catastrophe were to eradicate all the languages of Europe tomorrow, we would actually lose relatively little of the world's linguistic diversity. Europe, with its 200 some languages belonging to only six families has only about 3 percent of the world's linguistic diversity. Most European languages are also widely spoken elsewhere; six of the nine languages in figure 38.2 with speaker numbers of 100 million or more belong to the Indo-European family (Spanish, English, Hindi, Portuguese, Bengali, and Russian) and are structurally similar because they are related historically. If we were to lose the same number of languages in New Guinea or the Americas, the loss would be far more significant due to the greater degree of phylogenetic diversity, especially in South America (Nettle & Romaine 2000: 35–38). In addition, many of these languages remain undocumented. The population expansion of speakers of Eurasian languages has seriously skewed the typological distribution of the world's languages and our expectations concerning the nature of human language. Object-initial languages, for example, the rarest word-order type, were discovered only relatively recently (Derbyshire 1977), and are found only among small groups. Such languages were once thought not to exist because it was believed they violated a linguistic universal requiring the subject or verb to go first.

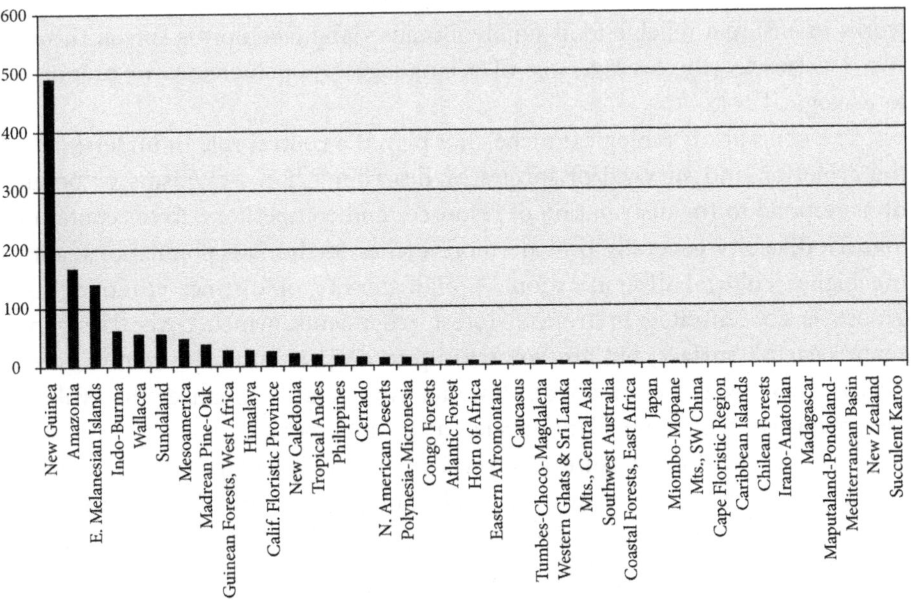

Figure 38.4 Number of languages spoken by fewer than 1000 speakers in high biodiversity regions

Source: Data based on Gorenflo et al. (forthcoming)

Explanations and Theories

Understanding of the ramifications of diversity in ecosystems, species, cultures and languages is in its infancy (Harmon 2002; Pretty et al. 2009). Recognizing a complex web of relationships and fundamental links between human languages and cultures, nonhuman species, and the earth's ecosystems, Nettle and Romaine (2000) argue that the explanation for the connections between biological and cultural-linguistic diversity will need to be sought in a sophisticated ecological theory that takes account of peoples' interactions with their environment. Ecological risk has a significant influence on the formation and persistence of linguistic groups. This factor refers to the amount of variation people face in their food supply over time, which in turn is related to other variables, such as climate, diversification of productive and income-generating activities, food storage, mobility, and patterns of social exchange. In areas where rainfall is continuous throughout the year and communities are able to produce their own food supply, they are not so dependent on their neighbors for subsistence. Nettle's (1999) study of the distribution of West African languages revealed a correlation between the length of the rainy season and the number of languages in a region. Only 20 languages are found in Niger, a vast, arid region, while farther south 430 languages are found in equally large but wetter Nigeria. These findings add weight to the conclusion that distinct languages may be more likely to evolve and be maintained in small, self-sufficient communities. The greater the ecological risk, the more people must develop larger social networks to ensure a reliable food supply. Because language norms spread through social networks, the average size of a language group increases in proportion to ecological risk.

The concept of "ecological niche" has played a central role in understanding the evolution and survival of species by describing how organisms or populations respond to the distribution of resources and competitors. Areas containing high biodiversity generally provide more niches for human populations, allowing higher cultural diversification. A high density of distinct ethnolinguistic groups is concentrated in tropical forest ecosystems, which cover just 7 percent of earth's surface, but are home to up to 90 percent of the world's species (Nettle 1999; Oviedo et al. 2000). A wetter climate also enhances the evolution and coexistence of more plant species of great important to humans. Barth's (1956) classic analysis of cultural groups in the river valleys and surrounding mountains in Swat in northwestern Pakistan showed how three distinct cultures developed and coexisted via niche partitioning and specialization. The Kohistanis, the oldest inhabitants, were herders and seasonal agriculturalists, the Pathans were sedentary agriculturalists who entered the region later, and the most recent inhabitants, the Gujars, were nomadic herders. Because these three lifestyles relied on different ways of utilizing resources, the groups were able to coexist by niche partitioning.

Ecological niche theory can be useful for understanding processes of diversification by providing a general framework for examining the interlocking matrix of political, geographical, and economic factors that support the maintenance of biological, linguistic, and cultural diversity. Such a theory can also help us to analyze some of the forces threatening to disrupt language ecologies (Romaine 2013). Nevertheless, the considerable variability in linguistic diversity with respect to biological diversity found across the hotspots examined by Gorenflo et al. (forthcoming) suggests that underlying reasons are very complex and may well differ in different areas. This would not be surprising, given the complexity of the natural environments and social-cultural settings in which different language groups exist. Hotspots are "hot" for different reasons, that is, they contain different kinds of biodiversity, not all of which provide equally useful resources favoring human niche diversification. Forest and woodland tend to support large numbers of species, particularly trees, while wetlands have lower levels of species and genetic diversity, but provide highly valuable water resources. The Caucasus biodiversity hotspot (spanning Georgia, Armenia, and Azerbaijan, the North Caucasian portion of the Russian Federation, the northeastern part of Turkey, and a part of northwestern Iran) with its 57 languages provides an example of an area whose linguistic diversity falls in the mid-range (Gorenflo et al. forthcoming). The distribution of small, highly localized languages such as Archi with fewer than 100 speakers correlates closely with locations close to the sources of streams (Comrie 2008). Mapping the utility value of various ecosystem types to humans as well as to the maintenance of global genetic diversity could further elucidate linkages between linguistic and biological diversity. Latin American ecoregions that make up tropical moist forest such as the Amazon Basin are not only the most rich in species and languages, but also rank highest in utility value, supporting the largest number of indigenous populations (334, or over two-thirds of the total diversity recorded for the whole of Latin America), while tropical dry forests supported 89 different indigenous groups (Wilcox & Duin 1995).

For various reasons, however, not all locales with high biodiversity display correspondingly high linguistic diversity. Linguistically speaking, Madagascar with its small number of languages contrasts sharply with the island of New Guinea, due to the vastly different time depth of human settlement. The island of Madagascar broke off from the African continent 160 to 180 million years ago, allowing highly distinctive flora and fauna to develop in relative isolation in a variety of major ecosystems including desert areas, rainforests, high mountains, and lowlands (Goodman & Benstead 2003), but human colonization occurred roughly only 2000 years ago, thus providing no such opportunity for linguistic evolution. Amid this rich biodiversity with high levels of genus- and family-level endemism all the languages spoken on Madagascar today are varieties of Malagasy (spoken by about 15 million people), with the exception of an enclave of Swahili speakers in the northwest (Blench 2006).

Meanwhile, Eurasia has a history of human settlement at least as ancient as New Guinea, going back 50,000 some years, yet has far fewer languages, due to the spread of agriculture and the rise of empires. Conventional explanations for the linguistic diversity of New Guinea as well as other areas like the Caucasus have typically invoked the rugged mountainous terrain as a significant factor impeding communication between groups. However, geographic barriers to the dispersion of groups and languages cannot on their own satisfactorily explain high levels of linguistic diversity. The areas of greatest linguistic diversity in New Guinea are concentrated in coastal regions such as the northeast facing coast and the islands to the east in the Bismarck Archipelago, while the highlands, by contrast, with some of the most isolated and rugged areas, are more uniform linguistically. The absence of state formation in New Guinea has generally inhibited the sustained spread of any one language group, while in the Highlands specifically, lower incidence of malaria has allowed a few large language groups like Enga and Huli with over 100,000 speakers to spread (see Fincher & Thornhill 2008 for discussion of variation in parasite intensity and species dispersion). Despite functioning as potential barriers, mountains also host high plant diversity. There is a significant linkage between high linguistic diversity and high numbers of vascular plant species, especially in montane regions. Indeed, from a global perspective the greatest number of languages is found in mountains (Stepp et al. 2004; Stepp, Castaneda, & Cervone 2005). Stepp, Castaneda, and Cervone (2005) identified a high clustering of languages in the highest zones of plant diversity on the island of New Guinea, with 70 percent of languages originating in mountain regions. In addition, the presence of pidgins/creoles as lingua francas, such as Tok Pisin in Papua New Guinea, has helped, at least until recently, to maintain linguistic diversity by facilitating intergroup communication.

The contrast between the linguistic situation in the Caucasus and New Guinea makes it necessary to consider a variety of factors affecting the nature and types of contact between groups. Speakers of a language are embedded in not just a natural but also a social environment, which means that we need to take into account the way in which differing social structures and communicative practices may lead to language convergence or divergence. Social factors have probably played at least as important a role as geography in the development of linguistic diversity in the Caucasus. Comrie (2008: 140–141), for example, points to endogamous marriage patterns preventing outsiders from gaining access to land in an area short of arable ground. This custom constrains membership of local speech communities and minimizes outside influence. A move away from endogamy would endanger small languages, as in the case of Hinukh, where increasing intermarriage with speakers of Bezhta and Tsez is leading to increased use of these languages. In quite a different context, among the Doga people of Milne Bay Province in Papua New Guinea, Landweer (2010) postulates a link between language choice and security of land tenure. The settlement patterns of formerly sea-faring nomadic

Doga have been dictated by the availability of land for subsistence and the necessity of accommodation to their land-based neighbors. As recent immigrants, they have married into the host society. The children of exogamous marriages gain access to land through their non-Doga parent and typically grow up speaking that parent's language rather than Doga. In this setting too, endogamy is strongly linked to language maintenance, and exogamy to language shift.

These examples show that understanding not only the correlation between biological and linguistic diversity but also possible mechanisms of causality will require research more geographically focused on the biodiversity and cultures occurring in particular localities.

Nevertheless, even if different processes gave rise to the diversification of languages, cultures, and species in different areas, similar practical forces are now driving biological extinctions and cultural/linguistic homogenization. Broad changes in the form of habitat loss due to large-scale human impact also represent potential risks to languages and their associated cultures. For many conservation priorities and languages, efforts to maintain particular biodiversity targets could affect one or more languages in the same geographic area, and vice versa. Looking at the larger picture of overlap between languages and species may help to identify instances where maintaining habitat and land use practices of people speaking a particular language might mutually benefit linguistic and biological diversity.

Regardless of the precise functional connections between linguistic and biological diversity, the tendency for both to be high in particular regions suggests that certain cultural systems and practices, represented by speakers of particular languages, tend to be compatible with high biodiversity. Independent evidence supports this contention. For example, analysis of satellite data shows that indigenous lands occupying one-fifth of the Brazilian Amazon (five times the area under protection in parks) currently are the most important barrier to Amazon deforestation, a major cause of biodiversity loss in the area. The inhibitory effect of indigenous lands on deforestation was not correlated with indigenous population density. Moreover, biodiversity is equal if not higher in anthropogenic than in non-anthropogenic areas (Nepstad et al. 2005). Given the capacity of humans to dominate, and in many cases eradicate, other species on our planet, the importance of the relationship between such groups and the natural environments they inhabit cannot be overstated for biodiversity conservation. Unfortunately, the opportunity to engage speakers of particular languages in biodiversity conservation is rapidly disappearing as languages are lost at an alarming rate.

The developed nations of the world are now rapidly destroying the habitats sustaining much of the world's biological and linguistic diversity. Resource extraction, the spread of mechanized agriculture, and development projects damage the environment at the same time as they displace and marginalize people from places they traditionally relied on for their food, shelter, cultural practices, and spiritual well-being. Since 1900, 90 of Brazil's 270 Indian tribes have completely disappeared. More than two-thirds of the remaining ones have fewer than 1000 members (Hemming 1978). Warfare also takes a huge toll on people and biodiversity. Over 90 percent of the major armed conflicts between 1950 and 2000 occurred within countries containing biodiversity hotspots, and more than 80 percent took place directly within Conservation International's hotspot areas, which are home to about one-third of the world's total population, among them many of the poorest and most marginalized people, who rely on natural resources for their daily survival (Hanson et al. 2009).

What Can Be Done to Preserve Linguistic and Biological Diversity?

Despite these challenges, and the lack of sufficient data, especially in the linguistic domain, a more precise mapping and assessment of language overlap with hotspots and conservation priorities defined at several geographic scales provides an important foundation for further work that may help to tease out the relationship between these linguistic and other kinds of diversity and sharpen our understanding of the evolutionary, ecological, and anthropogenic mechanisms underlying the origin and maintenance of diversity. Due to the fact that regions containing high biological diversity also represent areas of vital importance to maintaining linguistic and cultural diversity, conservation strategies that promote the persistence of economic and cultural systems likely will help sustain biological diversity in many settings as well. Setting realistic priorities is paramount because much typically needs to be done quickly with too few resources. The fact that there are significant differences from region to region calls for smaller scale field studies and the need for multiple indices of diversity to identify high priority areas for conservation. Even in the absence of satisfactory explanatory theories, the strong geographic intersection between biodiversity and languages in certain areas and the magnitude of the threat demands an integrated approach to the conservation of linguistic diversity and biodiversity. This requires collaboration between researchers focusing on biodiversity conservation and those concerned with linguistic and cultural conservation in particular regions. More practically speaking, a strategic alliance of professional expertise from diverse disciplines with common interests in conserving diversity (e.g., anthropologists, linguists, ecologists, human rights professionals, and indigenous peoples) is more likely to command attention from governments, NGOs, donors as well as the general public.

Extinctions in general, whether of languages or species, are part of a pattern of human activities contributing to radical alterations in our global ecosystem. If there is any "good" news here, then, it is that we are dealing with one large interconnected problem rather than several independent extinction crises. Because the historical causes of the threats facing the earth's languages, cultures, and biodiversity are the same, the solutions are also likely to come from the same place: empowering local people and communities. The maintenance of the world's many languages has a vital role to play in preserving biodiversity because the measures most likely to preserve small languages are the very ones that will help increase their speakers' standard of living in a long-term, sustainable way.

References

Barth, F. 1956. Ecologic relationships of ethnic groups in Swat, North Pakistan. *American Anthropologist* 58: 1079–089.

Blench, R. 2006. The Austronesians in Madagascar and on the east African coast: Surveying the linguistic evidence for domestic and translocated animals. Paper given at the International Conference on Austronesian Languages X, Puerto Princesa, Palawan.

Comrie, B.L. 2008. Linguistic diversity in the Caucasus. *Annual Review of Anthropology* 37: 131–43.

Crosby, A. 1994. *Ecological imperialism: The biological expansion of Europe, 900–1900.* Cambridge: Cambridge University Press.

Crystal, D. 2000. *Language death.* Cambridge: Cambridge University Press.

Crystal, D. 2003. *English as a global language*, 2nd ed. Cambridge: Cambridge University Press.

Davis, W. 2001. *Light at the edge of the world: A journey through the realm of vanishing languages.* London: Bloomsbury.

Derbyshire, D.C. 1977. Word order universals and the existence of OVS languages. *Linguistic Inquiry* 8: 590–99.

Fincher, C. L., & Thornhill, R. 2008. A parasite-driven wedge: Infectious disease may explain language and other biodiversity. *Oikos* 17: 1289–297.

Global Mapping International 2006. *World Mapping Language System.* Colorado Springs, CO.

Goodman, S. M., & Benstead J. P. (eds.) 2003. *The natural history of Madagascar.* Chicago: University of Chicago Press.

Gorenflo, L. J., Romaine, S., Mittermeier, R. A., & Painemiller, K. W. Forthcomng. *Linguistic diversity in high biodiversity hotspots and wilderness areas.* Washington, DC: Conservation International.

Hanson, T., Brooks, T. M., de Fonseca, G. A. B., Hoffman, M., Lamoreux, J., Machlis, G., Mittermeier, C. G., Mittermeier, R. A., & Pilgrim, J. D. 2009. Warfare in biodiversity hotspots. *Conservation Biology* 23(3): 578–87.

Harmon, D. 1996. Losing species, losing languages: Connections between biological and linguistic diversity. *Southwest Journal of Linguistics* 15(1/2): 89–108.

Harmon, D. 2002. *In light of our differences: How diversity in nature and culture makes us human.* Washington, DC: Smithsonian Institution Press.

Harrison, K. D. 2007. *When languages die: The extinction of the world's languages and the erosion of human knowledge.* New York: Oxford University Press.

Hemming, J. 1978. *Red gold: The conquest of the Brazilian Indians.* London: Macmillan.

Hviding, E. 2006. Knowing and managing biodiversity in the Pacific Islands: Challenges of environmentalism in Marovo Lagoon. *International Social Science Journal* 187: 69–85.

Krauss, M. E. 1992. The world's languages in crisis. *Language* 68: 4–10.

Krauss, M. E. 2007a. Keynote—Mass language extinction and documentation: The race against time. In O. Miyaoka, O. Sakiyama, & M. E. Krauss (eds), *The vanishing languages of the Pacific Rim*, 3–22. Oxford: Oxford University Press.

Krauss, M. E. 2007b. Classification and terminology for degrees of language endangerment. In M. Brenzinger (ed.), *Language diversity endangered*, 1–8. Berlin: Mouton de Gruyter.

Landweer, M. L. 2000. Indicators of ethnolinguistic vitality. Notes on Sociolinguistics 5(1): 5–22.

Landweer, M. L. 2010. Land-language link. In K.A. McElhanon & G. Reesink (eds.), *A mosaic of languages and cultures: Studies celebrating the career of Karl J. Franklin*, 351–80. Dallas, TX: SIL International.

Lewis, M. P. 2009. *Ethnologue: Languages of the world*. 16th ed. Dallas, TX: SIL International. Online version: http://www.ethnologue.com/.

Loh, J., & Harmon, D. 2005. A global index of biocultural diversity. *Ecological Indicators* 5: 231–41.

Maffi, L. ed. 2001. *On biocultural diversity: Linking language, knowledge, and the environment.* Washington, DC: Smithsonian Institution Press.

Maffi, L. 2005. Linguistic, cultural and biological diversity. *Annual Review of Anthropology* 29: 599–617.

Martí, F., Ortega, P., Idiazabal, I., Barrena, A., Juaristi, P., Junyent, C., Uranga, B., & Amorrortu, E. 2005. *Words and worlds: World languages review.* Clevedon: Multilingual Matters.

McConvell, P., & Thieberger, N. 2001. State of Indigenous languages in Australia—2001, Australia State of the Environment Second Technical Paper Series (Natural and Cultural Heritage), Department of the Environment and Heritage, Canberra.

McConvell, P., & Thieberger, N. 2006. Keeping track of indigenous language endangerment in Australia. In D. Cunningham, D. E. Ingram, & K. Sumbuk (eds.), *Language diversity in the Pacific: Endangerment and survival*, 54–84. Clevedon: Multilingual Matters.

Millennium Ecosystem Assessment 2005. *Ecosystems and human well-being.* Washington, DC: Island Press.

Mittermeier, R. A., Gil, P. R., Hoffmann, M., Pilgrim, J., Brooks, T., Mittermeier, C. G., Lamoreux, J., & de Fonseca, G. A. B. 2004. *Hotspots revisited: Earth's biologically richest and most threatened terrestrial ecoregions.* Monterrey, Mexico: CEMEX.

Myers, N., Mittermeier, R. A., Mittermeier, C. G., de Fonseca, G. A. B., & Kent, J. 2000. Biodiversity hotspots for conservation priorities. *Nature* 403: 853–58.

Nepstad, D., Schwartzman, S., Bamberger, B., Santilli, M., Ray, D., Schlesinger, P., Lefebvre, P., Alencar, A., Prinz, E., Fiske, G., & Rolla, A. 2005. Inhibition of Amazon deforestation and fire by parks and indigenous lands. *Conservation Biology* 20(1): 65–73.

Nettle, D. 1999. *Linguistic diversity.* Oxford: Oxford University Press.

Nettle, D., & Romaine, S. 2000. *Vanishing voices: The extinction of the world's languages.* New York: Oxford University Press.

Norris, M. J., & Jantzen, L. 2002. *From generation to generation: Survival and maintenance of Canada's aboriginal languages within families, communities and cities*. Ottowa: Indian and Northern Affairs. Canadian Heritage. Government of Canada.

Oviedo, G., Maffi, L., & Larsen, P.B. 2000. Indigenous and traditional peoples of the world and ecoregion conservation: An integrated approach to conserving the world's biological and cultural diversity. Gland, Switzerland: World Wildlife Foundation International & Terralingua.

Pretty, J., Adams, B., Berkes, F., de Athayde, S. F., Dudley, N., Hunn, E., Maffi, L., Milton, K., Rapport, D., Robbins, P., Sterling, E., Stolton, S., Tsing, A., Vintinner, E., & Pilgrim, S. 2009. The intersections of biological diversity and cultural diversity: Towards integration. *Conservation and Society* 7(2): 100–12.

Price, D. H. 1990. *Atlas of world cultures: A geographical guide to ethnographic literature*. London: Sage.

Romaine, S. 2007. The impact of language policy on endangered languages. In M. Koenig & P. De Guchteneire (eds.), *Democracy and human rights in multicultural societies*, 217–236. Aldershot: Ashgate/UNESCO.

Romaine, S. 2013. Language and ecology. In P. Binder & K. Smith (eds.), *The language phenomenon*. New York: Springer Verlag.

Skutnabb-Kangas, T., Maffi, L., & Harmon, D. 2003. *Sharing a world of difference. The earth's linguistic, cultural and biological diversity*. Paris: UNESCO, Terralingua, World Wide Fund for Nature.

Sponsel, L. E. ed. 2000. *Endangered peoples of Southeast and East Asia: Struggles to survive and thrive*. Westport, CT: Greenwood Press.

Stepp, J. R., Castaneda, H., & Cervone, S. 2005. Mountains and biocultural diversity. *Mountain Research and Development* 25(3): 223–27.

Stepp, J. R., Cervone, S., Castaneda, H., Lasseter, A., Stocks, G., & Gichon, Y. 2004. Development of a GIS for global biocultural diversity. *Policy Matters* 13: 267–70.

Sutherland, W. 2003. Parallel extinction risk and global distribution of languages and species. *Nature* 423: 276–77.

Task Force on Aboriginal Languages and Cultures 2005. *Towards a new beginning: A foundational report for a strategy to revitalize First Nation, Inuit and Métis languages and cultures*. Report to the Minister for Canadian Heritage. Ottawa: Aboriginal Languages Directorate. Canadian Heritage. Government of Canada.

UNEP [United Nations Environment Program] 2007. *Global environment outlook: Environment for development (GEO-4)*. Nairobi: UNEP.

UNESCO 2001. *World atlas of the world's languages in danger of disappearing*. Paris: UNESCO.

UNESCO Ad Hoc Expert Group on Endangered Languages 2003. Language vitality and endangerment. Paris: UNESCO.

Wilcox, B. A., & Duin, K. N. 1995. Indigenous cultural and biological diversity: Overlapping values of Latin American ecosystems. *Cultural Survival Quarterly* 18(4): 49–53.

Wilson, E.O. 1998. *Consilience: The unity of knowledge*. London: Abacus.

Wolfram, W., & Schilling-Estes, N. 1998. Endangered dialects: A neglected situation in the endangerment canon. *Southwest Journal of Linguistics* 14: 117–31.

CHAPTER 39

LANGUAGE REVITALIZATION

LENORE A. GRENOBLE

Revitalization as Response to Language Endangerment

The ongoing issues of language shift and attrition have evoked different responses from different groups. Linguists have become increasingly engaged in language documentation, working to record languages while they are still spoken. Speaker communities often turn to revitalization programs, attempting to strengthen the speaker base of their ancestral languages and make them vital again. The exact nature of such programs varies greatly, depending on the dynamics of the individual communities involved and on the specific sociolinguistic situations in which they find themselves. This chapter addresses the factors that enter into the decision of what kind of revitalization to pursue and then discusses different kinds of models for language revitalization.

Language revitalization, by definition, takes place in communities that are undergoing language shift. Thus, revitalization is necessarily situated within a complex context and, in order for revitalization efforts to have any hope of success, that context needs to be understood, and certain elements within it need to be addressed. Teaching the language is generally not enough to revitalize it; in general, programs need to address the underlying causes of language shift. Some of the factors in shift are generally beyond the control or influence of the speech community, such as the dominance of a language of wider communication in the government or in education. Yet an awareness of these factors and some adjustment of how community members react to them may be key to successful revitalization. Finally, it is important to recognize the differences between revitalization and maintenance. Although in practice it may be difficult to sharply differentiate between the two, revitalization programs are needed when the language is undergoing shift, with the single biggest indicator of attrition being that children—most or many—are no longer learning the language. In contrast, maintenance programs are intended to foster language use when there is already a speaker community in place but that community feels pressure from other languages.

One of the most influential theoretical frameworks for language revitalization is Joshua Fishman's (1991) work on Reversing Language Shift (RLS). The very first step, before beginning a revitalization program, is what Fishman calls *prior ideological clarification*, an important part of what I call *assessment* here (Grenoble & Whaley 2006). Dauenhauer and Dauenhauer (1998: 63) argue that one of the key obstacles to successful revitalization may be attitudes and beliefs held by community members about their language; failure to achieve prior ideological clarification—"an open, honest assessment of the state of the language and how people really feel about using and preserving it"—can be detrimental, even fatal, for revitalization. Dauenhauer and Dauenhauer point to a disparity between a community's expressed desire to revitalize their language and deep-rooted, or even unconscious, fears and biases about the language, often stemming from colonial attitudes, all of which can be serious impediments to revitalization. In addition, it is not uncommon to find a general sense that revitalization would be a good idea, without a full understanding of or commitment to the sustained level of effort required to actually achieve it. The Dauenhauers write about their firsthand experience in Alaska, but their observations apply to many communities elsewhere, and their work has been significant for reshaping how people confront such ideological issues.

Fishman's stages of reversing language shift are divided into two phases: the first to attain diglossia, the second to transcend diglossia (1991: 395). Fishman's definition of diglossia places genetically unrelated languages on a continuum of usage; he argues that bilingualism, and not diglossia, must be achieved in order to achieve RLS. These stages in RLS should be read from the bottom up; thus the first stage is to reconstruct the language, with Xish here used to represent the language being revitalized, and Yish the language that is encroaching upon it. This framework is intended as a general blueprint for RLS, not a rigid formula.

1 Education, work sphere, mass media, and governmental operations at higher and nationwide levels.
2 Local/regional mass media and governmental services.
3 The local/regional (i.e., non-neighborhood) work sphere, both among Xmen and Ymen.

4b Public schools for Xish children, offering some instruction via Xish, but substantially under Yish curricular and staffing control.
4a Schools in lieu of compulsory education and substantially under Xish curricular and staffing control.

II. RLS to transcend diglossia, subsequent to its attainment
5 Schools for literacy acquisition, for the old and for the young, and not in lieu of compulsory education.
6 The intergenerational and demographically concentrated home-family-neighborhood: the basis of mother tongue transmission.
7 Cultural interaction in Xish primarily involving the community-based older generation.
8 Reconstructing Xish and adult acquisition of XSL.

I. RLS to attain diglossia (*assuming prior ideological clarification)*

The role of linguists in reversing language shift can be complicated: linguists can make important contributions to reconstructing a language but are not well equipped to motivate communities to revitalize their language. One major change in the last 20 years or so since the publication of RLS has been the increasing awareness on the part of linguists of the need to partner with community members, applied linguists, and language pedagogues in order to accomplish this work.

Fishman's conceptualization of RLS has had a major impact for different communities working to revitalize their languages and has provided a framework for them to work with. The educational system is an integral part of his approach to RLS; the role of the schools begins at stage 4 and increases in the move to transcend diglossia. One of the important parts of his theory is that it explicitly lays out a series of stages to reverse shift, rather than suggesting that it can be an instantaneous kind of achievement. This means that communities can and should recognize achievements along the path to full revitalization. In fact, attaining Fishman's Level 1 is unrealistic for the overwhelming majority of endangered language communities, who cannot reasonably hope to get their language used in national governments or in national media, for example.

Just what kind of revitalization program is realistic depends on an interplay of available resources, commitment from community members who will be involved in revitalization, and their overall goals. All of these can and often do change over the course of time. Moreover, there is a great range of potential resources and obstacles. Resources here are understood broadly but include, first and foremost, speakers who can teach the language; finances for creating and publishing pedagogical and reference materials; funds for teacher training programs for hiring teachers; and dedicated community members to organize and harness these resources. On one end of the spectrum are communities where language shift is in its early stages, with relatively large numbers of fluent speakers across generations. If speakers in these communities are enthusiastic about language usage, have financial resources, and sufficient administrative and/or political influence to assure the creation and implementation of language policies that will address the causes of shift, it may be possible to institute larger, more ambitious revitalization programs. These aim more at arresting language shift before it has progressed further and (re)creating a situation where the language is fluently spoken across all generations and in all domains. From a global perspective, such circumstances are more the exception than the rule. In many more cases, however, communities are at the other end of the spectrum and lack at least some of these basic resources. Moreover, it is often the case that communities do not recognize the need for revitalization until attrition has advanced so that there are considerably fewer speakers for building a language program. Where basic resources—be they financial or human—are lacking, and/or there are serious impediments to language revitalization (such as hostile language laws or education policies), communities are often required to address these issues before beginning a revitalization program, and their initial goals are more modest than those of communities that are better positioned in terms of resources.

This points to a need to assess resources, attitudes, and obstacles at the very onset of language revitalization. A frank evaluation is invaluable to setting realistic language goals and building a successful program. The next section presents an overview of relevant factors and variables in moving from language shift to a vital language community.

From Shift to Revitalization

Many communities embarking on revitalization programs face similar issues from the outset, although the particulars of these issues, as well as the possible resolutions, can differ radically. One of the key challenges for language revitalization programs is changing, or at least offsetting, the factors that led to language shift in the first place. This is not always possible, as some of these factors may be the result of national or even international circumstances and are beyond the community's control. Much depends on how vital a language is when a community decides to start revitalization. If attrition is caught early and there are still many speakers across generations, the situation is quite different than when the language is spoken only by the oldest generation.

This section outlines some of the most common factors in language shift that need to be considered for revitalization efforts to move forward. They operate at different levels: global, extra-national, national, regional, and local (Grenoble & Whaley 1998, 2006). The strategies for working with or against them vary in accordance with these different levels. For example, the use of English as a global language puts pressure on many local languages; not much can be done by local communities to change this. This is an extreme example of the impact of a widespread, international lingua franca. Other examples at the extra-national (but not global) level include languages like Swahili in Africa, which has an estimated first-speaker population of just under 800,000, but some 30,000,000 people are cited as second language users (Lewis 2009). At a national level, language policies and laws and education laws can be favorable to local languages, hostile, or indifferent. Education policies of some countries, such as the No Child Left Behind Act of 2001 in the United States and the Unified State Exam (*edinyj gosudarstvennyj èkzamen*) in the Russian Federation, which require nationwide testing in English or Russian, respectively, are examples of legislation that is a serious impediment to the development of local languages. Such factors can also play out at a regional level, depending on how such policies are instated and implemented within an individual country.

Changing aspects of the context that have led to attrition may be beyond what an individual community can accomplish. Many groups have found that partnering with other indigenous groups has given them a more powerful voice, nationally and internationally, which can leverage more influence over governments. A number of international organizations have been working to promote better language attitudes and policies. One such set of actions promotes the use of indigenous languages as a basic human right; this is the position of the United Nations and is clearly articulated in its Declaration on the Rights of Indigenous Peoples, ratified September 2007 (United Nations 2007). UNESCO places safeguarding the use and documentation of endangered languages as part of its efforts to support Intangible Cultural Heritage.[1] In addition to such global organizations are more regional, but still transnational, groups. For example, the African Academy of Languages (or, Académie Africaine des Langues) has as one of its goals the promotion of the use of African languages. To that end, it fostered the International Year of African Languages (2006) and implemented a pan-African plan to strengthen the use of the native languages throughout the continent. Similarly, pan-Arctic organizations, such as the Inuit Circumpolar Council, which represents people living in Russia (Chukotka), the United States (Alaska), Canada, and Greenland, and the Nordic Council, promote the right to use Arctic indigenous languages.

These are just a sample of the kinds of organizations that encourage language use in regions cutting across national borders. We can now turn to the different factors that revitalization supporters must address to reverse language shift.

Language Attitudes

More often than not, language attitudes are a factor leading to language shift; they can be an issue at both the local level and the national level. Low prestige is common. Clearly, more positive attitudes toward the language tend to strengthen its usage; and more negative attitudes, to weaken it. But communities are often not homogenous in this regard (or many others), and there may be language activists and supporters, as well as those favoring exclusive use of the language of wider communication at the expense of the local language. Revitalization programs often need to confront these attitudes and the concomitant false beliefs that are often found with them, such as the belief that the endangered language is not a language, does not have a grammar, or is simply not as good as the language of the national government. This is an important part of ideological clarification.

Language Vitality

The overall vitality of the language, with specific attention to the numbers of speakers, the generational and geographic distribution of the speakers, and the domains where the language is used, is essential to understanding how to proceed with revitalization. Speakers are the single biggest resource a language has; an honest assessment of speakers is key to language revitalization. Historically, many communities have tended to overestimate the numbers of speakers, or rather, to underestimate the process of shift, and thus not recognize the need for revitalization programs until attrition has progressed beyond a point where it can be easily stopped.

Beyond the actual number of speakers across generations, language use across domains is important. In order for a language to be vital, it needs to be used by a community of speakers in a large number of domains. One of the key signs of language shift is the use of the language in dwindling domains; in order to revitalize it, the domains need to be increased. This is very challenging, as shift tends to occur when the local language has been replaced by the language of wider communication. The language of wider communication tends to be found in public domains such as government, education, and media. Where the community is embedded in a multilingual context, it is often the speakers of the local language who shift to the language of wider communication to accommodate the majority speakers. Such accommodation may be legislated or it may be voluntary; in either case, reversing it is very challenging. Revitalization programs need to carve out domains for language use and foster them intensely.

Financial Resources

Financial resources include the kinds of funding available both within and outside the community to support revitalization. In most places, funding is needed for creating pedagogical materials, paying teachers, training teachers, and so on. In some regions, money may be needed to build schools, equip classrooms, set up digital resources, and the like. If there is no funding available, that will fundamentally limit the kinds of revitalization programs that can be implemented. This does not mean that revitalization is impossible, but rather that the program needs to be developed with the financial constraints in mind. Models like the Master-Apprentice program (discussed later) have proven to be an accessible means for many communities with limited resources (financial or human) to start revitalization.

Codification

Language codification is one of the thorniest issues communities face if there is significant variation. Codification is often seen as privileging one variety over another (or all others) and thus can be perceived as a threat to dialect diversity. It almost always means some sort of compromise and, if not carefully implemented, can be divisive and undermine revitalization efforts.

A key issue in codification, and in other issues of so-called language development, is determining who has the authority to make decisions regarding the language. Some communities are administratively organized in ways that make this clear; a tribal council or some other governing body either has the authority to make decisions or the power to appoint a body that does. In many cases this is less clear, and in some cultures the notion of a language committee may go against accepted cultural norms.

Literacy

Literacy is an important component of many revitalization programs, and it is often mistakenly assumed to be a necessary part of them. This is not true for all programs: the Master-Apprentice program, for example, is built on the assumption that literacy is not only unnecessary, but is also an impediment to learning the language in a communicative setting, and uses an oral-only methodology for teaching and learning. But literacy can help raise the prestige of a language; in fact, speakers of many different languages have been reported to claim that what they speak is not a language since it has no written form, or that it has no grammar, for the same reason. Changing such attitudes is important for a successful revitalization program. In addition, school-based revitalization programs typically need to use a written form of the language in their curriculum; integral parts of building school curricula for many revitalization programs have included the development of textbooks and reference materials in the target language. Literacy is also important because it increases the domains in which a language can be used; for example, communities with computers and Internet access find the Internet a cheap, convenient way to create cyber communities of language users. Texting is another way of increasing language use, in particular among younger speakers, and requires some written form.

At the same time, the introduction of literacy can be problematic. It has been argued, most notably by Peter Mühlhäusler (1990), that literacy facilitates acquisition of the majority language, and the majority language will already be better established in all domains, including the Internet, so the local language will be competing with it there as elsewhere. But that said, it is difficult to imagine that literacy in the majority language is something for a minority population to avoid. This would favor absolute isolation; that is not necessarily sustainable, nor is it something that all communities want. Many groups have found themselves disadvantaged if they cannot communicate fluently with the majority population, with the people they come in contact with, and with political officials and leaders. So it is probably more constructive to think in terms of bilingualism and active literacy in more than one language.

Yet there are other issues with literacy that need to be taken into consideration. Moving from an oral culture to a literate culture involves major cultural change, and the potential repercussions should be carefully considered. The teaching of literacy presupposes a literate group who can serve as teachers, as the creators of written materials, and furthermore, literacy itself presupposes domains where it will be used; the failure to create and sustain domains of usage has resulted in the failure of written languages. Such is the case with many of the Siberian indigenous languages, for example. Linguists created orthographies and standard forms at the beginning of the Soviet period, in the 1920s and 1930s, as part of a larger Bolshevik literacy campaign. But because Russian was already so firmly entrenched as the language of written communication, these nascent written forms failed to catch on and have persisted only as artificial, textbook varieties. The norms that were created then continue in many cases to create barriers to actively learning and promoting the language, as they are seen as representing a "correct" form of the language that, in fact, no speaker actually uses. But this raises the larger issue of standardization that accompanies the creation of a written language. Decisions need to be made about what variety will become the standard, and such questions can be very divisive if one form is seen as being promoted over another. (Some communities address these concerns by incorporating different features from different dialects into the standard, but the extent to which this is feasible can only be locally determined, in large part depending on how similar the different varieties are to one another.)

Orthographic Systems

Orthography is an important part of the decision to develop literacy. Some endangered languages have orthographic systems that, for whatever reasons, are not used (but may be seen as part of the cultural wealth of the language). Some may be written in the same orthographic system as the national language or the language of wider communication; others may have a different writing system. Still many others—in fact more than half of all known languages—do not have any written form at all. For languages with an existing writing system, some communities prefer to use the orthographic system of the language of wider communication to facilitate its acquisition in revitalization; others prefer to use a different system to distinguish the two quite clearly. These are very important decisions and can be very political, even for majority languages—such as Croatian (written in the Roman alphabet) and Serbian (written in Cyrillic), or Hindi (written in Devanagari) and Urdu (written in Arabic script).

Many issues enter into orthography design. Linguists tend to prefer a one sound–one symbol system, where there is one and only one symbol for each phoneme of the language. But this may not be the system that speakers prefer, and their attitudes are often influenced by the writing system of the majority language. Most frequently the phonemic inventories of the local language and the majority language do not match up perfectly, but the strong writing tradition of the majority language can influence choices about writing in the other. For example, speakers of indigenous languages in contact with Spanish sometimes opt to distinguish only five vowels in writing, under the influence of Spanish orthography. Others, such as the Quechua, deliberately distinguish only three (see Grenoble & Whaley 2006, chapter 6, for discussion). Even communities whose languages have long-standing written traditions grapple with these issues. For example, the Nunavut Language Commission is currently struggling with variation among the Inuit varieties spoken in Canada and how they are to be written. Are these dialects of one language or separate languages? Should there be a unified, codified variety or multiple varieties? Should they (or it) be written in the syllabary, as is accepted practice for Inuktitut, or in the Roman alphabet, as is common for other Inuit varieties, as well as for the majority languages of the country, English and French?

Creating an orthographic system that is acceptable to all community members can bring revitalization programs to a halt if there is significant controversy among different constituents. Orthography is linked to spelling, and both are part of the larger issue of standardization. These issues often require prolonged discussion to be resolved. For these many reasons, some communities opt not to pursue literacy as part of the initial steps in revitalization.

Building the Lexicon

For some groups embarking on revitalization, there is no need to create new terminology as the language is still spoken by many speakers. But this is probably the exception rather than the rule. Often terminology is lacking for those domains where it is not used (e.g., government, technology, and education) and needs to be developed. The need for lexical development is even greater if the language has been dormant or has been used in only very limited domains (such as religious or ceremonial uses) for an extended period of time.

New vocabulary can be coined from language-internal sources, such as building new words from existing lexemes and morphemes. This is particularly well suited to languages with rich derivational morphology and a well-known strategy for polysynthetic languages, for example. Alternatively, new words can be borrowed from other languages. Generally, there is resistance to borrowing from the dominant language because revitalization is attempting to combat the influx of words from it into the endangered language, but it is sometimes possible to borrow words (or roots) from related languages. This is a common practice in Inuit languages, even in West Greenlandic (Kalaallisut), which is not endangered but has experienced loss of certain names due to Danish influence. Names are often borrowed from closely related Inuktitut (spoken in Canada) where necessary.

Models for Language Revitalization

Different approaches to language revitalization are being used throughout the world. Which is best suited to an individual community depends on a combination of factors, including the number of speakers, available resources and the goals of the community, but most revitalization programs face similar challenges. This section provides an overview of some of the models currently found in language revitalization programs, such as the Master-Apprentice Program, Language Nests, immersion programs, bilingual programs, and nomadic schools. Some of these models are in widespread use throughout the world; others are associated with specific regions, languages, or ways of life. There are a number of handbooks of language revitalization (e.g. Grenoble & Whaley 2006; Hinton & Hale 2001; Tsunoda 2005) that provide more information about these different models and general guidelines to establishing language revitalization programs.

Te Kōhanga Reo, the Language Nest

The language nest model is a particular kind of immersion program associated with the original language nest, *Te Kōhanga Reo*, Māori revitalization in New Zealand, established in the early 1980s. The language nest model emerged under recognition of ongoing shift away from Māori to English. It is founded on a principle of total immersion. The program was created in a stepwise fashion, beginning in the preschool by bringing fluent elders into the preschools to work with the young children in a total immersion environment, and creating the curriculum as the first class of children progressed through the school system. This plan was conceived based on the recognition of two facts: (1) at the time, the fluent speakers were primarily over 40; and (2) young children are the most proficient language learners. Thus the program was developed to take advantage of the existing resources and to target future learners as efficiently as possible. As a result of the success of the preschool program, the first immersion primary school (Kura Kaupapa Māori) was created in 1985. This stepwise creation of the program addresses the need for curricular development: it is impossible for programs to start from scratch and move to a fully fledged immersion curriculum overnight. The other issue is teacher training. Here, too, the program has stepwise training of teachers, building each new level on the successes of lower levels.

Master-Apprentice Program

The Master-Apprentice program (Hinton et al. 2002) pairs a language learner (the apprentice) with a fluent or highly proficient speaker (the master) for intensive immersion language learning. This program was devised for those situations where there are few remaining speakers and where there are individuals who are interested in learning the language in a one-on-one pairing. Those individuals may go on to revitalize the language among a larger community of potential speakers, or they may be the sole learners. It is aimed specifically at adult learners and has the advantage of not requiring formal pedagogical materials or a classroom setting. Instead, it sets about to teach the language in the natural setting in which it is used by the master, in the home and in everyday life. The method relies on oral communication only and has become very popular with communities; it offers a practical way for speakers and learners to take control of language learning without requiring massive financial resources. Although the program was originally designed to pay both the master and the apprentice for their time, as an incentive to carry out the work, it has been implemented in many communities without any kind of salaries or pay.

Nomadic Schools

Nomadic schools have been established in parts of Siberia among a few communities of reindeer herders, primarily in the Republic of Sakha (Yakutia) with support from UNESCO. In these communities, the local languages (such as Evenki, Chuckchi, and Dolgan) are spoken most robustly among the families who maintain a traditional lifestyle, which includes nomadic herding and hunting. Historically, children have been enrolled in boarding schools in the villages to receive their (Russian-based) education, facilitating shift. The nomadic schools were created in response to this situation to enable children to stay with their families and still receive formal education. There are several different models, depending on the needs and desires of local communities; the models vary as to whether the children spend a few initial years in the boarding school and then return to the herds; whether a teacher travels with the herds; or whether in some cases the teacher meets only periodically with the herds, and parents are responsible for day-to-day education. In some versions, instruction depends upon Internet access and computers, so that the children and teachers can maintain contact electronically. This model is not readily portable to other parts of the world, as it is specifically designed to address the issues of a nomadic lifestyle, but it has much to offer for other nomadic communities.

Language Reclamation Programs

Language reclamation refers to those instances where there are no remaining speakers of a language. In some cases there may be a few "rememberers," people who know only a few words (or phrases) of the language. In other cases, there may be no one left who has ever heard the language spoken; instead, perhaps all that has survived is some kind of documentation: a dictionary or even just a word list, perhaps a descriptive grammar, perhaps recordings. In such cases, the first task is to reconstruct the language as much as possible. Where the documentation is scant, such reconstruction often depends on knowledge from related languages.

A well-documented reclamation project is that of Kaurna, a Nunga language of South Australia that was reconstructed based on documentation dating to the middle of the nineteenth century (Amery 2000). The reclamation efforts have led to the reclamation of place names, traditional greetings, and welcoming speeches, and even to Kaurna language classes in the local schools. Another example is provided by Chochenyo, a Costanoan language of the Muwekma Ohlone people of California, which had not been spoken since the 1930s. Early reclamation efforts involved reconstructing as much of the language as possible from existing documentation, which included the field notes and recordings of the linguist J. P. Harrington, although many of the recordings were songs, with few words, and by comparing the existing materials to those of the Mikowk and Yokut languages, which were known to be phonetically and structurally similar. The community, working with linguist Juliette Blevins, was then in a position to create an orthographic system for Chochenyo and to build a word list, again, from existing materials, but also creating new words for missing ones, words for new items not used when Chochenyo was last spoken, and words to fill in some blanks in the historical records.

One of the more dramatic illustrations of language reclamation is the Myaamia Project, supported by the Miami Tribe of Oklahoma and Miami University. Like Chochenyo and Kaurna, Myaamia had not been spoken for many generations. The project has two goals: "to conduct in-depth research to assist tribal educational initiatives aimed at the preservation of language and culture" and "to expose undergraduate and graduate students at Miami University to tribal efforts in language and cultural revitalization," as defined by the program website (www.myaamiaproject.com). The project is directed by linguist and Miami tribal member Daryl Baldwin, who has worked closely with an external linguist, David Costa, to analyze the historical documentation and make Myaamia a viable modern language. Despite initial impressions to the contrary, there are significant written records and documentation of Myaamia. These records, along with comparison to living related Algonquian languages, have allowed Baldwin and Costa to revitalize the language and fill in lexical gaps. The program has been very successful in creating new speakers and stimulating interest in younger people to speak their language. It is seen as a key part of strengthening both language and culture.

Language Domains and Social Networks

(Re)learning the language, its lexicon and grammar, is only part of the process of revitalization. To move from endangerment to vital, the language needs to be used. Lack of use is what brings about language shift in the first place. Thus it is important for revitalization programs to take language usage into account; ideally they should strive to create opportunities to speak, read, and write the language (where literacy is part of revitalization). Creating domains of usage is challenging. It is very difficult to oust the language of wider communication in a given domain and replace it with the revitalized language. Moreover, the dominant language tends to spread to new domains of use: this feature is typical of vital languages and can be taken as one measure of vitality. One challenge for the Hawaiian revitalization program, for example, has been to create places for Hawaiian to be spoken outside the school. Without such places, it runs the danger of being a "school" language, much like foreign languages taught in high schools in the United States. In order to prevent this, or at least mitigate it, some programs have parents sign a contract that commits them to learning the language and speaking it at home with their children.

It is clear that more than domains are involved. Research on social networks shows that they play a critical role in language revitalization and maintenance (Milroy 2002; Sallabank 2011). Social networks, or "the aggregate of relationships contracted with others" (Milroy 2002: 549), can provide a theoretical framework for understanding how speakers interact and how those interactions can influence language and linguistic behavior. Work in language variation and change has used social networks to explain the kinds of social mechanism that support linguistic varieties or foster their change within given social groups. For example, social networks have been used to explain language change that results from urbanization. Networks made of strong ties can support the (continuing) use of localized norms. In networks with weak ties, or where previously strong ties have weakened, the result is often modifications in the social structure that are conducive to language change and shift.

Just as weakened ties can foster shift, so too can stronger ties offset change. For revitalization efforts it is thus important to build and strengthen ties. Social network theory makes explicit the perhaps obvious but often forgotten fact that language use and vitality is dependent upon speech communities. Community-based and community-driven revitalization programs are well placed to create social networks for language use because they directly involve the speakers themselves.

The Role of the External Linguist

One issue of much debate is the role of the external linguist in language revitalization. At some level the goals of linguists and communities are at odds: linguists are interested in documentation, description, and theoretical advances that can be achieved by access to unusual linguistic data. Linguists are often charged with being interested in languages, not language and its speakers. Communities are interested in revitalization, and often show only a secondary interest in the products of documentation and description insofar as they can further the development of pedagogical materials. These goals would appear to be at odds with one another, and yet the two groups havemore in common than might at first be apparent. Revitalization requires documentation and description. Linguistic description is critical for the creation of textbooks and reference materials such as dictionaries and reference grammars. Documentation is equally critical: it not only provides content for lessons and reference materials, but in many cases, what we know about languages today is due to earlier documentation. This is particularly true for languages that have not been spoken for years; reclamation of Kaurna or Wampanoag would have been impossible without documentation. By the same token, linguists cannot accomplish any of this work without speakers; they are completely dependent upon them. Current ethical guidelines for linguists call for collaboration at all stages of a project, and this often means that linguists need to spend part of their time jointly developing revitalization materials. Since many are not trained for such work, there is increasing tendency to include applied linguists in field projects, and to receive additional instruction in language pedagogy and materials development. (For further discussion and examples, see the papers in part 4 of Grenoble & Furbee 2010.)

Successful Revitalization: The Case of Hebrew

Hebrew is often held up as the most successful example of language revitalization. In the late nineteenth century, Hebrew revitalization slowly began in several agricultural settlements and colonies and was declared the only sanctioned public language in Tel Aviv. From this foundation it slowly spread, so that by the 1920s, Hebrew had become the first language for some. With the end of the Ottoman Empire in 1919 and the establishment of British rule, Hebrew usage spread in the educational systems established by the Jewish communities, who were allowed a fair amount of latitude. Classical Hebrew needed to be changed from a liturgical language to a modern, secular one; in this the Language Committee (later renamed the Hebrew Language Academy) played a critical role (Blau 1981). Since the state of Israel was created in 1948, the use of Hebrew as an official language and a language of the home has continually grown. (Arabic, English and Hebrew were all official languages prior to 1948 as part of British Mandatory law; English was dropped from this list with the establishment of Israel.) The growth of Hebrew is in large part due to two factors: an influx of Jewish immigrants with diverse first languages who opted to use a single lingua franca, and a political climate that was very favorable to establishing Hebrew as a unifying official language of Israel.

That said, it should be remembered that Hebrew presents a very particular case in time and was in an arguably unique position for revitalization. Its success comes in large part from the fact that revitalization was politically motivated and was seen as an integral part of the larger goal of creating a new Jewish state. (See Nahir 1998; Spolsky & Shohamy 1999 for more details.) Moreover, Hebrew is remarkable in that, although it had ceased to be used as a language for daily interaction, it continued (and continues) to be robustly used for religious purposes, so that even when it was no longer the primary or first language for most of the Jewish population, it continued to be transferred from one generation to another in one domain, religion. It was never completely dormant, although this specialized religious language could not meet the demands of daily interaction. Thus, when the decision was made to revitalize Hebrew and make it the first language of the emerging nation state of Israel, there were ample speakers with knowledge of the language, even though the language itself needed to be reinvigorated to handle the vast number of domains in which any national language is used, ranging from menial aspects of daily communication to government, law, and higher education.

The revival of Hebrew is thus unique in many respects, both sociocultural and sociolinguistic. The creation of the state of Israel, and subsequent massive Jewish immigration, resulted in a unique set of circumstances for fostering the revived use of Hebrew. Moreover, it was revived in "an acute communicative vacuum" (Nahir 1998: 340) where it was not competing with another language but became the primary language of communication. This distinguishes Hebrew from almost all other endangered languages today, in that it became the language of a nation-state. Kalaallisut (West Greenlandic) is possibly comparable in having national, official status, and it has been successfully revitalized since the implementation of Home Rule in 1979, which granted it official status in both education and in the government. The overwhelming majority of the world's local languages are not in this position, and for them it can be problematic to have the case of Hebrew as a role model.

Assessing Language Revitalization Programs

Despite decades of revitalization efforts, to date there has been little true assessment of the efficacy of these programs. At present we lack good survey data on exactly what kinds of programs are underway and where; numbers of participants (both students and teachers); and the duration of such programs. We also lack data about how successful (or not) they are, although there are indications that they may not be creating new communities of speakers. Reporting the results of a 2000 survey conducted by Indian Country Today, Berardo and Yamamoto (2007: 107) show that although 71 percent of respondents said that the language programs were offered by their tribes, only a very small percentage claim actual knowledge of the tribal language.

The reasons for lack of assessment are both political and practical. It takes a tremendous effort for a community to begin and maintain a revitalization program. A negative assessment could have a very detrimental impact on the morale of language supporters and on the status and credibility of the leaders of such efforts. From a practical standpoint, the goals and resources of individual programs are themselves in constant flux. Any assessment would necessarily need to determine what would constitute "successful" revitalization in a given community. Does it mean that the entire population or some percentage is fully fluent and functional in the revitalized language, or that some subset of the population has some knowledge of the language and can use it in ceremonial domains? There is a wide range of results that can be considered "successful." In many cases, simply maintaining the program on a daily (or yearly) basis is a victory. Any program assessment needs to take into account the status of the language when the program began and the group's goals; both are difficult to measure in any objective way. We often lack reliable data about language vitality at the onset of revitalization, so it is challenging to know how much progress has actually been made.

In addition, targets or goals can and do change as a revitalization program progresses. One prime example is Wampanoag (or Wôpanâak), an Algonqian language of eastern North America; the last known speaker, Chief Wild Horse, was recorded in 1961 by Gordon Day. There have been no fluent speakers for over 150 years and the language was considered "dormant" or extinct. At present, however, there is a very active language reclamation project, which is a collaborative effort of members of the Aquinnah (Gay Head), Mashpee Wampanoag Tribes and Assonet Band. The project made significant progress under the leadership of Jessie Little Doe Baird, who studied linguistics at MIT and has spearheaded a major reclamation project to recreate Wampanoag. Baird has worked extensively with legacy materials to reproduce Wampanoag in a form for today's purposes. Having taught herself the language, she is now raising her daughter to be the first fluent speaker of Wampanoag in many, many generations. Does such a program constitute success? Given the odds against any kind of Wampanoag reclamation, it should be considered a resounding success. Has Wampanoag replaced or even supplemented English among community members? Hardly. Thus, what by one measure is a tremendous victory may appear dubious by other measures; this underscores the need for an assessment metric that is sensitive to the particulars of very individualistic settings.

To address these problems, the Cherokee Nation of Oklahoma advocates Culturally Responsible Evaluation, which is sensitive to the local culture and respectful of the dignity and integrity of local stakeholders (Peter 2003). It challenges traditional evaluation measures, which are seen as overly dependent on quantitative data. Instead, it relies on ongoing evaluation, working closely with stakeholders to understand their perspectives and to develop and enlarge them. Negotiation and sharing of results are integral to Culturally Responsive Evaluation. The Cherokee Nation language revitalization is framed as an act of linguistic self-empowerment, and this different form of evaluation emerges from this sense of self-empowerment. It is one possible model for assessment of revitalization that might result in more effective, more successful programs.

Future Research in Revitalization

The existence of so many revitalization programs provides the opportunity and need for new and different kinds of research. These include scientific investigations into the linguistics processes and effects of both attrition and (re)acquisition, or revitalization. The situation with revitalization language is the reverse of that for many heritage languages. With heritage languages, the children learn a language at home with the (usually immigrant) parents and cease speaking it when they enter the school system. This results in what is termed *interrupted acquisition*: the children do not acquire full adult fluency and the language is replaced by another. In some cases, the acquisition pattern of indigenous languages is similar: children are raised in monolingual environments where only the indigenous language is spoken. They then shift to another language when they enter the school system or have extensive contact with speakers of the majority language. But often there are different patterns, more instances of forgetting than of interrupted acquisition. In such cases adult speakers of the language cease using it because they speak another language at work or when they move to an urban area, or because they make a conscious decision not to speak it to their children. (This is frequent in situations where speakers have been punished for using their language.) Thus the children are raised monolingually in the dominant language; the parent generation may be bilingual, but opts not to use the indigenous language. Over time, such speakers may forget their language, in particular if pressure to speak the dominant language is so great that the endangered language falls out of use. One result is real loss across a single generation, where what was formerly the parent generation has now become the elderly grandparent generation, and their children (now parents) have little to no knowledge of their ancestral language. This new parent generation is ill-equipped to teach the language to their children.

This raises several scientific questions with regard to the linguistic processes of attrition. At the same time, we should ask several questions about the linguistic processes of revitalization. At a very basic level, two (potentially) different forms of the language can be identified. First is the linguistic structure of the language when fluently spoken, i.e., from a time of pre-contact, or when children are raised by fluent speakers and themselves reach fluency. Second is the linguistic structure of the revitalized language, which may have been influenced by the contact language(s) and may also have been influenced by attrition. In many cases of revitalization, the instructors of the language (parents or formal teachers) are themselves not fluent in the language; they either learn it as adults as a second language or have partial acquisition as children. (In these instances it may be useful to distinguish between revitalized languages and reinvigorated languages, whose use is encouraged where there are still fluent speakers across generations. Until we have further research into these questions, we can theoretically assume that the input that children receive differs in the two cases.) In cases of reclamation, there are no speakers of a language and the linguistic structure is reinvented from extant documentation. Although linguists recognize that the structure of a reclaimed or revitalized language differs from earlier versions of the language, it is not yet clear if it differs in predictable ways, what is the contribution of the contact language(s) to the new structure and what, if any, impact does attrition have.

Notes

1. See the UNESCO website at http://www.unesco.org/culture/ich/index.php?lg=en&pg=00136. Accessed November 20, 2010.

References

Amery, R. 2000. *Warrabarna Kaurna! Reclaiming an Australian language.* Exton, PA: Swets & Zeitlinger.

Berardo, M., & Yamamoto, A. 2007. Indigenous voices and the linguistics of language revitalization. In O. Miyaoka, O. Sakiyama, & M. E. Krauss (eds.), *The vanishing languages of the Pacific Rim*, 107–17. Oxford: Oxford University Press.

Blau, J. 1981. *The emergence and linguistic background of Judaeo-Arabic: A study of the origins of Middle Arabic.* 2nd ed. Jerusalem: Ben-Zvi Institute for the Study of Jewish Communities in the East.

Dauenhauer, N. M., & R. Dauenhauer, R. 1998. Technical, emotional, and ideological issues in reversing language shift: Examples from southeast Alaska. In L. A. Grenoble and L. J. Whaley (eds.), *Endangered languages: Current issues and future prospects*, 57–98. Cambridge: Cambridge University Press.

Fishman, J. A. 1991. *Reversing language shift: Theoretical and empirical foundations of assistance to threatened languages.* Clevedon: Multilingual Matters.

Grenoble, L. A., & Furbee, N. L. (eds.) 2010. *Language documentation. Practice and values.* Amsterdam: John Benjamins.

Grenoble, L. A., & Whaley, L. J. 1998. Toward a typology of language endangerment. In L. A. Grenoble & L. J. Whaley (eds.), *Endangered languages: Current issues and future prospects*, 22–54. Cambridge: Cambridge University Press.

Grenoble, L. A., & Whaley, L. J. 2006. *Saving languages. An introduction to language revitalization.* Cambridge: Cambridge University Press.

Hinton, L., & Hale, K. (eds.). 2001. *The green book of language revitalization in practice.* San Diego: Academic Press.

Hinton, L., Vera, M., & Steele, N. 2002. *How to keep your language alive.* Berkeley, CA: Heyday Books.

Lewis, M. P. (ed.) 2009. *Ethnologue: Languages of the world.* 16th ed. Dallas, TX: SIL International.

Milroy, L. 2002. Social networks. In J. K. Chambers, P. Trudgill, & N. Schilling-Estes (eds.), *The handbook of language variatioin and change*, 549–72. Oxford: Blackwell.

Mühlhäusler, P. 1990. "Reducing" Pacific languages to writing. In J. E. Joseph & T. J. Taylor, (eds.), *Ideologies of language*, 189–205. London: Routledge.

Nahir, M. 1998. Micro language planning and the revival of Hebrew: A schematic framework. *Language in Society* 27: 335–57.

Peter, L. 2003. Assessing the impact of total immersion on Cherokee language revitalization: A culturally responsive, participatory approach. In J. Reyner, O. V. Trujillo, R. L. Carrasco, & L. Lockard (eds.), *Nurturing native languages*, 7–24. Flagstaff: Northern Arizona University.

Sallabank, J. 2010. The role of social networks in endangered language maintenance and revitalization: The case of Guernesiais in the Channel Islands. *Anthropological Linguistics* 52: 184–205.
Spolsky, B., & Shohamy, E. 1999. *The languages of Israel: Policy, ideology and practice.* Clevedon: Multilingual Matters.
Tsunoda, T. 2005. *Language endangerment and language revitalization: An introduction.* Berlin: Mouton de Gruyter.
United Nations. 2007. *Declaration on the rights of indigenous peoples.* Adopted 13 September 2007. http://www.un.org/esa/socdev/unpfii/en/declaration.html. Accessed October 16, 2010.

CHAPTER 40

SOCIOLINGUISTICS AND SOCIAL ACTIVISM

ANNE H. CHARITY HUDLEY

> Once social change begins, it cannot be reversed. You cannot uneducate the person who has learned to read. You cannot humiliate the person who feels pride. You cannot oppress the people who are not afraid anymore. We have seen the future, and the future is ours.
>
> —Cesar Chavez (1984)

This chapter examines the history of social activism in sociolinguistics, with a particular focus on efforts in the United States. Given the essential sociolinguistic premise that language is fundamentally a social action, sociolinguists are in a unique position to help scholars and practitioners across disciplines research issues that intersect with the societal consequences of language behavior and language policy. As such, I exemplify ways that the study of sociolinguistics is critical for increased social justice and social change, and demonstrate how sociolinguistic models might better reflect a social justice framework if they are co-constructed by linguists *and* the communities in which they learn and teach. Through such co-construction, sociolinguists might better exemplify Bolinger's definition of the socially minded linguist as "one who works to inform the public about linguistics with a mind to curbing the use of language as a *one sided instrument of power*" (1979: 407).

Sociolinguistics as a discipline has been served by the examination of not only language change and its social correlates, but also by the complimentary examination of social change and the interaction of language in both macro and micro social processes. Social justice–based frameworks of research and action fit naturally into the sociolinguistic model, as these frameworks call for respect and rights for every person and for a thorough respect for justice in all aspects of society (Skutnabb-Kangas 2009). At the heart of a linguistics-centered social justice framework is the most basic right of a speaker: the right to speak his or her language of choice at all times.

Language discrimination is one of the last acceptable forms of discrimination (Lippi-Green 2011) and has frequently been used as a way to discriminate against individuals and groups of people without overtly judging their inherent being, despite the fact that Title VII of the U.S. Civil Rights Act of 1964 prohibits workplace discrimination based on religion, national origin, race, color, or sex. Lippi-Green challenged linguists not only to affirm the languages that speakers use but, more importantly, to affirm the rights of the speakers to speak them. Otherwise, nonstandardized languages and language varieties and their speakers are relegated to positions of novelty and/or subordination rather than affirmed languages of status.

Macrolevel language policies have been used as a way to justify social and political divisions and to force speakers of nonstandardized varieties and languages to assimilate linguistically. Phillipson (2009) noted that unresolved tensions between language and nationalism further contribute to social constructions of language and linguistic hierarchies. Sociopolitical situations surrounding language rights often strongly correlate with access to literacy and education. For example, Slave Codes forbade the promotion of literacy among enslaved African Americans in the United States (Baugh 2000), and the struggle toward literacy among many Americans from the African Diaspora continues today (Rickford 1997). Struggles for civil rights that include linguistic self-determinism are still active around the world and in the United States, as exemplified by Arizona's proposed restrictions on teachers with accents, coupled with restrictions on what can be taught in classrooms (Linguistic Society of America 2010). The use of standardized testing to uphold the model of the U.S. meritocracy is a prime example of linguistic discrimination (Charity Hudley & Mallinson 2011; Hoover, Politzer, & Taylor 1995).

Crucial to positioning sociolinguistics in a social justice framework is knowing who the speakers and the researchers studying them are. Much sociolinguistic theory has centered on speakers of nonstandardized varieties of language. Baker (2010a, 2010b) examined how early anthropologists and linguists set the tone for who was worthy of linguistic study and why. Baker examined linguistics' early roots in anthropological models that privileged the examination of Native American language and culture over African American language and culture along an imagined continuum of *exotification* and *othering*:

> Beginning with Lewis Henry Morgan through John W. Powell and Frederic W. Putnam, and then continuing with Franz Boas and his students, the

> primary focus of academic anthropological inquiry in the United States was American Indian languages and customs. It was not until World War II that anthropology in the United States did much else. In the timeless words of Michel-Rolph Trouillot, "the 'scientific' study of the Savage qua Savage became the privileged field of academic anthropology." Anthropologists got the savage slot, and continued to fill it with descriptions of out-of-the-way others. (Baker 2010a)

Although hints of those early models still exist within both sociolinguistics and anthropology, sociolinguistics has made great advances in helping to demonstrate the links between language use and social justice across racial and cultural groups. Baker (2010a) noted that, in contrast, sociology "described in-the-way others, and focused on recent immigrants and African Americans; they rarely focused on American Indians. In general terms, sociologists were used to support broader ideas of cultural assimilation, while anthropologists were used to support ideas of cultural preservation and conservation." Across the social sciences, this tradition of what sociologists call "studying down" still exists: scholars tend to study people in statuses that are lower than their own. With a few exceptions, including Feagin (1979) and Kroch (1995), scholars rarely study how privileged people speak from a sociolinguistic perspective.

As sociolinguistics draws on models from multiple fields including but not limited to linguistics, sociology, anthropology, and psychology, there is often an undercurrent of tension in the ways that different groups have been represented in the literature. A social justice framework helps to rectify those tensions.

Motivations for Socially Just Sociolinguistics: Funding

Although many sociolinguists have been working within social justice frameworks, a greater focus on social justice in research priorities, even among those who study nonstandardized speakers, is still needed. For example, Rickford (1997) stated that while sociolinguistics has drawn heavily from African American communities, the return benefit to communities has been low. Sociolinguists can become even more socially engaged through social service and public outreach.

The U.S. National Science Foundation (NSF), a major source of funding for linguists, has responded to these needs in research modeling and has called for researchers to devote more time to a direct commitment to the public interest. NSF proposals must include a detailed explanation of the "broader impacts" of the proposed research activity. Under this mandate, the NSF requires responses to the following questions:

- How well does the activity advance discovery and understanding while promoting teaching, training, and learning?
- How well does the proposed activity broaden the participation of underrepresented groups (e.g. gender, ethnicity, disability, geographic, etc.)?
- To what extent will it enhance the infrastructure for research and education, such as facilities, instrumentation, networks, and partnerships?
- Will the results be disseminated broadly to enhance scientific and technological understanding?
- What may be the benefits of the proposed activity to society? (National Science Foundation 2007)

The NSF mandate asks for plans for immediate dissemination of the knowledge. This revision forces the researcher to be aware of and contemplate the relevance of the knowledge to be gained. The efficacy of and the compliance with the new broader impacts statement in linguistics research, however, have yet to be disseminated by the NSF. An attention to community needs in the design and implementation of sociolinguistic scholarship results in expanded funding sources. Many linguists have been supported by cultural and historical preservation funds as well as by funding from sources in related fields, including education, anthropology, and history.

Waves of Sociolinguistic Justice

Four waves of social justice–centered sociolinguistic scholarship have each approached calls to social justice in various ways that model and mirror changes that have occurred across academia, especially in the humanities and social sciences. The waves do not represent generations of scholars; rather, they reflect the natural and iterative progression of thought and action, such that a scholar can easily appear in all four waves of work and that scholars who remain active across a lifetime should expect to participate in three to four waves (For more information see Eckert, 2012).

First Wave: Bringing Issues to Light and Creating Theory

The first wave of sociolinguists approached sociolinguistic social justice by seeing their mission as getting ideas out into the academic and public sphere and then starting to test them through quantitative and qualitative measures. Labov (1982) recounted the education-centered motivations for his work in Harlem.

"Deficit studies" by researchers such as Bereiter and Engelmann (1966) argued that working-class minority children begin with little or no exposure to language. Sociolinguists, including Wolfram (1969) and Labov (1972), responded to this argument by showing that language difference—not language deficit—was at the heart of language variation among speakers of nonstandardized varieties of English. The implementation of the difference framework did a great deal to eliminate paucity arguments from studies of language and culture and gave further evidence to basic linguistic frameworks that centered around the reality that most humans have the ability to speak and that no language is superior to another in either form or function.

Even among the first wave of sociolinguists, there were definitely the underpinnings of direct action at the core. The explanations of early modern linguists in the 1950s, 1960s, and 1970s that all language varieties, both spoken and signed, were equal were acts of social justice into themselves. The U.S. Center for Applied Linguistics (CAL) was established in 1959 by a grant from the Ford Foundation to the Modern Language Association at the juncture of basic and applied research to "serve as a liaison between the academic world of linguistics and the practical world of language education and language-related concerns" (Center for Applied Linguistics 2010a). CAL has sponsored many projects and programs that have had great impact in the areas of language assessment, instruction, and access. In addition, CAL has had a special history of serving refugees to the United States who are English language learners and are in a position to learn English through the Cultural Orientation Resource Center (CAL 2010b).

First wave research is still an ongoing necessity to interweave sociolinguistic theory within a more globally centered social justice framework and to examine varieties that are not as represented or studied in the literature. For example, Alim, Ibrahim, and Pennycook (2009) demonstrated the influence that hip-hop music has had on African American and global cultures and shed light on the integral nature of language and music throughout the world.

Second Wave: Finding Applications and Extending Theoretical Models

The second wave of sociolinguists tested the initial hypotheses of the first generation and expanded the social context of the sociolinguistic finding that language is both internally and externally conditioned, such that the speakers in their local contexts were examined more deeply for both linguistic and social meaning. As described in the findings of many of the chapters in this handbook, second wave sociolinguists recognized that a true understanding of social categories provides a more comprehensive set of strategies that linguists can use to bring about linguistic and social justice. As such, the second wave brought about a greater emphasis on action research.

Labov (1982) described the linguistic community's commitment to the children of Ann Arbor, Michigan. The parents of the African American students represented in the Ann Arbor case sought equal educational protection under the law for their children's use of African American English in the classroom. In describing the situation that linguists faced in the Ann Arbor trial, Labov asserted that the objectivity linguists need for scientific research may often lie in opposition to their commitment to social action. He shows how reconciliation between the linguist as scientist and the scientist as activist may occur by bringing linguistic information to communities when they need it and by being committed to use information gathered from a community for that community's direct benefit.

Action research models integrate elements from both basic and applied research and recognize the immediacy of the need to make findings available for community use and knowledge (Gray 2009). Action research embodies a focus on simultaneous action and research in a participative manner. Research subjects are themselves researchers or are involved in a democratic partnership with a researcher, and data are generated from the direct input of the researcher and those being studied.

Research that focuses on social justice is another way to reconfigure and reconcile the basic and applied model, as all of the models are critically important for the advancement of theory and practice. Social justice research emphasizes the processes and conditions that allow for social justice and, as such, is basic, applied, *and* action-centered in nature. With a focus on building bridges between the traditional models, researchers who work in a social justice framework are freer to work across disciplines on social issues that are informed by both theory and process. Sociolinguistics is a natural fit for this model. Along these lines, Cameron and colleagues (1992) focused on empowerment of the communities served and not just sociolinguistic investigations of them.

Wolfram (1993 and this volume) introduced the principle of linguistic gratuity, proposing that linguists give back to the local communities where they conduct their studies. Wolfram (1998, 2000; see also chapter 37, this volume) evaluated his own public outreach measures to see in what ways efforts to give back to the local communities of North Carolina were successful or contested by local communities. Wolfram has coauthored numerous books and papers for non-linguistic readership (for examples see Wolfram, chapter 37, this volume).

As sociolinguistics has expanded its realm to include greater numbers of women, minorities, and scholars with physical differences, the focus of sociolinguists expanded as well. Rickford (1997) noted that AfricanAmerican linguists have often made homes in other departments that allow for cross intersection of the waves, especially with regard to outreach, and do not shy away from alliances with speech hearing sciences, communications, and education.

The second wave of linguistics has also demonstrated that sign language has variation just like any other language. Lucas, Bayley, and Valli (2003) demonstrated the variability in sign language, which demonstrated its comprehensiveness as a language and not just a finite set of signs. Baugh (2007) demonstrated that the distinctiveness of African American speech patterns and features has resulted in such discrimination as landlords denying housing to African Americans as early in the process as the initial telephone inquiries. Baugh has shown that just the way a speaker says, "Hello," can trigger racial identification, resulting in the landlord reporting that the apartment has been rented.

Third Wave: Direct Action That Informs Sociolinguistic Theory

The increased focus on community engagement and social justice is a movement that is happening across higher education (Boyer 1990). Traditional notions of basic research as the standard measure of academic excellence are being revisited to privilege research that both expands knowledge and includes models that acknowledge that applied research does indeed influence basic fundamental and theoretical questions (Gray 2008). Applied research that addresses the improvement of the human condition is now being seen as theoretical and fundamental. New classifications from the Carnegie Foundation emphasize universities' commitment to community engagement in addition to their research productivity.

As such, the third wave of social justice sociolinguistics expanded the social implications of the previous two waves of sociolinguistic work and is greatly adding to the dimensions of sociolinguistic activism such that it is not secondary to the research but central to the framing of key questions within sociolinguistic theory. The waves of research models are directly relevant in sociolinguistics as speakers of nonstandardized varieties help to negotiate the research priorities of sociolinguists who work with them. Granted, even traditional models set degrees of relevance based on the immediate usefulness of the information. As Rickford (1997) stated, for the benefit of speakers who are donating their time and energy to the research efforts, some immediacy of presentation of results and implications should be built into the research model. Rickford compelled linguists to improve the relationships between their universities and the communities in which they work. Labov's current work focuses on the production of teaching materials for struggling readers in the form of a tutoring program for grades 2 to 5 and a language arts intervention program for grades 4 to 8 maybe mention what he currently stated in his recent email to you, about 90 tutors working independent of any course (Labov et al. 2010). The programs use previous sociolinguistic knowledge to help struggling readers acquire greater literacy and the project also provided for a state of the art examination of language variation in African American, white, and Latina/o children in different areas of the United States.

Recent work in ASL, where the white Deaf community has been extensively studied, focuses on the understudied African American signing community (McCaskill, Lucas, Bayley, & Hill 2011). The information drawn from this work greatly informs the community and the interpters and others who serve them. Charity Hudley and Mallinson (2009) showed that the linguistic features that educators are concerned with at school are not always ones that have drawn the most interest from linguists, but they greatly affect students' assessment. Skutnabb-Kangas and colleagues (2009) put together an edited collection that worked to re-frame language and education policy through a social justice lens. It was one of the first texts in sociolinguistics and language policy to take that approach. The editors situated the text at the intersection of education, opportunity, and politics on a global scale, and through the case studies in the book, they wished to demonstrate how using several languages can contribute to social justice.

Batibo (2009) and Brenzinger (2009) addressed how poverty affects language survival and how differential access to economic resources is most often the fundamental determinant of language shift and language death. Along these lines, Magga et al. (2005) highlighted the inequalities that dominant language–medium instruction create. They showed how dominant language instruction prevents access to education because of linguistic, pedagogical, and psychological barriers; leads to language extinction; and does not present any method by which break the cycle of poverty created by lack of literacy and education. In this sense, the notion of *linguistic genocide* extends not just to death and physical injury based on the language that someone speaks but also to mental harm and detriment or destruction of the language among speakers. More needs to be done in sociolinguistic research lines to extend notions of linguistic insecurity and discrimination to focus on the actual harm done to speakers minority languages and language varieties.

What is critical in all of these models is that sociolinguistics is kept central in these larger conversations of social inequality; for sociolinguists of the fourth wave, this will be a continued component of sociolinguistic social justice work.

The Fourth Wave: The Scholarship of Dissemination

Across academia. Labov's principle of debt incurred applies not just to those outside of the field, but also to the future members of the field (Labov 1982). The greatest benefit of sociolinguistic research thus far has been to students of sociolinguistics: those who stay in the field of sociolinguistics, but more importantly, those who go on to influence society in a myriad of ways and who take their sociolinguistic information with them.

Many schools of education have relationships with local public schools that service-learning courses may be able to partner with. It is important to examine our own campuses to discover answers to the following questions:

- What is taught to linguistics students about education, culture, and diversity?

- What is taught to education students about language, culture, and diversity?
- What is taught to everyone else?

The answers to such questions call for cooperation across disciplines, excellent teaching and advising, and collective responsibility for sociolinguistic information outside what can be seen as the realm of sociolinguistics.

Service learning is a teaching and learning method that intentionally integrates academic content and learning objectives with projects designed to support and enhance the good of a specific community. The Corporation for National and Community Service describes service learning as a method of teaching where students learn and develop through active participation in thoughtfully organized community service. The service experience is integrated into and enhances the academic curriculum of the student. Service-learning courses provide structured time for the students to reflect on the service experience as it relates to their coursework, personal development, and civic involvement (Corporation for National and Community Service 2010). Service learning as an extension of collegiate volunteerism is an upward trend. At least a quarter of all higher education institutions and more than half of all community colleges have adopted service-learning programs (Corporation for National and Community Service 2010).

On campuses, service learning–based courses and community-based research present further venues for integrating sociolinguistic knowledge, research opportunities, and educational outreach in a range of different communities. Through community-based courses and community research, students and scholars have unique opportunities to connect academic learning and research with community needs, carrying linguistic knowledge back into schools and communities. Service learning is a way to make action a crucial component of linguistics as the study of people and their language is no longer confined to the classroom or the field researcher. Service learning is greatly beneficial to speakers from communities that sociolinguists have traditionally researched as well as for majority students who seek to learn more about communities that are not their own. García (2009) noted that the social justice principle of linguistics values the strength of students and communities and enables the creation of learning contexts that are not threatening to the students' identities while maintaining academic rigor (see Skutnabb-Kangas 2009).

Scholarly. It is critical to examine the practices of organizing bodies within sociolinguistics, including the funding sources, journals, and conferences that maintain the scholarship in the field. Journals such as *Linguistic Compass* and magazines such as *Language Magazine* serve to make research in sociolinguistics more accessible to a greater audience.

Off-campus. Rickford (1997) argued that the relationship between linguist and studied community is still not equal, as linguists benefit more directly and expediently from the research they conduct in communities than do the communities from linguistic research. Rickford (1997) challenged linguists to improve the relationships between themselves and the communities in which they gather information. Eleven years after Rickford, Queen, and Baptista (2008) stated that "in spite of these efforts, though, linguists have not achieved the desired impact on public understanding about the [language] variety or about its complex relationship to other languages and varieties of English." Sociolinguists are faced with questions as to how to disseminate all that we have researched and learned when met with the basic reality of the linguistically uninformed teacher, speech hearing scientist, psychologist, or school counselor.

While crucial information has been gathered by sociolinguists, the information often needs to be disseminated many times and in different formats in order to reach each generation of students and communities. Along these lines, Queen and Baptista noted:

> We believe linguists should do more to reach out to African American communities and to include working-, middle-, and upper-middle-class communities in our efforts to explain the benefits of a less prejudicial approach to AAE. Thus, in addition to our ongoing efforts to educate college students and public school teachers and students, we should also begin to promote a linguistically and socio-politically oriented approach to AAE in the very communities where its varied speakers live. (2008: 187)

Charity Hudley and Mallinson (2009) described the dissemination of linguistic knowledge in the professional development of teachers, where contrastive analysis (of African American English vs. standardized English) plays a major role. Taking lessons from the challenges presented in the Ebonics Debate (Baugh 2000), it is important to take notice of changes that have taken place in the school environment that might make contrastive analysis more acceptable as a teaching strategy but that also open the door for other discussions about language and multicultural education to take center stage in classrooms and other pedagogical settings. Charity Hudley and Mallinson (2010:254) presented a *linguistic awareness* model that is designed to facilitate the sharing of knowledge about language variation between researchers and community members:

- *to partner* with community members, particularly in underserved areas where universities may not already have such partnerships, including K-12 schools and others who provide for the educational, social, and health welfare of the community;
- *to communicate* sociolinguistic information about language variation to community members in ways that are effectively tailored to their skills and their needs;
- *to disseminate* accurate linguistic knowledge to community members, both to train them in the science of linguistics and to help them better serve dialectally diverse students;

- *to assess* the results of providing linguistic information to community members; and
- *to apply* these findings to public policy and social justice models.

Charity Hudley and Mallinson contended that more effort and energy should be spent on disseminating relevant information that has *already* been gathered about language variation, particularly when integrated with existing literature from education, sociology, psychology, and other related fields. It is crucial that researchers share knowledge while also adding to this body of information by continuing to document and analyze how language variation interacts in real-world educational settings, within the contexts of local communities. Linguists and related scholars should also be more involved in creating easy-to-implement and realistic language-based strategies to help educators and students facing larger social and educational issues. These strategies must both be linguistically and educationally informed; that is, they must be oriented toward helping students understand sociolinguistic concepts, and they must be practical enough to be implement in everyday settings.

At the January 2010 American Dialect Society Conference held in Baltimore, Maryland, a special panel session was held that was sponsored by the American Dialect Society Committee on Teaching. Entitled "Cultivating Socially Minded Linguists: Service Learning and Engaged Scholarship in Linguistics and Education," the panel session brought together linguists and practitioners who have implemented service-learning projects related to language and education in various forms including:

- models for an introductory undergraduate linguistics course that includes a service learning component on African American English (Charity et al. 2008);
- partnerships in Texas and Oklahoma that pair students with community agencies to serve nonnative English–speaking community members and Native American language communities (Fitzgerald 2009);
- an investigation into the effects of service learning on linguistically and culturally diverse college students enrolled in a first-year composition course, finding that nonnative English–speaking students may expect and gain more from service-learning activities than native English–speaking students (Wurr & Hellebrandt 2007).

As these projects demonstrate, engaged scholarship takes a wide variety of forms, and many practical challenges related to education can be addressed by applying linguistic knowledge to address community and educational needs.

The public at large. Deborah Tannen has brought sociolinguistic ideas to a larger public. Tannen (1990), which provided a public framework for communication issues about language and society that other scholars can model to share ideas with the greater public, has sold several million copies. Sociolinguists have participated in several popular video and television projects, which can be used to inform the public about key concepts, including *American Tongues* (Alvarez & Kolker 1988), *Do You Speak American?* (see Reaser & Adger 2007), and the North Carolina Language and Life Project (NCLLP). In *What's Your Sign For PIZZA: An Introduction to Variation in ASL*, Lucas, Bayley, & Clayton Valli (2003) present information in accessible language with an accompanying DVD with signing and voiceover. Walt Wolfram has set an excellent example for graduate student–level community involvement through the NCLLP (NCLLP n.d.). Kirk Hazen has followed that model with the formation of the West Virginia Dialect Project (2012), which is designed to conduct research on language variation to be used for educational purposes. Barbara Johnstone and Scott Keisling created a similar outreach page in the Pittsburgh Speech and Society Project (2008).

Sociolinguists have also appeared in the media to comment on linguistic issues. Controversies over federal investigators seeking Ebonics translators have re-sparked debates about African American English (see Cratty, Hayes, & Gast 2010) while the need for more translators in courtrooms remains an issue across languages as in the case of the *State of Maryland v. Mahamu D. Kanneh*, No. 94, September Term, 2007.

Sociolinguists on Facebook and Twitter provide sociolinguistic information for a wider audience than academic writing and conferences allow for (for a list of linguists on Twitter, see *Twitter* 2010). The Language Log Blog (2010) has a large following that has caused the authors to write a book based on the posts. Ben Zimmer writes "The Word" column for the *Boston Globe*, and New York University hosts a blog about African American English at: http://africanamericanenglish.com/. It is also critical to note that many lay readers turn to Wikipedia for information, so it is important to monitor the sociolinguistic information on the site for accuracy and completeness.

The Challenges of Community Co-construction

Advocating *for* a community instead of *with* a community may not be a situation that sociolinguists create on purpose. Rather, it may come about as a result of community members' own concerns or actions. Community members may not want to jeopardize relationships with the universities or community foundations with which the sociolinguist may be working, or community members may hope for other benefits by working with the linguists, and some community members may have unarticulated concerns but, due to the position of power of the linguists, may have a well-founded fear of not saying no to their intrusions into their communities.

Blommaert and Jie (2010) extended the co-construction model and stated that when working in communities, language as a social construct should be constantly reexamined. Bloomaert and Jie assert that concepts such as "English, French, and Chinese" are "folk ideologies that are popularized by institutional discourses," and that these concepts should be salient as objects of sociolinguistic inquiry rather than be taken for granted as the basis of accepted linguistic theory.

It is important that the goals of the sociolinguist (i.e., to preserve a language or language variety or to show how some linguistic ideologies are less desirable than others based on linguistic theory) are not imposed on the community even when the sociolinguist has the best intentions. Dobrin, Austin, and Nathan (2007) argued that endangered languages have become commodified outside of the purveyance of the community. Hinton (2002: 151–52, as cited in Dobrin et al. 2007) modeled the challenges of linguistic objectives as follows:

> As an outsider, I would feel very uncomfortable if I were to advocate to a speech community that it ought to try to keep its language alive. It is entirely up to the community or to individuals within a community as to whether they want to put in the effort to develop new speakers for their language. Community members have the right to advocate within their community for the survival of their language; someone from outside the community does not. The right to language choice includes the right to choose against a language. This is the logical result of believing that maintaining an indigenous language is a matter of human rights, a belief virtually all language advocates must share. The outside expert's role is to assist in providing the means for language survival or revival to motivated community members and perhaps to provide encouragement and a sense of hope that it can be done.

Hinton's model exemplified the type of co-construction that is needed throughout sociolinguistics in order for the next wave of scholarship to advocate not *for* languages but *with* communities.

Community-based research practices are also crucial to the methodological outcomes of those who are dedicated to basic sociolinguistic research. Wiley and de Klerk (2009) emphasized the importance of listening to youth as participants, not only in research, but also in the way that the research questions are structured and framed. Wiley and de Klerk recounted studies in indigenous communities where educators reported that they didn't hear indigenous languages used. Youth in the communities, however, reported vibrant use of language outside of the educational context. Wiley and de Klerk noted that the point of view of the person being interviewed is crucial to how language is used and in what contexts. Moreover, the students most often reported "speaking their culture" instead of just "speaking their language" (Wiley & de Klerk 2009: 136). Indeed, co-construction of models will challenge frameworks that center on one or a few sociolinguistic variables alone as driving forces in sociolinguistic speech communities and will call for work that examines complete linguistic and social systems. Such work will be a formidable task but will prove to drive both the practical and theoretical models presented in sociolinguistics thus far.

The Co-construction of Ethics

The Linguistic Society of America (LSA) approved an ethics statement in 2009 that calls for a greater recognition of the direct implications of linguistic research. The LSA's statement on ethics incorporates many of the concepts of community- and social justice–centered research.

> Other communities are eager to share their knowledge in the context of a long-term relationship of reciprocity and exchange. In all cases where the community has an investment in language research, the aims of an investigation should be clearly discussed with the community and community involvement sought from the earliest stages of project planning. (LSA 2009: 3)

Ethical considerations should also advise the way in which research is conducted with a mind toward how it is disseminated by researchers and others. The LSA ethics statement supports such considerations as follows:

- Linguists have a responsibility to consider the social and political implications of their research.
- Linguists should make the results of their research available to the general public, and should endeavor to make the empirical bases and limitations of their research comprehensible to nonprofessionals.
- Linguists should give consideration to likely misinterpretations of their research findings, anticipate the damage they may cause, and make all reasonable effort to prevent this. (LSA 2009: 4–5)

Rice (2006) noted that there has not much discussion in linguistics on ethics until very recently. Great care needs to be taken so that every sociolinguistics student receives protocols about standards within the discipline as well as the guidelines set by the LSA and each university's internal review board.

Greater ethical considerations would take into account how communities are entered and represented. Sociolinguists have used various methods to enter a community, from finding a local connection to entering through school systems or other large organizations.

The amount of due diligence a researcher has to do when attempting to represent a social and linguistic model of a community must also be of concern. There have been very few sociolinguistically informed full-scale samplings of communities due to the time and money needed to acquire large amounts of sociolinguistic information. But there is a danger in representing a class, race, or gender of a community based on very few samples. Even when smaller communities are represented, the researcher must be very specific in any report made about the size of the sample, not only in the demographic information, but also in how the title and other information about the study represent the research.

Sociolinguists also have a direct responsibility to ensure that communities are fully aware of the results of research. Academic papers should aggressively be made available to communities in which the research was conducted, as these are often difficult or impossible for many community members to access. In addition, research debriefings must not only take the form of academic papers but should also include talks in communities and websites that present information that is tailored to the linguistic and literacy needs of the participants (e.g., given at appropriate reading or comprehension levels).

It is also important to analyze the full spectrum of what a community gains, both short term and long term, when a sociolinguist enters a community to do research and, later, when that research is disseminated to a larger audience. With each new research endeavor, it is important to map out what status or opportunities the researchers gain as a result (e.g., publication, funding, awarding of a degree or tenure that then leads to further opportunities and income) and what the community gains (e.g., benefits from grant money, help with immediate or long-term social needs).

A crucial question, then, is what greater gains for the community could sociolinguists help to provide? Such gains might include better access to education or equitable funding for the time that researchers spend in a community, rather an abstract promise of future benefits from the research as a form of gift in kind. It is also critical to think about what a community risks (i.e., privacy, losing ownership of intellectual information) when undertaking research with an outside researcher. Even researchers with the best of intentions who have successfully passed the internal review procedures at their university put the anonymity of communities and community members in jeopardy, run the risk of having the linguistic and cultural information gathered taken out of context, and may bring about (among other things) ridicule due to the public nature of the dissemination. Even community members who are willing to take risks due to the potential gains from the research may not foresee what the information could come to symbolize once it is out of the community's hands.

Social Justice as an Interdisciplinary Necessity

As demonstrated in this chapter and in those in this volume by Wolfram (37), Romaine (38), and Grenoble (39), sociolinguists are in a unique position to help scholars and practitioners across disciplines research issues that intersect with the societal consequences of language behavior and language policy.

Future sociolinguistic work is best done on teams that include sociolinguists as well as scholars and activists from related disciplines, including but not limited to sociology, psychology, anthropology, education, law, government, ethnic studies, speech hearing and communication sciences, and medicine.

Many scholars who work in linguistics and education have been instrumental in bringing linguistic insights to major organizations such as the American Educational Research Association (AERA), the National Council of Teachers of English (NCTE), the American Federation of Teachers (AFT), and the Teaching of English as a Second or Other Language (TESOL)/Teaching Of English as a Foreign Language (TOEFL) communities.

Mohanty (2009) noted several international organizations that have heralded one's choice of language use as a basic human right and thus related to issues of everything from international relations to health. He cited UNESCO, UNPFII, and the UN Human Rights Council's Minority Forum as organizations that have set policies in place which the nation must now follow. Mohanty's descriptions mirrored efforts that have been highlighted in the U.S. sociolinguistics literature to produce proclamations on issues including the Ebonics Debate and the right of first nations to speak their own languages.

Nonetheless, it is alarming how often discussions of language are missing from the actual practices designed to mitigate social inequality in education, psychology, and sociology. Banks (2011) asserted, however, that it is easier for institutions and policy makers to state that students should have the right to speak their own language than it is for educators and administrators to make the broad policies a reality. Right now there are few guidelines on how to implement the idealistic policies of student rights in actual classrooms.

As Baugh (2000) described, no linguists served on the Oakland School Board's African American Education Task Force although linguist Ernie Smith was consulted and influenced the statement that Ebonics was not English. Despite the linguistic inaccuracy, Oakland was at least attempting to address the crucial, long-standing issue of dialect differences in the school system. A considerable amount of writing after the Ebonics debate was devoted to misunderstandings about what the educators and linguists who came to their aid were trying to say, yet with concentrated help from linguists working within the school system, the misunderstanding and backlash that ensued might have been different.

Conclusion

Shuy (2003) reported on the personal and intellectual decisions made by leaders in the field about the direction of sociolinguistics and what would be considered sociolinguistics. Future work must include a critical examination of who exactly gets to decide what sociolinguistics is among the next generation of scholars and how that definition is co-constructed between sociolinguists and the communities in which they teach and learn. Questions that are framed and asked in ways that directly benefit both the sociolinguists and those in the community who make such knowledge possible allow for greater creation of knowledge with a purpose for common good.

Through a continued dedication to the ways that sociolinguistic research can best contribute to social change and social justice, sociolinguists may best meet the charge of Bolinger (1979) charge to keep socially minded linguistics at the root of the sociolinguistic mission. There are several concepts that are key to both community engagement and sociolinguistic research: that we listen carefully, listen well, seek to understand, and then act.

Acknowledgment

This work was supported by the NSF under awards #9030522 and #0512005 and the William and Mary Professorship in Community Studies. I would like to thank Ms. Melissa Hogarty, Drs. Christine Mallinson, Monica Griffin, Regina Root, Joel Schwartz, and Kelly Whalon, as well as my linguistics and community studies courses: Introduction to Community Studies, fall '09 and '10; Language Attitudes, spring '09; Methods in Community Studies, spring '09; and Swahili Language and Culture, summer '10 for their discussions and feedback about the paper. Some of the material in this article is based on Charity (2009) and Charity Hudley and Mallinson (2010).

References

Alim, H. S., Ibrahim, A., & Pennycook, A. (eds.). 2009. *Global linguistic flows: Hip hop cultures, youth identities, and the politics of language*. London: Routledge.

Alvarez, L., & Kolker, A. (dirs.). 1988. *American tongues* [documentary]. PBS. United States: Center for New American Media.

Baker, L. 2010a. Anthropology and racial politics. Interview in *Inside Higher Education*. April 16. [online]. http://www.insidehighered.com/news/2010/04/16/baker.

Baker, L. 2010b. *Anthropology and the racial politics of culture*. Durham: Duke University Press.

Banks, J. A. 2011. Series introduction: Multicultural Education Series. In A. Charity Hudley & C. Mallinson, *Understanding English language variation in U.S. schools*, vii-xi New York: Teachers College Press.

Batibo, H. M. 2009. Poverty as a crucial factor in language maintenance and language death: Case studies from Africa. In W. Harbert, S. McConnell-Ginet, A. Miller, & J. Whitman (eds.), *Language and poverty*, 23–36. Clevedon: Multilingual Matters.

Baugh, J. 2000. *Beyond Ebonics: Linguistic pride and racial prejudice*. New York: Oxford University Press.

Baugh, J. 2007. Linguistic contributions to the advancement of racial justice within and beyond the African Diaspora. *Language and Linguistics Compass* 1: 331–49.

Bereiter, C., & Engelmann, S. 1966. *Teaching disadvantaged children in the preschool*. Englewood Cliffs: Prentice-Hall.

Blommaert, J., & Jie, D. 2010. *Doing ethnographic fieldwork: A beginner's guide*. Clevedon: Multilingual Matters.

Bolinger, D. 1979. The socially-minded linguist. *Modern Language Journal* 63: 404–07.

Boyer, E. L. 1990. *Scholarship reconsidered: Priorities of the professorate*. San Francisco: Jossey-Bass.

Brenzinger, M. 2009. Language diversity and poverty in Africa. In W. Harbert, S. McConnell-Ginet, A. Miller, & J. Whitman (eds.), *Language and poverty*, 37–49. Clevedon, UK: Multilingual Matters.

Cameron, D., Frazer, E., Harvey, P., Rampton, B. H., & Richardson, K. 1992. *Researching language: Issues of power and method*. Oxford: Routledge.

Center for Applied Linguistics (CAL). 2010a. *About CAL*. [online]. www.cal.org/about/index.html.

Center for Applied Linguistics (CAL). 2010b. *Cultural Orientation Resource Center*. [online]. www.cal.org/co/.

Charity, A. H. 2009. *Linguists as agents for social change. Language and Linguistics Compass* 2.923–39.

Charity Hudley, A. H., & Mallinson, C. 2009. *Language variation in the classroom: An educator's toolkit*. Summer Workshop Series. Richmond, VA: Virginia Commonwealth University.

Charity Hudley, A. H., & Mallinson, C. 2010. Communicating about communication: Multidisciplinary approaches to educating educators about language variation. *Language and Linguistics Compass*.4.245–57.

Charity Hudley, A. H., & Mallinson, C. 2011. *Understanding English language variation in U.S. schools*. New York: Teachers College Press.

Chavez, C. 1984. Address Before the Commonwealth Club of San Francisco. San Francisco, California.

Charity, A. H., Harris, J., Hayes, J., Ikeler, K., & Squires, A. 2008. Service learning as an introduction to sociolinguistics and linguistic equality. *American Speech* 83: 237–51.

Civil Rights Act. 1964. [online]. http://clerk.house.gov/library/reference-files/PPL_CivilRightsAct_1964.pdf.

Corporation for National and Community Service. 2010. *Corporation for National and Community Service*. [online]. www.nationalservice.gov/.

Cratty, C., Hayes, A., & Gast, P. 2010, August 24. DEA wants to hire Ebonics translators. *CNN*. [online]. http://articles.cnn.com/2010-08-24/us/dea.ebonics_1_ebonics-translators-language-form-linguistic-society?_s=PM:US.

Dobrin, L., Austin, P. K., & Nathan, D. 2007. Dying to be counted: The commodification of endangered languages in documentary linguistics. In P. K. Austin (ed.), *Language documentation and description*, vol. 6, 37–52. London: Hans Rausing Endangered Languages Project.

Eckert, P. 2012. Three waves of variation study: The emergence of meaning in the study of variation. Annual Review of Anthropology, 41: 87–100.

Feagin, C. 1979. *Variation and change in Alabama English: A sociolinguistic study of the white community*. Washington, DC: Georgetown University Press

Fitzgerald, C. M. 2009. Language and community: Using service learning to reconfigure the multicultural classroom. *Language and Education* 23: 1–15.

García, O. 2009. Education, multilingualism and translanguaging in the 21st century. In T. Skutnabb-Kangas, R. Phillipson, A.K. Mohanty, & M. Panda (eds.), *Social justice through multilingual education*, 140–58. Clevedon: Multilingual Matters.

Gray, D. 2009. *Doing research in the real world.* London: Sage.

Hinton, L. 2002. Commentary: Internal and external advocacy. *Journal of Linguistic Anthropology* 12: 150–56.

Hoover, M., Politzer, R., & Taylor, O. 1995. Bias in reading tests for black language speakers: A sociolinguistic perspective. In A. G. Hilliard (ed.), *Testing African American students*, 2nd ed., 51–68. Chicago: Third World Press.

Kroch, A. 1995. Dialect and style in the speech of upper class Philadelphia. In G. Guy, J. Baugh, D. Schiffrin, & C. Feagin (eds.), *Towards a social science of language: Papers in honor of William Labov*, vol. 1, 23–46. Philadelphia: John Benjamins.

Labov, W. 1972. *Language in the inner city: Studies in the Black English vernacular.* Philadelphia: University of Pennsylvania Press.

Labov, W. 1982. Objectivity and commitment in linguistic science: The case of the black English trial in Ann Arbor. *Language and Society* 11: 165–201.

Labov, W., Soto-Hinman, I., Dickson, S. V., Charity Hudley, A. H., & Thorsnes, B. 2010. *Portals to reading: Intensive intervention.* Boston: Houghton Mifflin Harcourt.

Language Log Blog. 2010. *Language log.* [online]. http://languagelog.ldc.upenn.edu/nll/.

Linguistic Society of America (LSA). 2009. *Ethics statement.* [online]. www.lsadc.org/info/pdf_files/Ethics_Statement.pdf.

Linguistic Society of America (LSA). 2010. *Resolution on the Arizona Teachers' English Fluency Initiative.* [online]. www.lsadc.org/info/lsa-res-arizona.cfm.

Lippi-Green, R. 2011. *English with an accent: Language, ideology, and discrimination in the United States.* London: Routledge.

Lucas, C., Bayley, R., & Valli, C. 2003. *What's your sign for PIZZA? An introduction to variation in American Sign Language* [book and DVD]. Washington, DC: Gallaudet University Press.

Magga, O. H., Nicolaisen, I., Trask, M., Dunbar, R., & Skutnabb-Kangas, T. 2005. *Indigenous children's education and indigenous languages.* Expert paper written for the United Nations Permanent Forum on Indigenous Issues. New York: United Nations.

McCaskill, C., Lucas, C., Bayley, R., & Hill, J. 2011. *The hidden treasure of Black ASL: Its history and structure* [book and DVD]. Washington, DC: Gallaudet University Press.

Mohanty, A. K. 2009. Multilingual education: A bridge too far? In T. Skutnabb-Kangas, R. Phillipson, A. K. Mohanty, & M. Panda (eds.), *Social justice through multilingual education*, 85–102. Clevedon: Multilingual Matters.

National Science Foundation (NSF). 2007. *Merit review broader impacts criterion: Representative activities.* [online]. www.nsf.gov/pubs/gpg/broaderimpacts.pdf.

NCLLP (North Carolina Language and Life Project). 2012. Homepage. [online]. http://www.ncsu.edu/linguistics/ncllp/.

Phillipson, R. 2009. The tension between linguistic diversity and dominant English. In T. Skutnabb-Kangas, R. Phillipson, A. K. Mohanty, & M. Panda (eds.), *Social justice through multilingual education*, 85–102. Clevedon: Multilingual Matters.

Pittsburgh Speech and Society Project. 2008. Homepage. [online]. http://english.cmu.edu/pittsburghspeech/.

Queen, R., & Baptista, M. 2008. African American English: Connecting linguistics' message with a mission. *Journal of English Linguistics* 36: 185–88.

Reaser, J., & Adger, C. T. 2007. Developing language awareness materials for non-linguists: Lessons learned from the *Do You Speak American?* project. *Language and Linguistic Compass* 1: 155–67.

Rice, K. 2006. Ethical issues in linguistic fieldwork: An overview. *Journal of Academic Ethics* 4: 123–55.

Rickford, J. R. 1997. Unequal partnership: Sociolinguistics and the African American speech community. *Language in Society* 26: 161–97.

Shuy, R. W. 2003. A brief history of American sociolinguistics 1949–1989. In C. Bratt Paulston & G. R. Tucker (eds.), *Sociolinguistics: The essential readings*, 4–16. Oxford: Blackwell.

Skutnabb-Kangas, T. 2009. Multilingual education for global justice: Issues, Approaches, Opportunities. In T. Skutnabb-Kangas, R. Phillipson, A. K. Mohanty & M. Panda (eds.), *Social justice through multilingual Education*, 85–102. Clevedon: Multilingual Matters.

Skutnabb-Kangas, T., Phillipson, R., Mohanty, A. K. & Panda, M. (eds.). 2009. *Social justice through multilingual education*. Clevedon: Multilingual Matters

State of Maryland v. Mahamu D. Kanneh, No. 94, September term, 2007.

Tannen, D. 1990. *You just don't understand: Women and men in conversation*. New York: William Morrow.

Twitter. 2010. *Langology index*. [online]. http://twitter.com/langology/world-language-teachers.

West Virginia Dialect Project. 2012. *West Virginia Dialect Project*. West Virginia University, Eberly College of Arts and Sciences. [online]. http://dialects.english.wvu.edu/. Accessed 8/16/12.

Wiley, T. G., & de Klerk, G. 2009. Common myths and stereotypes regarding literacy and language diversity in the multilingual United States. In M. Farr, L. Seloni, & J. Song (eds.), *Ethnolinguistic diversity and education: Language, literacy and culture*, 167–93. London: Routledge.

Wolfram, W. 1969. *A sociolinguistic description of Detroit Negro speech*. Washington, DC: Center for Applied Linguistics.

Wolfram, W. 1993. Ethical considerations in language awareness programs. *Issues in Applied Linguistics* 4: 225–55.

Wolfram, W. 1998. Black children are verbally deprived. In L. Bauer & P. Trudgill (eds.), *Language myths*, 103–12. London: Penguin Books.

Wolfram, W. 2000. Endangered dialects and social commitment. In Joy Peyton, Peg Griffin, Walt Wolfram, and Ralph W. Fasold (eds.), *Language in Action: New Studies of Language in Society*. Cresshill: Hampton Press. 19–39.

Wurr, A. J. & Hellebrandt, J. 2007. *Learning the language of global citizenship: Service learning in applied linguistics*. Bolton, MA: Anker.

Index

F

G

O

Lightning Source UK Ltd.
Milton Keynes UK
UKOW05f0257070516

273676UK00012B/160/P